McGraw-Hill Ryerson

CHEMISTRY 12

Authors

Christina Clancy
Dufferin-Peel Catholic District School Board

Katy Farrow
Thames Valley District School Board

Trevor Finkle
York Region District School Board

Lea Francis
York Region District School Board

Brian Heimbecker
Dufferin-Peel Catholic District School Board

Barbara Nixon-Ewing
Toronto District School Board

Mary Schroder
Dufferin-Peel Catholic District School Board

Trish Thomas
Ottawa-Carleton District School Board

Consultants

Tigist Amdemichael
Toronto District School Board

Anu Arora
Peel District School Board

Contributing Authors

Michelle Anderson
Science Writer

Jonathan Bocknek
Science Writer

Lois Edwards
Science Writer

Jim Gaylor
Avon-Maitland District School Board

Sara Goodchild
Science Writer

Kathy Hamilton
Science Writer

Tina Hopper
Science Writer

Michael Jansen
Crescent School
Toronto, Ontario

Kathryn Navarro
University of Ontario Institute of Technology

Ken Stewart
York Region District School Board

Christine Weber
Science Writer

Greg Wisnicki
Durham District School Board

Toronto   Montréal   Boston   Burr Ridge, IL   Dubuque, IA   Madison, WI   New York   San Francisco
St. Louis   Bangkok   Bogotá   Caracas   Kuala Lumpur   Lisbon   London   Madrid   Mexico City
Milan   New Delhi   Santiago   Seoul   Singapore   Sydney   Taipei

McGraw-Hill Ryerson

Copies of this book may be obtained by contacting:
McGraw-Hill Ryerson Limited

e-mail:
orders@mcgrawhill.ca

Toll-free fax:
1-800-463-5885

Toll-free call:
1-800-565-5758

or by mailing your order to:
McGraw-Hill Ryerson Limited
Order Department
300 Water Street
Whitby, ON L1N 9B6

Please quote the ISBN and title when placing your order.

Chemistry 12

Copyright © 2011, McGraw-Hill Ryerson Limited, a Subsidiary of The McGraw-Hill Companies. All rights reserved. No part of this publication may be reproduced or transmitted in any form or by any means, or stored in a data base or retrieval system, without the prior written permission of McGraw-Hill Ryerson Limited, or, in the case of photocopying or other reprographic copying, a licence from The Canadian Copyright Licensing Agency (Access Copyright). For an Access Copyright licence, call toll free to 1-800-893-5777.

The information and activities in this textbook have been carefully developed and reviewed by professionals to ensure safety and accuracy. However, the publisher shall not be liable for any damages resulting, in whole or in part, from the reader's use of the material. Although appropriate safety procedures are discussed and highlighted throughout the textbook, the safety of students remains the responsibility of the classroom teacher, the principal, and the school board district.

ISBN-13: 978-0-07-106010-3
ISBN-10: 0-07-106010-3

4 5 6 7 8 9 TCP 1 9 8 7

Printed and bound in Canada

Care has been taken to trace ownership of copyright material contained in this text. The publishers will gladly accept any information that will enable them to rectify any reference or credit in subsequent printings.

EXECUTIVE PUBLISHER: Lenore Brooks
PROJECT MANAGER: Jane McNulty
SENIOR PROGRAM CONSULTANT: Jonathan Bocknek
DEVELOPMENTAL EDITORS: Michelle Anderson, Vicki Austin, Jonathan Bocknek, Lois Edwards, Katherine Hamilton, Tina Hopper, Julie Karner, Charlotte Kelchner, Christine Weber
MANAGING EDITOR: Crystal Shortt
SUPERVISING EDITOR: Janie Deneau
COPY EDITORS: Dianne Brassolotto, May Look, Paul McNulty, Alexandra Venter
PHOTO RESEARCH/PERMISSIONS: Linda Tanaka
REVIEW COORDINATOR: Jennifer Keay
EDITORIAL ASSISTANT: Michelle Malda
EDITORIAL INTERN: Daniel McDonald
MANAGER, PRODUCTION SERVICES: Yolanda Pigden
PRODUCTION COORDINATOR: Sheryl MacAdam
SET-UP PHOTOGRAPHY: David Tanaka
COVER DESIGN: Vince Satira
INTERIOR DESIGN: Vince Satira
ELECTRONIC PAGE MAKE-UP: Word & Image Design Studio, Inc.
COVER IMAGES: ©Neil Beer, Getty Images; Dmitriy, Shutterstock Images

Acknowledgements

Pedagogical Reviewers

Sean Addis
Upper Canada District School Board

Richard Beddoe
York Catholic District School Board

Frank Behrend
Toronto District School Board

Meredith Cammisuli
Halton District School Board

Louise Cheung
Toronto Catholic District School Board

Debbie Freitag
Niagara Catholic District School Board

Stewart Grant
Toronto District School Board

Christine Hazell
Grand Erie District School Board

Ryan Imgrund
York Catholic District School Board

Antoni Jakubczak
Ottawa Catholic School Board

Diane Lavigne
Niagara Catholic District School Board

Sara McCormick
Peel District School Board

Karrilyn McPhee
Halton District School Board

Robert Miller
Ottawa Catholic School Board

Nadine Morrison
Hamilton-Wentworth District School Board

Chris Schramek
London District Catholic School Board

Sarah Vurma
Simcoe County District School Board

Accuracy Reviewers

R. Tom Baker
University of Ottawa

Dr. John Carran
Queen's University

Kevin M. Jaansalu
Royal Military College of Canada

Dr. Jeff Landry
McMaster University

Professor Yingfu Li
McMaster University

Safety Reviewer

Brian Heimbecker
Dufferin-Peel Catholic District School Board

Lab Testers

Katy Farrow
Thames Valley District School Board

Trevor Finkle
York Region District School Board

Antoni Jakubczak
Ottawa Catholic School Board

Philip Snider
Lambton-Kent District School Board

Bias Reviewer

Nancy Christoffer
Markham, Ontario

Catholicity Reviewer

Rado A. Krevs
Toronto Catholic District School Board

Answer Checkers

Tisha Barnes
District School Board of Niagara

Laura Benninger
University of Ontario Institute of Technology

Dr. Santo D'Agostino
St. Catharines, Ontario

Joe Engemann
Brock University

Sara McCormick
Peel District School Board

Special Feature Writers

Geula Bernstein

Emily Chung

Paul McNulty

Sharon Oosthoek

Christine Weber

Unit Project Writers

Katy Farrow

Christine Weber

Contents

Safety in the Chemistry Lab and Classroom xiv

Unit 1 Organic Chemistry 2

Unit 1 Preparation 4

Chapter 1 **Structure and Physical Properties of Organic Compounds** 6
    1.1 Introducing Organic Compounds 8
    1.2 Hydrocarbons 15
    1.3 Hydrocarbon Derivatives 42
    Chapter 1 Summary 86
    Chapter 1 Review 87
    Chapter 1 Self-Assessment 92

Chapter 2 **Reactions of Organic Compounds** 94
    2.1 Types of Organic Reactions 96
    2.2 Polymer Equations 116
    Chapter 2 Summary 136
    Chapter 2 Review 137
    Chapter 2 Self-Assessment 142

Unit 1 Project 144

Unit 1 Summary 146

Unit 1 Review 147

Unit 1 Self-Assessment 154

Unit 2 Structure and Properties of Matter 156

Unit 2 Preparation 158

Chapter 3 **Atomic Models and Properties of Atoms** 162
- **3.1** Developing a Nuclear Model of the Atom 164
- **3.2** The Quantum Mechanical Model of the Atom 174
- **3.3** Electron Configurations and the Periodic Table 181
- Chapter 3 Summary 198
- Chapter 3 Review 199
- Chapter 3 Self-Assessment 204

Chapter 4 **Chemical Bonding and Properties of Matter** 206
- **4.1** Models of Chemical Bonding 208
- **4.2** Shapes, Intermolecular Forces, and Properties of Molecules 228
- Chapter 4 Summary 252
- Chapter 4 Review 253
- Chapter 4 Self-Assessment 258

Unit 2 Project 260

Unit 2 Summary 262

Unit 2 Review 263

Unit 2 Self-Assessment 268

Unit 3   Energy Changes and Rates of Reaction ... 270

Unit 3 Preparation ... 272

Chapter 5   **Energy Changes** ... 276
    5.1 The Nature of Energy and Heat ... 278
    5.2 Thermochemical Equations and Calorimetry ... 292
    5.3 Hess's Law ... 312
    5.4 Energy Efficiency and Energy Resources ... 325
    Chapter 5 Summary ... 342
    Chapter 5 Review ... 343
    Chapter 5 Self-Assessment ... 350

Chapter 6   **Rates of Reaction** ... 352
    6.1 Chemical Reaction Rates ... 354
    6.2 Collision Theory and Factors Affecting Rates of Reaction ... 365
    6.3 Reaction Rates and Reaction Mechanisms ... 380
    Chapter 6 Summary ... 391
    Chapter 6 Review ... 392
    Chapter 6 Self-Assessment ... 398

Unit 3 Project ... 400

Unit 3 Summary ... 402

Unit 3 Review ... 403

Unit 3 Self-Assessment ... 410

Unit 4 Chemical Systems and Equilibrium ... 412

Unit 4 Preparation ... 414

Chapter 7 **Chemical Equilibrium** ... 418
- **7.1** Chemical Systems in Balance ... 420
- **7.2** The Effects of External Changes on Equilibrium ... 432
- **7.3** Calculating Equilibrium Constants ... 442
- **7.4** Applications of Equilibrium Systems ... 463
- **Chapter 7 Summary** ... 481
- **Chapter 7 Review** ... 482
- **Chapter 7 Self-Assessment** ... 488

Chapter 8 **Acid-Base Equilibrium Systems** ... 490
- **8.1** Understanding Acid-Base Equilibrium ... 492
- **8.2** Acid-Base Strength and Acid Dissociation ... 504
- **8.3** Base Ionization ... 519
- **8.4** Salts, Buffers, Titrations, and Solubility ... 528
- **Chapter 8 Summary** ... 558
- **Chapter 8 Review** ... 559
- **Chapter 8 Self-Assessment** ... 564

Unit 4 Project ... 566

Unit 4 Summary ... 568

Unit 4 Review ... 569

Unit 4 Self-Assessment ... 574

Unit 5 Electrochemistry 576

Unit 5 Preparation 578

Chapter 9   Oxidation-Reduction Reactions 582
    9.1 Characterizing Oxidation and Reduction 584
    9.2 Redox Reactions Involving Ionic Compounds 590
    9.3 Redox Reactions Involving Molecular Compounds 603
    Chapter 9 Summary 623
    Chapter 9 Review 624
    Chapter 9 Self-Assessment 630

Chapter 10   Electrochemical Cells 632
    10.1 Galvanic Cells 634
    10.2 Applications of Galvanic Cells 649
    10.3 Driving Non-spontaneous Reactions 660
    Chapter 10 Summary 676
    Chapter 10 Review 677
    Chapter 10 Self-Assessment 682

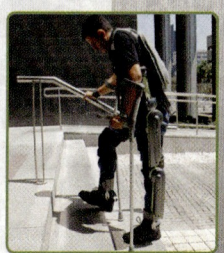

Unit 5 Project 684

Unit 5 Summary 686

Unit 5 Review 687

Unit 5 Self-Assessment 692

Guide to the Appendices 694

Appendix A: Science Skills 695

Appendix B: Useful References 730

Appendix C: Answers to Selected Questions and Problems 751

Glossary 796

Index 805

Credits 813

Activities and Investigations

Activities

Chapter 1
- 1.1 Organic Isomers 13
- 1.2 Sniffing Out Cancer 23
- 1.3 Rings Around You 39
- 1.4 CFCs: A Chilling Issue 46
- 1.5 Polybrominated Diphenyl Ethers 66

Chapter 2
- 2.1 Identifying Compounds Using Oxidation Reactions 113
- 2.2 Environmentally-friendly Alternatives to Polystyrene 124

Chapter 3
- 3.1 The "Birth" of Quanta and Photons 170

Chapter 4
- 4.1 Exploring the Packing Efficiency of Spheres 219
- 4.2 Applying VSEPR Theory 240
- 4.3 Canadian Contributions to Molecular Geometry 246

Chapter 5
- 5.1 Make Your Own Hot Pack or Cold Pack 287
- 5.2 Determining the Temperature of a Bunsen Burner Flame or Hot Plate 302
- 5.3 Comparing Propane-driven and Gasoline-driven Cars 330

Chapter 6
- 6.1 Calculating Reaction Rates 357
- 6.2 Chlorofluorocarbons as Catalysts in Ozone Depletion 376
- 6.3 Graphical Analysis of Reaction Rates vs. Concentration 382

Chapter 7
- 7.1 LeChâtelier's Principle: Response of an Equilibrium System to Stress ... 439
- 7.2 Data Analysis: Calculating an Equilibrium Constant 455
- 7.3 The Haber-Bosch Process: Synthesizing Ammonia 468

Chapter 8
- 8.1 The Chemistry of Oven Cleaning 524
- 8.2 Analyzing a Weak Acid-Strong Base Titration 540

Chapter 9
- 9.1 Using Lewis Structures to Assign Oxidation Numbers 607

Chapter 10
- 10.1 Make a Potato Clock 637
- 10.2 Modelling Corrosion Prevention 658

Investigations

Inquiry Investigation 1-A Modelling Organic Compounds 83
ThoughtLab Investigation 1-B Alternatives for Potentially Hazardous Products 84
Inquiry Investigation 2-A Oxidation of Alcohols 128
Inquiry Investigation 2-B Preparing Esters 130
Inquiry Investigation 2-C Modelling and Making Polymers 132
Inquiry Investigation 3-A Observing Spectra 195
Inquiry Investigation 3-B Electronic Structures for Period 3 Elements 196
ThoughtLab Investigation 3-C Extending the Periodic Table 197
Plan Your Own Investigation 4-A Predicting and Testing for Bonding in Solids 248
Plan Your Own Investigation 4-B Bonding in an Unknown Solid 249
Plan Your Own Investigation 5-A Determining the Enthalpy of a Neutralization Reaction 336
Inquiry Investigation 5-B Hess's Law and the Enthalpy of Combustion of Magnesium 338
Plan Your Own Investigation 6-A Examining Reaction Rates 388
Plan Your Own Investigation 6-B The Effect of a Catalyst on the Decomposition of H_2O_2 389
ThoughtLab 6-C Exploring Catalysts in Industry 390
Inquiry Investigation 7-A Simulating Dynamic Equilibrium 472
Plan Your Own Investigation 7-B How Does an Equilibrium System Respond to
Changing Conditions? 474
Inquiry Investigation 7-C Using Experimental Data to Determine an Equilibrium Constant 476
Inquiry Investigation 8-A Determining K_{sp} for Calcium Hydroxide 551
Inquiry Investigation 8-B Determining K_a for Ethanoic (Acetic) Acid 552
Inquiry Investigation 8-C Preparing a Buffer and Investigating Its Properties 554
Inquiry Investigation 9-A Testing Relative Oxidizing and Reducing Strengths of
Metal Atoms and Ions 618
Inquiry Investigation 9-B Redox Reactions and Balanced Equations 620
ThoughtLab Investigation 9-C Assessing Antioxidant Supplements 622
Inquiry Investigation 10-A Measuring Cell Potentials of Galvanic Cells 670
ThoughtLab Investigation 10-B Health and Safety Issues Involving Corrosion 672

STSE Special Features

Chemistry Connections

Green Chemistry and the Reduction of Hexane Use 40
Trans Fats in the Diet...114
Green Solvents 226
Deep Water Cooling 334
Inside a Catalytic Converter: Car Pollution Solution? 378
Chelation: Removing Heavy Metals from the Body 441
Hemoglobin Rises to the Challenge 479
How Green Is White Paper?..616

Case Studies

Organic Compounds in Everyday Life 134
Nanoparticles and Their Properties 250
Comparing Ethanol and Biodiesel 340
Site Remediation 556
Electrochemical Technologies 674

Canadian Research in Action

Producing Polyurethane from Plant-based Hydrocarbon Derivatives............81
Enhanced MRI Images and Epilepsy Research.................................194
Investigating the Thermodynamics of Aqueous Solutions 310
Applying Equilibrium Principles to Improve Cancer Treatment.................480
Energizing a Greener World 668

Safety in the Chemistry Lab and Classroom

To make the investigations and activities in *Chemistry 12* safe and enjoyable for you and others,

- become familiar with and use safety rules and procedures
- follow any special instructions from your teacher
- *always read* the safety notes before beginning each activity or investigation. Your teacher will tell you about any additional safety rules that are in place at your school.

WHMIS Symbols for Hazardous Materials

Look carefully at the WHMIS (Workplace Hazardous Materials Information System) safety symbols shown here. The WHMIS symbols and the associated safety data sheets (SDS) are used throughout Canada to identify dangerous materials. These symbols and the material safety data sheets help you understand all aspects of safe handling of hazardous materials. Your school is required to have these sheets available for all chemicals, and they can also be found by doing an Internet search.

Note: Symbols updated in 2016 to support WHMIS 2015 and GHS

Safety Symbols

Be sure you understand each symbol used in an activity or investigation before you begin.

	Disposal Alert This symbol appears when care must be taken to dispose of materials properly.
	Thermal Safety This symbol appears as a reminder to be careful when handling hot objects.
	Sharp Object Safety This symbol appears when there is danger of cuts or punctures caused by the use of sharp objects.
	Fume Safety This symbol appears when chemicals or chemical reactions could cause dangerous fumes.
	Electrical Safety This symbol appears as a reminder to be careful when using electrical equipment.
	Skin Protection Safety This symbol appears when the use of caustic chemicals might irritate the skin or when contact with micro-organisms might transmit infection.
	Clothing Protection Safety This symbol appears as a reminder that a lab coat or apron should be worn during the activity.
	Fire Safety This symbol appears as a reminder to be careful around open flames.
	Eye Safety This symbol appears when there is danger to the eyes and chemical safety goggles should be worn.
	Poison Safety This symbol appears when poisonous substances are used.
	Chemical Safety This symbol appears when chemicals could cause burns or are poisonous if absorbed through the skin.

General Precautions

- Always wear chemical safety goggles and a lab coat or apron in the laboratory. Wear other protective equipment, such as gloves, as directed by your teacher or by the Safety Precautions at the beginning of each investigation.

- Inform your teacher if you wear contact lenses. Generally, contact lenses should not be worn in the laboratory. If possible, wear eyeglasses instead of contact lenses, but remember that eyeglasses are not a substitute for proper eye protection. Always wear appropriate eye and face protection over your contacts or eye glasses when working in the laboratory.

- Know the location and proper use of the nearest fire extinguisher, fire blanket, fire alarm, first aid kit, eyewash station, and drench hose/shower. Read "Fire Safety" on

the next page and discuss with your teacher what type of fire-fighting equipment should be used on particular types of fires.
- Do not wear open-toed shoes or sandals in the laboratory. Accessories may get caught on equipment or present a hazard when working with a Bunsen burner. Ties, scarves, long necklaces, and dangling earrings should be removed before starting an investigation.
- Tie back long hair and any loose clothing before starting an investigation.
- Lighters and matches must not be brought into the laboratory.
- Food, drinks, and gum must not be brought into the laboratory.
- Inform your teacher if you have any allergies, medical conditions, or physical problems (including hearing impairment) that could affect your work in the laboratory.

Before Beginning Laboratory Investigations
- Listen carefully to the instructions that your teacher gives you. Do not begin work until your teacher has finished giving instructions.
- Obtain your teacher's approval before beginning any investigation that you have designed yourself.
- Read through all of the steps in the investigation before beginning. If there are any steps that you do not understand, ask your teacher for help.
- Be sure to read and understand the Safety Precautions at the start of each investigation.
- Always wear appropriate protective clothing and equipment, as directed by your teacher and the Safety Precautions.
- Be sure that you understand all safety labels on materials and equipment. Familiarize yourself with the material safety data sheets (MSDS) and WHMIS symbols for the materials used in the laboratory.
- Make sure that your work area is clean and dry.

During Laboratory Investigations
- Make sure that you understand and follow the safety procedures for different types of laboratory equipment. Do not hesitate to ask your teacher for clarification if necessary.
- Never work alone in the laboratory.
- Remember that gestures or movements that may seem harmless could have dangerous consequences in the laboratory. For example, tapping people lightly on the shoulder to get their attention could startle them. If they are holding a beaker that contains an acid, for example, the results could be very serious.
- Make an effort to work slowly and steadily in the laboratory. Be sure to make room for other students.
- Organize materials and equipment neatly and logically. For example, place materials where you will not have to reach behind or over a Bunsen burner to get them. Keep your bags and books off your work surface and out of the way.
- Never taste any substances in the laboratory.
- Never touch a chemical with your bare hands.
- Never draw liquids or any other substances into a pipette or a tube with your mouth.
- If you are asked to smell a substance, do not hold it directly under your nose. Keep the object at least 20 cm away from your nose. Gently waft the fumes towards your nostrils with your hands, taking care to not inhale deeply.
- Label all containers holding chemicals. Do not use chemicals from unlabelled containers.
- Hold containers away from your face when pouring liquids or mixing reactants.
- If any part of your body comes in contact with a potentially dangerous substance, report it to your teacher immediately. Wash the affected area immediately and thoroughly with water.
- If you get any material in your eyes, do not rub them. Wash your eyes immediately and continuously for 15 minutes at the nearest eyewash station, and make sure that your teacher is informed. A doctor should examine any eye injury. It is recommended not to wear contact lenses when working with chemicals and it would be better to take them out if possible prior to using an eyewash. Failing to do so may result in the contact lenses doing further damage to your eyes or having material become trapped behind the contact lenses. Flush your eyes with water for 15 minutes, as above.
- Do not touch your face or eyes while in the laboratory unless you have first washed your hands.
- If your clothing catches fire, STOP, DROP, and ROLL. Other students may use the fire blanket to smother the flames. Do not wrap the fire blanket around yourself while in a standing position. This could result in a "chimney effect," bringing fire directly into a person's face.

- Do not look directly into a test tube, flask, or the barrel of a Bunsen burner.
- If you see any of your classmates jeopardizing their safety or the safety of others, let your teacher know.

Heat Source Safety

- When heating any item, wear safety eyewear, heat-resistant safety gloves, and any other safety equipment that your teacher or the Safety Precautions suggest.
- Always use heat-proof, intact containers. Check that there are no large or small cracks in beakers or flasks.
- Never point the open end of a container, such as a test tube, that is being heated in a direction that could cause injury. The mouth of the container or test tube should point away from you and from others.
- Do not allow a container to boil dry unless specifically instructed to do so.
- Handle hot objects carefully. Be especially careful with a hot plate that may look as though it has cooled down, or glassware that has recently been heated.
- Before using a Bunsen burner, make sure that you understand how to light and operate it safely. Always pick it up by the base. Never leave a Bunsen burner unattended.
- Before lighting a Bunsen burner, make sure that there are no flammable solvents nearby.
- Always have the Bunsen burner secured to a utility stand.

Use EXTREME CAUTION around an open flame.

- If you do receive a burn, run cold water over the burned area immediately. Make sure that your teacher is notified.
- Remember that cold objects can also harm you. Wear appropriate gloves when handling an extremely cold object.

Electrical Equipment Safety

- Make sure that the work area and the area of the socket are dry.
- Make sure that your hands are dry when touching electrical cords, plugs, sockets, or equipment.
- When unplugging electrical equipment, do not pull the cord. Grasp the plug firmly at the socket and pull gently.
- Place electrical cords in places where people will not trip over them.
- Use an appropriate length of cord for your needs. Cords that are too short may be stretched in unsafe ways. Cords that are too long may tangle or trip people.
- Never use water to fight an electrical equipment fire. Severe electrical shock may result. Use a carbon dioxide or dry chemical fire extinguisher. (See "Fire Safety" below.)
- Report any damaged equipment or frayed cords to your teacher.

Glassware and Sharp Objects Safety

- Cuts or scratches in the chemistry laboratory should receive immediate medical attention, no matter how minor they seem. Alert your teacher immediately.
- Never use your hands to pick up broken glass. Use a broom and dustpan. Dispose of broken glass in the "Broken Glass Container." Do not put broken glassware into the garbage can.
- Cut away from yourself and others when using a knife or another sharp object.
- Always keep the pointed end of scissors and other sharp objects pointed away from yourself and others when walking.
- Do not use broken or chipped glassware. Report damaged equipment to your teacher.

Fire Safety

- Know the location and proper use of the nearest fire extinguisher, fire blanket, and fire alarm.
- Understand what type of fire extinguisher you have in the laboratory, and what type of fires it can be used on. (See details below.) Most fire extinguishers are the ABC type.

- Notify your teacher immediately about any fires or combustible hazards.
- Water should only be used on Class A fires. Class A fires involve ordinary flammable materials, such as paper and clothing. *Never use water* to fight an electrical fire, a fire that involves flammable liquids (such as gasoline), or a fire that involves burning metals (such as potassium or magnesium).
- Fires that involve a flammable liquid, such as gasoline or alcohol (Class B fires), must be extinguished with a dry chemical or carbon dioxide fire extinguisher.
- Live electrical equipment fires (Class C) must be extinguished with a dry chemical or carbon dioxide fire extinguisher. Fighting electrical equipment fires with water can cause severe electric shock.
- Class D fires involve burning metals, such as potassium and magnesium. A Class D fire should be extinguished using a class D extinguisher or by smothering it with dry sand. Adding water to a metal fire can cause a violent chemical reaction.
- If your hair or clothes catch on fire, STOP, DROP, and ROLL. Other students may use the fire blanket to smother the flames. Do not wrap the fire blanket around yourself while in a standing position. This would result in a "chimney effect," bringing fire directly into a person's face. Do not discharge a fire extinguisher at someone's head.

Clean-Up and Disposal in the Laboratory

- Small spills should be cleaned up immediately, as directed by your teacher.
- Large spills require clean-up by a trained individual with the aid of an appropriate spill control kit.
- If you spill acid or base on your skin or clothing, wash the affected area immediately with a lot of cool water.
- You can neutralize spills of acid solutions with sodium hydrogen carbonate (baking soda). You can neutralize spills of basic solutions with sodium hydrogen sulfate or citric acid.
- Clean equipment before putting it away, as directed by your teacher.
- Dispose of materials as directed by your teacher, in accordance with your local school board's policies. Do not dispose of materials in a sink or a drain. Always dispose of them in a special container, as directed by your teacher.
- Wash your hands thoroughly after all laboratory investigations.

Safety in Your On-line Activities

The Internet is like any other resource you use for research—you should confirm the source of the information and the credentials of those supplying it to make sure the information is credible before you use it in your work. Unlike other resources, however, the Internet has some unique pitfalls you should be aware of, and practices you should follow.

- When you copy or save something from the Internet, you could be saving more than information. Be aware that information you pick up could also include hidden, malicious soft ware code (known as "worms" or "Trojans") that could damage your computer system or destroy data.
- Avoid sites that contain material that is disturbing, illegal, harmful, and/or was created by exploiting others.
- *Never* give out personal information on-line. Protect your privacy, even if it means not registering to use a site that looks helpful. Discuss with your teacher ways to use the site while protecting your privacy.
- Report to your teacher any on-line content or activity that you suspect is inappropriate or illegal.

> **Instant Practice**
>
> 1. One of the materials you plan to use in a Plan Your Own Investigation bears the following symbols:
>
>
>
>   Describe the safety precautions you would need to incorporate into your investigation.
>
> 2. On-line research also comes with safety hazards. Describe the safety practices you would follow when conducting Internet research to find MSDS information on laboratory chemicals.

UNIT 1
Organic Chemistry

BIG IDEAS

- Organic compounds have predictable chemical and physical properties determined by their respective structures.
- Organic chemical reactions and their applications have significant implications for society, human health, and the environment.

Overall Expectations

In this unit, you will…

- **assess** the social and environmental impact of organic compounds used in everyday life, and **propose** a course of action to reduce the use of compounds that are harmful to human health and the environment
- **investigate** organic compounds and organic chemical reactions, and **use** various methods to represent the compounds
- **demonstrate** an understanding of the structure, properties, and chemical behaviour of compounds within each class of organic compounds

Unit Contents

Chapter 1
Structure and Physical Properties of Organic Compounds

Chapter 2
Reactions of Organic Compounds

Focussing Questions

1. What are the characteristics of organic compounds?
2. What are the general structures and physical properties of hydrocarbons and hydrocarbon derivatives?
3. What types of reactions do organic compounds undergo?

Go to **scienceontario** to find out more about organic chemistry

Scientists describe life on Earth as carbon-based. This description reflects the fact that the organic molecules that comprise living organisms are made of carbon atoms that are bonded to other carbon atoms, to hydrogen atoms, and to atoms of a few other elements such as oxygen and nitrogen. Organic molecules may define life, but there are many other non-life-related organic molecules. In addition, organic molecules are not limited to planet Earth. For example, analysis of meteorites like the one shown in the inset photograph has revealed the presence of organic molecules that include amino acids, nucleic acids, sugars, and carboxylic acids—all molecules that make up organisms. Other organic molecules detected in space include hydrocarbon molecules such as methane, and hydrocarbon derivatives, such as methanol and formaldehyde. Some of these organic molecules have even been detected in star systems millions of light years from Earth. For example, the galaxy shown in the photograph is 12 million light years from Earth and contains polycyclic aromatic hydrocarbons, molecules that are essential to life. As you investigate organic molecules and their interactions in this unit, think about their importance as the building blocks of living things as well as how the products derived from them affect your daily life.

As you study this unit, look ahead to the Unit 1 Project on pages 144 to 145. Complete the project in stages as you progress through the unit.

The Murchison meteorite, thought to be about 4.65 billion years old, hit Earth in Murchison, Australia in 1969. Since then scientists have extensively analyzed its chemistry, finding over 90 amino acids. To date, only nineteen of these amino acids can be found on Earth.

UNIT 1 Preparation

Safety in the Chemistry Laboratory and Classroom

- Always wear protective clothing, such as safety eyewear and a lab coat or apron, when using materials that could splash, shatter, or release dust.
- Know which safety equipment, such as a fire blanket, a fire extinguisher, and an eyewash station, are available and where they are located in your classroom.
- Know the proper procedures for using the available safety equipment. For example, if the hair or clothing of another student catches fire, that student should STOP, DROP, and ROLL while other students use the fire blanket to smother the flames.
- If you get something in your eyes, do not touch them. Use the eyewash station to flush your eyes with water for 15 min, and make sure that someone tells your teacher.
- Follow all instructions for proper disposal of broken glass and chemicals to prevent injury.
- WHMIS (Workplace Hazardous Materials Information System) symbols are used in Canadian schools and workplaces to identify dangerous materials.
- Always review any relevant MSDS (material safety data sheet) information before beginning an investigation.

1. Which safety equipment should you use if a chemical has splashed into your eyes?
   a. lab apron
   b. protective gloves
   c. fire blanket
   d. safety eyewear
   e. eyewash station

2. Which list of safety equipment includes only equipment that is used after an accident occurs?
   a. a lab apron and protective gloves
   b. protective gloves and a fire blanket
   c. a fire extinguisher and a lab apron
   d. safety eyewear and an eyewash station
   e. an eyewash station and a fire extinguisher

3. Draw a safety map of your classroom. Include a key that identifies the locations of lab aprons, safety eyewear, a fire blanket, a fire extinguisher, and an eyewash station.

4. Examine the fire extinguisher that is available in your classroom. Write a script for a short video that explains the steps needed to use the fire extinguisher.

5. An investigation involves testing how well common kitchen chemicals dissolve in water. Your lab partner thinks that safety eyewear and a lab apron are not necessary. Write an explanation you could use to persuade your lab partner of the necessity of wearing these two pieces of protective clothing.

6. Why is a special container for the disposal of broken glass important?

7. Which WHMIS symbol would you expect to see on a material that is corrosive?

   a.   d.

   b.   e.

   c.

8. Describe what you can do to reduce your risk of injury when working with the type of material represented by each WHMIS symbol in the answers to question 7.

9. Name the WHMIS symbol that would be used for each of the following chemicals.
   a. carbon monoxide
   b. gasoline
   c. hydrochloric acid
   d. helium

Chemical Bonds and Physical Properties

- A covalent bond forms when two atoms share one or more pairs of valence electrons.
- An ionic bond forms when a negatively charged ion and a positively charged ion are attracted to each other.
- The strength of the attractive forces acting between ions or molecules, referred to as intermolecular forces, determines the melting point and the boiling point of a compound.
- Ionic compounds usually have the highest melting points and boiling points. Polar molecules have intermediate melting points and boiling points, and non-polar molecules have the lowest melting points and boiling points.
- Ionic and polar compounds are likely to be soluble in water. Non-polar compounds are insoluble in water.

10. Define the following terms.
    a. covalent bond
    b. molecular compound
    c. ionic bond
    d. melting point
    e. boiling point

11. Which statement about the properties of compounds is true?
    a. A compound that has a very high melting point is a liquid at room temperature.
    b. Ionic bonds are stronger than intermolecular forces.
    c. Non-polar molecules experience no intermolecular forces.
    d. A compound that has a very low boiling point is a liquid at room temperature.
    e. Dipole-dipole forces are stronger than the force between oppositely charged ions.

12. Which compound is *most* likely to be soluble in water?
    a. a non-polar compound
    b. a slightly polar compound
    c. a polar compound
    d. an ionic compound
    e. all of the above

13. Explain why compounds consisting of polar molecules are likely to have a higher melting point than compounds consisting of non-polar molecules.

14. List the following compounds in the order of their boiling points, from lowest to highest, without knowing any exact boiling points. Explain your reasoning for your order, based on the structures given.

    methanol   chlorine   potassium oxide

Combustion Reactions

- A combustion reaction of a substance with oxygen produces one or more oxides. Energy, in the form of heat and light, is released.
- A hydrocarbon is a compound that is composed of only the elements hydrogen and carbon. The combustion of a hydrocarbon can be either complete or incomplete.
- The products of complete combustion reactions are carbon dioxide and water vapour.
- The products of incomplete combustion reactions include carbon, carbon monoxide, carbon dioxide, and water vapour.

15. In a laboratory investigation, what evidence might indicate that a combustion reaction is occurring?

16. Would the presence of excess oxygen cause hazardous products to be formed during combustion? Explain your reasoning.

17. What are the reactants in a complete combustion reaction?

18. The candle flame shown here is an example of incomplete combustion.
    a. Describe incomplete combustion.
    b. Explain why incomplete combustion is potentially hazardous.

CHAPTER 1
Structure and Physical Properties of Organic Compounds

Specific Expectations

In this chapter, you will learn how to …

- B1.1 **assess** the impact on human health, society, and the environment of organic compounds used in everyday life

- B2.1 **use** appropriate terminology related to organic chemistry

- B2.2 **use** International Union of Pure and Applied Chemistry (IUPAC) nomenclature conventions to **identify** names, **write** chemical formulas, and **create** structural formulas for the different classes of organic compounds

- B2.3 **build** molecular models for a variety of simple organic compounds

- B3.1 **compare** the different classes of organic compounds by describing the similarities and differences in names and structural formulas of the compounds within each class

- B3.2 **describe** the similarities and differences in physical properties within each class of organic compounds

- B3.5 **explain** the concept of isomerism in organic compounds and how variations in the properties of isomers relate to their structural and molecular formulas

The chemical composition of birch bark, the distinctly white bark of a paper birch tree, makes it useful for many things, including making canoes. Birch bark contains an organic compound called betulin that makes the bark waterproof—a fact that Canada's Aboriginal peoples have used to their advantage in the construction of canoes. More recently, chemists have been testing the medicinal properties of betulin and have found its antiviral properties to be effective against herpes simplex virus type 1 and type 2, as well as HIV. Birch bark also contains betulinic acid, a natural derivative of betulin. Research has shown that betulinic acid is effective at inhibiting the growth of melanoma cancer cells in humans. Scientists are working to synthesize potentially life-saving medications from betulin and its derivatives.

Another, more familiar organic compound, salicylic acid, was isolated from birch bark more than 100 years ago. In 1893, when Felix Hoffmann synthesized acetylsalicylic acid from salicylic acid, it was the first truly synthetic medication and the start of a multi-billion dollar global business. You likely know this drug better by its trade name, Aspirin®. How do chemists modify a natural compound to produce a synthetic compound? What are some of the risks and benefits of producing organic compounds? In this chapter, you will examine the nature of organic compounds and the features that determine their use.

Launch Activity

Organic or Inorganic: What's the Difference?

For hundreds of years scientists have classified compounds as organic or inorganic. Right now you are surrounded by various organic and inorganic compounds, such as plastics and water, and compounds in food and air. In this activity, you will try to identify the main differences between organic and inorganic compounds.

Materials
- structural diagrams of certain compounds
- molecular modelling kit (optional)

betulin

betulinic acid

ethane C_2H_6; water H_2O; carbon tetrachloride CCl_4; ammonia; propanal C_3H_6O; carbon dioxide CO_2; sulfur dioxide SO_2; propan-1-amine C_3H_9N

Procedure

1. Each of the compounds shown above is either organic or inorganic. Study the diagrams of each compound. If asked by your teacher, create a molecular model of each compound.
2. Work in pairs to create a definition of an organic compound and an inorganic compound based on your observations in step 1. Explain your reasoning.
3. Compare your definitions with those of other groups in your class.
4. Your teacher will reveal which of the compounds are organic and which are inorganic.
5. Revise your definitions based on the new information.

Questions

1. The term *organic* is used in several different contexts. Identify some of the contexts in which the term is used. How are all of these contexts related?
2. Which characteristics do you think scientists currently use to classify organic and inorganic compounds?
3. Why do you think it is important to have a standard definition for organic compounds and inorganic compounds as well as a unique way to classify compounds into these two categories?

SECTION 1.1 Introducing Organic Compounds

Key Terms

organic compound
inorganic compound
isomer
constitutional isomer
stereoisomer
diastereomer
enantiomer

For hundreds of years, up to and including the 1800s, many influential thinkers believed that an invisible "vital energy" was a key part of the compounds that make up living organisms. People used the term "organic" to describe matter that was or that came from living matter, and the term "inorganic" was used to describe matter that was or that came from non-living matter.

This distinction between organic matter and inorganic matter had a powerful influence on the thinking of scientists for several hundred years. Scientists commonly assumed that a different set of scientific laws governed the identity and behaviour of living matter compared to non-living matter. For example, most scientists believed that organic compounds could come only from living organisms. In 1828, however, laboratory evidence showed that this belief was mistaken.

A German chemist, Friedrich Wöhler, was attempting to synthesize ammonium cyanate by reacting one inorganic compound, silver cyanate, with another inorganic compound, ammonium chloride. He was surprised to find that this reaction produced a white, crystalline substance with none of the chemical or physical properties of ammonium cyanate. The properties of this crystalline compound, as well as its molecular formula, were identical to those of a compound that had been isolated from the urine of mammals many years before: urea, shown in **Figure 1.1A**. At that time, chemists considered (correctly) ammonium cyanate to be inorganic and urea to be organic. Thus, Wöhler's synthesis demonstrated that organic matter could be synthesized from inorganic matter—at that time, a truly amazing discovery. Soon after, other chemists began to synthesize many organic compounds—such as acetic acid, methane, and ethanol—from inorganic compounds. By the late 1800s, it was clear to most scientists that all matter, regardless of its source or classification, behaved according to the same scientific laws. Organic matter and inorganic matter, they realized, are *not* fundamentally different from each other.

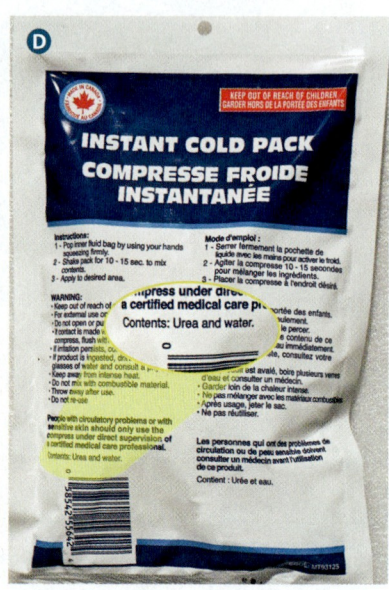

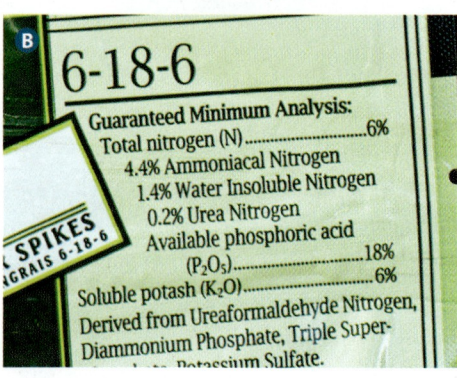

Figure 1.1 (**A**) Urea was the first organic compound to be synthesized from inorganic compounds, shattering the belief of scientists at the time that organic compounds could only come from living matter. Today, synthetic urea is used as (**B**) a fertilizer (due to the nitrogen it contains), in (**C**) hand creams to re-hydrate skin (because it binds with water), and in (**D**) instant cold packs (due to its endothermic reaction with ammonium chloride).

The Modern Definitions of Organic Compounds and Inorganic Compounds

As chemists developed a greater understanding of the organic compounds they were analyzing and synthesizing, they observed that all these compounds contained carbon atoms. The modern definition states that an **organic compound** is a type of compound in which carbon atoms are nearly always bonded to each other, to hydrogen atoms, and sometimes to atoms of a few specific elements. These elements are usually oxygen, nitrogen, sulfur, or phosphorus, as well as several others. This definition for organic compounds has several exceptions, however. These exceptions are carbonates (CO_3^{2-}), cyanides (CN^-), carbides (C_2^{2-}), and oxides of carbon (CO_2, CO). Even though these compounds contain carbon, they do not contain any carbon-carbon or carbon-hydrogen bonds. The exceptions, along with all compounds that do not contain carbon atoms, are classified as **inorganic compounds**.

organic compound
a type of compound in which carbon atoms are nearly always bonded to each other, to hydrogen atoms, and occasionally to atoms of a few specific elements

inorganic compound
a type of compound that includes carbonates, cyanides, carbides, and oxides of carbon, along with all compounds that do not contain carbon atoms

The Special Nature of the Carbon Atom

What is the nature of the carbon atom that allows it to form the foundation of all organic compounds and to be the basis of the thousands of molecules found in living organisms? Recall that a carbon atom has four valence electrons. Because it has exactly half of a filled outer shell of electrons and an intermediate electronegativity, a carbon atom is much more likely to share electrons than to gain or lose enough electrons to form ions. Having four valence electrons, a carbon atom can form covalent bonds with up to four other atoms. This property allows for a wide variety of molecules with differing structures and properties.

When a carbon atom is bonded to four different atoms, the resulting molecule has a specific shape that is often referred to as *tetrahedral*. **Figure 1.2** models this shape for the methane molecule in three common ways. **Figure 1.2A** is a ball-and-stick model. The blue lines connecting the hydrogen atoms form a tetrahedron. **Figure 1.2B** shows an easier way to sketch the shape. In both A and B, the carbon atom and the hydrogen atoms above and to the left of the carbon are in the same plane as the plane of the page. The lowest hydrogen atom is protruding from the page, and the hydrogen atom on the right is behind the page. **Figure 1.2C** is a space-filling model. When analyzing or drawing two-dimensional structural diagrams of organic compounds, keep the three-dimensional shape in mind, because it is the more accurate shape.

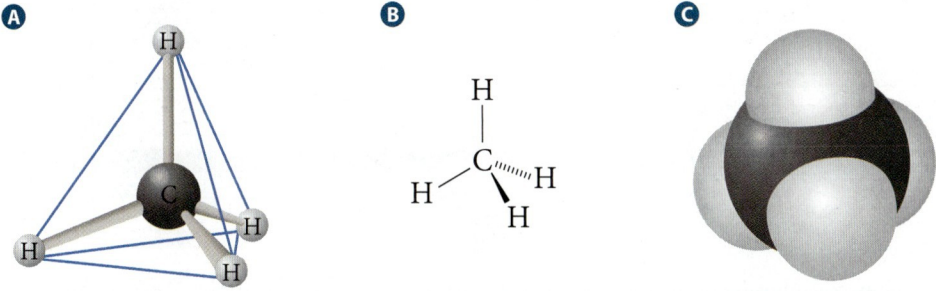

Figure 1.2 (**A**) In a tetrahedron, all of the sides, as well as the base, are identical equilateral triangles. For methane, shown here, the carbon atoms are at the centre of the tetrahedron, and the hydrogen atoms are on the vertices. (**B**) Notice that a dashed line is used to give the impression that an atom is behind the page, and a wedge is used to show an atom protruding from the page. (**C**) In this space-filling model of methane, the carbon atom is represented in black and the hydrogen atoms are in white.

Isomers

Carbon atoms can form bonds with each other, often resulting in very long straight or branched chains of carbon atoms. Each carbon atom in a chain is also bonded to hydrogen atoms or atoms of other elements. These structures provide the root for an extremely large number of compounds. For example, consider molecules containing five carbon atoms, all single-bonded to other carbon atoms or hydrogen atoms. **Figure 1.3** shows three different structures of molecules that can exhibit this combination of atoms. Notice that, despite being structurally different, these three molecules have the same molecular formula, because they have the same number of atoms of each element. Molecules that have the same molecular formula but with their atoms in a different arrangement are called **isomers** of each other. There are two main classes of isomers: constitutional isomers and stereoisomers.

isomers molecules that have the same molecular formula but their atoms are in a different arrangement

constitutional isomers molecules that have the same molecular formula but their atoms are bonded together in a different sequence

Constitutional Isomers

The isomers shown in **Figure 1.3** are constitutional isomers. **Constitutional isomers** are molecules that have the same molecular formula, but their atoms are bonded together in a different sequence. Another common term for constitutional isomer is *structural isomer*. For example, a molecule with 6 carbon atoms and 14 hydrogen atoms can form five constitutional isomers. A molecule with 10 carbon atoms and 22 hydrogen atoms can form 25 constitutional isomers. With 20 carbon atoms and 42 hydrogen atoms, 366 319 constitutional isomers are possible. And these data include only molecules with single bonds!

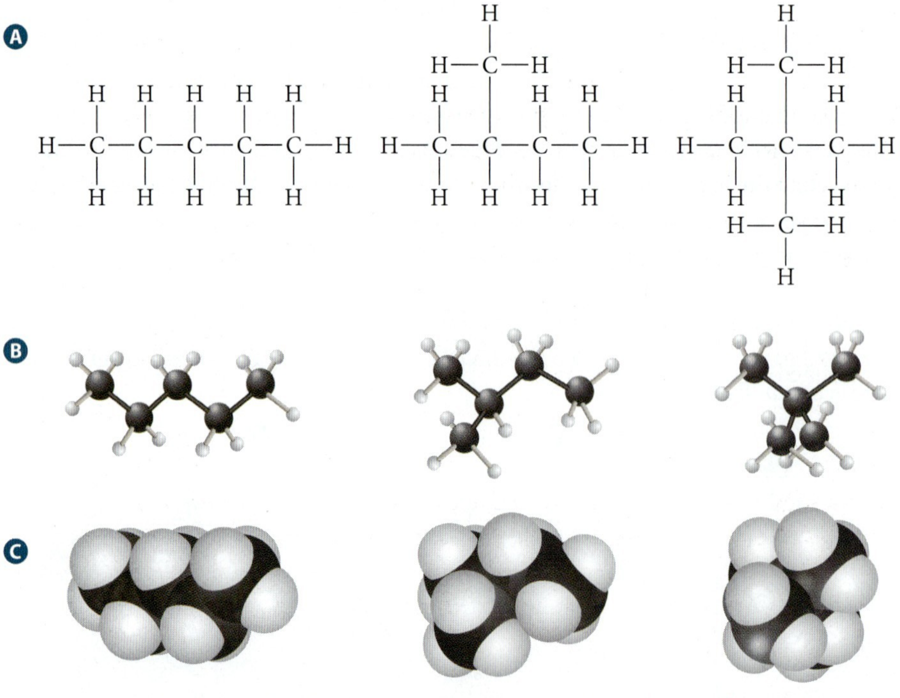

Figure 1.3 All of these molecules have the same molecular formula: C_5H_{12}. Because their atoms are bonded in a different sequence, they are constitutional isomers of each other. Their physical properties, such as boiling points, vary, as do their shapes. Structural diagrams are shown in (**A**). Ball-and-stick models are shown in (**B**), and space-filling models are shown in (**C**).

Now consider the molecules shown in **Figure 1.4**. Each of these molecules has five carbon atoms and 12 hydrogen atoms, but they are *not* isomers of the molecules in **Figure 1.3**. For example, **Figure 1.4A** is the same molecule as the middle one shown in **Figure 1.3A**. To see this, simply flip the image horizontally. Similarly, **Figures 1.4B** and **1.4C** are the same as the first molecule in **Figure 1.3A**, because atoms can freely rotate around a single bond.

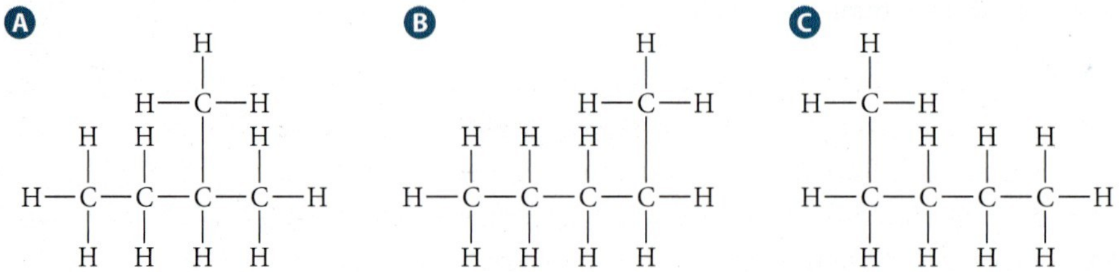

Figure 1.4 By flipping the molecule or rotating atoms around a single bond, you can see that these three structures are not isomers of the molecules shown in **Figure 1.3**.

In addition to straight or branched chains, carbon atoms also can form rings of three, four, five, six, or more atoms. **Figure 1.5** shows all possible ring structures that can be made with five carbon atoms. These molecules are all constitutional isomers of each other, as well as the molecules in **Figure 1.3**.

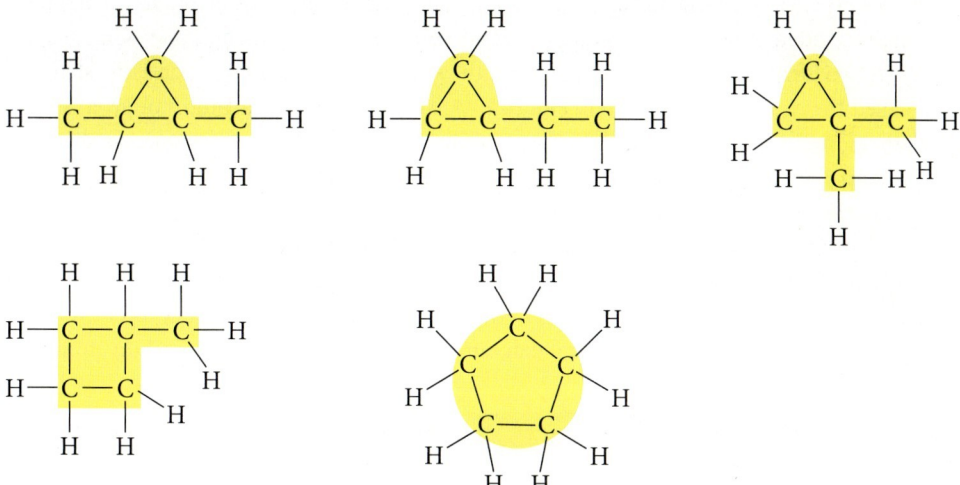

Figure 1.5 These five carbon molecules are all constitutional isomers. The coloured portions highlight the ring structures in these molecules. Ring structures are common in organic compounds.

Learning Check

1. Explain how the modern definition of the term *organic compound* differs from the definition this term had during the 1800s and earlier.
2. Describe the properties of a carbon atom that allow it to be the foundation of all organic compounds.
3. Using the modern definitions, explain what determines whether a carbon-containing molecule is classified as organic or inorganic.
4. Why do many organic compounds form a three-dimensional shape instead of a two-dimensional shape?
5. Draw two molecules that could be confused as constitutional isomers but are actually identical.
6. Draw all the constitutional isomers for a molecule with the formula C_7H_{16}.

Stereoisomers

Carbon atoms can form multiple bonds with other carbon atoms. **Figure 1.6** shows a structural diagram, a ball-and-stick model, and a space-filling model of a two-carbon compound with a double bond. An important property of this molecule is the inability of the atoms to rotate around the double bond. Therefore, this molecule is flat and rigid.

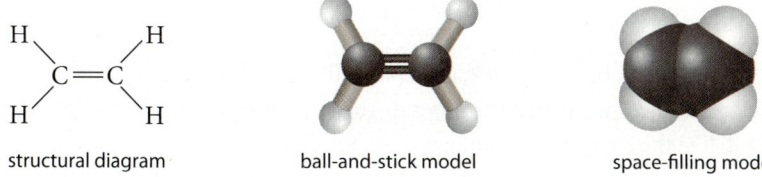

structural diagram   ball-and-stick model   space-filling model

Figure 1.6 Molecules with double bonds are flat and rigid, because their atoms cannot rotate around the double bond.

The rigidity of the structure of atoms around a double bond is one source of another type of isomer called a stereoisomer. **Stereoisomers** are molecules that have the same molecular formula and their atoms are bonded together in the same sequence. They differ, however, in the three-dimensional orientations of their atoms in space. There are two kinds of stereoisomers: diastereomers and enantiomers.

stereoisomers molecules that have the same molecular formula and their atoms are bonded together in the same sequence, but differ in the three-dimensional orientations of their atoms in space

Diastereomers

diastereomer a stereoisomer based on a double bond, in which different types of atoms or groups are bonded to each carbon in the double bond

Stereoisomers based on double bonds are called **diastereomers**. Diastereomers only form when each carbon atom involved in the double bond has different types of atoms or groups of atoms bonded to it. **Figure 1.7** shows the two diastereomers that can form when the double bond is in the middle of a four-carbon chain. Each carbon atom in the double bond is bonded to two unique atoms or groups: one hydrogen atom and one $-CH_3$ group. When two identical atoms or groups are on the same side of the double bond, the structure is called the *cis* isomer, as shown in **Figure 1.7A**. When two identical atoms or groups are on the opposite sides of the double bond, the structure is called a *trans* isomer, as shown in **Figure 1.7B**. If the double bonds were changed to single bonds, the atoms could rotate around the central C-C bond and the two molecules shown here would be identical.

All of the possible isomers containing five carbon atoms and ten hydrogen atoms are shown in **Figure 1.8**. Notice that structures A, B, and C do not form diastereomers. In each case, one of the carbon atoms involved in the double bond has identical atoms or groups bonded to it. In such cases, structural diagrams are often drawn with the carbon atoms in a straight line.

Figure 1.7 The double bonds prevent rotation around the carbon atoms, resulting in two separate orientations in space of the $-CH_3$ groups and H atoms. Thus, these molecules are diastereomers.

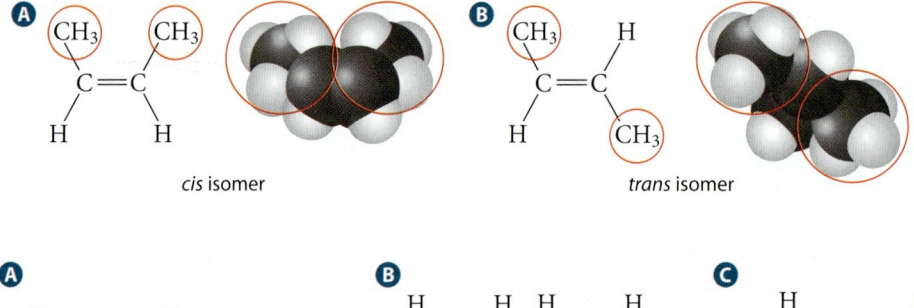

Figure 1.8 *Cis* (**D**) and *trans* (**E**) isomers can form only when each of the carbon atoms involved in the double bond has two different atoms or groups single bonded to it.

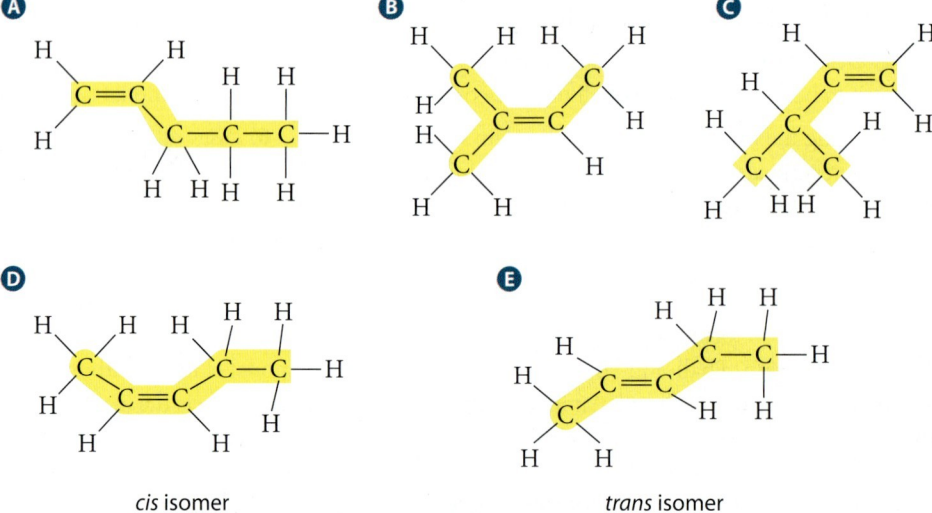

Figure 1.9 shows structural, ball-and-stick, and space-filling models of molecules in which two carbon atoms are joined with a triple bond. The structure around the triple bond is flat and rigid, like the structure around a double bond. Additionally, the triple bond structure is also linear. Therefore, diastereomers are not possible. However, longer chain molecules with triple bonds can still form constitutional isomers. **Figure 1.10** shows the constitutional isomers that can be formed from five carbon atoms and eight hydrogen atoms.

Figure 1.9 The structure around a triple bond is flat, rigid, and linear.

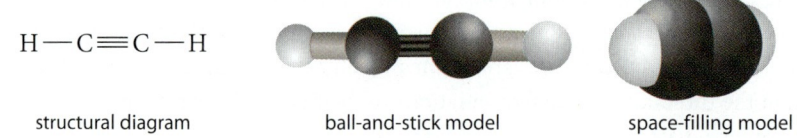

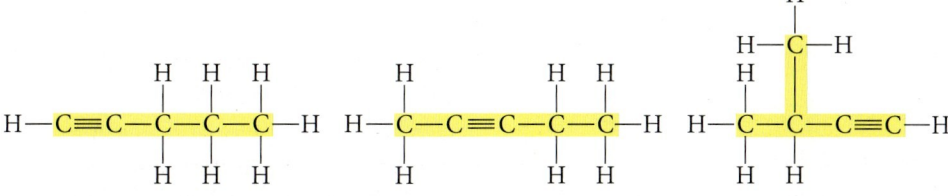

Figure 1.10 Although triple bonds do not form diastereomers, there are still three different possible constitutional isomers formed from five carbon atoms and eight hydrogen atoms.
Explain why triple bonds do not form diastereomers.

Enantiomers

Enantiomers are the second type of stereoisomers. **Enantiomers** are mirror images of each other around a single carbon atom. To form enantiomers, at least one carbon in the compound must be bonded to four different types of atoms or groups. **Figure 1.11A** shows a molecule with atoms of four different elements bonded to one carbon atom. Exchanging the hydrogen atom and the fluorine atom results in the enantiomer of this molecule, shown in **Figure 1.11B**. These molecules cannot be superimposed on each other—they are mirror images of each other, just as a person's two hands are mirror images of each other.

enantiomer a stereoisomer in which molecules are mirror images of each other around a single carbon atom bonded to four different types of atoms or groups

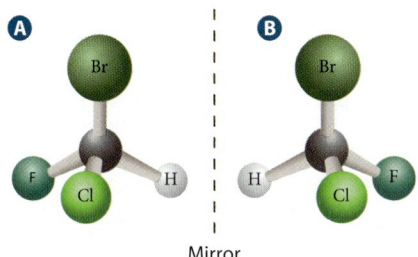

Figure 1.11 In each molecule, the carbon atom is bonded to a chlorine atom, a fluorine atom, a bromine atom, and a hydrogen atom. Because the locations of the hydrogen and fluorine atoms have been switched, the molecules are mirror images of each other and are enantiomers.

Note that enantiomers form only when the carbon atom is bonded to four different types of atoms or groups. For instance, if the fluorine atoms in the molecules in **Figure 1.11** are replaced with hydrogen atoms, the molecules are no longer enantiomers. In fact, as **Figure 1.12** shows, they are now identical.

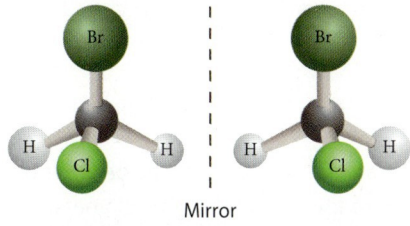

Figure 1.12 When the fluorine atoms from the previous example are replaced with hydrogen atoms, the molecules are no longer enantiomers. They are identical.

Activity 1.1 Organic Isomers

Unlike many elements, carbon can form branched, double, or triple bonded compounds. In this activity, you will build a variety of molecules in order to become more familiar with carbon compounds and the isomers they form.

Materials
- model-building kits

Procedure

1. Build all the possible constitutional isomers for the formula C_6H_{14}. Record each structure in a data table.

2. Build all the possible straight-chain isomers (no cyclical or branching structures) for the formula C_6H_{12}. Record each structure in your data table.

3. Build the diastereomers, *cis* and *trans*, for each of your double-bonded structures. Draw these structures in a data table.

4. Build, then draw, three possible structures that have the formula C_6H_{10}.

5. Build a molecule that has a chlorine, a fluorine, and two hydrogen atoms attached to a central carbon atom and build a molecule that has a chlorine, fluorine, bromine, and hydrogen attached to the central carbon atom. Build mirror images of these two molecules. Record each structure in a data table.

Questions

1. How did building three-dimensional models help you understand more about the different types of isomers carbon compounds can form?

2. Review your models and drawings of molecules for step 5. Identify which two molecules are enantiomers.

Section 1.1 Review

Section Summary

- In organic compounds, carbon atoms are almost always bonded to each other, to hydrogen atoms, and occasionally to atoms of a few specific elements.
- A carbon atom has four valence electrons, allowing it to form covalent bonds with up to four other atoms.
- Carbon atoms can bond with each other to produce straight or branched chain molecules that provide the root for a large number of organic compounds.
- Many organic compounds form isomers. The two main classes of isomers are constitutional isomers and stereoisomers.
- Diastereomers are stereoisomers in which different atoms or groups are bonded to each carbon involved in a double bond. Enantiomers are stereoisomers in which molecules are mirror images of each other around a single carbon atom bonded to four different types of atoms or groups.

Review Questions

1. **K/U** In the 1800s, organic compounds such as sugar, fats, and wood were classified as organic because they came from living organisms. How does this definition compare to the modern definition of organic compounds?

2. **A** The structure of carbonic acid (H_2CO_3) is shown below. Explain why it is considered inorganic even though it contains both hydrogen and carbon.

3. **A** Draw the Lewis structure and a three-dimensional shape of CH_4. What would be the consequences to living organisms if carbon only formed 90° angles with other atoms?

4. **C** Draw all the possible constitutional isomers for the following molecules.
    a. C_4H_8
    b. $C_2H_2Cl_2$

5. **K/U** Explain why cis and trans isomers normally are not possible around the following bonds.
    a. a single bond
    b. a triple bond

6. **C** The terms *transnational, transcontinental,* and *transatlantic* all have the same prefix. Explain what makes this prefix appropriate for describing one way of placing different groups around a double bond.

7. **A** Consider your left hand. If the palm is considered the centre, what are the parts of your left hand that make it a non-superimposable mirror image of your right hand?

8. **C** Use a Venn diagram to compare and contrast diastereomers and enantiomers.

9. **T/I** Predict how the physical and chemical properties of a pair of enantiomers would compare.

10. **K/U** Explain why the molecule shown below is not an example of a *cis* stereoisomer.

11. **T/I** The following ring structure can also form *cis* and *trans* isomers.

    a. Draw the three-dimensional shape of this molecule, showing both the *cis* and the *trans* isomers.
    b. What makes these structures different from linear *cis* and *trans* isomers, and why is this possible?

12. **A** How would you expect constitutional isomers to compare in terms of their boiling points and their chemical reactivity? Explain your answer.

13. **T/I** Friedrich Wöhler's accidental production of urea from inorganic compounds led to the modern definitions of organic and inorganic compounds. It also was considered the discovery of the existence of isomers. The structure of urea is shown below. Ammonium cyanate is a constitutional isomer of urea. Speculate and draw a possible structure for ammonium cyanate. (Hint: Begin by making a triple bond between the carbon atom and one of the nitrogen atoms.)

SECTION 1.2 Hydrocarbons

Hydrocarbons are organic compounds that contain only carbon atoms and hydrogen atoms. Examples of hydrocarbons include fossil fuels, such as gasoline and natural gas. In this section, you will learn how hydrocarbons are classified, as well as how to name and draw them. You will also read about some of their physical properties.

Alkanes

The simplest hydrocarbons are **alkanes**. They contain only single covalent bonds. Organic compounds that contain only single bonds, with no double or triple bonds between carbon atoms, are said to be **saturated hydrocarbons**. They are saturated because each carbon atom is bonded to as many other atoms as possible.

Methane is the simplest alkane, containing only one carbon atom and four hydrogen atoms. **Figure 1.13** shows the structure of methane and the next three members of the alkane family. Notice that each molecule differs from the previous molecule by the addition of the structural unit $-CH_2-$. Each carbon atom in the chain has a minimum of two hydrogen atoms bonded to it. As well, the two carbon atoms at the ends of the chain are bonded to an additional hydrogen atom. You can make a general statement about this pattern by saying that the number of hydrogen atoms in an alkane is two times the number of carbon atoms plus two more. If n represents the number of carbon atoms, then the general formula for all straight or branched chain alkanes is C_nH_{2n+2}. Therefore, if an alkane has 5 carbon atoms, its formula is $C_5H_{(2 \times 5)+2}$ or C_5H_{12}. Any set of organic compounds in which each member differs from the next by a $-CH_2-$ group is called a **homologous series**. Since all alkanes fit this pattern, all alkanes form a homologous series.

Key Terms

hydrocarbon
alkane
saturated hydrocarbon
homologous series
substituent group
root
prefix
suffix
alkyl group
alkene
unsaturated hydrocarbon
alkyne
cyclic hydrocarbon
benzene
aromatic hydrocarbon
aliphatic compound
phenyl group

methane   ethane   propane

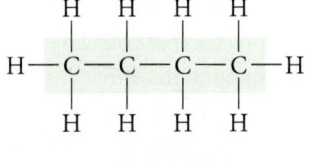

butane

Figure 1.13 The structure of methane and the next three alkanes.
Compare how these molecules are similar and how they are different.

hydrocarbon compound that contains only carbon atoms and hydrogen atoms

alkane a hydrocarbon molecule in which the carbon atoms are joined by single covalent bonds

saturated hydrocarbon hydrocarbon that contains only single bonds, and no double or triple bonds, that is, each carbon atom is bonded to the maximum possible number of atoms

homologous series series of molecules in which each member differs from the next by an additional specific structural unit

substituent group atom or group of atoms substituted in place of a hydrogen atom on the parent chain of an organic compound

Modelling Alkanes

The formula C_5H_{12} indicates only that the molecule has 5 carbon atoms and 12 hydrogen atoms. The formula says nothing about the structure of the molecule. Therefore, chemists have developed several ways to represent organic compounds to give a more complete picture of their structure. **Table 1.1**, on the next page, shows five different ways to represent the structures of alkanes, using C_5H_{12} as an example. Notice that the chain of carbon atoms in alkanes does not have to be a straight chain. Molecules can have branches in which one carbon atom is bonded to more than two other carbon atoms. These branches can be thought of as separate groups that have been substituted in the place of a hydrogen atom. The groups are called **substituent groups**. More commonly, they are referred to as *side groups*. Examine the structures in **Table 1.1** to confirm that the formula C_nH_{2n+2} applies even when branches are present in the carbon chain.

Table 1.1 Models Used to Represent Alkane Structures

Model	Description
Empirical molecular formula C_5H_{12}	An empirical formula shows the number and types of atoms present. This formula makes no attempt to specify structure, so it is not very useful for most applications.
Expanded molecular formula $CH_3CH(CH_3)CH_2CH_3$	An expanded molecular formula shows groupings of atoms. Brackets are used to indicate the locations of branched chains. In the formula on the left, a side chain consisting of $-CH_3$ is shown attached to the second carbon from the left end of the molecule. Bonds are assumed to exist between atoms.
Structural formula 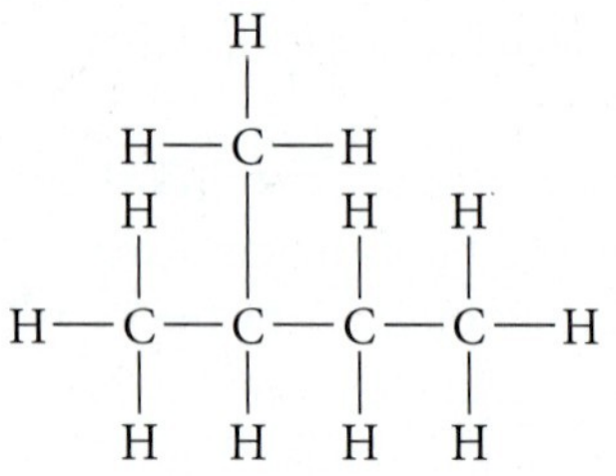 (structural diagram shown)	The structural formula gives a clear picture of all atoms and the locations of the bonds. Straight lines represent chemical bonds between atoms. Although detailed and accurate, this method requires a lot of space.
Condensed structural formula 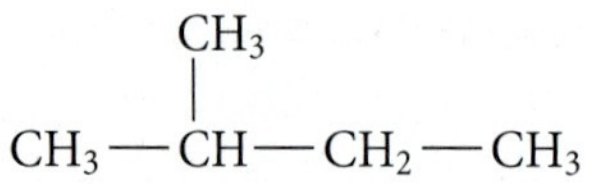 $CH_3-CH(CH_3)-CH_2-CH_3$	To save space, the condensed structural formula does not show the carbon-hydrogen bonds; they are assumed to be present. The model does show all other bonds. This method still specifies the location of the side branches but has the advantage of being much cleaner and clearer than a structural formula.
Line structural formula 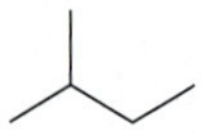 (line diagram shown)	This model uses lines to represent chemical bonds. Each end of a straight line represents a carbon atom (unless otherwise specified) and each carbon is assumed to have as many hydrogen atoms bonded to it as is necessary to give it four bonds.

Naming Alkanes

You are familiar with the International Union of Pure and Applied Chemistry (IUPAC) system of naming ionic compounds and simple molecular compounds. Despite the fact that there are millions of different organic compounds, the IUPAC system has rules for naming each of them based on its structure. As a result, the names are so precise that you can draw any structure from its name. The IUPAC name of any organic compound has three basic parts: a root, a prefix, and a suffix.

- The **root** denotes the number of carbon atoms in the longest continuous chain of carbon atoms.
- The **prefix** gives the positions and names of any branches from the main chain.
- The **suffix** indicates the series to which the molecule belongs. The suffix for alkanes is "-ane."

For this course, you will be responsible for learning the root names for chains of up to 10 carbon atoms and the names of side groups for up to six carbon atoms. These names are listed in **Table 1.2**. Note that the side groups on alkanes are basically alkanes with a missing hydrogen atom. For example, if the side group is a $-CH_3$ group, it looks like methane that is missing one hydrogen atom. A side group that is derived from an alkane is called an **alkyl group**. An alkyl group is named by using the same root that you would use for a main chain, but instead of adding the suffix "-ane" you add "-yl." For example, the $-CH_3$ group is called a methyl group.

---

root the part of the IUPAC name of any organic compound that denotes the number of carbon atoms in the longest continuous chain of carbon atoms for alkanes or the longest continuous chain that includes the functional group

prefix the part of the IUPAC name of any organic compound that gives the positions and names of any branches from the main chain

suffix the part of the IUPAC name of any organic compound that indicates the series to which the molecule belongs; sometimes includes position number of functional group

alkyl group a side group that is based on an alkane

Table 1.2 Root and Side Group Names for Alkanes

Number of Carbon Atoms	Root Name	Side Group Name	Number of Carbon Atoms	Root Name	Side Group Name
1	meth-	methyl-	6	hex-	hexyl-
2	eth-	ethyl-	7	hept-	
3	prop-	propyl	8	oct-	
4	but-	butyl-	9	non-	
5	pent-	pentyl-	10	dec-	

Table 1.3 outlines the steps to follow when naming alkanes. For each step, first read the description in the left column. Then study the example in the right column.

Table 1.3 Steps for Naming Alkanes

1. Identify the root. a. Identify the longest continuous chain.	$$\begin{array}{c} CH_3 \\ | \\ CH_3-CH_2-C-CH-CH_2-CH_3 \\ |\quad\; | \\ CH_3\; CH_2-CH_3 \end{array}$$
b. Find the root for the number of carbons in the chain.	The longest chain is six carbon atoms. The root for a six carbon chain is hex-.
2. Identify the suffix.	The compound is an alkane. The suffix is -ane.
3. Identify the prefix. The prefix indicates the position, number, and type of side groups on the main chain. To identify the prefix: a. Identify the number of carbon atoms in each side group. b. Determine the name of each side group according to the number of carbon atoms.	Two side groups have one carbon atom, and the third side group has two carbon atoms. $$\begin{array}{c} CH_3 \\ | \\ CH_3-CH_2-C-CH-CH_2-CH_3 \\ |\quad\; | \\ CH_3\; CH_2-CH_3 \end{array}$$ The side groups with one carbon atom are *methyl* groups. The other side group has two carbon atoms, so it is an *ethyl* group.
c. If there is more than one type of side group, write their names in alphabetical order. d. Find the position of each side group. Numbering must begin at the end of the main chain that will give the side groups the lowest possible numbers. A quick way to do this is to add up the numbers for each possibility.	Alphabetic order is ethyl and then methyl. $$\begin{array}{c} CH_3 \\ | \\ CH_3-CH_2-C-CH-CH_2-CH_3 \\ \;1\quad\;\;2\quad\;|3\;\;|4\quad\;5\quad\;\;6 \\ CH_3\; CH_2-CH_3 \end{array}$$ The compound is numbered from left to right. This gives the side groups the numbers 3, 3, 4.
e. Precede the name of each side group with the number of the carbon atom to which it is attached on the main chain. Use a hyphen to separate numbers and words, and use a comma to separate the numbers.	The ethyl group is on carbon atom 4. The methyl groups are on carbon atom 3. The prefix is now 4-ethyl-3,3-methyl-.
f. Use a prefix to indicate how many of each type of side group are present if there is more than one of the same side group. The prefixes *di-*, *tri-*, or *tetra-* are used when there are two, three, or four of the same side group present, respectively. Note that this additional prefix does not affect the alphabetical order established earlier.	There are two methyl groups. The complete prefix is 4-ethyl-3,3-dimethyl-.
4. Name the compound. Combine the prefix, root, and suffix to name the compound. Note that there is no hyphen or space between the prefix and the root or between the root and the suffix.	The root plus the suffix is hexane (hex- plus -ane). Therefore, after adding the prefix, the name of the compound is 4-ethyl-3,3-dimethylhexane.

The sample problem below shows two more examples of steps to follow when naming alkanes. In both examples, the side groups have the same number, no matter the direction in which the compound is numbered. If this occurs for an alkane, the compound must be numbered in the direction that gives the side group that comes first alphabetically the lowest number. After you study the Sample Problem, develop your naming skills by completing the Practice Problems.

Sample Problem

Naming Alkanes

Problem
Name the following alkanes.

a. 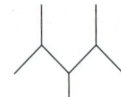   b.

What Is Required?
You must name two alkanes.

What Is Given?
You are given the structural formulas for the alkanes.

Plan Your Strategy	Act on Your Strategy
a. Find the root.	The longest chain has five carbon atoms, so the root is pent-.
Find the suffix.	Since the compound is an alkane, the suffix is -ane.
Find the prefix.	A methyl group is attached to the main chain on carbon atoms 2, 3, and 4. (This is the case if you start numbering at either end.) The prefix is 2,3,4-trimethyl-.
Write the name.	The full name is 2,3,4–trimethylpentane.
b. Find the root.	There are eight carbons in the longest chain. The root is oct-.
Find the suffix.	Since the compound is an alkane, the suffix is -ane.
Find the prefix. Number the side groups. The side groups have the same number, no matter which direction the compound is numbered. So the compound must be numbered in the direction that gives the side group that comes first alphabetically the lowest number.	Ethyl comes before methyl alphabetically. The compound is numbered from left to right to give the ethyl group the lowest number. The prefix is 4-ethyl-5-methyl-.
Write the name.	The full name is 4-ethyl-5-methyloctane.

Check Your Solution

a. The name indicates that the longest chain is five carbon atoms long, which it is. The name indicates that there are three methyl groups with one on each of carbon atoms 2, 3, and 4, which is correct.

b. The name indicates that the longest chain is eight carbon atoms long, which it is. The name indicates that there is an ethyl group on carbon atom 4 and a methyl group on carbon atom 5, which is correct.

Learning Check

7. Name four products that you use or encounter each day that are made from hydrocarbons.

8. An alkane is a saturated hydrocarbon. Explain what that means.

9. Explain the term homologous series as it applies to organic compounds. Include an example in your explanation.

10. What is the empirical molecular formula for an alkane that has 3 carbon atoms? 7 carbon atoms? 9 carbon atoms? 12 carbon atoms?

11. Draw a structural diagram of an alkane to show the meaning of the term *substituent group*.

12. Identify the root, the prefix, and the suffix for the compound 2-methylpentane.

Practice Problems

For the next five questions, name the molecules.

1.
$$H_3C-CH(CH_3)-CH_3$$

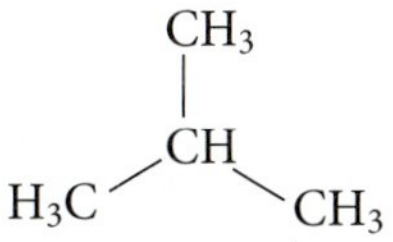

2. 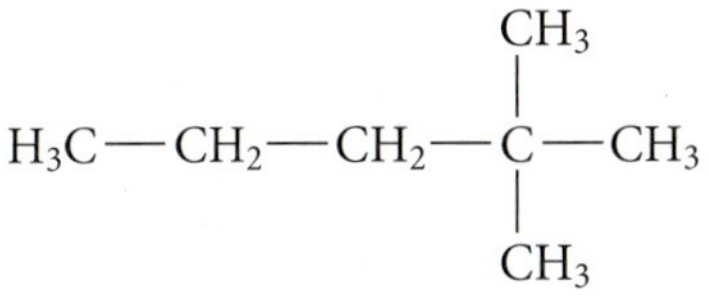
$$H_3C-CH_2-CH_2-C(CH_3)_2-CH_3$$

3.
(branched alkane structure with H_3C-CH_2, $CH_2-CH_2-CH-CH-HC-CH_2$, H_2C, CH_3, CH_3, CH_3)

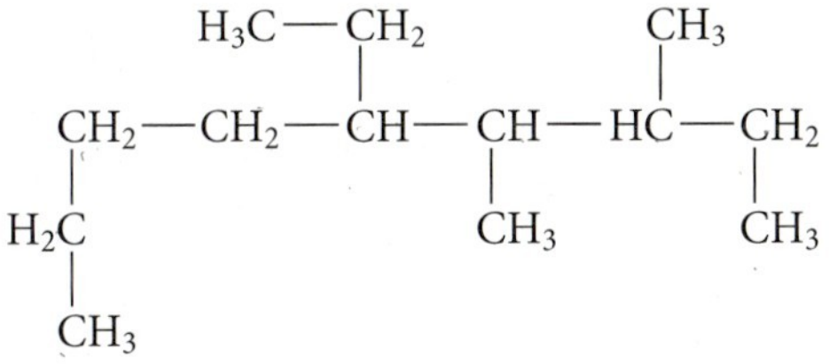

4.
$$H_3C-HC(CH_2CH_3)-CH_2-C(CH_3)(CH_2CH_3)-CH_3$$

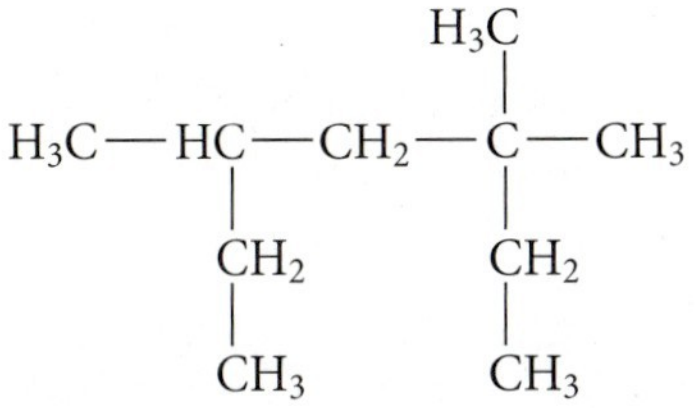

5.
$$HC(CH_3)(CH_3)-CH_2-CH_2-C(CH_3)_2-CH_3$$

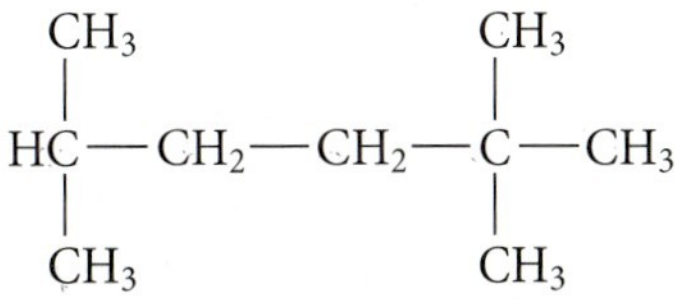

For the next three questions, identify any errors in the structures by drawing them. Rename them correctly.

6. 2-ethylpropane

7. 2,2,2-trimethylethane

8. 2-ethyl-2,4,4-trimethylpentane

For the next three questions, name the compounds.

9. (zigzag line structure — 4 carbons)

10. (zigzag structure with methyl branch)

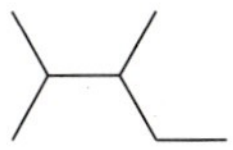

11. (zigzag structure with two methyl branches on same carbon)

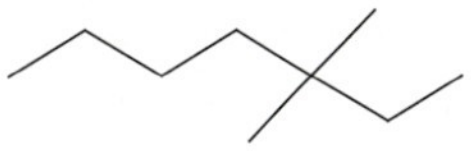

Drawing Alkanes

The IUPAC system also enables you to draw a structural formula for any organic molecule, given its name. The logic involved is the same as the logic used in naming the molecule. **Table 1.4** shows the steps for drawing alkanes, along with an example.

Table 1.4 Steps in Drawing Alkanes

1. Identify the root. The root of the name gives the number of carbon atoms in the main chain.	3-ethyl-3-methylpentane The root is pent-, so there are five carbon atoms in the main chain.
2. Identify the suffix. The suffix gives the structure of the carbon atoms in the main chain and the nature of the bonds between the carbons.	The suffix is -ane, so the compound is an alkane and has only single bonds.
3. Draw and number the main chain, but do not add any hydrogen atoms yet. This chain will be the base of the structure you draw. Add numbers to the carbon atoms.	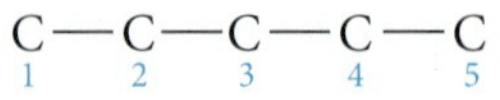 C—C—C—C—C 1 2 3 4 5
4. Identify the prefix and draw the side groups. The prefix will tell you what the side groups are and to which carbon atom of the main chain they are attached.	The prefix is 3-ethyl-3-methyl-. Therefore, there is an ethyl group and a methyl group attached to carbon atom 3 of the main chain. You can place the side groups on either side of the main chain.
5. Complete the condensed structural formula. Add the number of hydrogen atoms beside each carbon atom that will give each carbon four bonds.	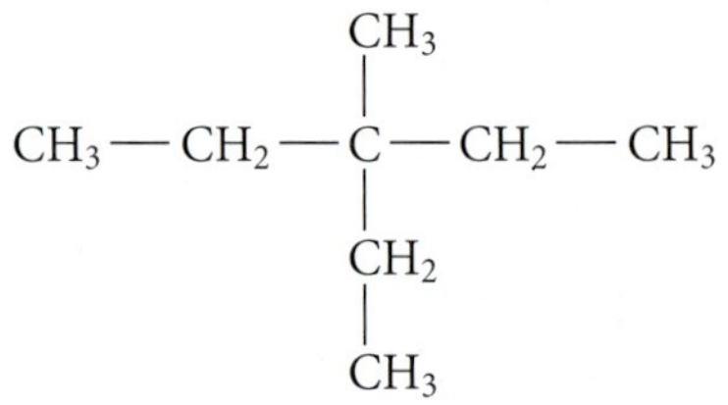 $CH_3-CH_2-\underset{\underset{CH_3}{\mid}}{\overset{\overset{CH_3}{\mid}}{C}}-CH_2-CH_3$ CH_2
6. Draw the line structural formula.	

The following Sample Problem will guide you through another example of drawing a structure from a name. After you are familiar with the process, use the Practice Problems to practice your drawing skills.

Sample Problem

Drawing an Alkane

Problem
Draw a condensed structural formula for 3-ethyl-2-methylheptane.

What Is Required?
You must draw a condensed structural formula for an alkane.

What Is Given?
You are given the name of the alkane.

Plan Your Strategy	Act on Your Strategy
Identify the root.	The root is hept-, which indicates that there are seven carbons in the main chain.
Identify the suffix.	The suffix is -ane, so the molecule is an alkane. There are only single bonds between carbon atoms.

Identify the prefix, and draw the side groups.	The prefix is 3-ethyl-2-methyl-, which indicates that there is an ethyl group on carbon atom 3 and a methyl group on carbon atom 2. 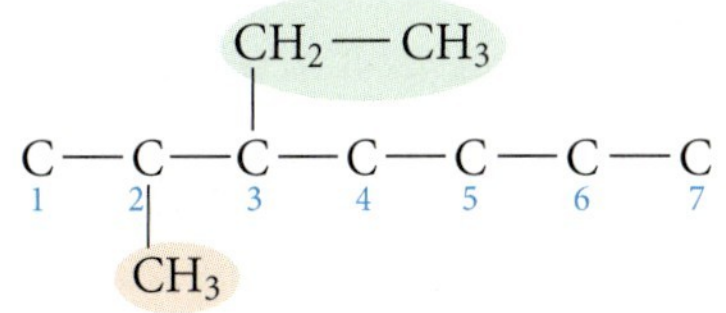	C—C—C—C—C—C—C with CH$_2$—CH$_3$ on C3 and CH$_3$ on C2 (carbons numbered 1–7)
Complete the condensed structural formula. Add enough hydrogen atoms to each carbon atom so that each has a total of four bonds.		CH$_3$—CH(CH$_3$)—CH(CH$_2$—CH$_3$)—CH$_2$—CH$_2$—CH$_2$—CH$_3$

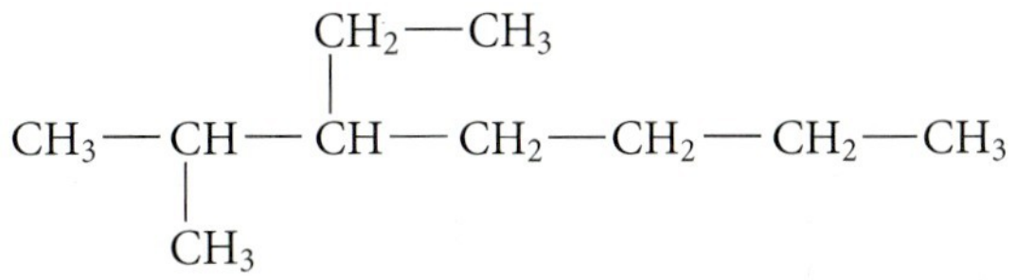

Check Your Solution

The seven carbon atoms in the main chain agree with the root hept-. The two-carbon chain attached to carbon atom 3 agrees with the prefix 3-ethyl-, and the single carbon atom attached to carbon atom 2 agrees with 2-methyl-. All bonds are single bonds.

Practice Problems

For the next three questions, draw the condensed formula for each structure.

12. 2-methylbutane

13. 3-ethyl-3-methylhexane

14. 4-(1,1-dimethylethyl)nonane

15. For each of the molecules in questions 12–14, draw a line structural formula.

In the next three questions, the name of each structure is incorrect. Draw the structure that each name describes. Rename each structure correctly.

16. 4-methylbutane

17. 3-propylheptane

18. 2,3,3 triethylpentane

For the next three questions, draw the complete structural formula for each molecule.

19. 2-methylbutane

20. 3,3,4-triethylnonane

21. 3,3,4,4-tetramethyldecane

22. Draw the line structure for the incorrectly named molecule 3,3 dipropyl hexane. Name it correctly.

Physical Properties of Alkanes

Since all alkanes are non-polar, they are not soluble in water. Alkanes are, however, soluble in benzene and other non-polar solvents. Small alkanes such as methane and propane are gases at standard temperature. Medium-length alkanes are liquids at standard temperature. The very large alkanes are waxy solids. In **Table 1.5** the boiling points of alkanes are given in ranges, because the shape and size of the molecules affect their boiling points. For example, highly branched chain molecules have lower boiling points than straight chain molecules.

Table 1.5 Sizes and Boiling Points of Alkanes

Size (number of carbon atoms per molecule)	Boiling Point Range (°C)	Examples of Uses
1 to 4	Below 30	Gases: used for fuels to heat homes and cook
5 to 16	30 to 275	Liquids: used for automotive, diesel, and jet engine fuels; also used as raw material for the petrochemical industry
16 to 22	Over 250	Heavy liquids: used for oil furnaces and lubricating oils
Over 18	Over 400	Semi-solids: used for lubricating greases and paraffin waxes to make candles, waxed paper, and cosmetics
Over 26	Over 500	Solid residues: used for asphalts and tars in the paving and roofing industries

Alkenes

All year long, fruits and vegetables such as the bananas shown in **Figure 1.14** are shipped over great distances from their point of origin. To prevent them from spoiling before they reach grocery stores and supermarkets, fruits and vegetables are usually picked before they are ripe and then refrigerated to slow the ripening process during transport. When they reach their destination, ethene gas—a plant hormone that causes plants to ripen—is pumped into their containers. Ethene is the simplest of the group of hydrocarbons called alkenes.

Figure 1.14 A hydrocarbon, ethene, enables you to have access to ripe fruits and vegetables throughout the year. Ethene is given off by many types of plants to cause them to grow during their life cycle.

Alkenes are hydrocarbons that have at least one double bond in the carbon chain. Since two carbons are involved in a double bond, all alkenes consist of at least two carbon atoms. The presence of a double bond gives alkenes the ability to bond to more atoms than are already present in the molecules. For example, **Figure 1.15** shows an alkene reacting with hydrogen and bonding to two more hydrogen atoms than were originally present. The result is the alkane, ethane. Since the carbon atoms in alkenes are not bonded to the maximum number of atoms possible, they are said to be **unsaturated hydrocarbons**.

alkene a hydrocarbon molecule that contains one or more carbon-carbon double bonds

unsaturated hydrocarbon hydrocarbon that contains carbon-carbon double or triple bonds, whose carbon atoms can potentially bond to additional atoms

Figure 1.15 An unsaturated hydrocarbon reacts with a hydrogen molecule and becomes a saturated hydrocarbon.
Explain *why the structure on the left side of the equation is unsaturated and why the structure on the right side of the equation is saturated.*

In **Figure 1.15**, you also can see that an alkene with one double bond has two fewer hydrogen atoms than an alkane with the same number of carbon atoms. Therefore, the general formula for straight and branched chain alkenes with one double bond is C_nH_{2n}. **Figure 1.16** shows the first three alkenes. Check the structures in **Figure 1.16** to ensure that they fit the formula.

Figure 1.16 These alkenes consist of two, three, and four carbon atoms.
Explain *why there are two different alkenes with four carbon atoms.*

ethene

propene

but-1-ene

but-2-ene

As shown in **Figure 1.16**, there is only one possible structure for the first two alkenes. Since there is only one double bond in ethene, only one structure can be drawn. Similarly, if the double bond in propene were between carbon atoms 2 and 3 (counted from the left) and flipped side to side, the molecule would still be identical to the structure in **Figure 1.16**. However, alkenes with at least four carbon atoms can have more than one structure, because the double bond can be in different positions. As more carbon atoms are added, the variety becomes even greater.

Modelling Alkenes

The same five types of formulas used to model alkanes can be used to model alkenes. The alkene with five carbon atoms, C_5H_{10}, is used as an example in **Figure 1.17**, which shows the formula types as they apply to alkenes.

Empirical molecular formula

C_5H_{10}

Structural formula

Expanded molecular formula

$CH_3C(CH_3)CHCH_3$

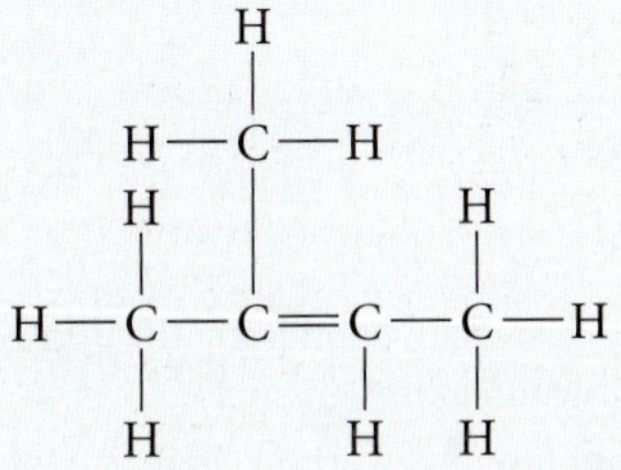

Condensed structural formula

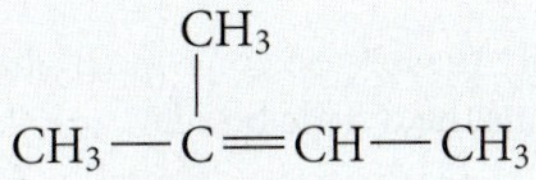

Line structural formula

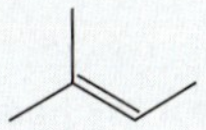

Figure 1.17 This example shows the five different types of formulas that can be used to model the five-carbon alkene, C_5H_{10}.

You would have to analyze the molecular formula and the expanded molecular formula at length to determine that the molecule is an alkene. It is not possible to determine the position of the double bond from the molecular formula. Similarly, you would have to analyze the expanded molecular formula to determine where the double bond is located. All of the structural formulas clearly show the double bond, but the condensed and the line structural formulas are the quickest to draw.

Activity 1.2 — Sniffing Out Cancer

Cancer has a better chance of being successfully treated if it is detected early. Regular screening for cancer is important, but current methods used to determine the presence of cancer cells may involve surgery or other invasive techniques. Researchers are constantly looking for better methods of detecting cancer and dogs may play a vital role in these methods in the future. Some dogs are able to detect the presence of alkanes in people's breath—alkanes that are created by cancerous tumours. Before a procedure becomes a clinical practice, the validity of the method must be supported by research and repeated, successful clinical trials. In this activity, you will find out more about using dogs for cancer detection.

Materials
- reference books
- computer with Internet access

Procedure

1. Research some of the current methods used to detect cancer. Record each method and a description of it in a table. As well, record information about the advantages and disadvantages of each method.

2. Find out why cancer tumours produce alkanes and how dogs are able to detect these compounds.

3. Summarize three studies that have been done regarding the efficacy of cancer-sniffing dogs. For each study, be sure to include information about the source, such as the author's name, date of publication, name of magazine or journal with issue and page numbers, or the site URL with the name of the site and publication organization.

Questions

1. Why are alkanes created by cancer tumours?
2. How are dogs able to detect these alkanes?
3. What are the advantages and disadvantages of using dogs to detect cancer?
4. Are the studies on cancer-sniffing dogs reliable? Evaluate the validity of your information using the guidelines in Appendix A.
5. Based on your research, do you think that dogs will be used to assist health care professionals in the detection of cancer in the near future? Why or why not?

Learning Check

13. Show five different ways that a four-carbon straight chain alkane can be represented.
14. Describe the solubility of alkanes.
15. State the range of carbon atoms in an alkane molecule that would be
    a. a liquid at room temperature.
    b. a gas at room temperature.
16. What is the general formula for an alkene containing one double bond?
17. Compare the similarities and differences between the alkenes in **Figure 1.16** and the first three alkanes.
18. Draw the condensed structures of alkenes that would have the same empirical molecular formula but different structural formulas.

Naming Alkenes

The IUPAC steps for naming alkenes are very similar to those used for naming alkanes. A few exceptions are shown in **Table 1.6**.

Table 1.6 Steps in Naming Alkenes

1. Identify the root.	
a. Identify the longest continuous chain that contains the double bond.	$CH_3-C=C-CH_2-CH_3$ with CH_3 groups on the two central carbons. The longest chain containing the double bond is five carbon atoms.
b. Find the root for the number of carbons in the chain. The root for a given chain in an alkene is the same as the root for a given chain in an alkane.	The root for a five-carbon chain is pent-.
2. Identify the suffix.	
a. Number the main chain by starting at the end of the chain nearest the double bond, giving the double bond the lowest possible carbon numbers. **Note:** For alkenes, this rule takes precedence over any numbering rule you learned for alkanes.	$CH_3-C=C-CH_2-CH_3$ numbered 1 2 3 4 5 with CH_3 branches. Numbering the main chain from left to right gives the double bond carbons the lowest possible numbers.
b. If the alkene contains four or more carbons, give the position of the double bond by indicating the number of the carbon atom that *precedes* the double bond. The suffix consists of a hyphen, the number, a hyphen, and -ene.	The compound is an alkene. It contains four or more carbons. The double bond lies between carbon atoms 2 and 3. The suffix is -2-ene.
3. Identify the prefix. Name the side groups on alkenes as you would for alkanes.	One methyl group is bonded to carbon atom 2. The other is bonded to carbon atom 3. The prefix is 2,3-dimethyl-.
4. Name the compound. Combine the prefix, root, and suffix, to name the compound. Note that there is no space or hyphen between the prefix and the root.	The compound is 2,3-dimethylpent-2-ene.

In some molecules, the chain containing the double bond is not the longest chain. Nevertheless, the root name must describe the chain that contains the double bond. The rule for placing the number that describes the position of the double bond was recently revised by IUPAC, so you might sometimes see the number in the prefix. Always use the new rule that puts the number in the suffix. For example, a six-carbon chain that has a double bond between the second and third carbon atom is named hex-2-ene.

Analyze the following Sample Problem to learn how to apply the rules. Then complete the Practice Problems to develop your skills.

Sample Problem

Naming Alkenes

Problem

Name the following alkenes.

a.
$$CH_3-\underset{\underset{CH_3}{|}}{\overset{\overset{CH_3}{|}}{C}}-\underset{\underset{CH_2-CH_3}{|}}{C}=CH-CH_2-CH_2-CH_3$$
(numbered 1, 2, 3, 4, 5, 6, 7)

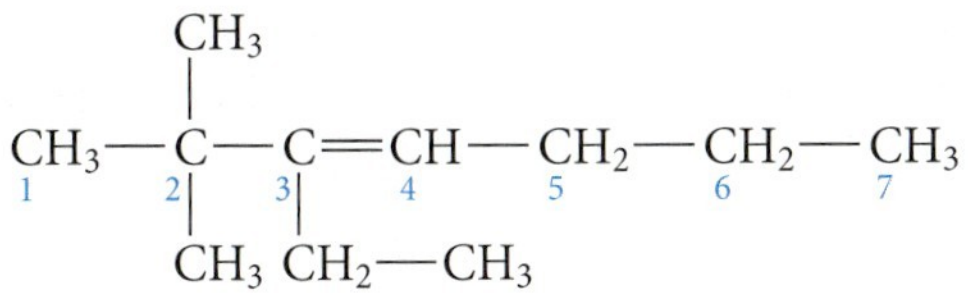

b. (skeletal structure with carbons numbered 1–6, a double bond between C1 and C2, methyl groups on C4 and C5, and an ethyl group on C4)

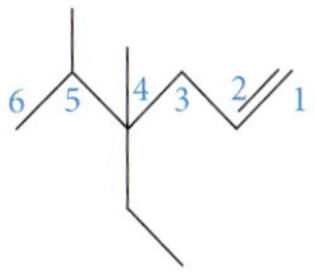

What Is Required?

You must name two alkenes.

What Is Given?

You are given the structural formulas of the alkenes.

Plan Your Strategy	Act on Your Strategy
a. Find the root.	The longest chain that includes the double bond has seven carbons. The root is hept-.
Determine the suffix.	Assign numbers to the carbon chain containing the double bond. Number from left to right so that the lowest number (3) is on the first carbon involved in the double bond, as shown below. (Numbering from right to left is incorrect, because the first carbon involved in the double bond would have been carbon atom 4.) 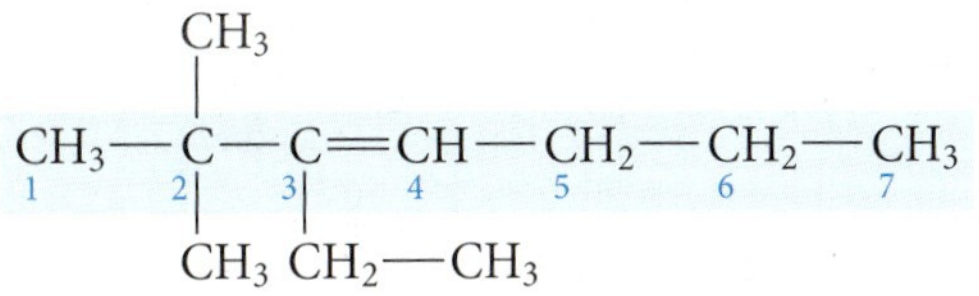 $$CH_3-\underset{\underset{CH_3}{|}}{\overset{\overset{CH_3}{|}}{C}}-\underset{\underset{CH_2-CH_3}{|}}{C}=CH-CH_2-CH_2-CH_3$$ (numbered 1, 2, 3, 4, 5, 6, 7) Because the molecule has one double bond between carbon atoms 3 and 4, the suffix is -3-ene.
Determine the prefix.	Two methyl groups are bonded to carbon atom 2. One ethyl group is bonded to carbon atom 3. The groups in the prefix must be in alphabetical order, and "e" comes before "m." Therefore, the prefix is 3-ethyl-2,2-dimethyl-. 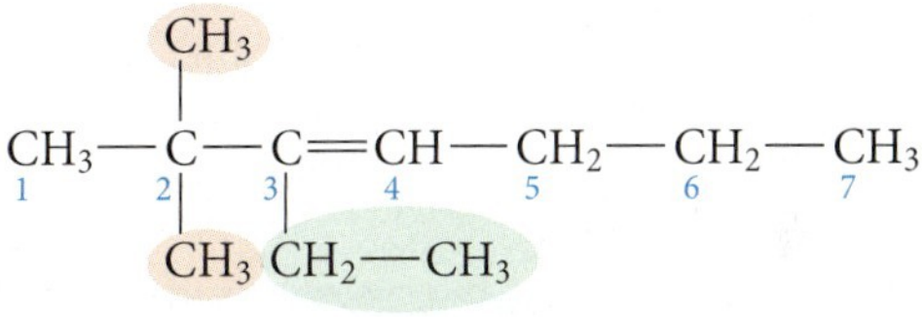
Write the name.	The name of the compound is 3-ethyl-2,2-dimethylhept-3-ene.
b. Find the root.	The longest chain that includes the double bond has six carbon atoms. The root is hex-.
Find the suffix.	Assign numbers to the carbon chain containing the double bond. Number from right to left so that the lowest number is on the first carbon involved in the double bond. 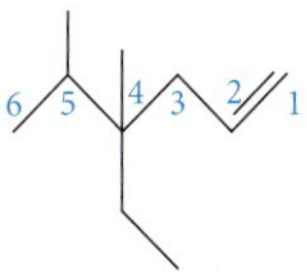 The molecule has one double bond that is between carbon atoms 1 and 2. Therefore, the suffix is -1-ene.
Determine the prefix.	One methyl group is bonded to carbon atom 4 and another is bonded to carbon atom 5. One ethyl group is bonded to carbon atom 4. Therefore, the prefix is 4-ethyl-4,5-dimethyl-.
Write the name.	The name of the compound is 4-ethyl-4,5-dimethylhex-1-ene.

Check Your Solution

In each case, the length of the main chain and the position and name of the side groups agree with the given structure.

Practice Problems

For the next five questions, name each alkene.

23. H₃C—CH=CH—CH₂—CH₃

24.
$$H_2C=CH-\underset{\underset{CH_3}{|}}{CH}-CH_3$$

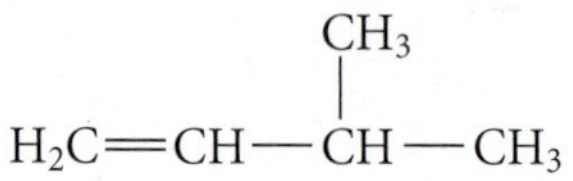

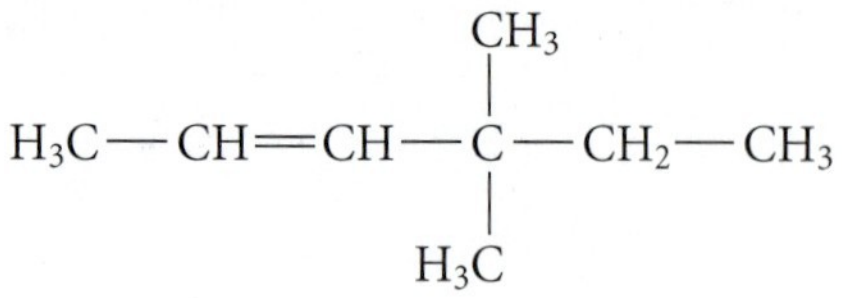

25.
$$H_3C-CH=CH-\underset{\underset{H_3C}{|}}{\overset{\overset{CH_3}{|}}{C}}-CH_2-CH_3$$

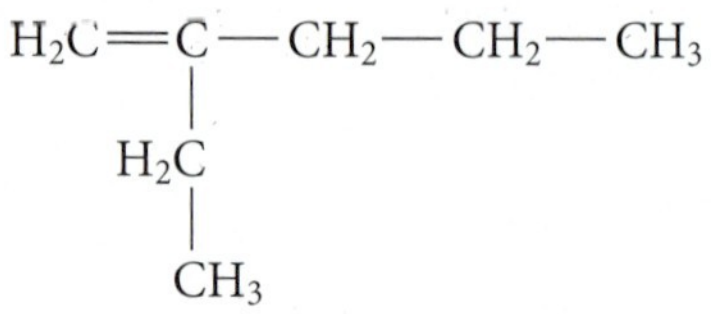

26.
$$H_2C=\underset{\underset{\underset{CH_3}{|}}{\underset{H_2C}{|}}}{C}-CH_2-CH_2-CH_3$$

27.
$$H_3C-CH=\underset{\underset{\underset{\underset{H_3C}{|}}{CH_2}}{|}}{\overset{\overset{CH_2-CH_3}{|}}{C}}-CH-CH_2-CH_3$$

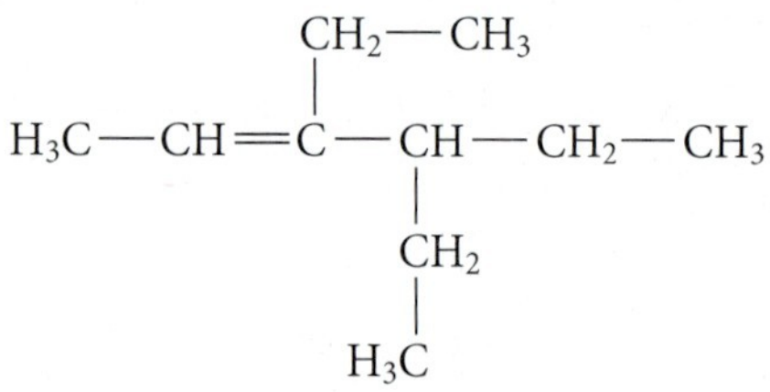

For the next four questions, identify any errors in each structure by drawing it. Rename the structure correctly.

28. but-3-ene
29. 2,3-dimethylhept-4-ene
30. 3-ethyl-4-methylhex-4-ene
31. 5-methyl-2-propyl-hex-3-ene

For the next three questions, name each compound.

32. 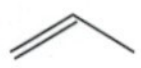 [skeletal structure of propene]

33. 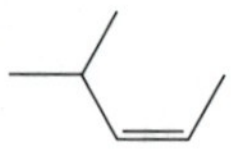 [skeletal structure]

34. 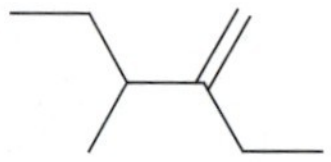 [skeletal structure]

Drawing Alkenes

The method for drawing alkenes is basically the same as that for drawing alkanes. The main difference is in placing the double bond in the correct place. Remember that the double bond comes after the carbon atom with the number stated in the suffix. Also, remember that the two carbon atoms that share the double bond have only two other bonds. When you have completed a structure, check to be sure that all carbon atoms have only four bonds.

Sample Problem

Drawing Alkenes

Problem
Draw a structural formula for 2-methylbut-2-ene.

What Is Required?
You must draw a structural formula.

What Is Given?
You are given the name of the compound.

Plan Your Strategy	Act on Your Strategy
Identify the root.	The root is but-, so there are four carbon atoms in the main chain.
Identify the suffix.	The suffix is -2-ene, so there is a double bond after carbon atom 2 in the main chain.
Draw and number the main carbon chain.	C—C=C—C 1 2 3 4

Identify the prefix and draw the side groups.	The prefix is 2-methyl-, so there is a methyl group on carbon atom 2.	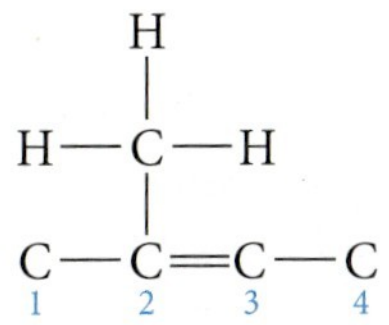
Complete the structural formula. Add enough hydrogen atoms so that each carbon atom has a total of four bonds.	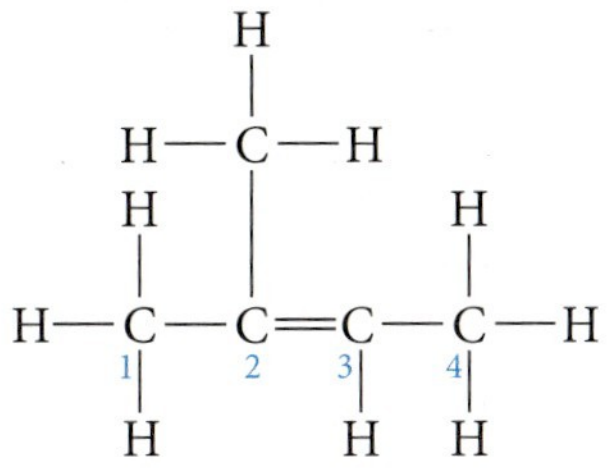	

Check Your Solution
The number of carbon atoms in the main chain, the position of the double bond, and the type and position of the side group in the structural formula all agree with the name.

Practice Problems

For the next four questions, draw the condensed structural formula for each alkene.

35. pent-2-ene

36. 3-propylhept-2-ene

37. 4,4-dimethylhex-2-ene

38. 4-ethyl-2,5-dimethyloct-3-ene

39. For each of the molecules listed in questions 35–38, draw a line structural formula.

In the next three questions, each name is incorrect. Draw each structure. Rename each structure correctly.

40. hex-4-ene

41. 3-propylhept-5-ene

42. 3,3-dimethylprop-2-ene

43. Draw the complete structural formula for the following.
   a. 2-methylbut-1-ene
   b. 4-ethyl-4,5-dimethylhex-1-ene

44. Draw the line structure for the incorrectly named molecule 3-methyl-4-ethyl-4-propyl-hex-5-ene. Name it correctly.

Physical Properties of Alkenes

The physical properties of alkenes are very similar to those of alkanes. Alkenes are non-polar, so they do not dissolve in water. If you were to try to dissolve an alkene, such as an industrial lubricating oil, in water, the two substances would separate almost instantly. Alkenes do not dissolve in water because the attractive forces between individual alkene molecules are stronger than the attractive forces between the alkene molecules and the water molecules. However, alkenes do dissolve in other non-polar solvents. The first three alkenes—ethene, propene, and butene—are all gases at standard temperature, while the intermediate size alkenes are liquids. However, the boiling points of the alkenes are slightly lower than those of the alkanes that have the same number of carbon atoms. For example, the boiling point of ethene is −103.8°C while that of ethane is −88.6°C.

As you know, when the number of carbon atoms in an alkene is four or greater, there is more than one possible position for the double bond. Even the slight differences in the shape of the molecules caused by the location of the double bond affect boiling point, as does the form of the diastereomer. For example, the boiling point of but-1-ene is −6.3°C, whereas the boiling point of *trans*-but-2-ene is 0.88°C, and that of *cis*-but-2-ene is 3.71°C.

Figure 1.18 The tool that gas welders use to join, cut, and shape metals uses pure oxygen combined with the fuel acetylene (properly called ethyne).

Alkynes

The fuel used by gas welders, such as the one in **Figure 1.18,** is commonly called acetylene, although its correct IUPAC name is ethyne, which is an example of an alkyne. **Alkynes** are hydrocarbons that have at least one triple bond. Like alkenes, the carbon atoms in alkynes are not bonded to the maximum number of other atoms, so they are also unsaturated hydrocarbons.

Figure 1.19 shows the first three alkynes. Notice that, for molecules with the same number of carbon atoms, alkynes have two fewer hydrogen atoms than alkenes do. Therefore, the general formula for straight or branched chain alkynes is C_nH_{2n-2}. For example, the alkyne that has five carbon atoms has a formula of $C_5H_{(2\times5)-2}$, or C_5H_8.

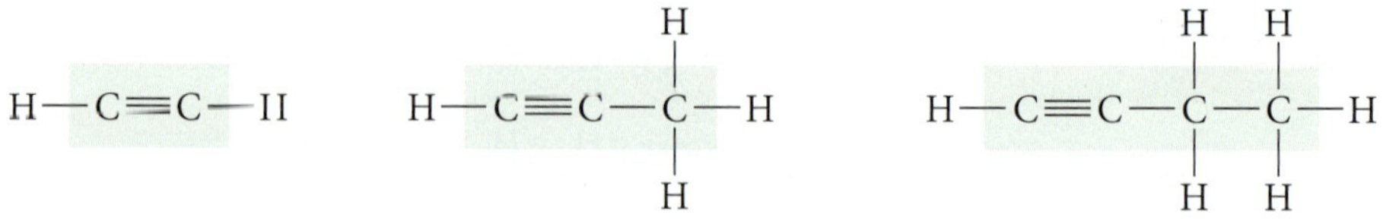

ethyne   propyne   but-1-yne

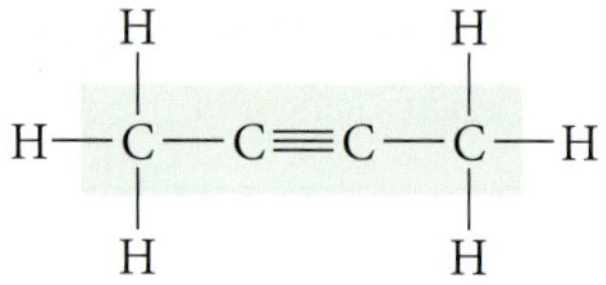

but-2-yne

Figure 1.19 These diagrams show the first three alkynes. Similar to the alkenes, alkynes with four or more carbon atoms can have more than one structure, because the triple bond can be in different positions.

alkyne a hydrocarbon molecule that contains one or more carbon-carbon triple bonds

Modelling Alkynes

You represent alkynes using the same variety of formulas that you used for alkanes and alkenes. **Figure 1.20** shows a five-carbon alkyne, C_5H_8, drawn using the five different formulas you are familiar with.

When you analyze the formulas in **Figure 1.20**, you can see that the molecular formula provides very little information about the molecule. The expanded molecular formula provides more information, but you must carefully count hydrogen atoms to determine whether the compound has any double or triple bonds. The three types of structural formulas provide the most information.

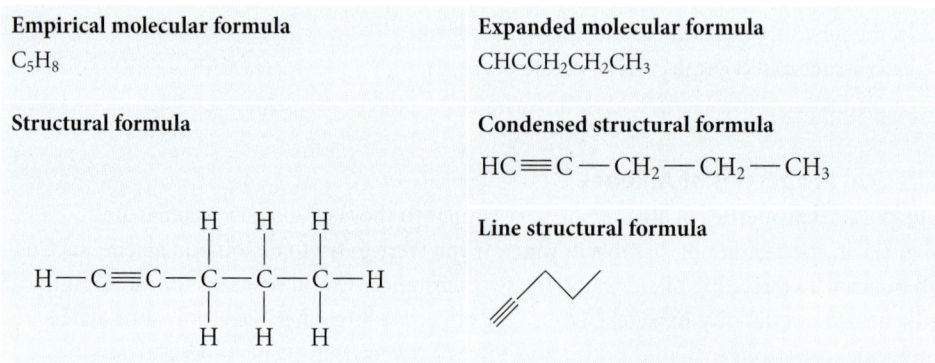

Empirical molecular formula
C_5H_8

Expanded molecular formula
$CHCCH_2CH_2CH_3$

Structural formula

Condensed structural formula
$HC\equiv C-CH_2-CH_2-CH_3$

Line structural formula

Figure 1.20 A five-carbon alkyne is represented using five different formulas.

Figure 1.21 Alkynes are always linear around the triple bond.

Naming and Drawing Alkynes

The naming of alkynes follows the rules for alkenes, except the suffix is -yne instead of -ene. Drawing alkynes is also very similar to drawing alkenes. However, when drawing alkynes, the lines representing bonds on either side of the triple bond are lined up with the triple bond, as shown in **Figure 1.21**. Use the next set of Sample Problems and Practice Problems to develop your skills for naming and drawing alkynes.

Sample Problem

Naming and Drawing Alkynes

Problem

Name the alkyne (a), and draw the alkyne (b).

a. 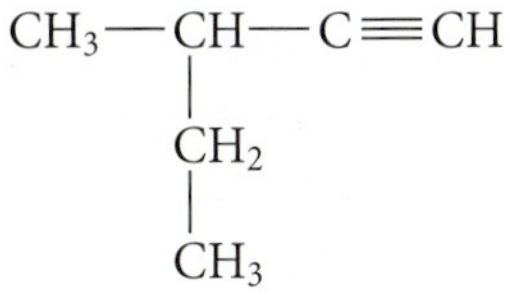 $CH_3-CH-C\equiv CH$
        $|$
       CH_2
        $|$
       CH_3

b. 4-ethylhex-2-yne

What Is Required?

You must name one alkyne and draw another alkyne.

What Is Given?

You are given a structure to name, and you are given a name for which you will draw a structure.

Plan Your Strategy	Act on Your Strategy
a. Identify the root.	The longest chain that includes the triple bond is five carbon atoms, so the root is pent-.
Identify the suffix.	Numbering starts at the end of the chain nearest the triple bond, giving the lowest possible numbers to the carbon atoms in this bond. The compound has one triple bond, so the suffix contains -yne. The triple bond is between carbon atoms 1 and 2. Using the lowest number, the suffix is -1-yne. 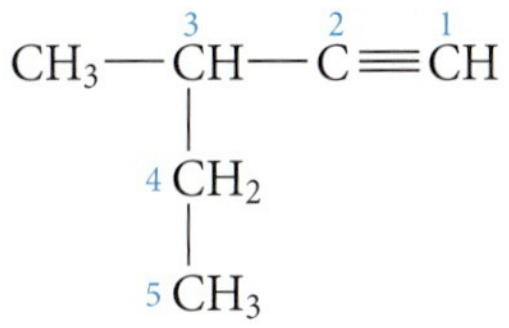 $CH_3-\overset{3}{C}H-\overset{2}{C}\equiv \overset{1}{C}H$ $\underset{4}{|}CH_2$ $\underset{5}{|}CH_3$
Identify the prefix.	There is a methyl group on carbon atom 3 so the prefix is 3-methyl-.
Name the compound.	The compound is 3-methylpent-1-yne.
b. Identify the root.	The root is hex-, so the main chain has six carbon atoms.
Identify the suffix.	The suffix is -2-yne, so there is a triple bond between carbon atoms 2 and 3.
Draw and number the main chain.	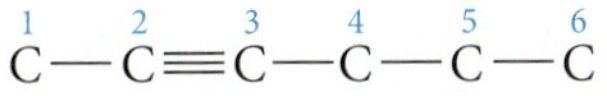 $\overset{1}{C}-\overset{2}{C}\equiv \overset{3}{C}-\overset{4}{C}-\overset{5}{C}-\overset{6}{C}$
Identify the prefix and draw any side groups	The prefix is 4-ethyl-. Draw an ethyl group on carbon atom 4. 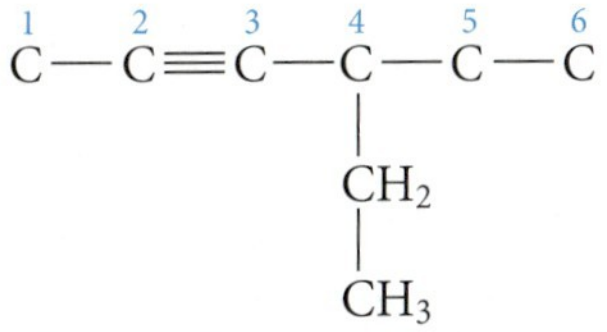 $\overset{1}{C}-\overset{2}{C}\equiv \overset{3}{C}-\overset{4}{C}-\overset{5}{C}-\overset{6}{C}$ $|$ CH_2 $|$ CH_3
Add enough hydrogen atoms to give each carbon atom four bonds.	$\overset{1}{CH_3}-\overset{2}{C}\equiv \overset{3}{C}-\overset{4}{CH}-\overset{5}{CH_2}-\overset{6}{CH_3}$ $|$ CH_2 $|$ CH_3

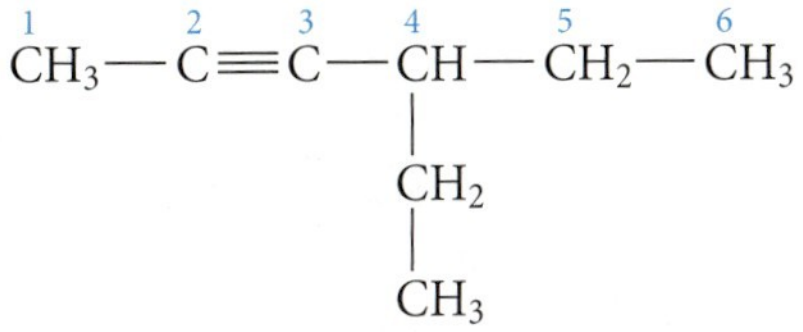

Check Your Solution

The number of carbon atoms in the main chains, the position of the triple bonds, and the type and position of the side groups in both structures are in complete agreement with the names.

Practice Problems

For the next four questions, name each alkyne.

45. H₃C—CH₂—C≡C—CH₂—CH₃

46. HC≡C—CH₂
         |
    H₃C—CH—CH₃

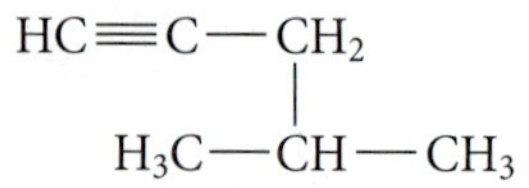

47.   H₂C—C≡C—CH₃
                    |
    H₃C—CH₂—CH₂—CH—CH₂—CH₃

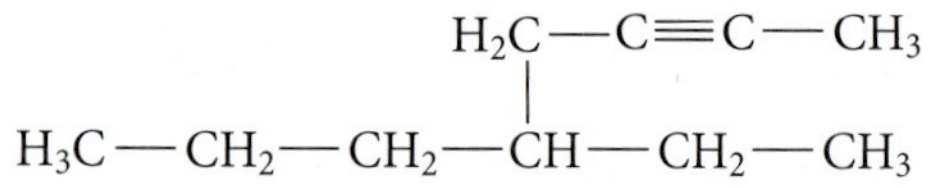

48.   CH₃ CH₃
       | |
   HC—C—CH₂—C≡CH
       | |
      CH₃ CH₃

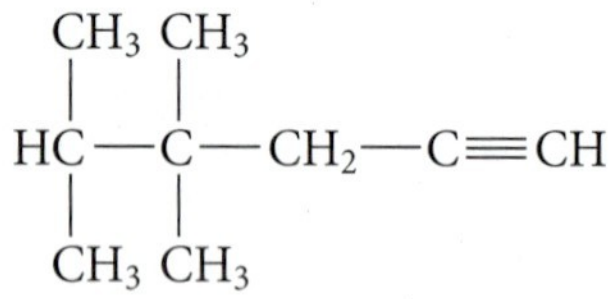

49. Draw the condensed structural formula for the following molecules.
    a. but-2-yne
    b. 4,5-dimethylhex-1-yne
    c. 4-ethyl-4-methylhept-2-yne
    d. 2,5,7-trimethylnon-3-yne

50. For each of the molecules listed in question 49, draw a line structural formula.

In the next four questions, each name is incorrect. Draw the structure that each name describes. After examining your drawings, rename each structure correctly.

51. 3-methylprop-1-yne
52. but-3-yne
53. 2-methylpent-3-yne
54. 2-methyl-4-propyl-4-ethylhex-5-yne

Physical Properties of Alkynes

Similar to the other hydrocarbons, alkynes are non-polar, so they are insoluble in water. Also, like the alkanes and alkenes, the first few alkynes exist as gases at standard temperature. An interesting property of hydrocarbons arises when you compare the boiling points of the lower-mass, straight-chain alkanes, alkenes, and alkynes that are listed in **Table 1.7**. (Note: The multiple bonds are all between carbon atoms 1 and 2.) As mentioned previously, the alkenes have lower boiling points than their corresponding alkanes. However, alkynes have a higher boiling point than the corresponding alkanes. The linear structure of alkynes and the nature of the triple bond cause them to attract one another more strongly than do the alkenes or alkanes. Consequently, it takes more energy to overcome these attractive forces.

Table 1.7 Boiling Points of Small Alkanes, Alkenes, and Alkynes

Alkanes	Boiling Point (°C)	Alkenes	Boiling Point (°C)	Alkynes	Boiling Point (°C)
Ethane	−89	Ethene	−104	Ethyne	−84
Propane	−42	Propene	−47	Propyne	−23
Butane	−0.5	Butene	−6.3	Butyne	8.1
Pentane	36	Pentene	30	Pentyne	39
Hexane	69	Hexene	63	Hexyne	71

Cyclic Hydrocarbons

cyclic hydrocarbon an aliphatic hydrocarbon chain that forms a ring (but not a benzene ring); compare *aromatic hydrocarbon*

Cyclic hydrocarbons are hydrocarbon chains that form rings. These compounds are the foundation of many biologically important molecules, including cholesterol and the steroid hormones testosterone and the estrogens. Cyclic hydrocarbons can be alkanes, alkenes, and alkynes. (However, cyclic alkynes are rare and are usually unstable.) The first four cyclic alkanes are shown in **Figure 1.22** as both structural formulas and line structural formulas.

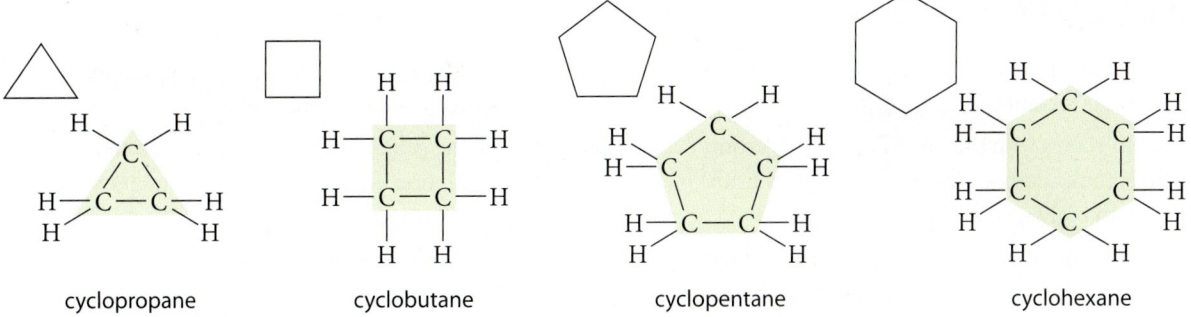

Figure 1.22 This figure shows the first four cyclic alkanes. Notice that a carbon chain must have at least three carbon atoms to form a ring. In cyclic alkanes, there are two hydrogen atoms for each carbon atom. Therefore, the general formula for cyclic alkanes is C_nH_{2n}.

Naming and Drawing Cyclic Hydrocarbons

All of the basic rules for naming hydrocarbons apply to cyclic hydrocarbons, along with a few additional rules such as the addition of *cyclo* preceding each name. The steps for naming cyclic hydrocarbons are listed in **Table 1.8**. To draw cyclic hydrocarbons, follow the same pattern that has been developed for naming. Sample Problems and Practice Problems follow **Table 1.8**.

Table 1.8 Steps in Naming Cyclic Hydrocarbons

1. Identify the root. Determine the number of carbon atoms in the ring in order to find the root. This is the same as the straight chain alkane, alkene, or alkyne with the same number of carbon atoms, preceded by cyclo-.	There are five carbon atoms in the ring. The root is cyclopent-.
2. Identify the suffix. Determine whether the molecule has all single bonds, at least one double bond, or at least one triple bond. The suffix is -ane, -ene, or -yne, respectively. It is not necessary to indicate the location of the double or triple bonds, because they are always assumed to be between carbon atoms 1 and 2.	The ring has one double bond, so the suffix is -ene.
3. Identify the prefix. Find the names for the alkyl prefixes as you would for straight chain hydrocarbons. However, there is a special set of rules for numbering the carbon atoms in the ring to which the side groups are attached: • If there are no side groups or only one side group on a cyclic alkane, the carbon atoms are not numbered. • If the molecule is a cyclic alkane and there are two or more side groups, the numbering must start with the side group and then proceed in the direction that gives the lowest possible numbers to all side groups. As is the case for alkanes, if the numbers are the same for two or more side groups no matter how the molecule is numbered, the side group that comes first alphabetically is assigned as carbon atom 1. • If the molecule is a cyclic alkene or cyclic alkyne, the multiple bond takes highest priority. The carbon atom on one side of the multiple bond is carbon atom 1, and the carbon atom on the other side is carbon atom 2. If there are side groups, the numbering starts in the position that will make the number of the carbon atoms bonded to the side groups as small as possible.	The molecule is a cyclic alkene. The carbon atoms on the two sides of the double bond must be numbers 1 and 2. The numbering must proceed so that the side groups have the lowest possible number. Therefore, the numbering must be as shown below. Because the numbering of the carbon atoms involved in the double bond must be 1 and 2, it is not necessary to specify these numbers in the name. There are two methyl groups on carbon atoms 3 and 4. The prefix is 3,4-dimethyl-.
4. Name the compound. Combine the prefix, root, and suffix to name the compound. Note that there is no hyphen or space between the prefix and the root or between the root and the suffix.	The name is 3,4-dimethylcyclopentene.

Learning Check

19. Draw all the possible structures of an alkene with the molecular formula of C_6H_{12}.
20. For molecules with the same number of carbon atoms, rank alkanes, alkenes, and alkynes from lowest to highest boiling points.
21. What features do alkynes possess that give them a different boiling point than alkanes and alkenes with the same number of carbon atoms?
22. Give two examples of steroid hormones that have cyclic hydrocarbons as their foundation.
23. Compare the general formulas for alkenes and alkynes with one multiple bond with straight chain and cyclic alkanes.
24. What is the minimum number of carbons to form a cyclic hydrocarbon and what would be the empirical molecular formula for the molecule?

Sample Problem

Naming Cyclic Hydrocarbons

Problem
Name the following hydrocarbons.

a.

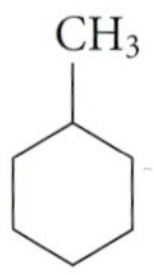

b.

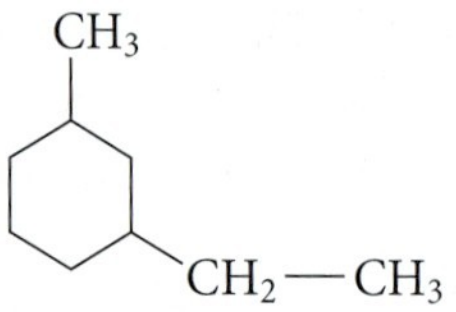

c.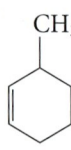

d.

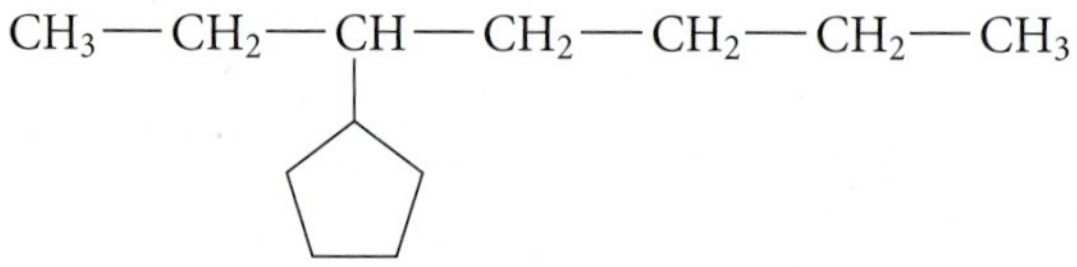

What Is Required?
You must write the names of four compounds that contain cyclic hydrocarbons.

What Is Given?
You are given four structural diagrams.

Plan Your Strategy	Act on Your Strategy
a. Find the root.	The ring has six carbons, so the root is cyclohex-.
Find the suffix.	There are no multiple bonds, so the structure is an alkane. Therefore, the suffix is -ane.
Find the prefix.	Because there is only one side group and the molecule is a cyclic alkane, it is not necessary to assign position numbers for the carbon atoms in the ring. The side group has one carbon atom, so the prefix is methyl-.
Write the name.	The name is methylcyclohexane.
b. Find the root.	The ring has six carbon atoms, so the root is cyclohex-
Find the suffix.	There are no multiple bonds, so the structure is an alkane. Therefore, the suffix is -ane.
Find the prefix.	The side groups have the same numbers, no matter the direction in which the compound is numbered. Thus, like other alkanes, the compound must be numbered in the direction that gives the side group that comes first alphabetically the lowest number. There is a methyl and an ethyl side group. The letter *e* comes before *m*. Therefore, the numbering must be as shown below. The prefix is 1-ethyl-3-methyl-. 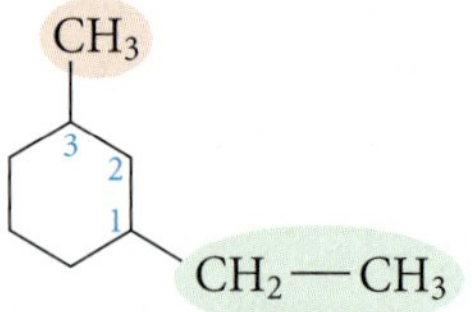
Write the name.	The name is 1-ethyl-3-methylcyclohexane.

c. Find the root.	The ring has six carbon atoms, so the root is cyclohex-.
Find the suffix.	The ring has one double bond, so the structure is an alkene. The suffix is -ene.
Find the prefix.	The carbon atoms on the two sides of the double bond must be numbers 1 and 2. The numbering must proceed so that the side group has the lowest possible number. Therefore, the numbering must be as shown below. 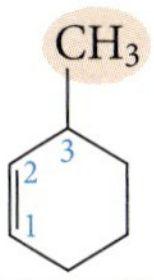 Because the numbering of the carbon atoms on the ends of the double bond must be 1 and 2, it is not necessary to specify these in the name. The side group is on carbon atom 3, so the prefix is 3-methyl-.
Write the name.	The name is 3-methylcyclohexene.
d. Find the root.	The longest continuous carbon chain is seven atoms long. 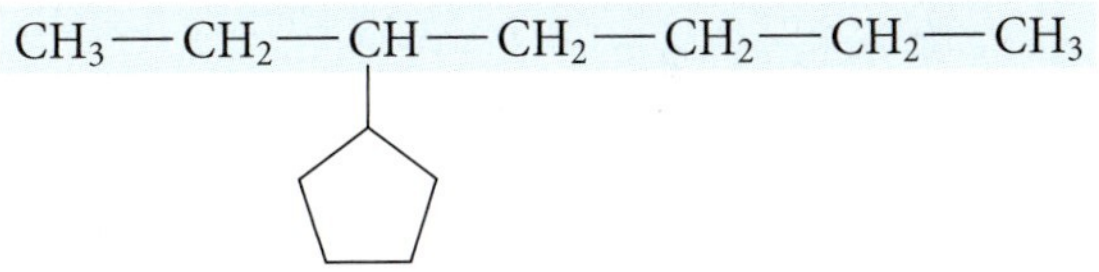 $CH_3-CH_2-CH-CH_2-CH_2-CH_2-CH_3$ The main chain is the straight chain alkane, not the cyclic alkane. Therefore, the root is hept-.
Find the suffix.	The structure is an alkane. Therefore, the suffix is -ane.
Find the prefix.	Number from left to right to give the carbon attached to the side group the lowest number. 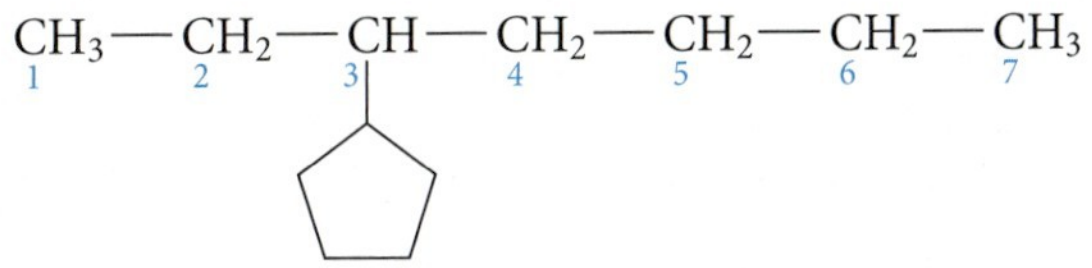 $CH_3-CH_2-CH-CH_2-CH_2-CH_2-CH_3$ 1 2 3 4 5 6 7 The five carbon ring is a side group on carbon atom 3 of the main chain. It is named as if it were a straight chain alkyl group, except cyclo- is included in the prefix. 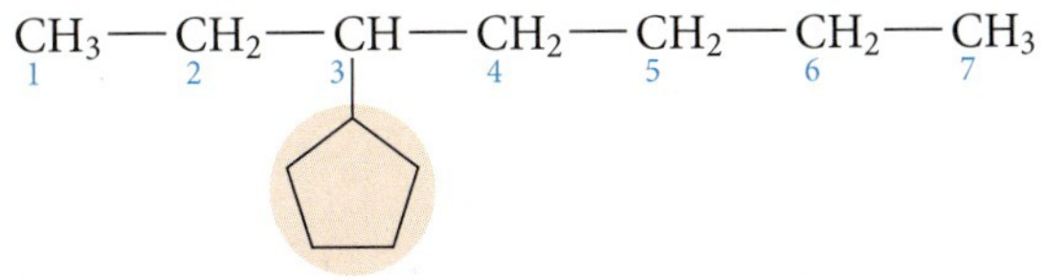 $CH_3-CH_2-CH-CH_2-CH_2-CH_2-CH_3$ 1 2 3 4 5 6 7 Thus, the prefix is 3-cyclopentyl-.
Write the name.	The name is 3-cyclopentylheptane.

Check Your Solution
In each case, the root, prefix, and suffix correctly describe the structure.

Sample Problem

Drawing Cyclic Hydrocarbons

Problem
Draw the structure of 4-ethyl-2-methylcyclopentene.

What Is Required?
You must draw the structure of a compound.

What Is Given?
You are given the name of the compound.

Continued on next page

Plan Your Strategy	Act on Your Strategy
Identify the root.	The root is cyclopent-, so the structure is based on a five carbon ring. 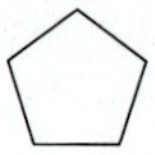
Identify the suffix.	The suffix is -ene, so there is a double bond in the ring. 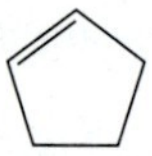
Number the carbon atoms in the ring.	The double bond must be between carbon atoms 1 and 2. 
Identify the prefix and draw the side group(s).	The prefix is 4-ethyl-2-methyl-1, so there is an ethyl group on carbon atom 4 and methyl group on carbon atom 2. 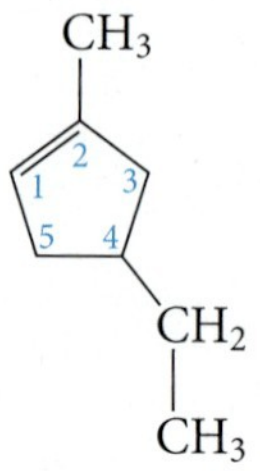
Write the name.	The name is 4-ethyl-2-methylcyclopentene.

Check Your Solution

The double bond is between carbon atoms 1 and 2, the methyl group is on carbon atom 2, and the ethyl group is on carbon atom 4, so the structure is correct.

Practice Problems

For the next five questions, name each cyclic hydrocarbon.

55.

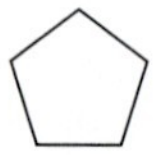

56.

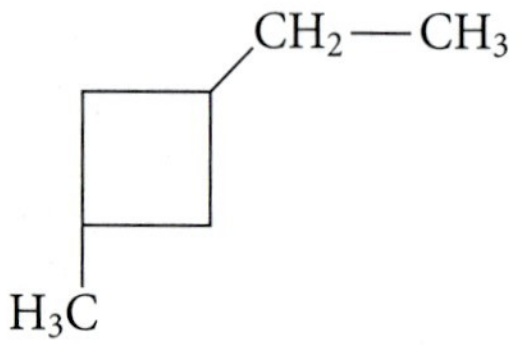

57.

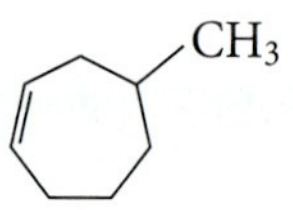

58.

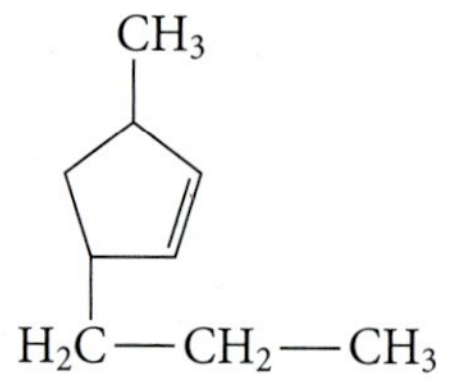

59.

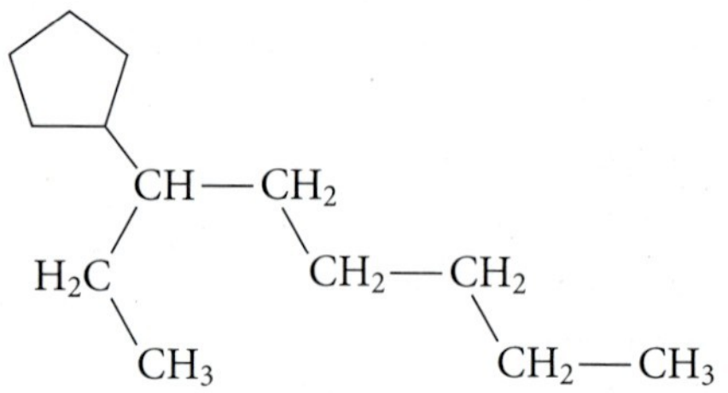

For the next five questions, draw a condensed structural formula for each compound.

60. methylcyclobutane

61. 1,2-dimethylcyclohexane

62. 3-methylcyclopentene

63. 2-ethyl-3-propylcyclohexene

64. 2-cyclobutylpentane

Properties of Cyclic Hydrocarbons

Cyclic hydrocarbons are non-polar and have physical properties similar to their straight chain counterparts. Note that all cyclic hydrocarbons are insoluble in water, with cyclopropane being the one exception. The boiling points and melting points of the cyclic hydrocarbons are slightly higher than straight chain hydrocarbons with the same number of carbon atoms. **Table 1.9** compares these data for a few alkanes and cyclic alkanes.

Table 1.9 Boiling Points and Melting Points of Some Alkanes and Cyclic Alkanes

Cyclic Alkane	Boiling Point (°C)	Melting Point (°C)	Alkane	Boiling Point (°C)	Melting Point (°C)
cyclopropane	−32.7	−127	propane	−42.1	−190
cyclobutane	12.0	−50.0	butane	−0.5	−138
cyclopentane	49.3	−93.0	pentane	36.1	−130
cyclohexane	80.7	6.6	hexane	68.9	−95.5

The Aromatic Hydrocarbons

A type of hydrocarbon that looks very much like a typical cyclic hydrocarbon has such unique properties that it forms the basis of an entire class of hydrocarbons: the aromatic hydrocarbons. Originally, the name was applied to naturally occurring plant compounds with intense aromas. For many years, chemists sought to explain two contradictory properties of these compounds. Aromatic hydrocarbons have a low hydrogen-to-carbon ratio and unusual stability. A low hydrogen-to-carbon ratio is usually associated with the presence of multiple bonds. However, multiple bonds tend to make compounds more reactive, not less reactive. How could a low hydrogen-to-carbon ratio be associated with stability? This question was answered with the discovery that naturally occurring aromatic compounds are all based on the presence of a benzene ring. A **benzene** ring is a single-carbon ring with one hydrogen atom bound to each carbon atom, thus having the formula C_6H_6. **Aromatic hydrocarbons** are hydrocarbons derived from the benzene ring. All of the compounds that you have been studying up to this point are called **aliphatic compounds** to distinguish them from the aromatics. In other words, aliphatic compounds are any compounds that do not contain a benzene ring.

Chemists originally drew the benzene ring with alternating single and double bonds, as shown in **Figure 1.23A**. However, experimental observations showed that all six carbon–carbon bonds are identical in length and in other properties. The length of the carbon–carbon bonds is intermediate between a single and a double bond. Chemists then realized that benzene was a resonance hybrid of the two structures shown in **Figure 1.23B**. A *resonance hybrid* is an average of two different Lewis structures, or a structure that is between two structures.

Chemists now realize that the electrons that make up the second bond in the "double bonds" are equally shared by all six carbon atoms. Electrons that behave in this way are called *delocalized electrons*. In any compound that has one single bond between two double bonds, the electrons are delocalized. The double bonds in this combination are called conjugated double bonds. Such structures are very stable, because the electrons are not readily available for chemical reactions. Based on this information about the structure, chemists now prefer to draw the benzene ring as shown in **Figure 1.23C**. In this model, there are single bonds between the carbon atoms and a circle within the carbon ring to represent the six delocalized electrons.

benzene a cyclic, aromatic hydrocarbon, C_6H_6, in which all six carbon-carbon bonds are intermediate in length between a single and double bond; delocalized electrons are shared by all six carbon atoms

aromatic hydrocarbon compound containing only carbon and hydrogen and based on the aromatic benzene ring

aliphatic compound compound containing only carbon and hydrogen in which carbon atoms form chains and/or non-aromatic rings

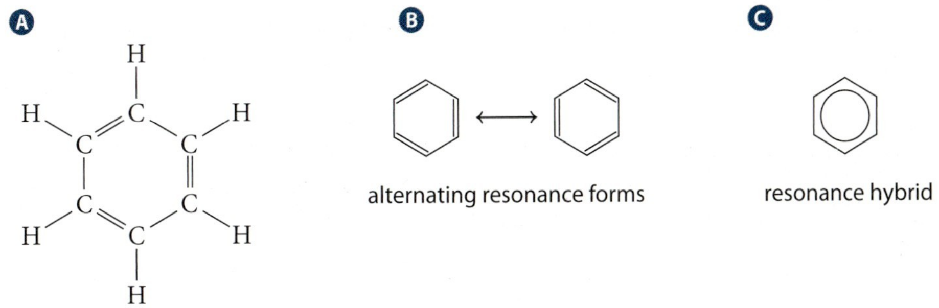

A [structure showing benzene with alternating single and double bonds, all H and C atoms drawn out]

B [two hexagonal benzene structures with alternating double bonds connected by a double-headed arrow]
alternating resonance forms

C [hexagonal benzene structure with circle inside]
resonance hybrid

Figure 1.23 Although the double bonds portray the correct number of electrons in the bonds (**A**), they do not portray the true chemical and physical properties of benzene, which is a hybrid between two alternating resonance forms (**B**). Benzene is best represented as a circle inside a carbon ring (**C**), which models that it is a resonance hybrid.

> **Learning Check**
>
> 25. Using **Table 1.9** compare the boiling and melting points of straight chain hydrocarbons with cyclic hydrocarbons. In which case is there a greater difference, boiling or melting points?
> 26. Compare and contrast aliphatic and aromatic hydrocarbons.
> 27. Compare cyclohexene with benzene in terms of reactivity and structure.
> 28. What evidence is there that benzene is a resonance hybrid?
> 29. What is meant by the term *delocalized electrons*?
> 30. Draw the preferred way to show a benzene ring.

Naming and Drawing Aromatic Hydrocarbons

Since benzene forms the basis of all aromatic hydrocarbons, the naming of simple aromatic hydrocarbons uses benzene as the root. The major steps in naming aromatic hydrocarbons are given in **Table 1.10**.

Table 1.10 Steps in Naming Aromatic Hydrocarbons

1. Identify the root. The root for an aromatic hydrocarbon is -benzene.	The root is -benzene.
2. Identify the prefix. **a.** Determine the position number of the side groups in order to write the prefix. The carbons in a benzene ring are numbered to locate the presence of more than one side group.	
b. Prioritize alkyl side groups with six or fewer carbon atoms in alphabetical order. Then continue to number in the direction of the nearest side group.	There are two methyl groups and one ethyl group. Because ethyl comes before methyl alphabetically, it should be numbered 1. Numbering must proceed in the direction that gives the side groups the lowest numbers. Therefore, proceed counterclockwise from the ethyl group.
c. Write the prefix as you would for any other hydrocarbon.	The prefix is 1-ethyl-2,3-dimethyl-.
3. Name the compound. Combine the prefix and root to name the compound. Note that there is no hyphen or space between the prefix and the root.	The compound is 1-ethyl-2,3-dimethylbenzene.

To draw aromatic hydrocarbons with side groups that have six or fewer carbon atoms in any given chain, draw the benzene ring, and then add the side groups as indicated. If a benzene ring is attached to a single hydrocarbon chain that is larger than the benzene ring itself (more than six carbon atoms), the benzene ring is considered to be the side group. In such cases, the attached benzene ring is called a **phenyl group**. Name the compound according to the steps for naming aliphatic hydrocarbons, and then name the benzene ring as a phenyl group, just as you would have named an alkyl group such as "methyl." The Sample Problems and Practice Problems that follow will help you apply the naming and drawing of aromatic hydrocarbons.

phenyl group term used for a benzene ring that forms a substituent group on a hydrocarbon chain

Sample Problem

Naming Aromatic Hydrocarbons

Problem

Name the following hydrocarbons.

a.

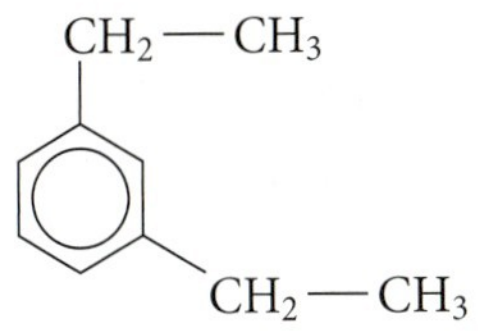
CH2—CH3
CH2—CH3

b.

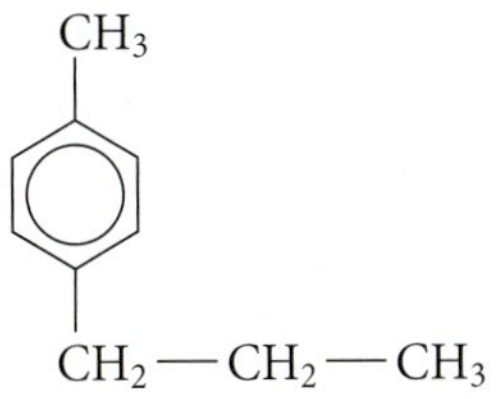
CH3
CH2—CH2—CH3

c.

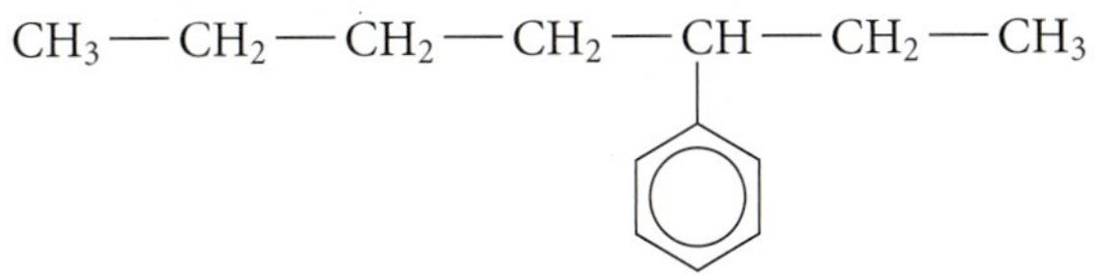
CH3—CH2—CH2—CH2—CH—CH2—CH3

What Is Required?

You must name three aromatic hydrocarbons.

What Is Given?

You are given the structural formulas of the hydrocarbons.

Plan Your Strategy	Act on Your Strategy
a. Identify the root.	The hydrocarbon chains have fewer than six carbon atoms, so the root is -benzene.
Identify the prefix.	Both side groups have two carbon atoms, so they are both ethyl groups. Either ethyl group can be chosen to be on carbon atom 1. Counting goes in the direction that will give the second group the smaller number. Therefore, the prefix is 1,3-diethyl-.
Write the name.	The compound is 1,3-diethylbeneze.
b. Identify the root.	The hydrocarbon chains have fewer than siz carbon atoms, so the root is -benzene.
Identify the prefix.	The side group at the top of the benzene ring is a methyl group. The side group with three carbon atoms is a propyl group. The methyl group comes first alphabetically, so it is on carbon atom 1. The propyl group will be on carbon atom 4 regardless of the direction of the numbering. Therefore, the prefix is 1-methyl-4-propyl-. 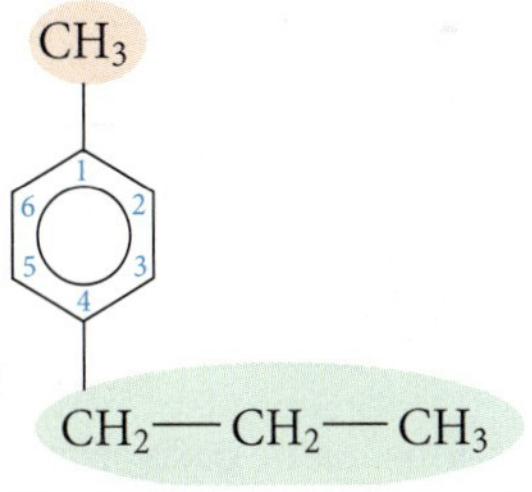 CH3 1 2 3 4 5 6 CH2—CH2—CH3
Write the name.	The compound is 1-methyl-4-propylbenzene.
c. Identify the root.	The hydrocarbon chain has seven carbon atoms, so the benzene ring is a side group. There are no multiple bonds in the main chain, so the root and suffix are -heptane.
Identify the prefix.	Benzene is the side group, so it is a phenyl group. The phenyl group is nearer the right end of the chain. Numbering goes from right to left and the side group is on carbon atom 3. 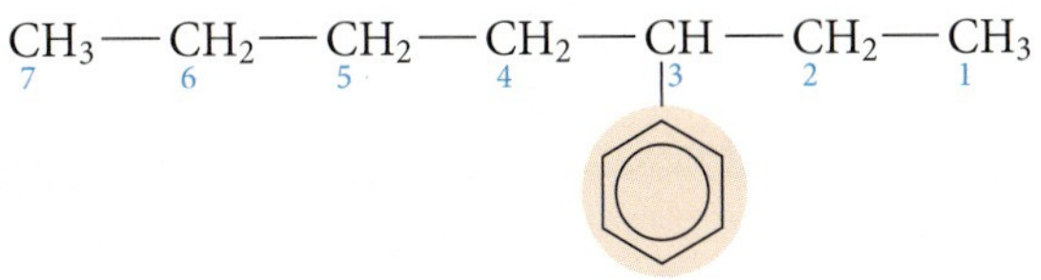 CH3—CH2—CH2—CH2—CH—CH2—CH3 7 6 5 4 3 2 1 The prefix is 3-phenyl-.
Write the name.	The compound is 3-phenylheptane.

Check Your Solution

In each case, the root, prefix, and suffix correctly describe the structure.

Sample Problem

Drawing Aromatic Hydrocarbons

Problem
Draw the structure of 1-ethyl-3-propylbenzene.

What Is Required?
You must draw the structure of a compound.

What Is Given?
You are given the name of the compound.

Plan Your Strategy	Act on Your Strategy
a. Identify the root.	The root is benzene, so the structure is based on a benzene ring. 
If there is more than one side group, number the carbon atoms in the ring.	There are two side groups, so the ring must be numbered. 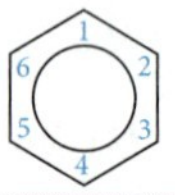
Identify the prefix, and draw the side groups.	The prefix is 1-ethyl-3-propyl-, so there is an ethyl group on carbon atom 1 and a propyl group on carbon atom 3. 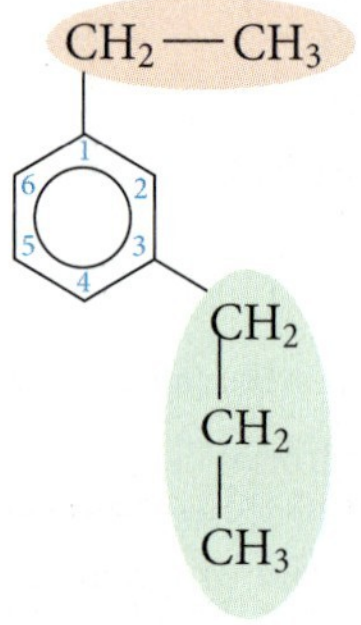

Check Your Solution
An ethyl group is on carbon atom 1 and a propyl group is on carbon atom 3 of the benzene ring, so the structure is correct.

Practice Problems

For the next four questions, name each aromatic hydrocarbon.

65.

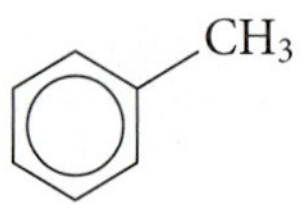

66.

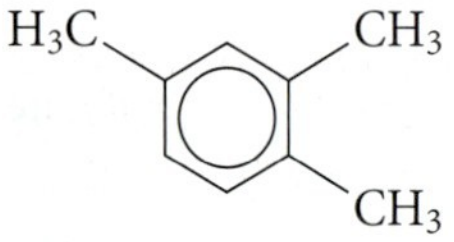

67.

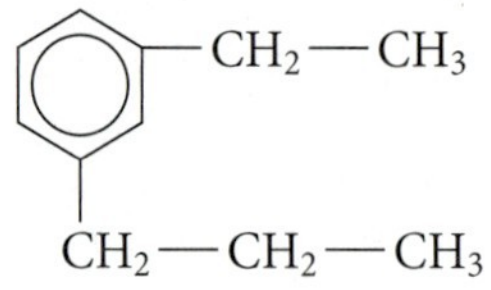

68.

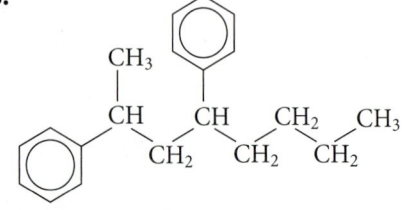

For the next five questions, draw the condensed structural formula for each aromatic hydrocarbon.

69. 1,3-diethyl-4-methyl-2-propylbenzene

70. 1,4-dimethylbenzene, historically known as para-xylene or p-xylene

71. 1-ethyl-3-propylbenzene

72. 1,2-diethyl-4,5-dimethylbenzene

73. 2-phenyl-5-propyloctane

74. The molecule 2-methyl-5-ethylbenzene is named incorrectly. Draw the line structural formula for the molecule and name it correctly.

38 MHR • Unit 1 Organic Chemistry

Physical Properties of Aromatic Compounds

Benzene is a liquid at standard temperature. If you compare the boiling points of simple aromatic hydrocarbons, you will see that they are very similar to those of the aliphatic hydrocarbons that have the same number of carbon atoms. Also, as the name *aromatic* implies, these compounds often have strong odours. Examples of aromatic compounds that have odours you may be familiar with are shown in **Figure 1.24**. In the next section, you will learn about some of the side groups that are part of these compounds.

Suggested Investigation

Inquiry Investigation 1-A, Modelling Organic Compounds

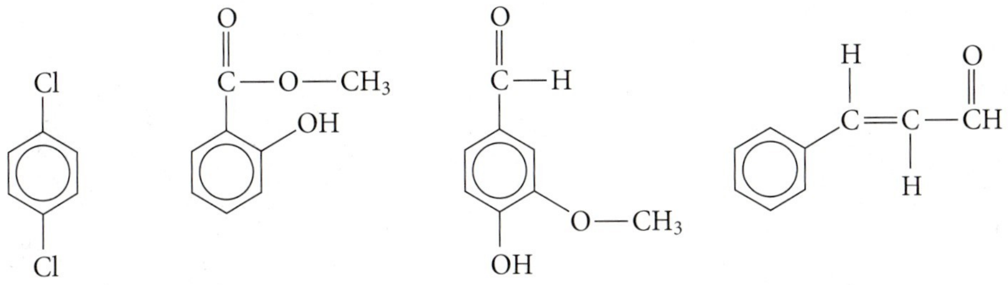

moth balls   wintergreen   vanilla   cinnamon

Figure 1.24 Substituted benzene rings form the basis of compounds with many familiar odours, such as those shown here.

Activity 1.3 Rings Around You

Did you know that many of the products around you contain aromatic compounds, a family of molecules based on the benzene ring? In fact, benzene is used in the manufacture of many products from plastics to pharmaceuticals. Vanilla flavouring and acetylsalicylic acid are just two examples of substances based on a ring structure that we consume regularly. Should you be concerned about aromatic compounds in the products around you and in your food? In this activity, you will research the ingredients found in products such as plastics and sunscreens in order to answer that question.

Materials
- reference books
- computer with Internet access

Procedure
1. Working in groups of four, have each group member select one of the following topics to research.
   - pharmaceuticals
   - artificial flavours
   - plastics and plasticizers
   - sunscreens
2. Research information about the topic you chose, using the following questions to guide your research.
   - What are examples of chemical ingredients in your products that contain benzene rings? Draw structures for two of these.
   - For the two chemicals you selected, how are these manufactured? What are the starting ingredients?
   - What are the uses of these chemicals?
   - How do these chemicals impact the environment as a result of their manufacture, use, or disposal? Provide a detailed description.
   - Identify any health effects associated with the use or manufacture of these chemicals.
   - Identify any alternatives to their use that are safer or more environmentally friendly, often referred to as "green substitutes."
3. Share and discuss the information you found with your group members.

Questions
1. Write a short report summarizing the environmental and/or health concerns associated with chemicals you researched.
2. Find a blog or posting on the Internet about your topic. Is the information correct based on your research? Write a critical review of the posting.
3. There are some concerns about the prevalence of products containing aromatics that we use daily. Comment on whether these concerns are justified based on your group's research.
4. Is it possible to live without compounds containing aromatic molecules? Discuss this in your group and share the results of your discussion with the class.

STSE
CHEMISTRY Connections

Green Chemistry and the Reduction of Hexane Use

Green chemistry involves redesigning chemical processes from the ground up, thus making industrial chemistry safer, cleaner, and more energy-efficient throughout a product's life cycle, from synthesis to clean-up to disposal. One important goal of green chemistry is to eliminate or reduce exposure to harmful substances. Green chemistry is especially effective when it solves more than one environmental problem. This is the case with the work of Queen's University chemistry professor Philip Jessop and his students based in Kingston, Ontario. They have determined how to replace hexane with carbon dioxide in the manufacture of cooking oil.

USES OF HEXANE Hexane, C_6H_{14}, is a volatile organic compound found in crude oil, gasoline, and natural gas. Hexane is widely used in the printing industry because it is a solvent that dissolves glue and ink. This organic compound can be found in adhesives, sealants, binders, fillers, lubricants, paints and coatings, rubber and rubber cements, brake cleaners, and degreasers. Hexane is also used to extract oil from crushed soybeans, sunflower seeds, corn, and other crops.

HEALTH AND ENVIRONMENTAL ISSUES Short-term exposure to hexane at high concentrations causes dizziness, headache, and a depression of the central nervous system. Long periods of exposure to hexane result in numbness in the extremities and muscular weakness. The most likely risk of exposure to hexane is in the workplace.

When hexane is used in the oil extraction process, most of it is contained and re-used. However, a small amount escapes into the environment. These small amounts accumulate over time, contributing to the formation of smog. According to Jessop, hexane solvent distillation during vegetable oil manufacture contributes more hexane to Canada's atmosphere than the oil, gas, coal, and oil sands industries combined. In addition, the oil extraction process itself involves distillation, which uses large amounts of energy.

SIDE-STEPPING THE USE OF HEXANE Jessop, who holds a Canada Research Chair in Green Chemistry, has synthesized a solvent that, when combined with carbon dioxide, extracts oil from soybeans. The solvent is hydrophobic, which means that it mixes with oil but not with water. However, when carbon dioxide is added, the solvent becomes hydrophilic, which means it mixes with water but not with oil.

Soybeans are crushed to extract oil. Currently, part of the extraction process involves the use of hexane as a solvent.

Therefore, when carbonated water (carbon dioxide and water) is added to a mixture made up of the solvent and soybeans, the oil is extracted. When the carbon dioxide is removed, the solvent switches back to its hydrophobic state, which is why Jessop calls it a "switchable" solvent.

There are three distinct advantages to this extraction system. It avoids the use of hexane, it recycles the greenhouse gas carbon dioxide, and it eliminates the need for the large amounts of energy required in the distillation process. In addition, the water and the solvent that are components of the improved extraction process can be re-used.

While it will be some years yet before the process can be used commercially, cooking oil companies have already expressed an interest in this breakthrough research.

Connect to the Environment

1. Identify an industrial chemical other than hexane that is potentially harmful, and research green chemistry alternatives to its use. Evaluate the effectiveness of those alternatives.

2. Advocates of green chemistry promote it as an innovative solution to the problem of using harmful substances in industrial processes. However, critics claim that green chemistry is simply public relations rather than effective management of exposure to harmful substances. Research both points of view and defend your opinion using specific examples.

Section 1.2 Review

Section Summary

- Hydrocarbons are compounds that contain only carbon atoms and hydrogen atoms.
- Alkanes are made up of single bonds only. Alkenes are hydrocarbons that have at least one double bond, while alkynes have at least one triple bond.
- Cyclic hydrocarbons include alkanes, alkenes, and alkynes in the shape of a ring. Aromatic hydrocarbons are ring structures that are derived from benzene.
- Hydrocarbons are insoluble in water but are soluble in non-polar solvents, such as benzene. They are ranked as follows from highest to lowest boiling point: aromatic and cyclic hydrocarbons, alkynes, alkanes, alkenes.
- All hydrocarbon names are based on the structure of the compound and follow IUPAC rules. The names are so precise that the structure of the compound can be drawn from them.

Review Questions

1. **K/U** What is a homologous series? Identify two examples of molecules that are part of the same homologous series.

2. **C** Draw a three-dimensional diagram of ethane.

3. **C** Using 2-methylheptane as an example, identify and explain the three basic parts to the naming of an organic molecule.

4. **K/U** Identify the general formula for each of the following.
   a. an alkane
   b. an alkene with one double bond
   c. an alkyne with one triple bond

5. **A** Identify four hydrocarbons encountered in everyday life. For each example, state the uses and appropriate expanded molecular formulas of the hydrocarbon.

6. **K/U** Compare and contrast unsaturated and saturated hydrocarbons. Describe one physical property that would be different between the two if they had the same number of carbons.

7. **T/I** Name each of the following compounds.
   a. $H_3C-CH_2-CH_2-HC-CH_2$ with CH_3 branches
   b.
   c.
   d.

8. **C** Draw a condensed structural formula for each of the following compounds.
   a. 2,4-dimethylpent-2-ene
   b. 3,5-diethyl-3,4,7,8-tetramethyl-5-propyldec-1-yne
   c. 1,3-dimethylcylobutene
   d. 4-ethyl-2-phenyloctane

9. **C** Draw a line structural formula for each of the following compounds.
   a. but-1-yne
   b. 3,5-dimethylhex-1-yne
   c. 3-cyclobutyl-4-ethylhexane
   d. 1,3-dimethylbenzene

10. **T/I** You are given samples of hexane, hex-1-ene, hex-1-yne, and cyclohexane.
    a. Design an investigation to distinguish these four liquids.
    b. Predict the results of the investigation. Refer to **Table 1.7** and **Table 1.9** for help.

11. **K/U** What is the general formula for a saturated cyclic hydrocarbon? What straight chain hydrocarbon has the same formula?

12. **A** Give an example of a naturally found:
    a. cyclic hydrocarbon.
    b. aromatic hydrocarbon.

13. **K/U** Why is it unnecessary to number the multiple bonds in the following molecules?
    a. propyne
    b. cyclobutene

14. **K/U** Why is a ring in the centre of the structural formula for benzene more appropriate than alternating single and double bonds?

SECTION 1.3
Hydrocarbon Derivatives

Key Terms

functional group
hydrocarbon derivative
alcohol
hydroxyl group
parent alkane
haloalkane
carbonyl group
formyl group
aldehyde
ketone
carboxylic acid
carboxyl group
ester
ether
alkoxy group
amine
amide

functional group in a molecule, a certain group of atoms responsible for chemical reactions that are characteristic of that molecule

hydrocarbon derivative a compound made up of carbon atoms and at least one other atom that is not hydrogen

Organic chemists classify chemical compounds according to their functional groups. A **functional group** is a special arrangement of atoms that is mainly responsible for the chemical behaviour of the molecule. Functional groups also determine some of the physical properties of the molecule. When one or more functional groups are attached to a hydrocarbon, the resulting compound is referred to as a **hydrocarbon derivative**. Hydrocarbon derivatives are compounds made up of carbon atoms and at least one other atom that is not hydrogen.

Table 1.11 lists some of the common functional groups. You have already learned how to name and draw alkanes, alkenes, and alkynes, and have learned about their physical properties. Throughout the remainder of this section, you will learn to recognize, name, and draw alcohols, haloalkanes, aldehydes, ketones, carboxylic acids, esters, ethers, amines, and amides. You will also learn about some of their physical properties.

Table 1.11 Organic Compounds and Functional Groups

Organic Compound	General Formula of Functional Group	Prefix or Suffix
Alcohol	R—OH (hydroxyl group)	-ol
Haloalkane	R—X (X = a halogen)	Prefix varies with halogen
Aldehyde	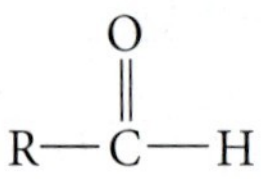 R—C(=O)—H (formyl group)	-al
Ketone	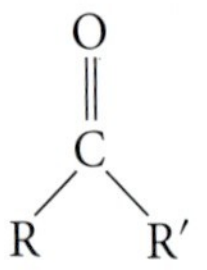 R—C(=O)—R' (carbonyl group)	-one
Carboxylic acid	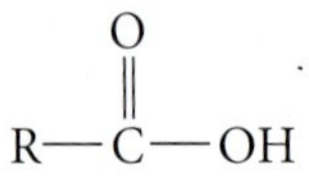 R—C(=O)—OH (carboxyl group)	-oic acid
Ester	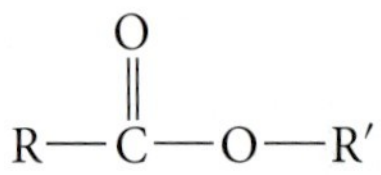 R—C(=O)—O—R'	-oate
Ether	R—O—R' (alkoxy group)	-oxy; -yl
Amine	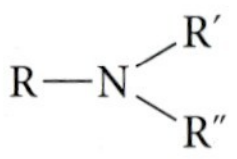 R—N(R')(R'')	-amine
Amide	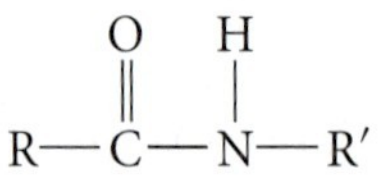 R—C(=O)—N(H)—R'	-amide

Note: In this table, R, R', and R" can represent hydrogen atoms or unspecified hydrocarbons in the rest of the molecule.

Alcohols

alcohol a hydrocarbon derivative that contains a hydroxyl group

hydroxyl group a functional group consisting of an oxygen atom and a hydrogen atom

An **alcohol** is a hydrocarbon derivative that contains a hydroxyl functional group. A **hydroxyl group** consists of an oxygen atom and a hydrogen atom (—OH). Alcohols are components of many commonly used products. **Table 1.12** summarizes a few common alcohols and some of their uses.

Table 1.12 Common Alcohols and Their Uses

IUPAC Name	Common Name(s)	Structure	Boiling Point (°C)	Use(s)
methanol	wood alcohol, methyl alcohol	CH_3-OH	64.6	• solvent in many chemical processes • component of automobile antifreeze • fuel
ethanol	grain alcohol, ethyl alcohol	CH_3-CH_2-OH	78.2	• solvent in many chemical processes • component of alcoholic beverages • antiseptic liquid • additive for fuel
propan-2-ol	rubbing alcohol, isopropyl alcohol, isopropanol	CH_3 $\searrow$ $CH-OH$ $\nearrow$ CH_3	82.4	• antiseptic liquid
ethane-1,2-diol	ethylene glycol	$HO-CH_2-CH_2-OH$	197.6	• main component of automobile antifreeze

Naming and Drawing Alcohols

The root of the name of an alcohol is based on the **parent alkane**, which is the alkane having the same basic carbon structure. The steps in **Table 1.13** will help you name alcohols. Draw alcohols according to the parent alkane, and then place the hydroxyl group on the correct carbon atom as determined by the number.

parent alkane the alkane having the same basic carbon structure as a hydrocarbon derivative

Table 1.13 Steps in Naming Alcohols

1. Identify the root. **a.** Identify the longest chain that includes the hydroxyl group(s). **b.** Name the parent alkane.	$CH_3-CH_2-CH_2-CH-CH-CH-CH_3$ with OH on carbons, and CH_2-CH_3 branch The longest chain containing the hydroxyl groups is seven carbon atoms long. The parent alkane is heptane.
2. Identify the suffix. **a.** Number the main carbon chain in the direction that gives the carbons bonded to the hydroxyl group(s) the lowest numbers. **b.** The suffix of an alcohol always ends with -ol. Indicate the position of each hydroxyl group by placing the number of the carbon atom bonded to each group in front of the -ol. **c.** If there is more than one hydroxyl group, place a prefix (di-, tri-, tetra-) at the beginning of the suffix to indicate the number of hydroxyl groups.	$CH_3-CH_2-CH_2-CH-CH-CH-CH_3$ 7 6 5 4 3 2 1, with CH_2-CH_3 branch Numbering the main chain from right to left gives the carbons bonded to the hydroxyl groups the lowest possible numbers. The compound is an alcohol. The hydroxyl groups are bonded to carbon atoms 2 and 3. The suffix contains -2,3-ol. There are two hydroxyl groups. The complete suffix is -2,3-diol.
3. Identify the prefix. Name and number any alkyl side groups on the main chain as you would for a hydrocarbon.	$CH_3-CH_2-CH_2-CH-CH-CH-CH_3$ 7 6 5 4 3 2 1, with CH_2-CH_3 branch An ethyl group is bonded to carbon atom 4. The prefix is 4-ethyl-.
4. Name the compound. Combine the prefix, root, and suffix to name the compound. If the suffix begins with a vowel, drop the -e on the end of the parent alkane. There is no space or hyphen between the prefix and the root.	The suffix begins with a consonant, so the $-e$ is not dropped. The compound is 4−ethylheptane-2,3-diol.

Recall from the previous section that the rule for placing the number that describes the position of the double bond was recently revised by IUPAC. IUPAC has similarly revised rules for naming molecules containing various functional groups, including alcohols and other hydrocarbon derivatives you will encounter in this section. While you may see these compounds named differently in other chemical literature, always use the new IUPAC rules when naming hydrocarbon derivatives. For example, a five-carbon chain with a hydroxyl group bonded to carbon atom 3 is named pentan-3-ol.

Sample Problem

Naming Alcohols

Problem

Name the following alcohols.

a. 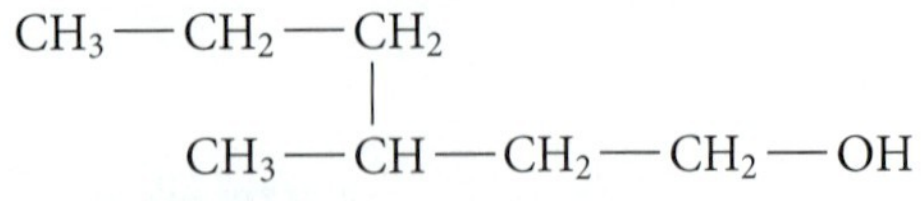 $CH_3-CH_2-CH_2$
   $|$
   $CH_3-CH-CH_2-CH_2-OH$

b. 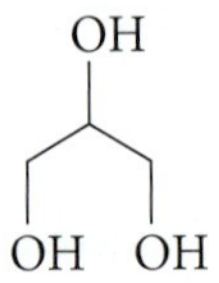 OH
    |
    CH
   / \
  OH OH
   (propane backbone with OH on carbons 1, 2, 3)

What Is Required?

You must name two alcohols.

What Is Given?

You are given the structures of the alcohols.

Plan Your Strategy	Act on Your Strategy
a. Identify the root.	The hydroxyl group is attached to a hydrocarbon chain having six carbon atoms. Therefore, the parent alkane is hexane. 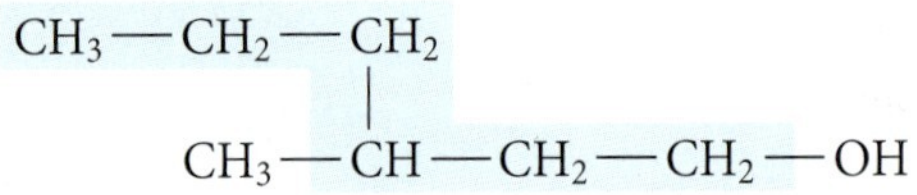
Identify the suffix.	There is one hydroxyl group and it is bonded to the end of the chain. Thus, the number of the carbon atom to which the hydroxyl group is attached is 1. The suffix is -1-ol. 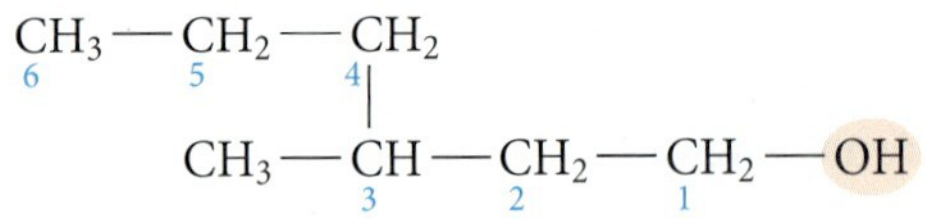
Identify the prefix.	There is a methyl group on carbon atom 3 so the prefix is 3-methyl-. 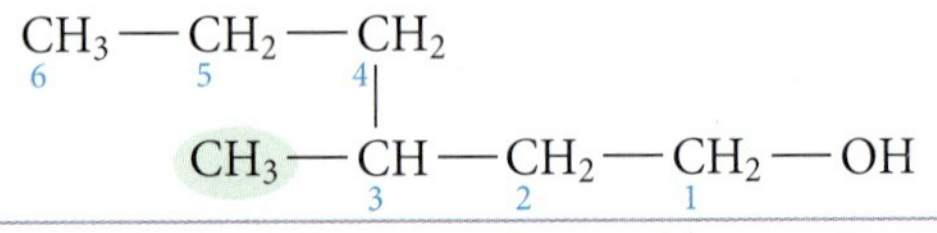
Write the name.	The suffix begins with a vowel, so omit the -e on the end of the parent alkane. The name of the alcohol is 3-methylhexan-1-ol.
b. Identify the root.	The hydroxyl groups are attached to a carbon chain that has three carbon atoms. Therefore, the parent alkane is propane.
Identify the suffix.	There are three hydroxyl groups so the suffix ends with -triol. There is one hydroxyl group on each of the three carbon atoms, so the suffix must contain -1,2,3-. The suffix is -1,2,3-triol.
Identify the prefix.	There are no other side groups on the main chain so there is no prefix.
Write the name.	The suffix starts with a consonant so do not remove the -e from the root. The name of the alcohol is propane-1,2,3-triol.

Check Your Solution

a. There are six carbons in the main chain, with a methyl group on carbon atom 3 and a hydroxyl group on carbon atom 1. The name correctly reflects this structure.

b. There are three carbon atoms in the main chain and a hydroxyl group on carbon atoms 1, 2, and 3. The name correctly reflects this structure.

Sample Problem

Drawing Alcohols

Problem
Draw the condensed structural formula for 4-methylpentane-1,2-diol.

What Is Required?
You must draw the condensed structural formula for a compound.

What Is Given?
You are given the name.

Plan Your Strategy	Act on Your Strategy
Identify the root.	The parent alkane is pentane. Therefore, the main chain has five carbon atoms.
Draw and number the main chain.	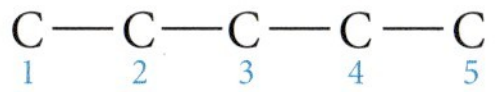 C—C—C—C—C 1 2 3 4 5
Identify the suffix and draw the side groups.	The suffix is -1,2-diol, so there is a hydroxyl group on carbon atoms 1 and 2. 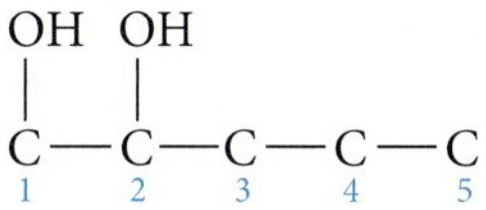 OH OH | | C—C—C—C—C 1 2 3 4 5
Identify the prefix and draw the side groups.	The prefix is 4-methyl-, so there is a methyl group on carbon atom 4. 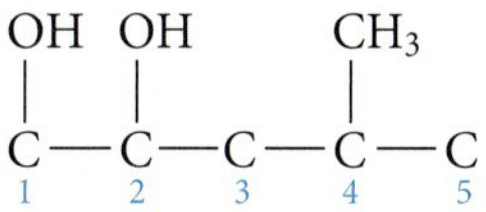 OH OH CH$_3$ | | | C—C—C—C—C 1 2 3 4 5
Add enough hydrogen atoms to give each carbon atom four bonds.	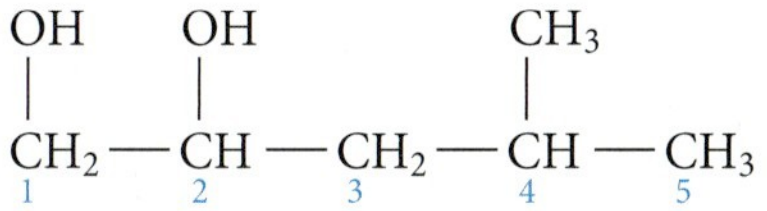 OH OH CH$_3$ | | | CH$_2$—CH—CH$_2$—CH—CH$_3$ 1 2 3 4 5

Check Your Solution
The main chain has five carbon atoms, there are hydroxyl groups on carbon atoms 1 and 2, and there is a methyl group on carbon atom 4, so the structure is in agreement with the name.

Practice Problems

For the next five questions, name each alcohol.

75.
  OH
  \|
H$_3$C—CH$_2$—CH—CH$_3$

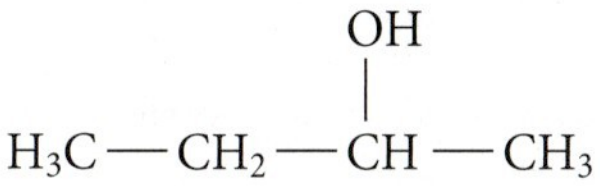

76.
  OH OH
  \| \|
H$_3$C—CH$_2$—HC—CH—CH$_3$

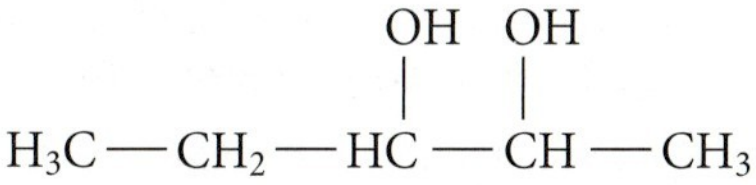

77.
(isopropyl structure with OH)

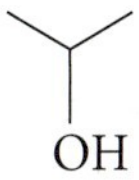

78.
  OH   OH
  \| \|
H$_2$C—CH$_2$—C—CH$_3$
              \|
              CH$_3$

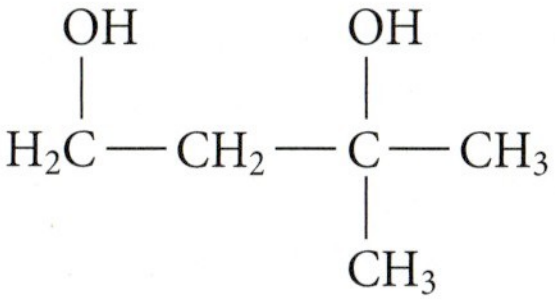

79.
(benzene ring with substituents, OH group)

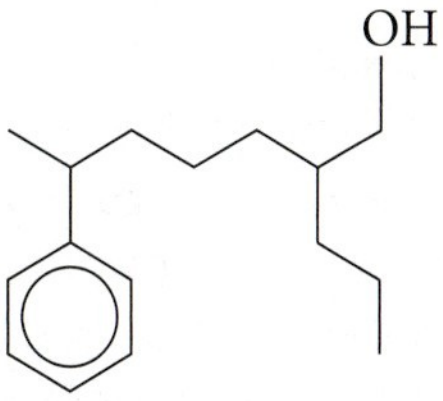

For the next five questions, draw the condensed structural formula for each alcohol.

80. ethanol
81. propan-1-ol
82. butane-1,3-diol
83. 3,4-dimethylhexan-2-ol
84. 2,3-diethylcyclohexanol

Physical Properties of Alcohols

The hydroxyl group is very polar, making the small alcohols polar as well. Consequently, the smallest alcohols, methanol and ethanol, are miscible (can be mixed in all proportions) with water. As the hydrocarbon chain becomes longer, the non-polar characteristics supersede the polarity of the hydroxyl group and the alcohols become less soluble in water.

The hydroxyl groups also allow the alcohols to hydrogen bond with one another. Therefore, the boiling points of the pure alcohols are much higher than are those of the corresponding alkanes. All straight chain alcohols with fewer than twelve carbon atoms are liquids at standard temperature.

All alcohols are toxic. Methanol can cause blindness or death. Although ethanol is consumed in alcoholic beverages, it too can cause death if excessive amounts are consumed.

Haloalkanes

haloalkane a hydrocarbon derivative that contains at least one halogen atom

A **haloalkane** is a hydrocarbon that contains at least one halogen atom. Haloalkanes are not found in living systems but are artificial. Trichloromethane, commonly known as chloroform, was once used as an anaesthetic. It is no longer used as such because it is now considered a possible carcinogen. Another familiar group of haloalkanes, chlorofluorocarbons (CFCs), were once used as refrigerants and as propellants in spray cans. In addition to being potent greenhouse gases, CFCs are responsible for damage to the ozone layer, such as that shown in **Figure 1.25**. The ozone layer in the stratosphere normally absorbs most ultraviolet light before it reaches Earth's surface. The reduction of the ozone layer permits dangerous levels of ultraviolet light from the Sun to reach the ground. Because serious health effects such as skin cancer, as well as crop damage, can result from exposure to ultraviolet light, CFCs are now banned substances.

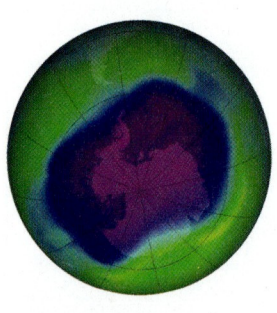

Figure 1.25 This satellite image, taken on September 24, 2006, shows the hole in the ozone layer over Antarctica. The ban of CFCs will enable the layer to re-form with time, although the process is taking longer than expected.
Speculate Even though CFC production has stopped, why might it take longer than expected for the ozone layer to re-form?

Activity 1.4 | CFCs: A Chilling Issue

Through the Montreal Protocol and Earth Summit gatherings, many countries—including Canada—have banned CFC production and use. Since phasing out the use of CFCs, a number of substitutes have been used, but these substitutes also have the potential to cause environmental problems.

Materials
- reference books
- computer with Internet access

Procedure
Research the chemicals that are currently being used as refrigerants and the alternative chemicals available to replace them. Use a table to organize the results of your research. Be sure to answer the following questions about each group of chemicals.
- What is their chemical structure?
- What are the advantages and disadvantages of these chemicals?

Questions
1. Hydrochlorofluorocarbons (HCFCs) were initially used to replace CFCs. Draw the structures for two examples of HCFCs: 2,2,-dichloro-1,1,1–difluoroethane and 2-chloro-1,1,1,2-tetrafluoroethane. Why were HCFCs only temporary replacements for CFCs?
2. Some governments are looking at HFO-1234yf as the coolant for the future. What costs are entailed in adopting this chemical as a refrigerant in cars?
3. Scientists are always looking for better refrigerants.
   a. What properties should a good refrigerant have?
   b. Why are refrigerants essential to our society?
4. Of the chemicals you researched, which is the most efficient and environmentally-friendly refrigerant? Why?
5. Propose a plan of action that could be taken to make sure that governments promote the most effective and most environmentally-friendly refrigerant.

Naming and Drawing Haloalkanes

Like alcohols, haloalkanes are named according to the parent alkane. The steps in **Table 1.14** will help you name and draw haloalkanes. For naming, notice that the suffix is the same as the alkane. Draw haloalkanes according to the parent alkane and add the halogens and any alkyl side groups to the correct carbons in the main chain as determined by their numbers.

Table 1.14 Steps in Naming Haloalkanes

1. Identify the root. **a.** Identify the longest chain that includes the halogen atom(s).	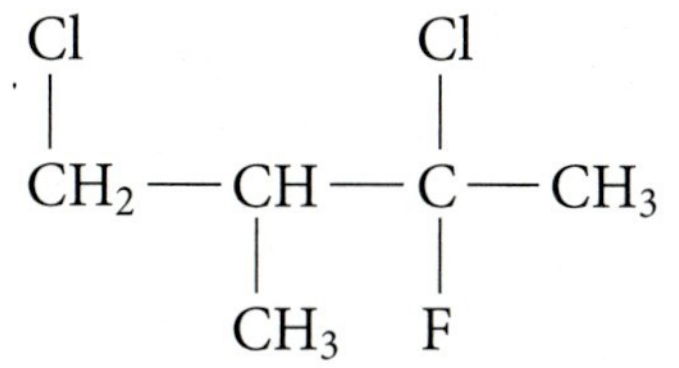 $CH_2-CH-C-CH_3$ with Cl on CH_2, Cl on C, CH_3 and F on the middle carbons The longest chain containing the halogen atoms is four carbon atoms long.
b. Name the parent alkane.	The parent alkane is butane.
2. Identify the prefix. **a.** Number the main carbon chain in the direction that gives the carbons bonded to the halogens the lowest numbers. Number a cyclic alkane by assigning the number 1 position to the carbon bonded to the halogen that provides the lowest possible numbers.	The carbons bonded to the halogen atoms have the lowest numbers when the structure is numbered from left to right. 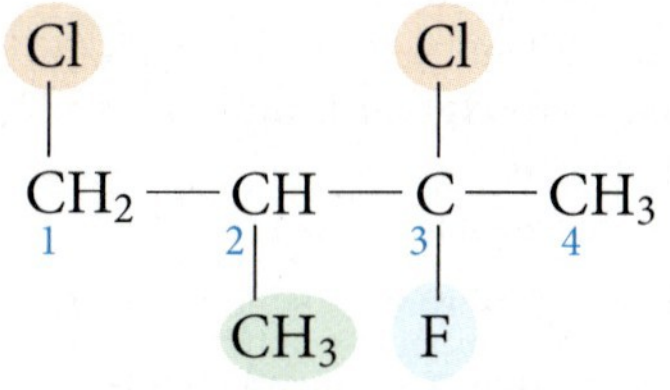 $\underset{1}{CH_2}-\underset{2}{CH}-\underset{3}{C}-\underset{4}{CH_3}$ with Cl, Cl, CH_3, F substituents
b. Use prefixes to identify the specific halogens (chloro-, fluoro-, bromo-, iodo-). Then determine the numbers of the carbon atoms bonded to the halogens. Write the prefixes alphabetically. If there are two or more of the same type of halogen, use a prefix (di-, tri-) to indicate the number. Recall that these prefixes are not considered when alphabetizing the terms.	There are two chlorine atoms (prefix chloro-) on carbon atoms 1 and 3 and a fluorine atom (prefix fluoro-) on carbon atom 3. Writing prefixes alphabetically, the prefix contains 1,3-dichloro-3-fluoro-.
c. Name and number any alkyl side groups on the main chain. Write all prefixes alphabetically.	There is a methyl group on carbon atom 2. The complete prefix, ordered alphabetically, is 1,3-dichloro-3-fluoro-2-methyl-.
3. Name the compound. Combine the prefix and root to name the compound. There is no space or hyphen between the prefix and the root.	The compound is 1,3-dichloro-3-fluoro-2-methylbutane.

Study the Sample Problems that follow to learn more about naming and drawing haloalkanes. Then apply your knowledge to complete the Practice Problems on naming and drawing haloalkanes.

Sample Problem

Naming Haloalkanes

Problem

Name the following haloalkanes.

a.
```
              Br      Br
              |       |
CH₃—CH₂—CH—CH—CH—CH₃
                 |
                 Cl
```

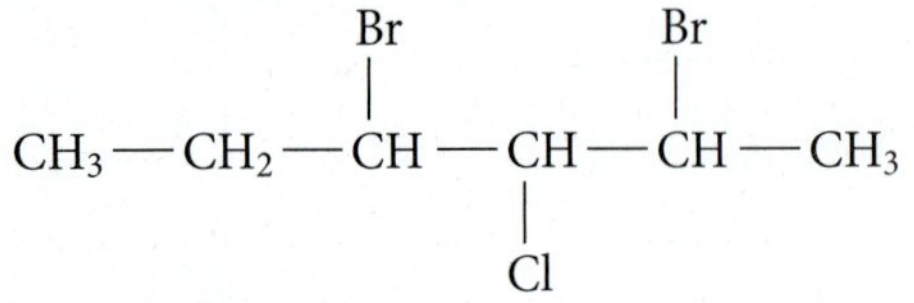

b. A cyclohexane ring with Br, Br, and CH₃ substituents.

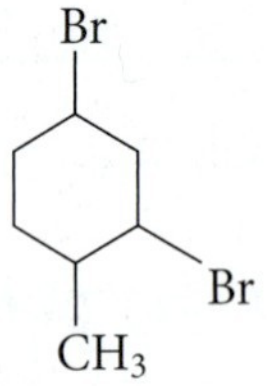

What Is Required?

You must name two haloalkanes.

What Is Given?

You are given the structures.

Plan Your Strategy	Act on Your Strategy
a. Identify the root.	The chain has six carbon atoms so the root is hexane.
Identify the prefix.	The halogen atoms have the lowest numbers when the structure is numbered from right to left. There are bromine atoms on carbon atoms 2 and 4 and a chlorine atom on carbon atom 3. Therefore, the prefix is 2,4-dibromo-3-chloro-. 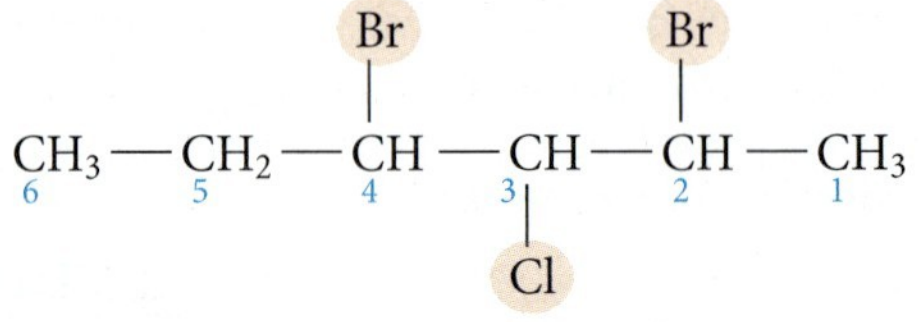
Name the compound.	The compound is 2,4-dibromo-3-chlorohexane.
b. Identify the root.	The structure is based on a six-membered ring so the root is cyclohexane.
Identify the prefix.	The halogen atoms have numbering priority so numbering should start with a bromine atom. Number so that the numbers are the lowest possible by labelling the carbon atom at the top as number 1 and then continue to number clockwise. There are bromine atoms on carbon atoms 1 and 3 and a methyl group on carbon atom 4. Therefore, the prefix is 1,3-dibromo-4-methyl-. 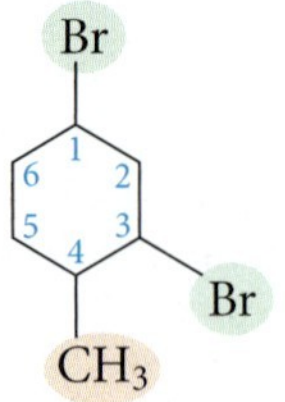
Name the compound.	The name of the compound is 1,3-dibromo-4-methylcyclohexane.

Check Your Solution

In both problems, the halogens received numbering priority and the numbering technique provides the lowest possible series of numbers.

Sample Problem

Drawing Haloalkanes

Problem

Draw a line structural formula for 4-bromo-2-chloro-3-fluoro-5-methylhexane.

What Is Required?

You must draw a line structural formula.

What Is Given?

You are given the name.

Plan Your Strategy	Act on Your Strategy
Identify the root.	The root is hexane so there are six carbon atoms in the main chain.
Draw and number the main chain.	
Identify the prefix and add the necessary structures.	The prefix is 4-bromo-2-chloro-3-fluoro-5-methyl, so there is a bromine atom on carbon atom 4, a chlorine atom on carbon atom 2, a fluorine atom on carbon atom 3, and a methyl group on carbon atom 5. In a line structural formula, you do not draw out a methyl group because a straight line implies that there is a carbon atom at the end of the line and it has enough hydrogen atoms to give a total of four bonds. 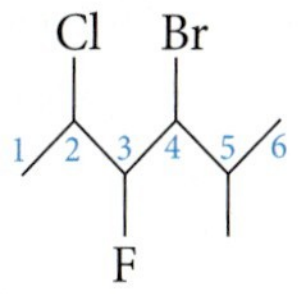

Check Your Solution
There is a chlorine atom on carbon atom 2, a fluorine atom on carbon atom 3, a bromine atom on carbon atom 4, and a methyl group on carbon atom 5. The structure agrees with the name.

Practice Problems

For the next five questions, name each haloalkane.

85. $H_3C-CH_2-HC(F)-CH_3$

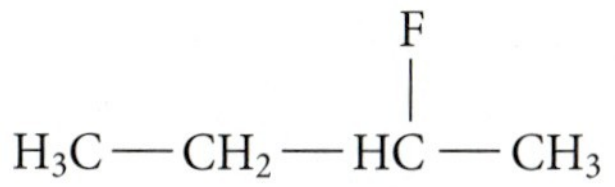

86. $H_3C-CH_2-C(Br)(CH_3)-CH_2-CH_3$

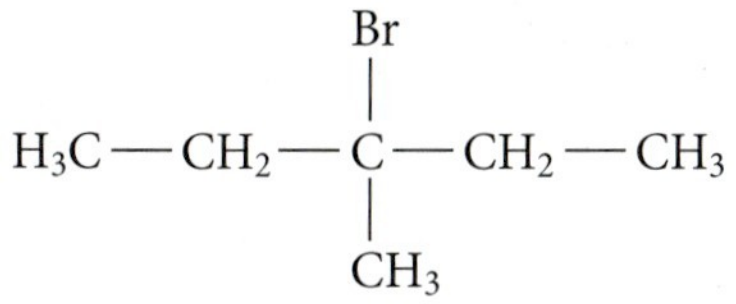

87. $H_3C-CH_2-CH(Cl)-CH_2-HC(CH_3)-CH_3$

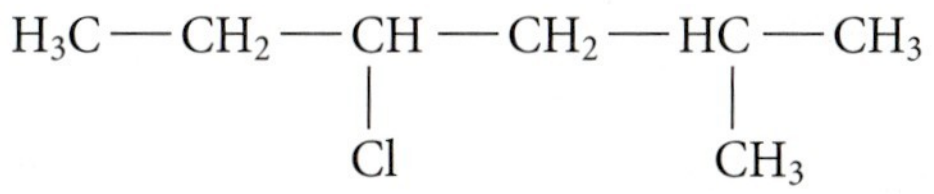

88. (line structure with Cl, Cl, F substituents)

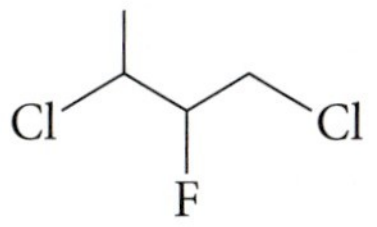

89. (cyclohexane with Br, Cl, Br substituents)

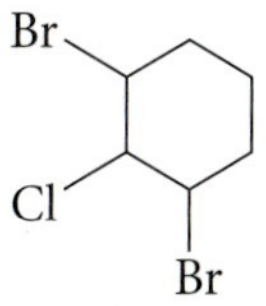

For the next five questions, draw the condensed structural formula for each haloalkane.

90. 1-iodopropane

91. 2-chloro-1-fluoroethane

92. 3-bromo-2,2-dimethylpentane

93. 2,4-dibromo-3-chlorohexane

94. 1,4-difluoro-2-propylcycloheptane

95. Identify any errors in the following names by drawing a line structure. Give the correct name for each haloalkane.
  a. 3-chlorobutane
  b. 4-chloro-3-bromohexane
  c. 2,4-dichlorocyclopentane
  d. 3-chloro-2,2-dimethylbutane

Physical Properties of Haloalkanes

Similar to the alkanes, only the smallest haloalkanes (fluoromethane, chloromethane, bromomethane, and iodomethane) are slightly soluble in water. All of the other haloalkanes are insoluble in water. In contrast, the boiling points of the haloalkanes differ greatly from those of alkanes with the same number of carbon atoms. For example, the boiling point of methane is −161°C, whereas the boiling point of chloromethane is −24.2°C and that of iodomethane is 42°C. The boiling point of propane is −42.1°C, whereas that of 1-chloropropane is 45.6°C and that of 1-iodopropane is 102.5°C.

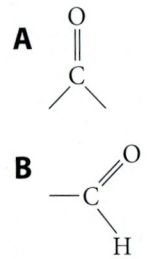

Figure 1.26 A carbonyl group **(A)** is a component of a formyl group **(B)**, as well as several other funtional groups.

carbonyl group
a functional group in which a carbon atom is double bonded to an oxygen atom

formyl group
a functional group in which a carbon atom is double bonded to an oxygen atom and single bonded to a hydrogen atom

aldehyde
a hydrocarbon derivative that contains a formyl group

Aldehydes

You may be familiar with the smell of the most common aldehyde, formaldehyde (methanal). A water solution of formaldehyde, called formalin, is often used to preserve organisms, such as frogs, for dissection in school laboratories. The federal government and several provincial governments have placed legal limits on human exposure to formaldehyde. As a result, the concentration of formaldehyde currently found in laboratories, such as those in Ontario classrooms, has been deemed safe. Nevertheless, researchers are trying to find alternatives to formalin because of its toxic effects at high concentrations.

Aldehydes, as well as several other hydrocarbon derivatives discussed later in this section, contain a carbonyl functional group. A **carbonyl group** (>C=O) is a functional group containing a carbon atom that is double bonded to an oxygen atom. The structure of this group is shown in **Figure 1.26A**. Carbonyl groups are components of several different functional groups. In aldehydes, a carbonyl group is part of a larger functional group that also contains a hydrogen atom bonded to the carbon atom. Called a **formyl group** (—CHO), this functional group is shown in **Figure 1.26B**.

By definition, an **aldehyde** is a hydrocarbon derivative that contains a formyl group. Notice that three bonds on the carbon atom in the formyl group are with the other atoms in the group. There is only one position available on the carbon atom to bond to other atoms. Therefore, this group is always found at the end of a hydrocarbon chain.

Naming and Drawing Aldehydes

Aldehydes are named in much the same way as alcohols are named. That is, the root of the name of an aldehyde is based on the parent alkane, the alkane having the same basic carbon structure. The steps in **Table 1.15** will guide you through the naming of aldehydes. To draw an aldehyde, draw the parent alkane and then place the hydrogen and oxygen atoms of the formyl group on the first carbon of the chain.

Table 1.15 Steps in Naming Aldehydes

1. Identify the root.		
		CH₃—CH(CH₃)—CH(CH₃)—CH₂—CHO
a. Locate the longest chain that includes the formyl group.		The longest chain containing the formyl group is five carbon atoms.
b. Name the parent alkane. Drop the -e on the parent alkane to get the root.		The parent alkane is pentane. The root is pentan-.
2. Identify the suffix. Write the suffix for the compound. For aldehydes, the suffix is -al. There are no numbers in the suffix because the formyl group is always on carbon atom 1.		The compound is an aldehyde. The suffix is -al.
3. Identify the prefix.		CH₃—CH(CH₃)—CH(CH₃)—CH₂—CHO (numbered 5-4-3-2-1)
a. Number the main carbon chain. The carbon atom in the formyl group is always carbon atom 1.		
b. Name and give the position of any alkyl side groups on the main chain as you would for a hydrocarbon.		There are methyl groups on carbon atoms 3 and 4. The prefix is 3,4-dimethyl-.
4. Name the compound. Combine the prefix, root, and suffix to name the compound. There are no spaces between the prefix, root, and suffix.		The compound is 3,4-dimethylpentanal.

Sample Problem

Naming Aldehydes

Problem

Name the following aldehydes.

a.
```
        CH₃
        |
        CH₂
        |
CH₃—CH—CH₂—CH₂—C(=O)H
```

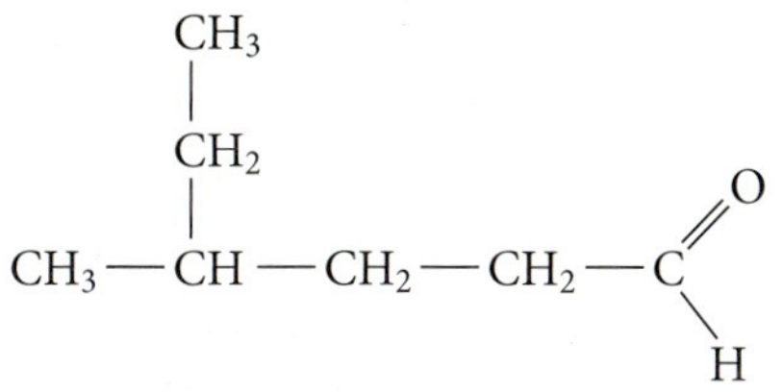

b. (branched aldehyde structure with methyl and ethyl substituents)

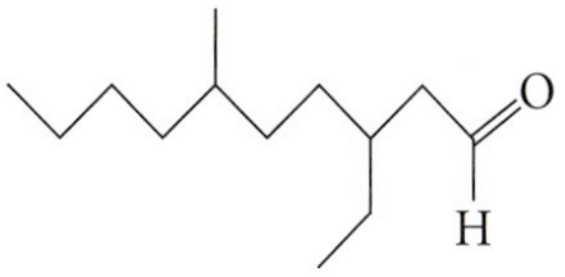

What Is Required?

You must name two aldehydes.

What Is Given?

You are given the structures.

Plan Your Strategy	Act on Your Strategy
a. Identify the root.	There are six carbon atoms in the longest chain including the formyl group, so the root is hexan-. 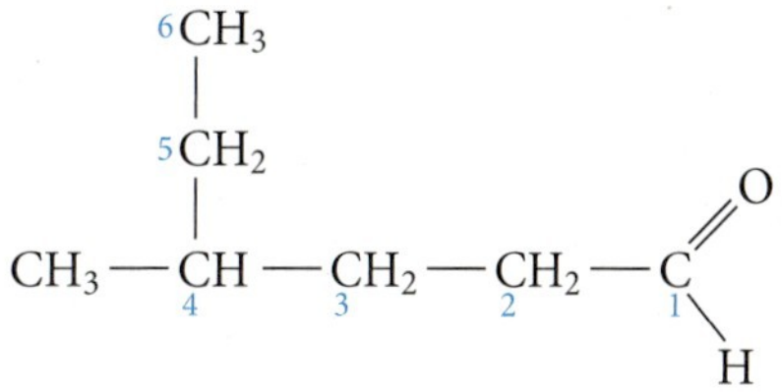 ⁶CH₃—⁵CH₂—CH₃—⁴CH—³CH₂—²CH₂—¹C(=O)H
Identify the suffix.	The compound is an aldehyde so the suffix is -al. There are no numbers in the suffix because the formyl group is always on carbon atom 1.
Identify the prefix.	There is a methyl side group on carbon atom 4. The prefix is 4-methyl-. 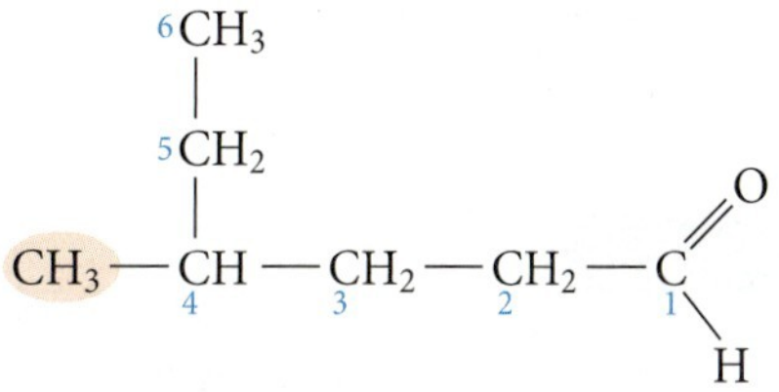 ⁶CH₃—⁵CH₂—**CH₃**—⁴CH—³CH₂—²CH₂—¹C(=O)H
Write the name.	The full name of the aldehyde is 4-methylhexanal.
b. Identify the root.	There are ten carbon atoms in the longest chain including the formyl group, so the root is decan-.
Identify the suffix.	The compound is an aldehyde so the suffix is -al.
Identify the prefix.	There is a methyl side group on carbon atom 6 and an ethyl side group on carbon atom 3, so the prefix is 3-ethyl-6-methyl-.
Write the name.	The full name of the aldehyde is 3-ethyl-6-methyldecanal.

Check Your Solution

a. The compound has a formyl group at the beginning of a six-carbon main chain, with a methyl group on carbon atom 4. The name correctly reflects this structure.

b. The compound has a formyl group at the beginning of a ten-carbon main chain. There is an ethyl group on carbon atom 3 and the methyl group on carbon atom 6 of the chain. The name correctly reflects this structure.

Sample Problem

Drawing Aldehydes

Problem
Draw a line structural formula for 5-ethyl-4-methyloctanal.

What Is Required?
You must draw a line structural formula for a compound.

What Is Given?
You are given the name.

Plan Your Strategy	Act on Your Strategy	
Identify the root and draw and number a line structure for the root.	The root of the name is octan- so there are eight carbon atoms in the chain.	
Identify the suffix and add the structure to the diagram.	The suffix is –al so it is an aldehyde. The carbon atom in the formyl group is always carbon atom 1. So, add a hydrogen atom and oxygen atom to carbon atom 1.	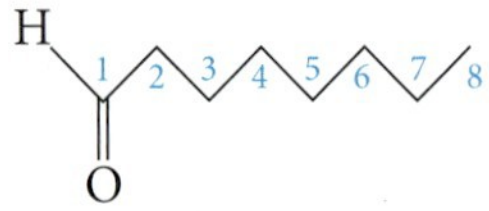
Identify the prefix and add any side groups to the line structure.	The prefix is 5-ethyl-4-methyl- so there is an ethyl group on carbon atom 5 and a methyl group on carbon atom 4.	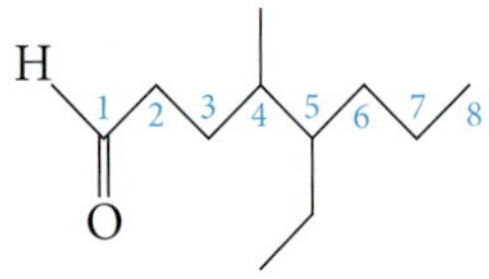

Check Your Solution
The carbon atom in the formyl group is carbon atom 1. A single line connected to the main chain at carbon atom 4 means that there is a methyl group bonded to that carbon. The bent line on carbon atom 5 means that there is an ethyl group bonded to that carbon. Each bend or end of a line represents a carbon atom. The structure agrees with the name.

Practice Problems

For the next four questions, name each aldehyde.

96. 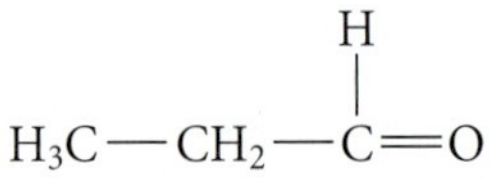 $H_3C-CH_2-\overset{\overset{H}{|}}{C}=O$

97. 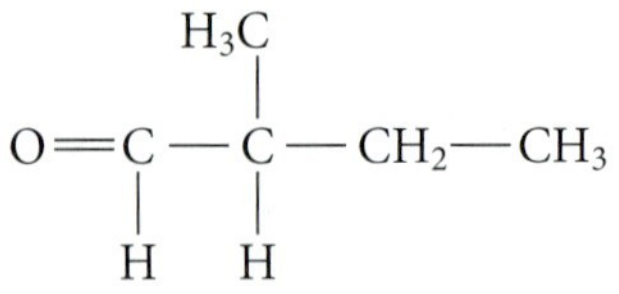 $O=\overset{\overset{H}{|}}{C}-\overset{\overset{H_3C}{|}}{\underset{\underset{H}{|}}{C}}-CH_2-CH_3$

98.

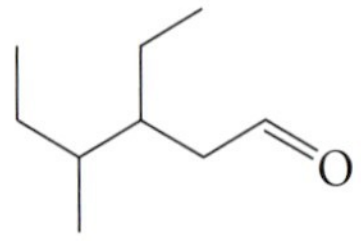

99.

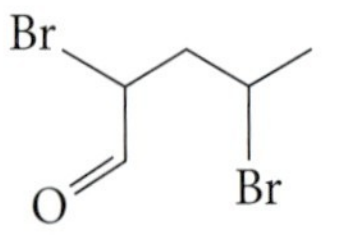

For the next five questions, draw the condensed structural formula for each aldehyde.

100. 3-methylbutanal

101. methanal (commonly known as formaldehyde)

102. 2-methylpropanal

103. 2-chloroethanal

104. 4,4-diethylhexanal

105. Explain why the following aldehydes are named incorrectly or cannot exist.

    a. 2-ethanal

    b. 5-ethylhexanal

    c. cyclobutanal

    d. 1-fluoropentanal

Physical Properties of Aldehydes

The carbonyl group of aldehydes is very polar but the carbon-hydrogen bonds are not. Thus, aldehydes cannot hydrogen bond with one another but they can hydrogen bond with water. Therefore, the strength of the attraction among aldehyde molecules is not as strong as that between alcohol molecules, which can bond with one another.

As a result, the boiling points of aldehydes are lower than those of alcohols having the same number of carbon atoms. Only methanal (formaldehyde) is a gas at room temperature. Ethanal has a boiling point of 20.1°C, which is very close to room temperature. So, it is either a very volatile liquid or a gas, depending on the exact temperature of the room. Aldehydes from three to 14 carbons long are liquids at room temperature, while those with carbon chains of 15 carbon atoms or longer are waxy solids.

The small aldehydes having one through four carbon atoms are soluble in water and those with five through seven carbon atoms are slightly soluble in water. When the carbon chain gets longer than seven carbon atoms, the insoluble nature of the hydrocarbon chain overcomes the solubility of the polar carbonyl group and the aldehydes are insoluble in water. Short chain aldehydes have a very pungent odour but, as the chain gets larger, the odour becomes more pleasant.

Ketones

Acetone is the common name for the ketone, propanone. Because it dissolves many compounds that are insoluble in water, it is used to remove nail polish from fingernails, ink stains from fingers, as well as price–tag stickers from glass, metal, or porcelain objects. However, it cannot be used on a plastic surface without dissolving the surface itself.

The smell of acetone may also indicate the presence of a serious health condition. Breath that smells like acetone can be a sign of a dangerous condition known as diabetic ketoacidosis. This condition occurs when a diabetic individual is unable to produce enough insulin to utilize glucose as a fuel source for the body. Instead, the body burns fatty acids. Ketones, a by–product of fatty acid metabolism, produce the scent of acetone on the breath. If not treated immediately, diabetic ketoacidosis can cause a diabetic coma and death.

A **ketone**, like an aldehyde, contains a carbonyl group (>C=O). Unlike aldehydes, the carbon atom in the carbonyl group of a ketone is bonded to two carbon atoms or carbon chains. **Figure 1.27** shows the structural diagram used to symbolize ketones. The R and R' groups represent carbon atoms or chains. They may be either the same or different from each other.

Because the carbonyl carbon in ketones must be bonded to two other carbon atoms, the smallest ketone must have at least three carbon atoms. **Figure 1.28** shows the structures of the two smallest ketones. Note that neither of these molecules requires a number to indicate the location of the carbonyl group. There is only one possible location for this group in each molecule. For butanone, flipping the molecule from side to side gives the same molecule as placing the carbonyl group between the two carbon atoms furthest to the right.

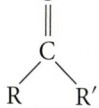

Figure 1.27 In ketones, the carbonyl group is bonded to the two carbon atoms or chains, R and R'.

ketone a hydrocarbon derivative that contains a carbonyl group that is bonded to two carbon atoms or carbon chains

propanone
(common name: acetone)

butanone
(common name: methylethylketone)

Figure 1.28 Acetone and methylethylketone are the common names for two of the smallest ketones, propanone and butanone. These well known solvents can dissolve many compounds that are insoluble in water. Methylethylketone (MEK) is a common industrial solvent used in paints, lacquers, industrial cements, and printing inks.

Naming and Drawing Ketones

Like alcohols and aldehydes, ketones are named according to the parent alkane. Thus, the root of the name of the ketone is the root of the alkane. The steps in **Table 1.16** will help you name ketones. Keep in mind that, to draw ketones, the number in the suffix refers to the carbon atom in the carbonyl group.

Table 1.16 Steps in Naming Ketones

1. Identify the root. a. Locate the longest chain that includes the carbonyl carbon atom. b. Name the parent alkane. Drop the -e on the parent alkane to get the root.	The longest chain containing the carbonyl carbon atom is five carbon atoms. The parent alkane is pentane. The root is pentan-. 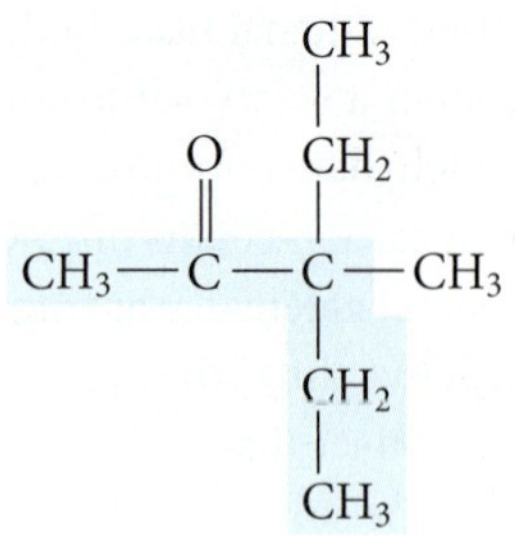	$CH_3-\overset{O}{\underset{\|}{C}}-\underset{\underset{CH_3}{\underset{\|}{CH_2}}}{\overset{\overset{CH_3}{\|}}{\overset{\|}{\underset{\|}{C}}}}-CH_3$
2. Identify the suffix. a. Start numbering at the end of the carbon chain that is nearest the carbonyl carbon atom. b. Determine the number of the carbonyl carbon atom. c. Write the suffix with a hyphen, the number of the carbonyl carbon atom, and -one.	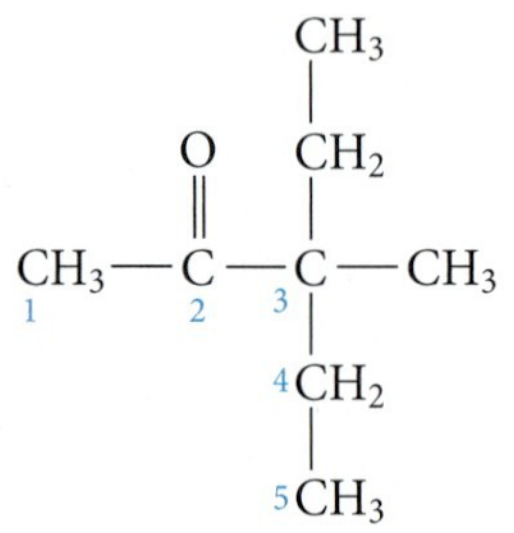 (numbered structure shown) The carbonyl carbon is carbon atom 2. The suffix is -2-one.	
3. Identify the prefix. Name and number any alkyl side groups on the main chain. The alkyl side groups are written just as they are for hydrocarbons.	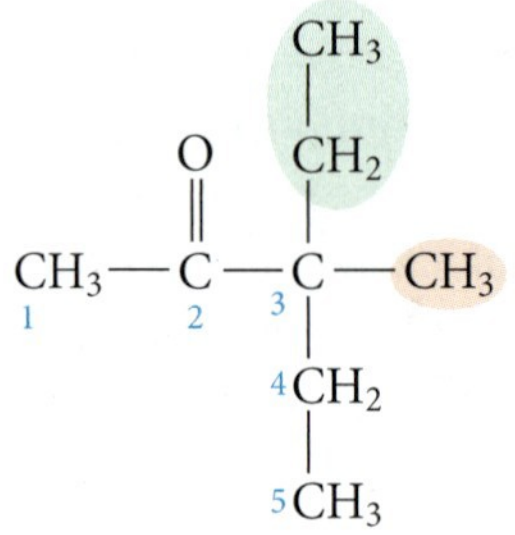 (structure with highlighted groups shown) There is a methyl and an ethyl group on carbon atom 3. The prefix is 3-ethyl-3-methyl-.	
4. Name the compound. Combine the prefix, root, and suffix. There is no space between the prefix and the root.	The compound is 3-ethyl-3-methylpentan-2-one.	

Sample Problem

Naming Ketones

Problem
Name the following ketones.

a. $CH_3-\underset{\underset{CH_2-CH_2-CH_3}{\|}}{\overset{\overset{CH_3}{\|}}{C}}-\overset{O}{\underset{\|}{C}}-CH_3$

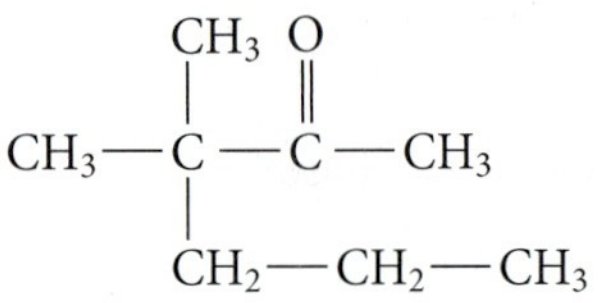

b. (skeletal structure of a ketone with a phenyl group)

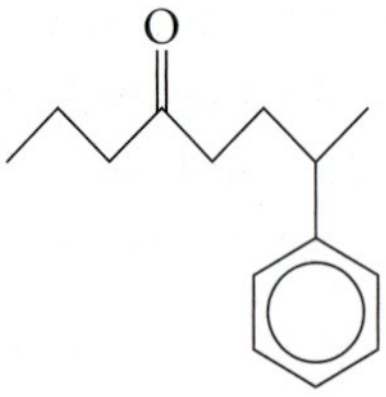

What Is Required?
You must name two ketones.

What Is Given?
You are given the structures.

Plan Your Strategy	Act on Your Strategy	
a. Identify the root.	The longest chain containing the carbonyl carbon is six carbon atoms long. The root is hexan-. 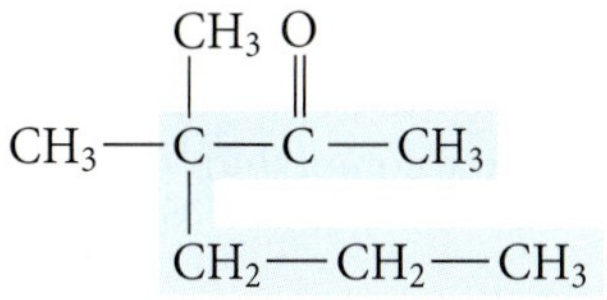	CH_3—C(—CH_3)(—CH_2—CH_2—CH_3)—C(=O)—CH_3
Identify the suffix.	The carbonyl carbon is carbon atom 2 and the compound is a ketone, so the suffix is -2-one. 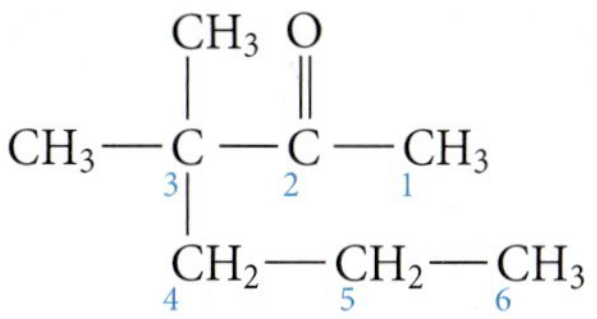	Numbered structure with carbonyl at C2
Identify the prefix.	There are two methyl groups on carbon atom 3, so the prefix is 3,3-dimethyl-. 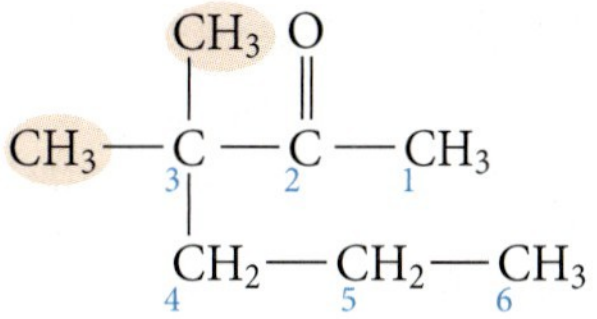	Numbered structure highlighting two CH_3 groups on C3
Write the name.	The name is 3,3-dimethylhexan-2-one.	
b. Identify the root.	The carbon chain containing the carbonyl carbon is eight carbon atoms long. The root is octan-. 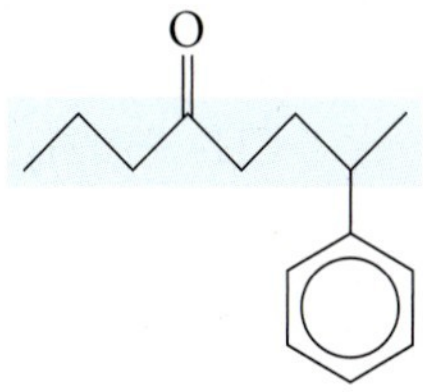	Skeletal structure of ketone with phenyl group
Identify the suffix.	The carbonyl carbon atom is nearer the left end, so start numbering there. This makes the carbonyl carbon atom 4. The suffix is -4-one. 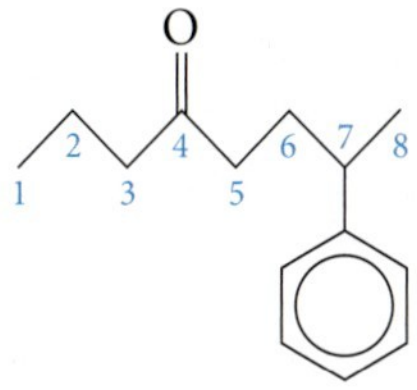	Numbered skeletal structure 1–8
Identify the prefix.	There is a benzene ring on carbon atom 7. As a side group, it is called a phenyl group. The prefix is 7-phenyl-. 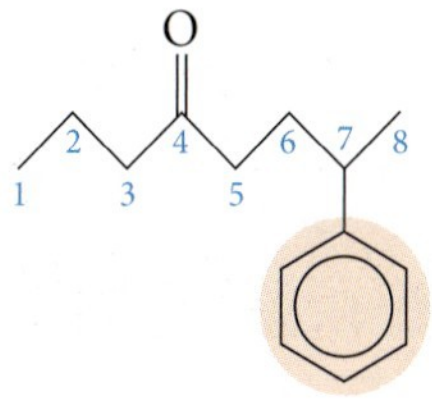	Numbered skeletal structure with phenyl highlighted on C7
Write the name.	The name of the compound is 7-phenyloctan-4-one.	

Check Your Solution
a. The compound has a carbonyl group on carbon atom 2 of a six-carbon main chain. It also has two methyl groups on carbon atom 3. The name correctly reflects this structure.

b. The compound has a carbonyl group on carbon atom 4 of an eight-carbon main chain. There is a phenyl group on carbon atom 7. The name correctly reflects this structure.

Sample Problem

Drawing Ketones

Problem
Draw a condensed structural formula for 5,5-dimethylheptan-3-one.

What Is Required?
You must draw a condensed structural formula.

What Is Given?
You are given the name of the compound.

Plan Your Strategy	Act on Your Strategy
Identify the root and draw and number the carbon atoms in the main chain.	The root is heptan-, so the main chain is seven carbon atoms long. C—C—C—C—C—C—C (numbered 1–7)
Identify the suffix and add any necessary structures to the main chain.	The suffix is -3-one, which means the compound is a ketone. Add the oxygen atom to make carbon atom 3 a carbonyl carbon. 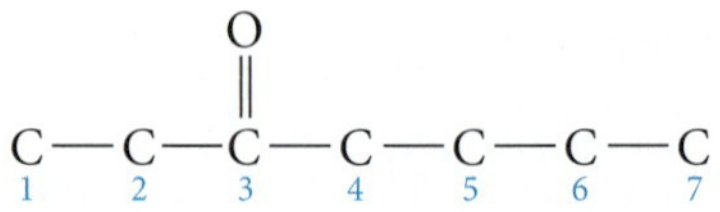
Identify the prefix and add any necessary structures to the main chain.	The prefix is 5,5-dimethyl-, so there are two methyl groups on carbon atom 5. 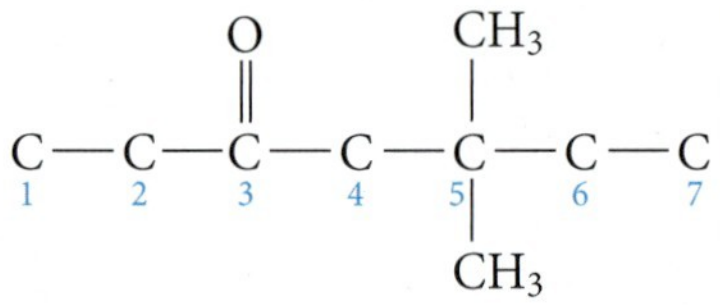
Add enough hydrogen atoms to the main-chain carbon atoms to give every carbon atom a total of four bonds.	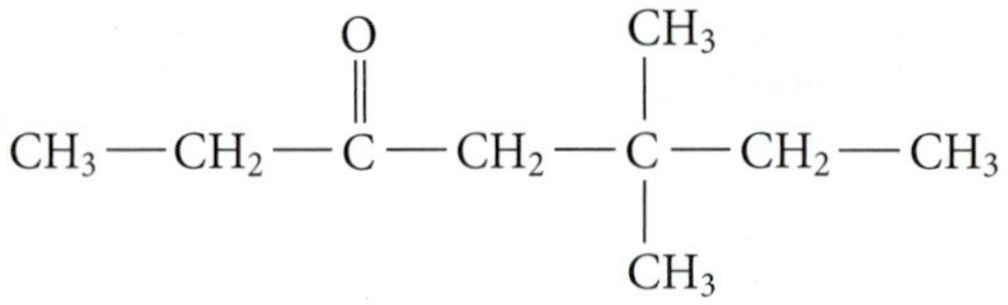 $CH_3-CH_2-C(=O)-CH_2-C(CH_3)_2-CH_2-CH_3$

Check Your Solution
The compound is a ketone, the carbonyl carbon is carbon atom 3, and there are two methyl groups on carbon atom 5. The structure is in agreement with the name.

Practice Problems

For the next three questions, name each ketone.

106. $H_3C-CH_2-C(=O)-CH_3$

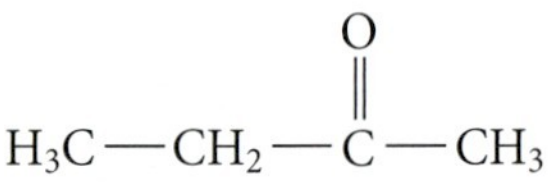

107. $H_3C-CH(CH_3)-C(=O)-CH_2-CH_3$

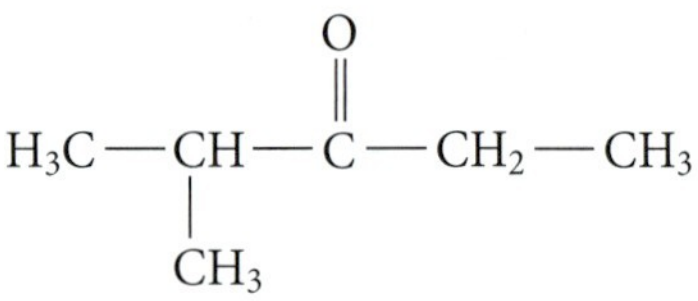

108. (structure shown)

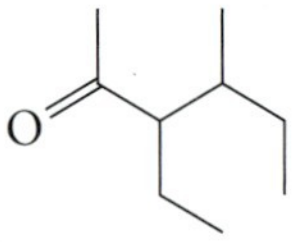

For the next three questions, draw the line structural formula for each ketone.

109. propanone (commonly known acetone)

110. 3-ethylhexan-2-one

111. 4,4-diethylhexane-2,3-dione

For the next four questions explain why each ketone is named incorrectly or cannot exist. If it can exist, give the proper name.

112. propan-1-one

113. pentan-4-one

114. 2-propylhexan-3,4-dione

115. benzen-1-one

Physical Properties of Ketones

Ketones, like aldehydes, have a carbonyl group that is very polar but have no hydrogen atoms bonded to strongly electronegative atoms. Thus, they cannot hydrogen bond with one another. However, they can hydrogen bond with water molecules. As a result, ketones have boiling points and solubilities similar to those of aldehydes. Like aldehydes, ketones that have carbon chains of 15 carbon atoms or longer are waxy solids at room temperature. However, all smaller ketones are liquid at room temperature.

Carboxylic Acids

Do you like vinegar with your French fries? Maybe you enjoy oil and vinegar dressings, such as those shown in **Figure 1.29**, on your salad. If so, you are eating ethanoic acid (acetic acid), a carboxylic acid found in vinegar. Similarly, if you eat oranges, you are consuming another carboxylic acid called 3-carboxy-3-hydroxypentanedioic acid, commonly known as citric acid. Tamarinds, the fruit of a tamarind tree, contain tartaric acid, another example of a carboxylic acid.

Figure 1.29 Carboxylic acids are found in many foods, including oil and vinegar (acetic acid) salad dressings, oranges (citric acid), and tamarinds (tartaric acid).

A **carboxylic acid** is a hydrocarbon derivative that contains a carboxyl group. A **carboxyl group** (-COOH) is made up of a carbonyl group with a hydroxyl group attached to it. **Figure 1.30** shows the structural formula for a carboxyl group and two examples of carboxylic acids.

$$\begin{array}{ccc}
\text{O} & \text{O} & \text{O} \\
\| & \| & \| \\
-\text{C}-\text{OH} & \text{HC}-\text{OH} & \text{CH}_3-\text{C}-\text{OH} \\
\text{carboxyl group} & \text{methanoic acid} & \text{ethanoic acid} \\
& \text{(common name: formic acid)} & \text{(common name: acetic acid)}
\end{array}$$

Figure 1.30 Methanoic acid and ethanoic acid, as well as all other carboxylic acids, contain a carboxyl group.

carboxylic acid a hydrocarbon derivative that contains a carboxyl group

carboxyl group a functional group made up of a carbonyl group with a hydroxyl group attached to it

Note that carboxylic acids are weak acids for which the ionization equation can be written as shown below.

$$-\text{COOH(aq)} \rightleftharpoons -\text{COO}^-(\text{aq}) + \text{H}+(\text{aq})$$

Naming and Drawing Carboxylic Acids

Notice that three bonds on the carbon atom in the carboxyl group are with the other atoms in the group. There is only one position available on the carbon atom to bond to other atoms. Therefore, the carboxyl group must always be on the end of a chain. The carbon atom of the carboxyl group is always given the number one. The steps in **Table 1.17**, on the next page, will allow you to name and draw simple carboxylic acids.

Chapter 1 Structure and Physical Properties of Organic Compounds

Table 1.17 Steps in Naming Carboxylic Acids

1. Identify the root.		
a. Locate the longest chain that includes the carboxyl carbon atom.		CH₃–CH₂–CH₂–CH(CH₂CH₃)–CH(CH₂CH₃)–COOH structure shown; longest chain of six carbons highlighted
	The longest chain containing the carboxyl carbon atom is six carbon atoms.	
b. Name the parent alkane. Drop the –e on the parent alkane to get the root.	The parent alkane is hexane. The root is hexan-.	
2. Identify the suffix. Write the suffix for the compound. For carboxylic acids, the suffix is –oic acid. There are no numbers in the suffix because the carboxyl group always involves carbon atom 1.	The suffix is -oic acid.	
3. Identify the prefix. Name and number any alkyl side groups on the main chain. The carbon atom of the carboxyl group is always carbon atom 1.	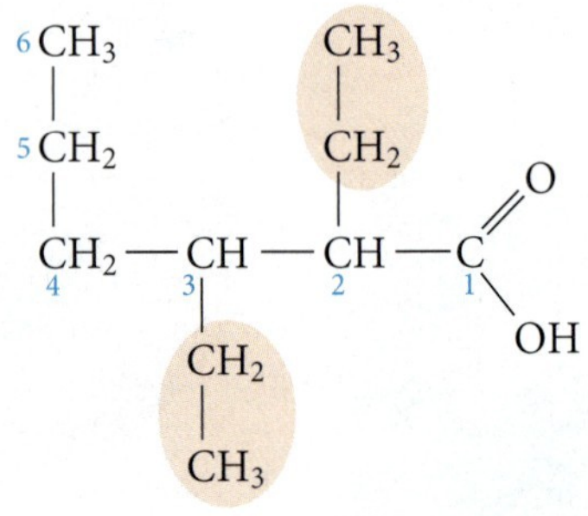 Same structure with carbons numbered 1–6 along main chain, and two ethyl side groups highlighted. The carboxyl carbon is always carbon atom 1, so no number is required to identify it. There are two ethyl groups, one on carbon atom 2 and the other on carbon atom 3. The prefix is 2,3-diethyl-.	
4. Name the compound. Combine the prefix, root, and suffix. There are no spaces between the prefix, root, and suffix.	The compound is 2,3-diethylhexanoic acid.	

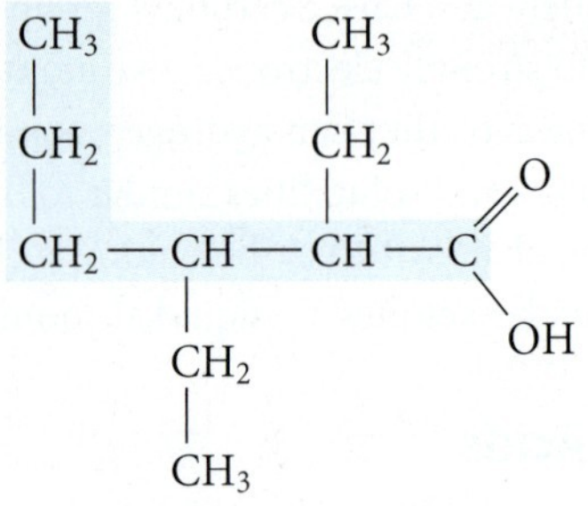

Sample Problem

Naming Carboxylic Acids

Problem
Name the following carboxylic acids.

a.
$$CH_3-CH_2-CH(CH_3)-CH_2-C(=O)-OH$$

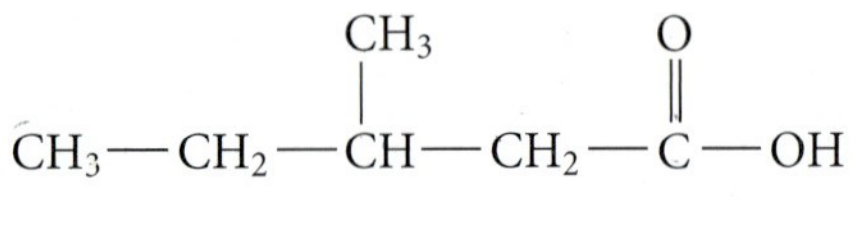

b.
$$CH_3-CH_2-CH_2-CH_2-CH(CH_2CH_3)-C(=O)-OH$$

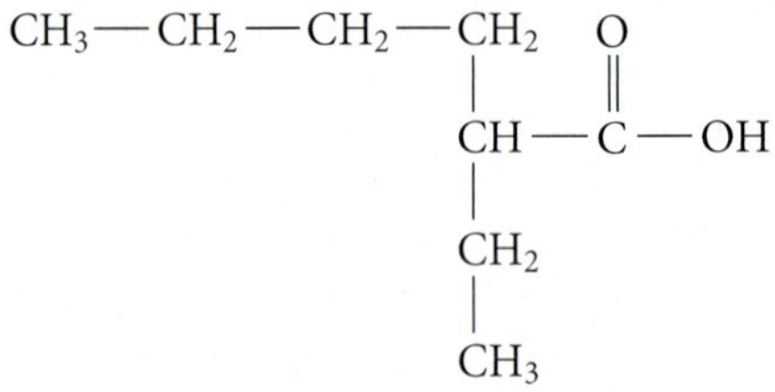

What Is Required?
You must name two carboxylic acids.

What Is Given?
You are given the structure of the carboxylic acid.

Plan Your Strategy	Act on Your Strategy
a. Identify the root.	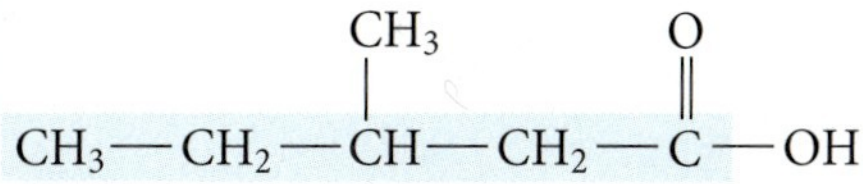 $CH_3-CH_2-\underset{\underset{CH_3}{\|}}{CH}-CH_2-\underset{\underset{}{\overset{\overset{O}{\|}}{C}}}-OH$ The longest chain that includes the carboxyl group has five carbon atoms including the carbon in the carboxyl group. Therefore, the root is pentan-.
Identify the suffix.	$CH_3-CH_2-\underset{\underset{CH_3}{\|}}{CH}-CH_2-\underset{\underset{}{\overset{\overset{O}{\|}}{C}}}-OH$ The compound is a carboxylic acid, so the suffix is -oic acid.
Identify the prefix.	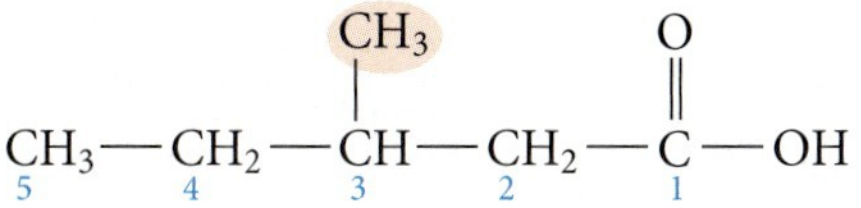 $\underset{5}{CH_3}-\underset{4}{CH_2}-\underset{3}{\underset{\underset{CH_3}{\|}}{CH}}-\underset{2}{CH_2}-\underset{1}{\underset{}{\overset{\overset{O}{\|}}{C}}}-OH$ Numbering always begins at the carbonyl carbon atom. There is a methyl group on carbon atom 3, so the prefix is 3-methyl-.
Name the compound.	Combine the prefix, root, and suffix. The name of the compound is 3-methylpentanoic acid.
b. Identify the root.	The longest chain that includes the carboxyl group has six carbon atoms including the carbon in the carboxyl group. Therefore, the root is hexan-. Notice that the longest carbon chain has seven carbon atoms but it does not contain the carbonyl carbon. 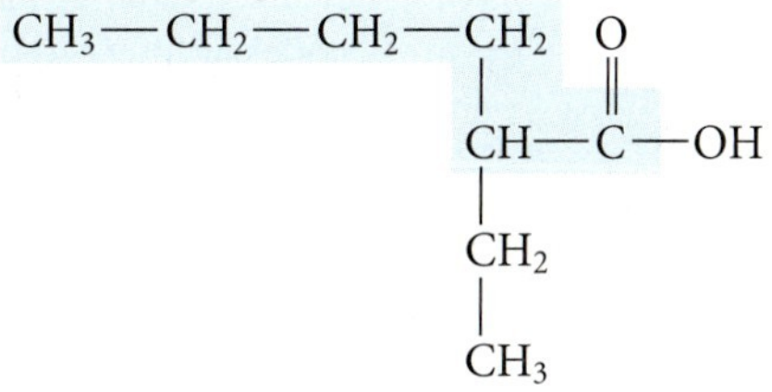
Identify the suffix.	The compound is a carboxylic acid, so the suffix is -oic acid. 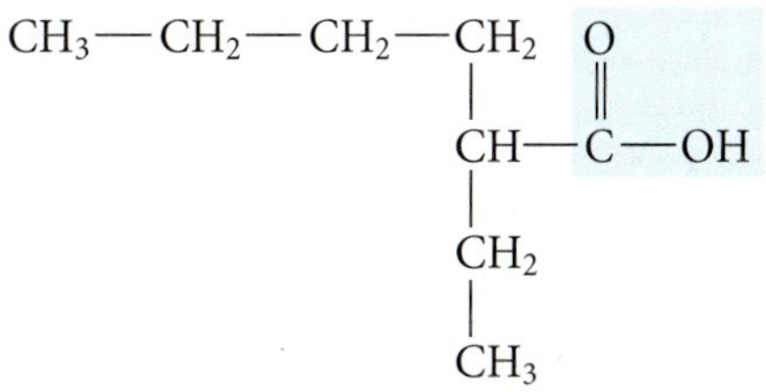
Identify the prefix.	Numbering always begins at the carbonyl carbon atom. There is an ethyl group on carbon atom 2, so the prefix is 2-ethyl-. 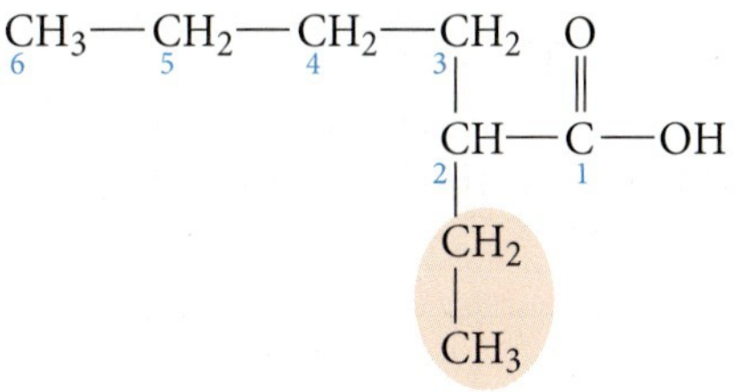
Name the compound.	Combine the prefix, root, and suffix. The name of the compound is 2-ethylhexanoic acid.

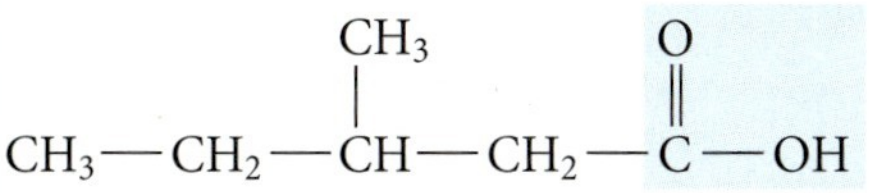

Check Your Solution

a. The compound has a carboxyl group at the beginning of a five-carbon main chain. It also has a methyl group on carbon atom 3. The name correctly reflects this structure.

b. The compound has a carboxyl group at the beginning of a six-carbon main chain. It also has an ethyl group on carbon atom 2. The name correctly reflects this structure.

Sample Problem

Drawing Carboxylic Acids

Problem
Draw a condensed structural formula for 2-ethylpentanoic acid.

What Is Required?
You must draw a condensed structural formula.

What Is Given?
You are given a name.

Plan Your Strategy	Act on Your Strategy
Identify the root and draw and number the carbon chain.	The root is pentan-, so the main carbon chain has five carbon atoms. C—C—C—C—C
Identify the suffix. Add the necessary atoms to the structure and number the carbon atoms.	The suffix is -oic acid, so it is a carboxylic acid. Add a double bonded oxygen atom and a hydroxyl group to the carbon atom at the end. The carboxyl carbon atom is always number 1. 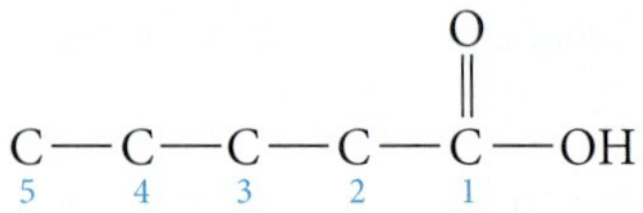 $\underset{5}{C}-\underset{4}{C}-\underset{3}{C}-\underset{2}{C}-\underset{1}{C}(=O)-OH$
Identify the prefix and add necessary atoms to the structure.	The prefix is 2-ethyl-, so there is an ethyl group on carbon atom 2. 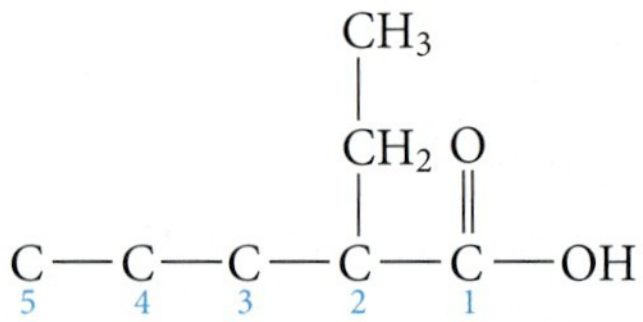 $\underset{5}{C}-\underset{4}{C}-\underset{3}{C}-\underset{2}{C}(CH_2CH_3)-\underset{1}{C}(=O)-OH$
Add enough hydrogen atoms to give each carbon atom a total of four bonds.	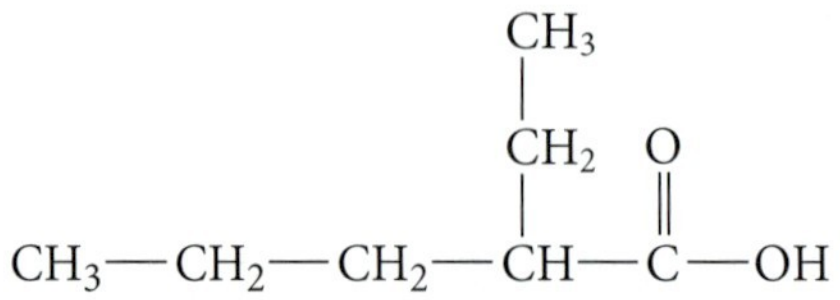 $CH_3-CH_2-CH_2-CH(CH_2CH_3)-C(=O)-OH$

Check Your Solution
There are five carbon atoms in the main chain and there is a carboxyl group, making the compound pentanoic acid. The carboxyl carbon must be numbered 1. The ethyl group is on the carbon beside the carbonyl carbon because that is carbon atom 2. The structure agrees with the name.

Practice Problems

For the next two questions, name each carboxylic acid.

116.

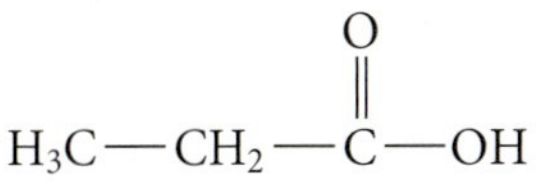

$H_3C-CH_2-\overset{\overset{O}{\|}}{C}-OH$

117.

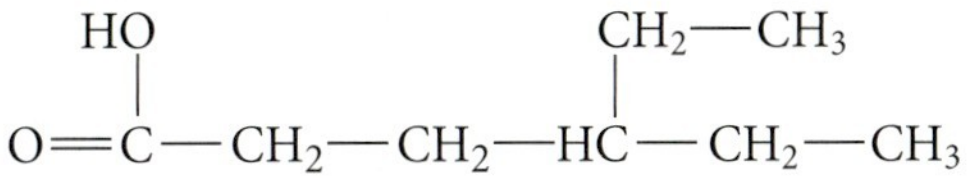

$O=\overset{\overset{HO}{|}}{C}-CH_2-CH_2-\overset{\overset{CH_2-CH_3}{|}}{HC}-CH_2-CH_3$

For the next four questions, draw the condensed structural formula for each carboxylic acid.

118. butanoic acid (common name: butyric acid)

119. 4-ethyloctanoic acid

120. 3-methyl-4-phenylhexanoic acid

121. pentandioic acid (common name: glutaric acid)

For the next four questions, explain why each carboxylic acid is named incorrectly or cannot exist. If it can exist, give the proper name.

122. hexan-6-oic acid

123. butan-2-oic acid

124. 3-butylpentanoic acid

125. cyclohexanoic acid

Physical Properties of Carboxylic Acids

The presence of both a >C=O group and the –OH group make the carboxyl group very polar, allowing carboxylic acid molecules to form hydrogen bonds with one another. Thus, the boiling points of carboxylic acids are much higher than those of other hydrocarbons and their derivatives with the same number of carbon atoms, as shown in **Table 1.18**.

Short-chain carboxylic acids are liquids at standard temperature while those with longer chains are waxy solids. The polarity of the carboxyl group makes the small carboxylic acids soluble in water. In fact, carboxylic acids with one to four carbon atoms are completely miscible with water. Those with chain lengths of five to nine carbon atoms are less soluble in water, while those with chains longer than ten carbon atoms are insoluble in water. Carboxylic acids are also weak acids and thus turn litmus paper red. As weak acids, they conduct electric current.

Table 1.18 Boiling Points of Carbon Compounds

Compound	Boiling Point (°C)
butane	−0.5
butanal	74.8
butan-2-one	79.6
butan-1-ol	117.2
butanoic acid	165.5

Esters

When you smell the aroma of fresh fruit such as raspberries, you probably do not think about what chemical compound might be producing the pleasant fruity odour. In many cases, the fruity odour is caused by a compound called an ester. An **ester** is a hydrocarbon derivative that contains the functional group shown in **Figure 1.31**.

The general formula for an ester is RCOOR′. The symbol R represents any hydrocarbon or just a hydrogen atom. The symbol R′ represents a hydrocarbon and, therefore, it must contain at least one carbon atom. To name an ester, it helps to think of it as a combination of a carboxylic acid and an alcohol because the names of those compounds are used in the name of the ester. The equation in **Figure 1.32** below illustrates the reaction that results in this combination.

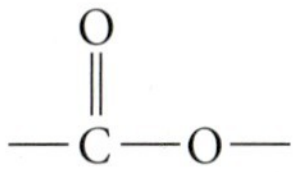

$\underset{\text{carboxylic acid}}{R-\overset{\overset{O}{\|}}{C}-OH} + \underset{\text{alcohol}}{HO-R'} \rightarrow \underset{\text{ester}}{R-\overset{\overset{O}{\|}}{C}-O-R'} + \underset{\text{water}}{HOH}$

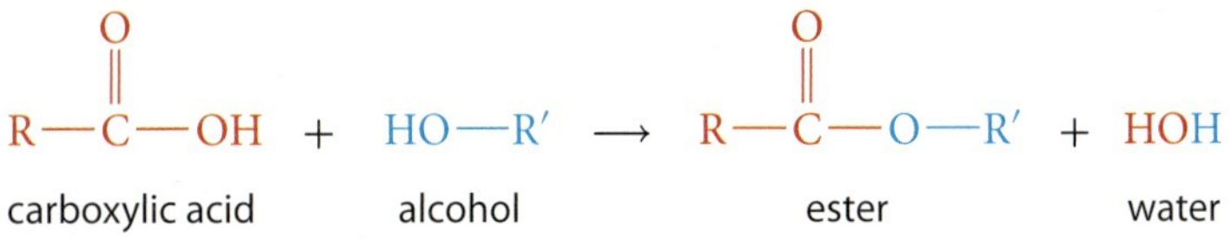

Figure 1.32 Esters can be thought of as the product of a reaction between a carboxylic acid and an alcohol.

$-\overset{\overset{O}{\|}}{C}-O-$

Figure 1.31 An ester contains a functional group in which a carbon atom is double bonded to one oxygen atom and single bonded to another.

ester a hydrocarbon derivative that contains a functional group with a carbon atom double bonded to one oxygen atom and single bonded to another

Naming and Drawing Esters

Refer to the equation above while you read through the steps for naming an ester in **Table 1.19**, on the next page. See **Figure 1.33** for a summary of the components involved in these steps. Then examine the Sample Problems and complete the Practice Problems.

Table 1.19 Steps in Naming Esters

1. Identify the root. a. Identify the part of the ester that contains the C=O group. This is the part of the ester that is red in the equation in **Figure 1.32**. It comes from the acid. Thus, the root for the ester is based on the name of the carboxylic acid. b. Name the parent carboxylic acid. Drop the suffix of the acid to form the root.	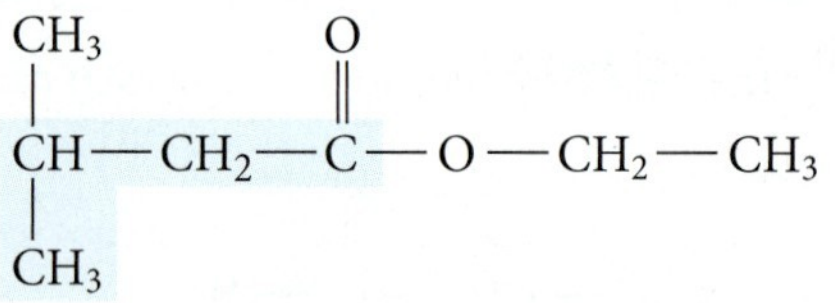 $$CH_3\text{—}CH\text{—}CH_2\text{—}\underset{\|}{\overset{CH_3}{C}}\text{—}\overset{O}{\underset{\|}{C}}\text{—}O\text{—}CH_2\text{—}CH_3$$ The >C=O group is part of a four carbon group, so the main chain has four carbon atoms. The parent carboxylic acid is butanoic acid. The root is butan-.
2. Identify the suffix. The suffix for an ester is –oate.	The compound is an ester. The suffix is -oate.
3. Identify the prefix. a. To form the prefix, first consider the part of the ester that is associated with the alcohol, the part in blue in the equation in **Figure 1.32**. Ignore the oxygen atom and name only the alkyl group to write the prefix. This part of the prefix is placed first when naming the ester.	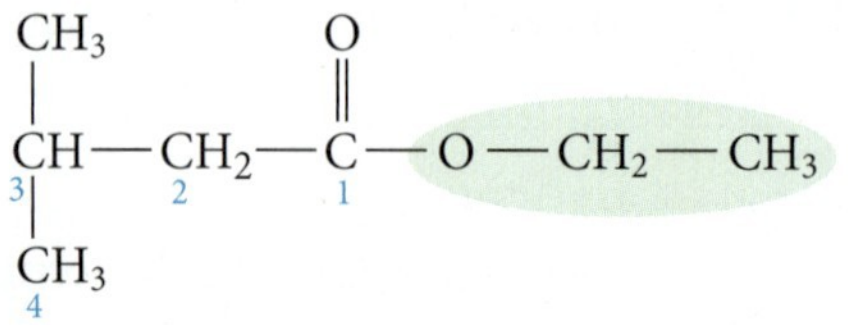 (structure with ethyl group highlighted) The prefix is the name of the alkyl group attached to the oxygen atom that is single bonded to the main chain. It has two carbon atoms, so the first part of the prefix is ethyl.
b. If there is a side group on the main chain, name it as a prefix the same way that you would in a simple hydrocarbon. This is the second part of the prefix.	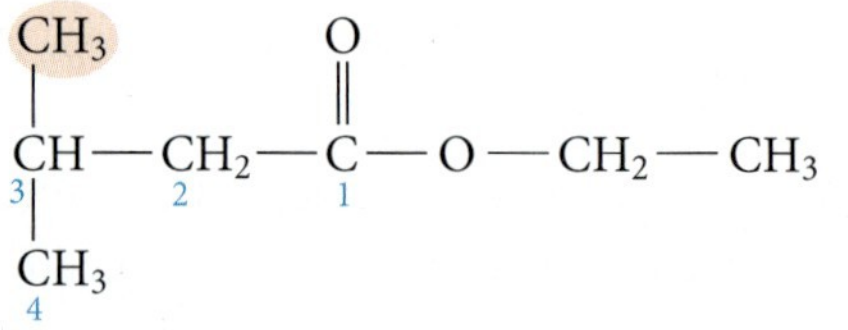 (structure with CH₃ side group highlighted) There is a methyl group on carbon atom 3 of the main chain, so 3-methyl- is the second part of the prefix.
c. Combine the two components of the prefix to get the complete prefix. Write the prefix that identifies the alkyl group bonded to the oxygen first and the prefix that gives the alkyl group bonded to the main chain second. Note that there is a space, not a hyphen, between the first part of the prefix and the number of the second part of the prefix.	The complete prefix is ethyl 3-methyl-.
4. Name the compound. Combine the prefix, root, and suffix. There is no space between the root and the suffix.	The compound is ethyl 3-methylbutanoate.

side group
3-methyl

$$CH_3\text{—}CH_2\text{—}CH_2\text{—}\underset{\|}{\overset{CH_3}{CH}}\text{—}\overset{O}{\underset{\|}{C}}\text{—}O\text{—}CH_2\text{—}CH_3$$

parent acid — butanoate   alkyl group — ethyl

ethyl 3-methylbutanoate

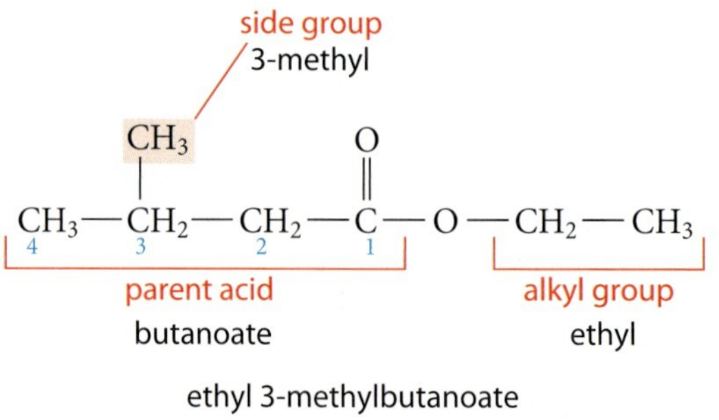

Figure 1.33 The highlighted groups in this structure summarize the components involved in naming an ester.

Sample Problem

Naming Esters

Problem

Name the following esters.

a.
$$CH_3CH_2\overset{\overset{O}{\|}}{C}-O-CH_3$$

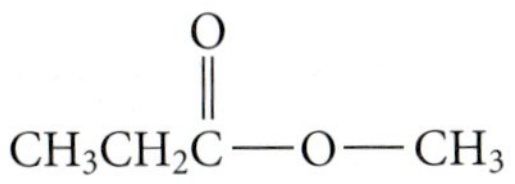

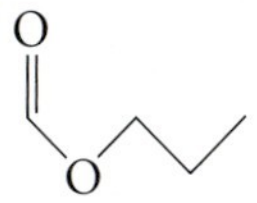

b.
$$\overset{O}{\underset{O}{\|}}\text{(HCOO-CH}_2\text{CH}_2\text{CH}_3\text{)}$$

c.
$$\begin{array}{c} CH_3 \\ | \\ CH_2 \\ | \\ CH-CH_2-\overset{\overset{O}{\|}}{C}-O-CH_2-CH_3 \\ | \\ CH_2 \\ | \\ CH_3 \end{array}$$

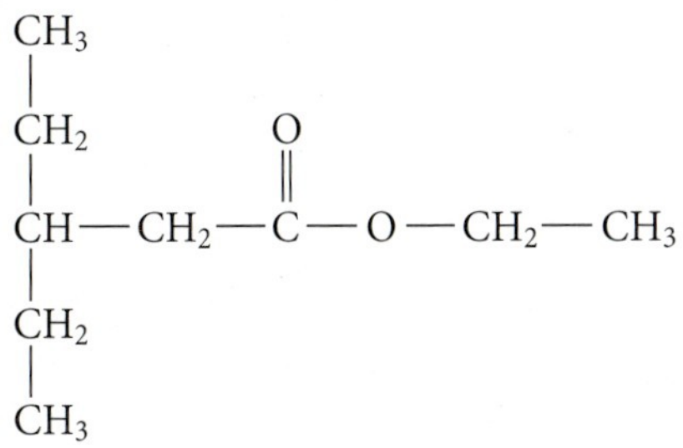

What Is Required?

You must name three esters.

What Is Given?

You are given the structures.

Plan Your Strategy	Act on Your Strategy
a. Identify the root.	The >C=O group is part of a three-carbon group. 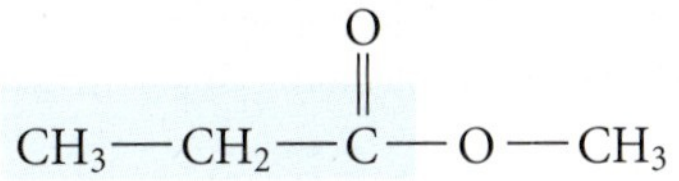 $$CH_3-CH_2-\overset{\overset{O}{\|}}{C}-O-CH_3$$ Thus, the parent acid is propanoic acid. The root is propan-.
Identify the suffix.	The compound is an ester, so the suffix is -oate.
Identify the prefix.	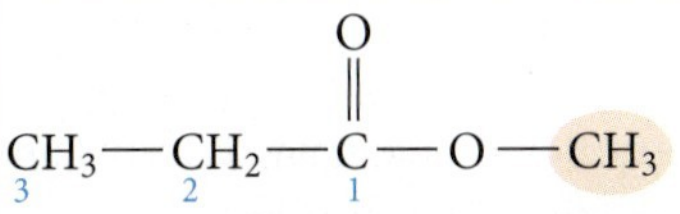 $$\underset{3}{CH_3}-\underset{2}{CH_2}-\underset{1}{\overset{\overset{O}{\|}}{C}}-O-CH_3$$ The prefix is the name of the alkyl group attached to the singly bonded oxygen atom. It has one carbon atom, so it is a methyl group. The prefix is methyl.
Write the name.	Combine the name of the prefix, root, and suffix. The name of the ester is methyl propanoate.
b. Identify the root.	The >C=O group is bonded directly to a hydrogen atom, making the parent acid methanoic acid. The root is methan-.
Identify the suffix.	The compound is an ester, so the suffix is -oate.
Identify the prefix.	The prefix is the name of the alkyl group attached to the oxygen atom. It has three carbon atoms so the prefix is propyl.
Write the name.	Combine the name of the prefix, root, and suffix. The name of the ester is propyl methanoate.

Continued on next page

c. Identify the root.	The longest carbon chain that includes the carbonyl carbon is five carbon atoms long. 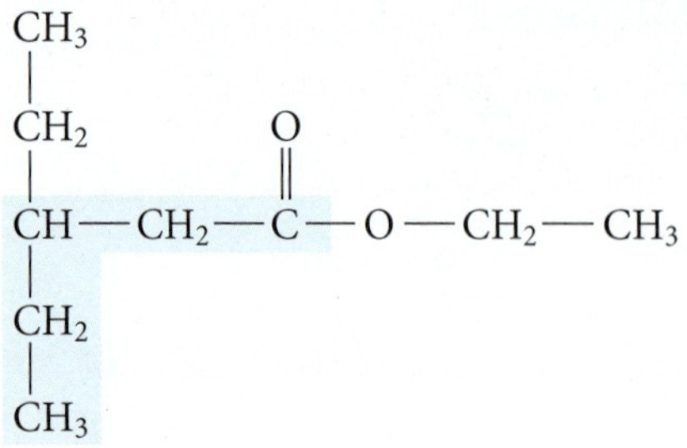 $$\begin{array}{c} CH_3 \\ | \\ CH_2 \quad\quad O \\ | \quad\quad\quad \| \\ CH-CH_2-C-O-CH_2-CH_3 \\ | \\ CH_2 \\ | \\ CH_3 \end{array}$$ Therefore, the root is pentan-.
Identify the suffix.	The compound is an ester, so the suffix is -oate.
Identify the prefix.	$$\begin{array}{c} CH_3 \\ | \\ CH_2 \quad\quad O \\ | \quad\quad\quad \| \\ _3CH-\underset{2}{CH_2}-\underset{1}{C}-O-CH_2-CH_3 \\ | \\ _4CH_2 \\ | \\ _5CH_3 \end{array}$$ The prefix has two parts. The first part of the prefix is based on the group attached to the single bonded oxygen atom. This group has two carbon atoms, so the prefix starts with ethyl. The second part of the prefix is based on the alkyl side group on the main carbon chain on carbon atom 3. The side group has two carbon atoms. Thus, the second part of the prefix is 3-ethyl-. The complete prefix is ethyl 3-ethyl-.
Write the name.	Combine the name of the prefix, root, and suffix. The name of the ester is ethyl 3-ethylpentanoate.

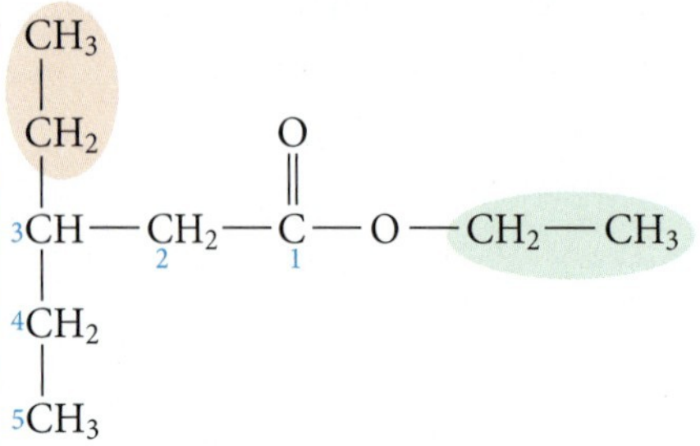

Check Your Solution

a. The compound has a >C=O group that is part of a three-carbon group. It has a methyl group attached to the singly bonded oxygen atom. The name correctly reflects this structure.

b. The >C=O group has a single carbon. The compound has a propyl group attached to the singly bonded oxygen atom. The name correctly reflects this structure.

c. The compound has a >C=O group that is part of a five-carbon group. It has one ethyl group attached to the singly bonded oxygen atom and another attached to carbon atom 3 on the main carbon chain. The name correctly reflects this structure.

Sample Problem

Drawing Esters

Problem
Draw a condensed structural formula for butyl propanoate.

What Is Required?
You must draw a condensed structural formula.

What Is Given?
You are given a name.

Plan Your Strategy	Act on Your Strategy
Identify the root of the name.	The root is propan-, so the carbon chain has three carbon atoms.
Identify the suffix. Draw the basic structure described by the root and the suffix.	The suffix is -oate, so the compound is an ester and related to propanoic acid. This means that the carbon atom on the end of the main chain is a carbonyl carbon. 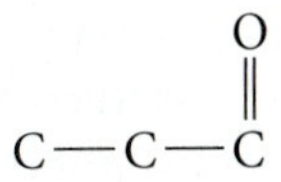 $$C-C-\overset{\overset{O}{\|}}{C}$$
Identify the prefix. Draw the basic part of the structure described by the prefix.	The prefix is butyl, which is related to the alcohol, butanol. Thus, the second part of the structure has four carbon atoms bonded to the single bonded oxygen atom. 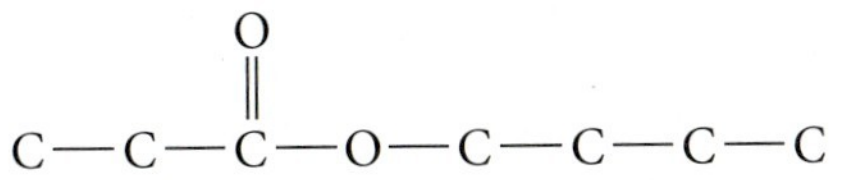 $$C-C-\overset{\overset{O}{\|}}{C}-O-C-C-C-C$$
Add enough hydrogen atoms to give each carbon atom a total of four bonds.	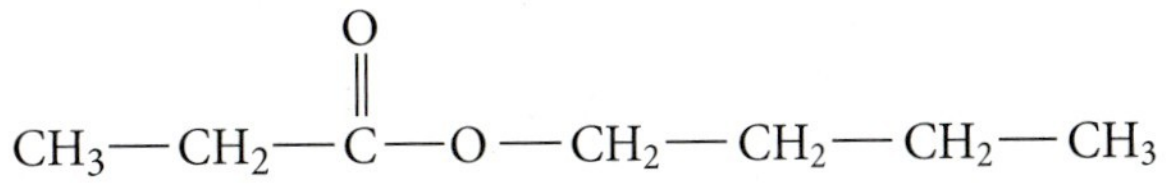 $$CH_3-CH_2-\overset{\overset{O}{\|}}{C}-O-CH_2-CH_2-CH_2-CH_3$$

Check Your Solution

If the ester bond was broken by the insertion of water, the products would be propanoic acid and butanol, as shown in the equation below. This is in agreement with the name.

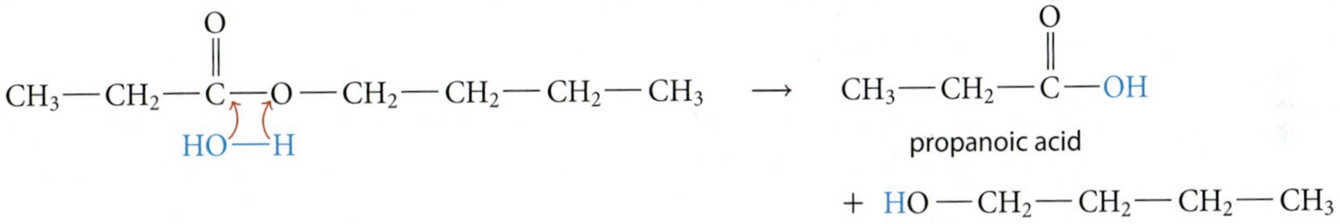

$$CH_3-CH_2-\overset{\overset{O}{\|}}{C}-O-CH_2-CH_2-CH_2-CH_3 \;+\; HO-H \;\rightarrow\; CH_3-CH_2-\overset{\overset{O}{\|}}{C}-OH \text{ (propanoic acid)} \;+\; HO-CH_2-CH_2-CH_2-CH_3 \text{ (butanol)}$$

Practice Problems

For the next three questions, name each ester.

126. $H_3C-O-\overset{\overset{O}{\|}}{C}-CH_3$

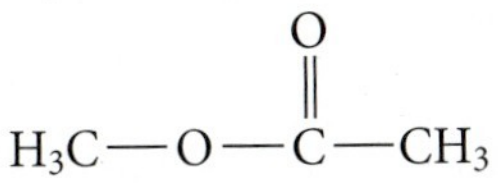

127. $H_3C-CH_2-O-\overset{\overset{O}{\|}}{CH}$

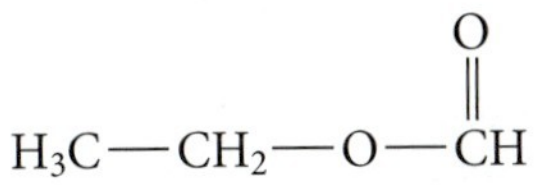

128. (line structure of 3-chlorobutanoate with butyl group)

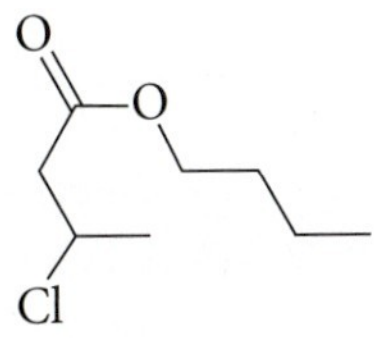

For the next three questions, draw the condensed structural formula for each ester.

129. butyl ethanoate

130. ethyl butanoate

131. ethyl 2-cyclobutylpropanoate

For the next four questions, draw the line structure of the ester formed from each reaction.

132. propanoic acid and ethanol

133. butanoic acid and propanol

134. 3-fluoropentanoic acid and methanol

135. butanol and 4-phenylhexanoic acid

Physical Properties of Esters

The presence of the >C=O group makes esters somewhat polar but without an —OH group, ester molecules cannot form hydrogen bonds with one another. Therefore, the boiling points are lower than the corresponding alcohols and carboxylic acids. The smaller esters are liquids at standard temperature while the longer chain esters are waxy solids. Esters with four or fewer carbon atoms are soluble in water while larger esters are insoluble. The most noticeable characteristic of esters is their volatility, which allows them to generate aromas.

Ethers

Before the 1840s, no anaesthetic was available for surgery patients. Very few surgeries were performed but the few that were done were extremely painful. In 1842, the first surgery was performed using ether (ethoxyethane or diethyl ether) as an anaesthetic. The field of surgery was transformed. However, ether is very flammable and causes severe nausea and vomiting. Doctors searched for other anaesthetics but ether remained in use for many years. Today, due to its low cost and availability, ether is still sometimes used for surgery in the developing world. As well, it is still often used in "fly labs" to anaesthetise fruit flies so genetics students can study their inheritance patterns.

Ether has other, numerous current uses, such as a starter for diesel engines in extremely cold weather. It is also used as an aerosol propellant, solvent, and plasticiser. One type of ether, methyl tertiary butyl ether (MTBE), is used as a gasoline additive. Although it helps gasoline to burn cleaner, spillage and leakage around gas stations have resulted in the pollution of ground water. Therefore, its use has been greatly decreased.

An **ether** is a hydrocarbon derivative in which an oxygen atom is single bonded to two carbon atoms. The functional group can be written as –O–. The general formula for all ethers can be expressed as R–O–R′, where R and R′ are alkyl groups.

> **ether** a hydrocarbon derivative in which an oxygen atom is single bonded to two carbon atoms
>
> **alkoxy group** a side group found in an ether that includes the oxygen atom and the shorter alkyl group bonded to it

Naming and Drawing Ethers

The IUPAC system of naming ethers identifies the longer carbon chain as the R group. The R group is designated as the main chain in the molecule and takes the name of the parent alkane. The oxygen and shorter carbon chain (–O–R′) group make up the side group. This side group is called an **alkoxy group**. This group is named by adding -oxy to the root name of the R′ group. For example, the alkoxy group in $CH_3–CH_2–CH_2–O–CH_3$ is methoxy-. The main chain is propane.

Table 1.20 will guide you through the process of naming and drawing ethers according to the IUPAC recommendations. See **Figure 1.34** for a summary of the components involved in these steps.

Activity 1.5 — Polybrominated Diphenyl Ethers

Polybrominated diphenyl ethers (PBDEs) are used as a fire retardant in products such as plastics, upholstery foam, and carpet textiles. Since they are added to the products after manufacture, PBDEs are continually released during the lifetime and disposal of the product. As a result, PBDEs are found in the air, water, and soil. PBDEs bioaccumulate readily in ecosystems and have been linked with cancer and adverse health effects on thyroid hormones, and the immune system. In 2010, Environment Canada proposed a ban on PBDEs, and PBDEs are listed as toxic substances under the Canadian Environmental Protection Act. However, the use of one type of PBDE is still allowed in Canada, and , PBDEs continue to leach out of older products and landfills into our lakes and rivers.

Materials
- reference books
- computer with Internet access

Procedure
Research more about the environmental and health issues associated with PBDEs. Use the questions below to help guide your research.
- What are PBDEs and their sources?
- What are current government regulations on the production of PBDEs and their disposal?
- How can PBDEs get into the environment and pollute freshwater systems?
- What regulations are in place to protect the Great Lakes?
- What additional regulations may be needed?

Questions
1. Use the results of your research to complete a risk-benefit analysis for the issue of reducing PBDEs in the environment. See Appendix A for assistance.
2. Based on your analysis, identify a possible solution to the issue of reducing PBDEs in the environment. Justify your solution using verifiable information.

Table 1.20 Steps in Naming Ethers

1. Identify the root.	
a. Locate the longest chain (the R group) that is bonded to the oxygen atom.	The longest chain bonded to the oxygen atom is six carbon atoms long. This is the main chain. CH₃—CH—CH—O—CH₂—CH₂—CH₃ with CH₂—CH₃ branch up from second CH and CH₂—CH₃ branch down from second CH
b. Name the parent alkane.	The parent alkane is hexane.
2. Identify the prefix.	
a. Number the carbon atoms in the main chain, starting at the end of the chain nearest the oxygen atom.	⁶CH₃—⁵CH₂—⁴CH(CH₃)—³CH—O—CH₂—CH₂—CH₃ with ²CH₂—¹CH₃ branch
b. The first part of the prefix involves the alkoxy group. The number of the carbon atom bonded to the oxygen atom is given first, followed by the name of the alkoxy group. To name the alkoxy group, identify the root of the shorter carbon chain (the R′ group). Then, add -oxy to the root.	The oxygen atom of the alkoxy group is bonded to carbon atom 3 of the main chain. The alkoxy group is three carbon atoms long, so the root is prop-. Add oxy- to the root. The first part of the prefix is 3-propoxy-.
c. If there are one or more alkyl side groups on the main chain, name them as you would name any alkane. This is the second part of the prefix.	There is a methyl group bonded to carbon atom 4 of the main chain. The second part of the prefix is 4-methyl-.
d. Combine the two components of the prefix to get the complete prefix. Write the prefix that identifies the alkoxy group first and the alkyl group second.	The complete prefix is 3-propoxy-4-methyl-.
3. Name the compound. Combine the prefix and root. There is no space between the prefix and the root.	The compound is 3-propoxy-4-methylhexane.

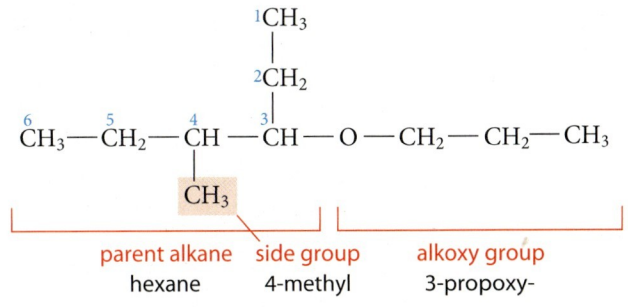

parent alkane: hexane
side group: 4-methyl
alkoxy group: 3-propoxy-

3-propoxy-4-methylhexane

Figure 1.34 The highlighted groups in this structure summarize the components involved in naming an ether.

Sample Problem

Naming Ethers

Problem

Name the following ethers.

a. 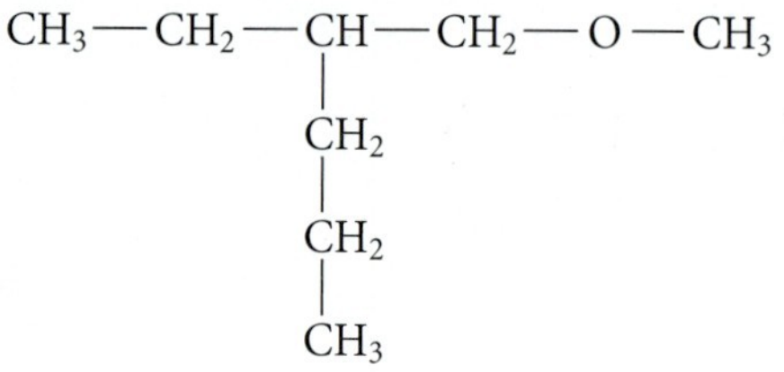
$$CH_3-CH_2-CH-CH_2-O-CH_3$$
$$|$$
$$CH_2$$
$$|$$
$$CH_2$$
$$|$$
$$CH_3$$

b. 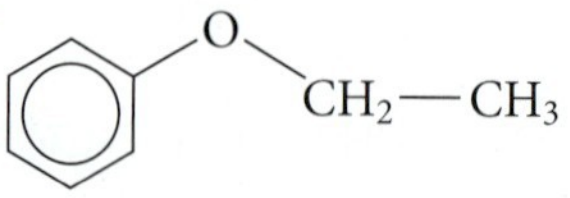 Phenyl—O—CH_2—CH_3

What Is Required?

You must name two ethers.

What Is Given?

You are given the structures.

Plan Your Strategy	Act on Your Strategy
a. Identify the root.	The longest chain bonded to the oxygen atom is five carbon atoms long. The parent alkane is pentane. 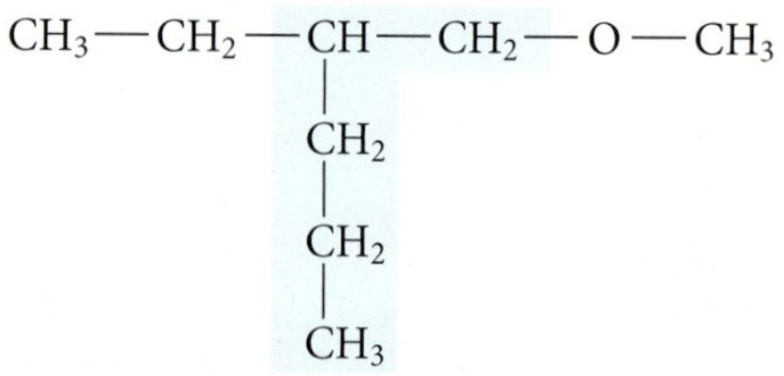 $CH_3-CH_2-CH-CH_2-O-CH_3$ with $CH_2-CH_2-CH_3$ branch (highlighted)
Identify the prefix.	The oxygen atom of the alkoxy group is bonded to carbon atom 1 of the main chain. The alkoxy group is one carbon atom long. The first part of the prefix is 1-methoxy-. 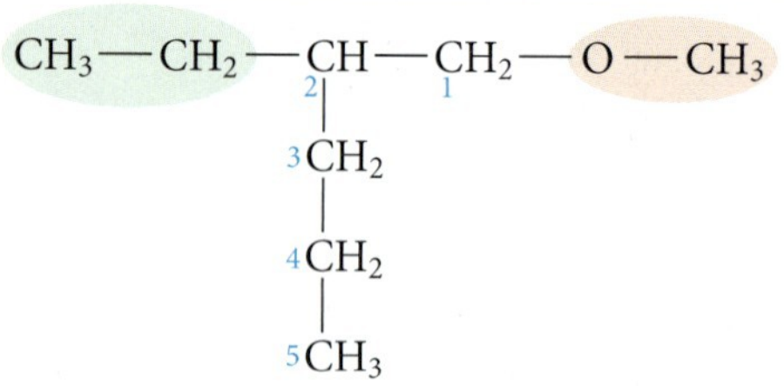 There is an ethyl group on carbon atom 2 of the main chain, so the second part of the prefix is 2-ethyl-. The complete prefix is 1-methoxy-2 ethyl-. $CH_3-CH_2-\underset{2}{CH}-\underset{1}{CH_2}-O-CH_3$ with $_3CH_2-_4CH_2-_5CH_3$
Write the name.	The name of the compound is 1-methoxy-2-ethylpentane.
b. Identify the root.	The larger carbon chain is a benzene ring. Because there are no other groups on the benzene ring, no numbering is needed.
Identify the prefix.	The alkoxy group is two carbon atoms long, so it is an ethyl group. The first part of the prefix is ethoxy-. There are no alkyl groups bonded to the benzene ring, so the prefix is complete.
Write the name.	The compound is ethoxybenzene.

Check Your Solution

a. The compound has an –O– group bonded to a five-carbon chain and a methyl group. There is an ethyl group on carbon atom 2 of the main chain. The name correctly reflects this structure.

b. The compound has an –O– group bonded to a benzene ring and an ethyl group. The name correctly reflects this structure.

Sample Problem

Drawing Ethers

Problem
Draw the condensed structural formula for 2-methoxy-4-methylpentane.

What Is Required?
You must draw a condensed structural formula.

What Is Given?
You are given the name.

Plan Your Strategy	Act on Your Strategy
Identify the type of compound.	The name has -oxy in it, so it is an ether.
Identify the root.	The parent alkane is pentane, so the main carbon chain has five carbon atoms.
Identify the first part of the prefix.	The first part of the prefix is 2-methoxy-. Thus, a methyl group is bonded to an oxygen atom, which is bonded to the main chain at carbon atom 2.
Draw the skeleton of the structure containing the oxygen atom. To simplify the drawing, make a bend in the main chain at the carbon atom that is bonded to the oxygen. Number the carbon atoms in the main chain.	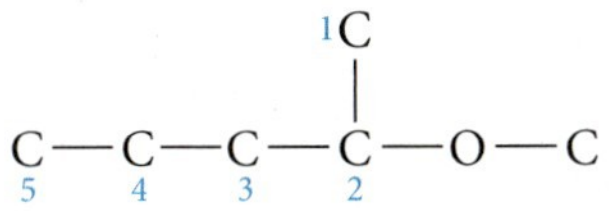 C—C—C—C—O—C (with 1C above C2; numbered 5 4 3 2)
Identify the second part of the prefix. Add necessary groups to the structure.	The second part of the prefix is 4-methyl-, so there is a methyl group on carbon atom 4 of the main chain. 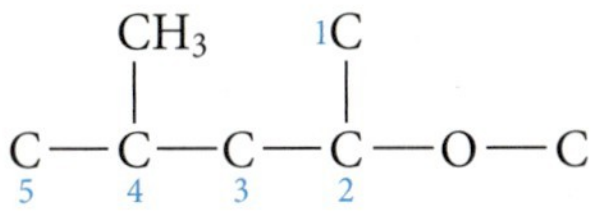 (structure with CH_3 on C4 and 1C on C2)
Add enough hydrogen atoms to give each carbon atom a total of four bonds.	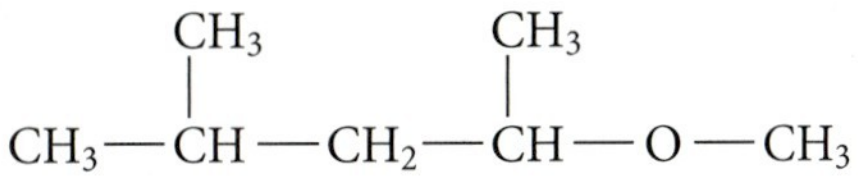 CH_3—CH—CH_2—CH—O—CH_3 with CH_3 groups on the two CH carbons

Check Your Solution
The longest chain has five carbon atoms and it is bonded to the oxygen atom at carbon atom 2. The smaller group on the oxygen is a methyl group, which is in agreement with the prefix methoxy-. There is a methyl group on carbon atom 4 of the longest chain. The structure is in agreement with the name.

Practice Problems

For the next three questions, name each ether.

136. H_3C—CH_2—O—CH_2—CH_2—CH_3

137. (structure: ethyl isopropyl ether)

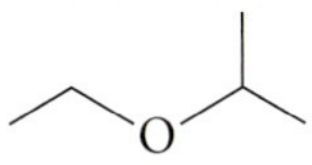

138. (structure: ethyl cyclohexyl ether)

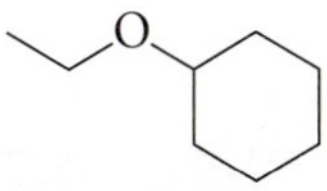

For the next four questions, draw the condensed structural formula for each ether.

139. methoxyethane

140. 2-propoxybutane

141. 3-ethoxy-4-methylhexane

142. 2-phenoxyheptane

For the next four questions, explain why each ether is named incorrectly or cannot exist. If it can exist, give the correct name.

143. ethoxymethane

144. 3-propoxybutane

145. 4-methoxy-4-methylbutane

146. 2-ethoxybenzene

Physical Properties of Ethers

The bond angle formed by the C–O bonds in ethers, shown in **Figure 1.35**, makes them slightly polar. If the bonds formed a straight line, the two bond dipoles would cancel each other. Nevertheless, ethers are not as polar as any of the other common hydrocarbon derivatives you have studied. As well, because ether molecules cannot form hydrogen bonds with one another, the attraction between them is small. As a result, ethers with a total of two or three carbon atoms are gases at room temperature while larger ethers are liquids.

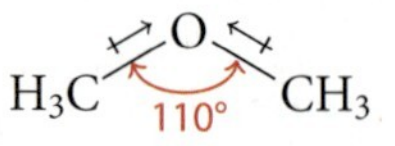

Figure 1.35 The bond angle between the two C–O bonds in ethers is 110° so the two dipoles do not cancel each other. This makes ethers slightly polar.

Ethers can form hydrogen bonds with water molecules. Thus, ethers with two or three carbon atoms are soluble in water. Straight chain ethers with a total of four to six carbon atoms are slightly soluble while all larger ethers are insoluble in water.

Amines

You may have noticed that fish dishes are often prepared or served with lemon, as shown in **Figure 1.36**. This is done to reduce the odour associated with fish. "That fishy odour" is due to the presence of amines, volatile hydrocarbon derivatives that tend to vapourize. The citric acid in the lemon juice neutralizes the amines, which are basic molecules. The acid converts the amines to their salt form, which is not volatile. Thus, lemon juice eliminates the odour.

Figure 1.36 The citric acid in lemon juice reacts with the amines in fish to eliminate its odour.
Explain what reaction occurs between the citric acid and the amine.

Amines have other practical uses, such as corrosion inhibitors in boilers, antioxidants in roofing asphalt, flotation agents in mining, and many more. Amines are also components of important biological molecules. When you are in a dangerous situation, a complex amine, adrenaline, is released into your blood. Once in your blood, adrenaline increases your heartbeat and respiration and helps to release more glucose into your bloodstream. In this way, it prepares your body for the "fight or flight" response to danger.

An **amine** is a hydrocarbon derivative that contains a nitrogen atom bonded to at least one carbon atom, although it may be bonded to up to three. Chemists separate amines into three categories depending on the number of carbon atoms bonded to the nitrogen atom. **Figure 1.37** shows examples of these three categories. *Primary amines* have one carbon atom bonded to the nitrogen, *secondary amines* have two, and *tertiary amines* have three.

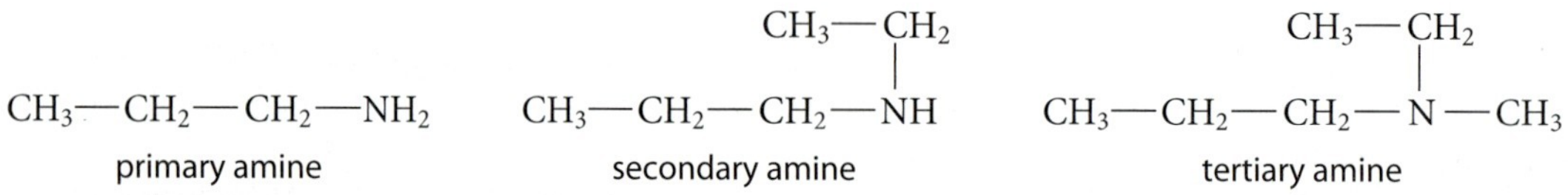

amine a hydrocarbon derivative that contains a nitrogen atom bonded to at least one carbon atom, although it may be bonded to up to three

$CH_3-CH_2-CH_2-NH_2$
primary amine

$CH_3-CH_2-CH_2-NH-CH_2-CH_3$
secondary amine

$CH_3-CH_2-CH_2-N(CH_3)-CH_2-CH_3$
tertiary amine

Figure 1.37 The three categories of amines are primary, secondary, and tertiary amines. Notice that the nitrogen atom in each type of amine always has three bonds. Any bonds that are not filled by a carbon atom are filled by a hydrogen atom.

Naming and Drawing Amines

The IUPAC system of naming amines considers the longer hydrocarbon group bonded to the nitrogen to be the main chain. Smaller hydrocarbons bonded to the nitrogen are dealt with as side groups. **Table 1.21** will guide you through the process of naming and drawing amines according to the IUPAC recommendations. **Figure 1.38** provides a summary of the components involved in the naming process.

Table 1.21 Steps in Naming Amines

1. Identify the root. a. Locate the longest chain that is bonded to the nitrogen atom. b. Name the parent alkane. Drop the -e on the end of the parent alkane to determine the root.	The longest carbon chain that is bonded to the nitrogen atom has seven carbon atoms. The parent alkane is heptane. The root is heptan-.
2. Identify the suffix. a. Number the carbon atoms in the main chain, starting with the carbon atom nearest the nitrogen atom. b. The suffix of an amine always ends with -amine. Indicate the position of the nitrogen atom if the main chain is three or more carbon atoms long. Do this by placing the number of the carbon atom bonded to the nitrogen atom in front of the -amine.	The main chain is three or more carbon atoms long. The suffix is -3-amine.
3. Identify the prefix. a. If the compound is a primary amine, there is no prefix. b. For secondary amines, name the smaller alkyl group bonded to the nitrogen atom. Write N, hyphen, and then the name of the alkyl group. c. For tertiary amines, both of the smaller alkyl groups are bonded to the nitrogen atom. Write an N in front of each group and order them alphabetically. If the two groups are the same, write N,N-di- and the name of the alkyl groups.	This is not a primary amine, so the prefix is not complete. This is not a secondary amine, so the prefix is not complete. This is a tertiary amine. There is one ethyl group and one propyl group bonded to the nitrogen atom, so the prefix is N-ethyl-N-propyl-.
4. Name the compound. Combine the prefix, root, and suffix to name the compound. There is no space between the prefix and the root.	The compound is N-ethyl-N-propylheptan-3-amine.

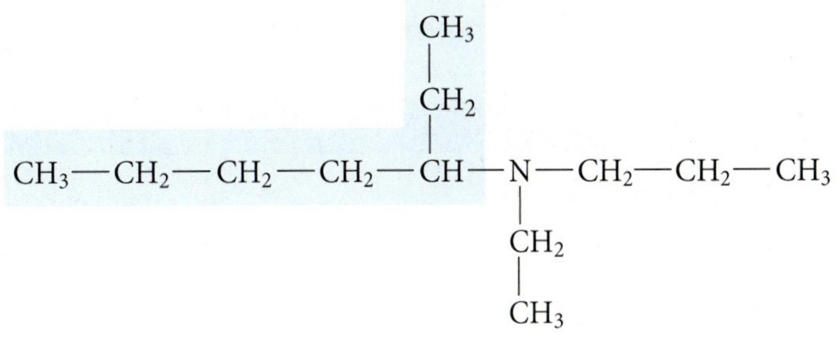

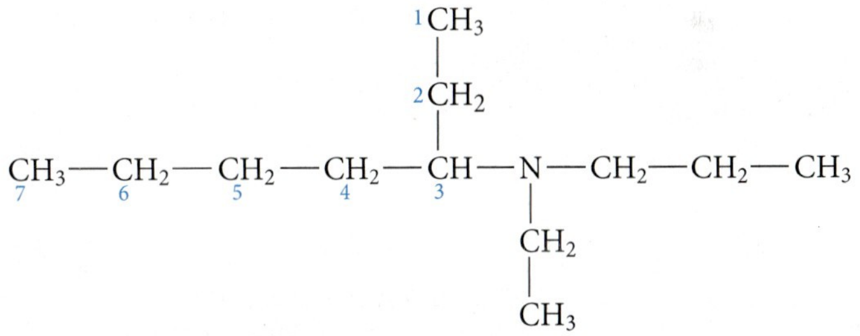

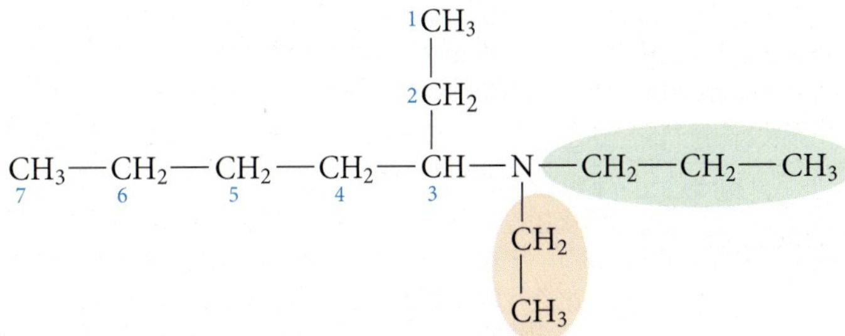

Figure 1.38 The highlighted groups in this structure summarize the components involved in naming an amine.

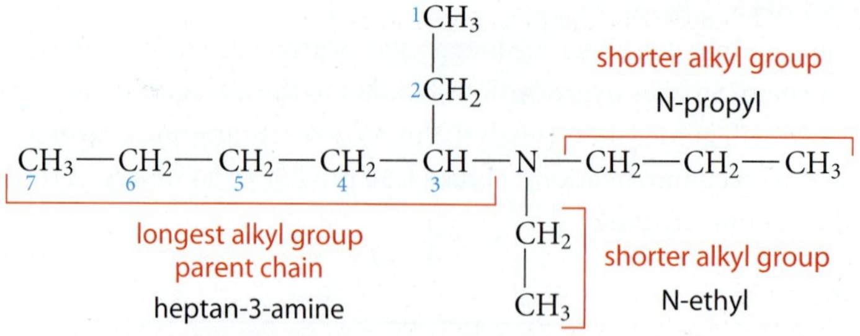

$$\underset{7}{CH_3}-\underset{6}{CH_2}-\underset{5}{CH_2}-\underset{4}{CH_2}-\underset{3}{CH}-N-CH_2-CH_2-CH_3$$

longest alkyl group / parent chain — heptan-3-amine

shorter alkyl group — N-propyl

shorter alkyl group — N-ethyl (CH₂—CH₃ branch on N)

N-ethyl-N-propylheptan-3-amine

Sample Problem

Naming Amines

Problem

Name the following amines.

a. $CH_3-CH_2-CH(CH_3)-NH_2$

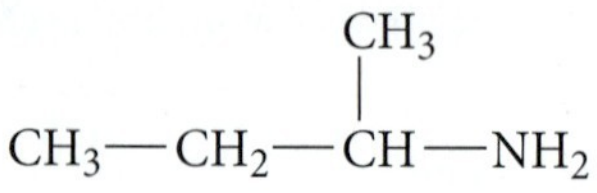

b. $CH_3-CH_2-N(CH_2CH_3)-CH(CH_3)-CH_3$

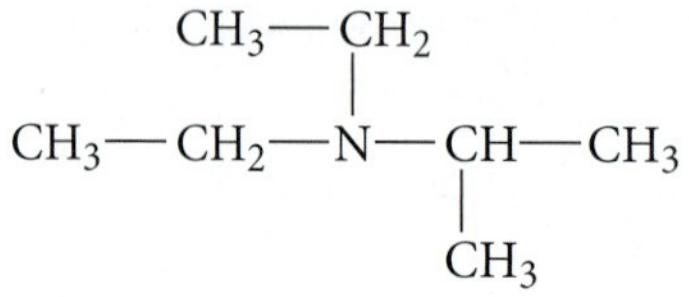

c. (structure of an N,N-disubstituted amine)

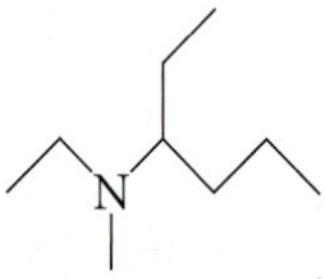

What Is Required?

You must name three amines.

What Is Given?

You are given the structures.

Plan Your Strategy	Act on Your Strategy
a. Identify the root.	The longest carbon chain has four carbon atoms, so the parent alkane is butane. The root is butan-. 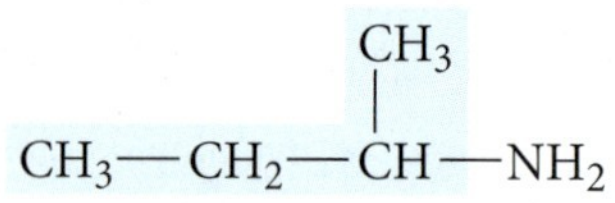
Identify the suffix.	Number the carbon atoms starting with the carbon atom nearest the nitrogen atom. Carbon atom 2 is bonded to the nitrogen, so the suffix is -2-amine. This is a primary amine so the name is complete. 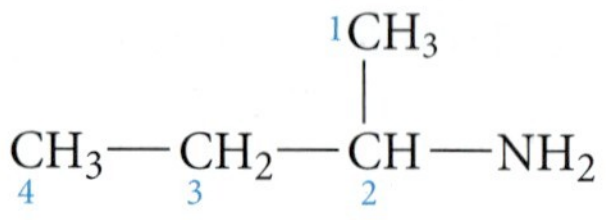
Write the name.	The compound is butan-2-amine.
b. Identify the root.	The longest chain has three carbon atoms, so the parent alkane is propane. The root is propan-. 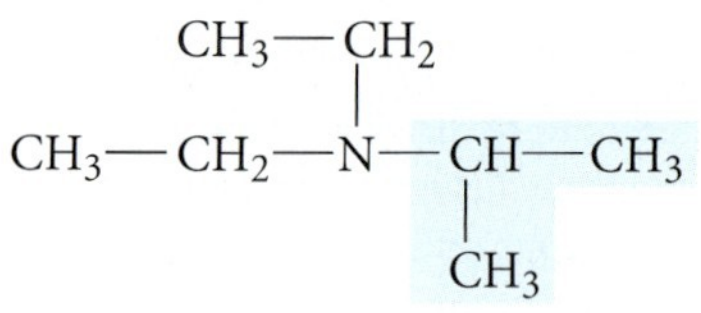
Identify the suffix.	Number the carbon atoms starting with the carbon atom nearest the nitrogen atom. Carbon atom 2 is bonded to the nitrogen, so the suffix is -2-amine. 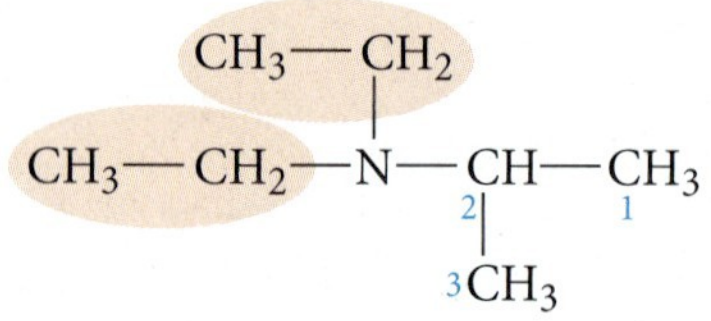
Identify the prefix.	There are two ethyl groups bonded to the nitrogen atom. So, the prefix is N,N-diethyl-.
Write the name.	The name of the compound is N,N-diethylpropan-2-amine.

72 MHR • Unit 1 Organic Chemistry

c. Identify the root.	The longest chain has six carbon atoms, so the root is hexan-.	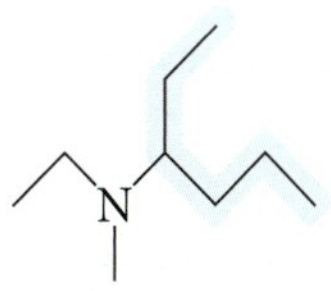
Identify the suffix.	Number the carbon atoms starting with the carbon atom nearest the nitrogen atom. Carbon atom 3 is bonded to the nitrogen atom, so the suffix is -3-amine.	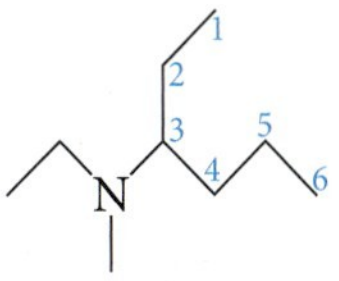
Identify the prefix.	There is one methyl group and one ethyl group bonded to the nitrogen atom, so the prefix is N-ethyl-N-methyl-.	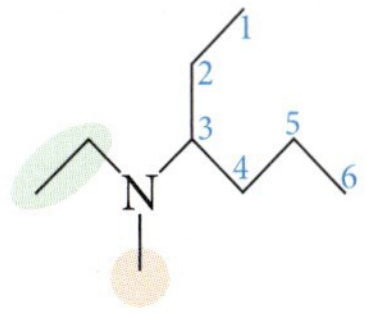
Write the name.	The compound is N-ethyl-N-methylhexan-3-amine.	

Check Your Solution
a. The compound has a nitrogen atom bonded to carbon atom 2 on a four-carbon atom chain. There are no side groups. The name reflects this.
b. In this compound, a nitrogen atom is bonded to carbon atom 2 on a chain that is three carbon atoms long. It is also bonded to two ethyl groups. The name correctly reflects the structure.
c. A nitrogen atom is bonded to carbon atom 3 on a six-carbon chain. It is also bonded to a methyl and an ethyl group. The name correctly reflects the structure.

Sample Problem

Drawing Amines

Problem
Draw a condensed structural formula for N-ethylpentan-3-amine.

What Is Required?
You must draw a condensed structural formula.

What Is Given?
You are given the name of the compound.

Plan Your Strategy	Act on Your Strategy
Identify the type of compound you are going to draw.	The name ends with -amine in it, so it is an amine.
Identify the root of the name.	The root is pentan-, so the longest carbon chain is five carbon atoms long.
Identify the suffix which indicates the position at which the nitrogen atom is bonded to the main chain. Draw the skeleton of the nitrogen atom and the main chain. To simplify the drawing, bend the chain at the carbon atom that is bonded to the nitrogen atom.	The suffix is 3-amine, which means that carbon atom 3 is bonded to the nitrogen atom. 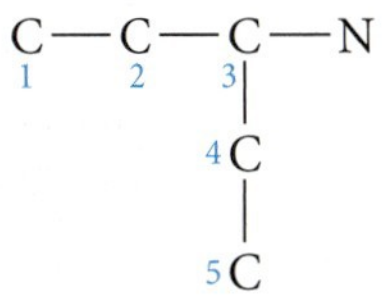

Continued on next page

Identify the prefix and draw the necessary atoms.	The prefix is N-ethyl-, which means that there is an ethyl group bonded to the nitrogen atom. There is only one N in the prefix, so there is only one side group bonded to the nitrogen atom. 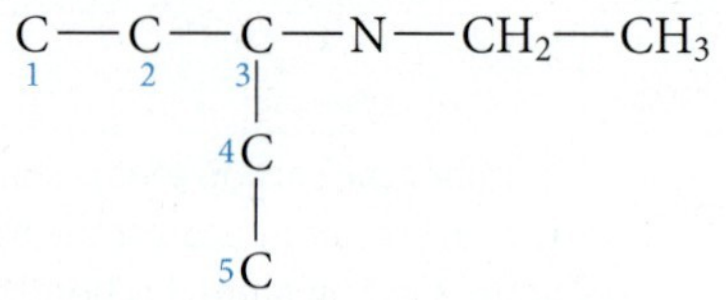
	
	C—C—C—N—CH$_2$—CH$_3$
	1 2 3
	            4 C
	            5 C

Add enough hydrogen atoms so that the nitrogen atom has a total of three bonds and each carbon atom has a total of four bonds.	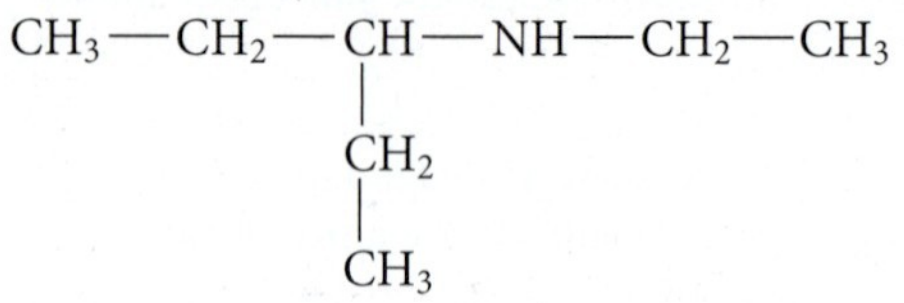 CH$_3$—CH$_2$—CH—NH—CH$_2$—CH$_3$
	                        CH$_2$
	                        CH$_3$

Check Your Solution

The longest carbon chain has five carbon atoms and carbon atom 3 is bonded to the nitrogen atom. There is an ethyl group bonded to the nitrogen atom, the nitrogen atom has three bonds, and each carbon atom has four bonds. The structure agrees with the name.

Practice Problems

For the next four questions, name each amine.

147. H$_3$C—CH$_2$—NH$_2$

148. 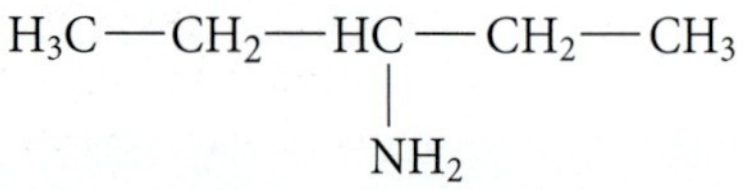 H$_3$C—CH$_2$—HC—CH$_2$—CH$_3$
                            |
                          NH$_2$

149. 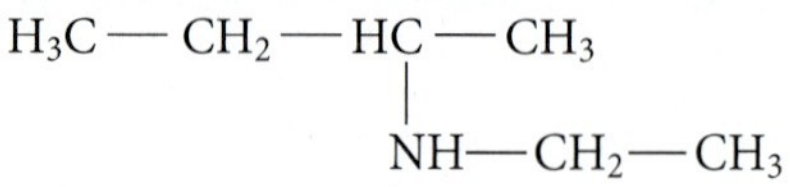 H$_3$C—CH$_2$—HC—CH$_3$
                        |
                      NH—CH$_2$—CH$_3$

150.
H$_3$C—CH$_2$—CH$_2$—CH$_2$—HC—CH$_3$
                                          |
H$_3$C—N—CH$_2$—CH$_2$—CH$_3$

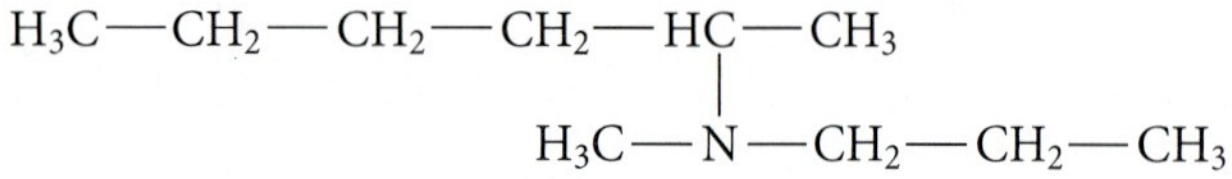

For the next four questions, draw the condensed structural formula for each amine.

151. methanamine

152. N-propylbutan-1-amine

153. hexan-1,4-diamine

154. N-ethyl-N-methylheptan-3-amine

For the next four questions, draw line structures of each amine.

155. propan-1-amine

156. N-ethyl-pentan-2-amine

157. N,N-dimethylbutan-2-amine

158. N-ethyl-N-propylhexan-3-amine

Physical Properties of Amines

The N-H bonds in primary and secondary amines are very polar. However, tertiary amines do not have N-H bonds. Thus, primary and secondary amines can hydrogen bond with themselves and with one another but tertiary amines cannot. Therefore, primary and secondary amines have relatively high boiling points compared to ethers and alkanes of a similar size. As well, they have higher boiling points than tertiary amines with the same number of carbon atoms. The boiling points of a few amines are listed in **Table 1.22**. Use the table to compare the boiling points of primary, secondary, and tertiary amines that have the same number of carbon atoms. For example, ethanamine, a primary amine, and N-methylmethanamine, a secondary amine, both have two carbon atoms and their boiling points differ by about 10°C. N,N-dimethylmethanamine, a tertiary amine, and propan-1-amine, a primary amine, both have three carbon atoms but their boiling points differ by more than 45°C.

All amines can hydrogen bond with water. Therefore, the smaller amines are very soluble in water.

Table 1.22 Boiling Points of Some Amines

Amine	Boiling Point (°C)
methanamine	−6.32
ethanamine	16.5
N-methylmethanamine	6.88
N,N-dimethylmethanamine	2.87
propan-1-amine	47.2
N-ethylethanamine	55.5
N,N-diethylethanamine	89.0
N-propylpropan-1-amine	109
N,N-dipropylpropan-1-amine	156

Amides

Have you ever had a headache and reached for a bottle containing pain reliever tablets? Unlike Aspirin® products, most other pain medications, like the one shown in **Figure 1.39**, contain acetaminophen, an amide. Penicillin is also an amide but it is very complex. It contains several other functional groups in addition to an amide group. Another amide, commonly called dimethylformamide, is a very commonly used organic solvent in industry. Most common commercial uses of amides, however, are in polymers such as nylon and polyacrylamide. You will learn about polymers in Chapter 2.

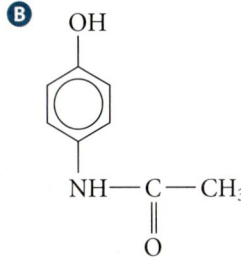

Figure 1.39 (A) The pain killer acetaminophen is an amide. (B) Its structural formula contains the functional group –CON–.

Amides are hydrocarbon derivatives containing the functional group, –CON–, which is a carbonyl group bonded to a nitrogen atom. One, or both, of the hydrogen atoms on the nitrogen atom can be replaced by alkyl groups. Similar to the case of amines, such replacements result in secondary and tertiary amides. **Figure 1.40** shows the general formula for amides and gives an example of a primary, secondary, and tertiary amide.

amide a hydrocarbon derivative that contains a carbonyl group bonded to a nitrogen atom

Figure 1.40 In the general formula, R, R′, and R″ can represent the same or different alkyl groups, but they can also represent hydrogen atoms. A primary amide has two hydrogen atoms bonded to the nitrogen atom. A secondary amide has one hydrogen and one alkyl group bonded to the nitrogen atom. A tertiary amide has two alkyl groups bonded to the nitrogen atom.

Recall that when studying esters, you were advised to think of an ester as the product of a reaction between a carboxylic acid and an alcohol. In the case of amides, you can think of them as the product of a reaction between a carboxylic acid and ammonia or a primary or secondary amine, as shown in **Figure 1.41**. If R′ and R″ are hydrogen atoms, the blue reactant is ammonia. If either R′ or R″ are alkyl groups, it is an amine.

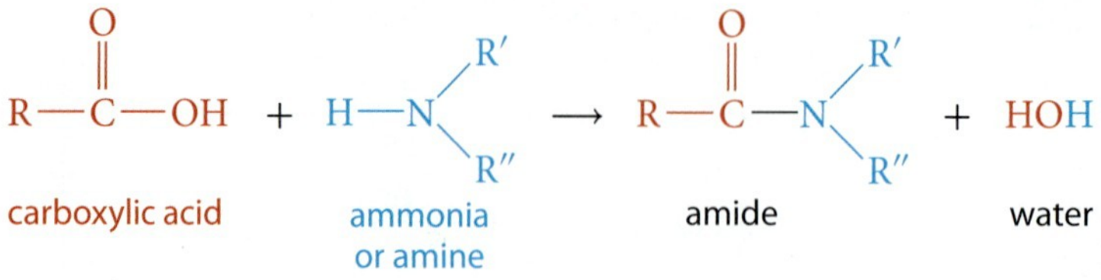

$$R-\underset{\text{carboxylic acid}}{\overset{\overset{\displaystyle O}{\|}}{C}-OH} + H-\underset{\text{ammonia or amine}}{N\diagdown \overset{R'}{R''}} \rightarrow R-\underset{\text{amide}}{\overset{\overset{\displaystyle O}{\|}}{C}-N\diagdown \overset{R'}{R''}} + \underset{\text{water}}{HOH}$$

Figure 1.41 Amides can be thought of as the product of a reaction between a carboxylic acid and ammonia or a primary or secondary amine.

Naming and Drawing Amides

The root of an amide comes from the part of the amide that contains the carbonyl carbon. For example, the root of the primary amide in **Figure 1.42** is propan- because the carbon chain containing the carbonyl carbon is made up of three carbon atoms. **Table 1.23** will guide you through the process of naming and drawing amides according to the IUPAC recommendations. **Figure 1.42** provides a visual summary of how an amide is named.

Table 1.23 Steps in Naming Amides

1. Identify the root. a. Determine the longest carbon chain that contains the carbonyl group.	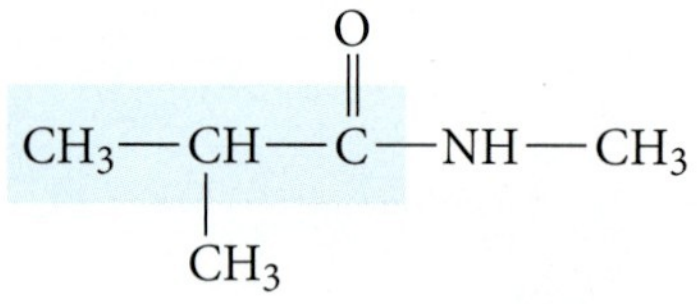 $CH_3-CH-\overset{\overset{\displaystyle O}{\|}}{C}-NH-CH_3$ $\vert$ CH_3 The longest carbon chain that contains the carbonyl carbon atom has three carbon atoms.
b. Name the parent alkane. The parent alkane comes from the longest carbon chain that contains the carbonyl carbon. Drop the last -e to create the root.	The parent alkane is propane. The root is propan-.
2. Identify the suffix. For amides, the suffix is always -amide.	The compound contains a –CON– functional group. The suffix is -amide.
3. Identify the prefix. a. Number the carbon atoms in the main chain. Always start with the carbonyl carbon atom.	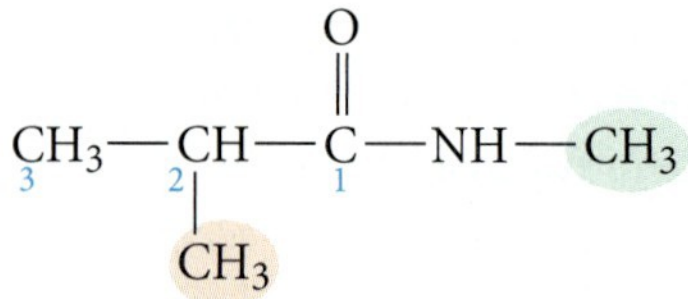 $\underset{3}{CH_3}-\underset{2}{CH}-\underset{1}{\overset{\overset{\displaystyle O}{\|}}{C}}-NH-CH_3$ $\vert$ CH_3 Number the carbon atoms starting with the carbonyl carbon atom.
b. If the main chain has any alkyl side groups, name them as you would for any hydrocarbon.	There is a methyl on carbon atom 2 of the main chain. The prefix contains 2-methyl-.
c. For secondary amides, determine the name of the alkyl group bonded to the nitrogen atom. Write N, hyphen, and the name of the alkyl group. This part of the prefix is placed before the prefix identifying the alkyl group attached to the main chain.	There is one methyl group bonded to the nitrogen atom. The prefix contains N-methyl-.
d. For tertiary amides, determine the names of the alkyl groups bonded to the nitrogen atom. This prefix is written as N-alkyl group-N-alkyl group-, with the groups in alphabetical order. If there are two identical groups, write N,N-di- and the name of the alkyl groups.	
e. Combine the two components of the prefix to get the complete prefix. Place the N component of the prefix first, followed by the component that describes any alkyl groups attached to the main chain.	The complete prefix is N-methyl-2-methyl-.
4. Name the compound. Combine the prefix, suffix, and root. There are no spaces between the prefix, root, and suffix.	The compound is N-methyl-2-methylpropanamide.

Figure 1.42 The highlighted groups in this structure summarize the components involved in naming an amide.

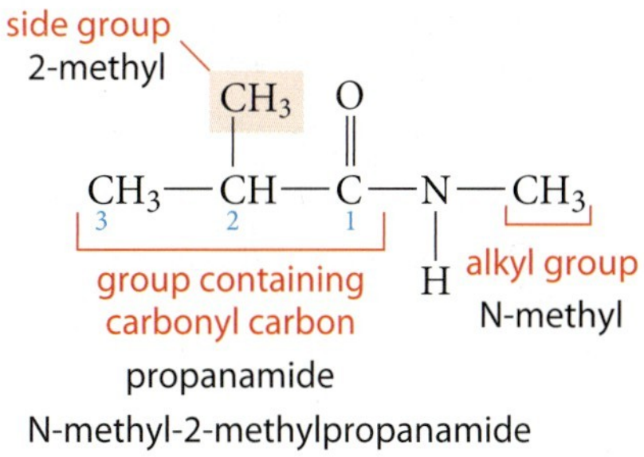

side group
2-methyl

$$CH_3-\underset{3}{CH}-\underset{2}{CH}(CH_3)-\underset{1}{C}(=O)-N(H)-CH_3$$

group containing carbonyl carbon — propanamide
alkyl group N-methyl

N-methyl-2-methylpropanamide

Sample Problem

Naming Amides

Problem

Name the following amides.

a. $CH_3-CH_2-CH_2-CH_2-C(=O)-N(H)-CH_2-CH_3$

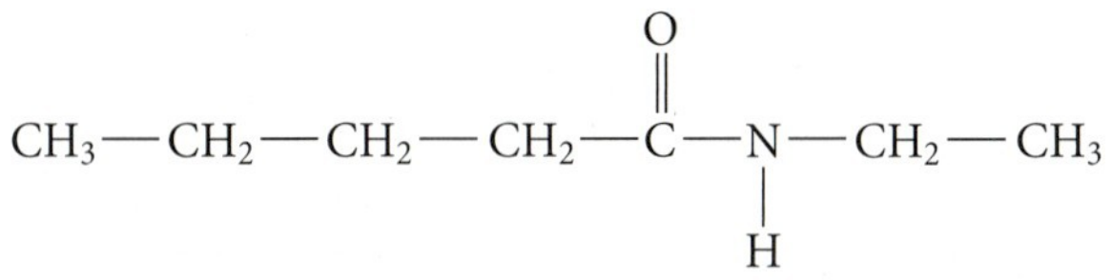

b. (structure shown)

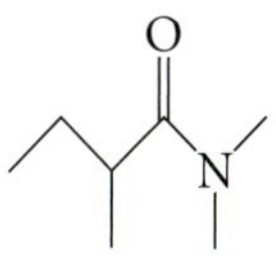

What Is Required?

You must name two amides.

What Is Given?

You are given the structures.

Plan Your Strategy	Act on Your Strategy
a. Identify the root.	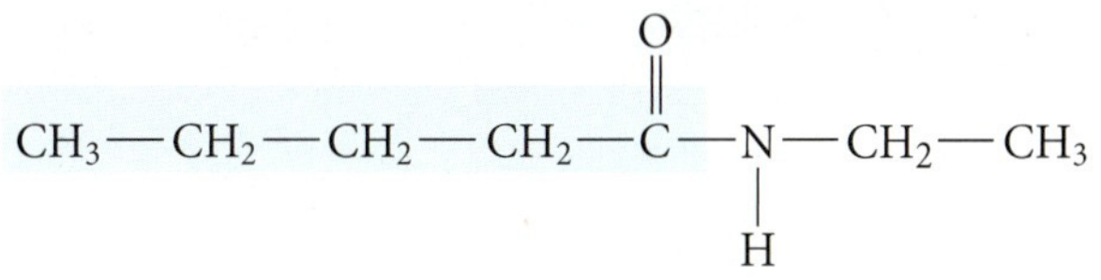 $CH_3-CH_2-CH_2-CH_2-C(=O)-N(H)-CH_2-CH_3$ The carbon chain containing the carbonyl group has five carbon atoms, so the root is pentan-.
Identify the suffix.	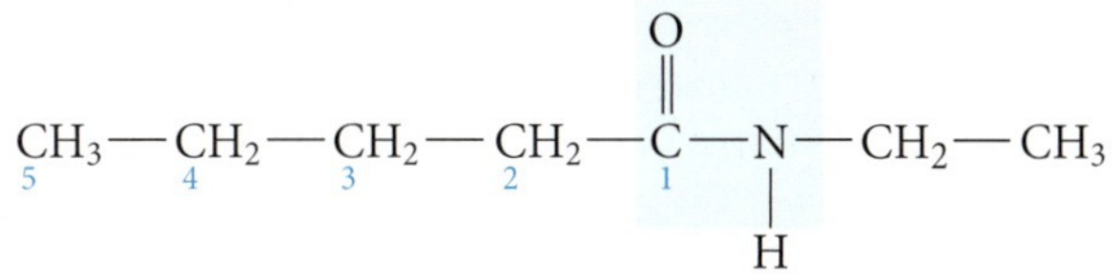 $\underset{5}{CH_3}-\underset{4}{CH_2}-\underset{3}{CH_2}-\underset{2}{CH_2}-\underset{1}{C}(=O)-N(H)-CH_2-CH_3$ The compound contains a –CON– functional group, so the suffix is –amide.
Identify the prefix.	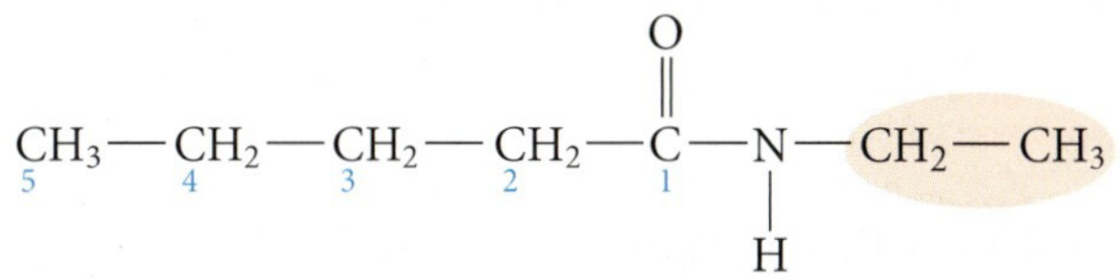 $\underset{5}{CH_3}-\underset{4}{CH_2}-\underset{3}{CH_2}-\underset{2}{CH_2}-\underset{1}{C}(=O)-N(H)-CH_2-CH_3$ There are no side groups on the main chain. There is an ethyl group bonded to the nitrogen atom. The prefix is N-ethyl-.
Write the name.	The compound is N-ethylpentanamide.

Continued on next page

b. Identify the root.	The carbon chain containing the carbonyl group has four carbon atoms, so the root is butan-.	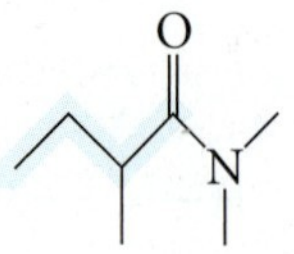
Identify the suffix.	The compound contains a –CON– functional group, so the suffix is -amide.	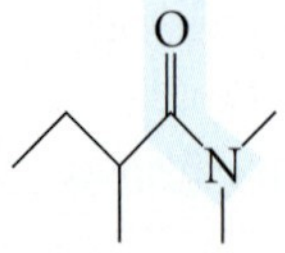
Identify the prefix.	There is a methyl on carbon atom 2 of the main chain. So, the prefix contains 2-methyl-.	
	There are two methyl groups bonded to the nitrogen atom. The prefix also contains N, N-dimethyl-. The complete prefix is N,N-dimethyl-2-methyl-.	
Write the name.	The compound is N,N-dimethyl-2-methylbutanamide.	

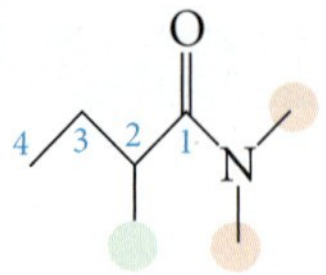

Check Your Solution
a. The compound contains a –CON– functional group. The >C=O group is part of a five-carbon chain. There is an ethyl group bonded to the nitrogen atom, but there are no side groups on the main chain. The name correctly reflects this structure.
b. The compound contains a –CON– functional group. The >C=O group is part of a chain of four carbon atoms. There are three methyl side groups. Two are bonded to the nitrogen atom and one to carbon atom 2. The name correctly reflects this structure.

Sample Problem

Drawing Amides

Problem
Draw a condensed structural formula for N,N-diethyl-2-ethylpentanamide.

What Is Required?
You must draw a condensed structural formula.

What Is Given?
You are given the name of the structure.

Plan Your Strategy	Act on Your Strategy
Identify the type of compound.	The suffix is -amide, so the compound is an amide.
Identify the root of the name. Draw the structure that is described by the root and suffix.	The root is pentan-, indicating that there are five carbons in the chain containing the carbonyl carbon of the amide group. 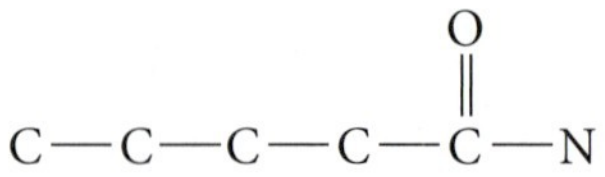

Identify the N component of the prefix. Draw the structure described by the prefix.	The N component of the prefix is N,N-diethyl-, which means that there are two ethyl groups bonded to the nitrogen atom.	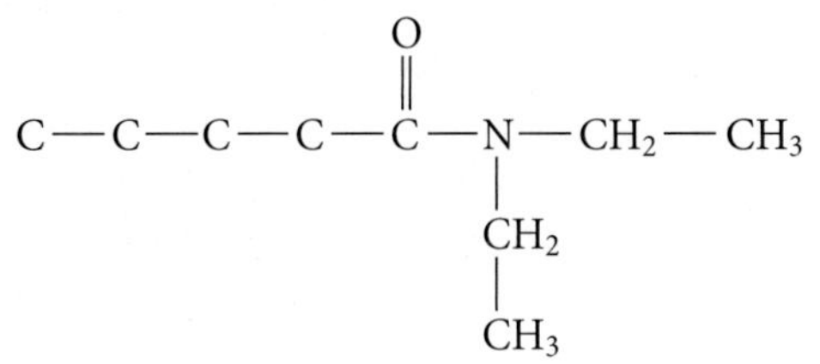 C—C—C—C—C(=O)—N(—CH₂—CH₃)—CH₂—CH₃
Determine whether there are any side groups on the main chain. If so, draw them.	The prefix ends in 2-ethyl-, so there is an ethyl group bonded to carbon atom 2 of the main chain. The numbering starts with the carbonyl carbon atom.	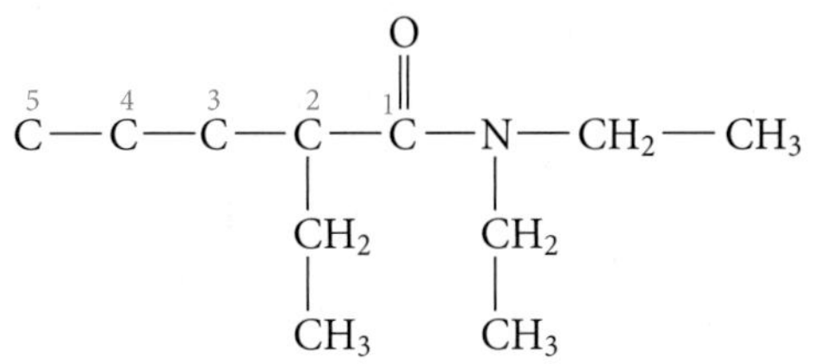 $\overset{5}{C}$—$\overset{4}{C}$—$\overset{3}{C}$—$\overset{2}{C}$(CH₂CH₃)—$\overset{1}{C}$(=O)—N(CH₂CH₃)—CH₂—CH₃
Add enough hydrogen atoms to give the nitrogen atom a total of three bonds and each carbon atom a total of four bonds.		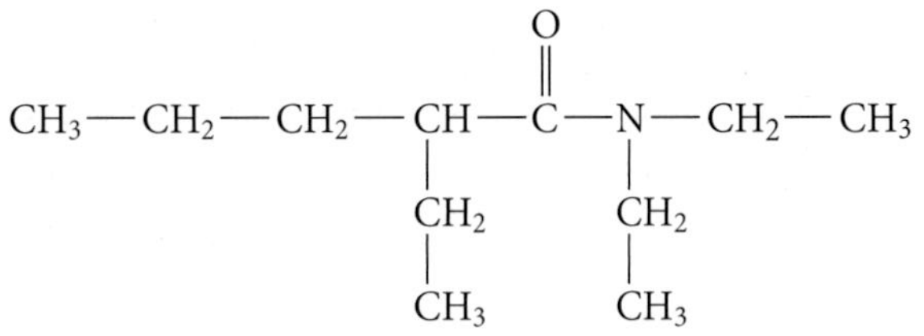 CH₃—CH₂—CH₂—CH(CH₂CH₃)—C(=O)—N(CH₂CH₃)—CH₂—CH₃

Check Your Solution
The chain containing the carbonyl carbon has five carbon atoms. There are two ethyl groups bonded to the nitrogen atom and there is an ethyl group bonded to carbon atom 2 of the main chain. The structure agrees with the name.

Practice Problems

For the next four questions, name each amide.

159. H₂N—CHO (formamide structure with H-N(H)-C(H)=O)

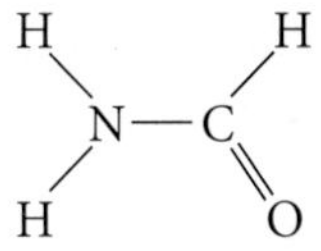

160. H₃C—CH₂—CH₂—CH(CH₂CH₃)—CH₂—C(=O)—NH₂

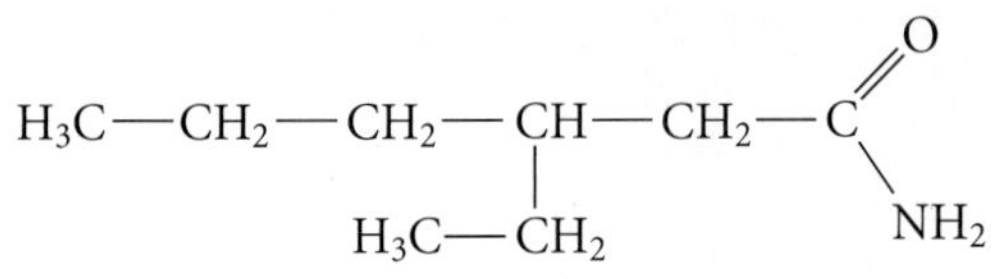

161. H₃C—CH₂—CH₂—CH₂—C(=O)—NH—CH₂—CH₂—CH₃

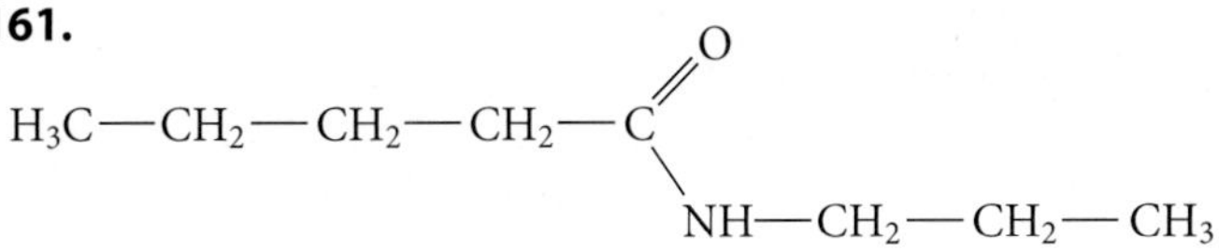

162. H₃C—CH₂—CH₂—C(=O)—N(CH₃)(CH₃)

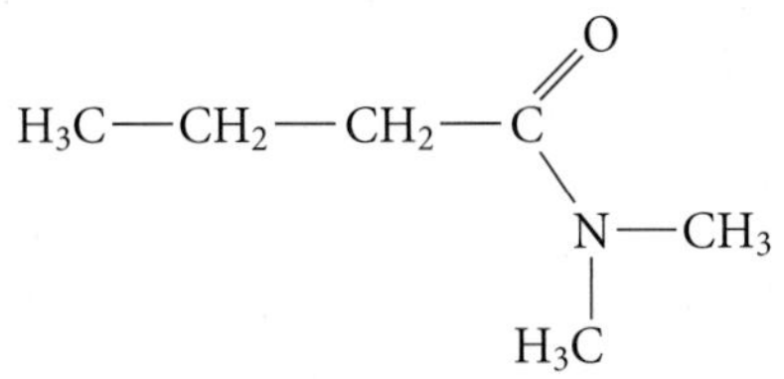

For the next four questions, draw the condensed structural formula for each amide.

163. ethanamide

164. 2-methylpropanamide

165. N,N-diethylhexanamide

166. N-ethyl-N-propyl-2-methylbutanamide

For the next three questions, name each amide.

167. CH₃CH₂—C(=O)—NH₂

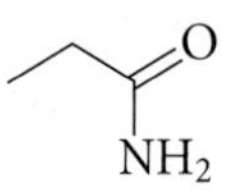

168. (CH₃)₂CH—C(=O)—NH—CH₂CH₃ (with methyl branching)

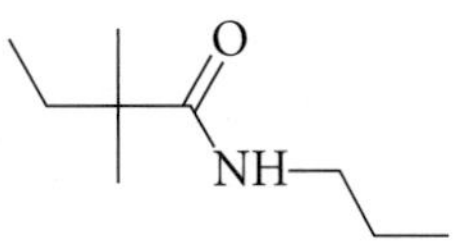

169. Structure with butyl and propyl chains on α-carbon, amide C(=O)—N(CH₃)— group

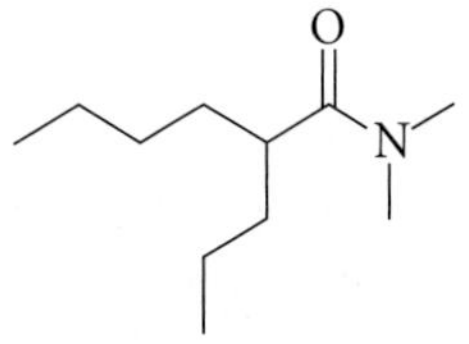

Suggested Investigation

ThoughtLab Investigation 1-B, Alternatives for Potentially Hazardous Products

Physical Properties of Amides

Amides have a polar carbonyl group and primary and secondary amides have at least one –NH group. Therefore, they can form strong hydrogen bonds among themselves. Consequently, their boiling points are much higher than those of other hydrocarbon derivatives of similar size. For example, **Table 1.24** lists the melting and boiling points of a two-carbon amide plus two other hydrocarbon derivatives that contain two carbon atoms.

Table 1.24 Melting and Boiling Points of Two Carbon Derivatives

Hydrocarbon Derivative	Melting Point (°C)	Boiling Point (°C)
ethanamide	80.16	222
ethanoic acid	16.64	117.9
ethanamine	−80.5	16.5

As you can see from the melting and boiling points, ethanamide is a solid at room temperature, ethanoic acid is a liquid, and ethanamine is a gas. The polarity and potential for forming hydrogen bonds makes a tremendous difference in the physical properties of the compounds. In general comparison, the order of the hydrocarbon derivatives of similar size in terms of their polarity, from greatest to least is:

amide > acid > alcohol > ketone ≅ aldehyde > amine > ester > ether > alkane

Because amides can form hydrogen bonds with water, the small amides are very soluble in water.

Hydrocarbon Derivatives with Multiple Functional Groups

Glucosamine, shown in **Figure 1.43A**, is an organic compound made up of a carbohydrate and an amino acid, called an amino sugar. Upon examining the structure of glucosamine in **Figure 1.43B**, you will find that it has a formyl group (−CHO), an amino group (−NH$_2$), and four hydroxyl groups (-OH). This combination of several functional groups is very common for organic compounds. Many of them have more than one type of functional group. The IUPAC priority list for naming these compounds is shown in Appendix B.

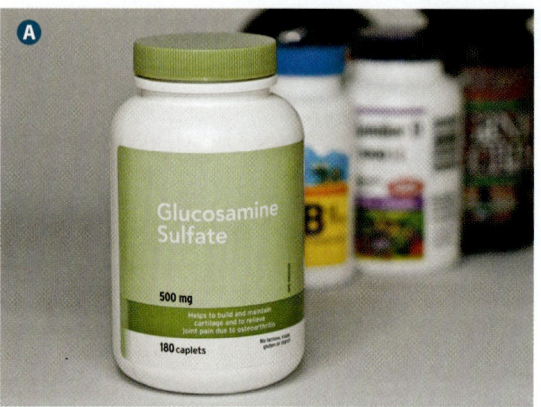
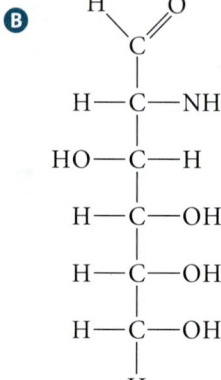

Figure 1.43 (**A**) Glucosamine is often found on the drugstore shelf, as a component of the substance that lubricates joints. However, controlled scientific studies have not shown any improvement for people who take the capsules. (**B**) The structure of glucosamine has a formyl group, an amino group, and four hydroxyl groups.
Speculate Is glucosamine an amine, an alcohol, or an aldehyde?

Benzene Derivatives with Substituted Functional Groups

In section 1.2, you studied benzene compounds that were substituted with alkyl side groups only. There are many other benzene derivatives substituted with different functional groups. Many benzene derivatives are commonly used in industry and in the laboratory. Consequently, their common names are widely used. These names are so well-established in chemical literature that IUPAC accepts them, though it does not recommend them as a first choice. Because the trivial names are IUPAC accepted, you are likely to encounter them in chemical literature. The trivial IUPAC accepted names, the IUPAC preferred names, and the structures of several common benzene derivatives you may encounter in your studies are shown in Appendix B.

Canadian Research in Action

Producing Polyurethane from Plant-based Hydrocarbon Derivatives

Dr. Leila Hojabri, an organic chemist at the Trent Centre for Biomaterials Research at Trent University in Ontario, is pictured here with research colleagues. Front row, left to right: Dr. Tamanna Sultana, Ling Yu, Ghazaleh Pourfallah, Dr. Suresh Narine, Dr. Leila Hojabri, Carolyn Virginia Payne, Dr. Laziz Bouzidi. Back row, left to right: Ali Mahdevari, Dr. Shaojun Li, Michael Floros, Rekha Singh, Jiaqing Zuo.

Related Career

Chemical engineers are involved in designing, building, operating, and maintaining equipment and machinery used in chemical reactions. These chemical reactions are generally used to make products or carry out processes that have practical applications in human lives. Many chemical engineers also apply green principles, in this case the principles of green engineering, to reduce the environmental impact of a process or a product. Chemical engineers generally have a university undergraduate degree in engineering, although they may have completed further studies as well. They may work in a variety of fields. On Dr. Hojabri's team, the scientist who calibrates and maintains all laboratory equipment is a chemical engineer.

Polyurethane is a flexible and durable hydrocarbon derivative. First produced in 1937, this plastic exists today in a variety of forms and has numerous uses, including being used to make insulation, mattresses, and adhesives.

While polyurethane's potential for new applications continues to grow, its production also has significant environmental impacts. Like other plastics, polyurethane is petroleum-based. The plastic is manufactured by combining two different types of hydrocarbon derivatives in a chemical reaction. One of these is a polyol, an alcohol that contains two or more hydroxyl groups. The other is a diisocyanate. Diisocyanates are hydrocarbon derivatives that contain two isocyanate functional groups (–N=C=O). The type of polyol and diisocyanate combined in the chemical reaction determines the properties of the resulting polyurethane. The polyols and diisocyanates that are normally used to synthesize polyurethane are derived from petroleum. Petroleum excavation and refining result in ecosystem disturbance, air pollution, waste water production, and other effects that are harmful to the environment. Additionally, the synthesis of petroleum-based diisocyanates uses carbonyl dichloride (phosgene), a highly toxic compound associated with significant health and safety concerns, as a reactant.

In light of these concerns, Dr. Leila Hojabri, an organic chemist at the Trent Centre for Biomaterials Research at Trent University in Peterborough, Ontario, has focussed her research on making polyurethane production greener—literally. Along with the members of her research team, she has successfully produced bio-based polyurethane from plants rather than from petroleum. Dr. Hojabri and her colleagues have studied how to synthesize both polyols and diisocyanates from plant-derived vegetable oils. For instance, they have synthesized diisocyanates from dicarboxylic acids, such as nonanedioic acid (azelaic acid), that are derived from these oils. The bio-based compounds are then used to produce various polyurethanes.

Dr. Hojabri's research goals are centred on the principles of green chemistry, a movement to improve safety and efficiency in chemical processes while reducing waste generation, along with energy and resource consumption. (Green chemistry is covered in greater detail in Appendix A in this textbook.) In future, Dr. Hojabri intends to "green" the reactions she uses to produce polyols and diisocyanates from vegetable oils by reducing the solvents and the energy used in the reaction process.

Questions

1. Nonanedioic acid is a dicarboxylic acid derived from vegetable oil that is used to synthesize diisocyanates for polyurethane production. Draw the condensed structural formula for nonanedioic acid.

2. Use Internet and/or print resources to compare and contrast the life cycles of bio-based polyurethane and petroleum-based polyurethane, evaluating how each life cycle adheres to the principles of green chemistry.

3. Use Internet and/or print resources to find another career related to the research covered in this feature. Briefly describe the nature of this career and any required training or education.

Section 1.3 Review

Section Summary

- Functional groups are chemically active groups of atoms. One or more functional groups attached to a hydrocarbon form a hydrocarbon derivative.
- Alcohols contain a hydroxyl group (–OH), a functional group made up of an oxygen atom and a hydrogen atom. Haloalkanes are synthetic hydrocarbon derivatives that contain one or more halogen atoms.
- Aldehydes and ketones are two hydrocarbon derivatives that contain a carbonyl group (>C=O). In ketones, the carbon atom in the carbonyl group is bonded to two carbon atoms or chains.
- Carboxylic acids contain a carboxyl group (–COOH), a carbonyl group with a hydroxyl group attached to it. Esters contain a carbon atom double bonded to one oxygen atom (a carbonyl group) and single bonded to another.
- Ethers are hydrocarbon derivatives in which an oxygen atom is single bonded to two carbon atoms (-O-).
- Amines have a nitrogen atom bonded to at least one carbon atom. Amides include the functional group, -CON-.

Review Questions

1. **K/U** Name four different uses for alcohols.
2. **T/I** Explain why propane, but not propan-1-ol, is suitable for use as a fuel in gas barbeques.
3. **A** Tetrachloroethene (C_2Cl_4), sometimes called perchloroethylene, is the most commonly used dry cleaning solvent. Dry cleaning involves the washing of clothes in the liquid solvent to remove non-polar fats and oils and then distilling the solvent to recover it. Why would tetrachloroethene be used instead of ethanol, which has the same number of carbons, is less expensive, and has lower toxicity?
4. **C** Use a table to compare aldehydes and ketones with regards to structure, naming, and physical properties.
5. **A** Short-chain carboxylic acids, such as propanoic acid and butanoic acid, have strong pungent odours. Butanoic acid, also known as butyric acid, has the original name derived from the smell of rancid butter. Why might strong cheeses and vomit both contain significant amounts of these compounds?
6. **K/U** Which functional group would you expect to conduct electricity and turn litmus paper red?
7. **T/I** Identify two substances that would react to form the following compounds.
   a. propylethanoate
   b. N-ethylpropanamide
8. **K/U** Consider the functional groups studied in this chapter.
   a. Which would you expect to form hydrogen bonds with identical molecules?
   b. What physical properties would you expect the functional groups in part a. to possess compared to the remaining functional groups?
9. **T/I** There are many constitutional isomers that have the formula $C_4H_{10}O$.
   a. How many isomers of ethers could have this formula? Explain your reasoning.
   b. What other types of substituted hydrocarbons could also have this formula?
   c. What differences in physical properties would you expect between the compounds determined in a. and b.?
10. **T/I** Name the following hydrocarbon derivatives.
    a.
    b.
    c.
11. **C** Draw the line structural formulas for following hydrocarbon derivatives.
    a. butan-2-ol
    b. ethane-1,2-diol
    c. propanoic acid
    d. methyl-2-methylpentanoate
    e. ethanamine

Inquiry INVESTIGATION

1-A

Skill Check
- Initiating and Planning
- ✓ Performing and Recording
- ✓ Analyzing and Interpreting
- ✓ Communicating

Materials
- paper and pencil
- molecular modelling kit

Modelling Organic Compounds

Three-dimensional models help scientists understand the structure of organic compounds. Chemists use models to help them predict the various ways in which a molecule might interact with other molecules. In this investigation, you will prepare molecular models to represent several organic compounds. You will also examine structural changes that result from the presence of an unsaturated bond.

Pre-Lab Questions
1. Why do scientists make three-dimensional models of molecules?
2. How do multiple bonds between atoms affect the characteristics of a molecule?

Question
How can you model the structure of various organic compounds?

Procedure
1. Construct three-dimensional models for each of the indicated series of molecules. As you complete each model, try to rotate each of the bonds in the molecules, and then draw a careful diagram of the structure. Your diagram might be similar to the one shown on the left.
   a. propane, propene, propyne
   b. methylcyclobutane, 3-methylcyclobutene, 3-methylcyclobutyne
   c. cyclohexane, cyclohexene, benzene
2. Build a model for hydrogen cyanide (HCN).

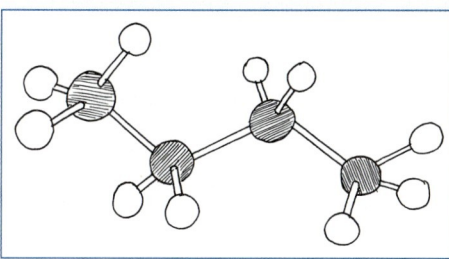

Analyze and Interpret
1. How did the addition of a multiple bond change the ability of a bond to rotate?
2. How did the addition of a multiple bond change the three-dimensional shape of each series of molecules?
3. Other than the presence of multiple double bonds, how do the structures of cyclohexane and benzene differ?

Conclude and Communicate
4. Were any molecules more difficult to construct than the others? Explain.
5. How would you describe to another student the effect on a molecule of an increasing number of multiple bonds?

Extend Further
6. **INQUIRY** Inspect your model of hydrogen cyanide. How is this compound different from the other compounds that you constructed in this exercise?
7. **RESEARCH** Use Internet resources to research information about the colour coding used in three-dimensional molecular models. Is there a standard colour system used by all chemists? Why or why not? What are some possible advantages and disadvantages to a standard colour system?

ThoughtLab INVESTIGATION 1-B

Skill Check
- Initiating and Planning
- ✓ Performing and Recording
- ✓ Analyzing and Interpreting
- ✓ Communicating

Suggested Materials
- reference books
- computers with Internet access

Go to Developing Research Skills in Appendix A for help with conducting research.

Alternatives for Potentially Hazardous Products

Throughout this chapter, you have been learning about families of organic molecules and the products they are found in. Suppose that the Chemical Institute of Canada has decided that people need to be more aware of the chemicals around them. The best way to do this is by having high school students participate in activities such as constructing websites, blogs, or creating brochures about organic chemicals found in everyday household products. Suppose your class has been asked to participate in these activities in order to inform your community about the hazards and benefits associated with organic chemicals and the "green" alternatives that are available. Green chemistry is a term used to refer to chemicals and processes that are sustainable, that reduce or eliminate pollution released into the environment, use renewable resources, and/or reduce or eliminate health hazards.

Pre-Lab Questions

1. What types of household products contain organic chemicals?
2. What is green chemistry?
3. List two reasons why people may choose to use "green" chemical products.

Question

What are the benefits and hazards associated with organic chemicals found in household products, and what alternative green products are available?

84 MHR • Unit 1 Organic Chemistry

Procedure

1. Select one of the following groups of products. Use print and/or Internet resources to identify three examples of organic chemicals found in those products. Before you begin your research, have your topic approved by your teacher.
   - pharmaceuticals
   - cosmetics
   - dietary supplements
   - food additives
   - plastics
   - pesticides

2. Describe each of the chemicals in detail including the chemical structure, why these chemicals are used, and the benefits of using each of these chemicals. Construct a table to help you organize the results of your research.

3. Research the health and environmental effects of the chemicals that are present in the product group you chose. Use the following questions to help guide your research. You may wish to add to your existing table or make a new graphic organizer to help organize the results of your research as you proceed with each remaining step.
   - What are the health effects associated with exposure to these chemicals?
   - What impact is there on the environment due to the manufacture, use, and disposal of these chemicals?
   - How much energy and raw materials are needed to manufacture these chemicals? What are the hazards associated with the raw materials?

4. Identify any "green" or alternative products or technologies that can replace potentially hazardous chemicals in the product group. Use the questions below to guide your research.
   - What characteristics must a product have in order for it to be considered "green"?
   - What is the chemical structure of the "green" alternative?
   - How are the "green" products manufactured?
   - Why are these alternatives considered to be "green"?
   - What advantages are associated with the use of the "green" products or technologies?

5. Research the health and environmental effects of the "green" alternatives. Use the questions below to help you in your research.
   - Are there any health effects or other issues associated with the use or ingestion of these alternative products?
   - What impact is there on the environment due to the manufacture and disposal of these alternatives? Consider how much energy and raw materials are needed to manufacture these chemicals and hazards associated with the raw materials.
   - Will these alternatives impact the environment as a result of how they are used?

Analyze and Interpret

1. Design a flow chart for each of the three chemicals you researched to show the impact of each one on human health and the environment.

2. Create a comparison chart that outlines the advantages and disadvantages of the green products/technologies compared to the three chemicals.

3. Summarize the advantages and disadvantages of green chemistry.

Conclude and Communicate

4. Are "green" alternatives always healthier for you and the environment?

5. Make a prediction about the future of our environment if we continue to use the same chemicals and processes that we currently use in household products.

Propose a Course of Action

6. Design a website, blog, or brochure to promote healthier alternatives to any of the harmful chemicals you researched.

7. Compose a letter to your Member of Parliament in which you outline your concerns about the future of our environment if we continue to use the same chemicals and processes that we currently use in household products.

Extend Further

8. **RESEARCH** Find out more information about government regulations regarding "green" products. Are government regulations strict enough in terms of whether or not products are designated as being "green"? What are the issues associated with the designation of "green" products?

9. **INQUIRY** Design a "green" alternative for one of the products in the group you chose. For example, you could identify the ingredients for a "green" sunscreen, flavouring, pesticide, or plastic.

Chapter 1 | SUMMARY

Section 1.1 Introducing Organic Compounds

Organic compounds consist of carbon atoms that are nearly always bonded to each other, to hydrogen atoms, or to atoms of a few specific elements, such as oxygen, nitrogen, sulfur, or phosphorus.

Key Terms

constitutional isomer
diastereomer
enantiomer
inorganic compound
isomer
organic compound
stereoisomer

Key Concepts

- In organic compounds, carbon atoms are almost always bonded to each other, to hydrogen atoms, and occasionally to atoms of a few specific elements.
- A carbon atom has four valence electrons, allowing it to form covalent bonds with up to four other atoms.
- Carbon atoms can bond with each other to produce straight or branched chain molecules that provide the root for a large number of organic compounds.
- Many organic compounds form isomers. The two main classes of isomers are constitutional isomers and stereoisomers.
- Diastereomers are stereoisomers in which different atoms or groups are bonded to each carbon involved in a double bond. Enantiomers are stereoisomers in which molecules are mirror images of each other around a single carbon atom bonded to four different types of atoms or groups.

Section 1.2 Hydrocarbons

Hydrocarbons consist of only carbon and hydrogen atoms, yet they have a wide variety of chemical and physical properties.

Key Terms

aliphatic compound
alkane
alkene
alkyl group
alkyne
aromatic hydrocarbon
benzene
cyclic hydrocarbon
homologous series
hydrocarbon
phenyl group
prefix
root
saturated hydrocarbon
substituent group
suffix
unsaturated hydrocarbon

Key Concepts

- Hydrocarbons are compounds that contain only carbon atoms and hydrogen atoms.
- Alkanes are made up of single bonds only. Alkenes are hydrocarbons that have at least one double bond, while alkynes have at least one triple bond.
- Cyclic hydrocarbons include alkanes, alkenes, and alkynes in the shape of a ring. Aromatic hydrocarbons are ring structures that are derived from benzene.
- Hydrocarbons are insoluble in water but are soluble in non-polar solvents, such as benzene. They are ranked as follows from highest to lowest boiling point: aromatic and cyclic hydrocarbons, alkynes, alkanes, alkenes.
- All hydrocarbon names are based on the structure of the compound and follow IUPAC rules. The names are so precise that the structure of the compound can be drawn from them.

Section 1.3 Hydrocarbon Derivatives

Hydrocarbon derivatives contain functional groups.

Key Terms

alcohol
aldehyde
alkoxy group
amide
amine
carbonyl group
carboxyl group
carboxylic acid
ester
ether
formyl group
functional group
haloalkane
hydrocarbon derivative
hydroxyl group
ketone
parent alkane

Key Concepts

- Functional groups are chemically active groups of atoms. One or more functional groups attached to a hydrocarbon form a hydrocarbon derivative.
- Alcohols contain a hydroxyl group (–OH), a functional group made up of an oxygen atom and a hydrogen atom. Haloalkanes are synthetic hydrocarbon derivatives that contain one or more halogen atoms.
- Aldehydes and ketones are two hydrocarbon derivatives that contain a carbonyl group (>C=O). In ketones, the carbon atom in the carbonyl group is bonded to two carbon atoms or chains.
- Carboxylic acids contain a carboxyl group (–COOH), a carbonyl group with a hydroxyl group attached to it. Esters contain a carbon atom double bonded to one oxygen atom (a carbonyl group) and single bonded to another.
- Ethers are hydrocarbon derivatives in which an oxygen atom is single bonded to two carbon atoms (–O–).
- Amines have a nitrogen atom bonded to at least one carbon atom. Amides include the functional group, –CON–.

Chapter 1 REVIEW

Knowledge and Understanding

Select the letter of the best answer below.

1. Which molecule is an example of an organic molecule?
   a. CO_2
   b. C_2H_4
   c. $CaCO_3$
   d. NaCN
   e. CaC_2

2. Isomers are molecules that have
   a. the same molecular mass but different number of atoms.
   b. the same number of atoms but different types of atoms.
   c. different three-dimensional structures with the same molecular formula.
   d. the same three-dimensional structures with a different molecular formula.
   e. different three-dimensional structures but the same types of physical and chemical properties.

3. Which molecule can form diastereomers?
   a. $C_2H_2F_2$
   b. $C_2H_4F_2$
   c. C_2H_2
   d. C_2H_4ClF
   e. $C_2H_4Cl_2$

4. Which molecule could exist as an enantiomer?
   a.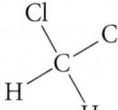
   b.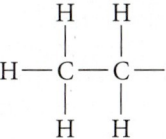
   c.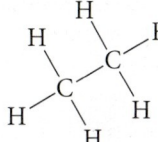
   d. 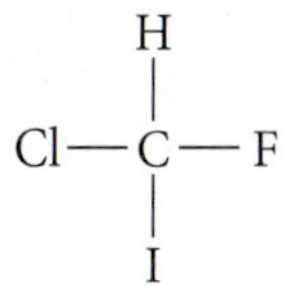
   $$Cl-\underset{I}{\overset{H}{C}}-F$$
   e.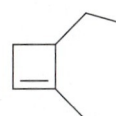

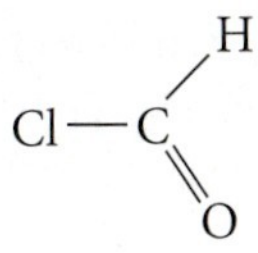

5. Which is a general formula for a straight chain or branched chain alkane?
   a. $C_{2n}H_n$
   b. $C_{2n}H_{2n}$
   c. C_nH_n
   d. C_nH_{2n}
   e. C_nH_{2n+2}

6. Which is the formula for hept-1-ene?
   a. C_6H_{10}
   b. C_6H_{12}
   c. C_6H_{14}
   d. C_7H_{14}
   e. C_7H_{16}

7. Which molecule would you expect to have the lowest boiling point?
   a. ethane
   b. ethene
   c. propane
   d. pentyne
   e. hexane

8. Which is the molecular formula for cyclohexane?
   a. C_6H_6
   b. C_6H_8
   c. C_6H_{10}
   d. C_6H_{12}
   e. C_6H_{14}

9. Which is the correct name for the following molecule?

   a. 2-methyl-3-ethylcyclobutane
   b. 2-ethyl-1-methylcyclobutyne
   c. 1-methyl-4-ethylcyclobutene
   d. 1-methyl-4-ethylcyclobutyne
   e. 3-ethyl-2-methylcyclobutene

10. In a benzene ring, the carbon to carbon bonds are
    a. single bonds.
    b. double bonds.
    c. alternating single and double bonds.
    d. the length of double bonds.
    e. intermediate length between single and double bonds.

11. Which is the name of the functional group shown below?

    R—OH

    a. alcohol
    b. haloalkane
    c. aldehyde
    d. ketone
    e. ester

Chapter 1 REVIEW

12. The functional group below is an example of a(n)

    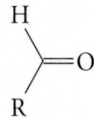

    a. alcohol.
    b. ketone.
    c. aldehyde.
    d. ether.
    e. carboxylic acid.

13. Which results from a reaction between an alcohol and a carboxylic acid?
    a. aldehyde
    b. ether
    c. amine
    d. amide
    e. ester

14. The prefix "phenyl" refers to a(n)
    a. alcohol.
    b. benzene ring.
    c. ether.
    d. ester.
    e. carboxylic acid.

Answer the questions below.

15. What aspects of the carbon atom make it suitable for forming the variety of organic molecules that exist?

16. What are isomers?

17. What makes stereoisomers different from other types of constitutional isomers?

18. What kinds of molecules can form diastereomers?

19. What is the name for a pair of molecules with the same molecular and structural formulas but that are non-superimposable mirror images? In terms of their properties, what makes them different from other types of isomers?

20. State the difference between a saturated and an unsaturated hydrocarbon.

21. What is the general formula for the following molecules?
    a. straight or branched chain alkanes
    b. alkenes with one double bond
    c. alkynes with one triple bond
    d. cyclic alkanes

22. What physical property do alkanes, alkenes, and alkynes share?

23. Compare and contrast cyclohexane and benzene.

24. What are two physical properties that distinguish ethanol from ethane?

25. What are the structural similarities and differences between aldehydes and ketones?

26. An ester can be thought of as the product of a reaction between what two other functional groups?

27. An amide can be thought of as the product of a reaction between what two other functional groups?

28. Explain why you are likely to encounter the common names for benzene derivatives in chemical literature.

Thinking and Investigation

29. Each alkane formula listed below has an error in it. Identify and state the error, then rewrite the formula correctly with the same number of carbon atoms.
    a. CH_5
    b. C_2H_3
    c. C_6H_7
    d. CH_2O

30. Explain why the molecule CH_2BrF could not form enantiomers.

31. Identify which of the following molecules can form diastereomers. Explain why the other two cannot.
    a. $C_2H_2Br_2Cl_2$
    b. $C_2H_2Br_2$
    c. C_2HI

32. Suppose you are given an alkane that may have the formula C_2H_6 or C_8H_{18}. Design an investigation in which you could test a physical property to determine which alkane you have.

33. Determine whether the following molecules are named correctly. If incorrect, provide the correct name.

    a. 4-methyl-3-ethylpentane

    b. 4-ethenylhexane

34. Hexane, cyclohexane, and benzene all have six carbons. How are they distinguished by their chemical formulas?

35. Research five molecules that contain a benzene ring. Draw, name, and cite a use for each substance. Use terms such as aromatic, phenyl, or benzyl to help you in your search.

36. How many constitutional isomers can be made with the formula C_4H_8? Explain your reasoning.

37. Research more information about *volatile organic compounds*, commonly known as VOCs.
    a. Define these compounds.
    b. State the benefits and risks of using VOCs.
    c. Identify and provide the structures of two VOCs that are naturally produced and four that are manufactured by humans.
    d. Choose one VOC and evaluate scientific evidence of its impact on human health. Discuss any strengths and weaknesses of the evidence.

38. Lactic acid is produced by anaerobic respiration and is incorrectly attributed to muscle soreness when exercising. Can the lactic acid molecule, shown below, form an enantiomer? Explain your reasoning.

39. Design an investigation that could help distinguish among samples of ethane, ethanol, and ethanoic acid.

40. Determine whether the following molecules are named correctly. If not, provide the correct names.
    a. hexan-3,4-diol
    b. 2,3-dimethyl-4-chloropentane
    c. 6-methyl-3-ethyldecan-2-al
    d. 2-methyl-2-ethylbutan-3-one

41. Use print and/or Internet sources to identify three inorganic compounds that are greenhouse gases and three organic compounds that are greenhouse gases.
    a. Write the molecular formula and draw the structure of each molecule.
    b. Identify the sources of each compound, natural and/or the result of human activities.
    c. How does each compound act as a greenhouse gas?
    d. If organic greenhouse gas molecules are much more effective than inorganic molecules at trapping heat, explain why we are more concerned with certain inorganic greenhouse gas molecules.
    e. Choose one compound that is being added to the atmosphere due to human activities. Identify three actions that could help reduce emissions.

42. The table below shows the boiling points for the first ten alkanes.

    Boiling Points of First Ten Alkanes

Name	Boiling Point (°C)
Methane	−162
Ethane	−89
Propane	−42
Butane	−0.5
Pentane	36
Hexane	69
Heptane	98
Octane	126
Nonane	151
Decane	174

    a. Use the data from the table to graph the boiling point versus the number of carbon atoms in the alkane chain.
    b. Predict the boiling points for straight-chain alkanes with 11 and 12 carbon atoms.

43. The leaves of the poison ivy plant, shown below, contain a chemical called Urushiol-3, which is a skin irritant. The structural diagram of Urushiol-3 is also shown below.

    a. Identify all the functional groups in Urushiol-3.
    b. Predict the range of temperatures at which you would expect it to boil. Explain your reasoning.
    c. Predict which type of solubility it would have. Explain your reasoning.
    d. Predict which type of isomers it could form. Explain your reasoning.

44. Determine whether the following molecules are named correctly. If not, provide the correct names.
    a. 2-ethylpropan-1-oic acid
    b. 2-phenyl-2-ethyloctan-6-one
    c. 1-ethoxypentan-1-one
    d. N-butyl-N-methylpropanamine

Chapter 1 REVIEW

45. BIG IDEAS Organic compounds have predictable chemical and physical properties determined by their respective structures.

  a. Rank the following molecules with similar numbers of carbons in terms of their boiling points: ethanoic acid, ethanamine, methoxymethane, ethane, ethanamide.
  b. Explain why you expect these differences.
  c. Predict which molecule would be a liquid at room temperature.

Communication

46. BIG IDEAS Organic chemical reactions and their applications have significant implications for society, human health, and the environment. Sugar replacers and substitutes are found as additives in many foods. Use print and/or Internet resources to help you complete the following. Organize your responses in a table.

  a. Draw the structures of saccharin, sucralose, mannitol, and aspartame.
  b. Identify the functional group(s) contained in each substance.
  c. Identify any benefits and/or risks associated with the use of each substance.

47. Organic molecules can be represented in various forms.

  a. Draw three different two-dimensional ways of representing pent-2-en-1-ol.
  b. What kind of isomers could it form? Explain your reasoning.

48. Draw line structural formulas for the following hydrocarbons.

  a. 3,4-dimethylheptane
  b. 3,4,6-triethyloct-1-ene
  c. 4,4-dipropylnon-2-yne

49. Name the following hydrocarbon derivatives.

  a. [structure with Cl, Cl, F substituents]
  b. [structure: $H_3C-CH_2-CH(CH_2)-CHO$ type aldehyde]
  c. [structure with NH_2, HO, and C=O groups]

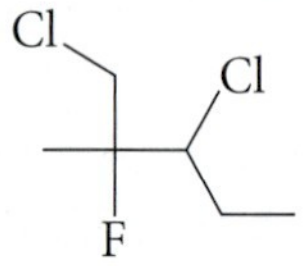

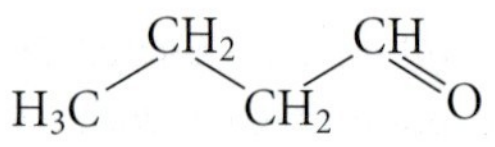

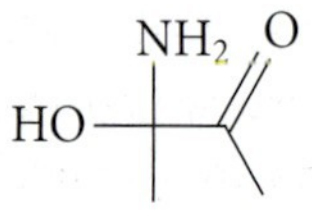

50. Use print and/or Internet resources to write the correct IUPAC name for these organic compounds.

  a. formaldehyde
  b. toluene
  c. ortho-xylene
  d. aniline
  e. chloroform

51. Summarize your learning in this chapter using a graphic organizer. To help you, the Chapter 1 Summary lists the Key Terms and Key Concepts. Refer to Using Graphic Organizers in Appendix A to help you decide which graphic organizer to use.

Application

52. BIG IDEAS Organic chemical reactions and their applications have significant implications for society, human health, and the environment. Many popular herbicides use the organic compounds 2,4-D (dichlorphenoxyacetic acid) or glyophosate (N-phosphonomethyl amino acetic acid).

  a. What are herbicides and why are they used?
  b. Identify which of the two molecules is shown below, 2,4-D or glyophosate? Justify your answer.

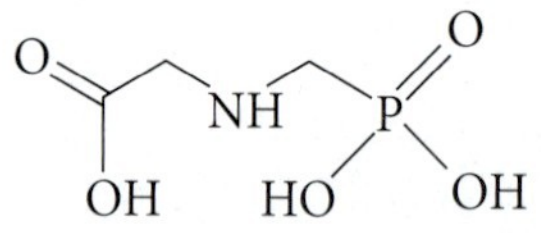

  [structure showing: HOOC-CH₂-NH-CH₂-P(=O)(OH)₂]

  c. Using print and/or Internet resources, identify why these substances may be harmful to the environment.
  d. Propose a personal course of action to reduce your use of such synthetic organic compounds around the home or garden by providing alternatives.

53. Putrescine and cadaverine are the common names of similar organic molecules that are breakdown products of proteins having an undesirable odour. They are shown below.

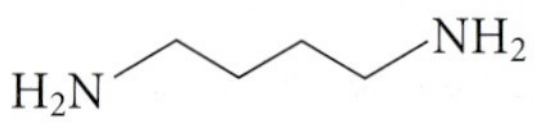

[structure: $H_2N-(CH_2)_4-NH_2$]
putrescine

[structure: $H_2N-(CH_2)_5-NH_2$]
cadaverine

  a. Provide the correct IUPAC name for each molecule.
  b. Speculate as to how each received its common name.
  c. What common household substances could be used to neutralize their disagreeable odours?

54. The widely used insect repellent DEET has its acronym based on the common name N,N-diethyl-m-toluamide. The structure of DEET is shown below. The common name for methylbenzene is toluene. Use your knowledge gained in this chapter and/or other resources to answer the following questions.

   a. Provide the correct IUPAC name for the compound.
   b. Suggest reasons for the common name.
   c. The molecule, which is a liquid at room temperature, has a mostly non-polar nature with some polar substituents. What types of solvents would you expect DEET to best dissolve in?
   d. Referring to your previous answer, what WHMIS symbols would you expect solutions containing DEET to have?
   e. Use a table to indicate the risks and benefits of the use of this insect repellent.
   f. What alternatives are there to using such a synthetic repellent?

55. Volatile organic compounds (VOCs) contribute to global warming and the creation of smog. Many, such as methane, propane, and hydrocarbons found in transportation and heating fuels, are significant contributors. What are some actions an individual could take to reduce their release into the atmosphere?

56. Formaldehyde has a low boiling point and is a gas at room temperature. Methanol is a liquid at room temperature with a similar molecular formula.
   a. Why is there such a difference between their boiling points?
   b. How can formaldehyde be used to preserve organisms, such as frogs used in laboratory dissections, if it is a gas at room temperature?

57. Fats and oils are an essential part of our diets. Much of their molecular structure consists of long hydrocarbon chains.
   a. What physical property can often be used to distinguish saturated and unsaturated fats?
   b. What is the difference between *cis* and *trans* fats? Use a sketch as part of your explanation.
   c. Research and explain why unsaturated fats are less detrimental to human health than saturated fats.

58. The hormone adrenaline is produced by the adrenal glands. It increases heart rate, constricts blood vessels, dilates air passages, and increases alertness. It is often referred to as the "fight or flight" hormone. Amphetamines are pharmaceutical drugs that have many side effects, including loss of appetite, restlessness, and dry mouth. Prolonged abuse of amphetamines can cause cardiac arrhythmias, dizziness, and convulsions. The structures of these two molecules are shown below.

   adrenaline   amphetamine

   a. Write the molecular formula for each substance.
   b. What are the similarities and differences in functional groups between the two molecules?
   c. If someone is having a severe allergic reaction, they may have to take an injection of adrenaline. Why might this help?
   d. Explain why amphetamines may be prescribed to someone suffering from narcolepsy, a disorder that causes excessive sleepiness and periods of extreme drowsiness, especially during the day.

59. Limonene can form enantiomers. Its structure is shown below. To form an enantiomer, four different functional groups are needed around a single, central carbon atom.

   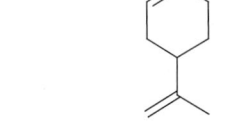

   a. Redraw the molecule showing all hydrogens to identify the central carbon atom.
   b. What types of foods would you expect limonene to be found in?
   c. Using print and/or Internet sources, research how the two enantiomers could be distinguished by smell.
   d. Besides being found in foods, limonene is used to replace toxic compounds such as methyl ethyl ketone and chlorofluorocarbons. What physical property in its structure allows it to do this?
   e. What other benefits does limonene have over synthetically produced organic compounds?

Chapter 1 | SELF-ASSESSMENT

Select the letter of the best answer below.

1. **K/U** Which molecule would be considered inorganic?
   a. H_2CO_3
   b. C_2H_2
   c. CH_4
   d. C_3H_6O
   e. C_2H_7N

2. **K/U** Stereoisomers have the same
   a. molecular formula but different connections between the atoms.
   b. molecular mass but different molecular formulas.
   c. molecular formula and connectivity between the atoms but differ in the three-dimensional orientation of the atoms.
   d. number of carbon atoms but differ in the number of hydrogen atoms.
   e. number of carbon and hydrogen atoms but differ in their substituents or functional groups.

3. **K/U** Which forms enantiomers?
   a. C_2H_6
   b. CH_3Cl
   c. $C_2H_2F_2$
   d. C_2H_2FCl
   e. $BrCHClF$

4. **K/U** Which statement is *true*?
   a. Alkenes contain only single-bonded carbons and alkynes contain at least one double bond.
   b. Alkanes contain only single-bonded carbons and alkynes contain at least one double bond.
   c. Alkynes contain only single-bonded carbons and alkenes contain at least one double bond.
   d. Alkynes contain only single-bonded carbons and alkenes contain at least one double bond.
   e. Alkanes contain only single-bonded carbons and alkynes contain at least one triple bond.

5. **K/U** Which is the general formula for a straight-chain saturated hydrocarbon?
   a. C_nH_n
   b. C_nH_{2n}
   c. $C_{2n}H_{2n}$
   d. C_nH_{2n+2}
   e. C_nH_{2n-2}

6. **K/U** The general formula C_nH_{2n-2} represents which type of hydrocarbon?
   a. alkane
   b. alkene
   c. alkyne
   d. benzene
   e. cyclic alkane

7. **K/U** Which is the *root* name for the following molecule?

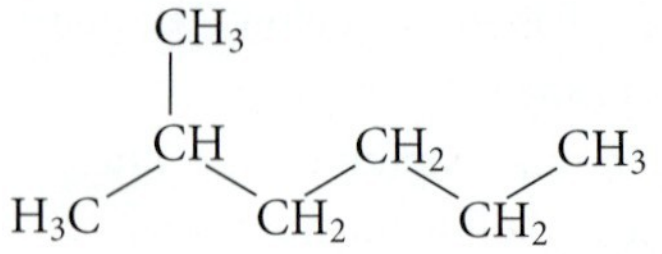

   a. hex-
   b. hept-
   c. pent-
   d. prop-
   e. sept-

8. **K/U** Into which group would the following molecule be classified?

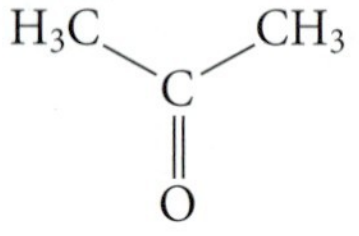

   a. alcohol
   b. aldehyde
   c. ketone
   d. ester
   e. ether

9. **K/U** Which functional group is shown below?

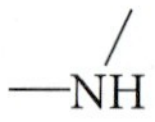

   —NH

   a. haloalkane
   b. primary amide
   c. secondary amine
   d. carboxylic acid
   e. secondary amide

10. **K/U** An amide can be thought to be the product of which two groups?
    a. carboxlic acid and ether
    b. amine and ether
    c. alcohol and amine
    d. ester and amine
    e. carboxylic acid and amine

Use sentences and diagrams as appropriate to answer the following questions.

11. **T/I** Would the two molecules represented below be considered constitutional isomers? Explain your reasoning.

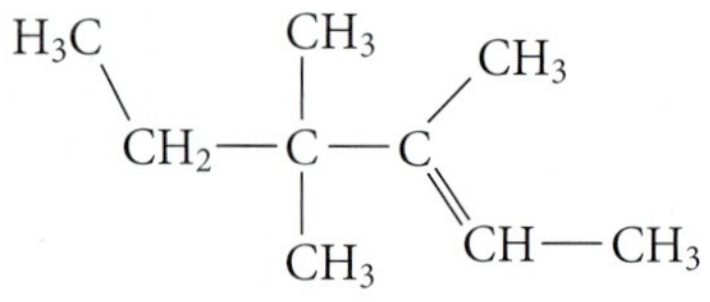

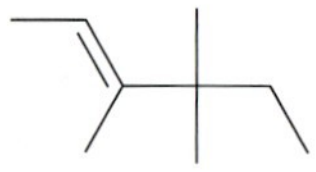

12. **C** Draw and name all the diastereomers that could be made using the formula C_6H_{12}.
13. **T/I** Identify which of the following molecules are named incorrectly. Explain your reasoning. Provide the proper name when necessary.
    a. 2-ethylpropane
    b. 3,4-dimethylpentane
    c. 3-ethyl-2-methyloctane
    d. 2-methyl-3-ethylhept-4-ene
14. **A** Identify an unsubstituted alkane in each state listed below that could be found in the home. What would each example you identified be used for and how long would you expect its carbon chain to be?
    a. solid
    b. liquid
    c. gas
15. **C** Name, draw, and write the molecular formula for a six-carbon chain for each type of hydrocarbon listed below.
    a. branched alkane
    b. cylic alkane
    c. branched alkyne
    d. cyclic alkene
    e. aromatic
16. **T/I** Explain why benzene is drawn differently than cyclic alkanes.
17. **C** Name the following molecules.
    a. 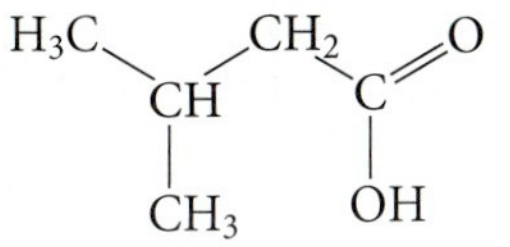 H_3C–CH(–CH_3)–CH_2–C(=O)–OH
    b. 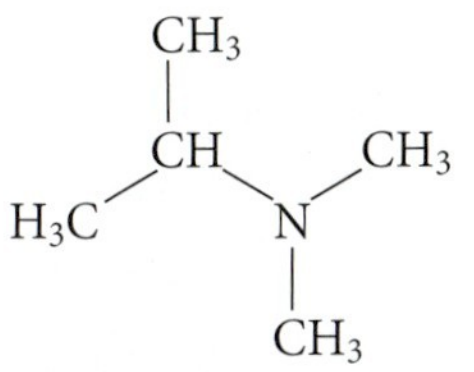 H_3C–CH(–CH_3)–N(–CH_3)–CH_3
18. **C** Draw condensed structural formulas for the following molecules.
    a. 3-ethylpentan-2-one
    b. 2-ethoxy-3-methylhexane
    c. N-propylethanamide
19. **K/U** Compare and contrast esters and amides in terms of their structures, how they are named, and their physical properties.
20. **A** Oxalic acid is found in the leaves of some plants, such as rhubarb. Its structure is shown on the right. 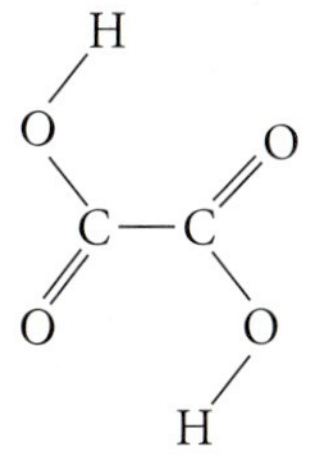
    a. Suggest a possible name using IUPAC terminology.
    b. What state of matter would you expect it to be at room temperature and why?
    c. What solvents would you expect it to dissolve in and why?
21. **T/I** Draw and name all the constitutional isomers that could have the molecular formula C_3H_8O.
22. **A** Is cyclopentane an isomer of pentane? Explain your reasoning.
23. **C** Prepare a 5-min presentation about alkanes, alkenes, and alkynes for a group of Grade 8 students. Assume students have basic knowledge of the periodic table and how atoms bond. Include diagrams as needed in your presentation.
24. **T/I** The common name for 2-propanol is isopropyl alcohol. It is also known as rubbing alcohol. 2-propanol is often added to gasolines in Canada to prevent ice from forming in fuel lines. Otherwise, ice forms as a result of condensed water that is naturally present in the air.
    a. Draw the molecule.
    b. Describe why it can mix with both a polar substance, such as water, and non-polar substances, such as the alkanes in gasoline.
    c. What precautions could one take to prevent water from condensing in gas tanks?
25. **A** Humans use hydrocarbons for many purposes.
    a. What is the source of hydrocarbons we use?
    b. Identify problems associated with using this source.
    c. What alternative sources could be used to achieve similar results?

Self-Check

If you missed question…	1	2	3	4	5	6	7	8	9	10	11	12	13	14	15	16	17	18	19	20	21	22	23	24	25
Review section(s)…	1.1	1.1	1.1	1.2	1.2	1.2	1.2	1.3	1.3	1.3	1.1	1.1	1.2	1.2	1.2	1.2	1.3	1.3	1.3	1.3	1.3	1.3	1.2	1.2	1.2

CHAPTER 2
Reactions of Organic Compounds

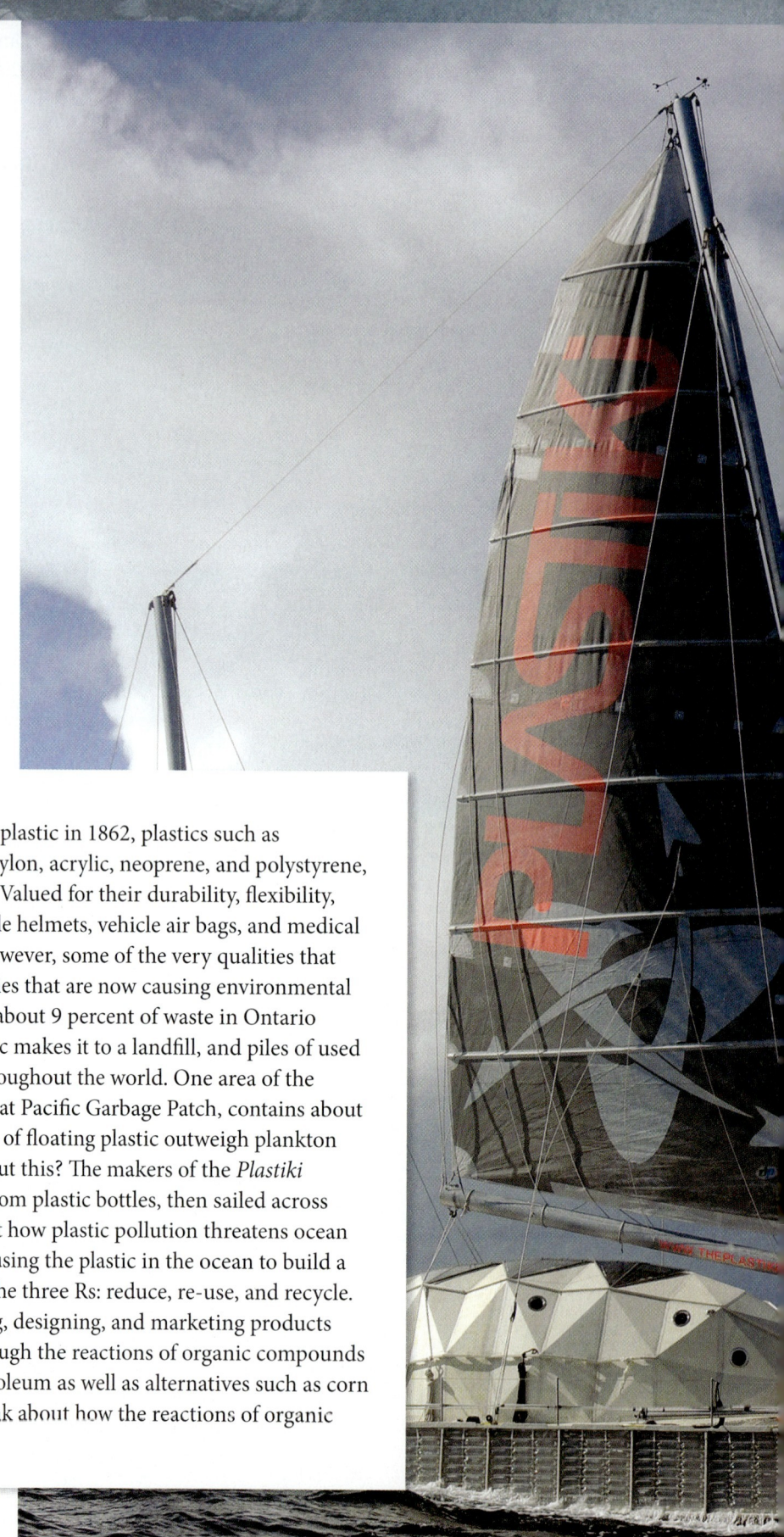

Specific Expectations

In this chapter, you will learn how to . . .

- B1.1 **assess** the impact on human health, society, and the environment of organic compounds used in everyday life

- B1.2 **propose** a personal course of action to reduce the use of compounds that are harmful to human health and the environment

- B2.1 **use** appropriate terminology related to organic chemistry

- B2.4 **analyze**, on the basis of inquiry, various organic chemical reactions

- B3.3 **explain** the chemical changes that occur during various types of organic chemical reactions, including substitution, addition, elimination, oxidation, esterification, and hydrolysis

- B3.4 **explain** the difference between an addition reaction and a condensation polymerization reaction

Since the production of the first type of plastic in 1862, plastics such as polyethylene, polyvinyl chloride (PVC), nylon, acrylic, neoprene, and polystyrene, have become an integral part of our lives. Valued for their durability, flexibility, and inexpensive cost, the plastics in bicycle helmets, vehicle air bags, and medical supplies help keep us safe and healthy. However, some of the very qualities that make plastic so useful are the same qualities that are now causing environmental problems. Discarded plastic accounts for about 9 percent of waste in Ontario landfills. However, not all discarded plastic makes it to a landfill, and piles of used plastic materials collect in many areas throughout the world. One area of the Pacific Ocean, often referred to as the Great Pacific Garbage Patch, contains about 2.8 million tonnes of plastic, where pieces of floating plastic outweigh plankton by a ratio of 6 to 1. What can be done about this? The makers of the *Plastiki* constructed the sailboat almost entirely from plastic bottles, then sailed across the Pacific Ocean to raise awareness about how plastic pollution threatens ocean ecosystems. One company has proposed using the plastic in the ocean to build a habitable, floating island. Then there are the three Rs: reduce, re-use, and recycle. Many companies are also now researching, designing, and marketing products made from alternative materials. It is through the reactions of organic compounds that we are able to make plastic from petroleum as well as alternatives such as corn or sugar cane. As you read Chapter 2, think about how the reactions of organic compounds affect your daily life.

Launch Lab

Plastic Reduction

Do you know how much plastic you use every day? Plastic is found in many things from our cars to our clothes and is so embedded in our daily life that it would be difficult for us to go a day without using plastic. Plastics make our lives easier, but they can also be harmful to us and to the environment. In this activity, you will inventory your plastic use and implement a reduction plan for one week in order to determine whether or not this is a viable solution.

These discarded toothbrushes, the handles and bristles of which are made of plastic, were all found during a beach clean-up in Honolulu, Hawaii.

Materials
- computers with Internet access

Procedure
1. Inventory the plastics that you use or encounter every day. Summarize your data in a table.
2. Design a feasible plan that will reduce your plastic use for a week. This plan should be based on reducing the plastics you encountered in your inventory and use every day. Have your summary table and plan checked by your teacher.
3. Implement your plan for one week. Keep a daily log to reflect on the successes and problems you encounter as you implement your plan.
4. At the end of the week, summarize the successes and problems you encountered with your plan.

Questions
1. Draw a conclusion about the feasibility of your plan based on your summary of successes and failures.
2. Research what environmentally friendly alternatives to plastic are available and currently being used. How does the price of products made from alternative materials compare to those made with conventional plastics?
3. Working with two or three other students, design a plan for reducing the impact of plastic on the environment based on your research and the success of your plastics reduction plan. Use a creative format, such as a skit, video, or song, to share your plan with the class.

SECTION 2.1

Types of Organic Reactions

Key Terms

addition reaction
elimination reaction
substitution reaction
condensation reaction
esterification reaction
hydrolysis reaction
oxidation
reduction
combustion reaction
complete combustion reaction
incomplete combustion reaction

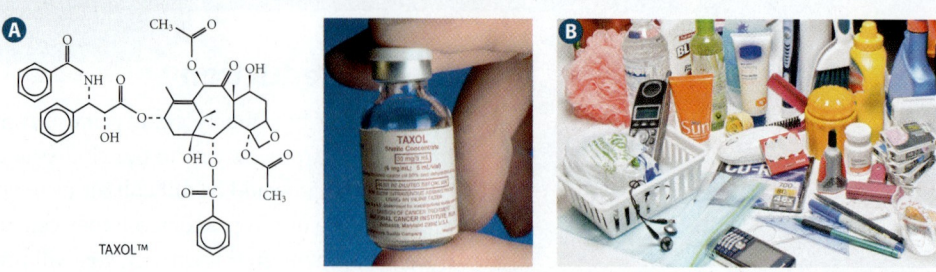

Figure 2.1 (**A**) TAXOL™ is synthesized through organic reactions from an organic compound found in the needles and twigs of the European yew tree. (**B**) Through organic reactions, molecules from petroleum are used to produce plastics, which are used to make many consumer products.

Organic chemists can use one or more of thousands of reactions to change one type of organic compound into a different organic compound. By using combinations of these organic reactions, scientists can convert simple molecules into large, complex molecules found in many important products. For example, TAXOL™, shown in **Figure 2.1A**, is an organic compound found in the bark of the Pacific yew tree. It has been approved for use in treating ovarian cancer. The bark of a large yew tree yields only enough TAXOL™ for a single treatment; however, cancer patients require repeated treatments over a long period. Organic chemists found a solution to this problem. The needles and twigs of a different yew tree, the European yew, contain an organic compound that is similar to TAXOL™. Using just a few organic reactions, scientists can transform this compound into TAXOL™. Through organic reactions, chemical industries also convert simple molecules from petroleum and natural gas into the into large, complex organic molecules found in many useful products; including the plastic bottles, bags, and phone casings shown in **Figure 2.1B**.

During chemical reactions, existing bonds are broken and new bonds are formed. Recall that the bonds in organic substances are covalent. Because covalent bonds are relatively strong, the rearrangement of bonds causes many reactions of organic compounds to be slow and require a continuous input of energy to keep molecules moving rapidly and colliding. In some cases, catalysts are be used to speed up organic reactions that could otherwise take days, months, or even longer to yield useful amounts of product. Often, bonds can break and re-form in several different positions. As a result, nearly all organic reactions result in a mixture of products. The unwanted products must then be separated from the expected product, a process that often takes time and further reactions.

This section introduces the main types of organic reactions: addition, elimination, substitution, condensation, esterification, hydrolysis, oxidation, and combustion. Section 2.2 then explains how these reactions are used to produce consumer products.

Addition, Elimination, and Substitution Reactions

Organic chemists use many different reactions to synthesize specific organic products. Many of these reactions can be classified into three categories: addition, elimination, and substitution reactions. Each type of reaction transforms certain organic compounds into other organic compounds.

Addition Reactions

Alkenes and alkynes characteristically undergo **addition reactions** in which atoms are added to a double or triple bond, as shown in **Figure 2.2**. To recognize an addition reaction, check whether the carbon atoms in the product(s) are bonded to *more* atoms than are the carbon atoms in the organic reactant.

addition reaction
reaction in which atoms are added to a carbon-carbon double or triple bond

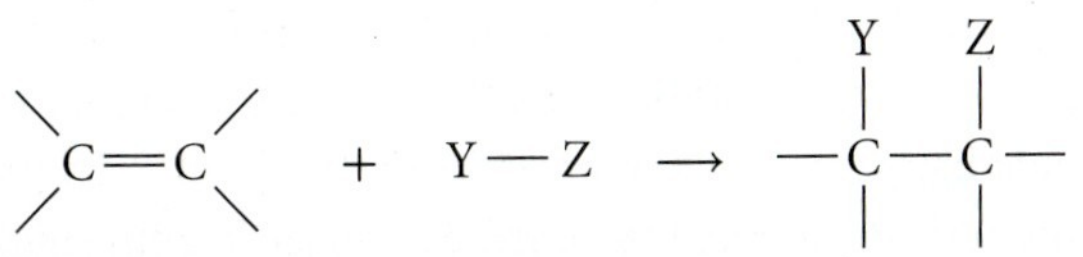

Figure 2.2 This general formula for an addition reaction shows that the carbon atoms in the product are bonded to more atoms than the carbon atoms in the organic reactant.

In a typical addition reaction, a small molecule is added to an alkene or alkyne. The small molecule is usually one of the following: H_2O (ℓ) (when the bonds of water break in a reaction, it is often written, HOH), H_2, HX, or X_2 (where X = F, Br, Cl, or I). The reaction results in one major product or two products that are isomers of each other. (Recall that isomers have the same molecular formula but different structures.) **Figure 2.3** shows some specific examples of addition reactions involving an alkene.

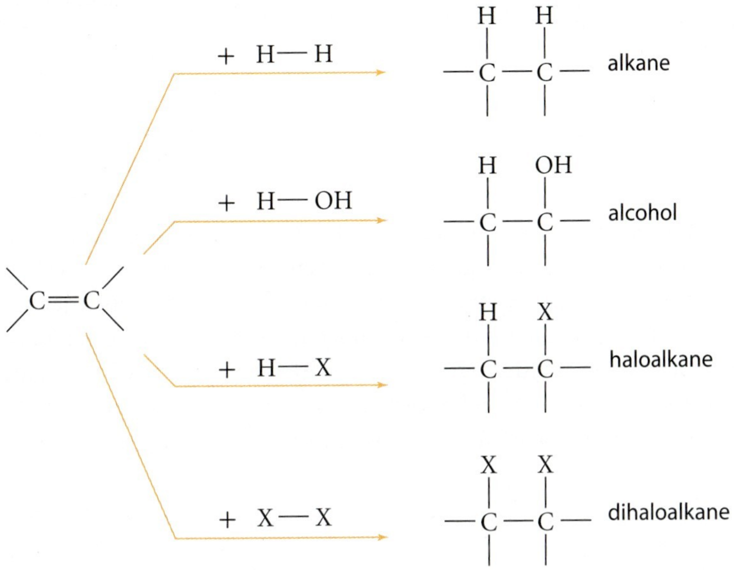

Figure 2.3 In each addition reaction shown here, the electrons from one of the double bonds are re-arranged and form two single bonds, one with each of the two additional atoms.
Compare the bonds of carbon atoms in the reactants to the bonds of carbon atoms in the products of an addition reaction.

The following equation is an example of an addition reaction in which chlorine gas reacts with but-2-ene. In this addition reaction, the double bond between the carbon atoms is replaced by single bonds with the chlorine atoms.

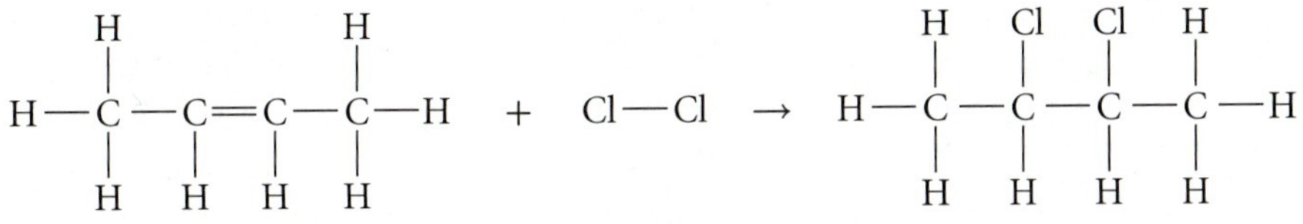

but-2-ene + chlorine → 2,3-dichlorobutane

Chemists use the addition reaction of bromine with an alkene or alkyne as a colour test for the presence of multiple (double or triple) bonds. When bromine is added to a compound with double or triple bonds, the bromine reacts with the multiple bonds and loses its brownish colour, as shown in **Figure 2.4A**. If no multiple bonds are present in the compound, the mixtures will remain a brownish yellow colour, as shown in **Figure 2.4B**.

Figure 2.4 (A) The loss of brownish colour indicates that the compound contains multiple bonds. **(B)** The retention of the brownish colour indicates that the compound is an alkane.

In an alkyne, a maximum of four bonding electrons can be re-arranged to form bonds with three new atoms, leaving a single bond between the two carbon atoms. Equation A, below on the left, shows what happens when excess chlorine is added to ethyne (acetylene). The triple bond between the carbon atoms in the ethyne is replaced with single bonds between the carbon atoms and between the carbons atoms and chlorine atoms.

If the amount of chlorine is limited, an alkene is formed, as shown in Equation B, below on the right. In contrast to the previous reaction, the triple bond between the carbon atoms is replaced with a double bond between the carbon atoms and single bonds between the carbon atoms and chlorine atoms.

Equation A

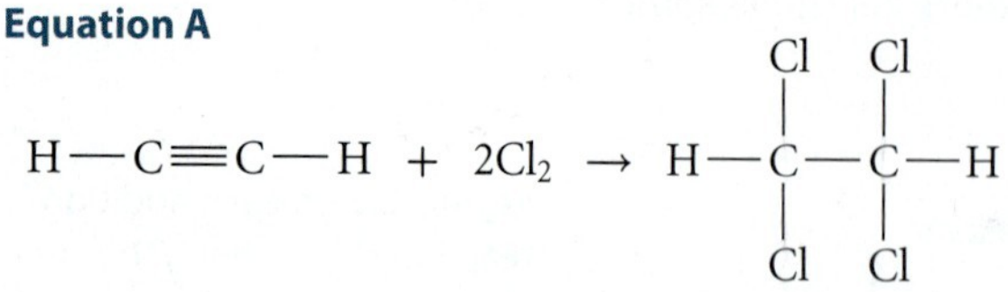

$$H-C\equiv C-H \;+\; 2Cl_2 \;\rightarrow\; \underset{\text{1,1,2,2-tetrachloroethane}}{H-\underset{\underset{Cl}{|}}{\overset{\overset{Cl}{|}}{C}}-\underset{\underset{Cl}{|}}{\overset{\overset{Cl}{|}}{C}}-H}$$

ethyne   chlorine (excess)   1,1,2,2-tetrachloroethane

Equation B

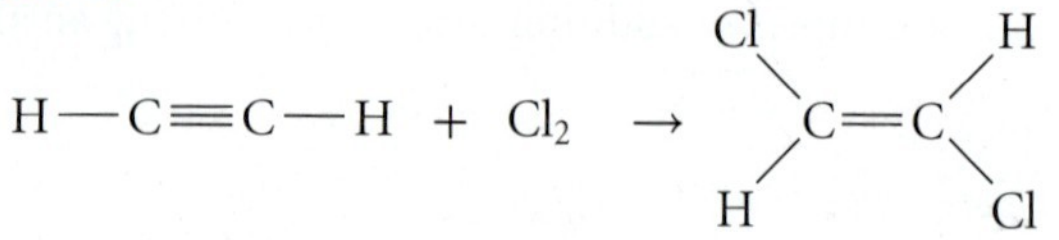

$$H-C\equiv C-H \;+\; Cl_2 \;\rightarrow\; \underset{H}{\overset{Cl}{}}C=C\underset{Cl}{\overset{H}{}}$$

ethyne   chlorine (limited)   1,2-dichloroethene

When alkenes and alkynes that contain more than two carbon atoms react with a small molecule, more than one product might form. For example, if hydrogen chloride, HCl(g), is added to pent-2-ene, two constitutional isomers will form as shown in the equation below. If the two atoms being added to the alkene are different, they each can be placed on either of the two carbons involved in the double bond. For example, when HCl(g) is added to pent-2-ene, the Cl can be added to either carbon 2 (with the H adding to carbon 3) or the Cl can be added to carbon 3 (with the H adding to carbon 2) forming two isomers as shown here.

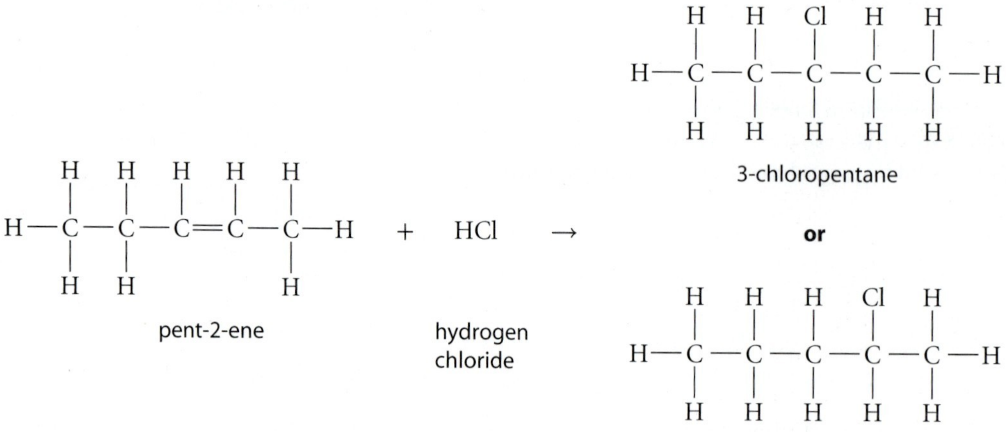

pent-2-ene + hydrogen chloride → 3-chloropentane **or** 2-chloropentane

When a small molecule is added to an asymmetric alkene, such as propene, it is possible to predict which isomer will be more abundant using Markovnikov's rule. According to this rule, the hydrogen atom of the small molecule will attach to the carbon of the double bond that is already bonded to the most hydrogen atoms. In the equation shown below, the major product is 2-chloropropane.

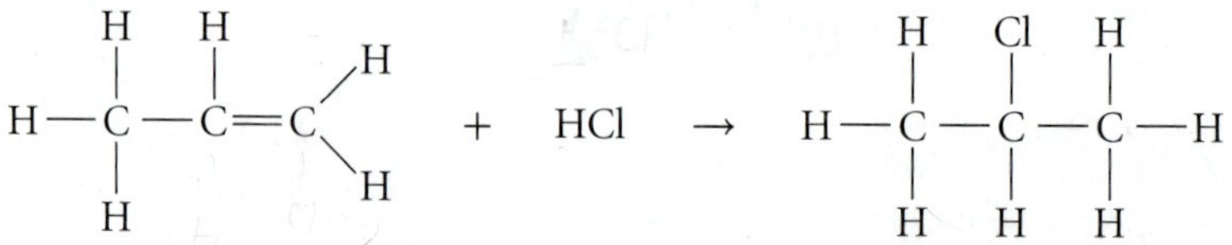

propene + hydrogen chloride → 2-chloropropane

Sample Problem

Addition Reactions

Problem
Complete the equation for the following addition reaction.
$$H_2C=CHCH_2CH_3 + H_2 \xrightarrow{Pt\ or\ Pd}$$

What Is Required?
You must complete a balanced chemical equation representing the reaction.

What Is Given?
You are given the reactants and the conditions of the reaction.

Plan Your Strategy	Act on Your Strategy
Determine the type of reaction that will occur when an alkene is combined with the small, diatomic molecule, H_2, in the presence of a platinum or palladium catalyst.	addition reaction
Write the reaction so a hydrogen atom is added to each of the two carbons forming the double bond. The bond becomes a single bond.	$H_2C=CHCH_2CH_3 + H_2 \xrightarrow{Pt\ or\ Pd} CH_3CH_2CH_2CH_3$
The equation is balanced. Name the reactants and product.	$H_2C=CHCH_2CH_3 + H_2 \xrightarrow{Pt\ or\ Pd} CH_3CH_2CH_2CH_3$ but-1-ene hydrogen butane

Check Your Solution
The type of reaction is an addition reaction. The double bond between the carbon atoms is replaced with a single bond between the carbon atoms and single bonds between the carbon atoms and the additional hydrogen atoms. The equation is balanced. The four carbons in the main chain agree with the root but-.

Practice Problems

1. Complete the equation for the following addition reaction:
$$H_3CCH=CHCH_3 + H_2 \xrightarrow{Pt\ or\ Pd}$$

2. Complete the equation for the following reaction if:
$$H_3CCH_2C\equiv CCH_3 + Br_2 \rightarrow$$
   a. A minimal amount of Br_2 is present
   b. An excess of Br_2 is present

3. For the following reaction, determine the product and explain why only one product is possible.
$$H_2C=CH_2 + HI \rightarrow$$

For the reactions in questions 4–6, determine the product(s) and indicate the more abundant product if more than one is formed.

4. $CH_3CH=CHCH_2CH_3 + Cl_2 \rightarrow$

5. $CH_3CHCH_2CH=CH_2 + H_2O \rightarrow$ H-OH
   |
   CH_3

6. $CH_3CHCH=CHCH_3 + HBr \rightarrow$
   |
   CH_3

7. Determine the products for the following reactions.
   a. 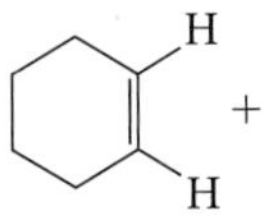 cyclohexene (with H's shown) + HBr →
   b. 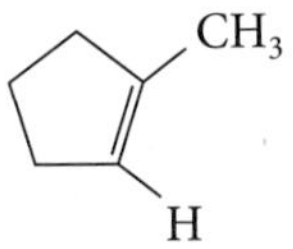 1-methylcyclopentene + HI →

8. Determine the major products for the following addition reactions.
   a. 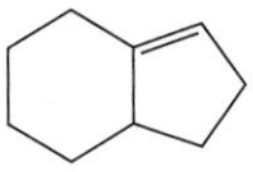 bicyclic alkene + H_2O →
   b. 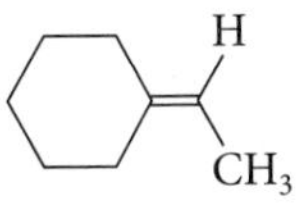 (cyclohexylidene)methane with CH_3 + HCl →

Continued on next page

9. Determine the reactants for the following reactions.
   a. ☐ + H$_2$ $\xrightarrow{\text{Pt or Pd}}$ H$_3$CCH$_2$CH$_2$CH$_3$

   b. ☐ + HCl → H$_3$CCHCH$_2$CH$_3$
                              |
                              Cl

10. Determine the product for the following reaction.
    (Hint: Draw the structure of sulfuric acid.)
    H$_3$CCH=CHCH$_3$ + H$_2$SO$_4$ →

11. For the following reaction, draw the reactants and product that would form.
    1-methylcyclohexene + hydrobromic acid →

Elimination Reactions

elimination reaction
reaction in which atoms are removed from an organic molecule to form a double bond

In an **elimination reaction**, atoms are removed from an organic molecule and a double bond forms between the two carbon atoms from which the atoms were removed, as shown in **Figure 2.5**. This type of reaction can be envisioned as the reverse of an addition reaction. One reactant usually loses two atoms, and two products are formed. A double bond is formed in the organic product. To recognize an elimination reaction, determine whether the carbon atoms in the organic product are bonded to *fewer* atoms than were the carbon atoms in the organic reactant.

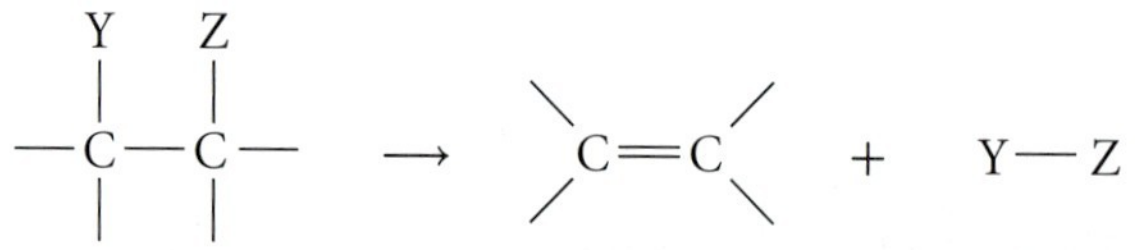

Figure 2.5 This general formula for an elimination reaction shows that the carbon atoms in the product are bonded to fewer atoms than the carbon atoms in the organic reactant.

The equation below illustrates an example of how alcohols can undergo elimination reactions to form alkenes when they are heated in the presence of a strong acid, such as sulfuric acid (H$_2$SO$_4$(aq)). The strong acid acts as a catalyst to speed up the reaction. A small, stable molecule, such as H$_2$O(ℓ), is formed as a second product.

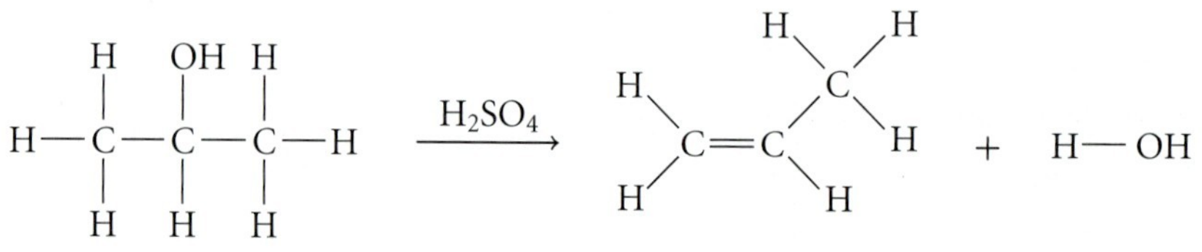

propan-2-ol → propene + water (H$_2$SO$_4$)

Haloalkanes can undergo elimination reactions to produce alkenes when they are heated in the presence of a strong base, such as sodium ethoxide (NaOCH$_2$CH$_3$) as shown in the equation below.

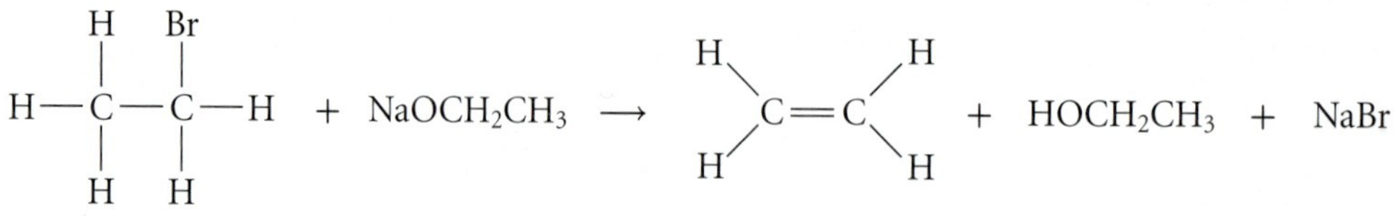

bromoethane + sodium ethoxide (strong base) → ethene + ethanol + sodium bromide

When an asymmetric molecule undergoes an elimination reaction, more than one constitutional isomer can be present among the products. For example, in the case of 2-bromobutane, a hydrogen atom can be removed from either the first carbon in the chain or the third carbon in the chain to form the double bond. As a general rule, the hydrogen atom is most likely to be removed from the carbon atom with the most carbon–carbon bonds. In this example, therefore, a hydrogen atom will be removed from the third carbon to form but-2-ene as the major product or from the first carbon to form but-1-ene as the minor product, as shown in the equations below. Note that the major product but-2-ene has a *cis* and a *trans* isomer. Only the *trans* isomer is shown here for simplicity.

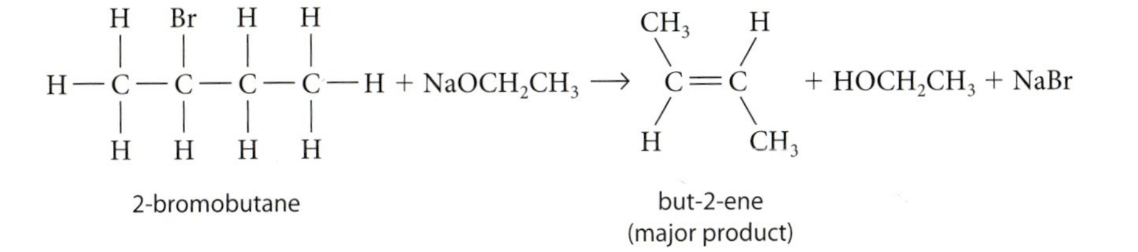

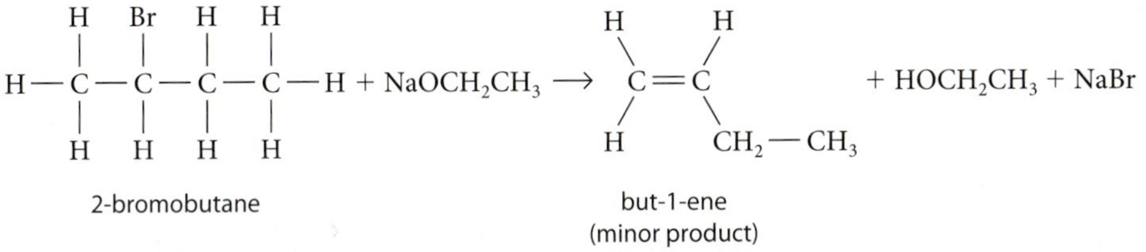

$$\text{2-bromobutane} + \text{NaOCH}_2\text{CH}_3 \rightarrow \text{but-2-ene (major product)} + \text{HOCH}_2\text{CH}_3 + \text{NaBr}$$

$$\text{2-bromobutane} + \text{NaOCH}_2\text{CH}_3 \rightarrow \text{but-1-ene (minor product)} + \text{HOCH}_2\text{CH}_3 + \text{NaBr}$$

Sample Problem

Elimination Reactions

Problem
Complete the equation for the elimination reaction.

$$\text{HO}-\text{CH}_2\text{CH}_2\text{CH}_3 \xrightarrow[\Delta]{\text{H}_2\text{SO}_4}$$

What Is Required?
You must complete a balanced chemical equation representing the reaction.

What Is Given?
You are given the reactants and the conditions of the reaction.

Plan Your Strategy	Act on Your Strategy
Determine the type of reaction that will occur when an alcohol is heated in the presence of a strong acid.	elimination reaction
Write the reaction so that the product has the same number of carbon atoms as the organic reactant, but with a double bond between the carbon atom that was bonded to the hydroxyl group and an adjacent carbon atom.	$\text{HO}-\text{CH}_2\text{CH}_2\text{CH}_3 \xrightarrow[\Delta]{\text{H}_2\text{SO}_4} \text{CH}_2=\text{CHCH}_3$
The reactant has one more oxygen atom and two more hydrogen atoms. Add a water molecule to the products. Name the reactants and products.	$\text{HO}-\text{CH}_2\text{CH}_2\text{CH}_3 \xrightarrow[\Delta]{\text{H}_2\text{SO}_4} \text{CH}_2=\text{CHCH}_3 + \text{HOH}$ propan-1-ol propene water

Check Your Solution
The type of reaction is an elimination reaction. A double bond forms between the first two carbon atoms. The hydroxl group is removed, along with one hydrogen atom, in order for the double bond to occur. The hydroxide ion and hydrogen ion combine to form water. The equation is balanced. The three carbons in the main chain agree with the root pro-.

Practice Problems

Determine the products for the elimination reactions in the next two questions.

12. H$_3$CCHCH$_2$OH $\xrightarrow[\Delta]{H_2SO_4}$
    |
    CH$_3$

13.
$$H-\underset{H}{\overset{H}{C}}-\underset{H}{\overset{Cl}{C}}-\underset{H}{\overset{H}{C}}-H + NaOCH_2CH_3 \xrightarrow{\Delta}$$

14. Determine the number of possible products for the following reaction. Explain your reasoning.

$$H-\underset{H}{\overset{H}{C}}-\underset{H}{\overset{H}{C}}-\underset{H}{\overset{Br}{C}}-\underset{CH_3}{\overset{H}{C}}-\underset{H}{\overset{H}{C}}-H \xrightarrow[\Delta]{NaOCH_2CH_3}$$

Determine the products for the elimination reactions in the next two questions.

15. H$_3$CCH$_2$CHCHCH$_3$ $\xrightarrow[\Delta]{H_2SO_4}$
     | |
     HO CH$_3$

16. H$_3$CCHCHCH$_3$ $\xrightarrow[\Delta]{NaOCH_2CH_3}$
     | |
     H$_3$C I

For the next two questions, determine the major product of the reactions.

17. [methylcyclohexane with Br] $\xrightarrow[\Delta]{NaOCH_2CH_3}$

18. [cyclopentane with ethyl and OH] $\xrightarrow[\Delta]{H_2SO_4}$

For the next two questions, determine the possible reactants of the reactions.

19. ? + H$_2$SO$_4$ $\xrightarrow{\Delta}$ $\underset{H}{\overset{H}{}}C=C\underset{CH_2CH_3}{\overset{H}{}}$

20. ? + NaOCH$_2$CH$_3$ $\xrightarrow{\Delta}$ $\underset{H}{\overset{H_3C}{}}C=C\underset{CH_3}{\overset{CH_2CH_2CH_3}{}}$

21. Determine the major product that would form from the following reaction.

    cyclobutanol + sulfuric acid →

22. Predict the final products of the following reaction. (Hint: Eliminate both Cl atoms.)

$$H-\underset{H}{\overset{H}{C}}-\underset{Cl}{\overset{Cl}{C}}-\underset{H}{\overset{H}{C}}-\underset{H}{\overset{H}{C}}-H \xrightarrow{NaOCH_2CH_3}$$

Learning Check

1. Compare and contrast addition and elimination reactions.
2. What is the purpose of adding sulfuric acid or sodium ethoxide in elimination reactions?
3. Consider elimination reactions.
   a. When is more than one product possible with elimination reactions?
   b. How do you determine which constitutional isomer is the major product?
4. What is Markovnikov's rule and when is it used?
5. When alkynes undergo addition reactions with an X-X, will the final product always be a substituted alkane? Explain your answer.
6. Explain why alkenes and alkynes undergo addition reactions but alkanes do not.

substitution reaction
reaction in which a hydrogen atom or functional group is replaced by a different atom or functional group

Substitution Reactions

In a **substitution reaction**, a hydrogen atom or a functional group is replaced by a different functional group, as shown in **Figure 2.6**. To recognize this type of reaction, look for the following two features:
- *two* compounds react to form two different compounds
- *carbon* atoms are bonded to the *same* number of atoms in the product as in the reactant

$$-\overset{|}{\underset{|}{C}}-Y \ + \ A-Z \ \rightarrow \ -\overset{|}{\underset{|}{C}}-Z \ + \ A-Y$$

Figure 2.6 This general formula for a substitution reaction shows that the carbon atoms in the product are bonded to the same number of atoms as the carbon atoms in the organic reactant and two new compounds have been formed.

Alcohols and haloalkanes commonly undergo substitution reactions. When an alcohol reacts with an acid that contains a halogen, such as hydrogen chloride or hydrogen bromide, the halogen atom is substituted for the hydroxyl group of the alcohol, as shown in the equation below. A haloalkane is produced.

$$CH_3-CH_2-OH \ + \ HCl \ \rightarrow \ CH_3-CH_2-Cl \ + \ H-OH$$

ethanol   hydrogen chloride   chloroethane   water

A haloalkane can undergo a substitution reaction with a hydroxide ion to produce an alcohol, as shown below.

$$CH_3-CH_2-Cl \ + \ OH^- \ \rightarrow \ CH_3-CH_2-OH \ + \ Cl^-$$

chloroethane   hydroxide ion   ethanol   chloride ion

Recall that haloalkanes can also undergo elimination reactions in the presence of a base. These reactions are not easily controlled, but for the purposes of this course, assume that the reaction of a haloalkane with a hydroxide ion will result in a substitution. Likewise, assume that when a haloalkane reacts with a base such as sodium ethoxide, the result will be an elimination reaction.

Alkanes also undergo substitution reactions. However, because they are relatively unreactive, considerable energy is required. The equation below illustrates how, in the presence of ultraviolet light (UV), alkanes react with chlorine or bromine to produce haloalkanes. If enough chlorine is present in a mixture of chlorine and methane, four possible organic products can form.

$$4CH_4 \ + \ 10Cl_2 \ \xrightarrow{UV} \ CH_3Cl \ + \ CH_2Cl_2 \ + \ CHCl_3 \ + \ CCl_4 \ + \ 10HCl$$

methane   chlorine   chloromethane   dichloromethane   trichloromethane   tetrachloromethane   hydrogen chloride
                             (methyl chloride)   (methylene chloride)   (chloroform)   (carbon tetrachloride)

Substitution reactions of alkanes are not very useful in the laboratory because they usually result in a mixture of products. Chemists generally use other reactions to obtain specific haloalkanes.

Like alkanes, most aromatic hydrocarbons are fairly stable. They will undergo substitution reactions with chlorine and bromine but only in the presence of a catalyst. In the equation representing the reaction between benzene and bromine shown below, iron(III) bromide is acting as the catalyst:

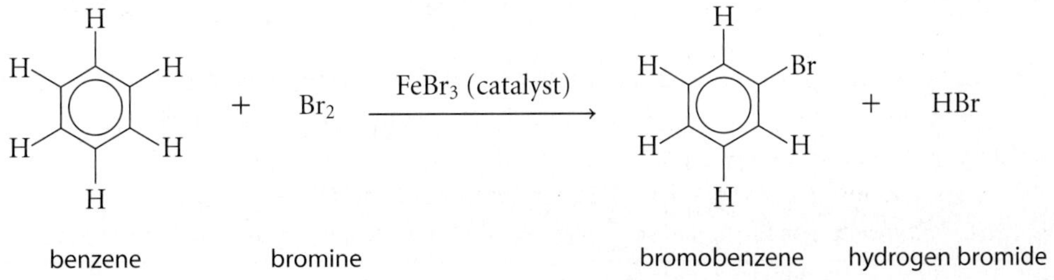

$$C_6H_6 \ + \ Br_2 \ \xrightarrow{FeBr_3 \ (catalyst)} \ C_6H_5Br \ + \ HBr$$

benzene   bromine   bromobenzene   hydrogen bromide

Sample Problem

Substitution Reactions

Problem
Complete the equation for the substitution reaction.
$$CH_3CH(CH_3)CH_2CH_3 + Br_2 \xrightarrow{UV\ light}$$

What Is Required?
You must complete a balanced chemical equation representing the reaction.

What Is Given?
You are given the reactants and the conditions of the reaction.

Plan Your Strategy	Act on Your Strategy
Determine the type of reaction that might occur when a halogen molecule is mixed with an alkane in the presence of ultraviolet light.	substitution
Addition of a halogen to an alkane is almost a random process. Depending on the concentration of the halogen, a few or all of the hydrogen atoms on the alkane could be substituted with a halogen. Just show one example.	$CH_3CH(CH_3)CH_2CH_3 + Br_2 \xrightarrow{UV\ light} CH_3CBr(CH_3)CH_2CH_3 + HBr$
The equation is balanced. Just name the reactants and products.	$CH_3CH(CH_3)CH_2CH_3 + Br_2 \xrightarrow{UV\ light} CH_3CBr(CH_3)CH_2CH_3 + HBr$ 2-methylbutane bromine 2-bromo-2-methylbutane hydrogen bromide

Check Your Solution
The alkane reacted with bromine in the presence of UV light. One of the hydrogen atoms bonded to a carbon atom was substituted with a bromine atom. A haloalkane was produced.

Practice Problems

23. Determine one possible product for the following substitution reaction.

$$H_3CCH_2CCH_3\ \substack{CH_3 \\ | \\ | \\ CH_3} + Cl_2 \xrightarrow{UV\ light}$$

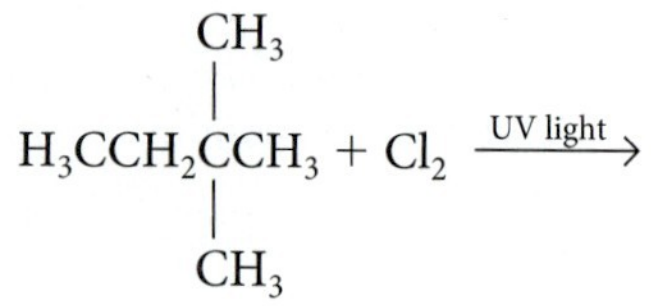

24. Determine how many possible products (not including HBr) may be formed in the following reaction.

$$H-\underset{\underset{H}{|}}{\overset{\overset{H}{|}}{C}}-\underset{\underset{H}{|}}{\overset{\overset{H}{|}}{C}}-H + Br_2 \xrightarrow{UV\ light}$$

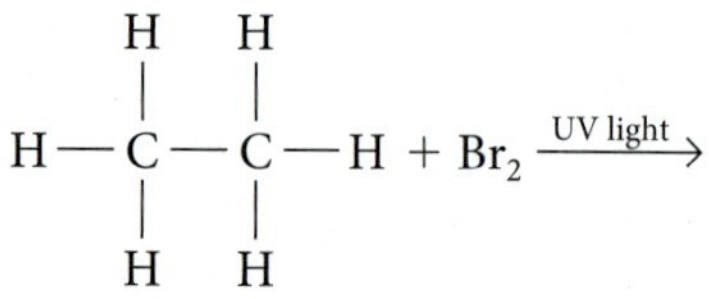

Complete the following substitution reactions.

25. 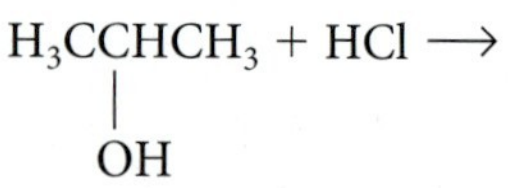 $H_3CCHCH_3 + HCl \rightarrow$
         |
        OH

26. phenol + HBr $\rightarrow$

27. benzene + $Br_2 \xrightarrow{FeBr_3}$

28. 2-chloropropane + $OH^- \rightarrow$

29. For the following reaction, determine the products and explain how you decided between a substitution reaction and an elimination reaction.

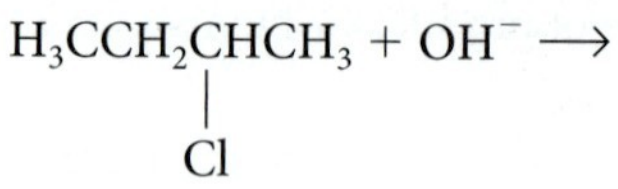

$$H_3CCH_2CHCH_3 + OH^- \rightarrow$$
          |
         Cl

Determine the missing reactants for the following equations.

30. 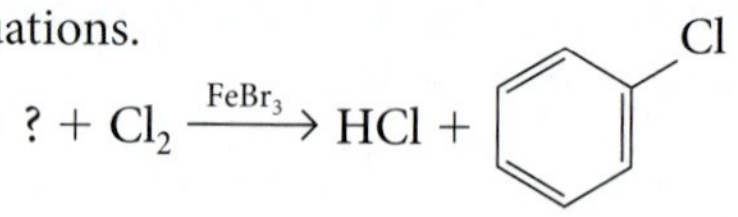 $? + Cl_2 \xrightarrow{FeBr_3} HCl +$ (chlorobenzene)

31. $? + ? \xrightarrow{UV\ light} CH_3CH_2CH_2{-}Br + HBr$

32. 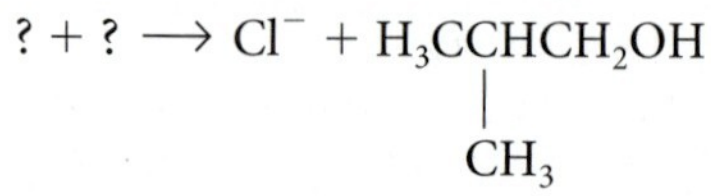 $? + ? \rightarrow Cl^- + H_3CCHCH_2OH$
                          |
                         CH_3

Condensation Reactions

A **condensation reaction** is a reaction in which two large molecules combine and form one larger molecule and a very small molecule, usually water. The reaction in **Figure 1.41**, which showed the formation of an amide, shown again here in **Figure 2.7**, is an example of a condensation reaction. The carboxylic acid and the amine are the large molecules that combine. The resulting amide is the larger molecule and water is the small molecule.

condensation reaction reaction in which two molecules combine to form a larger molecule, producing a small, stable molecule, usually water, as a second product or functional group

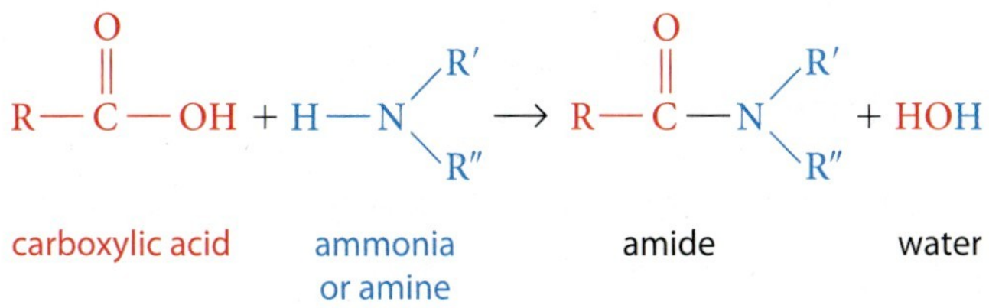

$$R-\underset{\underset{O}{\|}}{C}-OH + H-N\underset{R''}{\overset{R'}{\diagup}} \rightarrow R-\underset{\underset{O}{\|}}{C}-N\underset{R''}{\overset{R'}{\diagup}} + HOH$$

carboxylic acid   ammonia or amine   amide   water

Figure 2.7 In this example of a condensation reaction, the carboxylic acid and the amine combine to form a larger molecule, the amide, and a smaller molecule, water.

Condensation reactions are very important in all living systems. They are the type of reaction that forms most of the large biomolecules, such as proteins, carbohydrates, fats, and DNA. Recall that amino acids are the building blocks of proteins. Every amino acid has an amine group on one end, a carboxyl group on the other end, and what is called an R group, or variable side chain, in the middle, as shown in **Figure 2.8**. There are 20 different amino acids that make up all proteins and it is their R groups that distinguish them. It is the sequence of the amino acids that gives the protein its overall structure and function. Although the actual process is complex, the reaction in **Figure 2.9** summarizes the way that amino acids are combined to form proteins.

In **Figure 2.9**, the symbols R_1, R_2, and R_3 represent R groups of three different amino acids. The carboxyl group on one amino acid reacts with the amino group on another amino acid. The process continues and makes very long chains of amino acids to make a protein. The red boxes around atoms in the reactants show which atoms are removed and form the water molecules. The blue boxes around atoms in the products show the newly formed amide groups that link the amino acids together. In polymers, these groups are called *amide linkages*. When the polymer is a protein, the amide linkages are called *peptide bonds*. Section 2.2 will discuss polymers in greater detail.

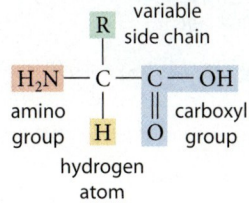

Figure 2.8 Amino acids consist of an amine group, a carboxyl group, and a variable side chain.

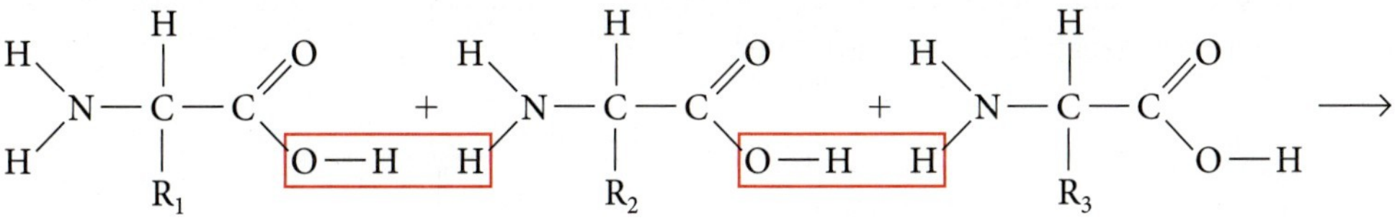

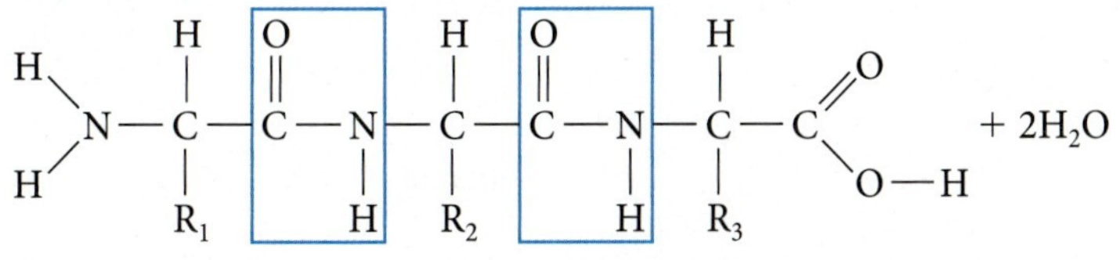

Figure 2.9 The amino group of one amino acid bonds to the carboxyl group of another amino acid to form a peptide bond.

esterification reaction
reaction of a carboxylic acid with an alcohol to form an ester and water; a specific type of condensation reaction

Esterification Reactions

An **esterification reaction** is a special type of condensation reaction in which a carboxylic acid reacts with an alcohol to form an ester and water. This reaction is shown in **Figure 2.10**. The chemical formula for sulfuric acid over the arrow indicates that the reaction is catalyzed by a strong acid.

Figure 2.10 In an esterification reaction, a carboxylic acid combines with an alcohol to form an ester and water.

Esterification reactions can be used to produce useful consumer products, such as acetylsalicyclic acid, commonly sold as Aspirin™. Many of the flavours and aromas of fruits and spices are due to the presence of esters. Through esterification reactions, chemists are able to duplicate natural esters. Synthesized esters are used to give artificial flavour to juices, candy, and many foods. **Figure 2.11** shows the compound responsible for the flavour of cherries.

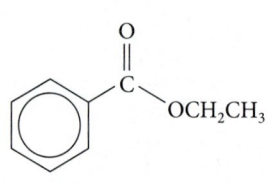

Figure 2.11 The organic compound responsible for the flavour of cherries is an ester named ethyl benzoate.

The equation below shows the esterification reaction that is used to form the cherry-flavour compound. Benzoic acid (a carboxyl acid) combines with ethanol (an alcohol) to form ethyl benzoate (an ester) and water.

Another esterification reaction, in which pentyl propanoate, a fruity-smelling compound found in apricots, is formed, is illustrated below.

$$CH_3CH_2-\underset{\underset{O}{\|}}{C}-OH + HO-(CH_2)_4CH_3 \rightarrow CH_3CH_2-\underset{\underset{O}{\|}}{C}-O(CH_2)_4CH_3 + HOH$$

propanoic acid   pentan-1-ol   pentyl propanoate   water

Learning Check

7. Explain how to identify substitution, condensation, and esterification reactions based on the reactants.
8. Use a Venn diagram to compare and contrast condensation and esterification reactions.
9. Why are condensation reactions so important to living systems?
10. List three examples of consumer products that esterification reactions are used to produce.
11. The reactants of a lab were all placed in a waste beaker. The reactants were methanol, ethanol, propan-1-ol, methanoic acid, ethanoic acid, and propanoic acid. Someone added sulfuric acid and heated the mixture. How many esters were formed? Explain your answer.
12. Indicate which type of reaction would be used to form the following products. Explain your reasoning.
    a. ethyl methanoate (rum flavouring)
    b. ethyl amide
    c. chlorocyclohexane

Hydrolysis Reactions

A **hydrolysis reaction** is essentially the reverse of a condensation reaction. The term *hydrolysis* means to "break apart using water." The compounds that are formed by condensation reactions can be broken down by hydrolysis reactions. The hydroxyl group in a water molecule is added to one side of a bond such as an ester bond or an amide bond and the hydrogen atom of the water molecule is added to the other side of the bond and the bond is broken. The diagram in **Figure 2.12** represents a simplified version of the process of hydrolysis.

hydrolysis reaction reaction in which a molecule is broken apart by adding the hydroxyl group from a water molecule to one side of a bond and the hydrogen atom of a water molecule to the other side of the bond

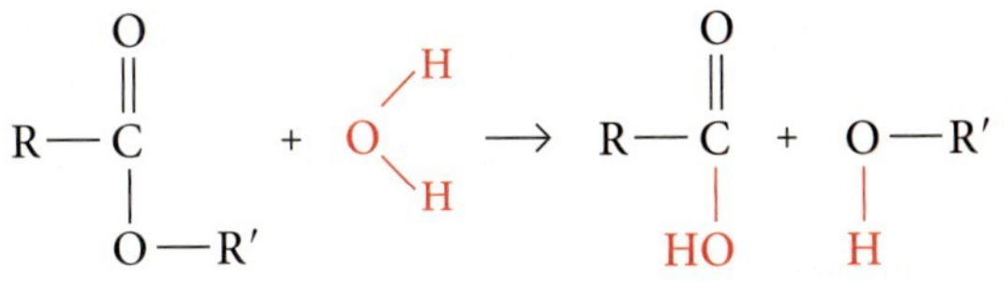

Figure 2.12 In this general example of a hydrolysis reaction, an ester is broken into a carboxylic acid and an alcohol.

This reaction appears to be the opposite of the reaction shown in **Figure 2.10** for forming an ester. Both the condensation reaction and the hydrolysis reaction are catalyzed by an acid. So, the reactions are reversible, as shown in the equation below. A double arrow can be drawn to represent a reversible reaction.

carboxylic acid   alcohol   ester   water

If a reaction is reversible, how can one influence the direction in which the reaction proceeds? Some reactant and some product will always be present after the reaction is carried out. However, the reaction will go further in one direction or the other by adjusting certain factors. For example, if the concentration of the reactants increases, the reaction will shift to the right and yields more products. Also, if a base is used to catalyze the hydrolysis of an ester, the conditions favour hydrolysis. In biological systems, condensation and hydrolysis reactions are performed in several steps and each set of steps is catalyzed by different enzymes, thus carefully controlling the directions of the reactions.

Sample Problem

Esterification Reactions

Problem

Complete the equation for the esterification reaction.

$$CH_3CH_2CH_2COOH + CH_3CH_2OH \xrightarrow{H_2SO_4}$$

What Is Required?

You must complete a balanced chemical equation representing the reaction.

What Is Given?

You are given the reactants and the conditions of the reaction.

Plan Your Strategy	Act on Your Strategy
Determine the type of reaction that occurs when a carboxylic acid and an alcohol are mixed in the presence of a strong acid.	esterification (a special type of condensation reaction)
During esterification, a hydroxyl group is removed from the carboxyl group of the acid and a hydrogen atom is removed from the hydroxyl group of the alcohol. These combine to form water. An ester bond forms between the remaining parts of the acid and alcohol. Write the reaction and identify the reactants and products.	$CH_3CH_2CH_2COOH + CH_3CH_2OH \xrightarrow{H_2SO_4}$ butanoic acid ethanol $CH_3CH_2CH_2COOCH_2CH_3 + HOH$ ethyl butanoate water

Check Your Solution

An esterification reaction occurred. A carboxylic acid combined with an alcohol to produce an ester and water. The number of carbons in the main chain reflects the root but-.

Practice Problems

For the next five questions, identify each reaction as an esterification reaction or a condensation reaction and determine the products.

33.

$$H_3CCH_2CH_2-\overset{\overset{O}{\|}}{C}-OH + NH_3 \longrightarrow$$

34.

$$H_3CCH_2CH_2-\overset{\overset{O}{\|}}{C}-OH + HO-CH_3 \xrightarrow{H_2SO_4}$$

35.

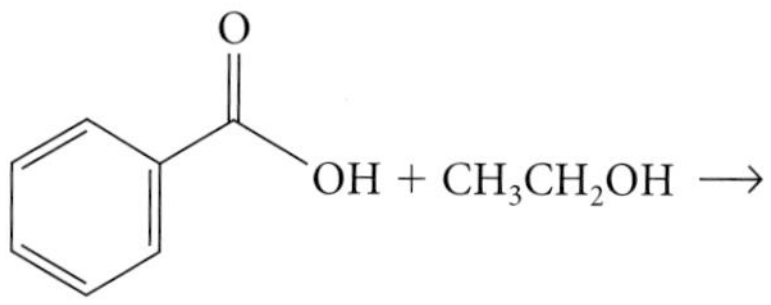

$$C_6H_5-\overset{\overset{O}{\|}}{C}-OH + CH_3CH_2OH \longrightarrow$$

36.

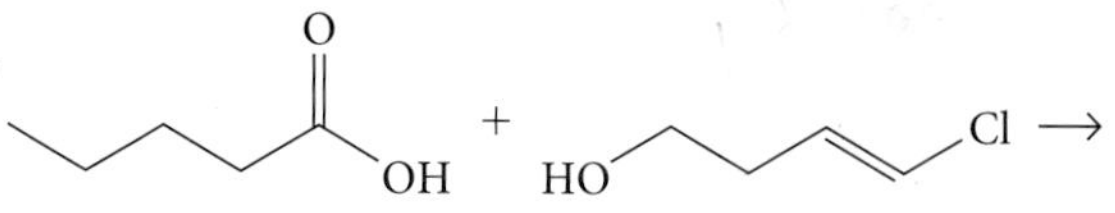

$$\text{pentanoic acid} -OH + HO-CH_2CH=CHCH_2Cl \longrightarrow$$

37.

$$\text{pentanoic acid} -OH + H_2N-CH_2CH_2CH_3 \longrightarrow$$

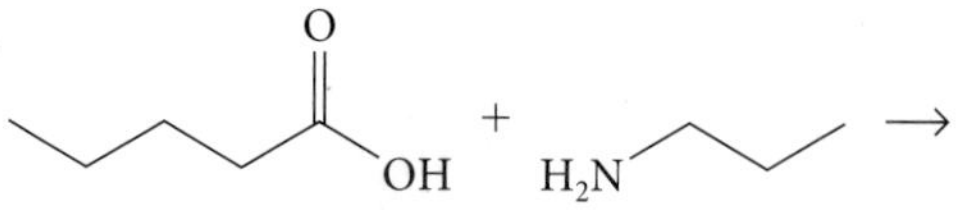

For the next five questions, name and draw the condensed structural formula of the reactants needed to produce each ester.

38.

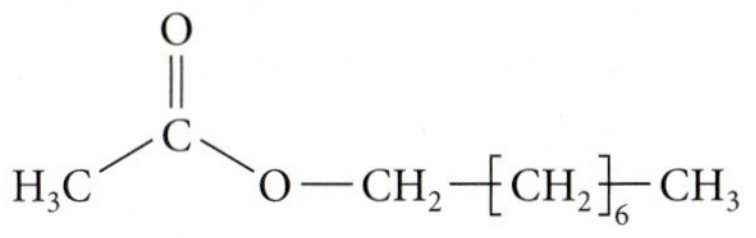

H₃C—C(=O)—O—CH₂—[CH₂]₆—CH₃

octyl ethanoate (orange flavour)

39.

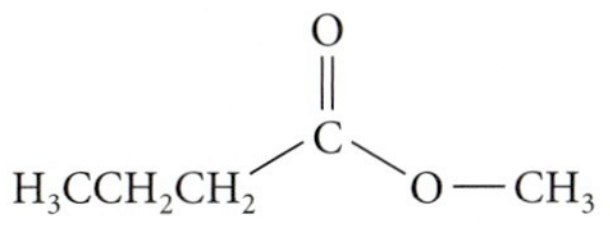

H₃CCH₂CH₂—C(=O)—O—CH₃

methyl butanoate (apple flavour)

40.

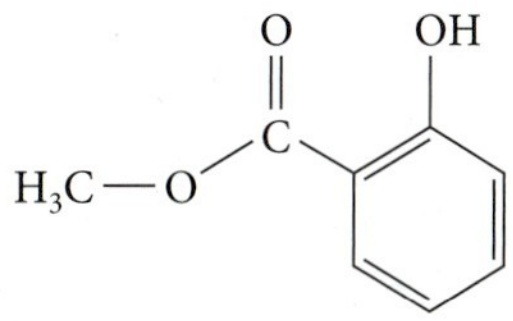

H₃C—O—C(=O)—(benzene ring with OH)

methyl salicylate (oil of wintergreen)

41. 2-hydroxypropyl 3,3-dimethylheptanoate

42. propyl butanoate

Oxidation and Reduction Reactions

An important type of organic reaction occurs when there is a change in the number of hydrogen or oxygen atoms that are bonded to carbon. In Unit 5, you will take a close look at oxidation-reduction reactions in terms of the transfer of electrons. As you will learn, oxidation and reduction always occur together. One reactant is oxidized while the other reactant is reduced. In this unit, however, you will focus on the organic reactant only. Therefore, you will deal with oxidation and reduction separately, as they apply to organic compounds. In organic chemistry, oxidation and reduction are defined by the changes of the bonds to carbon atoms in the organic reactant.

Oxidation

In organic chemistry, **oxidation** is defined as a reaction in which a carbon atom forms more bonds to oxygen, O, or fewer bonds to hydrogen, H. An oxidation that involves the formation of double C—O bonds may also be classified as an elimination reaction. For example, alcohols can be oxidized to produce aldehydes and ketones. Oxidation occurs when an organic compound reacts with an oxidizing agent. Common oxidizing agents include acidified potassium permanganate, $KMnO_4$, acidified potassium dichromate, $K_2Cr_2O_7$, and ozone, O_3. The symbol [O] is used to symbolize an oxidizing agent, as shown below. Note that equations for the oxidation of organic compounds are often left unbalanced. The purpose of the equation is to show the changes in the organic reactant only.

oxidation a reaction in which a carbon atom forms more bonds to oxygen atoms or fewer bonds to hydrogen atoms

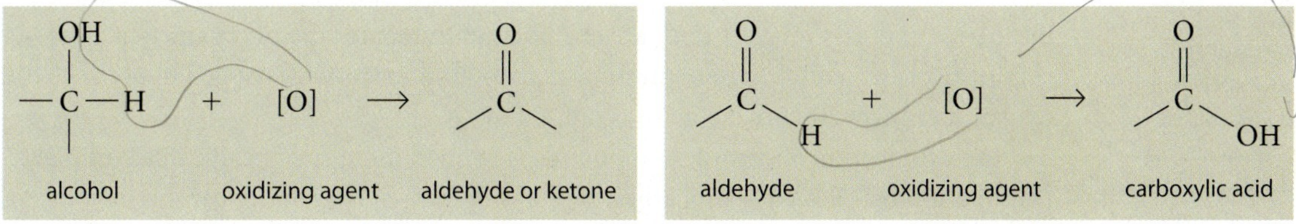

alcohol + [O] → aldehyde or ketone

aldehyde + [O] → carboxylic acid

To identify an oxidation, count and compare the number of C—H and C—O bonds in both the reactant and product. Try it for the following example.

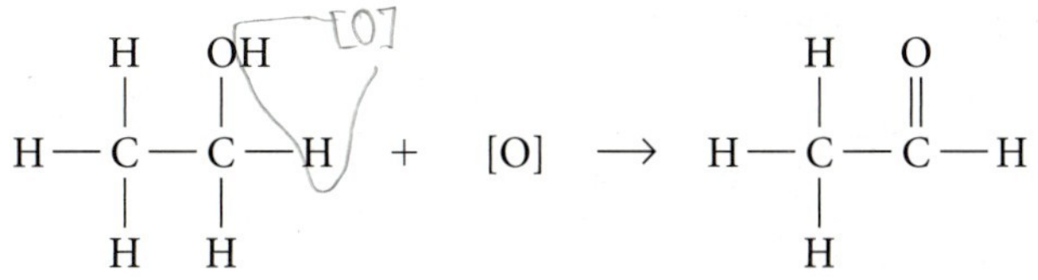

ethanol + [O] → ethanal

Chapter 2 Reactions of Organic Compounds • MHR **109**

Reduction

reduction a reaction in which a carbon atom forms fewer bonds to oxygen atoms or more bonds to hydrogen atoms

In organic chemistry, **reduction** is defined as a reaction in which a carbon atom forms fewer bonds to oxygen, O, or more bonds to hydrogen, H. Often, a C=O bond or C=C double bond is reduced to a single bond by reduction. A reduction that transforms double C=C or C=O bonds to single bonds may also be classified as an addition reaction. Aldehydes, ketones, and carboxylic acids can be reduced to become alcohols. Alkenes and alkynes can be reduced by the addition of H_2 to become alkanes.

Reduction occurs when an organic compound reacts with a reducing agent. Common reducing agents are lithium aluminum hydride, $LiAlH_4$, and hydrogen gas over a platinum catalyst, H_2/Pt. The symbol [H] is used to symbolize a reducing agent. As is the case for oxidation, equations showing the reduction of organic compounds are often left unbalanced.

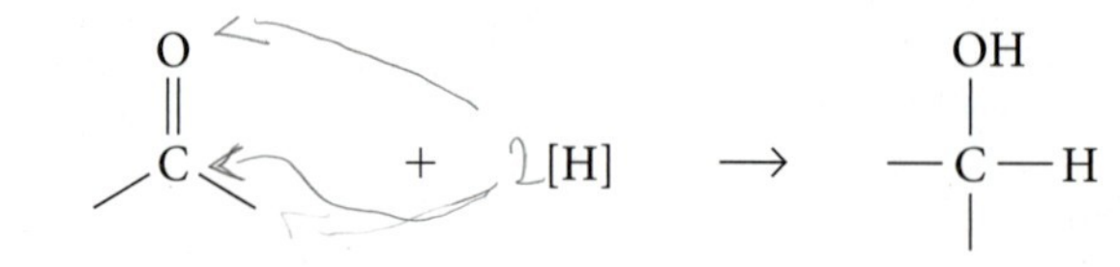

$$\underset{\text{aldehyde or ketone}}{\overset{O}{\underset{\|}{C}}} + \underset{\text{reducing agent}}{2[H]} \rightarrow \underset{\text{alcohol}}{\overset{OH}{\underset{|}{-C-H}}}$$

$$\underset{\text{alkene}}{C=C} + \underset{\text{reducing agent}}{[H]} \rightarrow \underset{\text{alkane}}{-\overset{H}{\underset{|}{C}}-\overset{H}{\underset{|}{C}}-}$$

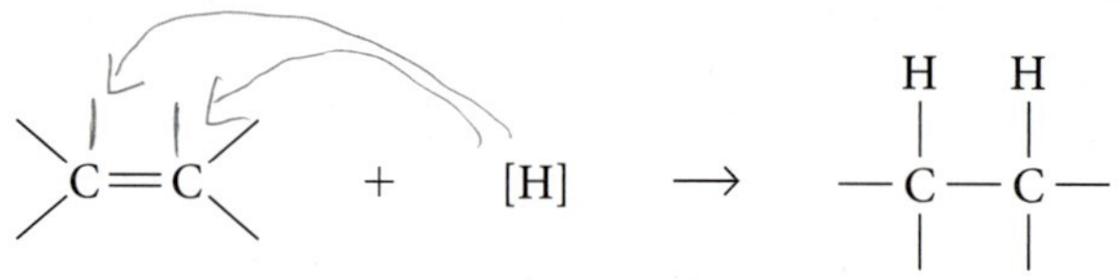

To identify a reduction, count and compare the number of C—H and C—O bonds in both the reactant and the product. Try it for the following example.

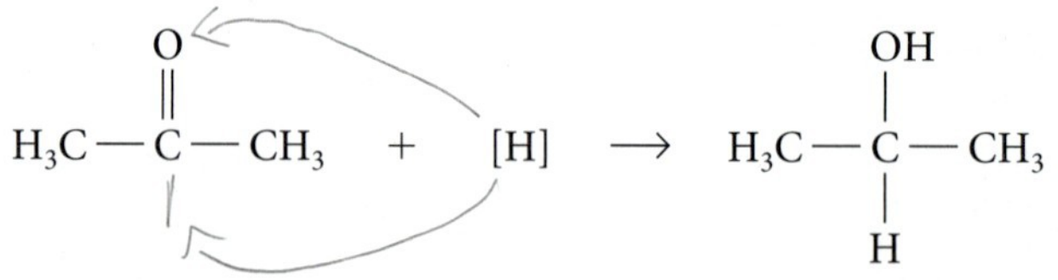

$$\underset{\text{propanone}}{H_3C-\overset{O}{\underset{\|}{C}}-CH_3} + [H] \rightarrow \underset{\text{2-propanol}}{H_3C-\overset{OH}{\underset{\underset{H}{|}}{\underset{|}{C}}}-CH_3}$$

Among the most common oxidation-reduction reactions are combustion reactions.

Combustion Reactions

combustion reaction a type of reaction in which a compound reacts with oxygen to produce the oxides of elements that make up the compound

complete combustion reaction an excess of oxygen reacts with a hydro-carbon and produces carbon dioxide and water vapour, and releases energy

The photograph in **Figure 2.13A** shows a person obtaining energy by eating a sandwich. **Figure 2.13B** shows the combustion of natural gas in a Bunsen burner flame. How are these two processes related? Both are examples of the same type of organic reaction—combustion. In a **combustion reaction**, a compound reacts with oxygen to produce the oxides of elements that make up the compound.

The combustion of organic compounds is defined more specifically. In a **complete combustion reaction**, a hydrocarbon reacts with oxygen to produce carbon dioxide and water vapour, and release energy. No matter how complicated the structure, if excess oxygen is present, *all hydrocarbons will burn completely to produce carbon dioxide and water vapour.* The following unbalanced chemical equation is an example of complete combustion in which a hydrocarbon burns in an excess of oxygen.

$$\text{hydrocarbon} + O_2(g) \rightarrow CO_2(g) + H_2O(g) + \text{energy}$$

 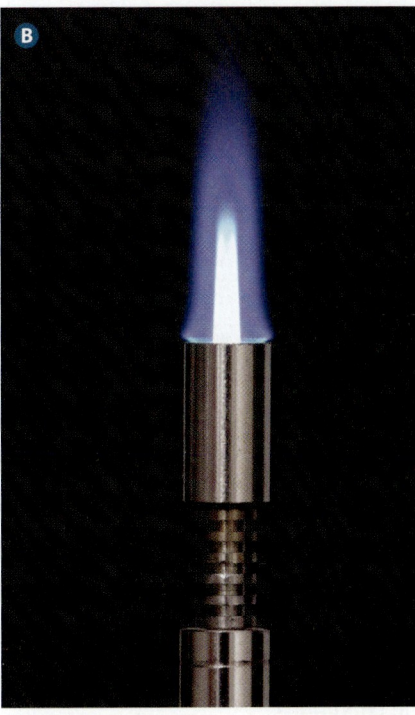

Figure 2.13 (**A**) Cellular respiration, the process your body uses to obtain energy from food, is a series of organic reactions that form carbon dioxide and water, and release energy. (**B**) These are the same products that result from the burning, or combustion, of natural gas.

The hydrocarbon in the previous equation may range from the fuel that runs vehicles to the methane burning in the Bunsen burner in **Figure 2.13B** to the food you ate for breakfast. Recall that through the process of cellular respiration, your body breaks down food in the presence of oxygen to obtain energy, while also producing carbon dioxide and water.

The blue flame of the Bunsen burner in **Figure 2.13B** indicates that the combustion of the fuel is complete. When insufficient oxygen is present, all of the elements in the fuel will not combine with oxygen to the greatest extent possible. The products contain some carbon monoxide and soot. Soot is made up of tiny pieces of unburned carbon. This process is an **incomplete combustion reaction**. The following unbalanced chemical equation represents incomplete combustion.

$$\text{hydrocarbon} + O_2(g) \rightarrow C(s) + CO(g) + CO_2(g) + H_2O(g) + \text{energy}$$

The orange flame of a burning candle indicates that the combustion of the candle wax is incomplete. The orange colour of the flame is the glow from particles of soot in the flame. You have probably heard or read warnings about not using camp stoves or heaters indoors. Likewise, you should never let a car run in a closed garage. Even a poorly ventilated fireplace can be dangerous. The reason that they are all dangerous is because the incomplete combustion forms carbon monoxide (CO), which is a poisonous gas. Carbon monoxide binds to the hemoglobin in blood 20 times more tightly than oxygen, preventing the hemoglobin from transporting oxygen.

Although it is important to understand incomplete combustion and its consequences, it is not possible to balance incomplete combustion equations. It is too difficult to predict how far the combustion process will go and what combination of products will be formed. In this course, when you work with combustion problems, the process will always be complete and the products will always be carbon dioxide and water vapour.

Recall that when you are balancing combustion reactions, there are sometimes an odd number of oxygen atoms in the products. There is no integer that you can place in front of O_2 to give an odd number of oxygen atoms in the reactants. To solve the problem, multiply all other coefficients by 2 and then balance the oxygen atoms.

incomplete combustion reaction reaction that occurs when insufficient oxygen is present; all of the elements in the fuel will not combine with oxygen to the greatest extent possible

Sample Problem

Oxidation and Reduction Reactions

Problem

Identify each reaction as an oxidation or reduction.

a.
$$CH_3CH_2CH_2\overset{\overset{O}{\|}}{C}H \rightarrow CH_3CH_2CH_2\overset{\overset{OH}{|}}{C}H_2$$

b.

A cyclohexanol ring with OH → a cyclohexanone ring with =O

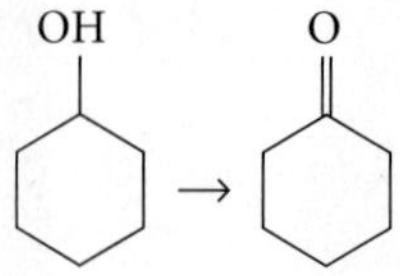

Complete and balance the following chemical equation and identify the products.

c.
$$CH_3-CH_2-CH_2-\overset{\overset{O}{\diagup}}{\underset{\diagdown H}{C}} + O_2 \rightarrow$$

What Is Required?
You must identify reactions as oxidation or reduction. You must complete and balance an oxidation equation.

What Is Given?
You are given the reactants and conditions.

Plan Your Strategy	Act on Your Strategy
a. Count the number of C—H bonds and C—O bonds in the reactant and the product.	$CH_3CH_2CH_2\overset{\overset{O}{\|}}{C}H \rightarrow CH_3CH_2CH_2\overset{\overset{OH}{\|}}{C}H_2$ Reactant: 8 C—H bonds, 2 C—O bonds (or 1 C=O) Product: 9 C—H bonds, 1 C—O bond
Examine how the number of C—H bonds and C—O bonds have changed.	The product has *gained* a C—H bond and *lost* a C—O bond. Thus, it is a reduction.
b. Count the number of C—H bonds and C—O bonds in the reactant and the product.	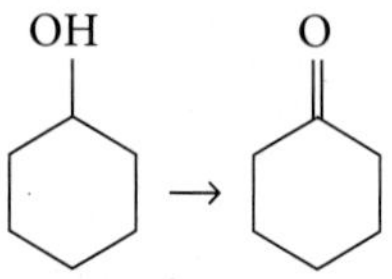 (cyclohexanol → cyclohexanone) Reactant: 11 C—H bonds, 1 C—O bonds Product: 10 C—H bonds, 2 C—O bond (or 1 C=O)
Examine how the number of C—H bonds and C—O bonds have changed.	The product has *lost* a C—H bond and *gained* a C—O bond. Thus, it is a oxidation.
c. This is a combustion reaction. Write the products, carbon dioxide and water.	$CH_3-CH_2-CH_2-CHO + O_2 \rightarrow CO_2 + H_2O$
Balance the equation according to the standard procedure.	$2CH_3-CH_2-CH_2-CHO + 11O_2 \rightarrow 8CO_2 + 8H_2O + energy$

Check Your Solution
In Part a, the product has one more C—H bond and one less C—O bond than the reactant. This agrees with the definition of reduction. In Part b, product has one less C—H bond and one more C—O bond than the reactant. This agrees with the definition of oxidation. In Part c, the hydrocarbon reacts with oxygen to form carbon dioxide and water, and release energy.

Practice Problems

For the next four questions, identify each reaction as an oxidation or a reduction. The oxidizing and reducing agents are not shown.

43.

CH₃—CH(CH₃)—CH(CH₂CH₃)—CH₂—CHO →

CH₃—CH(CH₃)—CH(CH₂CH₃)—CH₂—C(=O)—OH

44.

(CH₃CH₂)(H)C=C(CH₃)(CH₃) → CH₃CH₂CH₂CH(CH₃)CH₃

45.

cyclohexane-1,4-dione → cyclohexane-1,4-diol

46.

(CH₃)₂CH—C(=O)—H → (CH₃)₂CH—C(=O)—OH

For the next two questions, classify each reaction in two different ways: for example, as oxidation *and* as an elimination reaction.

47.

(CH₃)(H)C=C(H)(CH₂CH₃) + H_2 → $CH_3CH_2CH_2CH_2CH_3$

48. CH_3—C(=O)—OH + HO—CH_3 ⇌ CH_3—C(=O)—O—CH_3 + HOH

For the next three questions, write a balanced equation to show the complete combustion of the hydrocarbon given.

49. methane, CH_4

50. but-2-ene, C_4H_8

51. propane, C_3H_8

52. Although cellular respiration in the body is a complex process, the overall reaction can be reduced to the equivalent of a combustion reaction. Write and balance the chemical equation for the complete combustion of glucose, $C_6H_{12}O_6$.

Activity 2.1 — Identifying Compounds Using Oxidation Reactions

When the permanganate ion comes in contact with unsaturated compounds, a reaction occurs and the solution changes colour. When the permanganate ion comes in contact with saturated compounds, no reaction occurs.

Safety Precautions

- $KMnO_4$(aq) will stain your skin or clothing. If you accidentally spill $KMnO_4$(aq) on your skin, wash immediately with copious amounts of water. Remove the stain with a solution of sodium bisulfite.

Materials

- samples of vegetable oils, such as margarine, corn oil, and coconut oil
- samples of animal fats, such as butter and lard
- 5.0 mmol/L $KMnO_4$(aq)
- warm-water bath
- hot plate
- medicine droppers (one for each sample)
- test tubes
- test-tube rack
- stoppers

Procedure

1. Melt solids, such as butter, in their containers in a warm-water bath (40 °C–50 °C), and then test them as liquids. Using a different medicine dropper for each substance, place about two full medicine droppers of each test substance into a separate test tube.

2. Use a clean medicine dropper to add one full medicine dropper of potassium permanganate solution to each substance. Seal each tube with a clean rubber stopper and shake the test tube to thoroughly mix the reactants. Record your observations. Dispose of the reactants and products as directed by your teacher.

Questions

1. What physical properties account for the fact that some of the samples caused a change in the colour of the potassium permanganate solution and some did not?

2. Based on this observation, infer a relationship between the chemical structure and a physical property of the samples that you analyzed.

STSE
CHEMISTRY Connections

Trans Fats in the Diet

The next time you reach for your favourite snack, have a look at the nutrition label. Does this food contain *trans fats* or partially hydrogenated oils? If so, this tasty treat could be putting you at risk for heart disease and other disorders.

ALL FATS ARE NOT CREATED EQUAL Butter, margarine, olive oil, and hydrogenated soybean oil all contain fats. Why is olive oil liquid at room temperature while these other products are solid? Their state depends on the intermolecular forces between the molecules. Fats consist of three *fatty acids* bonded to glycerol. Fatty acids are long-chain carboxylic acids. Unsaturated fatty acids normally have a *cis* configuration around their double bonds, which gives them a bent or kinked structure, as shown in the space-filling models below. The kinks in the hydrocarbon chains prevent the chains from lining up close to one another thus limiting the forces of attraction between the chains. As a result, unsaturated fats tend to be liquid at room temperature. Saturated fatty acids have straight chains and thus can pack close together. The larger number of intermolecular forces make these fats more solid at room temperature.

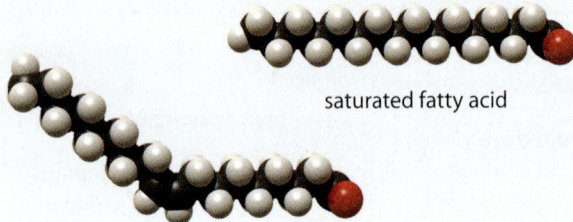

saturated fatty acid

unsaturated fatty acid

Unsaturated fats are readily oxidized and tend to become rancid more rapidly than do saturated fats. To extend the shelf life of foods containing unsaturated fats or to keep them from melting at room temperature, unsaturated fats can be hydrogenated (have hydrogen atoms added) to reduce the number of double bonds. However, under the conditions of hydrogenation, the normal *cis* configuration is changed to the *trans* configuration for those double bonds that do not become saturated. The hydrocarbon chains of trans fatty acids are straight, as shown in the diagram on the right, and behave similarly to saturated fatty acids because the hydrocarbon chains fit closely together.

A GROWING HEALTH CONCERN Fats are not only a source of energy but are also a major part of cell membranes. Fats are also precursors for some hormones. Health studies show, however, that trans fats do more harm than good.

Most enzymes cannot break down trans fats completely and they can become part of cell membranes. With their unusual trans configuration, trans fats reduce the ability of membranes to function properly.

Research also shows that trans fats affect the body's ability to manage cholesterol. Since cholesterol is insoluble in water, the body uses special complexes to transport fats and cholesterol in the blood. The two types of complexes are called low-density lipoproteins (LDL) and high-density lipoprotein (HDL). High levels of LDL contribute to the build-up of plaque in the arteries. In contrast, HDLs do not contribute to the formation of plaque. Trans fats are thought to raise levels of LDL ("bad cholesterol") and lower levels of HDL ("good cholesterol"), increasing the risk of heart disease.

Connect to Society

1. If fats were fully hydrogenated, there would be no trans fats. Why would food manufacturers choose to only partially hydrogenate fats?

2. Trans fats were used in foods for about 80 years before consumer groups became concerned about their adverse health effects. Why do you think it took this long for people to make the link between the consumption of trans fats and development of heart disease?

3. Do trans fats occur naturally in foods? Are all trans fats, such as conjugated linoleic acid, unhealthy? Research these topics on the Internet.

unsaturated fatty acid

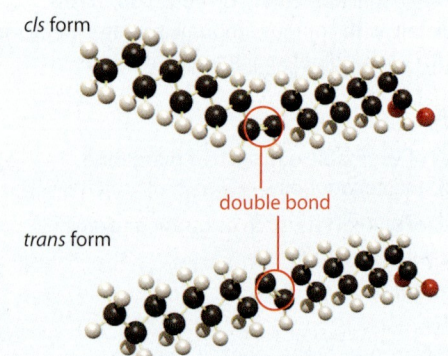

cis form

double bond

trans form

Section 2.1 Review

Section Summary

- An addition reaction is one in which atoms from a small molecule react with a double or triple bond in an organic molecule and become part of the molecule.
- An elimination reaction is one in which atoms or groups of atoms are removed from an organic molecule and a double bond is formed in the molecule.
- In a substitution reaction an atom or small group replaces another atom or small group on the organic molecule.
- In a condensation reaction two large molecules combine to form one larger molecule and a very small molecule, usually water.
- An esterification reaction is a special type of condensation reaction in which a carboxylic acid reacts with an alcohol to form an ester and water.
- A hydrolysis reaction is the reverse of a condensation reaction. The compounds that are formed by condensation reactions can be broken down by hydrolysis reactions.
- Oxidation is defined as a reaction in which a carbon atom forms more bonds to oxygen, O, or less bonds to hydrogen, H. Reduction is defined as a reaction in which a carbon atom forms fewer bonds to oxygen, O, or more bonds to hydrogen, H.
- A combustion reaction is a type of reaction in which a compound reacts with oxygen to produce the oxides of elements that make up the compound.

Review Questions

1. **K/U** Identify the following reactions as addition, elimination, condensation, esterification, substitution, oxidation, or reduction reactions.

   a. $CH_3-\underset{\underset{OH}{|}}{CH}-CH_2-CH_3 + H_2O + [O] \rightarrow CH_3-\underset{\underset{O}{\|}}{C}-CH_2-CH_3$

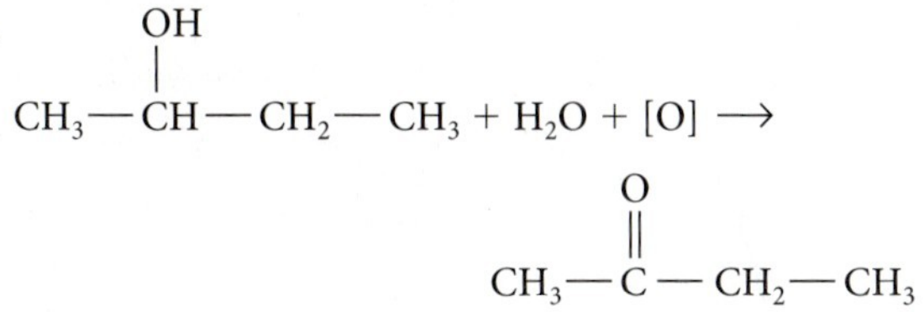

   b. $CH_3-CH_2-\underset{\underset{O}{\|}}{C}-OH + HO-CH_3 \xrightarrow{H_2SO_4} CH_3-CH_2-\underset{\underset{O}{\|}}{C}-O-CH_3 + H_2O$

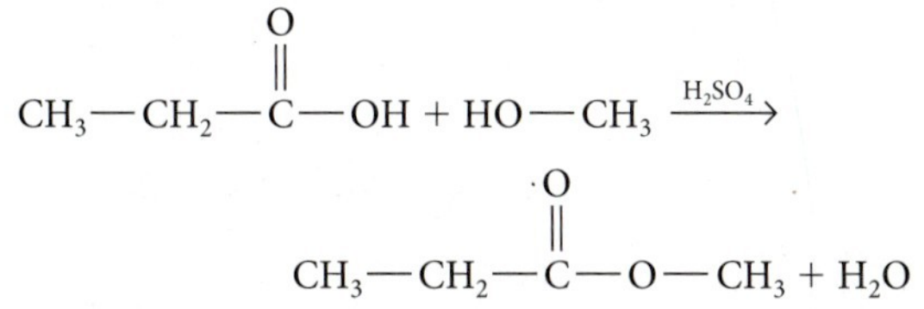

   c. $CH_3-CH_2-Cl + NaOCH_2CH_3 \rightarrow CH_2=CH_2 + HOCH_2CH_3 + NaCl$

2. **T/I** Determine the products for the following reactions.
   a. hexanoic acid + ethanol $\xrightarrow{H_2SO_4}$
   b. formaldehyde + [O] $\rightarrow$
   c. propan-2-ol + hydrobromic acid $\rightarrow$
   d. benzene + bromine $\xrightarrow{FeBr_3}$

3. **C** Create a flow chart outlining which reactions would be necessary to convert a haloalkane to a carboxylic acid. Make sure to include the products of each reaction.

4. **K/U** Which types of reactions can result in a major and minor product? How do you determine which is the major product?

5. **A** Write a balanced equation for the combustion of the following alkanes.
   a. propane
   b. butane
   c. kerosene ($C_{13}H_{28}$)

6. **T/I** Determine the products of the following addition and elimination reactions.
   a. $HO-CH_2-CH_2-CH_3 \xrightarrow{H_2SO_4}$
   b. $CH_3CH=CHCH_3 + Cl_2 \rightarrow$
   c. $CH_2=CHCH_3 + HBr \rightarrow$

7. **T/I** Identify the type of reaction and determine the products for the following reaction.

   $CH_3-\underset{\underset{CH_3}{|}}{CH}-CH_2-\underset{\underset{O}{\|}}{C}-O-CH_2-CH_3 + H_2O \rightarrow$

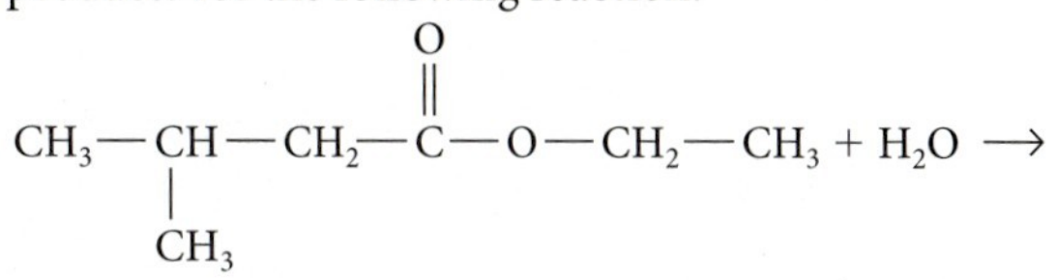

8. **T/I** Determine the missing organic reactants for the following equations.

   a. $? + [O] \rightarrow \underset{H}{\overset{O}{\underset{|}{\overset{\|}{C}}}}\underset{H}{}$

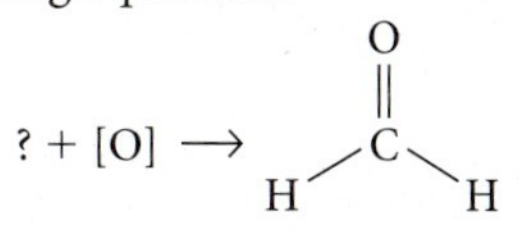

   b. $? + [H] \rightarrow CH_3-\underset{\underset{OH}{|}}{CH}-CH_3$

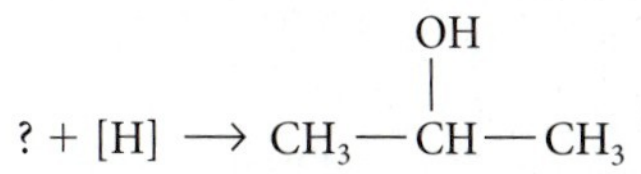

9. **T/I** Indicate the major and minor products that would result from reacting 2-methyloct-2-ene with hydrogen bromide.

10. **T/I** Why can incomplete combustion be harmful?

SECTION 2.2
Polymer Equations

Key Terms

polymer
monomer
plastics
addition polymerization
condensation polymerization
petrochemical

From grocery bags and plastic soft-drink bottles to furniture and computer equipment, plastics are an integral part of our homes, schools, and workplaces. Plastics, such as polyethylene terephthalate (PET) shown in **Figure 2.14A**, belong to a group of organic compounds called polymers. These useful organic compounds have a much larger molecular size than the compounds you have already studied in this unit.

Polymer Chemistry

A **polymer** is a very long molecule that is made by linking together many smaller molecules called **monomers**. To picture a polymer, imagine taking a handful of paper clips and joining them into a long chain. Each paper clip represents a monomer. The long chain of paper clips represents the polymer. Some polymers contain only one type of monomer, as is the case in the paper clip example. Polymers can also be made from a combination of two or more different monomers. **Figure 2.14B** shows an example of joined monomers in a polymer structure.

Figure 2.14 (A) Polyethylene terephthalate (PET) is a polymer that is used to make soft-drink bottles.
(B) A polymer, such as this one, can contain several thousand monomer units.
Use an analogy, besides a chain of paperclips, to describe a polymer.

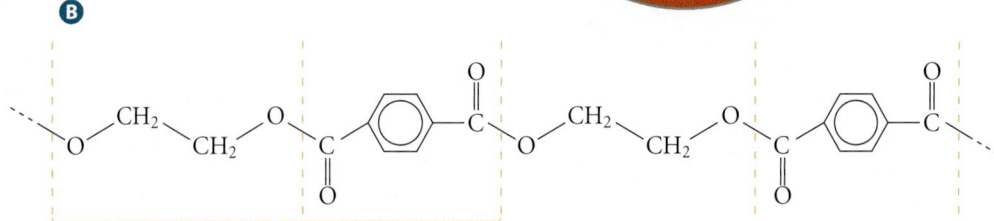

repeating unit made from two monomers

polymer
a large, long-chain molecule with repeating units of small molecules called monomers

monomer
a small molecule, linked covalently to others of the same or similar type to form a polymer

plastics
synthetic polymers that can be heated and moulded into specific shapes and forms

Polymers can be synthetic (produced by humans) or natural. Polymers that can be heated and molded into specific shapes and forms are commonly known as **plastics**. All plastics are synthetic polymers. Adhesives, chewing gum, and polystyrene are also made from synthetic polymers. The name of a synthetic polymer is usually written with the prefix poly- (meaning "many") before the name of the monomer.

The common name of the monomer is sometimes used instead of the proper IUPAC name. For example, the common name for ethene is ethylene. Thus, the name polyethylene is used for the polymer that is made from ethene. Polyethylene is used to make plastic bags, containers, and food wrap. Similarly, the polymer made from chloroethene (common name: vinyl chloride) is named polyvinylchloride (PVC). It is used to make numerous items, from adhesives to auto parts. Adding a *plasticizer* to PVC makes it an extremely flexible material that is used in items such as bendable hoses, inflatable objects, and wire insulation. Another common plastic, made from propene (common name: propylene) is called polypropylene. Among its many uses, polypropylene is used to make plastic items for laboratories and medical facilities, such as those shown in **Figure 2.15A**, since it can withstand the high temperatures required for sterilization.

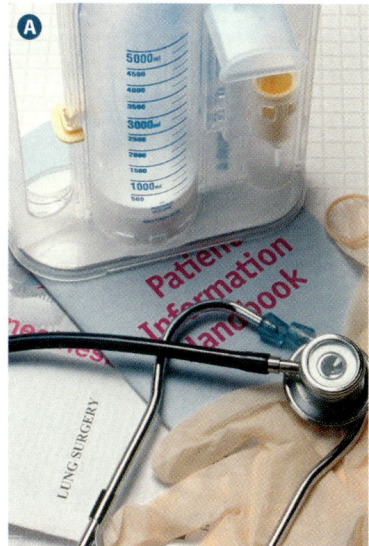  

Figure 2.15 (**A**) Polypropylene, a synthetic polymer, is used to make plastic medical supplies, among other products. (**B**) The kites used by these snowkiters are also made from a synthetic polymer. (**C**) Both synthetic and natural polymers are used to make clothing. Wool is a natural polymer that is used to knit warm clothing, such as toques and sweaters.

Some synthetic polymers can also be used to make fabrics. For example, rayon and polyester fabrics are made from synthetic polymers, as is the nylon fabric in the kite shown in **Figure 2.15B**. Natural polymers, polymers found in living systems, are also used to make fabrics. Cotton, linen, wool, and other natural polymers have been used for thousands of years to make clothing. Other natural polymers, such as starch and protein, will be discussed in greater detail later in this section.

Making Synthetic Polymers: Addition and Condensation Polymerization

Synthetic polymers are extremely useful and valuable. Many polymers and their manufacturing processes have been patented as corporate technology. Polymers are formed by two of the reactions that were covered in Section 1: addition reactions and condensation reactions.

Addition Polymerization

Addition polymerization is a reaction in which alkene monomers are joined through multiple addition reactions to form a polymer. Addition reactions are characterized by a reduction in the number of double bonds found on the polymer, as addition reduces a double bond to a single bond. **Figure 2.16** illustrates the addition polymerization of ethene to form polyethene. **Table 2.1**, on the next page, gives the names, structures, and uses of some common addition polymers.

addition polymerization reaction in which alkene monomers are joined through multiple addition reactions to form a polymer

$$H_2C=CH_2 + H_2C=CH_2 \longrightarrow -\underset{H}{\overset{H}{C}}-\underset{H}{\overset{H}{C}}-\underset{H}{\overset{H}{C}}-\underset{H}{\overset{H}{C}}- \xrightarrow{H_2C=CH_2} -\underset{H}{\overset{H}{C}}-\underset{H}{\overset{H}{C}}-\underset{H}{\overset{H}{C}}-\underset{H}{\overset{H}{C}}-\underset{H}{\overset{H}{C}}-\underset{H}{\overset{H}{C}}- \text{ etc.}$$

Figure 2.16 The polymer, polyethene, is made from ethene (commonly called polyethylene and ethylene, respectively). Notice that after the polymer is formed, there are no double bonds remaining. Nevertheless, the name sounds like it is an alkene. Polymers are named according to the structure of the monomer, which, in this case, is an alkene.

Table 2.1 Examples of Addition Polymers

Name	Structure of Monomer	Structure of Polymer	Uses
Polystyrene	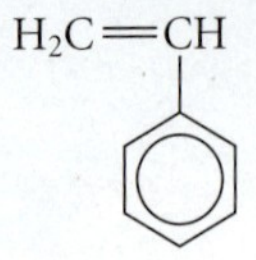 styrene ($H_2C=CH-C_6H_5$)	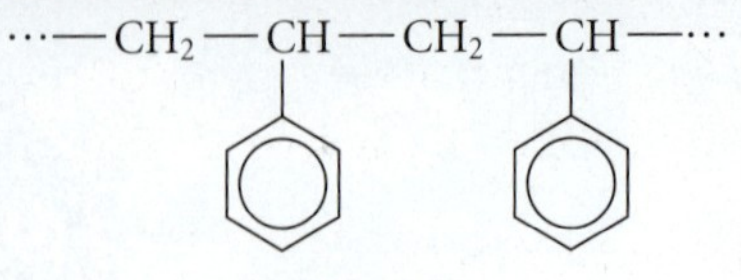 polystyrene ($-CH_2-CH(C_6H_5)-CH_2-CH(C_6H_5)-$)	• styrene and Styrofoam™ cups • insulation • packaging
Polyvinylchloride (PVC, vinyl)	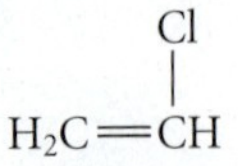 vinylchloride ($H_2C=CHCl$)	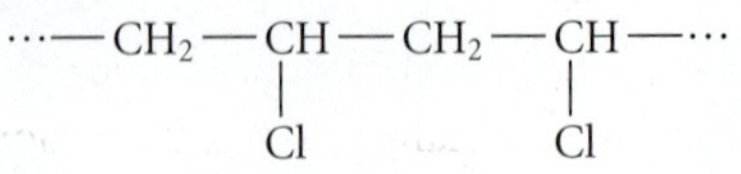 polyvinylchloride ($-CH_2-CHCl-CH_2-CHCl-$)	• construction materials • sewage pipes • medical equipment

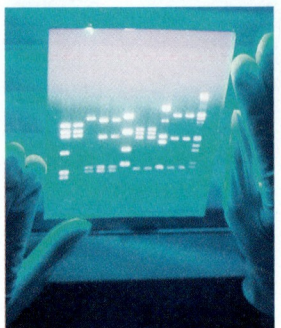

Figure 2.17 Gel electrophoresis is an important procedure used to analyze DNA. The results have many applications including being used as evidence in criminal cases and to diagnose genetic diseases.

An Addition Polymer: Polyacrylamide Gel

The results of the laboratory technique called *gel electrophoresis* are shown in **Figure 2.17**. Gel electrophoresis is used to separate and analyze samples of proteins and DNA fragments. The gel that is used to separate proteins is an addition polymer called polyacrylamide.

Polyacrylamide is a unique polymer because cross links can be made between the polymer chains, resulting in a three dimensional network. Cross linking is a process in which bonds are formed from one strand to another at several points along a polymer strand. Polyacrylamide is formed from the monomer shown in **Figure 2.18A**, which is commonly called acrylamide. **Figure 2.18B** shows the addition polymer that can be formed from this monomer in the same way that the addition polymers in **Table 2.1** are formed. The only difference is that polyacrylamide has an amide group as a side group.

The resulting polymer is a single chain. To create cross links between chains, another ingredient commonly called bisacrylamide must be added. As shown in **Figure 2.18C**, bisacrylamide looks like two acrylamide molecules that have been joined together by a —CH_2— group bound to the nitrogen atoms in each molecule. By adding some bisacrylamide to the mixture while the polymer is forming, cross linking is achieved. The amount of cross linking can be controlled by adjusting the ratio of bisacrylamide to acrylamide. Cross links can have important effects on polymers. A polymer that contains many crosslinks is stronger and less flexible than its straight-chain relative. In some cases, cross links allow a polymer to be stretched and still return to its original shape once the stretching force is removed.

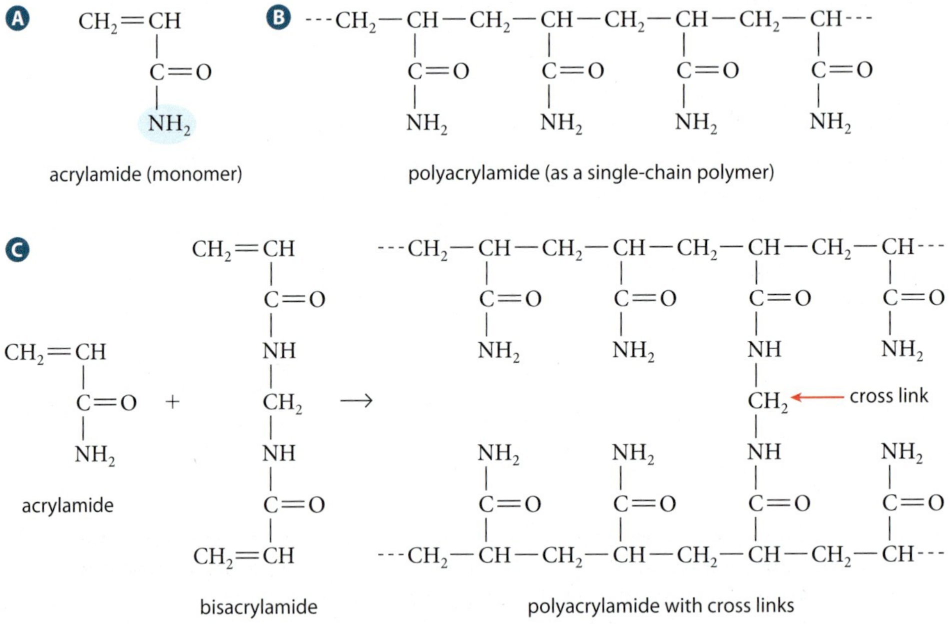

Figure 2.18 (A) The monomer acrylamide has an amide side group (circled in blue). (B) The straight-chain polymer polyacrylamide forms through addition polymerization reactions. (C) Cross links can form in the polyacrylamide if bisacrylamide is added as a reactant. The red arrow is pointing to a cross link.

Condensation Polymerization

In **condensation polymerization**, monomers are combined through multiple condensation reactions to form a polymer. A second, smaller product, usually water, is also produced in the reaction. For condensation polymerization to occur, each monomer must have two functional groups (usually one at each end of the molecule).

condensation polymerization reaction in which monomers are combined through multiple condensation reactions to form a polymer

Two Condensation Polymers: PET and Kevlar®

The previous section explained that esterification is one type of condensation reaction. The formation of a polymer by esterification reactions between two monomers is shown in **Figure 2.19**. Note that one of the monomers, terephthalic acid, has a carboxyl group on each end of the molecule. The second monomer, ethane-1,2-diol (commonly called ethylene glycol), has an alcohol group on each end. *Ester linkages* can thus form on both ends of each monomer, forming a long polymer chain. Condensation polymers that contain ester linkages are called polyesters. The resulting polyester in this case is called polyethylene terephthalate (PET). PET is often used to make soft-drink and water bottles. Note that water is also released in this condensation polymerization reaction.

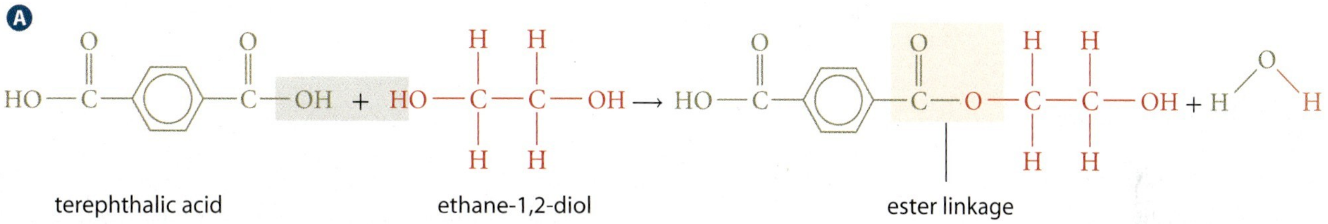

Figure 2.19 (A) Continued formation of ester linkages between monomers leads to the formation of polyethylene terephthalate (PET). **(B)** PET is used to make many plastics that are categorized from 1 to 7 for recycling purposes.

Polymers that contain repeating amide functional groups are also formed by condensation polymerization. Such polymers are formed from two different monomers. One monomer has a carboxyl group at both ends and the other monomer has an amine at both ends. Each carboxyl group on one monomer reacts with an amine group on the other monomer to form an *amide linkage*. Condensation polymers that contain amide linkages are called *polyamides* or *nylons*. In addition to a polyamide, water is also produced in this reaction. Polyparaphenylene terephthalamide, better known as Kevlar®, is an example of this type of polyamide. The chemical structures of the monomers 1,4-diaminobenzene and benzene-1,4-dicarboxylic acid and the polymer of Kevlar® are shown in **Figure 2.20A**. The most well known use of Kevlar® is for bulletproof vests, as shown in **Figure 2.20B**. It is also used in radial tires, boat hulls, bicycles, and even in helicopter blades.

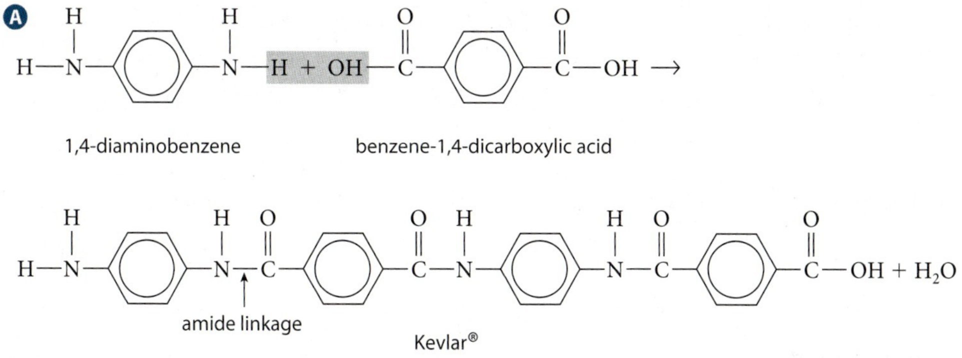

Figure 2.20 (A) The chemical structures of the monomers and the polymer of Kevlar® are shown here. Note that there is an amide linkage between each of the monomer units in the polymer. **(B)** Kevlar® is lightweight but strong and is highly resistant to heat.

Chapter 2 Reactions of Organic Compounds • MHR 119

Other Common Condensation Polymers

To determine whether condensation polymerization has occurred, look for the formation of ester or amide linkages in the product, along with a second smaller product, usually water. **Table 2.2** gives the names, structures, and uses of two condensation polymers. Notice that Dacron™ (a trade name for polyethylene terephthalate fibres) contains ester linkages between monomers. Nylon-6 contains amide linkages between monomers.

Table 2.2 Examples of Condensation Polymers

Name	Structure of Polymer	Uses
Dacron™ (a polyester)	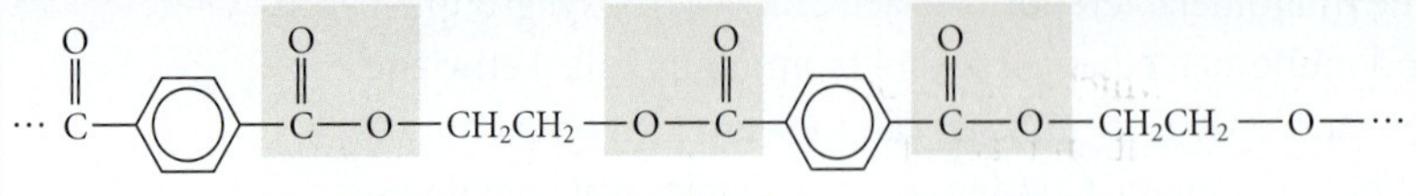 ···C—⌬—C—O—CH$_2$CH$_2$—O—C—⌬—C—O—CH$_2$CH$_2$—O—··· (ester bonds)	• synthetic fibres used to make fabric for clothing and surgery
Nylon-6 (a polyamide)	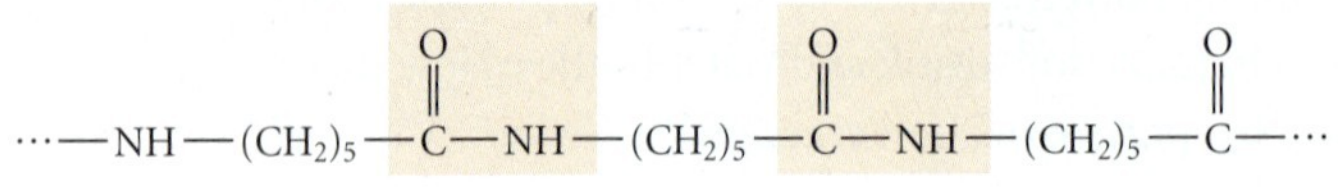 ···—NH—(CH$_2$)$_5$—C—NH—(CH$_2$)$_5$—C—NH—(CH$_2$)$_5$—C—··· (amide bonds)	• tires • synthetic fibres used to make rope and articles of clothing, such as stockings

Learning Check

13. Define *polymer* and list some common uses of polymers.
14. Use a Venn diagram to compare and contrast addition and condensation polymerization reactions.
15. Urethane is a monomer that is polymerized to make computer housing. Predict the name of the polymer formed from urethane monomers.
16. Identify features you would look for to help classify a polymer as an addition polymer or condensation polymer.
17. In Section 2.1 you saw that proteins, like polymers, are made through condensation reactions. What are the monomers of proteins?
18. Polyacrylamide contains crosslinks between polymer chains. How might cross-linking change the polymer's properties compared to single-chain polyacrylamide?

The following Sample Problem shows how to classify a polymerization reaction.

Sample Problem

Classifying a Polymerization Reaction

Problem
Tetrafluoroethene polymerizes to form the slippery polymer that is commonly known as Teflon™. Teflon™ is used as a non-stick coating in frying pans, among its other uses. Classify the following polymerization reaction to make Teflon™, and name the product. (The letter *n* indicates that many monomers are involved in the reaction.)

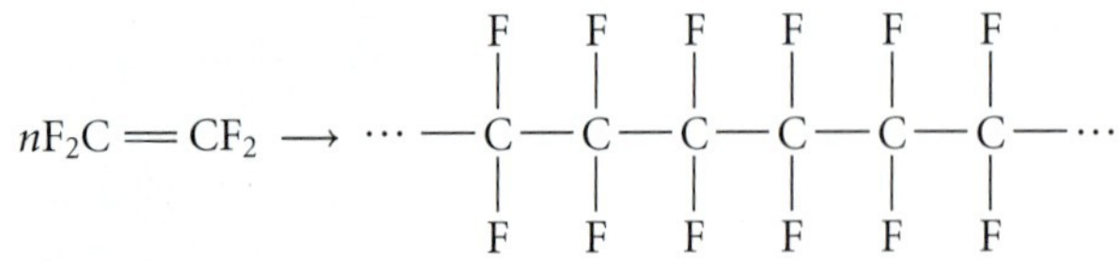

$$nF_2C = CF_2 \longrightarrow \cdots -\underset{F}{\overset{F}{C}}-\underset{F}{\overset{F}{C}}-\underset{F}{\overset{F}{C}}-\underset{F}{\overset{F}{C}}-\underset{F}{\overset{F}{C}}-\underset{F}{\overset{F}{C}}- \cdots$$

What Is Required?
You must classify the polymer that is made.
You must determine the name of the polymer.

What Is Given?
You are given a chemical equation representing the polymerization reaction.

Plan Your Strategy	Act on Your Strategy
Determine the type of polymer that is formed when a monomer with a double bond reacts to form a polymer that has no double bonds. As well, there are no small molecules formed.	addition polymer
To name the polymer, write poly in front of the monomer name.	polytetrafluoroethene

Check Your Solution

Addition polymerization is a reaction in which alkene monomers are joined through multiple addition reactions to form a polymer. Addition reactions are characterized by a reduction in the number of double bonds found in the polymer. In the formation of polytetrafluoroethene, the double bond that is between carbon atoms is broken and is replaced by single bonds.

Practice Problems

Identify the next three reactions as addition or condensation polymerization.

53. 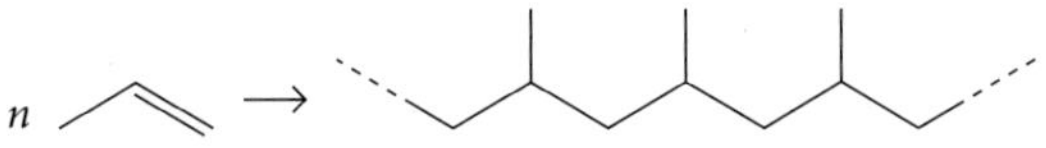 n CH$_2$=CH$_2$ → polymer chain

54. n CH$_2$=C(Cl)—CH=CH$_2$ → polymer chain

55. HO—C(=O)—C$_6$H$_4$—C(=O)—OH + H$_2$N—(CH$_2$)$_6$—NH$_2$ →
    ---C(=O)—C$_6$H$_4$—C(=O)—NH—(CH$_2$)$_6$—NH—C(=O)—C$_6$H$_4$—C(=O)---

For the next three questions, classify each polymer as a polyester or polyamide and draw the structure of the monomer.

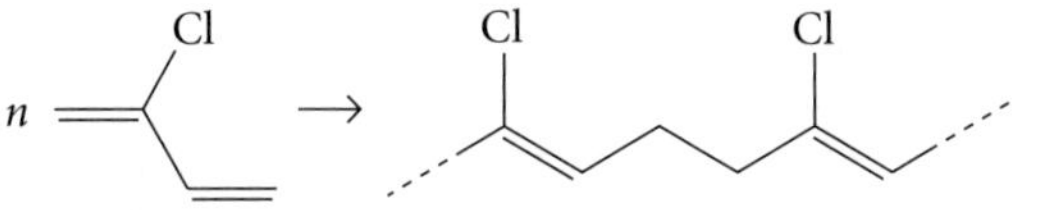

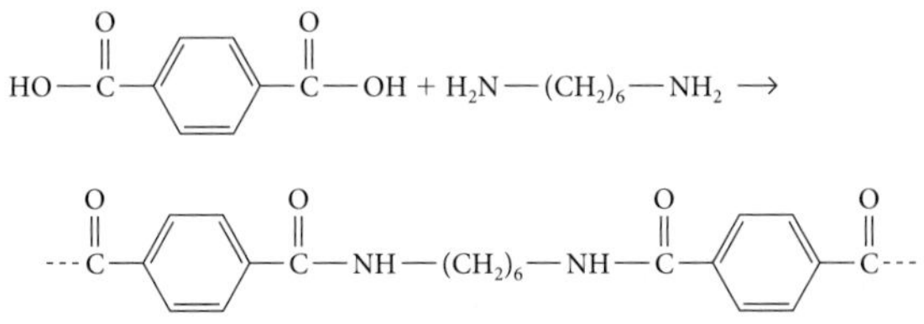

56. 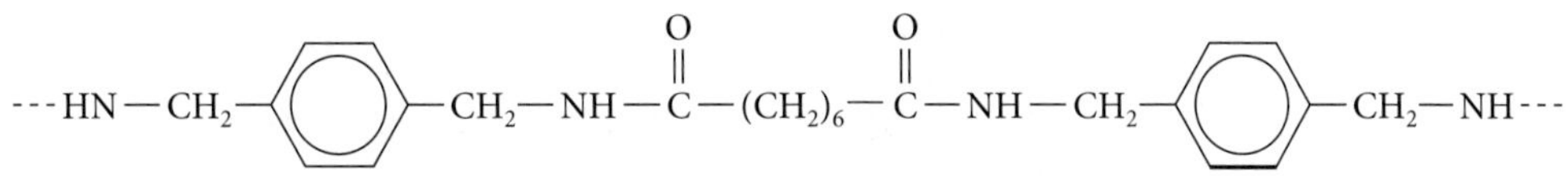 ---HN—CH$_2$—C$_6$H$_4$—CH$_2$—NH—C(=O)—(CH$_2$)$_6$—C(=O)—NH—CH$_2$—C$_6$H$_4$—CH$_2$—NH---

57. ----O—CH$_2$CH$_2$CH$_2$—O—C(=O)—CH$_2$—C(=O)—O—CH$_2$CH$_2$CH$_2$—O----

58. 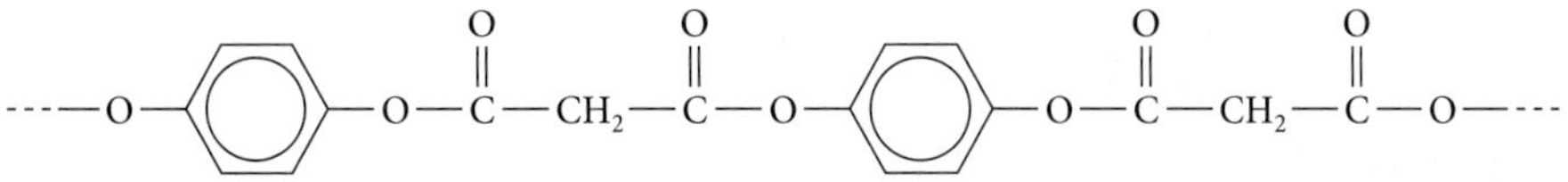 ----O—C$_6$H$_4$—O—C(=O)—CH$_2$—C(=O)—O—C$_6$H$_4$—O—C(=O)—CH$_2$—C(=O)—O----

59. How could you convert 1-bromoethane into polyethene? Write an equation for each step.

For the next three questions, draw the product of each polymerization reaction. Include at least two linkages.

60. HO—C(=O)—C$_6$H$_4$—C(=O)—OH + HO—CH$_2$—C$_6$H$_4$—CH$_2$—OH →

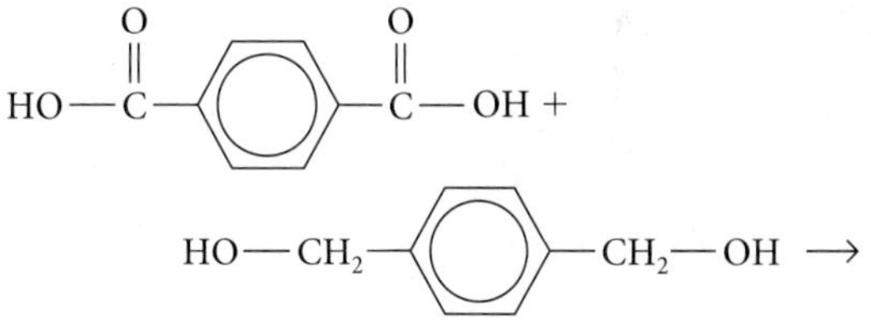

61. nCH$_2$=CH(CN) →

62. nHO—CH$_2$—C(=O)—OH →

Polymers and Industry

Industries use the properties of organic compounds to manufacture consumer products. The organic compounds that industries use to make polymers and other products start out mainly as *petroleum*, a fossil fuel that contains a mixture of hydrocarbons, such as alkanes and alkenes. Various organic reactions are used to convert the hydrocarbon components obtained from petroleum into **petrochemicals**, the organic compounds required by industry for the manufacture of plastics and other materials. For example, ethane is an important petrochemical. Ethene is produced on a large scale using a process known as cracking at plants such as the one shown in **Figure 2.21**. During this process, the ethane provided from petroleum refiners is heated to 800°C and undergoes the following catalytic cracking reaction to produce ethene:

$$C_2H_6(g) \xrightarrow{Pt} CH_2=CH_2(g) + H_2(g)$$

petrochemical product derived from petroleum; a basic hydrocarbon, such as ethene and propene, that is converted into plastics and other synthetic materials

The presence of the double bond makes ethene much more reactive than ethane. Through organic reactions, the petrochemical industry uses ethene to synthesize useful materials, such as ethylene glycol (used in antifreeze). Other related materials, such as polyethylene (used to make containers and food wrap) and polyvinyl chloride (PVC, used to make a wide variety of items from adhesives to car parts) were described earlier in this section.

The Manufacture of PVC

The manufacture of PVC illustrates the way in which organic reactions are used in the petrochemical industry. PVC is a type of plastic that is used in almost every industry. For example, the construction industry uses PVC for vinyl windows and doors, wall coverings, siding, PVC pipe, flooring, and fencing. In the manufacture of PVC, ethene is first reacted with chlorine in an addition reaction to produce 1,2-dichloroethane, as follows:

$$C_2H_4(g) + Cl_2(g) \rightarrow C_2H_4Cl_2(g)$$

Figure 2.21 Gas cracking occurs at petroleum refineries, such as this one in Sarnia, Ontario.

The 1,2-dichloroethane product is then cracked at high temperatures to produce chloroethene (vinyl chloride) and hydrogen chloride by the elimination reaction shown below:

$$C_2H_4Cl_2(g) \rightarrow C_2H_3Cl(g) + HCl(g)$$

The by-product of the cracking reaction, HCl(g), is reacted further with oxygen and more ethene to produce even more 1,2-dichloroethane to be cracked:

$$2C_2H_4(g) + 4HCl(g) + O_2(g) \rightarrow 2C_2H_4Cl_2(g) + 2H_2O(g)$$

The vinyl chloride is then reacted in an addition polymerization reaction to produce the polymer PVC:

$$n\text{H}_2\text{C}=\text{CHCl} \rightarrow \cdots-\text{CH}_2-\underset{\underset{\text{Cl}}{|}}{\text{CH}}-\text{CH}_2-\underset{\underset{\text{Cl}}{|}}{\text{CH}}-\text{CH}_2-\underset{\underset{\text{Cl}}{|}}{\text{CH}}-\cdots$$

chloroethene (vinylchloride)   polyvinylchloride

Polymer Production: Risks and Solutions

In the 1970s, workers at an American plastic manufacturing plant began to experience serious illnesses. Several workers died of liver cancer before the problem was traced to its source: prolonged exposure to vinyl chloride, a powerful carcinogen. Government regulations now restrict workers' exposure to vinyl chloride. Trace amounts of this dangerous chemical are still present, however, as pollution in the environment. Most vinyl chloride emissions enter the environment from gas emissions or through waste-water contaminants from manufacturing plants producing PVC plastics.

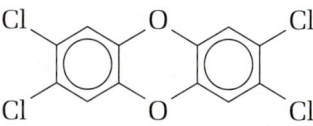

Figure 2.22 The dioxin TCDD, or 2,3,7,8-tetra-chlorodibenzo-p-dioxin, has been shown to be extremely toxic in animal studies. As well, it is suspected of causing reduced fertility and birth defects in humans.

The manufacture and disposal of PVC creates another serious problem. *Dioxins*, a class of chlorinated aromatic hydrocarbons, such as the one shown in **Figure 2.22**, are highly toxic chemicals. Dioxins are produced as an unwanted by-product during the manufacture and burning of PVC. Government regulations and voluntary industry efforts have significantly reduced the amount of dioxins being produced by the petrochemical industry. In fact, the largest human source of dioxin emissions now comes from garbage that people burn in their backyards.

Many synthetic polymers, including most plastics, do not degrade in the environment very easily or quickly. It is estimated that some plastics may take hundreds of years to degrade. What, then, can be done with plastic and other polymer waste? As mentioned above, burning plastic waste releases harmful compounds, such as dioxins, into the environment. Most people are already aware of one solution to the problem of polymer waste: recycling. Plastics make up approximately 7 percent by mass of the garbage we generate. Because plastics are strong and resilient, they can be collected, processed, and recycled into a variety of useful products, including clothing, bags, bottles, synthetic lumber, and furniture. For example, polyethylene terephthalate (PET) from pop bottles can be recycled to produce fleece fabric. This fabric is used by many clothing companies to make jackets and other clothing, as shown in **Figure 2.23**.

Figure 2.23 To produce this fleece fabric, plastic pop bottles, made of polyethylene terephthalate (PET), are cleaned and chopped into small flakes. These flakes are melted down and extruded as fibre, which is then knitted or woven into fabric.

Although it has many benefits, recycling does have significant costs that result from transporting, handling, sorting, cleaning, processing, and storing plastics. Along with recycling, it is essential that society learns to *reduce* its use of polymers and to develop ways of *re-using* polymer products. Together with recycling, these directives are known as the "three R's": reduce, re-use, and recycle.

Another solution that may complement the three R's is the development and use of *bioplastics*. These are polymers that break down more quickly than most traditional petroleum-based plastics when exposed to environmental conditions, such as light and bacteria. The polymer molecules that make up most synthetic plastics are too large and complex to be degraded by biological processes in a short period of time. Although chemical processes will eventually degrade plastics back into carbon, hydrogen, and oxygen, this may take many hundreds of years. Bioplastics, such as the one shown in **Figure 2.24**, are designed in such a way as to accelerate the rate at which this happens. Hydrobiodegradable bioplastic is produced from renewable, natural polymers, such as starch and cellulose from plants. Often, however, this bioplastic also contains a small amount of petroleum-based plastic. In comparison, oxobiodegradable bioplastic is composed of petroleum-based plastics, which are synthetic polymers. This type of bioplastic also contains a catalyst that increases the rate at which the plastic degrades.

Figure 2.24 This cup is made from a bioplastic that was derived from corn.

Activity 2.2 Environmentally-friendly Alternatives to Polystyrene

Polystyrene is found in many products because it is lightweight, a good insulator, and inexpensive. It is used to make insulation for houses and cups that keep beverages hot or cold as well as in shipping materials. However, the manufacture of polystyrene requires hazardous chemicals and also uses petroleum, a non-renewable resource.

Materials
- reference books
- computers with Internet access

Procedure
1. Research polystyrene in order to better understand what it is and how it is made. Use the questions below to guide your research.
   - What is the chemical structure of polystyrene and what is the chemical reaction for the production of polystyrene?
   - What properties of polystyrene make it hazardous to the environment?
   - What is the environmental impact of polystyrene on the environment through its manufacture, use, and disposal?
   - What is the impact of polystyrene on human health?
2. Find out how is polystyrene recycled. Are there industries in your community or in Ontario that recycle polystyrene?
3. Research alternatives that are available that could be used instead of polystyrene.

Questions
1. Summarize the advantages and disadvantages of the use of polystyrene.
2. Construct a table to show the advantages and disadvantages associated with recycling polystyrene.
3. Identify the advantages and disadvantages of the alternatives to polystyrenes.
4. Hold a debate in your class about whether or not the use of polystyrene should be banned in your community. Invite other classes to view the debate and judge the winners.

Learning Check

19. Identify and describe the chemical process used to convert petroleum into petrochemicals.
20. Why do manufacturers want to convert the components in petroleum into petrochemicals?
21. Use a graphic organizer to show the steps involved in converting ethene into PVC.
22. List the advantages and disadvantages to producing PVC.
23. What are dioxins?
24. Identify two ways you can reduce the amount of plastic waste generated in your home.

Natural Polymers

Natural polymers are found in almost every living system. Natural polymers include polysaccharides, proteins, and DNA. Polysaccharides, such as starch, are made up of sugar monomers and broken down to release energy by living things. Proteins are used by living things to build muscle and connective tissues and as enzymes to catalyze chemical reactions. DNA is the genetic material inside cells.

Polysaccharides

Polymers comprising sugar monomers (also called *saccharides*) are called *polysaccharides*. For example, the natural polymer *cellulose* provides most of the structure of plants. The monomer of cellulose is glucose, a sugar. Wood, paper, cotton, and flax are all composed of cellulose fibres. **Figure 2.25A** gives a close-up look at cellulose fibres. **Figure 2.25B** shows part of a cellulose polymer.

Starch, the energy storage unit in plants, shown in **Figure 2.26**, is also a polysaccharide. Humans can digest starch, but they cannot digest cellulose. What is the difference between these polymers? The orientation of individual glucose monomers differs in the two polymers. In cellulose the glucose monomers form *beta linkages* and in starch the glucose monomers form *alpha linkages*. The difference between the two linkages is difficult to visualize in a two-dimensional sketch, but chemists have agreed on a convention for drawing the alpha and beta linkages. In the beta linkage, the bond from the carbon atom to the oxygen atom is drawn upward, as shown by the red arrows in the cellulose in **Figure 2.25A**. In the alpha linkage, the bond from the carbon atom to the oxygen atom is drawn downward, as shown by the red arrows in the starch in **Figure 2.26**.

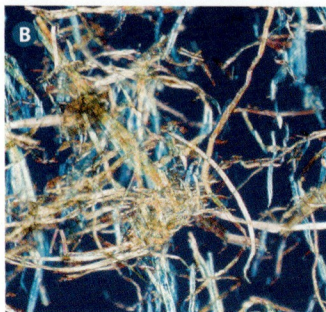

magnification: unknown

Figure 2.25 (**A**) Cellulose is the main structural fibre in plants and makes up the fibre in our diet. Red arrows point to beta linkages. (**B**) Cellulose forms fibres that can be viewed through a scanning electron microscope.

Enzymes in our bodies recognize and break down the alpha linkages in a starch molecule. However, animals, including human beings, have no enzymes that recognize the beta linkages. Thus, cellulose passes through our system. However, some animals, such as cows and termites, are host to bacteria that can digest beta linkages. In this manner, these animals can gain nutrients from cellulose.

Starch also differs from cellulose in that it can have branched chains. Straight-chain starch is called *amylose* and branched-chain starch is called *amylopectin*. After about every 24 to 30 glucose monomers in amylopectin, there is a branch such as the one in **Figure 2.26**. *Glycogen*, a third glucose polymer, is the energy storage unit in animals. Like starch, glycogen has an alpha linkage, so it can also be digested by humans. However, glycogen differs from starch in that it has many more branches. Glycogen branches at about every 8 to 12 glucose units. This extensive branching creates many free ends that allow enzymes to act on the glycogen polymer at many points simultaneously, thus increasing the rate at which glucose can be released from storage.

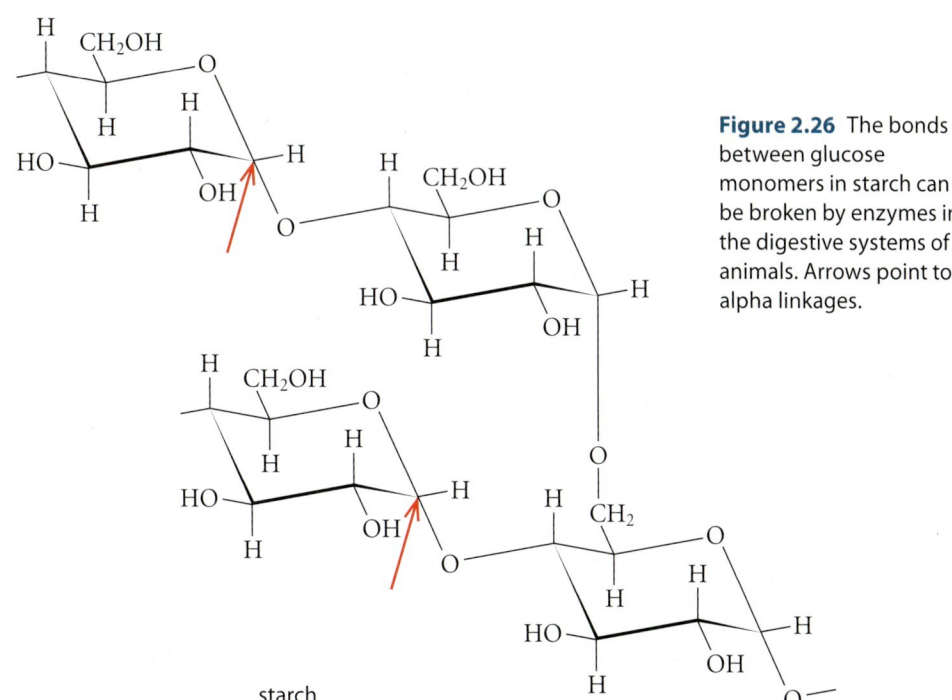

Figure 2.26 The bonds between glucose monomers in starch can be broken by enzymes in the digestive systems of animals. Arrows point to alpha linkages.

Proteins

As described earlier in Section 1, a protein is a natural polymer that is composed of monomers called amino acids. Proteins carry out many important functions in the body, such as speeding up chemical reactions (enzymes), transporting oxygen in the blood (hemoglobin), and regulating body responses (hormones). **Figure 2.27** shows two of the common 20 amino acids. During protein synthesis, a very complex process in living cells, amide linkages form between amino acids to make proteins. The cell's DNA determines the sequence of amino acids in proteins and this sequence determines the structure and function of the protein.

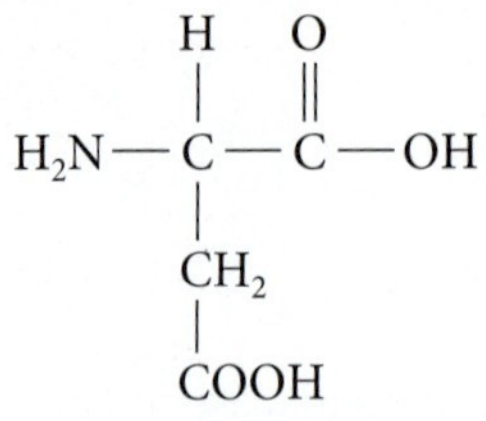

Figure 2.27 There are 20 common amino acids found in proteins, each with a different side group.

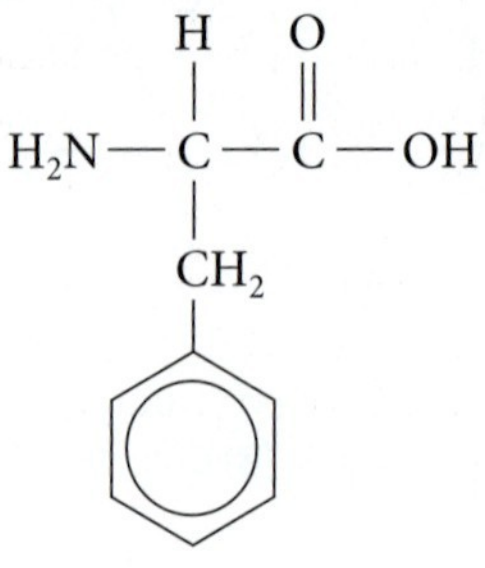

DNA

DNA (short for deoxyribonucleic acid) is a biological molecule found in cell nuclei that codes for the amino acid sequence in all proteins of an organism and ultimately controls cellular development and function. Each strand of DNA is a polymer composed of repeating units called *nucleotides*. As seen in **Figure 2.28**, nucleotides have three parts: a sugar (labelled S), a phosphate group (P), and a cyclic organic molecule containing nitrogen known as a nitrogenous base. Through condensation polymerization, the sugar of one nucleotide is linked to the phosphate group of the next to form a strand of DNA.

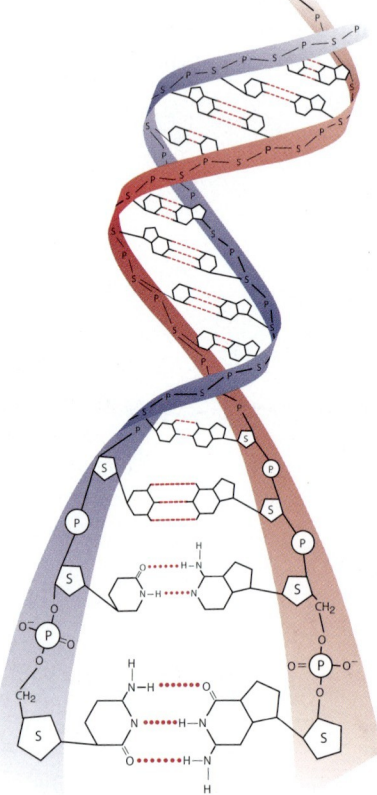

Figure 2.28 Four different bases are found in DNA. The sequence of these bases is the code that determines the sequence of amino acids in proteins. Hydrogen bonds link complementary nitrogenous bases in two strands of DNA to form a double helix.

Section 2.2 Review

Section Summary

- A polymer is a long molecule consisting of repeating units called monomers. Most polymers are formed by addition reactions or condensation reactions.
- Addition polymerization is a reaction in which alkene monomers are joined through multiple addition reactions to form a polymer. Addition reactions are characterized by a reduction in the number of double bonds found in the polymer, as addition reduces a double bond to a single bond.
- In condensation polymerization, a hydrogen atom is removed from one monomer and a hydroxyl group is removed from the next. The hydrogen atom and hydroxyl group form a water molecule and a bond forms between the two monomers.
- The organic compounds that industries use to make polymers and other products start out mainly as petroleum, a fossil fuel that contains a mixture of hydrocarbons, such as alkanes and alkenes.
- Many synthetic polymers, including most plastics, do not degrade in the environment. Reducing use, recycling, and using degradable plastics can help address this issue.
- Cellulose, starch, and glycogen are natural polymers consisting of glucose monomers. Proteins are natural polyamides. DNA is a natural polymer consisting of nucleotide monomers.

Review Questions

1. **K/U** Polymers can be synthetic or natural.
   a. Compare and contrast synthetic and natural polymers.
   b. List three examples of each type of polymer.
   c. Name the monomer for each type of polymer that you listed in part (b).

2. **K/U** What two reaction processes are used to form synthetic polymers?

3. **K/U** Which two functional groups react to form:
   a. a polyester?
   b. a polyamide (nylon)?

4. **C** The use of synthetic polymers has advantages and disadvantages.
   a. Describe three problems caused by society's use of synthetic polymers.
   b. What are some of the benefits we obtain from the use of synthetic polymers?
   c. In your opinion, do the benefits outweigh the risks?

5. **T/I** Draw the monomers for each of the following polymers and identify the polymers as polyamides or polyesters.

   a. $-\text{NH}-\overset{\overset{\text{O}}{\|}}{\text{C}}-(\text{CH}_2)_4-\overset{\overset{\text{O}}{\|}}{\text{C}}-\text{NH}-(\text{CH}_2)_6-\text{NH}---$

   b. $---\text{NH}-\text{CH}_2-\underset{\underset{\text{CH}_3}{|}}{\text{CH}}-\text{NH}-\overset{\overset{\text{O}}{\|}}{\text{C}}-\text{CH}_2-\overset{\overset{\text{O}}{\|}}{\text{C}}-\text{NH}-\text{CH}_2-\underset{\underset{\text{CH}_3}{|}}{\text{CH}}-\text{NH}---$

   c. $---\text{O}-\text{CH}_2-\text{C}_6\text{H}_4-\text{CH}_2-\text{O}-\overset{\overset{\text{O}}{\|}}{\text{C}}-\text{CH}_2-\overset{\overset{\text{O}}{\|}}{\text{C}}-\text{O}---$

6. **T/I** Draw the product of each polymerization reaction and classify the reaction.

   a. $n\text{H}_2\text{C}=\text{CH}_2 \rightarrow$

   b. $n\text{H}_2\text{C}=\text{CH}(\text{C}_6\text{H}_5) \rightarrow$

   c. $n\text{HO}-\overset{\overset{\text{O}}{\|}}{\text{C}}-(\text{CH}_2)_3-\overset{\overset{\text{O}}{\|}}{\text{C}}-\text{OH} + n\text{H}_2\text{N}-\underset{\underset{\text{CH}_3}{|}}{\text{CH}}-\text{NH}_2 \rightarrow$

   d. $n\text{HO}-\text{CH}_2-\text{OH} + n\text{HO}-\overset{\overset{\text{O}}{\|}}{\text{C}}-\text{C}_6\text{H}_4-\overset{\overset{\text{O}}{\|}}{\text{C}}-\text{OH} \rightarrow$

7. **C** Make a concept map to show how the petrochemical industry uses organic reactions to produce important compounds from fossil fuels. Include specific examples of reactions.

Inquiry INVESTIGATION 2-A

Skill Check
- Initiating and Planning
- ✓ Performing and Recording
- ✓ Analyzing and Interpreting
- ✓ Communicating

Safety Precautions

- Wear safety eyewear and a lab coat or apron throughout this activity.
- $KMnO_4(aq)$ will stain your skin or clothing. If you accidentally spill $KMnO_4(aq)$ on your skin, wash immediately with copious amounts of water. Remove the stain with a solution of sodium bisulfite.
- Alcohols are very flammable. Be sure there is no open flame in the laboratory.
- Sodium hydroxide and hydrochloric acid are corrosive to the eyes and skin and harmful if swallowed or inhaled. Wash any spills on your skin or clothing with plenty of cool water. Inform your teacher immediately if you spill hydrochloric acid or sodium hydroxide on yourself or on the lab bench or floor.

Materials
- ethanol
- 1-butanol
- 2-butanol
- 2-methyl-2-propanol
- 3 mol/L $H_2SO_4(aq)$
- 3 mol/L NaOH(aq)
- 0.01 mol/L $KMnO_4(aq)$
- concentrated (12 mol/L) HCl(aq) for demonstration use only
- distilled water
- 10 mL graduated cylinders or graduated medicine droppers
- test tubes
- test-tube rack
- rubber stoppers

Oxidation of Alcohols

There are three different types of alcohols, classified based on the number of carbon atoms attached to the hydroxyl carbon. In a primary alcohol, the carbon atom bonded to the hydroxyl carbon is only bonded to one other carbon atom, such as 1-butanol. In a secondary alcohol, the carbon atom bonded to the hydroxyl carbon is bonded to two other carbon atoms, such as 2-butanol. In tertiary alcohols, the carbon atom bonded to the hydroxyl carbon is bonded to three other carbon atoms, such as 2-methyl-2-butanol. Primary, secondary, and tertiary alcohols with the same number of carbon atoms are also structural isomers of each other but have different physical and chemical properties. In this experiment, you will investigate the reactions of primary, secondary, and tertiary alcohols in order to better understand and make predictions about the properties of alcohols.

Pre-Lab Questions
1. What is the difference among primary, secondary, and tertiary alcohols?
2. What information is listed in the material data safety sheets (MSDS) that would require special safety precaution when alcohols and sulfuric acid are used near potassium permanganate?
3. Describe oxidation reactions, oxidizing agents, and substitution reactions.

Question
What is the difference in reactivity of primary, secondary, and tertiary alcohols?

Procedure

Part 1: The reaction of ethanol with neutral, acidic, and basic solutions of potassium permanganate

1. Construct an observation table with the following headings.

Solution	Observations at 1 min	Observations at 5 min
Neutral solution		
Acidic solution		
Basic solution		

2. Label three medium size test tubes neutral, acidic, and basic. Place 2 mL of $KMnO_4$ in each.
3. Add 4 mL of distilled water to the neutral tube, 4 mL of 3 mol/L H_2SO_4 to the acidic tube, and 4 mL of 3 mol/L NaOH to the basic tube.
4. Add four drops of ethanol to each tube, stopper the tube, shake and note any colour changes. Add another drop or two of ethanol and observe any additional changes which take place after 5 minutes. Also note any differences in the rate of reaction.
5. Do not discard any solutions down the drain. Dispose of solutions as instructed by your teacher.

Part 2: The comparison of three isomeric alcohols reactions with potassium permanganate

6. Construct an observation table with the following headings.

Alcohol	Observations at 1 min	Observations at 5 min
1-butanol		
2-butanol		
2-methyl-2-propanol		

7. Place 2 mL of 0.01mol/L $KMnO_4$ in a test tube.
8. Add 2 mL of 1-butanol and 1 mL of distilled water. Place a stopper in the tube and shake.
9. Observe the colour of the permanganate solution over a five-minute period. Shake occasionally.
10. Repeat this test with the other isomeric alcohols.
11. Do not discard any solutions down the drain. Dispose of solutions as instructed by your teacher.

Part 3: Teacher Demonstration - The comparison of three isomeric alcohols reactions with concentrated HCl

12. Construct an observation table with the following headings.

Alcohol	Observations at 1 min
1-butanol	
2-butanol	
2-methyl-2-propanol	

13. Predict which alcohol(s) will react based on prior observations.
14. Your teacher will place 5 mL of 12 mol/L HCl into each of three test tubes. To the first tube, 1 mL of 1-butanol is added. A stopper is placed in the test tube, the test tube is shaken carefully, and then observed for the presence of cloudiness in the solution. This test is repeated with the other isomeric alcohols.

Analyze and Interpret

1. Identify one of the products of each of the reactions of ethanol in acidic, basic, and neutral solutions of $KMnO_4$ given the following information:
   - a green colour indicates the presence of MnO_4^{2-}
   - a light pink colour indicates Mn^{2+},
   - the brown precipitate is MnO_2

2. What type of reaction is the reaction of ethanol with $KMnO_4$? What is the other product in each of the ethanol reactions?

3. Which alcohols reacted with $KMnO_4$? Identify one of the products of each of the reactions of the isomers of butanol with solutions of $KMnO_4$ using the information in question 1.

4. What type of reaction is the reaction of the isomers of butanol with $KMnO_4$? What is the other product in each of the butanol reactions?

5. Which alcohol(s) reacted with the concentrated HCl (aq)? What type of reaction is this?

Conclude and Communicate

6. In the reactions involving the three isomeric alcohols with the formula C_4H_9OH, describe what each of the following tests showed about reactivity of the -OH group and reactions of 1°, 2°, and 3° alcohols.
   - the test with neutral $KMnO_4$
   - the test with concentrated HCl

7. Predict how the fourth alcohol with the formula $C_4H_{10}O$ would react if tested with:
   - neutral 0.01 $KMnO_4$
   - concentrated HCl at room temperature

Extend Further

8. **RESEARCH** Use your observations of the solutions formed in the previous experiments and your understanding of alcohols to complete a table like the one shown below. Research the melting and boiling points to verify your answers.

9. **INQUIRY** Design an experiment to check your predictions of solubility and litmus colour. Include a materials list, safety precautions, and a detailed procedure.

Properties of Alcohols

Alcohol	Structural Diagram	Melting Point	Boiling Point	Solubility in Mineral Oil	Solubility in Water	Colour with Litmus
Ethanol						
1-butanol						
2-butanol						
2-methyl-2-propanol						

Inquiry INVESTIGATION 2-B

Skill Check

Initiating and Planning
✓ Performing and Recording
✓ Analyzing and Interpreting
✓ Communicating

Safety Precautions

- Organic compounds are very flammable. Be sure that there is no open flame in the laboratory. Use a hot plate, not a Bunsen burner.
- Carry out all procedures in a well-ventilated area. Use a fume hood for all steps involving acids.
- Treat the acids with extreme care. Wear goggles, an apron, and gloves. If you spill any acid on your skin, immediately wash it with plenty of cold water and notify your teacher. If you spill the acids on the lab bench or floor, inform your teacher right away.

Suggested Materials

- ice
- distilled water
- ethanoic acid
- ethanol
- propan-1-ol
- 6 mol/L sulfuric acid
- 250 mL beakers (2)
- 50 mL small beakers (2)
- 100 mL beaker
- 10 mL graduated cylinder
- pipettes (2)
- watch glass
- hot plate
- thermometer (alcohol or digital)
- retort stand
- 2 clamps
- 4 plastic micropipettes
- medicine dropper
- stopper or paper towel

Preparing Esters

Chemists use esterification reactions to create artificial esters. Artificial esters are commonly used in a number of products, including foods, but often are made from reactants that are hazardous. In this investigation, you will synthesize two esters in order to become more familiar with the properties of esters and their impact on the environment. Make careful observations and see if you can recognize the aromas of these esters.

Pre-Lab Questions

1. Review the MSDS sheets for all chemicals you will be using in this investigation and summarize the appropriate safety precautions.
2. Describe the steps you should follow if you accidentally spill some ethanoic acid or propan-1-ol on your skin.

Question

What observable properties do esters have?

Procedure

1. Label two pipettes as shown below. Use the appropriate pipette for each of the two reactions.
   - ethanoic acid + ethanol
   - ethanoic acid + propan-1-ol

2. Prepare your equipment as follows:
   a. Be sure that all the glassware is clean, dry, and free of chips or cracks.
   b. Prepare a hot-water bath. Heat about 125 mL of tap water in a 250 mL beaker on the hot plate to 60°C. Adjust the hot plate so the temperature remains between 50°C and 60°C. Avoid touching the hot plate or beaker.
   c. Prepare a cold-water bath. Place about 125 mL of a mixture of water and ice chips in the second 250 mL beaker. The temperature of the cold-water bath will remain around 0°C.
   d. Place about 5 mL of distilled water in a 50 mL beaker. You will use this in Procedure step 9.
   e. Set up the retort stand beside the hot-water bath. Use one clamp to hold the thermometer in the hot-water bath. You will use the other clamp to steady the micropipettes when you place them in the hot-water bath.
   f. Cut off the bulb of the unlabelled micropipette, halfway along the wide part of the bulb. You will use this bulb as a cap to prevent vapours from escaping during the reactions.

3. **Note**: In this step, do not inhale any alcohol vapour directly. Use the graduated pipette to measure 1.0 mL of ethanol into the 50 mL beaker. As you do so, you may get a whiff of the odour of the alcohol. Record your observations.

4. **Note**: in this step, do not inhale any acid directly. While in a fume hood, use the graduated pipette to add 1.0 mL of ethanoic acid to the ethanol. As you do so, you may get a whiff of the odour of the acid. Record your observations.

130 MHR • Unit 1 Organic Chemistry

5. Your teacher will carefully add four drops of sulfuric acid to the alcohol/acid mixture.

6. Suction the mixture into the appropriately labelled micropipette. Invert the micropipette. Place it, bulb down, in the hot-water bath. (See the diagram below.) Place the cap over the tip of the pipette. Use a clamp to hold the pipette in place.

7. Leave the pipette in the hot water for about 10 min to 15 min. Use the thermometer to monitor the temperature of the hot water. The temperature should stay between 50°C and 60°C.

8. After 10 min to 15 min in the hot-water bath, place the pipette in the cold-water bath. Allow it to cool for about 5 min.

9. Carefully squeeze a few drops of the product onto a watch glass. Mix it with a few drops of distilled water. To smell the odour of the compound, use your hand to waft the aroma toward your nose. Do not inhale. Record your observations of the aroma.

10. Repeat Procedure steps 2 through 8 for the other reaction. **Note:** While the first reaction mixture is being heated, you may want to prepare the other mixtures and put them in the hot-water bath. Working carefully, you should be able to stabilize more than one micropipette with the clamp. If you choose to do this, make sure that your materials are clearly labelled. Also, remember to keep a record of the time at which each micropipette is placed in the hot-water bath.

11. Dispose of all materials as your teacher directs. Clean all glassware and wash your hands thoroughly with soap and water.

Analyze and Interpret

1. How do you know that a new product was formed in each reaction? Explain.

2. Describe the odour of the ester produced in each reaction and compare this to the initial odour of the reactants.

3. Explain why the synthesized ester does not always match the odour of the fragrance found in nature.

Conclude and Communicate

4. Describe the physical properties of each product that was formed.

5. What were the possible sources of error that occurred if a strong odour was not observed in each of your reactions? How could you improve your procedure to result in a better product?

6. Review the safety precautions necessary for this investigation and conclude whether the manufacture of esters is safe for the environment.

Extend Further

7. **RESEARCH** Should all hospitals and schools implement a scent-free policy? In order to answer this question, research the beneficial and negative effects that fragrances have on the environment. Consider the reactants used in the manufacture of fragrances and how the use of fragrances affects people's health. Find at least ONE current article (within the past 1-2 years) related to this issue. Draw conclusions about the impact of fragrances on the environment and the implementation of scent-free policies. Use a creative presentation to share this with the class.

8. **INQUIRY** Research the organic compounds that are responsible for the smell and taste of oranges, pears, oil of wintergreen, cherry, and apples. Find and record the chemical structure of each compound. What reactants are used to make these compounds? Design a procedure to produce one of these compounds. Make sure that you have included all safety precautions, materials, and a detailed listing of all the steps that you will follow.

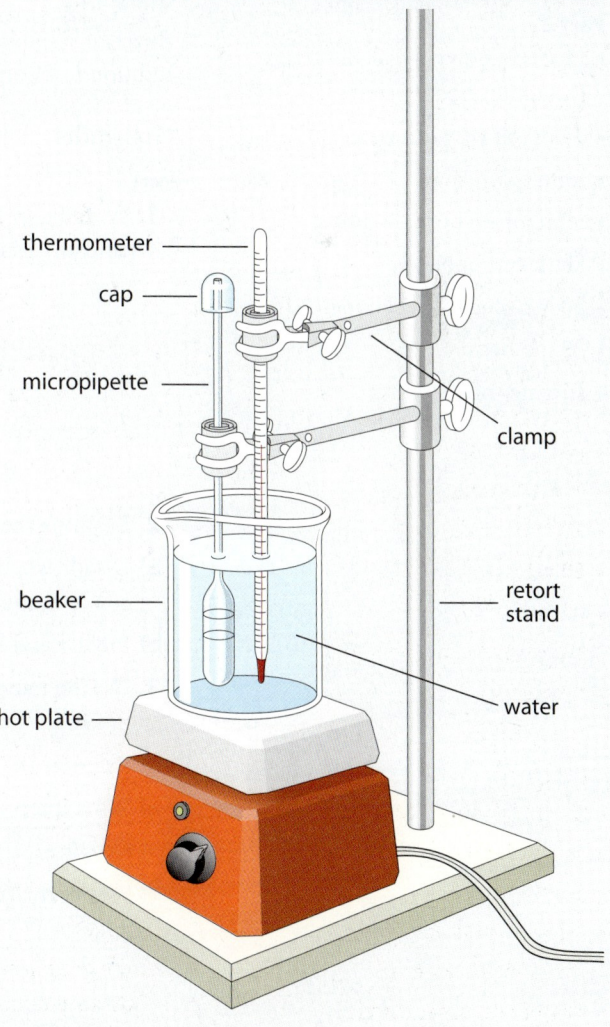

Inquiry INVESTIGATION 2-C

Skill Check
- Initiating and Planning
- ✓ Performing and Recording
- ✓ Analyzing and Interpreting
- ✓ Communicating

Safety Precautions

- Wear an apron, safety glasses, and gloves while completing Part 2 of this investigation.
- Wash your hands thoroughly after this investigation.

Materials

Part 1
- molecular model kit (1 per group)

Part 2
- pieces of polyvinyl alcohol bags (totalling about 20 cm^2)
- 10 mL of very hot water
- food colouring
- 5 mL of 4% borax solution
- kettle or hot plate
- 10 mL graduated cylinder
- 50 mL beaker
- stirring rod

Modelling and Making Polymers

Polyvinyl alcohol (PVA) is used to make a special type of plastic bag. In the first part of this investigation, you will build a structural model of a short strand of PVA. In the second part of this investigation, you will use PVA to make a different polymer product, "Slime." You will prepare "Slime" by *cross-linking* long strands of polyvinyl alcohol using borax, sodium tetraborate decahydrate, $Na_2B_4O_7 \cdot 10H_2O(aq)$. Recall that cross-linking means that bonds form from one strand to another at several points along the polymer strand.

Pre-Lab Questions

1. What can you learn about the properties of PVA from building a model of it?
2. What polymerization reaction appears to be responsible for the formation of PVA?
3. How are the polymers PVA and "Slime" similar? How are they different?

Questions

How can you use a model of PVA to predict whether PVA forms from an addition reaction or a condensation reaction?

Procedure

Part 1

1. Working in a group of four, use your molecular model kits to build four ethenol monomers, as illustrated below.

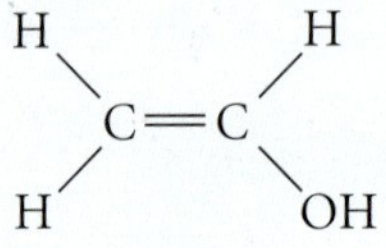

$$\begin{array}{c} H \quad\quad\quad H \\ \diagdown \quad\quad \diagup \\ C = C \\ \diagup \quad\quad \diagdown \\ H \quad\quad\quad OH \end{array}$$

ethenol
(vinyl alcohol)

2. Examine the models you have built.

   a) Decide whether they will react in an addition polymerization or a condensation polymerization reaction to form polyvinyl alcohol.

   b) Predict and draw the structure of PVA.

3. Use the four monomers to build a short strand of PVA with four repeating units.

4. Examine the polymer model.

   a) What intermolecular force(s) might operate between two strands of this polymer?

   b) Use your knowledge of the force(s) to predict whether this polymer would dissolve in water or not.

Part 2

1. Work with a partner. Before starting, examine the pieces of the polyvinyl alcohol bag. Record your observations.
2. Place 10 mL of near-boiling water into a 50 mL beaker. Be careful to avoid burning yourself.
3. Add the pieces of the polyvinyl alcohol bag to the hot water. Stir and poke the mixture using a stirring rod until the compound has dissolved.
4. Add a few drops of food colouring to the mixture, and stir again.
5. Add 5 mL of the borax solution and stir.
6. When it has cooled so it can be comfortably handled, examine the "Slime" you have produced. Record your observations.
7. While wearing eye protection and gloves manipulate the "Slime" sample. For example, roll it into a ball and drop it on the lab bench. Slowly pull it apart between your hands. Pull it apart quickly. Let the ball of "Slime" sit on the bench while you clean up. Record your observations.

Analyze and Interpret

1. Does PVA appear to be formed by an addition reaction or a condensation reaction? Give reasons to support your answer.
2. Explain why PVA dissolves in water, even though it is a very large molecule.
3. What happened when you manipulated the "Slime" in various ways? Suggest an explanation for what you observed.

Conclude and Communicate

4. How do you think a bag made of polyvinyl alcohol might be useful in the following settings?
   a. in a hospital
   b. as an adhesive
   c. in the cosmetics industry
5. How could you tell that changes to the polymer occurred when you added the borax solution to the dissolved solution of polyvinyl alcohol? Explain your observations.
6. Compare the properties of the polyvinyl alcohol polymer and the "Slime" cross-linked polymer you observed in this investigation. Were there any similarities? How were they different?

Extend Further

7. **INQUIRY** Construct a four-monomer strand of a condensation polymer of your choice. Next, take the model apart and use it to build four monomers. What additional atoms are required from the model kit to build the monomers? What does this tell you about a condensation reaction?
8. **RESEARCH** Although polyvinyl alcohol appears to form by a simple polymerization reaction of vinyl alcohol monomers, it does not. Vinyl alcohol is unstable and rearranges to form ethanal. Draw the structure of ethanal. Do library or electronic research to find out how polyvinyl alcohol is synthesized.

STSE
Case Study

Organic Compounds in Everyday Life
Assessing the Risk of Bisphenol A

Scenario

During Environment Week activities at your school, students have been challenged to develop a personal environmental action plan related to an issue that affects them in everyday life. You have been studying organic compounds in chemistry class, including compounds known or suspected to be harmful to human health and the environment. For example, bisphenol A (BPA) is the subject of continuing scientific and public policy debate about its potential risks. You decide to investigate some issues related to BPA and to create a personal action plan based on your research and analysis.

The BPA Debate

BPA, 2,2-bis(4-hydroxyphenyl) propane, is used to make epoxy resins and a hard plastic known as polycarbonate. Human exposure to BPA occurs mainly through food packaging and containers such as hard plastic bottles. BPA is also found in the protective lining of aluminum and other metal-based cans in which food and beverages are sold.

Numerous scientific assessments have indicated that human exposure to BPA has several possible effects. In animal studies, BPA has been linked to changes in reproductive systems (both male and female), in immune systems, and in body tissue associated with breast cancer. This compound can mimic estrogen in the body and it can act as an endocrine disruptor. Many functions in the human body are regulated by how molecular receptors attached to cells respond when they bind with signaling molecules such as peptides and hormones. In females, the hormone estradiol and other estrogen compounds are essential for sexual development and reproduction. BPA that mimics estrogen can interfere with these processes. Dr. Joe Schwarcz, a chemistry professor at McGill University in Montreal, has hypothesized that low exposure to BPA may be more problematic than high exposure. His hypothesis is based on a proposition that less "crowding" of BPA in the body may make it easier for individual molecules of the compound to attach to cell receptors.

Many environmental groups have called for a ban on BPA in food containers to minimize human exposure. In 2008, acting on its own assessment of potential at-risk groups such as infants and young children, Health Canada banned the importation, sale, and advertising of polycarbonate baby bottles containing BPA. Canada was the first jurisdiction to do so. Since then, the European Union has taken similar action, as have several states in the United States.

Canada's federal government has concluded that current dietary exposure to BPA through food packaging is not expected to pose a health risk to the general population. However, in 2010, the government declared BPA to be a toxic substance under the *Canadian Environmental Protection Act, 1999*. (See the news article on the following page.) This designation makes it easier to manage BPA-related issues as they arise, allowing the government to ban the compound in specific products through regulation rather than legislation. Health Canada states that it will continue to conduct and participate in studies to better understand the risks associated with BPA.

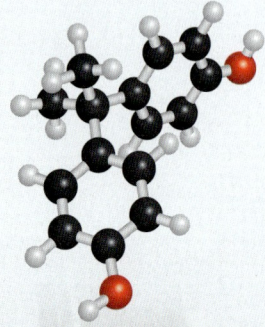

bisphenol A

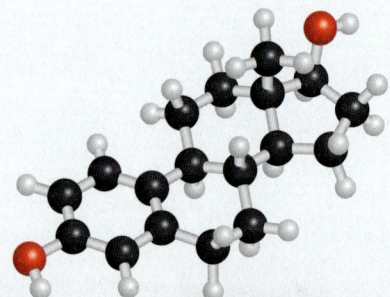

estradiol (estrogen)

Canada Declares BPA Toxic, sets stage for more bans

Thu, Oct 14 2010

By Louise Egan

OTTAWA (Reuters) - Canada has declared bisphenol A a toxic chemical, prompting calls for far-reaching curbs on the industrial chemical that is used in everything from the linings of aluminum cans to coatings on electronic till receipts.

Canada added the compound, known as BPA, to a list of substances deemed potentially harmful to health or the environment in a notice published in the Canada Gazette on Wednesday.

That makes it easier for Ottawa to regulate the use of the chemical, perhaps by limiting how much BPA can be released into air or water or perhaps with outright bans on its use in specific food containers.

"The risk assessment of BPA put together by our federal government is very strong in terms of its conclusions, so I think it's a foregone conclusion that it will drive further action rather quickly," said Rick Smith, executive director of Environmental Defense, which campaigned to ban BPA.

BPA is mass produced and has been used for decades to harden plastics. It is widely used to line food and beverage containers, and a recent government report said it was present in the bodies of 91 percent of Canadians.

"We are literally marinating in it on a minute-by-minute basis," said Smith.

The primary health concerns center on BPA's potential effects as an endocrine disruptor, which can mimic or interfere with the body's natural hormones and potentially damage development, especially of young children.

"Our science indicated that Bisphenol A may be harmful to both human health and the environment and we were the first country to take bold action in the interest of Canadians," Health Minister Leona Aglukkaq said in a statement.

CANADA LEADING CRACKDOWN

Smith said Canada has been a world leader in its crackdown on BPA. It promised the first steps to control use of the chemical in 2008, and in March this year banned plastic baby bottles that contain BPA. A next step could curb BPA use in the lining of baby formula tins, he added.

Canada could also limit BPA emissions by factories into the environment and work with industry to reduce exposure through the lining of canned goods.

But industry groups point to other research which has been inconclusive on the toxicity to humans, leading regulators in other countries to be more lenient on manufacturers.

The American Chemistry Council (AAC), an industry group, said the move to declare BPA toxic contradicted research by Canada's own health department and it said studies show BPA does not accumulate in the body.

It's not clear what substitute manufacturers could use to replace BPA.

(Editing by Janet Guttsman)

© Thomson Reuters 2011. All rights reserved.

Research and Analyze

1. Conduct research and prepare a summary of the current debate about the potential risks posed by BPA to human health and the environment. Examine the issue from multiple perspectives, for example, government regulators, manufacturers, food processing companies, consumers, and advocacy groups.

2. Make a list of items that you use or buy regularly that contain BPA or have BPA in the packaging. Think of possible substitutes, such as glass, ceramics, stainless steel, or polyethylene terephthalate (PET) and other plastics that do not contain BPA. Evaluate the potential health and environmental impacts of the items in your list, as well as the strengths and weaknesses of the various alternatives.

3. Construct a table to organize the results of your research. This table can help you assess whether you should limit your exposure to BPA based on your review of the debate about risk as well as on your analysis of substitute materials.

Take Action

1. **PLAN** Prepare a synopsis of each item you identified above and its possible alternatives. In each case, specify which item or its substitute is preferable in terms of BPA exposure and overall environmental impact. Justify each choice and use your choices to create a personal plan for buying and using products and packaging in your daily life.

2. **ACT** Prepare a presentation to your class about your research into BPA. Describe the current debate about the health and environmental risks of BPA. Then, describe your personal action plan and explain how you developed it based on your research and analysis.

Chapter 2 SUMMARY

Section 2.1 Types of Organic Reactions

Chemists commonly use reactions such as addition, elimination, and substitution to convert organic compounds derived from petrochemicals to other useful compounds.

Key Terms
- addition reaction
- combustion reaction
- complete combustion reaction
- condensation reaction
- elimination reaction
- esterification reaction
- hydrolysis reaction
- incomplete combustion reaction
- oxidation
- reduction
- substitution reaction

Key Concepts
- An addition reaction is one in which atoms from a small molecule react with a double or triple bond in an organic molecule and become part of the molecule.
- An elimination reaction is one in which atoms or groups of atoms are removed from an organic molecule and a double bond is formed in the molecule.
- In a substitution reaction, an atom or small group replaces another atom or small group on the organic molecule.
- In a condensation reaction, two large molecules combine to form one larger molecule and a very small molecule, usually water.
- An esterification reaction is a special type of condensation reaction in which a carboxylic acid reacts with an alcohol to form an ester and water.
- A hydrolysis reaction is the reverse of a condensation reaction. The compounds that are formed by condensation reactions can be broken down by hydrolysis reactions.
- Oxidation is defined as a reaction in which a carbon atom forms more bonds to oxygen, O, or fewer bonds to hydrogen, H. Reduction is defined as a reaction in which a carbon atom forms fewer bonds to oxygen, O, or more bonds to hydrogen, H.
- A combustion reaction is a type of reaction in which a compound reacts with oxygen to produce the oxides of elements that make up the compound.

Section 2.2 Polymer Reactions

Polymers, long molecules consisting of repeating monomers, can be synthetic, such as plastics, or natural, such as polysaccharides, proteins, and DNA.

Key Terms
- addition polymerization
- condensation polymerization
- monomer
- petrochemicals
- plastics
- polymer

Key Concepts
- A polymer is a long molecule consisting of repeating units called monomers. Most polymers are formed by addition reactions or condensation reactions.
- Addition polymerization is a reaction in which alkene monomers are joined through multiple addition reactions to form a polymer. Addition reactions are characterized by a reduction in the number of double bonds found in the polymer, as addition reduces a double bond to a single bond.
- In condensation polymerization, a hydrogen atom is removed from one monomer and a hydroxyl group is removed from the next. The hydrogen atom and hydroxyl group form a water molecule and a bond forms between the two monomers.
- The organic compounds that industries use to make polymers and other products start out mainly as petroleum, a fossil fuel that contains a mixture of hydrocarbons, such as alkanes and alkenes.
- Many synthetic polymers, including most plastics, do not degrade in the environment. Reducing use, recycling, and using degradable plastics can help address this issue.
- Cellulose, starch, and glycogen are natural polymers consisting of glucose monomers. Proteins are natural polyamides. DNA is a natural polymer consisting of nucleotide monomers.

Chapter 2 REVIEW

Knowledge and Understanding

Select the letter of the best answer below.

1. Which is *not* a small molecule often used in addition reactions?
   a. H-X
   b. H-H
   c. H-S
   d. X-X
   e. H$_2$O

2. In which type of reaction is an alcohol converted to an alkene and water when heated in the presence of a strong acid?
   a. oxidation
   b. hydrolysis
   c. polymerization
   d. elimination
   e. reduction

3. Which is a characteristic feature of a substitution reaction?
   a. Carbon atoms are bonded to the same number of atoms in the product as in the reactant.
   b. Carbon atoms are bonded to a smaller number of atoms in the product than in the reactant.
   c. Carbon atoms are bonded to a larger number of atoms in the product than in the reactant.
   d. Two compounds react to form one compound.
   e. There are fewer carbon-carbon bonds in the products than in the reactants.

4. Which two reactants could undergo a condensation reaction to produce an amide and water?
   a. an alcohol and an amine
   b. a carboxylic acid and an amide
   c. an acid and an amine
   d. a carboxylic acid and an amine
   e. an alcohol and an amide

5. Which are the two reactants in an esterification reaction?
   a. an alcohol and an amine
   b. a carboxylic acid and an amide
   c. an acid and an amine
   d. a carboxylic acid and an alcohol
   e. an alcohol and an amide

6. How could a chemist influence a condensation/hydrolysis reaction so that it favours hydrolysis?
   a. Increase the concentration of the reactants of hydrolysis (ester and water).
   b. Increase the concentration of the reactants of condensation (carboxylic acid and alcohol).
   c. Decrease the concentration of the reactants of hydrolysis (ester and water).
   d. Add more sulfuric acid.
   e. The reaction cannot be influenced so that it favours hydrolysis.

7. In an oxidation reaction
   a. a carbon will form fewer bonds to carbon.
   b. a carbon will form fewer bonds with oxygen or more bonds to hydrogen.
   c. a carbon will form more bonds with oxygen or fewer to hydrogen.
   d. two small molecules combine to form a large molecule.
   e. two large molecules react to form a large molecule and a small molecule.

8. In a reduction reaction
   a. a carbon will form fewer bonds to carbon.
   b. a carbon will form fewer bonds with oxygen or more bonds to hydrogen.
   c. a carbon will form more bonds with oxygen or fewer to hydrogen.
   d. two small molecules combine to form a large molecule.
   e. two large molecules react to form a large molecule and a small molecule.

9. Polymers can be made through which types of reactions?
   a. elimination and oxidation
   b. condensation and addition
   c. substitution and addition
   d. addition and reduction
   e. hydrolysis and elimination

10. Which statement explains why polyacrylamide is unique?
    a. It contains halogens.
    b. It contains cross links between polymer chains.
    c. It is made using an addition reaction.
    d. It contains C=O bonds.
    e. It is used in sewage and waste treatment.

11. In order for condensation polymerization to occur
    a. each monomer must have two functional groups.
    b. each monomer must have more than two functional groups.
    c. each monomer must have only one functional group.
    d. one monomer must have an alcohol and an amide as functional groups while the other monomer has no functional groups
    e. two different monomers must both have alcohol functional groups.

Chapter 2 REVIEW

12. A product derived from petroleum, such as ethane and propene, that is converted into plastics and other synthetic materials is known as
  a. cracking.
  b. a natural polymer.
  c. gasoline.
  d. a petrochemical.
  e. a monomer.

13. Why can the manufacturing and disposal of PVC be a problem?
  a. It releases PVC.
  b. It releases greenhouse gases.
  c. It releases ethane.
  d. It releases carbon monoxide.
  e. It releases dioxins.

14. Which is a monomer of natural polymers?
  a. cellulose
  b. DNA
  c. amino acid
  d. protein
  e. lipid

Answer the questions below.

15. Write the general reaction equation for each type of reaction and explain one way to identify each type of reaction.
  a. addition (give one example only)
  b. elimination
  c. substitution
  d. condensation
  e. esterification
  f. oxidation
  g. reduction
  h. combustion

16. Compare and contrast addition and elimination reactions.

17. During some reactions, more than one possible product may be obtained. One is the major and one is the minor product. How do you decide which will be the major product?

18. Why are substitution reactions of alkanes not very practical?

19. What are the similarities and differences between condensation and esterification reactions?

20. Explain what happens during a hydrolysis reaction.

21. Why does *polypropylene* end with –ene if it does not contain any double bonds?

22. Why are some natural molecules such as proteins and starches classified as polymers?

23. Identify the following reactions as addition, substitution, or elimination.
  a. $CH_3CH_2CH_2Br + NH_3 \rightarrow CH_3CH_2CH_2NH_2 + HBr$
  b. $CH_3CH_2OH \xrightarrow{H_2SO_4} CH_2=CH_2 + H_2O$
  c. $CH_2=CHCH_3 + H_2 \xrightarrow{Pt\ or\ Pd} CH_3\text{-}CH_2\text{-}CH_3$
  d. $CH_3CH_2CH_2CH_3 + Br_2 \xrightarrow{UV\ light} CH_3CH_2CH_2CH_2-Br + HBr$
  e. $H-C\equiv C-H + Br_2 \text{ (excess)} \rightarrow H-CBr_2-CBr_2-H$
  f. 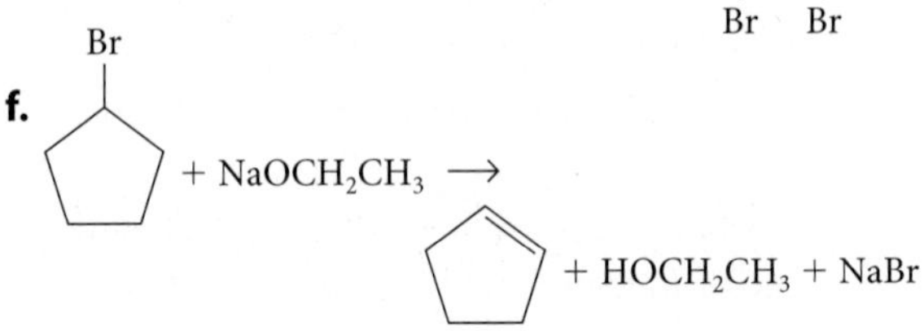 bromocyclopentane + $NaOCH_2CH_3 \rightarrow$ cyclopentene + $HOCH_2CH_3$ + NaBr

24. Identify the following reactions as oxidation or reduction. (Oxidizing and reducing agents are not shown.)
  a. 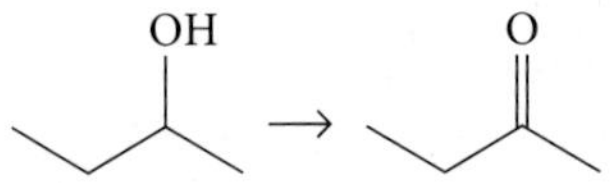 2-propanol → propanone (acetone)
  b. 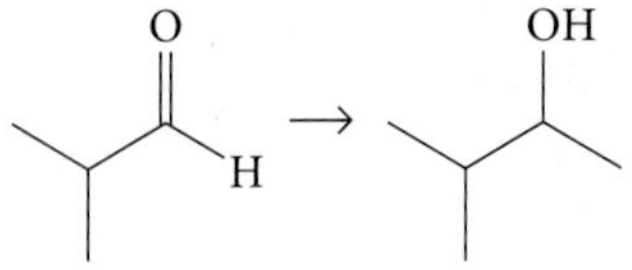 2-methylpropanal → 2-methyl-2-propanol (alcohol)
  c. 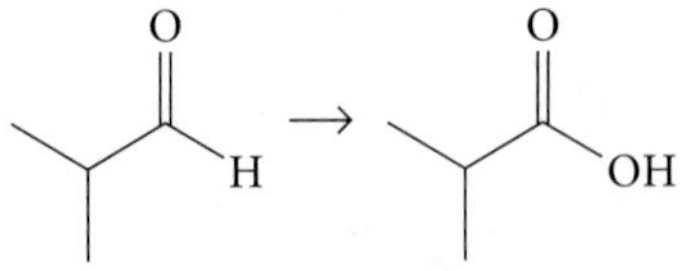 2-methylpropanal → 2-methylpropanoic acid

25. Identify the following reactions as esterification, condensation, or hydrolysis reactions.
  a. $CH_3CH_2CH_2-OH + CH_3-C(=O)-OH \xrightarrow{H_2SO_4} CH_3-C(=O)-O-CH_2CH_2CH_3 + H_2O$
  b. $CH_3CH_2CH_2-NH_2 + CH_3-C(=O)-OH \xrightarrow{H_2SO_4} CH_3-C(=O)-NH-CH_2CH_2CH_3 + H_2O$
  c. $CH_3-C(=O)-O-CH_3 + H_2O \rightarrow CH_3-OH + CH_3-C(=O)-OH$

26. A monomer called vinylacetate is polymerized in an addition reaction to make bouncing putty. What is the name of this polymer?

27. Use a Venn diagram to compare and contrast polyesters and polyamides.

28. Identify the following polymers as addition polymers or condensation polymers.

   a. —CH$_2$—CH$_2$—CH$_2$—CH$_2$—

   b. ---O—C(=O)—CH$_2$—C(=O)—O—CH$_2$CH$_2$—O—C(=O)—CH$_2$—C(=O)—O---

   c.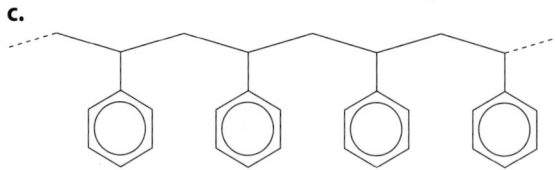

Thinking and Investigation

29. Identify the type of reaction that would accomplish each of the following changes. Justify your reasoning.
   a. alkyl halide → alkene
   b. alkene → alcohol
   c. alkane → carbon dioxide
   d. alcohol → alkyl halide

30. Determine the product for the following addition and elimination reactions. If applicable, identify which product will be the major product.

   a. CH$_3$—CH=CH—CH$_3$ + H$_2$O →

   b. CH$_3$—CH=C(CH$_3$)—CH$_3$ + HBr →

   c. CH$_3$CH$_2$CH$_2$—OH $\xrightarrow{H_2SO_4}$

   d. CH$_3$—CH(Br)—CH(CH$_3$)—CH$_2$—CH$_3$ + NaOCH$_2$CH$_3$ →

31. Identify the products of the following substitution and condensation reactions.

   a. CH$_3$CH$_2$CH$_2$—Br + OH$^-$ →

   b. CH$_3$—CH$_2$—C(=O)—OH + NH$_2$—CH$_2$CH$_3$ $\xrightarrow{H_2SO_4}$

32. Draw the products for the following polymerization equations.

   a. (proline) + (glycine, H$_2$N—CH$_2$—COOH) →

   b. $nF_2C=CF_2 \rightarrow$

   c. HO—C(=O)—C$_6$H$_4$—C(=O)—OH + H$_2$N—CH$_2$—CH$_2$—NH$_2$ →

33. Draw the monomers for each of the following polymers.

   a. ---C(=O)—CH$_2$—CH(CH$_3$)—O—C(=O)—CH$_2$—CH(CH$_3$)—O---

   b. ---CH$_2$—CH(CH$_2$CH$_3$)—CH$_2$—CH(CH$_2$CH$_3$)---

   c. ---NH—CH$_2$—CH(CH$_3$)—NH—C(=O)—CH$_2$—C(=O)---

34. Is a protein an example of a polyester or a polyamide? Justify your reasoning.

35. Write equations for the complete combustion of the following organic compounds.
   a. C$_2$H$_6$
   b. C$_2$H$_5$OH

36. Bromine water (Br$_2$(aq)) can be used to test for double bonds.
   a. Design a procedure using bromine water to test fats and oils for the presence of double bonds.
   b. Look up the WHMIS guidelines for bromine. What safety precautions will you include in your procedure?
   c. When bromine water is added to but-2-ene, the colour of the bromine solution changes. What type of reaction has occurred?
   d. Draw the structure for the product of the reaction in part (c).

37. How can alkenes be formed though an elimination reaction?

Chapter 2 REVIEW

38. Determine the missing components for the following reactions.

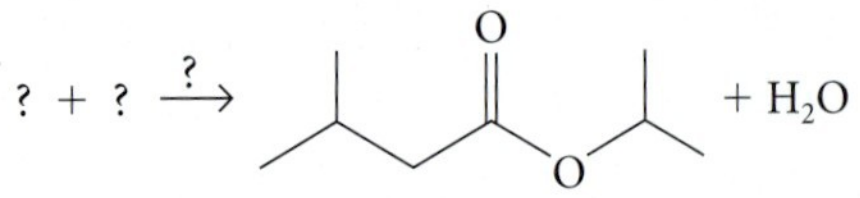

a.
$$? + ? \rightarrow \begin{array}{c} CH_3-CH_2 \quad\quad CH_3 \\ H-C-C-Cl \\ H \quad\quad CH_2-CH_3 \end{array}$$

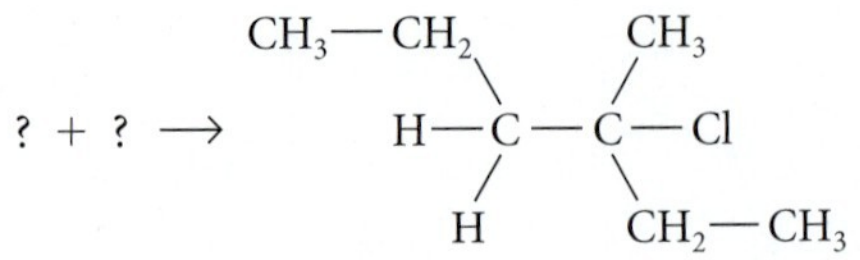

b.
$$? + ? \xrightarrow{?} \begin{array}{c} O \\ \parallel \\ \text{(isopropyl butanoate structure)} \end{array} + H_2O$$

c.
$$? + ? \rightarrow CH_3-\underset{\underset{CH_3}{|}}{\overset{\overset{CH_3}{|}}{C}}-Cl + HOH$$

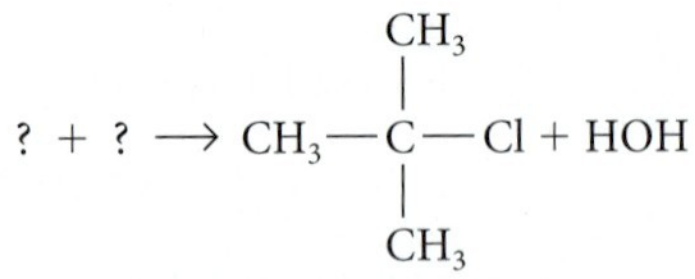

d.
$$? + Br_2 \text{ (excess)} \rightarrow CH_3-\underset{\underset{CH_3}{|}}{\overset{\overset{Br}{|}}{C}}-\overset{\overset{Br}{|}}{CH}-\overset{\overset{Br}{|}}{CH}-\underset{\underset{CH_3}{|}}{\overset{\overset{Br}{|}}{C}}-CH_3$$

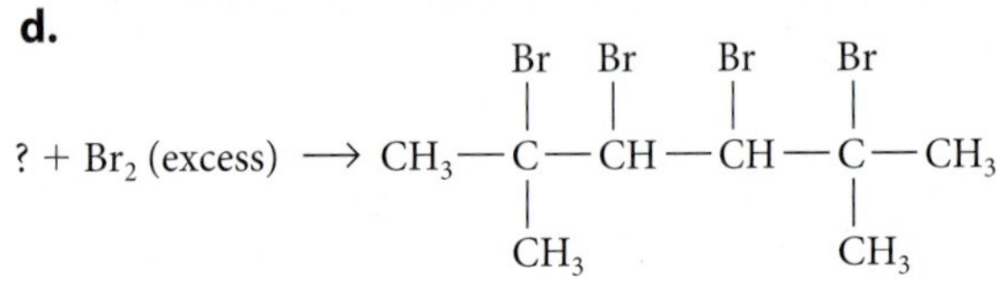

e.
$$? + ? \xrightarrow{UV\ light} H_3C-Cl + H_2-C-Cl + \underset{\underset{Cl}{|}}{\overset{\overset{Cl}{|}}{H-C}}-Cl + \underset{\underset{Cl}{|}}{\overset{\overset{Cl}{|}}{Cl-C}}-Cl + 10\ HCl$$

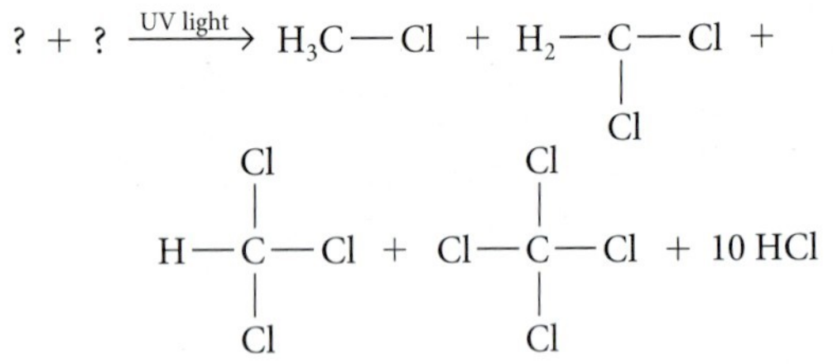

f. $? + [O] \rightarrow ? + [O] \rightarrow$ (2-methylpropanoic acid structure with OH)

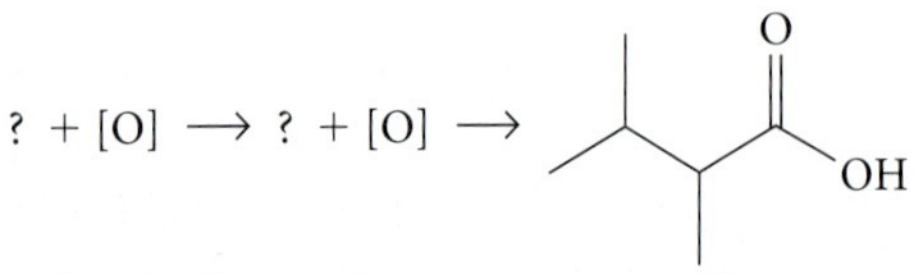

39. Design a short procedure to carry out the polymerization of but-2-ene. Your procedure should include:
- structural diagrams for the monomer and the expected polymer product,
- an appropriate solvent in which but-2-ene dissolves and in which the reaction will be carried out,
- the addition of a catalyst and heat to start the polymerization, and
- safety precautions for dealing with all the compounds used, including the solvent and product (use WHMIS information).

40. For the following reaction, determine all the products. Name the products and identify the major product.

$$H_2C=CH-CH_3 + HBr \rightarrow$$

41. Justify whether the statement below is true or false. The following reaction is a substitution reaction.

$$H_3C-CH_2-CH_3 + Br_2 \xrightarrow{UV\ light} H_3C-CH_2-CH_2-Br$$

42. Maltose is a common sugar formed by a condensation reaction of two glucose molecules. Write the chemical equation for this reaction.

43. Determine the carboxylic acid and alcohol that form the following esters.
   a. ethyl 2-phenylethanoate (fragrance of honey)
   b. ethyl butanoate (fragrance of pineapple)
   c. ethyl ethanoate (nail polish remover)

44. The following reaction is reversible. The reaction was left uncovered and the methanol began to evaporate. Predict what happened to the reaction.

$$CH_3CH_2COOH + CH_3OH \xrightarrow{H_2SO_4} CH_3CH_2COOCH_3 + H_2O$$

Communication

45. Bioplastics are polymers that break down over time when exposed to environmental conditions, such as light and bacteria. Write a short essay to answer the following questions.
   a. How could the use of bioplastics help our environment?
   b. Why might it be difficult to enforce the use of bioplastics around the world?

46. Use structural formulas and equations to help explain why addition of hydrogen bromide to hex-1-ene yields two different products but the addition of hydrogen bromide to hex-3-ene yields only one product.

47. Why can some reactions be classified as more than one type? Use an example to clarify your explanation.

48. Use a concept map to summarize all the reactions in this chapter, include a general example of each type of reaction in the concept map.

49. **BIG IDEAS** Organic compounds have predictable chemical and physical properties determined by their respective structures.
   a. Identify the properties of plastics that you have learned about in this chapter and observed in your life which make them so useful in our society.
   b. How are these properties related to their chemical composition and structure?

50. Use a spider map to show how DNA and proteins are related.

51. Explain why when a watch glass is slowly swept over a lit candle a black residue is left on the watch glass.

52. Use a flowchart to describe the development and manufacture of PET from the natural compounds from which it is formed.

53. Many grocery stores in Canada now charge five cents for each plastic bag used to carry items from the store. Many stores are trying to promote the use of reusable bags. Research why people are trying to reduce the number of plastic bags going into landfill sites. Use the following questions to help guide your research. Write an essay to summarize the results of your research.
   a. How long does it take for a plastic bag to degrade in a landfill?
   b. Are recycling programs offered for these plastic bags? Why or why not?
   c. What are the advantages to using reusable bags?
   d. Identify any disadvantages to using reusable bags.

54. Reducing our consumption of polymer products and re-using polymer products help to minimize polymer waste. Compile a list of suggestions for your school or community on ways to reduce and re-use polymer products.

55. Summarize your learning in this chapter using a graphic organizer. To help you, the Chapter 2 Summary lists the Key Terms and Key Concepts. Refer to Using Graphic Organizers in Appendix A to help you decide which graphic organizer to use.

Application

56. **BIG IDEAS** Organic chemical reactions and their applications have significant implications for society, human health, and the environment. BPA is commonly used to make plastics due to its high durability. In 2008 BPA became illegal to be used in the manufacturing of baby bottles. Research BPA and the polymerization reactions it is involved in to make plastics. Determine the benefits and consequences to using BPA.

57. Propose a synthesis for methyl octanoate from bromomethane and octan-1-ol and any other substances you may need.

58. By looking at the structure of Kevlar®, propose an explanation for its strength.

59. Propose a synthesis of the following polymer starting with bromoethane and propan-2-one.

60. Over 9 billion kilograms of plastic ends up in the ocean each year. Suspended on the top of the water, the plastic photodegrades into smaller and smaller particles.
   a. Identify the effects this could this have on aquatic organisms.
   b. List three things you can do as an individual to help reduce the amount of plastic waste going into our oceans.

61. Propose a synthesis for the product on the right, using carbonic acid and 2-methylprop-1-ene-1,3-diol as two of the reactants.

62. Suppose you are working in a lab and suddenly run out of carboxylic acid, which is necessary for the experiment you are performing. What could you look for in the lab to synthesize some replacement carboxylic acid?

63. Proteins are polymers formed from amino acids with two carbons plus a side chain. Show the reaction of three different amino acid monomers forming into a trimer. Research the amino acids and choose three.

64. Write the reaction for the formation of poly-6-hydroxyoctanoic acid starting from

65. Paper clips can be used to represent the repeating monomers in the chain structure of a polymer. Describe a way to represent the repeating units of a polymer that is formed from the combination of different monomers. Give one example of this type of polymer, and identify the two monomers it contains.

66. Gasoline, or octane, is used to run most motorized vehicles. It burns with oxygen to form carbon dioxide gas and water.
   a. Draw the complete structural diagram for octane.
   b. Write the balanced chemical equation for this reaction.
   c. Explain the environmental effects of this reaction.

Chapter 2 SELF-ASSESSMENT

Select the letter of the best answer below.

1. **K/U** Which reaction would be performed to convert an alkyne to alcohol?
   a. substitution
   b. elimination
   c. esterification
   d. addition
   e. hydrolysis

2. **K/U** Which reaction is used in industry to convert alkanes to alkenes?
   a. esterification
   b. polymerization
   c. cracking
   d. breaking
   e. elimination

3. **K/U** Which pair of reactions are the reverse of one another?
   a. addition and substitution
   b. hydrolysis and condensation
   c. elimination and substitution
   d. esterification and condensation
   e. oxidation and addition

4. **K/U** Identify the name of the major product for an addition reaction with the following reactants.

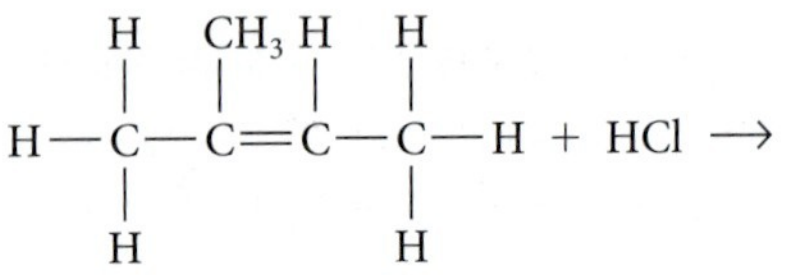

   $$H_3C-CH(CH_3)-CH=CH-CH_3 + HCl \rightarrow$$

   (structure shown: $H-\underset{H}{\overset{H}{C}}-\underset{H}{\overset{CH_3}{C}}=\underset{}{\overset{H}{C}}-\underset{H}{\overset{H}{C}}-H + HCl \rightarrow$)

   a. 2-methylbut-2-ene
   b. 2-chloro-3-methylbutane
   c. 3-chloro-2-methylbutane
   d. 2-chloro-2-methylbutane
   e. 2-chloro-3-methylbutene

5. **K/U** Which statement about oxidation reactions is *true*?
   a. Oxidation reactions can change an aldehyde to a carboxylic acid.
   b. Oxidation reactions can change a ketone to an alcohol.
   c. Oxidation reactions can change an alkene to an alkane.
   d. Oxidation reactions can change an alkyne to an alkene.
   e. Oxidation reactions can change an aldehyde to an alcohol.

6. **K/U** Which reaction would be used to convert an alkyl halide to an alcohol?
   a. reduction
   b. addition
   c. condensation
   d. elimination
   e. substitution

7. **K/U** Which is *not* a solution to petroleum-based plastics' inability to degrade easily?
   a. Reduce the use of plastics.
   b. Burn plastics when they are discarded.
   c. Re-use plastics as often as possible.
   d. Recycle plastics as often as possible.
   e. Replace petroleum-based plastics with degradable plastics.

8. **K/U** Which are the monomers of proteins?
   a. glucose
   b. alkanes
   c. nucleotides
   d. amino acids
   e. sucrose

9. **K/U** Which two functional groups react together in a condensation reaction to form an amide and water?
   a. an amine and an alcohol
   b. a carboxylic acid and an amine
   c. a carboxylic acid and an amide
   d. a carboxylic acid and an alcohol
   e. an ester and an alcohol

10. **K/U** Crosslinking is seen in which of the following polymers?
    a. polystyrene
    b. PVC
    c. polyacrylamide
    d. PET
    e. Kevlar®

Use sentences and diagrams as appropriate to answer the questions below.

11. **A** What monomer would you expect to be an active ingredient in muscle-building supplements? Explain your answer.

12. **T/I** Determine the products of the following condensation and esterification reactions.
    a. 2,2-dimethylbutanoic acid + 2-methylpropan-2-ol $\xrightarrow{H_2SO_4}$
    b. 3-chlorobutanoic acid + propan-1-amine $\xrightarrow{H_2SO_4}$

142 MHR • Unit 1 Organic Chemistry

13. **A** Propose a synthesis, including any necessary conditions, for cycloheptanone from an alkene.

14. **T/I** Determine the monomers for the following polymers and identify the polymers as addition or condensation polymers.

    a.

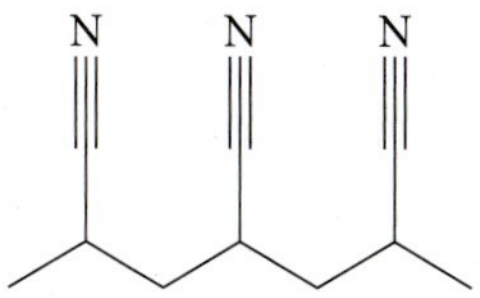

    b.

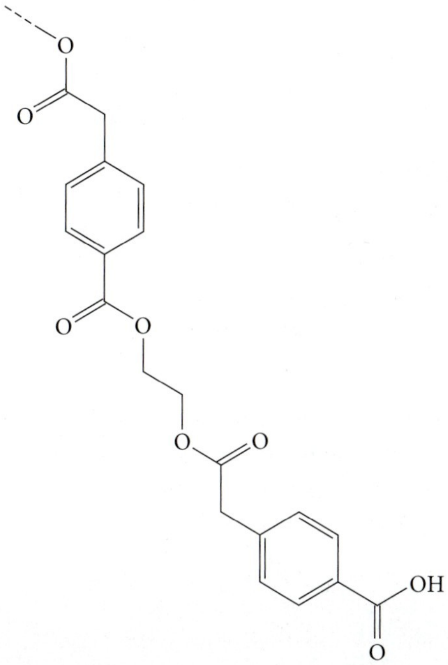

15. **K/U** What are the similarities and differences between cellulose and starch?

16. **T/I** Write a laboratory procedure (main reactions only) to perform an addition polymerization if your starting material is a carboxylic acid.

17. **T/I** Determine the products of the following addition and elimination reactions. Identify the major product in each case.
    a. hept-2-ene + HCl →
    b. 2-methylheptan-4-ol $\xrightarrow[\Delta]{H_2SO_4}$

18. **C** Write a short essay explaining how plastics contribute to your life. Include your opinion on whether the benefits outweigh the consequences of their use.

19. **T/I** Determine the products of the following reaction, then balance the equation.
    $(CH_3)_2CHCH=CHCH_3 + O_2 \rightarrow$

20. **T/I** Is a protein an example of a polyester or a polyamide? Explain your answer.

21. **K/U** Explain what happens during reduction of an organic molecule.

22. **T/I** Determine the products for the following reactions.
    a. $CH_3CH_2C\equiv CH + Cl_2 \rightarrow ? + Cl_2 \rightarrow ?$
    b. cyclopentanol $\xrightarrow[\Delta]{H_2SO_4}$
    c. $Cl-CH_2CH_2CH_3 + OH^- \rightarrow$

23. **A** Propose a synthesis, including any necessary conditions, for a four-carbon alkyl halide from butanone.

24. **T/I** Determine the reactants in the following reactions.
    a. ? + ? → propanoic acid + hexanol
    b. $\xrightarrow[\Delta]{H_2SO_4}$ cyclobutene + water

25. **A** Propose a one-step synthesis of the following compound from a non-cyclic reactant.

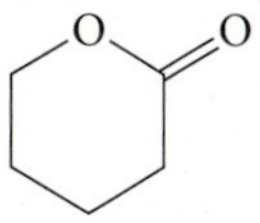

Self-Check

If you missed question …	1	2	3	4	5	6	7	8	9	10	11	12	13	14	15	16	17	18	19	20	21	22	23	24	25
Review section(s)…	2.1	2.2	2.1	2.1	2.1	2.1	2.2	2.2	2.1	2.2	2.2	2.1	2.1	2.2	2.2	2.2	2.1	2.2	2.1	2.2	2.1	2.1	2.1	2.1	2.1

Unit 1 Project

An Issue to Analyze

Evaluating Bioplastics

Bioplastic is plastic that is made from renewable resources or that can be degraded by micro-organisms. It presents a possible alternative to traditional petroleum-based plastic, which poses numerous environmental problems. Today, there are two types of bioplastic—hydrobiodegradable bioplastic and oxobiodegradable bioplastic. The names of these bioplastics indicate how they degrade. Hydrobiodegradable bioplastic is produced from renewable, natural polymers, such as starch and cellulose from plants. Often, however, this bioplastic also contains a small amount of petroleum-based plastic. The degradation of hydrobiodegradable bioplastic starts with a hydrolysis reaction. In comparison, oxobiodegradable bioplastic is composed of petroleum-based plastics, which are synthetic polymers. This type of bioplastic also contains a catalyst that increases the rate at which the plastic degrades. For this bioplastic, degradation begins with oxidation.

In this project, you will research hydrobiodegradable and oxobiodegradable bioplastics. You will evaluate the advantages and disadvantages associated with each and present one of these bioplastics as a suitable alternative to traditional petroleum-based plastic, using the results of your research and analysis to support your choice.

Which type of bioplastic—hydrobiodegradable bioplastic or oxobiodegradable bioplastic—is a suitable alternative to traditional petroleum-based plastic, and why?

Initiate and Plan

1. Establish how you will assess your information sources for accuracy, reliability, and bias. Go to "Developing Research Skills" in Appendix A for tips on evaluating the reliability of your sources.

Perform and Record

2. Use print and Internet resources to research the chemistry of hydrobiodegradable and oxobiodegradable bioplastics. Use the following questions to help guide your research.

   a. There are several different kinds of hydrobiodegradable and oxobiodegradable bioplastics. Name the polymers that form two different kinds of each bioplastic. Then identify the monomers that make up each polymer.

   b. Draw the structures of each monomer and polymer identified above.

   c. Classify and illustrate the polymerization reactions that produce each polymer.

   d. Describe the reaction process by which each bioplastic degrades.

3. Use the material in this unit, as well as other print and Internet resources, to answer the questions in Perform and Record step 2 for two different types of traditional, petroleum-based plastics.

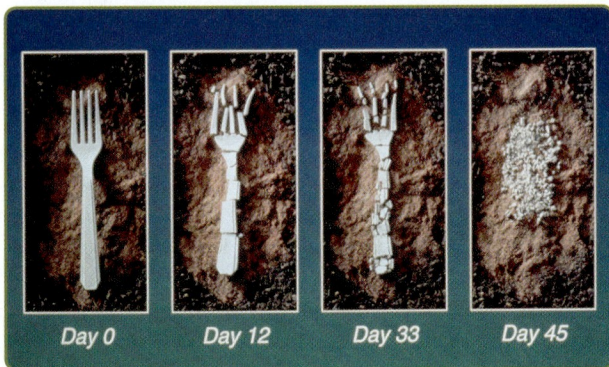

This photograph shows a bioplastic fork at different stages of degradation over time. The time required for bioplastic to degrade depends on the type of bioplastic and the environmental conditions to which it is exposed.

4. Research hydrobiodegradable and oxobiodegradable bioplastics, as well as traditional petroleum-based plastics, in greater detail. Consider the following questions to guide your research.

- What terms, such as *degradable, biodegradable,* and *transition metal salt,* do you need to define to better understand scientific writing about bioplastics?
- What effects does each bioplastic and plastic have on the environment, from production through to final degradation? How does each plastic adhere to the principles outlined in "Green Chemistry" and "Green Engineering" in Appendix A?
- How effective a solution is recycling in terms of solving the problems associated with petroleum-based plastic waste?
- Is each bioplastic truly biodegradable and how does it interact with current recycling and composting methods?
- How is each bioplastic used commercially, and what limits, if any, are related to this use?
- How economically feasible is the production and use of each bioplastic and why?
- Find out more about current research advances related to each type of bioplastic, focussing on Canadian research.
- What sources have you used to gather your information? How have you determined that these sources are scientifically valid?

Analyze and Interpret

1. Use appropriate graphic organizers to organize your research findings. "Using Graphic Organizers" in Appendix A may help you select suitable formats.

2. Evaluate the advantages and disadvantages associated with each bioplastic and assess how they compare to the positive and negative aspects of traditional petroleum-based plastic. Then determine which bioplastic is a suitable alternative to traditional petroleum-based plastic. Explain your reasoning, using your research findings to support your viewpoint.

Communicate Your Findings

3. Decide on the best way to present your evaluation, such as a poster, a computer presentation, or an interactive Web page. Be sure to consider the purpose of your presentation and your audience when choosing your mode of presentation. Your presentation should make use of suitable instructional visuals as well.

4. Prepare a presentation that summarizes your evaluation of hydrobiodegradable and oxobiodegradable bioplastics, as well as traditional petroleum-based plastic. Your presentation should include the following:

- an overview of the chemistry of each bioplastic and plastic, including details related to the production, uses, and degradation processes
- details supporting your evaluation of the advantages and disadvantages associated with each material and your conclusion as to which bioplastic is a suitable alternative to traditional petroleum-based plastic
- a brief discussion of current research advances related to each bioplastic, focussing on Canadian research
- a literature citation section that documents the sources you used to complete your research, using an appropriate academic format

Assessment Criteria

Once you complete your project, ask yourself these questions. Did you…

- ☑ **T/I** assess your information sources for accuracy, reliability, and bias?
- ☑ **K/U** describe the chemistry of different types of bioplastics and traditional petroleum-based plastics?
- ☑ **K/U** explain the production, uses, and degradation processes for each bioplastic and plastic?
- ☑ **A** identify the advantages and disadvantages associated with each bioplastic and plastic?
- ☑ **A** investigate current research advances related to each bioplastic, focussing on Canadian research?
- ☑ **C** use appropriate graphic organizers to organize your research findings?
- ☑ **T/I** evaluate which bioplastic is a suitable alternative to traditional petroleum-based plastic?
- ☑ **C** communicate your evaluation in a form that is appropriate to your audience and purpose, and that makes use of suitable instructional visuals?
- ☑ **C** document your sources using an appropriate academic format?

UNIT 1 SUMMARY

BIG IDEAS

- Organic compounds have predictable chemical and physical properties determined by their respective structures.
- Organic chemical reactions and their applications have significant implications for society, human health, and the environment.

Overall Expectations

In this unit, you learned how to…

- **assess** the social and environmental impact of organic compounds used in everyday life, and propose a course of action to reduce the use of compounds that are harmful to human health and the environment
- **investigate** organic compounds and organic chemical reactions, and **use** various methods to represent the compounds
- **demonstrate** an understanding of the structure, properties, and chemical behaviour of compounds within each class of organic compounds

Chapter 1: Structure and Physical Properties of Organic Compounds

Key Ideas

- In organic compounds, carbon atoms are almost always bonded to each other, to hydrogen atoms, and occasionally to atoms of a few specific elements.
- Carbon atoms can bond with each other to produce straight or branched chain molecules that provide the root for a large number of organic compounds.
- Many organic compounds form isomers—molecules that have the same molecular formula but a different arrangement of their atoms. The two main classes of isomers are constitutional isomers and stereoisomers.
- Hydrocarbons are compounds that contain only carbon atoms and hydrogen atoms. Alkanes are made up of single bonds only. Alkenes are hydrocarbons that have at least one double bond, while alkynes have at least one triple bond.
- Hydrocarbon chains can form rings. Cyclic hydrocarbons include alkanes, alkenes, and alkynes in the shape of a ring. Aromatic hydrocarbons are ring structures that are derived from benzene.
- All hydrocarbon names are based on the structure of the compound and follow IUPAC rules.
- Functional groups are chemically active groups of atoms. One or more functional groups attached to a hydrocarbon form a hydrocarbon derivative. Hydrocarbon derivatives with different functional groups have unique structures and physical properties.
- Hydrocarbon derivatives include alcohols, haloalkanes, aldehydes, ketones, carboxylic acids, esters, ethers, amines, and amides.

Chapter 2: Reactions of Organic Compounds

Key Ideas

- Reactions of organic compounds include addition, elimination, substitution, condensation, esterification, hydrolysis, oxidation, and combustion reactions.
- A polymer is a long molecule consisting of repeating units called monomers. Most polymers are formed by addition reactions or condensation reactions.
- Addition polymerization is a reaction in which alkene monomers are joined through multiple addition reactions to form a polymer. Addition reactions are characterized by a reduction in the number of double bonds found in the polymer, as addition reduces a double bond to a single bond.
- In condensation polymerization, a hydrogen atom is removed from one monomer and a hydroxyl group is removed from the next. The hydrogen atom and hydroxyl group form a water molecule and a bond forms between the two monomers.
- The organic compounds that industries use to make polymers and other products start out mainly as petroleum.
- Many synthetic polymers, including most plastics, take a significantly long time to degrade in the environment. Reducing use, recycling, and using bioplastics can help address this issue.
- Cellulose, starch, and glycogen are natural polymers consisting of glucose monomers. Proteins are natural polyamides. DNA is a natural polymer consisting of nucleotide monomers.

UNIT 1 REVIEW

Knowledge and Understanding

Select the letter of the best answer below.

1. Carbon atoms bonded to four other atoms form what shape?
   a. linear
   b. square
   c. tetrahedral
   d. triangular
   e. none of the above

2. Which molecule could form constitutional isomers?
   a. CH_4
   b. C_2H_3F
   c. C_2H_6O
   d. C_2H_5Cl
   e. CH_2Cl_2

3. Stereoisomers are molecules that have the same molecular formulas but have
   a. different functional groups.
   b. the same sequence of atoms, but their atoms are bonded differently in three-dimensional space.
   c. the same functional groups, but are bonded in a different sequence.
   d. multiple bonds instead of single bonds.
   e. different placement of their multiple bonds.

4. Which formula represents a molecule that can have diastereomers?
   a. C_nH_n
   b. C_nH_{2n}
   c. C_nH_{2n+2}
   d. C_nH_{4n}
   e. All of the above

5. Which of the following hydrocarbons has the highest boiling point?
   a. cyclohexane
   b. propyne
   c. ethane
   d. ethene
   e. ethyne

6. The use of compounds in which group of hydrocarbon derivatives led to a reduction of the ozone layer?
   a. alcohols
   b. aromatics
   c. ethers
   d. haloalkanes
   e. amides

7. Which is the correct root name for the molecule shown below?

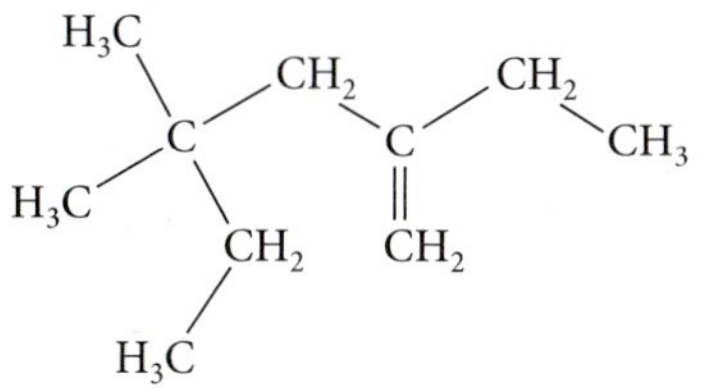

   a. hept-
   b. hex-
   c. meth-
   d. pent-
   e. pro-

8. The following functional group is a(n)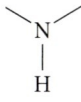
   a. ester.
   b. alcohol.
   c. ether.
   d. carboxylic acid.
   e. ketone.

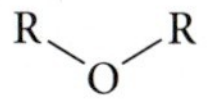

9. The following molecule is an example of a:
   a. primary amine.
   b. secondary amine.
   c. tertiary amine.
   d. primary amide.
   e. tertiary amide.

10. Which can be thought of as the product of a carboxylic acid and an alcohol?
    a. ether
    b. amide
    c. amine
    d. aldehyde
    e. ester

11. Which statement is correct regarding molecules that have the same number of carbon atoms?
    a. Alcohols have higher boiling points than ethers.
    b. Carboxylic acids are less soluble in water than haloalkanes.
    c. Amines are more soluble in water than amides.
    d. Esters have lower melting points than aromatics.
    e. None of the above are correct.

12. In which type of reaction is a molecule broken apart by adding the hydroxyl group from a water molecule to one side of a bond and the hydrogen atom of a water molecule to the other side of the bond?
    a. oxidation
    b. reduction
    c. elimination
    d. polymerization
    e. hydrolysis

13. Which is a monomer of proteins?
    a. amino acid
    b. ethene
    c. glucose
    d. nucleotide
    e. methane

14. Which is an example of a synthetic polymer?
    a. cellulose
    b. DNA
    c. polyethylene
    d. starch
    e. hemoglobin

UNIT 1 REVIEW

Answer the questions below.

15. Identify the type of hydrocarbon represented by each formula listed below.
  a. C_2H_4
  b. C_6H_{14}
  c. C_5H_{10}
  d. C_4H_6

16. Identify whether each pair of molecules below are constitutional isomers. Explain your reasoning.

  a.

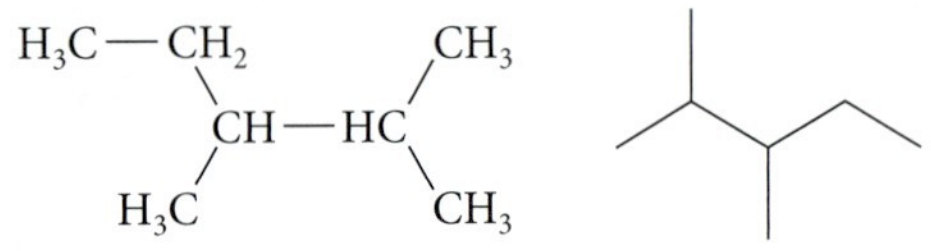

  b.

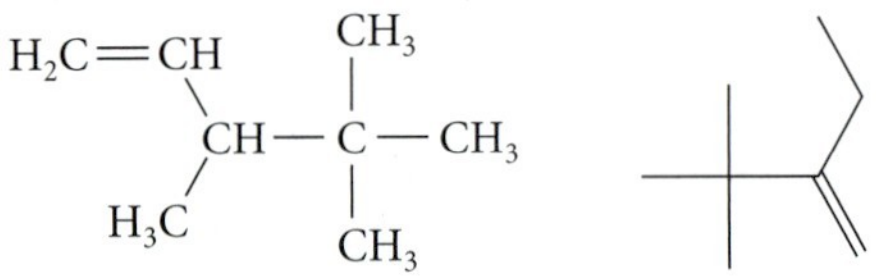

17. Compare and contrast diastereomers and enantiomers.

18. Identify each type of reaction listed below.
  a. haloalkane + hydroxide ion →
  b. alkyne + hydrogen $\xrightarrow{\text{Pt or Pd}}$
  c. carboxylic acid + amine →
  d. water + ester →
  e. alcohol $\xrightarrow{H_2SO_4}$
  f. alkane + oxygen →

19. Describe the terms *polymer* and *monomer* in your own words. Give an example of each.

20. Which would you expect to be most soluble in water: primary, secondary, or tertiary amides? Explain your reasoning.

21. Compare and contrast polyesters and polyamides.

22. Explain why it is sometimes possible to have two products with an addition reaction.

23. Define the term petrochemical. What are petrochemicals used for?

24. Identify the name of the monomer for each of the following polymers.
  a. polychloroprene
  b. polymethyl methacrylate

25. Identify the following polymer as an addition or condensation polymer.

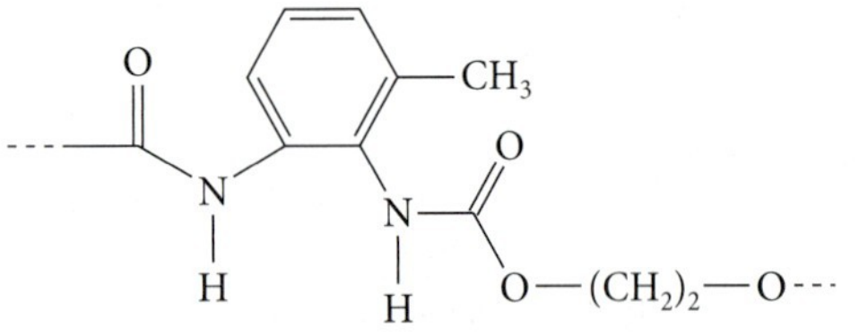

spandex

26. Identify the following reactions as combustion, addition, substitution, elimination, or condensation.

  a. $CH_3-C=CH-(CH_2)_3-CH_3 + HBr \rightarrow$
  with CH_3 branch, product shown with Br on carbon.

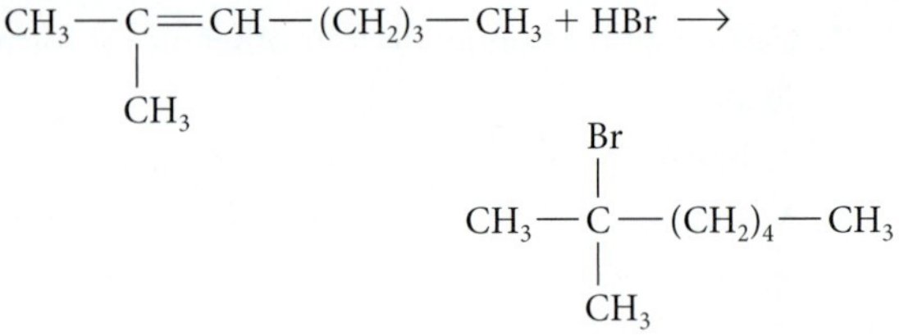

  b. (carboxylic acid + alcohol) $\xrightarrow{H_2SO_4, \Delta}$ ester $+ H_2O$

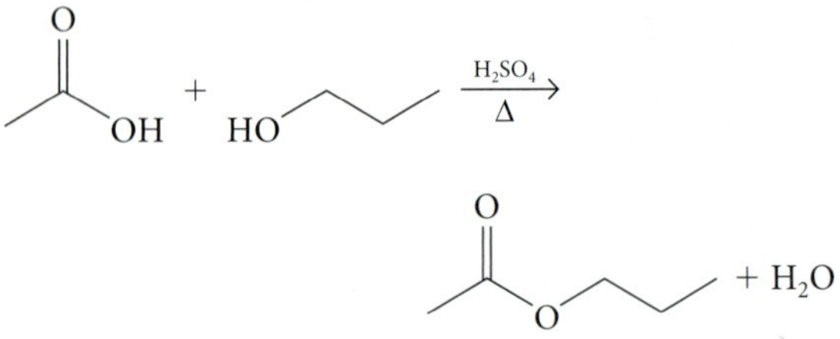

  c. $C_3H_8 + 5O_2 \rightarrow 3CO_2 + 4H_2O +$ energy

27. Identify the following reactions as oxidation or reduction. Oxidizing and reducing agents are not shown.

  a. aldehyde → carboxylic acid

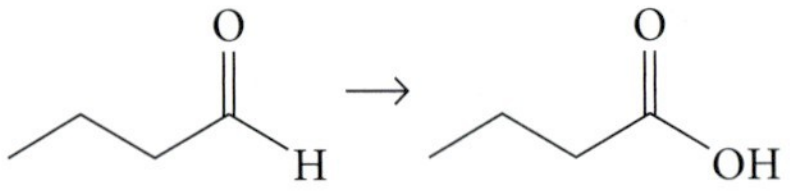

  b. alkene → alkane

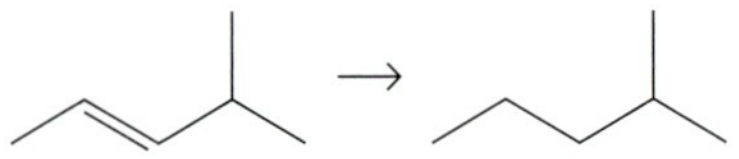

28. Identify the following reactions as esterification, condensation, or hydrolysis.

  a. ester $+ H_2O \rightarrow$ alcohol $+$ carboxylic acid

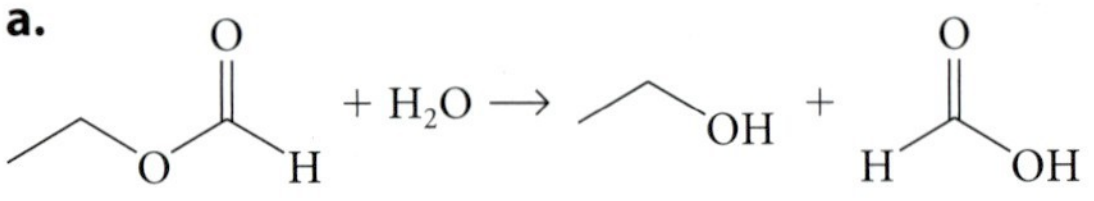

  b. alcohol $+$ carboxylic acid $\rightarrow$ ester $+ H_2O$

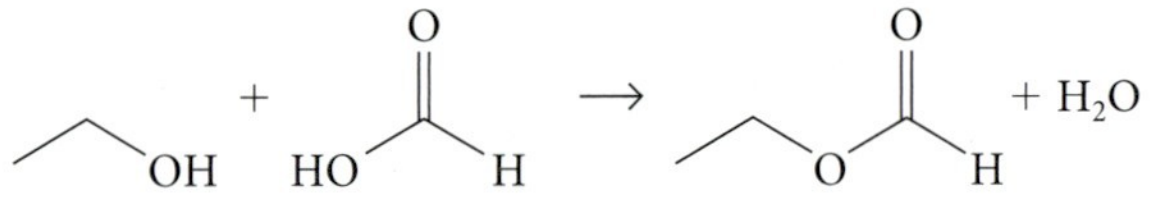

Thinking and Investigation

29. State the name of the product formed in each of the following reactions.
  a. ethanoic acid and butan-1-amine
  b. butanoic acid and cyclopentanol

30. Explain why each of the following molecules are named incorrectly. Provide the correct name for each.
  a. 4-methylbutane
  b. 3,4-dimethylpentane
  c. 2,2-dimethyl-3-ethylnonane
  d. 1-phenylpentane

31. Explain why the following molecules are named incorrectly. Provide the correct name.
   a. propan-2-al
   b. 2-chloro-3-bromocyclobutane
   c. 2-ethyloctan-6-ol
   d. butoxyethane
   e. 4-methenylhexane
   f. methyl-3-ethylbutanoate

32. You are given samples of propan-1-ol, propyne, and propanoic acid. Design an experiment to distinguish the physical properties among them.

33. Identify the reactions that the following molecule could undergo. Draw the equation for these reactions.

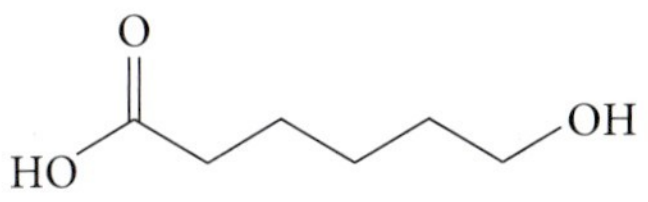

34. Propose a synthesis reaction for ethoxyethane from ethane.

35. Identify the products of the following substitution, condensation, or hydrolysis reactions.
   a. [structure] + H₂O →
   b. [structure] + HCl →
   c. [structure] + HO[structure] →

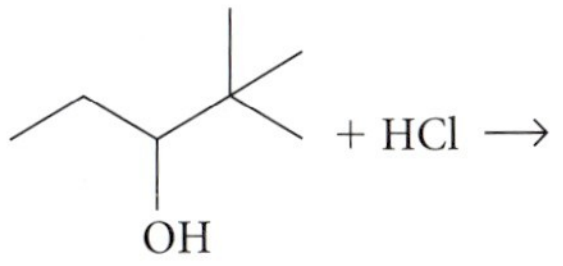

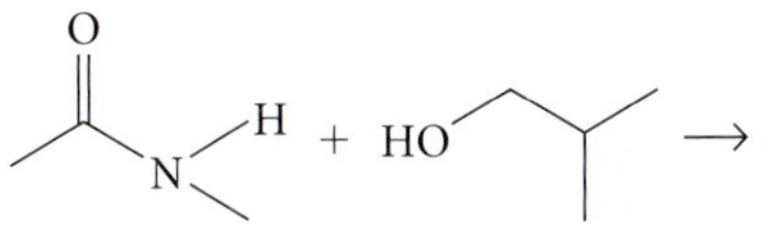

36. Suppose that you are working with four unknown compounds in a chemistry laboratory. Your teacher tells you that these compounds are ethane, ethanol, ethyl ethanoate, and ethanoic acid.
   a. Use the table of physical properties shown below to identify each unknown compound.
   b. Draw a structural formula for each compound.

37. Polychlorinated biphenyls (PCBs) were once used in electrical transformers. They were banned in 2001 by the Stockholm Convention because they were found to cause disruption of the human endocrine and nervous systems. An example of a PCB known as 2,2′,4,4′,5,5′-hexachlorobiphenyl is shown below.

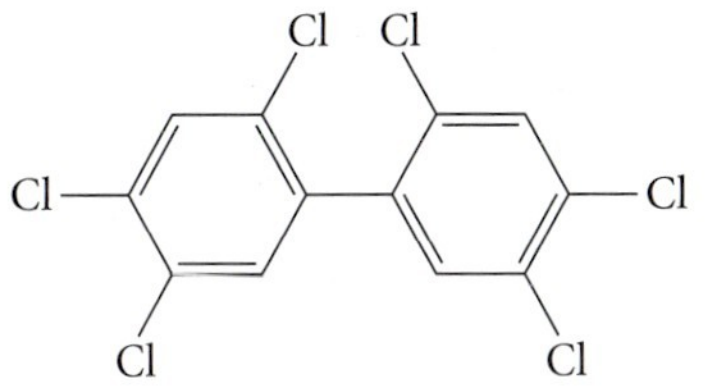

   Polybrominated biphenyls (PBBs) are used as flame retardants in plastic foams, home electrical appliances such as computers, cabinets, and certain textiles. An example is shown below.

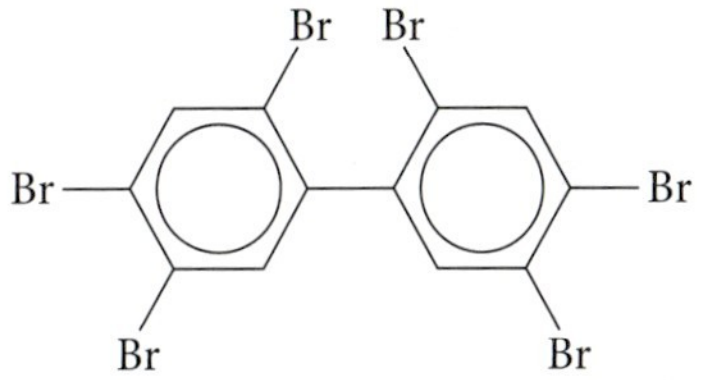

   a. Identify the functional groups PCBs and PBBs have that are similar.
   b. Relate these functional groups to the name of each compound.
   c. Predict the state of matter PCBs and PBBs would be in at room temperature. Explain your reasoning.
   d. Predict the solubility of these molecules.
   e. Infer other similarities these two molecules may have.

38. When a carboxylic acid and an alcohol react, an ester forms. What do you propose would be the product of two alcohols reacting?

39. Write a lab procedure to prepare 1,3-dibromobenzene from a hydrocarbon.

Hydrocarbon Data

Compound	Solubility in water	Hydrogen bonding	Boiling point	Odour	Molecular polarity
A	Not soluble	None	−89°C	Odourless	Non-polar
B	Soluble	Accepts hydrogen bonds from water but cannot form hydrogen bonds between its own molecules	77°C	Sweet	Polar
C	Infinitely soluble	Very strong	78°C	Sharp, antiseptic smell	Very polar
D	Infinitely soluble	Extremely strong	118°C	Sharp, vinegar smell	Very polar

UNIT 1 REVIEW

40. In the past, perfumes were made of extracts from flowers, but the organic molecules used in perfumes today are often produced synthetically. Shown below is geraniol, which has the fragrance of roses.

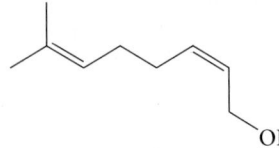

  a. Give the correct IUPAC name for geraniol.
  b. What physical properties would you expect geraniol to have?
  c. What solvent would you expect geraniol to be used in as a perfume? Justify your response.

41. Amino acids are the building blocks of proteins in living organisms. Glycine and alanine are shown below.

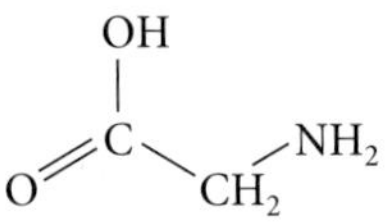

  glycine 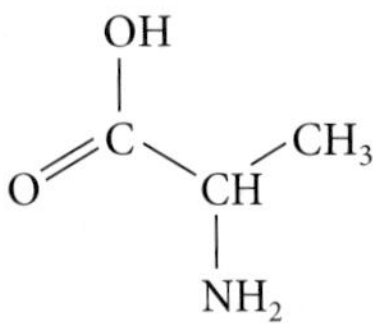   alanine

  a. Infer why these molecules are termed amino acids.
  b. What would be their proper names according to IUPAC terminology?
  c. Predict whether glycine or alanine would be more soluble in water. Explain your reasoning.

42. Ethoxyethane (diethyl ether) was used as an anaesthetic and is still used to help internal combustion engines to start by spraying it into air intakes.
  a. Draw the structure of ethoxyethane.
  b. Predict the physical properties of ethoxyethane.
  c. Infer why its use as an anaesthetic was discontinued.

43. Design a short procedure to carry out the polymerization of but-2-ene. Your procedure should include:
  - structural diagrams for the monomer and the expected polymer product,
  - an appropriate solvent in which but-2-ene dissolves and in which the reaction will be carried out,
  - the addition of a catalyst and heat to start the polymerization, and
  - safety precautions for dealing with all the compounds used, including the solvent and product (use WHMIS information).

44. Determine the products of the following oxidation and reduction reactions.
  a. 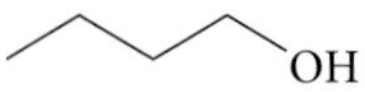 [structure] + [O] → ? + [O] → ?
  b. 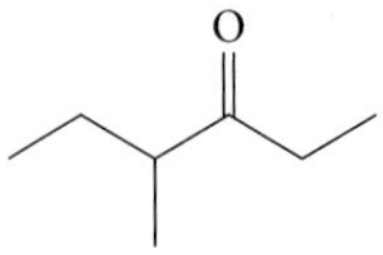 [structure] + [H] →

45. Determine the products for the following polymerization reactions.
  a. $n\text{CH}_2=\text{C}-\text{Cl}$ →
           |
           Cl
  b. 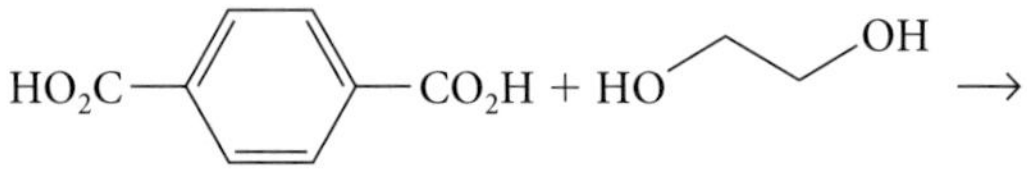 HO_2C—⟨benzene⟩—CO_2H + HO—[structure]—OH →

46. Bromine water, Br_2(aq), can be used to test for double bonds.
  a. Design a procedure to test oils and fats for the presence of double bonds.
  b. Look up the WHMIS guidelines for bromine. What safety precautions will you include in your procedure?
  c. When bromine water is added to but-2-ene, the colour of the bromine solution changes. What type of reaction has occurred?
  d. Draw the structure for the product of the reaction in part (c).

47. You are given three unlabelled test tubes that contain colourless liquids. One test tube contains benzene, another contains ethanol, and the third contains hex-2-ene.
  a. Design a procedure that will allow you to identify the contents of each test tube.
  b. Describe your expected observations. (Caution: Do not try your procedure in a lab. Benzene is carcinogenic.)

48. Use information in Appendix B to name the following molecules, which have more than one functional group.
  a. 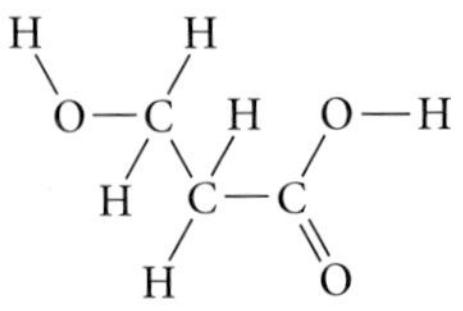 [structure]
  b. 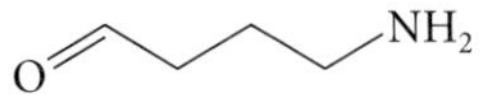 [structure with NH₂]

49. Study the table below. Compare the boiling points of the haloalkanes to those of the alkanes with the same number of carbons. Identify a pattern in how the boiling point of each haloalkane changes as the halogen changes from fluorine to chlorine, bromine, and iodine. Based on your observations, place the following substances in order of increasing boiling point.
- 2-chloropentane
- 3-methylpentane
- 2-iodopentane
- butane
- 1-bromohexane

Boiling Points of Alkanes and Haloalkanes

Compound	Boiling Point (°C)
methane	−161
chloromethane	−24
propane	−42
1-chloropropane	45.6
pentane	36
1-fluoropentane	62.8
1-chloropentane	108
1-bromopentane	130
1-iodopentane	155

50. Starting with ethanol and non-1-en-5-amine, propose a synthesis for:

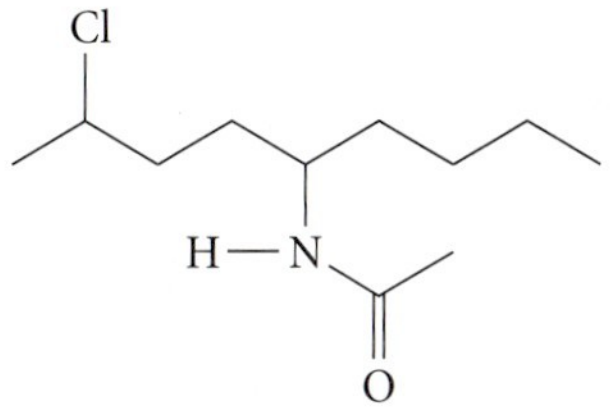

Communication

51. You have read about many uses or applications for alkanes, alkenes, alkynes, alcohols, haloalkanes, aldehydes, ketones, carboxylic acids, esters, ethers, amines, and amides. Write down each of the names of the classes of hydrocarbons or hydrocarbon derivatives. For each class, list as many ways as you can that you use or encounter these compounds in your everyday living. Read labels on foods, medications, cleaning solutions, and other common household items to find more examples of these classes of compounds.

52. Draw the simplest method for showing the 3-dimensional shape of chloromethane. Identify which atoms are above, below, or on the plane of the paper.

53. Draw and name the simplest hydrocarbon that could form *cis/trans* stereoisomers.

54. Using diagrams, show that the molecule 1-bromo-1-chloro-1-fluoroethane could or could not form enantiomers.

55. A large amount of clothing is made of synthetic material. Choose a natural fibre and a synthetic fibre. Research both types of fibre and compare them in terms of physical properties and manufacturing methods. Write a short editorial piece expressing your opinion as to whether you think natural or synthetic materials are better for manufacturing clothing, and why.

56. Use a Venn diagram to compare and contrast complete and incomplete combustion. Then explain why incomplete combustion can be dangerous.

57. Products, such as clothing, have been made from natural polymers, including cotton, wool, and silk, for thousands of years. The first synthetic polymer was produced in the late 1800s. Suppose you lived in the early 1800s, before the invention of synthetic polymers. Write a short story to describe how your life would have been different compared to your life today due to the lack of synthetic polymers.

58. Create a mind map or a flow chart to show how key terms in Unit 1 are related to one another.

59. Write a short paragraph to convince someone that we need to reduce the amount of plastics we use. Be sure to include a sentence that introduces the main idea, several sentences with details that support the main idea, and a conclusions sentence.

60. How are organic compounds important to your health and lifestyle? Write a short paragraph that describes any benefits you obtain from an organic compound.

61. Draw a concept map that summarizes the concepts that you have learned about organic chemistry. Include the following topics:
- functional groups
- reactions of organic compounds
- natural and synthetic polymers
- biological molecules and their functions
- petrochemicals

62. Use a flowchart to describe the development and manufacture of PET from the natural compounds from which it is formed.

UNIT 1 REVIEW

63. Many sources that compare the nature of organic and inorganic compounds state that organic substances have low solubility in water and do not conduct electricity. Write a short essay explaining whether you agree or disagree with this statement.

64. The photo below shows *Cerura vinula*, also known as the puss moth caterpillar. When threatened, the caterpillar sprays formic acid at its potential attacker. Carpenter ants spray formic acid into a wound after biting a would-be predator. The lemon ant, *Myrmelachista schumanni*, which is found in the Amazon rain forest, uses formic acid as an herbicide to keep certain plants from growing in their habitat. Research more information about insects that use formic acid for various purposes. Prepare a presentation for a Grade 6 class about formic acid and the organisms that use it. Use the following questions as a guide in your research.
    a. What is formic acid?
    b. What are some ways in which humans use formic acid?
    c. Which other species use formic acid?
    d. In what ways do other species use formic acid?

Application

65. Teflon® is commonly used in frying pans to create a non-stick surface. Research more information about Teflon®.
    a. Explain why this particular polymer exhibits the properties it does.
    b. What are some negative consequences of using these pans?
    c. Based on your answer to part (b), write a safety note that could be included in the information pamphlet that comes with newly purchased Teflon®-coated pots and pans.

66. Emulsifiers are molecules that can bind to non-polar molecules such as oils on one end as well as to polar molecules such as water on the other end.
    a. Draw a molecule that could possibly be used as an emulsifier.
    b. What use would non-toxic emulsifiers serve in the kitchen?

67. What are four careers, other than an organic chemist, in which knowledge of organic molecular structure would be essential? Choose two and research what kind of training would be required.

68. In April 2010, the Deep Water Horizon offshore oil drilling rig exploded and began leaking over 50 000 barrels of oil per day in the Gulf of Mexico. The following are some methods to control oil spills: using skimmers, burning the oil, and using dispersants, which break the oil into smaller droplets. Corexit® was the dispersant used to break up the crude oil. It was used under the water for the first time and not just on the surface. The ingredients were made public due to the concerns of residents and workers in this region. Some of its components are butoxyethanol and sorbitan monostearate. Its structure is shown below.

    a. Draw the formula for butoxyethanol.
    b. What WHMIS symbols would you expect Corexit® to have?
    c. What are the functional groups on sorbitan monosterareate and how would they account for its ability to break up oil into smaller droplets in water?
    d. What are some benefits and drawbacks of using the methods listed above in dealing with this type of disaster?
    e. Propose some personal courses of action to reduce such a disaster.

69. Determine the structure of the polymer formed by a condensation polymerization reaction with the following monomer.

70. Hexane has a boiling point of 68.7°C. Benzene has a boiling point of 80.1°C and cyclohexane, 80.7°C. Since both benzene and cyclohexane have lower molar masses than hexane, they might be expected to also have lower boiling points. Explain why this is not the case.

71. The cycle shown below becomes activated when acetyl-CoA is restricted from entering the tricarboxylic acid cycle because of a deficiency in nutrients (generally either phosphorus, nitrogen, or oxygen) needed by the cell to further metabolize acetyl-CoA for cell survival. Identify the type of reactions occurring in steps 1, 2, and 3.

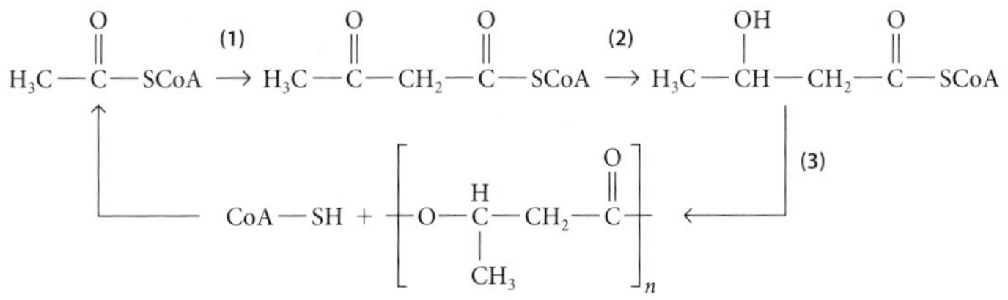

72. You are changing a long fluorescent bulb in your recreation room. You find that the fluorescent starter has leaked a very thick, tar-like substance onto the plastic covering for the light. You look around your home to find something that you might use to clean the plastic cover. You find some rubbing alcohol (propan-2-ol), some vinegar (5% ethanoic acid), and some vegetable oil (esters of medium length, with 14 to 18 carbons, and carboxylic acids with propane-1,2,3-triol). Which do you think would be the most likely product to dissolve the tar-like substance? Explain why.

73. During energy transport in cells, NADH is converted to NAD+ to release energy. The diagram below shows the molecular changes. What type of reaction is this? Explain your answer.

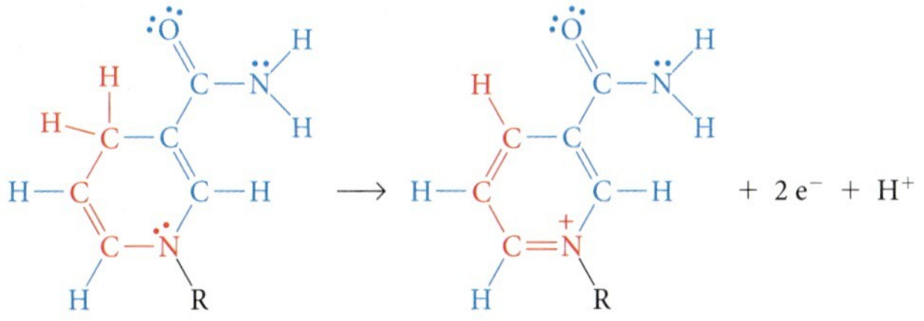

74. Alcohol consumption is prevalent in much of the world.
  a. What is the name and molecular formula of the alcohol that is commonly consumed?
  b. In which physical states would you expect most alcohols to exist?
  c. What WHMIS symbols would you expect to find on containers containing high percentages of all alcohols?

75. Many people rust-proof their cars, especially in winter, because the salt on the streets that mixes with water catalyzes the rusting reaction. Research and identify the type of reaction that occurs when rust forms. How do the reactants in the rust reaction differ from the reactants discussed throughout Unit 1?

76. Scientists who manufacture and market pesticides called pyrethroids (see structural formula below) are concerned about public opinion regarding these pesticides. Many people buy the natural pesticide pyrethrin (see below) even though it is more toxic than pyrethroids. Why do you think people make this choice? Do you think this happens for other synthetic organic products that have natural alternatives? Write a brief editorial outlining your opinions and advice to consumers to make informed choices.

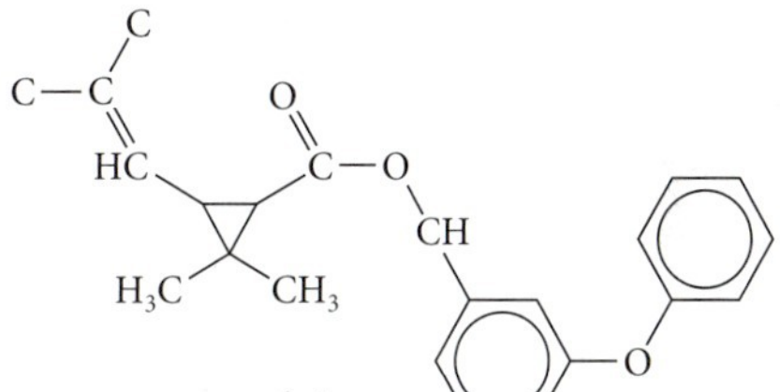

permethrin

Permethrin, shown here, is one example of the many synthetic pyrethroids that are used as insecticides.

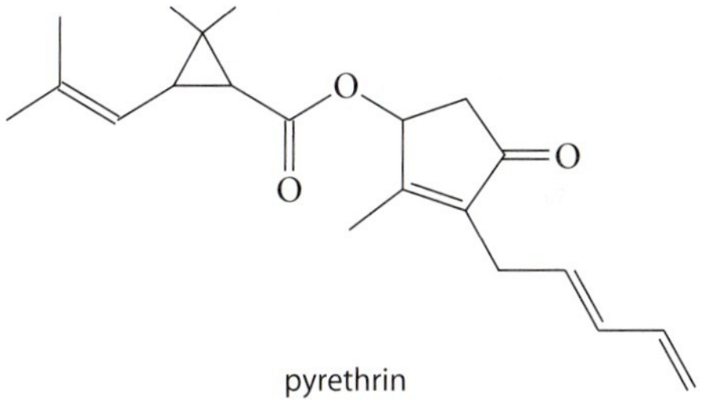

pyrethrin

There are two naturally occurring pyrethrins that have the base structure shown here. In pyrethrin I, the R group is a methyl group, $-CH_3$. In pyrethrin II, the R group is an acetyl group, $-COOCH_3$.

77. Organic solvents can dissolve many substances, such as paint, oil, and grease. Toluene and turpentine are commonly used as paint removers. Acetone is used to remove nail polish. Spot removers contain hexane.
  a. Research some of the advantages and disadvantages of organic solvents.
  b. Research potentially negative health or environmental effects that result from the use of these products.
  c. Organize the results of your research in a table.
  d. Identify ways in which the use of these products could be reduced.

UNIT 1 SELF-ASSESSMENT

Select the letter of the best answer below.

1. **K/U** Which term best describes molecules that have the same molecular formula but whose atoms are bonded in a different sequence?
   a. enantiomers
   b. constitutional isomers
   c. diastereomers
   d. optical isomers
   e. *cis/trans* isomers

2. **K/U** Which is the general formula for an alkyne with one unsaturated bond?
   a. C_nH_n
   b. C_nH_{2n}
   c. $C_{2n}H_{2n}$
   d. $C_{2n}H_{2n+2}$
   e. C_nH_{2n-2}

3. **K/U** Which molecule would you expect to have the lowest boiling point?
   a. pentane
   b. pent-1-ene
   c. pent-1-yne
   d. cyclopentane
   e. benzene

4. **K/U** What is the general name for the class of hydrocarbons with the following functional group?

   $$R-\overset{\overset{\displaystyle O}{\|}}{C}-H$$

   a. alcohol
   b. aldehyde
   c. ketone
   d. ether
   e. carboxylic acid

5. **K/U** Which molecule would you expect to be the most soluble in water?
   a. ethanol
   b. ethanal
   c. methoxymethane
   d. ethanamine
   e. ethanoic acid

6. **K/U** Which type of reaction is shown below?
   $$O_2 + C_3H_8 \rightarrow CO_2 + H_2O$$
   a. addition
   b. combustion
   c. elimination
   d. hydrolysis
   e. oxidation

7. **K/U** Which type of reaction is shown below?
   water + methyl acetate → methanol + ethanoic acid
   a. addition
   b. combustion
   c. elimination
   d. hydrolysis
   e. oxidation

8. **K/U** Which is a reaction in which a carboxylic acid reacts with an alcohol to form an ester and water?
   a. addition
   b. esterification
   c. polymerization
   d. oxidation
   e. substitution

9. **K/U** Which statement best describes Kevlar®?
   a. It is an addition polymer.
   b. It is a condensation polymer.
   c. It is a natural polymer.
   d. It results from a reaction in which alkene monomers are joined through multiple reactions.
   e. It results from a reaction in which a hydrocarbon reacts with oxygen to form carbon dioxide and water, and release energy.

10. **K/U** Which type of reaction is shown below?
    1-butene + chlorine → 1,2-dichlorobutane
    a. addition
    b. combustion
    c. elimination
    d. hydrolysis
    e. oxidation

Use sentences and diagrams as appropriate to answer the questions below.

11. **T/I** Using diagrams, illustrate what types of isomers the molecule C_4H_8 could form.

12. **C** Draw condensed structural formulas of the following molecules.
    a. 3-propylcyclobutene
    b. methoxybenzene
    c. 3-propylhexanoic acid
    d. but-2,3-dione
    e. pentylethanoate

13. **A** Describe four benefits and four drawbacks of the development of organic chemistry over the past 200 years with respect to its impact on technology and society.

14. **A** Vitamin C, also known as ascorbic acid, is a necessary nutrient for the prevention of scurvy. Its structure is shown below.

    a. Could vitamin C form enantiomers? Explain why or why not.
    b. What physical properties would you expect ascorbic acid to have and why?
    c. Does your answer to part b. confirm the fact that vitamin C cannot be stored in human fatty tissues?

15. **T/I** Name the molecules illustrated below.
    a. [structure]
    b. [structure with F and ethyl on benzene]
    c. [structure with OH]
    d. [structure with phenyl group]

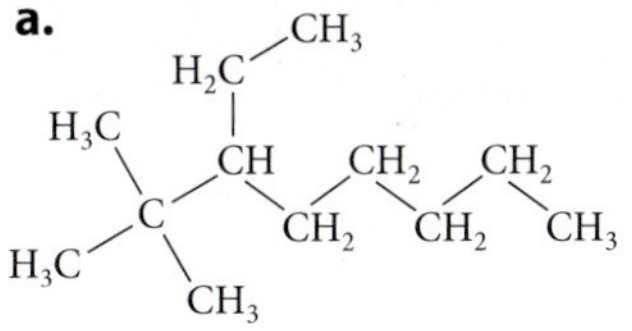

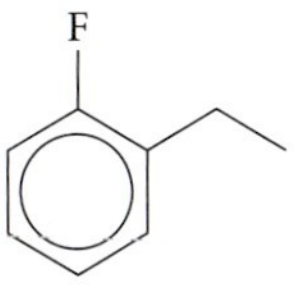

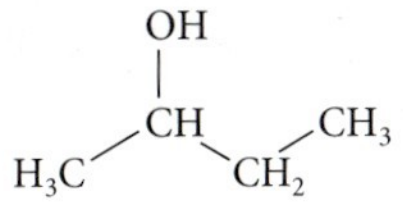

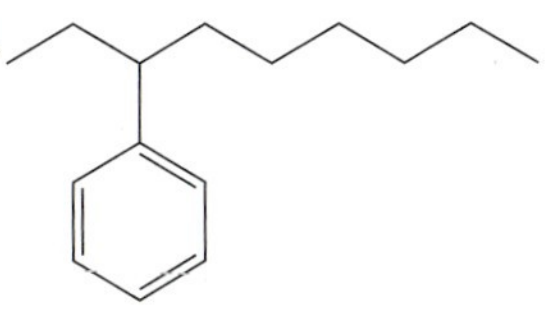

16. **A** What substances in your home or body might contain the following functional groups? Be as specific as possible.
    a. alkanes
    b. alcohols
    c. benzene rings
    d. carboxylic acids
    e. esters

17. **T/I** What reactions would an alkane have to undergo to cause the following changes?
    alkane → haloalkane → alcohol → carboxylic acid

18. **K/U** What features must a molecule have to be able to undergo polymerizations?

19. **A** Compare the two polymers below. Which one would you expect to be stronger? Explain your answer.

    Polymer A
    -CH₂-CH₂-CH₂-CH₂-CH₂-

    Polymer B
    [structure]

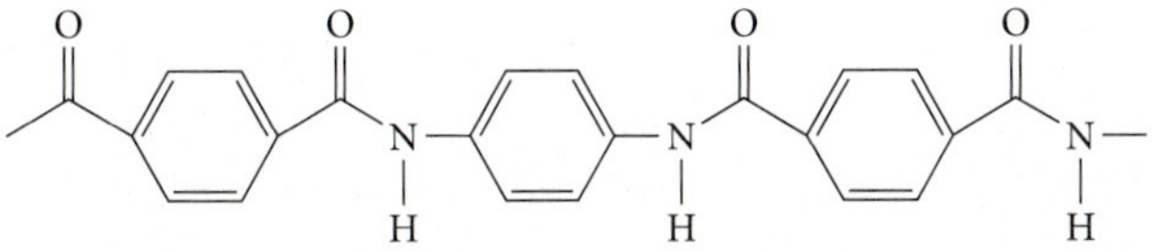

20. **C** Suggest some actions that your school could take to help reduce the amount of plastic waste it produces. Present your ideas in the form of a blog or poster.

21. **T/I** Determine the reactants for the following reactions.
    a. ? + ? → [structure with Cl] + H₂O
    b. ? —?→ [alkene structure]

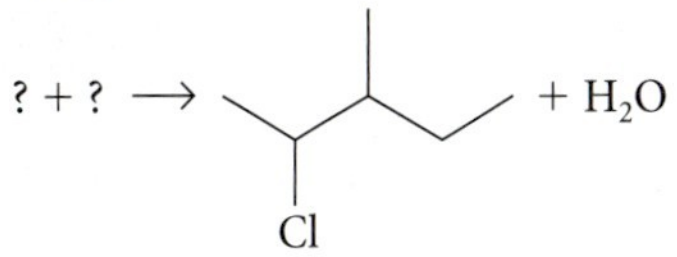

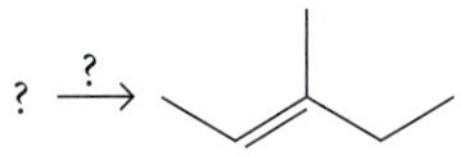

22. **T/I** Determine the monomers for the following polymer.
    [polymer structure]

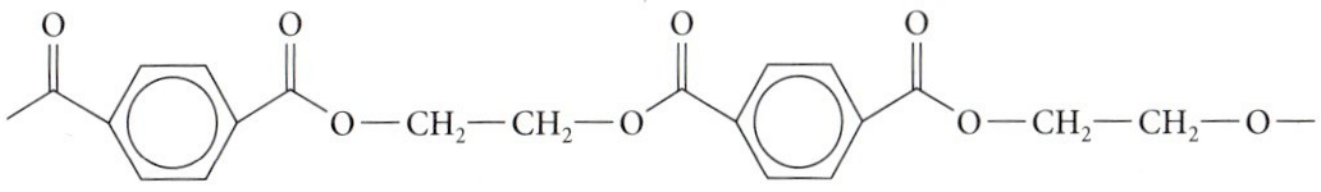

23. **T/I** Starting with but-3-en-2-amine and ethanol, propose reaction to synthesize the following compound.
    [structure]

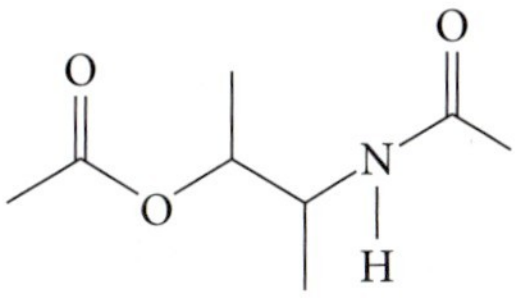

24. **T/I** Determine the products for the following reactions.
    a. [structure] + HBr →
    b. H₂O + [ester structure] →
    c. [structure with OH] + [O] →

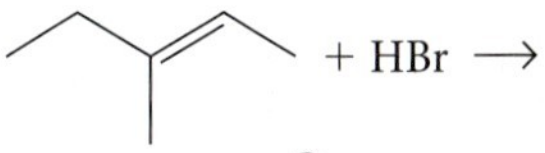

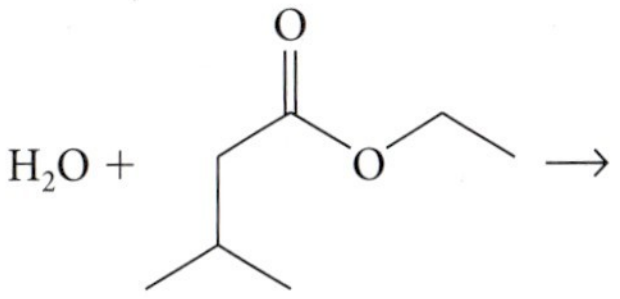

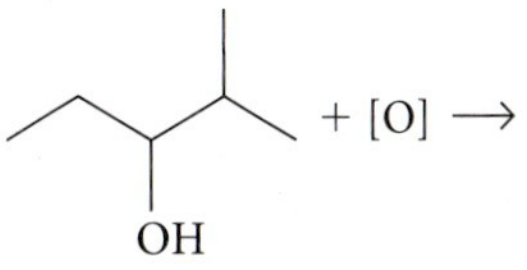

25. **A** Research why gasoline is made up mostly of carbon chains of between 5-12 carbons. What problems would combustion of smaller carbon chains present?

Self-Check

If you missed question …	1	2	3	4	5	6	7	8	9	10	11	12	13	14	15	16	17	18	19	20	21	22	23	24	25
Review section(s)…	1.1	1.2	1.2	1.3	1.3	2.1	2.1	2.1	2.2	2.1	1.1	1.2, 1.3	2.3	1.1, 1.3	1.2, 1.3	1.2, 1.3	2.1	2.2	2.2	2.2	2.1	2.2	2.1	2.1	2.1

UNIT 2: Structure and Properties of Matter

BIG IDEAS

- The nature of the attractive forces that exist between particles in a substance determines the properties and limits the uses of that substance.
- Technological devices that are based on the principles of atomic and molecular structures can have societal benefits and costs.

Overall Expectations

In this unit, you will…

- **assess** the benefits to society and **evaluate** the environmental impact of products and technologies that apply principles related to the structure and properties of matter
- **investigate** the molecular shapes and physical properties of various types of matter
- **demonstrate** an understanding of atomic structure and chemical bonding, and how they relate to the physical properties of ionic, molecular, covalent network, and metallic substances

Unit 2 Contents

Chapter 3
Atomic Models and Properties of Atoms

Chapter 4
Chemical Bonding and Properties

Focussing Questions

1. How do atomic structure and chemical bonding relate to the properties of elements and compounds?
2. How do the shapes of molecules influence the properties of molecular compounds?
3. How do intermolecular forces affect the properties of liquids and solids?

Go to **scienceontario** to find out more about the structure and properties of matter

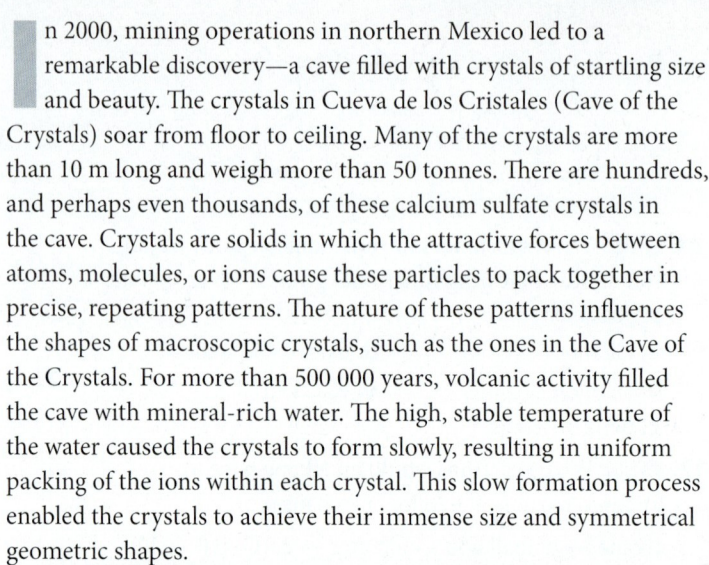

In 2000, mining operations in northern Mexico led to a remarkable discovery—a cave filled with crystals of startling size and beauty. The crystals in Cueva de los Cristales (Cave of the Crystals) soar from floor to ceiling. Many of the crystals are more than 10 m long and weigh more than 50 tonnes. There are hundreds, and perhaps even thousands, of these calcium sulfate crystals in the cave. Crystals are solids in which the attractive forces between atoms, molecules, or ions cause these particles to pack together in precise, repeating patterns. The nature of these patterns influences the shapes of macroscopic crystals, such as the ones in the Cave of the Crystals. For more than 500 000 years, volcanic activity filled the cave with mineral-rich water. The high, stable temperature of the water caused the crystals to form slowly, resulting in uniform packing of the ions within each crystal. This slow formation process enabled the crystals to achieve their immense size and symmetrical geometric shapes.

The chemical structure of crystals accounts for their unique properties. This is true for other compounds as well. As you study the structure and properties of matter in this unit, consider how the chemical structures of everyday compounds affect their properties. Consider also how the properties of these compounds would change if their chemical structures were altered.

As you study this unit, look ahead to the Unit 2 Project on pages 260 to 261. Complete the project in stages as you progress through the unit.

UNIT 2 Preparation

Safety in the Chemistry Laboratory and Classroom

- Be sure to read all safety information, including the material safety data sheet (MSDS) for each chemical required, before starting an investigation. Ensure you understand the meanings of all safety symbols and WHMIS symbols.
- Always wear appropriate protective clothing and equipment, as directed by your teacher and described in the Safety Precautions of each investigation.
- Immediately notify your teacher of any chemical spills, broken glassware, or broken equipment.
- On-line research also requires consideration of safety issues. Protect your privacy and never give out your personal information, even if this means not registering to use a site that may be helpful for your research.

1. Describe the hazards represented by the symbols below and the precautions associated with them.

   a.  b.

2. An investigation requires the use of a Bunsen burner. Describe the safety precautions that should be taken when using this equipment.

3. Describe the safety practices you should follow when conducting Internet research on a particular topic.

4. Which of the following types of fires should be extinguished using water?
   a. Class A, a fire that involves ordinary flammable materials
   b. Class B, a fire that involves flammable liquids, such as alcohol
   c. Class C, a fire that involves electrical equipment
   d. Class D, a fire that involves burning metal
   e. all of the above

Atomic Properties and Trends in the Periodic Table

- The sum of the protons and neutrons that make up the nucleus of an atom is the mass number for the atom. The atomic number of an atom represents the number of protons in the atom. Some elements have different isotopes, which are atoms that have the same number of protons but different numbers of neutrons.
- The Bohr-Rutherford model of the atom depicts a central core, called the nucleus, which is surrounded by electrons. The electrons exist in particular energy levels, or shells, which are often represented in models as rings around the nucleus. Lewis diagrams are simplified models for representing atoms. The chemical symbol for the element is used and dots, which represent the valence electrons, are placed around the symbol. Both paired and unpaired valence electrons are represented in Lewis diagrams.
- Trends occur within the periodic table according to the different properties of the atoms of each element. The placement of an element in the periodic table can predict the atomic radius, ionization energy, electron affinity, and electronegativity of the element, relative to other elements.

5. Copy and complete the table below.

Isotope Data

Name of Isotope	Notation for Isotope	Atomic Number	Mass Number	Number of Protons	Number of Electrons	Number of Neutrons
		35	81			
			22	10		
calcium-44						
				47		60

6. Define the term *valence electron* and explain the role these electrons play in chemical bonds.

7. In the Bohr-Rutherford model of the atom, Bohr showed that electrons can exist only in specific energy levels. The maximum number of electrons that can occupy an energy level can be determined by the formula
   a. n^2
   b. $2n^2$
   c. $A = N - Z$
   d. $N = A - Z$
   e. none of the above

8. Which of the following represents the correct Lewis diagram of sulfur?

   a., b., c., d. (Lewis diagrams of S)

   e. none of the above

9. Explain why the electrons depicted in the diagram below are placed as far apart as possible.

   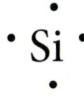

Use the diagram below to answer questions 10 to 12.

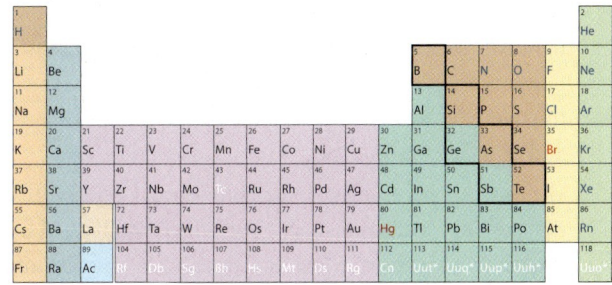

10. Define the following terms.
    a. atomic radius
    b. electron affinity
    c. electronegativity
    d. ionization energy

11. For each term in question 10, describe how the values of this property change
    a. down a group
    b. from left to right across a period

12. The colour codes in this periodic table divide elements into categories that highlight their unique chemical properties. Name the category highlighted by each colour below and describe the properties of the elements in this category.
    a. yellow
    b. purple
    c. brown

The Formation of Ionic and Covalent Bonds

- The octet rule can be used to predict the way in which bonds will form between many atoms.
- An ionic bond between two atoms forms due to the attraction between a negatively charged ion, called an anion, and a positively charged ion, called a cation.
- Ionic bonds form between metal and non-metal atoms. A compound held together by covalent bonds is referred to as a molecular compound. It exists as individual molecules. Molecular compounds consist of non-metals.
- Covalent bonds can be single, double, or triple bonds, depending on the number of shared electron pairs involved in the bond.

13. Write a caption to explain what is occurring in the following diagram.

    Na :Cl: → [Na]$^+$ [:Cl:]$^-$

    Mg :O: → [Mg]$^{2+}$ [:O:]$^{2-}$

14. Describe the octet rule and explain why certain elements do not follow this rule.

15. Draw Lewis diagrams for the following ionic compounds containing transition metals.
    a. Fe_2O_3
    b. $FeCl_2$

16. Which statement best describes a covalent bond?
    a. A bond that involves an uneven distribution of electrons.
    b. The electrostatic attraction between positively charged electrons and negatively charged nuclei.
    c. The attractive electrostatic force between a negative ion and a positive ion.
    d. The attraction between atoms that results from the sharing of electrons.
    e. none of the above

17. Compare and contrast the concepts of *lone pair* and *bonding pair*.

Writing Names and Formulas for Ionic and Molecular Compounds

- To name a binary ionic compound, begin with the name of the metal element. If necessary, use a roman numeral to indicate the charge on the ion. Then use the name of the non-metal element and change the end of the name to –*ide*.
- The formula for a binary ionic compound begins with the symbol for the metal element, which is followed by the symbol for the non-metal element. The number of atoms of each element in the compound is indicated be adding subscripts to the appropriate symbol.
- To name a binary molecular compound, begin with the name of the element with the lowest group number. Then the name of the element with the highest group number is added, with the end of the name changed to –*ide*. Prefixes are used to indicate the number of each element. If there is only one atom of the first element, a prefix is not used.
- The formula for a binary molecular compound begins with the symbol for the element with the lower group number, which is followed by the symbol for the element of the higher group number. The number of atoms of each element is indicated using subscripts on the appropriate symbol.

18. Identify whether each formula below represents an ionic compound or a molecular compound.
    a. NaCl
    b. SO_2
    c. CCl_4
    d. LiBr
    e. K_2CO_3

19. Name each polyatomic ion.
    a. NH_4^+
    b. CN^-
    c. CrO_4^{2-}
    d. CO_3^{2-}
    e. NO^{2-}

20. Titanium(IV) oxide is a white solid compound that is often found in sunscreen. Explain why the Roman numeral IV must be included in the name of this compound.

21. Identify each compound as ionic or molecular. Then write the name of the compound.
    a. Fe_2O_3
    b. PI_5
    c. N_2O
    d. CaI_2
    e. NaCNO

22. Identify each compound as ionic or molecular. Then write the chemical formula for the compound.
    a. zinc bromide
    b. sulfur hexafluoride
    c. copper(II) chromate
    d. dichlorine monoxide
    e. cesium chloride

23. Copy the table below, adding the missing prefixes for binary molecular compounds.

Prefixes of Binary Molecular Compounds

Number	Prefix
1	
2	
3	
4	
5	
6	
7	
8	
9	
10	

Comparing the Properties of Ionic and Molecular Compounds

- The strength of the attractive forces acting between ions or molecules determine physical properties of compounds, such as their melting points and boiling points.
- Boiling points and melting points are unique to each pure compound. Thus, they can provide important information about the characteristics of the compound.
- Ionic compounds tend to have very high melting points and boiling points. They also are good conductors of electricity and are likely to be soluble in water.
- Polar molecules have intermediate melting points and boiling points. They are likely to be soluble in water but do not conduct electricity. Non-polar molecules have the lowest melting points and boiling points. They are insoluble and non-conductive.
- The strong attractive forces in ionic compounds mean that each ion is strongly attracted to all adjacent ions of the opposite charge, resulting in a stable crystal lattice structure.
- The forces that act between molecules in molecular compounds are called intermolecular forces.

24. List the compounds shown below in the order of their boiling points, from lowest to highest (there is no need to know the exact boiling points of the compounds). Provide your reasoning.

methanol   chlorine   potassium oxide

25. The melting points and boiling points of a molecular compound are determined by its
  a. covalent bonds
  b. ionic bonds
  c. intermolecular forces
  d. solubility
  e. none of the above

26. Referring to the image below, explain why ionic compounds are good conductors of electricity while molecular compounds are not.

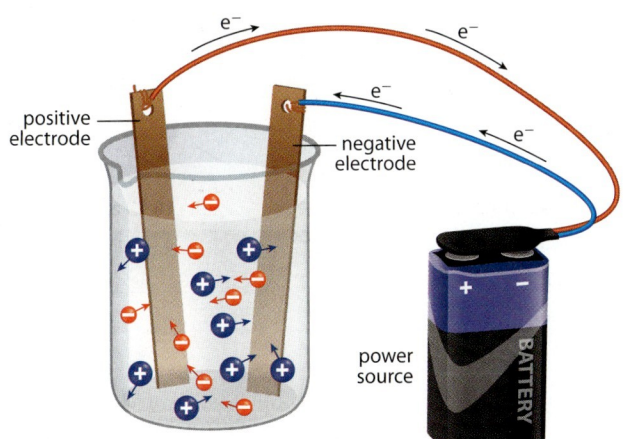

27. Examine the molecule below.
  a. Describe the polarity of the bonds in the molecule.
  b. Describe the overall polarity of the molecule.
  c. Would you expect this compound to be soluble in water? Explain your reasoning.

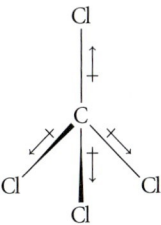

28. Refer to the structure of sodium chloride to explain why there are no specific pairs of sodium and chloride ions that could be identified as "molecules."

29. Compare and contrast intermolecular forces and covalent bonds.

30. Write a caption to explain the nature of the forces between the molecules in the diagram below.

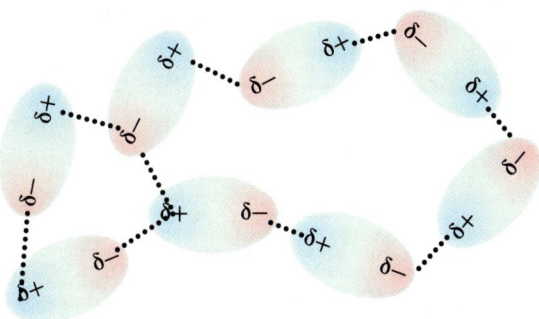

CHAPTER 3
Atomic Models and Properties of Atoms

Specific Expectations

In this chapter, you will learn how to . . .

- C1.1 **assess** the benefits to society of technologies that are based on the principles of atomic and molecular structures (3.3)

- C2.1 **use** appropriate terminology related to structure and properties of matter (3.1, 3.2, 3.3)

- C2.2 **use** the Pauli exclusion principle, Hund's rule, and the aufbau principle to **write** electron configurations (3.3)

- C3.1 **explain** how experimental observations and inferences made by Ernest Rutherford and Niels Bohr contributed to the development of the planetary model of the hydrogen atom (3.1)

- C3.2 **describe** the electron configurations of a variety of elements in the periodic table, using the concept of energy levels in shells and subshells, as well as the Pauli exclusion principle, Hund's rule, and the aufbau principle (3.2, 3.3)

- B3.3 **identify** the characteristic properties of elements in each of the *s*, *p*, and *d* blocks of the periodic table, and **explain** the relationship between the position of an element in the periodic table, its properties, and its electron configuration (3.2, 3.3)

Fossils of birds and their ancestors sometimes capture the shapes and textures of plumage. However, until recently, the colours of long-extinct birds were a matter for speculation, inference, and sometimes even flights of fancy. In 2011, researchers developed a technique for analyzing fossil feathers, using a particle accelerator called a synchrotron to produce a very intense, narrowly focussed X-ray beam. Specific wavelengths of X rays are absorbed by atoms of different elements. The researchers were able to identify copper atoms that, in conjunction with a pigment called eumelanin, are found in dark-coloured feathers. They compared their data from 120 million year old fossils of birds with feathers of modern birds and confirmed their results. The data allowed these researchers to determine colour patterns on the feathers of the oldest-known beaked bird, *Confuciusornis sanctus*, shown here in this artist's conception.

Launch Lab

Flame Tests to Identify Elements

When a compound containing a metal is heated in a flame, a distinctive colour is emitted that corresponds to that particular metal. In this activity, you will observe flame tests on solutions of metal-containing compounds and use your observations to identify the metal in an unknown compound.

Safety Precautions

- Wear safety eyewear throughout this activity.
- Tie back loose hair and clothing.
- Use EXTREME CAUTION when near an open flame.
- Use EXTREME CAUTION when using lithium hydroxide, as it is extremely corrosive.

Materials

- Bunsen burner
- heat-resistant pad
- wooden splint soaked in water
- labelled dropper bottles containing aqueous solutions of lithium hydroxide, sodium chloride, potassium chloride, calcium chloride, and strontium chloride
- labelled dropper bottle containing an unknown solution

Procedure

1. **Note:** Your teacher will demonstrate the flame tests with solutions of each of the known metallic compounds. Design a table to record your observations of the flame colour for each compound tested.
2. Obtain a sample of an unknown solution from your teacher.
3. Set up the Bunsen burner on the heat-resistant pad. Light the burner, and adjust the air supply to produce a hot flame with a blue cone.
4. Wet one end of a water-soaked wooden splint with a few drops of the unknown solution. Hold the wooden splint at the edge of the Bunsen burner flame. (You may need to hold the splint in the flame for up to 30 s until the solution vaporizes and mixes with the flame.)
5. Observe and record the colour of the flame.
6. Dispose of the used splint as instructed by your teacher.

Questions

1. Four of the known compounds tested contain chlorine, and one compound contains the hydroxide ion. Does this complicate the interpretation of the data? Explain your reasoning.
2. What is the identity of the unknown solution? Explain how you know.
3. Explain the importance of purity of the sample being tested. In what ways could contaminants affect the accuracy of the flame test?

SECTION 3.1
Developing a Nuclear Model of the Atom

Key Terms

nuclear model
electromagnetic radiation
frequency
photon
emission spectrum
line spectrum
quantum

The scientific concept of the atom as a physical component or constituent of matter is barely 200 years old. In that brief time, scientists' model of the atom has undergone remarkable changes—from a lawn-bowling ball, to a plum pudding, to a planetary system, to a quasi-particulate entity surrounded by even tinier fundamental entities that are neither particles nor waves and that can be described only by using mathematical equations. This last model, called the quantum mechanical model of the atom, will be introduced later, in Section 3.2.

To help you understand how and why the quantum mechanical model was developed, Section 3.1 will focus on the atomic models developed by two chemists, Ernest Rutherford and Niels Bohr, whose experiments, ideas, and insights were central to the conception of the quantum mechanical model. To set the stage, two earlier models, those of John Dalton and J.J. Thomson, are briefly reviewed first.

Reviewing the Atomic Models of Dalton and Thomson

John Dalton (1766–1844) was a schoolteacher and scientist whose atomic theory, published in 1808, marked the beginning of a new way to describe, explain, and visualize the nature of matter. Dalton's interest in the gases that make up Earth's atmosphere led him to investigate the composition and properties of substances such as carbon dioxide, water vapour, and nitrogen monoxide. In explaining some of his experimental results, Dalton compared the particles that make up matter to small, hard spheres, to which he gave the name atoms. **Figure 3.1** shows models of these spheres.

Figure 3.1 Dalton was an avid lawn-bowler, so it is not surprising that he visualized atoms in the form of tiny solid spheres. He likely also was influenced by Sir Isaac Newton's description of matter as being formed from "solid, massy, hard, impenetrable, movable particles" (from *Opticks*).

According to Dalton's model, the atom was indestructible and indivisible. However, a series of investigations beginning in the 1850s and extending into the early 1900s demonstrated that atoms are not indivisible—that they are made up of even smaller components. These investigations led to the discovery of electrons, protons, and neutrons, and contributed to scientists' understanding of atomic structure.

The first of these smaller components to be discovered was the electron, and the person who discovered it was Joseph John (J.J.) Thomson (1856–1940). Thomson, a physicist, was especially interested in studying electric currents in gas discharge tubes, which are glass tubes from which most of the air has been removed. The glass tubes, called cathode ray tubes, are fitted with metal electrodes that are sealed in place and connected to an external source of electrical energy. An example of a cathode ray tube is shown in **Figure 3.2**.

When the power is turned on, a "ray" emanates from the negative electrode (cathode) and travels to the positive electrode (anode). Because the nature of the "ray" was not known, they were simply called cathode rays. Thomson and other scientists who worked with cathode ray tubes observed that the results of their many experiments did not depend on the material from which the cathode was made. Cathode rays appeared to be a component even more fundamental than atoms and common to all matter. As well, when a magnet was placed near the tube, as demonstrated in **Figure 3.2**, the path of the ray curved in the direction that negative charges should move. Thomson determined in 1897 that the cathode rays were streams of negatively charged particles—electrons.

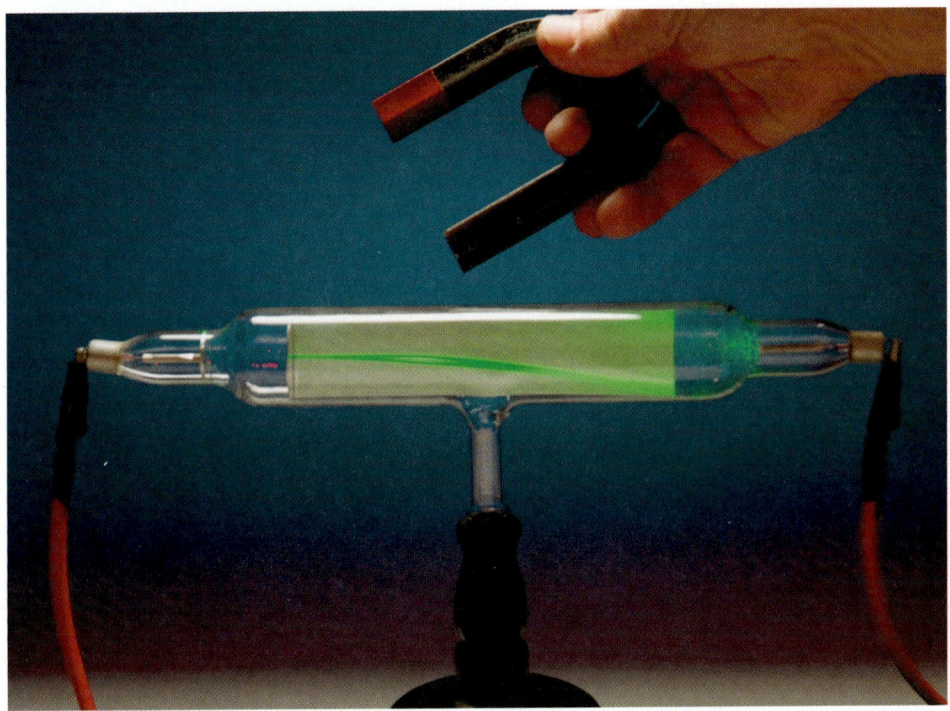

Figure 3.2 Cathode rays are invisible, but when they collide with the few remaining gas molecules in the tube, they excite atoms in the gas molecules. These excited atoms emit visible light, making the path of the cathode rays visible.

Based on his studies, Thomson proposed a model of the structure of the atom based on a plum pudding, a popular cake-like dessert that was common in England. (A plum pudding was originally made with dried plums and later evolved to use currants, raisins, or any other dried fruit.) This plum pudding model, shown in **Figure 3.3**, portrayed the atom as a positively charged, spherical mass in which negatively charged electrons (the "plums") were embedded and held by electrostatic forces.

Thomson presented his atomic model during a series of lectures in 1903 and later published his ideas in 1904. For the scientific community, however, this model was short-lived. By 1911, a more complete and accurate model of the atom was proposed by one of Thomson's students, a chemist and physicist named Ernest Rutherford.

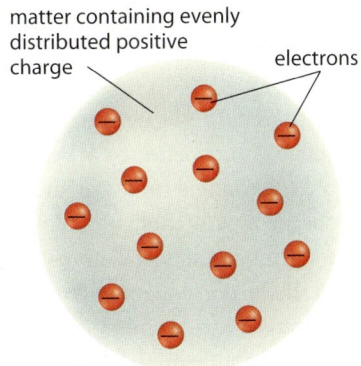

Figure 3.3 The Thomson model of the atom. **Analyze** Originally referred to as the "plum pudding model," Thomson's model is also called a "raisin bun model" or a "blueberry muffin model." How do comparisons like these help in communicating scientific ideas?

Rutherford's Experiments with Alpha Particles

At the end of the 19th century, French physicists Henri Becquerel and Marie and Pierre Curie discovered that certain elements are radioactive—they naturally emit positively charged particles (alpha particles), negatively charged particles (beta particles), and electromagnetic energy (gamma radiation). Between 1898 and 1907, New Zealand-born British chemist Ernest Rutherford (1871–1937) began intensive studies of the chemistry of radioactive elements while working at Montreal's McGill University. His efforts would lead to a Nobel Prize in chemistry in 1908.

In 1909, two of Rutherford's students reported observations that cast doubts on Thomson's atomic model. As part of ongoing investigations into the nature and properties of radioactive emissions, the students aimed alpha (α) particles at extremely thin sheets of gold foil. The gold foil was surrounded by a zinc sulfide-coated screen that produced a flash of light whenever it was struck by an alpha particle. By noting where the flashes occurred, the researchers could determine if and when the atoms in the gold foil deflected the alpha particles.

Based on Thomson's atomic model, the researchers expected to observe only minor deflections of the alpha particles. As shown in **Figure 3.4**, they expected the paths of the large, fast-moving alpha particles to be altered only slightly by a nearby encounter or collision with an electron. With Thomson's model of the atom in mind, Rutherford also believed that, because the positive charge within the gold atoms was uniformly distributed, it would not affect the paths of the alpha particles.

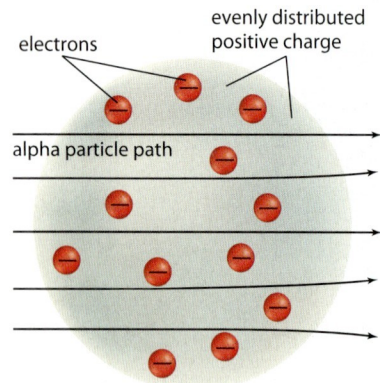

Figure 3.4 Rutherford and his students expected most of the large, highly energetic alpha particles to pass straight through the gold foil atoms. They also expected some alpha particles to be slightly deflected by the electrons in the gold foil atoms.

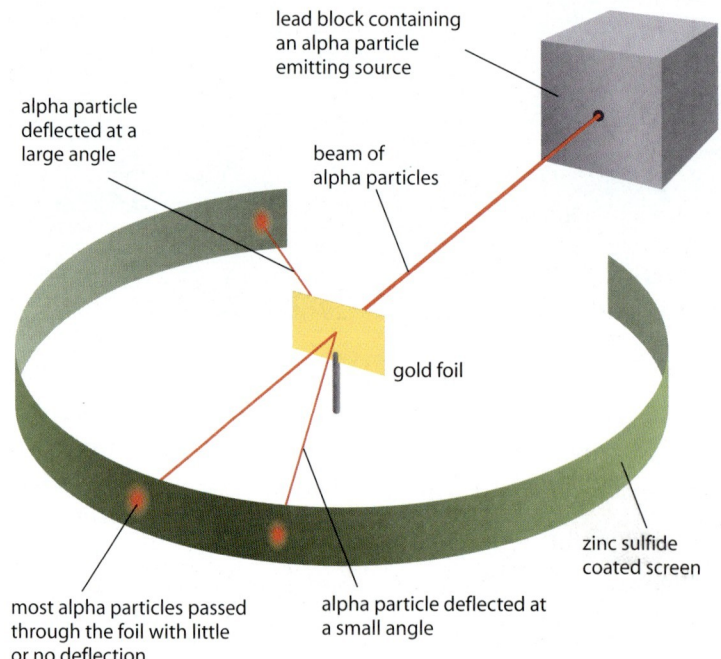

Figure 3.5 Rutherford's experiment was designed to measure the scattering of alpha particles when directed at a thin gold foil. Most of the alpha particles passed directly through the gold foil with little or no deflection. However, some were scattered at small angles, and a few alpha particles were deflected at very large angles.

After several days of testing, Rutherford and his students discovered that some of the alpha particles—about 1 in every 8000—were deflected at very large angles. About 1 in 20 000 were deflected from the gold foil at angles much greater than 90°, as shown in **Figure 3.5**. These observations were inconsistent with Thomson's atomic model. The researchers expected the alpha particles to pass through the metal atoms with deflections averaging $\frac{1}{200}$ of a degree, at most. Therefore, deflections of 90° *and more* strained the credibility of Thomson's model. Rutherford encouraged further investigation. Either their observations and the data were flawed, or Thomson's atomic model was invalid.

Rutherford's Atomic Model

In 1911, Rutherford published the results of the gold foil experiments undertaken by him and his students. Based on their experimental findings, Rutherford proposed that the observed deflections were caused by encounters between alpha particles and an intense electric field at the centre of the atom. Since these results were inconsistent with Thomson's model of the atom, Rutherford developed a new atomic model.

Given the properties of the alpha particles and electrons, and the frequency and the angles of the deflections that were observed, Rutherford calculated that all of the positive charge and most of the atom's mass were confined to a very small region at the centre of the atom, which he called the nucleus. Rutherford's atomic model, shown in **Figure 3.6**, depicts electrons in motion around an atomic nucleus, so chemists often call this the **nuclear model** of the atom. It is sometimes also referred to as a *planetary model*, because the electrons resemble planets in motion around a central body.

Figure 3.7 shows how Rutherford's nuclear model of the atom explained the results of the gold foil experiments. The repulsive force that occurred between the positive nucleus and the positive alpha particles caused the deflection of the alpha particles. When alpha particles *closely* approached the nucleus, they were deflected at small angles. However, when alpha particles *directly* approached the nucleus, they were deflected at very large angles. The nuclear model also explains the neutral nature of matter—that is, the positive charge of the nucleus balances the negative charge of the electrons. Despite these findings, however, Rutherford's model still could not account for all of the atom's mass. Another 20 years would pass before this discrepancy was finally explained by James Chadwick's discovery of the neutron.

nuclear model a model of the atom in which electrons move around an extremely small, positively charged nucleus; also called a *planetary model*

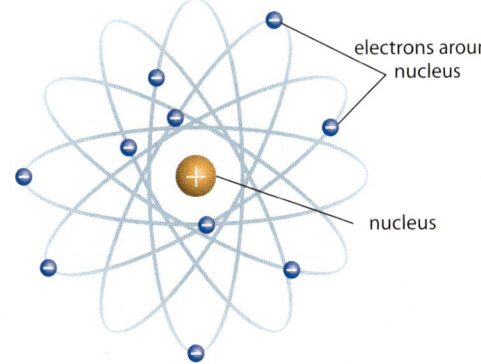

Figure 3.6 The atomic model that Rutherford proposed in 1911 is known as the nuclear, or planetary, model of the atom.

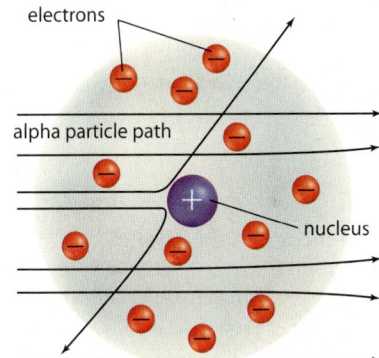

Figure 3.7 Rutherford's nuclear model explained the unexpected interactions of alpha particles with the gold foil. The strong repulsive force between the positively charged nucleus and the positively charged alpha particles caused their deflections.

The Limitations of Rutherford's Atomic Model

Rutherford's atomic model answered some of the questions arising from Thomson's atomic model, but it also raised others. First, an atomic nucleus composed entirely of positive charges should break apart as a result of electrostatic forces of repulsion. Second, until the discovery of the neutron 20 years later, Rutherford's nuclear atom could not adequately explain the total mass of an atom.

There was a more significant problem, however. According to the scientific laws and understandings of physics before the turn of the 20th century, an electron in motion around a central body *must* continuously emit radiation. Therefore, one would expect to observe a continuous spectrum, or "rainbow," of light energy as the electron gives off radiation. Because the electron should also lose energy as a result of this radiation, the radius of its orbit should continuously decrease in size until it spirals into the nucleus, obliterating the atom entirely. Since this does not occur, either the Rutherford model was incorrect or scientists' understanding was flawed—perhaps even both.

Science, as understood and explained by the physicists of the late 1800s, could not explain why Rutherford's model corresponded to a stable atom. The solution to this problem marked a turning point in the history of chemistry and physics, because it required scientists to think about energy and matter in a startlingly new way.

Learning Check

1. What evidence invalidated Dalton's atomic theory that atoms are indivisible?
2. If Thomson's model of the atom had been valid, what would Rutherford and his team have observed in the gold foil experiment, and why?
3. State one way the discovery of radioactive elements furthered the development of atomic theory.
4. Draw two labelled diagrams with captions to summarize Thomson's and Rutherford's atomic models.
5. Dalton enjoyed lawn-bowling, and plum pudding was a popular dessert in England long before Thomson was even born. What role do you think that personal interests and cultural history play in the kinds of models that scientists use to communicate their ideas? Use another example to explain your answer.
6. Explain why Rutherford and his students expected to observe only minor deflections of alpha particles, based on Thomson's model.

Rethinking Atomic Structure Based on the Nature of Energy

By the early 1900s, scientists were starting to gain a better understanding of chemical behaviour. For instance, they had long known that atoms could emit light when stimulated by an electric current. In fact, chemists knew that they could identify elements by the set of specific wavelengths of light that atoms of each element emit when stimulated. However, they had no idea how or why this occurred. To learn how chemists used this information, it will be necessary to review some key ideas about the nature of light.

Light is a form of energy called **electromagnetic radiation**. The light that you see—visible light—is only a small fraction of the wide range of electromagnetic radiation, which includes X rays, ultraviolet radiation, infrared radiation, microwaves, and radio waves. All these types of electromagnetic radiation travel through space in the form of waves and at the same speed, 3.0×10^8 m/s, which is the speed of light in a vacuum.

electromagnetic radiation oscillating, perpendicular electric and magnetic fields moving through space as waves

Characteristics of Electromagnetic Radiation

Figure 3.8 shows the characteristics that all waves have in common. *Wavelength* (λ) is the shortest distance between equivalent points on a continuous wave. Wavelength is most often expressed in metres or nanometres (1 nm = 1×10^{-9} m). **Frequency** (ν) is the number of wave cycles that pass a given point in a unit of time. Although f is often used to represent frequency, the Greek letter nu (ν) is commonly used when describing electromagnetic waves. One hertz (Hz), the SI unit of frequency, represents one cycle per second (s^{-1}).

frequency the number of complete wave cycles that pass a given point in a unit of time

Figure 3.8 (**A**) Three waves with different wavelengths (λ) and frequencies (ν) are shown. Note that as the wavelength decreases, the frequency increases. (**B**) The amplitude of a wave represents its intensity. For visible light, this is perceived as brightness of the light. Here, the two waves have the same wavelength but different amplitudes; therefore, each wave has a different brightness.

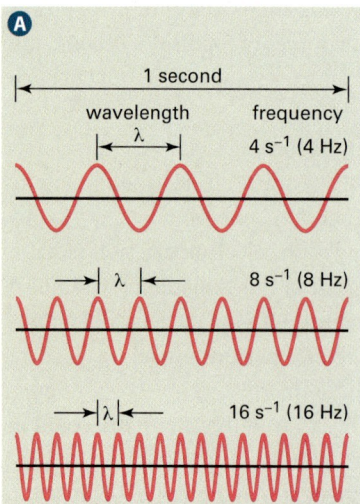

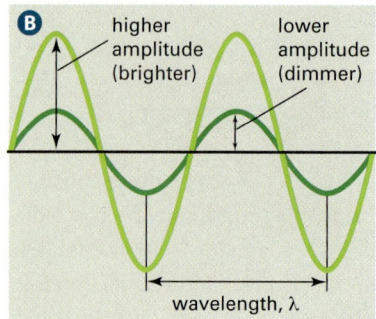

A labelled diagram of the electromagnetic spectrum is shown in **Figure 3.9**. Notice that as wavelength decreases, frequency increases. In other words, wavelength and frequency are inversely proportional.

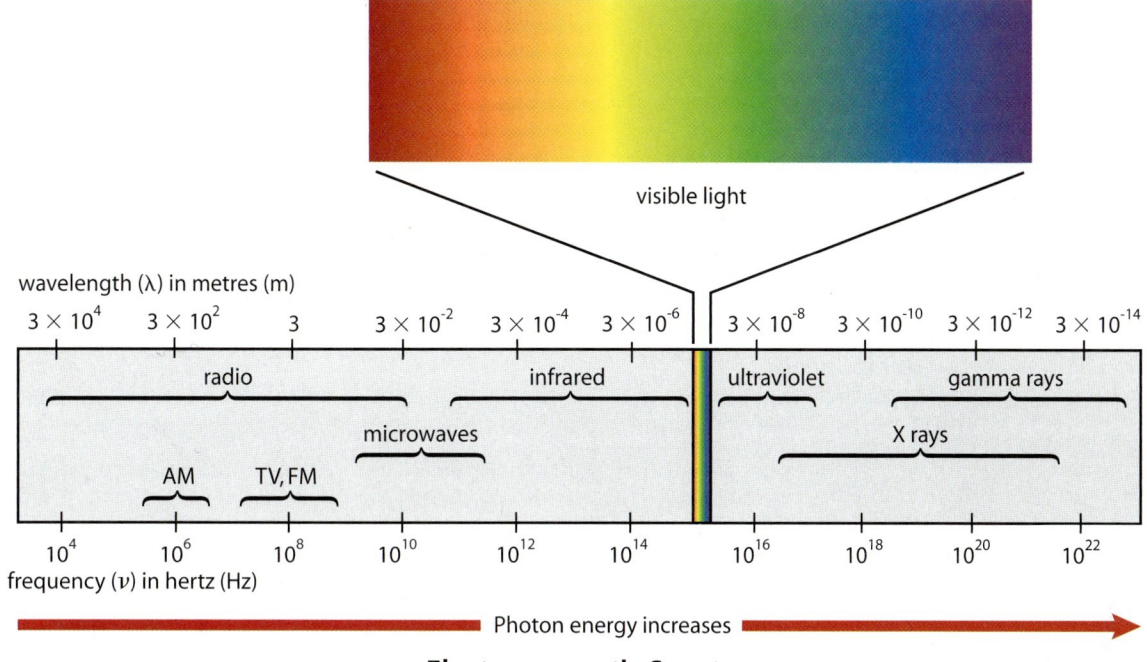

Electromagnetic Spectrum

Figure 3.9 The relatively narrow visible region of this electromagnetic spectrum has been expanded (and the scale made linear) to show the component colours.

The Energy of Light and other Types of Electromagnetic Radiation

When electromagnetic waves interact with matter, they do so in discrete packets, or quanta, of energy called **photons**. The energy, E, of a photon depends on the wavelength or frequency. Electromagnetic radiation of long wavelength and low frequency, such as radio waves, is composed of lower-energy photons. Short-wavelength radiation with high frequencies is composed of higher-energy photons. Photon energy is directly proportional to frequency and inversely proportional to wavelength.

photon a packet, or quantum, of electromagnetic energy

Mathematical relationships can be used to calculate the wavelength (λ), frequency (ν), and photon energy of electromagnetic radiation. The product of frequency and wavelength is a constant, c, which is the speed of light in a vacuum: $\nu\lambda = c$. This equation shows the inverse relationship between wavelength and frequency. Since the speed of light in a vacuum, c, is a constant, when frequency is large, wavelength must be small; when wavelength is large, frequency must be small. If the value of either wavelength or frequency is known, you can calculate the unknown value by rearranging the equation:

$$\nu = \frac{c}{\lambda} \text{ or } \lambda = \frac{c}{\nu}$$

The mathematical relationships between photon energy and frequency and between photon energy and wavelength are described by the following equations, where h is a constant with a value of 6.626×10^{-34} J·s:

$$E_{photon} = h\nu \qquad E_{photon} = \frac{hc}{\lambda}$$

(The constant, h, is called Planck's constant. You can investigate the significance of this constant and the scientist, Max Planck, who discovered it, in Activity 3.1.)

Activity 3.1   The "Birth" of Quanta and Photons

The concepts of the quantum and the photon developed mostly from the work of Max Planck and Albert Einstein as they attempted to understand and explain two phenomena: blackbody radiation and the photoelectric effect. In this activity, you will investigate these phenomena and the work of these two scientists.

Procedure

1. Do research to help you describe—verbally as well as visually—blackbody radiation and the photoelectric effect.

2. In the course of your research, refer to Planck, Einstein, and any other scientists whose work helped to inform their thinking. (In the case of Planck, one such scientist was Gustav Kirchhoff, for instance.)

Questions

1. Summarize the reasons why conventional physics could not explain these phenomena.

2. Explain how Planck's concept of the quantum and Einstein's concept of the photon could explain them.

Atomic Spectra

When visible light passes through a prism, it separates into its component colours. Sunlight produces a *continuous spectrum*, which includes all the wavelengths in the visible region of the electromagnetic spectrum, as shown in **Figure 3.10A**. The term *white light* refers to light from a light source that produces a continuous spectrum. Unlike white light, coloured light is not composed of all the wavelengths, so its spectrum is not continuous. A neon light, for example, consists of a tube containing only neon atoms under very low pressure. When an electric current is passed through the neon gas in the tube, neon atoms absorb energy and then emit it in the form of light. If this light is passed through a slit and then through a prism, the resulting spectrum has a set of distinct coloured lines, as shown in **Figure 3.10B**. Each coloured line represents a single wavelength of light, and the pattern of these lines is called an **emission spectrum** or a **line spectrum**.

When atoms of an element are excited (absorb energy), the energy can be emitted as light energy. The light that atoms of a given element produce in this way contains only specific colours, as shown by its line spectrum. The line spectrum for each element is unique, so it can be used to identify the element. You will see in the following paragraphs how a Danish chemist named Niels Bohr, who worked briefly in the laboratories of both J.J. Thomson and Ernest Rutherford, related the line spectrum for hydrogen to its atomic structure.

emission spectrum or **line spectrum**
a series of separate lines of different colours of light emitted by atoms of a specific element as they lose excitation energy

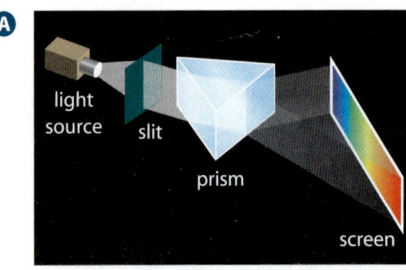
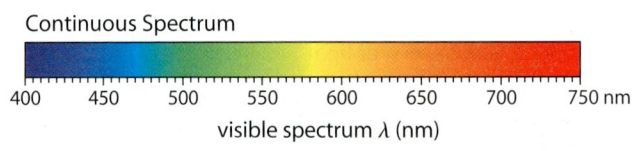
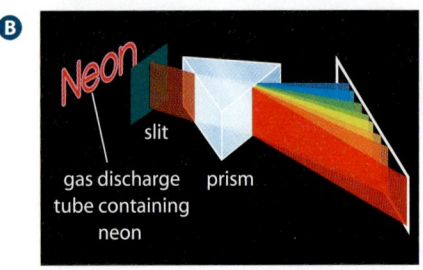
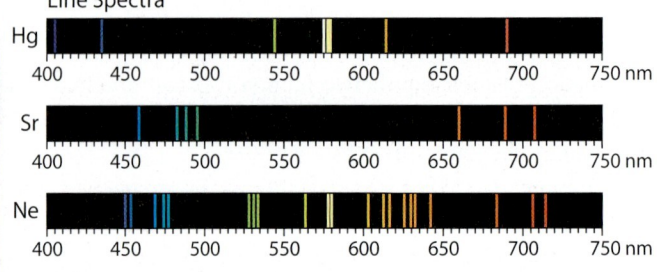

Figure 3.10 When white light passes through a prism, a continuous spectrum (**A**) is produced. The coloured light emitted by a substance, such as neon, produces a line spectrum (**B**) that is unique to that substance. Line spectra of various elements are shown here.

The Bohr Model of the Hydrogen Atom

One year after Rutherford published his nuclear model of the atom, Niels Bohr (1885–1962) came to work in his laboratory. Fascinated by this model, Bohr set out to explain the stability of the nuclear atom and why it appeared to contradict known laws of physics. He based his analysis on the recent work of Max Planck and Albert Einstein, as well as on the line spectra emitted by excited atoms. Bohr knew from a paper published by Plank in 1900 that hot matter emitted electromagnetic energy as discrete packets, or **quanta**, of energy. He knew from a paper published by Einstein in 1905 that when matter absorbs light energy, it can only absorb it in packets or photons in an "all or none" manner. In other words, matter cannot absorb or emit part of a photon or more than one photon in a single event. Bohr also knew that excited atoms emit specific wavelengths (photons) of light. He combined these ideas and reasoned that the total energy of each electron in an atom might also be quantized. Based on these concepts, Bohr developed a model of the atom based on the following postulates.

- Electrons exist in circular orbits, much like planetary orbits. The central force that holds them in orbit is the electrostatic force between the positive nucleus and the negative charge on the electrons, rather than a gravitational force.
- Electrons can exist only in a series of "allowed" orbits. Much like planets, electrons have different amounts of total energy in each orbit. Thus, these orbits can also be described as "energy levels." Because only certain orbits are allowed, only certain energy levels are allowed. This means that the energy of electrons in atoms is quantized.
- While an electron remains in one orbit, it does not radiate energy.
- Electrons can "jump" between orbits (energy levels) by absorbing or emitting photons carrying an amount of energy that is equal to the difference in the energy levels of the electrons.

By using the basic laws of physics and Planck's concepts, Bohr was able to calculate the energy and radii of the allowed orbits for the hydrogen atom. In Bohr's atomic model, the orbits are numbered with $n = 1$ as the orbit nearest the nucleus. Bohr's calculated radius of this orbit is $5.291\ 77 \times 10^{-11}$ m, which is now called the Bohr radius. Because that orbit has the lowest possible energy, it is called the *ground state* of the atom. Energy is required to move the electron farther from the nucleus due to the attractive force of the nucleus. A model of the Bohr atom, with six of its orbits, is shown in **Figure 3.11**. The radii of the orbits are not drawn to scale; the distance between the orbits gets larger with each orbit.

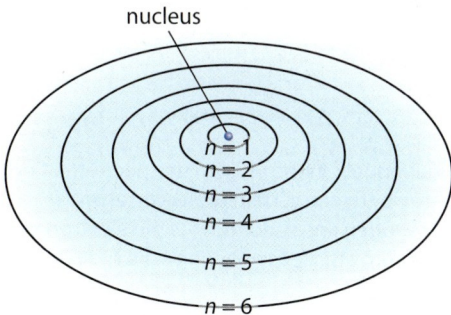

Figure 3.11 In the Bohr model of the hydrogen atom, the nucleus is at the centre of the atom, and the electron is located in one of the circular orbits, each with a specific energy and radius. Six orbits are shown here, but any number of orbits is possible.

According to Bohr's model, an atom can absorb energy and become excited in one of two ways. The atom can collide with a highly energetic particle such as an electron in an electric current passing through a gas. Alternatively, the atom can absorb a photon that has an amount of energy equal to the difference between the energy of the orbit it occupies and the energy of a higher orbit. Excited atoms quickly return to their ground state by emitting photons of an energy equal to the difference between the energy of the orbit it occupies and a lower orbit.

Suggested Investigation

Inquiry Investigation 3-A, Observing Spectra (Teacher Demonstration)

quantum an indivisible packet of energy that must be absorbed or emitted in an "all or none" manner (plural, quanta)

Bohr's Atomic Model Explains the Line Spectrum of Hydrogen

With the aid of this new atomic model and the idea that the energy of the photons emitted by excited atoms had to be equal to the difference between energy levels, Bohr calculated the possible energies of the photons that could be emitted by excited hydrogen atoms. By using Planck's equation relating the energy of photons to their wavelength, $E = hc/\lambda$, Bohr calculated the value of the wavelengths of the electromagnetic radiation. The wavelengths that fell in the visible range of the electromagnetic spectrum were the transitions from energy levels $n = 6, 5, 4$, and 3 to energy level $n = 2$. When he compared them with the wavelengths of the experimentally observed spectrum, they were in complete agreement. As shown in **Figure 3.12**, the transition from energy level $n = 6$ to $n = 2$ produces a photon with a wavelength of 410 nm, which is in the range of violet light. The transition from $n = 5$ to $n = 2$ produces a photon with a wavelength of 434 nm, which is the range of indigo light. The last two transitions produce photons with wavelengths of 486 nm and 656 nm, which are blue light and red light, respectively.

During the same period that Bohr was doing his theoretical work, other scientists discovered spectra from hydrogen atom that were in the infrared and ultraviolet regions of the spectrum. The wavelengths of the photons in these spectra were also in agreement with Bohr's predictions. Such excellent agreement between Bohr's theoretical predictions and observed data provided strong support for Bohr's basic tenets.

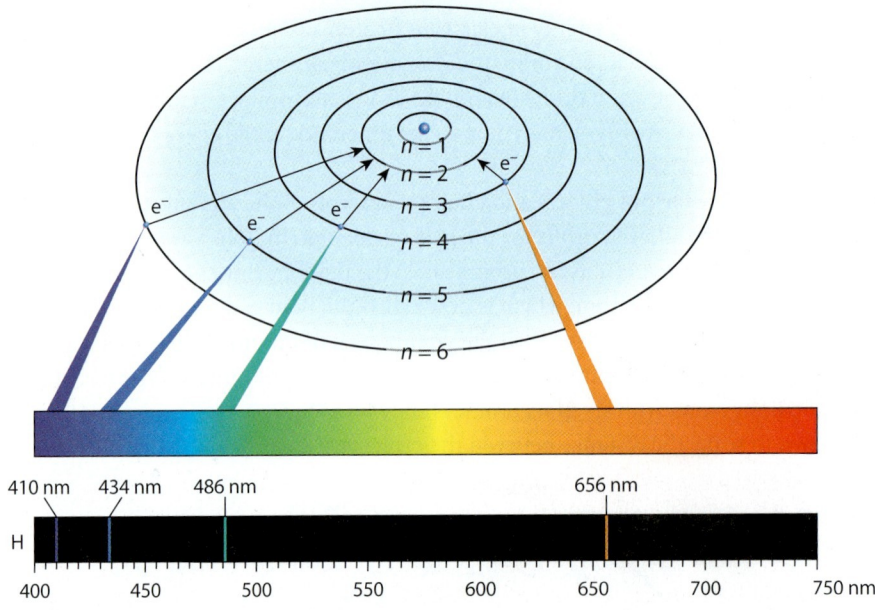

Figure 3.12 Four distinct lines appear in the visible line spectrum of hydrogen. In the Bohr model, the difference in energy between certain orbits corresponds to the photon energies of the lines that appear in the hydrogen line spectrum. As the electron moves from a higher-energy orbit to a lower-energy orbit, energy is released as light of a specific wavelength (and, therefore, of a specific colour).

The Limitations of Bohr's Atomic Model

Bohr's atomic model was successful in explaining the line spectrum of hydrogen. It also explained the line spectrum for single-electron ions such as He^+ and Li^{2+}. However, Bohr's model could not explain the line spectra for atoms that had two or more electrons, and so its value as a means for describing atomic structure was severely limited. Nevertheless, Bohr's ideas of quantized energy levels would prove to be of enormous benefit to other scientists working to solve the same fundamental problem of both describing and explaining atomic structure. In the next section, you will be introduced to the model that has resulted from their work: the quantum mechanical model of the atom.

Section 3.1 Review

Section Summary

- Historically, the development of and modifications to the atomic model have been the result of experimental evidence leading to new ideas about the nature of matter and energy.
- Thomson's discovery of the electron disproved Dalton's model of the atom as a solid, indivisible sphere. Instead, Thomson proposed that the atom existed as a positively charged sphere, with enough negatively charged electrons embedded in it to balance the overall charge on the atom.
- Observations and inferences made by Rutherford led to a nuclear model of the hydrogen atom. This model is still the most commonly depicted, with negatively charged electrons orbiting around a central positively charged nucleus.
- Bohr's model of the atom refined the Rutherford model, incorporating the concept that, like light, electrons in atoms could have only certain amounts of energy and, therefore, could exist in only specific orbits around the nucleus. Each allowed orbit had a specific amount of energy and a specific radius.

Review Questions

1. **C** Your friend is conducting Internet research on the history of atomic theory and e-mails you to ask why Thomson's model of the atom is sometimes called the "plum pudding" model. Write a brief e-mail reply to explain, and use a similar analogy that might be more familiar to your friend.

2. **A** Dalton's atomic theory represented a huge step forward for a scientific understanding of the nature of matter. One of its successes was explaining observations about mass relationships in chemical reactions.
    a. State and explain the law of conservation of mass in terms of Dalton's atomic model.
    b. State one shortcoming of Dalton's model of the atom.

3. **K/U** Rutherford could not account for all of the mass in the nucleus when he first made observations. Describe the discovery that provided an explanation.

4. **C** Draw a diagram to represent what Rutherford and his colleagues expected to happen when they fired alpha particles through a gold foil, based on Thomson's model of the atom.

5. **A** Suggest one reason why Rutherford and his colleagues chose gold as the substance through which to fire alpha particles.

6. **C** Compare Rutherford's model and Thomson's model of the atom using a Venn diagram.

7. **K/U** What is the key difference between Rutherford's model and Bohr's model, and what shortcoming of Rutherford's model does this key difference address?

8. **A** Why are only the transitions from $n = 3, 4, 5,$ and 6 to $n = 2$ shown in **Figure 3.12**?

9. **T/I** Arrange the following types of electromagnetic radiation from lowest energy to highest energy. For each type, state which has the highest and lowest frequency and the longest and shortest wavelength.
    a. gamma ray, microwave, visible light
    b. visible light, X ray, infrared light
    c. ultraviolet ray, X ray, radio wave

10. **K/U** According to 19th century physics, what type of radiation should an atom based on Rutherford's model emit? What were excited atoms observed to emit?

11. **T/I** When an electron in a hydrogen atom absorbs a photon of blue light with a wavelength of 434 nm, it moves from one energy level to another.
    a. What energy level did the electron occupy originally?
    b. What energy level does the electron occupy after emitting the photon?

12. **A** Dalton invented symbols such as those shown below to represent atoms and molecules. Suggest a reason why his symbols could represent carbon dioxide accurately but not water or methane.

    hydrogen   carbon dioxide
    carbon   water
    oxygen   methane

13. **K/U** How does the idea of quantized energy apply to Bohr's atomic model?

14. **C** A ladder and a ramp are one analogy for quantized vs. continuous theories of energy. Think of another analogy to compare the two theories and draw a diagram to represent it.

SECTION 3.2
The Quantum Mechanical Model of the Atom

Key Terms

quantum mechanical model of the atom
atomic orbital
quantum number
principal quantum number, n
shell
orbital-shape quantum number, l
sublevel
magnetic quantum number, m_l
spin quantum number, m_s
Pauli exclusion principle

While a graduate student at the Sorbonne in Paris, France, Louis de Broglie was doing an in-depth study of the recently published concepts in the particle theory of light. This theory suggested that light interacts with matter as individual photons. De Broglie reasoned that, if light waves have some properties of particles, then particles might have some properties of waves. He used some of the concepts involving light waves and applied them to particles such as electrons. He determined that the wavelength for particles should be $\lambda = h/mv$, where h is Planck's constant, m is the mass of the particle, and v is the speed of the particle. Using similar reasoning, de Broglie showed that the frequency of the matter wave should be $v = E_k/h$, where E_k is the kinetic energy of the particle.

Within three years after de Broglie published his theory of matter waves, two different groups of researchers performed experiments with electrons that supported de Broglie's theory. (One of the physicists who demonstrated the wave nature of electrons was George P. Thomson, the son of J.J. Thomson who had discovered the electron and showed that it is a particle.) The reason that the wave nature of particles had never been observed before de Broglie's work was that large objects have such small wavelengths that any influence that their wave nature might have on their motion is not detectable. For example, a 60 kg sprinter running 10 m/s would have a wavelength of 1.1×10^{-36} m.

De Broglie applied his concept of matter waves to the electrons in the Bohr model of the atom and obtained some remarkable results. He reasoned that the radius of the orbit would have to be equal to an integer number of wavelengths or the waves would cancel themselves out. When he applied his theory of matter waves to calculate the radii of allowed orbits, his results were identical to Bohr's results, lending support to Bohr's model of the atom. However, the more complex line spectra of multi-electron atoms remained unexplained.

The Quantum Mechanical Model of the Atom

De Broglie's matter waves stirred a great deal of interest among the chemists and physicists who were working on an improved model of the atom—one that could explain the line spectra of multi-electron atoms. Erwin Schrödinger, a Viennese physicist, realized that a wave theory and equations were needed for a complete treatment of these "matter waves." In 1926, Schrödinger published an equation that is now known as the Schrödinger wave equation.

When the Schrödinger wave equation is applied to the hydrogen atom, the solution to the equation is a mathematical function called a wave function. This wave function contains three variables that are called quantum numbers, and they are denoted as n, l, and m_l. When you substitute specific combinations of integers for each of these variables into the wave function, you have different solutions to the wave equation. Each solution describes a region in the space around the nucleus of an atom. Each of the quantum numbers represents a specific characteristic of the electrons occupying that space. The atomic model in which electrons are treated as waves is called the **quantum mechanical model of the atom**. Like Bohr's model, the quantum mechanical model limits the energy of an electron to certain discrete values. The region of space that is related to a wave function, or solution to Schrödinger's wave equation, is called an **atomic orbital**.

Shortly after Schrödinger introduced his wave equation, a debate arose among chemists and physicist about the meaning of these matter waves. The currently accepted interpretation was presented by German physicist, Max Born, who showed that the wave functions could be used to determine the probability of finding the electron at any point within the region of space described by the wave function. When the most probable distance from the nucleus is calculated for the electron in the lowest energy level in the hydrogen atom, the result is the same as the Bohr radius, giving validity to both

quantum mechanical model of the atom
an atomic model in which electrons are treated as having wave characteristics

atomic orbital
a region in space around a nucleus that is related to a specific wave function

approaches. As well, the energy of the electron in this lowest energy level, as determined by Schrödinger's wave equation, is the same as the energy calculated by Bohr. However, the solutions to the Schrödinger wave equation provide much more information about electrons in atoms. Nearly all of the observable characteristics of atoms, including their spectra, can be explained by these wave functions. Some refinements, including a fourth quantum number, were soon presented by other chemists and physicists.

Adding credence to the concept of matter waves, in 1927, Werner Heisenberg published a paper in which he mathematically showed that it is not possible to know both the position, x, and momentum (mass times velocity, mv) of a particle with precision. Known as the *Heisenberg uncertainty principle*, this concept can be expressed mathematically as $\Delta x \Delta mv \geq h/4\pi$, where $h/4\pi = 5.2728 \times 10^{-35}$ J·s. The Δ means "a range of values." In other words, you can know that the position, x, of an object is within a certain range Δx, and you can know that its momentum, mv, is within a certain range, Δmv, and the product of those two ranges is $h/4\pi$. As one range becomes smaller, meaning that you know it more precisely, the other range gets larger, to keep the product the same. For large objects, the mass, and thus the momentum, is so large that the ranges within which you can know the position and speed are so small that you can know them precisely. However, the mass of an electron is so small that you cannot know the position, x, or speed, v, with much precision. You can know *only* that the electron is within some region in space, which is essentially what a wave function describes.

You can visualize an atomic orbital as a fuzzy cloud in which the density of the cloud at any point is proportional to the probability of finding the electron at that point. **Figure 3.13** shows the probability map, or orbital, that describes the hydrogen atom in its ground state. Because the cloud has no definite boundary, the "surface" of the cloud is often defined as the region in which the electron spends 90 percent of its time.

Figure 3.13 The electron density diagram (**A**) for a hydrogen atom represents the likelihood of locating an electron at a particular point in the atom. The density of the dots at any point is proportional to the probability of finding the electron at that location. The circle (**B**) shows the region within which the electron spends 90 percent of its time.

Quantum Numbers Describe Orbitals

For the quantum mechanical model of the atom, **quantum numbers** describe electrons in atoms. Three quantum numbers are used to describe the distribution of electrons in the atom. The first quantum number, n, describes an orbital's energy level and relative size. The second quantum number, l, and the third quantum number, m_l, respectively describe an orbital's shape and orientation in space. A fourth quantum number, m_s, describes the behaviour of a specific electron in an orbital.

quantum numbers integers arising from the solutions to the wave equation that describe specific properties of electrons in atoms

The Principal Quantum Number, n

Recall that the Bohr atomic model uses the symbol n to represent electron orbits. In a similar manner, the quantum mechanical model assigns a **principal quantum number, n** that specifies the energy level, or **shell**, of an atomic orbital and its relative size. All orbitals that have the same value of n are said to be in the same shell. The value of n can range from $n = 1$ to $n = \infty$. The shell with $n = 1$ is called the *first shell*, the shell with $n = 2$ is the *second shell*, and so on. A higher value for n indicates a higher energy level. A greater n value also means that the size of the shell is larger, with a higher probability of finding an electron farther from the nucleus.

The Orbital-Shape Quantum Number, l

Chemists use a variety of names for the second quantum number. In this book, it is referred to as the **orbital-shape quantum number, l**, because it describes an orbital's shape. This quantum number refers to energy **sublevels**, or subshells, within each principal energy level. The values of l are dependent on the value of the principal quantum number, n. The values of l are positive integers that range in value from 0 to $(n - 1)$. So, if $n = 1$, $l = 0$ (that is, $1 - 1$). If $n = 2$, l can be either 0 or 1. If $n = 3$, l can be 0, 1, or 2. Notice that the number of possible values for l in a given energy level is the same as the value of n. In other words, if $n = 2$, then there are only two possible sublevels, or subshells (two types of orbital shapes), at this energy level.

Each value of l is identified by a specific letter—s, p, d, or f—that is used to help distinguish it from the principal quantum number.

- The $l = 0$ orbital has the letter s.
- The $l = 1$ orbital has the letter p.
- The $l = 2$ orbital has the letter d.
- The $l = 3$ orbital has the letter f.

To identify an energy sublevel, combine the value of n with the letter of the orbital shape. For example, the sublevel with $n = 3$ and $l = 0$ is called the $3s$ sublevel. The sublevel with $n = 2$ and $l = 1$ is the $2p$ sublevel. (There are additional sublevels beyond $l = 3$; however, for chemical systems known at this time, only the s, p, d, and f sublevels are required.)

The Magnetic Quantum Number, m_l

The **magnetic quantum number, m_l** indicates the orientation of the orbital in the space around the nucleus. The value of m_l depends on the value of l. For any given value of l, there are $(2l + 1)$ values for m_l ranging from $-l$ to $+l$. So, if $l = 0$, m_l can be only 0. If $l = 1$, m_l can have one of three values: -1, 0, or $+1$. In other words, for a given value of n, when $l = 0$, there is only one orbital, of s type.

For a given value of n, when $l = 1$, there are three orbitals of p type. Each of these p orbitals has the same shape and energy, but a different orientation around the nucleus, and are designated p_x, p_y, and p_z. The total number of orbitals for any energy level n is given by n^2. For example, if $n = 2$, it has a total of 4 (2^2) orbitals (one s orbital and three p orbitals).

Figure 3.14 shows the shape of the s, p, and d orbitals. The first row shows s orbitals for the first three energy levels, $n = 1$, $n = 2$, and $n = 3$. Notice that the size of the orbital increases as the energy increases, which indicates that the electron spends time farther from the nucleus when it has more energy. The second and third rows show the shapes of the p and d orbitals. (The f orbital shapes are beyond the scope of this chemistry course.)

Keep in mind that the *overall shape* of an atom is a combination of all its orbitals. Thus, the overall shape of an atom is spherical. Be careful, however, to distinguish between the overall spherical shape of the atom and the spherical shape that is characteristic of *only* the s orbitals.

---

principal quantum number, n a positive whole number (integer) that indicates the energy level and relative size of an atomic orbital

shell the main energy level associated with a given value of n (the principal quantum number)

orbital-shape quantum number, l an integer that describes the shape of atomic orbitals within each principal energy level

sublevel the energy subshell associated with a given value of l (the orbital-shape quantum number)

magnetic quantum number, m_l an integer that indicates the orientation of an orbital in the space around the nucleus

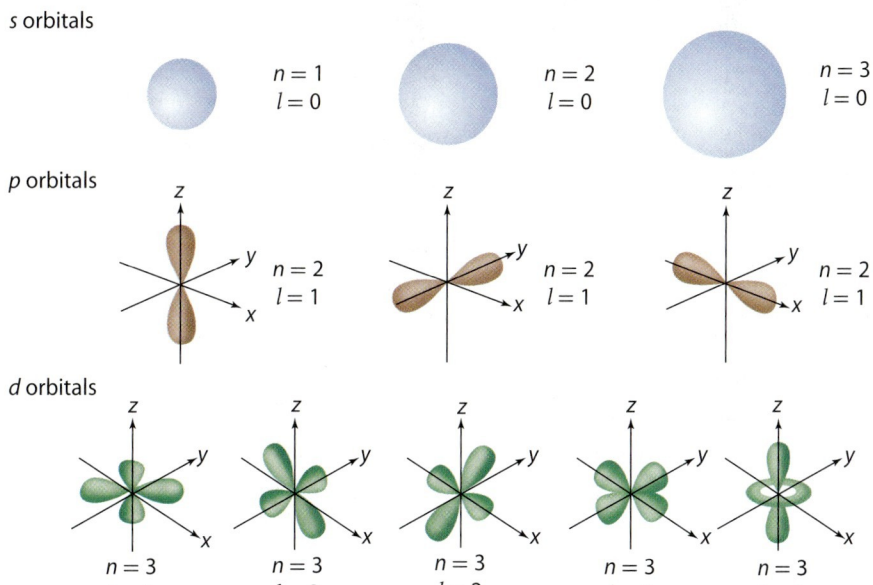

Figure 3.14 All s orbitals are spherical in shape. Each of these p orbitals has a double-lobed shape, but the orientation varies with m_l. Four of the d orbitals have a cloverleaf shape while the fifth looks like a dumbbell with a doughnut around it. These five shapes represent the five values of m_l.

It is also important to be clear that orbitals are solutions to mathematical equations. Those solutions, when manipulated, describe the location of the electron in terms of probabilities. Orbital diagrams in print and electronic resources make orbitals *appear* solid, which can lead to the *misconception* that orbitals are physical "containers" that are "occupied" by electrons. In some ways, this is unavoidable. However, keep in mind that orbitals are regions in space in which electrons *can* exist. When an electron is not there, nothing is there. The mathematical equations describe many possible orbitals for the electron in a hydrogen atom. However, at any one time, the electron occupies only one of those orbitals.

The Spin Quantum Number, m_s

The first three quantum numbers describe the energy, size, shape, and spatial orientation of an orbital. A fourth quantum number was derived from experimental observations and later verified mathematically, that could be explained by an electron spinning on its axis. Any spinning charge will generate a magnetic field. The effect is the same as if the axis of the electron is a bar magnet. The **spin quantum number, m_s** specifies the direction in which the axis of the electron is oriented and has only two possible values: $+\frac{1}{2}$ or $-\frac{1}{2}$. **Table 3.1** summarizes the four quantum numbers and their properties.

spin quantum number, m_s the quantum number that specifies the orientation of the axis on which the electron is spinning

Table 3.1 Summary of Quantum Numbers of Electrons in Atoms

Name	Symbol	Allowed Values	Property
Principal (shell)	n	Positive integers (1, 2, 3, etc.)	Orbital size and energy level
Orbital-shape (subshell)	l	Integers from 0 to $(n-1)$	Orbital shape (l values 0, 1, 2, and 3 correspond to s, p, d, and f orbitals)
Magnetic	m_l	Integers from $-l$, to $+l$	Orbital orientation
Spin	m_s	$+\frac{1}{2}$ or $-\frac{1}{2}$	Spin orientation

Identifying Electrons Using Sets of Quantum Numbers

In 1925, Austrian physicist, Wolfgang Pauli, proposed that *only two electrons of opposite spin could occupy an orbital*. This proposal became known as the **Pauli exclusion principle**. Thus, an orbital can have a maximum of two electrons only, each of which must have the opposite spin of the other. An orbital can also have only one electron of either spin or no electrons at all.

Another way of stating the Pauli exclusion principle is that *no two electrons in an atom can have the same four quantum numbers*. This means that each electron in an atom has its own unique set of four quantum numbers, each of which is limited by certain factors. A common analogy for this is a person's home address. The principal quantum number, n, represents a city. In the city, there are a finite number of streets. Each street is represented by the orbital-shape quantum number, l. On each street, there are a finite number of buildings (houses and apartment buildings), each with its own particular number. Each building number is represented by the magnetic quantum number, m_l. Finally, the spin quantum number, m_s, represents the name of a person living at the address. Just as the address for each person has its own unique set of identifiers, an electron in an atom has its own unique set of identifiers, which are its quantum numbers. In general, in any energy level, n, there can be no more than $2n^2$ electrons.

Table 3.2 provides the set of quantum numbers that distinguish between the ground-state hydrogen atom and helium atom. Recall that a helium atom has two electrons. Note also that the m_s quantum number is given as $+\frac{1}{2}$. It could just as easily have a value of $-\frac{1}{2}$. By convention, chemists usually use the positive value first.

Pauli exclusion principle a principle that states that a maximum of two electrons can occupy an orbital, and that the electrons must have opposite spins

Table 3.2 Quantum Numbers for Hydrogen and Helium

Atom	Electron	Quantum Numbers
hydrogen	Lone	$n = 1, l = 0, m_l = 0, m_s = +\frac{1}{2}$
helium	First	$n = 1, l = 0, m_l = 0, m_s = +\frac{1}{2}$
helium	Second	$n = 1, l = 0, m_l = 0, m_s = -\frac{1}{2}$

Sample Problem

Determining Quantum Numbers

Problem
a. What values of l and m_l are allowed for a principal quantum number, n, of 2? How many orbitals exist for $n = 2$?
b. Give the possible values for m_l if $n = 4$ and $l = 3$. What type of orbital is associated with these quantum numbers? How many orbitals are associated with these quantum numbers?
c. What is the set of quantum numbers for one electron in the 3s orbital?

What Is Required?
a. You need to determine the allowed values for l and m_l, and the number of orbitals that exist, for a principal quantum number of $n = 2$.
b. You need to determine the type of orbital, and the number of orbitals, associated with the quantum numbers $n = 4$ and $l = 3$.
c. You need to determine n, l, m_l, and m_s for an electron in the 3s orbital.

What Is Given?
a. You are given the value of the principal quantum number as $n = 2$.
b. You are given the values of the quantum numbers, $n = 4$ and $l = 3$.
c. You are given the electron orbital, 3s.

	Plan Your Strategy	Act on Your Strategy
a.	To determine the allowed quantum numbers, use the rules you have just learned in the textbook. The allowed values for l are integers from 0 to $(n-1)$. The allowed values for m_l are integers from $-l$ to $+l$, including 0. One m_l value is assigned to each orbital, so the total number of m_l values gives the number of orbitals.	Determining l values for $n = 2$: $l = 0, 1$ Determining m_l for each l value: for $l = 0$, $m_l = 0$ for $l = 1$, $m_l = -1, 0, +1$ There are four m_l values, so there are four orbitals with $n = 2$.
b.	To determine the type of orbital, combine the value for n with the letter used to identify l. You can determine the possible values for m_l from l. The total number of m_l values gives the number of orbitals.	Determining the type of orbital, the $l = 3$ orbital has the letter f. Since $n = 4$, the quantum numbers represent a $4f$ orbital. Determining the total number of orbitals, find m_l for $l = 3$: m_l may be $-3, -2, -1, 0, +1, +2, +3$. There are seven possible m_l values, so there are seven orbitals associated with the quantum numbers.
c.	To determine the four quantum numbers for the electron, begin by determining which are possible for the $3s$ orbital.	Since the orbital is $3s$: $n = 3$, $l = 0$, and $m_l = 0$. Since there is one electron and by convention it is assigned a $m_s = +\frac{1}{2}$, the set of quantum numbers for the electron is $n = 3$, $l = 0$, $m_l = 0$, and $m_s = +\frac{1}{2}$.

Check Your Solution

a. Since the total number of orbitals for any given n is n^2, when $n = 2$, the number of orbitals must be 4 (that is, 2^2).

b. The number of m_l values is equivalent to $2l + 1$: $2(3) + 1 = 7$. Since the number of orbitals equals the number of m_l values, the answer of 7 must be correct.

c. Since it is an s orbital, there can only be a maximum of 2 electrons. These would have the same first three quantum numbers and differ only by the spin quantum number, m_s.

Practice Problems

1. For the quantum number $n = 3$, what values of l are allowed, what values of m_l are possible, and how many orbitals are there?

2. If $n = 5$ and $l = 2$, what orbital type is this, what are the possible values for m_l, and how many orbitals are there?

3. What are the n, l, and possible m_l values for the following orbital types?
   a. $2s$
   b. $3p$
   c. $5d$
   d. $4f$

4. What orbital type can be described by the following sets of quantum numbers?
   a. $n = 2$, $l = 0$, $m_l = 0$
   b. $n = 5$, $l = 3$, $m_l = -2$

5. How many orbitals are associated with each of the following types?
   a. $1s$
   b. $5f$
   c. $4f$
   d. $2p$

6. What sets of quantum numbers are possible for a $4d$ orbital? List them.

7. What is one possible value for the missing number in each of the following sets?
   a. $n = 3$, $l = 1$, $m_l = ?$
   b. $n = 4$, $l = ?$, $m_l = -3$

8. Write two possible sets of quantum numbers for a $6p$ orbital.

9. The following sets of quantum numbers are not allowed. Identify the problem and change one number to give an allowed set.
   a. $n = 1$, $l = 2$, $m_l = -2$
   b. $n = 4$, $l = 1$, $m_l = -2$

10. Label each of the following sets of quantum numbers as *allowed* or *not allowed*. Identify the problem for each of the *not allowed* sets.
    a. $n = 3$, $l = 2$, $m_l = 0$
    b. $n = 1$, $l = 1$, $m_l = -1$
    c. $n = 0$, $l = 0$, $m_l = 0$
    d. $n = 5$, $l = 1$, $m_l = 3$

Section 3.2 Review

Section Summary

- According to the quantum mechanical model of the atom, electrons have both matter-like and wave-like properties.
- The position and motion of electrons cannot both be determined with certainty, so the position is described in terms of probabilities.
- An orbital represents a mathematical description of the volume of space around a nucleus in which an electron has a probability of being found.
- The first three quantum numbers describe the size, energy, shape, and orientation of an orbital. The fourth quantum number describes the orientation of the axis around which the electron is spinning.

Review Questions

1. **K/U** How does n in Bohr's atomic model compare to n in the quantum mechanical model of the atom?

2. **C** Draw a diagram to show the allowed values for l and m_l when $n = 4$.

3. **K/U** What is the name and symbol of the fourth quantum number, what values can it have, and what property does it represent?

4. **C** Construct and complete a table to show key characteristics of the quantum numbers n, l, m_l, and m_s.

5. **C** Think of visual analogies to help you remember the shapes of the s, p, and d orbitals. For example, the p orbital might remind you of barbells. Sketch a diagram to show your analogies.

6. **T/I** Agree or disagree with the following analogy, and support your opinion: An electron in an orbital is like a fly trapped in a glass jar.

7. **A** Label each of the following sets of quantum numbers as *allowed* or *not allowed*. Identify the problem for each of the *not allowed* sets.
   a. $n = 2, l = 2, m_l = 0$
   b. $n = 2, l = 0, m_l = -1$
   c. $n = 4, l = 0, m_l = 0$
   d. $n = 2, l = 3, m_l = -1$

8. **T/I** How many of each of the following types of orbitals are there in an atom?
   a. $3s$
   b. $7f$
   c. $4p$
   d. $7d$
   e. $2s$
   f. s

9. **T/I** How many sets of quantum numbers are possible for a $3p$ orbital? List them.

10. **T/I** What is wrong with each set of quantum numbers? Change one number to give an allowed set.
    a. $n = 0, l = 1, m_l = 0$
    b. $n = 3, l = 2, m_l = -3$

11. **C** A friend missed the class in which orbitals were discussed. Write a brief e-mail to explain what an orbital is.

12. **T/I** Examine **Figure 3.14**. In what key ways do d orbitals differ from s and p orbitals?

13. **A** A classmate says, "Since there are $2n^2$ electrons possible in each energy level, and the atom with the greatest number of electrons has 118 electrons, that must mean that 8 is the highest possible value for n, because a value of 7 gives $2n^2 = 98$ and a value of 8 gives $2n^2 = 128$."
    a. State two problems with this reasoning.
    b. How many energy levels are there for a given atom?

14. **K/U** If the $n = 1$ energy level is shown in a diagram as a sphere, what does this sphere represent?

15. **K/U** What is the Pauli exclusion principle and what consequence does it have in terms of quantum numbers?

16. **T/I** Is it possible for a hydrogen atom's one electron to have the following quantum numbers: $n = 2, l = 0, m_l = 0, m_s = +\frac{1}{2}$? Explain your answer.

17. **K/U** How does $n = 2$ compare with $n = 1$ in terms of its size and the energy of an electron moving in its volume?

18. **T/I** What is the greatest number of electrons possible in each of the following energy levels?
    a. $n = 1$
    b. $n = 2$
    c. $n = 3$
    d. $n = 4$

19. **K/U** Explain why there are $(2l + 1)$ values for m_l for any given value of l.

20. **A** Given the information that an electron is associated with $l = 0$, can you tell what the value of n is? Explain your answer.

SECTION 3.3
Electron Configurations and the Periodic Table

The single-electron atom, hydrogen, is unique with respect to the energies of its orbitals, because the energy for any given orbital depends only on n, the principal quantum number. For example, consider a situation in which a hydrogen atom is excited by an electric current in a gas discharge tube. As a result of this absorption of energy, the electron jumps to the $n = 4$ level. In the fourth energy level, there is no difference in the energy of the electron if it is in the $4s$, $4p$, $4d$, or $4f$ orbital. An electron in any orbital of the fourth energy level, or shell, will have the same energy. The situation is quite different, however, for atoms with two or more electrons. Electrons in different orbitals within the same energy level will have different energies.

Key Terms

electron configuration
orbital diagram
aufbau principle
Hund's rule
atomic radius
ionization energy
electron affinity

Atomic Orbital Energies for Many-Electron Atoms

To understand why the presence of more than one electron in an atom affects the energies of electrons in different orbitals within the same energy level, examine **Figure 3.15**. First look at **Figure 3.15A**, which shows the interaction between the nucleus and the electron in the single-electron atom, hydrogen. The attractive force between the positively charged nucleus and the negatively charged electron is the only interaction occurring in the atom. This interaction is incorporated into the Schrödinger wave equation when solving it for hydrogen. The solutions give results for all possible combinations of quantum numbers. Analysis shows that, regardless of the degree of excitation, there will be no difference in the energy of an electron whether it is in the s, p, d, or f orbitals for any specific n.

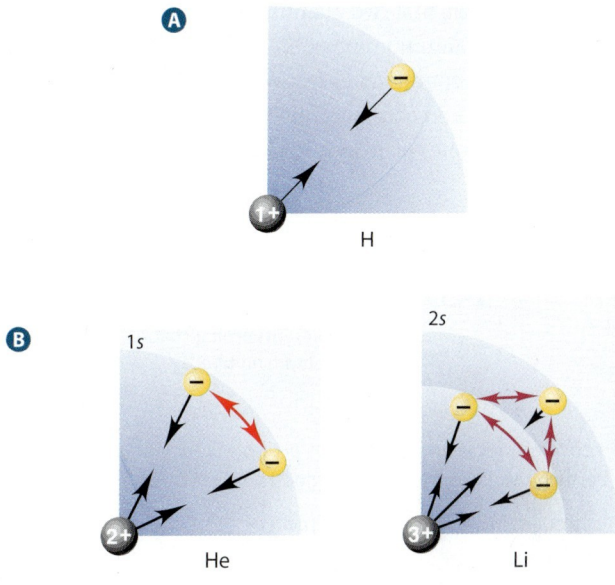

Figure 3.15 In the hydrogen atom (**A**), the only force affecting the electron is the attractive force between the nucleus and the electron. In helium (**B**) and Li (**C**) atoms, each electron is attracted by the nucleus and repulsed by the other electrons in the atom.

Now focus on **Figure 3.15B**, which shows the helium and lithium atoms. There are attractive forces between the nucleus and each of the electrons, as well as repulsive forces between each of the electrons of the atom. All of these interactions must be incorporated into the Schrödinger wave equation to solve it for these atoms. Not only the nucleus, but also all of the other electrons influence the energy of any individual electron in its orbital. As a result, the energies of the s, p, d, and f orbitals within the same shell (same value of n) are different. This difference in the energies of the orbitals is shown in what is called an energy level diagram for multi-electron atoms in **Figure 3.16**. One reason for the difference in the energies of electrons in these orbitals is that electrons in an s orbital—for example, the $2s$ orbital—spend more time closer to the nucleus than do the electrons in the $2p$ orbitals. Thus, the energy level of the $2s$ electrons is lower than that of the $2p$ electrons.

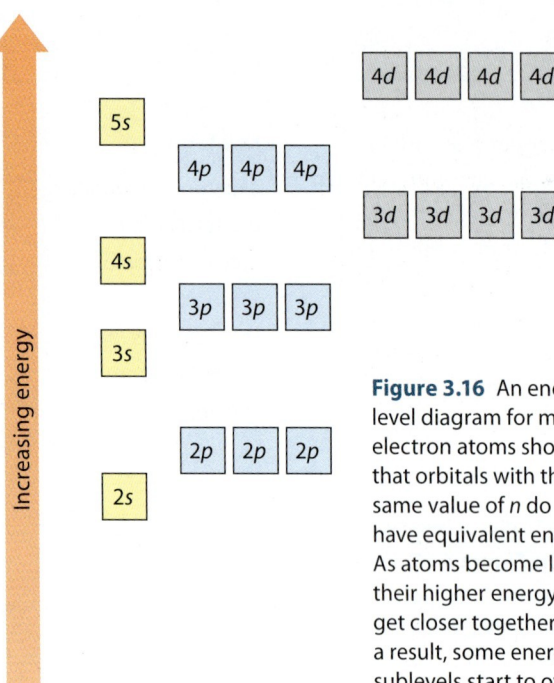

Figure 3.16 An energy level diagram for many-electron atoms shows that orbitals with the same value of n do not have equivalent energies. As atoms become larger, their higher energy levels get closer together. As a result, some energy sublevels start to overlap. *Identify which is higher in energy: a 3d orbital or the 4s orbital.*

As you can see, in the energy level diagram in **Figure 3.16**, the 2s orbital has a lower energy than the 2p orbitals. Similarly, the 3p orbitals are lower in energy than the 3d orbitals. Notice, however, that all the orbitals within a sublevel have the same energy. For example, the three p orbitals in the 3p sublevel have the same energy. As you learn to describe the distribution of electrons in many-electron atoms, refer to this diagram or the order of orbital energy below.

$$1s < 2s < 2p < 3s < 3p < 4s < 3d < 4p < 5s < 4d < 5p < ...$$

Representing Electrons: Electron Configurations and Orbital Diagrams

An atom's **electron configuration** shows the number and arrangement of electrons in its orbitals. Since the value of n ranges to infinity, each atom has an infinite number of possible electron configurations. By convention, electron configurations are drawn with the atoms in their lowest possible energy levels, because an atom's chemical properties are mainly associated with its ground-state electron configuration.

Electron configurations provide information about the first two quantum numbers, n and l. (Electron configurations reflecting the third quantum number, m_l, are beyond the scope of this chemistry course.) For example, the ground-state electron configuration for a hydrogen atom is shown in **Figure 3.17**. Its electron configuration is $1s^1$ (pronounced "one ess one"). The superscript 1 indicates that only one electron is in the s orbital.

electron configuration a shorthand notation that shows the number and arrangement of electrons in an atom's orbitals

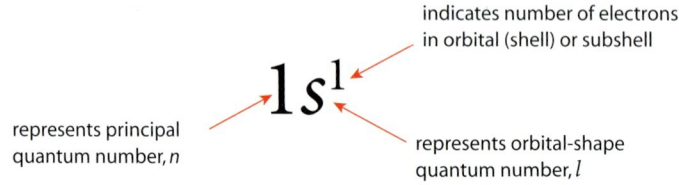

Figure 3.17 The electron configuration for hydrogen is pronounced "one ess one." Each number and letter in an electron configuration represents the electron distribution in an atom.

An orbital diagram often accompanies the electron configuration for an atom to represent the electron spin in each orbital. An **orbital diagram** uses a box for each orbital in any given principal energy level. (Some chemists use a circle or a line instead of a box.) An empty box represents an orbital with no electrons (an unoccupied orbital). A box that has a single arrow represents an orbital that is half-filled. A box with two oppositely pointing arrows represents a filled orbital. **Figure 3.18** shows how electron configuration and orbital diagrams are represented together.

orbital diagram a diagram that uses a box for each orbital in any given principal energy level

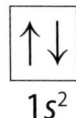

Figure 3.18 The ground-state electron configuration for a helium atom is $1s^2$ (pronounced "one ess two", not "one ess squared"). The superscript 2 indicates that there are two electrons in the s orbital. The opposite arrows in the orbital diagram indicate that the electrons are of opposite spins.

Describing the Electrons in Lithium

An orbital can have a maximum of two electrons, and they must have opposite spins. This principle applies when writing electron configurations and orbital diagrams. **Table 3.3** summarizes how electrons in lithium (Li), which has three electrons, are described using quantum numbers, electron configuration notation, and an orbital diagram.

For lithium, the first two electrons occupy the 1s orbital. According to the Pauli exclusion principle, the 1s orbital ($n = 1$) is full, because it contains the maximum number of electrons: 2. For lithium's third electron, n cannot equal 1. Therefore, the next principal energy level for the electron is $n = 2$. If $n = 2$, l may have a value of 0 or 1. Because an orbital with $l = 0$ (an s orbital) has a lower energy than an orbital with $l = 1$ (a p orbital), you would expect a high probability of finding lithium's third electron in the s orbital given by $n = 2, l = 0$. In fact, experimental evidence supports this expectation. You know that if $l = 0$, m_l has only one possible value: 0. Finally, by convention, m_s is $+\frac{1}{2}$. The electron configuration shows two of the electrons in the 1s orbital and the third in the next energy level, 2s. For the orbital diagram, the filled 1s orbital is shown as a pair of opposite arrows, and by convention the one electron in the 2s orbital is pointing upwards, which represents a positive m_s.

You may have noticed that the first few examples of electron configurations do not include information about the spin direction of the electron. Once you have seen the electron configurations for a variety of atoms, you will see that you can safely infer where electrons with opposite spins have been paired.

Table 3.3 Descriptions of Electrons in Lithium

Atom	Electron	Quantum Numbers	Electron Configuration	Orbital Diagram
lithium	First	$n = 1, l = 0, m_l = 0, m_s = +\frac{1}{2}$	$1s^2 2s^1$	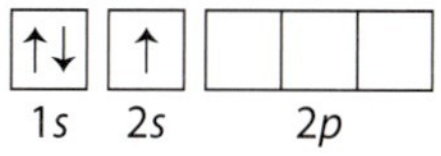 ↑↓ ↑ ☐☐☐ 1s 2s 2p
	Second	$n = 1, l = 0, m_l = 0, m_s = -\frac{1}{2}$		
	Third	$n = 2, l = 0, m_l = 0, m_s = +\frac{1}{2}$		

Learning Check

7. What is the key difference between the orbitals of a hydrogen atom and the orbitals of multi-electron atoms?

8. Write the following sets of orbitals in order from lowest to highest energy.
   a. 2s, 2p, 3s, 3p
   b. 3p, 3d, 4s, 4p
   c. 4d, 4f, 5s, 5p, 5d, 5f, 6s, 6p

9. What does it mean to say that an orbital is "full"?

10. How many electrons can occupy all possible orbitals with $n = 1$ and $n = 2$? Show two ways to arrive at the answer.

11. The orbital diagram for helium is given in **Figure 3.18**. Would drawing two arrows pointing in the same direction also be a correct orbital diagram? Explain your answer.

12. Draw an orbital diagram to represent each of the following:
    a. an "unoccupied" orbital
    b. an orbital with a single electron
    c. a filled orbital

Writing Electron Configurations and Orbital Diagrams

Electron configurations are closely related to the structure of the periodic table. To write electron configurations, start with the first element in the periodic table and "build up" its electronic configuration by adding an electron to its lowest available energy level. Then turn your attention to the next element, which has one more proton in the nucleus, and add an electron to the appropriate orbital. This process of building up the ground-state electronic structure for each atom, in order of atomic number, is called the aufbau principle. (*Aufbau* comes from a German word that means "to build up.") The **aufbau principle** states that *each electron occupies the lowest energy orbital available*.

aufbau principle a principle behind an imaginary process of building up the electronic structure of the atoms, in order of atomic number

To start representing the electron structures of atoms, you will use both electron configurations and orbital diagrams. Refer to the following guidelines and the relative energies of orbitals as you work your way through the information that follows.

> Guidelines for "Filling" Orbitals
>
> 1. Place electrons into the orbitals in order of increasing energy level.
> 2. Completely fill orbitals of the same energy level before proceeding to the next orbital or series of orbitals.
> 3. When electrons are added to orbitals of the same energy sublevel, each orbital receives one electron before any pairing occurs.
> 4. When electrons are added individually to different orbitals of the same energy, the electrons must all have the same spin.

Hund's rule a rule stating that the lowest energy state for an atom has the maximum number of unpaired electrons allowed by the Pauli exclusion principle in a given energy sublevel

Guidelines 3 and 4 reflect **Hund's rule**, which states that *single electrons with the same spin must occupy each equal-energy orbital before additional electrons with opposite spins can occupy the same orbitals*. For example, **Figure 3.19** shows the sequence in which six electrons occupy three *p* orbitals. One electron enters each of the three *p* orbitals before a second electron enters any orbitals.

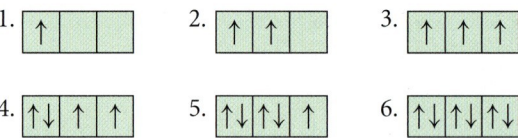

Figure 3.19 The three boxes represents each of the 2*p* orbitals. Electrons are "added" one at a time to each orbital. When each orbital has one electron, a second electron is added.

Filling Orbitals for Periods 1 and 2

Table 3.4 shows orbital diagrams and electron configurations for elements 1 to 10. Note the following:

- To draw orbital diagrams, place the electron in the first available box, from left to right.
- The energy of each orbital (or group of orbitals) increases from left to right.
- Boron's fifth electron goes into the 2*p* energy sublevel. Since $l = 1$, m_l may be -1, 0, or $+1$. The fifth electron can go into any of these orbitals, since they have the same energy.
- By convention, electrons are placed in the orbital boxes from left to right.
- With carbon, you must apply Hund's rule. That is, carbon's sixth electron must go into the next unoccupied 2*p* orbital. (Experimental evidence confirms this configuration.)
- The Pauli exclusion principle applies to oxygen. As with helium's 1*s* orbital and beryllium's 2*s* orbital, the last-added (eighth) electron is paired with a 2*p* electron of opposite spin.

Table 3.4 Orbital Diagrams and Electron Configurations for the First Ten Elements

Atomic Number (Z)	Element	Orbital Diagram	Electron Configuration	Orbital Shape*
1	H	↑ (1s)	$1s^1$	
2	He	↑↓ (1s)	$1s^2$	
3	Li	↑↓ ↑ ☐☐☐ (1s 2s 2p)	$1s^2 2s^1$	
4	Be	↑↓ ↑↓ ☐☐☐ (1s 2s 2p)	$1s^2 2s^2$	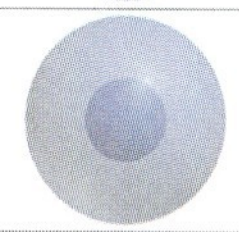
5	B	↑↓ ↑↓ ↑☐☐ (1s 2s 2p)	$1s^2 2s^2 2p^1$	
6	C	↑↓ ↑↓ ↑↑☐ (1s 2s 2p)	$1s^2 2s^2 2p^2$	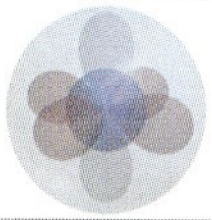
7	N	↑↓ ↑↓ ↑↑↑ (1s 2s 2p)	$1s^2 2s^2 2p^3$	
8	O	↑↓ ↑↓ ↑↓↑↑ (1s 2s 2p)	$1s^2 2s^2 2p^4$	
9	F	↑↓ ↑↓ ↑↓↑↓↑ (1s 2s 2p)	$1s^2 2s^2 2p^5$	
10	Ne	↑↓ ↑↓ ↑↓↑↓↑↓ (1s 2s 2p)	$1s^2 2s^2 2p^6$	

* Orbital occupancy is indicated with shading. The lighter colour indicates half-filled orbitals; the darker colour indicates filled orbitals.

Filling Orbitals for Period 3

Writing electron configurations and drawing orbital diagrams for atoms of Period 3 elements follows the same process as for Period 2. However, a *condensed electron configuration* is used to reduce the length of the electron configurations. This condensed notation places the electron configuration of the noble gas of the previous period in square brackets, using its atomic symbol only. Then you continue with the configuration of the next energy level being filled. For example, the condensed electron configuration for a nitrogen atom is [He]$2s^2 2p^3$. The notation [He] is used to represent $1s^2$. For a sodium atom ($Z = 11$), the condensed electron configuration is [Ne]$3s^1$. Here, [Ne] represents $1s^2 2s^2 2p^6$. Orbital diagrams that accompany these condensed electron configurations are also partial orbital diagrams. Only the valence electrons are represented in the diagrams.

For the transition and Group 12 elements, the "next energy level being filled" does not correspond to orbitals with the same principal quantum number. Referring to **Figure 3.16**, you can see that *d* electrons with one principal quantum number have energies between the *s* and *p* orbitals corresponding to the next principal quantum number. For example, for Period 4 elements, the energy levels being filled consist of the 4*s* electrons, the 3*d* electrons, and the 4*p* electrons in that order. For the transition elements, the $(n - 1)d$ electrons, as well as the *ns* electrons are considered valence electrons.

Suggested Investigation

Inquiry Investigation 3-B, Electronic Structures for Period 3 Elements

Filling Orbitals for Period 4

As discussed above, electrons start occupying 3d orbitals *only* when the 4s orbital has been filled. **Table 3.5** shows electron configurations and partial orbital diagrams for the Period 4 elements. The guidelines you have been using can help you write correct ground-state electron configurations for all elements up to and including vanadium (atomic number 23). After this point, two apparent exceptions occur: chromium and copper. Experimental evidence supports the idea that the energy of orbitals can change as electrons are added. In these cases, when all of the *d* orbitals are half-filled, as in chromium, or completely filled, as in copper, the atoms are more stable than if the *s* orbitals were filled. The correct configurations for chromium and copper, respectively, are $[Ar]4s^1 3d^5$ and $[Ar]4s^1 3d^{10}$. Similar situations arise for a number of atoms in the remaining periods.

Table 3.5 Orbital Diagrams and Electron Configurations for Period Four Elements

Atomic Number (Z)	Element	Orbital Diagram (4s, 3d, 4p)	Condensed Electron Configuration
19	K	↑	$[Ar]4s^1$
20	Ca	↑↓	$[Ar]4s^2$
21	Sc	↑↓ ↑	$[Ar]4s^2 3d^1$
22	Ti	↑↓ ↑ ↑	$[Ar]4s^2 3d^2$
23	V	↑↓ ↑ ↑ ↑	$[Ar]4s^2 3d^3$
24	Cr	↑ ↑ ↑ ↑ ↑ ↑	$[Ar]4s^1 3d^5$
25	Mn	↑↓ ↑ ↑ ↑ ↑ ↑	$[Ar]4s^2 3d^5$
26	Fe	↑↓ ↑↓ ↑ ↑ ↑ ↑	$[Ar]4s^2 3d^6$
27	Co	↑↓ ↑↓ ↑↓ ↑ ↑ ↑	$[Ar]4s^2 3d^7$
28	Ni	↑↓ ↑↓ ↑↓ ↑↓ ↑ ↑	$[Ar]4s^2 3d^8$
29	Cu	↑ ↑↓ ↑↓ ↑↓ ↑↓ ↑↓	$[Ar]4s^1 3d^{10}$
30	Zn	↑↓ ↑↓ ↑↓ ↑↓ ↑↓ ↑↓	$[Ar]4s^2 3d^{10}$
31	Ga	↑↓ ↑↓ ↑↓ ↑↓ ↑↓ ↑↓ ↑	$[Ar]4s^2 3d^{10} 4p^1$
32	Ge	↑↓ ↑↓ ↑↓ ↑↓ ↑↓ ↑↓ ↑ ↑	$[Ar]4s^2 3d^{10} 4p^2$
33	As	↑↓ ↑↓ ↑↓ ↑↓ ↑↓ ↑↓ ↑ ↑ ↑	$[Ar]4s^2 3d^{10} 4p^3$
34	Se	↑↓ ↑↓ ↑↓ ↑↓ ↑↓ ↑↓ ↑↓ ↑ ↑	$[Ar]4s^2 3d^{10} 4p^4$
35	Br	↑↓ ↑↓ ↑↓ ↑↓ ↑↓ ↑↓ ↑↓ ↑↓ ↑	$[Ar]4s^2 3d^{10} 4p^5$
36	Kr	↑↓ ↑↓ ↑↓ ↑↓ ↑↓ ↑↓ ↑↓ ↑↓ ↑↓	$[Ar]4s^2 3d^{10} 4p^6$

> **Learning Check**
>
> 13. Why do electrons fill the 5s orbital before the 4d?
> 14. Write full and condensed electron configurations and orbital diagrams for boron and neon.
> 15. Write the complete electron configuration for sulfur.
> 16. Draw a partial orbital diagram for silicon in the ground state.
> 17. Identify the elements with these condensed electron configurations, and write the complete forms.
>   a. [Ne]$3s^1$ b. [Ar]$4s^2 3d^3$
> 18. Identify the following element, and write a condensed electron configuration for it.
> $1s^2 2s^2 2p^6 3s^2 3p^6 4s^2 3d^2$

Using the Periodic Table to Predict Electron Configurations

The periodic table in **Figure 3.20** has segments colour-coded and labelled according to the type of orbital being filled. **Figure 3.20B** highlights the filling order, and therefore the energy order, of the orbitals when you read the periodic table from left to right. Note that Period 1 contains only s-block elements, Periods 2 and 3 contain both s- and p-block elements, Periods 4 and 5 contain s-, p-, and d-block elements, and Periods 6 and 7 contain s,-, p-, d-, and f-block elements.

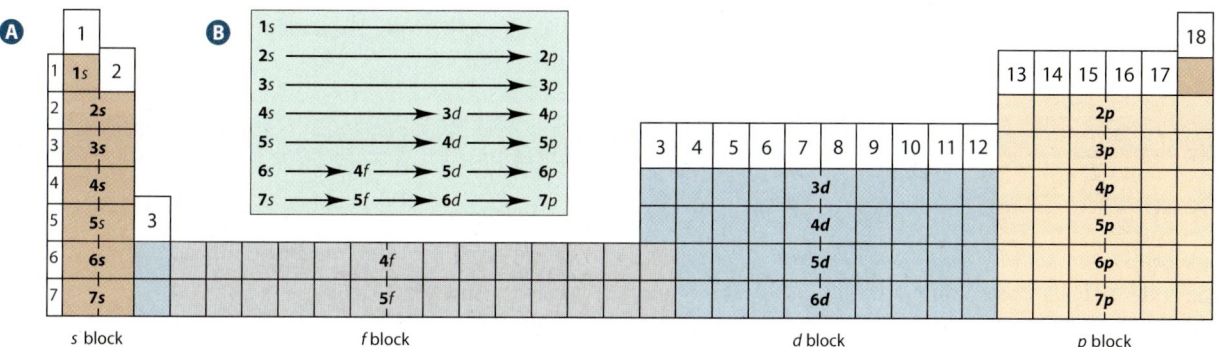

Figure 3.20 The periodic table can be divided (**A**) into four regions, the s block, p block, d block, and f block, according to the four energy sublevels. If you "read" the periods like the words on a page (**B**), the elements are arranged into sublevel blocks that occur in the order of increasing energy.

s-Block Elements
The s block consists of Groups 1 and 2. Valence electrons occupy only the s orbitals. Group 1 elements have partially filled s orbitals and electron configurations ending in ns^1. Group 2 elements have completely filled s orbitals and electron configurations ending in ns^2. Since the s orbitals can hold a total of two electrons, s block elements span two groups.

p-Block Elements
The p block contains Groups 13 to 18, and its elements have filled or partially filled p orbitals. The electron configuration of Group 18 elements takes the general form ns^2np^6, representing fully occupied s and p orbitals. Because the three p orbitals can hold a maximum of six electrons, the p block elements span six groups.

d-Block Elements
The d block contains the transition metal elements, as well as Group 12 of the main group elements. Apart from a few exceptions, d-block elements have filled s orbitals and filled or partially filled d orbitals of energy level $n - 1$. Because the five d orbitals can hold a maximum of 10 electrons, the d block spans 10 groups.

f-Block Elements
The f block includes the inner transition elements. These atoms have filled s orbitals in the outer energy levels and filled or partially filled 4f and 5f orbitals. In general, the notation for the orbital filling sequence for Period 6 and Period 7 is ns, followed by $(n - 2)f$, then $(n - 1)d$, and np. However, many exceptions make predictions difficult. Because there are seven f orbitals, with a maximum of 14 electrons, the f block spans 14 groups.

Group and Period Numbers Provide Patterns

Elements in a group have similar outer electron configurations and the same number of valence electrons, so they have similar chemical properties. This gives rise to three patterns:

- For main-group elements, the last numeral of the group number is the same as the number of valence electrons. For example, phosphorus in Group 15 has five valence electrons. Strontium in Group 2 has two valence electrons. The exception to this pattern is helium with its outermost energy level fully occupied by two valence electrons.
- The n value of the highest occupied energy level is the period number. For example, atoms of elements that have electrons with $n = 3$ appear in Period 3. Atoms of elements that have electrons with $n = 6$ appear in Period 6.
- The square of the n value (n^2) equals the total number of orbitals in that energy level. In addition, since each orbital can have a maximum of two electrons, the maximum number of electrons in any principal energy level is $2n^2$. For example, with $n = 2$, there are four orbitals: one $2s$ orbital and three $2p$ orbitals. Squaring the n value gives $2^2 = 4$. The total number of electrons in this energy level is *eight*, given by $2n^2$, and notice that there are *eight* elements in Period 2. For Period 3 elements, $n = 3$, and the number of orbitals is $n^2 = 9$. The number of electrons is $2n^2 = 18$. However, there are only eight elements in Period 3, because the $4s$ orbital has a lower energy than the $3d$ orbitals, so it fills first. The $3d$ orbitals fill after the $4s$ orbitals. Therefore, there are 18 elements in Period 4. Recall that the $4f$ orbitals do not fill until after the $6s$ orbital fills.

Sample Problem

Inferring the Characteristics of an Element

Problem
The condensed electron configuration for potassium is $[Ar]4s^1$. Without using a periodic table, identify the group number, period number, and orbital block for potassium.

What Is Required?
You need to use the condensed electron configuration to deduce the characteristics (group number, period number, and orbital block) of potassium.

What Is Given?
The condensed electron configuration for the potassium atom is given as $[Ar]4s^1$.

Plan Your Strategy	Act on Your Strategy
From the electron configuration, you can infer the energy level of the valence electrons, which tells you the period number for potassium. The number of valence electrons and their sublevel enable you to infer the group number and the block.	The configuration for the valence electrons, s^1, indicates that potassium is in Group 1. The value of 4 in $4s^1$ indicates that potassium is in Period 4. The notation s^1 means that potassium has one valence electron that is in an s orbital. Therefore, potassium must be in the s block.

Check Your Solution
All elements in Group 1 have electron configurations ending in the notation s^1. The link between n value and period number is correctly applied. Potassium has an electron configuration with the general notation of ns^1, which is characteristic of s block elements.

Practice Problems

11. Write complete and condensed electron configurations for yttrium, Y.

12. Write complete and condensed electron configurations for lead, Pb.

13. What elements have the valence electron configuration that is given by ns^2?

14. What elements have the valence electron configuration that is given by $ns^2(n-1)d^3$?

188 MHR • Unit 2 Structure and Properties of Matter

15. What are the two exceptions to the guidelines for filling orbitals in Period 4? Draw the partial orbital diagrams you would expect for them, based on the aufbau principle. Then draw partial orbital diagrams that represent their actual electron configurations. Finally, explain why the discrepancy arises.

16. The condensed electron configuration for strontium is [Kr]$5s^2$. Without using a periodic table, identify the group number to which strontium belongs. Show your reasoning.

17. Identify the following elements and write condensed electron configurations for atoms of each element.
    a. The *d*-block element in Period 4 with 10 valence electrons.
    b. The element in Period 6 with 3 valence electrons.

18. The condensed electron configuration for titanium is [Ar]$4s^2 3d^2$. Without a periodic table, identify the period number to which titanium belongs. Show your reasoning.

19. The condensed electron configuration for arsenic is [Ar]$4s^2 3d^{10} 4p^3$. Without using a periodic table, identify the orbital block in the periodic table to which arsenic belongs. Show your reasoning.

20. Without a periodic table, and based on the condensed electron configuration given below, identify the group number, period number, and orbital block to which each of the following elements belongs. Show your reasoning.
    a. francium, [Rn]$7s^1$
    b. tungsten, [Xe]$6s^2 4f^{14} 5d^4$
    c. antimony, [Kr]$5s^2 4d^{10} 5p^3$

Electron Configurations and Periodic Trends in Atomic Properties

Periodic trends involve properties such as atomic radius, ionization energy, metallic character, and electron affinity. These trends are related to patterns in electron configurations.

Atomic Radii

Chemists can determine the size of an atom—its **atomic radius**—by measuring the distance between the nuclei. For metals, the atomic radius is half the distance between neighbouring nuclei in a crystal. For elements that commonly occur as molecules, the atomic radius is half the distance between nuclei of identical atoms that are chemically bonded together. **Figure 3.21** shows the measured values of atomic radii for main-group elements.

Suggested Investigation

ThoughtLab Investigation 3-C, Extending the Periodic Table

atomic radius half the distance between the nuclei of two adjacent atoms; for metals, between atoms in a crystal, and for molecules, between atoms chemically bonded together

Group	1	2	13	14	15	16	17	18
	H 37							He 31
	Li 152	Be 112	B 85	C 77	N 75	O 73	F 72	Ne 70
	Na 186	Mg 160	Al 143	Si 118	P 110	S 103	Cl 99	Ar 98
	K 227	Ca 197	Ga 135	Ge 123	As 120	Se 117	Br 114	Kr 112
	Rb 248	Sr 215	In 166	Sn 140	Sb 141	Te 143	I 133	Xe 131
	Cs 265	Ba 222	Tl 171	Pb 175	Bi 155	Po 164	At 142	Rn 140

Increasing atomic radius →

Increasing atomic radius ↓

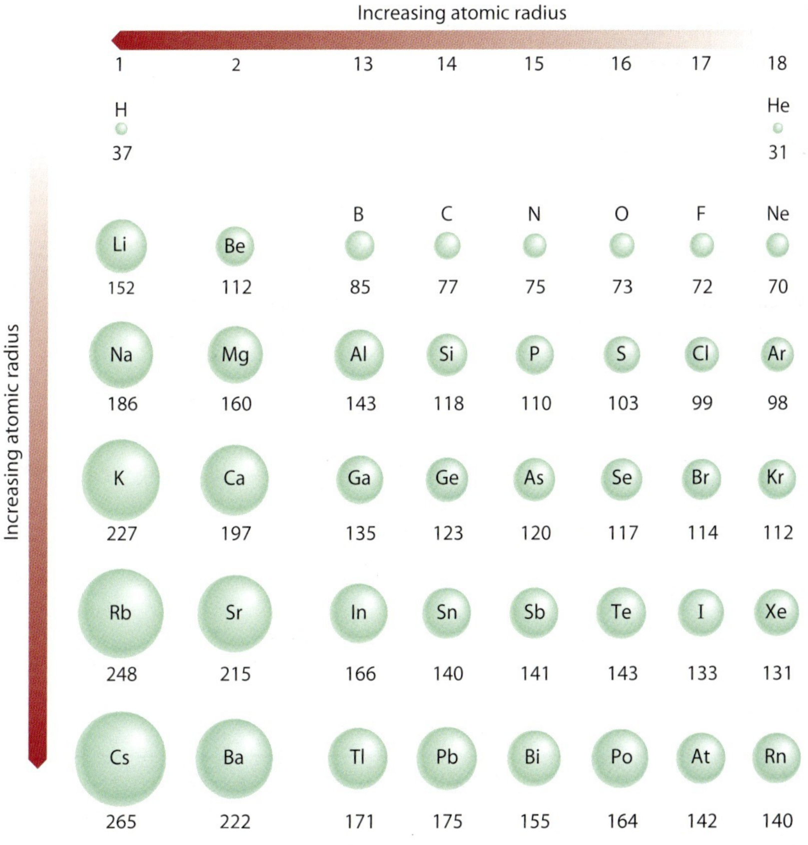

Figure 3.21 Atomic radii of the main-group elements generally decrease across a period, and increase down a group. This general trend applies to the entire periodic table. Values for atomic radii are given in picometres (pm), which is equivalent to 1×10^{-12} m.

Factors Affecting Atomic Radii

Two factors affect differences in atomic radii.

1. As n increases, there is a higher probability of finding electrons farther from their nucleus. Therefore, the atomic volume is larger. In other words, the atomic radius tends to increase with increasing n, and it tends to decrease with decreasing n.

2. Effective nuclear charge determines the *net* force of attraction between electrons and the nucleus. Only hydrogen's lone electron experiences the full charge of its nucleus, so the nuclear charge experienced by the electron in hydrogen is Z, its atomic number. For all other atoms, the nuclear charge that any given electron experiences is somewhat reduced by other electrons that are closer to the nucleus. Thus, the net force of attraction—the effective nuclear charge, Z_{eff}—is somewhat less than Z. As Z_{eff} increases, electrons are attracted more strongly, so the size of the atom decreases. As Z_{eff} decreases, there is a reduced force of attraction, and the size of the atom increases. Valence electrons, especially, experience a smaller Z_{eff} than inner electrons, because the inner electrons shield them from the attractive force of the nucleus.

For the main-group elements, the combined influences of n, Z_{eff}, and this shielding effect have the outcomes listed below and summarized in **Figure 3.22**.

- n governs the trend of increasing atomic radius down a group. Down a group, atoms of each subsequent element have one more level of inner electrons, increasing the shielding effect. The increase in atomic size, therefore, results from the increasing value of n.

- Z_{eff} governs the trend of decreasing atomic radius across a period. Across a period, atoms of each element have one more electron added to the same outer energy level—n does not change. However, one more proton increases the Z_{eff}, which pulls the electrons closer to the nucleus. The decrease in atomic size across a period, therefore, results from increasing Z_{eff}. A higher Z_{eff} means the electrons are more strongly attracted to the nucleus and so the atomic size of the atoms decreases as you move across a period.

Atoms of transition elements do not display the same general trend as the main-group elements, because shielding by the inner d electrons counteracts the usual increase in Z_{eff}. As a result, the atomic size remains fairly constant. (You will learn a more complete explanation for the atomic radii of transition-element atoms in future chemistry courses.)

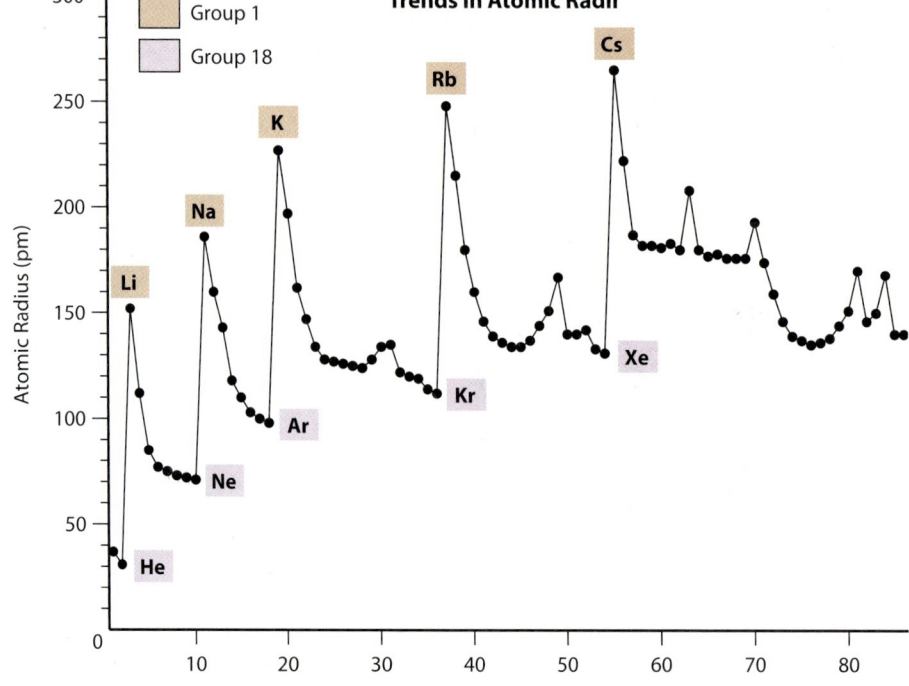

Figure 3.22 A plot of atomic radius vs. atomic number for elements of Periods 1 to 6 shows that the radius generally decreases through a period to the noble gas and then increases suddenly to the next alkali metal. Deviation from this trend occurs among the transition metals.

Ionization Energy

The formation of a positive ion (cation) requires the removal of an electron from a neutral atom. The energy needed to completely remove one electron from a ground-state gaseous atom is called the **ionization energy**. In order to remove an electron from an atom, energy is needed to overcome the force of attraction that is exerted on the electron by the nucleus. Therefore, in multi-electron atoms, more than one ionization energy exists. A gaseous atom's *first ionization energy* is the least amount of energy required to remove an electron from the outermost occupied energy level. The *second ionization energy* is always greater than the first ionization energy, because the electron must be removed from a positively charged ion. The same reasoning applies for successive ionization energies.

An atom's first ionization energy (IE_1) is closely linked to its chemical reactivity. Atoms with a low IE_1 tend to form cations during chemical reactions. **Figure 3.23** shows that the atoms with the lowest IE_1 are those belonging to Group 1 elements. These elements are among the most reactive elements in the periodic table. Atoms of elements with high IE_1 tend to form negatively charged ions (anions). The exception is the noble gases, which do not form ions naturally.

Figure 3.23 shows the overall periodic trends associated with ionization energy. Within a group, first ionization energies generally decrease as you move down the group. This trend is the inverse of the trend for atomic radius. The two trends are, in fact, linked. As the atomic radius increases, the distance of valence electrons from the nucleus also increases, so the force of attraction exerted by the nucleus on valence electrons decreases. As a result, less energy is needed to remove one such electron.

Within a period, first ionization energies generally increase from left to right. This trend is also linked to the atomic radius. Across a period, the atomic radius decreases because Z_{eff} increases. The increased effective nuclear charge of each successive element increases the attractive forces between the nucleus and valence electrons. Therefore, more energy is needed to remove one such electron.

There are several variations in the periodic trends associated with first ionization energies. These include boron and aluminum in Group 13 and oxygen and sulfur in Group 16. The observed drops in IE_1 can be explained in terms of the electron configurations for these atoms. Recall that atoms are most stable when orbitals are half-filled or completely filled. For B ($[He]2s^22p^1$) and Al ($[Ne]3s^23p^1$), removal of the only p orbital electron in each will produce more stable filled-orbital electron configurations for these atoms. For O ($[He]2s^22p^4$) and S ($[Ne]3s^23p^4$), removal of one p orbital electron in each will produce more stable half-filled orbital electron configurations for these atoms.

ionization energy the energy required to remove an electron from a ground-state atom in the gaseous state

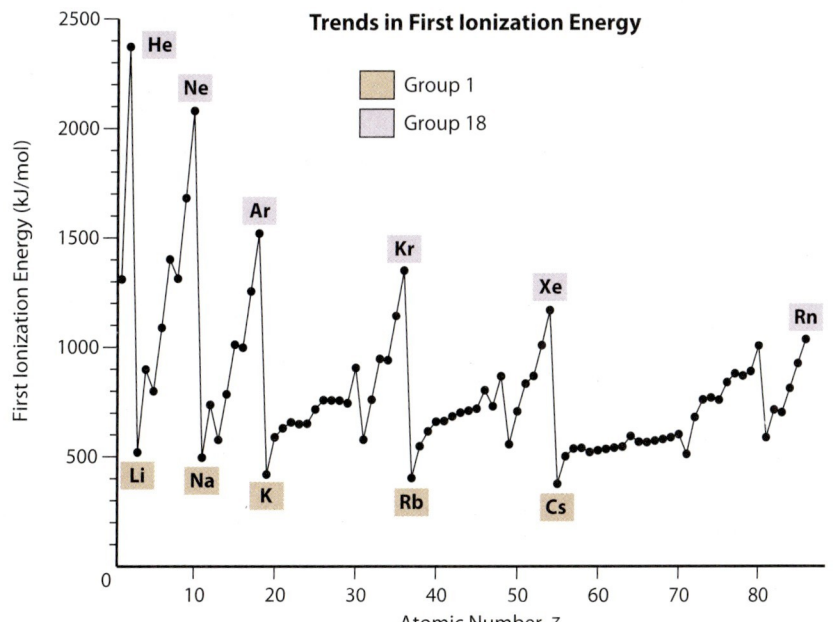

Figure 3.23 A plot of first ionization energy vs. atomic number for elements of Periods 1 to 6 shows that the lowest values occur for the alkali metals and the highest for the noble gases. This trend is the inverse of the trend in atomic size.

Reactivity of Metals

Periodic trends in ionization energy are linked to trends involving the reactivity of metals. Metals tend to readily lose electrons during chemical reactions, compared with non-metals. This is because of the low ionization energies of metals. In general, the chemical reactivity of metals increases down a group and increases from right to left across a period.

Electron Affinity

electron affinity a change in energy that accompanies the addition of an electron to an atom in the gaseous state

The energy change (in kJ/mol) that accompanies the addition of 1 mol of electrons to 1 mol of gaseous atoms or ions is known as **electron affinity**. As with ionization energy, there is a first electron affinity, a second electron affinity, and so on. The *first electron affinity* (EA_1) results in the formation of a gaseous anion with a charge of 1−. For example, when a neutral fluorine atom acquires an electron, the resulting electron configuration of the fluoride ion is the same as that of the noble gas, neon:

$$F(1s^22s^22p^5) + e^- \rightarrow F^-(1s^22s^22p^6) \qquad \Delta E = EA_1$$

Fluorine is very reactive, and the relative ease with which it gains an electron when it forms bonds is reflected in its high electron affinity. In most cases, energy is released when the first electron is added, because it is attracted to the atom's nuclear charge. Thus, EA_1 is usually negative. The second electron affinity (EA_2), on the other hand, is always positive, because energy must be absorbed in order to overcome electrostatic repulsions and add another electron to a negative ion. Large negative numbers mean a high electron affinity. Small negative numbers and positive numbers mean a low electron affinity. Some representative first electron affinities are shown in **Figure 3.24**.

Electron Affinities

1	2	3	4	5	6	7	8
H −72.8							He (0.0)
Li −59.6	Be ≤0	B −26.7	C −122	N +7	O −141	F −328	Ne (+29)
Na −52.9	Mg ≤0	Al −42.5	Si −134	P −72.0	S −200	Cl −349	Ar (+35)
K −48.4	Ca −2.37	Ga −28.9	Ge −119	As −78.2	Se −195	Br −325	Kr (+39)
Rb −46.9	Sr −5.03	In −28.9	Sn −107	Sb −103	Te −190	I −295	Xe (+41)
Cs −45.5	Ba −13.95	Tl −19.3	Pb −35.1	Bi −91.3	Po −183	At −270	Rn (+41)

Figure 3.24 This table of some representative first electron affinities shows the very large negative values for the Group 17 elements.

Trends for electron affinity are more irregular than those for atomic radius and ionization energy, because factors other than atomic size and Z_{eff} are involved. In future chemistry courses, you will learn about these factors and how they explain the irregularities. However, the property of electron affinity is still significant when considered in combination with ionization energy. Three main trends that result from this combination are important for chemical bonding.

1. *Reactive non-metals.* Atoms of elements in Group 17, and to a lesser degree Group 16, have high ionization energies and high electron affinities. As a result, it takes a great deal of energy to remove electrons from these atoms. However, these atoms attract electrons strongly, and form negative ions in ionic compounds.

2. *Reactive metals.* Atoms of elements in Group 1 and Group 2 have low ionization energies and low electron affinities. Atoms of these elements give up electrons easily, but attract them poorly. Therefore, they form positive ions in ionic compounds.

3. *Noble gases.* Atoms of elements in Group 18 have very high ionization energies and very low electron affinities. Therefore, in nature, they do not gain, give up, or share electrons at all. (Under laboratory conditions, only the larger Group 18 atoms can be made to form compounds.)

Section 3.3 Review

Section Summary

- For hydrogen, the relative energies of the atomic orbitals depend only on the principal quantum number, n. For many-electron atoms, other factors such as the orbital-shape quantum number, l, influence the relative energies of atomic orbitals.

- Electron configuration notation and orbital diagrams are two methods commonly used to represent or describe the distribution of electrons in atoms.

- Applying the Pauli exclusion principle, Hund's rule, and the aufbau principle, the electron configuration of atoms can be built up according to the position of the element in the periodic table.

- The modern, quantum mechanical model of the atom enables us to understand the elements, their positions in the periodic table, and their chemical and physical properties based on their electron configuration.

Review Questions

1. **K/U** Refer to **Table 3.5**. Draw a table that shows the quantum numbers, electron configuration, and orbital diagram for the electrons in nitrogen.

2. **K/U** A carbon atom has two electrons total in its $2p$ orbitals. If one of these electrons has an electron spin number of $+\frac{1}{2}$, what is the electron spin number of the other electron? Explain your answer in terms of Hund's rule.

3. **T/I** Examine the following orbital diagram for a neutral atom in its ground state.

↑↓	↑↓	↑↓	↑	↑
1s	2s	2p		

   a. What element is represented here? How do you know?
   b. Explain how Hund's rule applies to this orbital diagram.
   c. Explain how the Pauli exclusion principle applies to this orbital diagram.

4. **T/I** What is wrong with each of the following condensed electron configurations?
   a. $[Ne]4s^2$
   b. $[Kr]5s^25p^6$
   c. $[Br]5s^2$

5. **T/I** The condensed electron configuration for iodine is $[Kr]5s^24d^{10}5p^5$. Without using a periodic table, identify the group number to which iodine belongs. Show your reasoning.

6. **T/I** The condensed electron configuration for germanium is $[Ar]4s^23d^{10}4p^2$. Without using a periodic table, identify the group number, period number, and orbital block to which germanium belongs. Show your reasoning.

7. **K/U** Which elements have these valence electron configurations?
   a. ns^1
   b. ns^2np^6
   c. $ns^2(n-1)d^{10}np^4$

8. **T/I** Use Pauli exclusion principle, Hund's rule, and the aufbau principle to write condensed electron configurations for atoms of the following elements:
   a. potassium, K
   b. selenium, Se
   c. xenon, Xe

9. **K/U** The ns orbitals usually fill before the $(n-1)d$ orbitals. Why are there exceptions to this rule?

10. **T/I** Referring only to the periodic table at the back of your textbook, arrange the following sets of elements in order of increasing atomic radius. Briefly explain your reasoning.
    a. Be, Ca, Ba
    b. Na, Al, Cl
    c. Li, Rb, Sn

11. **C** Your friend Zen is studying for tomorrow's chemistry test and texts you to ask about the difference between Z and Z_{eff}. Write a text to explain, being as brief as possible while including all important information.

12. **K/U** First ionization energy is an important atomic property.
    a. What is first ionization energy and how does it relate to an atom's chemical reactivity?
    b. Briefly summarize and explain the periodic trends in first ionization energy.
    c. What is the relationship between ionization energy and atomic radius?

13. **C** Draw diagrams to illustrate why boron, aluminum, oxygen, and sulfur deviate from the periodic trends in ionization energy.

14. **A** The extremely reactive Group 1 metals are commonly stored in oil.
    a. What is the purpose of the oil?
    b. Suggest at least one safety precaution a chemist would need to take when working with Group 1 metals.
    c. Why are Group 1 metals so reactive?

Canadian Research in Action

Enhanced MRI Images and Epilepsy Research

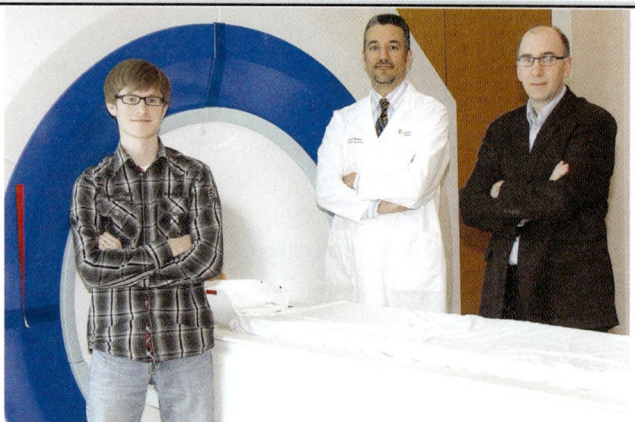

Dr. Jorge Burneo (cente) and his colleagues Dr. Rob Bartha (on the right) and Jake Penner (doctoral candidate, on the left) are shown here with the 7 Tesla MRI that they use in their research into epilepsy.

Related Career

MRI technicians are medical professionals who operate MRI machinery in hospitals or diagnostic imaging centres. MRI technicians undergo a two-year certification program that provides them with an understanding of MRI technology as well as a solid background in anatomy and physiology. In addition to strong technical skills, MRI technicians require skills in problem solving, communication, and team collaboration, as they work with other members of a diagnostic health-care team to provide patient care.

Four to five of every one thousand Canadians have epilepsy, a disorder characterized by sudden changes in brain function that often result in seizures. Thirty percent of individuals with epilepsy do not respond to medications and are diagnosed with *medically-intractable epilepsy*. Dr. Jorge Burneo of the University of Western Ontario in London, Ontario hopes to better understand the causes of this condition with the help of the newest addition to the university's research arsenal, a 7 Tesla MRI. MRI (magnetic resonance imaging) technology uses radio waves along with a powerful magnet and a computer to generate images of soft tissue. Like electrons, protons spin on their axes. However, the orientation of these axes is random. The strong magnetic field generated by the MRI magnet affects the protons in hydrogen atoms in body tissue, causing their axes to align with the same orientation. This is similar to how the needles in compasses adopt a north-south alignment when exposed to Earth's magnetic field. When exposed to radio waves at a specific frequency, certain protons are momentarily "knocked" out of this alignment. When the radio signal is removed, these protons re-align with the magnetic field, emitting their own radio waves as they do so. These signals are "read" by the computer to produce a detailed image of the body tissue. Image resolution depends on the strength of the magnet, which is measured in teslas, the SI unit of measurement for the concentration of a magnetic field. Used only for research purposes, the 7 Telsa is the world's most powerful MRI and the only one of its kind in Canada.

The 7 Tesla gives Dr. Burneo and his research team a glimpse into the brains of individuals with medically-intractable epilepsy in a way that less-powerful MRIs cannot. "We hope," Dr. Burneo states, "that with the use of the 7T technology, we will be able to identify structural abnormalities not seen in standard testing." Small changes within tissue can be detected by this powerful MRI. Dr. Burneo and his team are using a technique called magnetic resonance spectroscopy (MRS) to investigate metabolic changes in regions of the brain where seizures are generated. MRS uses special software to create a profile of all metabolites, both normal and abnormal, produced in these areas. The profile enables Dr. Burneo to study abnormal metabolic changes in these regions in individuals with medically-intractable epilepsy. In the past, these studies could only be completed by inserting electroscopes through a hole in the skull, a procedure associated with significant risk. Therefore, 7 Tesla technology provides Dr. Burneo with a safe and effective way to better understand medically-intractable epilepsy and, ultimately, help doctors treat this condition.

Questions

1. Explain the role that proton spin plays in magnetic resonance imaging.
2. During an MRI, when the radio signal is removed and the hydrogen protons re-align with the magnetic field, they emit their own radio waves. Suggest why this might occur.
3. Use Internet and/or print resources to find another career related to the research covered in this feature. Briefly describe the nature of this career and any required training or education.

Inquiry INVESTIGATION 3-A

Skill Check

Initiating and Planning
Performing and Recording
✓ Analyzing and Interpreting
✓ Communicating Results

Safety Precautions

- A very high voltage is required to operate the gas discharge tubes. Do not come into contact with the source while viewing the tubes.
- Do not work with the gas discharge tubes yourself. Your teacher will demonstrate them.

Materials

- spectroscope or diffraction grating
- incandescent bulb
- gas discharge tubes

Observing Spectra
(Teacher Demonstration)

When a high voltage current is passed through a glass tube that contains hydrogen gas at low pressure, the gas glows with a pinkish-purple colour. In this investigation, you will observe this gas discharge tube through a spectroscope or a diffraction grating to observe the line (emission) spectrum of hydrogen.

Pre-Lab Questions

1. Which part of the electromagnetic spectrum is visible to the human eye, and what range of wavelengths does it span?
2. Compare and contrast a continuous spectrum with a line spectrum.

Question

How can line spectra be used to identify specific elements?

Procedure

1. Practise using the spectroscope with an incandescent bulb. Point the slit toward the bulb; move the spectroscope until the spectrum is clearly visible.
2. Record the appearance of the spectrum from the incandescent bulb.
3. Your teacher will demonstrate the discharge tube apparatus for hydrogen.
4. Observe the hydrogen discharge tube, and note its colour when high-voltage current is applied to it.
5. With the lights dimmed, examine the hydrogen line spectrum with a spectroscope or diffraction grating. Make a sketch to record your observations.
6. Repeat steps 4 and 5 for the line spectra of other discharge tubes, if available.

Analyze and Interpret

1. Compare the spectrum of the incandescent bulb and the hydrogen discharge tube. If you observed other discharge tubes, compare their spectra with the spectrum from the hydrogen discharge tube.

Conclude and Communicate

2. Explain how spectra can be used to identify the presence of specific elements in a sample of a substance.

Extend Further

3. **INQUIRY** A fluorescent bulb is a type of gas discharge tube. However, the emissions of the gas are absorbed by a coating on the inside of the bulb; the excited atoms of the coating emit light when they return to their ground state. Predict what the line spectrum of a fluorescent light would look like. If you are not able to test your prediction, do research to verify it.

4. **RESEARCH** What is an atomic absorption spectrophotometer; for what it is used?

Inquiry Investigation 3-B

Skill Check
- Initiating and Planning
- ✓ Performing and Recording
- ✓ Analyzing and Interpreting
- ✓ Communicating Results

Materials
- periodic table in Appendix B

Electronic Structures for Period 3 Elements

In this investigation, you will use the Pauli exclusion principle, Hund's rule, and the aufbau principle to represent Period 3 elements of the periodic table.

Pre-Lab Questions

1. Explain, using an example, the Pauli exclusion principle.
2. Explain, using an example, Hund's rule.
3. Explain, using an example, the aufbau principle.

Question

How can you use the Pauli exclusion principle, Hund's rule, and the aufbau principle to represent elements of the periodic table?

Procedure

1. Use the periodic table in Appendix B to answer the following questions.

Analyze and Interpret

1. Write electron configurations and orbital diagrams for atoms of sodium, magnesium, aluminum, silicon, phosphorus, sulfur, chlorine, and argon.
2. Make a table with eight columns and two rows. In the first row, write the symbol, atomic number, and condensed electron configurations for the Period 2 elements.
3. Fill in the second row with the atomic number, atomic symbol, and electron configuration for the elements in question 1.

Conclude and Communicate

4. Describe two generalizations about the table that you created.
5. For atoms of any Group 1 element, a general electron configuration is ns^1, where n is the quantum number for the outermost occupied energy level. Use your answer to question 2 to predict general electron configurations for atoms in the following groups:
    a. 2
    b. 13
    c. 14
    d. 15
    e. 16
    g. 17
    h. 18

ThoughtLab INVESTIGATION 3-C

Skill Check
- Initiating and Planning
- ✓ Performing and Recording
- ✓ Analyzing and Interpreting
- ✓ Communicating

Extending the Periodic Table

Pekka Pyykkö at the University of Helsinki has predicted the position of elements up to 172. In this investigation, you will make predictions about the electron configurations of these large elements.

Pre-Lab Questions

1. List the order in which sublevels are filled in element 118.
2. If g is the next sublevel after f, what are the next three sublevels to be filled after $7p$ if the relative energies of atomic orbitals is $6d < 7p < 5g < 6f < 7d < 8p$.

Question
How should 172 elements be arranged in the periodic table?

Organize the Data

1. Complete shorthand electron configurations for elements 118 to 172.
2. Arrange these elements into groups so that they can be placed into the current periodic table. What criteria will you use?
3. Place these groups into the current periodic table. Redraw your table that now includes all 172 elements.

Analyze and Interpret

1. Describe the changes in the length of the periods and groups in each of the s, p, d, and f blocks of the periodic table.
2. Describe the properties of the elements in the groups that you arranged in step 2. Are you able to predict the properties of all of the groups? Explain.
3. Compare your periodic table (step 3) with that of your classmates. Which is best for accurately predicting the properties of the undiscovered elements?

Conclude and Communicate

4. Summarize the concepts about electron configurations of larger elements and the changes needed to accommodate 172 elements in the periodic table.
5. Experts cannot agree where the large elements beyond element 118 should go in the periodic table. What are the problems with arranging these elements?

Extend Further

6. **INQUIRY** Would a single periodic table with 172 elements be better for enabling chemists to make predictions about new elements? Explain.
7. **RESEARCH** How have Canadian scientists and/or scientists in Canadian laboratories advanced knowledge about the synthesis of new elements?

Chapter 3 SUMMARY

Section 3.1 The Nuclear Model of the Atom

Building on and extending from the work of scientists who came before them as well as their peers, Ernest Rutherford and Niels Bohr developed atomic models that, today, are referred to as nuclear and planetary models of the atom.

Key Terms

electromagnetic radiation
emission spectrum or line spectrum
frequency
nuclear model
photon
quantum

Key Concepts

- Historically, the development of and modifications to the atomic model have been the result of experimental evidence and new ideas about the nature of matter and energy.
- Thomson's discovery of the electron disproved Dalton's model of the atom as a solid, indivisible sphere. Instead, Thomson proposed that the atom existed as a positively charged sphere, with enough negatively charged electrons embedded in it to balance the overall charge on the atom.
- Observations and inferences made by Rutherford led to a nuclear model of the hydrogen atom. This model is still the most commonly depicted, with negatively charged electrons orbiting around a central positively charged nucleus.
- Bohr's model of the atom refined the Rutherford model, incorporating the concept that, like light, electrons in atoms could have only certain amounts of energy and, therefore, could exist in only specific orbits around the nucleus. Each allowed orbit had a specific amount of energy and a specific radius.

Section 3.2 The Quantum Mechanical Model of the Atom

New ideas and experimental evidence about the wave nature of particles led to a new, revolutionary atomic model—the quantum mechanical model of the atom.

Key Terms

atomic orbital
magnetic quantum number, m_l
orbital-shape quantum number, l
principal quantum number, n
Pauli exclusion principle
quantum mechanical model of the atom
quantum numbers
shell
spin quantum number, m_s
sublevel

Key Concepts

- According to the quantum mechanical model of the atom, electrons have both matter-like and wave-like properties.
- The position and momentum of atoms cannot both be determined with certainty, so the position is described in terms of probabilities.
- An orbital represents a mathematical description of the region of space in which an electron has a high probability of being found.
- The first three quantum numbers describe the size, energy, shape, and orientation of an orbital. The fourth quantum number describes the orientation of the axis around which the electron is spinning.

Section 3.3 Electron Configurations and the Periodic Table

The quantum mechanical model of the atom explains the experimentally determined, electronic structure of the periodic table and the properties of its elements.

Key Terms

atomic radius
aufbau principle
electron affinity
electron configuration
ionization energy
Hund's rule
orbital diagram

Key Concepts

- For hydrogen, the relative energies of the atomic orbitals depend only on the principal quantum number, n. For many-electron atoms, other factors such as the orbital-shape quantum number, l, influence the relative energies of atomic orbitals.
- Electron configuration notation and orbital diagrams are two methods commonly used to represent or describe the distribution of electrons in atoms.
- Applying the Pauli exclusion principle, Hund's rule, and the aufbau principle, the electron configuration of atoms can be built up according to the position of the element in the periodic table.
- The modern, quantum mechanical model of the atom enables us to understand the elements, their positions in the periodic table, and their chemical and physical properties based on their electron configuration.

Chapter 3 REVIEW

Knowledge and Understanding

Select the letter of the best answer below.

1. Which of the following best describes Rutherford's atomic model?
   a. indivisible (nothing smaller than the atom exists)
   b. has a very small nuclear core
   c. contains protons
   d. uses quantum physics to explain electron properties
   e. All of these are correct.

2. Which observation in the cathode ray tube experiments did not contribute to the conclusion that the electron is found in atoms of all matter?
   a. The beam travelled in straight lines.
   b. Changing the gases inside the cathode ray tube did not alter the path of the beam.
   c. Changing the metals of the electrodes did not change the path of the beam.
   d. Two of these are correct.
   e. All of these are correct.

3. The history of science records the discoveries and achievements of various scientists whose models of the atom helped to develop and further our understanding of the nature and behaviour of matter. Choose the correct historical sequence of atomic models from the following choices.
   a. Dalton, Rutherford, Thomson, Bohr
   b. Thomson, Rutherford, Bohr, Dalton
   c. Dalton, Thomson, Rutherford, Bohr
   d. Dalton, Bohr, Rutherford, quantum
   e. Dalton, Bohr, Thomson, quantum

4. The emission spectrum of an element
   a. has a dark background with bright-coloured lines.
   b. has a rainbow-coloured background with dark lines.
   c. has lines that represent the location of electrons inside the atom.
   d. has spaces between the lines that represent the distance between electrons inside the atom.
   e. is a continuous spectrum of visible light.

5. Which one of the following electron configurations represents an electron in an excited state?
   a. $[Ar]4s^2 3d^{10} 4p^3$
   b. $[Ar]4s^2 3d^{10} 4p^6$
   c. $[Ar]4s^2 3d^{10} 4p^2$
   d. $[Ar]4s^2 3d^{10} 4p^4$
   e. $[Ar]4s^2 3d^{10} 4p^3 5s^1$

6. Which of the following elements could have the following valence orbital diagram?

   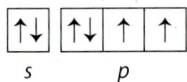

   a. carbon
   b. nitrogen
   c. boron
   d. sulfur
   e. neon

7. First ionization energy is
   a. the amount of energy an electron must gain to escape from a neutral atom.
   b. the amount of energy an electron must lose to escape from a neutral atom.
   c. the amount of energy an atom gains when it first becomes an ion.
   d. Two of these are correct.
   e. All of these are correct.

8. Electron affinity refers to
   a. the energy change accompanying the addition of 1 mol of electrons to 1 mol of gaseous atoms or ions.
   b. the attraction of the nucleus for electrons.
   c. the attraction of electrons for one another.
   d. the energy change of electrons of noble gas elements.
   e. none of the above.

9. In which period can you start to use condensed electron configurations?
   a. 1
   b. 2
   c. 3
   d. 4
   e. 5

10. Atomic radius decreases
    a. when the effective nuclear charge decreases.
    b. when the inner core decreases.
    c. down a group.
    d. across a period.
    e. in all of the above situations.

11. Which property changes in the same way that the atomic radius does in the periodic table?
    a. electron affinity
    b. atomic number
    c. ionization energy
    d. They all change in the same way.
    e. None of them change in the same way.

Chapter 3 REVIEW

12. Which two sets of quantum numbers describe electrons in the same sublevel?
    a. i, ii
    b. iii, v
    c. ii, iii
    d. iv, v
    e. ii, iv

	n	l	m_l	m_s
i.	2	1	0	$-\frac{1}{2}$
ii.	2	1	-1	$+\frac{1}{2}$
iii.	3	1	-1	$+\frac{1}{2}$
iv.	2	2	-1	$+\frac{1}{2}$
v.	3	2	-1	$+\frac{1}{2}$

13. When comparing the properties of carbon atoms and oxygen atoms, which statement is correct?
    a. Carbon and oxygen have the same spin quantum number, m_s.
    b. Carbon and oxygen have the same magnetic quantum number, m_l.
    c. Carbon and oxygen have the same principal quantum number, n.
    d. Carbon has a greater orbital-shape quantum number, l, than oxygen.
    e. Oxygen has a greater orbital-shape quantum number, l, than carbon.

14. Helium behaves like a noble gas because
    a. its valence shell is completely filled.
    b. its outermost orbital is completely filled.
    c. its outermost energy level is completely filled.
    d. Two of these are correct.
    e. All of these are correct.

Answer the questions below.

15. In what ways were Dalton's and Thomson's atomic models similar? In what ways were they different?
16. In what ways were Thomson's and Rutherford's models of the atom similar? In what ways were they different?
17. What is common to all atomic models, from Dalton's to Bohr's?
18. What property is common to all electromagnetic radiation?
19. Describe how the motion of an electron in Bohr's model of the atom is different from the motion of an electron in the quantum mechanical model of the atom.
20. Bohr's atomic model provides specific information about the energy and location of electrons in an atom. That is, the model predicts that both of these can be known with certainty. What structures (such as the nucleus) in the Bohr model are necessary to allow for these concepts?
21. Explain how periodic trends in ionization energy and electron affinity explain why atoms of elements in Group 1 and Group 2 tend to bond with other elements by forming positive ions in ionic compounds.
22. A nitrogen atom has a total of three electrons in its $2p$ orbitals. Are any of these electrons paired? Explain how you know.
23. The quantum mechanical model provides information about the atom that is certain and uncertain. Which information is certain? Which is uncertain?
24. What information do the quantum numbers provide about an orbital?
25. What two things does the principal quantum number, n, describe about an orbital and the electron in it?
26. Why does it make sense that an electron can be found farther away from the nucleus in an orbital of a higher energy level than in the same type of orbital in a lower energy level?
27. What is the Pauli exclusion principle, and how is it related to the spin quantum number, m_s?
28. What is Hund's rule and its significance?
29. Why does it make sense that electron configurations represent atoms in their ground state and not their many excited states?
30. What are the general trends for atomic radius down a group and across a period in the periodic table? Account for these trends.

Thinking and Investigation

31. If it had turned out that the cathode beam particle had a neutral charge, which experimental finding(s) would have remained the same in all of the cathode ray tube experiments?
32. Without consulting a periodic table, determine to which period, group, and block the element with the electron configuration $[Xe]6s^25d^{10}$ would belong.

33. Write the complete electron configuration for the element in Period 5 and Group 15.
34. List the 3s, 5s, 2p, 4p, 3d, and 5d orbitals in order, from the lowest energy to the highest energy.
35. List all possible values of m_l for electrons in the element having the electron configuration [Ar]$4s^2 3d^5$.
36. Use a basic periodic table, which does not contain electron configurations, to determine which element is defined by [Ar]$4s^2 3d^8$.
37. Use a basic periodic table, which does not contain electron configurations, to determine which element is defined by [Ne]$2s^2 2p^1$.
38. Use a basic periodic table, which does not contain electron configurations, to determine which element is defined by [Kr]$5s^2 4d^{10} 5p^4$.
39. If the last electron to be added to an atom was the seventh electron in the third energy level, what element would that be?
40. If the last electron to be added to an atom was the 44th electron in the atom, what element would that be?
41. If the last electron to be added to an atom was the sixth electron in the second energy level, what element would that be?
42. If the last electron to be added to an atom was the second electron in the sixth energy level, what element would that be?
43. Some chemists do not include the *d* electrons in the condensed electron configurations for large *p*-block elements. For example, they would write the condensed electron configuration for tin as [Kr]$5s^2 5p^2$. Why do you think this might be a valid way of writing the electron configurations?
44. Use Z_{eff} to predict which atom should be larger between boron and fluorine.
45. Use Z_{eff} to predict which atom should be larger between magnesium and silicon.
46. Use Z_{eff} to predict which atom should be larger between calcium and selenium.
47. The largest artificial element that scientists have been able to create to date has an atomic number of 118 and occupies the last available spot on the modern periodic table. Using only the organization of the periodic table, determine each of the following for element 118:
    a. condensed electron configuration
    b. set of quantum numbers for the last electron to be added to it
    c. physical state at room temperature
    d. reactivity

48. Referring only to a periodic table, arrange the following sets of elements in order of increasing first ionization energy. Briefly explain your reasoning.
    a. Na, Si, Ar
    b. Mg, Ca, Ba
    c. He, Li, Be
49. Consider the electron configuration: $1s^2 2s^2 2p^4$.
    a. Assume the electron configuration represents a neutral atom in its ground state. What element does it represent? Explain how you know.
    b. What information does this electron configuration notation provide?
    c. What information does this electron configuration notation *not* provide?

Communication

50. **BIG IDEAS** Technological devices that are based on the principles of atomic and molecular structures can have societal benefits and costs. Ultraviolet (UV) radiation technology is used in a wide variety of applications, including disinfection, curing of polymers and resins, detection of trace chemicals, and non-invasive testing. Research one of these and create a graphic organizer that lists the benefits, costs, and potential hazards to society.
51. **BIG IDEAS** Technological devices that are based on the principles of atomic and molecular structures can have societal benefits and costs. X rays were discovered "accidentally" when closed photographic plates were exposed near cathode ray tubes that were left operating. Cathode ray tubes are used in CRT computer monitors. Research the discovery of the X ray, and in a series of small paragraphs, describe how X rays can be released in cathode ray tubes, the precautions that are taken to prevent the unguarded release of X-ray radiation from the CRT computer monitor, and any other precautions or warnings that are necessary that extend from the use of a cathode ray tube in a computer monitor.
52. Use labelled diagrams to compare the concept of an orbit with the concept of an orbital. Be as detailed as possible in your answer.
53. The concept of orbitals overlapping in three-dimensional space to create an overall spherical atom is a difficult image for many people to construct in their minds. Suggest or build a model that can help to give this image more concrete substance to help people understand it better.

Chapter 3 REVIEW

54. Your friend is having a hard time understanding condensed electron configurations. Write an e-mail, giving one example of a condensed electron configuration, explaining why they are used, and helping to avoid any possible misconceptions.

55. Create a simple diagram of a main-group element that includes a nucleus, an inner core of electrons, and a valence shell. Use these terms to describe how the effective nuclear charge, Z_{eff}, is determined.

56. Create a diagram or graphic organizer to summarize all of the periodic trends described in this chapter.

57. This chapter presented ideas from several scientists who made significant contributions to the quantum mechanical model of the atom. These scientists include Bohr, Planck, Heisenberg, de Broglie, and Schrödinger. Other scientists whose work was integral for this model include Albert Einstein and Paul Dirac. Use this chapter as a starting point to conduct research about the roles played by each of these scientists in developing the quantum mechanical model of the atom. Present your findings in the form of a summary table or illustrated essay.

58. Summarize your learning in this chapter using a graphic organizer. To help you, the Chapter 3 Summary lists the Key Terms and Key Concepts. Refer to Using Graphic Organizers in Appendix A to help you decide which graphic organizer to use.

Application

59. Most of the scientists who developed atomic models or whose work was important in the development of atomic models were not chemists but were, rather, physicists and mathematicians.
    a. What skills and prior knowledge do you think the physicists and mathematicians contributed to complement the skills and knowledge of chemists?
    b. For what reasons do you think physicists in particular were interested in studying the atom?

60. The Thomson model of the atom is an example of a "continuum of matter," whereas the Rutherford model of the atom is an example of "quantized matter." Explain what you think this means.

61. Rutherford introduced three new structural features to the atomic model.
    a. Identify these three features.
    b. Explain how each of these features challenged the established concepts of science at the time (late 1800s and early 1900s).

62. The success of a theory or model is judged by how well it can explain and predict experimental findings. The Bohr model was at the same time highly successful and highly unsuccessful. Explain.

63. Interview a health-care professional in your community about infrared (IR) spectroscopy and near-infrared spectroscopy (NIRS), and determine the following:
    - Is it available in your area?
    - Is it commonly used?
    - Is the quality of this diagnostic application as good as other methods, such as MRIs?
    - Is the waiting period to have this diagnostic application done shorter, as long as, or longer than MRIs in your area?

64. Ultraviolet (UV) radiation is used in scanners to detect counterfeit money. Research what the special markers are that are embedded in legitimate bills that are meant to be detected by UV scanners. What is the science behind why these markers show up under the scanners?

65. The brightly coloured lights of fireworks are caused by the same principles as the emission spectra of elements. Research which elements are commonly responsible for red, green, blue, and purple in most firework displays. Use a table to summarize your findings.

66. The concepts of continuum versus quantum amounts can be challenging to understand without suitable analogies. With a classmate, brainstorm examples of continuous versus quantized versions of amounts, positions, or situations all around you. Record them in a chart like the one below.

Scenario	Example	
	Continuous Version	Quantized Version
Climbing	Using a ramp	Using a ladder or staircase
Paying an amount of money		
Getting down a snowy hill		

67. Create a new periodic table of the first 92 elements if the quantum numbers were as follows:

$n = 1, 2, 3 \ldots$
$l = 1, 2 \ldots n - 1$
$m_l = -n \ldots 0 \ldots +n$
$m_s = +\frac{1}{2}, -\frac{1}{2}$

68. Based on the periodic table you developed in the previous question, name the new noble gases.

69. Write a condensed electron configuration for an imaginary element X with atomic number 127.

70. The periodic table was originally organized into periods and groups according to the similarities and patterns of chemical behaviour that emerged by observing the known elements. Now it is apparent that the quantum mechanical model of the atom would organize the elements in a similar way. List four major patterns in the periodic table that correspond to the quantum mechanical model.

71. Lead and carbon are part of the same group on the periodic table, so they have the same number of valence electrons. However, their chemical and physical properties are dramatically different. Explain how and why this is the case.

72. Only two elements are liquids at 25°C: mercury and bromine. Chemists do not know the properties of all the elements, because some have never been prepared in quantities large enough for investigation. In these cases, chemists rely on periodic trends to predict their properties. One of the elements whose properties are predicted is francium (Fr). Its most stable isotope has a half-life of 21 min, so only traces of francium exist on Earth, and no measurable quantity has been prepared or isolated. Could francium be a liquid at 25°C? Do the following to make a prediction.

  a. Plot a graph of the Group 1 elements, with atomic number on the x-axis and melting point (in °C) on the y-axis. Use the following rounded values: Li, 181°C; Na, 98°C; K, 64°C; Rb, 39°C; Cs, 28°C.

  b. Determine by how much the melting point drops between successive pairs of elements (e.g., from lithium to sodium, from sodium to potassium, etc.).

  c. Use your graph and your answers for part (b) to infer a reasonable value for the melting point of francium.

  d. Predict whether francium will be a liquid at 25°C.

73. The history of the development of the quantum mechanical model of the atom, as well as subsequent advances in the application of quantum mechanics to chemistry, tends to focus on the achievements of male scientists. Because of the pivotal roles played by male scientists, one could easily get the impression that few or no female scientists were involved. This is certainly not the case. Do research to find out the achievements of the following female scientists in the history of quantum mechanics and quantum chemistry:

- Inga Fischer-Hjalmars (1918–2008)
- Maria Goeppert-Mayer (1906–1972)
- Sigrid Peyerimhoff (1937–##)
- Alberte Pullman (1920–2011)
- Hertha Sponer (1895–1968)

In communicating your findings, include information about challenges these scientists faced as women working in their fields, as well as any information that you, personally, found interesting or surprising.

Inga Fischer-Hjalmars

Maria Goeppert-Mayer

Sigrid Peyerimhoff

Alberte Pullman

Hertha Sponer

Chapter 3 | SELF-ASSESSMENT

Select the letter of the best answer below.

1. **K/U** Which of the following did Ernest Rutherford use in his gold foil experiment that helped to establish a new model for the atom?
   a. a beam of protons
   b. a cathode ray beam
   c. a beam of alpha particles
   d. a beam of X rays
   e. a beam of beta particles

2. **K/U** Which "feature" of atomic structure was discovered the earliest?
   a. the electron
   b. the proton
   c. the nucleus
   d. the orbit
   e. empty space

3. **K/U** Which aspect of Rutherford's and Bohr's orbits was different?
   a. Rutherford's orbits were elliptical and Bohr's were circular.
   b. Electrons were in constant motion in Rutherford's orbits but not in Bohr's.
   c. There was empty space between the orbits and the nucleus in Rutherford's model but not in Bohr's.
   d. Electrons gave off energy in Rutherford's orbits but not in Bohr's.
   e. Bohr's orbits could be called orbitals because they were quantized, but Rutherford's could not.

4. **K/U** As Bohr understood them, the dark spaces in the atomic spectrum of hydrogen corresponded to
   a. the energy between the energy levels inside the atom.
   b. the energy between the sublevels of energy within each energy level.
   c. the energy of the excited electrons that did not translate into a quantum leap.
   d. the space between the energy levels inside the atom; that is, where the electron could be.
   e. none of the above.

5. **K/U** Which one of the following means the same as "orbital"?
   a. orbit
   b. energy level
   c. shell
   d. wave function
   e. Two of these are correct.

6. **A** If the 24th electron is the last one filled in an element, which element is it?
   a. chromium
   b. titanium
   c. manganese
   d. zirconium
   e. molybdenum

7. **T/I** Which element, in its ground state, would not have an electron with the quantum numbers $n = 3$, $l = 1$, $m_l = 0$, $m_s = +\frac{1}{2}$ in their atoms?
   a. calcium
   b. bromine
   c. sulfur
   d. tin
   e. magnesium

8. **K/U** Which scientist is responsible for the rule that states only two electrons are allowed in one orbital?
   a. Bohr
   b. Schrödinger
   c. Aufbau
   d. Pauli
   e. Hund

9. **K/U** Which periodic trend increases down a group and decreases across a period?
   a. electron affinity
   b. ionization energy
   c. atomic radius
   d. atomic number
   e. None of these are correct.

10. **T/I** The condensed electron configuration for arsenic is
    a. $[Ar]4s^23d^{10}4p^3$.
    b. $[Ar]4s^24d^{10}4p^3$.
    c. $[Kr]4s^24d^{10}4p^3$.
    d. $[Kr]4s^24d^{10}4p^3$.
    e. $[Ar]3s^23d^{10}4p^3$.

Use sentences and diagrams as appropriate to answer the questions below.

11. **T/I** Answer the following questions in your notebook.
    a. What was the critical finding that suggested the atom contained a smaller particle?
    b. What was the critical finding that suggested that the particle was negatively charged?
    c. What was the critical finding that suggested that the same particle was found in all matter?

12. **A** Rutherford's model of the atom has been referred to as "the nuclear model," "the planetary model," and "the beehive model." What are the reasons behind each title? In your opinion, which title is the best one for Rutherford's model? Why?

13. **K/U** What is the difference between a continuous spectrum and a line spectrum?

14. **K/U** Explain how the meaning of n is similar and different in the Bohr and quantum mechanical models of the atom.

15. **A** Arrange the following in order from highest to lowest energy, and justify your answer: $n = 7$, $n = 2$, $n = 5$, $n = 4$, $n = 1$.

16. **K/U** List all of the sets of quantum numbers allowed for the first four energy levels.

17. **K/U** Explain how light and electrons each display characteristics of both particles and waves.

18. **T/I** Answer the following questions.
  a. Give the possible values for m_l if $n = 4$ and $l = 2$. What type of orbital is associated with these quantum numbers? How many orbitals are associated with these quantum numbers?
  b. Give the possible values for m_l if $n = 3$ and $l = 1$. What type of orbital is associated with these quantum numbers? How many orbitals are associated with these quantum numbers?
  c. Give the possible values for m_l if $n = 4$ and $l = 0$. What type of orbital is associated with these quantum numbers? How many orbitals are associated with these quantum numbers?

19. **C** Develop a flowchart to outline the steps of the aufbau principle.

20. **T/I** Using a basic periodic table that does not contain electron configurations, determine which element is defined by $[Kr]5s^14d^8$.

21. **T/I** The condensed electron configuration for a silicon atom is $[Ne]3s^23p^2$. Without using a periodic table, identify the group number, period number, and orbital block in the periodic table to which silicon belongs. Show your reasoning.

22. **K/U** Answer the following questions.
  a. What are s-block and p-block elements collectively known as?
  b. What are the d-block elements known as?
  c. What are the f-block elements known as?

23. **C** Using a graphic organizer such as a triple Venn diagram to record your answers, identify the models of the atoms shown below, name the scientists who developed them, and clearly indicate what the models have in common and how they differ.

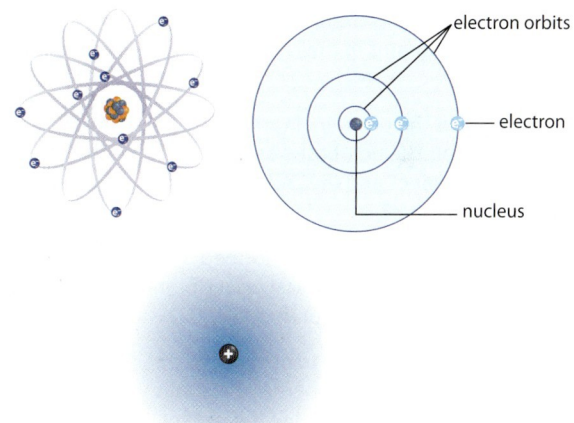

24. **K/U** Explain how the first ionization energy tends to change down a group and across a period in the periodic table?

25. **A** What other properties of elements vary the same way as first ionization energy down the groups and across the periods in the periodic table?

Self-Check

If you missed question …	1	2	3	4	5	6	7	8	9	10	11	12	13	14	15	16	17	18	19	20	21	22	23	24	25
Review section(s)…	3.1	3.1	3.1	3.1	3.2	3.2	3.2	3.3	3.3	3.3	3.1	3.1	3.2	3.1	3.2	3.2	3.2	3.3	3.3	3.1	3.1	3.3	3.1	3.3	3.3

CHAPTER 4
Chemical Bonding and Properties of Matter

Specific Expectations

In this chapter, you will learn how to ...

- C1.1 **assess** the benefits to society of technologies based on the principles of atomic and molecular structures (4.2)

- C1.2 **evaluate** the benefits to society, and the impact on the environment, of specialized materials created on the basis of research into the structure of matter and chemical bonding (4.2)

- C2.1 **use** appropriate terminology related to structure and properties of matter (4.1, 4.2)

- C2.3 **predict** the shapes of simple molecules and ions using the VSEPR model, and **draw** diagrams of their molecular shapes (4.2)

- C2.4 **predict** the polarity of various chemical compounds, based on their molecular shapes and the ΔEN values of the atoms (4.1, 4.2)

- C2.5 **predict** the type of solid formed by a given substance in a chemical reaction, and **describe** the properties of that solid (4.2)

- C2.6 **conduct** an inquiry to **observe** and **analyze** the physical properties of various substances and to **determine** the type of bonding in each substance (4.2)

- C3.4 **explain** how physical properties of a solid or liquid depend on their particles and the types of intermolecular and intramolecular forces (4.2)

- C3.5 **describe** a Canadian contribution to atomic and molecular theory (4.2)

Iron, in its pure form and as alloyed with other substances, is the most commonly used metal on Earth. Its strength makes it ideal for structures designed for support, such as buildings and bridges. A less obvious example of iron used for support, as well as for protection, is the horseshoe, which came into use in Europe more than 1000 years ago. Unlike gold, which is naturally quite soft, iron is malleable only when heated to temperatures close to its melting point of 1536°C. Pre-manufactured horseshoes are widely available today. However, many modern farriers, including Ontario's first female farrier, Cathy Lesperance, shown here, who began the trade more than 30 years ago, still work and shape horseshoes by hand. (Farriers are experts in the care of horses' hooves.) In this chapter, you will compare bonding in metals with bonding in ionic and covalent compounds. You will also learn how bonding influences the shapes of molecules and how molecular shape is related to the properties of substances.

Launch Lab

Applications of "Melt-away" Metals

Most pure, solid metals have melting points well above the boiling point of water, which suggests that the bonding between atoms in metals is quite strong. With the exception of lithium, the alkali metals would melt in hot or warm water if they did not react so violently with it. In 1701, Sir Isaac Newton reported a family of alloys of the metals bismuth, lead, and tin that would melt at or a few degrees below the boiling point of water. These alloys have since been called fusible alloys. Although popular as novelty ("joke") items—such as spoons that melt when used to stir hot beverages—fusible alloys have a wide range of industrial uses, and even a few applications in the home.

Materials
- computer with Internet access

Procedure
1. Conduct research into the nature and use of fusible alloys. The following questions can guide your research:
   a. Fusible alloys may involve two, three, four, or five metals in various proportions. Which metals tend to be the most commonly used?
   b. Which metals often used in fusible alloys are undesirable from an environmental perspective?
   c. What is lens blocking, and how are fusible metals used in this process?
   d. What is soldering, and why are fusible alloys useful in this process?
   e. Identify two home-based applications that make use of fusible alloys.

Questions
1. In your opinion, would lens blocking fit the definition of a green-chemical process? (Refer to Appendix A at the back of this textbook, if necessary, for a discussion on green chemistry.) Explain why or why not.
2. Why are fusible alloys useful in temperature-control and fire-protection devices?
3. Explain how and why fusible alloys can be useful alternatives to lead soldering and applications that involve mercury.

How might a fusible alloy be used in an automatic sprinkler system?

Chapter 4 Chemical Bonding and Properties of Matter • MHR **207**

SECTION 4.1
Models of Chemical Bonding

Key Terms

electronegativity
delocalized
electron-sea model
formula unit
valence bond theory
molecular orbital theory
hybrid orbital
allotrope
network solid

Why is gold the best substance for dental crowns and inlays? What makes copper the most practical substance for large-scale electrical conductors? How do different salts form crystals with such widely differing shapes? The answers to these questions lie in the nature of the bonds that form between the atoms of these substances.

All chemical bonds involve the electrons of atoms interacting with the other atoms of the same or different elements. Therefore, the electron configuration of any two atoms plays a significant role in the type of bond that forms between them. By grouping elements into two main categories based on electron configuration—metals and non-metals—three general types of bonding can be identified and described. You have investigated two of these, ionic and covalent bonding, for several years now in your chemistry studies. The third, metallic bonding, is introduced in this section. **Table 4.1** provides an overview and summary of the three types of chemical bonding. Each type will be investigated in greater depth as this section progresses.

Table 4.1 The Three Types of Chemical Bonding

Metal Bonded with Non-metal: Ionic Bonding	Non-metal Bonded with Non-metal: Covalent Bonding	Metal Bonded with Metal: Metallic Bonding
The metal atoms lose their electrons and become positive ions, and the non-metal atoms gain the electrons and become negative ions. The oppositely charged ions then attract one another and form a crystalline lattice. Each ion is attracted to many other oppositely charged ions. 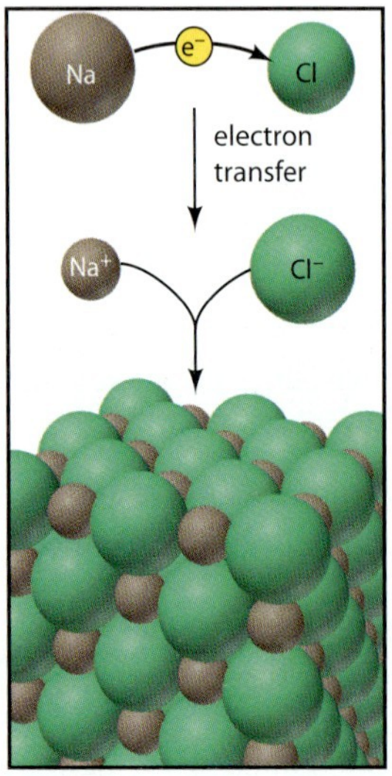	Non-metal atoms (excluding metalloids) have valence shells that are more than half-filled and can form filled shells most effectively by sharing electrons. These shared electrons constitute a covalent bond (represented here as a solid line). 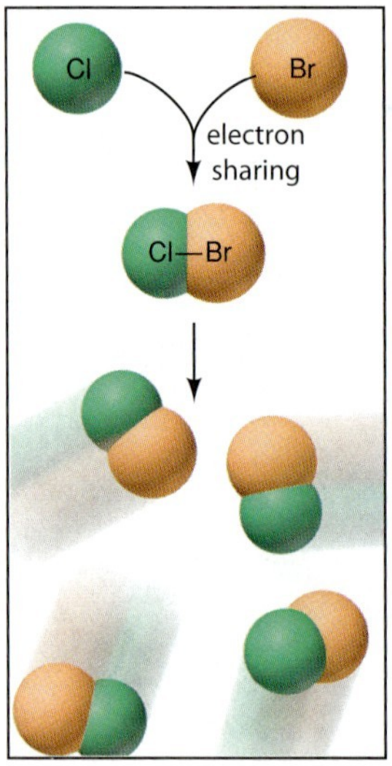	Metal atoms have valence shells that are less than half-filled, so two metal atoms cannot combine to form a filled shell or contribute electrons to each other to form filled shells. Instead, a "sea" of valence electrons of many metal atoms move freely among the atoms. The positively charged ions are all attracted simultaneously to many electrons. 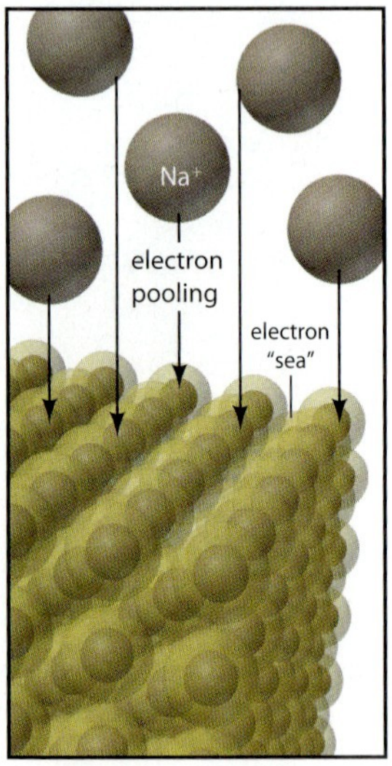

electronegativity the relative ability of the atoms of an element to attract shared electrons in a chemical bond

Electronegativity

Electronegativity, EN, is one of the most important concepts in chemical bonding. **Electronegativity** refers to the relative ability of an atom to attract shared electrons in a bond. **Figure 4.1** shows the electronegativity values of atoms of each element. The height of the bar representing each element is proportional to its electronegativity. (The noble gases are omitted, because their atoms do not share electrons or form bonds with other atoms in nature.)

In general, the electronegativity decreases as you go down through a group in the periodic table. The electronegativity increases from left to right along a period. Although the atomic numbers increase from left to right, the actual sizes of the atoms decrease. The reason for this trend is that all of the outer electrons of the atoms in a given period are in the same shell. The outer shell becomes smaller across a period because the effective nuclear charge increases, pulling the electrons closer to the nucleus. Note that these observations are trends and not rules. The transition metals, in particular, do not strictly follow these trends. For example, the precious metals (Groups 8 to 11 in Periods 5 and 6) have higher electronegativities than would be expected by the trends.

A comparison of the electronegativities of any two atoms that are bonded together reveals important information about the characteristics of the bond. To carry out this analysis, chemists use the electronegativity difference, ΔEN, between the bonding atoms. If the electronegativity difference between two bonded atoms is large, the atom with the higher electronegativity will attract shared electrons more than will the atom with the lower electronegativity. If the electronegativity difference between two bonded atoms is very small or zero, the two atoms will attract the electrons nearly equally. The ΔEN between the atoms with the highest electronegativity (F: $\Delta EN = 4.0$) and the lowest electronegativity (Fr: $\Delta EN = 0.7$) is 3.3, which is therefore the largest possible ΔEN.

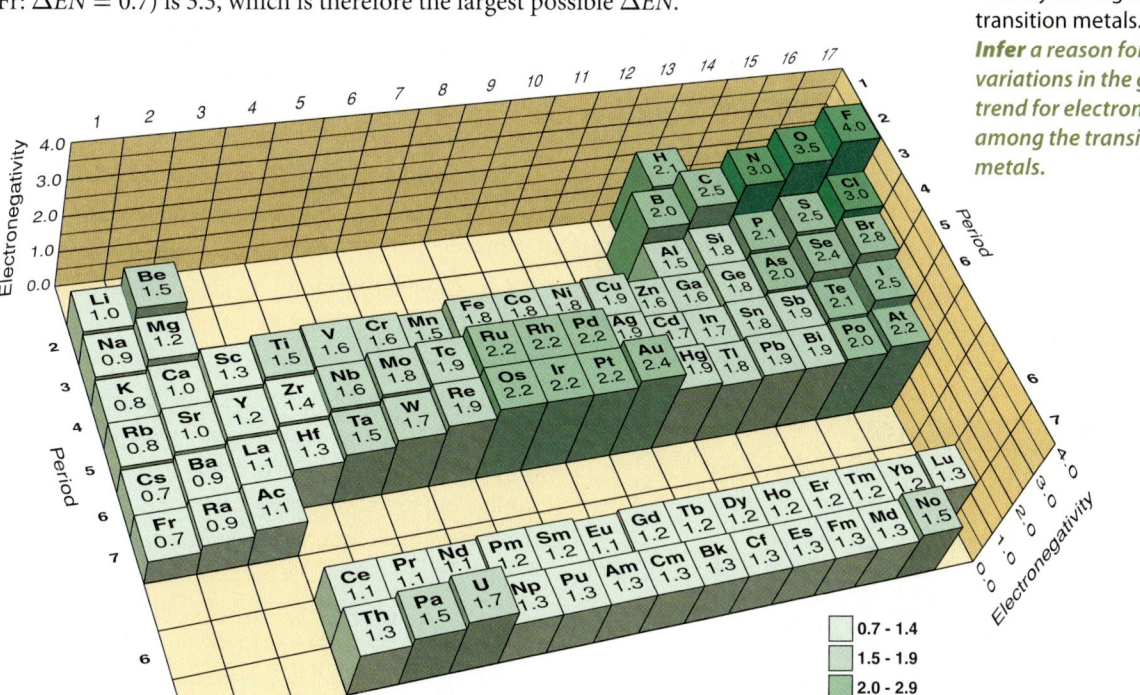

Figure 4.1 This three-dimensional periodic table represents trends in electronegativity. Notice that, although the general trend is for electronegativity to increase from left to right and from bottom to top, there are variations—notably among the transition metals.
Infer a reason for the variations in the general trend for electronegativity among the transition metals.

Electron Sharing and Electronegativity

Figure 4.2 on the next page shows electron density diagrams around bonds with low, medium, and high electronegativity differences. Notice that, when ΔEN is 0, most of the electron density is between the atoms. The shared electrons spend most of their time between the atoms and are equally shared between the atoms. When the ΔEN is 1.0, or intermediate, the shared electrons spend more time around the atom with the higher EN. The stronger pull by the more electronegative atom distorts the electron cloud, making one end slightly negatively charged and the other end slightly positively charged. The bond is said to be polar. When the ΔEN is high, there is a space between the atoms where electron density is very low. However, in all bonds, there is some sharing of electrons, even if it is a very small amount.

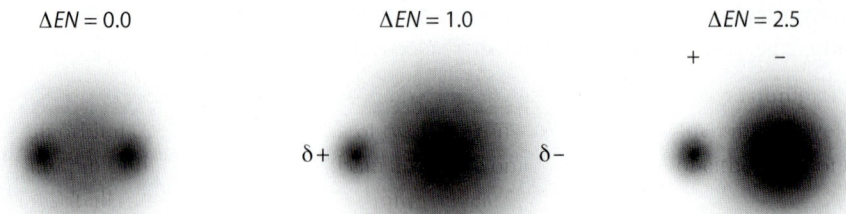

Figure 4.2 Comparing the distribution and density of electrons of atoms with three different electronegativity differences

The diagrams in **Figure 4.2** suggest that bonds form a continuum from equal sharing to minimal sharing of electrons. How can the concept of a bonding continuum be made consistent with the rigid-sounding definitions for covalent and ionic bonding? What is the cut-off point between ionic and covalent bonds? In fact, there is no natural cut-off point, so chemists have agreed on arbitrary ΔEN values. They have identified two points on the continuum of ΔEN values to define categories of bonds. **Figure 4.3** shows how chemists classify bonds based on the ΔEN of their atoms.

- Bonds with a ΔEN between 1.7 and 3.3 are classified as *mostly ionic*. Although there is some sharing of electrons, the compounds behave like ionic compounds.

- Bonds with a ΔEN between 0.4 and 1.7 are classified as *polar covalent*. Although there is some ionic character, the compounds with this type of bond behave like molecular compounds. However, the bond is polar. The arrow over the central molecule in **Figure 4.3** is the symbol that indicates a polar bond. The arrow points to the slightly negatively charged end of the bond and the tail of the arrow is made to look like a plus (+) sign to indicate that this end of the bond is slightly positively charged. The lower case deltas (δ) at the ends of the molecule are symbols that indicate that the plus and minus signs do not represent whole charges but, instead, represent partial charges.

- Bonds with a ΔEN between 0.0 and 0.4 are classified as *mostly covalent*. The electrons are almost equally shared by the two atoms. These bonds are sometimes called *non-polar covalent* because they have no significant separation of charge.

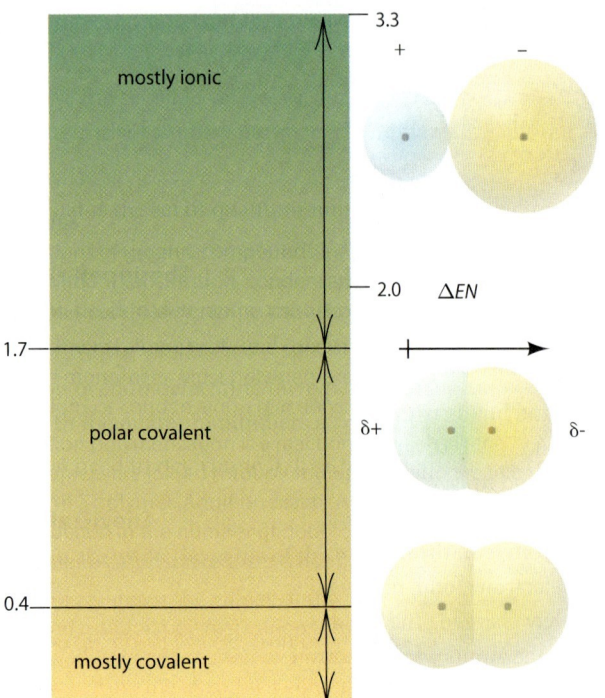

The bonding categories described are one of several different methods chemists have proposed to categorize bonds. Most of these methods yield similar, but not always identical, results. As well, the environment around the compounds can affect the nature of a bond. The hydrogen halides (HF, HCl, HBr, and HI) provide good examples. Their ΔEN values vary from 0.4 for HI to 1.9 for HF. In their gaseous form, all hydrogen halides behave like molecules with covalent bonds. However, they ionize in water to form strong acids, which suggests that their interaction with water molecules changes the nature of the bonds. Although the categorization of bonds based on ΔEN values is imperfect, it provides a good starting point for discussion and analysis.

Figure 4.3 Although chemical bonds range in character from mostly ionic to mostly covalent, they are arbitrarily divided into three categories.

Metallic Bonding

Metal atoms have low electronegativities, as well as valence shells that are less than half-filled. As a result, when metal atoms interact with atoms of the same or different metals, they cannot attract and hold electrons of other atoms well enough to form filled valence shells. Instead, metal atoms attract their own valence electrons so weakly that the valence electrons of solid or liquid metals can move somewhat freely from one atom to the next. The electrons are said to be **delocalized**, because they do not remain in one location or in association with one specific atom. To describe this delocalized condition, chemists use the **electron-sea model** of metals. This model visualizes a metal as a relatively ordered array of cations in a "sea" of freely moving electrons, with the positively charged ions all attracted to many of the electrons in the "sea" simultaneously.

delocalized as applied to the electron-sea model of metals, valence electrons that are not associated with a specific atom but move among many metal ions

electron-sea model a model of metallic bonding that proposes that the valence electrons of metal atoms move freely among the ions thus forming a "sea" of delocalized electrons that hold the metal ions rigidly in place

The Structure of Metals

The fact that all pure metals except mercury are solids at room temperature suggests that the atoms are held rigidly in place. In fact, most of the atoms of metals form a uniform crystalline pattern. This pattern typically is not visible at a macroscopic level. However, as shown in **Figure 4.4A**, microscopic observation reveals that metals are made up of aggregates of millions of tiny crystals. These crystals, called grains, range in size from a few nanometres to several millimetres, depending on the metal and the conditions under which it has formed. Not all the atoms that make up a metal are arranged in a regular manner, however. As shown in **Figure 4.4B**, the atoms of the crystals (grains) form precise, regularly repeating patterns, whereas the atoms at boundaries between grains are arranged randomly.

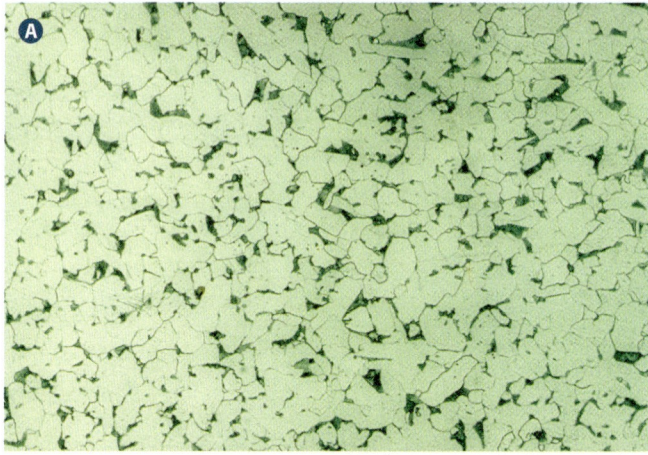 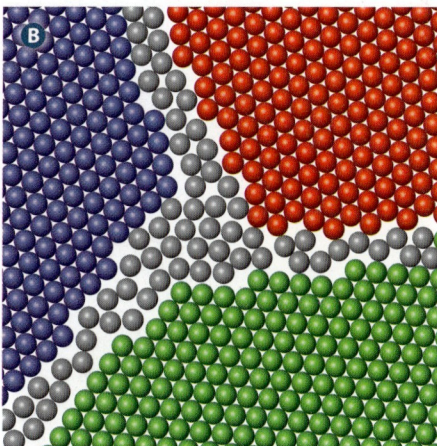

Figure 4.4 Micrographic observation (**A**) reveals the crystalline nature of metals. In (**B**), spheres all represent atoms of the same element. The different colours are used to help visualize the individual crystals of a metal and the grey spheres represent atoms in the boundaries.

Learning Check

1. Name and describe three general types of chemical bonding and identify what these three different types of bonding have in common.
2. What general trends do the electronegativity values of the atoms of the elements in the periodic table exhibit?
3. Describe three ways in which chemists classify bonds based on the electronegativity difference (ΔEN) of their atoms.
4. What happens when metal atoms interact with atoms of the same or different metals, and why?
5. Is the following statement true or false? If it is false, rewrite the statement to correct the error. "The electron-sea model of metals visualizes a metal as a relatively disordered array of cations in a 'sea' of freely moving electrons, with the positively charged ions all attracted to many of the electrons in the 'sea' simultaneously."
6. What does microscopic observation reveal about the structure of metals?

Properties of Metals

Typical properties of metals include melting point, boiling point, malleability, ductility, and electrical and thermal conductivity. The electron-sea model and basic information about the structure of metals can explain many of these properties.

Melting and Boiling Points

In order for a substance to be solid, its particles cannot have enough kinetic energy to pull away from their adjacent particles. As you know, the kinetic energy of the particles is directly related to the temperature of the substance. High melting and boiling points indicate that a large amount of kinetic energy is required to pull the particles apart. Thus, there is a strong correlation between the melting points and boiling points of pure metals and the strength of the bonding or attractive forces. The partial periodic table in **Figure 4.5** shows the melting points of many of the metals.

Melting Points of Metals (°C)

1	2	3	4	5	6	7	8	9	10	11	12	13
Li 180.5	Be 128.7											
Na 97.794	Mg 650											Al 660.32
K 63.38	Ca 842	Sc 1541	Ti 1668	V 1910	Cr 1907	Mn 1246	Fe 1538	Co 1495	Ni 1455	Cu 1084.6	Zn 419.53	Ga 29.77
Rb 39.30	Sr 777	Y 1522	Zr 1854.7	Nb 2477	Mo 2623	Tc 2157	Ru 2334	Rh 1964	Pd 1554.8	Ag 9612.2	Cd 321.1	In 156.6
Cs 28.44	Ba 727				W 3422		Os 3033		Pt 1768.2	Au 1064.2	Hg −38.83	

Figure 4.5 Displaying the melting points of many metal elements in the form of a periodic table reveals several trends.

Analysis of **Figure 4.5** reveals some trends involving melting point. For example, in Group 1, as the atomic number gets larger, the melting points decrease. Why? Because the atoms in each period have one more electron shell than atoms in the previous period, free valence electrons are progressively farther from the nucleus. Therefore, the strength of the attractive forces decreases.

Another trend is apparent across a period through the first six or seven groups: as the atomic numbers become larger across a period, the melting points increase. Why? The number of valence electrons increases across a period for the first several groups, and the ions have a larger positive charge. The larger number of electrons in the "electron sea" and the larger charge on the ions result in a stronger attractive force. Therefore, the ions are held in place more tightly. These trends do not continue across periods due to the complex nature of the electronic structure of the atoms as the d orbitals fill.

Examining Group 12 reveals another trend. Since d shells in Group 12 are filled, electrons cannot freely move away from the atom. Thus, there are fewer electrons in the "electron sea." The boiling points of Group 12 elements are influenced by the same characteristics that influence their melting points, and for much the same reason—how strongly the positively charged ions are attracted to the electrons in the "electron sea."

Electrical and Thermal Conductivity

Metals are good electrical conductors, because their valence electrons are free to move from one atom to another. Therefore, if a potential difference is applied to the ends of a piece of metal, the electrons are drawn toward the positive end and repelled from the negative end. Metals are good conductors of thermal energy for much the same reason. The freely moving electrons receive kinetic energy from the source of heat and pass it along readily to other electrons.

Malleability and Ductility

Malleability refers to the ability of metals to be hammered and shaped without breaking. Some metals, such as copper and aluminum, are malleable at room temperature. Other metals, such as iron shown at the start of this chapter, must be heated strongly to be malleable enough to hammer into a specific shape. Gold is probably the most malleable metal. One gram of gold, about the size of a small ball-bearing, can be hammered into a sheet that has an area of 1.0 m^2 and about 230 atoms thick.

Metals are also ductile, meaning that they can be drawn into fine wires without breaking. Gold not only is the most malleable metal, but also is the most ductile. One gram of gold can be drawn into a wire 20 μm thick and 165 m long.

As shown in **Figure 4.6**, the electron-sea model can explain the malleability and ductility of metals. **Figure 4.6** models what happens when a metal is hit by a hammer. The ions in the metal crystals can slide past each other because it causes little change in their environment. The delocalized electrons are always surrounding the ions.

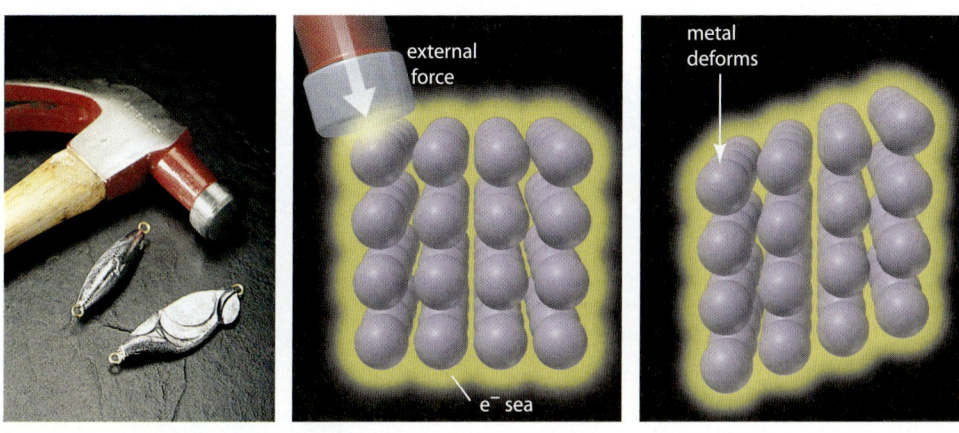

Figure 4.6 The electron-sea model is used to illustrate the deforming of metals.

Hardness

The hardness of a metal is its ability to resist scratching, denting, or bending. Although all metals can be scratched, dented, and bent, they vary greatly in their hardness. Gold is very soft, for example, whereas iron is much harder. However, different samples of the same metal can vary in hardness, depending on the size of their crystalline grains. In **Figure 4.6**, you saw that metals are malleable because the atoms in a crystal can slide over each other. The boundaries of grains resist this sliding, because the atoms are not aligned in layers that slide smoothly. Thus, a metal object that has a very large number of small crystals is harder than an object made of the same metal having a larger grain size. As well, with hardness comes brittleness. The atoms in boundaries around grains are not held as tightly and cracks can form along these boundaries. Controlling the grain size influences the hardness of a metal.

Metals can be hardened by heating them to the temperature at which they just begin to become soft and then cooling them very quickly. The heating causes the crystals to begin to melt, or lose their uniform array. Rapid cooling prevents the atoms from realigning and re-forming crystals. Pounding on a cold metal will also disrupt the crystalline structures. The metal is very hard but also brittle.

Tempering is a process in which a metal is softened but is also made less brittle. The metal is heated to a temperature that is lower than the temperature used for hardening so it does not begin to melt. Nevertheless, the metal atoms have enough energy to jostle around and in so doing, can settle into their uniform arrangement. The metal is then cooled very slowly to allow the crystals to grow and remain intact. The degree of hardening or tempering that a manufacturer chooses to do on a metal object depends on the intended purpose of the object.

Alloys

Most commonly used metals are alloys designed to have the precise properties for a specific task. An *alloy* is a solid mixture of two or more different types of metal atoms. In some cases, non-metal atoms such as carbon can be mixed with metal atoms in an alloy. The addition of even a small amount of a second metal with the main metal in an alloy can significantly change the physical properties of the metal. For example, pure gold is too soft for dental crowns and inlays. However, certain gold alloys have the same hardness that tooth enamel has.

The electron-sea model of metals helps to explain the structure of alloys. The electrons of the "sea" can attract any kind of positive metal ion, so ions of different metals can be held in the same "sea." If the metal atoms are similar in size, they usually form a *substitutional alloy* in which atoms of the second metal take the place of atoms in a pure metal, as shown in **Figure 4.7A**. If atoms of the second metal are much smaller than those of the first metal, they will fit into the spaces between the larger atoms, as shown in **Figure 4.7B**. Such alloys are called *interstitial alloys*.

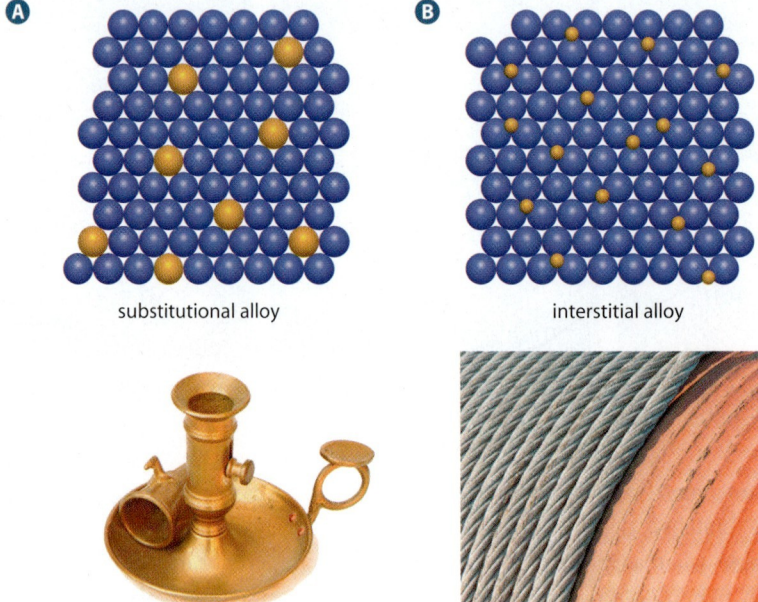

Figure 4.7 The difference between (**A**) substitutional and (**B**) interstitial alloys is illustrated here. The candle holder is an example of brass, an alloy which is mostly copper with varying amounts of tin and zinc. The extremely strong steel cables are an example of an interstitial alloy. Steel is mostly iron with varying amounts of carbon, manganese, silicon, and trace amounts of other metals.

Learning Check

7. Why is there a strong correlation between the melting points and the boiling points of pure metals and the strength of the bonding or attractive forces?
8. In a table, summarize some trends related to melting points and boiling points of metals and the reasons for those trends.
9. Explain why metals are good conductors of electric current and thermal energy.
10. Referring to the electron sea model of metals, explain the malleability and ductility of metals. Use drawings in your answer.
11. Give several reasons why metals can vary greatly in their hardness.
12. Draw a Venn diagram to compare and contrast a substitutional alloy and an interstitial alloy.

Ionic Bonding

Ionic bonding occurs when the electronegativity difference between atoms of two elements is greater than 1.7. This difference is found only between metals and non-metals. Although there is a small degree of sharing of electrons, one atom essentially loses one or more valence electrons, and the other atom gains the electrons. **Figure 4.8** shows three different ways to represent the transfer of an electron during the formation of two different ionic compounds.

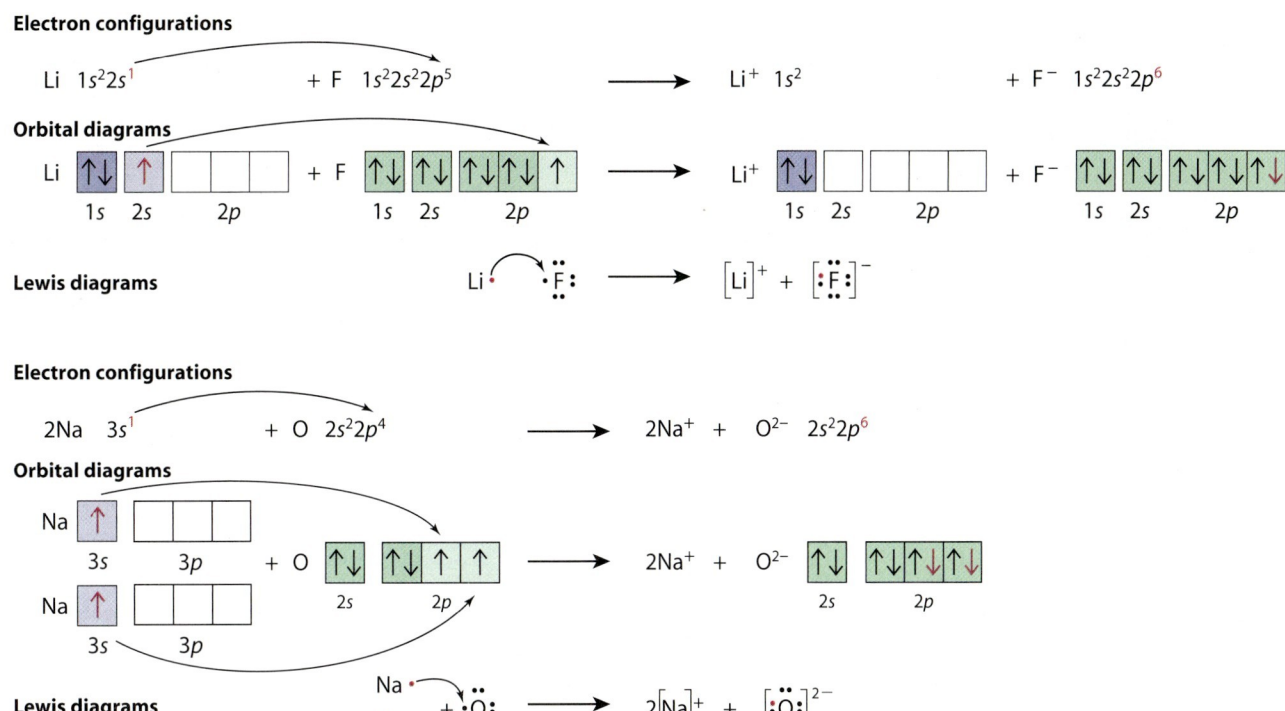

Figure 4.8 The formation of ionic compounds by the transfer of electrons is shown in the form of electron configurations, orbital diagrams, and Lewis diagrams.

Your past studies of ionic bonding have focussed on the ionization of individual atoms and the combinations of the ions that resulted in a net neutral charge. For example, one sodium ion and one chloride ion make a neutral unit of sodium chloride. In a crystal of solid sodium chloride, with a mass of approximately 1 mg, there are approximately 1×10^{21} sodium ions and the same number of chloride ions. Because an attractive force exists between positive and negative charges, the ions pack together tightly in a pattern similar to the structure shown in **Figure 4.9A**. This three-dimensional pattern of alternating positive and negative ions is called a *crystal lattice*. In NaCl(s), each sodium ion is adjacent to several chloride ions, and each chloride ion is adjacent to several sodium ions. The attractive forces between oppositely charged ions are represented by the sticks in **Figure 4.9B**. Notice that each chloride ion is attracted to six adjacent sodium ions, and each sodium ion is attracted to the six chloride ions adjacent to it. Each ion is attracted to *all* the adjacent ions of the opposite charge to the same extent. Thus, the formula, NaCl(s), means that the ratio of sodium to chloride ions is 1:1 throughout the crystal. Similarly, the formula CaF_2(s) means there is a ratio of one calcium ion to two fluoride ions in a crystal of calcium fluoride. The smallest whole number ratio of ions in a crystal is called a **formula unit.**

formula unit the smallest ratio of ions in a crystal

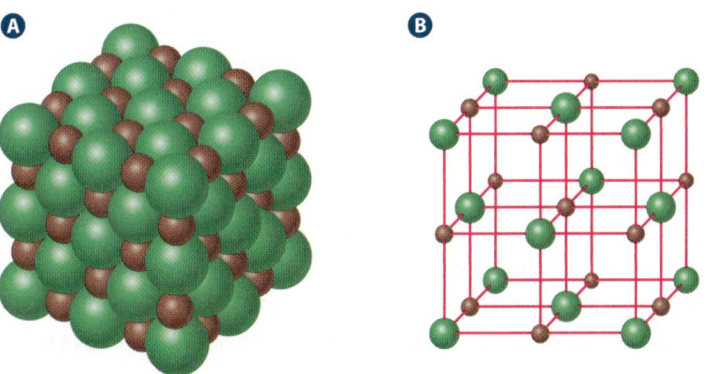

Figure 4.9 The green spheres in this crystal lattice structure of sodium chloride represent chloride ions and the brown spheres represent sodium ions.

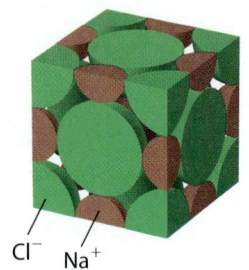

Figure 4.10 A space-filling sodium chloride unit cell

Ionic Crystals

Sodium chloride forms cubic crystals, whereas crystals of some ionic compounds appear needle-like, and others form hexagonal columns. The shape of macroscopic crystals is influenced by the way the individual ions pack together. Because oppositely charged particles attract one another, ions pack together so that oppositely charged ions are as close together as possible. The relative sizes and the charges of the ions also affect the pattern of the packing. If the crystals form very slowly, the packing of the ions will be very uniform, creating the repeating pattern that gives the crystals their symmetrical shape.

The smallest group of ions in a crystal for which the pattern is repeated over and over is called the *unit cell*. For example, the structure in **Figure 4.9B** represents a unit cell of sodium chloride. Since the ions on the sides of each unit cell are shared by the next unit cell, the depiction in **Figure 4.10** is a more realistic, space-filling model of a sodium chloride unit cell. Notice that the ions on the sides of the unit cell appear to be sliced into pieces. The other parts of the ions belong to an adjacent unit cell.

The relative sizes of the ions of a crystal is a factor that affects the pattern of their packing. For example, cesium chloride and sodium chloride form cubic-shaped crystals, but the way in which the ions are arranged in their respective crystals is different due to their size differences. The sodium ion is just over half as big as the chloride ion, whereas the cesium ion is more than twice as large as the chloride ion. The ball and stick model of cesium chloride in **Figure 4.11A** shows that layers of chloride ions alternate with layers of cesium ions. As well, the layers are offset—that is, the cesium and chloride ions are not directly above and below each other. As a result, each cesium ion is adjacent to eight chloride ions, and each chloride ion is adjacent to eight cesium ions. **Figure 4.11B** is a space filling model of the ions indicated in the outlined square from **Figure 4.11A**, which more clearly shows the eight chloride ions around one cesium ion.

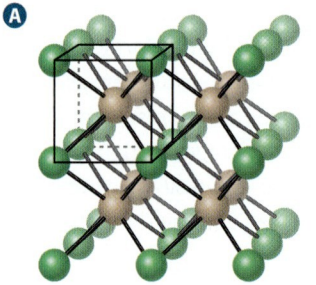
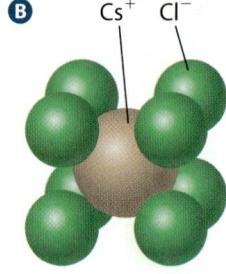

Figure 4.11 Ball-and-stick (**A**) and space-filling (**B**) models of cesium chloride

Another factor that affects the pattern of ions of a crystal is their relative charge. **Figure 4.12** shows the pattern of ions in a unit cell of calcium fluoride, CaF_2. Since calcium, Ca^{2+}, has a charge of 2+ and the fluoride ion, F^-, has only one negative charge, there must be two fluoride ions for each calcium ion.

Properties of Ionic Compounds

Although both metals and ionic compounds form crystals, the structure of the crystals and the bonding between ions is quite different in ionic compounds. As a result, these compounds have properties that are much different from those of metals.

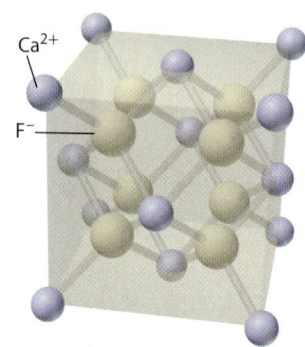

Figure 4.12 This unit cell of calcium fluoride is an example of a crystal that has twice as many negative ions as positive ions. (Keep in mind that all the calcium ions on the surface of the unit cell are shared with other unit cells.)

Melting and Boiling Points

Table 4.2 lists melting and boiling points of selected ionic compounds. These values are in roughly the same range as those of metallic substances. The attractions between oppositely charged ions are very strong. Nevertheless, the variations in melting and boiling points among ionic compounds provide some information about their properties.

Table 4.2 Melting and Boiling Points of Some Common Ionic Comounds

Substance	Melting Point (°C)	Boiling Point (°C)
CsBr(s)	+636	+1300
NaI(s)	+661	+1304
$MgCl_2$(s)	+714	+1412
NaCl(s)	+801	+1465
MgF_2(s)	+1263	+2227
MgO(s)	+2825	+3600

The most noticeable contrast among the melting and boiling points of the ionic compounds in the table is that MgO(s) has a much higher melting point and boiling point than those of the other ionic compounds. The magnesium and oxide ions are slightly smaller than most of the other ions, so they are packed more closely together than the ions in the other compounds, creating a somewhat stronger attractive force. However, the main reason for the higher melting and boiling points is the magnitude of the charges. Magnesium (2+) and oxide (2−) ions have larger charges than most of the other ions in the list. Larger charges create a much stronger attractive force between the ions.

Notice also that the melting point and boiling point of magnesium fluoride are much higher than those of magnesium chloride. The charges of fluoride and chloride are the same, but the fluoride ion is much smaller than the chloride ion. Therefore, the ions of magnesium fluoride can be packed much more closely together.

Solubility

For an ionic compound to be soluble in water, the attractive forces between the ions and water molecules must be stronger than the attractive forces among the ions themselves. As shown in **Figure 4.13**, when sodium chloride dissolves in water, the positive and negative poles of the water molecules exert attractive forces on the chloride and sodium ions and draw them apart, essentially breaking the ionic bonds. As the water molecules pack tightly around the ions, the water molecules are also drawn apart thus breaking the bonds between water molecules.

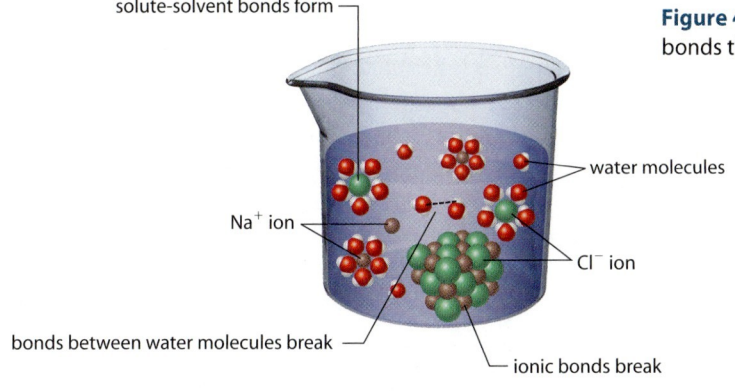

Figure 4.13 The effect of dissolving on the bonds that hold sodium chloride together

Some ionic compounds are not soluble in water because the attractive forces among the ions are very strong. **Table 4.3** shows the solubility of the ionic compounds from **Table 4.2**. A comparison of **Tables 4.2** and **4.3** shows that the order in which the melting points increase is nearly the same as the order in which the solubilities decrease. However, many factors affect the solubilities of compounds in water, so it is best to consult a solubility table such as the one in Appendix B to predict whether a particular ionic compound is soluble in water.

Table 4.3 Solubilities of Some Common Ionic Compounds

Substance	Solubility at 25°C (g/100 mL)
CsBr(s)	123
NaI(s)	184
$MgCl_2$(s)	56.0
NaCl(s)	36.0
MgF_2(s)	0.013
MgO(s)	very low

Mechanical Properties

Ionic compounds are hard and brittle, so they tend to break or shatter when subjected to stress such as being struck with a hammer. As shown in **Figure 4.14**, the force of the hammer blow can cause like charges to become aligned. When this happens, the crystal breaks along the line at which the like charges are repelling each other.

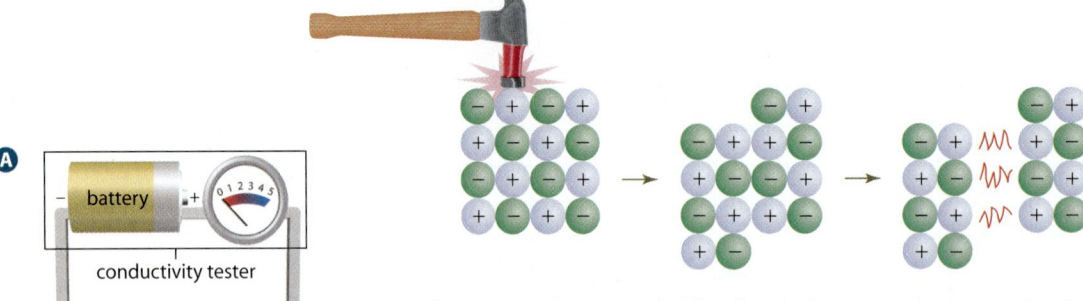

Figure 4.14 Ionic crystals often break along smooth planes. This diagram shows that, when crystals are stressed and when the ions move very slightly, opposite charges can become aligned in such a way that the repulsion forces are all on the same plane.

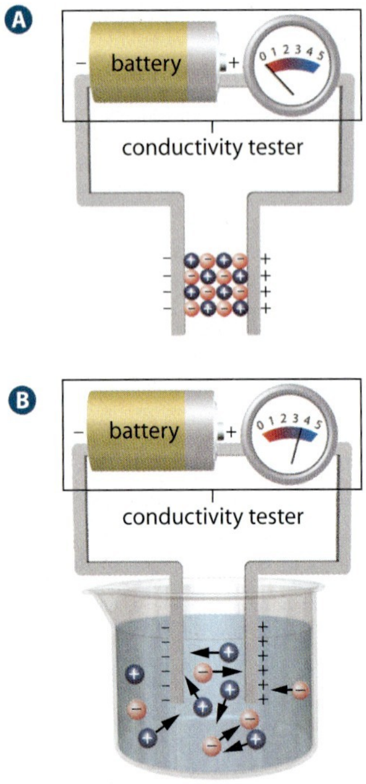

Conductivity

Electric current is the directional flow of charged particles—usually electrons or ions. If charged particles are free to move independently, they can be caused to do so by placing them between oppositely charged electrodes. The electrodes are charged by a battery or other power source. You can determine whether an electric current is flowing if you place a conductivity meter or light bulb in the circuit.

When the electrodes of a conductivity tester are placed on a piece of an ionic solid, no current will flow, as shown in **Figure 4.15A**. The attractive forces between the oppositely charged ions are so much stronger than electrical forces exerted by the electrodes in the conductivity tester that the ions in the compound will not move. A solid ionic compound does not conduct electric current.

If an ionic compound is dissolved in water, the ions are free to move past one another and will migrate to the electrodes, as shown in **Figure 4.15B**. As well, if an ionic compound is heated to the melting point, the ions will be able to move past one another and move toward the oppositely charged electrode. In either case, a current would register on the meter in the circuit.

Figure 4.15 In (**A**), both the positively and negatively charged ions remain in place in a solid ionic compound; no current registers on a conductivity tester. In (**B**), an aqueous solution of an ionic compound conducts an electric current. **Explain** the reading on the conductivity tester in (B).

Learning Check

13. What is a crystal lattice and how does it relate to the formula unit of an ionic compound?
14. What factors affect the way in which ions pack as they form crystals?
15. Compare and contrast the crystals formed by sodium chloride and cesium chloride.
16. Potassium fluoride, KF(s), is a water-soluble ionic compound. Describe in general what characteristics you would expect to see for each of the following properties of potassium fluoride.
    a. melting point and boiling point
    b. hardness
    c. malleability
    d. conductivity in aqueous solution
    e. conductivity in the solid state
17. Write a clarifying e-mail to a confused friend explaining why **Figure 4.10** represents a unit cell containing the equivalent of four sodium ions and four chloride ions.
18. Write a few sentences to explain why some ionic compounds are insoluble in water. Use a labelled diagram to enhance your explanation.

Activity 4.1 Exploring the Packing Efficiency of Spheres

Spherical objects such as oranges and baseballs can be stacked and packed together in a variety of ways, but some of these ways are more efficient than others. In this activity, you will determine the most efficient method to pack spheres into a volume.

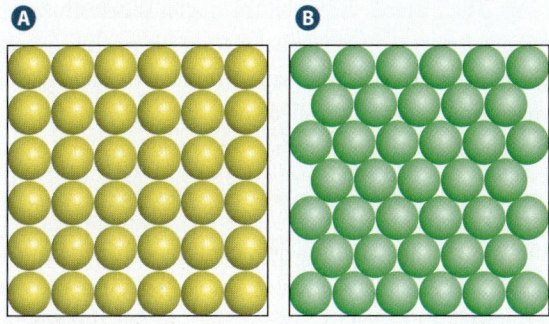

Procedure

1. Box A holds spheres arranged in a *square-packed* system. Box B holds spheres arranged in a *close-packed* system. Compare the number of spheres in the boxes. For a sphere in the middle of Box A, how many surrounding spheres are in contact with it? For Box B?

2. If each sphere in Box A is 1.0 cm in diameter, determine the volume of each sphere. If five more layers of spheres were added to Box A, giving six identical layers in a volume that is 6 cm × 6 cm × 6 cm, what is the total volume of the box? What is the total volume occupied by spheres? What is the percentage of total volume occupied by spheres—its *packing efficiency*?

3. Spheres are packed more efficiently in Box B, because the spheres of different layers fit into the spaces in the layer below. Either count the spaces in layer 1, or use spheres provided by your teacher, to determine the number of spheres that could be placed in layer 2.

4. There are two ways to stack layer 3. Spheres can be placed so they lie directly above those in layer A, resulting in an *abab* pattern of layers; or a unique layer can be created by placing the spheres in the spaces in layer 2, resulting in an *abcabc* pattern of layers. Both arrangements yield the same number of atoms in layer 3. Draw a diagram showing three layers of the stacking arrangement for patterns *abab* and *abcabc*. If possible, use spheres provided by your teacher to model the arrangements.

5. Calculate the total number of spheres that would be contained in a volume that is 6 cm × 6 cm × 6 cm. What is the total volume occupied by spheres? What is the packing efficiency of this arrangement?

Questions

1. Why is the square packing system (Box A) not usually used for packing fruit or atoms?

2. How many spheres surround one atom in a volume that is 6 cm × 6 cm × 6 cm for Box A and Box B?

3. Most metallic elements and ionic compounds crystallize in an arrangement like the one you made in step 4. This arrangement is called hexagonal closest packing for the *abab* pattern and cubic closest packing for the *abcabc* pattern. Explain the properties of metallic and ionic solids based on the concept of closest packing.

4. The greatest packing efficiency for closest packing solids is 74%. Explain any differences between your value and the accepted value.

Covalent Bonding

You know that covalent bonds arise from the sharing of electrons between atoms of non-metal elements, frequently in a way that results in an octet of electrons for the atoms. Although this idea forms the basis for understanding covalent bonding, there are exceptions that it cannot explain. For example, atoms of some elements can have more than eight electrons involved in bonds with other atoms. Also, it is possible for metal atoms to form covalent bonds with other atoms. To explain these and other exceptions, additional conceptual tools are necessary. In this section, you will apply the concept of electronegativity as well as the quantum mechanical model of the atom to extend your understanding of covalent bonding.

Recall that only compounds held together with covalent bonds consist of molecules. Covalent bonding can occur when the ΔEN between two atoms is less than 1.7. Chemists have defined two categories of covalent bonds: polar covalent and mostly (or non-polar) covalent. The atoms bound by polar covalent bonds do not share the electrons equally; instead, electrons spend much more time near the more electronegative atom. Conversely, the atoms bound by non-polar covalent bonds share the electrons almost equally. This range of electron-sharing results in molecules with widely differing properties.

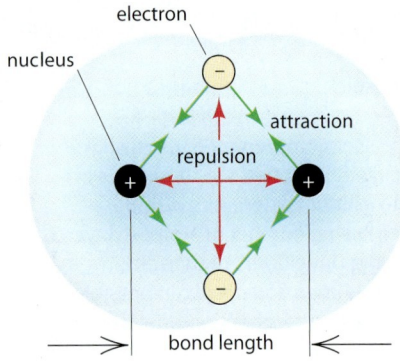

Figure 4.16 At an optimum distance between two hydrogen nuclei, attractive and repulsive forces are balanced. Shading represents electron density, which is greatest around and between the nuclei.

valence bond theory a quantum mechanically based theory that explains covalent bond formation and molecular shapes based on orbital overlap

molecular orbital theory a quantum mechanically based theory that explains covalent bond formation and molecular shapes based on the formation of new molecular orbitals

Forces in Covalent Bonds

In both metallic bonding and ionic bonding, there is a separation of positive and negative charges but in very different ways. Nevertheless, attractive forces between the positive and negative charges created the metallic and ionic bonding. In covalent bonds, electrons are shared by two atoms. How, then, are electrostic forces involved in covalent bonding?

Figure 4.16 shows that the nuclei of both atoms exert attractive force on both of the shared electrons. The distance between the nuclei is determined by a balance between the repulsive forces—positive nucleus against positive nucleus and negative electron against negative electron—and the attractive forces between the positive charges of nuclei and the electrons. Thus, electrostatic forces are involved in all types of bonding: metallic, ionic, and covalent.

Quantum Mechanics and Bonding

Your previous studies of the octet rule and Lewis structures provided a good foundation on which to build the concept of covalent bonding. However, many exceptions to the octet rule exist, and a more comprehensive model is needed to develop the concept further. Just as quantum mechanics provides much more information than the Bohr theory of the atom, quantum mechanics also provides more information about bonding.

Chemists employ two theories involving quantum mechanics to describe and explain chemical bonding and account for the shapes of molecules. The first, **valence bond theory**, is based on the principle that a covalent bond forms when the atomic orbitals of two atoms overlap to share a common region in space and a pair of electrons occupies that region of overlap. The second, **molecular orbital theory**, goes one step further by proposing that when atomic orbitals overlap, they combine to form new orbitals called molecular orbitals. These molecular orbitals have new shapes and energy levels and the electrons are delocalized throughout the new orbital.

Both valence bond (VB) theory and molecular orbital (MO) theory are valid applications of quantum mechanics. Chemists choose one or the other, depending on the problem to be solved. Discussions in this book will apply some fundamentals of molecular orbital theory only when it clarifies a concept.

There are three guiding principles, outlined below, that form the foundation of valence bond theory.

1. The region of orbital overlap has a maximum capacity of two electrons, and the electrons must have opposite spins. This is in accordance with the Pauli exclusion principle.

2. There should be maximum overlap of orbitals. The greater the orbital overlap, the stronger and more stable the bond. The extent of orbital overlap depends on the shapes and directions of the orbitals that are involved in bonding.

3. To help explain the observed molecular shapes of some molecules, the concept of atomic orbital hybridization is used. This process involves the combining or mixing of atomic orbitals to produce new atomic orbitals.

Explaining Single Bonds

First, consider the formation of some of the simplest single bonds—those of the hydrogen molecule, the hydrogen fluoride molecule, and the fluorine molecule. **Figure 4.17A** shows the s orbitals of two hydrogen atoms overlapping and then combining. When the new molecular orbital forms, the bond is called a σ (sigma) bond, which is defined as a bond that is symmetrical around the bond axis of the two nuclei. In other words, you could rotate the bond around the bond axis and nothing would change. This σ bond has an energy level that is lower than the energy of the s orbitals in the hydrogen atoms, making the hydrogen molecule more stable than the separate hydrogen atoms.

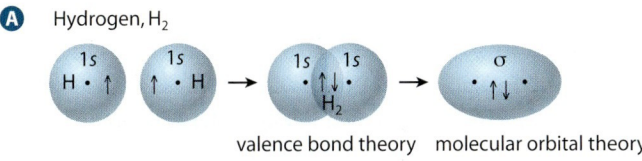
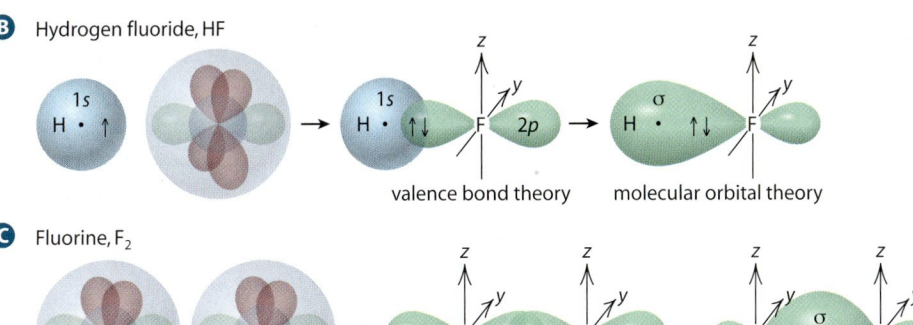

Figure 4.17 Using quantum mechanics (valence bond and molecular orbital theory) to explain bonding in three molecules

In **Figure 4.17B**, the half-filled s orbital of a hydrogen atom overlaps with the half-filled p orbital of fluorine. The fluorine atom that is depicted alone shows all of the orbitals. The 1s, 2s, and two of the 2p orbitals are filled. Only one of the 2p orbitals is half-filled and is shown in green. When orbitals are shown overlapping, only the orbitals involved in the bond are shown. Finally, the σ bond is shown. Although it has a different shape than the σ bond formed by two s orbitals, it is still a σ bond, because it is symmetrical around the line connecting the hydrogen and fluorine nuclei. **Figure 4.17C** shows the half-filled p orbitals in two fluorine atoms overlapping to form a fluorine molecule.

Not all single bonds are derived directly from the s and p atomic orbitals. Consider the case of methane, $CH_4(g)$. It is always portrayed as a completely symmetrical molecule with a tetrahedral shape and four identical bonds. Analytical studies have shown this is the correct configuration. However, recall that the electron configuration for carbon is $1s^22s^2p^2$. The 1s and 2s orbitals are filled, and two p orbitals are half-filled. There are only two half-filled p orbitals. Even if the 2s and all three 2p orbitals each had one electron and they each overlapped with the 1s orbital of a hydrogen atom, they would not form four identical bonds necessary for creating the tetrahedral shape of methane. This situation requires the use of hybrid orbitals from valence bond theory.

Hybrid orbitals are orbitals that are formed by the combination of two or more orbitals in the valence shell of an atom. To create four identical bonds with hydrogen atoms, the carbon atom must form four hybrid orbitals by combining the 2s orbital and the three 2p orbitals. Hybrid orbitals are named according to the atomic orbitals that are combined. Because there is one s orbital and three p orbitals combined in this case, the hybrid orbitals are called sp^3 orbitals. Note that the number of hybrid orbitals formed must be equal to the number of atomic orbitals combined. **Figure 4.18** shows the formation of sp^3 orbitals as, **A**, electron configuration diagrams and, **B**, a sketch, as well as, **C**, a methane molecule formed by the overlap of the 1s orbitals of four hydrogen atoms with one of the hybrid sp^3 orbitals of the carbon atom.

hybrid orbital an orbital that is formed by the combination of two or more orbitals in the valence shell of an atom

Figure 4.18 One s orbital and three p orbitals combine (**A**) to form four sp^3 orbitals (**B**) that can overlap with s orbitals to make four identical bonds (**C**).

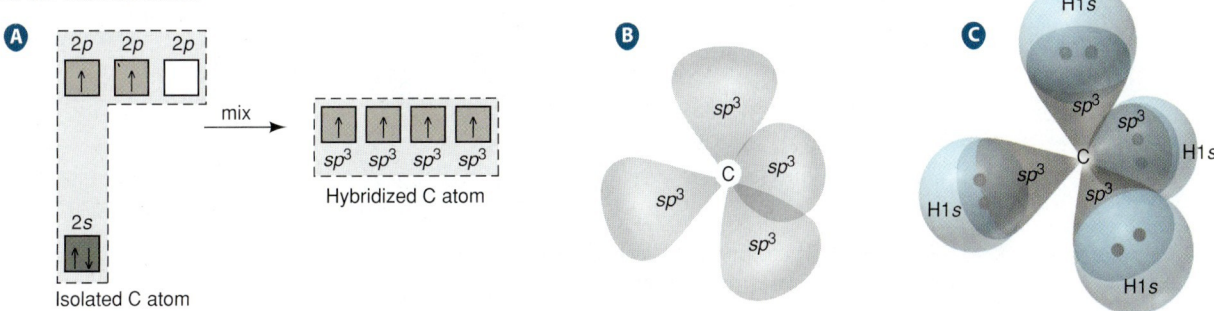

Explaing Double Bonds

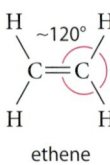

Figure 4.19 Bond angles in ethene

Hybrid orbitals are also required to explain the structure of ethene, $CH_2=CH_2$. Ethene is a planar molecule, which means that all of its atoms lie in the same plane. As shown in **Figure 4.19**, all of the bond angles in the molecule are approximately 120°. This structure implies that there are three orbitals of the carbon atoms that form a plane. This planar structure can only be explained by hybrid orbitals that are not sp^3 orbitals.

The hybrid orbitals of ethene are shown in **Figure 4.20A**. Note that the 2s orbital mixes with two of the 2p orbitals to form three similar orbitals, or sp^2 orbitals. In **Figure 4.20B**, you can see the shapes and configuration of these hybrid orbitals. They are in a plane and at angles of 120° with respect to each other. Each orbital is depicted in a different colour to show which lobes belong to a specific orbital. The remaining 2p orbital is not shown, but it is perpendicular to the plane of the three sp^2 orbitals. In other diagrams that contain more orbitals than just the sp^2 orbitals, the small lobes on the sp^2 orbitals are usually not visible.

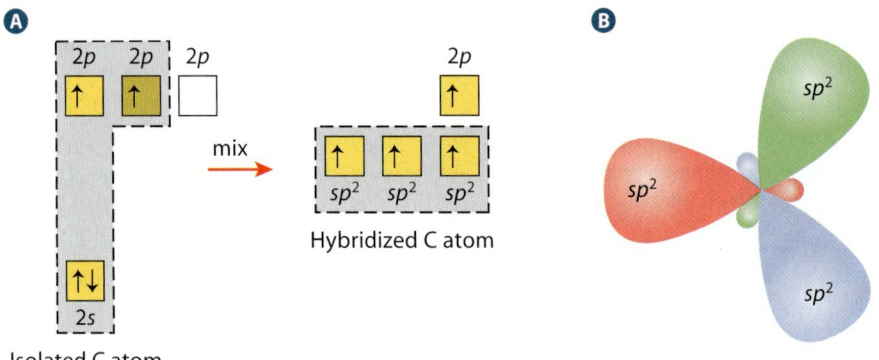

Figure 4.20 One s orbital and two p orbitals combine to form three sp^2 orbitals. This combination gives ethene its planar structure.

Figure 4.21 shows the formation of the bonds in ethene. In **Figure 4.21A**, one of the sp^2 orbitals of each carbon atom has overlapped and combined to form a σ bond. The two remaining sp^2 orbitals of each carbon atom have overlapped with the 1s orbital of a hydrogen atom and formed σ bonds. The 2p orbitals of each carbon atom are shown perpendicular to the plane formed by the nuclei of the atoms and the sp^2 orbitals. In **Figure 4.21B**, the σ bonds are shown as bars to avoid interfering with the visualization of the 2p orbitals that are overlapping. Recall that each p orbital has two lobes. You can see that both lobes are overlapping above and below the plane. In **Figure 4.21C**, you can see that the 2p orbitals have combined to form a π (pi) bond. A π bond has two lobes that are on opposite sides of the line joining the nuclei of the two atoms. Note that the two lobes, together, constitute one bond. Of the two bonds in a double bond, one is a σ bond and one is a π bond.

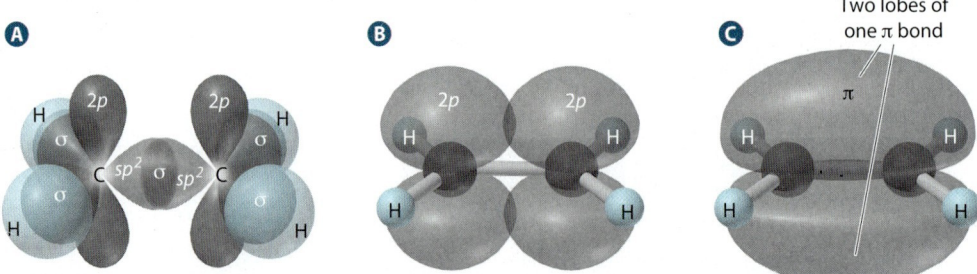

Figure 4.21 The σ bonds all lie in a plane whereas the π bond is symmetrical above and below the plane and prevents rotation around the axis between the carbon atoms.

Explaining Triple Bonds

To analyze a triple bond, consider the ethyne molecule, H–C≡C–H. The molecule is completely linear, meaning that both hydrogen nuclei and both carbon nuclei lie on a straight line. The angle between each H–C bond and one of the C–C bonds is 180°. Once again, hybrid orbitals are required to explain the structure of a triple bond. As shown in **Figure 4.22A**, the 2s orbital and one of the 2p orbitals of carbon mix to form two hybrid sp orbitals. The two remaining p orbitals remain unchanged. **Figure 4.22B** shows a carbon atom with all four of the orbitals. The two sp hybrid orbitals are in different colours to distinguish them.

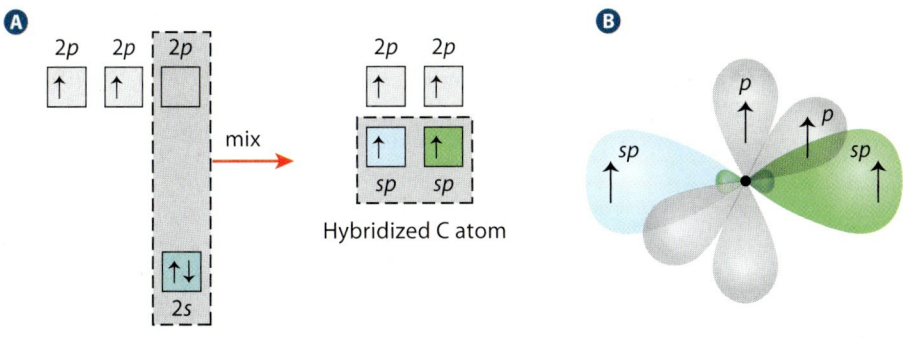

Figure 4.22 (**A**) One s orbital combines with one p orbital to form two sp orbitals. (**B**) The sp orbitals lie along the same line and are mutually perpendicular to the two p orbitals.

The formation of the ethyne molecule is shown in **Figure 4.23**. In **Figure 4.23A**, one of the sp orbitals in each carbon atom is overlapping with the 1s orbital of a hydrogen atom, forming a σ bond. The other sp orbitals of the two carbon atoms are overlapping with each other, forming a σ bond. In **Figure 4.23B**, the σ bonds are shown as bars to avoid confusion. The two p orbitals on each of the carbon atoms are overlapping with each other. **Figure 4.23C** shows the π bonds formed by the overlapping p orbitals. Note that each π bond has two lobes. The two π bonds are shown in different colours to distinguish them from each other. The triple bond between the two carbon atoms consists of one σ bond and two π bonds.

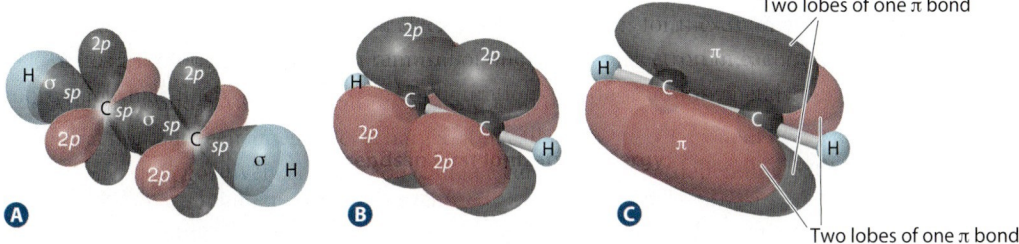

Figure 4.23 The formation of ethyne

> **Learning Check**
>
> 19. Describe forces involved in a covalent bond.
> 20. What are the characteristics of a σ bond? Give two examples as part of your answer.
> 21. For the tetrahedral molecule, silicon tetrachloride, $SiCl_4(s)$, write the condensed electron configuration of a lone silicon atom, predict the hybridization in the molecule, and write an electron configuration for the hybridized orbitals of the central silicon atom.
> 22. Describe the bonding in a molecule of ethene.
> 23. In biology, one meaning of *hybrid* is the offspring of two animals or plants from different species. How can this help you remember the meaning of *hybrid orbital*?
> 24. For the linear molecule hydrogen cyanide, HCN(g), draw a Lewis diagram to represent the molecule, predict the hybridization on the carbon atom, and identify the types of bonds between the carbon and nitrogen atoms, and the number of bonds of each type.

Types of Hybridization

Hybridization of orbitals can occur in atoms of many different elements. For atoms of elements in Period 3 and beyond, d orbitals can hybridize with s and p orbitals, as well. In every case, the name of the hybrid orbitals indicates the type and number of atomic orbitals that have combined to form the hybrid orbitals. For example, a sp^3d^2 orbital is a combination of one s orbital, three p orbitals, and two d orbitals. It is important to note that the number of hybrid orbitals that form is exactly the same as the number of atomic orbitals that combined to make the hybrid orbitals. **Figure 4.24** shows the shapes of the important hybrid orbitals. In each case, the orbitals shown are all hybrid orbitals, and each lobe is a different orbital. Each of these orbitals has a smaller lobe that is not shown. Depending on the type of hybrid orbital and the type of atom, some unchanged orbitals will still exist on the atom similar to those in the examples of ethene and ethyne. In Section 4.2, you will see many examples of hybrid orbitals and their influence on the shapes and functions of molecules.

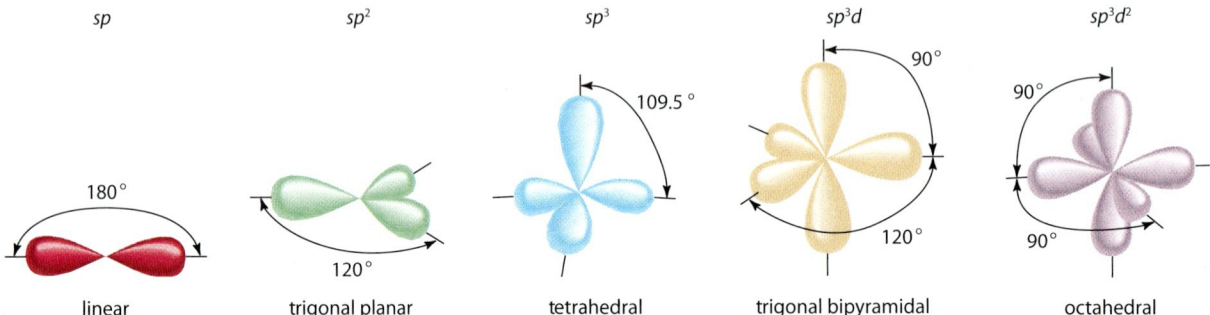

Figure 4.24 Types of hybrid orbitals. The label below each figure is the name of the overall shape of the hybrid orbital.

Allotropes

Carbon is a unique element because atoms of carbon can bond to as many as four other atoms of the same or different elements at once. In fact, pure carbon can take several structurally different forms that have different physical properties. Such compounds are called **allotropes**.

Pure carbon can be found in the form of the hardest substance on Earth—diamond. Pure carbon can also be found in the form of a slippery, black substance used in pencils and as a dry lubricant—graphite. How can the same pure element exist in such different forms? Covalent bonds can form among many carbon atoms in a variety of patterns. Four examples of allotropes of carbon are shown in **Figure 4.25**.

The carbon atoms in graphite (**Figure 4.25A**) have three short bonds with other carbon atoms. This array forms layers. The fourth bond on each carbon atom is longer and not as strong. As a result, this bond can be easily broken and re-formed with another atom, allowing the layers to slide past each other. This property gives graphite its slippery feel and its ability to act as a solid lubricant. The same property makes graphite a good substance to use in pencils. As you push the pencil across paper, the layers slide off the pencil and onto the paper.

In diamond (**Figure 4.25B**), each carbon atom is perfectly tetrahedral. Carbon–carbon bonds have their greatest strength in this configuration. This three-dimensional array of covalently bound carbon atoms makes diamond the hardest naturally occurring substance known. This structure also creates many planes of carbon atoms within diamonds, which reflect light and give diamonds their brilliance and sparkle.

allotrope one of two or more structurally different forms of the same element having different physical properties

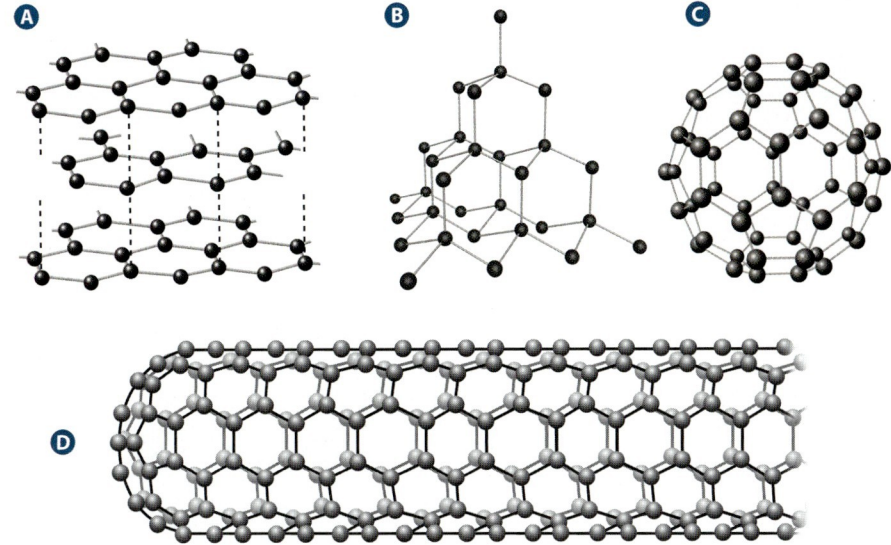

Figure 4.25 In graphite (**A**), the dotted lines represent bonds that are weak and can be broken and re-formed easily. In diamond (**B**), each carbon atom is perfectly tetrahedral, creating the strength and hardness of the gem. In "buckyballs" (**C**) and nanotubes (**D**), alternate bonds are double bonds, giving each carbon atom the requisite four bonds.

In 1985, chemists Robert F. Curl Jr., Richard E. Smalley, and Sir Harold W. Kroto discovered a class of spherical allotropes of carbon that they called *fullerenes*. One of these, buckminsterfullerene (C_{60}) is shown in **Figure 4.25C**; it is named after the architect R. Buckminster Fuller who designed geodesic dome structures that had an appearance similar to the fullerenes. The bonds in C_{60}, also called "buckyballs," form a pattern that is nearly the same as the stitching on a soccer ball. Notice the five-membered rings and six-membered rings of carbon atoms in **Figure 4.25C** and how each carbon atom appears to have only three bonds. However, alternate bonds are double bonds, giving each carbon atom four bonds. Chemists have also identified and studied C_{70}, C_{74}, and C_{82}, which have properties very similar to C_{60}.

The allotrope of carbon shown in **Figure 4.25D** is called a nanotube. Nanotubes are one of the first products of the new field of nanotechnology, which includes research and development of devices that have sizes ranging from 1 to 100 nanometres. Nanotubes with diameters of just a few nanometres and lengths in the range of micrometres have been assembled. Such nanotubes have great promise in the fields of microelectronics and medicine.

Covalent Network Solids

Two of the allotropes of carbon—diamond and graphite—have no natural beginning or end to the chains of carbon atoms. Such compounds are called **network solids**. Some network solids consist of two different elements instead of one. The most common compound in Earth's crust, silicon dioxide, $SiO_2(s)$, exists in the form of a network solid. Sand and quartz consist almost entirely of silicon dioxide (or silica). If you were asked to write the Lewis structure for silicon dioxide, you might draw a structure similar to carbon dioxide. Silicon, however, does not typically form double bonds with oxygen. Instead, silicon bonds to four oxygen atoms to form a tetrahedral shape around the silicon atom. Each oxygen atom is then bonded to another silicon atom to form a network, as shown in **Figure 4.26**. The network can be represented by the formula $(SiO_2)_n$, indicating that SiO_2 is the simplest repeating unit.

network solid
a substance in which all atoms are covalently bonded together in a continuous two or three dimensional array; no natural beginning or end exists

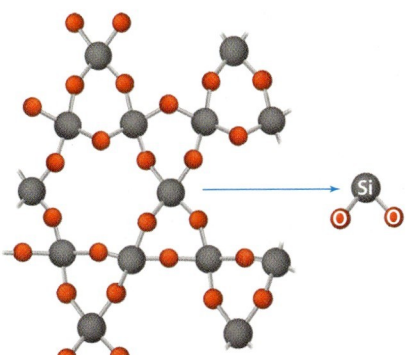

Figure 4.26 The repeating unit, SiO_2, is shown on the right. In the network solid, each oxygen atom in the SiO_2 unit is bonded to another silicon atom and each silicon atom is bonded to two other oxygen atoms.

STSE
CHEMISTRY Connections

Green Solvents

Society is shaped by molecular bonding and chemical reactions. The food people eat, the products people use to clean and paint their homes, and even the clothes people wear—all these products are based on chemical processes. Many of these processes use solvents that are dangerous to people and to the environment. Green chemistry is a movement to develop chemical processes that are more environmentally responsible. Scientists have been conducting research on ionic liquids and have found that they are excellent "green" solvents that help reduce the damage caused by standard industrial processes.

IONIC LIQUIDS TO THE RESCUE Room temperature ionic liquids, or RTILs, are salts that are liquid at room temperature. The lower melting points of RTILs result from their chemical composition. Ionic liquids, particularly RTILs, are made up of large bulky organic cations and inorganic anions. The resulting asymmetry decreases the energy needed to completely separate the ions in an ionic solid, and this in turn reduces the melting point. The composition and properties of ionic liquids depend on the cation and anion combinations, and there are billions of possibilities. This means that ionic liquids can be designed for specific purposes, with chemical and physical properties that achieve very specific tasks.

Most solvents used in industrial processes are called volatile organic compounds, or VOCs. The interest in ionic liquids for green chemistry is based on their non-measurable vapour pressure. Ionic liquids do not evaporate into the air. Therefore, unlike VOCs, ionic liquids can be easily contained and will not pollute the environment. The ability to contain ionic liquids also means that they can be recycled and re-used.

POTENTIAL APPLICATIONS Scientists are also hypothesizing about other ways to use and apply ionic liquids. For example, ionizing radiation does not seem to affect ionic liquids, so they might be useful in treating high-level nuclear waste. The ability of ionic liquids to dissolve specific gases means they could be used to purify the air in small vessels, such as spacecraft and submarines such as the one in the photograph. Laboratory experiments have shown promising results for ionic liquids that have been designed to remove mercury from contaminated water. The ionic liquid is water-insoluble, so when it comes in contact with contaminated water, the mercury ions are removed from the water and bond in the ionic liquid.

The air in this submarine must be continuously purified. Ionic solvents might be useful in the process.

Connect to Society

1. Most ionic salts have very high melting points and are unable to conduct electric current. Explain why ionic liquids are able to conduct electric current even though they are ionic salts. Conduct research to find one possible application for this conductivity.

2. What does green chemistry mean to you? Survey your friends and family to find out what they know about green chemistry. Do they think it is important? Why or why not?

3. Researchers are actively investigating the use of ionic liquids in connection with the development of fuels and other products made from underutilized lignocellulosic biomass—plant biomass such as wheat straw and corn husks that is made up of cellulose and lignin. Find out why lignocellulosic biomass is considered an alternative to petroleum for fuels and polymer materials and how ionic liquids may contribute in future to the economical and practical development of this alternative.

Section 4.1 Review

Section Summary

- The three types of chemical bonding are ionic bonding, covalent bonding, and metallic bonding.
- Bonds form a continuum from equal sharing to minimal sharing of electrons. Bonds with a ΔEN from 1.7 to 3.3 are mostly ionic; with a ΔEN from 0.4 to 1.7 are polar covalent; with a ΔEN from 0.0 to 0.4 are mostly covalent (or non-polar covalent).
- The electron-sea model visualizes a metal as a fairly ordered array of cations in a "sea" of freely moving electrons, with the positively charged ions all attracted to many of the electrons in the "sea" simultaneously.
- Metals and ionic compounds form crystals, but the structure of the crystals and the bonding between ions are different in ionic compounds, so their properties are different from those of metals.
- Valence bond (VB) theory proposes that a covalent bond forms when the atomic orbitals of two atoms overlap to share a common region in space and a pair of electrons occupies that region of overlap.
- Molecular orbital (MO) theory proposes that when atomic orbitals overlap, they combine to form new orbitals called molecular orbitals, which have new shapes and energy levels and delocalized electrons.
- Hybrid orbitals are formed by the combination of two or more orbitals in the valence shell of an atom.
- In network solids, a large number of atoms are bonded together by a repeating network of covalent bonds.

Review Questions

1. **K/U** Distinguish among the following terms: formula unit, unit cell, and molecule.

2. **K/U** Use the electron-sea model of metals to describe the structure of substitutional alloys and interstitial alloys.

3. **A** In the making of a facsimile samurai sword for a museum, a swordsmith plunges heated metal into a cool vessel of water.
   a. How does this action affect the properties of the metal sword?
   b. What step is likely to come next in the making of the sword and why?

4. **C** Make a table that compares the following characteristics for metals and ionic crystals: melting and boiling point, electrical conductivity, malleability, and hardness.

5. **C** A friend comments that sodium fluoride, NaF, consists of many molecules of one atom of sodium and one atom of fluorine bonded together. What is inaccurate about this statement? Write a brief e-mail to explain.

6. **K/U** "Ionic bonds tend to form between elements from opposite sides of the periodic table." Do you agree with this statement? If so, explain why. If not, explain why not.

7. **T/I** Predict which bond in the following groups is the most covalent in character. Calculate ΔEN for each to check your predictions.
   a. H–N, H–O, H–F
   b. O–O, O–N, O–C

8. **T/I** Classify the following bonds as ionic, polar covalent, or mostly covalent according to the location of the elements on the periodic table. Check your classifications by calculating ΔEN.
   a. K–F
   b. C–C
   c. C–N
   d. Ca–O

9. **A** Consider the hybrid orbital sp^3d.
   a. What type of orbitals and how many of each type combine to make sp^3d orbitals?
   b. How many hybridized sp^3d orbitals exist on the atom?
   c. What shape is characteristic of a molecule in which the central atom exhibits sp^3d hybridization?

10. **C** Draw a Venn diagram comparing ionic crystals and covalent network solids.

11. **K/U** Explain why graphite and diamond have such different properties despite both being pure carbon. Give one application for each allotrope.

12. **A** Characterize the hybridization of the orbitals in each of the following allotropes of carbon.
    a. diamond
    b. graphite
    c. C_{60}
    d. carbon nanotube

13. **C** Copy the following structure. Label each of the σ and π bonds and label each carbon atom with the hybridization its orbitals exhibit.

$$H_3C-\underset{\underset{CH_2}{\|}}{C}-C\equiv CH$$

SECTION 4.2 Shapes, Intermolecular Forces, and Properties of Molecules

Key Terms

co-ordinate covalent bond
expanded valence
resonance structure
bond angle
valence-shell electron-pair repulsion theory
intramolecular force
intermolecular force
dipole-dipole force
hydrogen bonding
ion-dipole force
dipole-induced dipole force
ion-induced dipole force
dispersion force

The structures of molecular compounds are much more varied than the structures of ionic compounds, in part because of the nature of covalent bonds. As their name indicates, molecular compounds are composed of individual units—molecules. To understand the structure and, therefore, the macroscopic properties of molecular compounds, you need to focus first on the structure of individual molecules. Keep in mind that the structure of a molecule involves more than just which atoms are bonded. Each atom, bonding pair of electrons, and lone pair of electrons takes up space and has its own position in space, relative to other atoms and electrons. Different forces of attraction and repulsion determine these positions, resulting in molecules with characteristic three-dimensional shapes. Chemists use different theories and models to predict these three-dimensional shapes.

Depicting Two-dimensional Structures of Molecules with Lewis Structures

The first step to predicting the three-dimensional shape of a molecule is to draw its two-dimensional Lewis structure. Drawing a Lewis structure for a molecule lets you see exactly how many electrons are involved in each bond, as well as how many, if any, lone pairs of electrons are present. To draw Lewis structures for simple molecules, as well as for polyatomic ions, that have a central atom with other atoms around it, follow the steps outlined below. In these Lewis diagrams, use lines for bonds and dots only for lone pairs of electrons.

Drawing Lewis Structures for Simple Molecules and Polyatomic Ions

Step 1 Position the least electronegative atom in the centre of the molecule or polyatomic ion. Draw a skeleton structure for the molecule by placing the other atoms around the central atom. Draw a single bond between each pair of atoms. Always place a hydrogen atom or a fluorine atom at an end position in the structure.

Step 2 Determine the total number of valence electrons (V) in all the atoms in the molecule. For polyatomic ions, add or subtract electrons to account for the charge. For example, for a cation with a charge of 2+ subtract two electrons from the total number of valence electrons that are calculated for the ion.

Step 3 Determine the total number of electrons (T) needed for each atom to achieve a noble gas electron configuration. For all atoms besides hydrogen this corresponds to the octet rule. For hydrogen, a complete valence shell is two electrons, not eight.

Step 4 Subtract the number of valence electrons (V) from the number of electrons needed to satisfy the octet rule (T). This represents the number of shared electrons (S) involved in bonding, $S = T - V$. Divide this number by 2 to give the number of bonds, bonds = $S/2$. Double bonds count as two bonds. Triple bonds count as three bonds.

Step 5 Subtract the number of shared electrons from the number of valence electrons to get the number of non-bonding electrons, $NB = V - S$. Add these electrons as lone pairs to the atoms to achieve a noble gas electron configuration for each atom.

Some Exceptions When Drawing Lewis Structures

Lewis structures and the octet rule can be used to explain the chemical bonding of many molecular compounds. However, some exceptions to the standard approach described above are required when writing Lewis structures for certain molecules and ions.

Co-ordinate Covalent Bonds

In all the examples of covalent bonds that you have seen so far, each of the two atoms involved has contributed one of the two electrons in the bond. In some cases, such as the ammonium ion, NH_4^+, in **Figure 4.27**, one of the atoms can contribute both the electrons. The bond in these cases is called a **co-ordinate covalent bond**. Once a co-ordinate covalent bond is formed, it behaves in the same way as any other single covalent bond. In other words, it is not possible to distinguish a co-ordinate covalent bond from any other covalent bond in that molecule. Thus, a co-ordinate covalent bond is not indicated in the Lewis structure. All covalent bonds are represented in the same manner.

Note that the Lewis structure for NH_4^+ does *not* indicate which atom provides each shared pair of electrons around the central nitrogen atom. However, the quantum mechanical model of the atom can explain the bonding around this nitrogen atom. The condensed electron configuration for nitrogen is $[Ne]2s^22p^3$. Each nitrogen atom has only three unpaired $2p$ electrons in three half-filled orbitals available for bonding. Since there are four covalent bonds shown around nitrogen in the Lewis structure, electrons in one of the bonds must have come from the filled orbitals of nitrogen. Therefore, one of the bonds around the central nitrogen atom must be a co-ordinate covalent bond.

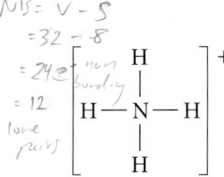

Figure 4.27 For the ammonium ion, one bond is a co-ordinate covalent bond. However, it is not distinguishable from any other covalent bond. It is important to note, however, that the covalent bonds in the ammonium ion are not identical to the covalent bonds in ammonia, $NH_3(g)$.

An Expanded Octet

Atoms of Period 2 elements obey the octet rule, because energy level $n = 2$ has a maximum of one s and three p orbitals with a maximum of two electrons each which limits the number of valence electrons to eight. However, atoms of the third period and higher can form hybrid orbitals that include the d orbitals because, when $n = 3$, l can have values of 0, 1, and 2 which represent s, p, and d orbitals, respectively. Therefore, for some molecules, bonding at the central atom is best explained by a model that shows more than eight electrons in the valence shell. The central atom in such compounds is said to have an **expanded valence**, or *expanded octet*. One example is sulfur hexfluoride, $SF_6(g)$, shown in **Figure 4.28**. The central sulfur atom forms six sp^3d^2, hybrid orbitals and each is occupied by one of the six valence electrons. Each of these hybrid orbitals forms a bond with the half filled p orbital of a fluorine atom.

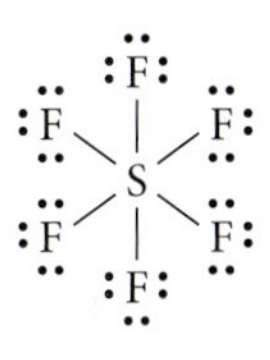

Figure 4.28 In sulfur hexafluoride, $SF_6(g)$, each of the six valence electrons of sulfur forms a covalent bond with a fluorine atom. Therefore, there are 12 electrons around the central sulfur atom.

An Incomplete Octet

Boron (B) and beryllium (Be) are unique metals in that they can form covalent bonds with the halogens such as boron trifluoride, $BF_3(g)$, and beryllium chloride, $BeCl_2(s)$. However, boron has only three valence electrons and beryllium has only two. Nevertheless, the physical data support the Lewis structures shown in **Figure 4.29**, giving boron a total of six valence electrons and beryllium a total of four valence electrons. These central atoms are said to have an *incomplete valence*.

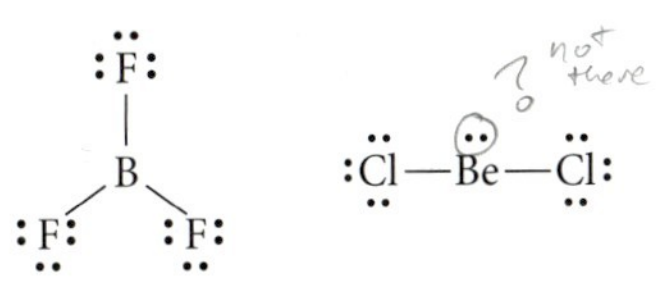

Figure 4.29 The halides of boron and beryllium have incomplete valences, nevertheless, they are stable molecules. Even molten beryllium chloride does not conduct electric current, supporting the concept that it does not dissociate into ions.

co-ordinate covalent bond a covalent bond in which one atom contributes both electrons to the shared pair of electrons

expanded valence a valence energy level of a central atom that has more than eight electrons

Resonance Structures

Sometimes, a Lewis structure that meets all the criteria is not supported by experimental observations. For example, the structure for ozone, $O_3(g)$, below fits all the criteria for an acceptable Lewis structure.

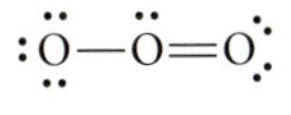

However, experimental measurements of bond lengths indicate that the bonds between the oxygen atoms are actually identical and have properties that are somewhere between a single bond and a double bond.

To communicate the bonding in O₃ more accurately, chemists draw two Lewis structures, as shown below.

$$\ddot{O}=\ddot{O}-\ddot{\underset{..}{O}}: \leftrightarrow :\ddot{\underset{..}{O}}-\ddot{O}=\ddot{O}$$

The double headed arrow indicates that the actual structure is between these two structures, not that the structure is changing back and forth. Each of these Lewis structures is called a **resonance structure**, which is one of two or more structures that differ only in the positioning of their bonding and lone pairs. An O₃ molecule is a combination—a *hybrid*—of its two resonance structures. It is more properly referred to as a *resonance hybrid*. The electrons that form the π bonds are delocalized and are shared by all three oxygen atoms.

Many other molecules and polyatomic ions are represented using resonance structures. An example of the latter, carbonate, is shown below.

resonance structure one of two or more Lewis structures that show the same relative position of atoms but different positions of electron pairs

$$:\ddot{\underset{..}{O}}-\overset{:O:}{\underset{\underset{..}{\ddot{O}}:}{C}}-\ddot{\underset{..}{O}}: \leftrightarrow \ddot{O}=\overset{:\ddot{O}:^-}{C}-\ddot{\underset{..}{O}}:^- \leftrightarrow {}^-:\ddot{\underset{..}{O}}-\overset{:\ddot{O}:^-}{C}=\ddot{O}$$

Learning Check

25. What are the advantages of drawing a Lewis structure as a first step to predicting three-dimensional shape?

26. In a Lewis structure, what does a line represent?

27. What is a co-ordinate covalent bond? Include labelled diagrams in your explanation.

28. What is an expanded valence? Include labelled diagrams in your explanation.

29. Could a carbon atom have an expanded valence as the central atom in a molecule? Explain why or why not.

30. How do chemists know that none of the individual Lewis structures of ozone are not accurate depictions of an ozone molecule, and how is this discrepancy addressed?

Sample Problem

Drawing Lewis Structures of Molecules

Problem
Draw a Lewis structure for the molecule nitrogen fluoride, NF₃(g).

What Is Required?
You need to draw a Lewis structure for $NF_3(g)$.

What Is Given?
The chemical formula tells you that the molecule consists of one nitrogen atom and three fluorine atoms.

Plan Your Strategy	Act on Your Strategy
Determine the least electronegative atom.	The least electronegative atom is nitrogen.

Draw a skeleton structure of the nitrogen atom with one single bond between it and each of the fluorine atoms.	F—N—F
	      |
	      F

Determine the total number of valence electrons in all the atoms of the molecule. The nitrogen atom has five valence electrons, and the fluorine atoms each have seven valence electrons.	$V = (1\ N\ atom \times 5e^-/N\ atom) + (3\ F\ atoms \times 7e^-/F\ atom)$ $= 5e^- + 21e^-$ $= 26e^-$
Determine the total number of electrons needed for each atom to achieve noble gas configuration.	$T = (1\ N\ atom \times 8e^-/N\ atom) + (3\ F\ atoms \times 8e^-/F\ atom)$ $= 8e^- + 24e^-$ $= 32e^-$

Determine the number of shared electrons and the resulting number of bonds.	$S = T - V$ $= 32\text{ e}^- - 26\text{ e}^- = 6\text{e}^-$ bonds $= \dfrac{S}{2} = \dfrac{6}{2} = 3$ covalent bonds
Determine the number of non-bonding electrons and add them as lone pairs to satisfy the octet rule for all atoms	$NB = V - S$ $= 26\text{ e}^- - 6\text{ e}^-$ $= 20\text{e}^-$
Complete the Lewis structure. There are 20 non-bonding electrons thus 10 lone pairs to place.	$:\!\ddot{\underset{..}{F}}\!-\!\ddot{N}\!-\!\ddot{\underset{..}{F}}\!:$ $\qquad\;\;\vert$ $\qquad:\!\ddot{\underset{..}{F}}\!:$

Check Your Solution

Each atom has achieved a noble gas configuration. The number of valence electrons is correct.

Sample Problem

Drawing a Lewis Structure That Includes a Co-ordinate Covalent Bond

Problem

Draw the Lewis structure for a hydronium ion, H_3O^+(aq).

What Is Required?

You need to draw the Lewis structure for H_3O^+(aq).

What Is Given?

The chemical formula shows that the hydronium ion has three hydrogen atoms, one oxygen atom, and a charge of 1+.

Plan Your Strategy	Act on Your Strategy
Draw a skeleton structure of the oxygen atom with one single bond between each of the hydrogen atoms. Since hydrogen atoms are always placed at an end position, the central atom must be oxygen.	$\text{H}-\text{O}-\text{H}$ $\qquad\;\;\vert$ $\qquad\text{H}$
Determine the total number of valence electrons in all the atoms of the molecule. The oxygen atom has six valence electrons and hydrogen atoms have one valence electron each. Subtract one electron to give the molecule its single positive charge.	$V = (1\text{ O atom} \times 6\text{e}^-/\text{O atom}) + (3\text{ H atoms} \times 1\text{e}^-/\text{H atom}) - \text{e}^-$ $= 6\text{e}^- + 3\text{e}^- - 1\text{e}^-$ $= 8\text{e}^-$
Determine the total number of electrons needed for each atom to achieve noble gas configuration.	$T = (1\text{ O atom} \times 8\text{e}^-/\text{O atom}) + (3\text{ H atoms} \times 2\text{e}^-/\text{H atom})$ $= 8\text{e}^- + 6\text{e}^-$ $= 14\text{e}$
Determine the number of shared electrons and the resulting number of bonds.	$S = T - V$ $= 14\text{ e}^- - 8\text{ e}^- = 6\text{e}^-$ bonds $= \dfrac{S}{2} = \dfrac{6}{2} = 3$ covalent bonds
Determine the number of non-bonding electrons, and add them as lone pairs to oxygen (hydrogen never has lone pairs).	$NB = V - S$ $= 8\text{ e}^- - 6\text{ e}^-$ $= 2\text{e}^-$
Complete the Lewis structure. Because the molecule has a charge of 1+, you must indicate this with square brackets and a plus sign as a superscript. There are 2 non-bonding electrons thus 1 lone pair.	$\left[\text{H}-\ddot{\underset{\vert}{O}}-\text{H}\right]^+$ $\qquad\;\;\text{H}$

Check Your Solution

Each atom has a noble gas configuration. The number of valence electrons is correct; the positive charge is included.

Practice Problems

1. Draw the Lewis structure for a molecule of carbon dioxide, $CO_2(g)$.
2. Draw the Lewis structure for a molecule of formaldehyde (methanal), $CH_2O(g)$.
3. Formic acid, or methanoic acid, $HCOOH(\ell)$, is found naturally in ant venom. Synthesized formic acid is used for its antibacterial and preservative properties in a variety of animal feeds, among other uses. Given that carbon is the central atom of the molecule, with hydrogen, oxygen, and hydroxide groups, draw its Lewis structure.
4. Draw a Lewis structure for a molecule of bromine pentafluoride, $BrF_5(\ell)$. The central bromine molecule has an expanded valence.
5. Draw a Lewis structure for a molecule of phosphorus pentachloride, $PCl_5(s)$.
6. Draw three resonance structures for the NO_3^- (aq) ion.
7. Draw two resonance structures for a molecule of sulfur dioxide, $SO_2(g)$. An expanded valence structure has been shown to better agree with experimental observations than resonance structures. Draw the Lewis structure for $SO_2(g)$ with an expanded valence.
8. Draw three resonance structures for phosgene, $CCl_2O(g)$, a toxic gas.
9. Compounds of Group 18 elements do not form in nature, but chemists can synthesize such compounds in the lab. One example is xenon tetroxide, $XeO_4(g)$, which contains co-ordinate covalent bonds. Draw the Lewis structure for a molecule of xenon tetroxide.
10. Draw a Lewis structure or structures for the carbonate ion. Consider the possibility of co-ordinate covalent bonds and/or resonance structures.

Predicting the Shapes of Molecules Using VSEPR Theory

A molecule's three-dimensional shape affects its physical and chemical properties. Factors that determine the shape of a molecule include bond lengths and bond angles. A **bond angle** is the angle formed between the nuclei of two atoms that surround the central atom of a molecule. Although such factors must be measured experimentally, there are models that can be used to predict the overall shape of a molecule or polyatomic ion.

As you know, Lewis structures show the arrangement of atoms and electrons in a molecule. Chemists can use this information to predict molecular shapes by applying the **valence-shell electron-pair repulsion theory**, or *VSEPR* (pronounced "vesper"). This theory was first developed in the mid-1950s by the English chemist Ronald Gillespie and an Australian chemist, Ronald Nyholm, while colleagues at University College in London, England. In 1958, Dr. Gillespie began a long and highly successful career as a professor in the Chemistry Department at McMaster University in Hamilton, Ontario.

VSEPR theory is based on the idea that the electron groups around an atom are positioned as far as possible from the others to minimize repulsions. An electron group is a single bond, double bond, triple bond, or lone pair. The result is a particular geometric arrangement of the electron groups. According to VSEPR theory, there are five basic electron-group arrangements, which are shown in **Figure 4.30**. The bars in the diagrams represent electron groups. Chemists can use this information to predict molecular shape. It is important, however, to distinguish between *electron-group arrangement*—the ways in which groups of valence electrons are positioned around a specific atom, and *molecular shape*—the relative positions of the atomic nuclei in an entire molecule.

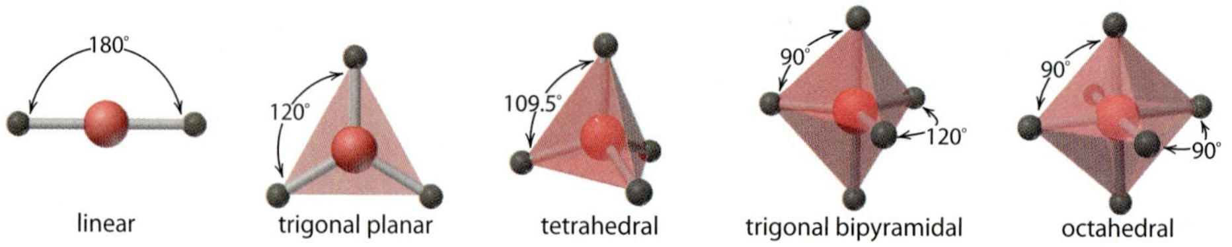

bond angle the angle formed between the nuclei of two atoms that surround the central atom of a molecule

valence-shell electron-pair repulsion theory a theory that proposes particular three-dimensional arrangements of electron groups around a central atom based on repulsions between the electron groups; a model used to predict molecular shapes

Figure 4.30 VSEPR theory predicts certain arrangements of electron groups about the central atom of a molecule. Each of these shapes has the same name as the electron-group arrangement.

linear (180°) — trigonal planar (120°) — tetrahedral (109.5°) — trigonal bipyramidal (90°, 120°) — octahedral (90°)

Electron Groups and Molecular Shapes

When all the electron groups around a central atom are bonding electrons (no lone pairs), a molecule will have a molecular shape that has the same name as the electron-group arrangement. **Table 4.4** shows some examples of molecules with these molecular shapes.

The class of molecule, in the first column, uses the letter A to represent the central atom and X to represent the surrounding atoms. The subscript on X indicates the number of surrounding atoms.

Table 4.4 Electron Arrangements and Shapes of Molecules with Central Atoms That Lack Lone Pairs

Class of Molecule	Number of Bonding Electron Groups	Arrangement of Electron Groups	Molecular Shape	Example
AX_2	2	linear	linear The bonding pairs are at opposite ends of a straight line. This results in a linear molecule with bond angles of 180°.	CO_2
AX_3	3	trigonal planar	trigonal planar The three bonds point to corners of an equilateral triangle. The atoms are in the same plane, and bond angles are 120°.	BF_3
AX_4	4	tetrahedral	tetrahedral There are four faces or sides to the molecule, forming a regular tetrahedron with bond angles of 109.5°.	CH_4
AX_5	5	trigonal bipyramidal	trigonal bipyramidal The five bonds extend from the central atom in a manner that generates two three-sided pyramids that are joined at their common triangular base.	PCl_5
AX_6	6	octahedral	octahedral The central atom is at a common square base and the surrounding atoms extend to six corners that generates two square pyramids with a common base.	SF_6

Note: Colours for the spheres are for atoms in general. For simplicity, only molecules composed of two different atoms are used as examples.

If one or more of the electron groups surrounding the central atom is a lone pair, the molecular shape is not given the same name as the electron group arrangement. In such molecules there are three types of repulsive forces: between bonding pairs (BP–BP), between lone pairs (LP–LP), and between a bonding pair and a lone pair (BP–LP). Lone pairs spread out more, so they take up more space than bonding pairs. As a result, they exert a greater repulsive force on neighbouring lone pairs and on bonding pairs. In general, according to the VSEPR model, the repulsive forces decrease in the following order:

LP–LP > LP–BP > BP–BP

For example, methane, water, and ammonia all have four electron groups on a central atom, so their electron group arrangement is tetrahedral. However, their classes (molecular shapes) are all different. Examine **Table 4.5** to see how lone pairs of electrons, represented by E, affect the shape of molecules that have a tetrahedral electron grouping. Methane, with no lone pairs, has a tetrahedral molecular shape, and all bond angles are 109.5°. Ammonia has one lone pair that has pushed the bonding pairs closer to each other, resulting in bond angles of 107.3°. Water has two lone pairs that push the bonding pairs closer together than one lone pair does. Consequently, the bond angle in water is 104.5°.

Table 4.5 Tetrahedral Electron Groups

Compound	CH_4	NH_3	H_2O
Class	AX_4	AX_3E	AX_2E_2
Structure	109.5°	107.3°	104.5°
Molecular shape	tetrahedral	trigonal pyramidal	bent

Summarizing Molecular Shapes

For every set of electron groups, the number of lone pairs can range from zero to two fewer than the total number of electron groups. The common molecular shapes are summarized in **Figure 4.31**, in which generic shapes are shown rather than specific molecules.

Figure 4.31 The common molecular shapes with two to six electron groups are shown here. Although molecules with shapes AX_3E_3 and AX_2E_4 are theoretically possible, no stables molecules having those shapes are known.

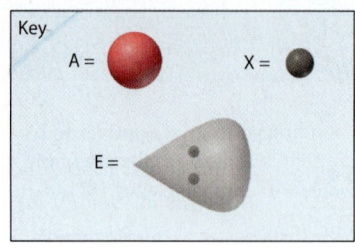

Key: A = (red), X = (black), E = (lone pair)

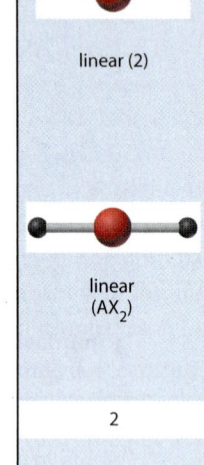
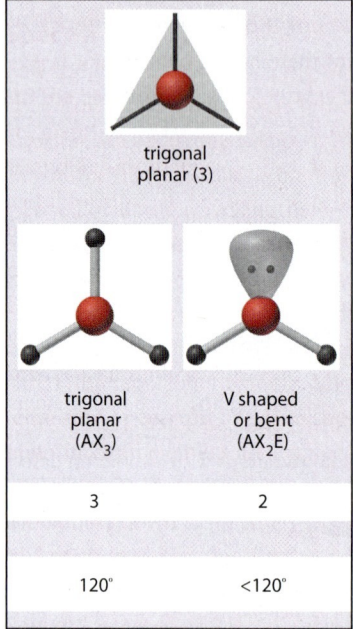
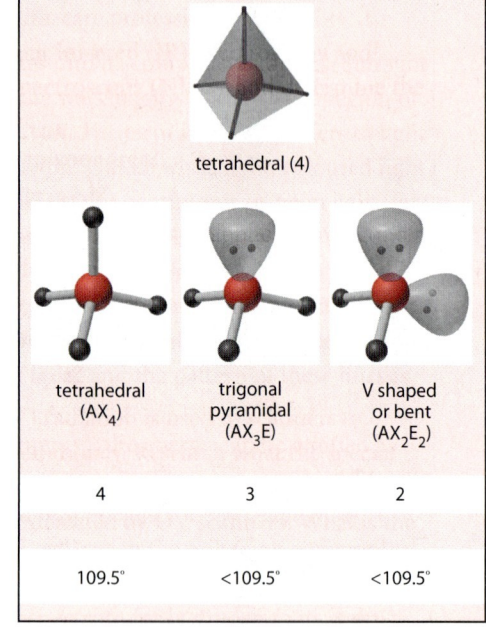

e⁻ Group arrangement (no. of groups)	linear (2)	trigonal planar (3)		tetrahedral (4)		
Molecular shape (class)	linear (AX_2)	trigonal planar (AX_3)	V shaped or bent (AX_2E)	tetrahedral (AX_4)	trigonal pyramidal (AX_3E)	V shaped or bent (AX_2E_2)
No. of bonding groups	2	3	2	4	3	2
Bond angle	180°	120°	<120°	109.5°	<109.5°	<109.5°

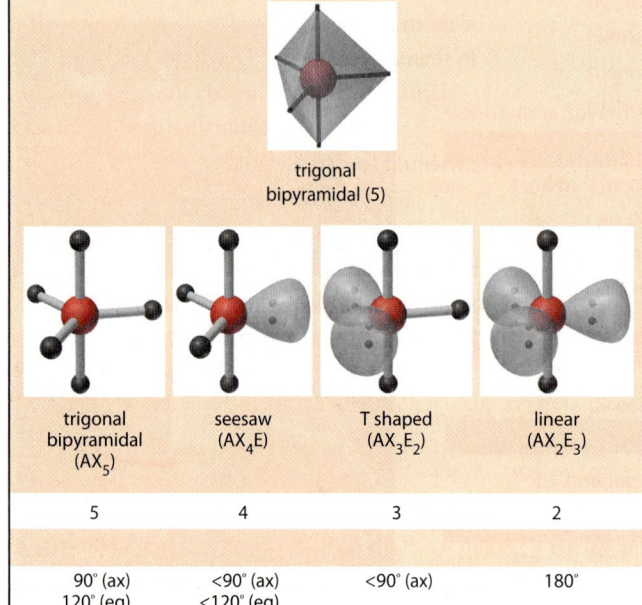
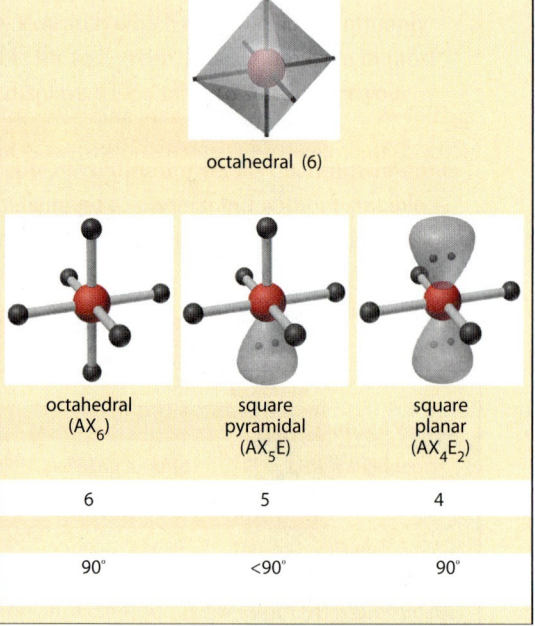

e⁻ Group arrangement (no. of groups)	trigonal bipyramidal (5)				octahedral (6)		
Molecular shape (class)	trigonal bipyramidal (AX_5)	seesaw (AX_4E)	T shaped (AX_3E_2)	linear (AX_2E_3)	octahedral (AX_6)	square pyramidal (AX_5E)	square planar (AX_4E_2)
No. of bonding groups	5	4	3	2	6	5	4
Bond angle	90° (ax) 120° (eq)	<90° (ax) <120° (eq)	<90° (ax)	180°	90°	<90°	90°

Guidelines for Using VSEPR Theory to Predict Molecular Shape

There are general guidelines that you can follow when using VSEPR theory to predict the shapes of simple molecules and polyatomic ions. Refer to the following steps, as well as the information in **Table 4.4** and **Figure 4.31**, as you work through the Sample Problems and Practice Problems that follow.

VSEPR Guidelines for Predicting Molecular Shape

1. Draw the Lewis structure of the molecule, considering only the electron pairs around the central atom.
2. Count the total number of electron groups around the central atom (bonding pairs and lone pairs), and account for any charge for ions. Treat double and triple bonds as though they were a single electron group.
3. Predict which of the five basic electron-group arrangements accommodates the total number of electron groups.
4. Predict the shape of the molecule based on the positions occupied by the electron groups and lone pairs of electrons. (See **Table 4.4** and **Figure 4.31**).
5. In predicting bond angles, note that a lone pair repels another lone pair or a bonding pair more strongly than a bonding pair repels another bonding pair. Keep in mind that, in general, there is no easy way to predict bond angles accurately when the central atom possesses one or more lone pairs

Sample Problem

Predicting the Shape of a Molecule

Problem
Use VSEPR theory to predict the shape of $PF_3(g)$.

What Is Required?
You must identify the molecular shape of $PF_3(g)$, based on the electron group arrangement that is proposed by VSEPR theory.

What Is Given?
You know from the chemical formula that the molecule has three fluorine atoms and one phosphorus atom.

Plan Your Strategy	Act on Your Strategy
Draw the Lewis structure.	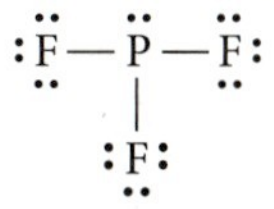 :F—P—F: | :F:
Determine the number of electron pairs surrounding the central atom. Predict the electron group arrangement based on this number.	There are four electron pairs around the P atom. Therefore, it has a tetrahedral arrangement of electron pairs.
Predict the geometry of the molecule.	With four electron groups, one of which is a lone pair, the shape is trigonal pyramidal.

Check Your Solution
The molecular shape corresponds to the VSEPR notation for this molecule, AX_3E. Since the electron arrangement is tetrahedral with one lone pair, bond angles should be less than 109.5°. (The repulsion from the bonding electron pairs by the lone pair on P is greater than the repulsion between bonding pairs.)

Sample Problem

Predicting the Shape of a Complex Molecule

Problem
Use VSEPR theory to predict the shape and bond angles of $SbCl_5(\ell)$.

What Is Required?
You need to identify the molecular shape and, based on this, the bond angles of $SbCl_5(\ell)$.

What Is Given?
You know from the chemical formula that the molecule has five chlorine atoms, and one antimony atom.

Plan Your Strategy	Act on Your Strategy
Draw the Lewis structure. Note that this structure has five bonds around the central atom. Therefore, the central atom has an expanded valence. The total number of valence electrons is 40e⁻. Ten electrons are used for the single bonds around Sb, leaving thirty electrons to distribute as lone pairs around the Cl atoms.	[Lewis structure of SbCl₅ showing Sb in the center bonded to five Cl atoms, each with lone pairs]
Determine the number of electron pairs surrounding the central atom. Predict the electron arrangement based on this number.	There are five electron pairs around the Sb atom. Therefore, it has a trigonal bipyramidal arrangement of electron pairs.
Predict the geometry and bond angles for the molecule.	There are no lone pairs around the central atom. Therefore the molecular shape is trigonal bipyramidal. Since there are no lone pairs, the bond angles are 90° and 120°.

Check Your Solution
The molecular shape corresponds to the VSEPR notation for this molecule, AX_5. Since the electron arrangement is trigonal bipyramidal and there are no lone pairs, the molecular shape is trigonal bipyramidal. Bond angles are predicted to be similar to the "ideal" values for this geometry, because the greater repulsion by lone pairs than bonding pairs is absent.

Practice Problems

11. What molecular shape is represented by each of the following VSEPR notations?
  a. AX_3
  b. AX_5E

12. What is the total number of valence electrons surrounding each of the atoms in the following compounds?
  a. $CF_4(g)$
  b. $NO_3^-(s)$

13. How many lone pairs and electron groups are associated with the central atom of the following molecules and ions? Remember that double and triple bonds count as only one electron group for the purpose of predicting molecular shape.
  a. $NH_4^+(s)$
  b. $HCN(g)$
  c. $XeF_4(s)$
  d. $PbCl_2$(vaporized)

14. Use VSEPR theory to predict the shape of $O_3(g)$.

15. Use VSEPR theory to predict the shape of $PH_3(g)$.

16. Use VSEPR theory to predict the shape of $SO_4^{2-}(s)$.

17. Use VSEPR theory to predict the shape and bond angles of $CH_2Cl_2(\ell)$.

18. Use VSEPR theory to predict the shape and bond angles of $CO_3^{2-}(s)$.

19. Consider the following fluorine-containing molecules to have the general formula XF_n. Arrange them in order of increasing F–X–F bond angles: $BF_3(g)$, $BeF_2(g)$, $CF_4(g)$, $NF_3(g)$, $OF_2(g)$.

20. Phosphorus pentachloride, used in synthetic chemistry to add chlorine to molecules, exists as molecules of $PCl_5(g)$ in the gas phase. As a solid, though, it exists as alternating ions $PCl_4^+(s)$ and $PCl_6^-(s)$. Predict the shapes of all three species: $PCl_5(g)$, $PCl_4^+(s)$, and $PCl_6^-(s)$.

Determining the Hybridization of the Central Atom of a Molecule or Ion

The concept of hybridization of orbitals (Section 4.1) extends the Lewis and VSEPR models. After using VSEPR to predict the shape of the electron groupings, you can match that shape to one of the forms of hybridization that matches the shape. Experimentally determined bond lengths and bond angles can then be used to verify the prediction. Follow the steps below to determine the hybrid orbitals for the central atom.

Guidelines for Predicting Hybridization of the Central Atom

1. Draw the Lewis structure of the molecule.
2. Predict the overall arrangement of the electron pairs (both bonding pairs and lone pairs) using the VSEPR model.
3. Deduce the hybridization of the central atom by matching the arrangement of the electron pairs with those of the hybrid orbitals in **Table 4.6**.

For example, in the Sample Problem above involving phosphorous trifluoride, $PF_3(g)$, the Lewis structure in **Figure 4.32A** shows that there are four electron groups around the phosphorous atom: three bonds and a lone pair. Therefore the electron-group arrangement is tetrahedral. Since sp^3 hybrid orbitals have a tetrahedral arrangement, phosphorous has an sp^3 hybridization. **Figure 4.32B** shows that the molecular shape is trigonal pyramidal. Because the tetrahedral electron group has one lone pair, you expect the bond angles to be smaller than 109.5°. The measured value for $PF_3(g)$ is 96.3°.

Figure 4.32 Lewis and molecular structures for phosphorous trifluoride

Table 4.6 Composition of Hybrid Orbitals

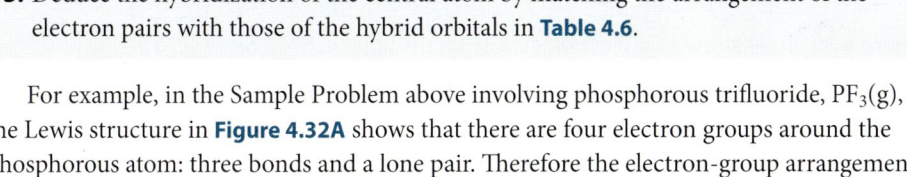

	Linear	Trigonal Planar	Tetrahedral	Trigonal Bipyramidal	Octahedral
Atomic Orbitals Mixed	one s one p	one s one p	one s one p	one s one p	one s one p
Hybrid Orbitals Formed	two sp	three sp^2	four sp^3	five sp^3d	six sp^3d^2
Unhybridized Orbitals Remaining	two p	one p	none	four d	three d
e⁻ Group Arrangement	180°	120°	109.5°	90°, 120°	90°, 90°

Learning Check

31. Refer to the Sample Problem on page 231, Drawing a Lewis Structure that Includes a Co-ordinate Covalent Bond. What is the hybridization of the oxygen atom in H_3O^+?

32. Refer to the Sample Problem on page 236, Predicting the Shape of a Complex Molecule. What is the hybridization of the antimony atom in the molecule $SbCl_5$?

33. What is the hybridization of the carbon atom in a molecule of formic acid (methanoic acid, $HCOOH(\ell)$)?

34. What is the hybridization of the nitrogen atom in each of the following, and what bond angles would you expect?
    a. $NH_3(g)$ **b.** $NH_4^+(s)$

35. Which hybrid orbitals and unhybridized orbitals are associated with the bromine atom in the molecule $BrF_5(\ell)$?

36. Which hybrid orbitals and unhybridized orbitals are associated with the chlorine atom in the molecule $ClF_3(g)$?

The Influence of Molecular Shape on Polarity

One of the most important effects that a shape of a molecule can have is on the polarity of the molecule. As you know, a covalent bond is polar when the two atoms involved have an electronegativity difference between 0.4 and 1.7. For the molecule of HF(g), shown in **Figure 4.33**, the fluorine atom is much more electronegative than the hydrogen atom. This results in the end of the bond near F developing a partial negative charge and the end of the bond near H developing a partial positive charge. This polarity in a bond is called a *bond dipole*. A vector is drawn over the Lewis structure of HF to show the direction of the dipole. The vector points towards the more electronegative atom.

$$\overset{\delta+}{H}-\overset{\delta-}{\underset{..}{\overset{..}{F}}}:$$
A

$$\overset{\longrightarrow}{H-\underset{..}{\overset{..}{F}}:}$$
B

Figure 4.33 In (**A**), the shift in electron density for the bond in HF(g) results in a partial positive charge that is associated with the hydrogen and a partial negative charge associated with the fluorine. In (**B**), the bond dipole is indicated using a vector that points in the direction of higher electron density (the atom with a higher electronegativity).

Determining Whether a Molecule is Polar

If a molecule includes one or more polar bonds, is it necessarily polar? To answer this question, the shapes of the molecules must be considered. Analyze the structures of carbon dioxide and water in **Figure 4.34**, both of which have two polar bonds. The polarity of a molecule as a whole can be determined by adding the vectors. In the water molecule, which has a bent geometry, the horizontal components of the vectors point toward each other, so they cancel each other. The vertical components of the vectors are added to give the final vector, labelled F_{total}. Thus, water is a polar molecule that has an oxygen atom with a partial negative charge and hydrogen atoms with a partial positive charge. The carbon dioxide molecule is linear, and the vectors representing the polarity of the bonds point directly away from each other. Because the bonds are identical, the polarities of the bonds are the same, and the polarity vectors cancel each other. The carbon dioxide molecule is not polar.

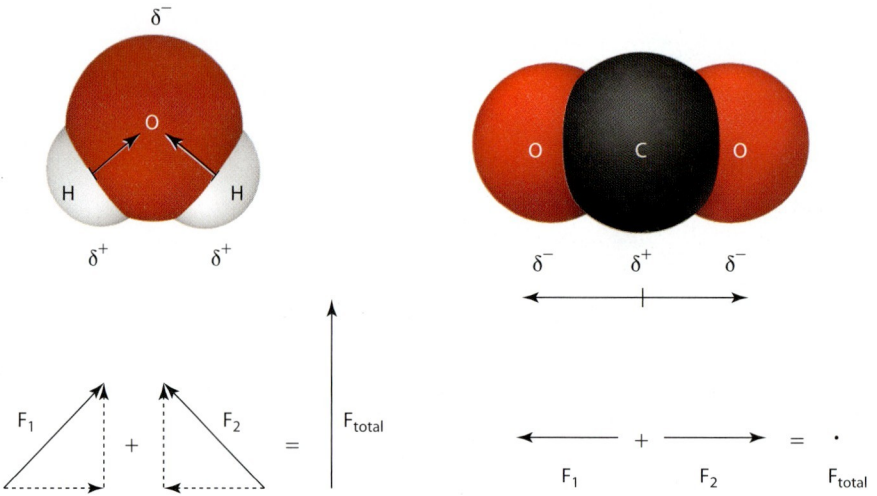

Figure 4.34 Both water and carbon dioxide are small molecules with two polar bonds. Water, with its bent configuration, is polar. The linear carbon dioxide molecule is not polar.

Some molecules are more complex, but one feature, symmetry, often helps in such cases. Consider the two molecules in **Figure 4.35**. Carbon tetrachloride, $CCl_4(\ell)$ is a symmetrical molecule, and all the polar C–Cl bonds are identical. Therefore, the polarities of the four bonds cancel one another, and the molecule is non-polar. If one of the chlorine atoms is replaced with hydrogen atom, the polar molecule trichloromethane, $CHCl_3(\ell)$, is produced. The C–Cl bond polarities cancel each other horizontally, but the polarities of all the vertical bonds point downward. The total polarity of $CHCl_3(\ell)$ is represented by an arrow from the hydrogen atom downward through the central carbon atom.

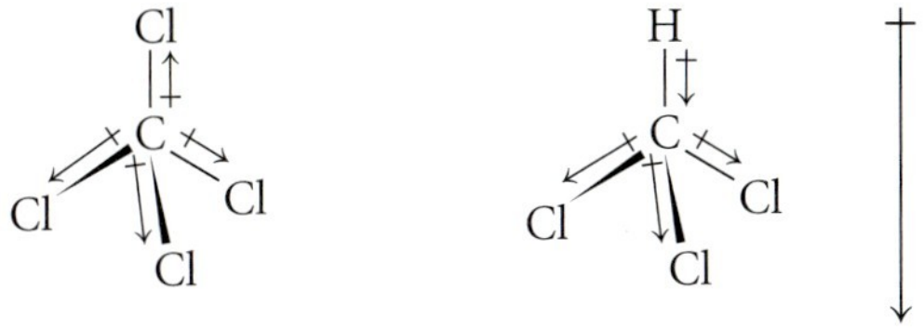

Figure 4.35 Replacing a chlorine atom with a hydrogen atom turns a non-polar molecule, $CCl_4(\ell)$, into a polar molecule, $CHCl_3(\ell)$. The identical bond dipoles in $CCl_4(\ell)$ produce a net zero molecular polarity. For $CHCl_3(\ell)$, there is net polarity.
Infer *whether the molecule CH_3OH is polar or non-polar, and explain why.*

Table 4.7 summarizes the combination of molecular shape and bond polarity for many simple molecules. In the table, the symbol "A" represents the central atom. Two different symbols, X and Y, are used to represent atoms of different elements bonded to the central atom to represent different magnitudes and directions of polarity of bonds.

Table 4.7 Molecular Shapes and Polarities

Molecular Shape	Polarity of Bond	Molecular Polarity
linear	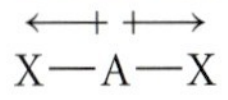 X—A—X	non-polar
linear	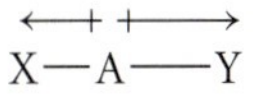 X—A—Y	polar
bent	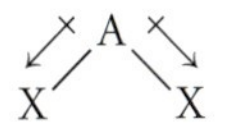 X, X with A	polar
trigonal planar	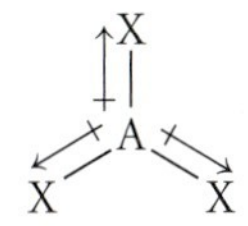 X (top), X, X	non-polar
trigonal planar	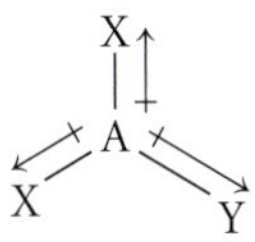 X (top), X, Y	polar
tetrahedral	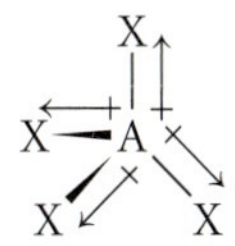 X, X, X, X	non-polar
tetrahedral	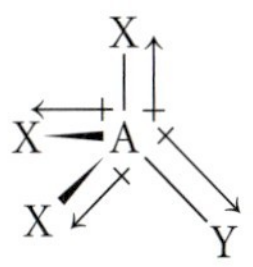 X, X, X, Y	polar
trigonal pyramidal	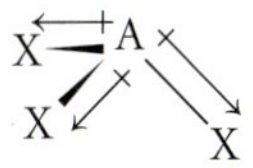 X, X, X	polar

Activity 4.2 | Applying VSEPR Theory

This activity will help to reinforce the use of VSEPR theory to predict the shapes, bond angles, and polarities of molecules. You will use simple materials such as erasers and straight pins (for which Styrofoam® spheres and toothpicks can be substituted easily) to create structures that represent a variety of molecules shapes. These shapes are based on the five basic electron-group arrangements predicted by VSEPR theory.

Safety Precautions

- Use EXTREME CAUTION when selecting and inserting very sharp straight pins into the erasers.

Materials

- pre-cut eraser pieces or suitable alternatives
- straight pins with coloured ends

Procedure

1. You will be supplied with 8 cubes, made by cutting erasers into equal-sized pieces, or with 8 suitable alternatives.

2. Use the pins and erasers to create the shapes shown below. When building these models, keep the following in mind.
   - The eraser represents the central atom, and the straight pins represent electron groupings. A coloured ball placed at the end of the pin represents an attached atom. If you keep the colours the same within each molecule, it will represent the same element, and therefore, an atom with the same electronegativity.
   - Your molecules are three-dimensional with particular angles between atoms and between atoms and lone pairs. All angles within the structures A to F and K to M are equal. Bond angles between the three atoms or electron pairs around the horizontal axis or equator in structures G to L are equal (similar to structure B).
   - Remember that VSEPR theory only predicts the arrangement of electron groupings in the valence shell of a central atom. Both the bonding and non-bonding electron pairs of the central atom need to be arranged to maximize the distance and minimize repulsive forces between them.

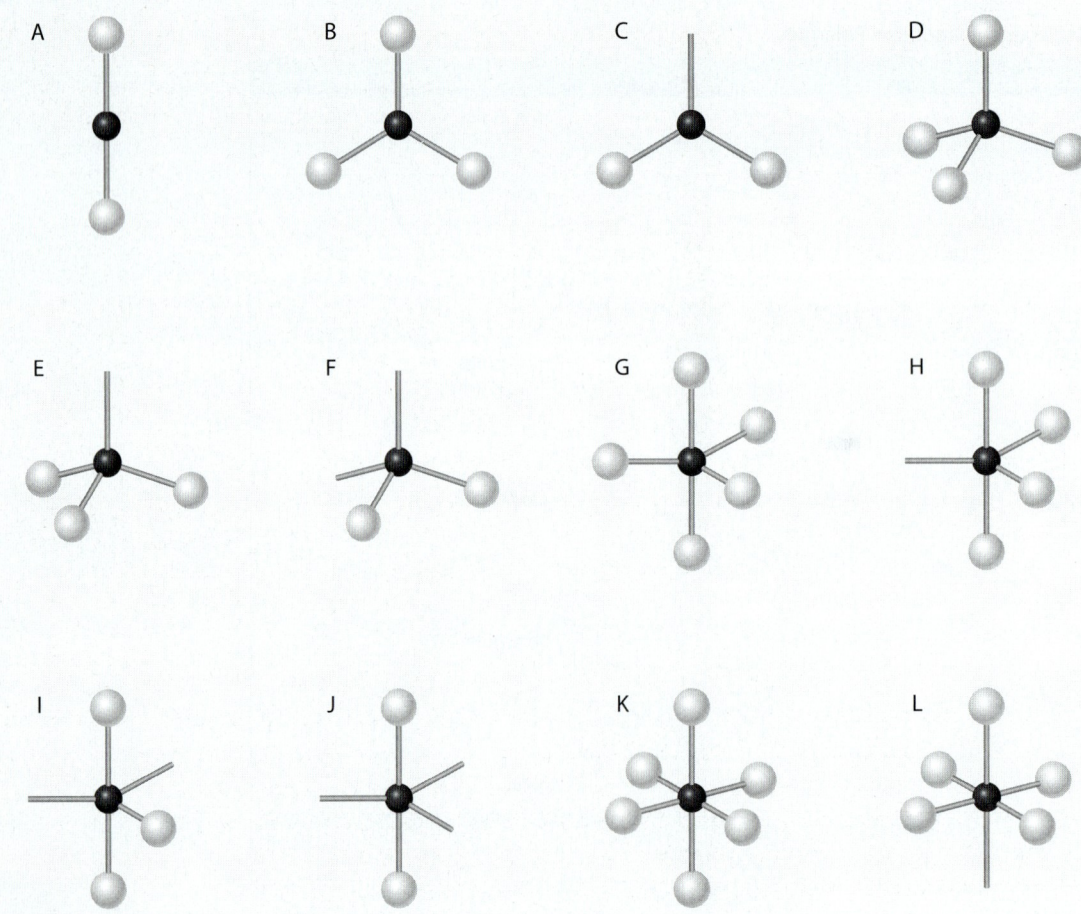

3. Construct a table like the one below, and complete it by filling in the information for each molecule. The first one is completed for you. Note that the second column, "Number of Electron groups", refers to the total number of groups (bonding and lone pairs) around the central atom.

Sketch of Molecular Shape	Number of Electron groups	Number of Lone Pairs	Number of Bonding Pairs	Electron-Group Arrangement	Name of Molecular Shape
	2	0	2	linear	linear

4. Predict the bond angles about the central atom in each structure. Compare your predictions with other students in the class. Explain why bond angles in structures E through M are estimations.

5. Use **Table 4.2** and **Table 4.3** to identify the names of the electronic shapes (formed by bonded and unbonded electron pairs) and molecular shapes (formed by bonded electron pairs only).

6. Determine if each shape would result in a polar or non-polar molecule, assuming the atoms surrounding the central atom are all the same.

Questions

1. Are your predicted bond angles correct? What common mistakes did you and other students make? Make sure that you have correct bond angles for all structures in your table. For angles that you had to estimate, use Internet or print resources to identify representative molecules and their bond angles.

2. A common error is to draw structures C and F as straight lines rather than bent or angular. Why are the correct structures bent? Why is there a difference in the bond angles of structures C and F?

3. For structure E, the molecular shape is trigonal pyramidal; for structure L, the molecular shape is square pyramidal. What is the difference between these two structures?

4. When are the names for the electronic geometry or VSEPR arrangement the same as the molecular shapes? In each case, what is the polarity of the molecule expected to be? Why?

5. VSEPR theory enables chemists to predict shapes based on the idea of arranging all electron pairs around the central atom (bonding and non-bonding) in a way that reduces repulsive forces. What is one shortcoming of the VSEPR theory? Explain your reasoning.

How Intermolecular Forces Affect the Properties of Solids and Liquids

The covalent bonding models that you have studied thus far focused on **intramolecular forces**—forces exerted *within* a molecule or polyatomic ion. Intramolecular forces influence the chemical properties of substances. Chemical changes involve overcoming these forces in order for bonds to break and new substances to be synthesized.

Intramolecular forces cannot account for many physical properties of molecular substances. Compare the data in **Table 4.8**. All three substances are molecular compounds of similar size, but they have very different physical properties. These differences are due in large part to the presence of other types of forces. Forces that influence the physical properties of substances are called **intermolecular forces**. These are forces of attraction and repulsion that act between molecules. They are categorized into the following groups, which will be discussed below in turn: dipole-dipole forces, ion-dipole forces, dipole-induced dipole forces, and dispersion forces. The dipole-dipole, dipole-induced dipole, and dispersion forces are also commonly referred to as van der Waals forces. This name recognizes the contributions of Dutch physicist Johannes van der Waals (1837–1923) to the understanding of these types of intermolecular attractions.

intramolecular force a force that holds atoms or ions together; in metals, a force between metal cations and free electrons; forms the basis of chemical bonding

intermolecular force a force that exists between molecules or between ions and molecules to influence the physical properties of substances

Table 4.8 Physical Properties of Some Molecular Compounds

Compound	Molar Mass (g)	Melting Point (°C)	Boiling Point (°C)
water	18.0	0	100
ammonia	17.0	−77.7	−33.3
methane	16.0	−182.5	−161.6

dipole-dipole force an intermolecular attraction between opposite partial charges of polar molecules

hydrogen bonding a strong intermolecular attraction between molecules with a hydrogen atom that is covalently bonded to a highly electronegative atom, often oxygen or nitrogen; a type of dipole-dipole attraction between partially positive hydrogen and partially negative atom, such as oxygen or nitrogen

Dipole-Dipole

In Section 4.1, you studied how a polar covalent bond has a bond dipole and that a polar molecule will have an overall dipole. This dipolar nature of polar molecules means they have a region that has a partial negative charge and another region that has a partial positive charge. These partial charges are permanent dipoles—they are always present in the molecule. As shown in **Figure 4.36**, this results in neighbouring molecules aligning themselves so that oppositely charged regions are directed toward each other. These forces of attraction between different polar molecules are called **dipole-dipole forces**, and they result in polar molecules being more attracted to each other than similarly-sized non-polar molecules. They are a main reason for the differences in melting points and boiling points for polar and non-polar molecules.

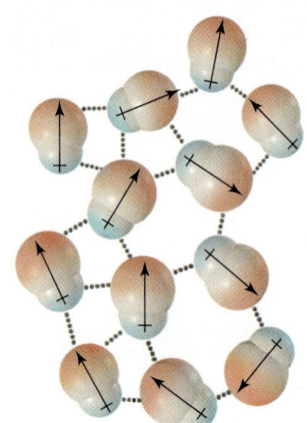

Figure 4.36 The dipoles of polar molecules cause neighbouring molecules to be oriented in such a manner that the oppositely charged regions are aligned.
Explain how dipole forces could differ in strength.

Hydrogen Bonds Are Dipole-Dipole Interactions

One specific dipole-dipole interaction that is often much stronger than other intermolecular forces is **hydrogen bonding**, shown in **Figure 4.37**. Because only a few elements can participate in hydrogen bonding, this type of interaction is often treated as a separate category. When a hydrogen atom is covalently bonded to a highly electronegative atom, such as oxygen or nitrogen, the electronegative atom draws the electrons away from the hydrogen. Because hydrogen has no electrons other than the bonding electrons, this leaves the positively charged nucleus nearly bare. A hydrogen bond is the electrostatic attraction between the strong partial positive charge of the hydrogen atom and the partial negative charge on the highly electronegative atom on an adjacent molecule. Lone pairs on the electronegative atom enhance the attractive force, which is often much stronger than other types of dipole-dipole interactions.

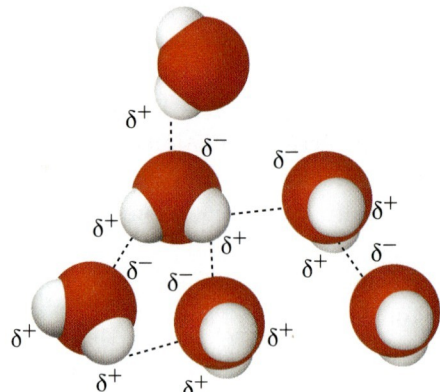

Figure 4.37 For molecules that have hydrogen atoms bonded to electronegative atoms such as oxygen, hydrogen bonding between molecules will occur. The hydrogen atoms have a partial positive charge and the electronegative atom it is bonded to has a partial negative charge. Hydrogen bonding of water molecules is shown here.

A hydrogen bond is only about 5 percent as strong as a single covalent bond. However, hydrogen bonding can have profound effects on the properties of substances. For example, many of the differences in physical properties in **Table 4.8** can be explained based on hydrogen bonding. Methane is a non-polar molecule and lacks hydrogen bonding. Therefore, these attractive forces are not helping to hold these molecules together. Much lower boiling and melting points are observed, compared with water and ammonia. So why is water a liquid at room temperature while ammonia is a gas? Both molecules are of similar size, are polar, and have hydrogen bonding. However, the forces holding the ammonia molecules together are weaker, because nitrogen is less electronegative than oxygen. This means the N–H bonds are less polar than the O–H bonds, resulting in weaker hydrogen bonds. In addition, the nitrogen atom in ammonia has only one lone pair whereas the oxygen atom in water has two.

Because water consists entirely of oxygen and hydrogen atoms and has two O–H bonds, hydrogen bonding is an important factor in the structure and properties of water. A single oxygen atom of one water molecule can be hydrogen-bonded to as many as six hydrogen atoms of different water molecules at the same time. The hydrogen bonding of water molecules, together with the bond angle between the oxygen and hydrogen atoms, gives snowflakes their characteristic six-sided shape.

In solid water, each water molecule is hydrogen-bonded to four other water molecules, as shown in **Figure 4.38A**. The molecules are farther apart in ice than in liquid water, so the hydrogen bonds are longer. Nevertheless, the hydrogen bonds are stronger because of the orientation of the atoms and the bonds. Hydrogen bonds are strongest when the molecules are oriented as shown in **Figure 4.38B**. Notice that the line from the oxygen atom through the hydrogen atom in that molecule and to the oxygen atom of the next water molecule is straight. In ice, all the hydrogen bonds have this orientation.

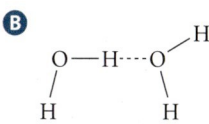

Figure 4.38 (A) The hydrogen bonds in ice are longer than they are in water, making ice less dense than water. **(B)** The orientation of the hydrogen bonds in ice gives them their maximum strength.

Ion-Dipole

Ions and dipoles are attracted to one another by electrostatic forces called **ion-dipole forces**. As you can see in **Figure 4.39**, there are two types of ion-dipole interactions: between a polar molecule and a cation, and between a polar molecule and an anion. The strength of this interaction depends on the charge and size of the ion and on the magnitude of the dipole and size of the molecule. The charges on cations are generally more concentrated, because cations are usually smaller than anions. Therefore, a cation interacts more strongly with dipoles than does an anion that has a charge of the same magnitude.

ion-dipole force an intermolecular attraction between partial charges of polar molecules and ions

Figure 4.39 Ion-dipole intermolecular forces involve an electrostatic attraction between either a cation and the partial negative charge of a polar molecule or an anion and the partial positive charge on a polar molecule.

The process of *hydration* involves ion-dipole forces. Hydration involves an ion or molecule being surrounded by water molecules that are arranged in a specific manner. For example, as **Figure 4.40** shows, NaCl(s) dissolves in water because the attractions between the Na^+ and Cl^- ions and the water molecules provide enough energy to overcome the forces that bind the ions together.

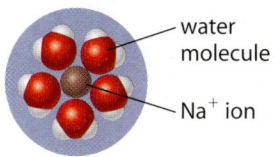 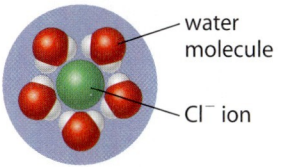

Figure 4.40 The negative end of water molecules attracts the sodium ion and the positive end of water molecules attracts the chloride ion.

Induced Dipoles

It is possible to induce the formation of dipoles in molecules that are classified as non-polar. Electrons in atoms and molecules are in constant, rapid motion. For a brief instant, the distribution of electrons can become distorted so that one point in a molecule is very slightly positive and another point is slightly negative. One way this charge induction can be accomplished is through the presence of another polar molecule. For **dipole-induced dipole forces**, the charge on a polar molecule is responsible for inducing the charge on the non-polar molecule that is nearby. These molecules are then attracted to each other, as shown in **Figure 4.41**. In a similar manner to dipole-induced forces, a nearby ion can induce a dipole in a non-polar molecule. Such attractive forces are called **ion-induced dipole forces**. **Figure 4.41** shows how dipoles can be induced in non-polar molecules by nearby ions or polar molecules.

dipole-induced dipole force an intermolecular attraction due to the distortion of electron density of non-polar molecule by a nearby polar molecule; a force of attraction between a polar molecule and a temporary dipole of a non-polar molecule

ion-induced dipole force an intermolecular attraction due to the distortion of electron density of a non-polar molecule caused by a nearby ion; a force of attraction between an ion and a temporary dipole of a non-polar molecule

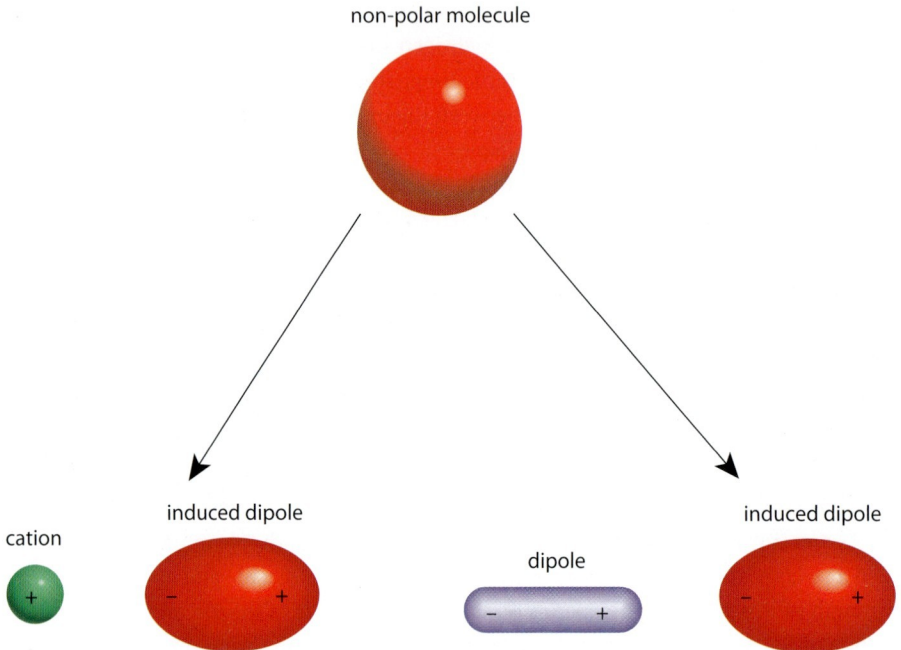

Figure 4.41 A dipole can be induced in a non-polar molecule. The electron distribution of the non-polar molecule is distorted by the force exerted by an ion or a polar molecule.

Dispersion Forces

The intermolecular forces discussed so far result from the partial charges at different points on polar molecules or charges on ions. Do non-polar molecules interact with each other? Consider the three photographs in **Figure 4.42**, taken under standard conditions of temperature and pressure. In increasing order of molar mass, the three halogens shown are chlorine, bromine, and iodine. All are diatomic molecules that are completely symmetrical and non-polar. Nevertheless, as the molar mass increases, the state of the substances goes from a gas to a liquid and then to a solid. In the gaseous state, there is very little interaction among the molecules. To form a liquid, the molecules must have some attraction for one another to remain close together. In a solid, such as iodine, the intermolecular forces must be relatively strong, because the molecules remain in the same positions relative to one another.

Figure 4.42 Under standard conditions of temperature and pressure, chlorine is a yellowish-orange gas (**A**), bromine is a reddish-brown liquid (**B**), and iodine is a violet-dark grey solid (**C**).

The attractive forces that act between non-polar molecules are called **dispersion forces**. Dispersion forces act between all molecules, but in non-polar molecules they are the only force. In honour of the German physicist Fritz London (1900–1954), who explained the force mathematically, dispersion forces are often called *London forces*. These attractive forces occur because non-polar molecules spontaneously form temporary dipoles. The shared pairs of electrons in covalent bonds are in constant motion. This motion, which is part of the normal condition of a non-polar molecule, causes momentary, uneven distributions of charge. In other words, a non-polar molecule becomes slightly polar for an instant, and this continues on a random but on-going basis. The momentary separation of charge (temporary dipole) induces a temporary dipole in the molecule beside it, which can induce another instantaneous dipole in another adjacent molecule. The process "disperses" through the substance, creating fleeting dipoles that attract one another. Each individual attractive force is extremely weak and lasts only an instant, but when many interactions occur at the same time, the overall effect is significant.

dispersion force a weak intermolecular attraction between all molecules, including non-polar molecules, due to temporary dipoles

Two factors affect the magnitude of dispersion forces. First, the attraction becomes larger as the mass of the molecules becomes larger. The basis for this increase in dispersion forces is the greater number of electrons. The probability that a temporary dipole will form increases as the number of electrons increases. This is evident in the halogen examples above. As the size increases, so do the dispersion forces, resulting in the difference in states at standard temperature and pressure. Iodine is the largest and its stronger dispersion forces result in it being a solid.

The shape of the molecule is the second factor that affects the strength of the dispersion forces. As you can see in **Figure 4.43**, the area of contact between two spherically-shaped molecules is very small, while the area of contact between linear molecules is larger. When two molecules have about the same number of electrons, dispersion forces are greater for the molecule with a linear shape.

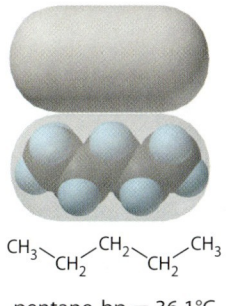

pentane, bp = 36.1°C

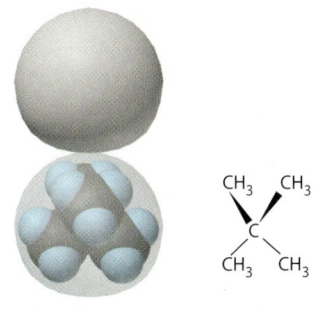

2,2-dimethylpropane, bp = 9.5°C

Figure 4.43 Both types of molecules have five carbon atoms and 12 hydrogen atoms, but their shapes are quite different. Dispersion forces are greater between the linear molecules than between the spherical molecules.

Activity 4.3 | Canadian Contributions to Molecular Geometry

Earlier you read that VSEPR was developed by Dr. Ronald Gillespie, associated with McMaster University in Hamilton, Ontario. Two other prominent Canadian scientists—Dr. Richard Bader, also of McMaster, and Dr. R. J. Le Roy, with the University of Waterloo in Waterloo, Ontario—have made significant contributions to the study of the shapes of molecules and the forces that hold them together. In this activity, you will research and report on their work.

Procedure

1. Work with two partners. Each of you will create a series of questions as if you were preparing to interview one of the three scientists, Gillespie, Bader, or Le Roy.

2. When you have completed your questions, exchange them with another member of your group. That student will research the scientist to find answers to the questions. Answers may be written as if that student is the scientist being investigated. As part of the process of research, record all sources of information used to answer the questions.

3. Exchange your completed research with the third member of your group (not the person who wrote the questions). That student will conduct follow-up research, using the source information as well as new, additional sources, to verify the information provided in step 2.

Questions

1. What skills and characteristics related to science do the three scientists have in common, and what science-related skills and characteristics distinguish each scientist from the others?

2. What, if any, other skills and characteristics (unrelated to science) helped influence the way each scientist thinks and the kinds of research interest he pursued?

3. What was the purpose and value of step 3, in which information was checked using the same, as well as additional, sources?

Dr. Ronald Gillespie

Dr. Richard Bader

Dr. R. J. Le Roy

Section 4.2 Review

Section Summary

- The structures of molecular compounds are much more varied than the structures of ionic compounds, in part because of the nature of covalent bonds.
- Different forces of attraction and repulsion determine the relative positions in space of atoms, bonding pairs of electrons, and lone pair of electrons, resulting in molecules with characteristic three-dimensional shapes. Chemists use different theories and models to predict these three-dimensional shapes.
- In a co-ordinate covalent bond, one atom contributes both electrons to the shared pair of electrons.
- In an expanded valence (expanded octet), a central atom has more than eight valence electrons.
- A resonance structure is a model in which two or more Lewis structures show the same relative position of atoms but different positions of electron pairs.
- VSEPR theory proposes that each of the electron groups around an atom is positioned as far as possible from the others to minimize repulsions. An electron group consists of a single bond, double bond, triple bond, or lone pair. The result is a particular geometric arrangement of the electron groups.
- Electron-group arrangement refers to the ways that groups of valence electrons are positioned around a specific atom. Molecular shape refers to the relative positions of the atomic nuclei in an entire molecule.
- Intermolecular forces are forces of attraction and repulsion that act between molecules and influence the physical properties of solids and liquids.

Review Questions

1. **K/U** Define a co-ordinate covalent bond and use Lewis structures to show the formation of a co-ordinate covalent bond between the molecule BF_3 and the ion F^- thus creating the polyatomic ion BF_4^-.

2. **C** What are resonance structures and when are they used? Write several sentences to explain, including one example and an accompanying diagram.

3. **K/U** Why is it necessary to draw a Lewis structure before predicting the shape of a molecule?

4. **T/I** Use VSEPR theory to predict the shape of the following molecules and polyatomic ions.
   a. $Br_2O(g)$
   b. $NBr_3(g)$
   c. $ClO_3^-(s)$
   d. $NO_2^+(s)$

5. **A** Using labelled diagrams, explain why $PF_5(g)$ is trigonal bipyramidal while $IF_5(\ell)$ is square pyramidal.

6. **T/I** For each of the following fluorine-containing molecules, draw a Lewis structure and then determine its shape.
   a. $BF_3(g)$
   b. $AsF_3(\ell)$
   c. $AsF_5(g)$

7. **T/I** For each of the following molecules, draw a Lewis structure, determine the molecule's shape, and predict whether it is a polar or non-polar molecule.
   a. $HCN(g)$
   b. $CH_3F(s)$
   c. $NOF(g)$
   d. $CS_2(\ell)$

8. **T/I** You are given two molecular compounds. You are told that one is composed of polar molecules and one is composed of non-polar molecules. Suggest three tests that could help you determine which is which.

9. **K/U** Compare and contrast sp hybridization and sp^2 hybridization. For each type, give an example of a molecule in which it is found.

10. **T/I** Consider the molecule $PF_3(g)$.
    a. Draw a Lewis structure for the molecule.
    b. Predict the overall arrangement of the electron pairs using the VSEPR model.
    c. Deduce the hybridization of the central atom.
    d. What is the shape of the molecule? Is it the same as the overall arrangement of the electron groups? Explain your answer.

11. **K/U** What is the most significant intermolecular force present in the solid phase of each of the following substances? Explain your answer in each case.
    a. $Ne(g)$
    b. $H_2O(\ell)$
    c. $CHCl_3(g)$
    d. $BF_3(g)$

12. **C** Compare and contrast an ion-dipole force and an ion-induced dipole force. Use diagrams.

13. **A** What intermolecular forces are at work when the following substances dissolve in water?
    a. sucrose, $C_{12}H_{22}O_{11}(s)$ (Hint: a molecule of sucrose has many —OH groups.)
    b. potassium chloride, $KCl(s)$

14. **K/U** What evidence supports the theory that dispersion forces exist?

Plan Your Own INVESTIGATION 4-A

Skill Check
✓ Initiating and Planning
✓ Performing and Recording
✓ Analyzing and Interpreting
✓ Communicating Results

Suggested Precautions

- Wear safety eyewear throughout this investigation.
- Tie back loose hair and clothing.
- Use EXTREME CAUTION when you are near an open flame.
- Wash your hands thoroughly when you are finished.

Suggested Materials
- samples of common products found in the home
- conductivity tester
- Bunsen burner or hot plate
- retort stand
- ring clamp
- wire gauze
- beakers
- test tubes
- melting point tubes
- thermometers
- split stopper

Predicting and Testing for Bonding in Solids

In this investigation, you will examine a common product in the home to predict its main type of bonding and to verify your prediction.

Pre-Lab Questions
1. Summarize these properties of ionic, polar covalent, non-polar covalent, and metallic solids: solubility in water, melting point, hardness, conductivity.
2. Explain, using your understanding of intermolecular forces, why salt and sugar dissolve well in water, while oil does not.
3. Draw sketches to compare the hardness and high melting point of ionic solids and the malleability and conductivity of metallic solids.

Question
What type of bonding is present in common household products?

Plan and Conduct
1. Working in pairs, select one of the products from the samples provided.
2. Predict the type of bonding in the product, and describe its properties based on your prediction.
3. Design an experiment to test the properties of the product. Ensure you have addressed all safety considerations. Your teacher must approve your procedure.
4. Perform your experiment, and record detailed observations.
5. Pool your results with those of other groups on a common summary table so that everyone has access to the predictions and observations for all the solids.
6. Put away equipment. Dispose of solutions and solids as your teacher instructs.

Analyze and Interpret
1. How accurate was your prediction? Explain why it was or was not accurate.
2. In terms of the whole class, which solid(s) had the most unexpected properties and did not match predictions? Explain.

Conclude and Communicate
3. How you can identify the bonding in a solid without doing an experiment?

Extend Further
4. **INQUIRY** What additional tests could be done to determine the type of bonding in solids? Explain how you could design an investigation using these tests on the solids with properties that did not match your predictions.
5. **RESEARCH** Examine a food-product label with five or more ingredients. Identify the type of bonding in each. Research those you are unfamiliar with.

Plan Your Own INVESTIGATION 4-B

Skill Check
✓ Initiating and Planning
✓ Performing and Recording
✓ Analyzing and Interpreting
✓ Communicating Results

Suggested Precautions

- Wear safety eyewear throughout this investigation.
- Tie back loose hair and clothing.
- Use EXTREME CAUTION when you are near an open flame.
- Wash your hands thoroughly when you are finished.

Suggested Materials
- sample of unknown substance (solid) from your teacher
- equipment from Investigation 4-A

Bonding in an Unknown Solid

In this investigation, you will receive an unknown solid from your teacher, and you will design an investigation to collect data about and analyse its physical properties to determine the type of bonding present.

Pre-Lab Questions
1. Review the Pre-Lab questions, and your answers, from Investigation 4-A.
2. What safety issues apply to the testing of an unknown substance?

Question
What type of bonding is present in an unknown substance?

Plan and Conduct
1. Your teacher will give you a sample of a solid that could contain ionic, polar covalent, non-polar covalent, or metallic bonds. Record as many visible properties as possible. Predict the main type of bonding present in your unknown solid.
2. Design an experiment that includes at least three tests to determine the properties of the unknown solid. Ensure you have addressed all safety issues. Your teacher must approve your procedure.
3. Perform your experiment, and record detailed observations.
4. Put equipment away. Dispose of solutions and solids as your teacher instructs.

Analyze and Interpret
1. Based on your observations, provide a detailed explanation of the type of bonding present in your unknown solid.
2. Were there any results that were inconclusive or uncertain? If so, Explain why.

Conclude and Communicate
3. How did your results compare with your predictions? Explain.
4. Find out from your teacher the identity of the solid and its bonding. Assess and explain the accuracy of your prediction.
5. What additional tests could be done to verify the type of bonding in your solid?

Extend Further

6. **INQUIRY** How did your experiences with Investigation 4-A assist you in planning and carrying out this investigation?
7. **RESEARCH** Determine at least two other solids—different from those used in this investigation and in Investigation 4-A—that could be used safely in a high school science laboratory to conduct experiments to determine the bonding of a solid substance. Explain your suggestions, paying special attention to how safety could be ensured.

STSE
Case Study

Nanoparticles and Their Properties
A Life-Cycle Approach to Risk Assessment

Scenario

Nanotechnology is a rapidly growing field focussed on the development and applications of materials that are so small that they measure between 1 and 100 nanometres (nm). That is only about 1/100 000 of the size of a human hair! While the creation of nanomaterials has captured the imagination of science fiction writers for decades, these substances are now real and are in widespread use in everyday life. They are found in hundreds of products available today, from sunscreens and cosmetics to golf clubs and cookware. Nanomaterials are used in medical therapies to combat cancer and other diseases, and they have many potential applications in diagnostic imaging and surgical robotics. Despite the many current and potential applications of nanomaterials, however, surveys conducted in Canada, the United States, and the United Kingdom report that the public is largely unaware of what nanotechnology and nanomaterials are, let alone the implications of their development.

What Are Nanoparticles and Why Are They Useful?

Scientists and engineers working in industry and research institutions create nanoparticles. Not only the size but also the shape of nanoparticles is important. A cube-shaped substance is a nanoparticle only when each of its sides measures between 1 nm and 100 nm. A sphere is considered a nanoparticle if its diameter also falls within this nanoscale-size range.

Nanoparticles are made up of tens, hundreds, or thousands of atoms. To form a nanoparticle, atoms are manipulated using chemical or physical processes. Nanoparticles are produced through a "bottom-up" or a "top-down" approach. In the "bottom-up" approach, atoms are assembled, sometimes one by one, to form a nanoparticle of the desired size and shape. In the "top-down" approach, a larger-sized, macroscopic (bulk) version of a material is shrunk to nanoparticle size, for example, by squeezing the atoms together very tightly. The properties of a nanoparticle depend on the arrangement of the atoms at its surface. The properties can also depend on the way the atoms are organized to form the interior or "core" of the nanoparticle. The arrangement and orientation of the atoms determine the activity of the nanoparticle, including the way it behaves, interacts, and bonds with other particles or biological molecules. Therefore, scientists can develop nanoparticles that have diverse and sometimes unexpected characteristics. For example, some nanoparticles are incredibly strong but very lightweight. Other nanoparticles are better conductors of electric current than the bulk forms of their material.

Nanoparticles can be designed so that their surface can have different functions compared to their inner core. As a result, the surface can be engineered for greater solubility, or equipped with contrast agents for high-resolution imaging. The surface can also be designed to allow the particle to target and bind to specific cells (for example, cancer cells), while the inner core is equipped with a lethal dosage of medication that, once delivered, will destroy diseased tissue. Nanoparticles may one day play a role in the development of renewable energy sources, new ways to store energy in batteries, or new ways to clean up polluted groundwater.

Potential Risks Associated with Nanoparticles

Subtle changes in the structure or size of nanoparticles can have enormous effects on their properties. This tendency may be an advantage in a controlled environment, such as the activation of nanoparticles in a localized area of the body to destroy cancer cells. In uncontrolled situations, however, such as the exposure of nanoparticles to the environment or biological systems in which the interactions are unknown, the effects of nanoparticles can be unpredictable. Therefore, a greater understanding of their physical and chemical properties is needed.

Nanomaterials may react with the environment and biological systems in different ways during the course of their life cycle (that is, from the time they are developed to their disposal/release into the environment). Therefore, a cautious approach is needed to monitor and assess risk at all stages. Government agencies such as Health Canada are responsible for putting safeguards in place to ensure that the public is not at risk from exposure to nanomaterials. However, if regulations are too strict and inflexible, they could curb new research developments.

Findings of the Expert Panel Report on Nanotechnology

In June 2007, an Expert Panel on Nanotechnology was formed in response to a request from Canada's Minister of Health. The panel was responsible for reporting on the level of knowledge of nanomaterial properties and risks. Panel members made the following key recommendations:

- A classification system should be devised at the same time that international organizations work to establish a standard terminology to distinguish among nanomaterials.
- Create regulatory "triggers" to signal when a nanomaterial or product is reviewed for health and environmental risks.
- Worker safety should be kept in mind by developing a standard approach to safe handling of nanomaterials.
- A method for measuring exposure to nanomaterials should be developed so that the effects on human health, workers, and the environment can be reliably monitored.

Fact Sheet — Benefits and Risks of Nanotechnology in Canada

Uses and Benefits	Concerns, Unknowns, and Hazards
Nanomaterials are incorporated into a vast array of consumer products, including sunscreens, clothing, and sports equipment.	A possibility of unexpected interactions in the environment and biological systems exist, with the potential for harm.
Unique properties of nanomaterials offer the potential for developing new products, therapies, devices, and other applications.	There is a need for greater understanding of the potential risks to human health and the environment.
Nanomaterials and nanoproducts (consumer products employing nanomaterials) may improve the quality of life for humans.	The public is generally uninformed and unaware of the implications of nanotechnology and nanomaterial development.
The nanotechnology industry is growing; in 2010, the federal government contributed $23.4 million to the National Institute of Nanotechnology.	Novel properties of nanoparticles are hard to predict based on larger-sized (bulk) form or atomic and molecular properties.
Nanomaterial properties can potentially be controlled.	Hazard identification is difficult due to limited knowledge of how changes in the environment may affect nanoparticle toxicity.
Uncertainties over risk assessment and management are common with the introduction of new technologies.	There is a lack of understanding of nanoparticle exposure levels and the resulting impact on biological systems.
Knowledge of the properties of nanomaterials is currently limited but is increasing at a fast pace.	Validated and standardized approaches to the measurement of nanoparticles are needed.

Research and Analyze

1. Select one example of a nanoparticle or nanotechnology of your choice that is being studied for use in diagnostic medical imaging, improved drug delivery, or surgical robotics or devices. Conduct research into the risks and benefits of developing this nanomaterial or technology for the treatment of patients.

2. Research the concept of a *life-cycle approach* to risk assessment. Use your findings to decide whether you agree with the recommendations of the Expert Panel on Nanotechnology to adopt an adaptive, life-cycle approach to risk assessment and management of nanomaterials.

3. What responsibility now resides with the government of Canada and affiliated organizations (the Council of Canadian Academies, Health Canada, and Environment Canada) to ensure that the findings of the Expert Panel are communicated to employers and consumers? What role might the Consumers Council of Canada play so that action is taken in response to the Expert Panel report? (The Consumers Council of Canada provided input into the report.) What next steps should Health Canada or Environment Canada take to address the Panel's findings and recommendations? How would you find out what kind of follow-up has taken place in response to this report?

Take Action

4. **PLAN** In a group, discuss the risks and benefits of nanotechnology and the four recommendations made by the Expert Panel. Decide whether Canada should apply the current regulations, or whether a new set of standards are needed for regulating nanomaterials. Share the results of the research and analysis you conducted in questions 1 to 3 above.

5. **ACT** Design a survey that will reveal misconceptions among members of the general public about nanotechnology and nanomaterials, and the implications of this technology for human health and the environment. Begin your survey by presenting an overview of the topic, including definitions, followed by multiple-choice questions that are based on the evidence you have uncovered in your research. Prepare a report based on your findings that could be posted on your school website, shared with your survey respondents, or sent to the Consumers Council of Canada.

Chapter 4 SUMMARY

Section 4.1 Models of Chemical Bonding

The type of bonds that form between atoms depends on the electron configuration of the two atoms. The large number of bond types that can form creates compounds with a wide variety of properties.

Key Terms

allotrope
delocalized
electronegativity
electron-sea model
formula unit
hybrid orbital
molecular orbital theory
network solid
valence bond theory

Key Concepts

- The three types of chemical bonding are ionic bonding, covalent bonding, and metallic bonding.
- Bonds form a continuum from equal sharing to minimal sharing of electrons. Bonds with a ΔEN from 1.7 to 3.3 are mostly ionic; with a ΔEN from 0.4 to 1.7 are polar covalent; with a ΔEN from 0.0 to 0.4 are mostly covalent (or non-polar covalent).
- The electron-sea model visualizes a metal as a fairly ordered array of cations in a "sea" of freely moving electrons, with the positively charged ions all attracted to many of the electrons in the "sea" simultaneously.
- Metals and ionic compounds form crystals, but the structure of the crystals and the bonding between ions are different in ionic compounds, so their properties are different from those of metals.
- Valence bond (VB) theory proposes that a covalent bond forms when the atomic orbitals of two atoms overlap to share a common region in space and a pair of electrons occupies that region of overlap.
- Molecular orbital (MO) theory proposes that when atomic orbitals overlap, they combine to form new orbitals called molecular orbitals, which have new shapes and energy levels and delocalized electrons.
- Hybrid orbitals are formed by the combination of two or more orbitals in the valence shell of an atom.
- In network solids, a large number of atoms are bonded together by a repeating network of covalent bonds.

Section 4.2 Shapes, Intermolecular Forces, and Properties of Molecules

Valence-shell electron-pair repulsion theory allows you to predict the shape of molecules. Together, the shape of the molecule and the polarity of the bonds allow you to predict the polarity of the molecule that is responsible for the type of intermolecular forces that occur between molecules.

Key Terms

bond angle
co-ordinate covalent bond
dipole-dipole force
dipole-induced dipole force
dispersion force
expanded valence
hydrogen bonding
intermolecular force
intramolecular force
ion-dipole force
ion-induced dipole force
resonance structure
valence-shell electron-pair repulsion theory

Key Concepts

- The structures of molecular compounds are much more varied than the structures of ionic compounds, in part because of the nature of covalent bonds.
- Different forces of attraction and repulsion determine the relative positions in space of atoms, bonding pairs of electrons, and lone pair of electrons, resulting in molecules with characteristic three-dimensional shapes. Chemists use different theories and models to predict these three-dimensional shapes.
- In a co-ordinate covalent bond, one atom contributes both electrons to the shared pair of electrons.
- In an expanded valence (expanded octet), a central atom has more than eight valence electrons.
- A resonance structure is a model in which two or more Lewis structures show the same relative position of atoms but different positions of electron pairs.
- VSEPR theory proposes that each of the electron groups around an atom is positioned as far as possible from the others to minimize repulsions. An electron group consists of a single bond, double bond, triple bond, or lone pair. The result is a particular geometric arrangement of the electron groups.
- Electron-group arrangement refers to the ways that groups of valence electrons are positioned around a specific atom. Molecular shape refers to the relative positions of the atomic nuclei in an entire molecule.
- Intermolecular forces are forces of attraction and repulsion that act between molecules and influence the physical properties of solids and liquids.

Chapter 4 REVIEW

Knowledge and Understanding

Select the letter of the best answer below.

1. The underlying reason why atoms ever form bonds at all is
   a. lower energy.
   b. greater stability.
   c. electrostatic forces.
   d. Two of the above are correct.
   e. All are correct.

2. An ionic bond will form between two types of atoms when the ΔEN value is
   a. less than 0.4.
   b. between 0.4 and 1.7.
   c. exactly 1.7.
   d. greater than 1.7.
   e. The value is dependent on the size and number of the atoms forming the bond.

3. In general, the melting points and boiling points of Group 1 metals are lower than Group 2 metals in the same period because
   a. Group 1 metals are smaller than Group 2 metals in the same period.
   b. Group 1 metals are more reactive than Group 2 metals.
   c. there are more valence electrons and a stronger positive charge in Group 2 metals.
   d. Two of the above are correct.
   e. All are correct.

4. Chemical bonding can best be predicted and explained by the properties of
   a. valence electrons.
   b. inner core electrons.
   c. the effective nuclear charge.
   d. the nuclear charge.
   e. the atomic radius.

5. Which of the following statements about electron pairs is false?
   a. They can be bonding or lone pairs of electrons.
   b. They arrange themselves around a central atom through three-dimensional space.
   c. Repulsive forces keep them spread apart.
   d. The repulsive force between all electron pairs is equal.
   e. Only the electron pairs in the valence shell of atoms are involved in bonding.

6. What information cannot be predicted by the Lewis structure of a molecule?
   a. electron arrangement in the valence shell of each atom
   b. molecular shape
   c. which electron pairs are lone pairs and which are bonding pairs
   d. which bonds are single, double, or triple bonds
   e. All of the above information can be predicted by Lewis structures.

7. The structure of metal objects consists of
   a. single large crystals.
   b. randomly arranged atoms.
   c. microscopic crystalline grains.
   d. alternating negatively and positively charged particles.
   e. All of the above are correct.

8. The smallest ratio of sodium ions to chloride ions in solid sodium chloride is called a
   a. unit cell.
   b. molecule.
   c. crystal.
   d. formula unit.
   e. None of the above are correct.

9. Which one of the following is an example of an intermolecular force?
   a. hydrogen bond
   b. covalent bond
   c. ionic bond
   d. metallic bond
   e. None are examples of intermolecular forces.

10. Oxygen gas and nitrogen gas are both non-polar molecules, but can dissolve, sparingly, in water because
    a. water is a universal solvent.
    b. of ion-induced dipole forces.
    c. of dipole-induced dipole forces.
    d. of dispersion forces.
    e. of the ability of every substance to dissolve in any solvent, however sparingly.

11. Which of the following is not a property of ionic compounds?
    a. conducts electric current in solution
    b. ductile
    c. brittle
    d. does not conduct electric current as a solid
    e. none of the above

Chapter 4 REVIEW

12. The ΔEN value between elements in a bond is 0.3. This makes the type of bond
    a. ionic.
    b. polar covalent.
    c. mostly covalent.
    d. metallic.
    e. mostly ionic.

13. Which type of hybrid orbitals is likely to exist for the sulfur atom in the bonds for the molecule sulfur hexafluoride, SF_6?
    a. sp^3d^2
    b. sp^3d
    c. sp^3
    d. sp^2
    e. sp

14. Which of the following statements about water molecules is false?
    a. One oxygen atom in a water molecule can bond with as many as six hydrogen atoms in other water molecules at the same time.
    b. Hydrogen bonds in solid water (ice) are longer than they are in liquid water.
    c. Water molecules are permanent dipoles.
    d. Hydrogen bonds are responsible for many unique properties of water.
    e. Hydrogen bonds in water are as strong as covalent bonds.

Answer the questions below.

15. Atoms of which combinations of elements tend to form ionic bonds? Why?

16. Atoms of which types of elements tend to form covalent bonds? Why?

17. Explain the process of hardening of a metal and why it works.

18. Electrons are said to be "delocalized" in metallic bonds.
    a. In your own words, describe what this means, and how it is different from the locations of valence electrons in ionic and covalent bonds.
    b. How does the "delocalization" of electrons in metallic solids explain "malleability," the property unique to all metals?

19. Explain why ionic solids are brittle.

20. Explain how single bonds form, based on quantum mechanical concepts.

21. What experimentally observed property of methane makes it necessary to invoke the concept of hybridization to explain the structure of methane?

22. List the five possible shapes of hybrid orbitals.

23. Describe two ways in which a non-polar molecule can temporarily become a dipole.

24. Explain why symmetrical molecules are non-polar and asymmetrical molecules can be polar.

25. If the polarity of the molecules of a substance is known, what other properties of that substance can also be known? List at least four properties.

26. List two properties of metallic and ionic (non-metal) solids that are
    a. the same.
    b. different.

27. List two properties of ionic solids and polar molecular solids that are
    a. the same.
    b. different.

28. Explain why a molecule such as boron trifluoride, BF_3, has no dipole, but a molecule such as water, H_2O, is polar, even though they are both symmetrical molecules.

Thinking and Investigation

29. The melting point of rubidium chloride is 718°C and its solubility in water is 91 g/100 mL. The melting point of rubidium bromide is 693°C and that for rubidium iodide is 646°C. Would you predict their solubility in water to increase or decrease as the melting point decreases? Why?

30. Use the periodic table to help you draw the orbital diagram (for the valence shell only) for the following elements and their most likely ions (if there is one):
    a. calcium
    b. nitrogen
    c. aluminum
    d. neon
    e. beryllium

31. Earlier in this chapter, ozone is pictured as a resonance structure as shown below:

    $$\ddot{\text{O}}=\ddot{\text{O}}-\ddot{\text{O}}: \longleftrightarrow :\ddot{\text{O}}-\ddot{\text{O}}=\ddot{\text{O}}$$

    a. Analyze the Lewis structures and apply VSEPR theory to predict the electron group arrangement and the molecular shape of the ozone molecule. Use Lewis resonance structures to roughly sketch the structure.
    b. Experimental evidence shows that the bond angle in the molecule is 116.8°. With this fact in mind, how likely is your answer to part (a) to represent the actual molecular structure?

32. Predict which bond in the following groups is the most ionic in character. Calculate ΔEN for each to check your predictions.
    a. H–Cl, H–Br, H–F
    b. Na–O, Li–O, K–O

33. Classify the following bonds as mostly ionic, polar covalent, or mostly covalent by looking at the location of the elements on the periodic table. Check your classifications by calculating ΔEN for each.
    a. Li–Cl
    b. S–S
    c. C–N
    d. Na–O

34. Use the periodic table to help you write the condensed electron configuration for the following elements and their most likely ion (if there is one):
    a. lithium
    b. argon
    c. chlorine
    d. phosphorus

35. Use VSEPR theory to identify the electron group arrangement (VSEPR shape), the molecular shape, and the bond angle of the following molecules whose central atoms have
    a. 4 bonding pairs and 1 lone pair.
    b. 6 bonding pairs and 0 lone pairs.
    c. 3 bonding pairs and 2 lone pairs.
    d. 3 bonding pairs and 0 lone pairs.
    e. 2 bonding pairs and 2 lone pairs.
    f. 4 bonding pairs and 2 lone pairs.

36. Determine whether each of the following compounds will be polar or non-polar.
    a. CO_2
    b. H_2S
    c. SiO_2
    d. PCl_3

37. In a lab, two liquids of 200 mL each are mixed together in a container. The resulting volume is 390 mL, even though none of the two liquids were spilled in the process. What must have happened for this to have occurred?

38. Describe an investigation that can be used to determine if an unknown liquid is polar or non-polar. Include the conclusions of this investigation that would allow you to determine the liquid to be polar or non-polar.

39. In Lewis structures, co-ordinate covalent bonds look the same as regular covalent bonds. How are they different from a regular covalent bond?

40. In the 1950s, the reaction of hydrazine, N_2H_4, with chlorine trifluoride, ClF_3, was used as a rocket fuel.
    a. Draw the Lewis structures for hydrazine and chlorine trifluoride.
    b. Identify the hybrid orbitals used in each one.
    c. Identify the molecular shape and polarity of chlorine trifluoride.

41. Perform an Internet search on the Mohs Hardness Scale for metals. Write a brief report on your findings and include some Mohs scale values for various metals.

42. Use VSEPR theory and Lewis structures to predict the number of bonding pairs and lone pairs around the central atom so that you can identify the VSEPR shape, molecular shape, and bond angle for the following molecules and ions:
    a. XeF_2
    b. BCl_4^-
    c. SF_5^+

43. Which compound in each of the following pairs has the higher boiling point? Explain your choice in each case.
    a. NH_3 or PH_3
    b. C_2H_6 or C_4H_{10}
    c. $SeCl_4$ or $SiCl_4$

44. For each of the following elements or compounds, predict which would have the higher boiling point and explain how you made your choice.
    a. O_2 or N_2
    b. ethanol (CH_3CH_2OH) or methoxymethane (CH_3OCH_3)
    c. heptane or 2,4-dimethyl pentane

Communication

45. Draw Lewis structures for the following compounds. (A resonance diagram might be required). In each case, count the number of lone pairs and bonding pairs.
    a. SbH_3
    b. $CFCl_3$
    c. HCN
    d. C_2H_2
    e. BeF_2

46. Create a list of standard tests that can be used to test and classify solids. For example, a lustrous, grey substance can conduct electricity in the solid state. Organize these tests in a flowchart and include directions that a classmate could use as a guide for carrying out the tests. Be sure that the order of the tests will minimize the amount of work necessary to draw a conclusion.

47. The structure of a glycerol molecule is shown here.

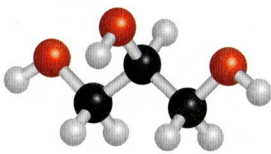

   a. Draw the Lewis structure for glycerol.
   b. Draw 3 to 4 Lewis structures for glycerol so that as many hydrogen bonds can form between the molecules as possible.

Chapter 4 REVIEW

48. A semiochemical is a molecule that delivers a specific message between individuals of the same or different species of plants or animals. Pheromones are the most well known of these chemicals. Research pheromones and prepare a brief report on your findings. Include a reference to the structure of the chemicals in your report.

49. The rules for drawing Lewis structures for simple molecules were based on molecules having a central atom. Many molecules do not have a central atom but are often written in a way that gives you clues about their structures. In some cases, symmetry allows you to draw half of the molecule and then put the two halves together. In other cases, the formulas are written in a way that reveals the grouping of atoms. You can isolate the groups, draw their structures, and then attach the groups. Draw Lewis structures for the following compounds by applying these concepts.
    a. NH_2CH_2COOH
    b. CH_3CH_2COOH
    c. CH_3CHF_2
    d. $(NH_2)_2CO$

50. **BIG IDEAS** The nature of the attractive forces that exist between particles in a substance determines the properties and limits the uses of that substance. Water alone cannot be used to remove greasy stains from fabrics or dishes. Detergents are made up of long molecules that have a water-soluble end (hydrophilic head) and a non-polar hydrocarbon (hydrophobic tail). The hydrophobic tails of the detergent molecules are attracted to the greasy stain and surround it, while the hydrophilic heads stick out, far away from the grease. The heads in turn are attracted to water and can mix with it. Therefore, water with detergent added can remove greasy stains. Draw a series of 2 to 3 simple diagrams to represent this process. Use a straight line with a small ball at the end to represent a detergent molecule.

51. Develop a flowchart or similar graphic organizer that can be used to create a Lewis structure for a molecule or polyatomic ion.

52. Make a series of sketches to show what happens when a positively charged ion approaches a neutral molecule. Explain the meaning of the sketches. For the neutral molecule, use a sphere with evenly distributed positive and negative charges.

53. A dry mixture contains the following solids, all very small (<1 mm diameter): shiny, light-grey nickel balls; shiny, colourless glass beads; wax shavings; and table salt. Draw a flowchart to show how you would separate the mixture into its four separate components. Use your knowledge of the properties of each type of solid to guide you. Your separated fractions should be dry at the end. On your flowchart, add a label to each solid to indicate the class to which each compound belongs.

54. Summarize your learning in this chapter using a graphic organizer. To help you, the Chapter 4 Summary lists the Key Terms and Key Concepts. Refer to Using Graphic Organizers in Appendix A to help you decide which graphic organizer to use.

Application

55. A photoelectric cell can be used as a "switch" to activate mechanical devices. Also known as an "electric eye" in this application, a photoelectric cell is an evacuated tube covered on one side with cesium metal. When light strikes the coating, electrons are ejected from the atoms and create an electric current. In the absence of light, the electric current is zero.
    a. Why do you think cesium is an effective metal to use in this application?
    b. Which other metals might be effective? Why?

56. Ethane-1,2-diol (common name: ethylene glycol), shown below, is commonly used as antifreeze in automobiles.

    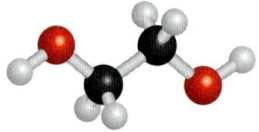

    a. Draw the Lewis structure for ethane-1,2-diol.
    b. Based on its structure, would you expect it to have a lower or higher boiling point than water? Explain your reasoning.
    c. Based on its structure, would you expect it to be able to dissolve in water? Explain your answer.
    d. How do the structural properties of ethane-1,2-diol prevent water from freezing?

57. Answer the following questions about the element antimony.
    a. Write the condensed electron configuration for antimony, Sb.
    b. Antimony can have a valence of −3, +3, or +5. Use condensed electron configurations to show how each of these valences must form. In each case, explain why that change makes sense.
    c. Antimony is a metalloid. Defend this claim using your answers to part (b) of this question.

58. Chemiluminescence is the ability of chemicals to emit light energy during a chemical reaction. Luminol, shown here, is a chemiluminescent molecular compound that is used at crime scenes to detect trace amounts of blood. When the compound luminol reacts with an oxidizing agent, such as the iron in blood hemoglobin, it emits a characteristic blue glow.

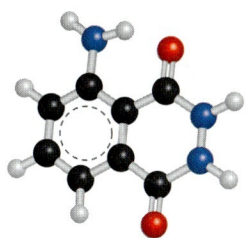

   a. Draw the Lewis structure for luminol.
   b. Luminol is usually applied as a spray onto a crime scene. Research luminol's polarity and discover what type of solvent would be required for dissolving luminol completely.
   c. Continue your research of luminol to discover what the drawbacks are to using such a versatile and sensitive compound at a crime scene. Make a list of some of these drawbacks.

59. Benzene, $C_6H_6(\ell)$, is a clear, colourless, and flammable liquid with a pleasant smell. It is now known to be a potent carcinogen. Before its carcinogenic properties were known, it was used for many applications that exposed it to the general public, such as for decaffeinating coffee, in high-school experiments, and even as an aftershave lotion. Today, it remains an important industrial chemical, but safety regulations govern its use.

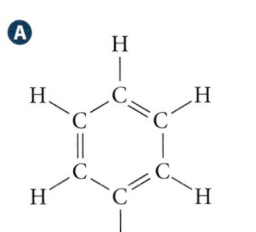 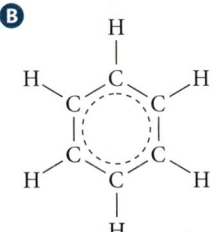

   a. A benzene ring, C_6H_6, has two resonance structures. One of them is shown here, labelled "A." Draw the other resonance structure.
   b. Chemists sometimes draw benzene as shown in the image labelled "B." What does the circular dashed line represent? How does this representation compare with the use of resonance structures? Which form do you think best portrays the structure of benzene?

60. Complete the chart for the following molecules:

Compound	Hybridization Notes	Hybrid Orbital Required	Bonding Groups	Lone Pairs	Electron Group Arrangement	Molecular Shape	Bond Angle	Polarity
SnF_2								
NH_3								
PF_5								
SF_6								

61. A lab technician pours sand into a container of marbles to help students visualize interstitial alloys. Explain why this demonstration is a good model for this type of alloy.

62. Molecules of the compound iodine heptafluoride, IF_7, have an unusual shape that is not listed in **Figure 4.31**. The shape is called pentagonal bipyramidal.
   a. Draw a Lewis structure for IF_7.
   b. Make a sketch to show what you think the molecule looks like. Include bond angles and explain your reasoning.

63. A unique black nail lacquer product forms cracks as it dries when it is applied overtop a layer of nail enamel that has already dried. The effect is stunning: the colour from the undercoat shows through the cracks of the black top coat. The cracks start to form when the top coat is close to being completely dried. Use your knowledge of solids and their properties to analyze the observations and inferences of this process, and form a possible explanation for how this product works.

64. A metal alloy is a solution of metals. Different metals can combine relatively easily with one another to form a homogeneous solid solution because of the nature of metallic bonds. Metal alloys often have a significantly different set of properties than the metals they contain. For example, gold is very soft and would wear away quickly over time. Ten carat gold, often used in jewellery, contains a mixture of gold (42%), silver (12% to 20%), and copper (38% to 46%) to make it more durable over time.
   a. In addition to preventing steel from rusting, the addition of nickel to steel has allowed the technology of wind turbines to be more viable in northern climates. Visit The Nickel Institute website to find out how.
   b. Cast iron is an alloy of iron that contains 3% to 4% carbon. Research how the properties of cast iron differ from those of pure iron.

Chapter 4 SELF-ASSESSMENT

Select the letter of the best answer below.

1. **K/U** If an ionic compound has small ions, then it will likely have
   a. a low melting point and low solubility.
   b. a high melting point and high solubility.
   c. a low melting point and high solubility.
   d. a high melting point and low solubility.
   e. There is not enough information provided to answer correctly.

2. **K/U** The difference between a mostly covalent bond and a polar covalent bond is that
   a. a polar covalent bond has a north and a south pole.
   b. the electron bond pair of a covalent bond is shared more or less equally.
   c. a polar covalent bond exists when the ΔEN is greater than 1.7 but less than 3.3.
   d. Two of the above are correct.
   e. All are correct.

3. **K/U** Helium behaves like a noble gas because
   a. its valence shell is completely filled.
   b. its outermost orbital is completely filled.
   c. its outermost energy level is completely filled.
   d. Two of the above are correct.
   e. All are correct.

For Questions 4 to 6, choose from the following electron group arrangements:

a. linear
b. trigonal planar
c. tetrahedral
d. trigonal bipyramidal
e. octahedral

4. **K/U** 4 bonding pairs, 2 lone pairs
5. **K/U** 120° bond angles
6. **K/U** $ClBr_2^-(g)$

7. **K/U** Which of the following bonds is the most polar?
   a. C–O
   b. Si–O
   c. C–Cl
   d. C–Br
   e. C–C

8. **T/I** Which of the following compounds does not have a bent molecular shape?
   a. $CO_2(g)$
   b. $H_2S(g)$
   c. $H_2O(\ell)$
   d. $SeH_2(g)$
   e. $XeCl_2(s)$

9. **K/U** Which type of hybridization is most likely to have occurred for the central atom in phosphorus pentachloride, $PCl_5(s)$?
   a. sp^3d^2
   b. sp^3d
   c. sp^3
   d. sp^2
   e. sp

10. **T/I** Which of the following compounds is non-polar?
    a. $H_2S(g)$
    b. $BrCl_3(\ell)$
    c. $SiH_3Cl(s)$
    d. $AsH_3(g)$
    e. $CCl_4(g)$

Use sentences and diagrams as appropriate to answer the questions below.

11. **T/I** Which compounds are not likely to occur (there can be more than one answer): $CaKr$, Na_2S, $BaCl_3$, MgF_2, PCl_5, NCl_5? Explain your choices.

12. **A** An unknown compound is a white solid at room temperature. It dissolves in water and is able to conduct an electric current in solution.
    a. Is this compound likely to contain ionic or covalent bonds? Explain your answer.
    b. Think of one common household substance that fits the description of the unknown compound.

13. **C** Use orbital diagrams to show how carbon and chlorine would bond. Write the chemical formula for the compound that forms.

258 MHR • Unit 2 Structure and Properties of Matter

14. **T/I** Which compound in each of the following pairs would have the higher melting point?
    a. CaO(s) or KI(s)
    b. KCl(s) or KBr(s)
    c. RbCl(s) or SrCl(s)

15. **T/I** Classify the following bonds as mostly ionic, polar covalent, or mostly covalent by calculating the difference in their electronegativity values.
    a. Mg–Cl
    b. Na–F
    c. Al–I
    d. O–O

16. **K/U** Briefly explain the term *co-ordinate covalent bond* and give an example to help illustrate your explanation. Include a diagram of your example.

17. **T/I** Determine which of the following molecules would be expected to dissolve in water. Explain your answers.
    a. ClF(g)
    b. NCl$_3$(ℓ)
    c. CH$_3$Cl(g)
    d. BF$_3$(g)
    e. CS$_2$(ℓ)

18. **T/I** Oxygen can form compounds with every Period 3 element except argon. Determine which would be ionic or covalent compounds, and draw Lewis diagrams to represent each one.

19. **K/U** Define *electronegativity, electron density,* and *bond dipole*.

20. **T/I** Use the terms in question 19 to describe a polar covalent bond that forms between hydrogen and chlorine.

21. **T/I** Use VSEPR theory to predict the shape of the following molecules and polyatomic ions:
    a. NF$_3$
    b. SO$_3$
    c. I$_3^-$
    d. SCl$_5$F

22. **T/I** Which molecules in question 21 would have a dipole? Explain your answer.

23. **A** Explain why C$_{20}$H$_{40}$ is a solid at room temperature, whereas C$_2$H$_4$ is a gas.

24. **A** Use your knowledge of the properties of compounds to predict the results of these two investigations.
    a. At $t = 0$ min, two clear and colourless liquids were combined in a beaker at room temperature. After 30 min, there were two distinct phases in the beaker: a clear, colourless liquid at the top and a white solid at the bottom. Explain what types of substances were likely inside each liquid at $t = 0$ min, and what information led you to that conclusion.
    b. At $t = 0$ min, two clear and colourless liquids were combined in a beaker at room temperature. After 30 min, there were two distinct phases in the beaker: each a clear and colourless liquid. Explain what types of substances were likely inside each liquid at $t = 0$ min.

25. **A** Diamond-encrusted sawblades are used to cut through very hard materials, because diamond is one of the hardest materials known. What is used to cut diamonds? Research your answer by asking a gemologist or a tool manufacturer.

Self-Check

If you missed question …	1	2	3	4	5	6	7	8	9	10	11	12	13	14	15	16	17	18	19	20	21	22	23	24	25
Review section(s)…	4.1	4.1	4.1	4.2	4.2	4.2	4.1	4.2	4.2	4.1	4.1	4.1	4.2	4.1	4.1	4.2	4.1	4.1	4.1	4.1	4.2	4.2	4.2	4.2	4.1

Unit 2 Project

Conduct an Inquiry

Comparing the Chemical Structure and Properties of a Specialized Material

In 1938, Dr. Roy Plunkett inadvertently created a compound that would one day result in the American chemist's induction into the Plastics Hall of Fame in Leominster, Massachusetts. While he was developing a new chlorofluorocarbon refrigerant, the tetrafluoroethylene he was working with spontaneously polymerized into a waxy solid. Dr. Plunkett had just synthesized polytetrafluoroethylene, the most slippery material ever created! Found in everything from cookware to space vehicles, polytetrafluoroethylene is better known by its brand name, Teflon®. Teflon® is a fluorocarbon, a compound made solely of carbon and fluorine. Its unique properties are related to its chemical structure. For instance, the high electronegativity of fluorine in the carbon-fluorine bond reduces dispersion forces to a negligible value, resulting in an extremely slippery polymer that makes an excellent lubricant. These bonds are also very strong, making Teflon® extremely non-reactive. As such, the material can be used to store or transport reactive materials.

In this project, you will assume the role of a summer student working for a chemical company that has just patented a new material. As part of your job, you must create a presentation that will introduce the company's financial investors to the concept of specialized materials such as Teflon®. Your presentation will help them understand the relationship between chemical structure (including any forces that act within the structure, and, for molecular compounds, any intermolecular forces) and the unique properties of specialized materials. To complete this presentation, you will research the relationship between the chemical structure and the properties of a specialized material of your choice. You will depict this material using drawings and a three-dimensional model. Additionally, you will assess the life cycle of the material and evaluate its impacts on society and the environment, noting any new research or possible future applications.

How does chemical structure relate to the properties of a specialized material and what are some impacts of this material on society and the environment?

Besides its many applications on Earth, Teflon® plays an important role in the space program. For instance, it is a component of the protective covering on the Mobile Servicing System (MSS), a robotic system that assists in the maintenance and repair of the International Space Station. The MSS, which includes the Canadarm shown here, was designed and built in Canada.

Initiate and Plan

1. Conduct a research overview of several specialized materials. These may also be suggested by your teacher. Choose one material that interests you to research in greater depth.

Perform and Record

2. Conduct preliminary research on your chosen material to gain an understanding of its unique properties, as well as information about its discovery.

3. Research the life cycle of your material, from production through applications to final degradation. Consider the following questions:

   • What applications does the material have? Consider its use in fields such as industry, science, and medicine. In what ways has the material benefited society?

- What effects does the material have on the environment throughout its life cycle? In what ways, if any, does the material's life cycle reflect the principles outlined in "Green Chemistry" and "Green Engineering" in Appendix A?
- What human health risks, if any, are associated with the material throughout its life cycle?
- What research advances are currently taking place in relation to the material, focussing on Canadian research?
- What possible applications of your material might arise in the future?

4. Refer to the quantum mechanical model of the atom to answer the questions that follow.

   a. Describe the electrons of the atoms of each element in your material. Include the quantum numbers for each electron, and the electron configuration and orbital diagram for each atom. You may wish to record your description in a table such as Table 3.4 Descriptions of Electrons in Lithium in section 3.3.

   b. Describe the following atomic properties for the atoms of each element in your material.
      i. atomic radius
      ii. ionization energy
      iii. reactivity
      iv. electron affinity
      v. electronegativity

5. Use what you learned in this unit, as well as information from other print and Internet resources, to describe the chemical structure of the material you have chosen.

6. Explain how any of the items you researched in Perform and Record steps 4 and 5 are related to the properties of your material.

7. Create drawings to depict the three-dimensional chemical structure of your material. Then use these drawings as a blueprint to make a three-dimensional model depicting the chemical structure of the material. If the material is molecular, use VSEPR theory to predict the shape of the molecules and their polarity.

Analyze and Interpret

1. Use appropriate graphic organizers to organize your research findings. "Using Graphic Organizers" in Appendix A may help you select suitable formats.

2. Compare the environmental and health impacts of your material with its societal benefits. Based on your comparison, do you conclude that your material has had a more positive or negative effect on society overall? Explain your reasoning.

3. Offer a recommendation about what you perceive to be the most promising new application or research direction for your material. Explain your reasoning, using your research findings to support your viewpoint. Discuss any obstacles that may stand in the way of this new application or research direction.

Communicate Your Findings

4. Choose an appropriate format to present your research, keeping your audience in mind. For instance, you may choose to create a video, a computer presentation, or a written report. Decide on the most effective way to integrate your model into your presentation.

5. If you display your model in the classroom, write a paragraph that explains the features of the model to someone observing it for the first time.

Assessment Criteria

Once you complete your project, ask yourself these questions. Did you…

- ☑ **K/U** research the unique properties and information related to the discovery of your chosen specialized material?
- ☑ **K/U** research the life cycle of the material?
- ☑ **T/I** assess your information sources for accuracy, reliability, and bias?
- ☑ **T/I** explain the relationship between the chemical properties and the structure of the material?
- ☑ **A** evaluate the environmental and societal impacts of the material?
- ☑ **A** make recommendations related to the most promising application or research direction of the material?
- ☑ **C** depict the three-dimensional structure of your material using drawings and a model?

UNIT 2 SUMMARY

BIG IDEAS

- The nature of the attractive forces that exist between particles in a substance determines the properties and limits the uses of that substance.
- Technological devices that are based on the principles of atomic and molecular structures can have societal benefits and costs.

Overall Expectations

In this unit, you learned how to…

- **assess** the benefits to society and **evaluate** the environmental impacts of products and technologies that apply principles related to the structure and properties of matter
- **investigate** the molecular shapes and physical properties of various types of matter
- **demonstrate** an understanding of atomic structure and chemical bonding, and how they relate to the physical properties of ionic, molecular, covalent network, and metallic substances

Chapter 3 Atomic Models and Properties of Atoms

Key ideas

- Historically, the development of and modifications to the atomic model have been the result of experimental evidence and new ideas about the nature of matter and energy.
- Thomson's discovery of the electron disproved Dalton's model of the atom as a solid, indivisible sphere. Instead, Thomson proposed that the atom existed as a positively charged sphere, with enough negatively charged electrons embedded in it to balance the overall charge on the atom.
- Observations and inferences made by Rutherford led to a nuclear model of the hydrogen atom. This model is still the most commonly depicted, with negatively charged electrons orbiting a central positively charged nucleus.
- Bohr's model of the atom refined the Rutherford model, incorporating the concept that, like light, electrons in atoms could have only certain amounts of energy and, therefore, could exist in only specific orbits around the nucleus. Each allowed orbit had a specific amount of energy and a specific radius.
- According to the quantum mechanical model of the atom, electrons have both matter-like and wave-like properties.
- The position and momentum of atoms cannot both be determined with certainty, so the position is described in terms of probabilities.

- An orbital represents a mathematical description of the region of space in which an electron has a probability of being found.

- The first three quantum numbers describe the size, energy, shape, and orientation of an orbital. The fourth quantum number describes the orientation of the axis around which the electron is spinning.
- For hydrogen, the relative energies of the atomic orbitals depend only on the principal quantum number, n. For many-electron atoms, other factors, such as the orbital-shape quantum number, l, influence the relative energies of atomic orbitals.
- Electron configuration notation and orbital diagrams are two methods commonly used to represent or describe the distribution of electrons in atoms.
- Applying the Pauli exclusion principle, Hund's rule, and the aufbau principle, the electron configuration of atoms can be built up according to the position of the element in the periodic table.
- The modern, quantum mechanical model of the atom enables us to understand the elements, their positions in the periodic table, and their chemical and physical properties based on their electron configuration.

UNIT 2 SUMMARY & REVIEW

Chapter 4: Chemical Bonding and Properties of Matter

Key ideas

- The three types of chemical bonding are ionic bonding, covalent bonding, and metallic bonding.
- Bonds form a continuum from equal sharing to minimal sharing of electrons. Bonds with a ΔEN from 1.7 to 3.3 are mostly ionic; with a ΔEN from 0.4 to 1.7 are polar covalent; and with a ΔEN from 0.0 to 0.4 are mostly covalent (or non-polar covalent).
- The electron-sea model visualizes a metal as a fairly ordered array of cations in a "sea" of freely moving electrons, with the positively charged ions all attracted to many of the electrons in the "sea" simultaneously.
- Metals and ionic compounds form crystals, but the structure of the crystals and the bonding between ions are different in ionic compounds, so their properties are different from those of metals.
- Valence bond (VB) theory proposes that a covalent bond forms when the atomic orbitals of two atoms overlap to share a common region in space, and a pair of electrons occupies that region of overlap.
- Molecular orbital (MO) theory proposes that when atomic orbitals overlap, they combine to form new orbitals called molecular orbitals, which have new shapes and energy levels and delocalized electrons.
- Hybrid orbitals are formed by the combination of two or more orbitals in the valence shell of an atom.
- In network solids, a large number of atoms are bonded together by a repeating network of covalent bonds.
- The structures of molecular compounds are much more varied than the structures of ionic compounds, in part because of the nature of covalent bonds.

- Different forces of attraction and repulsion determine the relative positions in space of atoms, bonding pairs of electrons, and lone pair of electrons, resulting in molecules with characteristic three-dimensional shapes. Chemists use different theories and models to predict these three-dimensional shapes.
- In a co-ordinate covalent bond, one atom contributes both electrons to the shared pair of electrons.
- In an expanded valence (expanded octet), a central atom has more than eight valence electrons.
- A resonance structure is a model in which two or more Lewis structures show the same relative position of atoms but different positions of electron pairs.
- VSEPR theory proposes that each electron group around an atom is positioned as far as possible from the others to minimize repulsions. An electron group consists of a single bond, double bond, triple bond, or lone pair. The result is a particular geometric arrangement of the electron groups.
- Electron-group arrangement refers to the way in which groups of valence electrons are positioned around a specific atom. Molecular shape refers to the relative positions of the atomic nuclei in an entire molecule.
- Intermolecular forces are forces of attraction and repulsion that act between molecules and influence the physical properties of solids and liquids.

Knowledge and Understanding

Select the letter of the best answer below.

1. Which of the following statements about electromagnetic radiation is false?
   a. All forms of electromagnetic radiation travel at a speed of 3×10^8 m/s in a vacuum.
   b. Radio waves and microwaves are found in the high-frequency region of the electromagnetic spectrum.
   c. The frequency and the wavelength of all forms of electromagnetic waves are inversely proportional to each other.
   d. The amplitude of an electromagnetic wave is related to the brightness or intensity of the wave.
   e. The energy of a photon of electromagnetic radiation is directly proportional to the frequency.

2. Which sets of quantum numbers describe electrons in the same energy sublevel?

	n	l	m_l	m_s
i.	2	1	0	$-\frac{1}{2}$
ii.	2	1	-1	$+\frac{1}{2}$
iii.	3	1	-1	$+\frac{1}{2}$
iv.	2	2	-1	$+\frac{1}{2}$
v.	3	2	-1	$-\frac{1}{2}$

   a. i, ii
   b. iii, v
   c. ii, iv
   d. ii, iii
   e. iv, v

3. Which of the following represents the orbital-shape quantum number?
   a. n
   b. m_l
   c. p
   d. l
   e. m_s

UNIT 2 REVIEW

4. Which of the following values can the magnetic quantum number have?
   a. from 0 to n
   b. $+\frac{1}{2}$ or $-\frac{1}{2}$
   c. from 0 to $n-1$
   d. from $-n$ to $+n$
   e. from $-l$ to $+l$

5. Which quantities have similar patterns of increase or decrease across and down the periodic table?
   i. atomic number
   ii. atomic radius
   iii. first ionization energy
   iv. electron affinity
   v. electronegativity

   a. i and ii
   b. i, iii, and iv
   c. i and v
   d. iii and iv
   e. iii, iv, and v

6. Which of the following is not a property of metals?
   a. low melting point
   b. conducts electric current
   c. ductile
   d. hard
   e. malleable

7. The molecule BF_3 is best represented as
   a. an incomplete octet.
   b. a resonance structure.
   c. an ionic compound.
   d. an expanded valence.
   e. None of the above are correct.

8. VSEPR theory allows you to predict
   a. the polarity of a simple molecule.
   b. whether a compound is ionic or molecular.
   c. the shape of a molecule around a central atom.
   d. the Lewis structure.
   e. the two-dimensional structure of a molecule.

For questions 9 to 15, choose from the answers below:
   a. ionic solid
   b. covalent network solid
   c. metallic solid
   d. molecular solid (polar molecules)
   e. molecular solid (non-polar molecules)

9. The solid is composed of positive ions sharing electrons with neighbouring positive ions.

10. All of the particles in the solid are bonded together covalently.

11. Only dispersion forces of attraction exist between the particles in this solid.

12. The melting points are usually very low.

13. The solid is a good conductor only when melted.

14. The solid is extremely hard, not malleable, and a poor conductor of electric current.

15. The solid is often soluble in water but does not conduct electric current in solution.

Answer the questions below.

16. How is the Rutherford model of the atom similar to the Thomson model of the atom? In what ways are these two models different?

17. Although Bohr's model was unable to explain some of the characteristics of atoms, it marked a shift in the importance of understanding the inner workings of the atom to other areas of chemistry and physics.
    a. What observations about atoms was Bohr's model able to explain?
    b. How did Bohr's model solve the problem created by the theory of electromagnetic radiation that an orbiting electron should emit radiation and spiral into the nucleus?
    c. What observations was the Bohr model not able to explain?

18. Explain why the atomic radii decrease across a period even though the atomic number increases?

19. Outline the steps to follow when filling orbitals to determine the electron configuration of an atom. Include the names of the principles involved in the process.

20. Answer the following with respect to electromagnetic radiation.
    a. List two types that have a higher frequency than visible light.
    b. Which colour in the visible spectrum is closest to the types that you listed in part (a)?
    c. List two types that have a lower frequency than visible light.
    d. What property of electromagnetic waves is common to all types?
    e. Which colour has a longer wavelength: red or blue?

21. Use the terms *electronegativity* and *continuum* to classify chemical bonds as mostly covalent, polar covalent, and mostly ionic.

22. What information about an electron inside an atom does the second quantum number, l, provide?

23. List at least three of the four postulates on which Bohr based his model of the atom.

24. What is meant by the tempering of steel and how is it done?

25. Identify the physical or chemical properties that can be explained by the following characteristics of bonding:
    a. delocalization of electrons in metallic bonds
    b. formation of cations and anions in ionic bonding
    c. covalent bonding throughout a solid, such as diamond

26. What properties of an ionic compound determine whether it is soluble in water?

27. What electrostatic forces are acting in a covalent bond?

28. Use VSEPR theory to identify the electron group arrangement (VSEPR shape), the molecular shape, and the bond angle of the following molecules whose central atoms have
    a. 5 bonding pairs and 1 lone pair.
    b. 4 bonding pairs and 1 lone pair.
    c. 2 bonding pairs and 3 lone pairs.
    d. 3 bonding pairs and 1 lone pair.
    e. 4 bonding pairs and 2 lone pairs.
    f. 4 bonding pairs and 0 lone pairs.

29. What evidence indicates that attractive forces exist among non-polar molecules?

30. What did each of the following Canadian scientists contribute to the better understanding of the structure and properties of matter?
    a. Richard F.W. Bader of McMaster University
    b. Robert J. LeRoy of the University of Waterloo
    c. Ronald J. Gillespie of McMaster University

Thinking and Investigation

31. Use the periodic table to help you write the condensed electron configuration for the following elements and their most likely ion (if there is one):
    a. boron
    b. magnesium
    c. sulfur
    d. potassium
    e. hydrogen

32. Using a periodic table, compare nitrogen and fluorine on the various properties given and choose
    (a) if nitrogen has the larger (or more positive) value.
    (b) if fluorine has the larger (or more positive) value.
    (c) if they have the same value.
    i. first quantum number, n, of the outermost electron
    ii. atomic size
    iii. first ionization energy
    iv. second quantum number, l, of the outermost electron
    v. electronegativity

33. Which elements are represented by the following electron configurations?
    a. $1s^2 2s^2 2p^1$
    b. $1s^2 2s^2 2p^5$
    c. $1s^2 2s^2 2p^6 3s^2 3p^6 3d^5 4s^2$
    d. $1s^2 2s^2 2p^6 3s^2 3p^6 4s^2$
    e. $1s^1$
    f. $1s^2 2s^2 2p^6 3s^2 3p^6$

34. Use a basic periodic table that does not contain electron configurations to determine which element is defined by $[\text{He}]2s^2 2p^2$.

35. Use a basic periodic table that does not contain electron configurations to determine which element is defined by $[\text{Kr}]5s^2 4d^{10} 5p^5$.

36. Consider the pattern of the periodic table.
    a. Find out which group element 119 would be in.
    b. Predict the following information about element 119:
        i. condensed electron configuration
        ii. set of quantum numbers for the last electron to be added to it
        iii. physical state at room temperature
        iv. chemical property

Use the table below to answer questions 37 through 40:

Compound	Melting Point (°C)	Solubility in Water (g/g H$_2$O, 25°C)
NaF	988	0.042
NaCl	801	0.357
NaBr	755	1.16
NaI	651	1.84

37. Explain why it makes sense that the melting point decreases from NaF to NaI.

38. Explain why it makes sense that the solubility increases from NaF to NaI.

39. Cesium fluoride has a melting point of 682°C and a solubility of 3.67 g/g H$_2$O at 25°C. Explain why it makes sense that these values differ from the corresponding values for NaF.

40. Use VSEPR theory to predict the molecular shape for $C_2H_2Cl_2(\ell)$ and draw a three-dimensional diagram for the compound. Indicate the polarity of the bonds on your diagram. Based on your sketch, is the molecule polar or non-polar? In reality, this molecule may be either polar or non-polar. Draw an additional diagram to illustrate this point.

UNIT 2 REVIEW

41. Use the periodic table to help you draw the orbital diagram (for the valence shell only) for the elements listed below, as well as their most likely ions (if there is one).
   a. boron
   b. magnesium
   c. sulfur
   d. potassium
   e. hydrogen

42. Which elements in the second period of the periodic table have paired electrons in their valence shell, according to
   a. their Lewis dot diagrams?
   b. the aufbau principle?

43. Classify the following bonds as mostly ionic, polar covalent, or mostly covalent (non-polar covalent) by looking at the location of the elements on the periodic table. Check your classifications by calculating ΔEN for each pair.
   a. Mg—S
   b. C—C
   c. P—O
   d. Na—F

44. An unknown compound is a white solid at room temperature. It does not dissolve in water, cannot conduct an electric current in any state, and melts readily, even when heated gently.
   a. What type of solid is it likely to be? Explain your answer.
   b. Think of one common household substance that fits the description of the unknown compound.

45. Use VSEPR theory and Lewis structures to predict the number of bonding pairs and lone pairs around the central atom so that you can identify the e^- group arrangement, molecular shape, and bond angle for the following molecules and ions:
   a. SnF_4
   b. H_3O^+
   c. AsF_5
   d. ICl_2^-

46. Which compound in each of the following pairs has the higher boiling point? Explain your choice in each case.
   a. H_2S or H_2O
   b. SCl_4 or $SiCl_4$
   c. propane (C_3H_8) or octane (C_8H_{18})

47. Compare and contrast the structures and physical properties of the covalent compounds propanol (C_3H_7OH), named for the alcohol group, —OH, attached to the carbon chain, and propanal (C_3H_6O), named for the carbonyl group, —C=O, at one end of the molecule.

Communication

48. Draw electron density maps for the following orbitals: $1s$, $2s$, $2p$, $3s$, $3p$, all of the $2p$ orbitals together. In each case, try to ensure that the orbitals get larger from each energy level to the next energy level.

49. Analyze the molecules of ammonia, $NH_3(g)$, and ethanal, $CH_3CHO(\ell)$, according to the following directions:
   a. Draw Lewis structures for the two molecules.
   b. Analyze the Lewis structures according to VSEPR theory to determine the electron group arrangements and molecular shapes. For ethanal, consider the shape around the formyl carbon atom only. Explain, in writing and using diagrams, how your Lewis structures led to the electron group arrangements and molecular shapes.
   c. Determine whether the molecules are polar or non-polar. Use arrows on your diagrams to indicate any polar bonds; if present, explain why polar bonds result in a polar molecule.

50. Draw a three-way Venn diagram to show the similarities and differences among polar covalent bonds, co-ordinate covalent bonds, and mostly (non-polar) covalent bonds.

51. Draw all of the resonance (Lewis) structures for SO_3.

52. What is the molecular shape of each molecule below?

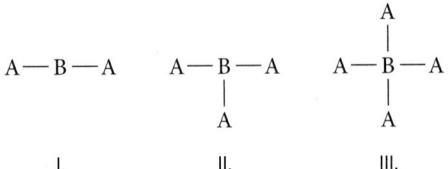

Assume the following:
   a. Each one has no lone pairs.
   b. Each one has one lone pair.
   c. Each one has two lone pairs.

Arrange your answer in a graphic organizer.

53. Use a table to summarize the distinguishing properties of ionic, covalent, metallic, and molecular (separate polar from non-polar) solids, including unit particle, type of attractions between particles, relative melting point, electrical conductivity (in solid, liquid, dissolved states), solubility (particular types of solvents), relative hardness/brittleness, and common examples.

54. **BIG IDEAS** The nature of the attractive forces that exist between particles in a substance determines the properties and limits the uses of that substance. If all of the pads of a gecko's feet were in contact with a surface, it could support a mass of more than 100 kg! Recently, scientists have determined how gecko feet are able to adhere to a surface. Many research teams are now trying to create materials that mimic the gecko foot. Research the way that gecko feet work and the state of the scientific research in duplicating this ability. What are some potential applications for this research?

Application

55. **BIG IDEAS** Technological devices that are based on the principles of atomic and molecular structures can have societal benefits and costs. Infrared (IR) radiation technology is used widely in astronomy, meteorology, biology, and art history, as well as in heating, communications, and military applications. Choose and research the training required for a job or profession that utilizes an infrared technology. Describe the technology and include information on its benefits and costs to society. Create a poster board to present your information to the class.

56. In 1835, French philosopher Auguste Comte declared that we could never know the chemistry of celestial bodies because we could not examine them directly. The founding scientists of modern spectroscopy would soon prove him wrong.
    a. Research how spectroscopy, from a position on Earth, is used to determine the chemical composition of celestial bodies.
    b. Helium was discovered on the Sun by Norman Lockyer and Pierre Janssen in 1869, but at the time helium was not known to exist on Earth. When, where, and by whom was helium discovered on Earth, and how was spectroscopy important in its identification?

57. Find tellurium on the periodic table and then answer the following questions:
    a. Write the condensed electron configuration for tellurium, Te.
    b. Tellurium can have a valence of −2, +4, or +6. Use condensed electron configurations to hypothesize how each of these valences might form. In each case, explain why that change makes sense.

58. Explain why the s, p, d, and f orbitals of many-electron atoms having the same n are at slightly different energy sublevels, whereas all of the orbitals having the same n in the hydrogen atom are all at the same energy sublevel of the hydrogen atom.

59. Compare SiF_4 and XeF_4 on the various aspects of molecular shape and related properties given, and choose
    (a) if the answer is only SiF_4.
    (b) if the answer is only XeF_4.
    (c) if the answer is both SiF_4 and XeF_4.
    (d) if the answer is neither SiF_4 nor XeF_4.
    i. polar molecule
    ii. symmetrical shape
    iii. contains lone pairs
    iv. has a larger bond angle
    v. flat, two-dimensional shape
    vi. would not dissolve in water
    vii. electron-group arrangement is the same as the molecular shape
    viii. the presence of double or triple bonds

60. Barium is a metal that gives a green colour to fireworks.
    a. Write the condensed electron configuration for barium.
    b. Classify barium according to group, period, and block in the periodic table.

61. The most abundant element, by mass, found on Earth is found in the d block.
    a. The last electron to load into one of its atoms has the quantum numbers $n = 3$ and $l = 2$. What is this element?
    b. Classify the element according to group and period.

62. Consider the second most abundant element, by mass, on Earth.
    a. Use a reliable source to discover what that element is.
    b. Write the condensed electron configuration for this element.
    c. Classify the element according to group, period, and block in the periodic table.

63. According to hybrid orbital theory, why can PCl_5 exist but NCl_5 cannot?

UNIT 2 SELF-ASSESSMENT

Select the letter of the best answer below.

1. **T/I** If the last electron to be added to an atom had the quantum numbers $n = 5$ and $l = 2$, which element could it be?
   a. technetium
   b. rhenium
   c. bismuth
   d. barium
   e. silver

2. **K/U** Which of the electron configurations could not represent an atom of a real element?
   a. $[He]2s^22p^3$
   b. $[Xe]6s^25d^{10}$
   c. $[Ar]4s^23d^{10}4p^5$
   d. $[Kr]3s^22d^7$
   e. $[He]2s^2$

3. **K/U** Which scientist is responsible for the rule that says one electron must be loaded into each degenerate orbital before they can be paired up?
   a. Bohr
   b. Schrödinger
   c. Aufbau
   d. Pauli
   e. Hund

4. **K/U** Which periodic trend below represents the energy required to produce a cation from a neutral atom?
   a. electron affinity
   b. ionization energy
   c. electronegativity
   d. electropositivity
   e. all of the above

5. **T/I** Which of the following is the condensed electron configuration for bromine?
   a. $[Kr]4s^23d^{10}4p^5$
   b. $[Ar]4s^14d^{10}4p^6$
   c. $[Ar]4s^23d^{10}4p^5$
   d. $[Kr]4s^24d^{10}4p^5$
   e. $[Ar]3s^23d^{10}4p^5$

6. **K/U** Which statement below is false?
   a. All waves travel at the speed of light, $c = 3.0 \times 10^8$ m/s.
   b. Frequency and wavelength are two properties of a wave.
   c. Frequency and wavelength are inversely proportional to each other.
   d. Sonar is related to sound energy; therefore, sonar is not found on the electromagnetic spectrum.
   e. None of the statements are false; all are true.

7. **T/I** Which of the following compounds would not be expected to dissolve in water?
   a. NH_3
   b. H_2S
   c. ICl_3
   d. CH_3OH
   e. BCl_3

8. **K/U** Which of the following elements is not capable of forming molecules in which one of the atoms has an expanded octet?
   a. Ga
   b. Br
   c. P
   d. C
   e. Xe

9. **T/I** Which ion is represented by $[Ar]4s^23d^{10}4p^6$?
   a. S^{2-}
   b. Se^{2+}
   c. Br^-
   d. Ca^+
   e. P^{3-}

10. **K/U** A substance that has a melting point of 1850°C and a boiling point of 2700°C is insoluble in water and is a good electrical insulator. The substance is most likely
    a. an ionic solid.
    b. a polar covalent solid.
    c. a metal.
    d. a network solid.
    e. a molecular solid.

Use sentences and diagrams as appropriate to answer the questions below.

11. **C** For each of the models of the atom below, answer the following questions.
    i. What model does it represent?
    ii. What features of the atom does it explain correctly?
    iii. Explain one way in which the model is inadequate and does not account for a certain property of atoms.

a.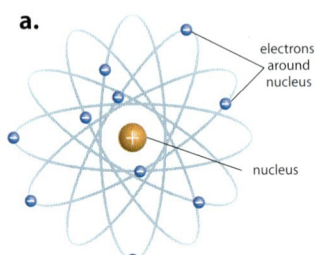

d.

b.

e.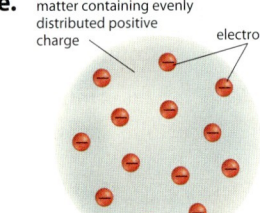

c.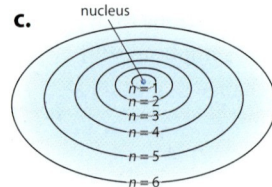

12. **K/U** Consider Rutherford's gold foil experiment.
    a. What was the evidence that suggested the atom contained a positive nuclear core?
    b. What was the evidence that suggested the atom contained mostly empty space?
    c. What was expected to happen based on Thomson's plum pudding model?

13. **A** Conduct research to find the difference between an emission spectrum and an absorption spectrum. If you were handed an atomic spectrum, how would you know if it was an emission spectrum or an absorption spectrum?

14. **T/I** Use a basic periodic table that does not contain electron configurations to determine which element is defined by $[Ar]4s^23d^7$.

15. **K/U** What information about an atom is *not* discernible from its electron configuration?

16. **T/I** An orbital has the values $n = 5$ and $l = 1$.
    a. Give the possible values for m_l.
    b. What type of orbital is associated with these quantum numbers?
    c. How many orbitals are associated with these quantum numbers?

17. **A** Lewis structures and VSEPR theory assist chemists in determining the detailed structure of molecules. However, they sometimes encounter molecules that could be one of two possibilities. For example, the molecule sulfur dioxide, $SO_2(g)$, could be a resonance structure or an expanded octet.
    a. Draw Lewis structures for each of these two possibilities.
    b. Describe the type of experimental evidence that chemists would use to best determine which of these two possibilities is the most likely structure.

18. **T/I** The condensed electron configuration for an indium atom is $[Kr]5s^24d^{10}5p^1$. Without using a periodic table, identify the group number, period number, and orbital block in the periodic table to which indium belongs. Explain your reasoning.

19. **C** Draw the Lewis structure for HCN. Include all structures if it is a resonance structure.

20. **C** Draw the Lewis structure for CO_3^{2-}. Include all structures if it is a resonance structure.

21. **K/U** Explain how the octet rule is connected to the noble gases.

22. **T/I** Write the following pairs of bonds in your notebook. Indicate the partial positive end and the partial negative end of each bond using the special symbols. In each pair, circle the bond that is more polar than the other.
    a. C—O, C—S
    b. C—F, C—N
    c. P—H, P—Cl

23. **C** Design a type of electron dot diagram that would obey the aufbau principle. Draft a set of rules that would accompany this type of diagram.

24. **T/I** You have been given five unknown solids to identify as being one of each of the five types of solids. You have been given only a limited supply of each.
    a. Describe the sequence of tests you would run to make your identification as efficiently as possible.
    b. Draw a flow diagram to represent the test procedure in part (a).

25. **A** The structural formula for acetonitrile, CH_3CN, is shown below:

$$H-\underset{H}{\overset{H}{\underset{|}{\overset{|}{C}}}}-C\equiv N$$

Examine the structure of the acetonitrile molecule. Identify the hybrid orbitals present in each carbon atom, and predict the shape of the molecule around each carbon atom based on the bond angles.

Self-Check

If you missed question …	1	2	3	4	5	6	7	8	9	10	11	12	13	14	15	16	17	18	19	20	21	22	23	24	25
Review section(s)…	3.3	3.2	3.3	3.3	3.3	3.1	4.1	4.2	3.3	4.1 4.2	3.1	3.1	3.1	3.3	3.2	3.2	4.2	3.3	4.2	4.2	4.2	4.1	3.3 4.2	4.1 4.2	4.2

UNIT 3: Energy Changes and Rates of Reaction

BIG IDEAS

- Energy changes and rates of chemical reactions can be described quantitatively.
- Efficiency of chemical reactions can be improved by applying optimal conditions.
- Technologies that transform energy can have societal and environmental costs and benefits.

Overall Expectations

In this unit, you will…

- **analyze** technologies and chemical processes that are based on energy changes, and evaluate them in terms of their efficiency and their effects on the environment
- **investigate** and **analyze** energy changes and rates of reaction in physical and chemical processes, and **solve** related problems
- **demonstrate** an understanding of energy changes and rates of reaction

Unit 3 Contents

Chapter 5
Energy Changes

Chapter 6
Rates of Reactions

Focussing Questions

1. How do physical changes, chemical reactions, and nuclear reactions differ in the amount of energy they release or absorb?
2. How can the energy change of a system be determined?
3. What factors affect the rate at which chemical reactions occur?

Go to **scienceontario** to find out more about energy changes and rates of reaction

The spine-covered reptile shown here is aptly named the thorny devil, *Moloch horridus*. This animal is native to the desert and scrubland of western and central Australia. Despite its thorny hide, which acts as a defence mechanism, this small reptile is vulnerable to larger predators. To remain safe, it darts quickly underneath small shrubs when a predator comes into view. This tactic is not always effective, however. The thorny devil's body temperature is not regulated internally. Instead, as for other reptiles, its body temperature varies with the temperature of its external environment. During the early part of the day, before the land and air have warmed significantly, the reptile's body temperature is cool. The energy-providing metabolic reactions that take place within its body occur more slowly at cool temperatures. Thus, the reptile is sluggish in the early part of the day. Until its body temperature rises, increasing the rate at which these metabolic reactions occur, the thorny devil is slower in responding to danger and is therefore at greater risk of being caught by a predator.

Temperature is one of several factors that influence the rate at which chemical reactions take place, both in living organisms and in the non-living environment. In this unit, you will learn about energy changes, rates of reaction, and factors that affect the rates at which chemical reactions occur.

As you study this unit, look ahead to the Unit 3 Project on pages 400 to 401. Complete the project in stages as you progress through the unit.

UNIT 3 Preparation

Safety in the Chemistry Laboratory and Classroom

- Know the meaning of WHMIS and safety symbols and adhere to any precautions they advise.
- Always review any relevant MSDS information before beginning an investigation.
- Handle caustic substances with care. If any part of your body comes in contact with a caustic substance, rinse the affected area immediately and thoroughly with water. Inform your teacher right away.
- Always follow heat source safety procedures when you are heating materials with a Bunsen burner or hot plate.
- Be sure to wear safety eyewear, heat-resistant safety gloves, and any other relevant safety equipment when heating an item.
- Use EXTREME CAUTION when working near an open flame.
- Be familiar with the location of any emergency equipment such as fire extinguishers and eyewash stations.

1. Describe the hazards represented by the symbols below and the precautions associated with them.

   a.

   b.

   c.

   d.

2. Indicate which of the symbols shown in question 1 would be applicable to an investigation in which the following procedures were carried out. Explain your reasoning.
   a. Magnesium oxide powder is added to a solution of hydrochloric acid.
   b. Copper metal is heated in the flame of a Bunsen burner.

3. An investigation that you are about to perform involves working with sodium hydroxide. Your teacher is discussing the safety procedures to follow when working with this base. As part of the discussion, your teacher asks the following question:

   "If the base is spilled on a student's arm, should the student neutralize it by applying an acid to the skin or flush the area immediately and thoroughly with water?"

   Explain how you would respond to this question. Provide your reasoning.

4. In an investigation, you are asked to use a Bunsen burner to heat water in a flask, as shown on the right.

   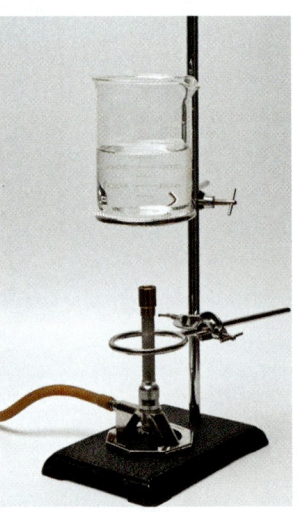

   a. Explain how you would set up the Bunsen burner and adjust it to produce a blue flame.
   b. Describe the method you would follow when heating the water. Include any safety precautions that are advised when performing this investigation.
   c. During the investigation, your laboratory partner drops the flask containing the water. The flask shatters on the floor. Explain how you and your partner should respond to this accident.

5. When working with an open flame in an investigation, which of the following is important to do?
   a. Use extreme caution.
   b. Tie back long hair and any loose clothing before starting the investigation.
   c. Make sure that there are no flammable solvents nearby.
   d. Place materials where you will not have to reach behind or over the flame to access them.
   e. all of the above

Forms and Transfer of Energy

- A force is a directional push or pull on an object. The SI unit for force is the newton, N.
- Work is the process of energy transfer to an object when the object is moved by a force.
- Energy is defined as the ability to do work. The SI unit for work and energy are the same—the joule, J. The joule is equal to the energy used when applying a force of one Newton over a distance of one metre (1 J = 1 N·m).
- Energy can be classified into two main types: kinetic energy and potential energy. Kinetic energy is energy of motion. Potential energy is energy that is stored by an object as a result of its composition or position.
- There are many different forms of energy. Energy can change from one form to another—for example, from chemical to electrical or from electrical to mechanical. In these conversions, energy is always conserved and never lost or destroyed.
- Heat is the energy transferred between two objects as a result of a difference in temperature between the objects.
- Thermal energy is the sum of the kinetic energies of all of the particles of an object or a substance.
- Temperature is a measure of the average kinetic energy of the particles of a substance or an object. Celsius and Kelvin are two temperature scales commonly used by scientists.

6. Read the following description and explain how each of the following terms applies: *work, force, energy,* and *kinetic energy*.

A crate is sitting on the floor. A person starts pushing the crate to move it across the floor.

7. Examine the images below.

a. Identify the image that represents each of the following. Explain your answers.
- gravitational potential energy
- gravitational potential energy and kinetic energy

b. Describe how the potential energy and the kinetic energy of the skier change as the skier progresses from the start of the course to the bottom of the course.

8. Describe where each of the following forms of energy is represented in the image below.
   a. chemical energy
   b. electrical energy
   c. electromagnetic energy
   d. thermal energy
   e. heat

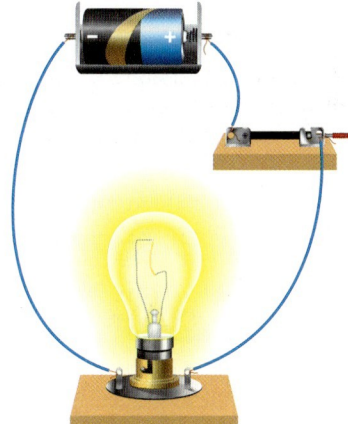

9. Which of the following represent(s) a measurement of energy?
   a. 14 V
   b. 6.7 N·m
   c. 46.5 J
   d. b and c
   e. none of the above

10. Describe the relationship among the terms *heat, temperature,* and *thermal energy*.

The Kinetic Molecular Theory

- The kinetic molecular theory can help describe the properties of matter and the behaviour of matter during a physical change.
- All matter is composed of particles. The state of a substance is determined by the energy of the particles, the distance between the particles, and the attractive forces between the particles.
- Particles at a higher temperature move faster, on average, than particles at a lower temperature.
- Energy is involved when matter changes state. Melting, vaporization, and sublimation from the solid state to the gaseous state involve the absorption of energy by particles. Freezing, condensation, and sublimation from the gaseous state to the solid state involve the release of energy from particles.

11. Describe briefly how you would design a computer-based presentation that could be used to explain the kinetic molecular theory to a class of Grade 8 students.

12. Vigorously beating their wings enables bees to adjust the air temperature of their beehive, such as the one shown below. Explain how this temperature change is achieved, making reference to the kinetic molecular theory in your answer.

13. According to the kinetic molecular theory, particles are constantly in motion. What does an increase in a particle's motion reflect?
  a. an increase in the particle's kinetic energy
  b. a decrease in the particle's kinetic energy
  c. an increase in the particle's potential energy
  d. a decrease in the temperature of the object that the particle is a component of
  e. none of the above

14. Create a graphic organizer that compares the particles of a substance in its solid, liquid, and gaseous states. Include the following properties and behaviours in your organizer.
  a. molecular motion
  b. distance between particles
  c. shape of the substance
  d. volume of the substance

15. Which statement best describes a substance in its solid state?
  a. The particles exhibit vibrational, rotational, and translational motions.
  b. The particles exhibit vibrational motion only.
  c. Particles of the substance interact with one another through numerous collisions.
  d. The substance always takes the shape of its container.
  e. The substance always fills the container it is in.

16. Draw diagrams and refer to the kinetic molecular theory to explain why a helium balloon appears to become partially deflated when it is taken outside in winter.

17. Methanol is a toxic, colourless liquid. At one time, its freezing point of −97.7°C made it an important component of antifreeze used in the engines of vehicles. However, because methanol boils away at the relatively low temperature of 65°C, it was eventually replaced by ethylene glycol in antifreeze. Referring to both kinetic energy and the postulates of the kinetic molecular theory, explain what happens to the particles in methanol when its temperature reaches
  a. −97.7°C
  b. 65°C

Math Skills

- When experimental data are collected and plotted in a line graph, information about the relationship between the independent and dependent variables can be gained from the shape and slope of the curve.
- The equation of a straight line is given by the equation $y = mx + b$, where y is the dependent variable, x is the independent variable, m is the slope of the line, and b is the y-intercept.
  - The equation for the slope of a straight line is
  $$\text{slope} = \frac{\text{rise}}{\text{run}}$$

In this unit, you will be required to perform the following:
- solve for a variable in a mathematical equation
- apply the rules for significant digits in mathematical calculations
- convert between mass and moles when determining the quantity of a substance

Use the diagram below to answer questions 18 to 23.

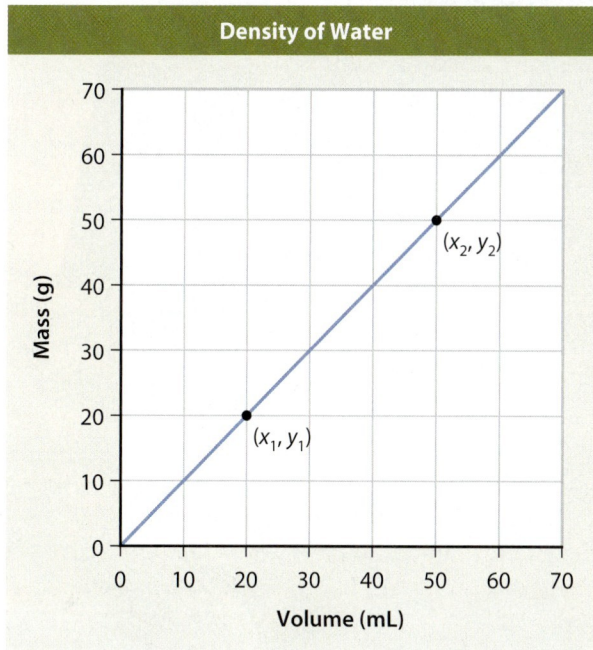

18. Explain what the rise and the run of the graph are.

19. Determine the coordinates of the points that are indicated on the graph.

20. Determine the slope of the line.

21. Determine the equation of the line.

22. Does this graph represent a direct relationship or an inverse relationship between the two variables? Explain your answer.

23. Describe how the relationship between the two variables would change if the slope was steeper compared with this one.

24. Use the graphs below to answer the following questions.

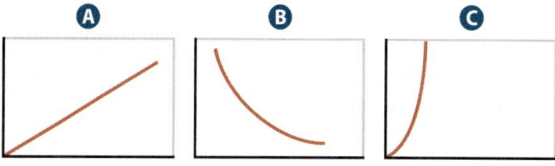

a. Which graph represents each of the following relationships between variables?
  - $y \alpha \frac{1}{x}$
  - $y \alpha x^n$ (n > 1)

b. Which graph represents a direct relationship between variables?

25. A student performed an experiment three times to determine the concentration of a substance. She recorded the following values from the three experiments: 0.54 mol/L, 0.491 mol/L, and 0.51 mol/L.

a. What is the mean value of concentration?

b. Using a the value calculated in part (a), determine the mass (in grams) of the substance present in a 25 mL volume, if its molar mass is 45.6 g/mol.

26. Solve each equation for the unknown variable.

a. $7 = \frac{21}{y}$

b. $14 = 6(2) + \left(\frac{2x^2}{4}\right)$

27. Perform the following calculations. Assume each number represents an experimentally determined measurement. Therefore, provide your answer with the correct number of significant digits.

a. $(0.652 \text{ L}) \left[\frac{(97.5 \text{ kPa})(273.15 \text{ K})}{(101.325 \text{ kPa})(294.15 \text{ K})} \right]$

b. $\frac{(7.5 \times 10^3 \text{ cm}) + (2.32 \times 10^3 \text{ cm})}{2.1 \text{ s}}$

CHAPTER 5

Energy Changes

Specific Expectations

In this chapter, you will learn how to . . .

- D1.1 **analyze** conventional and alternative energy technologies, and **evaluate** their efficiency and environmental impact (5.4)

- D2.2 **write** thermochemical equations, expressing the energy change as a ΔH value or as a heat term in the equation (5.2, 5.3)

- D2.3 **solve** problems involving analysis of heat transfer, using $Q = mc\Delta T$ (5.1, 5.2, 5.3)

- D2.4 **plan** and **conduct** an inquiry to calculate, using a calorimeter, the heat of reaction of a substance, compare the actual heat of reaction to the theoretical value, and suggest sources of experimental error (5.2)

- D2.5 **solve** problems using Hess's law (5.3)

- D2.6 **conduct** an inquiry to test Hess's law (5.3)

- D2.7 **calculate** the heat of reaction for a formation reaction, using a table of standard enthalpies of formation and applying Hess's law (5.3)

- D3.1 **compare** energy changes from physical changes, chemical reactions, and nuclear reactions (5.1)

- D3.2 **compare** the energy change from a reaction in which bonds are formed with one in which bonds are broken, and **explain** them in terms of endothermic and exothermic reactions (5.1, 5.2, 5.3)

- D3.3 **explain** how mass, heat capacity, and change in temperature of a substance determine the amount of heat gained or lost (5.2, 5.3)

- D3.4 **state** Hess's law, and **explain** how it is applied to find the enthalpy changes of a reaction (5.3)

In the world of competitive running, Sarah Reinertsen has just about done it all: 100 m, 200 m, 400 m, 5 km, 10 km, marathon, *and* triathlon. Her body—like yours and everyone else's—has a lot in common with the engine in a motor vehicle. Hydrocarbon combustion, the chemical reaction that takes place in a car engine, is similar to cellular respiration, the chemical reaction that takes place in body cells. Both processes react "fuel" with oxygen by breaking and forming chemical bonds, and both reactions release energy. In this chapter, you will investigate, measure, and analyze the energy involved in chemical reactions.

Launch Lab

Observing a Temperature Change

In a previous chemistry course, you may have heated a sample of copper(II) sulfate pentahydrate, $CuSO_4 \cdot 5H_2O(s)$, to drive off the waters of hydration. Here, you will react *anhydrous* $CuSO_4(s)$ with water. In terms of energy, how does this reaction compare with the removal of the waters of hydration of $CuSO_4 \cdot 5H_2O(s)$?

Copper(II) Sulfate

crystals of $CuSO_4 \cdot 5H_2O$ $CuSO_4$ powder

Safety Precaution

- Do not inhale the anhydrous $CuSO_4(s)$.
- Wear safety eyewear and protective clothing throughout this activity.
- Wash your hands thoroughly when you have completed this activity.

Materials

- 2 g of anhydrous $CuSO_4(s)$
- polystyrene cup
- stirring rod
- thermometer (alcohol or digital)
- 100 mL distilled water
- 100 mL graduated cylinder
- balance

Procedure

1. Add approximately 100 mL of water to the cup.
2. Record the temperature of the water.
3. Add about 2 g of anhydrous $CuSO_4$ to the water. Stir the solution.
4. Record the highest temperature attained by the solution.
5. Dispose of the chemicals as instructed by your teacher when you have completed the activity.

Questions

1. Does this reaction absorb or release heat? How do you know?
2. What do you think the temperature change for this reaction would have been if only one half of the quantity of anhydrous $CuSO_4(s)$ had been added to the same volume of water?
3. Given that energy has units of joules (J) and that temperature is measured in °C (or K), develop an equation that relates the energy (heat) obtained in this reaction to the observed temperature change, ΔT. (**Hint:** Recall what you learned about specific heat capacity in a previous science course.)

SECTION 5.1
The Nature of Energy and Heat

Key Terms

thermochemistry
open system
closed system
isolated system
thermal energy
temperature
specific heat capacity, c
first law of thermodynamics
enthalpy, H
endothermic
exothermic
second law of thermodynamics
enthalpy of solution, $\Delta H_{solution}$

During a fire such as the one shown in **Figure 5.1**, the matter that makes up wood is changed to other forms of matter—mostly ashes and various gases. At the same time, the energy content of the original wood decreases, and this change in energy content is released as other forms of energy—mostly heat and light. While many changes in matter involve the release of energy, other changes involve the absorption of energy. For example, energy is absorbed when an ice cube melts and when the chemical compounds in a therapeutic cold pack (water and ammonium chloride) chemically combine.

Figure 5.1 The chemical reaction that occurs when wood burns releases energy in various forms.

Whether they are chemical or physical, all changes in matter involve changes in the energy content of matter. Because energy-related technologies are so important to society, chemists and chemical engineers are especially interested in observing and measuring the amount of heat that is released during chemical and physical processes. In fact, an entire field of chemistry, called **thermochemistry**, is devoted to the study of heat involved in such changes. Over the next few pages, some foundational concepts for the study of thermochemistry are outlined. Several of these concepts, such as those associated with forms of energy, the transformation and transfer of energy, and the relationship between thermal energy and heat, are a brief review from previous science studies.

thermochemistry
the study of the energy changes involved in chemical and physical processes

Some Foundational Concepts for Thermochemistry

All forms of energy can be placed into one of two categories, kinetic energy and potential energy. Kinetic energy is the energy of motion. Anything that is moving has kinetic energy. Potential energy is the stored energy an object has a result of its condition (for example, the nature of its particles in relation to one another—chemical potential energy) or its position (for example, its location above or below another object—gravitational potential energy).

The derived SI unit for energy is the joule (J), which is equivalent to a kg·m^2/s^2. One joule is approximately the amount of energy necessary to lift one large kiwi (approximately 100 g) a distance of one metre. Since the amount of energy represented by a joule is very small, energy involving chemical reactions is often expressed in kilojoules (1 kJ = 1000 J).

System and Surroundings

Any sample under observation is referred to as a system. For example, the contents of the beaker in **Figure 5.2** can be considered to be a system. Everything that is not part of this system—that is, everything else in the entire universe—is considered the surroundings. These concepts can be expressed as an equation:

$$\text{universe} = \text{system} + \text{surroundings}$$

Figure 5.2 This photograph shows all the materials and equipment for a chemical analysis investigation. Once the contents of the beaker are defined as the system, everything else that is not the contents of the beaker become the surroundings. **Identify** at least three other examples of surroundings in this photograph. (Count the equipment as a single item.)

Usually, the parts of the surroundings that are relevant to the defined system are those that interact with it. Interactions between a system and its surroundings typically involve the exchange of energy and matter. Chemists have defined three types of systems with respect to such exchanges:

- An **open system** can exchange both energy and matter with its surroundings.
- A **closed system** can exchange energy, but not matter, with its surroundings.
- An **isolated system** cannot exchange energy or matter with its surroundings.

Figure 5.3 illustrates the three types of systems. An uncovered pot of potatoes boiling on the stove represents an open system. The system absorbs energy from the stove burner. The system loses both energy and matter when the water evaporates out of the pan in the form of steam. The pressure cooker with potatoes boiling on the stove represents a closed system because pressure cookers are sealed. The sealed lid prevents the loss of mass, or water in the form of steam, but heat can still enter the system through contact of the pot bottom with the stove. Finally, the pot of potatoes inside an insulated container represents an isolated system. The insulation prevents the exchange of any energy or matter between the system and its surroundings. It is difficult to completely isolate a system. Thus, some scientists claim that there is no truly isolated system except the universe itself.

open system a system that can exchange both matter and energy with the surroundings

closed system a system that can exchange only energy with the surroundings

isolated system a system that cannot exchange either energy or matter with the surroundings

Figure 5.3 Comparing open, closed, and isolated systems. **Explain** how the exchange of matter and energy is different in each situation.

Measurable and Calculated Variables of a System

thermal energy the sum of all the kinetic energies of all the particles of a sample of matter

temperature a measure of the average kinetic energy of all the particles of a sample of matter

specific heat capacity, c the amount of energy needed to increase the temperature of one gram of a substance by one degree Celsius

Certain properties of a system can be measured, and other properties cannot. For example, the **thermal energy** of a system—the sum of the kinetic energies of all the particles of the system—cannot be measured. However, you *can* measure the **temperature** of a system. The temperature of a system is directly related to the average kinetic energy of all of the particles of a system. You can also measure the volume of a system, the mass contained in a system, and the pressure that the system and surroundings exert on each other.

Measuring the temperature of a system before and after a process, such as a physical or chemical change, provides some of the data needed to calculate the amount of heat that has entered or left the system. Also needed for such a calculation is the mass of the system and an important property of the contents of the system, called specific heat capacity. The **specific heat capacity, *c*,** of a substance is the amount of energy needed to increase the temperature of one gram of the substance by one degree Celsius.

The specific heat capacity is a property that must be determined experimentally for every substance. Tables containing these data are readily available in print and online resources. A few examples are listed in **Table 5.1**. The specific heat capacity depends on the state of the substance. As well, temperature and pressure affect the specific heat capacity. The values in tables are usually reported for SATP, standard ambient temperature and pressure, which are defined as 25°C and 100 kPa.

Table 5.1 Specific Heat Capacities of Some Common Substances and Materials

Substance	Specific Heat Capacity (J/g·°C at SATP)	Substance	Specific Heat Capacity (J/g·°C at SATP)	Substance	Specific Heat Capacity (J/g·°C at SATP)
Elements		**Compounds**		**Mixtures**	
aluminum	0.897	Ammonia (liquid)	4.70	Air	1.01
carbon (graphite)	0.709	Ammonia (gas)	2.06	Concrete	0.88
copper	0.385	Ethanol	2.44	Glass	0.84
gold	0.129	Water (solid)	2.00	Granite	0.79
hydrogen (gas)	14.304	Water (liquid)	4.19	Wood	1.26
iron	0.449	Water (gas)	2.02		

Calculating the Amount of Heat Entering and Leaving a System

The amount of heat that enters or leaves an object when it is being heated or cooled can be calculated using the equation shown in **Figure 5.4**. The Greek letter delta, Δ, before the T represents a change in the temperature—that is, the final temperature minus the initial temperature: $\Delta T = T_{final} - T_{initial}$.

If ΔT is positive (if the final temperature is higher than the initial temperature), then Q is positive. A positive value for Q means that heat entered the system. If ΔT is negative, the initial temperature was higher than the final temperature, indicating that the temperature of the system decreased during the process. This would make Q negative, meaning that heat left the system. Practise using this formula by studying the following Sample Problem and completing the Practice Problems.

Figure 5.4 This equation enables you to calculate the amount of heat absorbed or released by a substance.

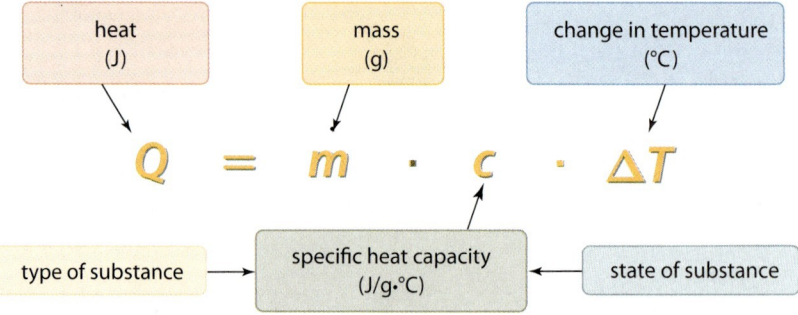

Sample Problem

Calculating the Absorption of Heat

Problem
When a 1.25 kg sample of water was heated in a kettle, its temperature increased from 16.4°C to 98.9°C. How much heat did the water absorb?

What Is Required?
You need to calculate the amount of heat absorbed by the water.

What Is Given?
You know the mass of water: $m = 1.25$ kg
You know the initial temperature: $T_{initial} = 16.4$°C
You know the final temperature: $T_{final} = 98.9$°C
You have the specific heat capacity of liquid water from **Table 5.1**: $c = 4.19$ J/g·°C

Plan Your Strategy	Act on Your Strategy
Determine the change in temperature of the water.	$\Delta T = T_{final} - T_{initial}$ $= 98.9°C - 16.4°C = 82.5°C$
Determine the amount of heat absorbed by the water. Use the formula $Q = mc\Delta T$. Because the mass was given in kilograms, be sure to convert to grams, because the specific heat capacity includes grams.	$Q = mc\Delta T$ $= (1.25 \text{ kg}) \left(\dfrac{1000 \text{ g}}{\text{kg}}\right) \left(4.19 \dfrac{\text{J}}{\text{g·°C}}\right) (82.5°C)$ $= 4.32 \times 10^5$ J The water absorbs 432 kJ of heat.

Check Your Solution
The solution has the correct number of significant digits. The units are correct.

Practice Problems

1. How much heat must be added to a 36.2 g sample of iron to increase its temperature by 250.0°C?

2. How much heat must be added to 128.62 g of steam at 126.0°C to increase its temperature to 189.5°C?

3. A 1.00×10^2 g sample of ethanol at 25.0°C is heated until it reaches 50.0°C. How much thermal energy does the ethanol gain?

4. Beaker A contains 50 g of liquid at room temperature. The beaker is heated until the liquid increases in temperature by 10°C. Beaker B contains 100 g of the same liquid at room temperature. The beaker is also heated until the liquid increases in temperature by 10°C. In which beaker does the liquid absorb more heat? Explain your answer.

5. How much heat is released when the temperature of 789 g of liquid ammonia decreases from 82.7°C to 25.0°C?

6. A solid substance has a mass of 250.00 g. It is cooled by 25.00°C and loses 4.937 kJ of heat. What is the specific heat capacity of the substance? Identify the substance using the values in **Table 5.1**.

7. The specific heat capacity of a compound used in fireworks is 0.800 J/g·°C. If it takes 8.04×10^3 J to heat this material from 20.0°C to 925.0°C, what mass of compound was used?

8. One litre of water at 1.00°C is warmed by the addition of 4.00 kJ of heat. What is the final temperature of the water? (1.00 L of water has a mass of 1.00 kg.)

9. On a warm day, how much solar energy does a 3.982 kg piece of concrete absorb as heat if its temperature increases from 13.60°C to 14.50°C?

10. You have samples of air and hydrogen gas at room temperature, both having a mass of 10.00 g.
    a. Compare the change in temperature of these two samples if each gains 500.0 J of thermal energy.
    b. Suggest a reason for the difference in the temperature changes.

The First Law of Thermodynamics: Energy Is Conserved

When a system absorbs energy, the surroundings release it. Similarly, when a system releases energy, the surroundings absorb it. This exchange or transfer of energy between a system and its surroundings can be in the form of heat, chemical energy, mechanical (kinetic) energy, or any other form of energy. In fact, energy is usually transformed from one form to another during an energy transfer. For example, the combustion of gasoline in a car engine releases forms of energy that include kinetic energy of the car's moving parts, chemical energy of the battery, electrical energy of the dashboard components, radiant energy of the headlights, and thermal energy that warms the parts of the car and areas within it. The sum of these forms of energy equals the change in energy between the reactants and products as the gasoline undergoes combustion.

In this example, as well as in all other situations involving energy transformations, energy is neither created nor destroyed; it is transformed from one type of energy to another or transferred from one object to another. You might recognize this idea from earlier studies as the *law of conservation of energy*, which is also the first law of thermodynamics. Essentially, the **first law of thermodynamics** states that the total energy of the universe is constant. In the form of an equation, the law is as follows:

$$E_{universe} = \text{constant}$$

You could also say that the change in the energy of the universe is zero:

$$\Delta E_{universe} = 0$$

Since, when defining a system, the surroundings consist of everything else in the universe you could also say that the system plus the surroundings equals the universe:

$$\text{universe} = \text{system} + \text{surroundings}$$

From this equation, the total energy of the universe is equal to the total energy of the system plus the total energy of the surroundings:

$$E_{universe} = E_{system} + E_{surroundings}$$

Similarly, any change in the total energy of the universe must be equal to the change in the total energy of the system plus the change in the total energy of the surroundings. Since the change in the total energy of the universe is equal to zero, the following applies:

$$\Delta E_{universe} = \Delta E_{system} + \Delta E_{surroundings} = 0$$

By re-arranging this equation, any change in the total energy of the system must be equal and opposite to the change in the total energy of the surroundings:

$$\Delta E_{system} = -\Delta E_{surroundings}$$

In terms of practical situations such as warming soup on a stove, thawing ice, and any laboratory situation involving physical and chemical changes, the implications of the first law of thermodynamics are relatively straightforward: for any system that gains energy, the energy must come from the surroundings; conversely, if any system loses energy, that energy must enter the surroundings.

Enthalpy, H

To express thermochemical changes, chemists need a system variable that is not affected by the conditions under which the process occurs. One such variable is called the **enthalpy**, H, of the system. Enthalpy, sometimes called the *heat content* of the system, is defined as the total energy of the system plus the pressure times the volume, or $H = E + PV$. It is not possible to measure the total enthalpy of a system, but it is possible to measure the *change* in the enthalpy of a system.

The symbol for an enthalpy change is ΔH. The enthalpy change of a system depends only on the initial state (condition) and on the final state of the system and is represented

---

first law of thermodynamics a law stating that energy can be converted from one form to another but cannot be created or destroyed; can be represented as $E_{system} = -E_{surroundings}$

enthalpy, H the total energy of the system plus the pressure times the volume, or $H = E + PV$

as $\Delta H = \Delta E + \Delta(PV)$. For reactions of solids and liquids in solutions that take place in, for example, an open beaker in a laboratory, we assume that there is no change in pressure or volume. The work done by the reaction on the surroundings, which is represented by $\Delta(PV)$, is zero. The heat exchanged between the system and the surroundings is equal to the enthalpy change of the system ($\Delta H = \Delta E = Q$).

Note, however, that the enthalpy change at one pressure is different from the enthalpy change at another pressure, because the initial and final states of the system are different at different pressures. In thermochemistry, atmospheric pressure is usually chosen with enthalpy, because it is easy to achieve; also, the specific heat capacity of substances is reported for atmospheric pressure.

If heat enters the system during a process, the enthalpy change is positive, because the enthalpy of the system has increased. The process is said to be **endothermic**. If heat leaves a system during a process, the enthalpy change is negative, because the enthalpy of the system has decreased. The process is said to be **exothermic**.

The Second Law of Thermodynamics

All processes always result in some amount of energy that does not and cannot do useful work. This is the fundamental fact behind the **second law of thermodynamics**. There are many ways to state this law, but the result is always the same—no process is completely, 100 percent efficient. The statement of the second law of thermodynamics that is critical in thermochemical experiments is that, *when two objects are in thermal contact, heat is always transferred from the object at a higher temperature to the object at a lower temperature until the two objects are at the same temperature.*

Figure 5.5 illustrates the second law of thermodynamics. The length of the arrows represents the relative amount of kinetic energy of each particle. When a hot object and a cold object are separated by an insulator, their temperatures remain constant. When the objects are placed in thermal contact, the high-energy (hot) particles are able to collide with the low-energy (cold) particles. With each collision, the high-energy particle transfers some of its energy to the low-energy particle. Eventually, the energy is equally distributed among all the particles in the two systems. When two systems have reached the same temperature, they are in *thermal equilibrium*. (In fact, the particles have a range of energies, but their average energy is intermediate between that of the original hot and cold objects, and the particles with different energies are equally distributed throughout the combined systems.)

endothermic describes the process during which heat enters a system

exothermic describes the process during which heat leaves a system

second law of thermodynamics a law stating that when two objects are in thermal contact, heat is always transferred from the object at a higher temperature to the object at a lower temperature until the two objects are at the same temperature

no thermal contact
hot object   cold object

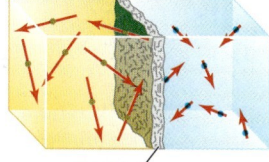

insulator

thermal equilibrium

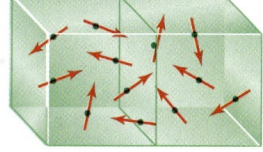

Figure 5.5 Two systems will eventually reach thermal equilibrium if they are in thermal contact.

Learning Check

1. Describe three examples from daily life in which an object in thermal contact with another object can transfer heat to it.
2. In what ways can a closed system exchange energy with its surroundings?
3. Under what conditions does the enthalpy change of a system equal the heat exchanged between the system and the surroundings?
4. The combustion of fuels in automobiles is an exothermic reaction. Thermal equilibrium is not achieved between the enthalpy of combustion from automobiles and the surroundings. Is this an exception to the second law of thermodynamics? Explain your answer.
5. Explain the difference between an endothermic and an exothermic process.
6. A compound such as calcium carbonate can decompose by absorbing energy. This reaction can be written as shown:

    $CaCO_3(s) + \text{energy} \rightarrow CaO(s) + CO_2(g)$

    a. Identify which has the greater potential energy: the reactants or the products.
    b. Is the enthalpy of the system increasing or decreasing? Is the reaction endothermic or exothermic? Is the enthalpy change positive or negative?

Comparing Categories of Enthalpy Changes

Any type of process is accompanied by a change in the enthalpy of the system. There are three fundamental types of processes for which enthalpy changes are considered: physical changes, chemical changes, and nuclear changes.

Physical Changes

Recall that a physical change in a substance is a change in its condition that does not change its chemical properties. There are two physical changes in systems that are associated with significant changes in the enthalpy of a system. One such change occurs when one substance dissolves in another. The most common situation is the dissolving of a solid in water. The second commonly encountered physical change that is accompanied with a large enthalpy change is the phase change.

Enthalpy of Solution

Three steps, each involving an enthalpy change, must occur for a solute to become dissolved in water or in another solvent.

- Bonds between molecules or ions of a solute must be broken to make room for the solvent molecules.
- Bonds between solvent molecules must be broken to make room for the solute molecules.
- Bonds must form between the solvent molecules and solute molecules or ions. These bonds can be intermolecular bonds, ionic bonds, dipole-dipole bonds, or any other type of bond between molecules or ions.

enthalpy of solution, $\Delta H_{solution}$ the enthalpy change associated with a solute dissolving in a solvent

An enthalpy change is associated with each of these processes. The sum of all of these enthalpy changes is called the **enthalpy of solution, $\Delta H_{solution}$**.

Enthalpies of solution can be endothermic or exothermic, depending on the nature of the solute and the solvent. Examples of each are shown in **Figure 5.6**. Note that in both processes, the enthalpies associated with separating both solute and solvent particles (ions or molecules), $\Delta H_{solvent}$ and ΔH_{solute}, are positive. Energy is always required to break bonds. The enthalpy associated with mixing solute and solvent particles, ΔH_{mix}, is negative. Energy is always released when bonds form. The factor that determines whether the overall process is endothermic or exothermic is the relative sizes of the enthalpy of mixing and the sum of the enthalpies of separating the particles, $\Delta H_{solvent} + \Delta H_{solute}$.

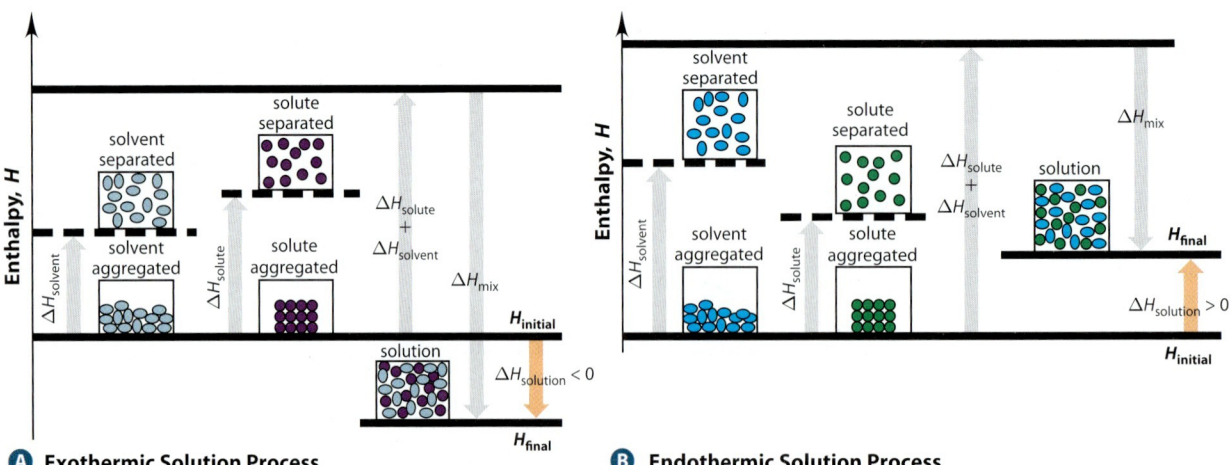

Figure 5.6 The three processes that occur when a substance is dissolved are represented here. Notice that $\Delta H_{solvent}$ and ΔH_{solute} are added together and placed in a single upward arrow in order to compare this sum with the ΔH_{mix}. The orange arrows show the size and direction of the arrow representing the overall enthalpy change for dissolving the substance. Enthalpies of solution can be exothermic (**A**) or endothermic (**B**).

Enthalpy of Phase Changes

In chemistry, a phase is any physically distinct, homogenous part of a system. The physical state of a substance—whether it is a solid, liquid, or gas—is an example of a phase. Phase changes are physical changes for which the enthalpy change is well-defined and thus can be easily studied.

A significant amount of heat must be added to or removed from a substance to change its phase. **Figure 5.7** defines the symbols for enthalpy changes that accompany phase changes. Subscripts are added to the symbol, ΔH, to identify the type of phase change. The superscripted symbol "°" is called "nought," and it represents standard conditions. Because enthalpy changes vary with pressure, the values are reported for standard atmospheric pressure. The four phase changes represented in **Figure 5.7** are summarized below.

- Energy needed to change a solid into a liquid is called *enthalpy of melting* and is symbolized $\Delta H°_{melt}$.
- Energy needed to change a liquid into a gas is called *enthalpy of vaporization* and is symbolized $\Delta H°_{vap}$.
- Energy released when a gas becomes a liquid is called *enthalpy of condensation* and is symbolized $\Delta H°_{cond}$.
- Energy released when a liquid becomes a solid is called *enthalpy of freezing* and is symbolized $\Delta H°_{fre}$.

Notice that the magnitudes of $\Delta H°_{melt}$ and $\Delta H°_{fre}$ are equal, but the directions are opposite. Therefore, one phase change is the negative of the other. The same is true for $\Delta H°_{vap}$ and $\Delta H°_{cond}$:

$$\Delta H°_{melt} = -\Delta H°_{fre}$$
$$\Delta H°_{vap} = -\Delta H°_{cond}$$

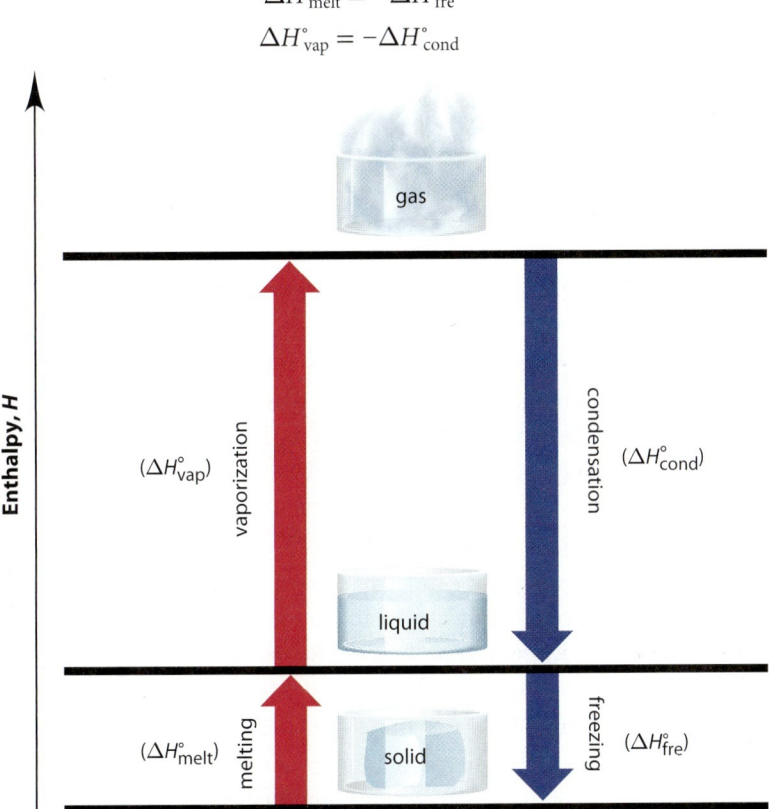

Figure 5.7 Enthalpy changes that accompany melting, vaporization, condensation, and freezing.

Terminology Differences with Enthalpy

The terminology used to describe enthalpy changes differs among textbooks and other information resources, so it is helpful to be aware of the other terms. Many resources use the term "heat" instead of "enthalpy." For example, the enthalpy of vaporization is sometimes called the heat of vaporization. In older textbooks, it is called the latent heat of vaporization. As well, most advanced chemistry textbooks use only two symbols: one for the transition between a solid and a liquid and another for the transition between a liquid and a gas. The symbol $\Delta H°_{vap}$ is used for both vaporization and condensation. You just use the positive value for vaporization and the negative value for condensation. Similarly, both $\Delta H°_{melt}$ and $\Delta H°_{fre}$ are symbolized $\Delta H°_{fus}$ and called the enthalpy of fusion.

Enthalpy and the Heating Curve of Water

Table 5.2 lists enthalpies of melting and vaporization for selected substances. Enthalpies for phase changes are typically reported in kilojoules per mole, kJ/mol.

Table 5.2 Enthalpies of Melting and Vaporization for Selected Elements and Compounds

Substance	$\Delta H°_{melt}$ (kJ/mol)	$\Delta H°_{vap}$ (kJ/mol)
Water	6.01	40.7
Mercury	2.30	19.2
Oxygen	0.44	6.82
Methane	0.94	8.19
Acetic acid	11.7	23.7
Ethoxyethane	7.19	26.5

You now have all of the information needed to analyze the changes when water is transformed from a solid to a gas. **Figure 5.8**, called a heating curve for water, shows how much heat must be added to 1 mol of water to increase its temperature from −25°C to 125°C.

- Between points A and B on the graph, the water is solid and is absorbing enough heat to increase the temperature from −25°C to 0°C. You could calculate the amount of heat added to the solid water by using $Q = mc\Delta T$. Note, however, that c for solid water is different from c for liquid water.

- Between points B and C on the graph, 6.01 kJ of heat are added to the 1 mol of water with no change in temperature. All of the energy is being used to break the intermolecular bonds between water molecules. The heat added in this region of the graph is the enthalpy of melting. When all of the solid water has melted, intermolecular bonds still exist between water molecules, but the molecules have enough energy to break away and then bond with another molecule. The water is in its liquid state.

- Between points C and D on the graph, the heat gained by the water increases the temperature of the water. You could calculate the amount of heat needed in this range by using $Q = mc\Delta T$. Remember, however, that the specific heat capacity is usually given in joules per gram. You would have to convert 1 mol of water to grams of water to use the formula. (Did you calculate a value of 8.18 kJ for Q?)

- Between points D and E on the graph, 40.7 kJ of heat are added to the 1 mol of water with no change in temperature. All of the heat is used to completely break all intermolecular bonds between water molecules and allow the molecules to escape from the liquid. This amount of heat is equal to the enthalpy of vaporization.

- Finally, between points E and F on the graph, the heat that is added to the water increases the temperature of the gaseous water. Once again, you could calculate this amount of heat by using $Q = mc\Delta T$, where c is the specific heat capacity of gaseous water.

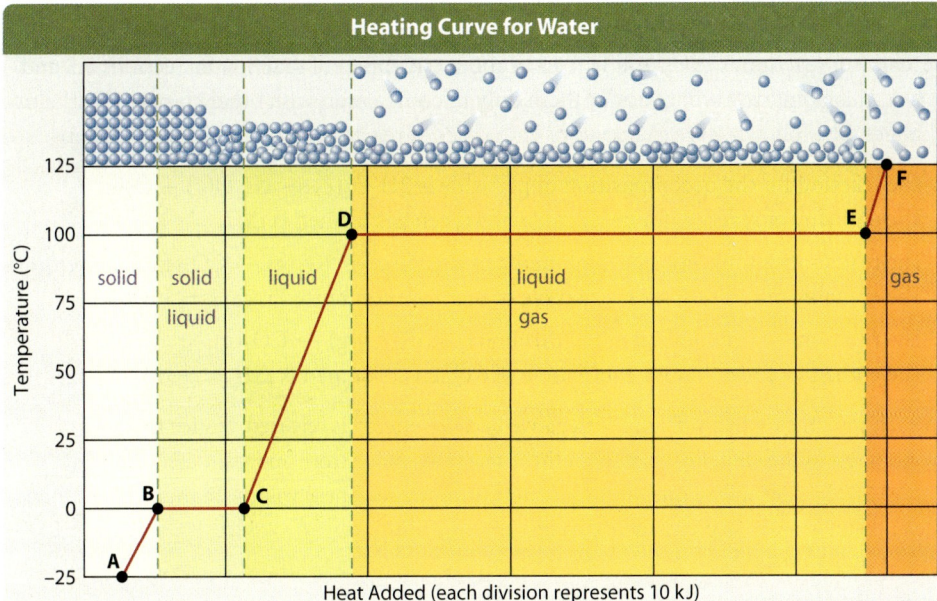

Figure 5.8 The illustrations above this heating curve for water represent water molecules as they interact with one another in different states and in transition between states.

Activity 5.1 | Make Your Own Hot Pack or Cold Pack

Commercially available hot and cold packs are useful for first-aid treatment when hot water or ice is not readily available. Also, hot packs are used by hikers and mountaineers in cases of extreme cold. You can make a simple hot pack or cold pack using a sealable plastic bag containing a solid compound, usually ionic. When water is added, the reaction either absorbs heat or gives off heat. In this activity, you will prepare either a hot pack or a cold pack using only these materials.

Safety Precautions

- Wear safety eyewear throughout this activity.
- Wear a lab coat or apron throughout this activity.
- Wear gloves when handling the chemicals.
- Wash your hands when you have finished this activity.

Materials

- a variety of water-soluble compounds—for example, NH_4NO_3, NH_4Cl, $CaCl_2$, $NaCl$, $NaCH_3CO_2$ (anhydrous), CaO (anhydrous), $MgSO_4$ (anhydrous), urea (H_2NCONH_2)
- distilled water
- resealable plastic bags (small and large)
- balance
- thermometer
- 100 mL graduated cylinder
- 100 mL beaker

Procedure

1. With your group, devise an initial design for your hot pack or cold pack that will allow you to quantitatively test at least one compound for its effectiveness at absorbing or releasing heat.
2. Construct a data table to record appropriate data.
3. Test your design with one of the available compounds. If necessary, refine your design.
4. Using your refined design, test one of the compounds for its suitability as a hot pack or a cold pack.
5. If time permits, repeat this investigation using another compound.
6. Dispose of the waste as directed by your teacher.

Questions

1. Based on your data or class data, which compound would make the best hot pack? Why? Which would make the best cold pack? Why? Use the terms *endothermic* or *exothermic*, and *system* and *surroundings* in your answers.
2. If you were to prepare a hot pack or a cold pack for commercial use, what safety concerns should you consider? Explain how you could use material safety data sheets to obtain safety information.
3. If you were to prepare these hot packs or cold packs commercially, what design changes would you like to make?
4. What economic factors would you take into account before preparing a commercial hot pack or cold pack?

Chemical Changes

Every chemical reaction has an enthalpy change associated with it. The symbol for the enthalpy of reaction is ΔH_r. You will learn about enthalpies of reaction in Sections 5.2 and 5.3. At this point, you will consider them only in comparison with other classes of enthalpy changes. The following are examples of enthalpies of reaction for a few simple reactions.

- The reaction for the decomposition of peroxide is $2H_2O_2(\ell) \rightarrow 2H_2O(\ell) + O_2(g)$.
  The enthalpy of reaction for every mole of oxygen gas formed is $\Delta H_r = -196.4$ kJ.
- The reaction for the combustion of methane is $CH_4(g) + 2O_2(g) \rightarrow CO_2(g) + 2H_2O(g)$.
  The enthalpy of reaction for every mole of methane combusted is $\Delta H_r = -890$ kJ.
- The reaction for the combustion of carbon is $C(s) + O_2(g) \rightarrow CO_2(g)$.
  The enthalpy of reaction for every mole of oxygen consumed is $\Delta H_r = -393.5$ kJ.

In each case, the enthalpy change is negative because energy is released. Notice that the magnitudes of the enthalpy changes of these reactions range from approximately 200 kJ to almost 900 kJ per mole of one of the reactants or products. These values are much larger than the enthalpies associated with phase changes.

Nuclear Changes

Atoms of some elements spontaneously emit particles from their nuclei and are transformed into other elements. Two different particles can be emitted. The nuclei of some radioactive isotopes emit beta (β) particles, which are identical to electrons. The nuclei of other radioactive elements emit alpha (α) particles, which are identical to helium nuclei (two protons and two neutrons). As well, the total mass of the products is measurably smaller than the mass of the original nucleus. The missing mass is converted into energy according to Einstein's equation, $E = mc^2$, where m is the amount of mass that was converted into energy and c is the speed of light.

Alpha Decay

When a nucleus emits an α particle, the resulting nucleus has two fewer protons and two fewer neutrons. Therefore, its mass number is reduced by 4 and its atomic number is reduced by 2. For example, radium-223 emits an α particle and becomes a radon-219 atom. The nuclear reaction can be written as shown here, where the α particle is written as a helium atom.

$$^{223}_{88}Ra \rightarrow {}^{4}_{2}He + {}^{219}_{86}Rn + \text{energy}$$

When 1 mol of radium-223 decays into radon-219, 5.64×10^8 kJ of energy is released.

Beta Decay

When a nucleus emits a β particle, a neutron in the nucleus becomes a proton. Therefore, the new nucleus has one less neutron and one more proton. For example, cesium-137 emits a β particle and becomes barium-137. This nuclear reaction can be written as shown below, where the β particle is written as an electron.

$$^{137}_{55}Cs \rightarrow {}^{0}_{-1}e + {}^{137}_{56}Ba + \text{energy}$$

When 1 mol of cesium-137 decays into barium-137, 1.13×10^8 kJ of energy is released.

Nuclear Fission

Nuclear fission is a process in which a heavier nucleus is split into smaller, lighter nuclei with the release of energy. For example, bombarding uranium-235 with neutrons causes the uranium-235 nucleus to split into two smaller nuclei. The two smaller nuclei can vary among many combinations of elements. One example is shown as an equation below and it is also shown in **Figure 5.9**.

$$^{235}_{92}U + {}^{1}_{0}n \rightarrow {}^{141}_{56}Ba + {}^{92}_{36}Kr + 3{}^{1}_{0}n + \text{energy}$$

The sum of the masses of the products is 0.215 u (atomic mass units) or 3.57×10^{-28} kg less than the mass of a uranium atom. When 1 mol of uranium-235 fissions, the amount of mass that is converted into energy is 2.15×10^{-4} kg. You can calculate the amount of energy released when 1 mol of uranium-235 fissions, using $E = mc^2$ as shown below.

$$\begin{aligned} E &= mc^2 \\ &= (2.15 \times 10^{-4} \text{ kg})\left(3.00 \times 10^8 \, \frac{\text{m}}{\text{s}}\right)^2 \\ &= 1.93 \times 10^{13} \text{ J} \end{aligned}$$

(**Note:** The unit kg·m²/s² is equivalent to the J.)

Thus, approximately 2×10^{10} kJ of energy is released when 1 mol of uranium-235 fissions. The products of nuclear fission are very radioactive.

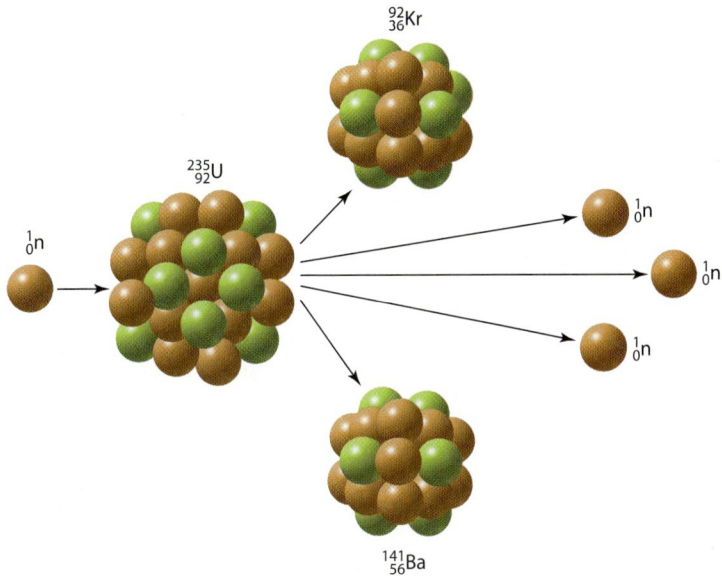

Figure 5.9 In this example, when a uranium-235 nucleus absorbs a neutron, it splits into a krypton-92 nucleus and a barium-141 nucleus and three neutrons. The krypton and barium isotopes are radioactive.

Nuclear Fusion

Another nuclear reaction occurs in the Sun. This process is called *nuclear fusion*. Two very small nuclei combine, or fuse, to form a slightly larger nucleus. The reaction that occurs most frequently in the Sun is the fusion of deuterium ($^2_1$H) and tritium ($^3_1$H), to form a very unstable helium-5 ($^5_2$He), which immediately breaks down into helium-4 ($^4_2$He) and a neutron ($^1_0$n). The reaction is shown below and is also illustrated in **Figure 5.10**. The helium-4 that is produced is stable, and thus fusion does not produce radioactive materials.

$$^2_1\text{H} + ^3_1\text{H} \rightarrow ^5_2\text{He} \rightarrow ^4_2\text{He} + ^1_0\text{n} + \text{energy}$$

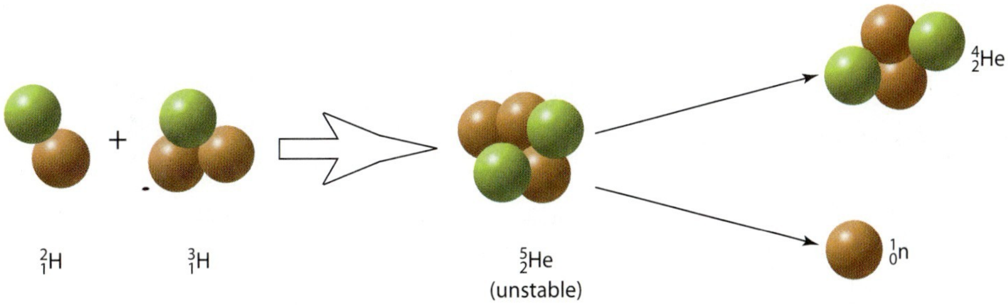

Figure 5.10 Many small nuclei undergo fusion to form a larger nucleus. This reaction is the most common reaction in the Sun.

The sum of the masses of helium-4 and the neutron is less than the sum of the masses of deuterium and tritium, and thus some mass has been converted into energy. When 1 mol of deuterium and 1 mol of tritium fuse, 1.7×10^9 kJ of energy is released. This value is approximately 10 times smaller than the energy released when 1 mol of uranium-235 fissions. However, the sum of the masses of deuterium and tritium is about 47 times smaller than the mass of uranium-235. Therefore, the energy released per unit mass is much larger for nuclear fusion than for nuclear fission. As well, nuclear fusion does not produce radioactive products.

In order for two small atoms to undergo nuclear fusion, they must collide with a tremendous amount of kinetic energy. The extremely high temperature and pressure in the Sun give the atoms enough energy. With every fusion reaction, more energy is released that maintains the high temperature, and therefore the fusion reactions continue to occur. For more than 50 years, scientists have been searching for methods to give deuterium and tritium sufficient energy to undergo fusion under controlled conditions. These reactions have occurred but cannot yet be sustained. Thus far in the research, more energy has been used to cause the reactions than has been released by the reactions under controlled conditions. Nevertheless, teams in several locations throughout the world are continuing to conduct research to find a way to accomplish controlled fusion. **Figure 5.11** shows a facility in California where fusion research is being carried out. If this research is successful, new nuclear fusion reactors will provide vast amounts of energy without producing radioactive by-products or greenhouse gases.

Comparing Enthalpy Changes

Table 5.3 lists the ranges in the values of enthalpy changes for physical, chemical, and nuclear changes. Notice that enthalpy changes associated with physical changes are the smallest. Enthalpy changes associated with chemical changes are greater than those of physical changes but less than those of nuclear reactions. Enthalpy changes associated with nuclear changes are much greater than any other type of change.

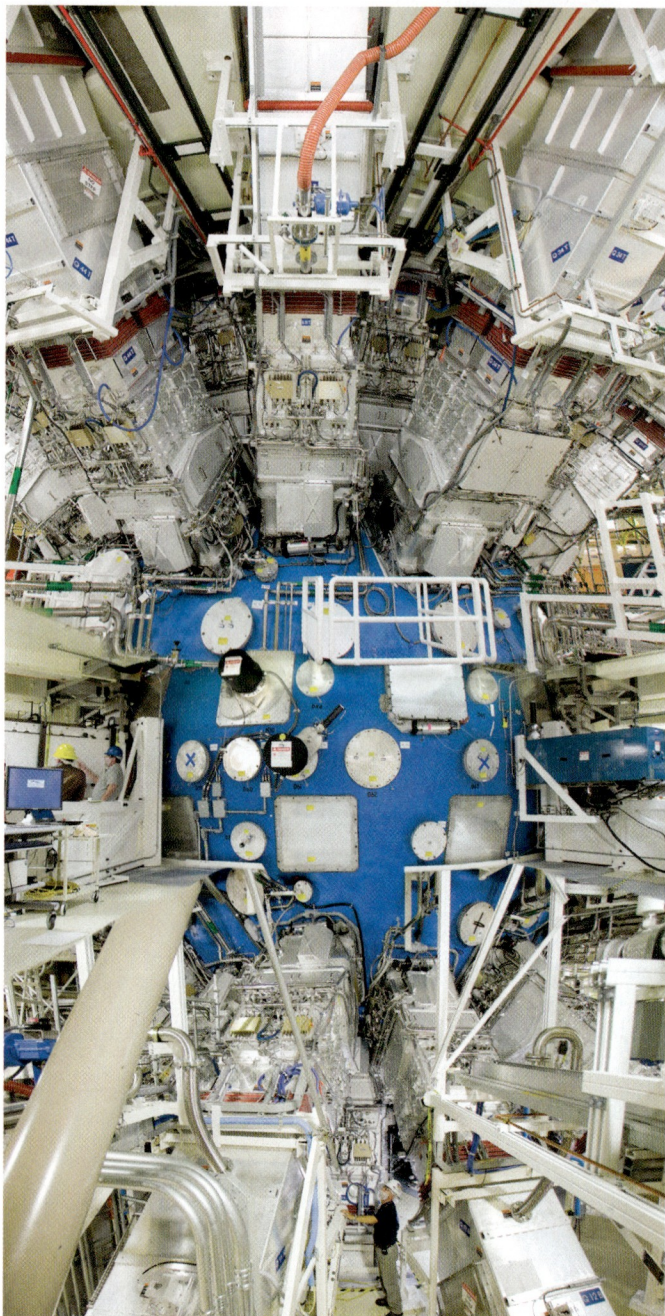

Figure 5.11 In March 2009, at the National Ignition Facility at the Lawrence Livermore National Laboratory in Livermore, California, a laser beam delivered 1.1 million joules of ultraviolet light to the target chamber where fusion experiments are conducted. This was the first time a fusion laser had delivered an amount of energy greater than one megajoule.

Table 5.3 Range of ΔH Values of Selected Examples of Physical, Chemical, and Nuclear Changes

Type of Change	Range of ΔH Values (kJ/mol)
Physical	± 0.44 to ± 40.7
Chemical	± 196.4 to ± 890
Nuclear	-1.13×10^8 to -2×10^{10}

Note: The $\pm$ signs indicate that the values can be positive or negative, depending on the direction of the change.

Section 5.1 Review

Section Summary

- A system is the object or substance being studied, and the surroundings are everything else in the universe. Systems can be open, closed, or isolated.
- Open and closed systems can exchange energy with the surroundings by doing work on the surroundings, or by the surroundings doing work on the system.
- The first law of thermodynamics states that energy cannot be created or destroyed but can be transformed from one type of energy to another type of energy or transferred from one object to another object.
- The second law of thermodynamics states that, when two objects are in thermal contact, heat will be transferred from the object at a higher temperature to the object at the lower temperature until they reach thermal equilibrium.
- An enthalpy change in a system, occurring at constant pressure, is the same as the amount of heat that is exchanged between the system and its surroundings. Enthalpy changes can be positive or negative and depend only on the initial and final states of the system.
- The range of enthalpy changes is lowest for physical changes, intermediate for chemical changes, and highest for nuclear changes.

Review Questions

1. **K/U** When a system consisting of solid calcium chloride, $CaCl_2(s)$, is dissolved in a beaker containing 100 mL of water, the temperature of the solution increases. Is the system gaining or losing thermal energy? Explain your answer.

2. **T/I** How much thermal energy is required to warm 350.0 g of ethanol, $C_2H_5OH(\ell)$, from $-6.4°C$ to $21.7°C$?

3. **T/I** Recall that in the symbol ^A_ZX, A is the mass number, Z is the atomic number, and X is the chemical symbol. Balance the nuclear equations below with the appropriate nuclear particle (^1_0n, $^0_{-1}e$, ^1_1p).
   a. $^{14}_6C \rightarrow {}^{14}_7N + $ _____
   b. $^1_0n \rightarrow $ _____ $ + {}^0_{-1}e$
   c. $^{55}_{26}Fe + $ _____ $ \rightarrow {}^{55}_{25}Mn + $ energy

4. **A** Ethoxyethane, $C_2H_5OC_2H_5(\ell)$, is a solvent that is slightly polar. Table salt, NaCl(s), is an ionic solid. Ethanol, $C_2H_5OH(\ell)$, is moderately polar. Compare the mixing of table salt and ethanol with ethoxyethane. In which compound would you predict the solute-solvent attractions to be greater? How would this affect the enthalpy of solution, $\Delta H_{solution}$? Explain your answers in a few sentences.

5. **T/I** The melting point of $O_2(s)$ is $-219°C$. Determine the amount of thermal energy that must be removed to completely freeze 15.0 mol $O_2(\ell)$ at this temperature.

6. **T/I** A piece of gold having a mass of 15.55 g is warmed to $14.7°C$ by the addition of 164.7 J of thermal energy. What was the initial temperature of the gold?

7. **T/I** By how much will the temperature of 2.00 kg of air change if it absorbs all of the heat given up when 1.00 kg of water cools from $40.0°C$ to $20.0°C$?

8. **K/U** State the first law of thermodynamics and express the law as an equation.

9. **T/I** A system does 500 J of work on its surroundings. At the same time, 500 J of energy enters the system. What is the change in energy of the system, ΔE_{system}?

10. **A** For each of the processes listed, define a system and state the sign of the enthalpy change for the system. Explain your reasoning for each answer.
    a. natural gas burning in a furnace
    b. water boiling
    c. moving from a seated position to a standing position
    d. melted wax solidifying
    e. hydrogen atoms undergoing nuclear fusion in the Sun

11. **C** Frost forms on the windshield of a car on a cold winter morning. This frost disappears with no evidence that liquid water forms. Draw an enthalpy diagram to illustrate the change.

12. **A** Refer to **Figure 5.8**. Explain the significance of the difference in the region between B and C compared with that between D and E. Use diagrams to support your explanation.

13. **K/U** Compare nuclear reactions with chemical reactions with respect to the following:
    a. identity of the atoms in the reactants and products
    b. type of atomic particles involved
    c. energy change

SECTION 5.2 Thermochemical Equations and Calorimetry

Key Terms

calorimeter
calorimetry
simple calorimeter
bomb calorimeter

In Section 5.1, you were introduced briefly to the enthalpy changes of chemical reactions. In this section and the next, you will focus on chemical reactions in more detail. First, consider the reason that enthalpy changes occur when a chemical reaction takes place. Although chemical reactions do not occur exactly as described below, it is valid to visualize a chemical reaction as happening in two steps.

In the first step of a chemical reaction, all chemical bonds are broken. In the second step, new bonds are formed. Energy is always needed to break bonds, so bond-breaking is endothermic. Energy is always released when bonds form, so bond-forming is exothermic. The amount of energy released or required varies greatly depending on the types of atoms and their bonding. For example, when a bond forms between a carbon atom and a hydrogen atom, the amount of energy released is quite different from the amount of energy released when a bond forms between an oxygen atom and a hydrogen atom. **Figure 5.12** shows the amount of energy needed to break all the bonds in a methane molecule and in two oxygen molecules. It also shows the energy released when bonds form between the same atoms in a different arrangement. A carbon dioxide molecule and two water molecules form. The difference between the total amount of energy used to break bonds and the total energy released when the bonds reform is equal to the enthalpy change of the reaction.

$$CH_4(g) + 2O_2(g) \rightarrow CO_2(g) + 2H_2O(\ell)$$

Under standard conditions, 890.8 kJ of heat is released when 1 mol of methane is combusted in 2 mol of oxygen, forming 1 mol of carbon dioxide and 2 mol of liquid water. As discussed on the next page, chemists have devised two different ways to include the enthalpy change in a chemical equation. In addition, you will see how an enthalpy diagram can help to visualize information related to enthalpy change.

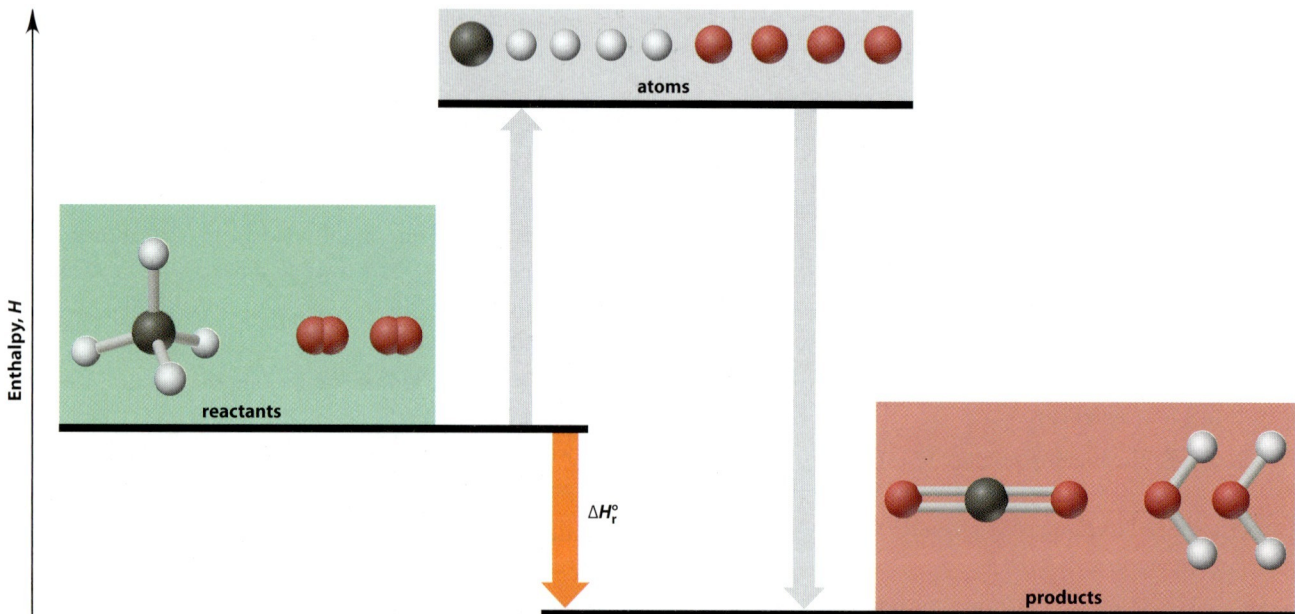

Figure 5.12 It takes less energy to break all of the bonds in a methane molecule and in two oxygen molecules compared with the energy that is released when the same atoms form a carbon dioxide molecule and two water molecules.

Thermochemical Equations

You have seen equations that include the word "energy," such as the equation below, which indicates energy is released in this reaction.

$$CH_4(g) + 2O_2(g) \rightarrow CO_2(g) + 2H_2O(\ell) + \text{energy}$$

To write a thermochemical equation, instead of writing "energy," write the numerical value for the enthalpy change of the reaction, as shown.

$$CH_4(g) + 2O_2(g) \rightarrow CO_2(g) + 2H_2O(\ell) + 890.8 \text{ kJ}$$

If energy is required to make a reaction proceed in the direction in which it is written, the enthalpy change term is on the left side of the equation. For example, the energy in lightning causes formation of nitrogen dioxide from oxygen and nitrogen in the air. The thermochemical equation is written as follows:

$$N_2(g) + 2O_2(g) + 66.4 \text{ kJ} \rightarrow 2NO_2(g)$$

It is critical to correctly interpret the meaning of the energy indicated in a thermochemical equation. The total enthalpy change of a reaction depends on the amounts of reactants that are converted into products. Obviously, 1 mol of methane gas combusted in oxygen will not produce as much heat as will 50 mol of methane when combusted in oxygen. Thermochemical equations are written with the assumption that the coefficients of the reactants and products represent the amount in moles of each substance that is involved in the reaction. The second form of the equation above in which methane is combusted in oxygen reads, "1 mol of methane and 2 mol of oxygen react to produce 1 mol of carbon dioxide, 2 mol of water, and 890.8 kJ of heat." A simpler way to read the equation uses the phrase "as written," which implies that the coefficients represent the amount in moles of reactants and products. The equation above could be read, "The enthalpy change of the reaction between methane and oxygen, as written, is −890.8 kJ."

ΔH Notation

You may also write the enthalpy term beside the chemical equation as shown here.

$$CH_4(g) + 2O_2(g) \rightarrow CO_2(g) + 2H_2O(\ell) \qquad \Delta H_r = -890.8 \text{ kJ}$$

$$N_2(g) + 2O_2(g) \rightarrow 2NO_2(g) \qquad \Delta H_r = +66.4 \text{ kJ}$$

The subscript "r" means that this value represents the enthalpy change of a *reaction*. The ΔH notation also implies that the coefficients represent the amount in moles of the reactants and products that are involved in the reaction. Normally, you would not include the plus sign in the notation, but it is used in this example and throughout this textbook to emphasize the nature of the reaction being discussed.

Enthalpy Diagrams

Enthalpy diagrams can help you to visualize the relative enthalpies of the reactants and products and whether the reaction is endothermic or exothermic. The two diagrams in **Figure 5.13** (on the next page) represent the same reactions that you have seen above. Notice that the *y*-axis is the Enthalpy axis. It does not have a zero point, because it is not possible to know the absolute enthalpy of the compounds involved in the reaction. Only *changes in enthalpy* can be measured and therefore represented in a diagram. Also note that there is no *x*-axis in an enthalpy diagram, because the enthalpy change of a system depends only on the initial and final states of the system and is not affected by anything that occurs during the process.

When a reaction is exothermic (has a negative enthalpy change) the reactants have a larger enthalpy than the products and are therefore drawn above the products, as shown in **Figure 5.13A**. The arrow representing the enthalpy change points downward. When a reaction is endothermic (has a positive enthalpy change), the products have a larger enthalpy than the reactants. Therefore, the products are drawn above the reactants and the arrow representing the enthalpy change points upward, as shown in **Figure 5.13B**.

Figure 5.13 Chemists use the concept of enthalpy because it depends only on the initial and final states of a system that undergoes a process. Therefore, enthalpy diagrams need to represent only the initial and final conditions of the compounds in a chemical reaction. The processes that occur during the reaction do not affect the enthalpy change.

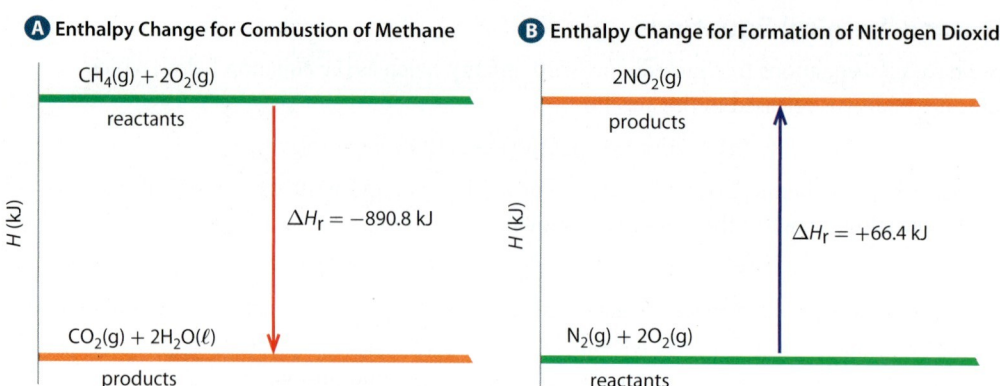

Molar Enthalpy of Combustion

Combustion reactions are so important in thermochemistry that they are given their own symbol: ΔH_{comb}. You can find standard molar enthalpies of combustion ($\Delta H°_{comb}$) in reference tables and many other sources of chemical data. Before you use these data, however, it is important to understand how to interpret the values. You know that the term "standard" means that the values are given for a temperature of 25°C and a pressure of 100 kPa. Since combustion reactions release a large amount of heat and the products are extremely hot, how can the values represent a reaction taking place under standard conditions? In determining the values, chemists have accounted for all of the steps that occur between the reactants at 25°C and 100 kPa of pressure, the combustion process, and products returning to 25°C and 100 kPa of pressure.

Another question arises when you consider the coefficients in reaction equations for combustion. For example, examine the following examples of combustion reactions:

$$C_5H_{12}(\ell) + 8O_2(g) \rightarrow 5CO_2(g) + 6H_2O(\ell)$$
$$2CH_3OH(\ell) + 5O_2(g) \rightarrow 2CO_2(g) + 8H_2O(\ell)$$
$$CH_3COCH_3(\ell) + 4O_2(g) \rightarrow 3CO_2(g) + 3H_2O(\ell)$$
$$2C_4H_{10}(g) + 13O_2(g) \rightarrow 8CO_2(g) + 10H_2O(\ell)$$

If you interpret the coefficients as the amount in moles of substances involved in the reaction, you see that a widely varying amount in moles of reactants and products can be involved in a single reaction. Values for standard molar enthalpies of combustion listed in tables refer only to the compound that is undergoing combustion. For example, in the first equation above, the value that you would find in a table such as **Table 5.4** represents the enthalpy change that occurs when 1 mol of pentane, C_5H_{12}, is combusted. The amount in moles of the other reactant and the products are not considered in the enthalpy of combustion for a specific compound.

The values for enthalpy changes in a thermochemical equation or beside the equation with the ΔH notation are the values for the equation "as written." In the second and fourth equations above, the methanol and the butane both have coefficients of 2. However, the $\Delta H°_{comb}$ values in tables represent the combustion of 1 mol of the compound undergoing combustion. Thus, they do not fit the equations above "as written." For that reason, you will sometimes see equations written with fractional coefficients, so the compound under consideration can be written with a coefficient of 1. For example, the second and fourth equations might be written as shown here, where all of the coefficients have been divided by 2.

$$CH_3OH(\ell) + \frac{5}{2}O_2(g) \rightarrow CO_2(g) + 4H_2O(\ell)$$

$$C_4H_{10}(g) + \frac{13}{2}O_2(g) \rightarrow 4CO_2(g) + 5H_2O(\ell)$$

No matter how an equation is written, the values in reference tables are always molar values. Some typical values of standard molar enthalpies of combustion are listed in **Table 5.4**.

Table 5.4 Some Representative Values of Standard Molar Enthalpy of Combustion*

Compound	Formula	$\Delta H°_{comb}$ (kJ/mol)
Methane	$CH_4(g)$	−890.8
Ethane	$C_2H_6(g)$	−1560.7
Propane	$C_3H_8(g)$	−2219.2
Butane	$C_4H_{10}(g)$	−2877.6
Pentane	$C_5H_{12}(\ell)$	−3509.0
Hexane	$C_6H_{14}(\ell)$	−4163.2
Heptane	$C_7H_{16}(\ell)$	−4817.0
Octane	$C_8H_{18}(\ell)$	−5470.3
Methanol	$CH_3OH(\ell)$	−726.1
Ethanol	$C_2H_5OH(\ell)$	−1366.8
Glycerol	$CH_2OHCHOHCH_2OH(\ell)$	−1655.4
Acetone	$CH_3COCH_3(\ell)$	−1789.9
Benzoic acid	$C_7H_6O_2(s)$	−3228.2
Ammonia	$NH_3(g)$	−382.8
Dinitrogen monoxide	$N_2O(g)$	−82.1

Note: Because these are *standard* values, meaning that the reactants started at 25°C and the products ended at 25°C, the products are $H_2O(\ell)$ and $CO_2(g)$. Many tables provide values that are not *standard* values.

Learning Check

7. The standard molar enthalpy of combustion, $\Delta H°_{comb}$, of a hydrocarbon is always a negative value. Is the enthalpy term included as a reactant or a product in thermochemical equations representing combustion reactions? How do you know?

8. For the reaction shown below, which has more potential energy: the reactants or the products? State a reason for your choice.
   $CH_4(g) + 2O_2(g) \rightarrow CO_2(g) + 2H_2O(g) + 802.5$ kJ

9. When ethane, $C_2H_6(g)$, undergoes complete combustion to form carbon dioxide and water, the standard molar enthalpy of combustion, $\Delta H°_{comb}$, is −1560.7 kJ/mol. Write the thermochemical equation for the combustion of ethane.

10. Sketch an enthalpy diagram for the combustion of cyclopropane, $C_3H_6(g)$.
    $C_3H_6(g) + \frac{9}{2}O_2(g) \rightarrow 3CO_2(g) + 3H_2O(\ell)$
    $\Delta H°_{comb} = -2091.3$ kJ/mol

11. The complete combustion of benzoic acid, $C_7H_6O_2(s)$, is represented by the equation shown below.
    $2C_7H_6O_2(s) + 15O_2(g) \rightarrow$
    $\qquad 14CO_2(g) + 6H_2O(\ell) + 6456.4$ kJ
    What is the standard molar enthalpy of combustion, $\Delta H°_{comb}$, per mole of benzoic acid?

12. The equations representing complete combustion of the esters methyl methanoate, $C_2H_4O_2(\ell)$, and methyl ethanoate, $C_3H_6O_2(\ell)$, are as follows:
    $C_2H_4O_2(\ell) + 2O_2(g) \rightarrow$
    $\qquad 2CO_2(g) + 2H_2O(\ell) + 972.6$ kJ
    $2C_3H_6O_2(\ell) + 7O_2(g) \rightarrow$
    $\qquad 6CO_2(g) + 6H_2O(\ell) + 3184.4$ kJ
    What is the standard molar enthalpy of combustion, $\Delta H°_{comb}$, for the ester having the greater value for this property?

Reactant Amounts and Enthalpy of Reaction

A roaring bonfire releases more thermal energy than does a burning matchstick. The reaction is the same, but the quantities involved are different. *The enthalpy change associated with a reaction depends on the amounts of the reactants involved.* For example, the thermochemical equation for the combustion of pentane indicates that 3509.0 kJ of energy is released when 1 mol of pentane is combusted. The combustion of 2 mol of pentane releases twice as much energy, or 7018.0 kJ.

$$C_5H_{12}(\ell) + 8O_2(g) \rightarrow 5CO_2(g) + 6H_2O(\ell) + 3509.0 \text{ kJ}$$
$$2C_5H_{12}(\ell) + 16O_2(g) \rightarrow 10CO_2(g) + 12H_2O(\ell) + 7018.0 \text{ kJ}$$

The enthalpy of a reaction is directly proportional to the amounts of the substances that react. That is, if the amounts of the reactants double, the enthalpy change also doubles. In other words, when you multiply the stoichiometric coefficients of a thermochemical equation by any factor, you must multiply the enthalpy term by the same factor.

If you know the thermochemical equation for a reaction, you can multiply the enthalpy term by the appropriate stoichiometric factor to predict the enthalpy change associated with the reaction for any amount of products or reactants. The enthalpy change for a reaction is equal to the amount in moles of a specified reactant or product times the enthalpy change for 1 mol of the specified reactant or product. Thus, the enthalpy change for a reaction can be expressed as follows:

> The enthalpy change of a reaction is equal to the amount in moles, n, of a specified reactant or product multiplied by the standard molar enthalpy change for the specified reactant or product.
>
> $$\Delta H_r = n\Delta H_r^\circ$$

If you know the enthalpy of a reaction, you can use it to determine the amounts of the reactants or products involved, as shown in the Sample Problems below.

Sample Problem

Calculating an Enthalpy Change

a. What is the enthalpy change when a 50.00 g sample of methane undergoes complete combustion according to the equation $CH_4(g) + 2O_2(g) \rightarrow CO_2(g) + 2H_2O(\ell)$?

b. What is the enthalpy of the reaction per mole of $O_2(g)$ consumed, $CO_2(g)$ produced, and $H_2O(\ell)$ produced?

Many people prefer gas stoves because it is easier to control the temperature of the food being cooked. Gas stoves burn natural gas, which is mostly methane.

What Is Required?
You need the enthalpy of combustion, ΔH_{comb}, for 50.00 g of methane.
You need the enthalpy of the reaction, ΔH_r, per mole of $O_2(g)$, $CO_2(g)$, and $H_2O(\ell)$.

What Is Given?
You are given the mass of methane: $m = 50.00$ g

You are given the balanced chemical equation: $CH_4(g) + 2O_2(g) \rightarrow CO_2(g) + 2H_2O(\ell)$

You know that $\Delta H°_{comb} = -890.8$ kJ/mol for methane (from **Table 5.4**)

Plan Your Strategy	Act on Your Strategy
a. Determine the amount of methane by using its mass and its molar mass.	$n = \dfrac{m}{M}$ $= \dfrac{50.00 \text{ g}}{16.05 \dfrac{\text{g}}{\text{mol}}}$ $= 3.115$ mol
Multiply the standard molar enthalpy of combustion by the amount of methane to determine the enthalpy change associated with the combustion of 50.00 g of methane.	$\Delta H_{comb} = n\Delta H°_{comb}$ $= (3.115 \text{ mol})\left(\dfrac{-890.8 \text{ kJ}}{\text{mol}}\right)$ $= -2.775 \times 10^3$ kJ

Plan Your Strategy	Act on Your Strategy
b. Use the mole ratio of $O_2(g)$, $CO_2(g)$, and $H_2O(g)$ to $CH_4(g)$ to find the enthalpy of reaction per mole of the three compounds.	$\Delta H_r \text{ (per mol } O_2\text{)} = \left(\dfrac{n_{CH_4}}{n_{O_2}}\right)\left(\dfrac{\Delta H°_{comb}}{n_{CH_4}}\right)$ $= \left(\dfrac{1 \text{ mol CH}_4}{2 \text{ mol O}_2}\right)\left(\dfrac{-890.8 \text{ kJ}}{1 \text{ mol CH}_4}\right)$ $= -445.4$ kJ $\Delta H_r \text{ (per mol } CO_2\text{)} = \left(\dfrac{n_{CH_4}}{n_{CO_2}}\right)\left(\dfrac{\Delta H°_{comb}}{n_{CH_4}}\right)$ $= \left(\dfrac{1 \text{ mol CH}_4}{1 \text{ mol CO}_2}\right)\left(\dfrac{-890.8 \text{ kJ}}{1 \text{ mol CH}_4}\right)$ $= -890.8$ kJ $\Delta H_r \text{ (per mol } H_2O\text{)} = \left(\dfrac{n_{CH_4}}{n_{H_2O}}\right)\left(\dfrac{\Delta H°_{comb}}{n_{CH_4}}\right)$ $= \left(\dfrac{1 \text{ mol CH}_4}{2 \text{ mol H}_2O}\right)\left(\dfrac{-890.8 \text{ kJ}}{1 \text{ mol CH}_4}\right)$ $= -445.4$ kJ

Check Your Solution
The units are correct. The sign of the enthalpy change is negative, which makes sense because a hydrocarbon combustion reaction is always exothermic. The enthalpy change for the reaction is about three times as great as the molar enthalpy of combustion, which makes sense because about 3 mol of methane was combusted.

Sample Problem

Using Enthalpy Data to Determine the Mass of Products

Problem

When methane is combusted, along with the heat produced, oxygen is consumed. Determine the mass of oxygen consumed if the total change in enthalpy of the reaction is -2.50×10^2 kJ, given the equation:

$$CH_4(g) + 2O_2(g) \rightarrow CO_2(g) + 2H_2O(\ell)$$

What Is Required?

You need to determine the mass of oxygen consumed in a reaction in which the total enthalpy change is -2.50×10^2 kJ.

What Is Given?

You know the chemical equation for the reaction: $CH_4(g) + 2O_2(g) \rightarrow CO_2(g) + 2H_2O(\ell)$

You know that $\Delta H°_{comb} = -890.8$ kJ/mol for methane (from **Table 5.4**).

You also know the total enthalpy change for the given reaction: $\Delta H_r = -2.50 \times 10^2$ kJ

Plan Your Strategy	Act on Your Strategy
Determine the amount in moles of methane combusted by using the formula $\Delta H_r = n\Delta H°_{comb}$.	$\Delta H_r = n\Delta H°_{comb}$ $n = \dfrac{\Delta H_r}{\Delta H°_{comb}}$ $= \dfrac{-2.50 \times 10^2 \text{ kJ}}{-890.8 \dfrac{\text{kJ}}{\text{mol}}}$ $= 0.2806$ mol
Find the amount in moles of oxygen consumed from the ratio of coefficients and the calculated amount in moles of methane combusted.	$\dfrac{n_{O_2}}{n_{CH_4}} = \dfrac{n_{O_2 \text{ consumed}}}{n_{CH_4 \text{ combusted}}}$ $\dfrac{2 \text{ mol } O_2}{1 \text{ mol } CH_4} = \dfrac{n_{O_2 \text{ consumed}}}{0.2806 \text{ mol } CH_4}$ $n_{O_2 \text{ consumed}} = \left(\dfrac{2 \text{ mol } O_2}{1 \text{ mol CH}_4}\right)(0.2806 \text{ mol CH}_4)$ $= 0.5612$ mol O_2
Find the mass of oxygen by using its molar mass and of its amount in moles.	$n = \dfrac{m}{M}$ $m = nM$ $= (0.5612 \text{ mol})\left(32.00 \dfrac{\text{g}}{\text{mol}}\right)$ $= 17.9584$ g $= 18.0$ g Therefore, 18.0 g of oxygen is consumed when the total enthalpy change of the combustion of methane is -2.50×10^2 kJ.

Check Your Solution

The units are correct. The mass of oxygen produced is less than the mass of 2 mol $O_2(g)$, which is 64 g. This makes sense, because the enthalpy change of the reaction was less than $\Delta H°_{comb}$.

Practice Problems

11. Pentane reacts with an excess of oxygen to produce carbon dioxide and water vapour. What is the enthalpy change of the reaction per mole of each of the following gases? The enthalpy of combustion for pentane, $C_5H_{12}(\ell)$, is −3509.0 kJ/mol.
   a. oxygen
   b. carbon dioxide
   c. water

12. What is the enthalpy change when 4.608 g of ethanol, $C_2H_5OH(\ell)$, undergoes complete combustion?
$$C_2H_5OH(\ell) + 3O_2(g) \rightarrow 2CO_2(g) + 3H_2O(\ell) + 1366.8 \text{ kJ}$$

13. Determine the thermal energy released by the combustion of each of the following samples of hydrocarbons to $CO_2(g)$ and $H_2O(\ell)$.
   a. 56.78 g of hexane, $C_6H_{14}(\ell)$
   b. 1.36 kg of octane, $C_8H_{18}(\ell)$
   c. 2.344×10^4 g of heptane, $C_7H_{16}(\ell)$

14. What is the enthalpy change for the combustion of a 1.00 g sample of methane, $CH_4(g)$, under standard conditions?

15. Naphthalene, $C_{10}H_8(s)$, is an organic compound used in the manufacture of dyes, plastics, and some insecticides. What mass of this compound will release 500.0 kJ of thermal energy when burned in an excess of oxygen?
$$C_{10}H_8(s) + 12O_2 \rightarrow 10CO_2(g) + 4H_2O(\ell) + 5156 \text{ kJ}$$

16. What mass, in kilograms, of methanol must be combusted to generate 5.39×10^5 kJ of thermal energy?

17. Answer the questions for the combustion of propene, $C_3H_6(g)$, using the following equation:
$$2C_3H_6(g) + 9O_2(g) \rightarrow 6CO_2(g) + 6H_2O(\ell) + 4116.0 \text{ kJ}$$
   a. Determine the standard molar enthalpy of combustion of propene.
   b. What is the maximum amount of thermal energy available from the combustion of 5.00 g of $C_3H_6(g)$?

18. When 0.050 mol of a hydrocarbon undergoes complete combustion, 110.95 kJ of heat is given off.
   a. What is the enthalpy of combustion for this hydrocarbon?
   b. Refer to **Table 5.4** and identify the hydrocarbon.

19. What mass of butane, $C_4H_{10}(g)$, must undergo complete combustion to produce 1.00 MJ of heat according to the following equation?
$$C_4H_{10}(g) + \frac{13}{2}O_2(g) \rightarrow 4CO_2(g) + 5H_2O(\ell) + 2877.6 \text{ kJ}$$

20. The standard molar enthalpy of combustion of propan-2-ol, $CH_3CH(OH)CH_3(\ell)$, is −2006 kJ/mol.
   a. Write the thermochemical equation for the combustion of 1 mol of this compound to form carbon dioxide and water.
   b. How much heat is given off when 25.00 g of water is produced?

Using Calorimetry To Study Energy Changes

A **calorimeter** is a device that is used to measure the heat released or absorbed by a physical or chemical process taking place within it. **Calorimetry** involves the use of a calorimeter to study the energy changes associated with physical processes and chemical reactions. The term *calorimeter* comes from the word *calorie*, which was the original unit for heat transferred from one object to another.

A calorie is defined as the amount of heat needed to increase the temperature of one gram of water by one degree Celsius. A calorie is not an SI unit, so most scientists no longer use it. However, many dieticians and nutritionists still use the calorie to communicate the amount of energy available in foods. When you see "Calories" written on food labels, it has a capital C, which means 1000 calories. One calorie is equal to 4.184 J and 1 Calorie is equal to 4.184 kJ.

calorimeter a device used to measure the heat released or absorbed during a chemical or physical process occurring within it

calorimetry the technological process of measuring the heat released or absorbed during a chemical or physical process

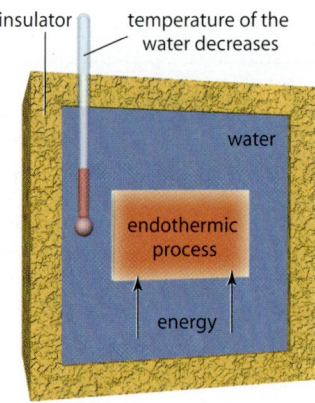
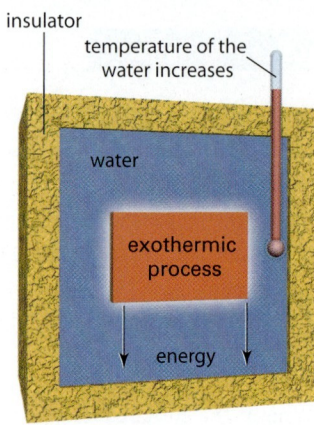

Figure 5.14 If an endothermic process occurs, heat will be transferred from the water to the system in which the process occurs. Because heat was lost, the temperature of the water is reduced.

Figure 5.15 If an exothermic process occurs in the calorimeter, heat will be transferred from the process to the water. Because heat was gained by the water, the temperature increases.

Ideally, a calorimeter is an isolated system, which does not allow products to escape or thermal energy to be transferred to the air or other materials surrounding it. **Figures 5.14** and **5.15** model how a calorimeter works. You can consider the water to be one system and the container in which the process is occurring as another system. The two systems are in thermal contact, but they are isolated from the surroundings.

The Theoretical Basis of Calorimetry

Calorimetry is based on the two laws of thermodynamics. Recall that the first law of thermodynamics, also known as the law of conservation of energy, states that the energy of the universe is constant. This law ensures that any energy added to a system came from the surroundings and, likewise, any energy lost by a system went to the surroundings. In relationship to calorimetry, the most useful statement of the second law of thermodynamics is stated in the following box.

> **Second Law of Thermodynamics**
> *Thermal energy is spontaneously transferred from an object at a higher temperature to an object at a lower temperature until the two objects reach the same temperature.*

This law ensures that the temperature that you measure after a process has taken place is the equilibrium temperature of all systems that are in thermal contact. It follows then that as energy is released (or absorbed) by a chemical reaction in a calorimeter, it will result in a change in the temperature of the calorimeter surrounding the reaction. Therefore, the enthalpy of a reaction can be calculated based on the thermal energy transfer in the calorimeter.

Using a Simple Calorimeter

simple calorimeter a calorimeter made of two stacked vessels covered by a lid with holes in the top just large enough for a thermometer and a stirrer

A **simple calorimeter** consists of two stacked vessels such as polystyrene cups covered with a lid, as shown in **Figure 5.16**. This type of calorimeter can yield reasonably accurate results if used carefully. The reaction occurs in the inner cup, which contains a known mass of water. The polystyrene cups prevent the escape of thermal energy because they are excellent insulators. The air trapped between the inner cup and the outer cup provides additional insulation. Liquid products remain inside the inner cup. However, gases can escape because the lid has holes for the thermometer and stirrer. Because the calorimeter allows gases to escape (or enter) it, this calorimeter measures the thermal energy changes of processes at a constant pressure.

Assumptions That Are Made

When using a simple calorimeter, the process that you are studying often involves compounds that are dissolved directly in the water. You are measuring the temperature change of the water in which a process such as a chemical reaction is occurring. To calculate the amount of heat transferred from the chemical reaction to the water, you must use the specific heat capacity of the water. Therefore, the solution must be dilute so that the presence of the reactants and the products does not significantly change the specific heat capacity of the water. When using a simple calorimeter, you must make the following assumptions:

- The system is isolated. (Any thermal energy that is exchanged with the surroundings outside the calorimeter is small enough to be ignored.)
- The thermal energy that is exchanged with the calorimeter polystyrene cups, thermometer, lid, and stirring rod is small enough to be ignored.
- If something dissolves or reacts with the water in the calorimeter, the resulting solution retains the properties of water. (For example, density and specific heat capacity remain the same.)
- The process takes place under constant pressure.

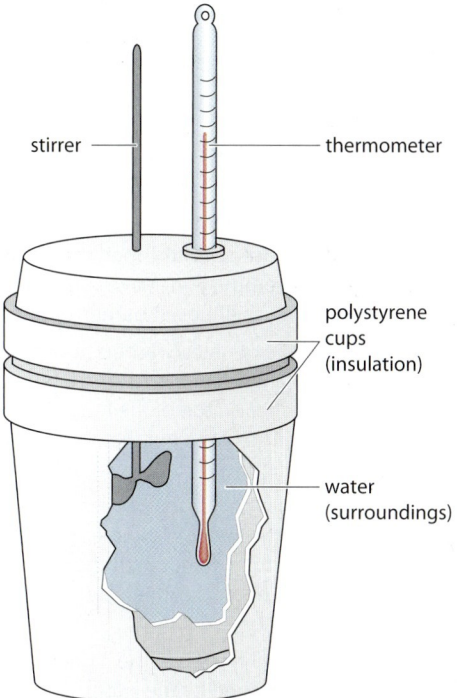

Figure 5.16 A simple calorimeter can be made from stacked polystyrene cups. It is helpful to place the calorimeter in a beaker to reduce the chance that it will tip over. **Infer** *why it is important to keep the holes in the lid for the stirrer and thermometer as small as possible.*

Once you make these assumptions, the following equations apply:

thermal energy released by the system = −thermal energy absorbed by the surroundings

heat lost (or gained) by the system = −heat gained (or lost) by the surroundings

The system is the chemical reaction (or physical change) that you are studying. The surroundings consist of the water in the calorimeter. When a chemical reaction releases or absorbs thermal energy in a calorimeter, the change in temperature is measured by a thermometer in the water. If you know the mass of the water and its specific heat capacity, you can calculate the change in thermal energy caused by the chemical reaction by using the equation $Q = mc\Delta T$.

How To Use a Simple Calorimeter

A simple calorimeter can measure thermal energy changes during chemical reactions, such as neutralization or displacement reactions, or during physical processes that involve a change in temperature. The following four steps outline how to use a simple calorimeter.

1. Ensure that the water in the calorimeter and all other solutions are equilibrated to room temperature before starting any investigation. Measure the initial temperature of the water in the calorimeter.

2. Add the reactants to the calorimeter. The water surrounds, and is in direct contact with, the chemical reaction (or physical change) that releases or absorbs thermal energy.

3. Allow the reaction to proceed. Stir the solution to ensure an even temperature throughout. The system is at a constant pressure because it is open to the air. Record the changing temperature of the water as the reaction proceeds. Identify the maximum or minimum temperature recorded. This temperature is the final temperature.

4. For an exothermic reaction, the final temperature is the maximum temperature recorded. It is used to calculate the thermal energy released. For an endothermic reaction, the final temperature is the minimum temperature recorded. It is used to calculate the thermal energy absorbed.

Activity 5.2 Determining the Temperature of a Bunsen Burner Flame or Hot Plate

In this activity, you will heat a sample of copper, contained within two pennies, in a Bunsen burner flame or on a hot plate. Once the copper is at the same temperature as the source of heat, you will transfer the copper to a known amount of water, at a known temperature. The heat lost by the copper is equal to the heat gained by the water.

Safety Precautions

- Wear safety eyewear and a lab coat or apron.
- Tie back hair or any loose clothing.
- Use EXTREME CAUTION when you are near an open flame.

Materials
- two pre-1997 Canadian copper pennies or copper washers
- 100 mL water
- simple calorimeter (see **Figure 5.16**; two nested polystyrene cups in a 250 mL beaker, with a two-holed polystyrene lid)
- 100 mL graduated cylinder
- thermometer (alcohol or digital)
- electronic centigram balance
- Bunsen burner with igniter, or electric hot plate
- metal tongs (or tweezers if using a hot plate)
- stirring rod

Procedure
1. Read the procedure and prepare a suitable data table.
2. Using the 100 mL graduated cylinder, carefully measure out 100 mL of water and pour this volume into your calorimeter. Record the volume of water in the calorimeter as well as the initial temperature of the water, $T_{initial}$, to the 10th of a degree.
3. Record the mass of the two pennies.
4. After igniting the Bunsen burner, open the air vents to achieve optimal combustion. Make sure that your calorimeter is next to the Bunsen burner, or hot plate.
5. Using tongs, hold the pennies/washers above the inner blue "cone" of the flame. (If you are using a hot plate, lay each penny/washer on top of the hot plate until the maximum temperature of the hot plate is reached.)
6. After about 1 min, when the pennies/washers are at the same temperature as the Bunsen burner flame, quickly immerse them into the water in the calorimeter. Release them slowly, so that they do not melt the sides of the calorimeter. Also, do not touch the water with the tongs or tweezers.
7. Stir the water thoroughly; record the highest temperature, T_{final}, reached by the water.

Questions
1. At the end of the experiment, what is the temperature of the copper relative to the temperature of the water?
2. Define T_{final}, $T_{initial}$, and ΔT.
3. How does the temperature of the copper compare with that of the Bunsen burner flame (or hot plate surface) after the copper and the flame have been in contact for 1 min?
4. Use your data to calculate the temperature of the Bunsen burner flame or of the surface of the hot plate. The specific heat capacity of water is 4.19 J/g·°C; the specific heat capacity of copper is 0.385 J/g·°C; the density of water is 1.00 g/mL. (**Hint:** Set up the equation: $\Delta H_{Cu} = -\Delta H_{H_2O}$.)
5. What assumptions did you make in your calculations?

Using Calorimetry Data To Determine the Enthalpy of Reaction

A simple calorimeter is well suited to determine the enthalpy changes of reactions in dilute aqueous solutions. The water in the calorimeter absorbs or provides the energy that is released or absorbed by a chemical reaction. When carrying out an experiment in a dilute solution, *the solution itself* absorbs or releases the energy. You can calculate the quantity of thermal energy that is absorbed or released by the solution using the equation $Q = mc\Delta T$. The mass, m, is the mass of the water or solution. *If the solution is dilute, you can assume the solution has the same specific heat capacity as water.* This assumption cannot be made for a concentrated solution because the specific heat capacity decreases when the concentration of a solute increases. For example, **Figure 5.17** shows a graph of the concentration of sodium chloride versus the specific heat capacity of the solution.

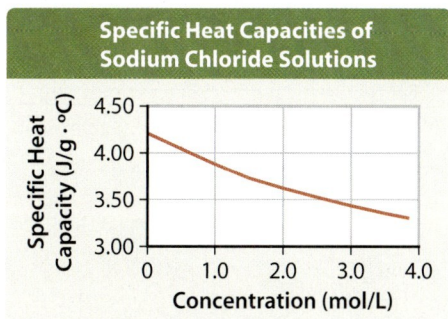

Figure 5.17 As the concentration of sodium chloride increases, the specific heat capacity of the solution decreases.

$Q = m_w c_w \Delta T_w$ is used to determine the quantity of thermal energy absorbed or released by the water in the calorimeter. To find the quantity of thermal energy released or absorbed by the system, just change the sign of the calculated value for Q.

You can use the data collected from a calorimetry experiment to determine the molar enthalpy of reaction, ΔH_r, for a reaction that has taken place in the calorimeter. In a simple calorimeter, the reaction takes place at constant pressure; therefore, the heat, Q, exchanged by the system and the water is equal to the experimental enthalpy change of the system (the compounds involved in the reaction), ΔH. To find the molar enthalpy change of the reaction, solve for ΔH_r in the equation:

$$\Delta H = n\Delta H_r$$

$$\Delta H_r = \frac{\Delta H}{n}$$

Recall that n is the amount in moles of the specified reactant or product.

The following Sample Problem shows how calorimetry data can be used to calculate the enthalpy change of a chemical reaction in solution. Notice that all the materials in the calorimeter in the Sample Problem have the same final temperature.

Suggested Investigation

Plan Your Own Investigation 5-A, Determining the Enthalpy of a Neutralization Reaction

Sample Problem

Determining the Enthalpy Change of a Reaction

Problem

Aqueous copper(II) sulfate, $CuSO_4(aq)$, reacts with sodium hydroxide, $NaOH(aq)$, in a double displacement reaction. A precipitate of copper(II) hydroxide, $Cu(OH)_2(s)$, and aqueous sodium sulfate, $Na_2SO_4(aq)$, is produced:

$$CuSO_4(aq) + 2NaOH(aq) \rightarrow Cu(OH)_2(s) + 2Na_2SO_4(aq)$$

A 50.00 mL volume of 0.300 mol/L $CuSO_4(aq)$ is mixed with 50.00 mL of $NaOH(aq)$ solution that contains an excess of $NaOH(aq)$. The initial temperature of both solutions is 21.40°C. After mixing the solutions in a simple calorimeter, the highest temperature reached is 24.60°C. Determine the enthalpy change for the reaction as written and write the reaction's thermochemical equation.

Continued on next page

What Is Required?
You need to calculate ΔH_r for the reaction as written.
You need to write the thermochemical equation for the reaction.

What Is Given?
You know the volume of $CuSO_4(aq)$ = 50.00 mL
You know the concentration of $CuSO_4(aq)$ = 0.300 mol/L
You know the volume of $NaOH(aq)$ = 50.00 mL
You know that there is an excess of $NaOH(aq)$
You know the initial temperature, $T_{initial}$ = 21.40°C
You know the final temperature, T_{final} = 24.60°C
You have the specific heat capacity of $H_2O(\ell)$: 4.19 J/g·°C (see **Table 5.1**)

Plan Your Strategy	Act on Your Strategy
Determine the total volume of the $CuSO_4(aq)$ solution and the $NaOH(aq)$ solution in the calorimeter.	$V_{total} = V_{CuSO_4} + V_{NaOH}$ = 50.00 mL + 50.00 mL = 100.0 mL
Determine the mass of the solution in the calorimeter, assuming the density is the same as the density of water (1.00 g/mL).	$m = Vd$ $= (100.0 \text{ mL})\left(1.00 \dfrac{g}{mL}\right)$ = 100.0 g
Determine the amount in moles of $CuSO_4(aq)$ present.	$n = cV$ $= \left(0.300 \dfrac{mol}{L}\right)(50.00 \text{ mL})\left(\dfrac{1 L}{1000 \text{ mL}}\right)$ = 0.0150 mol
Determine the change in thermal energy of the surroundings (water).	$Q = m_{solution} \, c_{solution} \, \Delta T_{solution}$ $= (100.0 \text{ g})(4.19 \dfrac{J}{g \cdot °C})(24.60°C - 21.40°C)$ $= 1.341 \times 10^3$ J = 1.341 kJ
Determine the ΔH of the system (the compounds in the reaction). Change the sign of Q to find the change in thermal energy of the system. This value is equivalent to the ΔH of the system.	$\Delta H_{system} = -Q_{solution}$ $mc\Delta T$ = -1.341 kJ
Find ΔH_r by using the formula $\Delta H = n\Delta H_r$. Use the amount in moles of $CuSO_4(aq)$.	$\Delta H = n\Delta H_r$ $\Delta H_r = \dfrac{\Delta H}{n}$ $= \dfrac{-1.341 \text{ kJ}}{0.0150 \text{ mol}}$ = -89.4 kJ/mol
Write the thermochemical equation for the reaction. Because the coefficient of $CuSO_4(aq)$ is 1, ΔH_r represents the enthalpy change when 1 mol of copper(II) sulfate reacts with an excess of sodium hydroxide.	$CuSO_4(aq) + 2NaOH(aq) \rightarrow$ $Cu(OH)_2(s) + 2Na_2SO_4(aq) + 89.4$ kJ

Check Your Solution
The solution has the correct number of significant digits. The units are correct. You know that the reaction was exothermic, because the temperature of the solution increased. The calculated value of ΔH is negative, which is correct for an exothermic reaction.

Practice Problems

21. A pellet of potassium hydroxide, KOH(s), having a mass of 0.648 g, is dissolved in 40.0 mL of water in an insulated cup. The temperature of the water increases from 22.6°C to 27.8°C. What is the molar enthalpy of solution, $\Delta H_{solution}$, for KOH(s)? Assume that the solution has a density and a specific heat capacity equal to that of water.

22. When 5.022 g of sodium hydrogen carbonate, NaHCO$_3$(s), reacts completely with 80.00 mL of acetic acid, CH$_3$COOH(aq), the temperature increases from 18.6°C to 28.4°C.

$$CH_3COOH(aq) + NaHCO_3(s) \rightarrow$$
$$CH_3COONa(aq) + CO_2(g) + H_2O(\ell)$$

Assume that the acid solution has the same density and specific heat capacity as water and that the mass of the final solution is 80.00 g. Calculate the molar enthalpy of reaction, ΔH_r.

23. Sodium reacts violently to form sodium hydroxide when placed in water, as shown in the following equation:

$$2Na(s) + 2H_2O(\ell) \rightarrow 2NaOH(aq) + H_2(g)$$

Determine an experimental value for the molar enthalpy of reaction for sodium given the following data:

mass of sodium, Na(s): 0.37 g

mass of water in calorimeter: 175 g

initial temperature of water: 19.30°C

final temperature of mixture: 25.70°C

24. In a simple calorimeter, 250.0 mL of 0.120 mol/L barium chloride, BaCl$_2$(aq), is mixed with 150.0 mL of 0.200 mol/L sodium sulfate, Na$_2$SO$_4$(aq). A precipitate of barium sulfate, BaSO$_4$(s), forms. The initial temperature of the two solutions is 20.00°C. After mixing, the final temperature of the solutions is 20.49°C. Calculate the enthalpy of reaction, in kilojoules per mole, of Na$_2$SO$_4$(aq). Assume that the solutions have densities and specific heat capacities equivalent to those of water.

$$BaCl_2(aq) + Na_2SO_4(aq) \rightarrow 2NaCl(aq) + BaSO_4(s)$$

25. A neutralization reaction occurs when 100.0 mL of 0.200 mol/L aqueous ammonia, NH$_3$(aq), and 200.0 mL of 0.200 mol/L hydrochloric acid, HCl(aq), are mixed in an insulated cup.

$$NH_3(aq) + HCl(aq) \rightarrow NH_4Cl(aq) + 53.6 \text{ kJ}$$

Assuming that the two solutions have the same density and specific heat capacity as water, what temperature change is expected after mixing?

26. In a simple calorimeter, 150.0 mL of 1.000 mol/L NaOH(aq) is mixed with 150.0 mL of 1.000 mol/L HCl(aq). If both solutions were initially at 25.00°C and after mixing the temperature increased to 30.00°C, what is the enthalpy of reaction as written? Assume that the solutions have a density of 1.000 g/mL and a specific heat capacity of 4.19 J/g·°C.

$$HCl(aq) + NaOH(aq) \rightarrow NaCl(aq) + H_2O(\ell)$$

27. The enthalpy of solution for sodium hydroxide, NaOH(s), is given as −55.0 kJ/mol. A chemist prepares 250.0 mL of a 0.100 mol/L solution of NaOH(aq). Assuming that this solution has the same specific heat capacity and density as water, by how much should the water temperature increase as the NaOH(s) dissolves?

28. A neutralization reaction occurs when 120.00 mL of 0.500 mol/L LiOH and 160.00 mL of 0.375 mol/L HNO$_3$(aq) are mixed in an insulated cup. Initially, the solutions are at the same temperature. If the highest temperature reached during mixing was 24.5°C, what was the initial temperature of the solutions?

$$LiOH(aq) + HNO_3(aq) \rightarrow$$
$$LiNO_3(aq) + H_2O(\ell) + 53.1 \text{ kJ}$$

Assume that both of these solutions have a density of 1.00 g/mL and a specific heat capacity of 4.19 J/g·°C.

29. Peroxides will react to release oxygen when added to water. By how much would the water temperature change if 7.800 g of sodium peroxide, Na$_2$O$_2$(s), is added to 110.00 mL of water?

$$2Na_2O_2(s) + 2H_2O(\ell) \rightarrow 4NaOH(aq) + O_2(g)$$
$$\Delta H° = -285.0 \text{ kJ}$$

30. In an insulated calorimeter, 200.0 mL of 1.00 mol/L potassium hydroxide, KOH(aq), is mixed with an equal volume of 1.00 mol/L sulfuric acid, H$_2$SO$_4$(aq). The temperature increases by 6.50°C. Assume that the solutions have the same density and specific heat capacity as water.

$$H_2SO_4(aq) + 2KOH(aq) \rightarrow K_2SO_4(aq) + 2H_2O(\ell)$$

What is the molar enthalpy of neutralization?

Using Flame Calorimetry To Determine the Enthalpy of Combustion

You can use a flame calorimeter, such as the one shown in **Figure 5.18**, to determine the enthalpy of combustion of a substance that is burning. Unlike a simple calorimeter, a flame calorimeter is fire-resistant. It does, however, absorb a significant amount of energy; therefore, the heat absorbed by the calorimeter itself must be included in energy calculations. The fuel being tested is burned under a small can, heating both the can and the water inside.

For pure substances, the molar enthalpy of combustion is used. For substances that are not pure, such as most foods, the enthalpy of combustion is expressed in kJ/g rather than kJ/mol. Another appropriate way to express the enthalpy of combustion for food is in kJ/serving.

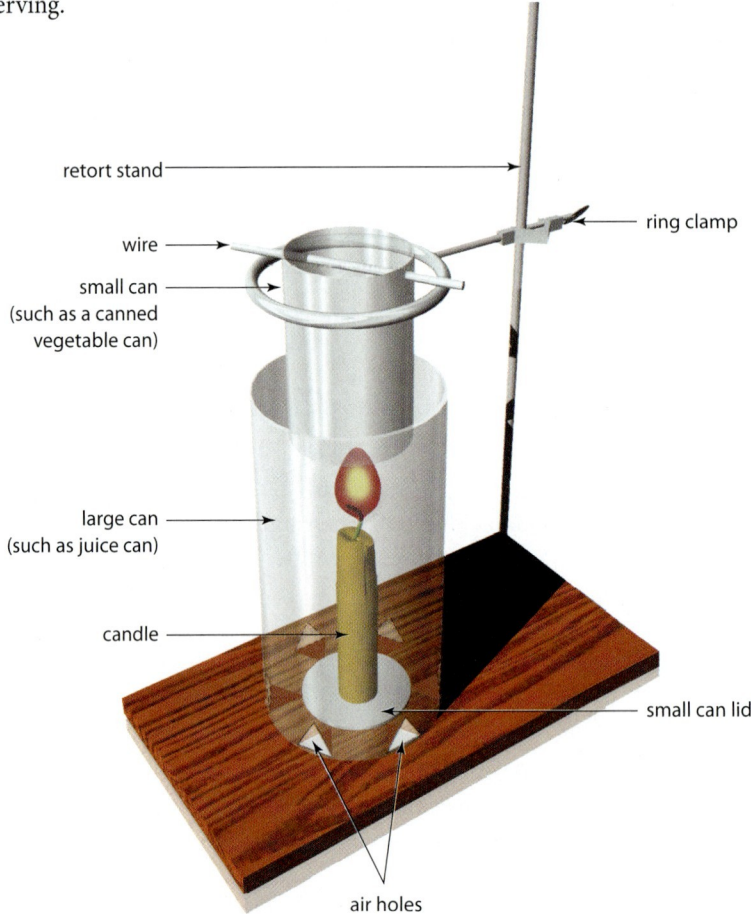

Figure 5.18 A flame calorimeter is commonly made from a small can suspended on a ring stand by a rod or wire. A large can with air holes surrounds the fuel source to direct the heat upward to minimize the loss of thermal energy to the surroundings. Nevertheless, there will be some loss of heat to the surroundings.
Analyze why the tip of the flame should just touch the bottom of the small can.

Using Bomb Calorimetry To Measure Enthalpy Changes during Combustion

To precisely and accurately measure the enthalpy changes of combustion reactions, chemists use a calorimeter called a **bomb calorimeter**, shown in **Figure 5.19**. A bomb calorimeter measures enthalpy changes during combustion reactions at a constant volume.

The bomb calorimeter works on the same general principle as the simple calorimeter. The reaction, however, takes place inside an inner metal chamber, called a *bomb*. This bomb contains pure oxygen. The reactants are ignited using an electric coil. A known quantity of water surrounds the bomb and absorbs the energy released by the reaction.

bomb calorimeter a device that measures heat released during a combustion reaction at a constant volume

A bomb calorimeter has many more parts than a simple calorimeter has. All these parts can absorb or release small quantities of energy. Therefore, you cannot assume that the heat lost to these parts is small enough to be negligible. To obtain precise heat measurements, you must know or find out the heat capacity, C, of the entire bomb calorimeter. A bomb calorimeter is calibrated for a constant mass of water. Because the mass of the other parts remains constant, there is no need for mass units in the heat capacity value. The units of C are joules per degree Celsius, or J/°C, because the mass of all parts of the calorimeter are included in C. The heat capacity of a bomb calorimeter takes into account the heat that *all* parts of the calorimeter can lose or gain, as shown by the equation below:

$$C_{\text{bomb calorimeter}} = C_{\text{water}} + C_{\text{thermometer}} + C_{\text{stirrer}} + C_{\text{container}}$$

The value of the heat capacity for a particular calorimeter is generally provided by the manufacturer. Because the heat capacity (C) accounts for the mass of the calorimeter, C is equivalent to mc in the equation $Q = mc\Delta T$. Therefore, when performing calculations involving data from a bomb calorimeter, you can write the equation as $Q = C\Delta T$.

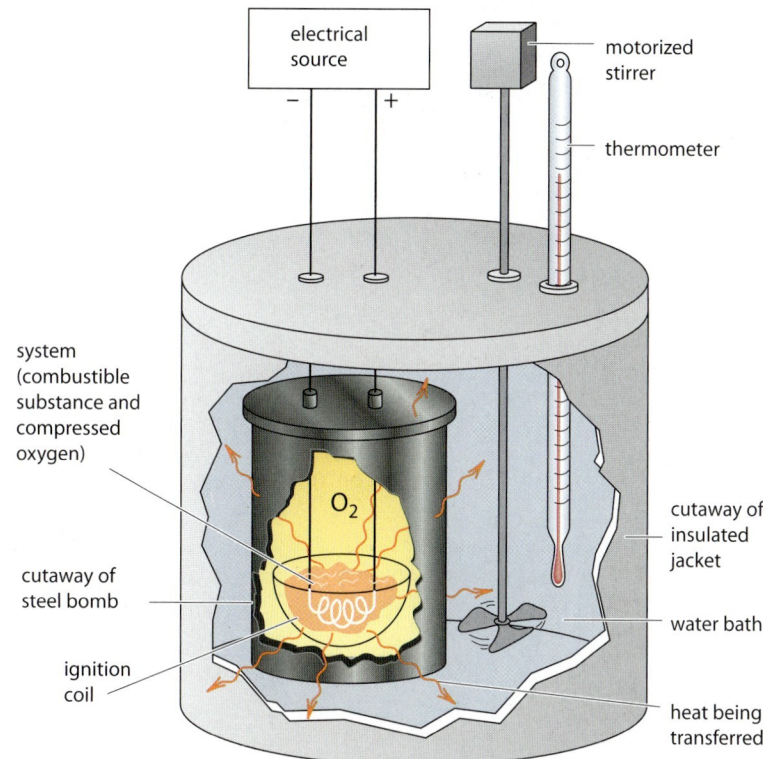

Figure 5.19 A bomb calorimeter is more sophisticated than a simple calorimeter or a flame calorimeter because it is an isolated system—the products of combustion cannot escape.

Another important aspect of a bomb calorimeter is that it is a closed system under pressure. In a bomb calorimeter, processes occur at constant volume but not constant pressure. Because the pressure can change significantly, the amount of heat transferred from the system to the calorimeter is not the same as the change in enthalpy of the system. If chemists want to find the enthalpy of a substance tested in a bomb calorimeter, they must make corrections to account for the change in pressure conditions. A correction factor is introduced into the calculations and the equation used is $Q = C\Delta T + RT\Delta n_{\text{(gas)}}$. R is the universal gas constant and $\Delta n_{\text{(gas)}}$ is the change in total moles of gas. However, for the purposes of the bomb calorimeter calculations you will perform, assume that the total moles of gas of reactants and products remains the same. As such, you can use the equation $Q = C\Delta T$. The following Sample Problem illustrates how to use the heat capacity of a bomb calorimeter in your calculations.

Sample Problem

Calculating Thermal Energy in a Bomb Calorimeter

Problem

A laboratory was contracted to test the energy content of a sample of peanut butter. A technician placed a 16.0 g sample of peanut butter in the steel bomb of a bomb calorimeter, along with sufficient oxygen to combust the sample completely. He ignited the mixture and took temperature measurements. The heat capacity of the calorimeter was previously determined to be 8.28 kJ/°C. During the experiment, the temperature increased by 50.5°C.

A chemist prepares a sample for testing in a bomb calorimeter.

a. What was the amount of thermal energy released by the sample of peanut butter?
b. How much heat was released per gram of the peanut butter combusted?

What Is Required?

You need to calculate the thermal energy lost by the peanut butter.
You need to calculate the heat released per gram of peanut butter combusted.

What Is Given?

You know the mass of peanut butter, $m = 16.0$ g
You know the heat capacity of the calorimeter, $C = 8.28$ kJ/°C
You know the change in temperature, $\Delta T = 50.5$°C

Plan Your Strategy	Act on Your Strategy
Calculate the amount of heat, Q, absorbed by the calorimeter.	$Q = C\Delta T$ $= \left(8.28 \, \dfrac{\text{kJ}}{\cancel{°C}}\right)(50.5 \, \cancel{°C})$ $= 418.14$ kJ
Determine the amount of thermal energy released by the peanut butter sample, which is equal to the amount of heat, Q, absorbed by the calorimeter but opposite in sign.	$Q_{\text{peanut butter}} = -Q_{\text{calorimeter}}$ $= -418$ kJ
To find the heat released per gram, divide the amount of thermal energy released by the mass of the sample.	$\dfrac{Q}{m} = \dfrac{-418.14 \text{ kJ}}{16.0 \text{ g}}$ $= -26.1 \, \dfrac{\text{kJ}}{\text{g}}$ The heat released per gram of peanut butter is 26.1 kJ/g.

Check Your Solution

Thermal energy was released by the peanut butter, so it makes sense that the thermal energy value is negative.

Practice Problems

31. Predict the final temperature of a 5.00×10^2 g iron ring that is initially at 25.0°C and is heated by combusting 4.95 g of ethanol, $C_2H_5OH(\ell)$; ΔH_{comb} for ethanol is −1234.8 kJ/mol. (**Note:** These are not standard conditions.)

32. Calculate the molar enthalpy of combustion of octane if 0.53 g of the fuel increased the temperature of a coffee can calorimeter (13 g of aluminum and 2.50×10^2 mL of water) by 17.2°C. Remember to include the heat gained by not only the water but also by the aluminum can.

33. How much propane (in grams) would have to be combusted to increase the temperature of 3.00×10^2 mL of water from 20.00°C to its boiling point? (The molar enthalpy of combustion of propane can be found in **Table 5.4**).

34. A lab technician places a 5.00 g food sample into a bomb calorimeter with a heat capacity of 9.23 kJ/°C. The initial temperature of the calorimeter system is 21.0°C. After burning the food, the final temperature of the system is 32.0°C. How much thermal energy is released by the combustion of the food in kilojoules per gram?

35. Determine the enthalpy of combustion of an unknown fuel if a 2.75 g sample increased the temperature of 5.00×10^2 mL of hot chocolate ($c = 3.75$ J/g·°C) in a 1.50×10^2 g glass mug ($c = 0.84$ J/g·°C) from 10.00°C to 45.00°C. Express the value for enthalpy of combustion in appropriate units.

36. Urea, $NH_2CONH_2(s)$, is widely used in various aspects of fertilizer manufacturing. A 4.28 g sample of urea is burned in a flame calorimeter. The calorimeter is made of aluminum and has a mass of 40.3 g. The 125.0 mL volume of water inside the calorimeter is at an initial temperature of 5.5°C. After the urea is completely combusted, the water temperature is 96.0°C. Use this information to calculate the enthalpy of combustion, ΔH_{comb}, for urea. Refer to **Table 5.1** for the specific heat capacity of aluminum.

37. When a sample of ethene gas, $C_2H_4(g)$, is burned the heat produced warms 50.0 g of water by 63.0°C. The mass of $C_2H_4(g)$ burned was 0.268 g.
   a. What is the standard molar enthalpy of combustion for $C_2H_4(g)$ in kilojoules per mole?
   b. Write the thermochemical equation for this combustion reaction.

38. Diborane, $B_2H_6(g)$, is a highly reactive compound that has been used as a reducing agent in rocket propellants. It can react with chlorine gas as written below.

$B_2H_6(g) + 6Cl_2(g) \rightarrow 2BCl_3(g) + 6HCl(g) + 755$ kJ

A 2.85 g sample of $B_2H_6(g)$ reacts with an excess of chlorine gas in a bomb calorimeter, which is calibrated to 8.82 kJ/°C. What change in temperature will occur when the sample reacts?

39. The equation below represents the burning of carbon disulfide, $CS_2(\ell)$, in a calorimeter. What mass of $CS_2(\ell)$ must have burned to increase the temperature of 1.00 kg of water by 15.5°C?

$CS_2(\ell) + 3O_2(g) \rightarrow CO_2(g) + 2SO_2(g) + 1690$ kJ

40. A sample of acetone having a mass of 1.920 g undergoes complete combustion in an insulated calorimeter holding 400.0 mL of water. It is determined that the water and calorimeter together absorb 58.829 kJ of heat energy from this combustion. Based upon this information, what is the standard molar enthalpy of combustion for acetone in kilojoules per mole?

Acetone is a common ingredient in nail polish remover.

Canadian Research in Action

Investigating the Thermodynamics of Aqueous Solutions

Dr. Hakin's research relies on techniques such as calorimetry to study the thermodynamics of aqueous systems.

> **Related Career**
>
> **Nuclear engineers** design, develop, and maintain nuclear power plants. They must understand the processes that produce nuclear energy, including the properties of radiation and the science of thermodynamics. In Canada, many nuclear engineers have undergraduate degrees in engineering or science and graduate degrees in nuclear engineering.

Dr. Andrew Hakin, a professor at the Department of Chemistry and Biochemistry, University of Lethbridge, Alberta, is a world-renowned specialist in the field of experimental thermodynamics. "More specifically," he comments, "I specialize in utilizing techniques of calorimetry and densimetry to probe the thermodynamic properties of aqueous electrolyte systems." Dr. Hakin leads one of the few research groups in the world that take high-precision heat capacity measurements of aqueous solutions. In 2003, he received the Stig Sunner Memorial Award for his contributions to the field of calorimetry.

Dr. Hakin's team was one of the first to build a densimeter, a device that measures the properties of aqueous systems under high temperature and pressure. These measurements are critical in a number of different fields. One example is in designing nuclear power plants in which hot radioactive water is pumped at high pressure through thousands of metres of tubing. The radioactive water flowing through the tubes heats non-radioactive water on the outside of the tubes, producing steam that runs turbines to generate electricity. Engineers who design these tubes must understand the properties of radioactive water at high temperature and pressure.

Dr. Hakin's densimeter, which took about four years to build, can increase the temperature of an aqueous system to 523 K and the pressure exerted on it to 300 times atmospheric pressure. When Dr. Hakin and his team published results from their first experiment with the densimeter in 1998, they turned a long-held idea in the field of thermodynamics on its head. At the time, scientific models predicted that in aqueous solution, glycine—the most basic of amino acids—would behave like a typical non-electrolyte when subjected to extreme temperature and pressure. Dr. Hakin's studies showed that under extreme temperature and pressure, glycine behaves not like a typical non-electrolyte, but more like a simple electrolyte, such as sodium chloride.

"We thought we had got it wrong, and so we repeated the experiment a number of times," recalls Dr. Hakin. "Eventually, we convinced ourselves that we were correct. It was a good achievement. We asked questions about some fundamental thermodynamic properties, designed an instrument [a densimeter] to achieve our goals, and got a result that made our community sit back and think."

In striving to find out whether he could verify the results of an accepted model with experimental data, Dr. Hakin discovered that he could not, and in the process made an important discovery. "Models are very useful and usually point us in the right direction, but there is no substitute for real experimental data," he explains. Other scientists have since repeated the experiment and achieved similar results, thus backing up Dr. Hakin's findings.

QUESTIONS

1. How do the laws of thermodynamics provide the framework for the research that Dr. Hakin conducts into the properties of aqueous solutions at extreme temperature and pressure?

2. Use the Internet and/or print resources to assess the impact that the calorimeter has had on the study of thermodynamics.

3. Use Internet and/or print resources to find another career related to the research covered in this feature. Briefly describe the nature of this career and any training or education required.

Section 5.2 Review

Section Summary

- When a process takes place under conditions of constant pressure, the enthalpy change of a system is equal to the amount of heat gained or heat lost by the system.
- The standard enthalpy of a reaction as written ($\Delta H_r°$) is the enthalpy change for the amount in moles of each reactant and product as determined by the coefficient of the term in the chemical equation.
- A process taking place in a simple calorimeter occurs at constant pressure. Therefore, the amount of heat that is exchanged between the calorimeter and the system is equal to the change in the enthalpy of the system.
- Temperature data from a simple calorimetry experiment can be used to calculate the enthalpy of a chemical reaction.
- The standard enthalpy of combustion ($\Delta H°_{comb}$) of a compound is the enthalpy change that occurs when 1 mol of a compound reacts completely with oxygen under the conditions that the reactants started out at 25°C and 100 kPa of pressure and the products cooled to 25°C and 100 kPa of pressure after the reaction was complete.
- A process taking place in a bomb calorimeter occurs at constant volume but not constant pressure.

Review Questions

1. **K/U** What is the main characteristic of a calorimeter that allows you to determine the thermal energy change?

2. **K/U** Why is polystyrene a good material to make a simple calorimeter?

3. **T/I** A reaction in a calorimeter containing 80.0 g of water at 20.0°C causes the temperature to fall by 1.5°C. What is the thermal energy change of the water?

4. **K/U** The enthalpy of reaction for a neutralization reaction is to be determined by mixing dilute solutions of an acid and a base in a polystyrene coffee cup. What data must be recorded to complete this activity? What assumptions are made to complete the calorimetric calculations?

5. **K/U** In solving calorimetry problems, the assumption is usually made that the specific heat capacity of a dilute solution is equal to that of water. This is not a valid assumption for concentrated solutions. Suggest a reason why this assumption would not apply for concentrated solutions.

6. **K/U** The enthalpy change of a reaction, ΔH_r, that is calculated when a solid dissolves in water is −10.0 kJ/mol. Has the temperature of the water increased or decreased in this process? State a reason for your answer.

7. **C** You have learned about three types of calorimeters in this section. Use a Venn diagram to communicate the similarities and differences in these types of calorimeters. Include sources of error for each type of calorimeter in your summary.

8. **A** A chemist mixes 100.00 mL of 0.050 mol/L aqueous potassium hydroxide, KOH(aq), with 100.00 mL of 0.050 mol/L nitric acid, HNO_3(aq). The temperature of the reactants is 21.01°C. The temperature after the reaction is complete is 21.34°C.
   a. Determine the molar enthalpy of neutralization for this reaction.
   b. Write the thermochemical equation and draw an enthalpy diagram for the reaction.

9. **C** Calorimetry is based upon the first and second laws of thermodynamics. Explain this relationship in a brief paragraph supported by a diagram.

10. **K/U** A bomb calorimeter is classified as an isolated system because neither mass nor energy is exchanged with the surroundings. What type of system describes a flame calorimeter?

11. **T/I** A 6.60 g sample of a biscuit is burned in a bomb calorimeter having a heat capacity of 11.6 kJ/°C. After the burning is complete, the temperature has increased by 8.41°C. What amount of thermal energy was released per gram of biscuit?

12. **A** In order to study a person's energy expenditure and ability to burn different fuels such as carbohydrates or fats, a "whole-room calorimeter" is used. Research this topic and write a brief report that describes the design of the room and the measurements that must be taken.

13. **K/U** Provide an example of a thermochemical equation for a chemical reaction that requires energy to proceed. In your own words, describe how someone would read the equation.

SECTION 5.3

Hess's Law

Key Terms

Hess's law
standard molar enthalpy of formation, ΔH_f°
thermal stability

Many reactions release too much energy to be performed safely with a simple calorimeter. Also, simple calorimeters are usually used only for processes involving dilute aqueous solutions. In addition, many reactions occur too violently or too slowly for the calorimetric method to be practical. However, chemists can determine the enthalpy change of nearly any reaction by using some accumulated data and **Hess's law**, which is stated in the box below.

> **Hess's Law**
> The enthalpy change of a physical or chemical process depends only on the initial and final conditions of the process. The enthalpy change of a multistep process is the sum of the enthalpy changes of its individual steps.

Hess's law a law stating that the enthalpy change of a physical or chemical process depends only on the initial and final conditions of the process; the enthalpy change of the overall process is the sum of the enthalpy changes of its individual steps

In 1840, Russian chemist Germain Henri Hess (1802–1850) stated the law that now bears his name. To understand Hess's law, analyze the example below, which shows that carbon dioxide can form from carbon and oxygen by one step or by two steps.

Two Steps
$$2C(s) + O_2(g) \rightarrow 2CO(g)$$
$$2CO(g) + O_2(g) \rightarrow 2CO_2(g)$$

One Step
$$C(s) + O_2(g) \rightarrow CO_2(g)$$

According to Hess's law, the sum of the enthalpy changes for the two reactions on the left should be the same as the enthalpy change for the single reaction on the right. However, notice that if you determine the enthalpy changes for the reactions on the left as written, you obtain the enthalpy change for the formation of 2 mol of carbon dioxide. The enthalpy change for the reaction on the right, as written, represents the formation of 1 mol of carbon dioxide. To compare the reactions, you must compare the same amount in moles of product. Therefore, you must divide the coefficients of the two reactions on the left by 2, as shown in the equations below under the title, Two Steps.

Keep in mind also that comparing enthalpy changes of chemical reactions requires carrying out the reactions under the same conditions. Chemists have agreed to use the standard enthalpy change, ΔH°, which implies conditions at SATP. For chemical reactions in solution, the standard state also includes a concentration of exactly 1 mol/L. Now you can compare the two pathways by which carbon dioxide could form from carbon and oxygen. Notice that the standard enthalpy change for the two pathways is the same. You can also represent this comparison with an enthalpy diagram, as shown in **Figure 5.20**.

Two Steps

$$C(s) + \tfrac{1}{2}O_2(g) \rightarrow CO(g) \quad \Delta H^\circ = -110.5 \text{ kJ}$$

$$CO(g) + \tfrac{1}{2}O_2(g) \rightarrow CO_2(g) \quad \underline{\Delta H^\circ = -283.0 \text{ kJ}}$$
$$\Delta H^\circ = -393.5 \text{ kJ}$$

One Step

$$C(s) + O_2(g) \rightarrow CO_2(g) \quad \Delta H^\circ = -393.5 \text{ kJ}$$

Figure 5.20 Carbon dioxide can be formed by the reaction of carbon with oxygen via two different pathways. The enthalpy change of the overall reaction is the same for either pathway.

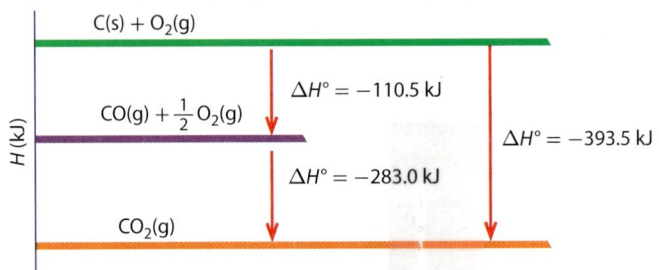

Two Pathways, One Change

One way to think about Hess's law is to compare the energy changes that occur in a chemical reaction with the changes in the potential energy of a mountain biker on hilly terrain. This comparison is shown in **Figure 5.21**. Hess's law is valid because enthalpy change is determined only by the initial and final conditions of the system. It is not dependent on the pathway of the system. Hess's law allows you to calculate the enthalpy change of a chemical reaction when it is not practical to use a calorimeter to find the enthalpy change of a reaction. You can, however, use a calorimeter to find the enthalpy changes of other reactions. You can combine the equations of these reactions to arrive at the equation of the reaction in which you are interested.

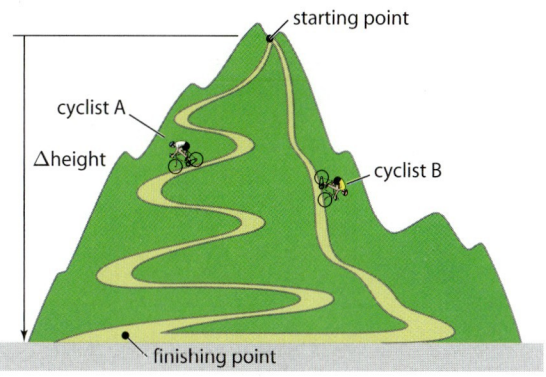

Figure 5.21 The routes that cyclists take to get from the starting point to the finishing point have no effect on the net change in the cyclists' gravitational potential energy. Similarly, enthalpy change is not dependent on the pathway of a system.

Combining Sets of Chemical Equations

You can use Hess's law to find the enthalpy change of any reaction as long as you know the enthalpy changes for any set of reactions that add up to the overall reaction in which you are interested. For example, the first two steps in the industrial synthesis of sulfuric acid are shown below and the entire process is depicted in **Figure 5.22**.

(1) $S_8(s) + 8O_2(g) \rightarrow 8SO_2(g)$ (2) $2SO_2(g) + O_2(g) \rightarrow 2SO_3(g)$

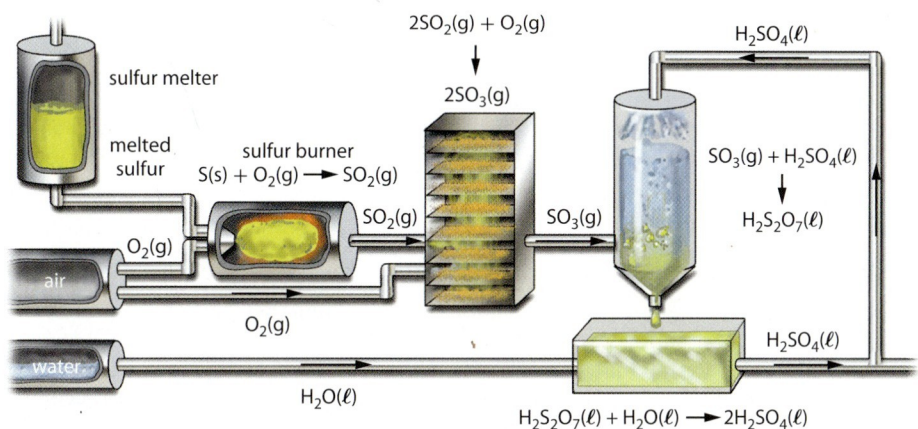

Figure 5.22 The industrial production of sulfuric acid shown here is called the contact process. The second step, the oxidation of sulfur dioxide, is very slow. Therefore, the system is designed to cause the gases to come in contact with a catalyst (illustrated by the box containing many layers), which speeds up the reaction.

Suppose you want to find the enthalpy change for the formation of sulfur trioxide from sulfur and oxygen. You must examine the equations and decide whether you need to divide the coefficients by a constant. Because you want 1 mol of sulfur trioxide in the final step, you want only 1 mol of sulfur dioxide in the first step, thus you need to divide the first equation by 8.

$$\frac{1}{8}S_8(s) + O_2(g) \rightarrow SO_2(g)$$

You must also divide the second equation by 2.

$$SO_2(g) + \frac{1}{2}O_2(g) \rightarrow SO_3(g)$$

Write the two equations with their arrows aligned, write their known standard enthalpy changes beside the equations, and add the equations and the standard enthalpy changes.

$$\frac{1}{8}S_8(s) + O_2(g) \rightarrow SO_2(g) \qquad \Delta H° = -296.8 \text{ kJ}$$
$$SO_2(g) + \frac{1}{2}O_2(g) \rightarrow SO_3(g) \qquad \Delta H° = -99.2 \text{ kJ}$$

$$\frac{1}{8}S_8(s) + O_2(g) + SO_2(g) + \frac{1}{2}O_2(g) \rightarrow SO_2(g) + SO_3(g) \qquad \Delta H° = (-296.8 \text{ kJ}) + (-99.2 \text{ kJ})$$

Examine the final equation to find any compounds occurring on both sides. These compounds will cancel each other. Also, look for any compounds that occur more than once on the same side, and add them together.

$$\frac{1}{8}S_8(s) + (1 + \frac{1}{2})O_2(g) + \cancel{SO_2(g)} \rightarrow \cancel{SO_2(g)} + SO_3(g) \qquad \Delta H° = (-296.8 \text{ kJ}) + (-99.2 \text{ kJ})$$
$$\frac{1}{8}S_8(s) + \frac{3}{2}O_2(g) \rightarrow SO_3(g) \qquad \Delta H° = -396.0 \text{ kJ}$$

The enthalpy diagram representing the process of synthesizing sulfur trioxide is shown in **Figure 5.23**.

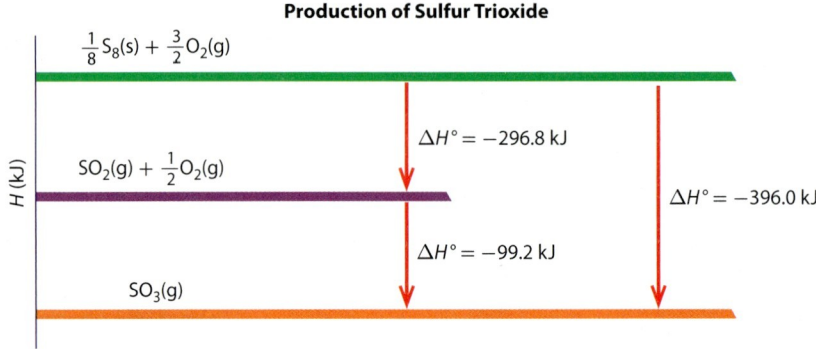

Figure 5.23 This enthalpy diagram shows the first two steps in the industrial production of sulfuric acid. It also shows that the enthalpies of these reactions can be added to determine the enthalpy change of the overall reaction.

Techniques for Manipulating Equations

You will often need to manipulate the equations before adding them, as was done above. There are two key ways you can manipulate an equation:

1. *Reverse an equation* so that the products become reactants and the reactants become products. When you reverse an equation, you need to change the sign of ΔH (multiply by -1). When a reaction is written in reverse, the enthalpy change has the opposite sign.

2. *Multiply each coefficient* in an equation by the same integer or fraction. When you multiply an equation, you need to multiply ΔH by the same number. Recall that the enthalpy change is directly related to the amount of the substances involved in a reaction. If two candles are burned instead of one, then twice as much heat and light will be produced.

When the same reactant or product is present in equations that you are manipulating, do not use that reactant or product to decide how to manipulate the equations. Always start with a reactant or product that is present in only one of the equations and that is also present in the overall equation.

Examine the following Sample Problem to see how to manipulate equations so that they add to the overall equation. Try the Practice Problems that follow to practise finding the enthalpy change by adding equations.

Suggested Investigation

Inquiry Investigation 5-B, Hess's Law and the Enthalpy of Combustion of Magnesium

Sample Problem

Using Hess's Law To Determine Enthalpy Change

Problem

One of the methods used in the steel industry to obtain metallic iron is to react iron(III) oxide, $Fe_2O_3(s)$, with carbon monoxide, $CO(g)$, as shown in the balanced equation below:

$$Fe_2O_3(s) + 3CO(g) \rightarrow 3CO_2(g) + 2Fe(s)$$

Determine the enthalpy change of this reaction, given the following equations and their enthalpy changes.

(1) $CO(g) + \frac{1}{2}O_2(g) \rightarrow CO_2(g)$ $\quad \Delta H° = -283.0$ kJ

(2) $2Fe(s) + \frac{3}{2}O_2(g) \rightarrow Fe_2O_3(s)$ $\quad \Delta H° = -824.2$ kJ

What Is Required?

You need determine the enthalpy change of a reaction by using two other reactions.

What Is Given?

You are given the overall equation and the two chemical equations and their corresponding enthalpy changes.

Plan Your Strategy	Act on Your Strategy
Examine equations (1) and (2) to see how they compare with the overall equation. Because oxygen gas is present in both equations, do not use $O_2(g)$ to decide on how to manipulate the equations.	Equation (1) has $CO(g)$ as a reactant and $CO_2(g)$ as a product, as does the overall equation. The stoichiometric coefficients do not match the coefficients of the overall equation. To achieve the same coefficients, multiply equation (1), including the $\Delta H°$ value, by 3. $3 \times$ eq. (1): $3CO(g) + \frac{3}{2}O_2(g) \rightarrow 3CO_2(g)$ $\quad \Delta H° = 3(-283.0$ kJ$)$ Equation (2) has the required stoichiometric coefficients, but $Fe(s)$ and $Fe_2O_3(s)$ are on the wrong sides of the equation. Reverse equation (2) and, therefore, change the sign of the $\Delta H°$ value. $-1 \times$ eq. (2): $Fe_2O_3(s) \rightarrow 2Fe(s) + \frac{3}{2}O_2(g)$ $\quad \Delta H° = -1(-824.2$ kJ$)$
Write the manipulated equations so that their equation arrows line up. Add the reactants and products on each side, and cancel substances that appear on both sides in equal amounts. Ensure that the manipulated equations add to the overall equation.	$3CO(g) + \frac{3}{2}O_2(g) \rightarrow 3CO_2(g)$ $Fe_2O_3(s) \rightarrow 2Fe(s) + \frac{3}{2}O_2(g)$ ――――――――――――――――― $3CO(g) + \cancel{\frac{3}{2}O_2(g)} + Fe_2O_3(s) \rightarrow 3CO_2(g) + 2Fe(s) + \cancel{\frac{3}{2}O_2(g)}$ $Fe_2O_3(s) + 3CO(g) \rightarrow 3CO_2(g) + 2Fe(s)$
Add the manipulated enthalpy values for the equations.	$\Delta H° = 3(-283.0$ kJ$) + (-1(-824.2$ kJ$))$ $= -849.0$ kJ $+ 824.2$ kJ $= -24.8$ kJ
Write the overall equation and enthalpy change.	$Fe_2O_3(s) + 3CO(g) \rightarrow 3CO_2(g) + 2Fe(s)$ $\quad \Delta H° = -24.8$ kJ

Check Your Solution

The equations added correctly to the overall equation. Check to ensure that you adjusted $\Delta H°$ accordingly for each equation. Because you added the $\Delta H°$ values, the final answer will be as precise as the least precise number used in the calculation. The final answer has one digit after the decimal point, which is correct.

Practice Problems

41. Nitrogen dioxide, $NO_2(g)$, is an emission resulting from the burning of gasoline in air in an automobile engine. Nitrogen dioxide contributes to the formation of smog and acid rain. It can be converted to dinitrogen tetroxide as shown below:

$$2NO_2(g) \rightarrow N_2O_4(g)$$

a. Use Hess's law and the following equations to determine the enthalpy change for this reaction.

(1) $N_2(g) + 2O_2(g) \rightarrow 2NO_2(g)$ $\Delta H° = 66.4 \text{ kJ}$
(2) $N_2(g) + 2O_2(g) \rightarrow N_2O_4(g)$ $\Delta H° = 11.1 \text{ kJ}$

b. Write the thermochemical equation for the overall reaction.

42. Ethyne, $C_2H_2(g)$, can be converted to benzene, $C_6H_6(\ell)$, over a palladium catalyst.

$$3C_2H_2(g) \xrightarrow{Pd} C_6H_6(\ell)$$

Determine the enthalpy of reaction for this process from the equations below that show the combustion of $C_2H_2(g)$ and $C_6H_6(\ell)$ at standard conditions.

(1) $C_2H_2(g) + \frac{5}{2}O_2 \rightarrow 2CO_2(g) + H_2O(g)$
$\Delta H° = -1301.1 \text{ kJ}$
(2) $C_6H_6(\ell) + \frac{15}{2}O_2 \rightarrow 6CO_2(g) + 3H_2O(g)$
$\Delta H° = -3267.6 \text{ kJ}$

43. Hydrazine, $N_2H_4(\ell)$, is a high-energy compound used as a rocket propellant. Use Hess's law to determine the enthalpy of reaction when this compound reacts as follows:

$$N_2H_4(\ell) + 2H_2O_2(\ell) \rightarrow N_2(g) + 4H_2O(\ell)$$

Use the following information:

(1) $H_2(g) + \frac{1}{2}O_2(g) \rightarrow H_2O(\ell)$ $\Delta H° = -285.8 \text{ kJ}$
(2) $N_2H_4(\ell) + O_2(g) \rightarrow N_2(g) + 2H_2O(\ell)$
$\Delta H° = -622.0 \text{ kJ}$
(3) $H_2(g) + O_2(g) \rightarrow H_2O_2(\ell)$ $\Delta H° = -188.0 \text{ kJ}$

44. Synthetic rubber can be manufactured from the hydrocarbon buta-1,3-diene, $C_4H_6(g)$. This compound reacts with hydrogen to produce butane, $C_4H_{10}(g)$, as shown in the equation below:

$$C_4H_6(g) + 2H_2(g) \rightarrow C_4H_{10}(g)$$

Use Hess's law and the equations that follow to determine the enthalpy change for this reaction.

(1) $C_4H_6(g) + \frac{11}{2}O_2(g) \rightarrow 4CO_2(g) + 3H_2O(g)$
$\Delta H° = -2541.5 \text{ kJ}$
(2) $C_4H_{10}(g) + \frac{13}{2}O_2(g) \rightarrow 4CO_2(g) + 5H_2O(g)$
$\Delta H° = -2877.6 \text{ kJ}$
(3) $H_2(g) + \frac{1}{2}O_2(g) \rightarrow H_2O(g)$ $\Delta H° = -241.8 \text{ kJ}$

45. Ethene, $C_2H_4(g)$, is commonly used as an agent to hasten the ripening of fruit, such as bananas. It can also be used to prepare 1,2-dichloroethane, $C_2H_4Cl_2(\ell)$, which is used to make vinyl chloride. Use Hess's law to determine the enthalpy of reaction for the preparation of $C_2H_4Cl_2(\ell)$.

$$C_2H_4(g) + Cl_2(g) \rightarrow C_2H_4Cl_2(\ell)$$

Given:
(1) $4HCl(g) + O_2(g) \rightarrow 2Cl_2(g) + 2H_2O(\ell)$
$\Delta H° = -202.4 \text{ kJ}$
(2) $2HCl(g) + C_2H_4(g) + \frac{1}{2}O_2(g) \rightarrow$
$C_2H_4Cl_2(\ell) + H_2O(\ell)$
$\Delta H° = -320.8 \text{ kJ}$

46. Carbon monoxide, $CO(g)$, can react with hydrogen, $H_2(g)$, to produce methane, $CH_4(g)$, and water vapour.

$$CO(g) + 3H_2(g) \rightarrow CH_4(g) + H_2O(g)$$

Given the following equations, use Hess's law to determine the enthalpy of reaction.

(1) $H_2(g) + \frac{1}{2}O_2(g) \rightarrow H_2O(g)$ $\Delta H° = -241.8 \text{ kJ}$
(2) $CO(g) + \frac{1}{2}O_2(g) \rightarrow CO_2(g)$ $\Delta H° = -283.0 \text{ kJ}$
(3) $2CO(g) + 2H_2(g) \rightarrow CH_4(g) + CO_2(g)$
$\Delta H° = -247.1 \text{ kJ}$

47. The following thermodynamic equations have been obtained from reference sources:

(1) $H_2(g) + \frac{1}{2}O_2(g) \rightarrow H_2O(\ell) + 285.8 \text{ kJ}$
(2) $H_2(g) + S(s) \rightarrow H_2S(g) + 20.6 \text{ kJ}$
(3) $S(s) + O_2(g) \rightarrow SO_2(g) + 296.8 \text{ kJ}$

Use Hess's law to determine the enthalpy change for the reaction below:

$$2H_2S(g) + 3O_2(g) \rightarrow 2SO_2(g) + 2H_2O(\ell)$$

48. The reaction to convert $SO_2(g)$ to $SO_3(g)$ is a two-step process:

Step 1: $SO_2(g) + 299 \text{ kJ} \rightarrow S(s) + O_2(g)$
Step 2: $S(s) + O_2(g) + \frac{1}{2}O_2(g) \rightarrow SO_3(g)$

The enthalpy diagram below is a graphical representation of the process. Use this diagram to determine the enthalpy change for step 2.

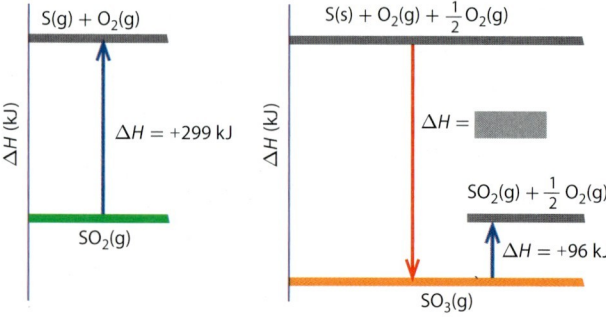

49. Ethene, $C_2H_4(g)$, is used in the manufacture of many polymers. If ethene could be formed from the elements carbon and hydrogen, the equation would be as follows:

$$2C(s) + 2H_2(g) \rightarrow C_2H_4(g)$$

Use Hess's law and the equations given below to determine the molar enthalpy of formation from its elements for $C_2H_4(g)$.

(1) $C(s) + O_2(g) \rightarrow CO_2(g) \quad \Delta H° = -393.5 \text{ kJ}$

(2) $H_2(g) + \frac{1}{2}O_2(g) \rightarrow H_2O(\ell) \quad \Delta H° = -285.8 \text{ kJ}$

(3) $C_2H_4(g) + 3O_2(g) \rightarrow$
$\quad 2CO_2(g) + 2H_2O(\ell) \quad \Delta H° = -1411.2 \text{ kJ}$

50. From the following equations, determine the molar enthalpy of formation from its elements for $HNO_2(aq)$, as shown below in the overall equation:

$$\frac{1}{2}H_2(g) + \frac{1}{2}N_2(g) + O_2(g) \rightarrow HNO_2(aq)$$

(1) $NH_4NO_2(aq) \rightarrow N_2(g) + 2H_2O(\ell)$
$\quad \Delta H° = -320.1 \text{ kJ}$

(2) $NH_3(aq) + HNO_2(aq) \rightarrow NH_4NO_2(aq)$
$\quad \Delta H° = -37.7 \text{ kJ}$

(3) $2NH_3(aq) \rightarrow N_2(g) + 3H_2(g)$
$\quad \Delta H° = +169.9 \text{ kJ}$

(4) $H_2(g) + \frac{1}{2}O_2(g) \rightarrow H_2O(\ell) \quad \Delta H° = -285.8 \text{ kJ}$

Learning Check

13. State Hess's law, and explain why it is useful.

14. Under what standard conditions is $\Delta H°$ measured?

15. What factor must be kept constant when comparing the enthalpy change between two reactions?

16. Figure 5.20 shows an enthalpy diagram for the formation of $CO_2(g)$. Sketch an enthalpy diagram for the reverse process: the decomposition of $CO_2(g)$ to $C(s)$ and $O_2(g)$.

17. How can data be obtained for the simpler steps that an overall reaction can take to apply Hess's law? For a reaction that can be represented by two or more simpler steps, must each step be experimentally carried out in order to use Hess's law? Explain your answer.

18. What statement can be made that validates that the steps (the pathway) between initial reactants and final products do not affect enthalpy change?

19. Use Hess's law to calculate the enthalpy of reaction for the reaction between ethene and water to form ethanol, as shown.

$$C_2H_4(g) + H_2O(\ell) \rightarrow C_2H_5OH(\ell)$$

Use the enthalpies of combustion of ethene and ethanol shown below.

$$\Delta H°_{comb}(C_2H_4(g)) = -1441.2 \text{ kJ}$$
$$\Delta H°_{comb}(C_2H_5OH(\ell)) = -1366.8 \text{ kJ}$$

After completing the calculation, draw an enthalpy diagram for the reactions.

Standard Molar Enthalpies of Formation

You have learned how to add equations for reactions with known standard enthalpy changes to find the enthalpy change of another reaction. Chemists have measured and calculated the standard enthalpy changes for thousands of chemical reactions. If you could find the right set of equations, you could calculate the standard enthalpy change for almost any reaction. How can you find these known enthalpy changes? Chemists have collected and organized data for one specific type of reaction that allow you to generate equations for almost any reaction. This type of reaction is a specific class of synthesis reaction in which the compound must be formed from its elements and not from any other compound.

The enthalpy change of formation for a compound at SATP is called the standard molar enthalpy of formation. The **standard molar enthalpy of formation, $\Delta H°_f$**, is the change in enthalpy when 1 mol of a compound is formed directly from its elements in their most stable state at SATP (25°C and 100 kPa). Because elements in their most stable state have been selected as a reference, the standard enthalpy of formation of the elements has been arbitrarily set at zero.

> **standard molar enthalpy of formation, $\Delta H°_f$** the change in enthalpy when 1 mol of a compound is formed directly from its elements in their most stable state at standard ambient temperature and pressure (SATP: 25°C and 100 kPa) and all solutions have a 1.0 mol/L concentration

Working with Standard Molar Enthalpies of Formation

Some molar enthalpies of formation are listed in **Table 5.5**. Additional molar enthalpies of formation are found in Appendix B. Notice that many of the formation equations include fractions. It is often necessary to use fractions in formation equations, because, by definition, they show the formation of exactly 1 mol of the product compound. For example, the following equation shows the formation of calcium oxide under standard conditions:

$$\text{Ca(s)} + \frac{1}{2}\text{O}_2\text{(g)} \rightarrow \text{CaO(s)} \qquad \Delta H_f^\circ = -634.9 \text{ kJ/mol CaO(s)}$$

To produce 1 mol CaO(s), you need 1 mol Ca(s) and 0.5 mol O_2(g). If you were to eliminate the fractions by multiplying the coefficients by 2, the equation would show the formation of 2 mol CaO(s), not 1 mol.

Table 5.5 Selected Standard Molar Enthalpies of Formation

Compound	Formation Equation	ΔH_f° (kJ/mol)
CO(g)	$C(s) + \frac{1}{2}O_2(g) \rightarrow CO(g)$	−110.5
CO_2(g)	$C(s) + O_2(g) \rightarrow CO_2(g)$	−393.5
CH_4(g)	$C(s) + 2H_2(g) \rightarrow CH_4(g)$	−74.6
$CH_3OH(\ell)$	$C(s) + 2H_2(g) + \frac{1}{2}O_2(g) \rightarrow CH_3OH(\ell)$	−239.2
$C_2H_5OH(\ell)$	$2C(s) + 3H_2(g) + \frac{1}{2}O_2(g) \rightarrow C_2H_5OH(\ell)$	−277.6
$C_6H_6(\ell)$	$6C(s) + 3H_2(g) \rightarrow C_6H_6(\ell)$	+49.1
$C_6H_{12}O_6$(s)	$6C(s) + 6H_2(g) + 3O_2(g) \rightarrow C_6H_{12}O_6(s)$	−1273.3
$H_2O(\ell)$	$H_2(g) + \frac{1}{2}O_2(g) \rightarrow H_2O(\ell)$	−285.8
H_2O(g)	$H_2(g) + \frac{1}{2}O_2(g) \rightarrow H_2O(g)$	−241.8
$CaCl_2$(s)	$Ca(s) + Cl_2(g) \rightarrow CaCl_2(s)$	−795.4
$CaCO_3$(s)	$Ca(s) + C(s) + \frac{3}{2}O_2(g) \rightarrow CaCO_3(s)$	−1207.6
NaCl(s)	$Na(s) + \frac{1}{2}Cl_2(g) \rightarrow NaCl(s)$	−411.2
HCl(g)	$\frac{1}{2}H_2(g) + \frac{1}{2}Cl_2(g) \rightarrow HCl(g)$	−92.3
HCl(aq)	$\frac{1}{2}H_2(g) + \frac{1}{2}Cl_2(g) \rightarrow HCl(aq)$	−167.5

Some elements exist in more than one form under standard conditions. For example, two forms of carbon are graphite and diamond, as shown in **Figure 5.24**. The enthalpy of formation of an element in its most stable state under standard conditions is arbitrarily set at zero. Graphite is the standard state of carbon. Therefore, the standard molar enthalpy of formation of graphite carbon is 0 kJ/mol. The standard molar enthalpy of formation of diamond is +1.9 kJ/mol.

Figure 5.24 Two forms of carbon under standard conditions are graphite (**A**), used in pencil leads, and diamond (**B**). Carbon can, however, have only one standard state. Carbon's standard state is graphite.

Analyze how you can use standard molar enthalpy of formation values to determine whether graphite or diamond is more stable at SATP.

Formation Reactions and Thermal Stability

Formation reactions can provide information about how stable a substance is. The ability of a substance to resist decomposition when heated is known as its **thermal stability**. The reverse of a formation reaction is a decomposition reaction. The opposite sign of the enthalpy change of a formation reaction, therefore, is the enthalpy change of a decomposition reaction. The greater the enthalpy change of a decomposition reaction, the more energy input is required to decompose a substance into its elements. In other words, the greater the enthalpy change of a decomposition reaction, the greater is its thermal stability. For example, compare the enthalpies of decomposition of calcium carbonate, $CaCO_3(s)$, and methane, $CH_4(g)$. (Use the enthalpies of formation from **Table 5.5** and multiply by -1.)

thermal stability the ability of a substance to resist decomposition when heated

- Methane's enthalpy of decomposition is $+74.6$ kJ/mol.

$$C(s) + 2H_2(g) \rightarrow CH_4(g) \quad \Delta H_f° = -74.6 \text{ kJ/mol}$$
$$CH_4(g) \rightarrow C(s) + 2H_2(g) \quad \Delta H_r° = +74.6 \text{ kJ/mol (decomposition reaction)}$$

- Calcium carbonate's enthalpy of decomposition is $+1207.6$ kJ/mol.

$$Ca(s) + C(s) + \frac{3}{2}O_2(g) \rightarrow CaCO_3(s) \quad \Delta H_f° = -1207.6 \text{ kJ/mol}$$
$$CaCO_3(s) \rightarrow Ca(s) + C(s) + \frac{3}{2}O_2(g) \quad \Delta H_r° = +1207.6 \text{ kJ/mol (decomposition reaction)}$$

Calcium carbonate requires a far greater energy input to decompose into its elements; therefore, calcium carbonate is considered more thermally stable.

Using Enthalpies of Formation and Hess's Law

A variation of Hess's law allows you to calculate the enthalpy change of a chemical reaction by adding the enthalpies of formation of the products and subtracting the sum of the enthalpies of formation of the reactants. The following equation can be used to determine the enthalpy change of a chemical reaction:

$$\Delta H_r° = \Sigma(n\Delta H_f° \text{ products}) - \Sigma(n\Delta H_f° \text{ reactants})$$

where n represents the stoichiometric coefficient for each substance and Σ means "the sum of."

As usual, you need to begin with a balanced chemical equation. Consider, for example, the complete combustion of methane, $CH_4(g)$:

$$CH_4(g) + 2O_2(g) \rightarrow CO_2(g) + 2H_2O(g)$$

Using the equation for the enthalpy change and the standard molar enthalpies of formation in Appendix B, you can calculate the enthalpy change for this reaction, as written.

$$\Delta H_r° = \Sigma(n\Delta H_f° \text{ products}) - \Sigma(n\Delta H_f° \text{ reactants})$$
$$= [(1 \text{ mol})(\Delta H_f°CO_2(g)) + (2 \text{ mol})(\Delta H_f°H_2O(g))] - [(1 \text{ mol})(\Delta H_f°CH_4(g)) + (2 \text{ mol})(\Delta H_f°O_2(g))]$$

$$= \left[(1 \text{ mol})\left(-393.2 \frac{\text{kJ}}{\text{mol}}\right) + (2 \text{ mol})\left(-241.9 \frac{\text{kJ}}{\text{mol}}\right)\right] - \left[(1 \text{ mol})\left(-74.6 \frac{\text{kJ}}{\text{mol}}\right) + (2 \text{ mol})\left(0 \frac{\text{kJ}}{\text{mol}}\right)\right]$$

$$= (-877.1 \text{ kJ}) - (-74.6 \text{ kJ})$$
$$= -802.5 \text{ kJ}$$

Note: Oxygen gas, $O_2(g)$, at SATP is an element in its most stable state. Therefore, its standard enthalpy of formation is zero. Therefore,

$$CH_4(g) + 2O_2(g) \rightarrow CO_2(g) + 2H_2O(g) \quad \Delta H_r° = -802.5 \text{ kJ}$$

Relating Enthalpies of Formation and Hess's Law

Why does this method of adding and subtracting enthalpies of formation work, and how does this method relate to Hess's law? Consider the equations for the formation of each compound involved in the reaction of methane with oxygen:

(1) $H_2(g) + \frac{1}{2} O_2(g) \rightarrow H_2O(g)$ $\quad\quad \Delta H_f^\circ = -241.8$ kJ/mol
(2) $\quad C(s) + O_2(g) \rightarrow CO_2(g)$ $\quad\quad \Delta H_f^\circ = -393.5$ kJ/mol
(3) $\quad C(s) + 2H_2(g) \rightarrow CH_4(g)$ $\quad\quad \Delta H_f^\circ = -74.6$ kJ/mol

There is no equation for the formation of oxygen, because oxygen is an element in its most stable state. By adding the formation equations and their enthalpy changes, you can obtain the overall equation. Notice that you must reverse equation (3) and multiply equation (1) by a factor of 2.

$2 \times$ (1) $\quad 2H_2(g) + O_2(g) \rightarrow 2H_2O(g)$ $\quad \Delta H_r^\circ = 2(-241.8$ kJ/mol$)$
(2) $\quad\quad\quad \cancel{C(s)} + O_2(g) \rightarrow CO_2(g)$ $\quad \Delta H_r^\circ = -393.5$ kJ/mol
$-1 \times$ (3) $\quad\quad CH_4(g) \rightarrow \cancel{C(s)} + 2H_2(g)$ $\quad \Delta H_r^\circ = -1(-74.6$ kJ/mol$)$

$\quad\quad\quad\quad\quad CH_4(g) + 2O_2(g) \rightarrow CO_2(g) + 2H_2O(g)$ $\quad \Delta H_r^\circ = -802.5$ kJ/mol

This value of ΔH_r° is the same as the value obtained by adding and subtracting enthalpies of formation. Therefore, using enthalpies of formation to determine the enthalpy of a reaction is consistent with Hess's law. In fact, using the formula in the box on the previous page makes it unnecessary to look for equations to add and carry out all of the extra steps. **Figure 5.25** shows the general process for determining the enthalpy of reaction from enthalpies of formation.

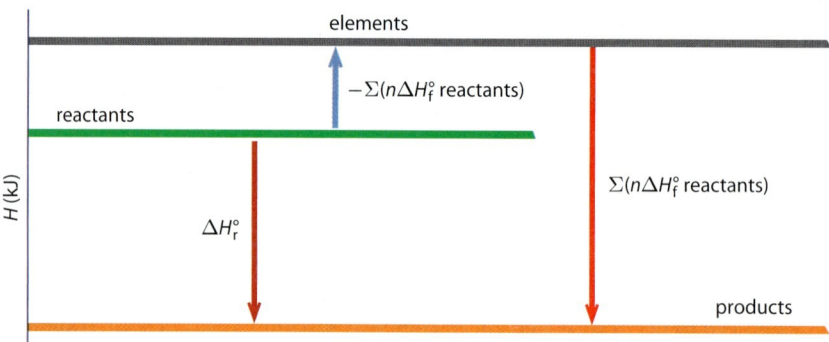

Figure 5.25 When using enthalpies of formation and Hess's law, you can visualize the overall reaction by imagining the reactants decomposing entirely into their elements and then the elements combining to form the products.

When using enthalpies of formation, remember that *the reactants do not actually break down into their elements and then react to form products*. Nevertheless, the method gives correct results because, according to Hess's law, the enthalpy change is the same, regardless of the pathway. The Sample Problem on the opposite page shows how to use enthalpies of formation to determine the enthalpy change of a reaction. Examine the second Sample Problem to learn how to determine enthalpy of formation using a known enthalpy of reaction. Then try the Practice Problems that follow.

Sample Problem

Using Enthalpies of Formation

Problem

Iron(III) oxide reacts with carbon monoxide to produce elemental iron and carbon dioxide. Determine the enthalpy change of this reaction by using known enthalpies of formation:

$$Fe_2O_3(s) + 3CO(g) \rightarrow 3CO_2(g) + 2Fe(s)$$

Iron ores are rocks that are rich in iron oxide and are an economical source of metallic iron.

What Is Required?

You need to find ΔH_r° for the given chemical equation by using ΔH_f° data.

What Is Given?

From Appendix B, you can find the molar enthalpies of formation:

ΔH_f° of $Fe_2O_3(s)$ = −824.2 kJ/mol

ΔH_f° of $CO(g)$ = −110.5 kJ/mol

ΔH_f° of $CO_2(g)$ = −393.5 kJ/mol

ΔH_f° of $Fe(s)$ = 0 kJ/mol (by definition, because Fe(s) is elemental iron in its most stable state)

Plan Your Strategy
Substitute the known values for enthalpies of formation into the equation: $\Delta H_r^\circ = \Sigma(n\Delta H_f^\circ \text{ products}) - \Sigma(n\Delta H_f^\circ \text{ reactants})$
Act on Your Strategy
$\Delta H_r^\circ = \Sigma(n\Delta H_f^\circ \text{ products}) - \Sigma(n\Delta H_f^\circ \text{ reactants})$ $= [(3 \text{ mol})(\Delta H_f^\circ \, CO_2(g)) + (2 \text{ mol})(\Delta H_f^\circ \, Fe(s))] - [(1 \text{ mol})(\Delta H_f^\circ \, Fe_2O_3(s)) + (3 \text{ mol})(\Delta H_f^\circ \, CO(g))]$ $= \left[(3 \text{ mol})\left(-393.5 \, \frac{kJ}{mol}\right) + (2 \text{ mol})\left(0 \, \frac{kJ}{mol}\right)\right] - \left[(1 \text{ mol})\left(-824.2 \, \frac{kJ}{mol}\right) + (3 \text{ mol})\left(-110.5 \, \frac{kJ}{mol}\right)\right]$ $= (-1180.5 \text{ kJ} + 0 \text{ kJ}) - (-824.2 \text{ kJ} - 331.5 \text{ kJ})$ $= -1180.5 \text{ kJ} + 1155.7 \text{ kJ}$ $= -24.8 \text{ kJ}$ Therefore, $Fe_2O_3(s) + 3CO(g) \rightarrow 3CO_2(g) + 2Fe(s) \quad \Delta H_r^\circ = -24.8 \text{ kJ}$

Check Your Solution

A balanced chemical equation was used in the calculation. The answer is correctly expressed to the same precision as ΔH_f°, with one digit after the decimal point. The units are also correct.

Sample Problem

Using an Enthalpy of Combustion to Determine an Enthalpy of Formation

Problem

Octane, $C_8H_{18}(\ell)$, one of the major components in gasoline, burns completely with oxygen, producing carbon dioxide and water vapour. The molar enthalpy of combustion of octane in these conditions is −5074.1 kJ/mol. Determine the molar enthalpy of formation of octane.

What Is Required?

You need to write a balanced chemical equation for the reaction. You need to find ΔH_f° of octane by using the given molar enthalpy of combustion for octane and ΔH_f° data.

What Is Given?

ΔH_{comb}° of $C_8H_{18}(\ell) = -5074.1$ kJ/mol

From Appendix B, you can obtain the molar enthalpies of formation.

ΔH_f° of $O_2(g) = 0$ kJ/mol (by definition)

ΔH_f° of $CO_2(g) = -393.5$ kJ/mol

ΔH_f° of $H_2O(g) = -241.8$ kJ/mol

Plan Your Strategy
a. Write a chemical equation representing the combustion of octane in an open system. **b.** Use the available ΔH_f° data and the ΔH_{comb}° (enthalpy of combustion of octane) to substitute into the equation $\Delta H_r^\circ = \Sigma(n\Delta H_f^\circ \text{products}) - \Sigma(n\Delta H_f^\circ \text{reactants})$, multiplying by the molar coefficients. **c.** Solve for the unknown ΔH_f° for octane.
Act on Your Strategy
a. Write and balance the chemical equation for the combustion of 1 mol of octane: $$C_8H_{18}(\ell) + \frac{25}{2} O_2(g) \rightarrow 8CO_2(g) + 9H_2O(g)$$ **b.** (**Note:** The overall reaction is a combustion reaction, so use ΔH_{comb}° for ΔH_r°.) $\Delta H_r^\circ = \Sigma(nH_f^\circ \text{ products}) - \Sigma(nH_f^\circ \text{ reactants})$ $\Delta H_{comb}^\circ\, C_8H_{18}(\ell) = \left[(8 \text{ mol})(\Delta H_f^\circ CO_2(g)) + (9 \text{ mol})(\Delta H_f^\circ H_2O(g))\right] - \left[(1 \text{ mol})(\Delta H_f^\circ C_8H_{18}(\ell)) + \left(\frac{25}{2} \text{ mol}\right)(\Delta H_f^\circ O_2(g))\right]$ $-5074.1 \text{ kJ} = \left[(8 \text{ mol})\left(-393.5 \frac{\text{kJ}}{\text{mol}}\right) + (9 \text{ mol})\left(-241.8 \frac{\text{kJ}}{\text{mol}}\right)\right] - \left[(1 \text{ mol})(\Delta H_f^\circ C_8H_{18}(\ell)) + \left(\frac{25}{2} \text{ mol}\right)\left(0 \frac{\text{kJ}}{\text{mol}}\right)\right]$ $-5074.1 \text{ kJ} = (-3148.0 \text{ kJ} - 2176.2 \text{ kJ}) - (1 \text{ mol})(\Delta H_f^\circ C_8H_{18}(\ell))$ **c.** $(1 \text{ mol})(\Delta H_f^\circ C_8H_{18}(\ell)) = +5074.1 \text{ kJ} - 3148.0 \text{ kJ} - 2176.2 \text{ kJ}$ $\Delta H_f^\circ C_8H_{18}(\ell) = \dfrac{-250.1 \text{ kJ}}{1 \text{ mol}}$ $= -250.1 \dfrac{\text{kJ}}{\text{mol}}$ The enthalpy of formation of octane, $C_8H_{18}(\ell)$, is −250.1 kJ/mol.

Check Your Solution

A balanced chemical equation was used in the calculation with appropriate molar coefficients. The answer is and should be expressed to the same precision as ΔH_f°, with one digit after the decimal point. The units are also correct.

Practice Problems

Refer to Appendix B for data on molar enthalpies of formation.

51. The complete combustion of ethanol, $C_2H_5OH(\ell)$, yields carbon dioxide and water vapour.

   a. Write the balanced chemical equation for this reaction.

   b. Use enthalpies of formation to determine the enthalpy of combustion, $\Delta H°_{comb}$, in kilojoules per mole of $C_2H_5OH(\ell)$.

52. A reagent bottle containing concentrated aqueous ammonia, $NH_3(aq)$, is accidentally left open near a bottle of concentrated hydrochloric acid, $HCl(aq)$. The cloud of white smoke that forms in the air near the two containers is ammonium chloride, $NH_4Cl(s)$. The following reaction occurs in the air:

$$NH_3(g) + HCl(g) \rightarrow NH_4Cl(s)$$

Use the standard molar enthalpies of formation to calculate the enthalpy of reaction.

53. A piece of zinc reacts completely with hydrochloric acid, $HCl(aq)$, to produce an aqueous solution of zinc chloride, $ZnCl_2(aq)$, and hydrogen gas.

   a. Use the data shown below to determine the enthalpy of reaction per mole of zinc.
   $\Delta H°_f$ of $HCl(aq) = -167.2$ kJ/mol
   $\Delta H°_f$ of $ZnCl_2(aq) = -488.2$ kJ/mol
   $$Zn(s) + 2HCl(aq) \rightarrow ZnCl_2(aq) + H_2(g)$$

   b. What mass of zinc must be used for 123 kJ of heat to be given off?

54. Ammonia reacts with oxygen according to the following unbalanced equation:

$$NH_3(g) + O_2(g) \rightarrow NO(g) + H_2O(g)$$

Use standard molar enthalpies of formation to find the enthalpy of reaction for this reaction.

55. Consider the following equation representing the reaction of methane and chlorine to form chloroform, $CHCl_3(g)$:

$$CH_4(g) + 3Cl_2(g) \rightarrow CHCl_3(g) + 3HCl(g)$$
$$\Delta H° = -305.0 \text{ kJ}$$

Use standard molar enthalpies of formation to determine the molar enthalpy of formation for chloroform.

56. The molar enthalpy of combustion for heptane, $C_7H_{16}(\ell)$, in a bomb calorimeter is -4816.7 kJ/mol of heptane. Using this and $\Delta H°_f$ data, determine the molar enthalpy of formation of heptane.

$$C_7H_{16}(\ell) + 11O_2(g) \rightarrow 7CO_2(g) + 8H_2O(\ell)$$

57. A double displacement reaction occurs when solutions of magnesium chloride, $MgCl_2(aq)$, and silver nitrate, $AgNO_3(aq)$, are mixed. Assume that the reaction goes to completion and that all of the silver chloride that forms precipitates as $AgCl(s)$.

$$MgCl_2(aq) + 2AgNO_3(aq) \rightarrow Mg(NO_3)_2(aq) + 2AgCl(s)$$

Use the given enthalpy of formation data to determine the enthalpy of reaction.

$\Delta H°_f$ of $MgCl_2(aq) = -801.2$ kJ/mol
$\Delta H°_f$ of $Mg(NO_3)_2(aq) = -881.6$ kJ/mol
$\Delta H°_f$ of $AgCl(s) = -127.0$ kJ/mol
$\Delta H°_f$ of $AgNO_3(aq) = -101.8$ kJ/mol

58. Hydrogen gas reacts with propene gas, $C_3H_6(g)$, in an addition reaction to produce propane, $C_3H_8(g)$.

$$C_3H_6(g) + H_2(g) \rightarrow C_3H_8(g) + 124.2 \text{ kJ}$$

Use enthalpy of formation data and the information given in the above equation to determine the enthalpy of formation of propene.

59. The complete combustion of hexane, $C_6H_{14}(\ell)$, can be represented by the following equation:

$$C_6H_{14}(\ell) + \frac{19}{2}O_2(g) \rightarrow 6CO_2(g) + 7H_2O(\ell) + 4163.2 \text{ kJ}$$

One possible reaction for the incomplete combustion of $C_6H_{14}(\ell)$ is as follows:

$$C_6H_{14}(\ell) + 5O_2(g) \rightarrow CO_2(g) + CO(g) + 4C(s) + 7H_2O(\ell)$$

Determine the amount of energy lost per mole of $C_6H_{14}(\ell)$ when combustion is incomplete as written. The standard molar enthalpy of formation for $C_6H_{14}(\ell)$ is -198.7 kJ/mol.

60. Ethanol, $C_2H_5OH(\ell)$, reacts with a 1.00 mol/L solution of acetic acid to produce ethyl ethanoate, a solvent used to make protective coatings such as polyurethane.

$$C_2H_5OH(\ell) + CH_3COOH(aq) \rightarrow CH_3COOC_2H_5(aq) + H_2O(\ell)$$

Calorimetry experiments determine that the enthalpy of reaction is 43 kJ. Use this information and the enthalpy of formation data to calculate the enthalpy of formation of ethyl ethanoate. The enthalpy of formation for 1.00 mol/L $CH_3COOH(aq)$ is -486.0 kJ/mol.

Section 5.3 Review

Section Summary

- Hess's law states that the enthalpy change of a physical or chemical process depends only on the initial and final conditions. The enthalpy change of the overall process is the sum of the enthalpy changes of its individual steps.
- You can add any number of chemical equations to obtain an equation that you need, and the enthalpy change of the overall reaction is the sum of the enthalpy changes of the individual reactions.
- You can manipulate chemical equations to make them fit into another set of reactions by multiplying the equation by a constant or by reversing the equation. If you multiply by a constant, you must multiply the enthalpy change by that same constant. If you reverse an equation, you must change the sign of the enthalpy change.
- The standard enthalpy of formation of a compound (ΔH_f°) is the enthalpy change for the formation of 1 mol of the compound from its elements in their most stable state under standard conditions.
- The enthalpy of formation of an element in its most stable state under standard conditions is arbitrarily set at zero.
- You can calculate the enthalpy change for any reaction by applying the formula

$$\Delta H_r^\circ = \Sigma(n\Delta H_f^\circ \text{ products}) - \Sigma(n\Delta H_f^\circ \text{ reactants})$$

Review Questions

1. **K/U** What is the difference between the standard molar enthalpy of formation for a compound and the standard enthalpy change for a reaction in which that compound is a product?

2. **T/I** The standard molar enthalpy of formation for ammonium hydrogen carbonate, $(NH_4)HCO_3(s)$, is −849.4 kJ/mol. Write the thermochemical equation to show the formation of this compound.

3. **T/I** The standard molar enthalpy of formation of sulfuric acid, $H_2SO_4(\ell)$, is −814.0 kJ/mol. The standard state for sulfur is orthorhombic sulfur, $S_8(s)$. Write the thermochemical equation to represent the enthalpy of formation for $H_2SO_4(\ell)$.

4. **A** Use Hess's law and the equations shown below to determine the enthalpy of reaction for

$$2NOCl(g) \rightarrow N_2(g) + O_2(g) + Cl_2(g)$$

(1) $\frac{1}{2}N_2(g) + \frac{1}{2}O_2(g) \rightarrow NO(g)$ $\Delta H^\circ = +90.5$ kJ

(2) $NO(g) + \frac{1}{2}Cl_2(g) \rightarrow NOCl(g)$ $\Delta H^\circ = -39.0$ kJ

5. **T/I** Use the given information and Hess's law to show how the enthalpy of reaction can be determined for the following reaction:

$$P_4O_{10}(s) + 6PCl_5(s) \rightarrow 10Cl_3PO(g)$$

(1) $P_4(s) + 6Cl_2(g) \rightarrow 4PCl_3(\ell)$ $\Delta H^\circ = -1272$ kJ

(2) $P_4(s) + 5O_2(g) \rightarrow P_4O_{10}(s)$ $\Delta H^\circ = -2915$ kJ

(3) $PCl_3(\ell) + Cl_2(g) \rightarrow PCl_5(s)$ $\Delta H^\circ = -125$ kJ

(4) $PCl_3(\ell) + \frac{1}{2}O_2(g) \rightarrow Cl_3PO(g)$ $\Delta H^\circ = -267$ kJ

6. **T/I** 21.9 kJ of energy is released when 5.48 g of barium is oxidized to barium oxide, BaO(s). What is the enthalpy of formation of BaO(s)?

$$Ba(s) + \frac{1}{2}O_2(g) \rightarrow BaO(s)$$

7. **K/U** The standard molar enthalpy of formation for oxygen gas, $O_2(g)$, is zero. The enthalpy of formation for atomic oxygen, O(g), is +250 kJ/mol. Why is there a difference in these values?

8. **T/I** Arrange the following compounds in decreasing order of thermal stability, and explain the basis for determining thermal stability: $CrCl_3(s)$, $CaCl_2(s)$, AgCl(s), NaCl(s).

9. **A** Consider the process below.

$$3Fe_3O_4(s) + 8Al(s) \rightarrow 9Fe(s) + 4Al_2O_3(s)$$

a. What is the enthalpy of reaction for this process?

b. What amount of heat would be released when 1.000×10^3 kg of iron is produced?

10. **C** Refer to the enthalpy of formation of hydrazine, $N_2H_4(\ell)$, in Appendix B. Would you expect this to be a thermally stable compound? Write your answer as an e-mail to a classmate who does not understand the concept.

11. **T/I** Use the enthalpy of formation data in Appendix B to determine the enthalpy of formation for chlorine trifluoride, $ClF_3(g)$.

$$2ClF_3(g) + 2NH_3(g) \rightarrow$$
$$N_2(g) + 6HF(g) + Cl_2(g) + 1.200 \times 10^3 \text{ kJ}$$

12. **C** As your part of a group presentation to the class, prepare a discussion that includes an enthalpy diagram that explains the significance of a positive sign for the enthalpy of formation for a compound.

13. **A** How much heat is required to decompose 500.0 g of calcium carbonate, $CaCO_3(s)$, into calcium oxide, CaO(s), and carbon dioxide?

$$CaCO_3(s) \rightarrow CaO(s) + CO_2(g)$$

SECTION 5.4
Energy Efficiency and Energy Resources

In the context of energy transfer and transformations, **efficiency** is the ratio of useful energy produced (*energy output*) to energy used in its production (*energy input*), expressed as a percentage. This definition can be expressed mathematically as shown in the box below. When you use this definition, however, you need to be clear about what you mean by "energy used." **Figure 5.26** shows factors to consider when calculating efficiency or analyzing efficiency data.

$$\text{efficiency} = \frac{\text{energy output}}{\text{energy input}} \times 100\%$$

Key Terms

efficiency
heat content

efficiency the ratio of useful energy produced (energy output) to energy used in its production (energy input), expressed as a percentage

Energy output
- energy delivered to consumer in usable form
- actual work done
- calculate using $Q = mc\Delta t$, $\Delta H = n\Delta H_x$
- **Note:** x can be f, comb, r, vap, or melt

Energy input
- ideal energy content of fuel
- energy used to extract and transport fuel
- solar energy used to create fuel (e.g., biomass)
- energy used to build and maintain power plant
- calculate using Hess's law and $\Delta H = n\Delta H_x$

Figure 5.26 Efficiency is expressed as a percentage. Always specify what is included in the "energy input" part of the ratio.

It is often difficult to determine how much energy is used and exactly how much useful energy is produced. For example, consider the preparation of the meal shown in **Figure 5.27**. Should you include the fuel used in the transportation of the vegetables and meat to market? Should you include the fuel used by the farmer in his tractors to plow, plant, fertilize, and harvest the vegetables? What about the energy used to heat the stove to cook the meat and vegetables? What do you include when calculating the energy efficiency of a process?

Figure 5.27 This is a healthy meal, but how much energy was used to prepare it?

Often, an efficiency percentage only takes into account the energy output of a system, based on the theoretical energy content of the fuel. The efficiency of a thermal energy conversion (heating) system is often calculated by using calorimetry data (energy output) and a calculation for energy input, which is a theoretical quantity (usually determined by Hess's law). The energy output takes into account only the useful energy for a particular process. The energy input includes that energy plus all of the "wasted" energy that is used to heat the oven, the air in the oven, and the kitchen. Examine the following Sample Problem to learn how to determine energy efficiency. Try the Practice Problems that follow to practise calculating efficiency.

Sample Problem

The Efficiency of a Propane Barbecue

Problem

Propane, $C_3H_8(g)$, is a commonly used barbecue fuel. Determine the efficiency of the barbecue as a heating device if 5.10 g of propane is required to change the temperature of 250.0 g of water contained in a 500.0 g stainless steel pot ($c = 0.503$ J/g·°C) from 25.0°C to 75.0°C.

What Is Required?

You need to find the amount of energy released by the combustion of the propane.
You need to find how much energy was absorbed by the water and the pot.
You then need to use those values to determine the efficiency of the barbecue.

What Is Given?

$m_{\text{propane used}} = 5.10$ g

$m_{\text{water}} = 250.0$ g

$m_{\text{steel pot}} = 500.0$ g

$c_{\text{water}} = 4.19$ J/g·°C

$c_{\text{stainless steel}} = 0.503$ J/g·°C

Initial temperature, $T_{\text{initial}} = 25.0$°C

Final temperature, $T_{\text{final}} = 75.0$°C

Plan Your Strategy
Energy input **a.** Write a balanced chemical equation for the complete combustion of propane, and calculate $\Delta H°_{\text{comb}}$ by using enthalpies of formation. **b.** Calculate the amount in moles of propane combusted from the mass and determine the theoretical energy content of the fuel. *Energy output* **c.** Determine how much energy was absorbed by the pot and the water by using $Q = mc\Delta T$. *Efficiency* **d.** Calculate the efficiency.

Act on Your Strategy

Energy input

a. $C_3H_8(g) + 5O_2(g) \rightarrow 3CO_2(g) + 4H_2O(g)$

$\Delta H°_{\text{comb}} = \Sigma(n\Delta H°_f \text{ products}) - \Sigma(n\Delta H°_f \text{ reactants})$

$= [(3 \text{ mol})(\Delta H°_f \, CO_2(g)) + (4 \text{ mol})(\Delta H°_f \, H_2O(g))] - [(1 \text{ mol})(\Delta H°_f \, C_3H_8(g)) + (5 \text{ mol})(\Delta H°_f \, O_2(g))]$

$= \left[(3 \text{ mol})\left(-393.5 \dfrac{\text{kJ}}{\text{mol}}\right) + (4 \text{ mol})\left(-241.8 \dfrac{\text{kJ}}{\text{mol}}\right)\right] - \left[(1 \text{ mol})\left(-103.8 \dfrac{\text{kJ}}{\text{mol}}\right) + (5 \text{ mol})\left(0 \dfrac{\text{kJ}}{\text{mol}}\right)\right]$

$= -2043.9 \text{ kJ}$

Therefore, the molar enthalpy of combustion of propane is $\Delta H°_{\text{comb}} = -2043.9$ kJ/mol.

b. The amount in moles of $C_3H_8(g)$ combusted is

$n = \dfrac{m}{M}$

$= \dfrac{5.10 \text{ g}}{44.11 \dfrac{\text{g}}{\text{mol}}}$

$= 0.11562 \text{ mol}$

Therefore, the energy content of the propane is

$\Delta H = n\Delta H°_{\text{comb}}$

$= (0.11562 \text{ mol})\left(-2043.9 \dfrac{\text{kJ}}{\text{mol}}\right)$

$= -236 \text{ kJ}$

Energy output

c. $Q_{total} = Q_{water} + Q_{steel}$
$= mc\Delta T_{water} + mc\Delta T_{steel}$
$= (250.0 \text{ g})\left(4.19 \dfrac{\text{J}}{\text{g} \cdot °\text{C}}\right)(75.0°\text{C} - 25.0°\text{C}) + (500.0 \text{ g})\left(0.503 \dfrac{\text{J}}{\text{g} \cdot °\text{C}}\right)(75.0°\text{C} - 25.0°\text{C})$
$= 6.50 \times 10^4 \text{ J}$
$= 65.0 \text{ kJ}$

Efficiency

d. efficiency $= \dfrac{\text{energy output}}{\text{energy input}} \times 100\%$

$= \dfrac{65.0 \text{ kJ}}{236 \text{ kJ}} \times 100\%$

$= 27.5\%$

As a heating device, the barbecue was 27.5% efficient.

Check Your Solution

The units are correct. The efficiency is significantly less than 100%, which makes sense. Much of the thermal energy is transferred to the surrounding air and to the barbecue itself, rather than to the pot and to the water being heated.

Practice Problems

61. Using the data for the molar enthalpy of combustion of butane from **Table 5.4**, determine the efficiency of a lighter as a heating device if 0.70 g of butane is required to increase the temperature of a 250.0 g stainless steel spoon ($c = 0.503$ J/g·°C) by 45.0°C.

62. A solid camping fuel has a stated energy content (energy released per gram of fuel burned) of 50.0 kJ/g. Determine its efficiency if a 2.50 g piece of the fuel was required to increase the temperature of 500.0 g of soup ($c = 3.77$ J/g·°C) in a 50.0 g aluminum pot by 45.0°C.

63. Determine the efficiency of a heating device that burns methanol, $CH_3OH(\ell)$, given the following information:

Data for Determining the Efficiency of a Methanol-burning Heater

Quantity Being Measured	Data
Initial mass of burner	38.37 g
Final mass of burner	36.92 g
Mass of aluminum can	257.36 g
Mass of aluminum can and water	437.26 g
Initial temperature of water	10.45°C
Final temperature of water	23.36°C
$\Delta H°_{comb}$ (CH_3OH)	−726.1 kJ/mol

64. What mass of pentane, $C_5H_{12}(g)$, would have to be burned in an open system to heat 2.50×10^2 g of hot chocolate ($c = 3.59$ J/g·°C) from 20.0°C to 39.8°C if the energy conversion is 45.0% efficient?

65. Heat from burning a fuel is absorbed by a copper calorimeter. The calorimeter has a mass of 81.34 g and contains 200.00 g of water initially at 21.00°C.

 a. How much heat was absorbed by the calorimeter and the water if the final temperature of the water is 36.40°C? Refer to **Table 5.1** for the required specific heat capacities.

 b. The absorption of heat by the system is 45.00% efficient. How much heat was lost to the surroundings?

66. A furnace outputs 5.000×10^4 kJ of heat to an empty room. The following information is given:

dimensions of room: 10.0 m × 10.0 m × 10.0 m

density of air: 1.290 kg/m³

specific heat capacity of air: 1.01 J/g·°C

initial air temperature: 12.0°C

final air temperature: 26.0°C

 a. Calculate the quantity of heat gained by the air in this room.

 b. Determine how much heat was lost from the room, and calculate an efficiency rating for the retention of heat for this room.

Continued on next page

67. A steel steam boiler has a mass of 1.50×10^3 kg and contains 255.00 kg of water at 35.00°C. Heat absorption by the boiler is 75.45% efficient. How much heat is required to increase the temperature of the system to the boiling point of water? The specific heat capacity of steel is 0.488 J/g·°C. The answer may be expressed in megajoules (1 MJ $= 1 \times 10^6$ J).

68. A flame calorimeter is used to determine the heat content (energy released per gram of fuel burned) of wood. The aluminum can in the apparatus has a mass of 180.51 g and holds 1.000 kg of water initially at 15.6°C. After 5.50 g of wood is burned, the water temperature increases to 20.7°C.

  a. Calculate the energy output that is absorbed by the calorimeter and the water.

  b. An estimate of the recoverable heat content for the wood is 6.5 kJ/g. How much heat could be available in the sample of wood?

  c. Determine the efficiency of the system in measuring the heat content of the wood.

69. Refer to **Tables 5.3** and **5.4** to obtain data necessary for the following questions.

  a. What mass of methane must burn to warm 60.00 g of water from 25.0°C to its boiling point and then turn it into steam at 100.0°C? (**Hint:** Two steps are involved: warming of the water to 100.0°C, and then change of the liquid water to a vapour at 100.0°C).

  b. If the transfer of heat is 56.5% efficient, what quantity of heat must come from the burning of methane?

  c. What mass of methane must be burned at this efficiency rating?

70. Ethanol, $C_2H_5OH(\ell)$, is used as a fuel in an alcohol burner. A glass beaker that has a mass of 386.00 g and a specific heat capacity of 0.880 J/g·°C is filled with 125.00 g of water initially at 15.5°C. The beaker of water is placed over the burner. When 1.24 g of ethanol burns, the water temperature in the beaker increases to 48.7°C. What is the efficiency of the transfer of heat to the beaker and the water? The enthalpy of combustion of ethanol is 1366.8 kJ/mol.

Using Energy Efficiently

Figure 5.28 summarizes energy use in Canadian homes by category. Canadians also use a great deal of energy getting from place to place. Forms of transportation account for 25 percent of all energy use. According to the first law of thermodynamics, energy is not destroyed, only transformed. You also know, from the second law of thermodynamics, that no process is completely efficient. Therefore, the challenge in developing more efficient technology is to find ways to convert more of the input energy into a useful form.

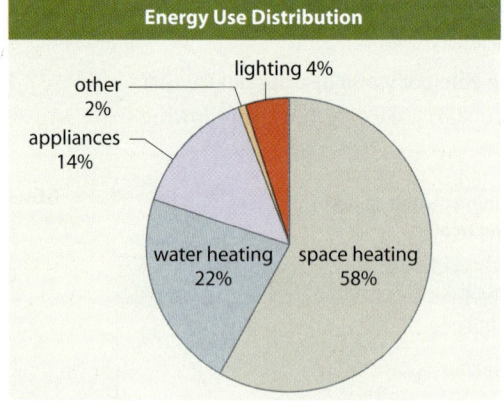

Figure 5.28 Most of the energy used in Canadian homes is for heating.

When assessing the efficiency of appliances, manufacturers focus on a single energy conversion—the input of electrical energy versus the output of useful energy. When looking at the bigger picture of energy efficiency, you also need to think about the source of the electricity. Consider, for example, natural gas. Natural gas is primarily methane. Therefore, you can estimate an ideal value for energy input by using the enthalpy of combustion of methane, $CH_4(g)$:

$$CH_4(g) + 2O_2(g) \rightarrow CO_2(g) + 2H_2O(g) \qquad \Delta H°_{comb} = -802.5 \text{ kJ/mol}$$

The Efficiency of Natural Gas

When natural gas is used directly to provide heat, its efficiency can be as high as 97% (the efficiency of a high-efficiency furnace). Thus, for every mole of natural gas burned, you get about 778 kJ of energy (0.97 × 802.5 kJ). If natural gas is used to produce electrical energy in a power plant, however, the efficiency is much lower—about 37%. Why? The heat from burning the natural gas is used to boil water. The kinetic energy of the resulting steam is transformed to mechanical energy for turning a turbine, which generates the electrical energy. Each step has an associated efficiency that is less than 100%. Thus, at each step, the overall efficiency of the fuel decreases. **Figure 5.29** shows the difference between the home furnace and the power plant.

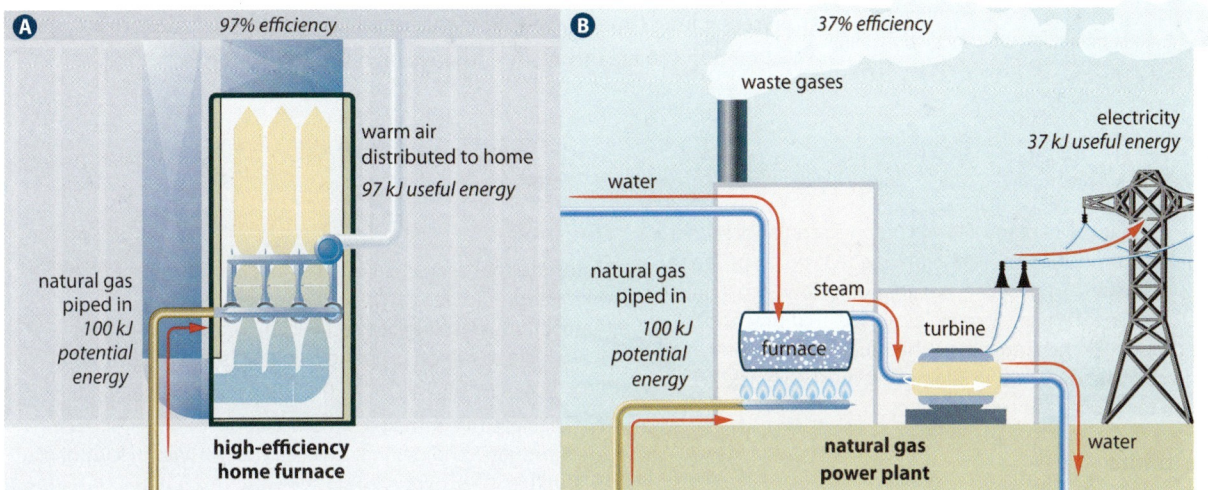

Figure 5.29 Natural gas is a far more efficient fuel when used to heat a home furnace than when it is used to generate electrical energy. There is only one energy conversion step in a high-efficiency furnace. Natural gas is burned, and the energy released heats air, which is distributed throughout the home (**A**). In a power plant, there are several energy conversions, and "waste" energy is released to the surroundings at each step (**B**).

The efficiencies of natural gas furnaces currently in use vary from 60% to 97%. The most energy-efficient gas furnaces on the market today are condensing furnaces. They, alone, can achieve efficiencies of 90% to 97% by using not only heat from the combustion of natural gas but also heat from the condensation of water vapour produced in the combustion process. When natural gas is burned, it produces a mixture of hot gases and water vapour. One of the main products of the combustion of natural gas is water vapour. The enthalpy of condensation of water is quite large, so when this water condenses, a large amount of energy is released. In older furnaces, the water vapour escaped out the exhaust. In the condensing furnace, a heat exchanger condenses the water vapour and the released heat adds to the heating of the house. The liquid water is released down a drain.

Energy Sources and the Environment

For many decades, people have become increasingly conscious of the effects of energy technologies on the environment. In evaluating the impact of energy sources on the environment, more and more people are asking themselves questions, such as:

- *Are any waste products or by-products of the energy production process harmful to living things or the environment?* Any process in which a hydrocarbon is burned produces carbon dioxide, a greenhouse gas. Greenhouse gases temporarily trap heat in Earth's atmosphere and delay the escape of heat into outer space. Many scientists have concluded that a build-up of greenhouse gases in the atmosphere is leading to an increase in global temperatures, known as global warming. In addition, any combustion process provides the heat required to form oxides of nitrogen from nitrogen gas. Oxides of nitrogen contribute to acid precipitation. Nuclear fission does not produce greenhouse gases, but it does leave behind radioactive waste that remains a danger for thousands of years.

- *Is obtaining or harnessing the fuel harmful to living things or the environment?* For example, strip coal mines and oil wells destroy habitats and harm living organisms. Although hydroelectric power plants produce very little in the way of emissions in the production of power, ecosystems both upstream and downstream of the plant are affected by their construction and presence.

- *Will using the energy source permanently remove the fuel from the environment?* A non-renewable energy source (such as coal, oil, or natural gas) is effectively gone once it is depleted. Non-renewable energy sources take millions of years to form and are used at a much faster rate than they can be replenished. A renewable energy source such as solar energy and wind energy can be replenished in a relatively short period of time. A somewhat renewable energy source is wood. Trees can be grown to replace those cut down. It takes trees a long time to grow, however, and habitats are often destroyed or permanently altered in the meantime by activities involved in logging.

Activity 5.3 Comparing Propane-driven and Gasoline-driven Cars

Vehicles that travel many kilometres on a regular basis, such as airline limousines and some taxis, often run on propane, $C_3H_8(g)$, instead of gasoline, because of its lower cost. In North America, however, vehicles are not manufactured to use propane—they must have their fuel systems converted to do so. What distance, in kilometres, must a vehicle be driven to recover the conversion cost?

Procedure

To begin to answer the above question, work in small groups to consider the following information. Also consider additional data that are needed to answer the question. Refer to Appendix B as necessary. Then use the points below to determine the distance needed to recover the conversion cost.

- Propane is a gas, but it is delivered to vehicles as a liquid under pressure. Gasoline is a mixture of hydrocarbons. For simplicity, assume that gasoline is pure octane, $C_8H_{18}(\ell)$.
- Automobiles are not manufactured to run on propane; they must be converted to be able to combust propane.
- Assume that both fuels, gasoline and propane, undergo complete combustion.
- Assume that the automobile travels a fixed distance per amount of energy, regardless of the fuel used to produce that energy.
- Assume the same efficiency of combustion for propane and gasoline.
- Assume that maintenance costs for a propane-powered car are the same as for a gasoline-powered car.

Questions

Note: You must calculate the distance, in kilometres, that a vehicle would need to be driven using propane, rather than octane (gasoline), to recover the cost of converting the vehicle to run on propane. You may solve the problem directly, or use the following points as a guide.

1. Calculate the enthalpy of combustion, ΔH_{comb}, for each of propane and octane. Express your answer in kJ/mol of the fuel.

2. a. Using the gasoline (octane) consumption of the vehicle, calculate the energy required to travel 100 km.
   b. Use your answer to part (a) to calculate the volume of liquid propane required for the vehicle to travel 100 km.

3. a. Calculate the cost to travel 100 km using octane.
   b. Calculate the cost to travel 100 km using propane.
   c. Calculate the price difference between propane and octane, per 100 km travelled.
   d. Use your answers to calculate the required distance, in kilometres, to travel before the fuel system conversion cost is recovered.
   e. If an airport limousine travels an average of 200 km per day, how long would it take to recover the conversion cost?

4. Other than the fuel cost, what considerations could influence someone's decision to convert his or her vehicle to run on propane?

5. a. What mass of $CO_2(g)$ is released into the atmosphere per 100 km of travel using octane?
   b. What mass of $CO_2(g)$ is released into the atmosphere per 100 km of travel using propane?

Conventional Energy Sources in Ontario

Ontario has three main conventional sources of electrical energy: nuclear power plants, power plants that burn fossil fuels, and hydroelectric generating stations. The single largest source of electrical energy in Ontario in 2010 was nuclear power, as shown in **Figure 5.30**. Generating electrical energy using nuclear energy produces no greenhouse gases. However, uranium mining damages the environment, and radioactive nuclear waste products must be stored safely because they remain hazardous for thousands of years.

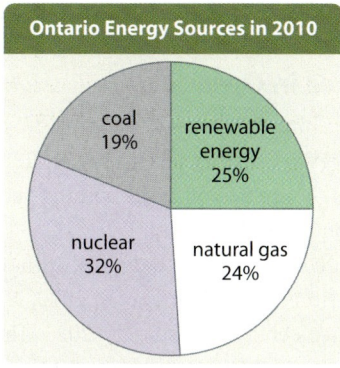

Figure 5.30 This graph shows the distribution of energy sources in Ontario in 2010. By 2025, renewable energy sources are projected to increase to 40 percent.
***Analyze** what percentage of Ontario's energy came from fossil fuels in 2010.*

Another large source for generating electrical energy in Ontario is fossil fuels. Their main advantages are low costs, the large available supply of coal and natural gas, and the ability of power plants that burn fossil fuels to respond quickly to increased demand for electrical energy during hours of peak use. But the plants are only about 30% efficient, and the environmental costs are considerable, including carbon dioxide emissions. **Figure 5.31** summarizes issues associated with the use of fossil fuels.

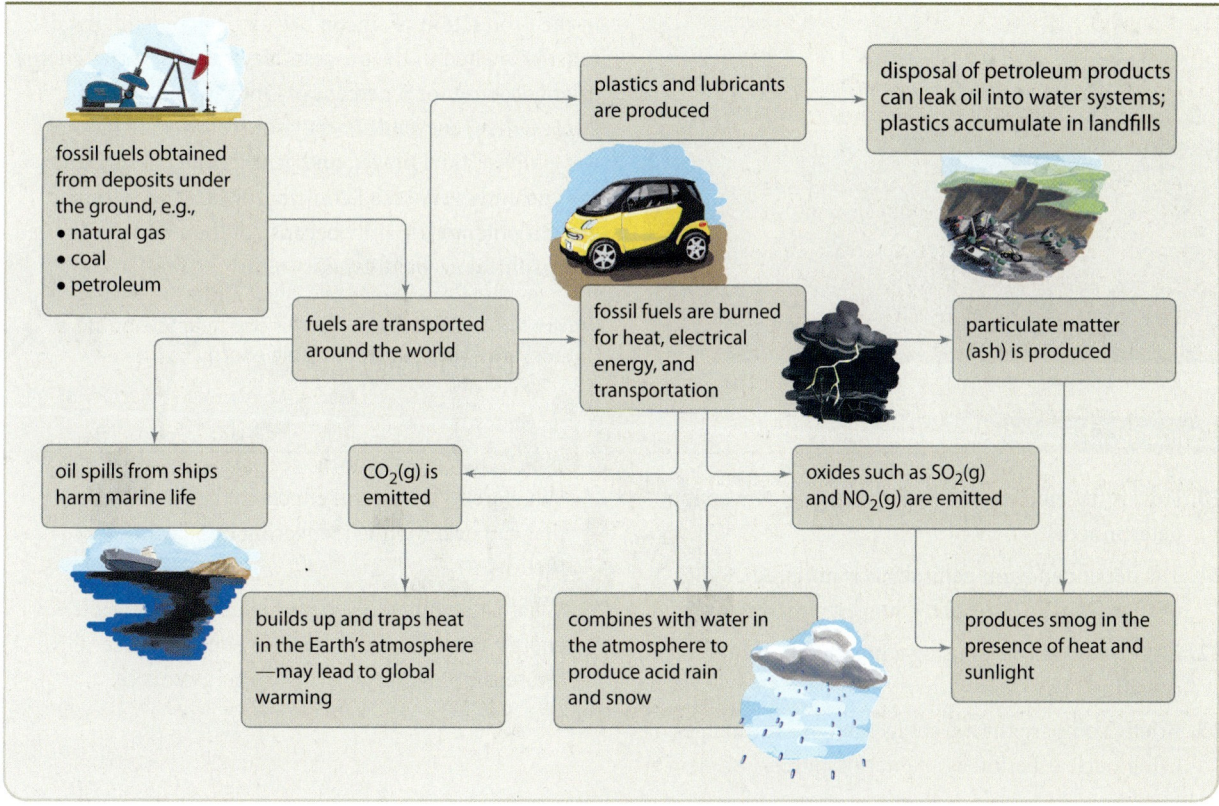

Figure 5.31 This concept map shows the interrelated issues that arise from the use of fossil fuels.

Hydroelectric Power: A Renewable Energy Resource

The third conventional source of energy comes from hydroelectric generating stations. Unlike nuclear power or fossil fuels, hydroelectric power is a renewable energy resource. Advantages of hydroelectric power are that there are no fuel costs, no combustion emissions, low operating costs, and it has high efficiency (about 90%). Disadvantages include the environmental effects of building dams, including the flooding of land and disruption of habitat. Once a dam is built, it does not use combustion of fossil fuels. However, the building of a dam is a tremendous task. The heavy equipment used during the construction of the dam uses large amounts of fossil fuels.

Alternative Renewable Energy Sources in Ontario

In 2010, renewable energy sources accounted for about 25 percent of energy production in Ontario. The major source of this renewable energy was hydroelectric power. Renewable energy sources are projected to become increasingly important in the coming years, perhaps reaching 40 percent of energy production by 2025.

One factor in the increase in renewable energy sources is wind energy. Although wind energy contributed only about 1 percent of Ontario's electrical energy in 2010, it might grow to provide 15 percent or more of the province's energy capacity by 2025. The cost of operating wind farms, such as the one shown in **Figure 5.32**, is very low, and they do not produce any chemical pollutants. The chief disadvantages are the great variation in winds at any site, the noise pollution produced, and the danger to birds that fly too near.

Solar energy is directly converted into electrical energy by solar cells. The primary advantage is that the energy is free and virtually unlimited in supply. However, solar energy has a low concentration at any particular location. Although the technology is improving, solar cells are not very efficient, and solar energy systems are expensive. In addition, large amounts of energy are used in the production of silicon because silicon and metal must be melted in the process. Nevertheless, solar energy might account for 5 percent of Ontario's energy by 2025. Other renewable energy sources include biomass, wave power, tidal power, and geothermal energy. All are currently very small contributors and have limited growth potential, mainly because of their costs or limited geographical availability.

Figure 5.32 Winds farms like this one near Shelburne, Ontario, are a source of renewable energy.

Learning Check

20. How is the efficiency of thermal energy conversion determined?
21. The dependency on natural gas is not predicted to change from 2010 to 2025. Suggest a reason for this.
22. List disadvantages of using a hydrocarbon source as a heating fuel.
23. Briefly compare the advantages and disadvantages of using nuclear fission as an energy source.
24. What are four harmful effects to the environment that can occur while recovering or using a source of fuel?
25. What is the difference between a non-renewable energy source and a renewable energy source? Give four examples of each type of energy source.

What Is a "Clean" Fuel?

Not all fossil fuels have the same impact on the environment, either during their recovery or in their use. Some fossil fuels are considered cleaner than others, meaning that their emissions are lower than those of others for an equivalent amount of energy produced. **Table 5.6** summarizes the carbon dioxide emissions for a variety of fuels in grams of $CO_2(g)$ per megajoule of energy produced.

Table 5.6 Fuel Source and Carbon Dioxide Emissions

Fuel	Carbon Dioxide Emissions (g/MJ of energy produced)
Anthracite coal	108.83
Lignite coal	103.08
Subbituminous coal	101.79
Bituminous coal	98.25
Municipal solid waste (landfill gas)	95.64
Wood and wood waste (biomass)	93.32
Tires/tire-derived fuel	90.71
Oil	78.48
Kerosene	76.35
Gasoline	74.86
Jet fuel	74.78
Propane	66.61
Flare gas	57.77
Natural gas (pipeline)	56.03
Methane	55.16
Nuclear	0.00
Renewables (solar, thermal, and photovoltaic; geothermal; wind; hydroelectric)	0.00

As you can see from **Table 5.6**, renewable energy sources, such as wind power and solar power, produce no carbon dioxide in their operation. However, coal and natural gas produce a significant amount of carbon dioxide. Other emissions, such as particulates (ash particles) and oxides that combine with water to produce acid rain and snow, should also be factored in when evaluating a fuel source. From **Table 5.7**, it is clear that the levels of other pollutants produced in the combustion of three commonly used fossil fuels—coal, oil, and natural gas—vary widely.

Table 5.7 Common Fossil Fuels and Harmful Emission Levels

Pollutant	Emission Levels (mg/MJ of energy produced)		
	Natural Gas	Oil	Coal
Carbon monoxide	19.14	15.79	99.54
Nitrogen monoxides	44.03	214.40	218.70
Sulfur dioxide	0.48	536.95	1239.96
Particulates	3.35	40.20	1313.18

The **heat content** of a fuel is the amount of energy released per kilogram of the fuel. To fairly assess a fuel, its heat content, along with other factors that include its environmental impact and its cost, must be considered.

heat content of a fuel, is the amount of energy released per kilogram of the fuel

STSE
CHEMISTRY Connections

Deep Water Cooling

New technologies are using deep water cooling as an alternative to conventional air conditioning systems in office towers, thus significantly reducing energy use and its environmental impact. Deep water cooling takes advantage of the fact that at standard atmospheric pressure, water is most dense at 3.98°C, which causes it to sink. The bottom of any deep body of water is therefore at a constantly chilly temperature of 3.98°C, even during the hottest summers. Deep water cooling applies the second law of thermodynamics, which states that when two objects are in thermal contact, heat is always transferred from the object at a higher temperature to the object at a lower temperature until the two objects are at the same temperature.

The system works by pumping chilly water from the bottom of a lake into a heat transfer station. At the transfer station, the intake pipes come into thermal contact with a separate closed system of pipes containing a liquid—often water. Because the water in the closed system is warmer than the water in the intake pipes, thermal energy from the warmer water transfers to the cold lake water. The closed system of pipes—along with its now substantially colder water—leads into commercial buildings. Within the buildings' heat transfer systems, thermal energy from the surroundings is transferred to the cold water in the pipes, thereby cooling the buildings.

THE WORLD'S LARGEST DEEP WATER COOLING SYSTEM Toronto-based Enwave Energy Corporation launched its deep water cooling system within the downtown Toronto-Dominion Centre in August 2004. The city is ideally situated to take advantage of Lake Ontario's cold deep-bottom water because the lake bed drops quickly and deeply within a few kilometres off shore. Enwave's three intake pipes draw water from 5 km off the shore of the lake at a depth of 83 m below the surface.

The cold deep-lake water is piped to the city's John Street Pumping Station, where it comes into thermal contact with Enwave's separate closed system of water pipes. At the station, heat exchangers transfer heat from the separate closed system to the lake water, in an exothermic process during which heat leaves the water of the closed system.

The pipes containing the newly chilled water then run from the transfer station into more than 60 of Toronto's downtown office towers, including the Air Canada Centre, the Royal Bank Plaza, and City Hall. Thermal energy from the buildings is transferred to the water in Enwave's closed pipes, cooling the buildings. The water inside Enwave's network of pipes then returns to the John Street Pumping Station to repeat the cycle. After it has absorbed thermal energy at the John Street Pumping Station, the now warmer lake water is piped to the city's filtration plants and is used as part of the municipal drinking water supply.

THE BENEFITS OF DEEP WATER COOLING Enwave estimates that deep water cooling has led to decreased emissions of the greenhouse gas carbon dioxide by 79 000 tonnes annually, which is the equivalent of taking 15 000 cars off the road. The system has reduced emissions of the pollutants nitrogen oxide and sulfur oxide, both by-products of coal-fired power plants. Additionally, because Toronto uses the deep-lake water for its drinking supply, deep water cooling avoids having to return the warmed water to Lake Ontario, where it could harm numerous species adapted to living in cold water.

Enwave Energy Corporation uses the cold water of Lake Ontario for its deep water cooling system. For Toronto buildings using this system, there is about an 80 percent reduction in summertime energy consumption, compared with conventional air conditioning.

Connect to Society

1. What ideal conditions are required for a deep water cooling system to operate at maximum efficiency?
2. Who developed the concept of deep water cooling? What other cities use it?

Section 5.4 Review

Section Summary

- The efficiency of a chemical, physical, or nuclear process can be expressed as

$$\text{efficiency} = \frac{\text{energy output}}{\text{energy input}} \times 100\%$$

- Every energy-conversion step in a process reduces its efficiency.
- Energy-conversion processes that involve boiling water into steam and using the steam to turn a turbine have low efficiencies.
- Fossil fuels are non-renewable resources. The burning of fossil fuels contributes to global warming, acid rain, and pollution of the environment.
- Renewable energy resources include hydroelectric power, solar energy, and wind energy. The use of renewable energy resources in Ontario to generate electricity is projected to increase substantially by 2025.

Review Questions

1. **K/U** What factors make natural gas more efficient as a fuel for home heating compared with its use as a fuel for a power plant?

2. **A** Heating and transportation uses come to mind when thinking of our dependency on fossil fuels. In what other ways do fossil fuels impact our life?

3. **K/U** Summarize the issues related to the use of fossil fuels. Suggest ways that you could contribute to reducing the use of fossil fuels.

4. **T/I** Compare the use of a wood waste biomass fuel with natural gas. Which fuel emits more $CO_2(g)$ per kJ energy produced? Express as a percent.

5. **A** The cost of a propane barbecue is 90% of the cost of a natural gas barbecue. A hibachi, which burns charcoal, costs only 10% the cost of the gas barbecue. From an environmental and economic perspective, which type of barbecue would you choose? Justify your answer.

6. **A** A car has a calculated fuel consumption of 10.0 L/100 km (city) and 7.1 L/100 km (highway) according to the EnerGuide information. Overall, the actual fuel consumption has averaged 10.5 L/100 km.
   a. Is this better or worse than the calculated fuel consumption?
   b. Provide three reasons why the actual fuel consumption may be different from the calculated consumption.
   c. List three ways in which the fuel consumption could be improved.

7. **A** You have probably noticed that a lot of heat is generated by the compressor of your refrigerator. Design a system that could apply this and other sources of "waste heat" in your home for some useful purpose.

8. **A** You are about to purchase a new washing machine. As an energy-conscious consumer, what information would you look for to assess its efficiency?

9. **C** What is meant by a "clean" fuel? Are there really any clean fuels? Justify your answer in a brief, well-reasoned paragraph.

10. **K/U** Identify the products of combustion associated with the following environmental issues:
    a. global warming
    b. acid rain or snow
    c. smog

11. **K/U** Differentiate between the *heat content* and *enthalpy of combustion* of a fuel. Which term is more useful in evaluating fuels? Why?

12. **T/I** The complete combustion of 1.00 mL of octane increases the temperature of 250.00 g of water by 22.7°C. The density of octane is 0.70 g/mL. What is the efficiency of the octane in heating the water?

13. **T/I** Based on the data below, is octane or ethanol a better fuel per unit volume?

    For octane:
    density = 0.70 g/mL; $\Delta H°_{comb} = -44.5$ kJ/g
    efficiency of heat to mechanical energy = 20.0%

    For ethanol:
    density = 0.79 g/mL; $\Delta H°_{comb} = -29.7$ kJ/g
    efficiency of heat to mechanical energy = 25.0%

14. **T/I** The complete combustion of methane is represented in the following equation:

    $CH_4(g) + 2O_2(g) \rightarrow CO_2(g) + 2H_2O(g) + 802.5$ kJ

    Assume that natural gas is essentially methane. The emission level of carbon dioxide, $CO_2(g)$, from the burning of natural gas is 56.03 g/MJ of energy produced. What mass of $CO_2(g)$ will be emitted when 100.0 g of natural gas is burned?

Plan Your Own INVESTIGATION 5-A

Skill Check
- ✓ Initiating and Planning
- ✓ Performing and Recording
- ✓ Analyzing and Interpreting
- ✓ Communicating

Safety Precautions

- If you get any hydrochloric acid or sodium hydroxide solution on your skin, immediately flush with plenty of cold water.
- Wear safety eyewear throughout this investigation.
- Wear a lab coat or apron throughout this investigation.

Suggested Materials
- 1.00 mol/L HCl(aq) at room temperature
- 1.00 mol/L NaOH(aq) at room temperature
- simple calorimeter (two nested polystyrene cups in a 250 mL beaker, with a two-holed polystyrene lid)
- 100 mL graduated cylinder
- thermometer (alcohol or digital)
- stirring rod

Go to Organizing Data in a Table in Appendix A for information about designing data tables.

Determining the Enthalpy of a Neutralization Reaction

As you have learned, the reaction between an acid and a base is often called a neutralization reaction. In a neutralization reaction, the acid is considered to counteract (or neutralize) the properties of the base, and the base counteracts the properties of the acid. As shown below, for a neutralization reaction between an Arrhenius acid and an Arrhenius base, the hydrogen ions from the acid, H^+(aq), react with the hydroxide ions, OH^-(aq), of the base to produce water. The metal cation of the base and the anion from the acid combine to form a salt.

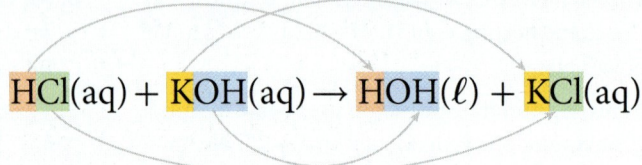

In this investigation, you will study the reaction between a hydrochloric acid solution and a sodium hydroxide solution. This neutralization reaction is represented by the following equation:

$$HCl(aq) + NaOH(aq) \rightarrow NaCl(aq) + H_2O(\ell)$$

Using a simple calorimeter, you will determine the enthalpy change for this reaction.

Pre-Lab Questions

1. Explain the benefit of letting the solutions of HCl(aq) and NaOH(aq) sit overnight.

2. When using the same graduated cylinder to measure the volumes of HCl(aq) and NaOH(aq), it is important to rinse the cylinder with water and a small amount of the second reactant before measuring the volume of the second reactant. Explain why this is important for this investigation.

3. Describe how to perform each of the following safely:
   - diluting a strong acid solution with water
   - dissolving a solid base in water
   - adding a solution of base to a solution of acid

4. If acid comes in contact with your skin, why must you flush the area with plenty of cold water, rather than neutralizing the acid with a base?

Question

What is the enthalpy of neutralization for the reaction between solutions of HCl(aq) and NaOH(aq)?

Plan and Conduct

1. Write a complete and detailed procedure for performing this investigation. Make sure to include all safety precautions that must be followed.

2. Prepare a table to record your observations. Decide at what time intervals you will record your observations.

3. Use **Figure 5.16**, which is also represented below for easy reference, to build a simple calorimeter. Be sure that the lid has two holes—one for the thermometer and one for the stirring rod. The holes should be as small as possible to minimize thermal energy exchange with the surroundings. Also, be sure to place the calorimeter within the 250 mL beaker to help secure it in an upright position.

4. Have your teacher approve your procedure, as well as the calorimeter you have assembled, before proceeding with the investigation.

5. If time permits, carry out a duplicate trial.

6. Dispose of any chemicals as instructed by your teacher.

7. Compare data from other classmates with your own data.

Analyze and Interpret

1. Calculate the quantity of thermal energy absorbed by the solution in the calorimeter and the quantity of thermal energy released by the reaction. State any assumptions you made in order to carry out your calculations.

2. Calculate the amount in moles of HCl(aq) and of NaOH(aq) involved in the reaction.

3. Use the answers to questions 1 and 2 to calculate the ΔH for the given neutralization reaction, in units of kilojoules per mole of the limiting reagent. (If HCl(aq) and NaOH(aq) are present in equimolar amounts, either one can be considered to be the limiting reagent.)

4. Is the neutralization reaction exothermic or endothermic? What is the sign—positive or negative—of ΔH?

Conclude and Communicate

5. Write the thermochemical equation for the neutralization reaction.

6. Compare the enthalpy of neutralization that you determined with those of your classmates.

7. Your teacher will provide you with the enthalpy of neutralization value that is reported in the literature. How does this value compare with your experimentally determined value?

8. Discuss possible sources of error for this investigation, which could have contributed to the discrepancies between values determined within your class and between your value and the reported value.

Extend Further

9. **INQUIRY** Write the thermochemical equation for the neutralization of HCl(aq) using solid sodium hydroxide, NaOH(s), instead of NaOH(aq). Would you expect the ΔH value to differ from that obtained using NaOH(aq)? Explain briefly.

10. Design an investigation to determine if using solid NaOH instead of NaOH(aq) will have any effect on the ΔH value for the neutralization reaction. If your teacher approves your procedure, carry out the investigation.

11. Design an experiment to determine if the acid involved in a neutralization investigation has any effect on the ΔH of the reaction. If your teacher approves your procedure, carry out the investigation.

12. **RESEARCH** On August 5, 2005 a CN train derailment north of Squamish, British Columbia, released about 40 000 L of a 73% (m/v) solution of sodium hydroxide into the Cheakamus River. Use Internet resources to determine the immediate effects of this spill on the local ecosystem. How was the spill eventually cleaned up? How did officials know that their clean-up efforts were successful?

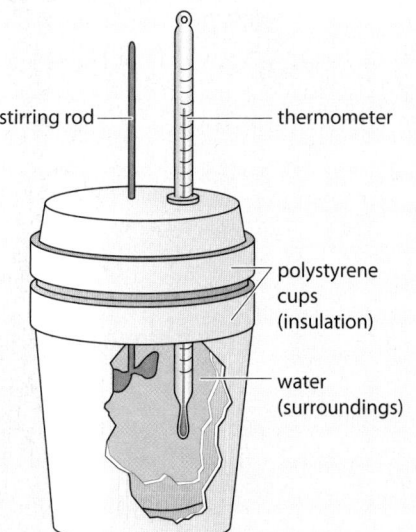

This simple calorimeter can be used to measure the enthalpy change for the neutralization reaction between HCl(aq) and NaOH(aq)

INQUIRY INVESTIGATION 5-B

Skill Check
- Initiating and Planning
- ✓ Performing and Recording
- ✓ Analyzing and Interpreting
- ✓ Communicating

Safety Precautions

- Hydrochloric acid is corrosive. Use care when handling it. Hydrochloric acid fumes also cause burning to the linings of the nose and throat when inhaled.
- Be careful not to inhale the magnesium oxide powder.

Materials
- 1.00 mol/L HCl(aq)
- MgO(s) powder
- Mg ribbon (or Mg turnings)
- simple calorimeter
- 100 mL graduated cylinder
- scoop
- electronic balance
- thermometer (alcohol or digital)
- sandpaper or emery paper

Hess's Law and the Enthalpy of Combustion of Magnesium

Magnesium ribbon burns in air in a highly exothermic combustion reaction. (See equation (1) below.) A very bright flame accompanies the production of magnesium oxide. It is impractical and dangerous to use a simple calorimeter to determine the enthalpy change for this reaction:

(1) $Mg(s) + \frac{1}{2}O_2(g) \rightarrow MgO(s)$

Instead, you will determine the enthalpy changes for two other reactions (equations (2) and (3) below). You will use these enthalpy changes, along with the known enthalpy change for another reaction (equation (4) below), to determine the enthalpy change for the combustion of magnesium.

(2) $MgO(s) + 2HCl(aq) \rightarrow MgCl_2(aq) + H_2O(\ell)$

(3) $Mg(s) + 2HCl(aq) \rightarrow MgCl_2(aq) + H_2(g)$

(4) $H_2(g) + \frac{1}{2}O_2(g) \rightarrow H_2O(\ell) + 285.8 \text{ kJ}$

Notice that reactions represented in equations (2) and (3) occur in aqueous solution. You can use a simple calorimeter to determine the enthalpy changes for these reactions. Equation (4) represents the formation of water directly from its elements in their standard state.

Pre-Lab Questions

1. Explain how Hess's law allows you to determine the enthalpy of a reaction without carrying out the reaction.
2. What type of data do you need in order to use Hess's law?
3. Describe the safety precautions you must follow when working with a strong acid.

Question

What is the molar enthalpy of combustion of magnesium?

When magnesium ribbon burns in air a very bright white flame is produced. The lower part of the ribbon shown here has been converted to the solid, white magnesium oxide product.

Procedure

Part 1: Determining ΔH of Reaction (2)

1. Read the Procedure for Part 1. Prepare a data table to record mass and temperature data.
2. Set up the simple calorimeter. Using a graduated cylinder, add 100 mL of 1.00 mol/L HCl(aq) to the calorimeter.
3. Record the initial temperature, T_{initial}, of the HCl(aq), to the nearest tenth of a degree.
4. Find the mass of no more than 0.80 g of MgO(s) powder. Record the exact mass.
5. Add the MgO(s) powder to the calorimeter containing the HCl(aq). Swirl the solution gently, recording the highest temperature, T_{final}, reached.
6. Dispose of the reaction solution as directed by your teacher.

Part 2: Determining ΔH of Reaction (3)

1. Read the Procedure for Part 2. Prepare a data table to record mass and temperature data.
2. Using a graduated cylinder, add 100 mL of 1.00 mol/L HCl(aq) to the calorimeter.
3. Record the initial temperature, T_{initial}, of the HCl(aq) to the nearest tenth of a degree.
4. If you are using magnesium ribbon (as opposed to turnings), sand the ribbon. Accurately determine the mass of no more than 0.50 g of magnesium. Record the exact mass.
5. Add the Mg(s) to the calorimeter containing the HCl(aq). Swirl the solution gently, recording the highest temperature, T_{final}, reached.
6. Dispose of the solution as directed by your teacher.

Analyze And Interpret

1. Determine the enthalpy of reactions for reactions (2) and (3). List any assumptions you make and explain why they are valid assumptions.
2. Write thermochemical equations for reactions (2) and (3) using ΔH notation. Ensure the signs you use are correct.
3. Algebraically combine equations (2), (3), and (4), and their corresponding ΔH values, to find equation (1) and the molar enthalpy of combustion of magnesium.
4. Draw an enthalpy diagram showing the combining of equations (2), (3), and (4) to form equation (1) and the molar enthalpy of combustion of magnesium.
5. Compare your experimental value of the molar ΔH_{comb} for magnesium. Calculate your percent error.
6. Suggest some sources of error in the procedure. In what ways could you improve the procedure?

Conclude and Communicate

7. Explain how the thermochemical equation for the combustion of magnesium that you obtained in question 4 relates to the equation that corresponds to ΔH_f of MgO(s).

Extend Further

8. **INQUIRY** Design an investigation to test Hess's law by using the following equations:

   (1) NaOH(s) → NaOH(aq)
   (2) NaOH(s) + HCl(aq) → NaCl(aq) + H₂O(ℓ)
   (3) NaOH(aq) + HCl(aq) → NaCl(aq) + H₂O(ℓ)

   Assume you have a simple calorimeter, NaOH(s), 1.00 mol/L HCl(aq), 1.00 mol/L NaOH(aq), and standard laboratory equipment. Write a step-by-step procedure for the investigation. Then outline a plan for analyzing your data. Be sure to include appropriate safety precautions. If time permits, obtain your teacher's approval and carry out the investigation.

9. **RESEARCH** Burning magnesium not only creates a very bright light but it also burns at a very high temperature. Research ways in which people have used the bright light and high temperatures in the past and currently.

STSE Case Study

Comparing Ethanol and Biodiesel
Is One Option Greener?

Scenario

You are an energy analyst for Natural Resources Canada. You have been asked to ensure that various federal government policies result in the greatest benefits for the environment. The government is seeking to reduce greenhouse gas emissions by boosting the production and use of biofuels. Biofuels are fuels made from plant and animal materials. Some examples of biofuels include ethanol, which can be made from corn or wheat, and biodiesel, which can be made from tallow (animal fat) or canola.

Replacing Fossil Fuels

Each biofuel burns in an engine in a way that is similar to the combustion of a certain kind of fossil fuel. Ethanol has a boiling point similar to that of gasoline. Thus, it can be mixed with gasoline and then burned in a regular car engine. Diesel has a higher boiling point than gasoline, so diesel engines use a different method to ignite fuel compared with gasoline engines. Biodiesel has a boiling point similar to that of diesel. Therefore, it can replace diesel in a diesel engine.

Unlike fossil fuels, biofuels are renewable. They will not run out because they can be replenished when farmers grow more plants or raise more animals. Additionally, plants and animals take in carbon from the environment as they grow, thereby compensating for the carbon dioxide that is released into the atmosphere when biofuels are burned. This balancing of carbon absorption and emission means that biofuels have no net effect on the amount of carbon in the atmosphere. Biofuels are therefore sometimes described as "carbon neutral."

However, that description does not take into account the extra energy inputs required to produce and distribute biofuels. These energy inputs include the fuel consumed by farm machinery and by the trucks that deliver ethanol to gas stations. Other energy inputs involved in the manufacture of ethanol and biodiesel include the energy in the chemical reactions used to convert raw corn and canola into ethanol and biodiesel.

The steps in the manufacturing process are all part of the life cycle of a biofuel. Scientists use computer models called "life-cycle assessments" to add up the values for all the energy inputs involved in producing a particular fuel. They then compare the total energy input with the energy output—the amount of energy released when the fuel is burned. They can do similar calculations involving greenhouse gas inputs and outputs. By comparing the life cycles of two fuels, such as ethanol and gasoline, scientists can determine the extent to which greenhouse gas emissions will change if one fuel replaces another.

How Are Ethanol and Biodiesel Manufactured?

In Canada, ethanol begins its life cycle as either corn or wheat (Canada's most plentiful crop). The corn or wheat is harvested and transported by truck or by train to a factory. There, sugars in the grains are fermented (converted into liquid alcohol) by the action of yeast according to the following chemical reaction:

$$C_6H_{12}O_6 \rightarrow 2CH_3CH_2OH + 2CO_2$$
$$\text{glucose} \qquad \text{ethanol}$$
$$\text{(sugar)}$$

The ethanol is distilled off, and the solid material left behind is used for animal feed.

Biodiesel is made of molecules called fatty esters. In a factory, a chemical reaction called transesterification can convert almost any plant and animal fats and oils into fatty esters (and therefore biodiesel). The chemical process that results in this conversion involves mixing plant and animal fats made of molecules called triglycerides with methanol (a type of alcohol) in the presence of a catalyst.

Each triglyceride contains three chains of carbon and hydrogen atoms (called fatty acid chains and labelled R_1, R_2, and R_3 as shown in the equation below). The transesterification reaction breaks each triglyceride into three fatty esters (one for each fatty acid chain) and one molecule of glycerol, a type of alcohol used in many foods, cosmetics, and drugs.

$$\underset{\text{triglyceride}}{\begin{matrix} CH_2-O-\overset{O}{\underset{\|}{C}}-R_1 \\ | \\ CH-O-\underset{\|}{\overset{O}{C}}-R_2 \\ | \\ CH_2-O-\underset{\|}{\overset{O}{C}}-R_3 \end{matrix}} + \underset{\text{methanol}}{3\,CH_3OH} \xrightarrow{\text{(Catalyst)}} \underset{\text{mixture of fatty esters}}{\begin{matrix} CH_3-O-\overset{O}{\underset{\|}{C}}-R_1 \\ \\ CH_3-O-\underset{\|}{\overset{O}{C}}-R_2 \\ \\ CH_2-O-\underset{\|}{\overset{O}{C}}-R_3 \end{matrix}} + \underset{\text{glycerol}}{\begin{matrix} CH_2-OH \\ | \\ CH-OH \\ | \\ CH_2-OH \end{matrix}}$$

Since 2010, a law has stipulated that all gasoline in Canada must contain 5 percent ethanol. Starting in 2011, all heating oil must contain 2 percent biodiesel. Currently, the Canadian federal government is trying to decide how and where to target new rules and incentives to boost the production of biofuels. In your role as energy analyst, you must assess whether ethanol is greener than biodiesel or vice versa. You need to compare the energy required to produce these biofuels, as well as the greenhouse gases that these biofuels release during their life cycle, against the fossil fuels they replace.

From: Renewable Fuels Research Group <renewables@nrcan.gc.ca>
Subject: Life Cycle Assessments for 4 Fuels
To: "Sarah Chang" <sarahchang@nrcan.gc.ca>
Received: Tuesday, January 25, 2012, 2:34 PM

Hi Sarah,

As requested, here are the data from our life-cycle assessments of different fuels to help you with your analysis of their environmental impacts.

Comparison of Energy Input and Energy Output of Selected Fuels

	Gas	Ethanol	Diesel	Biodiesel
Energy input (MJ/L)	9.96	16.16	9.85	8.33
Energy output (MJ/L)	34.69	23.58	38.65	36.9

The energy output of each fuel is the amount of energy released when 1 L of the fuel is burned. The energy input of each fuel is the amount of energy consumed to produce 1 L of the fuel.

Sincerely,
Carlo Singh
Renewable Fuels Research Group

Research and Analyze

1. Conduct research to determine the steps that are involved in the life cycle of ethanol and biodiesel, from planting the crop to burning the fuel in your car engine or home. What energy inputs are required? Which steps in each life cycle consume energy and which steps release energy? Which steps consume or release greenhouse gases?

2. Conduct research to determine the steps that are involved in the life cycle of gasoline and diesel. Which steps in their life cycle are similar to those of biofuels? Which steps are different?

3. Analyze the energy efficiencies of diesel, biodiesel, gasoline, and ethanol by answering the following questions. Use the data in the email at left.

   a. The net energy ratio describes the energy output (in joules) for each joule of energy input involved in making and distributing a fuel. This ratio can be a measure of efficiency. Use this equation to calculate the net energy ratio for each fuel:

   $$\text{net energy ratio} = \frac{\text{output}}{\text{input}}$$

   b. Calculate the energy input (in megajoules) to produce 7 L of gasoline—enough to fuel a Toyota Matrix for 100 km. (Hint: What is the energy input (in megajoules) to produce 1 L of gas?). Assume that the car always requires the same energy output to travel the same distance, no matter what fuel it is using. Determine the energy input (in megajoules) to produce enough diesel, biodiesel, or ethanol to fuel the car for 100 km.

Take Action

1. **PLAN** In a group, discuss how diesel compares with biodiesel and how ethanol compares with gasoline in terms of efficiency. How do biodiesel and ethanol compare with each other in terms of efficiency? Think about the processes involved in producing these fuels. Suggest some ways to use other "side products" such as heat. Describe energy inputs that could be changed to make the process more energy efficient.

2. **ACT** Write a report to your supervisor explaining whether you think replacing gasoline with ethanol made from corn or replacing diesel with biodiesel made from canola would have a more positive impact on the environment.

Chapter 5 | SUMMARY

Section 5.1 | The Nature of Energy and Heat

All chemical reactions and nuclear reactions, and many physical processes, are accompanied by changes in energy that can be measured.

Key Terms

closed system
endothermic
enthalpy, H
enthalpy of solution, $\Delta H_{solution}$
exothermic
first law of thermodynamics
isolated system
open system
second law of thermodynamics
specific heat capacity, c
temperature
thermal energy
thermochemistry

Key Concepts

- A system is the object or substance being studied, and the surroundings are everything else in the universe. Systems can be open, closed, or isolated.
- Open and closed systems can exchange energy with the surroundings by exchanging heat with the surroundings, by doing work on the surroundings, or by the surroundings doing work on the system.
- The first law of thermodynamics states that energy cannot be created or destroyed but can be transformed from one type of energy to another type of energy or transferred from one object to another object.
- The second law of thermodynamics states that, when two objects are in thermal contact, heat will be transferred from the object at a higher temperature to the object at the lower temperature until they reach thermal equilibrium.
- An enthalpy change in a system, occurring at constant pressure, is the same as the amount of heat that is exchanged between the system and its surroundings. Enthalpy changes can be positive or negative and depend only on the initial and final states of the system.
- The range of enthalpy changes is lowest for physical changes, intermediate for chemical changes, and highest for nuclear changes.

Section 5.2 | Thermochemical Equations and Calorimetry

When a process such as a chemical reaction takes place at constant pressure, the enthalpy change of the process is equal to the amount of heat exchanged between the system and its surroundings.

Key Terms

bomb calorimeter
calorimeter
calorimetry
simple calorimeter

Key Concepts

- When a process takes place under conditions of constant pressure, the enthalpy change of a system is equal to the amount of heat gained or heat lost by the system.
- The standard enthalpy of a reaction as written (ΔH_r°) is the enthalpy change for the amount in moles of each reactant and product as determined by the coefficient of the term in the chemical equation.
- A process taking place in a simple calorimeter occurs at constant pressure. Therefore, the amount of heat that is exchanged between the calorimeter and the system is equal to the change in the enthalpy of the system.
- Temperature data from a simple calorimetry experiment can be used to calculate the enthalpy of a chemical reaction.
- The standard enthalpy of combustion (ΔH_{comb}°) of a compound is the enthalpy change that occurs when 1 mol of a compound reacts completely with oxygen under the conditions that the reactants started out at 25°C and 100 kPa of pressure and the products cooled to 25°C and 100 kPa of pressure after the reaction was complete.
- A process taking place in a bomb calorimeter occurs at constant volume but not constant pressure.

Section 5.3 | Hess's Law

According to Hess's law, if a series of chemical equations are added together, then the enthalpy of reaction for the final equation is the sum of the enthalpy changes for the series of equations.

Key Terms

Hess's law
standard molar enthalpy of formation, ΔH_f°
thermal stability

Key Concepts

- Hess's law states that the enthalpy change of a physical or chemical process depends only on the initial and final conditions. The enthalpy change of the overall process is the sum of the enthalpy changes of its individual steps.
- You can add any number of chemical equations to obtain an equation that you need, and the enthalpy change of the overall reaction is the sum of the enthalpy changes of the individual reactions.

Chapter 5 SUMMARY & REVIEW

- You can manipulate chemical equations to make them fit into another set of reactions by multiplying the equations by a constant or by reversing the equations. If you multiply by a constant, you must multiply the enthalpy change by that same constant. If you reverse an equation, you must change the sign of the enthalpy change.

- The standard enthalpy of formation of a compound, $\Delta H_f°$, is the enthalpy change for the formation of 1 mol of the compound from its elements in their most stable state under standard conditions.
- The enthalpy of formation of an element in its most stable state under standard conditions is arbitrarily set at zero.
- You can calculate the enthalpy change for any reaction by applying the formula

$$\Delta H_r° = \Sigma(n\Delta H_f° \text{ products}) - \Sigma(n\Delta H_f° \text{ reactants})$$

Section 5.4 Energy Efficiency and Energy Resources

Energy sources are not and cannot be 100% efficient, and energy sources vary greatly in their environmental, societal, and economic impacts.

Key Terms
efficiency
heat content

Key Concepts
- The efficiency of a chemical, physical, or nuclear process can be expressed as

$$\text{efficiency} = \frac{\text{energy output}}{\text{energy input}} \times 100\%$$

- Every energy-conversion step in a process reduces its efficiency.

- Energy-conversion processes that involve boiling water into steam and using the steam to turn a turbine have low efficiencies.
- Fossil fuels are non-renewable resources. The burning of fossil fuels contributes to global warming, acid rain, and pollution of the environment.
- Renewable energy resources include hydroelectric power, solar energy, and wind energy. The use of renewable energy resources in Ontario to generate electricity is projected to increase substantially by 2025.

Knowledge and Understanding

Select the letter of the best answer below.

1. Hot soup is kept in a closed, insulated bottle at 60.0°C. The bottle is left near a heat source where the surrounding temperature is 35.0°C. Select the statement that correctly describes the bottle and its contents after 2 h.
   a. closed system, temperature greater than 60.0°C
   b. isolated system, temperature at 60.0°C
   c. open system, temperature less than 60.0°C
   d. closed system, temperature less than 60.0°C
   e. isolated system, temperature less than 60.0°C

2. Select the correct statement from the following:
   a. Thermal energy is the sum of the potential energies of all the particles in a sample.
   b. For an isolated system we can say:
      universe = system
   c. The particles in two samples of the same material at the same temperature have the same average kinetic energy.
   d. Melting an ice cube by holding it in your bare hand results in a decrease in the kinetic energy of particles of $H_2O(s)$.
   e. The use of a wood stove to heat a room is an example of a closed system.

3. The standard molar enthalpy of formation of a compound represents
   a. the thermal energy released when 1 mol of a compound decomposes.
   b. the enthalpy change when 1 mol of a compound is formed from its element at standard conditions.
   c. the enthalpy change when 1 mol of an element changes to a compound.
   d. the heat energy released when 1 mol of a compound undergoes complete combustion.
   e. the enthalpy change when 1 mol of a compound undergoes a phase change.

Chapter 5 REVIEW

4. Which of the following represents the enthalpy of solution?
   a. $\Delta H_{solvent} + \Delta H_{solute}$
   b. $\Delta H_{solvent} + \Delta H_{mix}$
   c. $\Delta H_{solvent} + \Delta H_{solute} + \Delta H_{mix}$
   d. $\Delta H_{solvent} + \Delta H_{solution}$
   e. none of the above

5. What is the missing particle in the nuclear reaction written below?
$$^{27}_{13}Al + ^{4}_{2}He \rightarrow ^{30}_{15}P + \underline{\hspace{1cm}}$$
   a. $^{1}_{1}H$
   b. $^{0}_{-1}e$
   c. $^{1}_{0}n$
   d. $^{0}_{+1}e$
   e. $^{1}_{1}P$

6. You have a sample of oxygen gas at SATP. To increase the total thermal energy you could
   a. decrease the temperature of the sample at constant pressure.
   b. increase the pressure on the sample at constant temperature.
   c. insulate the sample from the surroundings.
   d. change the specific heat capacity of the sample to a higher value.
   e. increase the mass of the sample.

7. Which combination of statements is correct for the reaction below?
$$2NO_2(g) \rightarrow N_2(g) + 2O_2(g) + 66.4 \text{ kJ}$$
   a. exothermic, potential energy greater in reactants
   b. exothermic, potential energy greater in products
   c. endothermic, potential energy greater in products
   d. endothermic, potential energy less in reactants
   e. endothermic, potential energy less in products

8. Identify the correct expression that can be used to determine the change in thermal energy for the following reaction:
$$C_4H_{10}(g) + \frac{13}{2}O_2(g) \rightarrow 4CO_2(g) + 5H_2O(\ell) + \text{heat}$$
   a. $\Delta H^\circ_r = \left[(4 \text{ mol})(\Delta H^\circ_f CO_2(g)) + (5 \text{ mol})(\Delta H^\circ_f H_2O(\ell))\right] + \left[(1 \text{ mol})(\Delta H^\circ_f C_4H_{10}(g)) + \left(\frac{13}{2} \text{ mol}\right)(\Delta H^\circ_f O_2(g))\right]$
   b. $\Delta H^\circ_r = \left[(1 \text{ mol})(\Delta H^\circ_f C_4H_{10}(g)) + \left(\frac{13}{2} \text{ mol}\right)(\Delta H^\circ_f O_2(g))\right] - \left[(4 \text{ mol})(\Delta H^\circ_f CO_2(g)) + (5 \text{ mol})(\Delta H^\circ_f H_2O(\ell))\right]$
   c. $\Delta H^\circ_r = \left[(1 \text{ mol})(\Delta H^\circ_f C_4H_{10}(g)) + \left(\frac{13}{2} \text{ mol}\right)(\Delta H^\circ_f O_2(g))\right] + \left[(4 \text{ mol})(\Delta H^\circ_f CO_2(g)) + (5 \text{ mol})(\Delta H^\circ_f H_2O(\ell))\right]$
   d. $\Delta H^\circ_r = \left[(4 \text{ mol})(\Delta H^\circ_f CO_2(g)) + (5 \text{ mol})(\Delta H^\circ_f H_2O(\ell))\right] - \left[(1 \text{ mol})(\Delta H^\circ_f C_4H_{10}(g)) + \left(\frac{13}{2} \text{ mol}\right)(\Delta H^\circ_f O_2(g))\right]$
   e. $\Delta H^\circ_r = \left[(1 \text{ mol})(\Delta H^\circ_f CO_2(g)) + \left(\frac{4}{5} \text{ mol}\right)(\Delta H^\circ_f H_2O(\ell))\right] - \left[(1 \text{ mol})(\Delta H^\circ_f C_4H_{10}(g)) + \left(\frac{13}{2} \text{ mol}\right)(\Delta H^\circ_f O_2(g))\right]$

9. Electrical energy used to heat a building can be generated by the following sequence of steps:
   (1) Kinetic energy of water flowing in a river turns turbines to generate electricity.
   (2) Electrical energy is sent through transmission lines.
   (3) Electrical energy is used to operate a heating unit.

   Which statement about this energy flow is correct?
   a. The first law of thermodynamics holds for steps (1) and (2) but not for step (3).
   b. The overall efficiency is less than 100% because energy is lost to the surroundings in each step.
   c. The second law of thermodynamics holds only for step (3).
   d. The potential energy of the system increases in step (1) and decreases in steps (2) and (3).
   e. The potential energy of the system increases in steps (2) and (3).

10. Which equation correctly represents the standard molar enthalpy of formation, ΔH°_f, for aluminum sulfate, $Al_2(SO_4)_3(s)$?
   a. $Al_2(SO_4)_3(s) \rightarrow 2Al(s) + \frac{3}{8}S_8(s) + 12O(g)$
   b. $2Al(s) + \frac{1}{8}S_8(s) + 6O_2(g) \rightarrow Al_2(SO_4)_3(s)$
   c. $Al_2(SO_4)_3(s) \rightarrow 2Al(s) + 3S(s) + 12O_2(g)$
   d. $2Al(s) + \frac{3}{8}S_8(s) + 6O_2(g) \rightarrow Al_2(SO_4)_3(s)$
   e. $Al(s) + \frac{1}{8}S_8(s) + O_2(g) \rightarrow Al_2(SO_4)_3(s)$

11. The development of which one of the following energy sources has the *least* negative impact on the environment?
   a. solar
   b. coal
   c. biomass
   d. natural gas
   e. hydroelectricity

12. You are using a bomb calorimeter that is calibrated at 7.8 kJ/°C to measure the energy content of food in kJ/g. Select the piece of information *not* required to complete the calculation for energy content.
   a. initial temperature
   b. heat capacity of the calorimeter
   c. mass of water in the calorimeter
   d. mass of food
   e. final temperature

13. When two compounds are compared, the one having the more negative value for its enthalpy of formation will be the more thermally stable. This is true because
   a. bonds are broken in decomposition but are made during formation.
   b. formation reactions use elements and decomposition involves compounds.
   c. formation is the reverse of decomposition; more energy given off during formation means more energy to be added for decomposition.
   d. formation reactions are exothermic and decomposition reactions are endothermic.
   e. compounds have more potential energy compared with their elements.

14. A condensing furnace fuelled by natural gas is more efficient than a conventional furnace using the same fuel because
   a. a condensing furnace allows for comparatively more complete combustion of natural gas.
   b. the ideal mixture of air and natural gas can be adjusted.
   c. carbon dioxide gas can be compressed into a liquid.
   d. energy is recovered from the water vapour.
   e. water vapour is allowed to escape.

Answer the questions below.

15. What is the meaning of the term *energy*? State the law of conservation of energy.

16. You are given the following equation:

$$_0^1 n + {}_{92}^{235}U \rightarrow {}_{52}^{137}Te + {}_{40}^{97}Zr + 2\,_0^1 n + energy$$

   a. Classify the reaction represented by this equation.
   b. What is the source of the energy released in this reaction?

17. Water at 90.0°C is heated to 110.0°C at standard pressure. Describe the energy conversions that occur and what is happening at the molecular level during these changes.

18. A wax candle is lit and is allowed to burn until the air temperature in the room increases by 0.50°C.

   a. Use this example to explain the difference between the terms *system* and *surroundings*.
   b. Express the first law of thermodynamics in words and by means of a mathematical equation.

19. One reaction occurs at constant pressure and another reaction occurs at constant volume. What does the amount of heat exchanged between the system and its surroundings represent for these two reactions?

20. On which two laws of thermodynamics is calorimetry based? Briefly outline how each of these laws makes calorimetric calculations possible.

21. For calculations using a bomb calorimeter, why is the heat capacity of the calorimeter used rather than the specific heat capacity?

22. Consider the reaction $N_2(g) + 2O_2(g) + 11\text{ kJ} \rightarrow N_2O_4(g)$.
   a. Which has more potential energy: the reactants or the product?
   b. Explain what this means in terms of the bonding in the reactant and product molecules.

23. An investigation to determine the heat content of an alcohol is carried out. The heat released is collected in an aluminum can that is holding water, which is acting as a flame calorimeter. After the investigation, black soot on the bottom of the calorimeter can be seen.
   a. What does this black soot indicate?
   b. How will this affect the accuracy of your calculations?
   c. What information must be recorded to determine the heat content of the alcohol?

24. For an exothermic reaction, are there more and/or stronger bonds in the reactants or in the products? Explain using the complete combustion of methane as an example.

Chapter 5 REVIEW

25. List five activities in your daily life that depend on the use of fossil fuels. Name the fuel.

26. When using the expression for the calculation of efficiency, give examples of what could be included as input energy and output energy.

27. A crop such as corn can be used to produce ethanol. Ethanol is a fuel with an enthalpy of combustion of 278 kJ/mol. Is ethanol produced in this way a renewable resource? Give reasons for your answer.

28. When ammonium chloride, $NH_4Cl(s)$, is dissolved in water, moisture is observed to condense on the side of the beaker, and a short time later, ice has formed that freezes the beaker to the table top. Briefly explain what has happened.

Thinking and Investigation

29. Define each word in the term *standard molar enthalpy of formation*. Use the equation as written below to determine the standard molar enthalpy of formation for $Cr_2O_3(s)$.

$$2Cr_2O_3(s) + 2256.8.4 \text{ kJ} \rightarrow 4Cr(s) + 3O_2(g)$$

30. Use the information listed below to determine $\Delta H°$ for the reaction as written:
$$Ca^{2+}(aq) + 2OH^-(aq) + CO_2(g) \rightarrow CaCO_3(s) + H_2O(\ell)$$
    (1) $CaO(s) + H_2O(\ell) \rightarrow Ca(OH)_2(s)$ $\Delta H° = -65.2$ kJ
    (2) $CaCO_3(s) \rightarrow CaO(s) + CO_2(g)$ $\Delta H° = +178.1$ kJ
    (3) $Ca(OH)_2(s) \rightarrow Ca^{2+}(aq) + 2OH^-(aq)$ $\Delta H° = -16.2$ kJ

31. Equal masses of water and an unknown liquid are heated by the same heat source for the same period of time. The temperature of the unknown liquid increases twice as much as the temperature of the water. What conclusion can be drawn from this information?

32. The molar enthalpy of formation for copper(II) nitrate, $Cu(NO_3)_2(s)$, is −302.9 kJ/mol.
    a. Write the thermochemical equation for the decomposition of $Cu(NO_3)_2(s)$ to its elements.
    b. Calculate the amount of thermal energy required to produce 37.9 g of copper metal.

33. Given the information
$$N_2O_4(g) \rightarrow 2NO_2(g) \quad \Delta H_r° = +57.2 \text{ kJ}$$
is the following correct? Briefly explain your reasoning.
$$NO_2(g) \rightarrow \tfrac{1}{2}N_2O_4(g) \quad \Delta H_r° = -57.2 \text{ kJ}$$

34. A 62.16 g sample of molten lead solidifies, exchanging 98.1 kJ of energy with the surroundings.
    a. What is the enthalpy of melting, $\Delta H°_{melt}$, for lead?
    b. Write the thermochemical equation for the solidification of $Pb(\ell)$.

35. A 10.0 g sample of phosphorus, $P_4(s)$, is reacted with chlorine gas to form phosphorus trichloride, $PCl_3(g)$. The enthalpy change for the reaction is −23.2 kJ. Write the equation for the standard molar enthalpy of formation, $\Delta H_f°$, for $PCl_3(g)$.

36. Use the given equations and Hess's law to determine the enthalpy of reaction when propyne, $C_3H_4(g)$, reacts with hydrogen gas, $H_2(g)$, to form propane, $C_3H_8(g)$.
    (1) $H_2O(\ell) \rightarrow H_2(g) + \tfrac{1}{2}O_2(g)$ $\Delta H° = +285.8$ kJ
    (2) $C_3H_4(g) + 4O_2(g) \rightarrow 3CO_2(g) + 2H_2O(\ell)$ $\Delta H° = -1936.8$ kJ
    (3) $C_3H_8(g) + 5O_2(g) \rightarrow 3CO_2(g) + 4H_2O(\ell)$ $\Delta H° = -2219.2$ kJ

37. Calculate the standard molar enthalpy of formation, $\Delta H_f°$, for nickel tetracarbonyl, $Ni(CO)_4(g)$, given the following reaction:
$$Ni(s) + 4CO(g) \rightarrow Ni(CO)_4(g) + 159.6 \text{ kJ}$$

38. Calculate the standard enthalpy of reaction for the reaction as written:
$$2C_2H_5OH(\ell) \rightarrow C_4H_6(g) + 2H_2O(g) + H_2(g)$$
$\Delta H_f°$ for $C_4H_6(g) = -391.1$ kJ/mol and refer to Table 5.5.

39. The table below shows the $\Delta H°_{comb}$ for compounds that contain a chain of three carbon atoms. They differ in the number of −OH groups attached to this chain of carbon atoms.

Standard Molar Enthalpies of Combustion, $\Delta H°_{comb}$

Name	Formula	$\Delta H°_{comb}$ (kJ/mol)
Propane	$CH_3CH_2CH_3(g)$	−2219
1-Propanol	$CH_2(OH)CHCH_3(\ell)$	−2021
1,2-Propylene glycol	$CH_2(OH)CH(OH)CH_3(\ell)$	−1828
Glycerol	$CH_2(OH)CH(OH)CH_2(OH)(\ell)$	−1655

   a. Plot a graph of enthalpy of combustion, $\Delta H°_{comb}$, vs. number of −OH groups. Plot the vertical axis from 1000 kJ/mol to 2400 kJ/mol and the horizontal axis from zero −OH groups to five −OH groups.
   b. What trend in $\Delta H°_{comb}$ is evident from this graph?
   c. The alcohol propylphycite, $(C_3H_4)(OH)_4(s)$, has been synthesized. Use your graph to predict $\Delta H°_{comb}$ for this compound.

40. A mixture of ammonia, $NH_3(g)$, and methane, $CH_4(g)$, is burned in an excess of oxygen in a bomb calorimeter. The heat released during this combustion reaction is 1377.65 kJ. If the calorimeter has a heat capacity of 15.6 kJ/°C, by how much will the calorimeter and its contents change in temperature?

41. In a student investigation, a 1.20 g sample of zinc metal is added to a paper cup containing 90.00 mL of dilute hydrochloric acid, $HCl(aq)$. The temperature of the solution increases from 22.44°C to 24.65°C. Assume that the solution has the same specific heat capacity and density as water.
    a. Use this information to calculate the enthalpy of reaction, ΔH_r, per mole of zinc.
    b. A reference text gives the enthalpy of reaction as −155 kJ/mol of zinc. Suggest one major reason for the difference in the experimental result and the reference value.
    c. Calculate the efficiency of this experimental set-up to determine the standard molar enthalpy of reaction.

42. The equation below represents the burning of carbon disulfide, $CS_2(\ell)$, in a calorimeter. What mass of $CS_2(\ell)$ must have combusted to increase the temperature of 1.00 kg of water by 15.5°C?
    $$CS_2(\ell) + 3O_2(g) \rightarrow CO_2(g) + 2SO_2(g) + 1077 \text{ kJ}$$

43. The reaction written below shows the combustion of cyanogen, $C_2N_2(g)$.
    $$C_2N_2(g) + 2O_2(g) \rightarrow 2CO_2(g) + N_2(g)$$
    $$\Delta H°_{comb} = -1096 \text{ kJ/mol}$$
    a. Calculate the enthalpy of formation of $C_2N_2(g)$.
    b. Write the thermochemical equation for the thermal decomposition of $C_2N_2(g)$.

44. At constant pressure, a calorimetry experiment is to be set up to determine the enthalpy of reaction, in kilojoules per mole, when 250.0 mL of 0.500 mol/L $HCl(aq)$ reacts with 50.0 mL of 1.0 mol/L $NaOH(aq)$. In determining $\Delta H°_r$, a student intends to base the calculation on the amount in moles of $HCl(aq)$.
    a. After calculating the quantity of heat, Q, absorbed by the solutions, what step must be included in the calculation before determining the enthalpy of reaction using the equation $\Delta H_r = \frac{Q}{n}$?
    b. If this step is not included, will the error lead to an answer that is too large or too small for ΔH_r?

45. The temperature of 50.0 g of water changes from 28.5°C to 26.9°C when 1.00 g of ammonium bromide, $NH_4Br(s)$, dissolves. What is the molar enthalpy of solution, $\Delta H_{solution}$, for this compound?

46. Fat has an energy content of 41.0 kJ/g. When a 0.68 g sample of fat is burned in a bomb calorimeter, the temperature of the calorimeter increases by 2.9°C. How efficient is the calorimeter at measuring the energy transfer if it has a rating of 8.7 kJ/°C?

Communication

47. The standard molar enthalpy of combustion of ethane, $C_2H_6(g)$, is −1560.7 kJ/mol. Sketch an enthalpy diagram to summarize this information.

48. Your class is reviewing the main ideas about thermochemistry. You and your lab partner must demonstrate to the class the distinction between the terms heat and temperature. Suggest a simple demonstration to illustrate the difference in the terms to the class.

49. **BIG IDEAS** Technologies that transform energy can have societal and environmental costs and benefits. A manufacturing company currently uses coal as a fuel to heat its building. It is considering a switch to burning municipal waste as a fuel source. Examine the information available to the company regarding this new fuel source. Organize the data into a Plus, Minus, Interesting (PMI) chart to help decide if using municipal waste is a good decision.

Data Regarding New Fuel Source
- new equipment must be purchased and installed
- estimated energy content from coal is 26 kJ/g
- unknown costs to monitor emissions
- cost saving over using coal, since a municipality wants to get rid of this product
- estimation that $CO_2(g)$ emission would be reduced 30% compared with coal
- health risk of using a fuel containing plastics including polyvinyl chlorides (PVCs)
- waste is not of uniform and consistent energy content
- company will be seen as environmentally friendly, leading to potential increased sales of their product
- diversion of waste from landfill sites
- estimated energy content from current waste is 13 kJ/g

Chapter 5 REVIEW

50. You have a product that you want to market as a portable food warmer for use by campers. You plan to prepare an advertisement that can be used for a print medium such as a newspaper or for use on a Web site for potential customers to read. What main points would you stress to make this an appealing product?

51. On an outdoor winter class trip, your teacher cautions against using snow as a source of drinking water. Your friend says that this is only common sense because there is no way of knowing what unhealthy material could be mixed in with the snow. What thermochemical reason can you give as another explanation for the teacher's instruction?

52. From an environmental point of view, hydrogen gas is an ideal fuel because the product of its combustion is water. A great deal of energy is needed to extract $H_2(g)$ from water by electrolysis, the process of passing a direct electric current through water.
    a. Research some of the ways in which technology is trying to develop the potential of hydrogen energy.
    b. Use a fishbone diagram graphic organizer to organize and present the pros and cons of using hydrogen as a fuel source. Refer to Appendix A for a model of a fishbone diagram.

53. You are a chemist in a power plant that produces nuclear energy. You are invited to speak to members of a local service club in the city where you live.
    a. Outline some of the points you would make to the group that would emphasize the positive aspects of this energy source while minimizing the negative aspects.
    b. Refer to Appendix A for a description of graphic organizers. Select one of the graphic organizers and organize the information for your presentation as a handout.

54. Transportation and heating top the list of ways in which people depend on fossil fuels.
    a. For your family, think of the ways that fossil fuels have been used to make what you use on a daily basis. Consult other family members, if possible, for their input. Select a graphic organizer from Appendix A to help you form a "picture" of how fossil fuels are part of daily living.
    b. Use a pie chart to compare your family's dependency on fossil fuels in four areas: transportation, heating, electricity, and a fourth area, "other products."

55. Select a graphic organizer from Appendix A to outline the questions that could be asked when considering the characteristics of a fuel.

56. There is a significant difference in the temperature of beach sand and that of the nearby water on a hot sunny day. This difference in temperature is less noticeable on a hot cloudy day.

    Demonstrate your knowledge of thermochemistry using the terms *specific heat capacity* and *the first and second laws of thermodynamics*, as well as the expression for calculating the quantity of heat, Q, to explain these observations to a friend.

57. A reporter is preparing to write a feature article on alternative energy sources that could reduce dependency on fossil fuels. The plan is to interview business people in the community who are directly involved with the development and distribution of energy sources.
    a. Make a list of 10 questions that the reporter might prepare before interviewing these people.
    b. Assume that you are a business person who advocates the use of geothermal energy to heat a home. Research this energy source and respond to the questions that the reporter plans to ask.

58. Summarize your learning in this chapter using a graphic organizer. To help you, the Chapter 5 Summary lists the Key Terms and Key Concepts. Refer to Using Graphic Organizers in Appendix A to help you decide which graphic organizer to use.

Application

59. Refer to the standard enthalpy of formation data given in Appendix B. Which of the three oxides of iron that are listed is the most thermally stable? Give a reason for your answer.

60. Both methane, $CH_4(g)$, and hydrogen gas, $H_2(g)$, are effective fuels. Their thermal energy can be expressed in energy units per unit of mass or per unit of volume. Use the equations as written below to compare these fuels in terms of available energy in
    a. kilojoules per gram.
    b. kilojoules per litre.

    $CH_4(g) + 2O_2(g) \rightarrow CO_2(g) + 2H_2O(\ell) + 890.8 \text{ kJ}$
    $H_2(g) + \frac{1}{2}O_2(g) \rightarrow H_2O(\ell) + 285.8 \text{ kJ}$

61. Determine the energy of combustion, in kilojoules per gram, for an alcohol burner containing 30% butan-1-ol and 70% ethanol by mass.
$C_2H_5OH(\ell) + 3O_2(g) \rightarrow 2CO_2(g) + 3H_2O(\ell) + 1366.8$ kJ
$C_4H_9OH(\ell) + 6O_2(g) \rightarrow 4CO_2(g) + 5H_2O(\ell) + 2758.6$ kJ

62. **BIG IDEAS** Energy changes and rates of chemical reactions can be described quantitatively. From the first law of thermodynamics, you know that in a chemical reaction energy is conserved but can be converted from one form to another. For example, a microwave oven uses electrical energy to emit microwaves of a frequency that specifically is absorbed by and heats only water. A microwave oven uses electrical energy at a rate of 1.100×10^3 J/s for 2.00 min. The oven converts this electrical energy to microwaves with an efficiency of 81.02%. The efficiency with which 500.0 g of water in a Pyrex™ bowl inside the oven absorbs the microwaves is 98.3%.
   a. What is the expected temperature change of the water?
   b. Suggest an explanation as to why the observed temperature change was 42.6°C.
   c. Suggest reasons why the electrical energy is not converted completely to microwaves.

63. A calorimetry experiment is set up to determine the enthalpy of solution, $\Delta H°_{solution}$. The following occurs:
   - 4.10 g of sodium acetate, $NaC_2H_3O_2(s)$, is dissolved in 100.0 mL of water in a double-insulated coffee cup calorimeter.
   - The temperature of the water increases from 19.6°C to 21.1°C.
   - For the calculations, it is assumed that for the solution formed, the specific heat capacity is 4.19 J/g·°C and the density is 1.0 g/mL.

   For each description given below, explain whether the calculated $\Delta H°_{solution}$ will be larger or smaller than the theoretical value.
   a. After adding the $NaC_2H_3O_2(s)$, the solution was stirred once and left standing during the dissolving process.
   b. The initial temperature was incorrectly recorded as 16.9°C.
   c. The actual specific heat capacity and the density of the solution are both slightly greater than the values accepted for water.

64. Which would give more accurate results for the determination of an enthalpy of combustion reaction: a bomb calorimeter using a constant volume system or a flame calorimeter using a constant pressure system? Explain your reasoning in a few sentences.

65. In an article on the Internet, you read the statement, "27 m³ of natural gas is equivalent to a gigajoule (GJ) of energy." Realizing that many Internet sources are not reliable, you are skeptical and want to verify it. Decide what information you need, research it, and determine whether the statement is accurate.

66. A thermal generating station is phasing out the use of coal and converting to the use of biomass pellets. What are some pros and cons of this change?

67. **BIG IDEAS** Technologies that transform energy can have societal and environmental costs and benefits. Hybrid cars have been called "the car of the future." They have two engines: a traditional gasoline engine, and an electric motor and batteries. Research the topic of hybrid vehicles and report on the advantages and disadvantages from an environmental and economic perspective.

68. Your task is to determine the thermal heat content in a food product by carrying out a combustion of the food in a bomb calorimeter. Before combustion, you oven-dried the food. Why would this step be important in order to obtain accurate results?

69. **BIG IDEAS** Technologies that transform energy can have societal and environmental costs and benefits. Controversy continues over the construction of wind turbines at various locations on the shores of the Great Lakes in Ontario. Research this topic and be prepared to present arguments for and against the development of this energy source.

70. Hydrogen gas is a very environmentally friendly fuel source. One factor that is important in determining whether it is used as a fuel source is the cost of production. Use the two equations below to evaluate which reaction requires more energy to produce 1 mol of $H_2(g)$. Reaction (1) as written produces $H_2(g)$ from methane and is 80.5% efficient. The production of $H_2(g)$ by electrolysis of water, as shown in reaction (2), is 49.1% efficient.

   (1) $CH_4(g) + H_2O(\ell) \rightarrow 3H_2(g) + CO(g)$
   $\Delta H°_r = +205.9$ kJ
   (2) $H_2O(\ell) \rightarrow H_2(g) + \frac{1}{2}O_2(g)$
   $\Delta H°_r = +285.8$ kJ

Chapter 5 SELF-ASSESSMENT

Select the letter of the best answer below.

1. **K/U** Which one of the following gases is considered a greenhouse gas and a major contributor to global warming?
   a. hydrogen chloride
   b. sulfur dioxide
   c. hydrogen
   d. carbon dioxide
   e. nitrogen

2. **K/U** Which one of the following has a non-zero value for enthalpy of formation?
   a. $N_2(g)$
   b. $Ne(g)$
   c. $Na^+(aq)$
   d. $Cl_2(g)$
   e. $He(g)$

3. **K/U** Which equation represents the formation of $(C_{17}H_{35}COO)_2Ca(s)$?
   a. $17C(s) + \frac{35}{2}H_2(g) + O_2(g) + Ca(s) \rightarrow (C_{17}H_{35}COO)_2Ca(s)$
   b. $18C(s) + 35H_2(g) + 2O_2(g) + Ca(s) \rightarrow (C_{17}H_{35}COO)_2Ca(s)$
   c. $34C(s) + 2O_2(g) + 2O_2(g) + Ca(s) \rightarrow (C_{17}H_{35}COO)_2Ca(s)$
   d. $36C(s) + 35H_2(g) + 2O_2(g) + Ca(s) \rightarrow (C_{17}H_{35}COO)_2Ca(s)$
   e. $18C(s) + 17H(g) + O_2(g) + Ca(s) \rightarrow (C_{17}H_{35}COO)_2Ca(s)$

4. **T/I** What amount of heat must be removed from 10.0 g of water at 1.00°C so that the water reaches the freezing point (but does not freeze)?
   a. 0.419 J
   b. 41.9 J
   c. 0.00419 J
   d. 419 J
   e. 4190 J

5. **T/I** When a 2.00 g sample of a substance is combusted in a bomb calorimeter that has a heat capacity of 2.337 kJ/°C, the temperature increases by 3.03°C. How much heat was released during the combustion?
   a. 6.06 kJ
   b. 7.08 kJ
   c. 14.2 kJ
   d. 0.771 kJ
   e. 3.54 kJ

6. **T/I** What is the efficiency of a system in which 200.0 g of water absorbs 40.0 kJ of thermal energy from a heater that emits 50.0 kJ of heat?
   a. 40.0%
   b. 90.0%
   c. 80.0%
   d. 180.0%
   e. 12.5%

7. **K/U** In which one of the following situations does the greatest absorption of thermal energy occur?
   a. 10.0 g of water freezes
   b. 10.0 g of ice melts
   c. 10.0 g of water vapour condenses
   d. 10.0 g of water evaporates
   e. 10.0 g of water heats up by 10.0°C

8. **T/I** Determine the value of $\Delta H°$ for the reaction $2C + B \rightarrow BC_2$, given the following information:
   (1) $AC_2 \rightarrow A + 2C$ $\Delta H° = +50$ kJ
   (2) $AC_2 + B \rightarrow BC_2 + A$ $\Delta H° = -20$ kJ
   a. −70 kJ
   b. −30 kJ
   c. +20 kJ
   d. −50 kJ
   e. +30 kJ

9. **K/U** You have a sample of water at 65°C. When it is warmed to a temperature of 125°C at standard pressure, how has the energy of the water changed?
   a. Only potential energy increases.
   b. Only kinetic energy increases.
   c. Potential energy remains the same and kinetic energy increases.
   d. Potential energy increases and kinetic energy stays the same.
   e. Both potential energy and kinetic energy increase.

10. **T/I** Given the reaction below, how much thermal energy is required to decompose 123.9 g of $Ag_2S(s)$?
    $$2\,Ag(s) + S(s) \rightarrow Ag_2S + 31.8\text{ kJ}$$
    a. 15.9 kJ
    b. 63.6 kJ
    c. 31.8 kJ
    d. 7.95 kJ
    e. 42.7 kJ

Use sentences and diagrams as appropriate to answer the questions below.

11. **K/U** You have two samples of water, one at 25°C and another at 40°C. What does this information tell you about the energy of the particles and the total energy of the samples?

12. **K/U** Although heating and transportation are the major uses of fossil fuels, it has been estimated that almost 5% of the air pollution in Canada is produced by the use of electric or gas-powered garden and lawn equipment. List some items used for home lawn and garden work and suggest ways in which the items could be modified to have less impact on the environment.

13. **T/I** How much energy can be recovered by a condensing furnace that is 97% efficient, from the combustion of natural gas that contains 2.0×10^6 g of methane?

350 MHR • Unit 3 Energy Changes and Rates of Reaction

14. **A** When 6.85 g of aluminum chloride, $AlCl_3(s)$, is dissolved in 255.0 mL of water, the final temperature of the solution is 48.7°C. What was the initial temperature of the water?

$$AlCl_3(s) \rightarrow Al^{3+}(aq) + 3Cl^-(aq) + 373.8 \text{ kJ}$$

15. **T/I** The enthalpy diagram below shows the relative potential energy of iodine in each of its three states. Write the thermochemical equation for the process indicated by the grey box.

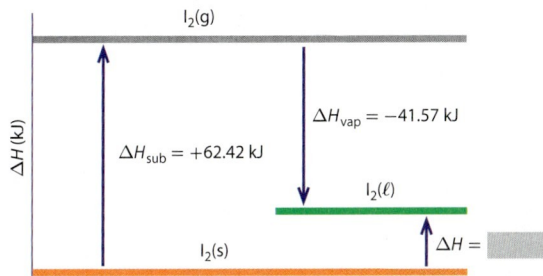

16. **A** Refer to the table of standard molar enthalpies of formation in Appendix B to determine the enthalpy of reaction, ΔH_r°, for calcium carbide, $CaC_2(s)$, and water.

$$CaC_2(s) + 2H_2O(\ell) \rightarrow C_2H_2(g) + Ca(OH)_2(s) + 128.0 \text{ kJ}$$

17. **A** For the following reaction

$$HNO_3(aq) + KOH(aq) \rightarrow$$
$$H_2O(\ell) + KNO_3(aq) + 55.31 \text{ kJ}$$

when 400.0 mL of 0.0500 mol/L $HNO_3(aq)$ is added to an unknown volume of 0.0500 mol/L $KOH(aq)$, the temperature increases from 18.67°C to 19.00°C. Assuming that both solutions have a specific heat capacity of 4.19 J/g·°C and a density of 1.000 g/mL, what volume of $KOH(aq)$ was used?

18. **T/I** Use the equations below to determine the enthalpy of reaction, ΔH_r°, for

$$2NO_2(g) + \frac{1}{2}O_2(g) \rightarrow N_2O_5(g)$$

(1) $2N_2O_5(g) \rightarrow 4NO(g) + 3O_2(g) \quad \Delta H^\circ = +447.4 \text{ kJ}$
(2) $2NO(g) + O_2(g) \rightarrow 2NO_2(g) \quad \Delta H^\circ = -114.2 \text{ kJ}$

19. **C** On a calm winter day, it begins to snow and the air temperature increases. Explain this increase based on thermodynamics at a level that could be understood by a younger sibling interested in chemistry.

20. **C** When propane, $C_3H_8(g)$, undergoes complete combustion to $CO_2(g)$ and gaseous water, $H_2O(g)$, the enthalpy of combustion, ΔH_{comb}, is -2043.9 kJ/mol. With a partner, discuss whether the value of ΔH_{comb} would change if the product was liquid water, $H_2O(\ell)$.

21. **T/I** How much heat must a stove burner release in order to raise the temperature of 1.245 kg of water from 24°C to the boiling point, if the water is in a pot on the stove? Assume that the transfer of the heat from the burner to the water is 34.5% efficient.

22. **A** A bomb calorimeter has a heat capacity of 5923 J/°C. When a 0.7450 g sample of fat is burned, the temperature increases from 18.45°C to 22.62°C.
    a. What is the enthalpy of combustion, in kilojoules per gram, for this sample of fat?
    b. It is estimated that 9.48% of the energy in this sample of fat is used in digestion. How much of the energy in this fat will be available as heat and as energy for muscle activity?

23. **A** What mass of propane would have to be burned to heat a 5.0 kg iron barbecue from 25°C to 190°C if the heat transfer is 45% efficient? The specific heat capacity of iron is 0.46 J/g·°C.

24. **T/I** Refer to the standard molar enthalpies of formation in Appendix B and determine whether it is the reactants or the products in the reaction below that have more potential energy.

$$4FeS_2(s) + 11O_2(g) \rightarrow 2Fe_2O_3(s) + 8SO_2(g)$$

25. **C** Develop a step-by-step procedure for comparing the standard molar enthalpies of combustion of alkanes with their corresponding alkenes having one double bond and the same number of carbon atoms. Include the following:
    - all of the data required and a description of how the data is used for the comparison
    - a flowchart that could act as a guide for the comparison
    - a description of how a graph could be used to display comparisons for compounds with two to ten carbon atoms

Self-Check

If you missed question …	1	2	3	4	5	6	7	8	9	10	11	12	13	14	15	16	17	18	19	20	21	22	23	24	25
Review section(s)…	5.4	5.2	5.2	5.2	5.2	5.4	5.2	5.3	5.1	5.2	5.1	5.4	5.2, 5.4	5.2	5.1	5.3	5.2	5.3	5.1	5.3	5.2, 5.4	5.2, 5.4	5.2, 5.4	5.3	5.3

CHAPTER 6
Rates of Reaction

Specific Expectations
In this chapter, you will learn how to . . .

- D1.2 **analyze** the conditions required to maximize the efficiency of some common natural or industrial chemical reactions (6.2)

- D2.1 **use** appropriate terminology related to energy changes and rates of reaction (6.1, 6.2, 6.3)

- D2.8 **plan** and **conduct** an inquiry to determine how various factors affect the rate of a chemical reaction (6.2)

- D3.5 **explain**, using collision theory and potential energy diagrams, how factors such as temperature, the surface area of the reactants, the nature of the reactants, the addition of catalysts, and the concentration of the solution control the rate of a chemical reaction (6.2)

- D3.6 **describe** simple potential energy diagrams of chemical reactions (6.2, 6.3)

- D3.7 **explain**, with reference to a simple chemical reaction, how the rate of a reaction is determined by the series of elementary steps that make up the overall reaction mechanism (6.3)

Fireflies, a common sight on summer nights in Ontario, are members of the beetle family that send out flashes of bright light to attract a mate. A firefly's brightness is referred to as its bioluminescent intensity and is determined by the rate (speed) at which a specific chemical reaction occurs in its abdomen. Various factors affect the rate of a reaction. For example, the rate of the bioluminescent reaction in fireflies is increased by the enzyme *luciferase*. The greater the concentration of this enzyme, the faster the reaction occurs. The concentration of the reactants involved also affects the reaction rate. As the concentration of reactants increases, so does the rate of the reaction. Scientists can determine the rate at which the reaction takes place by measuring the firefly's bioluminescent intensity, which is directly related to the rate at which photons of light are emitted by the insect.

Launch Lab

Factors That Affect Reaction Rate

How do different factors affect the rate of a reaction? In this activity, you will measure the time for a piece of magnesium to "disappear" under various reaction conditions and convert reaction time to reaction rate.

Safety Precautions

- Wear safety eyewear and protective clothing throughout this activity.
- If any HCl(aq) gets on your skin, immediately flush with plenty of cold water.

Materials

- 60 mL 1.0 mol/L HCl(aq)
- 6 - 1 cm pieces of clean magnesium ribbon
- small magnesium pieces cut from magnesium ribbon
- small piece of zinc (same mass as magnesium)
- 30 mL of water
- ice water for cooling
- 7 test tubes
- 400 mL beaker
- 10 mL graduated cylinder
- timing device that measures seconds
- thermometer

Procedure

1. Prepare solutions of hydrochloric acid as outlined in the table below.
2. Carry out each reaction. In each trial, measure and record the time for the metal to "disappear." Measure and record the temperature of each trial.
3. Your teacher will tell you the mass of 100 cm of magnesium. Use this to determine the mass of magnesium used.

Questions

1. For each trial, convert reaction time to reaction rate of metal in mol/s.
2. What was the effect on reaction rate of **a.** using different concentrations of acid? **b.** using magnesium pieces instead of a strip? **c.** changing temperature? **d.** using zinc rather than magnesium?
3. Summarize the effects of concentration, temperature, and nature of reactants with respect to the rate at which the reaction occurred.

Data Table

Trial	Volume of 1.0 mol/L HCl(aq) (mL)	Volume of Water (mL)	Total Volume of HCl(aq) (L)	Concentration of HCl (mol/L)	Metal Reacted	Reaction Time (s)	Temperature (°C)
1	10	0			1 cm Mg		room temperature
2	7	3			1 cm Mg		room temperature
3	5	5			1 cm Mg		room temperature
4	3	7			1 cm Mg		room temperature
5	10	0			1 cm Mg		5
6	10	0			Mg pieces		room temperature
7	10	0			equal mass zinc		room temperature

SECTION 6.1
Chemical Reaction Rates

Key Terms

reaction rate
average rate of reaction
instantaneous rate of reaction

Some processes, such as the complete hardening (curing) of concrete and the conversion of graphite to diamond, can take years, or even millions of years, to complete. Others, such as the reaction in **Figure 6.1**, occur so quickly that they are measured in femtoseconds—one millionth of one billionth of a second, 10^{-15} s. What accounts for differences in the rate at which reactions occur? What factors affect reaction rates? Chemists investigate such questions. On a practical level, chemists also investigate reaction rates to design medications, improve techniques to control pollution, and develop more efficient methods in the food processing industry.

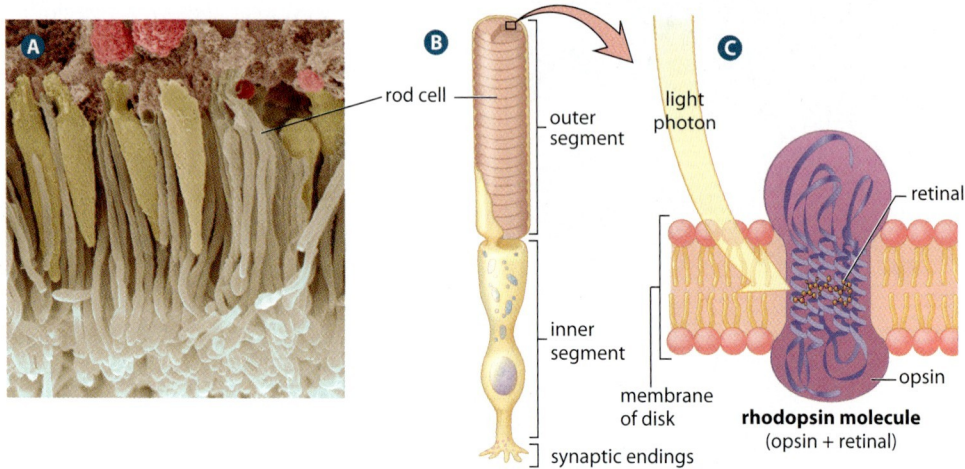

Figure 6.1 The retina, shown in this micrograph as a cross section (**A**), is located in the back of the eye. The rod cells of the retina (**B**) contain rhodopsin molecules, which are made up of the protein opsin and light-absorbing retinal (**C**). The first chemical event in vision occurs as rhodopsin absorbs a photon of light. This causes a portion of retinal to twist, changing its shape and triggering a series of reactions that lead to vision.

The field of chemistry that investigates the rate at which reactions occur is called *chemical kinetics*. You know the word "kinetics" from your study of thermodynamics. In the context of this chapter, kinetics refers to **reaction rates**—the change in the amount of reactants consumed or products formed over a given time interval. (Note that the term "rate of reaction" is often used when referring to reaction rates. Both mean the same thing.)

reaction rate the speed at which a reaction occurs, or the change in the amount of reactants consumed or products formed over a given time interval

Determining Reaction Rates

A rate is a description of a change in a quantity over a given time interval:

$$\text{rate} = \frac{\Delta \text{quantity}}{\Delta t}$$

For example, an Olympic male speed skater can skate a 5000 m race in about 6 min 15 s (6.25 min). This results in an average skating rate of 5000 m/6.25 min or 800 m/min (13.3 m/s). The rate in this case is determined based on the distance travelled divided by the time interval. The rate of a chemical reaction is the amount of reactants consumed or products formed divided by the time interval during which the change took place.

The reaction rate is usually given as a change in the concentration of a reactant or product per unit time. The symbol for the concentration of a compound in units of mol/L is a pair of square brackets, [ ], placed around the chemical formula. The reaction rate can be expressed as follows:

$$\text{reaction rate} = \frac{[A]_{\text{final}} - [A]_{\text{initial}}}{t_{\text{final}} - t_{\text{initial}}}$$

$$= \frac{\Delta[A]}{\Delta t}$$

Chemists determine the rate of a reaction by measuring the *increase* in concentration of a product or the *decrease* in concentration of a reactant. **Figure 6.2** shows the progress of a reaction in which compound A is converted into compound B. Each dot represents 1.0 mmol and the volume represents 1.0 L. Since there are 40 black dots in the first box, the initial concentration is 40 mmol/L (4.0×10^{-2} mol/L). Counting the black dots as the reaction progresses gives the data in **Table 6.1**.

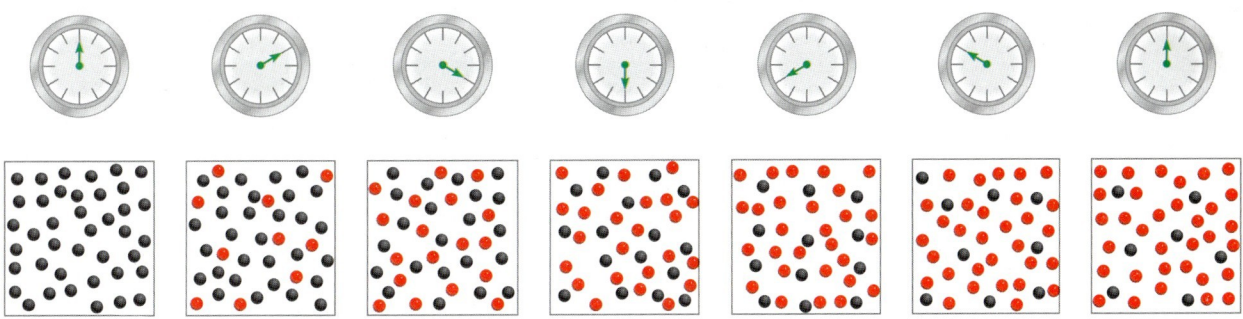

A ● B ●

Figure 6.2 The black spheres represent 1.0 mmol of compound A, and the red spheres represent 1.0 mmol of compound B. The boxes show the progress of the reaction A → B every 10 s for an interval of 60 s.

Table 6.1 Concentration of A in Millimoles per Litre

Time (s)	[A] (mmol/L)
0.0	40.0
10.0	30.0
20.0	22.0
30.0	17.0
40.0	12.0
50.0	9.0
60.0	7.0

Figure 6.3 is a graph of the data in **Figure 6.2**. The concentrations of A and B are plotted against time. The reaction rate in terms of both the decrease in A and the increase in B can be obtained from the graph.

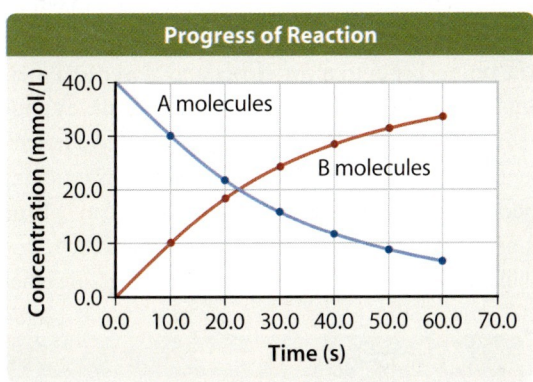

Figure 6.3 As the reaction A → B progresses, the number of molecules of A decreases, and the number of molecules of B increases. This graph represents the rate of the chemical reaction in an easily observable way.

The reaction rate in terms of the increase in the concentration of compound B can be expressed as follows:

$$\text{reaction rate} = \frac{\Delta[B]}{\Delta t}$$

Because the concentration of A is decreasing, the value of $\Delta[A]$ will be negative. To represent the reaction rate as a positive number, $\Delta[A]$ must be multiplied by -1. Therefore, the reaction rate in terms of the reactant, A, is expressed as follows:

$$\text{reaction rate} = -\frac{\Delta[A]}{\Delta t}$$

Average and Instantaneous Reaction Rates

Notice from the data on the previous page that the reaction rate between 10.0 s and 20.0 s is lower than the reaction rate between 0.0 s and 10.0 s. Because these two reactions occur over a period of time, both are considered **average rates of reaction**. A reaction rate calculated for any time interval is an average rate of reaction. As shown in **Figure 6.4**, an average rate of reaction is equal to the slope of a line drawn between the two points that define the time interval.

average rate of reaction the change in the concentration of a reactant or product per unit time over a given time interval as a chemical reaction proceeds

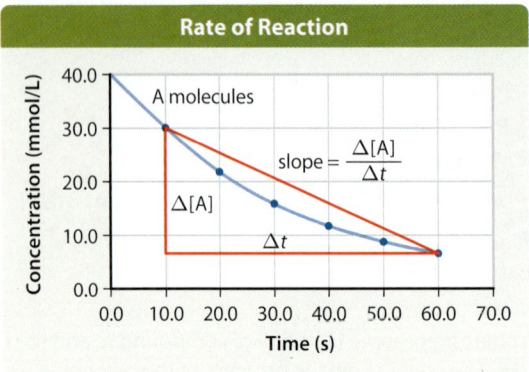

Figure 6.4 The average rate of a reaction is equal to the slope of a line between two points on the curve. The slope of a line is defined as the rise (vertical change) over the run (horizontal change).

Examine the slope drawn between 10.0 s and 30.0 s in **Figure 6.5**. Notice that as the line is drawn between points that are closer together than they are in **Figure 6.4**, the slope gets closer to the curve. Now imagine that the points at 40.0 s and 60.0 s have a slope drawn between them and the points begin to move closer and closer together. Eventually they will converge on the point at 50.0 s. The line will just touch the curve at one point. A line such as this, which is touching the curve at only one point, is called a tangent. The slope of the tangent gives the rate of the reaction at the point at which it is touching the curve. This is called the **instantaneous rate of reaction** at that point. You can calculate the instantaneous rate by measuring the length of the lines forming the sides of the triangle and dividing the length of the side labelled $\Delta[A]$, the rise, by the length of the side labelled Δt, the run.

instantaneous rate of reaction the rate of a chemical reaction at a particular point in time

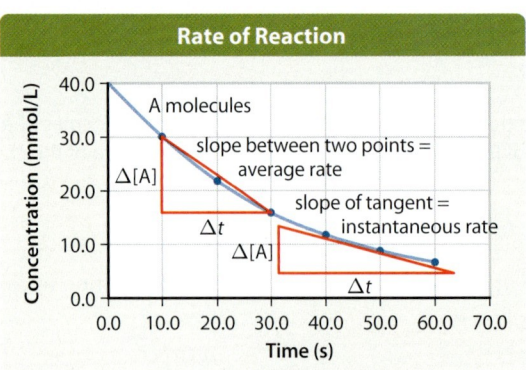

Figure 6.5 The slope of a line between two separate points on a concentration vs. time curve is the average rate of reaction. When a slope is drawn between two points and then the points are brought closer together until they converge to one point, the line becomes a tangent and the slope is the instantaneous rate of reaction.

Learning Check

1. What type of data could be used to determine the rate of the reaction for the chemical change that occurs when acid rain dissolves limestone and releases carbon dioxide?

2. What information about a chemical reaction is not given by the balanced equation?

3. To determine the average rate of a chemical reaction, a technician determined that the concentration of a substance was 0.25 mol/L at 0.50 min. At 2.00 min, the concentration of the substance was 0.420 mol/L. Was the technician using a reactant or a product to measure the rate of the reaction? Explain your answer.

4. Draw a graph of concentration versus time that shows the formation of a product. Near the centre of your graph, draw a tangent to the curve. Explain how you would use the tangent to find the instantaneous rate of the reaction at the time indicated by the tangent.

5. Refer to **Figure 6.2**, which shows information about the rate of the reaction A → B.

    a. If each dot represents one molecule, how many molecules of A remain after the first 10.0 s has elapsed? How many molecules of B have formed after the first 10.0 s?

    b. How can this information be used to determine the average rate of the reaction?

    c. Compare the rate of change in the number of molecules of A with the rate of change in the number of molecules of B at $t = 10.0$ s.

6. The manager of a grocery store is concerned about the length of time that fresh fruit can be kept on the store shelves. Would the manager be concerned about the instantaneous rate or the average rate at which the fruit spoils? Explain your answer.

Activity 6.1 Calculating Reaction Rates

In this activity, you will examine rate of reaction data for the decomposition of chlorine oxide, ClO(g), which is involved in the depletion of ozone in Earth's upper atmosphere. At room temperature, chlorine oxide decomposes rapidly according to the following equation:

$$2ClO(g) \rightarrow Cl_2(g) + O_2(g)$$

Procedure

1. For the data provided in the table below, use graph paper or spreadsheet software to plot (and print) a labelled graph of the concentration of chlorine oxide (y-axis) vs. time (x-axis). Provide a descriptive title for your graph.

Reaction Data

Time (s)	[ClO] (mol/L)
0.12×10^{-3}	8.49×10^{-6}
0.96×10^{-3}	7.10×10^{-6}
2.24×10^{-3}	5.79×10^{-6}
3.20×10^{-3}	5.20×10^{-6}
4.00×10^{-3}	4.77×10^{-6}

2. On your graph, draw a straight line from the point at $t = 0.12 \times 10^{-3}$ s to the point at $t = 4.00 \times 10^{-3}$ s.

3. Additionally, draw a *tangent* to the curve at $t = 0.12 \times 10^{-3}$ s and at $t = 4.00 \times 10^{-3}$ s.

4. Determine the slope of the line drawn in step 2, with proper units; pay attention to significant digits. Calculate and record the *average* rate of the reaction over the given time interval.

5. Determine the slope of each tangent, with proper units. Calculate and record the instantaneous reaction rate at $t = 0.12 \times 10^{-3}$ s and at $t = 4.00 \times 10^{-3}$ s?

Questions

1. Explain how you know that this is a very fast reaction.

2. Why are the units for the average rate and the instantaneous rate of the reaction the same?

3. Explain how it is possible that two students could use the table data to determine different average reaction rates.

4. Propose an explanation for the different instantaneous reaction rates obtained at $t = 0.12 \times 10^{-3}$ s and at $t = 4.00 \times 10^{-3}$ s.

5. Why does the graph become more level as the reaction progresses?

Expressing Reaction Rates in Terms of Reactants or Products

By measuring the rate of change in the quantity of just one reactant or product in a chemical reaction, you can calculate the rate of change of all the other reactants and products involved in the reaction. The calculation is based on the coefficients in the balanced chemical equation that give the mole ratios for the components in the reaction. Consider, for example, hydrazine, $N_2H_4(\ell)$, which can decompose as follows:

$$3N_2H_4(\ell) \rightarrow 4NH_3(g) + N_2(g)$$

Note that for every 3 mol $N_2H_4(\ell)$ consumed per unit time in the reaction, 1 mol of nitrogen, $N_2(g)$, and 4 mol of ammonia, $NH_3(g)$, are formed. Mathematically, this can be stated as follows:

$$\frac{\text{rate of consumption of } N_2H_4(\ell)}{\text{rate of production of } N_2(g)} = \frac{3}{1} = \frac{-\frac{\Delta [N_2H_4]}{\Delta t}}{\frac{\Delta [N_2]}{\Delta t}}$$

$$\frac{\frac{\Delta [N_2]}{\Delta t}}{1} = \frac{-\frac{\Delta [N_2H_4]}{\Delta t}}{3}$$

or

$$\frac{\Delta [N_2]}{\Delta t} = -\left(\frac{1}{3}\right)\left(\frac{\Delta [N_2H_4]}{\Delta t}\right)$$

Similarly, for every 3 mol $N_2H_4(\ell)$ consumed in the reaction, 4 mol $NH_3(g)$ is formed. The mole ratio of ammonia to hydrazine is therefore 4:3. Using the same reasoning as was used above, you can express the rate of formation of $NH_3(g)$ relative to $N_2H_4(\ell)$:

$$\frac{\Delta [NH_3]}{\Delta t} = -\left(\frac{4}{3}\right)\left(\frac{\Delta [N_2H_4]}{\Delta t}\right)$$

Use the Sample Problem and Practice Problems below to practise calculating reaction rates.

Sample Problem

Calculating an Average Reaction Rate

Problem
In a reaction between butyl chloride, $C_4H_9Cl(aq)$, and water, the concentration of butyl chloride is 2.2×10^{-1} mol/L at the beginning of the reaction. At 4.00 s, the concentration of butyl chloride is 1.0×10^{-1} mol/L. Calculate the average reaction rate, in terms of butyl chloride, over the first 4.00 s of the reaction.

What Is Required?
You need to calculate the average rate at which butyl chloride is consumed during the first 4.00 s of the reaction between butyl chloride and water.

What Is Given?
You know the initial time: $t_{\text{initial}} = 0.00$ s
You know the final time: $t_{\text{final}} = 4.00$ s
You know the initial concentration of butyl chloride: $[C_4H_9Cl]_{\text{initial}} = 2.2 \times 10^{-1}$ mol/L
You know the final concentration of butyl chloride: $[C_4H_9Cl]_{\text{final}} = 1.0 \times 10^{-1}$ mol/L

Plan Your Strategy	Act on Your Strategy
Write the equation for the average rate of decrease of butyl chloride.	$\text{average rate} = -\dfrac{\Delta [C_4H_9Cl]}{\Delta t} = -\dfrac{[C_4H_9Cl]_{\text{final}} - [C_4H_9Cl]_{\text{initial}}}{t_{\text{final}} - t_{\text{initial}}}$
Substitute the numerical values into the equation. Solve the equation.	$= -\left(\dfrac{1.0 \times 10^{-1} \,\frac{\text{mol}}{\text{L}} - 2.2 \times 10^{-1} \,\frac{\text{mol}}{\text{L}}}{4.00 \text{ s} - 0.00 \text{ s}}\right)$ $= -\left(\dfrac{-1.2 \times 10^{-1} \,\frac{\text{mol}}{\text{L}}}{4.00 \text{ s}}\right)$ $= 3.0 \times 10^{-2} \,\dfrac{\text{mol}}{\text{L} \cdot \text{s}}$ The average rate at which butyl chloride is consumed during the reaction is 3.0×10^{-2} mol/L·s.

Check Your Solution

The average reaction rate is reasonable given the initial and final concentrations of butyl chloride. The answer is correctly expressed in two significant digits. The answer is expressed in units of mol/L·s, which is correct.

Sample Problem

Determining Reaction Rates in Terms of Products and Reactants

Problem

Dinitrogen pentoxide, $N_2O_5(g)$, decomposes to form nitrogen dioxide and oxygen, according to the following equation: $2N_2O_5(g) \rightarrow 4NO_2(g) + O_2(g)$
$NO_2(g)$ is produced at a rate of 5.00×10^{-6} mol/L·s.
a. What is the rate of decomposition of $N_2O_5(g)$?
b. What is the corresponding rate of formation of $O_2(g)$?

What Is Required?

Because $N_2O_5(g)$ is a reactant, you need to calculate its rate of decomposition.
$O_2(g)$ is a product, so you need to determine its rate of formation.

What Is Given?

You know the rate of formation of nitrogen dioxide: $\text{rate} = \dfrac{\Delta [NO_2]}{\Delta t} = 5.00 \times 10^{-6}$ mol/L·s
You know the balanced chemical equation for the reaction.

Plan Your Strategy	Act on Your Strategy
a. Determine the ratio of $N_2O_5(g)$ to $NO_2(g)$.	2 mol N_2O_5 is decomposed for every 4 mol NO_2 formed, or $\dfrac{N_2O_5}{NO_2} = \dfrac{2}{4} = \dfrac{1}{2}$
Use the coefficients in the balanced chemical equation to determine the relative rate of decomposition of $N_2O_5(g)$.	For every mole of NO_2 that is formed, $\dfrac{1}{2}$ mol N_2O_5 is decomposed.
Write the equation for the rate of decomposition of $N_2O_5(g)$ relative to the rate of formation of $NO_2(g)$.	$\dfrac{\Delta [N_2O_5]}{\Delta t} = \dfrac{1}{2}\left(\dfrac{\Delta [NO_2]}{\Delta t}\right)$
Substitute the numerical values into the equation and solve the equation.	$\dfrac{\Delta [N_2O_5]}{\Delta t} = \dfrac{1}{2}\left(5.00 \times 10^{-6} \,\dfrac{\text{mol}}{\text{L} \cdot \text{s}}\right)$ $= 2.50 \times 10^{-6} \,\dfrac{\text{mol}}{\text{L} \cdot \text{s}}$ The rate of consumption of $N_2O_5(g)$ is 2.50×10^{-6} mol/L·s.

Continued on next page

b. Determine the ratio of $O_2(g)$ to $NO_2(g)$.	1 mol O_2 is formed for every 4 mol NO_2 formed, or $\dfrac{O_2}{NO_2} = \dfrac{1}{4}$
Use the coefficients in the balanced equation to determine the rate of formation of $O_2(g)$ relative to the rate of formation of $NO_2(g)$.	For every mole of NO_2 formed, $\dfrac{1}{4}$ mol O_2 is formed.
Write the equation for the rate of formation of $O_2(g)$ relative to the rate of formation of $NO_2(g)$.	$\dfrac{\Delta [O_2]}{\Delta t} = \dfrac{1}{4}\left(\dfrac{\Delta [NO_2]}{\Delta t}\right)$
Substitute the numerical values into the equation and solve the equation.	$\dfrac{\Delta [O_2]}{\Delta t} = \dfrac{1}{4}\left(5.0 \times 10^{-6}\,\dfrac{\text{mol}}{\text{L}\cdot\text{s}}\right)$ $= 1.25 \times 10^{-6}\,\dfrac{\text{mol}}{\text{L}\cdot\text{s}}$ The rate of production of $O_2(g)$ is 1.25×10^{-6} mol/L·s.

Check Your Solution

From the coefficients in the balanced chemical equation, you can see that the rate of decomposition of $N_2O_5(g)$ is $\dfrac{2}{4}$ or $\dfrac{1}{2}$, which is also the rate of formation of $NO_2(g)$. The rate of formation of $O_2(g)$ is $\dfrac{1}{2}$ the rate of decomposition of $N_2O_5(g)$.

Practice Problems

1. In the reaction A + 2B → 3C + 4D, the initial concentration of A was 0.0415 mol/L, and after 14.7 min the concentration of A was 0.0206 mol/L. What is the average rate of consumption in moles per litre per second of reactant B?

2. Calculate the average rate of a reaction, given the following data:

   Reaction Data

Time (s)	Concentration (mol/L)
60	5.00×10^{-2}
85	3.25×10^{-2}

3. For the reaction shown below, the average rate of formation of $CO_2(g)$ is 5.50×10^{-4} mol/s.
   $Br_2(aq) + HCOOH(aq) \rightarrow$
   $\qquad 2Br^-(aq) + 2H^+(aq) + CO_2(g)$
   a. What amount in moles of $CO_2(g)$ is formed in 5.00 min?
   b. How does this compare with the amount of $Br_2(aq)$ that reacts in the same time?

4. The concentration of a reactant is 4.0×10^{-2} mol/L at $t = 2.0$ min. If the average rate of consumption of the reactant from $t = 1.5$ min to $t = 2.0$ min was 0.045 mol/L·s, what was the concentration of this reactant at $t = 1.5$ min?

5. A zinc electrode is immersed in dilute sulfuric acid at 35.0°C and the following reaction occurs:
   $Zn(s) + H_2SO_4(aq) \rightarrow ZnSO_4(aq) + H_2(g)$
   The volume of $H_2(g)$ present at $t = 1.0$ min is 30.0 mL and at $t = 1.4$ min is 42.0 mL. What is the average rate of formation of $H_2(g)$ over this period of time measured in litres per second?

6. For the reaction shown below, the instantaneous rate of formation of $Br^-(aq)$ is 0.12 mol/L·s at $t = 2.0$ min.
   $3BrO^-(aq) \rightarrow BrO_3^-(aq) + 2Br^-(aq)$
   What are the instantaneous rates of formation of $BrO_3^-(aq)$ and consumption of $BrO^-(aq)$?

7. The data in the table below were obtained for the following reaction:
   $4HBr(g) + O_2(g) \rightarrow 2Br_2(g) + 2H_2O(g)$

   Reaction Data

Time (s)	[HBr] (mol/L)	[Br_2] (mol/L)
0.00	0.42	0.00
50.0	0.26	?

   a. What is the average rate of consumption of HBr(g) over 50.0 s?
   b. What is the molar concentration of $Br_2(g)$ at $t = 50.0$ s?

8. Consider the following reaction:
   $4NH_3(g) + 5O_2(g) \rightarrow 4NO(g) + 6H_2O(g)$
   Over a period of 1.80 min, the average rate of formation of NO(g) is 1.04 mol/L·s.
   What was the amount in moles of $O_2(g)$ consumed over this period of time?

9. A mass of 0.50 g of sodium metal reacts with water in 90.0 s.

$$2Na(s) + 2H_2O(\ell) \rightarrow 2NaOH(aq) + H_2(g) + \text{heat}$$

  a. Express the rate of consumption of Na(s) in moles per second.

  b. Calculate the rate at which $H_2(g)$ is generated, in litres per second, at 30.0°C and 102.4 kPa. Assume that hydrogen is an ideal gas.

10. For the reaction shown below, the instantaneous change in concentration of NO(g) is 1.4 mol/L·s.

$$2NO(g) + Cl_2(g) \rightarrow 2NOCl(g)$$

What is the rate at which $Cl_2(g)$ is consumed and the rate at which NOCl(g) is formed at this time?

Methods for Measuring Rates of Reaction

Chemists collect the data required to determine a reaction rate in a variety of ways, but all methods involve monitoring the rate at which a reactant is consumed or the rate at which a product is formed. The choice of method to be used depends on which reactant or product is measurable. For example, if a reactant or product has a specific colour, its consumption or formation can be measured quantitatively with a spectrophotometer, an instrument that measures the absorbance of light at any specific wavelength. If a gaseous product is formed, the gas can be collected and the volume measured. The mass of the non-gaseous compounds can be measured using a balance as a gaseous product escapes.

For example, consider the chemical reaction between calcium carbonate, $CaCO_3(s)$, and hydrochloric acid, 2HCl(aq). One of the products of this reaction is carbon dioxide, as shown in the following chemical equation:

$$CaCO_3(s) + 2HCl(aq) \rightarrow CaCl_2(aq) + H_2O(\ell) + CO_2(g)$$

Measuring the Volume of Gas Produced

One method of measuring the rate of this reaction is to collect the carbon dioxide being formed and measure its volume. **Figure 6.6** shows one method for measuring a gas as it is being formed by a chemical reaction. The reaction vessel (flask) has been connected to a syringe with tubing. When the reaction begins, the plunger of the syringe is pushed all the way in. As the gas escapes, it goes into the syringe, pushing the plunger back. The scale on the syringe shows how much gas has been collected.

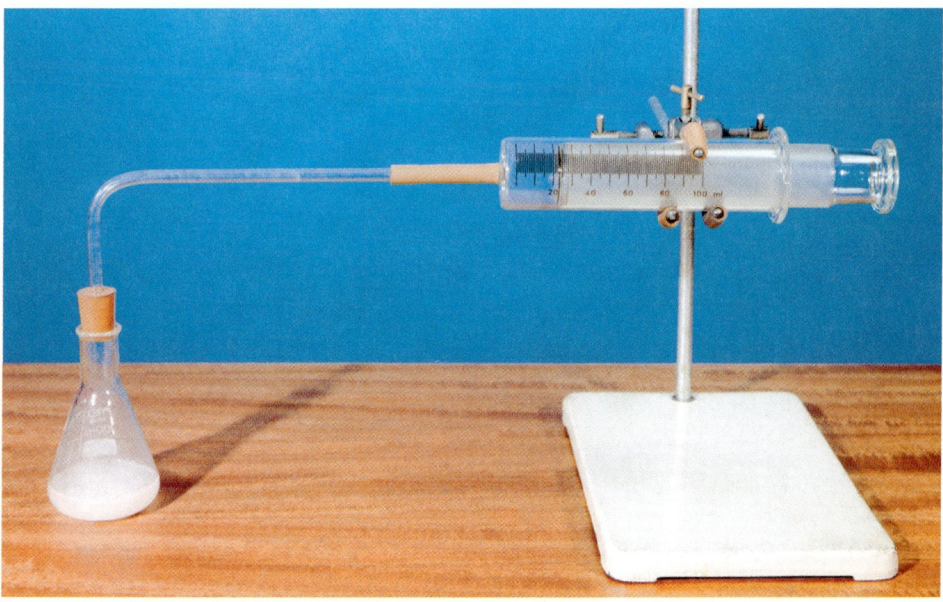

Figure 6.6 By measuring the increase in the volume of gas collected over time, the reaction rate can be determined.

Measuring the Remaining Mass

Another method for determining the rate of the chemical reaction between calcium carbonate and hydrochloric acid is to measure the decrease in mass that occurs as carbon dioxide escapes from an open container, as shown in **Figure 6.7**. The cotton wool in the opening of the flask prevents any liquid from splashing out as the solution bubbles up, but carbon dioxide easily escapes through the cotton wool. In general, the method shown in **Figure 6.7** works well for reactions that generate carbon dioxide or oxygen, but not for reactions that generate hydrogen, which has a much lower mass.

Table 6.2 summarizes some common methods for measuring reaction rates. Regardless of the method used to collect data, the rate would be reported in moles per second, requiring a conversion from the quantity measured into unit of moles.

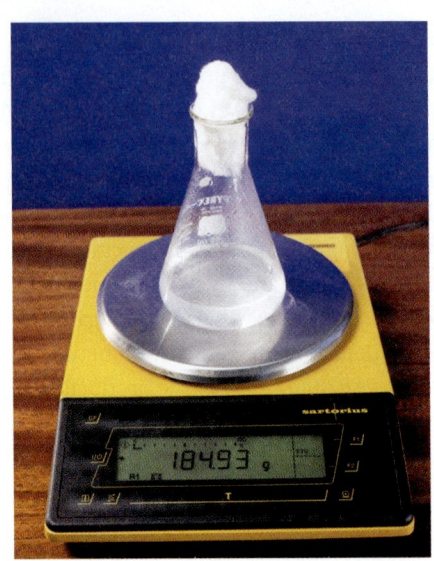

Figure 6.7 Calcium carbonate and hydrochloric acid are reacting in this flask. By measuring the loss in mass over time as carbon dioxide escapes, the reaction rate can be determined.
Analyze how the measurement of the rate of reaction might be affected if cotton wool were not used?

Table 6.2 Methods for Measuring Rates of Chemical Reactions

Property Measured	Type of Data Collected	Typical Equipment Used	Equation for Determining Rate
Volume	Volume of gas formed	Gas syringe	rate = $\frac{\Delta \text{volume}}{\Delta t}$
Mass	Change in mass of a reactant or a product	Balance	rate = $\frac{\Delta \text{mass}}{\Delta t}$
Temperature	Increase in temperature as an exothermic reaction proceeds or decrease in temperature as an endothermic reaction proceeds	Thermometer	rate = $\frac{\Delta \text{temperature}}{\Delta t}$
Pressure	Change in pressure in a closed container as a gas is formed or consumed	Pressure sensor	rate = $\frac{\Delta \text{pressure}}{\Delta t}$
Colour	Change in the amount of light of a specific wavelength absorbed by a chemical compound; changes with the concentration of the compound	Spectrophotometer	rate = $\frac{\Delta \text{absorbance}}{\Delta t}$
pH	Change in concentration of H_3O^+ or OH^- ions as a reaction proceeds	pH meter	rate = $\frac{\Delta \text{pH}}{\Delta t}$
Electrical conductivity	Change in the concentration of dissolved ions as a reaction proceeds	Electrical conductivity probe	rate = $\frac{\Delta \text{conductivity}}{\Delta t}$

Calculating Reaction Rates from Experimental Data

After data have been collected, it must be used to calculate the reaction rate. For example, suppose that a technician measures both the volume of carbon dioxide released and the mass of the remaining solution for the reaction above, between calcium carbonate and hydrochloric acid. Because volumes of gases are affected by the temperature and pressure, the technician recorded these values when taking data. The following data were recorded:

$$T = 291 \text{ K} \qquad \Delta m_{solution} = -47.0 \text{ mg}$$
$$P = 102.1 \text{ kPa} \qquad \Delta t = 5.00 \text{ min}$$
$$V_{CO_2} = 25.3 \text{ mL}$$

The calculations below show how to determine the average rate of the reaction from both the volume data and the mass data.

Calculating the rate from the volume of CO_2:
- Convert volume from mL to L.

$$25.3 \text{ mL} \left(\frac{1 \text{ L}}{1000 \text{ mL}}\right) = 0.0253 \text{ L}$$

- To find the amount in moles of a gas from a volume, use the ideal gas law and solve for n.

$$PV = nRT$$
$$n = \frac{PV}{RT}$$
$$n = \frac{(102.1 \text{ kPa})(0.0253 \text{ L})}{\left(\frac{8.314 \text{ kPa·L}}{\text{mol·K}}\right)(291 \text{ K})}$$
$$= 1.0677 \times 10^{-3} \text{ mol}$$

- Use the amount in moles and the time to calculate the rate in mol/s.

$$\text{rate} = \frac{\Delta n}{\Delta t}$$
$$= \frac{1.0677 \times 10^{-3} \text{ mol}}{5 \text{ min}\left(\frac{60 \text{ s}}{\text{min}}\right)}$$
$$= 3.559 \times 10^{-6} \frac{\text{mol}}{\text{s}}$$
$$= 3.56 \times 10^{-6} \frac{\text{mol}}{\text{s}}$$

Calculating the rate from the change in the mass of the solution:
- The decrease in the mass of the solution is the mass of the $CO_2(g)$ that escaped. Therefore, the mass of the $CO_2(g)$ was 47.0 mg.
- Determine the molar mass of $CO_2(g)$.

$$M_{CO_2} = M_C + 2M_O$$
$$= 12.01 \frac{\text{g}}{\text{mol}} + 2\left(16.00 \frac{\text{g}}{\text{mol}}\right)$$
$$= 44.01 \frac{\text{g}}{\text{mol}}$$

- Determine the amount in moles from the mass and the molar mass.

$$n = \frac{m}{M}$$
$$= \frac{(47.0 \text{ mg})\left(\frac{1 \text{ g}}{1000 \text{ mg}}\right)}{44.01 \frac{\text{g}}{\text{mol}}}$$
$$= 0.0010679 \text{ mol}$$

- Use the amount in moles and the time to calculate the rate in moles per second.

$$\text{rate} = \frac{\Delta n}{\Delta t}$$
$$= \frac{1.0679 \times 10^{-3} \text{ mol}}{5 \text{ min}\left(\frac{60 \text{ s}}{\text{min}}\right)}$$
$$= 3.5597 \times 10^{-6} \frac{\text{mol}}{\text{s}}$$
$$= 3.56 \times 10^{-6} \frac{\text{mol}}{\text{s}}$$

Notice that the same answer is obtained with both types of data. These data can be used to find the rate in terms of either the hydrochloric acid or calcium carbonate.

To use the other forms of data listed in **Table 6.2**, information that relates the form of data to amount in moles or concentration must be used. For example, when using absorbance data from a spectrophotometer, the absorbance of standard solutions of known concentrations will be measured at the wavelength at which the solution absorbs the most light. These measurements will be used to find the correct conversion factor for absorbance versus concentration. Similar methods can be found for the other forms of data.

Section 6.1 Review

Section Summary

- A reaction rate is the speed at which a chemical reaction proceeds. A reaction rate is measured by the change in the amount of reactants consumed or products formed over a given time interval.
- A reaction rate is always expressed as a positive value.
- The instantaneous rate of a reaction is the rate of the reaction at a particular point in time.
- The average rate of a chemical reaction is the change in the concentration of a reactant or product per unit time over a given time interval.
- Any measurable property that is related to a change in the amount of a reactant consumed or product formed during a chemical reaction can be used to determine the reaction rate.

Review Questions

1. **K/U** List four applications where an understanding of the rate of a reaction can benefit society.

2. **K/U** Answer the questions about reaction rates.
   a. Distinguish between the terms *instantaneous* rate of reaction and *average* rate of reaction.
   b. The concentrations of a product measured in mol/L are collected over time measured in seconds. How can these data be used to determine the instantaneous and average rates of the reaction?
   c. What are the units for the instantaneous rate and average rate that would come from using these data?

3. **T/I** A solution of copper(II) sulfate, $CuSO_4(aq)$, has a concentration of 0.50 mol/L. A piece of zinc metal is placed in the solution. After 280 s, the concentration of the $CuSO_4(aq)$ is 0.42 mol/L. At what average rate is the concentration of $CuSO_4(aq)$ changing over this period of time?

4. **T/I** A piece of metal initially has a mass of 6.29 g. Exactly 2 days later, it has corroded and the mass of the metal is now 6.18 g. Express the rate at which the metal corroded over this period of time in grams per second.

5. **T/I** As potassium chlorate decomposes, oxygen gas is released. The total volume of $O_2(g)$ produced is 88.4 mL. If the average rate of the formation of oxygen over the course of the reaction is 0.670 mL/s, how long did the reaction last?

6. **T/I** A graph of concentration vs. time for the formation of a product in a reaction has been plotted. The slope of the tangent to this graph was measured at two different time points: $t = 2.0$ min and $t = 5.0$ min. One slope is 4.5×10^{-2} mol/L·min and the other is 9.2×10^{-2} mol/L·min.
   a. What does the tangent represent?
   b. Which slope was measured at $t = 5$ min? Give a reason for your answer.
   c. Is it possible that these measurements could represent the consumption of the reactant? Give a reason for your answer.

7. **C** You and your lab partner are designing an investigation to determine the rate of the reaction between magnesium ribbon and a dilute acid.
   a. What questions would you ask in order to decide which is easier to measure: the instantaneous rate or the average rate of reaction?
   b. Which do you believe would be easier: determining the instantaneous rate or the average rate? Give a reason for your answer.

8. **K/U** Refer to **Figure 6.3**. What is happening in the reaction at the point in time where the two lines intersect?

9. **C** For the reaction shown below, all of AB is consumed.
$$AB \rightarrow A + B$$
Sketch a graph of concentration vs. time for the reactant and products as the reaction proceeds to completion.

10. **C** While working in groups to review the concepts related to rates of reactions, a statement is made that as a reaction slows down, the instantaneous rate and the average rate of a reaction are essentially the same. Do you agree with this statement? Explain your answer using a graph of concentration of product vs. time.

11. **K/U** In order to use the rate of change in the quantity of one substance in a reaction to determine the rate of change of another, what information must be known?

12. **A** For the reaction shown below, NO(g) is produced at a rate of 0.080 mol/L·s.
$$4NH_3(g) + 5O_2(g) \rightarrow 4NO(g) + 6H_2O(g)$$
At this same point in time, what is the rate of consumption of $O_2(g)$ and the rate of formation of $H_2O(g)$?

SECTION 6.2 Collision Theory and Factors Affecting Rates of Reaction

Chemists propose that, for a reaction to occur, reacting particles (atoms, molecules, or ions) must collide with one another. This proposition, known as **collision theory**, is supported by the kinetic molecular theory of gases. Consider, for example, a 1 mL sample of gas at room temperature and standard atmospheric pressure. Chemists estimate that approximately 10^{28} collisions among gas molecules take place in the sample every second. If each collision resulted in a reaction, however, all the reactions would be complete in about a nanosecond (10^{-9} s). In fact, these reactions can occur much more slowly than this. Thus, it is reasonable to infer that only a small fraction of collisions between reactants results in a reaction.

Key Terms

collision theory
activation energy, E_a
activated complex
catalyst
enzyme

Effective Collisions

For a collision between reactants to result in a reaction, the collision must be *effective*. An effective collision—one that results in the formation of products—must satisfy both of the criteria (conditions) outlined below.

For a collision between reactant particles to be effective
1. the orientation of the reactants (the collision geometry) must be favourable; and
2. the collision must occur with sufficient energy.

collision theory the theory that a reaction occurs between two particles (atoms, molecules, or ions) if they collide at the correct orientation and with certain minimum energy

Effective Collision Criteria 1: The Correct Orientation of Reactants

In order for a reaction to occur, reacting particles must collide with the proper orientation relative to one another. This is known as having the correct *collision geometry*. The importance of proper collision geometry can be illustrated by the following reaction:

$$NO(g) + NO_3(g) \rightarrow 2NO_2(g)$$

Figure 6.8 shows five of the many possible ways in which nitrogen monoxide, NO(g), and nitrogen trioxide, NO_3(g), can collide. Only *one* of the five possibilities has the correct collision geometry for a reaction to occur. As shown in the diagram, only a specific orientation of the two reactants before collision leads to the formation of two molecules of nitrogen dioxide, NO_2(g). Notice that, in the effective collision, the angle at which the nitrogen atom in the nitrogen monoxide molecule is approaching the oxygen atom in the nitrogen trioxide molecule is the same angle as that formed in the nitrogen dioxide molecules.

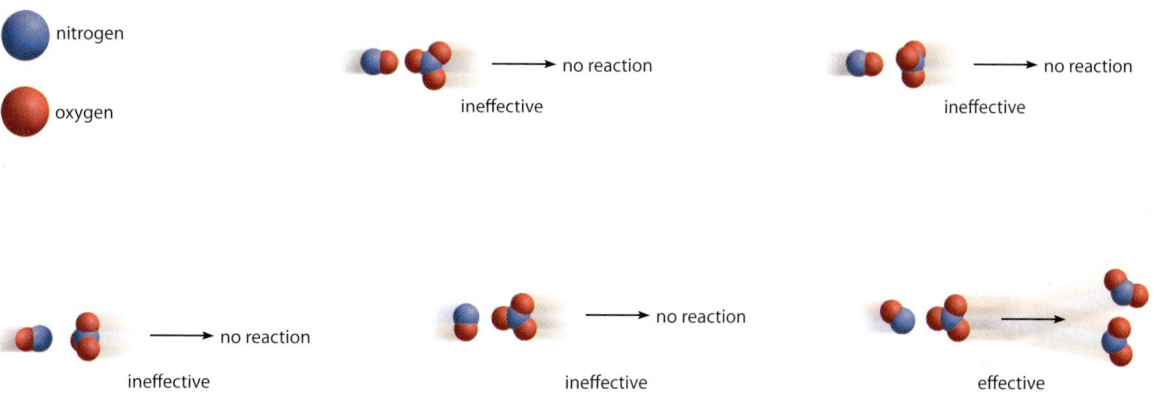

Figure 6.8 Only one of these possible orientations of NO(g) and NO_3(g) relative to each other will lead to the formation of the product, NO_2(g).
Explain *why all but one of the collisions shown here are ineffective.*

activation energy, E_a
the minimum amount of energy (collision energy) required to initiate a chemical reaction

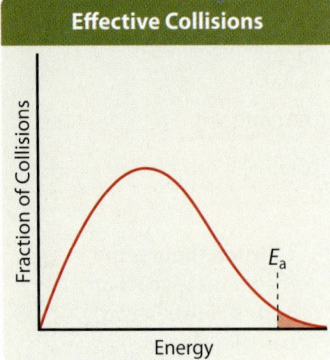

Figure 6.9 The area under a Maxwell-Boltzmann distribution curve represents the distribution of the kinetic energy of collisions at a given temperature. At any given temperature, only a small fraction of the molecules in a sample have enough kinetic energy to react.

Figure 6.10 Potential energy diagrams for an exothermic reaction (**A**) and an endothermic reaction (**B**). In both cases, a reaction can occur only if molecules collide with enough kinetic energy to overcome the barrier represented by the activation energy.

Effective Collision Criteria 2: Sufficient Activation Energy

In addition to having the correct collision geometry, reactant particles must collide with one another with sufficient energy for a reaction to occur. In most reactions, only a small fraction of the total collisions have sufficient energy for a reaction to occur. The **activation energy**, E_a, of a reaction is the minimum collision energy required for the reaction to take place.

The collision energy depends on the kinetic energy of the colliding particles. Plotting the number of collisions between the particles in a substance at a given temperature against the kinetic energy of each collision gives a curve like the one in **Figure 6.9**. This type of distribution is called a *Maxwell-Boltzmann distribution*. The dotted line indicates the activation energy. The shaded part of the graph indicates the fraction of the total collisions that have energy equal to or greater than the activation energy. The activation energy is independent of temperature—that is, it does not change when temperature changes.

Suppose that a particular set of reactants collide 10 000 times per second, and the fraction of effective collisions is 1 reaction/50 collisions. The reaction rate could be expressed as 10 000 collisions/s × 1 reaction/50 collisions, or 200 reactions/s. This rate would change if either the number of collisions per second or the fraction of effective collisions changed. For example, if the fraction of effective collisions increased to 1 reaction/25 collisions, the reaction rate would double to 400 reactions/s.

Representing the Progress of a Chemical Reaction

The changes in potential energy during a chemical reaction can be represented using a potential energy diagram, as shown in **Figure 6.10**. On the left side of the curve, the reactants are approaching each other. Moving from left to right of the curve, the potential energy increases as the reactants get closer to each other. If the collision energy is not as great as the maximum potential energy at the top of the curve, the reactants cannot get close enough to have an effective collision, so they instead "bounce off" each other ineffectually. The small fraction of reactants that have sufficient kinetic energy will change in configuration and are then said to be in their *transition state*, somewhere between reactants and products. From the transition state, the process can go forward to form products or go backward and re-form the reactants. The products or the re-formed reactants will move apart. The collisions are effective only if the compound in the transition state breaks apart in the way that forms products.

In **Figure 6.10A**, the products have a lower energy than the reactants have. This decrease in potential energy means that energy was released in the reaction, so the reaction was exothermic. In **Figure 6.10B**, the products have more potential energy; thus, the reaction is endothermic, because it absorbed energy. The difference between the potential energy of the reactants and the maximum potential energy is the activation energy, E_a. The difference between the potential energy of the reactants and the potential energy of the products is the enthalpy change, ΔH.

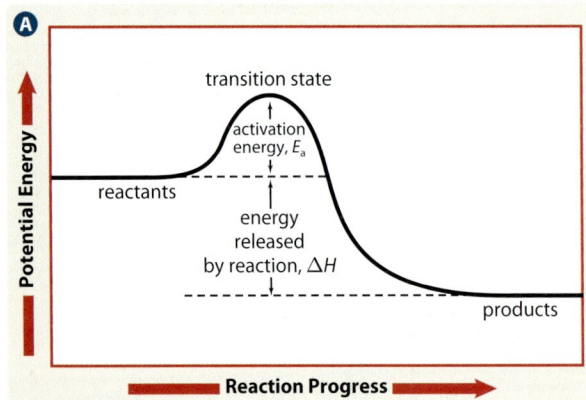
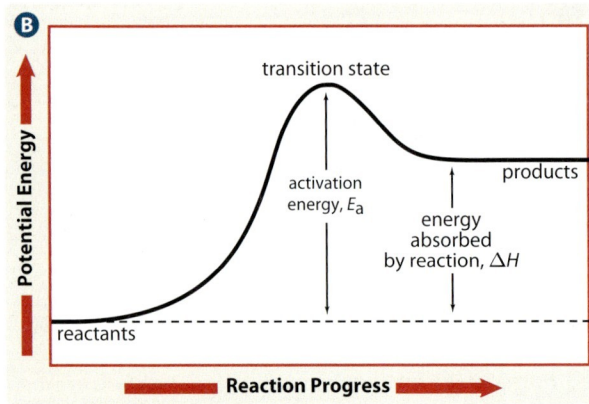

Learning Check

7. What criteria must be met in order to have an effective collision between reactant particles?

8. In 1 mL of a gas, there can be about 10^{28} collisions per second between reactant particles. With such a high number of collisions, you might expect all chemical reactions to go to completion instantaneously. Why does this not happen?

9. In order to have an effective collision, why is it necessary for the reactant particles to be properly oriented relative to one another?

10. Explain how you would know whether a reaction was exothermic or endothermic by examining a potential energy diagram that had no labels on it.

11. Answer these questions about activation energy.
    a. What is the meaning of the term *activation energy*, E_a?
    b. Reactions with a high E_a are generally slow at room temperature. Use collision theory to suggest an explanation for this statement.

12. List at least three characteristics of a reaction that you can determine from a potential energy diagram. Explain how you can determine those characteristics.

Activation Energy and Enthalpy

There is no way to predict the activation energy of a reaction from its enthalpy change. A highly exothermic reaction can have a very high activation energy and occur very slowly at room temperature. Conversely, a reaction may release very little heat, or even be endothermic, and still occur rapidly at room temperature. The enthalpy change of a reaction is determined only on the basis of the difference in the potential energy of the reactants and the products; it is independent of any process that occurs during the reaction.

The activation energy of a reaction is determined by analyzing the reaction rate at various temperatures. In general, reactions with low activation energies tend to proceed quickly at room temperature, regardless of whether they are endothermic or exothermic. However, exothermic or endothermic reactions with high activation energies tend to proceed slowly at room temperature.

Since gasoline is highly flammable, why does it not burst spontaneously into flames? The answer is that gasoline, which is mostly octane, requires a spark—a small *energy input*—to initiate combustion. The spark provides enough energy for a few octane and oxygen molecules to overcome the activation energy barrier. Once ignited, the gasoline continues to burn, because the energy released increases the kinetic energy of many other molecules, which can then overcome the activation energy barrier. Notice in **Figure 6.11** that the activation energy is relatively small compared with the enthalpy change.

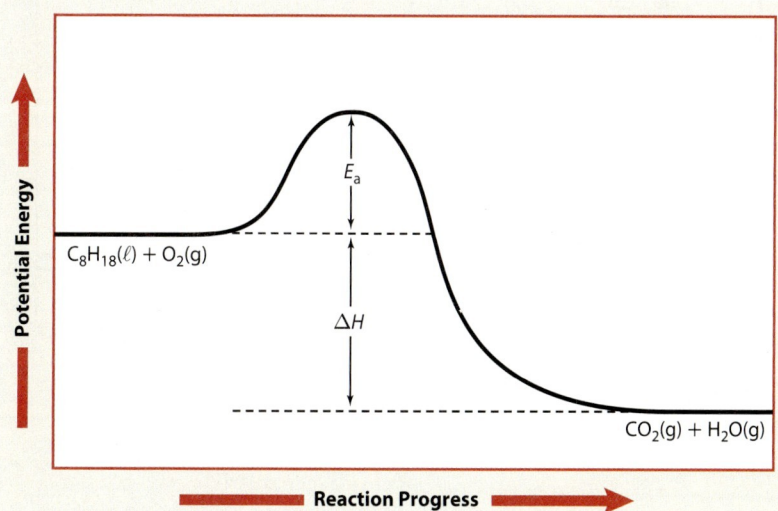

Figure 6.11 This potential energy diagram for the combustion of gasoline shows that gasoline does not burst into flame, because an activation energy is needed to initiate the reaction.

Activation Energy for Reversible Reactions

Many reactions can proceed in two directions: forward and reverse. For example, carbon monoxide and nitrogen dioxide react to form carbon dioxide and nitrogen monoxide, NO(g). This reaction, like many others, is reversible. Carbon dioxide and nitrogen monoxide can react to form carbon monoxide and nitrogen dioxide. The forward and reverse chemical equations are written below. Recall from Chapter 5 that when you write an equation with the ΔH_r notation, you must change the sign of ΔH_r for the equation of the reverse reaction.

Forward: $CO(g) + NO_2(g) \rightarrow CO_2(g) + NO(g)$ $\qquad \Delta H_r = -226.1$ kJ
Reverse: $CO_2(g) + NO(g) \rightarrow CO(g) + NO_2(g)$ $\qquad \Delta H_r = +226.1$ kJ

A potential energy diagram can represent the reaction in both the forward and reverse directions, as shown in **Figure 6.12**. To follow the forward reaction, go from left to right on the diagram. To follow the reverse reaction, go from right to left. Because the activation energies for the forward and reverse directions differ, add the subscript (fwd) to the activation energy for the forward direction: $E_{a(fwd)}$. Similarly, add the subscript (rev) to the activation energy for the reverse direction: $E_{a(rev)}$. Using this graph, you can see the relationships among the activation energies for the forward and reverse directions as well as the enthalpy change. The equation below also represents the relationship between these three terms.

$$E_{a(fwd)} - E_{a(rev)} = \Delta H_r$$

Thus, for exothermic reactions, ΔH_r is negative and the activation energy of the forward reaction is less than the activation energy for the reverse reaction. Conversely, for endothermic reactions, ΔH_r is positive and the activation energy of the forward reaction is larger than the activation energy of the reverse reaction.

Also included in **Figure 6.12** is the chemical species that exists at the top of the activation energy barrier, or in the transition state. It is referred to as an **activated complex**. An activated complex is neither a product nor a reactant. It is a temporary arrangement of atoms that form as bonds are breaking and new bonds are forming. Because the activated complex contains partial bonds, it is highly unstable. It can break down either to form products or to re-form reactants. The activated complex is like a rock teetering on top of a mountain. It could fall either way.

activated complex a chemical species temporarily formed by the colliding reactant molecules before the final product of the reaction is formed

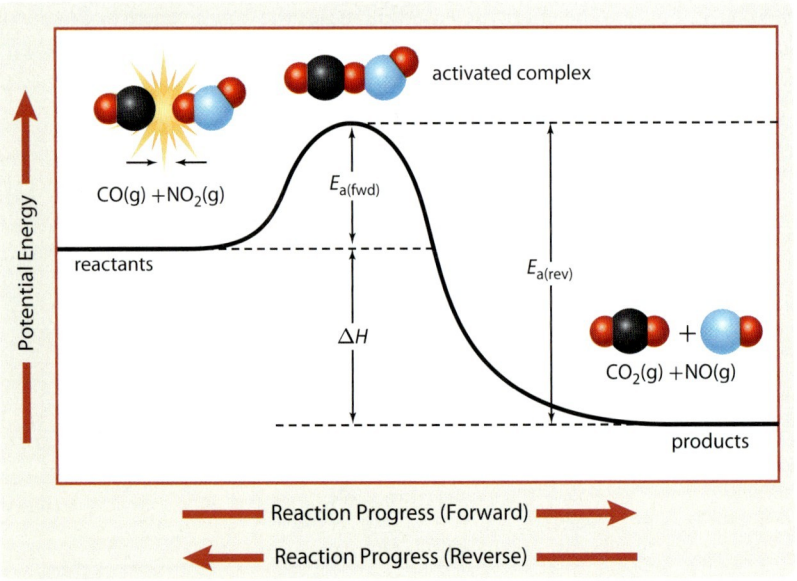

Figure 6.12 This potential energy diagram shows both a forward reaction between carbon monoxide and nitrogen dioxide and the reverse reaction between carbon dioxide and nitrogen monoxide. Atoms of the molecules shown are represented as follows: carbon is black, nitrogen is blue, and oxygen is red.

Learning Check

13. How does the magnitude of the activation energy generally affect the rate of a reaction?

14. Use collision theory to answer the following questions.
  a. Why is it necessary to use a lit match or other small flame to ignite a piece of paper?
  b. After lighting a barbecue that is fuelled by natural gas, the flame continues to burn on its own. Why is it not necessary to continually ignite the flame?

15. The enthalpy change for the conversion of graphite to diamond is +1.9 kJ/mol.

$$C_{graphite} + 1.9 \text{ kJ} \rightarrow C_{diamond}$$

This small energy difference suggests this conversion is very simple. What information is not shown by the equation that would help explain why this conversion is not a simple process?

16. Answer the following questions about activated complexes.
  a. Explain what an activated complex is.
  b. Examine **Figure 6.8** and make a sketch of the activated complex for this reaction.

17. Given the data for a reaction, $E_{a(fwd)} = +45$ kJ, $E_{a(rev)} = +50$ kJ, is the reaction endothermic or exothermic? What is the magnitude of ΔH_r?

18. The decomposition of carbon disulfide, $CS_2(\ell)$, into its elements is represented by the equation shown below. Sketch the potential energy diagram corresponding to the *formation* equation for carbon disulfide.

$$CS_2(\ell) \rightarrow C(s) + 2S(s) + 89.0 \text{ kJ}$$

Analyzing Reactions Using Potential Energy Diagrams

Consider the substitution reaction between a hydroxide ion and bromomethane:

$$BrCH_3(aq) + OH^-(aq) \rightarrow CH_3OH(aq) + Br^-(aq)$$

Figure 6.13 is a potential energy diagram that represents this reaction. It includes depictions at particular times of the reactants, the activated complex, and the products as the reaction proceeds.

For a reaction to take place, the bromomethane molecule and the hydroxide ion must collide. If the collision occurs at a favourable orientation with sufficient kinetic energy, the kinetic energy of the colliding particles is converted into potential energy. This potential energy is stored in the partial bonds of the activated complex, which is in transition between the reactants and the products. When the partial bonds of the activated complex re-form as chemical bonds, the potential energy that was stored is converted back into kinetic energy as the particles again separate. This conversion results in a decrease in potential energy with respect to the activated complex.

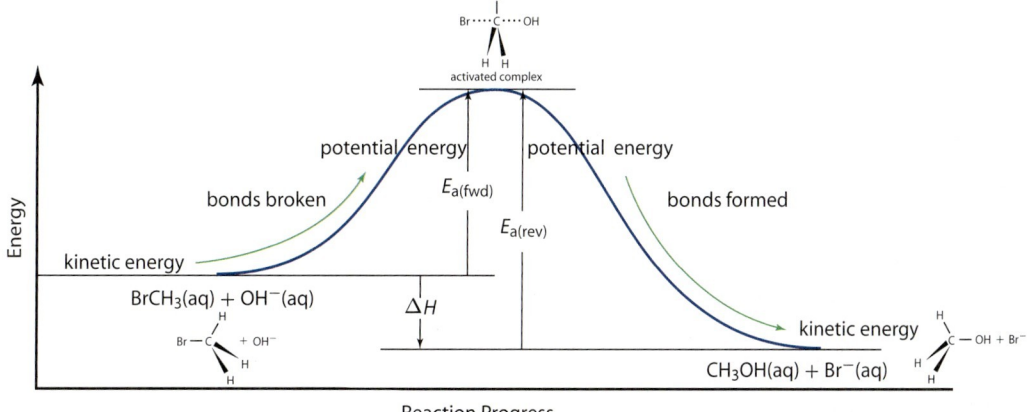

Figure 6.13 As the reactants collide, chemical bonds break and form. This potential energy diagram represents the reactants, the activated complex, and the products in the reaction.

Sample Problem

Representing a Reaction with a Potential Energy Diagram

Problem
Carbon dioxide, $CO_2(g)$, reacts with nitrogen monoxide, $NO(g)$. Carbon monoxide, $CO(g)$, and nitrogen dioxide, $NO_2(g)$, are formed. Draw a potential energy diagram to illustrate the progress of the reaction. (You do not need to draw your diagram to scale.) Label the axes, the transition state, and sketch and label the reactants, the products, and the activated complex. Indicate the activation energy of the forward reaction, $E_{a(fwd)} = +361$ kJ, as well as $\Delta H_r = +226$ kJ. Calculate the activation energy of the reverse reaction, $E_{a(rev)}$, and show it on the graph.

What Is Required?
You need to draw a potential energy diagram for the reaction, labelling the x-axis and y-axis, and the transition state. You also need to include sketches and labels for the reactants, the products, and the activated complex, and indicate the activation energy and ΔH_r of the forward reaction. You then need to calculate the activation energy of the reverse reaction and show it on the graph.

What Is Given?
Activation energy of the forward reaction: $E_{a(fwd)} = +361$ kJ

Enthalpy change of the forward reaction: $\Delta H_r = +226$ kJ

Plan Your Strategy	Act on Your Strategy
Determine the activation energy of the reverse reaction using the formula $E_{a(fwd)} - E_{a(rev)} = \Delta H_r$.	$E_{a(rev)} = E_{a(fwd)} - \Delta H_r$ $= +361$ kJ $- (+226$ kJ$)$ $= +135$ kJ

Draw and label the potential energy diagram for the reaction.

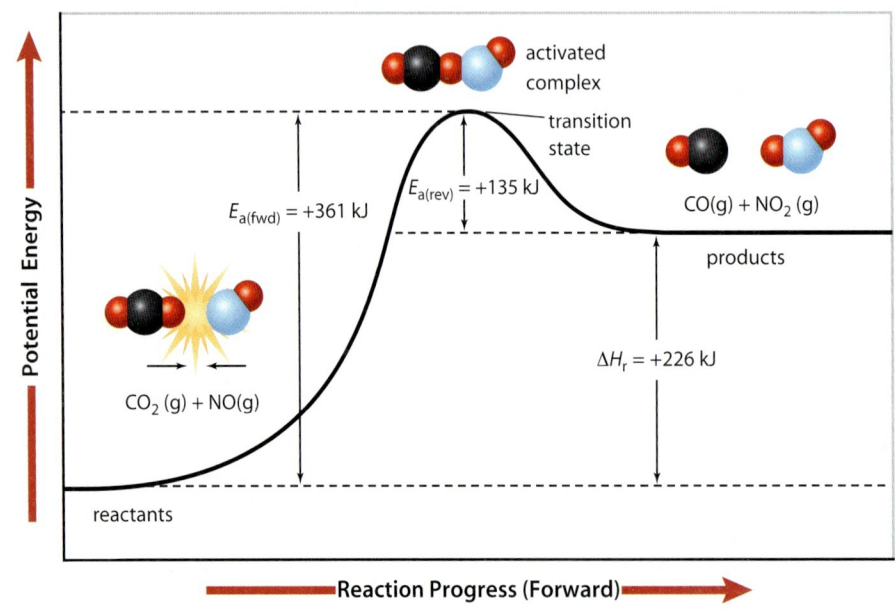

Check Your Solution
Look carefully at the potential energy diagram. Check that you have labelled it completely. Because the forward reaction is endothermic, the reactants should be shown at a lower energy level than the products, and they are. Using the potential energy diagram, you can confirm that the activation energy of the reverse reaction is +135 kJ.

Practice Problems

11. Complete the following potential energy diagram by adding the following labels: an appropriate label for the x-axis and y-axis, $E_{a(fwd)}$, $E_{a(rev)}$, ΔH_r.

  a. Is the forward reaction endothermic or exothermic?

  b. Which has the higher potential energy, the reactants or the products?

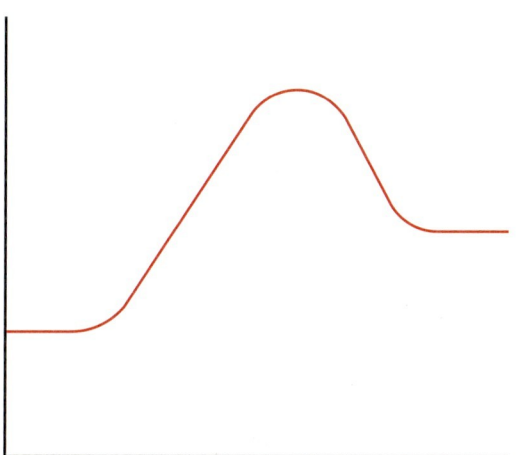

12. Consider the following reaction:

$$AB + C \rightarrow AC + B \quad \Delta H_r = +65 \text{ kJ}, E_{a(rev)} = +34 \text{ kJ}$$

Draw and label a potential energy diagram for this reaction. Calculate and label $E_{a(fwd)}$.

13. Consider the reaction below:

$$C + D \rightarrow CD \quad E_{a(fwd)} = +61 \text{ kJ}, E_{a(rev)} = +150 \text{ kJ}$$

Draw and label a potential energy diagram for this reaction. Calculate and label ΔH_r.

14. Using the potential energy diagram below, estimate the values for $E_{a(fwd)}$, $E_{a(rev)}$, and ΔH_r. Is the reaction endothermic or exothermic?

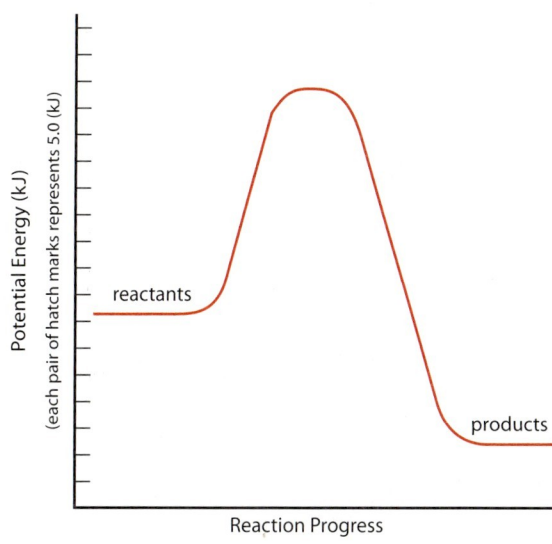

15. In the upper atmosphere, oxygen exists as $O_2(g)$, as ozone, $O_3(g)$, and as individual oxygen atoms, $O(g)$. Ozone and atomic oxygen react to form two molecules of oxygen gas. The enthalpy change is −392 kJ and the activation energy is +19.0 kJ. Draw and label a potential energy diagram. Include a value for $E_{a(rev)}$.

16. For a reaction, on an arbitrary scale, the potential energies are as follows: activated complex, +112 kJ; reactants, +36 kJ; products, +78 kJ.

  a. Determine the activation energy and the enthalpy change for the reaction.

  b. Draw a labelled potential energy diagram for the reaction, indicating the relative energies of the reactants, products, and activated complex.

17. Refer to the list of molar enthalpies of combustion for hydrocarbons in **Table 5.4**.

  a. Write the balanced thermochemical equation for the combustion of methane gas, $CH_4(g)$.

  b. Draw a potential energy diagram that would reasonably represent this combustion reaction. Indicate the ΔH_{comb} and a molecular structure that could represent an activated complex in this potential energy diagram.

18. When steam is passed over hot iron, a reaction occurs as shown below.

$$3Fe(s) + 4H_2O(g) \rightleftharpoons Fe_3O_4(s) + 4H_2(g)$$
$$\Delta H_r = -151.2 \text{ kJ}$$

The activation energy for the reverse reaction, $E_{a(rev)}$, is +200.71 kJ.

  a. Calculate the activation energy for the forward reaction.

  b. Draw a labelled potential energy diagram showing the enthalpy change, and the activation energies for the forward and reverse reactions.

19. The decomposition of dinitrogen tetroxide(g), $N_2O_4(g)$, to nitrogen dioxide, $NO_2(g)$, is a reversible reaction. The activation energy for the decomposition reaction is +58.6 kJ.

$$N_2O_4(g) + 55.3 \text{ kJ} \rightarrow 2NO_2(g)$$

Draw a potential energy diagram for the reaction showing appropriate labels for both axes, $E_{a(fwd)}$, $E_{a(rev)}$, and ΔH_r.

20. What is $E_{a(fwd)}$ for the reaction represented below that has $E_{a(rev)} = +235$ kJ?

$$A + 2CD + 85 \text{ kJ} \rightarrow G$$

Factors Affecting Reaction Rate

An understanding of collision theory contributes to an understanding of the factors that affect the rate at which a chemical reaction proceeds. In general, any factor that increases the frequency of collisions between particles also increases the rate of a chemical reaction, and any factor that decreases the frequency of collisions between particles also decreases the reaction rate. These factors include the following:

- nature of the reactants
- concentration of a solution
- temperature
- pressure of gases
- surface area of the particles of a solid reactant
- presence of a catalyst

A **catalyst** is a substance that increases a reaction rate without being consumed during the reaction. The following pages discuss how each factor, including the presence of a catalyst, can change the rate of a chemical reaction.

catalyst a substance that increases the rate of a chemical reaction without being consumed by the reaction

The Nature of the Reactants Influences the Reaction Rate

The reaction rate depends in part on the nature, or types, of the reactants involved and the types of chemical bonds that are breaking and forming during a chemical reaction. Reactions between ions in solution tend to have a rapid reaction rate, for two reasons. The first is that no bonds must be broken before new substances can form, because ions dissolve in water and move freely. The second reason is that positive and negative charges attract each other.

In general, like the reactions between ions, the reactions between acids and bases, which form salts, proceed rapidly because the acids and bases are often oppositely charged and thus attract each other.

Rates of reactions for molecules are usually slower than for ions. In molecular reactions, existing bonds must be broken before new bonds can form. During a particular chemical reaction, if the molecules of the reactants are large, must break apart, or have strong covalent bonds, then the reaction rate is generally slow. However, if the reaction is highly exothermic, like the reaction between octane and oxygen, and there is an external source of activation energy, then a few molecules will react. The energy released will give more reactant molecules enough kinetic energy to react, and the reaction will go to completion.

Concentration Influences the Reaction Rate

When a reaction occurs in solution, increasing the concentration of reactants leads to a greater number of collisions per unit time, because there are more particles in the same volume, as shown in **Figure 6.14**. Therefore, a greater number of effective collisions are likely to occur, and so the reaction rate increases. However, as the reaction progresses and the concentration of products increases, the reaction rate tends to decrease because the remaining reactants are more likely to collide with a product rather than with another reactant.

Figure 6.14 As the concentration of reactant particles increases, the rate of collision between the reactants also increases. Therefore, the rate of reaction increases.

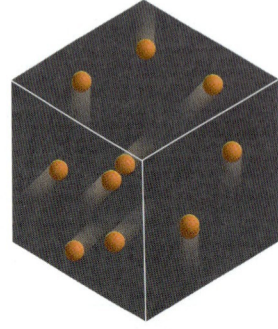
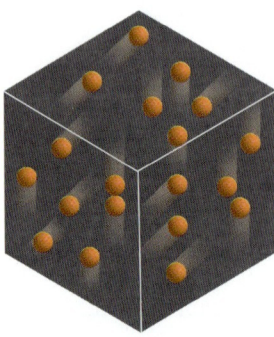

Temperature Influences the Reaction Rate

The distribution of kinetic energy of the individual particles of a substance changes as the temperature of the substance changes. When temperature increases, particles have more kinetic energy. As a result, the frequency of collisions increases, and the number of effective collisions increases per unit of time. **Figure 6.15** shows the distribution of kinetic energy in a sample of reacting gases at two different temperatures, T_1 and T_2, where $T_2 > T_1$. The activation energy is indicated by the dashed vertical line. Two observations are apparent from the graph:

- At both temperatures, a relatively small fraction of collisions have enough energy for a collision to result in a reaction. ("Enough energy" means greater than or equal to activation energy.)
- As the temperature of a sample increases, the fraction of collisions with energy equal to or greater than the activation energy increases significantly.

These observations explain why, for most reactions, the reaction rate will increase at higher temperatures. At higher temperatures, more collisions are effective.

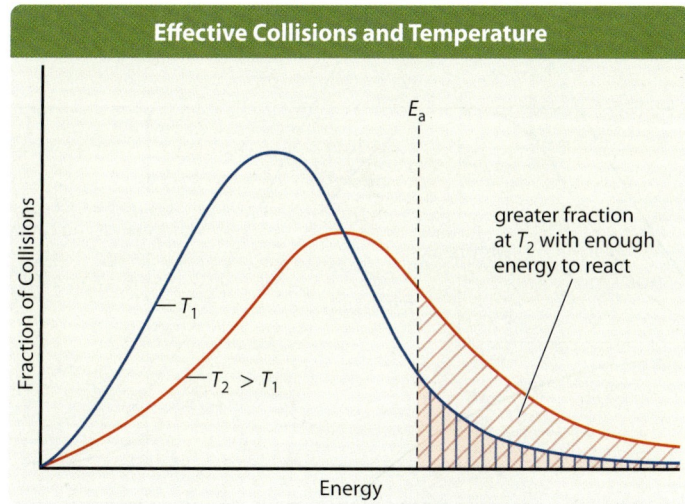

Figure 6.15 At increased temperatures, more particles collide with enough energy to react with one another. Therefore, increasing temperature speeds up the rate of a chemical reaction. *Explain* how the relative number of collisions having sufficient activation energy is displayed for the two curves.

Pressure Influences the Reaction Rate

For reactants that are gases, increasing the pressure increases the number of collisions per unit time, which increases the reaction rate. In accordance with Boyle's law, pressure can be increased by adding more reactant gas particles to the fixed volume in which a reaction is taking place, or by reducing the volume of the reaction container.

Surface Area Influences the Reaction Rate

To understand the effect of surface area of solid reactants on the rate of reaction, think about the process of sugar dissolving in a hot beverage. The greater the surface area, the faster the sugar dissolves. For example, powdered sugar dissolves faster than granular sugar, which dissolves faster than rock candy.

Smaller pieces of reactants have a greater amount of exposed surface area compared with larger pieces that have the same total mass. Therefore, the chances of effective collisions increase, and the rate of the reaction increases. However, this increase in reaction rate is not always desirable. Powdered materials, for example, are highly combustible, because they have a very large surface area. For example, coal dust in mines, flour dust in mills, or sawdust in a lumber mill can explode if a spark sets off a combustion reaction.

Suggested Investigation

Plan Your Own Investigation 6-A, Examining Reaction Rates

A Catalyst Influences the Reaction Rate

For some chemical reactions, the activation energy is so high that the reaction will either not occur at all or will occur very slowly, over days or even years. However, it is possible to increase the rate of a reaction by adding a particular substance known as a catalyst. A catalyst is a substance that increases the rate of a chemical reaction by lowering the activation energy. When the activation energy is lowered, a larger fraction of reactants have a kinetic energy equal to or greater than the activation energy. Speeding up reactions to make them practical and profitable for industrial applications is important, and it is often achieved by means of catalysts.

A *catalyzed reaction* is a reaction in which a catalyst has been used. The potential energy diagram in **Figure 6.16** compares the activation energy for an uncatalyzed reaction and the activation energy for the same reaction with the addition of a catalyst.

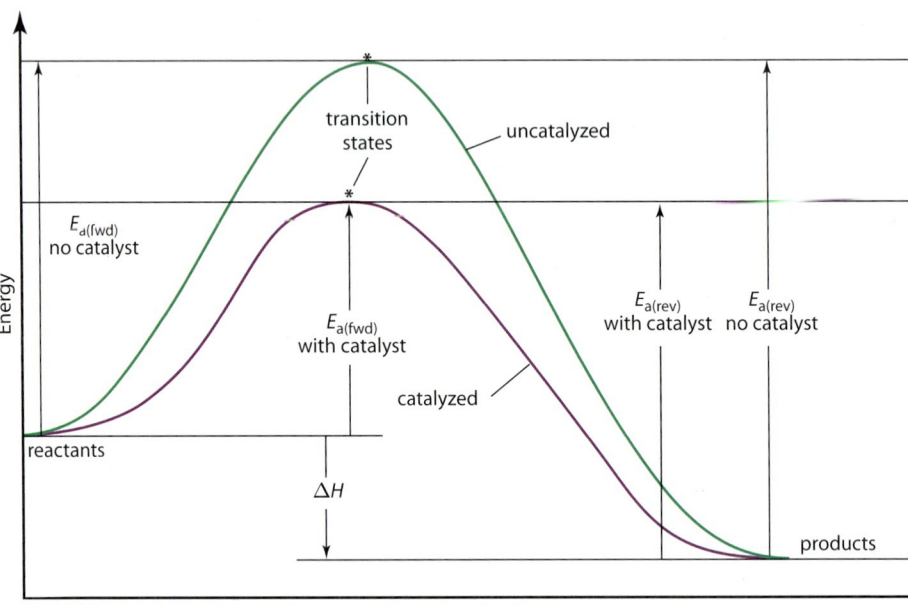

Figure 6.16 A catalyst causes the activation energy to be lower for a chemical reaction. A catalyst also increases the rate of the reverse reaction. **Analyze** what effect a catalyst has on ΔH.

Although the catalyzed reaction has the same reactants, products, and enthalpy change (ΔH) as the uncatalyzed reaction, the catalyzed reaction has a lower activation energy and therefore proceeds at a faster rate. The catalyst sometimes takes part in the reaction. However, even if the catalyst is changed during the reaction, it returns to its original condition by the time the overall reaction has reached completion.

Learning Check

19. How does collision theory explain a change in the rate of a chemical reaction?

20. Identify at least four factors that can alter the rate of a chemical reaction.

21. Use collision theory to explain the effect of a decrease in temperature on the reaction below:

$$CO(g) + \frac{1}{2}O_2(g) \rightarrow CO_2(g) \quad \Delta H_r = -283 \text{ kJ}$$

22. Iron, Fe(s), will rust as shown by the equation below:

$$Fe(s) + \frac{1}{2}O_2(g) + H_2O(\ell) \rightarrow Fe(OH)_2(s)$$

Using this equation and collision theory, explain how the rate at which rusting occurs could be slowed down.

23. Biomass fuels are now commonly manufactured as compressed pellets from waste products such as sawdust and plant material. In terms of collision theory, is there an advantage to burning this type of fuel as pellets rather than as sawdust or bulk plant material? Explain your answer.

24. The reaction $X(g) + Y(g) \rightarrow Z(s)$ occurs only at very high temperatures. Of the factors that affect the rate of reaction, which one would you expect to be the most effective in increasing the rate of the reaction? Explain your reasoning.

Catalysts in Industry

More than 3 000 000 t of catalysts are produced annually in North America. Newly discovered catalysts are patented by their manufacturers and kept as closely guarded secrets. Many reactions that produce useful compounds proceed too slowly to be used in industries. Some reactions need to be carried out at high temperatures or pressures to proceed quickly without a catalyst. These conditions, however, are expensive and dangerous to maintain. Therefore, when it is possible, chemists and engineers use catalysts to obtain products at a reasonable rate and under reasonable conditions.

The Production of Ammonia

Figure 6.17 illustrates the use of a catalyst to produce ammonia, $NH_3(g)$. Ammonia has numerous industrial applications, including the production of fertilizers and explosives. The formation of ammonia from nitrogen and hydrogen is exothermic, as shown below:

$$N_2(g) + 3H_2(g) \rightarrow 2NH_3(g) \qquad \Delta H_r^\circ = -92.6 \text{ kJ/mol}$$

However, the reaction proceeds very slowly at room temperature. Increasing the temperature increases the reaction rate somewhat, but an increase in temperature also increases the decomposition of ammonia back into nitrogen and hydrogen. For the reaction to be useful on an industrial scale, it must proceed at a reasonably fast rate and generate a large quantity of the desired product.

Early in the twentieth century, German chemist Fritz Haber discovered that the reaction proceeds rapidly at about 500°C when a catalyst composed of iron and a small amount of potassium oxide and aluminum oxide is used. A German chemical engineer, Carl Bosch, then determined how to apply the reaction to produce ammonia on an industrial scale. In this technique, known as the Haber-Bosch process, molecules of nitrogen and hydrogen break apart when they come in contact with the metal catalyst. The atoms of nitrogen and hydrogen are highly reactive, and they quickly combine to produce molecules of ammonia.

Suggested Investigation

Plan Your Own Investigation 6-B, The Effect of a Catalyst on the Decomposition of $H_2O_2(aq)$

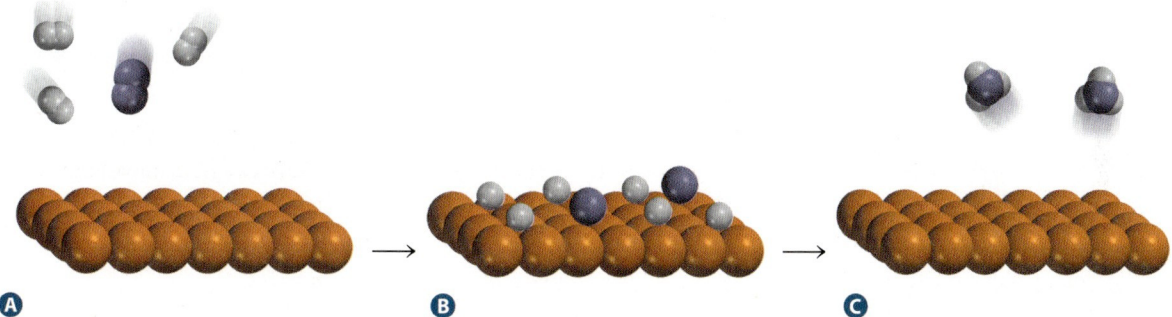

Figure 6.17 The synthesis of ammonia proceeds rapidly in the Haber-Bosch process as a result of the use of a catalyst.
Interpret what is represented in parts A, B, and C of this diagram.

The Production of Sulfuric Acid

Sulfur can be converted into sulfuric acid, an extremely important industrial acid used in such applications as manufacturing chemicals, refining ores, and processing waste water. The conversion process, called the *contact process*, uses vanadium(V) oxide, $V_2O_5(s)$, as a catalyst of one step in the process, as shown below. Without the catalyst, the reaction in step 2 would decrease the overall reaction rate. Notice that the catalyst is written above the reaction arrow, because it is not consumed during the reaction.

Step 1: $S_8(s) + 8O_2(g) \rightarrow 8SO_2(g)$
Step 2: $2SO_2(g) + O_2(g) \xrightarrow{V_2O_5(s)} 2SO_3(g)$
Step 3: $SO_3(g) + H_2SO_4(aq) \rightarrow H_2S_2O_7(aq)$
Step 4: $H_2S_2O_7(aq) + H_2O(\ell) \rightarrow 2H_2SO_4(aq)$

Suggested Investigation

ThoughtLab Investigation 6-C, Exploring Catalysts in Industry

The Production of Nitric Acid

Another important industrial acid, nitric acid, $HNO_3(aq)$, is produced using the Ostwald process. One major use of nitric acid is as a starting material for the production of ammonium nitrate, $NH_4NO_3(s)$, a fertilizer. The reaction steps of the Ostwald process are shown below. The first step is catalyzed using a platinum-rhodium catalyst (Pt-Rh) at 800°C. A photograph of the catalyst is shown in **Figure 6.18**. Notice that both nitric acid and nitrous acid are formed in step 3. When heated, nitrous acid is converted to nitric acid.

Step 1: $4NH_3(g) + 5O_2(g) \xrightarrow{Pt-Rh, 800°} 4NO(g) + 6H_2O(g)$
Step 2: $2NO(g) + O_2(g) \rightarrow 2NO_2(g)$
Step 3: $2NO_2(g) + H_2O(\ell) \rightarrow HNO_2(aq) + HNO_3(aq)$
Step 4: $3HNO_2(aq) \rightarrow HNO_3(aq) + H_2O(\ell) + 2NO(g)$

The manufacture of catalysts for industrial applications has seen incredible growth in recent years because of environmental regulations surrounding acceptable levels of air pollution. In Ontario, the Ministry of the Environment has set regulations on industrial emissions of pollutants. These regulations have become more stringent and are being applied to more industries over time. Stricter standards applying to such facilities as petroleum refineries and iron and steel mills went into effect in 2010. As of 2013, application of these standards has extended to paper mills and factories that produce transportation equipment. All facilities must comply with the standards by 2020.

Catalysts are often used to convert pollutants in industrial emissions to less harmful forms. Regulated emissions include those of sulfur dioxide, $SO_2(g)$, and nitrogen oxides, $NO_x(g)$. A major source of both is the combustion of fossil fuels. The use of catalysts to convert sulfur dioxide into hydrogen sulfide, $H_2S(g)$, can reduce emissions of sulfur dioxide by up to 50 percent, and the use of catalysts to convert nitrogen oxides to nitrogen gas and water can reduce emissions of nitrogen oxides by up to 95 percent.

Figure 6.18 The platinum-rhodium catalyst, shown here, is in the form of a gauze or mesh to maximize its surface area.
Explain why it is important that the catalyst has a large surface area.

Activity 6.2 Chlorofluorocarbons as Catalysts in Ozone Depletion

In the absence of human-made compounds, the concentration of UV-absorbing ozone, $O_3(g)$, in the stratosphere is constant. That is, its rates of formation and decomposition are equal. A simplified explanation for ozone formation is given as follows:

Reaction 1: $O_2(g) \xrightarrow{UV} O(g) + O(g)$
Reaction 2: $O(g) + O_2(g) \rightarrow O_3(g)$

In addition, ozone can decompose upon absorbing UV light:

Reaction 3: $O_3(g) \xrightarrow{UV} O_2(g) + O(g)$

The introduction of chlorofluorocarbons ($C_xCl_yF_z$) into the atmosphere has affected the balance of ozone formation and decomposition. Once these CFCs diffuse into the stratosphere, they decompose in the presence of UV radiation:

Reaction 4: $CF_2Cl_2(g) \xrightarrow{UV} CF_2Cl\cdot(g) + Cl\cdot(g)$

The reactive chlorine atoms ($Cl\cdot$) produced in reaction 4 are called chloride radicals. All radicals are highly reactive and react with ozone in the following two-step process:

Reaction 5: $Cl\cdot(g) + O_3(g) \rightarrow ClO\cdot(g) + O_2(g)$
Reaction 6: $ClO\cdot(g) + O(g) \rightarrow Cl\cdot(g) + O_2(g)$

Procedure

1. Algebraically combine reactions 1 and 2 to arrive at their sum.

2. Algebraically combine reactions 5 and 6 to arrive at their sum.

Questions

1. What does the sum of reactions 1 and 2 represent?

2. How does the rate of the overall reaction from question 1 compare with the rate of reaction 3?

3. What causes the reaction represented by reaction 4?

4. What does the sum of reactions 5 and 6 represent?

5. Does $Cl\cdot(g)$ appear in the sum of reactions 5 and 6? Explain why $Cl\cdot(g)$ is a catalyst in the overall reaction.

6. Does $ClO\cdot(g)$ appear in the overall equation? Explain why $ClO\cdot(g)$ is *not* a catalyst in this reaction; explain its role in the reaction.

7. Discuss the overall effect of the presence of CFCs in the upper atmosphere.

Learning Check

25. How can the use of a catalyst in an industrial process be an advantage for a company?

26. What property of a substance is most important in determining if it will be suitable for use as a catalyst in an industrial process?

27. In the contact process for producing sulfuric acid, the catalyst vanadium(V) oxide, $V_2O_5(s)$, will increase the rates of the forward and reverse reactions for the following system:

$$2SO_2(g) + O_2(g) \rightleftharpoons 2SO_3(g) + \text{heat}$$

  a. Draw a labelled potential energy diagram that could represent this process.

  b. Use collision theory to explain why the rates of the forward and the reverse reactions increase when the catalyst vanadium(V) oxide is present.

  c. How does the catalyst affect ΔH_{fwd} and ΔH_{rev}?

28. What industries are most affected by stricter government emission standards? What is the reason that these industries are targeted for strict emission controls?

29. In the Haber-Bosch process, ammonia gas, $NH_3(g)$, is produced in a catalyzed, exothermic reaction at a high temperature.

  a. Write the balanced thermochemical equation for the formation of ammonia from its elements.

  b. Why is a very high temperature used for the reaction? What problem is caused by the use of a higher temperature?

  c. What catalyst is used in this process? How does it increase the rate of reaction?

30. Explain how Haber and Bosch separately contributed to the development of the process that bears their names. Why is it important for industries to have teams of people solving problems and developing new catalysts instead of individual scientists working alone?

The Use of Biological Catalysts (Enzymes) in Paper Production

In industrial applications, as you have learned, chemists often use an increase in temperature to increase the rate of a chemical reaction, with or without a catalyst. In a living organism, however, all chemical reactions must proceed under conditions appropriate for sustaining life. In the human body, for example, reactions must take place at body temperature, 37°C. Living organisms depend on reactions that are catalyzed by amazingly efficient biological catalysts called **enzymes**. Enzymes are usually proteins that are specialized to catalyze only one or a few specific reactions.

Many types of enzymes are used in industrial processes. Consider the manufacture of paper, which is made by separating plant fibres from other plant material and then compressing the moist fibres into thin sheets and drying them. A substance called xylan that is present in plant fibres makes it more difficult to remove the natural brown colour from the fibres. Unless the fibres are bleached, paper will be brown, as shown in **Figure 6.19**. Therefore, chlorine-based bleaches, which can be damaging to the environment, are often used in the production of white paper. However, a class of enzymes called xylanases break down xylan. Xylanases are naturally produced by organisms such as fungi and some bacteria that can degrade the cell walls of plants. During paper production, the addition of xylanases allows for much smaller concentrations of bleach to be used to produce white paper. The waste water that is released into the environment from paper manufacturing plants therefore contains reduced concentrations of bleach. Besides lessening the environmental impact, the use of biocatalysts in producing paper also means that fewer chemicals are needed in the process and less energy is consumed in the process as well.

Another type of enzyme used to produce paper is called amylase. This enzyme is used in the production of the starch that can be added to paper. The starch improves the strength of the paper and increases its ability to withstand the friction of erasers.

enzyme a biological catalyst (usually a protein)

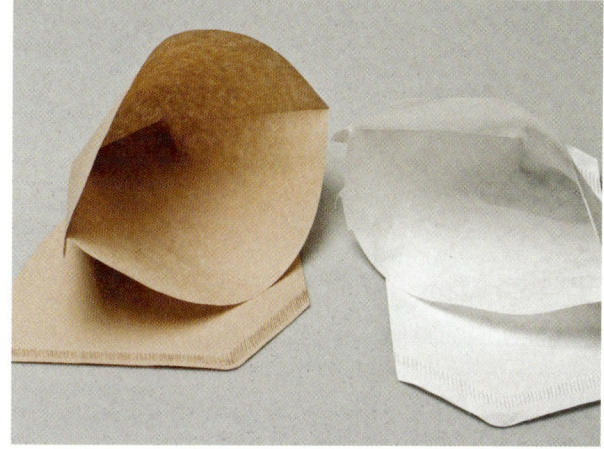

Figure 6.19 Unbleached paper is naturally light tan to brown in colour, depending on the types of fibres used to make the paper. To manufacture white paper, the colour of the fibres must be removed. The use of enzymes can greatly reduce the amount of bleach needed to decolourize plant fibres.

STSE
CHEMISTRY Connections

Inside a Catalytic Converter: Car Pollution Solution?

Since the introduction of catalytic converters in 1975, they have become mandatory for all new vehicles. When car engines burn fuel, they produce exhaust, made up primarily of nitrogen gas, carbon dioxide gas, and water vapour. Although carbon dioxide is a greenhouse gas that contributes to global warming, it is not the most harmful emission. Because combustion in an engine is not complete, car engines also produce smaller amounts of the poisonous gas carbon monoxide, CO(g), as well as hydrocarbons and nitrogen oxides, NO(g) and NO_2(g). Each of these substances contributes to the formation of smog and acid precipitation.

Three Stages of Conversion

Most modern vehicles are equipped with a three-way catalytic converter that is located in the exhaust system and exposed to the exhaust stream. Most three-way catalytic converters consist of a honeycomb-shaped structure, shown in the illustration below, coated with the metal catalysts platinum, palladium, and rhodium. As engine exhaust gases flow through the exhaust pipe into the honeycomb passageways of the catalytic converter, they come into contact with the metal catalysts, as shown in the illustration below.

Three-way catalytic converters reduce emissions of carbon monoxide, hydrocarbons, and nitrogen oxides in three stages:

Stage 1: The platinum and rhodium catalyze reactions that convert nitrogen oxides and carbon monoxide into nitrogen gas and carbon dioxide.

$$2NO(g) \xrightarrow{Pt(s),Rh(s)} O_2(g) + N_2(g)$$
$$2NO_2(g) \xrightarrow{Pt(s),Rh(s)} 2O_2(g) + N_2(g)$$

Stage 2: The platinum and palladium catalyze the complete combustion of the hydrocarbons and carbon monoxide, producing water vapour and carbon dioxide.

$$C_xH_y(g) + O_2(g) \xrightarrow{Pt(s),Pd(s)} CO_2(g) + H_2O(g)$$
$$2CO(g) + O_2(g) \xrightarrow{Pt(s),Pd(s)} 2CO_2(g)$$

Stage 3: For complete combustion to take place, the correct concentration of oxygen must be present in the exhaust. During the third stage, an oxygen sensor mounted between the car's engine and the three-way catalytic converter determines the amount of oxygen that there is in the exhaust and relays this information to the engine computer. The engine computer can control the amount of oxygen in the exhaust by adjusting the air-to-fuel ratio.

An Imperfect Solution

The catalytic converter can eliminate up to 95 percent of hydrocarbons, carbon monoxide, and nitrogen oxides, but it is not perfect. The exhaust still contains carbon dioxide, which contributes to global warming. Moreover, the three-way catalytic converter only begins to work at a relatively high temperature. It begins to operate at around 288°C, and efficient conversion starts at 399°C. Thus, when you start your car on a cold day, harmful gases escape with the exhaust until the catalytic converter heats up. Using a block heater in vehicles during the colder months of the year helps to combat this problem.

Connect to Technology

1. Research the environmental effects of the chemicals that are emitted in vehicle exhaust.
   a. What level of risk from the emission of these chemicals do you think is acceptable? Use a risk-benefit analysis chart to support your answer.
   b. Research which level of government regulates vehicle emissions in Ontario and what it is doing to reduce vehicle emissions.
2. Catalytic converters can produce dinitrogen monoxide, N_2O(g), commonly known as "laughing gas," which makes up about 7.2 percent of greenhouse gases. Although the industry proposes re-designing the catalytic converter, environmentalists argue that this is another reason to move away from gasoline-powered cars to electric or hybrid cars. Which do you think is the better solution to the problem? Give research-based reasons to support your answer.

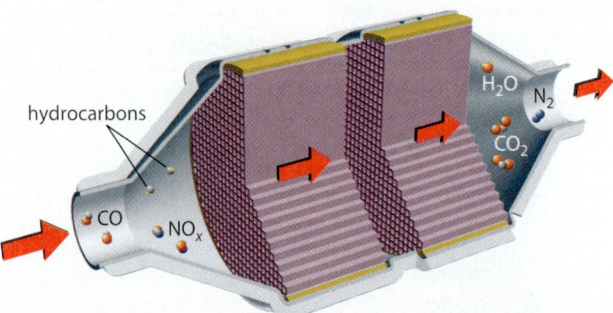

Chemical reactions occurring in a three-way catalytic converter change carbon monoxide to carbon dioxide, nitrogen oxides to nitrogen gas, and hydrocarbons to water vapour and carbon dioxide. As a result, the emission of pollutants is greatly reduced.

Section 6.2 Review

Section Summary

- According to collision theory, a reaction will occur only if the reactants collide with the correct orientation and with energy equal to or greater than the activation energy, E_a.
- When reactants collide with sufficient energy to overcome the activation energy barrier, they form an activated complex, which is an unstable transition state.
- A potential energy diagram can represent reversible reactions. For the reverse reaction, follow the curve from right to left.
- Factors that affect the rate of a chemical reaction include the nature of the reactants, the concentration of a solution, temperature, the pressure of gaseous reactants, the surface area of solid particles of the reactants, and the presence of a catalyst.
- A catalyst is a substance that increases the rate of a reaction but is itself unchanged at the end of the reaction.
- Biological catalysts are called enzymes and are specialized to catalyze only one or a few specific reactions. Enzymes can be used in industrial applications to reduce the use of chemicals that can adversely affect the environment.

Review Questions

1. **K/U** Describe the energy conversions that take place during a chemical reaction. Use the terms *kinetic energy*, *potential energy*, *bonds breaking*, and *bonds forming* in your answer.

2. **K/U** What information can be obtained from a potential energy diagram?

3. **K/U** What criteria must be met to create an effective collision between reactant particles?

4. **K/U** Is the activated complex a reactant or a product in a reaction? Explain your answer.

5. **T/I** An activated complex has been compared to a boulder sitting on the peak of a mountain. Explain why this is an appropriate comparison.

6. **T/I** A forward reaction has an activation energy of +45 kJ and an enthalpy change of -45 kJ. Sketch a potential energy diagram for the reaction. Label $E_{a(fwd)}$, $E_{a(rev)}$, and ΔH_r.

7. **C** Using collision theory and diagrams, explain to a friend how surface area can affect the rate of a reaction.

8. **C** Your lab partner argues that it is not possible for reactions that have a high activation energy to have a rapid rate of reaction. What example of a reaction could you give to dispute this argument? Explain your answer.

9. **T/I** You are designing an experiment to determine the effect of concentration on the rate of the reaction between hydrochloric acid and marble chips by measuring the volume of carbon dioxide gas produced over a period of time.

    $2HCl(aq) + CaCO_3(s) \rightarrow CaCl_2(aq) + H_2O(\ell) + CO_2(g)$

    As the concentration of acid is changed for several trials, what factors would you control in each trial to ensure that the acid concentration is the only factor affecting the reaction rate?

10. **A** A company is looking for the optimum conditions to produce hydrogen gas using the reaction between dilute sulfuric acid and magnesium metal. Predict whether the rate of reaction will increase, decrease, or remain the same when each one of the following changes is made. Support your answer with reference to collision theory.

    $Mg(s) + H_2SO_4(aq) \rightarrow MgSO_4(aq) + H_2(g)$

    a. The temperature of $H_2SO_4(aq)$ is decreased by 20°C.
    b. Magnesium powder is used rather than the equivalent mass of cubes of metal.
    c. The reaction is carried out in a closed vessel in which the pressure is increased.
    d. The concentration of $H_2SO_4(aq)$ is increased from 3 mol/L to 6 mol/L.

11. **T/I** A catalyst has been found to lower the activation energy of an exothermic reaction in the forward direction by 50 percent. Use this information with the data below to calculate the enthalpy change of the forward reaction. Sketch your results using a reasonable scale in a potential energy diagram.

    $E_{a(fwd)} = +160$ kJ (uncatalyzed)
    $E_{a(rev)} = +240$ kJ (catalyzed)

12. **C** Consider the following reaction:

    $A_2(g) + B_2(g) \rightarrow 2AB(g)$
    $E_{a(fwd)} = +143$ kJ
    $E_{a(rev)} = +75$ kJ

    a. Is the reaction endothermic or exothermic in the forward direction?
    b. Draw and label a potential energy diagram for this reaction. Include a value for ΔH_r.

SECTION 6.3
Reaction Rates and Reaction Mechanisms

Key Terms

initial rate
reaction mechanism
elementary step
intermediate
rate-determining step

As you know from Section 6.2, the rate of a reaction depends in part on the concentration of the reactants. When the concentration of reactants increases, the reaction rate tends to increase, because a greater number of collisions occur per unit time within the same volume. The increase in the number of collisions increases opportunities for effective collisions to take place. In this section, you will look more closely at the effect of concentration of reactants and products on rates of reactions in order to develop an understanding of reaction mechanisms—the detailed steps that occur during reactions.

Measuring the Effect of Concentration on Reaction Rate

Several concepts from Section 6.1 are reviewed in **Figure 6.20**, which shows three examples of lines tangent to the curve, with triangles formed from the slopes. The slopes are equal to $\frac{\Delta[A]}{\Delta t}$ at one instant in time. The slopes of these tangents therefore represent the instantaneous rate of the reaction for those instants in time. As time progresses, the slopes become smaller, because the concentration is decreasing. Therefore, the reaction rates become smaller.

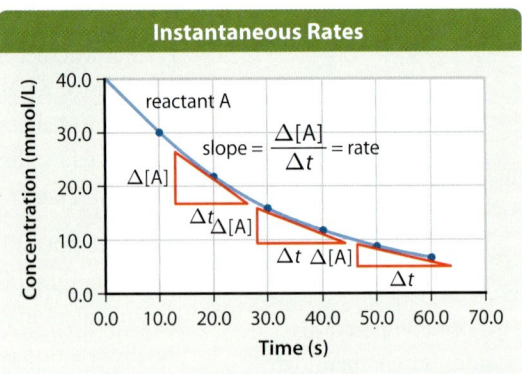

Figure 6.20 To find the instantaneous rate of a reaction at any point in time, draw a line tangent to the curve at that time point and calculate the slope of the tangent.

As soon as a reaction starts, products begin to form. The presence of products allows reverse reactions to take place. Thus, the observed rate of a reaction, measured at any time after time zero, is affected by the rate of the reverse reaction. The only accurate datum for the relationship between the concentration of a reactant and the reaction rate is the point at which there is no product present—at time zero. This point is called the **initial rate**, and can be determined by drawing a line tangent to the curve at time zero, as shown in **Figure 6.21**.

initial rate the rate of a chemical reaction at time zero

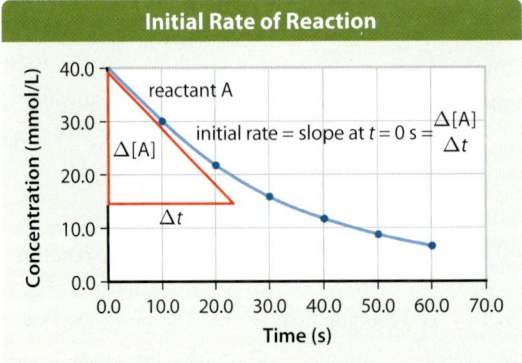

Figure 6.21 The initial rate of a reaction is found by drawing a line tangent to the curve at time zero and determining the slope of the line. Thus, the instantaneous rate of a reaction at $t = 0$ s is the initial rate of the reaction.

Graphing Reaction Rate in Terms of Concentration

To observe the effects of concentration on the rate of a reaction, several experiments are carried out, each one starting with a different concentration of reactant. Graphs are drawn and the initial rate for each curve is determined, as shown in **Figure 6.22A**. Each of the five curves represents data from a different experiment, and each experiment uses a different starting concentration of the reactant. **Figure 6.22B** is a graph of the initial rates determined from graph A and plotted against the starting concentrations of each of the experiments.

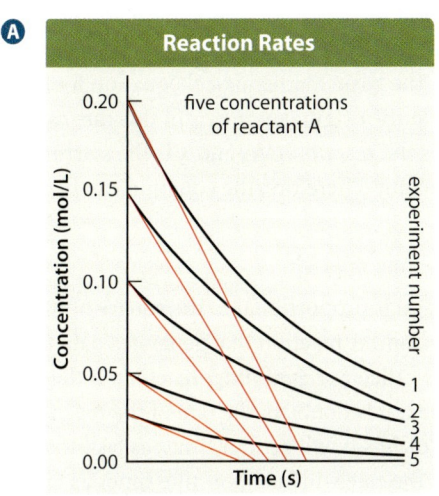
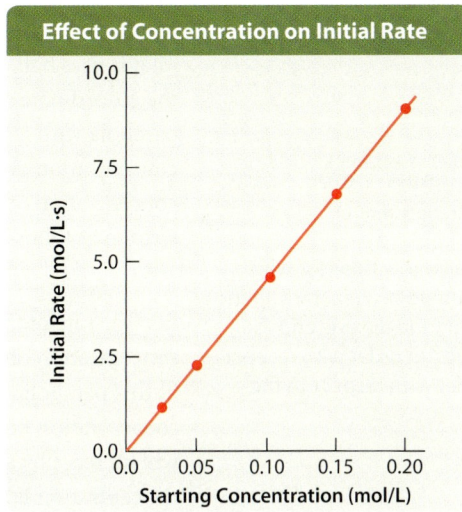

Figure 6.22 In graph (**A**), rate curves for five concentrations of reactant A are plotted and the initial rates are calculated. In graph (**B**), the initial rates for each concentration are plotted against the starting concentration.

The graph in **Figure 6.22B** shows that, in this case, the relationship between the initial rate of the reaction and the starting concentration of reactant A is a straight-line plot. Recall that the general equation for a straight line is $y = mx + b$. In **Figure 6.22B**, y is the initial rate of the reaction, x is the starting concentration, and m is the slope. The constant b is the point at which the line crosses the y-axis, which is zero in this case. Therefore, the results can be expressed mathematically: initial rate $= m[A]$. In chemistry, the slope of this line is usually represented by the symbol k, and the initial rate is usually simply called the rate. Therefore, this relationship is as follows:

$$\text{rate} = k[A]$$

First-order Reactions

In a linear equation such as this, k is the proportionality constant. Without even knowing the value of k, you know that the rate is proportional to the concentration of A. Therefore, if the concentration is doubled, the rate will double. If the concentration is tripled, the rate will triple. Because the rate of the reaction is directly proportional to the first power of the concentration, reactions that fit this linear relationship are called *first-order reactions*.

In many decomposition reactions, the rate is directly proportional to the concentration of the single reactant. For reactions with more than one reactant, rate vs. concentration experiments can be carried out on each reactant individually. For example, consider this general reaction:

$$A(aq) + 2B(aq) \rightarrow 3C(aq) + 4D(aq)$$

Experiments would be performed with an excess of reactant B, so its effect on the rate would be negligible; also, concentrations of A would be varied. Then further experiments would be performed with an excess of A, and the concentration of B would be varied. A rate vs. concentration relationship would be determined for each reactant. If each set of experiments with each reactant resulted in a linear relationship, you would say that the reaction is first order with respect to reactant A and first order with respect to reactant B.

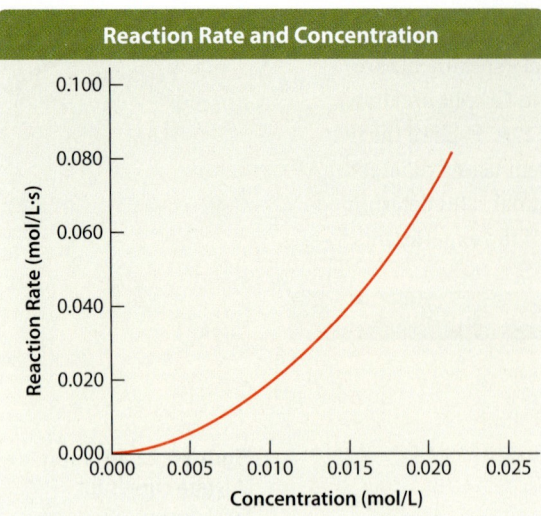

Figure 6.23 This graph represents reactions for which the rate is proportional to the square of a reactant. In the case of the reaction between chlorine dioxide and the hydroxide ion, the reaction is second order with respect to chlorine dioxide, but first order with respect to the hydroxide ion.

Second-order Reactions

However, many reactions are not first-order reactions with respect to a certain reactant. For example, in the reaction between chlorine dioxide and a hydroxide ion, a mixture of chlorate and chlorite ions are produced, as shown below.

$$2ClO_2(aq) + 2OH^-(aq) \rightarrow ClO_3^-(aq) + ClO_2^-(aq) + H_2O(\ell)$$

Data from experiments on various concentrations of chlorine dioxide in an excess of hydroxide ions generate a graph like the one shown in **Figure 6.23**. The shape of this curve is parabolic. That is, it is half of a parabola, with its vertex at the origin of the co-ordinate system. The basic mathematical equation for a parabola with its vertex at the origin is $y = kx^2$. In this rate vs. concentration graph, y is the reaction rate, and x is the starting concentration of the reactant. Therefore, the equation can be written as follows:

$$\text{rate} = k[A]^2$$

The rate of the reaction is proportional to the square of the concentration of the reactant. A reaction that generates data that fit this parabolic curve is called a *second-order reaction*. If the concentration of the reactant is doubled, the rate of the reaction will increase by a factor of 2^2—it will be four times as fast. If the concentration is tripled, the rate will be 3^2, or nine times as fast.

Activity 6.3 — Graphical Analysis of Reaction Rates vs. Concentration

In this activity, you will graph data for two different chemical reactions and then analyse the graphs to obtain a mathematical relationship between the reaction rate and the starting concentration of the reactant.

Consider the following two experiments.

Experiment 1 investigated this chemical reaction:
$$C_2H_5Br(g) + \text{heat} \rightarrow C_2H_4(g) + HBr(g)$$

Five trials were done for five different concentrations of bromoethane; the initial rates were determined from the graphs and the data in Table 1 were obtained.

Experiment 2 investigated this chemical reaction:
$$2NO_2(g) + \text{heat} \rightarrow 2NO(g) + O_2(g)$$

Five trials were done for five different concentrations of nitrogen dioxide. The rates were determined from the graphs and the data in Table 2 were obtained.

Table 1 Data Obtained from Experiment 1

$[C_2H_5Br]$ (mol/L)	Reaction Rate (mol/L·s)
1.00×10^{-3}	3.33×10^{-6}
2.00×10^{-3}	6.67×10^{-6}
3.00×10^{-3}	1.00×10^{-5}
4.00×10^{-3}	1.33×10^{-5}
5.00×10^{-3}	1.67×10^{-5}

Table 2 Data Obtained from Experiment 2

$[NO_2]$ (mol/L)	Reaction Rate (mol/L·s)
2.50×10^{-3}	4.69×10^{-8}
5.00×10^{-3}	1.88×10^{-7}
7.50×10^{-3}	4.22×10^{-7}
10.0×10^{-3}	7.50×10^{-7}
12.5×10^{-3}	1.17×10^{-6}

Procedure
For each set of data, draw a graph with reaction rate on the y-axis and starting concentration on the x-axis.

Questions
1. For each reaction, analyze the shape of the graph and determine the order of the reaction. Record your answer.
2. Write the general rate equation for each reaction, based on the orders of the reactions that were determined in question 1.
3. Calculate k for each experiment using representative data from each.
4. Write the rate equation for each reaction, based on your answers to questions 2 and 3.

The Rate Law

It is possible, although not common, for reactions to have an order of zero or a fraction such as $\frac{1}{2}$ or $\frac{3}{4}$. For example, a catalyzed reaction could be zero order with respect to one or all reactants if the catalyst was saturated. That is, a reaction rate would not change even with an increase in the amount of reactant, because there would be no more sites on the catalyst to which a reactant molecule could bind, if all sites were full (or saturated).

In general, the relationship between reaction rates and the concentration of reactants for the overall reaction can be written as follows:

$$\text{rate} = k[A]^m[B]^n$$

In this equation, m is the order of the reaction with respect to reactant A, and n is the order of the reaction with respect to reactant B. The proportionality constant, k, is called the *rate constant*. This equation is often called the *rate law*. Each reaction has its own rate law, with a specific value for the rate constant k, and for the order of the reaction, m and n, for each reactant, A and B. The order of the overall reaction is $m + n$. Note that some reactions have only one reactant whereas others have more than two reactants. Nevertheless, the form of the rate law is basically the same. Each constant—k, m, and n—must be calculated from experimental data. These constants can be determined graphically as discussed above or calculated mathematically. Mathematical methods for finding the rate law for specific reactions from experimental data are provided in Appendix B.

Learning Check

31. It would be tempting to use one graph of concentration versus time and measure the rate at different times and then use those data to plot a rate vs. concentration graph. Explain why this method could provide different results from the method you have learned.

32. What is the meaning of the term *initial rate*?

33. How is an initial rate measured? Explain the experimental procedure.

34. Explain how to obtain the data needed to make a plot of initial rate vs. starting concentration.

35. Describe the type of information that can be obtained from a plot of initial rate vs. starting concentration.

36. Given the general rate law, rate $= k[A]^m[B]^n$, explain the meaning of the constants, k, m, and n, and describe the methods for determining their value.

Reaction Mechanisms

The relationship between the concentration and the rate of a reaction can provide some general information about the **reaction mechanism**—a series of steps that occur during the process of converting reactants into products of a chemical reaction. In the discussion about activation energy, you read about an activated complex that was neither reactant nor product but a chemical species in between the two. In many reactions, there can be more than one activated complex, which means that the reaction takes place in more than one step. Each individual step in a multistep reaction is called an **elementary step**. The overall reaction, described by the balanced chemical equation, is a series of elementary steps that describe the progress of the overall reaction at the molecular level. How can the reaction order—the relationship between rate and concentration—reveal information about a reaction mechanism?

reaction mechanism a series of elementary steps that add to the overall reaction

elementary step a step in a series of simple reactions that represent the progress of the overall chemical reaction at the molecular level

Determining Reaction Mechanisms

A reaction between 2-bromo-2-methylpropane and sodium hydroxide, NaOH(aq) occurs as follows:

$$(CH_3)_3CBr(aq) + Na^+(aq) + OH^-(aq) \rightarrow (CH_3)_3COH(aq) + Na^+(aq) + Br^-(aq)$$

Omitting the spectator ion, Na^+, the overall equation is:

$$(CH_3)_3CBr(aq) + OH^-(aq) \rightarrow (CH_3)_3COH(aq) + Br^-(aq)$$

Experiments that measure reaction rates using different concentrations of reactants show that this reaction is first order with respect to 2-bromo-2-methylpropane and zero order with respect to the hydroxide ion. The observation that changing the concentration of the hydroxide ion has no effect on the rate of the reaction is a strong indication that the reaction is not a simple, one-step reaction involving the hydroxide ion colliding with the other reactant. However, experiments cannot reveal the steps that take place on the molecular level.

Femtochemistry

In the 1980s, chemists began using laser pulses to monitor chemical reactions. These pulses are extremely short—in the order of magnitude of femtoseconds. One technique involves a series of pairs of pulses. The wavelength of the laser light and the time between pulses can be varied. In each pair of pulses, the first pulse supplies the activation energy to initiate a reaction. The absorbance of the second pulse can be measured to determine the absorbance characteristics of any activated complexes or intermediate chemical species created by the reaction. In this way, researchers can identify some chemical species that exist only momentarily. For example, activated complexes generally exist for only 10 to 1000 fs.

Data from laser pulses that occur every few femtoseconds show changes in the chemical bonds. This information allows chemists to determine reaction mechanisms as well as how the rate of a reaction is affected by different factors. The development of the femtosecond laser has led to a field of study called femtochemistry. A goal of femtochemistry is to determine reaction mechanisms in sufficient detail so that chemists are better able to develop techniques for controlling reaction rates and increasing the yield of desired products that can have industrial, environmental, and medical applications.

An example of a reaction that chemists have studied in detail is the decomposition of dinitrogen monoxide to form nitrogen and oxygen. The overall reaction is as follows:

$$2N_2O(g) \rightarrow 2N_2(g) + O_2(g)$$

However, nitrogen gas and oxygen gas are not formed directly. Instead, an oxygen atom, which is not represented in the balanced chemical equation, is briefly produced in the first elementary step of the overall reaction. (Note that states of matter are generally not shown in chemical equations showing elementary steps.)

$$N_2O \rightarrow N_2 + O$$

The oxygen atom can then react with another molecule of dinitrogen monoxide to produce nitrogen and oxygen. This reaction is the second elementary step of the overall reaction:

$$N_2O + O \rightarrow N_2 + O_2$$

The overall chemical reaction is the sum of the elementary steps:

Step 1: $\quad N_2O \rightarrow N_2 + O$
Step 2: $\quad N_2O + O \rightarrow N_2 + O_2$
Sum of reactions: $2N_2O + \cancel{O} \rightarrow 2N_2 + \cancel{O} + O_2$
Overall reaction: $\quad 2N_2O \rightarrow 2N_2 + O_2$

The oxygen atom that is briefly produced in the first elementary step is called an **intermediate**, because it appears in the elementary steps but not in the balanced equation that represents the overall chemical reaction. An intermediate formed in an earlier elementary step is always consumed in a subsequent elementary step.

intermediate a chemical species that appears in the elementary steps of a chemical reaction but not in the overall balanced chemical equation

The Rate-determining Step

The rate of a reaction that has more than one elementary step is determined by the rate at which the slowest elementary step proceeds. Consider a line of vehicles on a road that is too narrow for one vehicle to safely pass another, as shown in **Figure 6.24**. The entire line of vehicles can proceed only as fast as the slowest vehicle is travelling. Similarly, the overall rate of a chemical reaction is dependent on the rate at which the slowest step occurs. The slowest elementary step is often called the *rate-limiting step* or the **rate-determining step**.

rate-determining step the slowest step among all the elementary steps in a specific multistep reaction, and which determines the rate of the overall chemical reaction

Figure 6.24 The overall rate of travel for these vehicles is limited by the speed of the car at the front of the line of traffic. In a similar way, the overall rate of a chemical reaction cannot be faster than its slowest elementary step.

An example of a three-step reaction, that of nitrogen monoxide with hydrogen gas to form nitrogen gas and water, is shown below:

$$2NO(g) + 2H_2(g) \rightarrow N_2(g) + 2H_2O(g)$$

Of the three elementary steps that make up the overall chemical reaction, the first and third proceed relatively quickly, but the second elementary step proceeds slowly.

Step 1: $2NO \rightarrow N_2O_2$ (fast)
Step 2: $N_2O_2 + H_2 \rightarrow N_2O + H_2O$ (slow) $r = k[N_2O_2]^1[H_2]^1$
Step 3: $N_2O + H_2 \rightarrow N_2 + H_2O$ (fast)

Therefore, the second step is the rate-determining step. Each elementary step has its own activation energy, as shown in **Figure 6.25**. Because the activation energy for step 2 is higher than for steps 1 or 3, step 2 determines the rate at which the overall reaction proceeds.

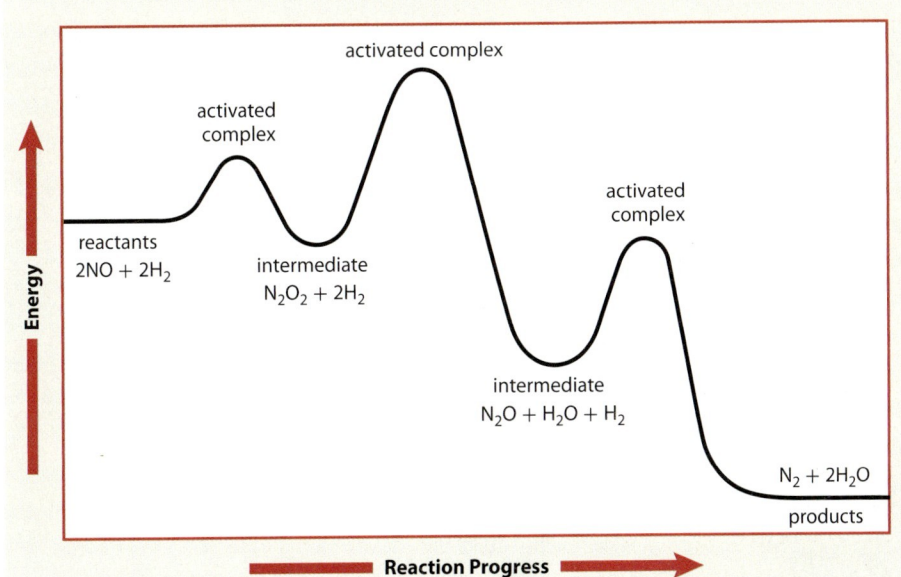

Figure 6.25 The three "hills" in this potential energy diagram represent the activation energies for the three elementary steps that make up the overall reaction. The second hill is highest, indicating that the second elementary step has the highest activation energy and is therefore the rate-determining step.

A Proposed Reaction Mechanism

A basic understanding of multistep reactions and rate-determining steps makes it possible to analyze the earlier reaction between 2-bromo-2-methylpropane and the hydroxide ion to find out how a reaction can be zero order with respect to one reactant.

The mechanism of the reaction is shown in **Figure 6.26**. The first step involves only the 2-bromo-2-methylpropane, which ionizes. This step is very slow relative to the second step. The second step, during which the hydroxide ion forms a covalent bond with the positively charged ion from the first step, is extremely fast. This reaction is so fast that increasing the concentration of the hydroxide ion has no effect on the overall speed of the reaction, because, in a sense, the hydroxide ions that are present are "waiting" for positively charged ions to form. The addition of more hydroxide ions will not speed up the formation of the positively charged ion from the first step. The instant that this positively charged ion forms, it reacts with either a bromide ion or a hydroxide ion. When the final product 2-methylpropan-2-ol is formed, it is quite stable, because the activation energy for the reverse reaction is so large that the reaction is essentially irreversible.

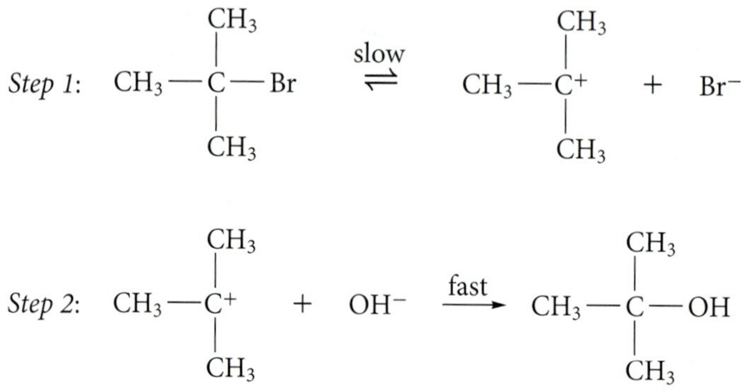

$$\text{Step 1:} \quad (CH_3)_3C-Br \; \rightleftharpoons \; (CH_3)_3C^+ \; + \; Br^- \quad \text{slow}$$

$$\text{Step 2:} \quad (CH_3)_3C^+ \; + \; OH^- \; \xrightarrow{\text{fast}} \; (CH_3)_3C-OH$$

Figure 6.26 The rate-determining step is the first step, which involves only the 2-bromo-2-methylpropane. Thus, doubling the concentration doubles the speed of step 1, making it a first-order reaction. Step 2 is so fast that it is dependent on the completion of step 1 and independent of the concentration of hydroxide ions. Therefore, the reaction is zero order with respect to hydroxide ions.

In comparison, the reaction between bromoethane, $CH_3CH_2Br(aq)$, and the hydroxide ion might be expected to follow the same process.

$$CH_3CH_2Br(aq) + OH^-(aq) \rightarrow CH_3CH_2OH(aq) + Br^-(aq)$$

However, this reaction is first order with respect to both the bromoethane and the hydroxide ion. Once again, the reaction mechanism explains why. The activation energy for the ionization of bromoethane is so high that the reaction virtually does not occur, as shown in **Figure 6.27**. Nevertheless, the carbon–bromide bond is polar, leaving the carbon atom slightly positively charged. The negatively charged hydroxide ion approaches the carbon atom and "pushes" the bromide away. The reaction occurs in one smooth step.

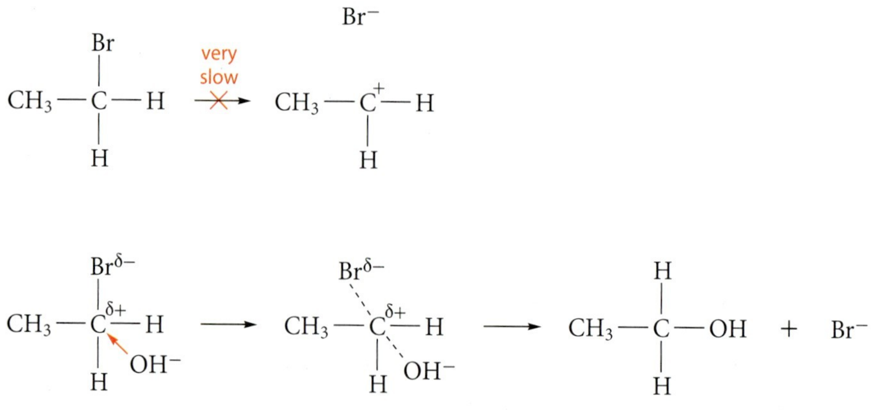

Figure 6.27 Doubling the concentration of bromoethane would double the rate of the reaction, and doubling the concentration of the hydroxide ion would also double the rate. Therefore, doubling the concentration of both reactants would quadruple (2 × 2 = 4) the reaction rate.

Section 6.3 Review

Section Summary

- To determine the relationship between the rate of a reaction and the concentration of reactants, several experiments must be carried out and the initial rates of each reaction determined.
- The rate of a reaction can be directly proportional to the concentration of a reactant, or proportional to the square of the concentration of a reactant.
- The rate law for a chemical reaction is a mathematical relationship that must be experimentally determined.
- Elementary steps are a series of simple reactions that describe the progress of an overall reaction at the molecular level.
- The slowest elementary step in a chemical reaction determines the rate of the overall reaction.
- Femtochemistry allows chemists to observe the properties of activated complexes and intermediates in chemical reactions and thus to determine reaction mechanisms.

Review Questions

1. **K/U** Which of the factors that affect the rate of a reaction is put into quantitative terms in the rate law expression?
2. **K/U** What does a balanced chemical equation indicate about the rate law for a reaction?
3. **C** Refer to **Figure 6.25**. Write your own caption for this diagram. The caption should also include an explanation that clearly distinguishes between the terms *activated complex* and *intermediate*.
4. **K/U** Explain what an initial rate is.
5. **C** You must plan an investigation to determine how to double the rate of a reaction. You have been told that the rate law for the reaction below is rate = $k[A]^2$.

    $2A(aq) + B(s) \rightarrow$ product

    Your partner suggests that the rate law does not need to be used. Doubling the surface area of reactant B would double the reaction rate. What response would you give to this suggestion?
6. **T/I** A two-step reaction mechanism is proposed for a reaction. One step is exothermic, but the overall reaction is endothermic. When a catalyst is introduced, the activation energy of the rate-determining step is reduced by 50%. Sketch a potential energy diagram that could represent this information.
7. **K/U** In a reaction mechanism, one step is referred to as being rate-determining. What does this mean? Why is it important to know this step?
8. **K/U** In a reaction mechanism, can the activated complex be the same as the reaction intermediate? Explain your answer.
9. **A** When a chemist is proposing a new reaction mechanism, each elementary step will ideally involve the collision of two particles. Why is this type of collision an important characteristic of elementary reactions?
10. **T/I** The reaction mechanism below has been proposed by a chemist working to convert chloroform to carbon tetrachloride.

    Step 1: $Cl_2 \rightarrow 2Cl$
    Step 2: $Cl + CHCl_3 \rightarrow HCl + CCl_3$
    Step 3: $Cl + CCl_3 \rightarrow CCl_4$

    a. Write the overall equation for this reaction mechanism.
    b. Is there a catalyst in this reaction? Give a reason for your answer.
    c. Identify any intermediates in this mechanism. Give a reason for your answer.
    d. The rate law for the overall reaction is rate = $k[CHCl_3]$. Which step would likely be the rate-determining step? Give a reason for your answer.
11. **T/I** Examine the potential energy diagram below and answer the following questions.
    a. Which letter(s) represents an activated complex?
    b. What is $E_{a(rev)}$ for step 2?
    c. Which letter(s) represents a reaction intermediate?
    d. What is $E_{a(fwd)}$ for step 3?
    e. What is ΔH_{fwd} for the endothermic step?
    f. What is ΔH_{fwd} for the overall reaction?

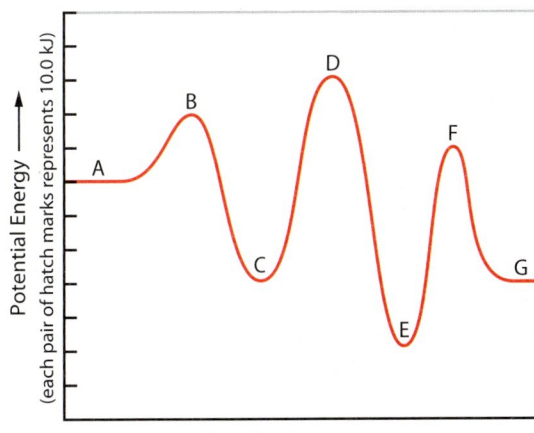

Plan Your Own INVESTIGATION 6-A

Skill Check
- ✓ Initiating and Planning
- ✓ Performing and Recording
- ✓ Analyzing and Interpreting
- ✓ Communicating

Safety Precautions

- Wear safety eyewear throughout this investigation.
- Wear a lab coat or apron throughout this investigation.
- Beware of electrical shock hazard if an electric kettle or hot plate is used.

Suggested Materials
- vinegar (5.0% (m/v), or 0.83 mol/L)
- $NaHCO_3$(s) or $CaCO_3$(s)
- 500 mL of 0.83 mol/L HCl(aq)
- additional materials and equipment appropriate to your experimental method

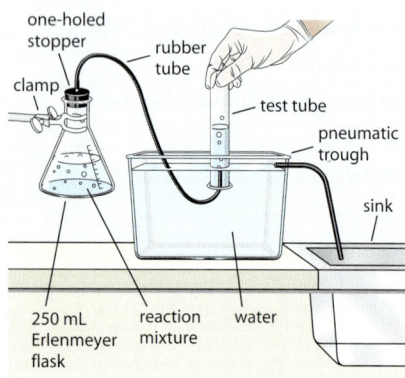

Go to Organizing Data in a Table in Appendix A for information about designing data tables.

Examining Reaction Rates

You will design an investigation to determine factors affecting the rate of this reaction:

$$CH_3COOH(aq) + NaHCO_3(aq) \rightarrow NaCH_3COO(aq) + CO_2(g) + H_2O(g)$$

These factors may include, but are not limited to, concentration of reactants, temperature of reactants, nature of reactants, and surface area.

Pre-Lab Questions

1. Aside from collecting carbon dioxide by downward displacement of water, as shown in the diagram, how else could you monitor the rate of CO_2 production in this investigation?
2. If you use the method illustrated in the diagram, why must the water be saturated with CO_2?

Question

What factors affect the rate of a chemical reaction?

Plan and Conduct

1. Decide on a method to measure the amount of CO_2 "lost" per unit of time. Write up a complete, detailed procedure and, with your teacher's permission, collect and set up the apparatus you will need.
2. Prepare a table to record observations. Remember to manipulate only one variable at a time. Collaborate with other groups who are measuring the CO_2 in the same manner and pool your results. Also, exchange results with other groups that are testing different factors.
3. Carry out as many trials as time permits.
4. Clean up your work area as instructed by your teacher.

Analyze and Interpret

1. Explain quantitatively how the factors that you investigated affected the reaction rate.

Conclude and Communicate

2. Make a general statement about the effect of each factor on the reaction rate.

Extend Further

3. **INQUIRY** One of the products of the reaction is a gas. Would changing the pressure of the system affect the rate of the reaction? Design an investigation that would measure the rate of the reaction under various pressures.
4. **RESEARCH** Find out about industrial processes carried out under pressure. What is the effect of pressure, and why is the method used?

Plan Your Own INVESTIGATION 6-B

Skill Check
- ✓ Initiating and Planning
- ✓ Performing and Recording
- ✓ Analyzing and Interpreting
- ✓ Communicating

Safety Precautions

- The reaction mixture will get hot. Handle all glassware with care.
- 6% hydrogen peroxide, H_2O_2(aq), is an irritant. Wear safety eyewear, gloves, and a laboratory apron.

Materials
- 40 mL of 6% (m/v) H_2O_2(aq)
- 20 mL of 1.0 mol/L NaI(aq)
- masking tape or grease pencil
- 100 mL beakers
- 10 mL graduated cylinders
- 250 mL Erlenmeyer flask
- clock with a second hand or stopwatch
- water
- one-holed stopper, fitted with a piece of glass tubing (must be airtight)
- rubber tubing to fit glass tubing (must be airtight)
- large test tube
- pneumatic trough or large beaker
- electronic balance accurate to 0.001 g

Go to Constructing Graphs in Appendix A for help with drawing graphs.

The Effect of a Catalyst on the Decomposition of H_2O_2(aq)

You will investigate the effect of the I^-(aq) ion as a catalyst on the decomposition of hydrogen peroxide, H_2O_2(aq). The gas produced can be measured as a decrease in mass of the system or by the downward displacement of water.

Pre-Lab Questions
1. Write the chemical equation for the decomposition reaction in this investigation.
2. How can you deal with the reaction vessel heating up during the reaction?
3. What factors could affect the rate of this reaction?

Prediction
Predict the effects of changing the concentration of a catalyst and the concentration of hydrogen peroxide on the rate of decomposition of hydrogen peroxide.

Plan and Conduct
1. Write a detailed procedure to test your prediction. Consider which variables will be constant and which will be changed. Include a data table.
2. Check your plan to ensure that all safety requirements are addressed.
3. Your teacher must approve your procedure before you can begin the experimental work.
4. Clean up your work area when you are finished.

Analyze and Interpret
1. Was there any evidence of a gas being produced before the catalyst was added? Explain.
2. Plot a graph of rate of formation of gas (in mL or g) vs. [I^-] for the trials you conducted.
3. What does the graph in question 2 indicate about the effect of the iodide ion on the reaction rate?
4. Plot a graph of the formation of gas (in mL or g) vs. [H_2O_2] for the trials you conducted.
5. What does the graph in question 4 indicate about the effect of the concentration of hydrogen peroxide on the reaction rate?
6. Evaluate the method you used. What changes or additions would you make if you could repeat the investigation?

Conclude and Communicate
7. Explain the effects of changing the concentration of iodide catalyst and changing the concentration of the reactant, hydrogen peroxide, on the rate of the decomposition of hydrogen peroxide.

Chapter 6 Rates of Reaction • MHR 389

Thought Lab INVESTIGATION 6-C

Skill Check
- Initiating and Planning
- ✓ Performing and Recording
- ✓ Analyzing and Interpreting
- ✓ Communicating

Exploring Catalysts in Industry

Catalysts are widely used in many industries. The petroleum industry uses catalysts for many processes, including the refining of oil for fuels and for the synthesis of polymers to make plastics and fibres. Other areas of industry that depend on catalysts include the food industry, pollution control, environmental protection, health, and new sources of energy.

Biological catalysts—enzymes—are also used in industry. The discovery of one particular enzyme with the right characteristics opened up the world of DNA research and such applications as DNA fingerprinting.

Question
What are the social and industrial benefits of a specific catalyst and what characteristics make this catalyst useful?

Organize the Data
1. Work in groups of 3 or 4. Each student should research a variety of catalysts used in industry.
2. Narrow your research to focus on one specific catalyst or catalyzed process. Suggest this catalyst to your group as a topic for your presentation.
3. As a group, review the suggested topics from each member and agree on one to study in more detail. Assign each member a task to complete.

Analyze and Interpret
1. Your research and report should include as many of the following topics as can be applied to your chosen catalyst or catalyzed process.
    - What is the chemical nature of your catalyst? For example, is it an inorganic compound containing a transition metal, is it an enzyme, or is it some other compound?
    - Is your catalyst a heterogeneous catalyst or a homogenous catalyst? (If you have not encountered these terms, find out what they mean.)
    - What is the mechanism of action of your catalyst? That is, how does it speed the reaction(s) involved in the overall process of manufacturing the product?
    - What product(s) is your catalyst used to manufacture?
    - How is your catalyst beneficial to the industry that uses it?
    - How is your catalyst beneficial to society or the environment?
2. What was the most interesting fact that you learned while researching and compiling your topic?

Conclude and Communicate
3. Organize the information that your group compiled into a multimedia presentation, a Web page, or a news item. Make your presentation available to your class for discussion and assessment.

Chapter 6 | SUMMARY

Section 6.1 Rates of Reaction

Reaction rates are determined by the activation energy, but not by the amount of energy gained or lost during the reaction.

Key Terms
average rate of reaction
instantaneous rate of reaction
reaction rate

Key Concepts
- A reaction rate is the speed at which a chemical reaction occurs. A reaction rate is measured by the change in the amount of reactants consumed or products formed over a given time interval.
- A reaction rate is always expressed as a positive value.
- The instantaneous rate of a reaction is the rate of the reaction at a particular point in time.
- The average rate of a chemical reaction is the change in the concentration of a reactant or product per unit time over a given time interval.
- Any measurable property that is related to a change in the amount of a reactant or product during a chemical reaction can be used to determine the reaction rate.

Section 6.2 Collision Theory and Factors Affecting Rates of Reaction

For a reaction to occur, reactants must collide in the correct orientation and with enough kinetic energy to overcome the activation energy barrier. The rate of a reaction is affected by factors that include the nature of the reactants, temperature, concentration, surface area of solid particles, and the presence of a catalyst.

Key Terms
activated complex
activation energy, E_a
catalyst
collision theory
enzyme

Key Concepts
- According to collision theory, a reaction will occur only if the reactants collide with the correct orientation and energy equal to or greater than the activation energy, E_a.
- When reactants collide with sufficient energy to overcome the activation energy barrier, they form an activated complex, which is an unstable transition state.
- A potential energy diagram can represent reversible reactions. For the reverse reaction, follow the curve from right to left.
- Factors that affect the rate of a chemical reaction include the nature of the reactants, the concentration of a solution, temperature, the pressure of gaseous reactants, the surface area of solid particles of the reactants, and the presence of a catalyst.
- A catalyst is a substance that increases the rate of a reaction but is itself unchanged at the end of the reaction.
- Biological catalysts are called enzymes and are specialized to catalyze only one or a few specific reactions. Enzymes can be used in industrial applications to reduce the use of chemicals that can adversely affect the environment.

Section 6.3 Reaction Rates and Reaction Mechanisms

The relationship between the rate of a reaction and the concentration of the reactants for any given reaction is indicated by the exponent of the concentration of the reactions in the expression rate $= k[A]^m$. Many overall reactions are the sum of several elementary steps.

Key Terms
elementary step
initial rate
intermediate
rate-determining step
reaction mechanism

Key Concepts
- To determine the relationship between the rate of a reaction and the concentration of reactants, several experiments must be carried out and the initial rates of each reaction determined.
- The rate of a reaction can be directly proportional to the concentration of a reactant, or proportional to the square of the concentration of a reactant.
- The rate law for a chemical reaction is a mathematical relationship that must be experimentally determined.
- Elementary steps are a series of simple reactions that describe the progress of an overall reaction at the molecular level.
- The slowest elementary step in a chemical reaction determines the rate of the overall reaction.
- Femtochemistry allows chemists to observe the properties of activated complexes and intermediates in chemical reactions and thus to determine reaction mechanisms.

Chapter 6 REVIEW

Knowledge and Understanding

Select the letter of the best answer below.

1. Which expression could be a unit for the measurement of rate of reaction?
   a. $\dfrac{mol^2}{L^2}$
   b. $\dfrac{L \cdot min}{mol}$
   c. $\dfrac{mol}{L}$
   d. $\dfrac{mol}{L \cdot s}$
   e. s^{-1}

2. Which one of the following features of a chemical reaction is the best indicator as to whether the reaction will proceed quickly at room temperature?
   a. reaction mechanism
   b. activation energy
   c. balanced equation
   d. rate law equation
   e. ΔH

3. For the reaction represented as $A + B \rightarrow C$, which statement is correct concerning the formation of product C?
   a. C forms half as fast as the reactants A and B are used up.
   b. C forms twice as fast as the reactants A and B are used up.
   c. C forms at the same rate as each of A and B are used up.
   d. C forms at a rate independent of the rate of change in reactants A and B.
   e. C forms at a rate equal to the sum of the rate at which reactants A and B are used up.

4. Which property cannot be used to measure the rate of the reaction given by the equation below?
   $$CaC_2(s) + H_2O(\ell) \rightarrow Ca(OH)_2(aq) + C_2H_2(g)$$
   a. change in concentration of reactants
   b. change in pH
   c. change in mass of $CaC_2(s)$
   d. change in volume of $C_2H_2(g)$
   e. change in concentration of $Ca^{2+}(aq)$

5. A decrease in temperature will decrease the rate of a reaction principally because
   a. the particles have less potential energy at the lower temperature.
   b. the particles in the reactants move closer together at a lower temperature.
   c. the activation energy for the reaction increases with a decrease in temperature.
   d. the activation energy for the reaction decreases with a decrease in temperature.
   e. fewer particles have energy equal to or greater than the activation energy.

6. Which graph correctly shows the change in amount of product as the reaction shown below proceeds to completion?
   $$S_8(s) + 8O_2(g) \rightarrow 8SO_2(g)$$

   a.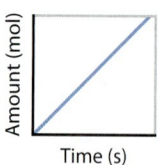

   b.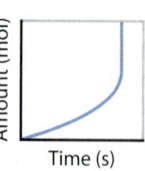

   c.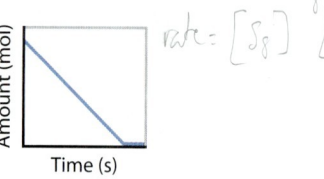

   d.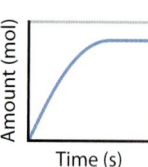

   e.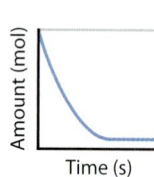

7. A reaction is exothermic in the forward direction. Which statement is correct with regard to the activation energy of the reverse reaction?
   a. $E_{a(rev)} = E_{a(fwd)} + \Delta H_r$
   b. $E_{a(rev)} = 2E_{a(fwd)} + \Delta H_r$
   c. $E_{a(rev)} = E_{a(fwd)} - 2\Delta H_r$
   d. $E_{a(rev)} = E_{a(fwd)} - \Delta H_r$
   e. $E_{a(rev)} = 2E_{a(fwd)} - \Delta H_r$

8. The expression for the rate law may be written in the general form:
   $$rate = k[A]^m[B]^n$$
   Experimental evidence indicates that for a particular reaction, $m = 2$ and $n = \dfrac{1}{2}$. What is the overall order of the reaction?
   a. 1
   b. $2\dfrac{1}{2}$
   c. 4
   d. $1\dfrac{1}{2}$
   e. $\dfrac{3}{2}$

9. Examine the potential energy diagram shown below. Identify the letter that represents the position(s) of a reaction intermediate.

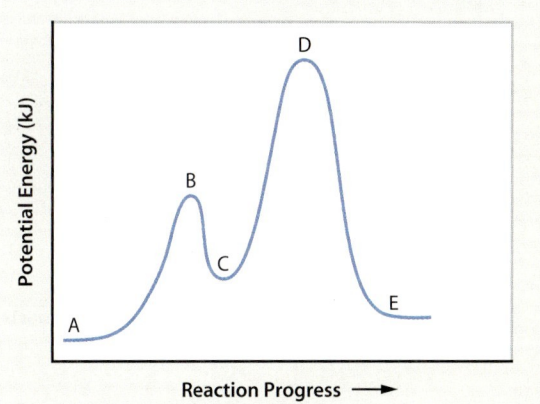

a. E
b. B and D
c. B, C, and D
d. C
e. A

10. Which of the following statements about an activated complex is accurate?
a. It always breaks down to form product molecules.
b. It occurs only in endothermic processes.
c. It has lower chemical potential energy than reactants or products.
d. It is a stable substance.
e. It occurs at the transition state of the reaction.

11. Which of the following most closely applies to collision theory?
a. kinetic molecular theory
b. the first law of thermodynamics
c. Boyle's law
d. atomic theory
e. the law of definite proportions

12. For the single displacement reaction,
$$Zn(s) + CuSO_4(aq) \rightarrow Cu(s) + ZnSO_4(aq)$$
select the factor from the list below that would have the greatest effect on the rate of reaction.
a. increase the amount of Zn(s)
b. increase the amount of Cu(s)
c. stir the reaction
d. increase the concentration of $CuSO_4(aq)$
e. increase the pressure on the system

13. A catalyst will increase the rate of a reaction by
a. decreasing ΔH for both the forward and reverse reactions.
b. increasing the number of collisions between particles.
c. providing an alternate reaction mechanism having a lower activation energy.
d. eliminating the rate-determining step in the reaction mechanism.
e. acting as an intermediate in the reaction mechanism.

14. Two test tubes, A and B, contain samples of zinc that are equal in mass and have the same surface area. Equal concentrations and amounts of sulfuric acid are added to the test tubes. A catalyst is added to test tube A. Why must the zinc samples have identical surface areas?
a. Test tube B is the control.
b. Surface area is another factor that could affect the rate of the reactions.
c. Test tube A is the control.
d. Both (a) and (b) are correct.
e. Both (b) and (c) are correct.

Answer the questions below.

15. State a quantitative definition of rate of reaction.
16. What would be a possible unit for measuring the rate of reaction for each of the following?
a. $O_2(g)$ is produced in a reaction.
b. Gases are produced in a closed container.
c. Acid is used up during a reaction.

17. How does the total pressure on a system affect the rate of reaction between
a. two reactants in the gas state?
b. two reactants in an aqueous solution?

18. Suggest two reasons why some reactions are difficult to start.

19. There are several important concepts related to the rates of reactions.
a. At what point in a chemical reaction does the initial reaction rate occur?
b. How can the initial rate of a chemical reaction be determined?
c. Is it possible, during a reaction, for the instantaneous and average rates of reaction to have the same value? How would you know if this is the case?

Chapter 6 REVIEW

20. Catalysts can significantly alter the rates of many chemical reactions.
   a. How does a catalyst speed up the rate of a reaction?
   b. The net ionic equation for the reaction between lead(II) ions, Pb^{2+}(aq), and carbonate ions, CO_3^{2-}(aq), is shown below as it occurs in aqueous solution. Would a catalyst affect the rate of this reaction? Give a reason for your answer.
   Pb^{2+} (aq) + CO_3^{2-}(aq) → $PbCO_3$(s)

21. A reaction is carried out between two gases in a closed system of fixed volume. Why does an increase in the partial pressure of a gaseous reactant increase the rate of reaction?

22. In terms of collision theory, how does stirring affect the rate at which a solid dissolves in water?

23. What is the difference between the activation energy and the activated complex in a reaction?

24. One way to determine the relationship between the reaction rate and the concentration is to determine the initial rates of reactions at different concentrations. Describe how this type of study is performed.

25. Each elementary step in a reaction mechanism usually occurs between two particles. Why is this important for each step in a reaction mechanism?

26. Name factors that would affect the ability of a substance to catalyze a reaction. How does each factor affect the catalytic process?

27. For a reaction at room temperature, a plot of the rate of reaction vs. concentration of reactant gives a straight line.
   a. How are the rate of reaction and concentration related?
   b. What does the slope of the graph of rate vs. concentration represent?
   c. What is the order of the reaction represented by this straight line relationship?

28. The rate law for the reaction
$2NO(g) + O_2(g) → 2NO_2(g)$ is rate = $k[NO][O_2]$.
   a. If the concentration of each reactant is reduced by 50%, what will be the overall effect on the value of the rate constant?
   b. A proposed mechanism for the reaction has two steps:
   Step 1: $NO + O_2 → NO_3$
   Step 2: $NO_3 + NO → 2NO_2$
   What label is given to NO_3 in this reaction mechanism?

Thinking and Investigation

Use the potential energy diagram below to answer questions 29 to 35.

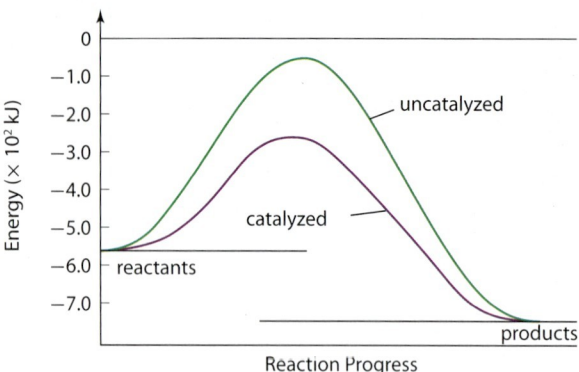

29. What is the $E_{a(fwd)}$ of the uncatalyzed reaction?
30. What is the $E_{a(fwd)}$ of the catalyzed reaction?
31. Which reaction is faster? Why?
32. What is the $E_{a(rev)}$ of the uncatalyzed reaction?
33. What is the $E_{a(rev)}$ of the catalyzed reaction?
34. What is the ΔH_r of the forward reaction?
35. What is the ΔH_r of the reverse reaction?
36. For the decomposition reaction $2AB → A_2 + B_2$, the concentration of A_2 after 4.4 min = 0.52 mol/L and after 5.6 min its concentration is 0.68 mol/L. What is the average rate of change in the concentration of AB over this period of time?
37. The reaction between copper and 1.0 L of nitric acid, HNO_3(aq), is written as follows:
$Cu(s) + 4HNO_3(aq) →$
$Cu(NO_3)_2(aq) + 2H_2O(\ell) + 2NO_2(g)$
The concentration of the HNO_3(aq) changes by 0.10 mol/L over a period of 1.5 min. What is the rate of change in the mass of the copper expressed in g/s?
38. Identify the potential energy diagram(s) that represent each of the following reactions. The reaction that
   a. has the largest $E_{a(fwd)}$
   b. has the smallest ΔH_r
   c. is endothermic
   d. occurs the fastest

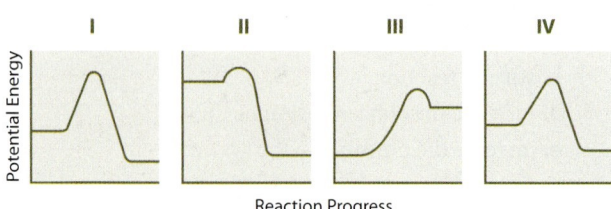

39. Consider the following reaction:
$$4HBr(g) + O_2(g) \rightarrow 2Br_2(g) + 2H_2O(g)$$
Explain using words and an equation how the rate of decomposition of HBr (in mol/L·s) compares with the rate of formation of Br_2 (in mol/L·s).

40. Consider the following reaction:
$$MgCO_3(s) + 2HCl(aq) \rightarrow MgCl_2(aq) + H_2O(\ell) + CO_2(g)$$
It is determined that 0.48 g of $MgCO_3(s)$ reacts in 5.8 min. Calculate the rate at which $CO_2(g)$ is generated in moles per second.

41. Consider the following reaction:
$$2H_2(g) + 2NO(g) \rightarrow N_2(g) + 2H_2O(g)$$
A proposed mechanism for this reaction is
Step 1: $H_2 + NO \rightarrow H_2O + N$ (slow)
Step 2: $N + NO \rightarrow N_2 + O$ (fast)
Step 3: $O + H_2 \rightarrow H_2O$ (fast)
If a catalyst was used with this reaction, which potential energy diagram shown below would most accurately show the catalytic action on the mechanism? Explain why it would.

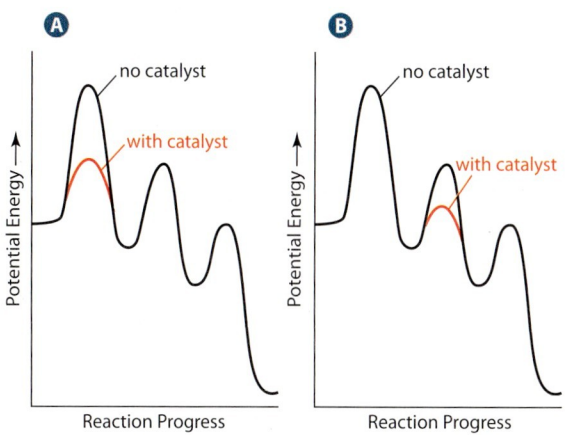

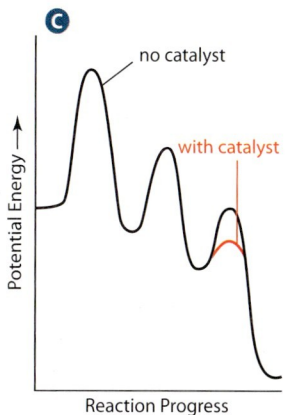

42. The enthalpy change, ΔH, for an endothermic reaction is +25 kJ. The activation energy for the forward reaction, $E_{a(fwd)}$, is +45 kJ.
  a. What is the activation energy for the reverse reaction, $E_{a(rev)}$?
  b. If the reaction was exothermic with an enthalpy of reaction of –25 kJ, and the forward reaction still had an activation energy of +45 kJ, would the reverse reaction have the same activation energy as in (a)? Show your reasoning with a calculation.

43. Examine the potential energy diagram shown below and answer the questions that follow.

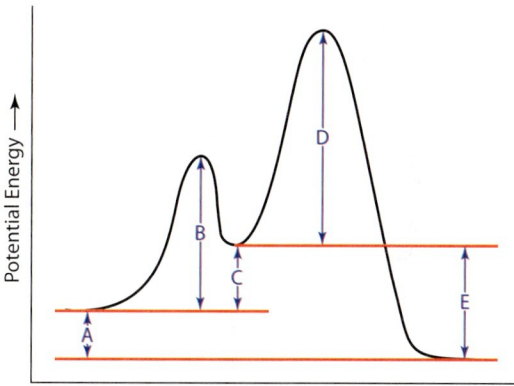

  a. How many steps are in this reaction?
  b. What quantity would represent the overall activation energy for the reaction?
  c. Is the overall reaction exothermic or endothermic?
  d. What does the quantity B represent?
  e. What does the quantity E represent?

44. The rate laws for two reactions are compared. For reaction A, rate = $k[R]^2$, and for reaction B, rate = $k[R][S]$.
  a. What is the overall order of each reaction?
  b. What is the effect on each reaction of doubling the molar concentration of R?

45. Identify the role of each of the following in the reaction mechanism below.
  a. P_2 **b.** PQ **c.** P_2Q_2 **d.** Q_2
  Step 1: $P_2 + Q_2 \rightarrow 2PQ$
  Step 2: $2PQ \rightarrow P_2Q_2$
  Step 3: $P_2Q_2 \rightarrow P_2 + Z$

46. Two gases, $X_2(g)$ and $Y_2(g)$, react in a closed container. The rate law for the reaction is rate = $k[X_2]$. If the volume of the container is reduced to half the original volume, how will the rate be affected?

Chapter 6 REVIEW

47. A mechanism has been proposed for the reaction below:
$$C_2H_5Br + C_6H_6 \rightarrow HBr + C_2H_5C_6H_6$$
Step 1: $C_2H_5Br + AlBr_3 \rightarrow AlBr_4^- + C_2H_5^+$
Step 2: $C_2H_5^+ + C_6H_6 \rightarrow C_6H_6C_2H_5^+$ (slow)
Step 3: $C_6H_6C_2H_5^+ + AlBr_4^- \rightarrow$
$$AlBr_3 + HBr + C_2H_5C_6H_6$$

  a. Identify the rate-determining step.
  b. Identify any intermediates that occur in this mechanism.
  c. Is there a catalyst shown in this mechanism? Explain your answer.

Communication

48. In planning an experiment to measure and compare the rate of reaction using different metals with dilute hydrochloric acid, you must decide whether to measure the decrease in mass of metal or the increase in volume of hydrogen gas produced in the reaction. If you use the change in mass of the metal, how would you present the data in your report so that the comparison between metals is valid?

49. Use a concept organizer to summarize the units that are appropriate for measuring the rate in the change in the amount of gaseous products in a reaction.

50. The nature of activation energy is debated in your group. The statement that has been challenged is "*Activation energy depends on the frequency of collision between particles.*" Is this statement correct? Explain your reasoning.

51. Two measurements were made of a reaction to determine the instantaneous rate of reaction at different times. One measurement gave the rate of disappearance of reactants as 3.6×10^{-2} mol/L·s. Another measurement gave the rate of disappearance of reactants as 3.6×10^2 mol/L·s. In your report of these results, explain how the two calculated instantaneous rates can be so widely different for the same reaction.

52. You are asked if a catalyst changes the rate of reaction in the same way that temperature changes the rate of reaction. How would you explain the difference?

53. The reaction between magnesium and dilute hydrochloric acid was used to illustrate the effect of surface area on the rate of reaction. In the first trial, the volume of hydrogen produced over 1 min was measured when a cube of magnesium having a known surface area reacted. The reaction was repeated using two identical cubes of magnesium, each with the same surface area as the cube used in the first trial. In this trial, twice as much hydrogen gas was collected in 1 min.

One person claims that the results demonstrate that the rate of reaction increases with an increase in surface area. Another person states that this is not a case of more surface area and the results do not illustrate the relationship between surface area and rate of reaction. Which person is correct? Give a reason for your answer, using a diagram to support your answer.

54. Two reactions occur at the same temperature and are between two reactants. Both reactions have an activation energy of +60 kJ but one is endothermic and the other is exothermic. Explain to someone in your class why the two reactions will not necessarily have the same rate of reaction.

55. Use a graphic organizer to summarize the factors to consider when selecting a catalyst for a reaction.

56. When demonstrating the effect of surface area on the rate of reaction, your instructor first ignites a pile of flour on a wire gauze pad and then blows powdered flour into a flame. The piled-up flour is not easily ignited and burns slowly. The flour blown into the flame ignites immediately and burns in a burst of flame. Draw a potential energy diagram for both burnings and relate this to collision theory to explain the difference in the rate of burning.

57. Draw a graphic organizer to summarize the ways in which the rate of reaction between two gases can be increased.

58. **BIG IDEAS** Efficiency of chemical reactions can be improved by applying optimal conditions. Reactions that must be carried out at high temperatures or at high pressures can be costly for industry. If carried out close to normal conditions, the reaction becomes more cost-efficient. The use of a catalyst can achieve this efficiency. Create a display or construct a concept map that answers the following questions:
  a. How does a catalyst change the rate of a reaction?
  b. How does a catalyst affect the rate of the forward and reverse reactions?
  c. Why is only a small amount of a catalyst necessary?
  d. Will any material act as a catalyst for a reaction?
  e. Give two industrial examples that rely on a catalyst to increase the efficiency of the reaction.

59. Summarize your learning in this chapter using a graphic organizer. To help you, the Chapter 6 Summary lists Key Terms and Key Concepts. Refer to Using Graphic Organizers in Appendix A to help decide which graphic organizer to use.

Application

60. In the contact process to make sulfuric acid, sulfur dioxide, $SO_2(g)$, is needed. This gas can be made by heating pyrite, $FeS_2(s)$.
$$4FeS_2(s) + 11O_2(g) \rightarrow 2Fe_2O_3(s) + 8SO_2(g)$$
  a. What would be an appropriate unit to measure the rate of decomposition of $FeS_2(s)$?
  b. What would be an appropriate unit to measure the rate of formation of $SO_2(g)$?
  c. How can the rate of decomposition of $FeS_2(s)$ and the rate of formation of $SO_2(g)$ be compared? How do the two rates compare?

61. In the Hall-Heroult process, molten cryolite, Na_3AlF_6, decomposes as shown by the equation below:
$$Na_3AlF_6(\ell) \rightarrow 3Na(\ell) + Al(\ell) + 3F_2(g)$$
If the average rate of formation of $F_2(g)$ is 0.85 mol/s, what is the average rate of decomposition of Na_3AlF_6, in grams per second?

62. BIG IDEAS Energy changes and rates of chemical reactions can be described quantitatively.
A company produces ammonia to make fertilizer using the combination reaction below:
$$N_2(g) + 3H_2(g) \rightarrow 2NH_3(g) + 91.8 \text{ kJ}$$
  a. Use the concentration vs. time data in the table below to graphically determine the average rate of formation of $NH_3(g)$ over the first 130 s of the reaction.

Data for Production of Ammonia

Time (s)	Concentration (mol/L)
0	0.000
20	0.0500
60	0.100
90	0.125
130	0.148
160	0.160
200	0.160

  b. For the $NH_3(g)$ to be produced at this rate in the process, will the reactants $N_2(g)$ and $H_2(g)$ be used up at this same rate? Explain your reasoning using calculations to support your answer.

63. In an industrial process, dinitrogen pentoxide, $N_2O_5(g)$, is used at a rate of 5.00×10^2 kg per hour. The equation for the process is given below:
$$2N_2O_5(g) \rightarrow 4NO_2(g) + O_2(g)$$
What is the rate at which $NO_2(g)$ is produced in moles per minute?

64. In the Haber-Bosch process, it is estimated that in the catalyzed reaction, often only 15% of the nitrogen and hydrogen convert to ammonia for one pass of the gases through the reactor. Suggest a reason why the percentage conversion is so low in the presence of a catalyst. What could be done to improve the conversion?

65. To increase the efficiency of production of a product, a manufacturer investigates the effect of temperature on the process. A suggestion is made by the chemist that the reaction temperature be increased. The rate of the reaction between two gases that occurs in one step is 1.43×10^{-3} mol/L·s at $T_1 = 18.0°C$. For this reaction, the activation energy is 20 kJ and the enthalpy change is −30 kJ. At $T_2 = 28.0°C$, the reaction rate almost doubles to 2.50×10^{-3} mol/L·s.
  a. Using a graph, explain why the increase in temperature increased the rate of reaction.
  b. Sketch a potential energy diagram to illustrate any change that is expected in the activation energy and the enthalpy change at the higher temperature.
  c. What other cost factor must be considered if the temperature is changed?

66. A reaction between substances D and E is found to be first order with respect to both D and E. Examine two proposed mechanisms for this reaction and explain which is more likely to be correct. Can it be stated with certainty that either of these mechanisms is correct? Explain your answer.
Mechanism 1
Step 1: $D \rightarrow G + H$ (slow)
Step 2: $E + G \rightarrow I$ (fast)
Mechanism 2
Step 1: $D + E \rightarrow DE$ (slow)
Step 2: $DE \rightarrow H + I$ (fast)

67. In an industrial process that is highly exothermic, a new, less costly, compound is to be substituted for an existing reactant. However, the process is difficult to initiate with the new material. Suggest a reason that may explain this difficulty in starting up the reaction. What other change could be introduced to allow the new reactant to be used?

68. Transition metals are frequently used as catalysts for industrial reactions. Use your knowledge of atomic structure to suggest why this type of metal is a good choice for a catalyst.

69. For what type of reaction is the number of collisions between reactants not a factor? Give an example.

Chapter 6 SELF-ASSESSMENT

Select the letter of the best answer below.

1. **K/U** Consider the reaction shown below:
   $$Mg(s) + 2CH_3COOH(aq) \rightarrow Mg(CH_3COO)_2(aq) + H_2(g)$$
   The rate of reaction can be calculated over a period of time by determining the change in the
   a. pH of the solution.
   b. concentration of Mg(s).
   c. colour.
   d. temperature.
   e. volume of the solution.

2. **T/I** Reactant A(g) has a concentration of 0.39 mol/L at the beginning of a reaction. After 3.2 min the concentration of A(g) is 0.023 mol/L. What is the average rate of change of A(g) over this time?
   a. $5.0 \times 10^{-2} \frac{mol}{L \cdot s}$
   b. $1.1 \times 10^{-1} \frac{mol}{L \cdot s}$
   c. $3.9 \times 10^{-1} \frac{mol}{L \cdot s}$
   d. $3.9 \times 10^{-2} \frac{mol}{L \cdot s}$
   e. $1.9 \times 10^{-3} \frac{mol}{L \cdot s}$

3. **K/U** For a reaction in aqueous solution, an increase in the concentration of the reactant(s) increases the rate of reaction because
   a. the potential energy of the chemical bonds is decreased.
   b. there are more collisions between reactant particles.
   c. the intermolecular attractions between water and the aqueous ions increase.
   d. the kinetic energy of the reactant particles increases.
   e. a greater percentage of the aqueous ions have energy equal to or in excess of the activation energy.

4. **K/U** Consider the potential energy diagram in question 23. Which of the following is the activation energy for the forward reaction in step 2?
   a. B
   b. H
   c. K
   d. J
   e. E

5. **K/U** The rate law expression for a reaction is rate = $k[B]^0[C]$. Based on this rate law, which statement is correct?
   a. The reaction is zero order overall.
   b. The reaction is second order overall.
   c. The reaction is first order with respect to B and C.
   d. The reaction is first order overall.
   e. The rate determining step must involve B.

6. **T/I** For a reaction having $\Delta H_r = +58$ kJ, the activation energy for the forward reaction, $E_{a(fwd)}$, is +89 kJ. What is $E_{a(rev)}$?
   a. +114 kJ
   b. +37 kJ
   c. +73 kJ
   d. −89 kJ
   e. +31 kJ

7. **T/I** Given the reaction mechanism shown below, for which substance would a change in concentration have the greatest effect on the overall rate of reaction?
   Step 1: A → B + C (fast)
   Step 2: C + D → F (slow)
   Step 3: F + B → G (fast)
   a. A
   b. A + B
   c. D
   d. C + D
   e. F

8. **K/U** For any chemical reaction, which of the following is most closely related to the overall rate?
   a. the average rate of all the steps in the reaction mechanism
   b. the number of steps in the reaction mechanism
   c. the overall reaction
   d. the slowest step in the reaction mechanism
   e. the fastest step in the reaction mechanism

9. **A** A reaction mechanism is suggested for an industrial process.
   Step 1: A_2 → 2A (slow)
   Step 2: 2A + B → C + D (fast)
   Step 3: D + G → DG (fast)
   Step 4: DG → F + G (fast)
   Which statement about this mechanism is false?
   a. G is a catalyst.
   b. There will be four transitional states in this mechanism.
   c. Step 1 is the rate-determining step.
   d. There are two reaction intermediates in this mechanism.
   e. The overall reaction is $A_2 + B \rightarrow C + F$.

10. **K/U** Which property listed below does not apply to a catalyst?
    a. lowers the overall activation energy of a reaction
    b. increases the number of collisions
    c. reacts in one step but is regenerated in another step
    d. provides an alternate path for the reaction
    e. increases the rate of the rate-determining step in a reaction mechanism

Use sentences and diagrams as appropriate, to answer the questions below.

11. **K/U** For a reaction that is endothermic,
   a. how is $E_{a(fwd)}$ related to $E_{a(rev)}$ and ΔH_r?
   b. how do $E_{a(fwd)}$ and $E_{a(rev)}$ compare in magnitude?

12. **C** A reaction between two gases occurs in a closed container that is fitted with a piston that can be moved to adjust the total volume. Explain how you would use diagrams of the apparatus to explain to a group how the rate of reaction between the gases increases with a decrease in volume.

13. **A** A company is testing potassium chlorate as an accelerant in the manufacture of a firecracker.

$$2KClO_3(s) + heat \rightarrow 2KCl(s) + 3O_2(g)$$

If 0.20 g of $KClO_3(s)$ decomposes in 2.8 s, at what rate is oxygen, $O_2(g)$, released over this time at SATP?

14. **A** A box is labelled *Explosives*, yet it does not explode. Explain why.

15. **C** Prepare a graphic presentation that illustrates to the class how collision theory can account for a doubling of the rate of reaction when the temperature increases by 20°C.

16. **T/I** Sketch a potential energy diagram based on the data below and determine the overall enthalpy change for the reaction.
   Step 1: $E_{a(fwd)} = +11$ kJ, $E_{a(rev)} = +31$ kJ
   Step 2: $E_{a(fwd)} = +61$ kJ, $\Delta H_{fwd} = +31$ kJ
   Step 3: $E_{a(fwd)} = +31$ kJ, $\Delta H_{fwd} = -75$ kJ

17. **A** For the reaction shown below, it was determined by experiment that nitrous oxide, NO(g), was reacting at an initial rate of 0.050 mol/L·s. Was $H_2O(g)$ used up at an equal rate? Explain your reasoning.

$$4NO(g) + 6H_2O(g) \rightarrow 4NH_3(g) + 5O_2(g)$$

18. **C** The following reaction is known to be second order with respect to $NO_2(g)$ and zero order with respect to CO(g). Propose a mechanism for this reaction.

$$NO_2(g) + CO(g) \rightarrow CO_2(g) + NO(g)$$

19. **T/I** Consider the following reaction:

$$2AgNO_3(aq) + CuCl_2(aq) \rightarrow 2AgCl(s) + Cu(NO_3)_2(aq)$$

The concentration of $Ag(NO_3)_2(aq)$ at $t = 30.0$ s is 0.42 mol/L. At $t = 60.0$ s its concentration is 0.28 mol/L. What is the change in [Cl$^-$] during this time?

20. **T/I** An exothermic reaction carried out at 10°C has an activation energy of +65 kJ and enthalpy change $\Delta H_r = -80$ kJ. How would these two properties change when the concentration of the reactants are altered to double the rate of reaction? Explain your answer.

21. **K/U** A reaction follows the rate law rate $= k[Br_2]^2$. Is this a first-order or second-order reaction? Explain your answer.

22. **T/I** A reaction produces 0.20 mol/L of product per minute at 25°C. Explain how you could get the same reaction to produce 0.50 mol/L of product per minute without changing the contents of the reaction vessel.

23. **K/U** Examine the potential energy diagram for a reaction mechanism and answer the questions that follow.

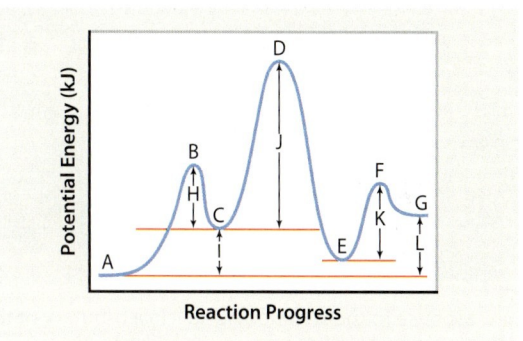

a. How many steps are involved? Explain.
b. Identify each label in this potential energy diagram.
c. Overall, is a net amount of energy added or released?

24. **A** Explain what femtosecond technology is and how it is used to study reaction mechanisms.

25. **C** Explain how an increase in temperature affects the rate of a reaction. Sketch a graph to use as the basis for your explanation.

Self-Check

If you missed question …	1	2	3	4	5	6	7	8	9	10	11	12	13	14	15	16	17	18	19	20	21	22	23	24	25
Review section(s)…	6.1	6.1	6.2	6.2	6.3	6.2	6.3	6.3	6.3	6.2	6.2	6.2	6.1	6.2	6.2	6.2	6.3	6.3	6.1	6.2	6.3	6.2	6.2	6.3	6.2

Unit 3 Project

Conduct an Inquiry

Neutralizing a Sulfuric Acid Spill

In 2007, a train derailment caused approximately 150 000 L of sulfuric acid to spill into a tributary of the Blanche River just north of North Bay, Ontario. Sulfuric acid has many applications in chemical industries, including the manufacture of paper, soap, and batteries. It is highly corrosive and its fumes are extremely harmful if inhaled. Numerous organisms were harmed as a result of the North Bay spill because the pH of the river water had dropped significantly before workers were able to neutralize the acid. Sulfuric acid also undergoes a violent exothermic reaction when mixed with water. The resulting change in water temperature may have harmed organisms as well.

In this project, you will assume the role of a hazardous materials consultant who is hired by the Ontario government to determine the most suitable method for neutralizing a sulfuric acid spill in a river. You will experimentally determine the temperature change that occurs when sulfuric acid is added to water. Then you will determine the suitability of various neutralizing agents, taking into account several factors, including the change in river water temperature after each neutralization reaction. Finally, you will present your findings and recommendation to the government.

Which neutralizing agent is the most suitable for neutralizing a sulfuric acid spill in a river?

A rapid response to the sulfuric acid spill in a tributary of the Blanche River near North Bay, Ontario in 2007 helped to reduce environmental damage. This response included adding a neutralizing agent to the river water.

Initiate and Plan

1. Use print and Internet resources to research factors that will help you evaluate which neutralizing agent is the most suitable for neutralizing sulfuric acid that has spilled into a river. The neutralizing agents you will consider are calcium carbonate, $CaCO_3(s)$; sodium carbonate, $Na_2CO_3(s)$; sodium hydrogen carbonate, $NaHCO_3(s)$; and calcium oxide, $CaO(s)$.

   - What terms, such as *thermal pollution*, do you need to define to better understand the scientific material you are reading?
   - How can a change in water temperature affect aquatic ecosystems?
   - What other factors, such as cost, might affect the suitability of a neutralizing agent?

2. Design an investigation that uses a simple calorimeter to measure the temperature change that occurs when sulfuric acid is added to water.

   - Write a brief overview of your experimental design.
   - Draw a diagram of the calorimeter you will use, labelling its components clearly.
   - List the chemicals and equipment you will need. You will be using a dilution of concentrated sulfuric acid that is approved for use in a school laboratory.
   - Describe all necessary safety precautions. Refer to any relevant material safety data sheets (MSDS) to explain why you must use a dilution of concentrated sulfuric acid in your investigation.
   - Write a step-by-step procedure for your investigation.

3. Have your teacher approve your experimental design, materials, procedure, and safety precautions.

Perform and Record

4. Conduct your investigation, repeating it at least once.
5. Use a table to record measurements and observations.

Analyze and Interpret

1. Your teacher will provide you with the temperature change that occurs when concentrated sulfuric acid is added to water. Compare and contrast this temperature change with the temperature change you measured in your investigation.

2. Use the temperature change for concentrated sulfuric acid to calculate the temperature of the river water immediately after the acid spill. Create a table to summarize your calculations.

   - Assume that the initial temperature of the river water was 10°C.
   - Assume that the area of river water affected by the acid spill was approximately 15 m wide, 500 m long, and 10 m deep.
   - Assume that the specific heat capacities of the sulfuric acid solution and the water are the same.
   - Use the following density values: 1 g/mL for the density of water, and 1.84 g/mL for the density of the concentrated sulfuric acid.

3. Write balanced equations for the reaction of sulfuric acid with each of the neutralizing agents below. (**Hint:** Assume that the products are a solid salt, liquid water, and carbon dioxide gas for all reactants except for (d).)

   a. $CaCO_3(s)$
   b. $Na_2CO_3(s)$
   c. $NaHCO_3(s)$
   d. $CaO(s)$

4. Calculate the enthalpy of reaction for the neutralization of sulfuric acid with each of the four reactants. Then use these values and the temperature of the river water immediately after the acid spill to calculate the temperature of the river water after each neutralization reaction. Create a table summarizing your calculations for each neutralization reaction. The following tips will help you complete your calculations.

   - Use Hess's law and standard molar enthalpies of formation to determine the enthalpy of reaction for each neutralization reaction. To complete your calculations, use the table "Selected Standard Molar Enthalpies of Formation" in Appendix B, as well as additional values provided by your teacher.
   - Calculate the temperature change and the final temperature of the river water after each neutralization reaction. Assume that this water includes both the water in the river and the water produced in the neutralization reaction. Also assume that the heat produced by each reaction is absorbed by both sources of water.

5. Use your research and calculations to evaluate which reaction is the most suitable for neutralizing sulfuric acid. Explain your reasoning.

Communicate Your Findings

6. Decide on the best way to present your findings and recommendation to the government, such as a computer presentation, a written report, or an interactive Web page.

7. Prepare a presentation that includes the following:
   - a summary of your experimental design and results
   - tables summarizing the calculations you performed
   - your evaluation of the most suitable method for neutralizing a sulfuric acid spill in a river and an explanation of the factors you took into account
   - a literature citation section that documents the sources you used to complete your research, using an appropriate academic format

Assessment Criteria

Once you complete your project, ask yourself these questions. Did you…

- ✓ **T/I** assess your information sources for accuracy and reliability?
- ✓ **K/U** describe your experimental design, including any safety precautions?
- ✓ **T/I** conduct your investigation, repeating your procedure at least once?
- ✓ **C** use tables to record your measurements and calculations?
- ✓ **A** use your research and calculations to evaluate which reaction is the most suitable for neutralizing a sulfuric acid spill in a river?
- ✓ **C** communicate your findings in a format that is appropriate to your audience and purpose, using suitable instructional visuals and scientific vocabulary?
- ✓ **C** document your sources using an appropriate academic format?

UNIT 3 SUMMARY

BIG IDEAS

- Energy changes and rates of chemical reactions can be described quantitatively.
- Efficiency of chemical reactions can be improved by applying optimal conditions.
- Technologies that transform energy can have societal and environmental costs and benefits.

Overall Expectations

In this unit, you learned how to…

- **analyze** technologies and chemical processes that are based on energy changes, and **evaluate** them in terms of their efficiencies and their effects on the environment
- **investigate** and **analyze** energy changes and rates of reaction in physical and chemical processes, and **solve** related problems
- **demonstrate** an understanding of energy changes and rates of reaction

Chapter 5 Energy Changes

Key ideas

- A system is the object or substance being studied, and the surroundings are everything else in the universe. Systems can be open, closed, or isolated.
- The first law of thermodynamics states that energy cannot be created or destroyed but can be transformed from one type of energy to another type of energy or transferred from one object to another object.
- The second law of thermodynamics states that, when two objects are in thermal contact, heat will be transferred from the object at a higher temperature to the object at the lower temperature until they reach thermal equilibrium.
- An enthalpy change in a system, occurring at constant pressure, is the same as the amount of heat that is exchanged between the system and its surroundings. Enthalpy changes can be positive or negative and depend only on the initial and final states of the system.
- The standard enthalpy of a reaction as written, $\Delta H_r°$, is the enthalpy change for the amount in moles of each reactant and product as determined by the coefficients in the chemical equation.
- A process taking place in a simple calorimeter occurs at constant pressure. The amount of heat that is exchanged between the calorimeter and the system is equal to the change in the enthalpy of the system.

- Hess's law states that the enthalpy change of a physical or chemical process depends only on the initial and final conditions. The enthalpy change of the overall process is the sum of the enthalpy changes of its individual steps.
- The standard enthalpy of formation of a compound, $\Delta H_f°$, is the enthalpy change that results from synthesizing 1 mol of the compound from its elements in their most stable state under standard conditions.
- You can calculate the enthalpy change for any reaction by applying the formula

$$\Delta H_r° = \Sigma(n\Delta H_f° \text{ products}) - \Sigma(n\Delta H_f° \text{ reactants})$$

- The efficiency of a chemical, physical, or nuclear process can be expressed as

$$\text{efficiency} = \frac{\text{energy output}}{\text{energy input}} \times 100\%$$

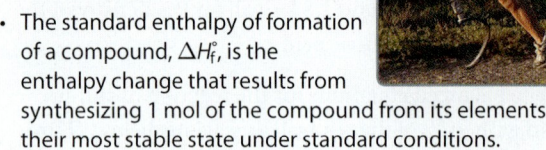

- Fossil fuels are non-renewable resources, which contribute to global warming, acid rain, and pollution of the environment. Renewable energy resources include hydroelectric power, solar energy, and wind energy.

Chapter 6 Rates of Reaction

Key ideas

- A reaction rate is the speed at which a chemical reaction occurs. A reaction rate is measured by the change in the amount of reactants consumed or products formed over a given time interval.
- The instantaneous rate of a reaction is the rate of the reaction at a particular point in time.
- The average rate of a chemical reaction is the change in the concentration of a reactant or a product per unit time over a given time interval.

- According to collision theory, a reaction will occur only if the reactants collide with the correct orientation and with energy equal to or above the activation energy, E_a.
- When reactants collide with sufficient energy to overcome the activation energy barrier, they form an activated complex, which is an unstable transition state.

UNIT 3 SUMMARY & REVIEW

- Factors that affect the rate of a chemical reaction include the nature of the reactants, the concentration of a solution, the temperature, the pressure of gaseous reactants, the surface area of solid particles of the reactants, and the presence of a catalyst.
- A catalyst is a substance that increases the rate of a reaction but is itself unchanged at the end of the reaction.
- To determine the relationship between the rate of a reaction and the concentration of reactants, several experiments must be carried out and the initial rates of each reaction determined.
- The rate of a reaction can be directly proportional to the concentration of a reactant, or proportional to the square of the concentration of a reactant.
- The rate law for a chemical reaction is a mathematical relationship that must be determined experimentally.
- Elementary steps are a series of simple reactions that describe the progress of an overall reaction at the molecular level.
- The slowest elementary step in a chemical reaction determines the rate of the overall reaction.

Knowledge and Understanding

Select the letter of the best answer below.

1. The total kinetic energy of all the particles in a sample represents the _____ of a sample.
   a. thermal energy
   b. potential energy
   c. enthalpy of formation
   d. activation energy
   e. enthalpy

2. Which source of energy for production of electricity has the least negative impact on the environment?
   a. coal
   b. natural gas
   c. oil
   d. solar
   e. propane

3. A match is not needed to keep a fire burning because the
   a. reaction is endothermic and heat energy is constantly absorbed.
   b. heat dissipates quickly.
   c. reaction is exothermic and the heat given off is used to supply kinetic energy to the fuel.
   d. oxygen provides thermal energy to maintain the reaction.
   e. heat from the match lowers the activation energy.

4. A kettle uses 925 kJ of electrical energy to heat a given mass of water by 40.0°C. In terms of energy efficiency, what does this quantity of energy represent?
   a. energy input
   b. the minimum efficiency
   c. the EnerGuide rating
   d. the maximum efficiency
   e. energy output

5. The sum of the enthalpies of formation of the reactants in a reaction is 300 kJ and the sum of the enthalpies of formation of the products is 250 kJ. Which statement about the reaction is correct?
   a. The reaction cannot occur.
   b. The ΔH is 300 kJ.
   c. The reaction is exothermic.
   d. The thermal energy given off is 550 kJ.
   e. The ΔH_r° is 550 kJ.

6. Which factor will not affect the rate of the reaction shown below?
   $$Ca(s) + H_2O(\ell) \rightarrow Ca(OH)_2(aq) + H_2(g)$$
   a. use of a catalyst
   b. increase in pressure
   c. increase in surface area of $Ca(s)$
   d. increase in water temperature
   e. decrease in water temperature

7. Which of the following statements about the chemical reaction represented by the potential energy diagram below is correct?

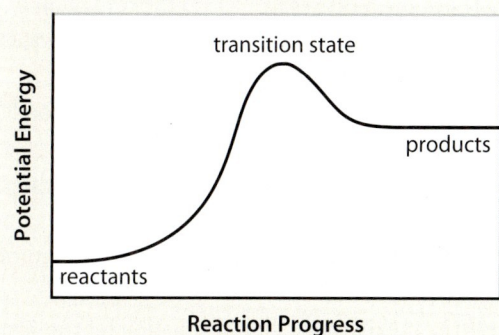

   a. The forward reaction is exothermic.
   b. $E_{a(fwd)}$ is less than $E_{a(rev)}$.
   c. ΔH_{rev} is a positive quantity.
   d. ΔH_{fwd} is a negative quantity.
   e. ΔH_{rev} is equal in magnitude to ΔH_{fwd}.

UNIT 3 REVIEW

8. Which of the following represents the units for the rate constant for a reaction that is second order in one reactant and zero order in another reactant?
   a. mol·s/L^2
   b. mol^2·s/L^2
   c. L·s/mol
   d. L/mol·s
   e. L/mol^2·s

9. What is the overall order of reaction for a chemical reaction that has the following rate law:
   rate = $k[A]^1[B]^0$
   a. 0
   b. 1
   c. 2
   d. 3
   e. cannot be determined

10. Which statement is predicted by collision theory?
    a. Twice as many collisions result in twice the rate of reaction.
    b. All collisions between particles with kinetic energy equal to the activation energy lead to product formation.
    c. Collisions between particles at a favourable orientation, but with energy less than the activation energy, are effective.
    d. The kinetic energy of at least one of the reactants must equal the potential energy of the activated complex.
    e. Only collisions between particles at the correct orientation and with kinetic energy equal to or in excess of the activation energy can lead to product formation.

Answer the questions below.

11. How do the average kinetic energy and the thermal energy of the particles in a glass of water and in a bathtub of water compare, if both samples of water are at 25°C?

12. A change of state occurs when water vapour condenses to form dew on grass.
    a. Is thermal energy added or removed from the system for this change of state?
    b. Is the enthalpy change positive or negative for this change of state?
    c. Write the thermochemical equation for this change of state. Refer to **Table 5.2**.

13. Define the term *activation energy*, E_a. What is the main factor that affects the magnitude of the activation energy for a reaction?

14. Does the magnitude of the activation energy for a reaction depend upon whether or not the reaction is endothermic or exothermic? Explain your answer.

15. **K/U** Examine the potential energy diagram below.

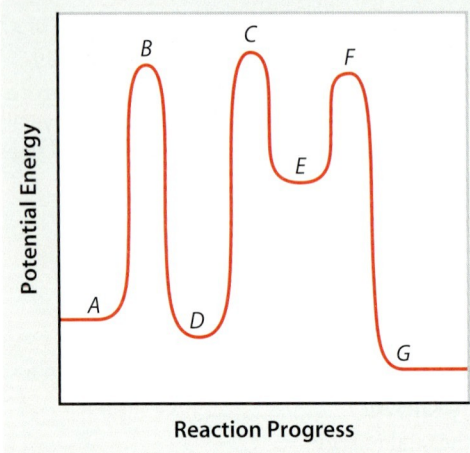

   a. How many steps are represented in this energy diagram? Give a reason for your answer.
   b. For which step does the enthalpy change have the greatest magnitude?
   c. The difference between which two letters represents the activation energy for the reverse of step 2?
   d. Which letters correspond to transition states?
   e. What does the energy between E and F represent?

16. Consider the following reaction:
    $2HCl(aq) + Li_2CO_3(s) \rightarrow 2LiCl(aq) + CO_2(g) + H_2O(\ell)$
    a. What quantities could be measured to determine the average rate of reaction?
    b. Would the instantaneous rate be determined in the same way? Give a reason for your answer.

17. The rate of a particular reaction between two gases was found to double when the temperature was increased. How do collision theory and kinetic molecular theory explain this change in reaction rate?

18. Several industrial catalysts are listed below. Copy the chart into your notebook and complete it by providing the names of the products for the applications. Where applicable, also name the industrial process.

Applications of Some Catalysts

Catalyst	Product	Process
Fe, K$_2$O, Al$_2$O$_3$		
V$_2$O$_5$		
Pt/Ir		
Xylanase		
Amylase		

19. How does a catalyst change the rate of a reaction?
20. A reaction mechanism is a proposed series of elementary steps that describe the progress of a reaction.
    a. What is an elementary step?
    b. What is the rate-determining elementary step?
    c. With respect to potential energy, what is a consistent characteristic of the rate-determining step in the reaction?
    d. How is the rate-determining step related to the rate law for the overall reaction?
21. What information can be learned from knowing the rate constant, k, for a reaction?
22. Is a measurement of temperature change an effective way to monitor the rate of reaction for reactions in aqueous solution? Give a reason for your answer.
23. An exothermic and an endothermic reaction both have the same high value for E_a. Can it be stated that this indicates that over the same period of time, the average rate of reaction for each reaction would be the same? Explain your reasoning.
24. A 10°C increase in temperature will almost double the rate of reaction for many reactions between gases. This is not true for reactions in aqueous solution. Explain the reason for this difference.
25. Potential energy diagrams for a reaction with and without a catalyst are shown below. Is the information shown possible? Give a reason for your answer.

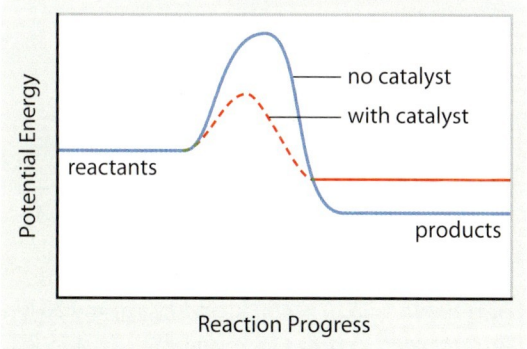

Thinking and Investigation

26. The standard molar enthalpy of formation, $\Delta H_f°$, for ozone, $O_3(g)$, is +142.7 kJ/mol. What is the enthalpy of reaction for the reaction below?
    $2O_3(g) \rightarrow 3O_2(g)$

27. Use the enthalpy changes given below to write the thermochemical equation for each reaction.
    a. Dissolving of ammonium nitrate, $NH_4NO_3(s)$, $\Delta H_{solution} = +25.69$ kJ/mol
    b. Complete combustion of 1-pentanol, $C_5H_{11}OH(\ell)$, $\Delta H°_{comb} = -3330.9$ kJ/mol
    c. Enthalpy of formation for phenol, $C_6H_5OH(s)$, $\Delta H_f° = -164.9$ kJ/mol
28. Ammonia, $NH_3(s)$, melts at −78°C. This change of state can be represented by the following equation:
    $NH_3(s) + 5.66 \text{ kJ} \rightarrow NH_3(\ell)$
    What amount of heat is given off when 6.46 g of $NH_3(\ell)$ solidifies?
29. Refer to the data for methane, $CH_4(g)$, in **Table 5.2**.
    a. Write the thermochemical equation for the condensation of methane.
    b. What amount of thermal energy is absorbed by 100.0 g of methane when it changes from a liquid to a gas?
30. The enthalpy change for the following reaction, as written, is −906 kJ.
    $4NH_3(g) + 5O_2(g) \rightarrow 4NO(g) + 6H_2O(g)$
    What is the molar enthalpy change for each reactant and product?
31. What is the final temperature of a 324 g sample of liquid that has a specific heat capacity of 2.8 J/g·°C when it absorbs 2.56 kJ of thermal energy? The initial temperature of the liquid is 5.0°C.
32. An experiment indicates that the burning of 0.26 mol of a fuel emitted 355.4 kJ of thermal energy.
    a. What is the molar enthalpy of combustion of the fuel?
    b. Refer to **Table 5.4** to identify the fuel.
33. Consider the following reaction:
    $NH_4HSO_3(s) + 768.6 \text{ kJ/mol} \rightarrow$
    $\frac{5}{2}H_2(g) + \frac{1}{2}N_2(g) + S(s) + \frac{3}{2}O_2(g)$
    a. What process is represented by the equation?
    b. What mass of S(s) would be formed when 2690.1 kJ is used in this reaction?
34. The heating value of diesel fuel has been reported as 44.80 MJ/kg, and for gasoline the value is 47.30 MJ/kg, assuming that the products of combustion are $CO_2(g)$ and $H_2O(\ell)$. How much more water, expressed in kilograms, could be converted to steam at 100°C by heating with 1.00 kg of gasoline rather than 1.00 kg of diesel fuel? Refer to **Table 5.2** for additional data to perform this calculation.

UNIT 3 REVIEW

35. For which of the following reactions will the enthalpy of reaction be a negative value?
   a. sulfur burning in a crucible
   b. NaI(s) dissolving in water, causing the temperature to increase
   c. the process of photosynthesis, where $CO_2(g)$ and $H_2O(\ell)$ combine in the presence of sunlight to form glucose and $O_2(g)$
   d. adding concentrated sulfuric acid to water, causing the temperature to increase from 15°C to 75°C
   e. iron rusting
   f. $CO_2(g) \rightarrow CO_2(s)$
   g. $MgCO_3(s) \rightarrow MgO(s) + CO_2(g)$

36. A methanol lamp is used to heat 500.0 g of water. When 1.84 g of methanol is burned, the temperature of the water increases from 18.4°C to 30.7°C.
   a. What amount of thermal energy did the water gain?
   b. Use the data for the molar enthalpy of combustion of methanol, $CH_3OH(\ell)$, from **Table 5.4** to determine the amount of thermal energy given off during the burning.
   c. Identify the energy input and the energy output for this system.
   d. Calculate the efficiency of the methanol lamp as it heated the water.

37. Ethylene glycol, $C_2H_6O_2(\ell)$, has a range of uses from antifreeze in cooling and heating systems and deicer of airport runways and aircraft to the formulations of printers' inks and inks for ballpoint pens. The complete combustion of this compound is shown below.

$$C_2H_6O_2(\ell) + \frac{5}{2}O_2(g) \rightarrow 2CO_2(g) + 3H_2O(\ell) + 1190 \text{ kJ}$$

Use this information and the enthalpy of formation data in Appendix B to calculate the enthalpy of formation of ethylene glycol.

38. The enthalpy of combustion of natural gas is found to be 54.0 kJ/g. Refer to **Table 5.7** for the emission levels of fossil fuels. When 1.00 kg of natural gas is burned, what mass of particulate matter is released into the atmosphere?

39. Use the given equations to determine the enthalpy change for the reaction below:

$$2SO_3(g) \rightarrow 2SO_2(g) + O_2(g)$$

(1) $S(s) + O_2(g) \rightarrow SO_2(g)$ $\Delta H°_{comb} = -296.8$ kJ
(2) $S(s) + \frac{3}{2}O_2(g) \rightarrow SO_3(g)$ $\Delta H°_{comb} = -395.7$ kJ

40. The enthalpy of combustion of sucrose, $C_{12}H_{22}O_{11}(s)$, is −5650 kJ/mol. A 3.00 g sample of this sugar is burned in 38.0 s in a bomb calorimeter that has a heat capacity of 1284 J/°C.
   a. What amount of heat will be given off during the burning?
   b. What amount of heat will the calorimeter absorb?
   c. By how much will the temperature of the calorimeter increase?
   d. Express the rate of burning of sucrose, in moles per second.

41. Fe(s) will displace Ag^+ from solution, according to the equation below:

$$Fe(s) + 2AgNO_3(aq) \rightarrow Fe(NO_3)_2(aq) + 2Ag(s)$$

Over a period of 25.0 min, the concentration of a $AgNO_3(aq)$ solution decreases from 0.200 mol/L to 0.185 mol/L.
   a. What is the rate of change in the concentration of $Ag^+(aq)$ measured in moles per litre per second?
   b. What is the rate of formation of $Fe^{2+}(aq)$ over this same period of time?

42. A graph of concentration vs. time is shown below. Reproduce this graph in order to determine the instantaneous rates of reaction at $t = 0$ s and $t = 30.0$ s and the average rate of reaction from $t = 0$ s to $t = 30.0$ s.

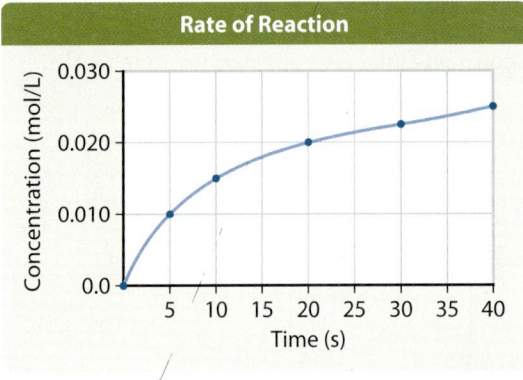

Rate of Reaction

43. For reaction 1, $\Delta H = -50$ kJ and $E_{a(fwd)} = +25$ kJ. For reaction 2, $\Delta H = +50$ kJ and $E_{a(rev)} = +25$ kJ. Compare the value of $E_{a(fwd)}$ for reaction 2 with the $E_{a(rev)}$ for reaction 1.

44. An average rate of reaction for the consumption of $BrO_3^-(aq)$ is 1.28 g/L·s, in the reaction shown below:

$$BrO_3^-(aq) + 5Br^-(aq) + 6H^+(aq) \rightarrow 3Br_2(\ell) + 3H_2O(\ell)$$

What is the average rate of formation of $Br_2(\ell)$?

45. The reaction mechanism outlined below occurs in an aqueous solution to which a small amount of ethanol has been added. The ethanol does not participate in the reaction but is added because of its properties as a solvent. $I_2(s)$ dissolves in alcohol to give a reddish-brown solution.

Step 1: $H_2O_2(aq) + I^-(aq) \rightarrow$
$\quad\quad\quad HIO(aq) + OH^-(aq)$ (slow)
Step 2: $OH^-(aq) + H^+(aq) \rightarrow H_2O(\ell)$ (fast)
Step 3: $HIO(aq) + H^+(aq) + I^-(aq) \rightarrow$
$\quad\quad\quad I_2(aq) + H_2O(\ell)$ (fast)

a. What is the overall equation that is represented by this reaction mechanism?
b. Suggest two properties that could be used to monitor the rate of reaction over time. Explain your choices of properties.

46. Consider the reaction mechanism outlined below:
Step 1: $H_2(g) + NO(g) \rightarrow H_2O(g) + N(g)$ (fast)
Step 2: $N(g) + NO(g) \rightarrow N_2O(g)$ (slow)
Step 3: $N_2O(g) + H_2(g) \rightarrow N_2(g) + H_2O(g)$ (fast)

a. Is a catalyst present? Give a reason for your answer.
b. Identify the intermediates in the reaction.
c. Write the overall reaction equation.

47. The rate law for a reaction is rate = $k[A]^{\frac{1}{3}}$. Determine the unit for the rate constant.

48. Distinguish between the meaning of the terms *reaction intermediate* and *catalyst*, using the two-step reaction mechanism shown below. Write the overall balanced chemical equation for the reaction.
Step 1: $Fe^{3+}(aq) + 2I^-(aq) \rightarrow Fe^{2+}(aq) + I_2(aq)$
Step 2: $S_2O_8^{2-}(aq) + Fe^{2+}(aq) \rightarrow 2SO_4^{2-}(aq) + Fe^{3+}(aq)$

49. At 950 K and a pressure of 70.0 kPa, the rate of formation of hydrogen gas, $H_2(g)$, is 4.8×10^{-3} mol/L·s. If all gases are measured at this same temperature and pressure, at what rate will phosphine, $PH_3(g)$, be consumed?
$$PH_3(g) \rightarrow P(g) + \frac{3}{2}H_2(g)$$

50. For the reaction below, the rate doubles if [NO] doubles and quadruples if $[H_2]$ doubles.
$$NO(g) + H_2(g) \rightarrow \frac{1}{2}N_2(g) + \frac{3}{2}H_2O(g)$$
a. What is the rate law for this reaction?
b. How will the rate of reaction be affected if both [NO] and $[H_2]$ double at the same time?

51. Apply Hess's law using the equations below to determine the enthalpy change for the following reaction:
$$2H_3BO_3(aq) \rightarrow B_2O_3(s) + 3H_2O(\ell)$$
(1) $H_3BO_3(aq) \rightarrow HBO_2(aq) + H_2O(\ell) \quad \Delta H° = -0.020$ kJ
(2) $2B_2O_3(s) + H_2O(\ell) \rightarrow H_2B_4O_7(s) \quad \Delta H° = -17.5$ kJ
(3) $H_2B_4O_7(s) + H_2O(\ell) \rightarrow 4HBO_2(aq) \quad \Delta H° = -11.3$ kJ

52. The table below shows rate of reaction data for the following reaction:
$$2A + B \rightarrow A_2B$$

Data

Experiment	Initial Concentration of A (mol/L)	Initial Concentration of B (mol/L)	Initial Rate (mol/L·s)
1	0.46	0.34	1.32
2	0.92	0.34	2.64
3	0.46	1.02	3.96

a. Use this information to determine the rate law expression for the reaction.
b. What is the overall order of the reaction?

Communication

53. The decomposition of magnesium carbonate, $MgCO_3(s)$, occurs according to the following reaction:
$$MgCO_3(s) \rightarrow MgO(s) + CO_2(g) \quad \Delta H_r = +117.3 \text{ kJ}$$
Sketch an enthalpy diagram for the reaction.

54. Outline how you would use a simple laboratory heating device, such as an alcohol lamp or Bunsen burner, to demonstrate the difference between potential energy and kinetic energy.

55. A classmate is having difficulty understanding why, when using thermochemical data to calculate energy changes for a change of state, ΔH_{fre} is a negative value. In one or two sentences, provide an explanation that is at a level that could help your classmate understand this concept.

56. *Enthalpy change* is a term that is used for more than one application. Use a concept map to summarize and indicate the difference between the different uses of the ΔH notation.

57. Research the use of catalysts in the refining of crude oil. Write a one-page report that outlines the cracking, reformation, and isomerization processes and how catalysts are used in these processes.

58. BIG IDEAS Technologies that transform energy can have societal and environmental costs and benefits. Draw a flowchart to represent the production of $NH_3(\ell)$ in the Haber-Bosch process.

UNIT 3 REVIEW

59. Platinum is used as a catalyst in many processes. Research the use of this metal as a catalyst. Using diagrams with descriptive captions, summarize key information about three industrial processes in which platinum is used. Your summary should indicate the characteristics of platinum that make it useful as a catalyst, and include the names of the processes or reactions and the reactants and products in the reactions.

60. Consider the following reaction:
$$2X + 3Y + 45 \text{ kJ} \rightarrow 3Z$$
Prepare a presentation to illustrate to your class that this reaction cannot proceed in the way the balanced equation indicates. List the points you would include in the presentation. What is a more likely occurrence for this reaction?

61. Using a graphic organizer, summarize information about rates of reaction in terms of the following: *reaction mechanism*, *rate-determining step*, *overall rate*, *role of a catalyst*, *activation energy*, and *order of a reaction*.

62. Develop a graphic representation to illustrate how the number of particles present at two different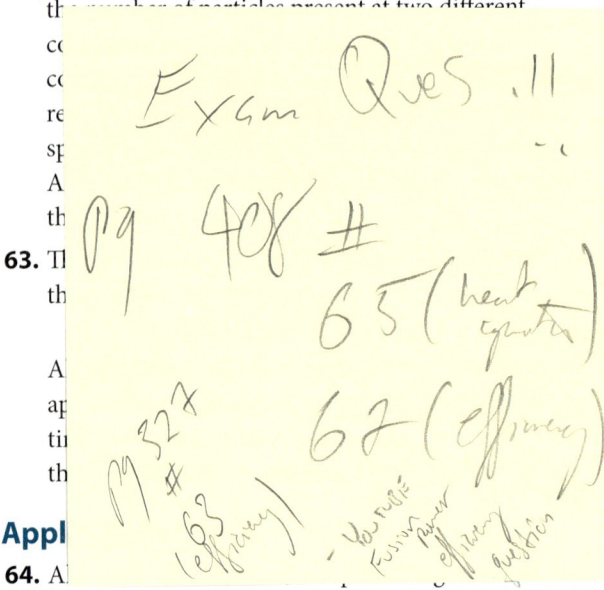

63. [obscured]

Appl[ications]

64. A[luminum is used to] make doors, windows, and siding for houses. It reacts quickly with $O_2(g)$ to form an impervious coating of aluminum oxide, $Al_2O_3(s)$, that prevents $O_2(g)$ from reacting any further with the aluminum. This reaction is unnoticeable even though the reaction shown below indicates a large enthalpy change. Why is the enthalpy of reaction not detectable?
$$4Al(s) + 3O_2(g) \rightarrow 2Al_2O_3(s) + 3351.4 \text{ kJ}$$

65. Pieces of three different metals, each having a mass of 12.5 g, are warmed to 150.0°C in an oil bath. They are individually transferred to 100.0 mL of water that is initially at 20.0°C. The final temperature of the water is recorded in the table below.

Data

Metal	Final Temperature (°C)
1	21.5
2	23.4
3	21.7

a. Why is the final temperature of the water different for each metal?
b. Calculate the specific heat capacity of each metal, and use the data in **Table 5.1** to identify the three metals.

66. There are many common examples of reactions that are beneficial to use by increasing the rate of reaction. Compile a list of at least four reactions that are of benefit to our everyday living, in which a *reduction* in the rate of reaction is desired.

67. BIG IDEAS Energy changes and rates of chemical reactions can be described quantitatively.
A butane burner is used to heat a pot of water at a camp site. The efficiency of heat transfer from the flame is 45.0%.
a. Use the data below to calculate the mass of butane that must be burned to bring the water to 100.0°C.
mass of water = 882 g
$c_{H_2O(\ell)} = 4.19$ J/g·°C
initial temperature of water = 15.0°C
final temperature of water = 100.0°C
mass of iron pot = 1208 g
$c_{iron} = 0.449$ J/g·°C
$\Delta H°_{comb}(C_4H_{10}) = -2877.6$ kJ/mol
b. If it takes 1 hour and 15 minutes to heat this water, at what rate, in moles per minute, is the butane burned?

68. BIG IDEAS Efficiency of chemical reactions can be improved by applying optimal conditions.
Acetylene is used as a fuel for a torch to cut through metal. When a worker first lights the torch, the flame is orange and there is noticeable black soot. To use the torch for cutting, the acetylene-air mixture is adjusted and the flame becomes blue and much hotter.
a. What type of combustion is occurring when the fuel is first lit compared with when it is used to cut through metal?

b. Compare the enthalpy change for the complete combustion and the incomplete combustion of acetylene, $C_2H_2(g)$, using the equations below and the enthalpies of formation listed in Appendix B.

$$C_2H_2(g) + \frac{5}{2}O_2(g) \rightarrow 2CO_2(g) + H_2O(g)$$

$$C_2H_2(g) + O_2(g) \rightarrow \frac{1}{2}CO_2(g) + \frac{3}{2}C(s) + H_2O(g)$$

c. Compare the availability of chemical energy from acetylene for complete combustion vs. incomplete combustion.

69. Ethylene, $C_2H_4(g)$, can be converted to ethanol, $C_2H_5OH(\ell)$, with an efficiency of 95% using a phosphoric acid catalyst. Use Hess's law to determine the enthalpy of reaction for the equation shown below:

$$C_2H_4(g) + H_2O(\ell) \rightarrow C_2H_5OH(\ell)$$

(1) $C_2H_5OH(\ell) + 3O_2(g) \rightarrow 2CO_2(g) + 3H_2O(\ell)$
$\Delta H = -1367$ kJ

(2) $C_2H_4(g) + 3O_2(g) \rightarrow 2CO_2(g) + 2H_2O(\ell)$
$\Delta H = -1411$ kJ

70. Nitryl chloride, NO_2Cl, is a strong oxidizing agent and a potential pollutant in the upper atmosphere. Research conducted to gather data about this molecule has proposed the following mechanism for its formation. The first and last steps in the mechanism and the overall reaction are shown below:

Step 1: $NO_2 + Cl_2 \rightarrow NO_2Cl_2$
Step 2:
Step 3: $Cl + NO_2 \rightarrow NO_2Cl$
Overall: $2NO_2 + Cl_2 \rightarrow 2NO_2Cl$

a. What is the equation for step 2?
b. How do you know which species is an intermediate? Identify the intermediate(s) in the mechanism.
c. Is step 2 likely the slow step in the mechanism? Give a reason for your answer.
d. Research nitryl chloride and provide a summary of its harmful effects on the environment. Present your findings in the format of your choice.

71. You are performing an investigation that involves the reaction represented below:

$$2A + B \rightarrow products$$

For this reaction, the following information is known:
rate law: rate $= k[A][B]$
original concentration of A $= 0.40$ mol/L
original concentration of B $= 0.60$ mol/L
rate of reaction $= 4.5 \times 10^{-2}$ mol/L·s, at 35°C
You have completed one trial. You decide for the second trial to use twice the concentration of reactant A.

a. Explain why the concentration of B must also change if the rate of reaction is to be unchanged at this temperature.
b. If the rate of reaction is to be the same as in the first trial, what concentration of reactant B must be used?
c. Calculate the value of the rate constant.
d. Confirm your answer to part (b) by calculating the rate, using the new values for [A] and [B].

72. Graphs of rate of reaction vs. concentration for two reactions are plotted. Each is a straight line but one has a steeper slope. What can be concluded about the rates of these reactions?

73. **BIG IDEAS** Energy changes and rates of chemical reactions can be described quantitatively. Hydrogen peroxide is used as an antiseptic and antibacterial agent. In the bottle and on our skin, it breaks down very slowly but it does not foam. On a scrape or a cut, bubbling action is observed as the hydrogen peroxide decomposes rapidly in the presence of a catalyst.

$$H_2O_2(aq) \rightarrow H_2O(\ell) + \frac{1}{2}O_2(g)$$

a. Using print or Internet sources, identify the catalyst that causes this action.
b. Use the molar enthalpy of formation data in Appendix B to determine the enthalpy change for this decomposition.
c. The activation energy for the uncatalyzed decomposition of hydrogen peroxide has been measured at 25°C to be 75 kJ/mol. Sketch a potential energy diagram, using an appropriate scale, to show $E_{a(fwd)}$ and ΔH. If it is estimated that there will 80% more collisions that are effective in the presence of the catalyst, show the path of the catalyzed reaction on the potential energy diagram.
d. What is ΔH for the reverse reaction? Does this quantity represent the enthalpy of formation, ΔH_f, for hydrogen peroxide? Give a reason for your answer.

74. For a reaction that occurs in the gaseous phase, the rate of reaction doubles when the concentration of reactant X is doubled. There is no change in the rate of reaction when the concentration of reactant Y is changed.

$$2X + \frac{1}{2}Y \rightarrow W + 2Z$$

If the volume of the container is doubled, what change would be expected in the rate of reaction? Give an explanation for your answer.

UNIT 3 SELF-ASSESSMENT

Select the letter of the best answer below.

1. **K/U** The enthalpy change in a reaction comes from the
   a. difference between the kinetic energy of the products and the reactants.
   b. sum of the potential energies of the reactants and products.
   c. sum of the thermal energies of the reactants and products.
   d. sum of the enthalpies of formation of the reactants and products.
   e. difference in the energy [...] breaking bonds in the reactants and th[...] hen bonds are formed in [...]

2. **T/I** Use the given [...] enthalpy change for [...]

   2SO[...]

   (1) S(s) + O_2(g[...]
   (2) S(s) + $\frac{3}{2}$ O[...]

   a. −98.9 k[...]
   b. +346.[...]
   c. −49.[...]

3. **T/I** [...]
   HCl(g, [...]

   4HCl(g) + O_2(g, [...]

   a. −457.6 kJ/mol
   b. −114.4 kJ/mol
   c. −28.6 kJ/mol

4. **T/I** The temperature of a calorimeter incre[...] from 15.6°C to 31.4°C as it gains 488.8 kJ of heat. W[...]at is the heat capacity of the calorimeter?
   a. 489 kJ/°C
   b. 30.9 kJ/°C
   c. 31.3 kJ/°C
   d. 10.4 kJ/°C
   e. 15.6 kJ/°C

5. **A** A sample of butane, C_4H_{10}(g), having a mass of 0.58 g was completely combusted to produce carbon dioxide, water vapour, and 27 kJ of thermal energy. Which thermochemical equation correctly shows this information per mole of C_4H_{10}(g)?
   a. $C_4H_{10}(g) + \frac{13}{2}O_2(g) \rightarrow 4CO_2(g) + 5H_2O(g) + 2700$ kJ
   b. $C_4H_{10}(g) + 13O_2(g) \rightarrow 4CO_2(g) + 5H_2O(g) + 270$ kJ
   c. $2C_4H_{10}(g) + 13O_2(g) \rightarrow 8CO_2(g) + 10H_2O(g) + 2700$ kJ
   d. $2C_4H_{10}(g) + O_2(g) \rightarrow 4CO_2(g) + 5H_2O(g) + 5400$ kJ
   e. $C_4H_{10}(g) + \frac{13}{2}O_2(g) \rightarrow 4CO_2(g) + 5H_2O(g) + 27$ kJ

6. **A** The rate law for a particular reaction is first order with respect to two reactants. If the concentrations of both reactants are doubled, the rate of the reaction would be expected to
   a. double.
   b. not change.
   c. triple.
   d. quadruple.
   e. increase by a factor of 1.5.

7. **A** Which statement regarding the potential energy diagram below is correct?

   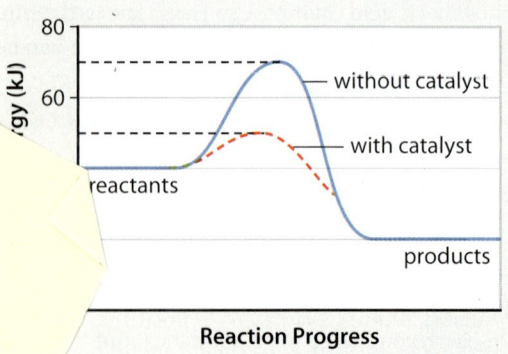

   a. The activation energy for the uncatalyzed reaction in the forward direction, $E_{a(fwd)}$, is +20 kJ.
   b. For the catalyzed reaction in the reverse direction, ΔH_{rev} is +20 kJ.
   c. The potential energy of the activated complex for the catalyzed reaction is +70 kJ.
   d. The catalyst lowers the activation energy of both the forward and reverse reactions by 30 kJ.
   e. For the uncatalyzed reaction in the forward direction, ΔH_{fwd} is +20 kJ.

8. **T/I** For the decomposition of potassium chlorate, $KClO_3$(s), 4.4 g of this compound reacted in 2.3 min. What is the average rate of reaction in moles per second?
   a. 1.7
   b. 3.2×10^{-2}
   c. 1.6×10^{-2}
   d. 2.6×10^{-4}
   e. 5.9×10^{-4}

9. **K/U** Which reaction is most likely to occur rapidly at room temperature?
   a. $Zn(s) + S(\ell) \rightarrow ZnS(s)$
   b. $H_2SO_4(aq) + 2NaOH(aq) \rightarrow Na_2SO_4(aq) + H_2(g)$
   c. $H_2O(\ell) \rightarrow H_2 + \frac{1}{2}O_2(g)$
   d. $2Fe(s) + 2H_2O(\ell) + O_2(g) \rightarrow 2Fe(OH)_2(s)$
   e. $Cd(s) + NiO_2(s) + 2H_2O(\ell) \rightarrow Cd(OH)_2(s) + Ni(OH)_2(s)$

10. **T/I** A hypothetical reaction mechanism is outlined below. For which substance(s) would a change in concentration have the greatest effect on the overall reaction rate?

   Step 1: $2A \rightarrow B + 2C$ (slow)
   Step 2: $B + C \rightarrow E$ (fast)
   Step 3: $C + D \rightarrow F$ (fast)

   a. A + D
   b. D
   c. A
   d. B + C
   e. C

Use sentences and diagrams, as appropriate, to answer the questions below.

11. **K/U** What information is given by the equation below?

    $$Cu(s) + Cl_2(g) \rightarrow CuCl_2(s) \qquad \Delta H_r^\circ = -220.1 \text{ kJ}$$

12. **T/I** The standard molar enthalpy of formation, ΔH_f°, for liquid benzene, $C_6H_6(\ell)$, is +49.1 kJ/mol and for benzene vapour, $C_6H_6(g)$, is +82.9 kJ/mol. Apply Hess's law to determine the standard molar enthalpy of vaporization, ΔH_{vap}°, for benzene.

13. **K/U** What assumptions are made when using a simple calorimeter?

14. **C** Your lab partner writes the equation for the enthalpy of formation, ΔH_f°, for $CO_2(g)$ as the following:

    $$CO(g) + \tfrac{1}{2}O_2(g) \rightarrow CO_2(g)$$

    How would you explain that this is incorrect? Write the correct enthalpy of formation equation.

15. **A** Air temperature is observed to increase when a rain shower occurs. What amount of thermal energy is given off into the air when 9.83×10^{10} kg of water vapour condenses?

16. **T/I** Calculate the amount of heat given off when 1 mol $SO_2(g)$ forms in the reaction as written below:

    $$CS_2(\ell) + 3O_2(g) \rightarrow CO_2(g) + 2SO_2(g)$$

17. **T/I** A 250.0 g sample of ethanol is heated until its temperature increases by 30.0°C. If 27.3 kJ of thermal energy was added to the sample, how efficient was the heat transfer? The specific heat capacity of ethanol is 2.44 J/g·°C.

18. **A** The following reaction is performed in duplicate:

    $$2H_2(g) + O_2(g) \rightarrow 2H_2O(\ell)$$

    In the first trial, the volume ratio used for $H_2(g):O_2(g) = 2:1$. In the second trial, the volume ratio used for $H_2(g):O_2(g) = 1:1$. For each trial, sketch a graph of concentration vs. time, for the reactants only, as the reaction proceeds to completion.

19. **C** The following decomposition reaction occurs:

    $$2HgO(s) \rightarrow 2Hg(\ell) + O_2(g)$$

    When the heat source is removed, the decomposition stops. The reaction begins again when the heat source is turned on. Develop a 2 to 3 min oral presentation that explains these observations.

20. **K/U** Reactions between ions in aqueous solution to form a precipitate occur in an instant at room temperature. Does this mean that, for these reactions, $E_a = 0$? Explain your reasoning.

21. **C** Develop a flowchart that summarizes how to use Hess's law to determine the enthalpy change of a reaction. Include an example.

22. **T/I** Examine the following reaction mechanism:

    Step 1: $NO_2(g) + Br_2(g) \rightarrow NO_2Br(g) + Br(g)$ (slow)
    Step 2: $NO_2(g) + Br(g) \rightarrow NO_2Br$ (fast)

    a. What is the overall reaction?
    b. Which is the rate-determining step?
    c. If rate = $k[NO_2][Br_2]$, what is the order of the reaction with respect to $Br_2(g)$?

23. **T/I** For the reaction mechanism shown below, the rate law is rate = $k[NO]^2[O_2]$. Is the proposed mechanism possible for this rate law? Explain.

    $$2NO(g) + O_2(g) \rightarrow 2NO_2(g)$$

    Step 1: $2NO + O_2 \rightarrow N_2O_4$ (fast)
    Step 2: $N_2O_4 \rightarrow 2NO_2$ (slow)

24. **K/U** Compare the energy changes associated with physical, chemical, and nuclear processes. Give one example of each process.

25. **K/U** Summarize the projected use of renewable energy sources in Ontario by 2025. Describe the advantages and disadvantages of these energy sources.

Self-Check

If you missed question …	1	2	3	4	5	6	7	8	9	10	11	12	13	14	15	16	17	18	19	20	21	22	23	24	25
Review section(s)…	5.1 5.2	5.3	5.2	5.2	5.2	6.3	6.2	6.1	6.3	6.3	5.2	5.3	5.2	5.3	5.1	5.3	5.4	6.1	6.2	6.2	5.3	6.3	6.3	5.1	5.4

UNIT 4

Chemical Systems and Equilibrium

BIG IDEAS

- Chemical systems are dynamic and respond to changing conditions in predictable ways.
- Applications of chemical systems at equilibrium have significant implications for nature and for industry.

Overall Expectations

In this unit, you will…

- **analyze** chemical equilibrium processes, and **assess** their impact on biological, biochemical, and technological systems
- **investigate** the qualitative and quantitative natures of chemical systems at equilibrium, and **solve** related problems
- **demonstrate** an understanding of the concept of dynamic equilibrium and the variables that cause shifts in the equilibrium of chemical systems

Unit 4 Contents

Chapter 7
Chemical Equilibrium

Chapter 8
Acid-Base Equilibrium Systems

Focussing Questions

1. When is a chemical system at equilibrium, and what characteristics do these chemical systems have?
2. What are the optimal conditions for a specific chemical equilibrium process, and what happens if those conditions change?
3. What are some examples of chemical equilibrium systems in nature and in industry?

Go to **scienceontario** to find out more about chemical systems and equilibrium

Kawah Ijen Lake in East Java, Indonesia, is located on top of an active volcano that belches out hot gases, including hydrogen sulfide, H_2S, that bubbles up through the lake water. The volcanic gases react with water to form many substances, including sulfuric acid, $H_2SO_4(aq)$. The acids that form cause the pH in this lake to drop to an extremely low level of 0.4. Reactions between metals dissolved in the acidic water and hydrogen sulfide from the thermal vent precipitate solid minerals that collect in the lakebed. These minerals include pyrite, FeS_2, enargite, Cu_3ArS_4, and elemental sulfur. The highly prized elemental sulfur is mined for its global use in industrial processes such as rubber and sugar processing, as well as in the manufacture of sulfuric acid for numerous applications in the agricultural, electronics, and textile industries.

As you study this unit, look ahead to the Unit 4 Project on pages 566 to 567. Complete the project in stages as you progress through the unit.

UNIT 4 Preparation

Safety in the Chemistry Laboratory and Classroom

- Be certain that you understand the meaning of WHMIS symbols, and use appropriate safety precautions when you see them on containers during an investigation.
- Know the meaning of the safety symbols used in activities and investigations in *Chemistry 12* and follow all precautions that the symbols advise.
- Always wear protective clothing, such as safety eyewear and a lab coat or apron, when performing investigations.
- Be sure that you know the location of the eyewash station, first aid kit, and other safety equipment in your classroom, as well as how to properly use them.
- EXTREME CAUTION should be used when working with concentrated acids and bases. Take care to follow proper procedures when diluting or disposing of a concentrated acid or base.

1. Why should strong acids and strong bases be neutralized by your teacher before disposal?
2. An investigation involves working with and diluting concentrated acids. A calculation tells you that a mixture of 5.00 mL of the concentrated acid and 45.00 mL of water needs to be made.
   a. Outline the proper procedure that must be followed for making this dilution.
   b. Describe the procedure you should follow if you get any acid in your eyes or on your clothing during the investigation.
   c. When using chemicals, such as acids, in the laboratory, why is it important to use only the minimum amount necessary?
3. An investigation requires you to mix a solution of lead(II) nitrate with a solution of sodium chloride. A solid forms in the resulting mixture.
   a. What safety considerations must you follow when dealing with the disposal of the resulting mixture once the investigation is over?
   b. Why is it important not to wash solid materials down the drain?
4. In one investigation in this unit, you use a straw to blow air into a mixture.
   a. Why should only clean fresh straws be used for each student?
   b. Why is it important to wear safety eyewear and to blow gently into the straw?

Preparing Solutions in the Laboratory

- Solutions of a needed concentration can be made by dissolving a solid into solution or by diluting a more concentrated solution.
- Knowledge of the relationships among moles, mass, volume, and concentration is essential in preparing solutions for an investigation.

5. For each of the solutions below, describe how each is made from the solid material.
   a. 225 mL of a 1.50 mol/L potassium chloride solution from solid potassium chloride
   b. 75.0 mL of a 0.85 mol/L solution of sodium hydroxide from solid sodium hydroxide
   c. 1.75 L of a 2.15 mol/L solution of tin(II) nitrate solution from solid tin(II) nitrate

6. For each of the solutions below, describe how each is made by diluting a more concentrated solution.
   a. 200.0 mL of 0.35 mol/L hydrochloric acid from 1.50 mol/L HCl(aq)
   b. 12.5 mL of 0.100 mol/L nitric acid from 5.00 mol/L HNO_3(aq)
   c. 1.10 L of 0.200 mol/L sulfuric acid from 12.00 mol/L H_2SO_4(aq)

Balancing Chemical Equations in Aqueous Solutions

- A chemical equation is a condensed method of representing a chemical reaction using numbers, symbols, and chemical formulas.
- A balanced equation shows that the numbers of each type of atom involved in the chemical reaction remains unchanged in the process. These numbers accurately reflect the ratios of the substances involved in the chemical reaction.
- Subscripts in chemical formulas cannot be changed, but coefficients can be changed when balancing chemical equations.
- When balancing chemical equations, begin by balancing the substance with the greatest number of atoms on each side of the equation first. If the polyatomic ions remain unchanged in the process, count polyatomic ions as a single item rather than counting the atoms within them.
- When spectator ions are removed from an overall ionic equation, the result is the net ionic equation.

7. For each of the following reactions, predict the products and balance the reaction. Assume that each reaction will occur.
   a. lithium hydroxide and hydrochloric acid
   b. potassium chloride and lead(II) nitrate
   c. sodium sulfide and silver nitrate

8. Under what condition will a solid form when two aqueous solutions are mixed?
   a. The solution is cooled.
   b. One of the possible products is insoluble in solution.
   c. The reaction is endothermic.
   d. The solution is slightly acidic.
   e. One of the reactants is insoluble in solution.

9. What results when an acid and a base combine?
   a. a neutral solution
   b. a solution that forms a solid precipitate
   c. an acidic solution
   d. a basic solution
   e. a solution that is less acidic or less basic than either of the original solutions

10. Consider the reaction below:
    $$2Ag^+(aq) + 2NO_3^-(aq) + 2Na^+(aq) + CrO_4^{2-}(aq) \rightarrow Ag_2CrO_4(s) + 2Na^+(aq) + 2NO_3^-(aq)$$
    a. List the spectator ions.
    b. Identify the precipitate that forms.
    c. Name and write the formula for a polyatomic ion in this reaction.
    d. Write the net ionic equation.

11. The colourless solution of silver nitrate in the test tube on the left is mixed with the yellow solution of sodium chromate in the test tube in the middle. The test tube on the right shows the result of this mixture.

   a. What evidence is there that a chemical reaction has occurred?
   b. Write and balance the overall ionic equation and the net ionic equation for the reaction that occurred.

12. A double displacement reaction occurs when a solution of hydrobromic acid, HBr(aq), is added to a solution of potassium hydroxide, KOH(aq).
    a. Write the ionic equation for this reaction.
    b. Write the net ionic equation for this reaction.
    c. Hydrobromic acid is a strong acid and potassium hydroxide is a strong base. What type of reaction does this represent?

Calculations Related to Chemical Reactions

- Determining the amount of product that forms requires determining the limiting reactant in a chemical reaction.
- The limiting reactant is the reactant that is completely consumed in the chemical reaction, whereas the reactant that remains is called the excess reactant.
- The volume, concentration, and amount in moles of a substance are related by the equation $c = \frac{n}{V}$.
- The activity series of metals helps predict whether a single displacement reaction between a metal and an ionic compound will take place.

13. Determine the amount (in moles) of hydroxide ions that are present in 25.00 mL of a 0.254 mol/L solution of potassium hydroxide.
14. What amount (in moles) of protons is contained in 38.42 mL of a 0.125 mol/L solution of hydrochloric acid?
15. What volume of 0.125 mol/L sodium sulfate is needed to supply 0.425 mol of sulfate ions in a solution?
16. What concentration of solution is needed to have 0.385 mol of chloride ions present in 225 mL of solution?
17. When 50.0 mL of a 0.200 mol/L sodium sulfate solution is mixed with 80.0 mL of a 0.100 mol/L solution of lead(II) acetate, what mass of lead(II) sulfate forms?
18. When potassium chromate, K_2CrO_4, reacts with lead(II) nitrate, a solid forms. The reaction is shown in the photograph on the right.
    a. What is the identity of this solid?
    b. Write the overall equation and the net ionic equation for this reaction.
    c. If 2.23 g of potassium chromate is added to 15.00 mL of a 0.120 mol/L solution of lead(II) nitrate, what mass of solid forms?

Acids and Bases

- An Arrhenius acid dissociates in water to produce hydrogen ions in solution.
- An Arrhenius base dissociates in water to produce hydroxide ions in solution.
- When an acid and a base combine, the neutralization reaction produces water and a salt.
- Acids have pH values less than 7, whereas bases have pH values greater than 7. Mixtures with a pH of 7 are neutral solutions.
- Titration is a process that is used to determine the concentration of an unknown acid or base.

19. Explain the difference between a concentrated acid and a dilute acid.
20. Explain the difference between a weak base and a strong base.
21. "Weak bases can be concentrated." Is this statement true or false? Explain your answer.
22. When 18.5 mL of a hydrochloric acid solution of unknown concentration is titrated with a 0.150 mol/L sodium hydroxide solution, 22.5 mL of the base is used to neutralize the acid. Determine the original concentration of the acidic solution.
23. Use the diagram below to help explain why sulfuric acid is a strong acid, but the hydrogen sulfate ion is a weak acid.

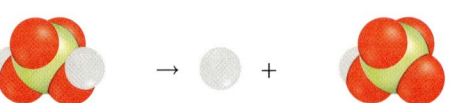

The Quadratic Formula, Scientific Notation, Exponents, and Logarithms

- When a quadratic equation in the form $ax^2 + bx + c = 0$ cannot be factored to solve, the quadratic formula must be used. The quadratic formula is as follows:

$$x = \frac{-b \pm \sqrt{b^2 - 4ac}}{2a}$$

- Scientific notation, using exponents with base 10, is an easier way to write numbers that are either very large or very small.

- Rules for exponents include the following:

$$b^n \times b^m = b^{n+m} \qquad \frac{b^n}{b^m} = b^{n-m}$$

- A logarithm is a useful way to represent numbers using powers of 10.
- Rules for logarithms include the following:

$$\log_b b^n = n$$
$$\log_b(xy) = \log_b x + \log_b y$$
$$\log_b\left(\frac{x}{y}\right) = \log_b x - \log_b y$$

24. Use the quadratic formula to solve each of the following equations to two decimal places.
  a. $x^2 + x - 4 = 0$
  b. $x^2 - 4x - 8 = 0$
  c. $3x^2 + 5x - 1 = 0$

25. Determine the positive root of each of the following equations.
  a. $3x^2 + 5x = 8$
  b. $x^2 + (2.25 \times 10^{-6})x - (1.77 \times 10^{-7}) = 0$

26. Simplify each of the following expressions.
  a. $\dfrac{2^3 \times 2^7}{2^4}$
  b. $\dfrac{a^9 \times a^{-2}}{a^{-5} \times a^2}$
  c. $\dfrac{(x^2 y^3)(x^3 y^2)}{xy}$
  a. $\dfrac{27^2 \times 3^2}{9^2}$

27. Simplify each of the following logarithmic expressions.
  a. $\log_2 8$
  b. $\log_3 81$
  c. $\log_{10} 1000 + \log_{10} 100\,000$
  d. $\log_{10}\left(\dfrac{100 \times 100\,000}{10^{-5}}\right)$
  e. $\log_{10}\left(\dfrac{1}{100\,000}\right) - \log_{10}(10\,000\,000)$

28. Express each number in scientific notation and to three significant digits.
  a. 287.2
  b. 0.005 945
  c. 1 789 435
  d. 0.000 000 412

29. Consider the function keys LOG and 10^x on the calculator shown below:

  a. Explain the difference between the two operations in terms of logarithms.
  b. Write two sample equations for which you would use each of these functions.
  c. Describe how the pH scale for acids and bases and logarithms are related.

CHAPTER 7
Chemical Equilibrium

Specific Expectations

In this chapter, you will learn how to . . .

- E1.1 **analyze** the optimal conditions for a specific chemical process related to the principles of equilibrium (7.4)

- E1.2 **assess** the impact of chemical equilibrium processes on various biological, biochemical, and technological systems (7.2, 7.4)

- E 2.1 **use** appropriate terminology related to chemical systems and equilibrium (7.1, 7.2, 7.3, 7.4)

- E2.2 **predict** how various factors would affect a chemical system at equilibrium and **conduct** an inquiry to test those predictions (7.2)

- E2.3 **conduct** an inquiry to **determine** the value of an equilibrium constant for a chemical reaction (7.3)

- E2.4 **solve** problems related to equilibria by performing calculations involving concentrations (7.2, 7.3)

- E3.1 **explain** the concept of dynamic equilibrium, using examples of physical and chemical equilibrium systems (7.1)

- E3.2 **explain** the concept of chemical equilibrium and how it applies to the concentrations of reactants and products in a chemical reaction at equilibrium (7.1)

- E3.3 **explain** Le Châtelier's principle and how it applies to changes to a chemical reaction at equilibrium (7.2)

- E3.4 **identify** common equilibrium constants (7.3)

Ammonia is an important industrial compound that is used as a crop fertilizer and as an essential raw material in other processes, such as manufacturing paint like the type that is used to protect these silos.

Many of the chemical reactions that you have studied proceed in only one direction. The reactants chemically combine and form products. Some overall reactions involve more than one reaction, however. For example, one of the chemical reactions that occurs in the production of ammonia is

$$N_2(g) + 3H_2(g) \rightarrow 2NH_3(g)$$

As the reaction proceeds, another reaction is also occurring:

$$2NH_3(g) \rightarrow N_2(g) + 3H_2(g)$$

In the same reaction vessel, the reactants are combining and forming ammonia while ammonia is decomposing and re-forming the reactants. In this chapter, you will learn more about this type of reaction and some chemical processes that use them.

Launch Lab

The Chemical Blues

In this demonstration, you will observe an example of a reversible change that involves a colour change.

Safety Precautions

- Wear safety eyewear throughout this activity.
- Your teacher will use extreme care when handling the materials.

Materials

- 5% glucose solution, $C_6H_{12}O_6$(aq) (5 g/100 mL)
- 8 mol/L sodium hydroxide solution, NaOH(aq)
- methylene blue indicator
- 1 L Erlenmeyer flask with stopper

Procedure

This activity is a teacher demonstration. Students should not perform it.

1. **Warning! Wear safety eyewear and protective gloves when performing this deomonstration.** Your teacher prepared the above solutions in advance. The solutions should be in stoppered flasks. Each of the following solutions will be added to a 1 L flask: 250 mL of glucose solution; 7.5 mL of 8 mol/L NaOH; and 1 to 2 drops of methylene blue. Place a stopper in the flask.

2. **Warning! All students should be wearing safety eyewear. Make sure students are standing a safe distance from the containers of sodium hydroxide.** Record the appearance of the solution in the flask. As a class, discuss the nature of each component of the solution.

3. **Warning! Keep your thumb on the stopper while shaking to prevent the stopper from coming out. Do shake the flask near students.** The teacher will give the flask a few vigorous shakes.

4. Observe and record the appearance of the solution in the flask.

5. Discuss possible explanations for the solution's colour change.

6. Wait until the solution in the flask changes colour again.

7. As a class, propose an explanation for the observed solution's colour changes.

Questions

1. What evidence do you have that the reaction you observed was reversible?
2. How do you think shaking the flask affected the reaction?
3. How could you determine if energy, in the form of heat, played a role in either the forward or reverse reaction? Explain your answer.

SECTION 7.1

Chemical Systems in Balance

Key Terms

reversible reaction
chemical equilibrium
dynamic equilibrium
homogeneous equilibrium
heterogeneous equilibrium
law of chemical equilibrium or law of mass action
equilibrium constant, K_{eq}

Previously, when you used stoichiometry to calculate the mass of a product, you assumed that the only factor limiting the amount of product formed was the presence of a limiting reactant. In those calculations, you assumed that the reactants formed products until one of the reactants was completely consumed. When there is an almost complete conversion of reactants to products or when the reaction proceeds until the limiting reactant is gone, the reaction goes to completion. However, many reactions do not proceed to completion, and in this section, you will learn why this is the case.

Reversible Reactions and Chemical Equilibrium

Consider the reaction that produces ammonia, $NH_3(g)$. This reaction consists of a forward reaction and a reverse reaction. A **reversible reaction** is a chemical reaction that proceeds in both forward and reverse directions. In the *forward direction* (reading the reaction from left to right), the reactants form products. In the *reverse direction* (reading the reaction from right to left), the product decomposes to re-form the reactants. In ammonia production, the forward and reverse reactions are as follows:

$$N_2(g) + 3H_2(g) \rightleftharpoons 2NH_3(g)$$

reversible reaction a chemical reaction that proceeds in both the forward and reverse directions

Consider what happens when 1 mol of nitrogen, $N_2(g)$, is added to 3 mol of hydrogen, $H_2(g)$, in a closed system. Recall that in a *closed system*, energy can cross the system boundary, but matter cannot. Initially, the concentrations of nitrogen and hydrogen are high and the concentration of ammonia is zero, as shown in **Figure 7.1**. As the reaction proceeds in the forward direction, the concentrations of nitrogen and hydrogen decrease and the concentration of ammonia increases.

Notice that to the right of the dashed line in the graph, the concentrations of substances no longer change over time. Remember that the reverse reaction is occurring simultaneously along with the forward reaction. Some of the ammonia is decomposing and re-forming the reactants. The portion of the graph to the right of the dashed line represents a chemical system in equilibrium. *Equilibrium* (plural *equilibria*) occurs when opposing forces or processes are in balance. In a chemical system, when the forward reaction and the reverse reaction are balanced and the reactions are occurring at the same rate, the system is said to be in **chemical equilibrium.**

chemical equilibrium a state in a chemical system in which the forward reaction and the reverse reaction are occurring at the same rate

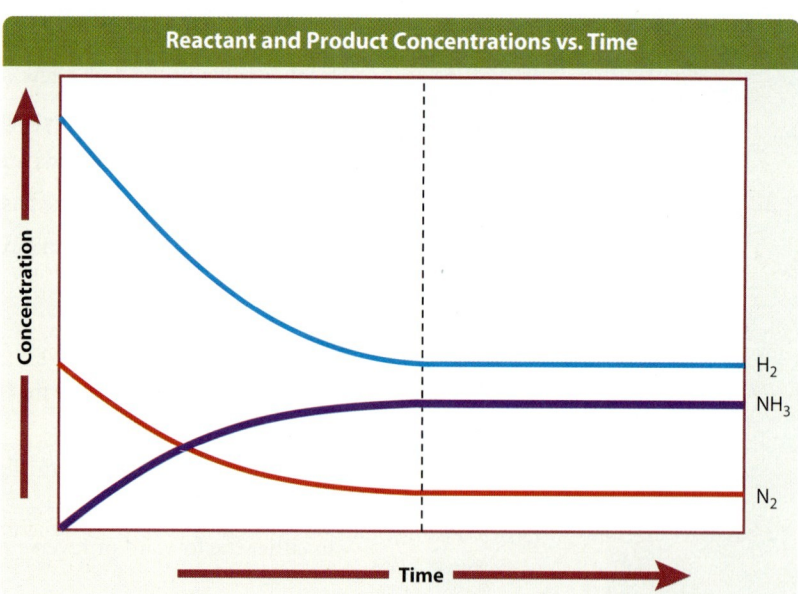

Figure 7.1 At equilibrium, the concentrations of the reactants and the products are constant and the rate of the forward reaction equals the rate of the reverse reaction.

Describe what is occurring on the molecular level in terms of collisions as the reversible reaction proceeds.

Chemical Equilibrium and Dynamic Equilibrium

One way to visualize chemical equilibrium is to think about a rope-pull competition, as shown in **Figure 7.2**. When the two men pull on the rope with the same force but in opposite directions, the forces are balanced. The system consisting of the two men and the rope is in equilibrium. It is important to note that while it looks like the men in the competition are static or inactive, they are not. Each man is actively pulling on the rope with equal force in opposite directions. In other words, the actions of the men are competing.

Figure 7.2 Sometimes during a rope-pull competition, both sides pull with equal force in opposite directions.

The same is true of chemical equilibrium—reactions are proceeding in both directions, but at the same rate, so there is no net change in the concentrations of reactants or products. In the ammonia production process, the molecules do not stop combining and decomposing. Instead, the process is dynamic or changing. The nitrogen and hydrogen molecules continue to combine while, at the same time, ammonia molecules decompose. The forward reaction and the reverse reaction occur at the same rate, so the overall concentrations of the molecules remain constant in the closed system.

This chemical system at equilibrium has the macroscopic property of constant concentrations of the reactants and product. A *macroscopic property* is an observable or measurable property such as concentration, colour, temperature, pressure, and pH. When a system is changing at the molecular level, but its macroscopic properties remain constant, the system is said to be in **dynamic equilibrium**. In the chemical equilibrium system involved in ammonia production, the system looks static because the concentrations are constant, but the system is dynamic because the molecules continuously react to form product and decompose to form reactants.

Look at the graph in **Figure 7.1** again. Notice that none of the concentrations in the equilibrium system is the same. Each substance stabilizes at a different concentration. In chemical systems at equilibrium, the concentrations of the reactants and the products are constant, but they are not necessarily equal.

dynamic equilibrium a chemical system at equilibrium that is changing at the molecular level, while its macroscopic properties remain constant

Writing Equilibrium Equations

Chemists use a simplified method for writing equations for reversible reactions like the one that produces ammonia. Chemists combine the two equations that represent a reversible reaction into a single equation such as this one:

$$N_2(g) + 3H_2(g) \rightleftharpoons 2NH_3(g)$$

Reading the chemical equation from left to right shows the forward reaction. Reading the chemical equation from right to left shows the reverse reaction. The double arrows ($\rightleftharpoons$) indicate that the chemical reaction is proceeding in both directions.

Learning Check

1. What is a reversible reaction?
2. What do the double arrows ($\rightleftharpoons$) mean in a chemical equation?
3. Explain why a rope-pull competition is similar to chemical equilibrium.
4. During an investigation, your lab partner states that a chemical system is not at equilibrium because the concentrations of the reactants and products are not equal. Explain why this statement might be incorrect.
5. The term *dynamic equilibrium* literally means "balanced change." Explain why this term describes a chemical system in equilibrium.
6. Carbon monoxide, $CO(g)$, and hydrogen, $H_2(g)$, react to form methane, $CH_4(g)$, and water, $H_2O(g)$. Write the chemical equation that represents this reversible reaction at equilibrium.

Equilibrium Involving Physical Systems

The chemical equilibrium system that produces ammonia consists of two different kinds of molecules (nitrogen and hydrogen) reacting and forming a third kind of molecule (ammonia). Chemical equilibrium involves different substances that react and form new substances. Some equilibrium systems, however, consist of one substance in two physical states. Consider what happens when water changes state at constant temperature.

A small amount of water left in an open flask, like the one in **Figure 7.3A**, disappears after a day or two. What happens to the water on the molecular level? The flask of water is an open system. Recall that an *open system* is a system in which matter and energy cross the system boundary. At the surface of the water, at least some of the water molecules have enough kinetic energy and are moving in the right direction to overcome the intermolecular attractions of the other water molecules. These fast-moving water molecules vaporize and escape into the air above the water in the flask, and then eventually move up the neck of the flask and into the room. (Recall that vapour is the gaseous state of a substance that is usually a solid or a liquid at room temperature.) Nearby water molecules in the flask move into the gap left by each vaporized molecule. The process repeats itself until all of the water evaporates from the flask.

Now consider a stoppered flask at constant temperature, like the one in **Figures 7.3B** and **C**. It contains water with a vacuum above the surface of the water. Some of the molecules at the surface of the liquid are moving fast enough and in the right direction to escape the intermolecular forces of the other water molecules and thus vaporize. As more and more water molecules vaporize, the pressure of the vapour above the liquid increases. Some of the water vapour molecules collide with molecules at the surface of the liquid. If the kinetic energy of the water vapour molecules is too low, they cannot escape the attractive forces of the water molecules at the surface of the liquid. They condense and form liquid. Eventually, the rate of condensation equals the rate of vaporization and the system reaches equilibrium.

Macroscopically, the system looks static because the amount of water vapour is constant and the amount of liquid is constant. However, the system is in dynamic equilibrium, because at the molecular level the system is constantly changing. The graph below in **Figure 7.3D** illustrates this process.

Figure 7.3 In an open system **(A)**, water molecules vaporize and escape into the room. If the system is closed with a stopper and air is removed from the flask **(B)**, water vapour cannot escape into the room. Over time **(C)**, equilibrium occurs between the water vapour molecules and the water molecules. A plot of Vapour Pressure vs. Time, under constant temperature, **(D)** shows that, at equilibrium, the rate of vaporization equals the rate of condensation.

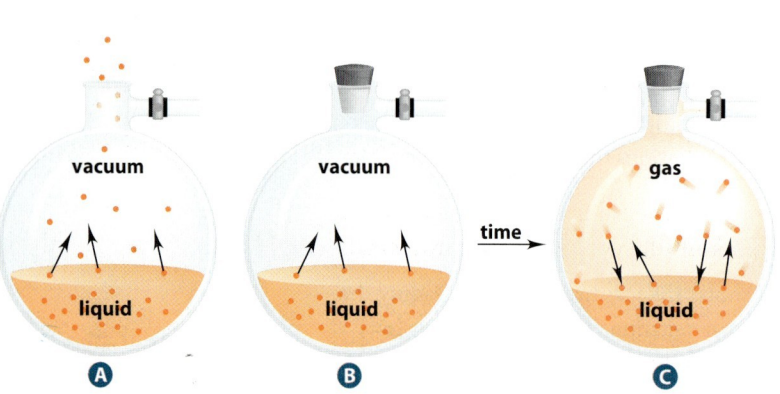
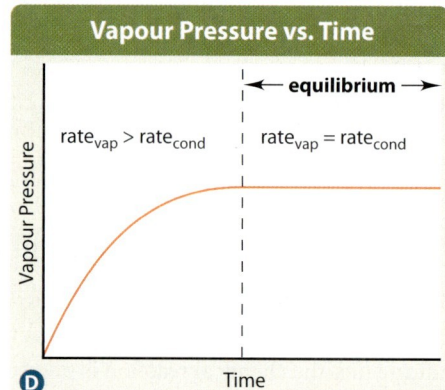

Another example of equilibrium involving physical processes is shown in **Figure 7.4**. Iodine crystals, $I_2(s)$, are placed in a closed flask, and the crystals undergo sublimation—that is, they change directly from the solid state to the gaseous state. The gaseous iodine particles with low enough kinetic energy undergo the reverse process. They undergo deposition—that is, the particles change directly from the gaseous state to the solid state without going through the liquid state. In this closed system, equilibrium occurs between the solid iodine crystals and the gaseous iodine molecules, $I_2(g)$. The equation below represents this process:

$$I_2(s) \rightleftharpoons I_2(g)$$

Conditions Necessary to Establish Equilibrium

In order for a system to reach equilibrium, the system must be a closed system. Consider the water in the flasks in the previous examples. In the open flask, the water vapour molecules with enough kinetic energy eventually move up the neck of the flask and into the air around the flask. Very few vapour molecules condense. In the closed flask, the vapour molecules are trapped. They build up *vapour pressure* and many molecules condense back into liquid. Because the vapour molecules are trapped in the flask, which is a closed system, the dynamic process of the molecules vaporizing and condensing is able to occur. The rate of the forward reaction and the rate of the reverse reaction eventually equalize.

Thermal Energy Requirements of Reversible Reactions

Consider the thermal energy requirements of reversible reactions. In a reversible reaction in which the reaction in one direction is exothermic and the reaction in the opposite direction is endothermic, changing the temperature alters the rates of the forward and reverse reactions. A temperature increase adds thermal energy to the chemical system. Additional thermal energy causes the reaction that absorbs thermal energy to proceed at a faster rate than the reaction that releases thermal energy. The rates of the forward and reverse reactions are no longer equal. The opposite is true if the temperature is lowered in a chemical system. When the temperature decreases, thermal energy is removed from the system. When thermal energy is removed from the system, the exothermic reaction proceeds at a faster rate. Because the rate of the forward reaction and the rate of the reverse reaction are no longer equal, the system is no longer at equilibrium. You will learn more about the effects of temperature on equilibrium in Section 7.2.

Figure 7.4 Iodine is a colourful example of equilibrium involving a physical process.

Describe *what is occurring at the molecular level during this process, using a diagram with labels.*

Homogeneous and Heterogeneous Equilibria

Systems in equilibrium can be classified according to the components in the system. A chemical system in equilibrium in which all of the components are in the same physical state is known as **homogeneous equilibrium.** The production of ammonia represents this type of equilibrium because all of the components are in the gaseous state, as shown below:

$$N_2(g) + 3H_2(g) \rightleftharpoons 2NH_3(g)$$

The previous example of water in equilibrium is an example of heterogeneous equilibrium. **Heterogeneous equilibrium** is a chemical system in equilibrium in which the components are in different physical states, as shown below:

$$H_2O(\ell) \rightleftharpoons H_2O(g)$$

Although this example features one substance in two physical states, the components in heterogeneous equilibrium do not have to be the same substance. For example, in a system where limestone, $CaCO_3(s)$, decomposes and forms quicklime, $CaO(s)$, and carbon dioxide, $CO_2(g)$, heterogeneous equilibrium occurs. This system represents heterogeneous equilibrium because the system contains two components in the solid state and one component in the gaseous state, as shown below:

$$CaCO_3(s) \rightleftharpoons CaO(s) + CO_2(g)$$

homogeneous equilibrium a chemical system in equilibrium in which all of the components are in the same physical state

heterogeneous equilibrium a chemical system in equilibrium in which the components are in different physical states

Suggested Investigation

Inquiry Investigation 7-A, Simulating Dynamic Equilibrium

Common Factors in Equilibrium Systems

As you learned about equilibrium systems, you might have noticed that they share some common factors:

- A system is in equilibrium when the rate of the forward process equals the rate of the reverse process.

- The macroscopic properties, such as colour, pressure, concentration, and pH, of an equilibrium system are constant. At equilibrium, there is no overall change in the properties that depend on the total quantity of matter in the system.

- Equilibrium can only be reached in a closed system, in which matter cannot cross the system boundary. To establish true equilibrium, a system should be a closed isolated system, in which neither matter nor energy can cross the system boundary. However, small changes to the components of a system are sometimes negligible, so equilibrium principles can be applied, even though the system is not completely closed and isolated.

- Equilibrium can be established from either direction. For example, in the reaction shown below of the decomposition of limestone to quicklime and carbon dioxide, equilibrium can be established regardless of whether the reaction starts with only reactants, such as limestone, or with only products, such as quicklime and carbon dioxide.

$$CaCO_3(s) \rightleftharpoons CaO(s) + CO_2(g)$$

The Equilibrium Constant Expression

You have read that many chemical systems do not proceed to completion. Instead, the system reaches equilibrium. At chemical equilibrium, both reactants and products are present in the reaction vessel. How can you predict and express the conditions of a chemical system that is in equilibrium?

The Law of Chemical Equilibrium

Chemists studied this question in the 19th century. Two Norwegian chemists, Cato Guldberg (1836–1902) and Peter Waage (1833–1900), studied many reactions, and in 1864, Guldberg and Waage independently proposed the **law of chemical equilibrium**, which is also called the **law of mass action**.

law of chemical equilibrium or **law of mass action** a law that states that in a chemical system at equilibrium, there is a constant ratio between the concentrations of the products and the concentrations of the reactants

> **Law of Chemical Equilibrium or Law of Mass Action**
> In a chemical system at equilibrium, there is a constant ratio between the concentrations of the products and the concentrations of the reactants.

The Equilibrium Constant, K_{eq}

To better understand Guldberg's and Waage's findings, consider a chemical reaction that changes colour as the reaction proceeds. Dinitrogen tetroxide, $N_2O_4(g)$, is a colourless gas that is important in space flight, as shown in **Figure 7.5**. Nitrogen dioxide, $NO_2(g)$, is a brown gas that is one of the components of air pollution caused by burning fossil fuels. You can observe the decomposition of dinitrogen tetroxide into nitrogen dioxide, because the colourless gas turns to a brown colour as the reaction proceeds. The reaction is represented by the equation below:

$$N_2O_4(g) \rightleftharpoons 2NO_2(g)$$
colourless   brown

Figure 7.5 Spacecraft use monomethyl hydrazine, CH_3NHNH_2, as the fuel and dinitrogen tetroxide, N_2O_4, as the oxidizer to provide thrust for their orbital maneuvering systems. This Russian Soyuz space capsule is maneuvering to dock with the International Space Station.

Suppose that a small quantity of dinitrogen tetroxide is placed in a capped bottle (a closed system) at 100°C, as shown in **Figure 7.6**. Notice in the graph that the initial rate of the forward reaction is relatively fast, while the initial rate of the reverse reaction is zero, because no product has formed. As the reaction proceeds, the rate of the forward reaction decreases. At the same time, the rate of the reverse reaction increases. Finally, at equilibrium, the rate of the forward reaction equals the rate of the reverse reaction, as demonstrated by the zero slopes of the lines on the graph.

You can visually observe the progress of the reaction because the colourless gas slowly darkens to a brown colour. Recall that at equilibrium, macroscopic properties such as colour and concentration remain constant. The molecular diagrams show how the mixture changes at the molecular level as the reactions proceed.

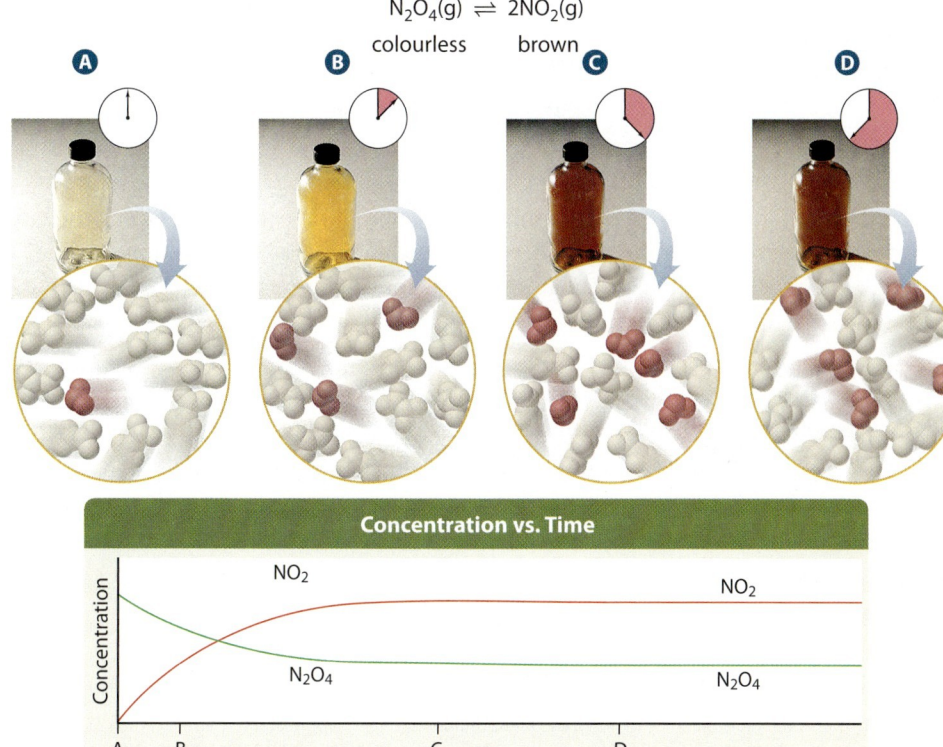

Figure 7.6 At the beginning of the reaction, the rate of the forward reaction decreases and the rate of the reverse reaction increases. At equilibrium, the rate of the forward reaction is equal to the rate of the reverse reaction, and the macroscopic properties of the system are constant. ***Describe** the changes that are taking place at the molecular level.*

Deriving the Equilibrium Constant, K_{eq}

When a chemical system reaches equilibrium, the rate of the forward reaction equals the rate of the reverse reaction:

$$\text{rate}_{fwd} = \text{rate}_{rev}$$

Both reactions are elementary steps, so their rate laws can be written from the balanced chemical equation. Recall that an elementary step is a simple reaction that represents a single molecular event in a reaction mechanism. The subscript "eq" denotes the concentrations at equilibrium, and k_{fwd} and k_{rev} are the forward and reverse rate constants, respectively.

$$k_{fwd}[N_2O_4]_{eq} = k_{rev}[NO_2]^2_{eq}$$

The rate law equations can be written as a ratio:

$$\frac{k_{fwd}}{k_{rev}} = \frac{[NO_2]^2_{eq}}{[N_2O_4]_{eq}}$$

equilibrium constant, K_{eq} the ratio of equilibrium concentrations for a particular chemical system at a particular temperature

The ratio of rate law equations is called the equilibrium constant and its symbol is K_{eq}. The new expression becomes

$$K_{eq} = \frac{[NO_2]^2_{eq}}{[N_2O_4]_{eq}}$$

The **equilibrium constant, K_{eq}**, is equal to the ratio of equilibrium concentrations at a particular temperature for a particular chemical system. Each of the molar concentration values is divided by a reference state and each is a unitless number. Thus, K_{eq} is also a unitless number. You will learn more about these units and reference states in a later course.

You can write a general equilibrium reaction as shown.

$$aA + bB \rightleftharpoons cC + dD$$

Based on this equation, the general form of the equilibrium constant expression, K_{eq}, can be written as shown below.

The Equilibrium Constant Expression

$$K_{eq} = \frac{[C]^c[D]^d}{[A]^a[B]^b}$$

where [A], [B], [C], and [D] represent the concentrations of the reactants and products after the reaction has reached equilibrium and the concentrations are no longer changing. The exponents, a, b, c, and d, are the stoichiometric coefficients from the balanced chemical equation at equilibrium. K_{eq} is the equilibrium constant for a chemical system at equilibrium.

The numerical value of the equilibrium constant tells you the relative concentration of products compared with the concentration of reactants at equilibrium. The equilibrium constant is always written with the product terms divided by the reactant terms.

$$K_{eq} = \frac{[\text{products}]}{[\text{reactants}]}$$

Therefore, a value of K_{eq} greater than 1 means that the concentration of products is larger than the concentration of reactants, as shown in **Figure 7.7**.

Figure 7.7 The numerical value of K_{eq} tells you the relative concentration of products and reactants.

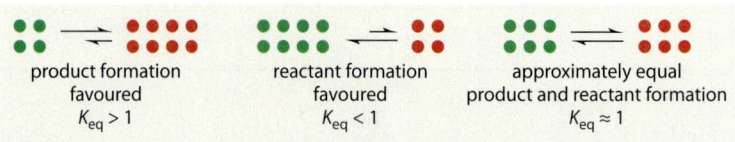

When referring to a reaction with a value of K_{eq} greater than 1, chemists often say that the *position of equilibrium* lies to the right (in the direction of the forward reaction) or that it favours product formation. Similarly, if K_{eq} is less than 1, the concentration of reactants is larger than the concentration of products at equilibrium. The position of equilibrium lies to the left (in the direction of the reverse reaction). That is, it favours reactant formation. Thus, the following general statements are true:

- When $K_{eq} > 1$, product formation is favoured. The equilibrium lies to the right (in the direction of the forward reaction). Reactions in which K_{eq} is greater than 10^{10} are usually regarded as proceeding to completion.
- When $K_{eq} \approx 1$, there are approximately equal concentrations of reactants and products at equilibrium.
- When $K_{eq} < 1$, reactant formation is favoured. The equilibrium lies to the left (in the direction of the reverse reaction). Reactions in which K_{eq} is smaller than 10^{-10} are usually regarded as not taking place at all and only reactants are in the reaction container.

Learning Check

7. A drinking glass and a tightly sealed jar are sitting on the kitchen counter. Both are half-filled with water and are undisturbed for several hours. Will the liquid and water vapour establish equilibrium in either container? Explain your answer.

8. Compare and contrast homogeneous equilibrium and heterogeneous equilibrium.

9. Explain what would occur to the equilibrium system in **Figure 7.4** if the stopper were removed.

10. Explain how the law of chemical equilibrium (the law of mass action) and the equilibrium constant are related.

11. If a chemical system is *not* at equilibrium, is it accurate to write an equilibrium constant expression or an equilibrium constant for the chemical system? Explain your answer in terms of rate laws.

12. A classmate does not understand how to interpret the value of the equilibrium constant to determine if products or reactants are favoured in a chemical system in equilibrium. Write an explanation for the student that explains what $K_{eq} > 1$, $K_{eq} \approx 1$, and $K_{eq} < 1$ mean.

Expressions for Homogeneous Equilibrium

For chemical systems at homogeneous equilibrium, you can use the balanced chemical equation to write the equilibrium constant expression, as shown in the Sample Problem on the next page for sulfuric acid. Sulfuric acid is a chemical used in many manufacturing processes; such as the production of rayon. Rayon is a material used to make many everyday products, such as the ones shown in **Figure 7.8**.

Figure 7.8 Sulfuric acid is used to make many products, including textiles such as rayon.

Sample Problem

Equilibrium Constant Expressions for Homogeneous Chemical Systems

Problem

Sulfuric acid is produced through the contact process, which involves the catalytic oxidation of sulfur dioxide as an intermediate reaction: $2SO_2(g) + O_2(g) \rightleftharpoons 2SO_3(g)$.
Write the equilibrium expression for this process.

What Is Required?

You need to determine an expression for K_{eq}.

What Is Given?

You know the balanced chemical equation.

Plan Your Strategy	Act on Your Strategy
The expression for K_{eq} is a fraction. The concentration of the product is in the numerator and the concentrations of the reactants are in the denominator. Each concentration term must be raised to the power of its coefficient in the balanced chemical equation.	The equation for the equilibrium constant expression is $$K_{eq} = \frac{[SO_3]^2}{[SO_2]^2\,[O_2]}$$

Check Your Solution

The square brackets indicate concentration terms. The product is in the numerator, and each term is raised to the power of its coefficient in the chemical equation. The usual practice in chemistry of not writing a coefficient or power of 1 is followed.

Practice Problems

Write the equilibrium constant expression for each equilibrium system.

1. The reaction at 200°C between ethanol and ethanoic acid to form ethyl ethanoate and water:

   $CH_3CH_2OH(g) + CH_3COOH(g) \rightleftharpoons$
   $\qquad CH_3COOCH_2CH_3(g) + H_2O(g)$

2. The reaction between nitrogen gas and oxygen gas at high temperatures is given by the following balanced chemical reaction:

   $N_2(g) + O_2(g) \rightleftharpoons 2NO(g)$

3. The reaction between hydrogen gas and oxygen gas to form water vapour:

   $2H_2(g) + O_2(g) \rightleftharpoons 2H_2O(g)$

4. The oxidation of ammonia (one of the reactions in the manufacture of nitric acid):

   $4NH_3(g) + 5O_2(g) \rightleftharpoons 4NO(g) + 6H_2O(g)$

5. Hydrogen sulfide reacts with methane and forms hydrogen gas and carbon disulfide as represented by the following reaction:

   $2H_2S(g) + CH_4(g) \rightleftharpoons 4H_2(g) + CS_2(g)$

6. Antimony pentachloride, $SbCl_5(g)$, decomposes into antimony trichloride, $SbCl_3(g)$, and chlorine gas, $Cl_2(g)$, in an equilibrium reaction.

7. Hydrogen gas displaces nitrogen from nitrogen monoxide gas to form nitrogen gas and water vapour according to the following reaction:

   $2H_2(g) + 2NO(g) \rightleftharpoons N_2(g) + 2H_2O(g)$

8. Sulfur trioxide gas, $SO_3(g)$, decomposes into sulfur dioxide gas, $SO_2(g)$, and oxygen gas, $O_2(g)$, in an equilibrium reaction.

   a. Write the balanced chemical equation for the equilibrium reaction.

   b. Write the equilibrium constant expression.

9. Nitrogen monoxide gas reacts with oxygen gas in an equilibrium reaction where nitrogen dioxide gas forms.

   a. Write the balanced chemical equation for the equilibrium reaction.

   b. Write the equilibrium constant expression.

10. Oxygen gas displaces chlorine from hydrogen chloride gas in an equilibrium reaction where chlorine gas and water vapour form.

    a. Write the balanced chemical equation for the equilibrium reaction.

    b. Write the equilibrium constant expression.

Expressions for Heterogeneous Equilibrium

Recall that a chemical system at heterogeneous equilibrium includes substances that are not in the same physical state. For example, consider ethanol, which is a common fuel and fuel additive, as well as an important industrial compound that is manufactured in Ontario, as shown in **Figure 7.9.** When ethanol is placed in a stoppered flask (a closed system), dynamic liquid-vapour equilibrium is soon established in the flask, as represented by the equation below:

$$C_2H_5OH(\ell) \rightleftharpoons C_2H_5OH(g)$$

You can use the general form of the equilibrium constant expression to write the expression for this reaction:

$$K_{eq} = \frac{[C]^c[D]^d}{[A]^a[B]^b} \qquad K = \frac{[C_2H_5OH(g)]}{[C_2H_5OH(\ell)]}$$

In the equilibrium expression above, K represents a temporary equilibrium expression.

Notice that liquid ethanol is in the denominator in the above expression. Liquid ethanol is a pure substance. Because ethanol's concentration is constant, the concentration is included in the term for the equilibrium constant. Both sides of this expression are multiplied by the term $[C_2H_5OH(\ell)]$ so that both sides of the expression remain equal and the terms with changing concentrations are isolated on one side of the equation. The equilibrium constant expression for this system becomes

$$[C_2H_5OH(\ell)] \times K = \frac{[C_2H_5OH(g)]}{\cancel{[C_2H_5OH(\ell)]}} \times \cancel{[C_2H_5OH(\ell)]}$$

The expression reduces to

$$[C_2H_5OH(\ell)]K = [C_2H_5OH(g)]$$

The concentration of the pure substance, liquid ethanol, is combined with K and it becomes the equilibrium constant, K_{eq}, for the heterogeneous equilibrium system. *Notice that the equilibrium constant depends only on the concentration of the gaseous ethanol.*

$$K_{eq} = [C_2H_5OH(g)]$$

In this example, the pure substance is a liquid. Solids are also pure substances with constant concentrations. The same procedure is used to determine the equilibrium constant expression for heterogeneous equilibrium chemical systems that contain solids. Use the Sample Problem and Practice Problems on the following pages to practise writing equilibrium constant expressions for heterogeneous chemical systems.

Figure 7.9 This facility in Ontario uses corn to make ethanol for fuel.

Sample Problem

Equilibrium Constant Expressions for Heterogeneous Chemical Systems

Problem

Limestone, or calcium carbonate, $CaCO_3(s)$, decomposes and forms quicklime, $CaO(s)$, and carbon dioxide, $CO_2(g)$, as represented in the equation: $CaCO_3(s) \rightleftharpoons CaO(s) + CO_2(g)$.
Write the equilibrium constant expression.

What Is Required?

You need to determine an expression for K and determine K_{eq}.

What Is Given?

You know the balanced chemical equation and the physical states of each component in the system.

Plan Your Strategy	Act on Your Strategy
The concentration of the products are in the numerator and the concentrations of the reactant is in the denominator. Each concentration term must be raised to the power of its coefficient in the balanced chemical equation.	The equation for the equilibrium constant expression is $$K = \frac{[CaO(s)][CO_2(g)]}{[CaCO_3(s)]}$$
Identify the pure substances in the expression and isolate them on the left side of the equation.	$$\frac{[CaCO_3(s)]}{[CaO(s)]} \times K = \frac{[\cancel{CaO(s)}][CO_2(g)]}{[\cancel{CaCO_3(s)}]} \times \frac{[\cancel{CaCO_3(s)}]}{[\cancel{CaO(s)}]}$$
The terms on the left side of the equation are combined and become K_{eq}.	$K_{eq} = [CO_2(g)]$

Check Your Solution

The square brackets indicate a concentration term. All of the pure substances are deleted from the expression. The usual practice in chemistry of not writing a coefficient or power of 1 is followed.

Practice Problems

Write the equilibrium constant expressions.

11. In the decomposition of solid ammonium chloride, $NH_4Cl(s)$, the products ammonia gas, $NH_3(g)$, and hydrogen chloride gas, $HCl(g)$, form:
$$NH_4Cl(s) \rightleftharpoons NH_3(g) + HCl(g)$$

12. Hydrogen gas and liquid sulfur react and form hydrogen sulfide gas:
$$H_2(g) + S(\ell) \rightleftharpoons H_2S(g)$$

13. Barium oxide and carbon dioxide react:
$$BaO(s) + CO_2(g) \rightleftharpoons BaCO_3(g)$$

14. Solid carbon and carbon dioxide gas react and form carbon monoxide:
$$C(s) + CO_2(g) \rightleftharpoons 2CO(g)$$

15. Solid sodium hydrogen carbonate, $NaHCO_3(s)$, decomposes into solid sodium carbonate, $Na_2CO_3(s)$, carbon dioxide gas, $CO_2(g)$, and water vapour, $H_2O(g)$:
$$2NaHCO_3(s) \rightleftharpoons Na_2CO_3(s) + CO_2(g) + H_2O(g)$$

16. When ammonia gas reacts with water, ammonium ions, NH_4^+, and hydroxide ions, OH^-, form according to the following reaction:
$$NH_3(g) + H_2O(\ell) \rightleftharpoons NH_4^+(aq) + OH^-(aq)$$

17. Solid iron reacts with water vapour as represented by the following reaction:
$$3Fe(s) + 4H_2O(g) \rightleftharpoons Fe_3O_4(s) + 4H_2(g)$$

18. In a closed container, solid magnesium and oxygen gas react to form magnesium oxide on the surface of the magnesium. This process is an equilibrium process. Write the equilibrium constant expression for this process.

19. In the synthesis of hydrogen iodide gas, $HI(g)$, hydrogen gas reacts with solid iodine in an equilibrium process. Write the equilibrium constant expression.

20. Solid carbon reacts with oxygen gas to form carbon dioxide gas in an equilibrium reaction. Write the equilibrium constant expression for this process.

Section 7.1 Review

Section Summary

- A reversible reaction is a chemical reaction that proceeds in both forward and reverse directions.
- Chemical equilibrium is the state of a chemical system in which the forward reaction and the reverse reaction are balanced and occur at the same rates.
- When a chemical system at equilibrium is changing at the molecular level, but its macroscopic properties are constant, the system is said to have dynamic equilibrium.
- In a chemical system at equilibrium, there is a constant ratio between the concentrations of the products and the concentrations of the reactants and this ratio is the equilibrium constant, K_{eq}.
- Because K_{eq} is a ratio of product concentration to reactant concentration, a value of K_{eq} greater than 1 means that the concentration of products is greater than the concentration of reactants. A value of K_{eq} less than 1 means the concentration of reactants is greater than the concentration of products. When K_{eq} is equal to 1, there are equal concentrations of reactants and products.

Review Questions

1. **T/I** Describe two physical processes and two chemical processes that are examples of reversible reactions that are *not* at equilibrium.

2. **K/U** What conditions must be taken into account when setting up an experiment to demonstrate equilibrium in which the reactants and products are in the gaseous state?

3. **C** For the reaction $H_2(g) + I_2(g) \rightleftharpoons 2HI(g)$, sketch a possible graph to illustrate the concentration vs. time from the start of the reaction, where the initial reactant concentrations are 1 mol/L and the initial product concentration is zero. Include the point in time on the graph at which equilibrium is reached, and label this point on the graph.

4. **K/U** Is the following statement true or false? If it is false, rewrite it to make it true. "If a chemical system at equilibrium in a closed container is heated, the system will remain at equilibrium." Explain your answer.

5. **C** Create a flowchart or similar graphic organizer that can be used as a checklist in determining if a reaction is capable of reaching equilibrium.

6. **A** A chemist places a mixture of nitrogen monoxide, NO(g), and bromine gas, $Br_2(g)$, in a closed flask. After a period of time, the flask contains a mixture of nitrogen monoxide, bromine gas, and nitrosyl bromide, NOBr(g).
   a. Explain this observation in two or three well-reasoned sentences.
   b. Is this a homogeneous equilibrium or a heterogeneous equilibrium? Explain your reasoning.

7. **K/U** Is the following statement true or false? If it is false, rewrite it to make it true. "In a chemical system at equilibrium, the concentration of reactants is equal to the concentration of products."

8. **K/U** What is the meaning of the double arrow, $\rightleftharpoons$, in a chemical equation?

9. **A** Use the concepts in this section to answer the following questions.
   a. When a damp towel is hung on a clothesline in fair weather, it will dry. The same towel left in a gym bag will remain damp. Use equilibrium principles to explain the difference.
   b. Is an operating clothes dryer an open system or a closed system? Explain your answer.

10. **A** A sealed carbonated drink bottle contains a liquid with a space above it. The space contains carbon dioxide at a pressure of about 400 kPa.
    a. What changes are taking place at the molecular level?
    b. Which macroscopic properties are constant?

11. **T/I** Copy the following balanced chemical equations into your notebook, and label each system as a homogeneous equilibrium or a heterogeneous equilibrium. Write the K_{eq} expression for each.
    a. $PCl_5(g) \rightleftharpoons PCl_3(g) + Cl_2(g)$
    b. $CaCO_3(s) \rightleftharpoons CaO(s) + CO_2(g)$
    c. $N_2O_3(g) \rightleftharpoons NO_2(g) + NO(g)$
    d. $C(s) + CO_2(g) \rightleftharpoons CO(g)$

12. **K/U** The photograph shown here is of a beaker of water being heated and forming water vapour.
    a. Explain why this system can never reach equilibrium.
    b. Explain why placing a tightly-fitting lid on this container is *not* a solution for establishing equilibrium.

SECTION 7.2
The Effects of External Changes on Equilibrium

Key Terms

Le Châtelier's principle

Le Châtelier's principle a principle stating that if a chemical system in a state of equilibrium is disturbed, the system will undergo a change that shifts its equilibrium position in a direction that reduces the effect of the disturbance

Le Châtelier's Principle

A system at equilibrium must be closed. At equilibrium, the concentrations of reactants and products remain the same, the volume and pressure of the system are constant, and the temperature does not change. What happens to a system at equilibrium if one or more of these factors change? In 1888, a French chemist, Henri Le Châtelier, answered this question and proposed what is now known as **Le Châtelier's principle.**

Le Châtelier's Principle
If an external stress (a change in concentration, pressure, volume, or temperature) is applied to a chemical system at equilibrium, the rates of the forward and reverse reactions are temporarily unequal because the stress affects the reaction rates. However, equilibrium is eventually restored in the chemical system.

The Effects of Concentration Changes on Equilibrium

Consider what happens if the concentration of reactants or products changes. This question has practical importance, because many manufacturing processes are continuous. Products can be removed and more reactants can be added without stopping a manufacturing process. For example, consider the Haber-Bosch process to manufacture ammonia that you read about in Chapter 6:

$$N_2(g) + 3H_2(g) \rightleftharpoons 2NH_3(g)$$

Ammonia can be removed from the mixture of gases by cooling, as shown in **Figure 7.10**. When the temperature is decreased, ammonia liquefies before nitrogen or hydrogen does. As the ammonia liquefies, it is pumped out of the reaction vessel. What happens to an equilibrium mixture if some ammonia is removed?

Look at the chemical reaction representing the Haber-Bosch process shown above. If ammonia is removed from the reaction vessel, there are fewer molecules of ammonia in the reaction vessel. Because there are fewer ammonia molecules that can decompose, the equilibrium temporarily shifts to the right. The reaction proceeding from left to right (ammonia synthesis) occurs at a faster rate than the reaction proceeding from right to left (ammonia decomposition). As ammonia concentration increases, the rate of its decomposition increases. Eventually, equilibrium is restored in the reaction vessel when the rate of the forward reaction equals the rate of the reverse reaction. In other words, the system is in equilibrium again when the synthesis of ammonia occurs at the same rate as the decomposition of ammonia.

Similarly, if additional nitrogen, hydrogen, or both are added, the rate of the forward reaction (ammonia synthesis) increases, or the equilibrium temporarily shifts to the right. If there are more reactant molecules in the reaction vessel, more collisions occur, and more product forms. The reaction rate for ammonia synthesis is temporarily faster than the reaction rate of ammonia decomposition. As the reactants are consumed, the rate of ammonia synthesis slows down. Eventually, the rate of ammonia synthesis equals the rate of ammonia decomposition and equilibrium is restored.

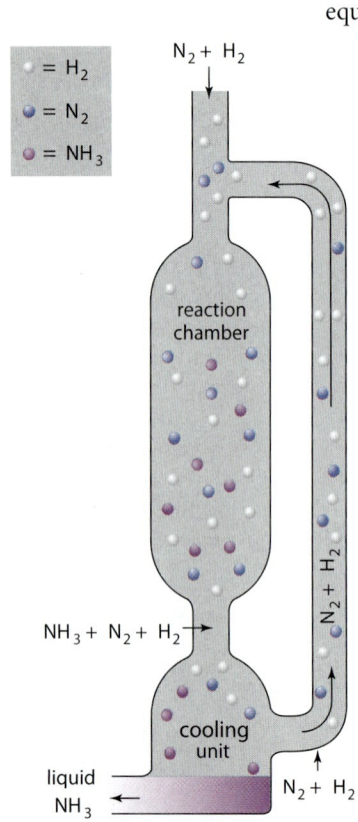

Figure 7.10 When ammonia is removed from the reaction vessel, there are fewer ammonia molecules that can decompose. The rate of ammonia synthesis becomes temporarily faster than the rate of ammonia decomposition.

Consider the equilibrium between dinitrogen tetroxide gas and nitrogen dioxide gas.

$$N_2O_4(g) \rightleftharpoons 2NO_2(g)$$

Figure 7.6 in Section 7.1 showed you how equilibrium was established in this particular chemical system. Now imagine that you inject more dinitrogen tetroxide gas into the system, as shown in the graph in **Figure 7.11**. Notice that the concentration of dinitrogen tetroxide gas instantly increases with the injection of more gas. Then the concentration immediately begins to drop. The rate of the reverse reaction also begins to increase as more nitrogen dioxide molecules combine and form dinitrogen tetroxide. Soon, a new equilibrium is established with new concentrations of reactants and products. *The ratio of the new concentrations of products to reactants, however, is the same as the original ratio.* The equilibrium constant does not change for a chemical system at constant temperature.

What happens if one or more of the components in the chemical system are a solid or a liquid? Recall that the concentration of a solid or a liquid is constant. The concentration does not depend on the amount of the substance present. Remember that according to the collision theory of chemical reactions involving a solid, collisions occur only at the exposed surface of the solid. The same surface area is exposed to both the forward and reverse reactions, and the reaction rates increase or decrease at the same rate, if they change at all. The effects of concentration changes on a chemical system at equilibrium are summarized in the blue box below:

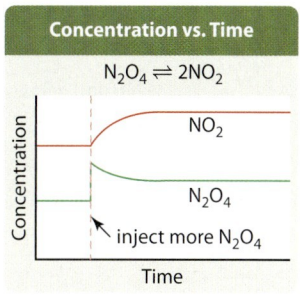

Figure 7.11 If you inject more dinitrogen tetroxide (a reactant) into the equilibrium system, there are more reactant molecules than product molecules. Temporarily, more product is produced until the reverse reaction rate increases and equilibrium is restored.

- Increasing the concentration of a product causes a shift to reactant formation.
- Decreasing the concentration of a product causes a shift to product formation.
- Increasing the concentration of a reactant causes a shift to product formation.
- Decreasing the concentration of a reactant causes a shift to reactant formation.
- K_{eq} is not affected by changes in the product or reaction concentrations, because the ratio of product to reactants is the same.

An example of the effects of concentration changes is found in your body, as shown in **Figure 7.12**. Your blood contains carbonic acid, $H_2CO_3(aq)$, that is in equilibrium with carbon dioxide, $CO_2(aq)$, and water, as represented by the reaction below:

$$H_2CO_3(aq) \rightleftharpoons CO_2(aq) + H_2O(\ell)$$

Your body controls the concentration of carbonic acid in your blood by removing carbon dioxide when you exhale. Removing carbon dioxide from this equilibrium system causes a shift in the reaction rates. The shift toward product formation causes a decrease in concentration of carbonic acid (the reactant) in your blood. Thus, your body maintains a safe level of carbonic acid in your blood by removing carbon dioxide through your lungs when you exhale.

Figure 7.12 During and following exercise, your body controls the amount of carbonic acid in your blood by removing carbon dioxide from your bloodstream through your lungs.

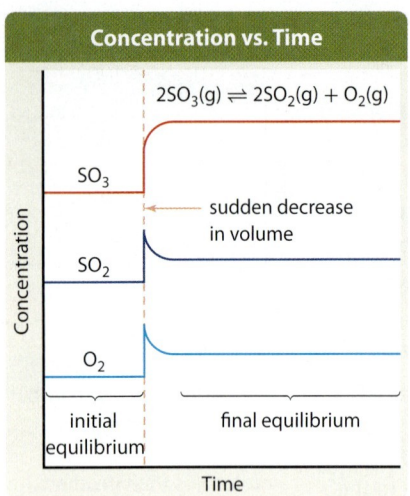

Figure 7.13 When the volume of the reaction vessel decreases, the concentration of each gas in the mixture increases. Initially, the system is no longer at equilibrium. When equilibrium is restored, the concentrations of the gases are not the same as they were before the volume decreased, but K_{eq} remains the same.

The Effects of Volume and Pressure Changes on Equilibrium

Changes in volume and pressure in a reaction vessel have no effect on solids and liquids. Recall that the volumes of solids and liquids are constant. Pressure also has no effect on solids and liquids because they are almost incompressible. However, changes in volume or pressure do have an effect on equilibrium systems that contain gases. When the volume of a mixture of gases decreases, the pressure of the gases increases, in agreement with Boyle's law. Boyle's law states that the volume of a fixed amount of gas at a constant temperature varies inversely with the pressure, $V \propto \frac{1}{P}$. Consider an equilibrium chemical system in which sulfur trioxide, $SO_3(g)$, decomposes and forms sulfur dioxide, $SO_2(g)$, and oxygen gas, $O_2(g)$.

$$2SO_3(g) \rightleftharpoons 2SO_2(g) + O_2(g)$$

When the volume of the reaction vessel suddenly decreases and the pressure increases, the system is no longer at equilibrium, as shown in **Figure 7.13**. When the pressure of a gas increases, the concentration of the molecules increases, because the same number of molecules occupies a smaller volume, as shown in **Figure 7.14**. Because the concentrations of the reactant gases increase, the number of collisions between molecules increases, and both the forward and reverse reaction rates increase. The equilibrium position can shift; however, the ratio of product concentrations to reactant concentrations, K_{eq}, does not change.

Gas pressure is caused by gas particles striking the walls of the reaction vessel. If the number of particles or molecules increases, gas pressure increases. To restore equilibrium, the reaction temporarily shifts in the direction that decreases the number of molecules and at the same time decreases the pressure in the system. For example, in the reaction represented below, there are three molecules of gas formed in the forward reaction and two molecules of gas formed in the reverse reaction. To reduce pressure in the system, the reverse reaction is favoured because there are fewer molecules formed.

$$2SO_3(g) \rightleftharpoons 2SO_2(g) + O_2(g)$$

Conversely, if the pressure decreases (volume increases), the reaction temporarily shifts in the direction that increases the number of molecules. In the above reaction, the rate of the forward reaction increases. As more molecules form, the pressure in the container increases and the system shifts back toward equilibrium.

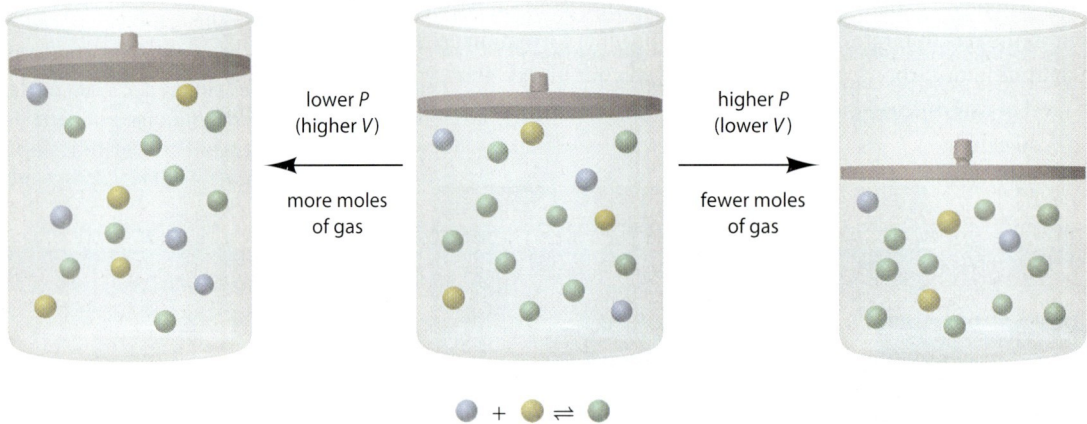

Figure 7.14 When pressure decreases and volume increases, the reaction shifts in the direction that produces more particles. When pressure increases and volume decreases, the reaction shifts in the direction that produces fewer particles.

What if both the forward reaction and the reverse reaction involve the same number of molecules? The increase of the forward reaction rate equals the increase in the reverse reaction rate and there is no effect on equilibrium.

Another possible way to change the pressure in a chemical system at equilibrium is to add an inert gas. An inert gas does not react with any of the components of the system. The only effect is to increase the total pressure. Because there is no change in volume, the partial pressures of the gases do not change and the system remains at equilibrium.

The effects of pressure or volume changes on a chemical system at equilibrium are summarized below:

- If pressure increases (and therefore volume decreases), the reaction shifts so that the total number of particles decreases, which decreases the pressure in the system.
- If pressure decreases (and therefore volume increases), the reaction shifts so that the total number of particles increases, which increases the pressure in the system.
- An inert gas added to a chemical system at equilibrium does not cause a shift in either direction in a reversible reaction.
- K_{eq} is not affected by a change in pressure or volume because the ratio of products to reactants is the same.

An example of equilibrium changes due to pressure changes is used in the process of freeze-drying foods for preservation, as shown in **Figure 7.15**. The first step in freeze-drying foods is to freeze the foods so that the water in the food becomes ice. Then the container is pressurized. When pressure decreases, the water in the food sublimes, as represented by the equation below. As you learned previously, sublimation is the change of state directly from the solid state to the gaseous state.

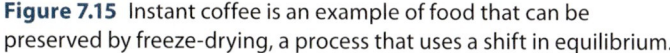

$$H_2O(s) \rightleftharpoons H_2O(g)$$

Decreasing the pressure causes the equilibrium to shift to the right in favour of water vapour formation. The water vapour is removed from the reaction vessel to reinforce the shift of equilibrium to the right. At the end of the process, the moisture content of the food is very low. Removing moisture from foods helps to preserve them.

Figure 7.15 Instant coffee is an example of food that can be preserved by freeze-drying, a process that uses a shift in equilibrium.

Learning Check

13. Explain Le Châtelier's principle in your own words.
14. How does increasing the concentration of a reactant affect a chemical system at equilibrium?
15. Explain how your body controls the concentration of carbonic acid in your blood.
16. How does the addition of an inert gas affect a chemical system at equilibrium?
17. Describe the changes that occur in a system at equilibrium when the pressure increases and when the pressure decreases.
18. What effects do the following changes have on the numerical value of the equilibrium constant, K_{eq}, for a chemical system at equilibrium?
    a. increasing the concentration of a reactant
    b. removing a product from the reaction chamber
    c. increasing the pressure in the reaction chamber
    d. increasing the concentration of a product
    e. decreasing the pressure in the reaction chamber
    f. adding an inert gas to the reaction chamber

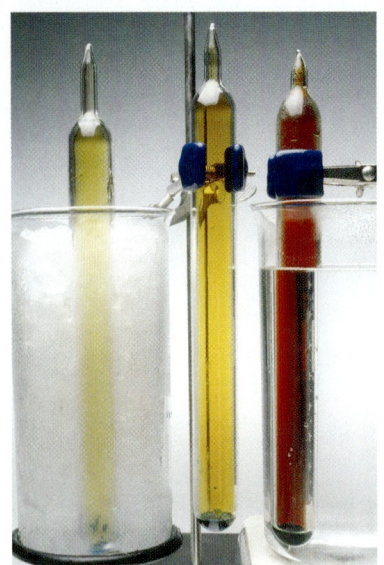

Figure 7.16 The dinitrogen tetroxide and nitrogen dioxide reaction illustrates how a temperature change causes equilibrium to shift in response to the amount of thermal energy in the system.

The Effects of Temperature Changes on Equilibrium

What happens when temperature changes in a chemical system? When a system is cooled, thermal energy is removed from the system. When a system is heated, thermal energy is added to the system. To evaluate how energy changes affect reaction rates, it is helpful to include the energy requirements of the reaction as a reactant or product in the chemical reaction. Recall that in an endothermic reaction, thermal energy is absorbed, and in an exothermic reaction, thermal energy is released. For example, the decomposition of dinitrogen tetroxide, $N_2O_4(g)$, is endothermic. So, the energy term can be written as a reactant.

$$N_2O_4(g) + 58.0 \text{ kJ/mol} \rightleftharpoons 2NO_2(g)$$
$$\text{colourless} \qquad \qquad \text{brown}$$

If this chemical system is cooled, the energy in the system decreases. There is less energy available for the forward reaction to occur. The net result is that the reverse reaction occurs at a faster rate than the forward reaction. That is, the reaction shifts to the left. You would observe an increase in reactant concentration in the reaction vessel.

When the reaction shifts to the left, not only is the concentration of dinitrogen tetroxide increasing, but the amount of energy in the system is increasing too. As energy increases in the system, the forward reaction rate increases. Eventually, the rates of the reverse reaction and the forward reaction equalize and equilibrium is restored. The photograph in **Figure 7.16** shows how temperature affects the reaction rates in this system. The forward reaction is favoured at high temperature. The light-brown sealed tube on the left contains mostly dinitrogen tetroxide, which is a colourless gas. The sealed tube on the right contains mostly nitrogen dioxide, which is dark brown. The sealed tube in the centre contains a more equal mixture, demonstrated by its intermediate colour intensity.

When the temperature increases, the endothermic reaction (left to right) is favoured (increased [NO_2] and decreased [N_2O_4]). Consequently, K_{eq} increases. When the temperature is lowered, the exothermic reaction (right to left) is favoured (decreased [NO_2] and increased [N_2O_4]). Consequently, K_{eq} decreases. These changes are shown graphically in **Figure 7.17**.

Of the system changes that can occur—concentration, pressure/volume, and temperature—only temperature changes affect the equilibrium constant. The effects of temperature changes on a chemical system at equilibrium are summarized below:

- A temperature increase (addition of thermal energy) favours the endothermic (heat-absorbing) reaction, whereas a temperature decrease (removal of thermal energy) favours the exothermic (heat-releasing) reaction.
- In an endothermic system, an increase in temperature increases K_{eq}.
- In an exothermic system, an increase in temperature decreases K_{eq}.

Figure 7.17 **(A)** When the temperature increases in a system in which the forward reaction is endothermic, equilibrium shifts toward product formation. **(B)** When the forward reaction is exothermic, reactant formation is favoured and equilibrium shifts to the left.
Explain how the addition or removal of thermal energy affects endothermic and exothermic reactions.

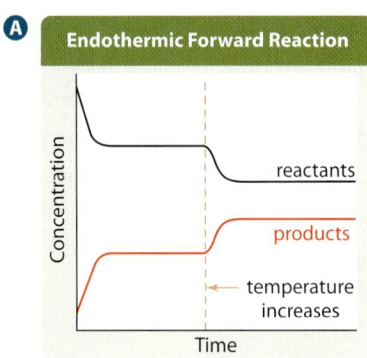
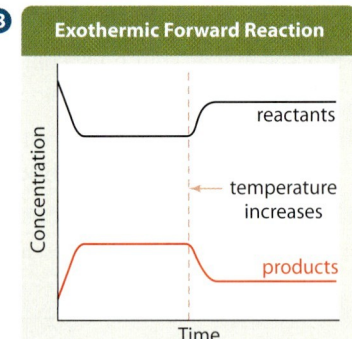

The Effect of a Catalyst on Equilibrium

Catalysts are often used in chemical processes to speed up a chemical reaction. As you learned in Chapter 6, a catalyst is a substance that increases the rate of a chemical reaction by lowering the activation energy without being consumed by the reaction. When a catalyst is added to a chemical system involving a reversible reaction, the catalyst increases the rates of the reactions in both directions—toward product formation and toward reactant formation. Therefore, the system reaches equilibrium more quickly, but the catalyst does not shift the equilibrium in either direction.

> The presence of a catalyst does not shift equilibrium in either direction.

Suggested Investigation

Inquiry Investigation 7-B, How Does an Equilibrium System Respond to Changing Conditions?

Summary of the Effects of Changing Conditions on a System at Equilibrium

When a chemical system is at equilibrium, the macroscopic properties of reactant and product concentrations, pressure, volume, and temperature are constant. In a reversible reaction at equilibrium, the rates of the forward and reverse reactions are equal. When these macroscopic properties of a system change, the opposing chemical reactions are affected and the rates of the opposing reactions are temporarily unequal. Over time, equilibrium is restored in the system. **Table 7.1** summarizes the effects of changing conditions on a system.

Use the Sample Problem on the next page to test your understanding of Le Châtelier's principle and use the Practice Problems to practise the application of this principle.

Table 7.1 The Effects of Changing Conditions on a System at Equilibrium

Change or Stress	Equilibrium Shift	Effect on K_{eq}
Increasing product concentration	Toward reactant formation	No effect
Decreasing product concentration	Toward product formation	No effect
Increasing reactant concentration	Toward product formation	No effect
Decreasing reactant concentration	Toward reactant formation	No effect
Pressure increase (volume decrease)	Toward fewer particle formation	No effect
Pressure decrease (volume increase)	Toward greater particle formation	No effect
Pressure increase with inert gas	No shift	No effect
Temperature increase	Toward endothermic reaction (heat-absorbing reaction)	Endothermic forward reaction—K_{eq} increases Exothermic forward reaction—K_{eq} decreases
Temperature decrease	Toward exothermic reaction (heat-releasing reaction)	Endothermic forward reaction—K_{eq} decreases Exothermic forward reaction—K_{eq} increases
Catalyst present	No shift	Equilibrium is reached more quickly, but the catalyst does not shift the equilibrium in either direction.

Learning Check

19. Compare and contrast endothermic and exothermic reactions.
20. Suppose a chemical system is at equilibrium and the forward reaction is endothermic.
    a. Describe what happens on the molecular level if the system is heated.
    b. Explain the changes in reactant concentration and product concentration when the system is heated.
21. Describe the effect of adding a catalyst to a chemical system at equilibrium.
22. What changes occur to K_{eq} when a catalyst is added to a chemical system at equilibrium? Explain your answer.
23. Suppose a chemical system is at equilibrium and the forward reaction is exothermic.
    a. Describe what happens on the molecular level if this system is heated.
    b. Explain the changes in reactant concentration and product concentration when this system is heated.
24. How is K_{eq} affected in questions 20 and 23? Explain your answers.
25. Which macroscopic property is used in the dinitrogen tetroxide and nitrogen dioxide chemical system, described in the preceding text, to indicate a shift in equilibrium?

Sample Problem

Using Le Châtelier's Principle

Problem

The following equilibrium is established in a closed, rigid container:

$$PCl_5(g) + \text{heat} \rightleftharpoons PCl_3(g) + Cl_2(g)$$

In which direction does the reaction shift as a result of each of the following changes?
a. adding additional phosphorus pentachloride gas, $PCl_5(g)$; **b.** removing chlorine gas, $Cl_2(g)$; **c.** decreasing the temperature; **d.** increasing the pressure by adding helium gas (an inert gas); **e.** using a catalyst

What Is Required?

You need to determine whether each change causes the reaction to shift to the left or the right, or whether each change has no effect.

What Is Given?

You know the chemical equation. You know the forward reaction is endothermic.

Plan Your Strategy	Act on Your Strategy
Identify the change that is imposed. Then identify how the system temporarily shifts before equilibrium is restored.	**a.** Phosphorus pentachloride is a reactant. Increasing a reactant stimulates product formation. The reaction shifts to the right.
	b. Chlorine gas is a product. Decreasing a product stimulates product formation. The reaction shifts to the right.
	c. Decreasing the temperature causes the reaction to shift in the direction of the exothermic reaction. If the forward reaction is endothermic, the reverse reaction is exothermic. The reaction shifts to the left.
	d. Helium is an inert gas. An inert gas added to the system increases the pressure, but it does not cause a shift in the reaction. The system remains at equilibrium.
	e. Adding a catalyst to a system at equilibrium causes the reaction rates in both directions to increase at the same rate. There is no shift in the system. The system remains at equilibrium.

Check Your Solution

Use **Table 7.1** to check your answers.

Practice Problems

21. In which direction does the following reaction shift if the temperature increases? Explain why.

$$2HI(g) \rightleftharpoons H_2(g) + I_2(g) + 52 \text{ kJ}$$

In the gaseous equilibrium systems in problems 22–25, the volume of the container is increased, causing a decrease in pressure. In which direction does each reaction shift? Explain why for each case.

22. $CO_2(g) + H_2(g) \rightleftharpoons CO(g) + H_2O(g)$

23. $2NO_2(g) \rightleftharpoons N_2O_4(g)$

24. $2CO_2(g) \rightleftharpoons 2CO(g) + O_2(g)$

25. $CH_4(g) + 2H_2S(g) \rightleftharpoons CS_2(g) + 4H_2(g)$

26. Toluene, $C_7H_8(\ell)$, is an important organic solvent. It is made industrially from methylcyclohexane $C_7H_{14}(g)$:

$$C_7H_{14}(g) + \text{heat} \rightleftharpoons C_7H_8(g) + 3H_2(g)$$

State three different changes to an equilibrium mixture of these reacting gases that would shift the reaction toward greater production of toluene.

27. In which direction does the following reaction shift as a result of each of the following changes?

$$2NO(g) + 2H_2(g) \rightleftharpoons N_2(g) + 2H_2O(g) + \text{heat}$$

a. increasing the pressure of gases in the reaction vessel by decreasing the volume

b. increasing the pressure of gases in the reaction vessel by adding inert argon gas while keeping the volume of the vessel constant

c. increasing the temperature

28. In question 27, how do each of the changes affect K_{eq}? Explain your answers.

29. The following reaction is endothermic when read from left to right: $N_2O_4(g) \rightleftharpoons 2NO_2(g)$

In which direction does the reaction shift as a result of each of the following changes?

a. adding $NO_2(g)$

b. adding a catalyst

30. In question 29, how do each of the changes affect K_{eq}? Explain your answers.

Activity 7.1 Le Châtelier's Principle: Response of an Equilibrium System to Stress

In this activity, you will use your knowledge of Le Châtelier's principle and explain the effects caused by the changes to the following system in equilibrium:

$$N_2O_4(g) \rightleftharpoons 2NO_2(g)$$
$$\text{colourless} \quad \text{brown}$$

Procedure
Use **Figure 7.16** to answer questions 1 and 2. Use the photographs below to answer question 3 and 4.

Questions
1. Given that $NO_2(g)$ is brown and that $N_2O_4(g)$ is colourless, what is the effect on the concentrations of $NO_2(g)$ and $N_2O_4(g)$ when the mixture is cooled?

2. What is the effect on the concentrations of $NO_2(g)$ and $N_2O_4(g)$ when the mixture is heated?

3. In the photographs below, the sealed syringe contains a mixture of $NO_2(g)$ and $N_2O_4(g)$. The photograph on the left illustrates an equilibrium mixture at atmospheric pressure. The centre photograph shows the contents of the syringe immediately after the plunger has been pushed down. The photograph on the right shows the same plunger several seconds later.

a. Explain why the gas changed colour when the plunger was pushed down.

b. Propose an explanation for the very light colour of the mixture in the photograph on the right.

4. Explain why this equilibrium system is *homogeneous*.

5. In terms of Le Châtelier's principle, summarize your conclusions from this activity.

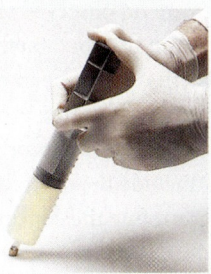

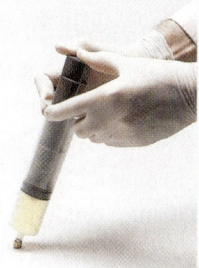

Section 7.2 Review

Section Summary

- Le Châtelier's principle states that if an external stress (a change in concentration, pressure, volume, or temperature) is applied to a chemical system at equilibrium, the rates of the forward and reverse reactions are temporarily unequal because the stress affects the reaction rates. However, equilibrium is eventually restored in the chemical system.

- Only a temperature change affects K_{eq}. In a system that is endothermic in the forward direction, a temperature rise increases K_{eq}. If the forward reaction is exothermic, a temperature rise decreases K_{eq}.

- Adding a catalyst causes a system to reach equilibrium more quickly, but it does not shift the equilibrium in either direction.

Review Questions

1. **K/U** Describe how you can increase the pressure on a system of gases at equilibrium without changing the volume.

2. **K/U** How does the change to the system in question 1 affect equilibrium?

3. **C** Draw a graph to represent the concentration of reactant and product gas molecules over time for the equilibrium system below. In the graph, show the points in time of when equilibrium is initially established; when more A is introduced to the system; and when the new position of equilibrium is established. Be sure to label the graph.

    $$A(g) + B(g) \rightleftharpoons 2AB(g)$$

4. **A** At one time, methanol, $CH_3OH(g)$, was obtained by heating wood without allowing the wood to burn. The products were collected, and methanol (sometimes called "wood alcohol") was separated by distillation. Today, methanol is manufactured by reacting carbon monoxide with hydrogen gas:

    $$CO(g) + 2H_2(g) \rightleftharpoons CH_3OH(g)$$

    At 210°C, K_{eq} for this reaction is 14.5. Is this temperature favourable for the formation of methanol? Explain.

5. **K/U** It is known that changing the temperature of a reaction at equilibrium will alter the K_{eq} value for the reaction. Summarize, in two sentences, how the value for K_{eq} is altered for both exothermic and endothermic reactions.

6. **T/I** In which direction does the reaction shift as a result of the change in each homogeneous equilibrium system in (a) to (d)?
    a. Adding $Cl_2(g)$: $2Cl_2(g) + O_2(g) \rightleftharpoons 2Cl_2O(g)$
    b. Removing $N_2(g)$: $2NO_2(g) \rightleftharpoons N_2(g) + 2O_2(g)$
    c. Using a catalyst:
       $$CH_4(g) + 2H_2O(g) \rightleftharpoons CO_2(g) + 4H_2(g)$$
    d. Increasing the temperature:
       $$CO(g) + 3H_2(g) \rightleftharpoons CH_4(g) + H_2O(g)$$
       $$\Delta H = -230 \text{ kJ}$$

7. **C** Draw a cause-and-effect diagram that describes changes to a chemical system at equilibrium. Include the concepts of changes in concentration, changes in pressure, changes in temperature, and changes in volume. Explain why the addition of a catalyst does not have to be in your diagram.

8. **A** Kidney stones form in an equilibrium process where calcium ions, $Ca^{2+}(aq)$, react with oxalate ions, $C_2O_4^{2-}(aq)$ (from oxalic acid found in many of the foods we eat), to form solid calcium oxalate, $CaC_2O_4(s)$, represented by the following equation:

    $$Ca^{2+}(aq) + C_2O_4^{2-}(aq) \rightleftharpoons CaC_2O_4(s)$$

    Explain how the formation of calcium carbonate might be prevented, using Le Châtelier's principle.

9. **T/I** For each reversible reaction, determine whether high temperatures or low temperatures favour the forward reaction:
    a. $2ICl(g) \rightleftharpoons I_2(g) + Cl_2(g)$ $\Delta H_r = -35$ kJ
    b. $2CO_2(g) + 566 \text{ kJ} \rightleftharpoons 2CO(g) + O_2(g)$
    c. $2HF(g) \rightleftharpoons H_2(g) + F_2(g)$ $\Delta H_r = -536$ kJ

10. **T/I** A student adds phosphorus trichloride gas, $PCl_3(g)$, and chlorine gas, $Cl_2(g)$, to a closed container and allows the reaction to occur at a constant temperature to form phosphorus pentachloride, $PCl_5(g)$. Phosphorus trichloride gas and phosphorus pentachloride gas are clear and colourless, whereas chlorine gas has a light greenish-yellow colour. After several minutes, there are no observed changes in macroscopic properties in the container. The student concludes that the reaction has gone to completion and has stopped occurring. Suggest three procedures that could be conducted to either support or refute the student's conclusion. Include the outcome that would allow you to support or refute the conclusion for each procedure.

STSE
CHEMISTRY Connections

Chelation: Removing Heavy Metals from the Body

Lead is a soft, heavy metal that is found naturally in the environment. Even at low levels of exposure, lead can have adverse effects on human health. Because of this potential for toxicity, the Canadian government and manufacturers have taken action during the past 40 years to reduce lead levels in products, such as in household paints, in the material to seal the seams of food cans, and in gasoline. In Canada, lead exposure is more likely to result from airborne lead dust that settles onto food crops, lead in water pipes, and lead in consumer goods such as lead-based paint, toys, costume jewellery, and ceramics.

LEAD BODY BURDEN Doctors can measure the amount of lead in a person's blood by means of a simple blood test. This measure of blood lead level (BLL) can reveal recent exposure to lead, but it does not reveal information about the accumulation of lead in body tissues. Over time, soft tissues, such as brain, liver, kidney, and bone marrow, absorb lead from the blood. Hard tissues such as bone also absorb lead, over time.

CHELATION THERAPY Removing sources of lead exposure is the most effective way to reduce the risk of toxicity. For people already affected by a very high BLL and severe toxicity, chelation therapy, shown below, may be an option.

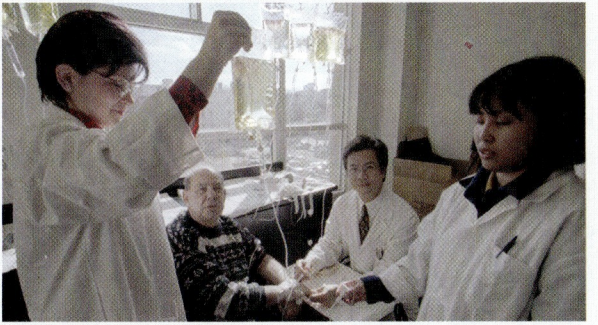

Chelation is carried out by experienced physicians in a hospital. The process removes metals from the body before permanent organ damage can occur.

EDTA (ethylenediamine tetraacetic acid), shown in the diagram at the top of the next column, is one type of chelating agent that is used to treat lead poisoning in humans. When EDTA is injected into the blood of a person who has severe lead toxicity, the functional groups of the chelating agent (2NH$_2$ and 4COOH) form complexes with the lead in the body. This reaction results in an equilibrium shift, in which lead is displaced from the molecular sites in the body as a result of the formation of chelates.

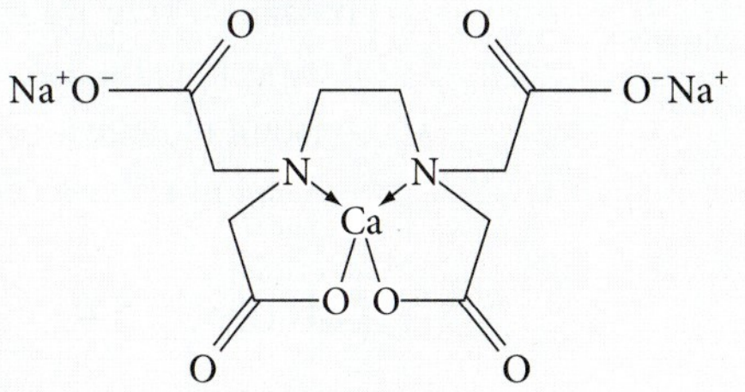

CaNa$_2$EDTA

This form of EDTA (calcium disodium ethylenediamine tetraacetic acid) ensures that the body's supply of calcium is not depleted when chelation therapy is administered.

Chelate formation depends on the location of metal ions in the body. EDTA preferentially forms complexes with the lead in the blood as opposed to the lead found in bone. Chelate formation also depends on the metal's stability constant (an equilibrium constant related to formation of the chelate). The higher the stability constant, the more successfully a metal can compete against other metals in binding to the chelating agent. The higher stability constant of lead allows for preferential removal of this potentially toxic metal over metals that are needed by the body, such as zinc and manganese.

Calcium is also essential for body functions. Even though calcium has a lower stability constant compared with lead, the calcium concentration in body fluids is high and so it may preferentially bind to EDTA. Because of this risk of calcium depletion from the body, EDTA is usually injected as calcium disodium ethylenediamine tetraacetic acid (CaNa$_2$EDTA). Upon injection of CaNa$_2$EDTA, the lead in the blood displaces the Ca from CaNa$_2$EDTA. The PbNa$_2$EDTA chelate formed is then excreted from the body in the form of urine, thus preventing excessive depletion of the calcium that our bodies need.

Connect to Society

1. Conduct further research into the advantages and disadvantages of using EDTA for chelation therapy in cases of acute (short-term) and chronic (long-term) lead exposure, and present a brief report on your findings to the class.

2. Many chelation kits are available for sale on the Internet. Research one of these kits and evaluate the safety of the product.

SECTION 7.3
Calculating Equilibrium Constants

Key Terms

quadratic equation
quadratic formula
reaction quotient

You have read how changes to an equilibrium system can affect the equilibrium constant, K_{eq}, in general terms. Now, you will learn how to determine the numerical value of that constant. The equilibrium constant expression is used to calculate the equilibrium constant. There are several ways to calculate the equilibrium constant using different kinds of experimental data. As you will learn in this section, you can also use the equilibrium constant to determine unknown quantities, such as the concentration of a reactant or a product in a chemical system.

Calculating K_{eq}

To calculate the equilibrium constant, K_{eq}, consider again the homogeneous equilibrium reaction between dinitrogen tetroxide, $N_2O_4(g)$, and nitrogen dioxide, $NO_2(g)$. **Table 7.2** lists data from four experiments performed on this chemical equilibrium system, involving different initial concentrations of reactants and products at a constant temperature. The graphs in **Figure 7.18** represent the same data. In Experiment 1, there is initially only dinitrogen tetroxide in the flask. In Experiment 2, there is initially only nitrogen dioxide in the flask. In Experiments 3 and 4, both dinitrogen tetroxide and nitrogen dioxide are present in the initial reaction mixture. The last column shows that although the equilibrium concentrations are different in the four experiments, the ratio of product concentrations to reactant concentrations is constant, within experimental error.

Table 7.2 Investigating the Decomposition of $N_2O_4(g)$

Experiment	Initial $[N_2O_4(g)]$ (mol/L)	Initial $[NO_2(g)]$ (mol/L)	Equilibrium $[N_2O_4(g)]$ (mol/L)	Equilibrium $[NO_2(g)]$ (mol/L)	Ratio: $\dfrac{[NO_2]^2}{[N_2O_4]}$
1	0.1000	0.0000	0.0491	0.1018	0.211
2	0.0000	0.1000	0.0185	0.0627	0.212
3	0.0500	0.0500	0.0332	0.0837	0.211
4	0.0750	0.025	0.0411	0.0930	0.210

Hundreds of experiments on this chemical equilibrium system show that these results are consistent at 100°C. Equilibrium is established regardless of the initial concentrations of the reactant and the product. The balanced equation for the chemical equilibrium system and the results of experiments are summarized as follows:

$$N_2O_4(g) \rightleftharpoons 2NO_2(g)$$

$$K_{eq} = \frac{[NO_2]^2}{[N_2O_4]} = 0.211$$

Develop your skills in calculating equilibrium constants for equilibrium systems by examining the Sample Problems and completing the Practice Problems on the following pages.

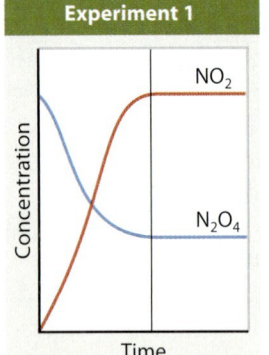
Experiment 1

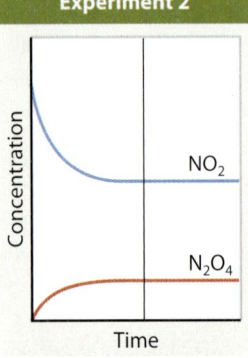
Experiment 2

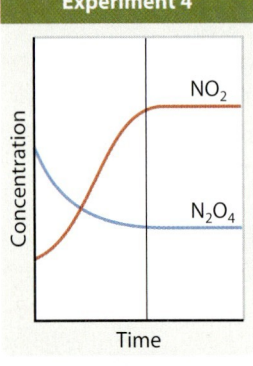
Experiment 4

Figure 7.18 These graphs show the experimental results of Experiments 1, 2, and 4. Although the starting concentrations were different in the three flasks, analysis of the mixture at equilibrium showed that the value of the equilibrium constant was approximately the same.
Describe Experiment 3 by drawing its graph and explaining why the graph looks as it does.

Sample Problem

Calculating an Equilibrium Constant for a Homogeneous Chemical System

Problem

A 5.0 L flask at constant temperature contains nitrogen, $N_2(g)$, chlorine, $Cl_2(g)$, and nitrogen trichloride, $NCl_3(g)$. The chemical equilibrium system is represented by the following reaction: $N_2(g) + 3Cl_2(g) \rightleftharpoons 2NCl_3(g)$

When the equilibrium system is analyzed, it contains 0.0070 mol $N_2(g)$, 0.0022 mol $Cl_2(g)$, and 0.95 mol $NCl_3(g)$. Calculate the equilibrium constant for this reaction.

What Is Required?

You need to calculate the value of K_{eq}.

What Is Given?

You know the balanced chemical equation and the amount of each substance.

Plan Your Strategy	Act on Your Strategy
Calculate the molar concentration of each compound at equilibrium, using the formula for concentration, $c = \frac{n}{V}$. The reaction takes place in a 5.0 L flask.	$[N_2] = \frac{0.0070 \text{ mol}}{5.0 \text{ L}} = 1.4 \times 10^{-3}$ mol/L $[Cl_2] = \frac{0.0022 \text{ mol}}{5.0 \text{ L}} = 4.4 \times 10^{-4}$ mol/L $[NCl_3] = \frac{0.95 \text{ mol}}{5.0 \text{ L}} = 1.9 \times 10^{-1}$ mol/L
Write the equilibrium constant expression. Then substitute the equilibrium molar concentrations into the expression. Each molar concentration is divided by the reference state of 1 mol/L and the concentration values are now unitless.	$K_{eq} = \frac{[NCl_3]^2}{[N_2][Cl_2]^3} = \frac{(1.9 \times 10^{-1})^2}{(1.4 \times 10^{-3})(4.4 \times 10^{-4})^3} = 3.0 \times 10^{11}$

Check Your Solution

The equilibrium constant expression has the product terms in the numerator and the reactant terms in the denominator. The exponents in the constant equilibrium expression match the corresponding coefficients in the balanced chemical equation. The final value of K_{eq} is correctly shown without units.

Calculating Molar Concentrations at Equilibrium

The equilibrium constant expression can also be used to determine the molar concentration of one or more components in the chemical system when you know the value of K_{eq}. The Sample Problem below shows how to do this. Use the Practice Problems that follow to practise calculating the numerical value of the equilibrium constant.

Sample Problem

Calculating the Molar Concentration of a Substance Using the Equilibrium Constant

Problem

Nitrogen, $N_2(g)$, and hydrogen, $H_2(g)$, gases are mixed in a closed 3500 mL flask. They react and form ammonia, $NH_3(g)$, as shown below. At equilibrium, the mixture contains 0.25 mol of ammonia gas and 0.080 mol of hydrogen gas. The equilibrium constant for this reaction is $K_{eq} = 5.81 \times 10^5$. What amount of nitrogen gas is present at equilibrium?

$$N_2(g) + 3H_2(g) \rightleftharpoons 2NH_3(g)$$

Continued on next page

What Is Required?

You need to calculate the amount of nitrogen gas at equilibrium.

What Is Given?

You know the balanced chemical equation.

You know the equilibrium constant, and the amounts of ammonia and hydrogen at equilibrium: $K_{eq} = 5.81 \times 10^5$; $n_{H_2} = 0.080$ mol; $n_{NH_3} = 0.25$ mol

You know the volume of the container: $V = 3500$ mL $= 3.5$ L

Plan Your Strategy	Act on Your Strategy
Calculate the molar concentrations of each compound at equilibrium, using the formula for concentration, $c = \dfrac{n}{V}$.	$[NH_3] = \dfrac{0.25 \text{ mol}}{3.5 \text{ L}} = 0.07143 \dfrac{\text{mol}}{\text{L}} = 7.143 \times 10^{-2}$ mol/L $[H_2] = \dfrac{0.080 \text{ mol}}{3.5 \text{ L}} = 0.02286 \dfrac{\text{mol}}{\text{L}} = 2.286 \times 10^{-2}$ mol/L
Write the equilibrium expression for the equation. Check for any solid or liquid substances in the expression. Because there are no solid or liquid pure substances, all of the concentrations remain in the equilibrium constant expression.	$K_{eq} = \dfrac{[NH_3]^2}{[H_2]^3[N_2]}$
Isolate the term for the concentration of nitrogen gas at equilibrium and solve for it.	$\dfrac{[N_2]}{K_{eq}} \times K_{eq} = \dfrac{[NH_3]^2}{[H_2]^3 [N_2]} \times \dfrac{[N_2]}{K_{eq}}$ $[N_2] = \dfrac{[NH_3]^2}{[H_2]^3 K_{eq}}$
Substitute in known values and calculate $[N_2]$.	$[N_2] = \dfrac{[NH_3]^2}{[H_2]^3 K_{eq}} = \dfrac{(0.07143 \text{ mol/L})^2}{(0.02286 \text{ mol/L})^3 (5.81 \times 10^5)}$ $\approx 7.4 \times 10^{-4}$ mol/L
Use the formula for concentration, $c = \dfrac{n}{V}$ (or $n = cV$), and solve for n. Substitute in the known values and solve for the numerical value of n (the amount in moles) of N_2.	$n = cV = (7.3512 \times 10^{-4} \dfrac{\text{mol}}{\text{L}})(3.5 \text{ L}) = 2.5729 \times 10^{-3}$ mol $\approx 2.6 \times 10^{-3}$ mol There is 2.6×10^{-3} mol of nitrogen in the flask at equilibrium.

Check Your Solution

The equilibrium expression was written correctly. The resulting values are reasonable.

Practice Problems

31. When 1.0 mol of ammonia gas is injected into a 0.50 L flask at a given temperature, the following reaction proceeds to equilibrium:

$$2NH_3(g) \rightleftharpoons N_2(g) + 3H_2(g)$$

At equilibrium, the mixture contains 0.30 mol $H_2(g)$, 0.10 mol $N_2(g)$, and 0.80 mol $NH_3(g)$.

a. Write the equilibrium expression for the reaction.
b. What is the value of the equilibrium constant?

32. Phosphorus trichloride, $PCl_3(g)$, reacts with chlorine, $Cl_2(g)$, to form phosphorus pentachloride, $PCl_5(g)$, as follows:

$$PCl_3(g) + Cl_2(g) \rightleftharpoons PCl_5(g)$$

When 0.75 mol each of $PCl_3(g)$ and $Cl_2(g)$ were placed into an 8.0 L reaction vessel at 500 K, the equilibrium concentration of the mixture was determined to contain 0.035 mol/L of $PCl_3(g)$ and $Cl_2(g)$. The value of K_{eq} at 500 K is 49. Calculate the equilibrium concentration of $PCl_5(g)$.

33. Iodine, $I_2(g)$, and bromine, $Br_2(g)$, react to form iodine monobromide, $IBr(g)$:

$$I_2(g) + Br_2(g) \rightleftharpoons 2IBr(g)$$

At 150°C, an equilibrium mixture in a 2.0 L flask contains 0.024 mol of iodine, 0.050 mol of bromine, and 0.38 mol of iodine monobromide. Determine K_{eq} for this reaction.

34. For the synthesis of ammonia, the equilibrium reaction is as follows:

$$N_2(g) + 3H_2(g) \rightleftharpoons 2NH_3(g)$$

At 475 K, $K_{eq} = 625$. The equilibrium mixture is analyzed and found to contain a nitrogen gas concentration of 2.11 mol/L and a hydrogen gas concentration of 1.74 mol/L. What is the equilibrium concentration of ammonia gas in this mixture?

35. Hydrogen sulfide, $H_2S(g)$, is a pungent, poisonous gas. At 1400 K, an equilibrium mixture contains 0.013 mol/L of hydrogen, $H_2(g)$, 0.18 mol/L of hydrogen sulfide, and an undetermined amount of sulfur, $S_2(g)$. The reaction is

$$2H_2S(g) \rightleftharpoons 2H_2(g) + S_2(g)$$

If the value of K_{eq} at 1400 K is 2.4×10^{-4}, what concentration of $S_2(g)$ is present at equilibrium?

36. Methane, $CH_4(g)$, ethyne, $C_2H_2(g)$, and hydrogen, $H_2(g)$, form the following equilibrium mixture:

$$2CH_4(g) \rightleftharpoons C_2H_2(g) + 3H_2(g)$$

While studying this reaction, a chemist analyzed a 4.0 L sealed flask containing an equilibrium mixture of the gases at 1700°C and found 0.64 mol of ethyne and 0.92 mol of hydrogen gas. If $K_{eq} = 0.15$ for the reaction at 1700°C, what is the expected concentration of methane gas at equilibrium?

37. Nitrogen gas and oxygen gas are present in large quantities in the atmosphere. At a certain temperature, the value of K_{eq} is 4.2×10^{-8} for the following reaction:

$$N_2(g) + O_2(g) \rightleftharpoons 2NO(g)$$

What can you infer about the equilibrium concentration of $NO(g)$ at this temperature?

38. At high temperatures, carbon dioxide gas, $CO_2(g)$, decomposes into carbon monoxide gas, $CO(g)$, and oxygen gas, $O_2(g)$. The concentrations of the gases at equilibrium are $[CO_2] = 1.2$ mol/L, $[CO] = 0.35$ mol/L, and $[O_2] = 0.15$ mol/L. Determine K_{eq} at the equilibrium temperature.

39. The following reaction took place in a sealed flask at 250°C: $PCl_5(g) \rightleftharpoons PCl_3(g) + Cl_2(g)$

At equilibrium, the gases in the flask had the following concentrations:

$[PCl_5] = 1.2 \times 10^{-2}$ mol/L

$[PCl_3] = 1.5 \times 10^{-2}$ mol/L

$[Cl_2] = 1.5 \times 10^{-2}$ mol/L

Calculate the value of the equilibrium constant at 250°C.

40. Hydrogen iodide gas decomposes into hydrogen gas and iodine gas according to the following equation:

$$2HI(g) \rightleftharpoons H_2(g) + I_2(g)$$

A 2.25 L container containing this equilibrium system is analyzed and found to contain 2.34 mol of hydrogen iodide and 1.76 mol of hydrogen gas. If the K_{eq} for the reaction is 2.86×10^{-2}, what amount (in moles) of iodine gas is present in the system?

The Equilibrium Constant, K_p

Often, it is more convenient to express the equilibrium constant for a homogeneous chemical system composed only of gases using gas partial pressures than it is using molar concentrations, because partial pressures are more easily measured than molar volumes. As long as each gas behaves as an ideal gas, the ideal gas law can be used to derive the equilibrium constant using gas partial pressures. The ideal gas law is $PV = nRT$, where P is the pressure of the gas, R is the universal gas constant, T is the temperature of the gas in Kelvin, n is the amount in moles of gas, and V is the volume of the gas. If the ideal gas law is rearranged, the expression becomes $\frac{P}{RT} = \frac{n}{V}$.

Notice that $\frac{n}{V}$ is the molar concentration of the gas. For an individual gas, its molar concentration is equal to its partial pressure divided by RT.

Calculating K_p

Examine the reaction below:

$$CO(g) + 3H_2(g) \rightleftharpoons CH_4(g) + H_2O(g)$$

In this reaction, the molar concentrations are replaced with the partial pressure of each gas, and the equilibrium constant becomes the following:

$$K_p = \frac{P_{CH_4} P_{H_2O}}{P_{CO} P_{H_2}^3}$$

When the equilibrium constant is expressed in terms of partial pressure, the constant is called K_p. The units for gas partial pressure are usually atmospheres, pascals, or torr. The partial pressure values are also divided by a reference state before they are used to calculate K_p. Thus, K_p is written without units. For the generic equation $aA + bB \rightleftharpoons cC + dD$, the generic form of K_p is as follows:

$$K_p = \frac{P_C^c P_D^d}{P_A^a P_B^b}$$

Frequently, the numerical values of K_{eq} and K_p differ for the same system. However, the following equation can be used to convert between the two different equilibrium constants. The units of R must be consistent with the units for the partial pressures.

$$K_p = K_{eq}(RT)^{\Delta n}$$

The term Δn is the sum of the coefficients of gas products minus the sum of the coefficients of gas reactants in the balanced chemical equation. The derivation of this equation will be covered in a higher level chemistry course. Study the following Sample Problem and practise calculating equilibrium constants using partial pressures in the Practice Problems that follow.

Sample Problem

Calculating Equilibrium Constants Using Gas Partial Pressures

Problem

Chloromethane, or methyl chloride, $CH_3Cl(g)$, is formed naturally in the oceans and it is also produced commercially. One of its uses is in the production of silicones, which are often used as sealants. One process that forms chloromethane is as follows:

$$CH_4(g) + Cl_2(g) \rightleftharpoons CH_3Cl(g) + HCl(g)$$

At 1500 K, the mixture contains the following: $P_{CH_4} = 0.13$ atm; $P_{CH_3Cl} = 0.24$ atm; $P_{HCl} = 0.47$ atm. What is the numerical value of the equilibrium constant, K_p?

What Is Required?

You need to calculate the value of K_p.

What Is Given?

You know the balanced chemical equation and you know the partial pressures of the gases in the equilibrium mixture: $P_{CH_4} = 0.13$ atm; $P_{CH_3Cl} = 0.24$ atm; $P_{HCl} = 0.47$ atm

Plan Your Strategy	Act on Your Strategy
Write the equilibrium expression for the equation. Check for any solid or liquid substances in the expression. Because there are no solid or liquid pure substances, all of the concentrations remain in the equilibrium constant expression.	$K_p = \dfrac{P_{CH_3Cl} P_{HCl}}{P_{CH_4} P_{Cl_2}}$
Each partial pressure value is divided by the reference state of 1 atm and the partial pressure values are now written without units. Substitute the partial pressures of the gases into the expression and solve for K_p.	$K_p = \dfrac{(0.24)(0.47)}{(0.13)(0.035)} = 24.79 = 25$

Check Your Solution

The equilibrium constant expression has the product terms in the numerator and the reactant terms in the denominator. The exponents in the constant equilibrium expression match the corresponding coefficients in the chemical equation. Partial pressure values at equilibrium were substituted into the expression. The final value of K_p is correctly shown without units.

Practice Problems

41. In the decomposition of water vapour, equilibrium is established according to the following equation:
$$2H_2O(g) \rightleftharpoons 2H_2(g) + O_2(g)$$
At a given temperature, the partial pressures are found to be as follows:
$P_{H_2O} = 0.63$ atm, $P_{H_2} = 1.15$ atm, and $P_{O_2} = 2.67$ atm. Determine the value of the equilibrium constant, K_p.

42. What is the numerical value of the equilibrium constant, K_p, for the system below?
$$2SO_2(g) + O_2(g) \rightleftharpoons 2SO_3(g)$$
$P_{SO_2} = 0.54$ atm, $P_{O_2} = 0.58$ atm, and $P_{SO_3} = 2.67$ atm.

43. A system is represented by the following reaction:
$$2HBr(g) + Cl_2(g) \rightleftharpoons 2HCl(g) + Br_2(g)$$
At 500 K, the partial pressures of this system at equilibrium were found to be as follows:
$P_{HBr} = 1.74$ atm, $P_{Cl_2} = 1.06$ atm, $P_{HCl} = 2.48$ atm, and $P_{Br_2} = 1.95$ atm.
Calculate the numerical value of the equilibrium constant, K_p, at this temperature.

44. Hydrogen sulfide, $H_2S(g)$, is an extremely poisonous gas that has a characteristic foul smell similar to that of rotten eggs. It is used in many chemical applications, including the process of separation of heavy water from a sample of water. Heavy water is used to help control the release of energy in a CANDU nuclear reactor.

The synthesis of hydrogen sulfide gas involves an equilibrium system in which sulfur gas, $S_2(g)$, reacts with hydrogen gas, $H_2(g)$, according to the following equation: $S_2(g) + 2H_2(g) \rightleftharpoons 2H_2S(g)$

At a given temperature, the following partial pressures were found to exist in an equilibrium mixture of the gases:
$P_{S_2} = 1.37$ atm, $P_{H_2} = 0.88$ atm, and $P_{H_2S} = 1.68$ atm.
What is the numerical value of the equilibrium constant, K_p, at this temperature?

45. A system consisting of 18% carbon dioxide gas, 33% carbon monoxide gas, and oxygen gas has a total pressure of 5.45 atm. Determine the K_p value for this system: $2CO_2(g) \rightleftharpoons 2CO(g) + O_2(g)$

46. A system of hydrogen chloride gas, $HCl(g)$, hydrogen gas, $H_2(g)$, and chlorine gas, $Cl_2(g)$, has a total pressure of 5.88 atm. It is determined that the pressure composition is 30% $H_2(g)$, 28% $Cl_2(g)$, and the remaining pressure exerted by $HCl(g)$. Determine the K_p value for the following reaction:
$$2HCl(g) \rightleftharpoons H_2(g) + Cl_2(g)$$

47. At a given temperature, the system
$$N_2(g) + O_2(g) \rightleftharpoons 2NO(g)$$
is at equilibrium with $K_p = 4.15$. The system has the following partial pressures: $P_{N_2} = 1.23$ atm and $P_{NO} = 5.35$ atm. Determine the partial pressure of the oxygen gas present in this equilibrium mixture.

48. At 435 K, $K_p = 21.3$ for the following reaction:
$$H_2(g) + CO_2(g) \rightleftharpoons CO(g) + H_2O(g)$$
The system is analyzed and found to have the following partial pressures:
$P_{H_2} = 0.84$ atm, $P_{CO_2} = 1.31$ atm, and $P_{CO} = 5.35$ atm.
Determine the partial pressure of the water vapour present in this equilibrium mixture.

49. At 1000 K, the following reaction occurs:
$$NO(g) + SO_3(g) \rightleftharpoons SO_2(g) + NO_2(g)$$
When this system reaches equilibrium at 1000 K, $K_p = 7.18$. A container of these gases at 1000 K is analyzed and found to have the following partial pressures:
$P_{SO_3} = 0.32$ atm, $P_{SO_2} = 2.39$ atm, and $P_{NO_2} = 2.24$ atm.
Determine the partial pressure of the nitrogen monoxide gas present in this system.

50. At a given temperature, $K_p = 1.54$ for the following reaction: $2NO_2(g) \rightleftharpoons 2NO(g) + O_2(g)$
The system is analyzed and found to have the following partial pressures:
$P_{NO} = 1.13$ atm and $P_{O_2} = 2.31$ atm.
Determine the partial pressure of the nitrogen dioxide gas present in this equilibrium mixture at this temperature.

Using ICE Tables to Determine Equilibrium Information

Sometimes it is helpful to organize the known and unknown information about a chemical system in an ICE table. If the system information is organized in a table, it is easier to see the relationships among the components and it is easier to see what information is missing. The letter "I" represents the **i**nitial molar concentrations of the reactants and products. The letter "C" represents the amount of **c**hange in each reactant and product from initial conditions to equilibrium. The letter "E" represents the molar concentrations of the reactants and products at **e**quilibrium.

Suppose that you are in the following situation:

> You want to experimentally determine the equilibrium constant for the decomposition of hydrogen iodide, HI(g), at 453°C. You fill an evacuated 2.0 L flask with 0.200 mol of hydrogen iodide at 453°C. You let the hydrogen iodide gas decompose into hydrogen gas, H_2(g), and iodine gas, I_2(g), until it reaches equilibrium. You determine that the concentration of hydrogen iodide gas is 0.078 mol/L at equilibrium, but you do not know the concentrations of the hydrogen or iodine gases.

You can use an ICE table to organize your information and to write the mathematical relationships among the components in the system. Use the following steps to set up an ICE table. New additions to the table are printed in blue type.

Step 1
Write out the equilibrium equation and make a column below each reactant and product. Then label the rows with Initial, Change, and Equilibrium.

$$2HI(g) \rightleftharpoons H_2(g) + I_2(g)$$

	[HI] mol/L	[H_2] (mol/L)	[I_2] (mol/L)
Initial			
Change			
Equilibrium			

Step 2
Add the known values to the table. You know the volume of the flask is 2.0 L and there is 0.200 mol of hydrogen iodide in the flask. Therefore, there is 0.200 mol/2.00 L, or 0.100 mol/L, in the flask. Add this value to the table. Initially, there is 0 mol/L of hydrogen and iodine in the flask because the hydrogen iodide has not started to decompose.

$$2HI(g) \rightleftharpoons H_2(g) + I_2(g)$$

	[HI] mol/L	[H_2] (mol/L)	[I_2] (mol/L)
Initial	0.100	0	0
Change			
Equilibrium			

Step 3
Let x represent a change in one concentration, and then express the other concentrations in terms of the change to x. Use a plus sign to show that a substance forms in the reaction or is increasing and a minus sign to show that a substance is consumed in the reaction or is decreasing. Recall that the coefficients in the balanced chemical equation show the molar relationships of the components in the reaction. For example, 2 mol of hydrogen iodide is consumed in this specific chemical reaction for every 1 mol of hydrogen gas and 1 mol of iodine gas formed. You can use $+x$ to represent the changes in concentration for hydrogen and iodine. Then use $-2x$ to represent the change in concentration of hydrogen iodide.

	2HI(g)	⇌	H_2(g)	+	I_2(g)
	[HI] (mol/L)		[H_2] (mol/L)		[I_2] (mol/L)
Initial	0.100		0		0
Change	$-2x$		$+x$		$+x$
Equilibrium					

Step 4
You know that the equilibrium concentration of each component equals the initial concentration plus or minus the change in concentration. You can show this relationship mathematically in the table by determining the sum of the initial concentration and the change. Add these expressions to the table.

	2HI(g)	⇌	H_2(g)	+	I_2(g)
	[HI] (mol/L)		[H_2] (mol/L)		[I_2] (mol/L)
Initial	0.100		0		0
Change	$-2x$		$+x$		$+x$
Equilibrium	$0.100 - 2x$		x		x

Step 5
You also measured the equilibrium concentration of hydrogen iodide to be 0.078 mol/L. Therefore, $0.100 - 2x = 0.078$ mol/L. Solve for x.

$$0.100 \text{ mol/L} - 2x = 0.078 \text{ mol/L}$$
$$-2x = 0.078 \text{ mol/L} - 0.100 \text{ mol/L}$$
$$\frac{-2x}{-2} = \frac{-0.022 \text{ mol/L}}{-2}$$
$$x = 0.011 \text{ mol/L}$$

Step 6
Now that you know the value of x, you can fill in the equilibrium concentrations for hydrogen and iodine in the ICE table. The concentrations of hydrogen and iodine at equilibrium are 0.011 mol/L.

Step 7
Now solve for the equilibrium constant by using the information you just calculated.

$$K_{eq} = \frac{[H_2][I_2]}{[HI]^2}$$
$$= \frac{(0.011)(0.011)}{(0.078)^2}$$
$$= \frac{0.000121}{0.006084}$$
$$= 0.019888$$
$$\approx 0.020$$

Use the following Sample Problem and Practice Problems to practise using ICE tables.

Sample Problem

Using Stoichiometry and K_{eq} to Calculate Equilibrium Concentrations

Problem

Hydrogen gas is considered to be a non-polluting, sustainable fuel source. It can be used in internal combustion engines and in fuel cells to produce thermal energy and electricity. Hydrogen gas can be produced in several different ways. The following reaction illustrates one method using carbon monoxide and water:

$$CO(g) + H_2O(g) \rightleftharpoons H_2(g) + CO_2(g)$$

At 700 K, the equilibrium constant is 0.83. Suppose that you start with 1.0 mol CO(g) and 1.0 mol H_2O(g) in a 5.0 L container. What amount of each substance will be present in the container when the gases are in equilibrium at 700 K?

What Is Required?

You need to determine the amount (in moles) of CO(g), H_2O(g), H_2(g), and CO_2(g) at equilibrium.

What Is Given?

You know the balanced chemical equation. You know the initial amount of each gas, the volume of the container, and the equilibrium constant. Because each of the molecules in the balanced equation has a coefficient of 1, you know that the initial amount of CO(g) is equal to the initial amount of H_2O(g).

Plan Your Strategy	Act on Your Strategy
Calculate the initial concentrations using the equation $c = \dfrac{n}{V}$.	$c_{CO} = c_{H_2O} = \dfrac{n}{V} = \dfrac{1.0 \text{ mol}}{5.0 \text{ L}} = 0.2 \text{ mol/L}$
Set up an ICE table. Record the initial concentrations you calculated in your ICE table. Let the change in molar concentrations of the reactants be represented by x. Use a minus sign to indicate that a component is consumed and a plus sign to indicate that a component is formed. Use the stoichiometry of the chemical equation to write and record expressions for the equilibrium concentrations. In this balanced chemical equation, all of the coefficients are 1. Determine the sum of the initial concentrations and the change in concentrations and write the expressions in the ICE table in the correct column.	$CO(g) + H_2O\ (g) \rightleftharpoons H_2(g) + CO_2(g)$ 		[CO] (mol/L)	[H_2O] (mol/L)	[H_2] (mol/L)	[CO_2] (mol/L)
---	---	---	---	---
Initial	0.20	0.20	0	0
Change	$-x$	$-x$	$+x$	$+x$
Equilibrium	$0.20 - x$	$0.20 - x$	x	x	
Write the equilibrium expression and substitute the expressions for the equilibrium concentrations into the expression for K_{eq}. Solve the equilibrium expression for x.	$K_{eq} = \dfrac{[H_2][CO_2]}{[CO][H_2O]}$ $0.83 = \dfrac{(x)(x)}{(0.20-x)(0.20-x)} = \dfrac{(x)^2}{(0.20-x)^2}$ $\sqrt{0.83} = \sqrt{\dfrac{x^2}{(0.20-x)^2}}$ $0.9110 = \dfrac{(x)}{(0.20-x)}$ $0.9110\,(0.20-x) = x$ $0.1822 - 0.9110x = x$ $0.1822 = x + 0.9110x$ $0.1822 = 1.919x$ $x = 0.095\,34$

Plan Your Strategy	Act on Your Strategy
Use the value you determined for x to calculate the equilibrium concentration for each component of the system. Then use the volume of the container to determine the amount (in moles) of each gas present at equilibrium.	The concentrations of the reactants at equilibrium are as follows: $[H_2] = [CO_2] \approx 0.095\,34$ mol/L $[CO] = [H_2O] \approx 0.2000$ mol/L $- 0.095\,34$ mol/L $\approx 0.104\,66$ mol/L Round to two significant figures: $[H_2] = [CO_2] \approx 0.095$ mol/L $[CO] = [H_2O] \approx 0.10$ mol/L To determine the amount of each gas, multiply the concentration of each gas by the volume of the container (5.0 L). Amount of $H_2(g) = CO_2(g) = 0.48$ mol Amount of $CO(g) = H_2O(g) = 0.50$ mol

Check Your Solution

The equilibrium expression has product concentrations in the numerator and reactant concentrations in the denominator. The concentration of each chemical present at equilibrium is given in mol/L. Check K_{eq} by substituting these concentrations back into the equation.

$$K_{eq} = \frac{(0.09534)^2}{(0.10466)^2} \approx 0.83.$$ The calculated value of K_{eq} is equal to the K_{eq} value given in the initial problem. The solution appears to be correct.

In the previous problem, the right side of the equilibrium equation is a perfect square in step 3. Noticing perfect squares, and then taking the square root of both sides, makes solving the equation easier. Also, when you use an answer to one part of a problem as datum in another calculation, always use the unrounded value. If you round numbers at every step, the error will become quite large. For example, if you had rounded every step in the solution to this Sample Problem to two significant digits, your answer for K_{eq} would have been 0.75, which is an error of about 10 percent. Use the Practice Problems that follow to practise using ICE tables.

Practice Problems

51. At 1100 K, hydrogen, $H_2(g)$, and iodine, $I_2(g)$, combine to form hydrogen iodide:

$H_2(g) + I_2(g) \rightleftharpoons 2HI(g)$. At equilibrium in a 1.0 L reaction vessel, the mixture of gases contained 0.30 mol of hydrogen, 1.3 mol of iodine, and 3.4 mol of hydrogen iodide. Determine the value of K_{eq}.

52. At 25°C, the following reaction takes place:

$$I_2(g) + Cl_2(g) \rightleftharpoons 2ICl(g)$$

K_{eq} for the reaction is 82. If 0.83 mol of iodine gas, $I_2(g)$, and 0.83 mol of chlorine gas, $Cl_2(g)$, are placed in a 10 L container at 25°C, what are the concentrations of the various gases at equilibrium?

53. A chemist is studying the following reaction at a certain temperature:

$$SO_2(g) + NO_2(g) \rightleftharpoons NO(g) + SO_3(g)$$

In a 1.0 L container, the chemist adds 0.17 mol of sulfur dioxide, $SO_2(g)$, to 0.11 mol of nitrogen dioxide, $NO_2(g)$. At equilibrium, the concentration of sulfur trioxide, $SO_3(g)$, is 0.089 mol/L. What is the value of K_{eq} for the reaction at this temperature?

Continued on next page

54. Hydrogen bromide, HBr(g), decomposes at 700 K, as represented by the following reaction:

$$2HBr(g) \rightleftharpoons H_2(g) + Br_2(g)$$

K_{eq} is 4.2×10^{-9} for this reaction. If 0.090 mol of hydrogen bromide is placed into a 2.0 L reaction vessel and heated to 700 K, what is the equilibrium concentration of each gas?

55. For the reaction of phosphorus trichloride, $PCl_3(g)$, and nitrogen dioxide, $NO_2(g)$, an equilibrium is established according to the following equation:

$$PCl_3(g) + NO_2(g) \rightleftharpoons POCl_3(g) + NO(g)$$

Initially, 1.24 mol of each reactant is placed into a 1.0 L container and equilibrium is established. If $K_{eq} = 3.77$ for the reaction, what are the equilibrium concentrations of all reactants and products?

56. When nitrogen gas reacts with oxygen gas, nitrogen monoxide gas forms: $N_2(g) + O_2(g) \rightleftharpoons 2NO(g)$ Initially, 0.30 mol of each reactant is placed into a 2.0 L container and equilibrium is established. If $K_{eq} = 52.1$ for the reaction, what are the equilibrium concentrations of all reactants and products?

57. In the reaction of hydrogen gas reacting with iodine gas to form hydrogen iodide gas, $K_{eq} = 49.6$ at 730 K. The reaction is as follows: $H_2(g) + I_2(g) \rightleftharpoons 2HI(g)$ Initially, 3.51 mol of each reactant is placed into a 3.0 L container and equilibrium is established. Determine the amount in moles of each substance that will be present when the system reaches equilibrium at 730 K.

58. Initially, 2.25 mol of carbon monoxide gas, CO(g), and 2.25 mol of water vapour, $H_2O(g)$, are placed into a 1.50 L container and the following equilibrium is established, with a K_{eq} value of 4.2:

$$CO(g) + H_2O(g) \rightleftharpoons CO_2(g) + H_2(g)$$

What is the amount in moles of each reactant and product at equilibrium?

59. Bromine gas and chlorine gas establish equilibrium when they react to form bromine chloride gas. The K_{eq} for this reaction at 450 K is 28.8.

$$Br_2(g) + Cl_2(g) \rightleftharpoons 2BrCl(g)$$

When 8.70 mol of each reactant is placed into a 5.00 L container, what is the amount in moles of each reactant and product at equilibrium?

60. Ozone, $O_3(g)$, reacts with nitrogen monoxide, NO(g), and forms nitrogen dioxide, $NO_2(g)$, and oxygen, $O_2(g)$. At 325 K, K_{eq} for the reaction is 6.70. The reaction is:

$$O_3(g) + NO(g) \rightleftharpoons NO_2(g) + O_2(g)$$

If 1.62 mol of each reactant is placed into a 2.00 L container, what is the amount in moles of each reactant and product at equilibrium?

Learning Check

26. What experimental data are used to calculate K_{eq}?

27. The concentrations of the reactant and product varied during the investigation as shown in **Table 7.2**. What did the investigation reveal about the equilibrium constant?

28. What does the variable K_p represent?

29. What experimental data are used to calculate K_p?

30. How do you know which value of the universal gas constant, R, to use when calculating K_p?

31. When is it appropriate to use an ICE table to solve equilibrium problems?

---

quadratic equation an algebraic equation in the form $ax^2 + bx + c = 0$, where a, b, and c are real numbers and $a \neq 0$

quadratic formula an algebraic equation used to determine the possible solutions to algebraic equations in the form $ax^2 + bx + c = 0$, where a, b, and c are real numbers and $a \neq 0$

Using the Quadratic Formula to Determine Equilibrium Information

Many problems do not involve perfect squares. Algebraic equations in the form $ax^2 + bx + c = 0$ are called **quadratic equations**. You can solve quadratic equations using the **quadratic formula** below:

$$x = \frac{-b \pm \sqrt{b^2 - 4ac}}{2a}$$

A quadratic equation may have up to two solutions, or roots. In the case of two roots, you must evaluate each solution to determine which one is the solution to your particular problem. One solution should be impossible or improbable and the other solution will be your answer. The Sample Problem on the next page demonstrates how to use the quadratic formula. Complete the Practice Problems that follow to practise using the quadratic formula.

Sample Problem

Using the Quadratic Equation to Determine Equilibrium Information

Problem

The following reaction has an equilibrium constant of 25.0 at 1100 K.

$$H_2(g) + I_2(g) \rightleftharpoons 2HI(g)$$

If 2.00 mol of hydrogen gas, $H_2(g)$, and 3.00 mol of iodine gas, $I_2(g)$, are placed in a 1.00 L reaction vessel at 1100 K, what is the equilibrium concentration of each gas?

What Is Required?

You need to determine $[H_2]$, $[I_2]$, and $[HI]$ at equilibrium.

What Is Given?

You know the balanced chemical equation. You know the equilibrium constant for the reaction, $K_{eq} = 25.0$. You also know the initial amounts of the reactant gases added to the reaction vessel: 2.00 mol $H_2(g)$ and 3.00 mol $I_2(g)$. You know the volume of the reaction vessel: 1.00 L.

Plan Your Strategy	Act on Your Strategy
Set up an ICE table. Because an equal amount in moles of hydrogen and iodine react, let x represent the change in their molar concentrations. Use plus and minus signs to indicate if a component is being consumed or formed. Use the stoichiometry of the chemical equation to write expressions for the equilibrium concentrations. Record these expressions in your ICE table.	$H_2(g) + I_2(g) \rightleftharpoons 2HI(g)$ 			
		$[H_2]$ (mol/L)	$[I_2]$ (mol/L)	$[HI]$ (mol/L)
	Initial	2.00	3.00	0
	Change	$-x$	$-x$	$+2x$
	Equilibrium	$2.00 - x$	$3.00 - x$	$+2x$
Write the equilibrium expression. Substitute the expressions for the equilibrium concentrations from the ICE table into the expression.	$K_{eq} = \dfrac{[HI]^2}{[H_2][I_2]}$ $25.0 = \dfrac{(2x)^2}{(2.00-x)(3.00-x)}$
This equation does not involve a perfect square. It must be re-arranged into a quadratic equation.	$0.840x^2 - 5.00x + 6.00 = 0$
Use the quadratic formula to solve for x. $x = \dfrac{-b \pm \sqrt{b^2 - 4ac}}{2a}$	$x = \dfrac{-(-5.00) \pm \sqrt{25.0 - 20.16}}{1.68}$ $= \dfrac{5.00 \pm 2.2}{1.68}$ $x = 4.28571$ and $x = 1.66667$
Evaluate the two possible answers and determine which one is possible.	The value $x = 4.28571$ mol/L is not physically possible because this number is greater than the values of both initial concentrations. Therefore, x must equal 1.66667 mol/L.
Substitute x into the equilibrium row of the ICE table to determine the equilibrium concentrations.	$[H_2] = 2.00$ mol/L $- 1.66667$ mol/L $= 0.333$ mol/L $[I_2] = 3.00$ mol/L $- 1.66667$ mol/L $= 1.33$ mol/L $[HI] = 2(1.66667$ mol/L$) = 3.33$ mol/L

Check Your Solution

To check your concentrations, substitute them back into the equilibrium expression: $K_{eq} = \dfrac{(3.33)^2}{(0.333)(1.333)} = 25.0$

The calculated value of K_{eq} is equal to the given value.

Practice Problems

61. When solid carbon reacts with water vapour, hydrogen gas and carbon dioxide gas form according to the following equation:

$$C(s) + H_2O(g) \rightleftharpoons H_2(g) + CO(g)$$

When 2.25 mol of water vapour is reacted with solid carbon in a 1.0 L container, and equilibrium is established, what concentration of each reactant and product in the gas phase will be present at equilibrium if K_{eq} equals 23.4?

62. Dinitrogen tetroxide, $N_2O_4(g)$, reversibly decomposes into nitrogen dioxide, $NO_2(g)$, according to the following equation:

$$N_2O_4(g) \rightleftharpoons 2NO_2(g)$$

This reaction has resulted in one of the most important rocket propellant processes that researchers have developed. At 325 K, the K_{eq} value is 0.91. Initially, 0.34 mol $N_2O_4(g)$ is placed into a 1.00 L container and equilibrium is established. Determine the equilibrium concentration of each gas in the container.

63. In an equilibrium process, ethene, $C_2H_4(g)$, is reacted with hydrogen gas to produce ethane, $C_2H_6(g)$. At a given temperature, the K_{eq} value is 1.04 for the following reaction:

$$C_2H_4(g) + H_2(g) \rightleftharpoons C_2H_6(g)$$

Initially, 0.34 mol $C_2H_4(g)$ and 0.53 mol $H_2(g)$ are placed into a 1.00 L container and equilibrium is established. Determine the equilibrium concentration of each gas in the container.

64. When 1.88 mol of hydrogen gas and 2.86 mol of iodine gas are placed in a 2.00 L container, an equilibrium is reached with hydrogen iodide gas such that the K_{eq} value is 55.3 at 700 K. Determine the amount in moles of each reactant and product in the container when equilibrium is established.

65. Carbonyl chloride gas, also called phosgene, $COCl_2(g)$, was used during World War I as a chemical weapon. Now, it is used in a process to manufacture plastics such as the ones used to make lenses in eyeglasses. It is formed by reacting carbon monoxide gas with chlorine gas in the following equilibrium system: $CO(g) + Cl_2(g) \rightleftharpoons COCl_2(g)$

The K_{eq} for this reaction at 1000 K is 24.0. If 2.35 mol $CO(g)$ and 1.14 mol $Cl_2(g)$ are placed into a 1.00 L container, what concentration of each gas will exist at equilibrium at 1000 K?

66. Phosphoryl chloride, $POCl_3(g)$, is used in the manufacturing of flame retardants. It is manufactured in an equilibrium process in which phosphorus trichloride reacts with nitrogen dioxide to form $POCl_3(g)$ and $NO(g)$ according to the following equation:

$$PCl_3(g) + NO_2(g) \rightleftharpoons POCl_3(g) + NO(g)$$

The K_{eq} for this reaction at 800 K is 1.82. If 1.86 mol $PCl_3(g)$ and 1.64 mol $NO_2(g)$ are placed into a 2.00 L container, what is the amount in moles of each gas at equilibrium at 800 K?

67. In the reaction

$$PCl_3(g) + Cl_2(g) \rightleftharpoons PCl_5(g)$$

the K_{eq} value at 305 K is 14.15. Initially, 0.81 mol $PCl_3(g)$ and 1.37 mol $Cl_2(g)$ are placed into a 1.00 L container and allowed to reach equilibrium. What are the equilibrium concentrations of all these substances?

68. The synthesis of nitrogen monoxide, $NO(g)$, is an equilibrium reaction, as shown below:

$$N_2(g) + O_2(g) \rightleftharpoons 2NO(g)$$

Initially, 1.33 mol of nitrogen gas and 2.80 mol of oxygen gas are placed into a 2.50 L container and allowed to reach equilibrium. What is the amount in moles of each gas at equilibrium at 200 K, if K_{eq} is 8.68 at this temperature?

69. Carbon monoxide reaches equilibrium with water vapour as they react to form hydrogen gas and carbon dioxide gas. At 300 K, K_{eq} is equal to 0.52 for the reaction:

$$CO(g) + H_2O(g) \rightleftharpoons H_2(g) + CO_2(g)$$

When 1.45 mol of carbon monoxide and 2.22 mol of water vapour are combined in a 1.00 L flask, equilibrium is established. What concentration of each reactant and product will be present at equilibrium?

70. Sulfuryl chloride, $SO_2Cl_2(g)$, is used in a process to produce pesticides. It is also used as a convenient source of chlorine gas, because it can be cooled to form a pourable liquid that is easier to store and dispense. To generate this compound, the following reaction can be used, with a K_{eq} value of 0.45 at 650 K:

$$SO_2(g) + Cl_2(g) \rightleftharpoons SO_2Cl_2(g)$$

Initially, 3.15 mol $SO_2(g)$ and 2.14 mol $Cl_2(g)$ are placed into a 1.00 L container and allowed to reach equilibrium. What are the equilibrium concentrations of all these substances?

Activity 7.2 — Data Analysis: Calculating an Equilibrium Constant

Ethyl ethanoate, $CH_3CH_2CO_2CH_3$(aq), also known as ethyl acetate, is an important ester. It is used as a solvent and is the principal ingredient in certain types of nail polish remover. It has also been used to extract caffeine from coffee beans or tea leaves. Ethyl ethanoate is prepared by the reaction of ethanoic acid, CH_3COOH(aq), with ethanol, CH_3CH_2OH(aq), in a homogeneous equilibrium reaction, which is catalyzed by hydrochloric acid:

$$CH_3COOH(aq) + CH_3CH_2OH(aq) \rightleftharpoons CH_3COOCH_2CH_3(aq) + H_2O(\ell)$$

A group of students investigated this reaction by using the following method.

Procedure

1. A known mass of ethanoic acid was placed in a flask. Then ethanol was measured and added to the flask.

2. A measured volume of hydrochloric acid of known concentration was added to the mixture of ethanoic acid and ethanol.

3. The flask was sealed with a stopper and placed in a water bath to keep the temperature of the mixture constant at 20°C. The flask was left for a week to allow the mixture to reach equilibrium.

4. After leaving the flask for a week, the volume of the solution was measured. Then the solution was titrated against a freshly prepared standardized solution of sodium hydroxide, using phenolphthalein as an indicator.

Questions

Using the titration data, the total amount of ethanoic acid and hydrochloric acid present at equilibrium was calculated. Because hydrochloric acid is a catalyst, its amount remains constant throughout the reaction. By subtracting the amount of hydrochloric acid from the total amount of acid, the amount of ethanoic acid at equilibrium was determined. The data at the top of the next column were obtained from five different trials.

The Equilibrium Reaction to Form Ethyl Ethanoate at 20°C

Experiment	Initial CH_3COOH(aq) (mol)	Initial CH_3CH_2OH(aq) (mol)	Equilibrium CH_3COOH(aq) (mol)	Total volume (mL)
1	0.220	0.114	0.125	38.1
2	0.184	0.115	0.0917	40.3
3	0.152	0.121	0.0631	39.4
4	0.214	0.132	0.110	42.6
5	0.233	0.137	0.122	41.5

1. Enter the data into a spreadsheet program and use the software to calculate the initial [CH_3COOH], the initial [CH_3CH_2OH], and the equilibrium [CH_3COOH].

2. The ICE table for trial 1 is partially filled in below. One more digit has been carried to reduce rounding error. Check that your spreadsheet returns the values shown in the ICE table for trial 1.

3. Add calculations to your spreadsheet program to calculate the terms missing from the ICE table for each of the five trials.

4. Use your spreadsheet program to calculate the equilibrium constant, K_{eq}, for each of the five trials.

5. The five calculations of K_{eq} should be the same within experimental error. Comment on the results of the investigation.

6. Explain how this investigation illustrates a *closed system*.

7. Explain why a *closed system* is a requirement for chemical equilibrium.

8. Explain, in terms of the rate of the forward reaction and the rate of the reverse reaction, why the trials were left for one week before the titrations were carried out.

9. Explain why you needed to know the total volume of the system before any calculations could be made.

	CH_3COOH(aq)	+	CH_3CH_2OH(aq)	$\rightleftharpoons$	$CH_3COOCH_2CH_3$(aq)	+	$H_2O(\ell)$
	[CH_3COOH] (mol/L)		[CH_3CH_2OH] (mol/L)		[$CH_3COOCH_2CH_3$] (mol/L)		[H_2O] (mol/L)
Initial	5.774		2.992		0		0
Change							
Equilibrium	3.281						

Solving Problems with a Small Equilibrium Constant

When you have an expression that requires the quadratic equation to solve, you can sometimes make an approximation that will simplify the equation. If the equilibrium constant for a reaction is very small, then a very small concentration of product is present at equilibrium. The concentration of reactant at equilibrium is almost the same as the initial concentration

For example, assume that the initial concentration of a reactant is 0.065 mol/L and the change in the concentration of reactant is 0.000032 mol/L. The concentration of reactant present at equilibrium would be 0.065 mol/L − 0.000032 mol/L = 0.064968 mol/L. The rule for significant digits when adding or subtracting tells you that the sum or difference cannot have any more decimal places than the data with the fewest number of decimal places. The number 0.065 has three decimal places so you must round the answer to three decimal places. When you round 0.064968 mol/L to three decimal places, the result is 0.065 mol/L. Your result is identical to the initial concentration of the reactant. Therefore, when your equilibrium constant is very small, you can make the approximation that the concentration of the reactant at equilibrium is the same as the initial concentration.

To decide whether to use approximation, chemists often compare certain quantities in the data. *An approximation may be made if the initial concentrations of reactants are at least 1000 times greater than K_{eq}.* The Sample Problem below will show you how to use this approximation method.

Sample Problem

Using the Approximation Method in Equilibrium Calculations

Problem
The atmosphere contains large amounts of nitrogen gas, $N_2(g)$, and oxygen gas, $O_2(g)$. These two gases do not react at ordinary temperatures; however, they do react at high temperatures, such as those produced by a lightning flash or inside a running car engine. In fact, nitrogen oxides from exhaust gases are a serious pollution problem.
An environmental chemist is studying the following equilibrium reaction:

$$N_2(g) + O_2(g) \rightleftharpoons 2NO(g)$$

At the temperature of the exhaust gases from a particular engine, the value of K_{eq} is 4.2×10^{-8}. The chemist puts 0.085 mol of nitrogen and 0.038 mol of oxygen in a rigid 1.5 L cylinder. What is the concentration of nitrogen monoxide gas, NO(g), in the mixture at equilibrium?

What Is Required?
You need to determine the concentration of nitrogen monoxide gas at equilibrium.

What Is Given?
You know the balanced chemical equation. You know the value of K_{eq} and the following initial concentrations: $[N_2] = 0.057$ mol/L and $[O_2] = 0.025$ mol/L

Plan Your Strategy	Act on Your Strategy
Set up an ICE table. Let x represent the change in $[N_2]$ and $[O_2]$. Because $N_2(g)$ and $O_2(g)$ are consumed in the reaction, you use a minus sign. Because 2 mol NO(g) forms for every 1 mol $N_2(g)$ and 1 mol $O_2(g)$ that react, the change in concentration, x, must be multiplied by 2. Use a plus sign for NO(g), because it forms in the reaction.	$N_2(g)$ + $O_2(g)$ $\rightleftharpoons$ 2NO(g) 			$[N_2]$ (mol/L)	$[O_2]$ (mol/L)	$[NO]$ (mol/L)		**I**nitial	0.057	0.025	0		**C**hange	$-x$	$-x$	$+2x$		**E**quilibrium	$0.057 - x$	$0.025 - x$	$2x$

Plan Your Strategy	Act on Your Strategy
Write the equilibrium expression. Substitute the expressions for the equilibrium concentration of the system components (from the ICE table) into the expression for K_{eq}.	$K_{eq} = \dfrac{[NO]^2}{[N_2][O_2]}$ $4.2 \times 10^{-8} = \dfrac{(2x)^2}{(0.057-x)(0.025-x)}$ $4x^2 + (3.444 \times 10^{-9})x - (5.985 \times 10^{-11}) = 0$ A quadratic equation is obtained when the equation is expanded.
If a quadratic equation is required to solve for x, test to see whether you can use the approximation method. If the initial concentrations of the reactants are more than 1000 times greater than K_{eq}, then the change in the concentrations of the reactants will be negligible. The initial concentrations of the reactants can be used to represent the equilibrium concentrations of the reactants.	To find out whether you can use an approximation, multiply K_{eq} by 1000 and compare it with the initial concentrations of the reactants. $1000 \times (4.2 \times 10^{-8}) = 4.2 \times 10^{-5}$ $[N_2] = 0.057$ mol/L $[O_2] = 0.025$ mol/L $1000 \times K_{eq}$ is much less than the initial concentration of either reactant. Therefore, you can make the approximation below: $0.057 - x \cong 0.057$ $0.025 - x \cong 0.025$
Solve for x.	$4.2 \times 10^{-8} = \dfrac{(2x)^2}{(0.057)(0.025)}$ $4x^2 = 5.985 \times 10^{-11}$ $x^2 = 1.49625 \times 10^{-11}$ $x = \sqrt{1.49625 \times 10^{-11}}$ $= 3.9 \times 10^{-6}$ or -3.9×10^{-6}
The value for x cannot be a negative number. So you know the value for x is 3.9×10^{-6} mol/L. Using the value for x, calculate [NO] at equilibrium.	$[NO] = 2x$ $= 2(3.9 \times 10^{-6}$ mol/L$)$ $= 7.8 \times 10^{-6}$ mol/L The concentration of NO(g) at equilibrium is approximately 7.8×10^{-6} mol/L.

Check Your Solution
Check the equilibrium values: $K_{eq} = \dfrac{(7.8 \times 10^{-6})^2}{(0.057)(0.025)} = 4.3 \times 10^{-8}$

This calculated value of K_{eq} is equal to the value of K_{eq} given in the initial problem, within rounding errors.

Practice Problems

71. The following equation represents the equilibrium reaction for the decomposition of phosgene gas, $COCl_2(g)$:

$$COCl_2(g) \rightleftharpoons CO(g) + Cl_2(g)$$

At 100°C, the value of K_{eq} for this reaction is 2.2×10^{-8}. The initial concentration of phosgene in a closed container at 100°C is 1.5 mol/L. What are the equilibrium concentrations of carbon monoxide gas, CO(g), and chlorine gas, $Cl_2(g)$?

72. Hydrogen sulfide, $H_2S(g)$, is a poisonous gas with a characteristic offensive odour. At 1400°C, the gas decomposes, and K_{eq} is equal to 2.4×10^{-4}:

$$2H_2S(g) \rightleftharpoons 2H_2(g) + S_2(g)$$

If 4.0 mol of hydrogen sulfide gas is placed in a 3.0 L container, what is the equilibrium concentration of hydrogen gas, $H_2(g)$, at 1400°C?

Continued on next page

73. At a particular temperature, K_{eq} for the decomposition of carbon dioxide gas, $CO_2(g)$, is 2.0×10^{-6}: $2CO_2(g) \rightleftharpoons 2CO(g) + O_2(g)$

    If 3.0 mol of carbon dioxide gas is put in a 5.0 L container, calculate the equilibrium concentration of each gas.

74. At a certain temperature, the value of K_{eq} for the following reaction is 3.3×10^{-12}:
    $$2NCl_3(g) \rightleftharpoons N_2(g) + 3Cl_2(g)$$
    A certain amount of nitrogen trichloride gas, $NCl_3(g)$, is put in a 1.0 L reaction vessel at this temperature. At equilibrium, 4.6×10^{-6} mol of nitrogen gas, $N_2(g)$, is present. What amount of nitrogen trichloride was put in the reaction vessel?

75. At a certain temperature, the value of K_{eq} for the following reaction is 4.2×10^{-8}:
    $$N_2(g) + O_2(g) \rightleftharpoons 2NO(g)$$
    If 0.45 mol of nitrogen gas, $N_2(g)$, and 0.26 mol of oxygen gas, $O_2(g)$, are put in a 6.0 L reaction vessel, what is the equilibrium concentration of nitrogen monoxide, $NO(g)$, at this temperature?

76. For the reaction in question 75, K_{eq} changes to 1.0×10^{-5} at 1500 K. What equilibrium concentration of nitrogen oxide gas exists in the container at this new temperature?

77. At 300 K, K_{eq} is 1.43×10^{-26} for the following reaction: $2SO_3(g) \rightleftharpoons 2SO_2(g) + O_2(g)$

    Initially, 1.18 mol of sulfur trioxide, $SO_3(g)$, is placed into a 1.00 L container and equilibrium is established. What concentrations of $SO_2(g)$ and $O_2(g)$ exist in the container at equilibrium?

78. Carbon dioxide decomposes into carbon monoxide and oxygen gases with a K_{eq} value of 6.4×10^{-7} at 2300 K: $2CO_2(g) \rightleftharpoons 2CO(g) + O_2(g)$

    Initially, 0.95 mol of carbon dioxide, $CO_2(g)$, is placed into a 1.00 L container and equilibrium is established. What concentrations of carbon monoxide gas and oxygen gas exist in the container at equilibrium at this temperature?

79. At 2400 K, $K_{eq} = 1.0 \times 10^{-7}$ for the reaction below:
    $$2H_2(g) + O_2(g) \rightleftharpoons 2H_2O(g)$$
    If 0.18 mol of hydrogen gas, $H_2(g)$, and 0.23 mol of oxygen gas, $O_2(g)$, are put in a 1.0 L reaction vessel, what is the equilibrium concentration of the water vapour at this temperature?

80. When nitrogen gas and chloride gas react to form nitrogen trichloride gas, an equilibrium is established in which $K_{eq} = 4.15 \times 10^{-5}$ at a given temperature. The reaction is as follows:
    $$N_2(g) + 3Cl_2(g) \rightleftharpoons 2NCl_3(g)$$
    If 2.74 mol of nitrogen gas, $N_2(g)$, and 0.84 mol of chlorine gas, $Cl_2(g)$, are put in a 2.0 L reaction vessel, what is the equilibrium concentration of the nitrogen trichloride gas at this temperature?

Learning Check

32. What is a quadratic equation?
33. How will you know when to use the quadratic formula to solve an equilibrium problem?
34. How do you know which root of a quadratic equation is the correct answer?
35. When can you use the approximation method to solve equilibrium calculations?
36. What is the general rule related to initial concentrations and K_{eq} that chemists use to determine when to use the approximation method?
37. Give an example of a scenario where it would be appropriate to use the approximation method.

Measuring Equilibrium Concentrations Using Colour

You can calculate equilibrium concentrations if you know the initial concentrations of the system components and the concentration of one reactant or product at equilibrium. Experimentally, this means that a reaction mixture must reach equilibrium, at which point one or more properties are measured. The concentrations cannot be measured directly. Instead, other properties are measured and concentrations are determined indirectly. Common examples of properties that can be measured include the colour of the mixture, pH in aqueous solution, and partial pressure of a gaseous reaction. Measurements of these properties at equilibrium allow you to calculate the equilibrium concentrations of the system components. These concentrations are then substituted into the equilibrium expression to calculate the value of K_{eq}.

When a reaction involves a coloured substance, the change in colour intensity can be measured and used to determine the equilibrium constant for the reaction. For example, an aqueous mixture of iron(III) nitrate, $Fe(NO_3)_3(aq)$, and potassium thiocyanate, $KSCN(aq)$, reacts to form iron(III) thiocyanate, $Fe(SCN)^{2+}(aq)$. The reactant solutions are nearly colourless. The product solution ranges in colour, from light orange to blood red, depending on the concentration. The nitrate and potassium ions are spectator ions, so the net ionic equation is as follows:

$$Fe^{3+}(aq) + SCN^-(aq) \rightleftharpoons Fe(SCN)^{2+}(aq)$$
nearly colourless   orange/blood red

> **Suggested Investigation**
>
> Inquiry Investigation 7-C, Using Experimental Data to Determine an Equilibrium Constant

Because the reaction involves a colour change, you can determine the concentration of $Fe(SCN)^{2+}(aq)$ by measuring the intensity of the colour. From the measurements of colour intensity, you can calculate the equilibrium concentration of $Fe(SCN)^{2+}(aq)$. Then knowing the concentration of each solution, you can calculate the equilibrium concentration of each ion by using the chemical equation.

Suppose, for instance, that the initial concentration of $Fe^{3+}(aq)$ is 6.4×10^{-3} mol/L and the initial concentration of $SCN^-(aq)$ is 1.0×10^{-3} mol/L, as shown in the ICE table below. When the solutions are mixed, the orange/red iron(III) thiocyanate ion forms. By measuring the intensity of its colour, you are able to determine that the concentration of $Fe(SCN)^{2+}(aq)$ is 4.5×10^{-4} mol/L. From the stoichiometry of the equation, each mole of $Fe(SCN)^{2+}(aq)$ forms when equal amounts of $Fe^{3+}(aq)$ and $SCN^-(aq)$ react. So, if there is 4.5×10^{-4} mol/L of $Fe(SCN)^{2+}(aq)$ at equilibrium, then 4.5×10^{-4} mol/L of both $Fe^{3+}(aq)$ and $SCN^-(aq)$ must have reacted.

The equilibrium concentration of any reacting species is the sum of its initial concentration and the change that results from the reaction. For instance, the initial concentration of $Fe^{3+}(aq)$ was 6.4×10^{-3} mol/L. The change in the concentration of $Fe^{3+}(aq)$ as a result of the reaction was -4.5×10^{-4} mol/L. The value is negative because $Fe^{3+}(aq)$ was used up in the reaction. Therefore, the concentration of $Fe^{3+}(aq)$ at equilibrium is $(6.4 \times 10^{-3} - 4.5 \times 10^{-4})$ mol/L = 5.95×10^{-3} mol/L, or 6.0×10^{-3} mol/L. You can determine the equilibrium concentration of $SCN^-(aq)$ in the same way. The completed ICE table is shown below.

$$Fe^{3+}(aq) + SCN^-(aq) \rightleftharpoons Fe(SCN)^{2+}(aq)$$

	$[Fe^{3+}]$ (mol/L)	$[SCN^-]$ (mol/L)	$[Fe(SCN)^{2+}]$ (mol/L)
Initial	6.4×10^{-3}	1.0×10^{-3}	0
Change	-4.5×10^{-4}	-4.5×10^{-4}	4.5×10^{-4}
Equilibrium	6.0×10^{-3}	5.5×10^{-4}	4.5×10^{-4}

Finally, you can calculate K_{eq} by substituting the equilibrium concentrations into the equilibrium expression.

The Reaction Quotients, Q_{eq} and Q_p

So far, all of the reactions that you have read about are at equilibrium. If a chemical system is at equilibrium, you know that K_{eq} or K_p is constant. However, before a reaction reaches equilibrium, this ratio is not constant. For these situations, in which the system is *not* at equilibrium, the equilibrium constant expressions for K_{eq} and K_p can yield important information about the ratio of products to reactants. A **reaction quotient**, Q_{eq} or Q_p, has the same formula as K_{eq} or K_p, but the chemical system may or may not be at equilibrium. The formula that you use depends on the kind of data that are available, just as it does for the equilibrium constant.

reaction quotient a numerical value determined by using the same formula as the equilibrium constant using data for a reversible reaction that may or may not be at equilibrium

If concentration data are available, you use the first formula shown below. If partial pressure data are available, you use the second formula shown below. Other reaction quotients exist that have different formulas. You will learn more about these in the next chapter and in later courses.

$$Q_{eq} = \frac{[C]^c[D]^d}{[A]^a[B]^b} \qquad Q_p = \frac{P_C^c P_D^d}{P_A^a P_B^b}$$

The reaction quotient can be used to predict in which direction a chemical reaction shifts to reach equilibrium. For example, if $Q < K$, for Q to equal K, the value of Q must get larger. Therefore, the numerator in the equation must get larger and the denominator in the equation must get smaller, or product concentrations must increase and reactant concentrations must decrease. There are three possible situations that occur when using the reaction quotient to predict reaction behaviour.

- If $Q_{eq} < K_{eq}$ (or $Q_p < K_p$), the ratio of products to reactants is less than K_{eq}. To reach equilibrium, more products must form and reactants must be consumed. The reaction shifts to the right (toward product formation) to reach equilibrium.
- If $Q_{eq} = K_{eq}$ (or $Q_p = K_p$), the system is at equilibrium.
- If $Q_{eq} > K_{eq}$ (or $Q_p > K_p$), the ratio of products to reactants is greater than K_{eq}. Products must be converted into reactants to reach equilibrium. The reaction shifts to the left (toward reactant formation) to reach equilibrium.

Study the following Sample Problem to learn how to determine the reaction quotient and how to use the reaction quotient to predict the shift in the reaction prior to equilibrium. Use the Practice Problems to practise this skill.

Sample Problem

Calculating and Using a Reaction Quotient

Problem
In the Haber-Bosch process for manufacturing ammonia, nitrogen and hydrogen combine in the presence of a catalyst:

$$N_2(g) + 3H_2(g) \rightleftharpoons 2NH_3(g)$$

At 500°C, the value of K_{eq} for this reaction is 0.40. The following concentrations of gases are present in the container at 500°C: $[N_2] = 0.10$ mol/L, $[H_2] = 0.30$ mol/L, and $[NH_3] = 0.20$ mol/L. Is this mixture of gases at equilibrium? If not, in which direction will the reaction shift to reach equilibrium?

What Is Required?
You need to calculate Q_{eq} and use it to predict in which direction the reaction will shift to reach equilibrium.

What Is Given?
You know the balanced chemical equation. You know K_{eq} for the reaction is 0.40. You know the concentration of the gases involved in the reaction:
$[N_2] = 0.10$ mol/L, $[H_2] = 0.30$ mol/L, and $[NH_3] = 0.20$ mol/L

Plan Your Strategy	Act on Your Strategy
Write the expression for the reaction quotient, Q_{eq}.	$Q_{eq} = \dfrac{[NH_3]^2}{[N_2][H_2]^3}$

Plan Your Strategy	Act on Your Strategy
Substitute the known values into the equation and calculate the value of Q_{eq}. Each of the molar concentration values are divided by the reference state of 1 mol/L before they are inserted into the formula. Thus, they are also written without units.	$Q_{eq} = \dfrac{(0.20)^2}{(0.10)(0.30)^3} = 15$
Compare Q_{eq} with K_{eq} and decide if the chemical system is at equilibrium. If the system is not at equilibrium, the reaction will shift to the right if $Q_{eq} < K_{eq}$. The reaction will shift to the left if $Q_{eq} > K_{eq}$.	$Q_{eq} > K_{eq}$; $15 > 0.40$ The system is not at equilibrium. Because the reaction quotient value is so high, the concentration of the products must be much greater than the concentration of the reactants. The product will temporarily decompose at a higher rate than the reactants will form the product. The reaction shifts to the left in favour of reactant formation.

Check Your Solution

Check your calculations of Q_{eq}. The value of Q_{eq} can only have two significant digits based on the number of significant digits in the concentration data.

Practice Problems

For questions 81 to 87, determine if the reactions are at equilibrium. If they are not at equilibrium, then determine the direction in which the reaction is favoured.

81. At 300 K, $K_{eq} = 35.5$ for the reaction below:
$$3C(s) + 3H_2(g) \rightleftharpoons CH_4(g) + C_2H_2(g)$$
The following concentrations are found to be present at a particular point in time: $[H_2] = 0.34$ mol/L, $[CH_4] = 2.13$ mol/L, and $[C_2H_2] = 1.77$ mol/L.

82. A 3.00 L reaction vessel contains 9.00 mol of hydrogen iodide gas, 6.00 mol of hydrogen gas, and 4.50 mol of iodine gas. At a given temperature, the K_{eq} value for the reaction below is 50.0.
$$H_2(g) + I_2(g) \rightleftharpoons 2HI(g)$$

83. At 525 K, $K_{eq} = 0.041$ for the following reaction:
$$PCl_5(g) \rightleftharpoons PCl_3(g) + Cl_2(g)$$
At one point in time, measurements were taken and the following concentrations were measured:
$[PCl_5] = 0.77$ mol/L, $[PCl_3] = 1.21$ mol/L, and $[Cl_2] = 0.49$ mol/L.

84. Consider the following reaction:
$$N_2(g) + 3H_2(g) \rightleftharpoons 2NH_3(g)$$
$K_{eq} = 6.0 \times 10^{-2}$ at 875 K. At a point just after nitrogen gas and hydrogen gas are injected into a container, the concentrations of each reactant and product are $[N_2] = 1.50 \times 10^{-5}$ mol/L, $[H_2] = 0.354$ mol/L, and $[NH_3] = 2.00 \times 10^{-4}$ mol/L.

85. In the reaction of phosphorus trichloride, $PCl_3(g)$, and ammonia, $NH_3(g)$, the products are hydrogen chloride gas, HCl(g), and $P(NH_2)_3(g)$:
$$PCl_3(g) + 3NH_3(g) \rightleftharpoons P(NH_2)_3(g) + 3HCl(g)$$
At 600 K, this reaction has an equilibrium constant, K_{eq}, that is 142.3. A system of these gases was analyzed and the following concentrations were determined:
$[PCl_3] = 2.15$ mol/L, $[NH_3] = 1.21$ mol/L, $[P(NH_2)_3] = 5.74$ mol/L, and $[HCl] = 2.04$ mol/L.

86. At 865 K, $K_p = 2.11$ for the reaction below:
$$P_4(s) + 6Cl_2(g) \rightleftharpoons 4PCl_3(g)$$
At one point in time, measurements were taken and the following partial pressures were measured:
$P_{Cl_2} = 1.21$ atm and $P_{PCl_3} = 3.04$ atm.

87. At 660 K, $K_p = 25.2$ for the reaction below:
$$N_2(g) + O_2(g) \rightleftharpoons 2NO(g)$$
At one point in time, measurements were taken and the following partial pressures were measured:
$P_{N_2} = 2.37$ atm, $P_{O_2} = 2.27$ atm, and $P_{NO} = 3.74$ atm.

88. If 1.00 mol of each reactant and product in the reaction below are placed into a 1.00 L container and if the system is kept at 700 K, in what direction will the reaction shift to reach equilibrium, if K_{eq} is 5.10?
$$CO(g) + H_2O(g) \rightleftharpoons CO_2(g) + H_2(g)$$

Section 7.3 Review

Section Summary

- The numerical value of the equilibrium constant is calculated by using the equilibrium constant expression.
- In a chemical equilibrium system composed of gases, the partial pressures of the gases can be used to calculate the equilibrium constant if the gases behave like ideal gases.
- You can determine information about an equilibrium system by organizing known information into an ICE table.
- If the equilibrium constant for a reaction is very small, you can make assumptions that will simplify the mathematical calculations for predicting the resultant concentrations of components in a chemical system.
- You can experimentally measure the macroscopic properties of an equilibrium system, such as colour intensity, and use them to calculate the equilibrium concentration of a product or a reactant.

Review Questions

1. **K/U** Write equilibrium expressions for each reaction.
   a. $2H_2S(g) + CH_4(g) \rightleftharpoons 4H_2(g) + CS_2(g)$
   b. $P_4(g) + 3O_2(g) \rightleftharpoons 2P_2O_3(g)$
   c. $7N_2(g) + 2S_8(g) \rightleftharpoons 2N_3S_4(g) + 4N_2S_2(g)$

2. **T/I** At 225 K, the equilibrium constant, K_{eq}, for the reaction of hydrogen sulfide gas decomposing to form sulfur gas and hydrogen gas is 18.5. The reaction is as follows:
   $$2H_2S(g) \rightleftharpoons 2H_2(g) + S_2(g)$$
   At equilibrium, the hydrogen sulfide gas concentration was found to be 1.18 mol/L and the sulfur gas concentration was found to be 2.34 mol/L. Determine the concentration of the hydrogen gas in this equilibrium mixture.

3. **T/I** The following is an ICE table for a reaction that started with 0.200 mol/L concentrations of hydrogen gas and chlorine gas:

	$H_2(g)$	+	$Cl_2(g)$	$\rightleftharpoons$	$2HCl(g)$
	$[H_2]$ mol/L		$[Cl_2]$ mol/L		$[HCl]$ mol/L
Initial	0.200		0.200		0
Change	$-x$		$-x$		$+x$
Equilibrium	$0.200 - x$		$0.200 - x$		x

   Is this table filled in properly? Explain your answer.

4. **T/I** At a certain temperature, K_{eq} equals 4.8 for the following reaction between sulfur dioxide, $SO_2(g)$, and nitrogen dioxide, $NO_2(g)$:
   $$SO_2(g) + NO_2(g) \rightleftharpoons NO(g) + SO_3(g)$$
   If sulfur dioxide and nitrogen dioxide have initial concentrations of 0.36 mol/L, what amount of sulfur trioxide, $SO_3(g)$, is present in a 5.0 L container at equilibrium?

5. **A** Hydrogen gas, $H_2(g)$, has several advantages and disadvantages as a potential fuel. Hydrogen can be obtained by the thermal decomposition of water at high temperatures:
   $$2H_2O(g) \rightleftharpoons 2H_2(g) + O_2(g)$$
   $$K_{eq} = 7.3 \times 10^{-18} \text{ at } 1000°C$$
   a. The initial concentration of water in a reaction vessel is 0.055 mol/L. What is the equilibrium concentration of hydrogen gas at 1000°C?
   b. Evaluate the practicality of thermal decomposition of water to obtain hydrogen gas.

6. **K/U** Write the K_p expressions for each of the following reactions:
   a. $CO(g) + H_2(g) \rightleftharpoons C(s) + H_2O(g)$
   b. $H_2(g) + I_2(g) \rightleftharpoons 2HI(g)$
   c. $CO(g) + H_2O(g) \rightleftharpoons CO_2(g) + H_2(g)$
   d. $C(s) + 2H_2(g) \rightleftharpoons CH_4(g)$

7. **C** Create a flowchart or similar graphic organizer that can be used to write an equilibrium constant expression, K_{eq}, for a reaction of gases in which the unbalanced equation is given.

8. **A** Arsenic can be removed from materials by first reacting the material with oxygen in a process called roasting. The oxide that forms is $As_4O_6(s)$, which is then reacted with solid carbon to form $As_4(g)$ and carbon monoxide according to the reaction:
   $$As_4O_6(s) + 6C(s) \rightleftharpoons As_4(g) + 6CO(g)$$
   a. Write the equilibrium constant for this reaction.
   b. If $[As_4] = 2.77$ mol/L and $[CO] = 1.33$ mol/L, what is the value of K_{eq}?
   c. Would you expect the K_{eq} value to increase or decrease if the volume were to decrease? Explain your answer using concepts studied in this section as well as in Section 7.2.

Section 7.4 Applications of Equilibrium Systems

Equilibrium systems are not just a topic to study in chemistry class. Equilibrium processes are abundant in nature. In fact, your body contains many processes that must remain in balance to sustain your life. Breathing air is an example of a body process that uses equilibrium, and scuba diving is an example of when that equilibrium can shift, causing unfortunate results for the diver.

Key Terms

hemoglobin
syngas

Biochemical Equilibrium Processes

In situations in which your body is subjected to abnormal conditions, such as while scuba diving, extra precautions must be taken to keep your body's systems in equilibrium, or serious consequences, and even death, can occur. Your body must maintain a delicate balance of pH and of the concentration of gases in the blood. Maintaining these properties in balance involves both physical and chemical equilibria.

Decompression Sickness and Scuba Diving

The scuba diver shown in **Figure 7.19** must understand the importance of several gas laws to safely enjoy diving. One of these laws is related to the physical equilibrium of gases dissolved in the diver's blood.

The total pressure exerted on a diver increases by one atmosphere for every 10 m descent below the surface. The diver's lungs would collapse if they were not supplied with air from the tank that is at the same pressure as the surrounding water. Because the total pressure of the air that the diver breathes has increased, the partial pressure of each of the gases present has increased proportionately. The solubility of a gas in a liquid increases as the pressure of that gas above the liquid increases. Therefore, as the diver descends, an increasing amount of nitrogen and oxygen dissolves in the blood.

High concentrations of nitrogen gas in the blood impair the conduction of electrical signals along the nerves. The effect of this impairment, called nitrogen narcosis, begins at depths below about 30 m. For every additional 15 m below the surface, a diver experiences an effect that is similar to consuming an alcoholic drink. Thus, at 60 m below the surface, a diver would experience the impaired judgment, confusion, and drowsiness of a person who had consumed too many alcoholic drinks. At depths of 90 m, nitrogen narcosis can lead to hallucinations and unconsciousness.

Figure 7.19 As depth increases, the diver must breathe air at greater pressure.

As a diver returns to the surface, the solubility of gases in the blood decreases. The gases flow out of the blood like carbon dioxide bubbles flow out of a freshly opened soft-drink bottle. A diver returning to the surface must do so slowly enough to allow nitrogen to be breathed out so that the body can safely maintain equilibrium. If the diver's ascent is too rapid, bubbles will form in the blood and nitrogen gas may collect in the joints and other parts of the body. This condition is called decompression sickness. The pain caused by increased gas pressure in the joints is called "the bends." Nitrogen bubbles in the blood vessels can cause damage to any of the tissues or organs where the bubbles collect. If a diver remains at a depth of less than 20 m, there is little danger of getting the bends. As divers descend deeper, however, the bends can occur at shorter and shorter time intervals.

What about the effect of dissolved oxygen gas on the scuba diver? Oxygen is toxic at the increased concentration in the blood caused by deep dives or dives where oxygen-enriched gas is breathed. Toxic levels of oxygen can lead to a seizure. Again, the diver must regulate oxygen levels so that chemical equilibrium is maintained in the body.

Carbon Monoxide Poisoning

Another example of biochemical equilibrium in the body is carbon monoxide poisoning. Carbon monoxide, $CO(g)$, is a poisonous gas that is formed when incomplete combustion of a hydrocarbon occurs. Burning fuel with a limited air supply forms carbon monoxide gas, which is colourless and odourless. The structure of carbon monoxide is similar to that of oxygen, $O_2(g)$, such that carbon monoxide is able to bind to the protein **hemoglobin** (Hb), which normally carries oxygen in the blood. The equilibrium constant for the reaction of hemoglobin with carbon monoxide is about 250 times greater than the equilibrium constant for the reaction of hemoglobin with oxygen:

$$HHb(aq) + CO(aq) \rightleftharpoons H^+(aq) + HbCO^-(aq)$$

hemoglobin
a protein in the blood of vertebrates that aids in the transport of oxygen to cells

Because hemoglobin binds more readily with carbon monoxide than with oxygen, the blood contains too little oxygen. Breathing even small concentrations of carbon monoxide can be deadly. Arterial blood pumped from the heart to the cells and organs carries too little oxygen. The cells do not get enough oxygen to carry out their life processes. As a result, cells die. If too many cells die, the person cannot recover and the person can die.

People who have carbon monoxide poisoning or decompression sickness from scuba diving often are treated in hyperbaric chambers, like the one shown in **Figure 7.20**. When a person is placed in a high-pressure, high-oxygen concentration environment, the equilibrium process shifts, and toxic gases are removed from the blood.

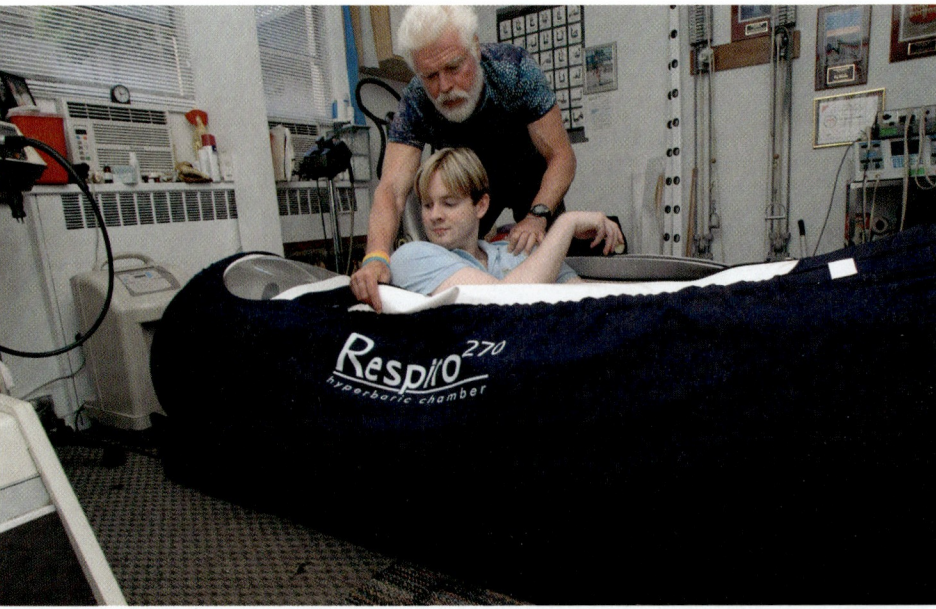

Figure 7.20 Hyperbaric chambers force an equilibrium shift that removes the harmful gases from the blood.

Biological Equilibrium Processes

One example of a biological equilibrium process in nature is the formation of a coral reef. Coral reefs, like the one shown in **Figure 7.21**, are diverse ecosystems that protect fish and provide natural breakwaters to protect coastlines. Tiny organisms, called polyps, which feed on small particles floating in the water, form coral reefs. These polyps also absorb nutrients and sugars from tiny photosynthetic algae that live inside the coral. A coral colony may consist of thousands of polyps that leave behind a hard, branching structure made of calcium carbonate when they die. The algae that live in the coral cement various corals and shells together with calcium compounds to create the coral reefs.

Many factors affect the health of coral, but increasing amounts of carbon dioxide, $CO_2(g)$, in the atmosphere present a long-term threat. The burning of fossil fuels releases about 25 billion tonnes of carbon dioxide into the atmosphere each year. Increased levels of atmospheric carbon dioxide enhance the greenhouse effect over time and, consequently, result in global warming. Higher global temperatures ultimately raise the temperature of the world's oceans. Even a small increase in seawater temperature causes coral to be stressed and to take on a bleached appearance.

Chemical reactions in the seawater involve equilibrium processes. Carbon dioxide gas dissolves in water to form carbonic acid, $H_2CO_3(aq)$, a weak acid. This creates an equilibrium system in seawater, involving three different reversible reactions:

$$CO_2(g) + H_2O(\ell) \rightleftharpoons H_2CO_3(aq)$$
$$H_2CO_3(aq) + H_2O(\ell) \rightleftharpoons H_3O^+(aq) + HCO_3^-(aq)$$
$$HCO_3^-(aq) + H_2O(\ell) \rightleftharpoons H_3O^+(aq) + CO_3^{2-}(aq)$$

The equilibrium in seawater can be simplified to

$$CO_2(g) + CO_3^{2-}(aq) + H_2O(\ell) \rightleftharpoons 2HCO_3^-(aq).$$

This equilibrium is very important to the chemistry of the ocean and the health of coral reefs around the world.

Carbon dioxide is not very soluble in water. However, as the concentration of carbon dioxide in the atmosphere increases, more carbon dioxide gas dissolves in ocean water. As more carbon dioxide gas dissolves in the oceans, Le Châtelier's principle predicts a shift to the right, and the concentration of carbonate ion, $CO_3^{2-}(aq)$, decreases. The decrease in carbonate ion affects the amount of dissolved calcium carbonate that is available to coral polyps for making shells:

$$CaCO_3(s) \rightleftharpoons Ca^{2+}(aq) + CO_3^{2-}(aq)$$

With less calcium carbonate available, corals grow more slowly. The slow growth of the corals affects the entire ecosystem, because it limits the success of the other organisms that depend on the coral reef for food and shelter. Today, many groups are working together to conserve and restore coral reefs, including the World Wildlife Fund and the Coral Reef Alliance.

Figure 7.21 Coral reefs are slow-growing ecosystems that are affected by changes to their environment. These ecosystems provide food and shelter to many organisms, as well as absorb about one third of the carbon dioxide gas released by fossil fuel combustion.

Learning Check

38. What are the symptoms of a higher than normal concentration of nitrogen in the blood?
39. What must a diver do to avoid getting the bends?
40. Why is inhaling carbon monoxide dangerous?
41. How does the equilibrium constant for the reaction of carbon monoxide with hemoglobin compare with the equilibrium constant for the reaction of oxygen with hemoglobin?
42. Explain how a hyperbaric chamber restores the gases in the blood to normal levels when a person has decompression sickness or carbon monoxide poisoning.
43. How do increasing amounts of carbon dioxide in the atmosphere affect coral polyps and coral reefs?

Technological Equilibrium Systems

Some industrial processes involve equilibrium systems. Three industrial chemicals, ammonia, sulfuric acid, and methanol, are discussed in greater depth in this section. Recall that you read about the catalysts used to produce ammonia and sulfuric acid in Chapter 6.

Manufacturing Ammonia

The Haber-Bosch process for manufacturing ammonia was the first application of modern chemical principles to produce a chemical in very large quantities. Before the work of Fritz Haber (1868–1934), a German chemist, sodium nitrate was imported to Germany from Chile and made into fertilizers and explosives. Sodium nitrate was an important resource and the supply from Chile could easily be interrupted or cut off. Several chemists undertook the challenge of finding a replacement for sodium nitrate that was not dependent on overseas sources. In 1909, Haber produced an equilibrium system consisting of nitrogen, hydrogen, and ammonia:

$$N_2(g) + 3H_2(g) \rightleftharpoons 2NH_3(g) + 92 \text{ kJ/mol} \qquad \text{At } 25°C, K_{eq} = \frac{[NH_3]^2}{[N_2][H_2]^3} = 4.1 \times 10^8$$

The large equilibrium constant suggests that the reaction proceeds to completion. However, the position of equilibrium is only one of several factors important in chemical reactions. Another factor in chemical reactions is the rate of the reaction. At 25°C, the rate of reaction between nitrogen and hydrogen is so slow that there is essentially no ammonia formed.

Haber knew that he could increase the rate of reaction by raising the temperature of the reacting gases. However, he also knew that the reaction is exothermic, so Le Châtelier's principle would predict a shift to the left (favouring reactant production) at higher temperature. **Table 7.3** shows that the value of K_{eq} falls very rapidly as temperature increases. As explained previously, a lower K_{eq} means that there is a larger concentration of reactants than products, because K_{eq} is a ratio of product concentrations to reactant concentrations.

Table 7.3 The Effect of Temperature Change on K_{eq} for the Reaction to Manufacture Ammonia

Temperature (°C)	25	100	200	300	400	500	600
K_{eq}	4.1×10^8	2.3×10^5	4.4×10^2	7.3	0.41	0.05	9.5×10^{-3}

Again, using Le Châtelier's principle, Haber knew that he could shift the position of equilibrium back toward the right by running the reaction at high pressure, which favours the production of fewer particles.

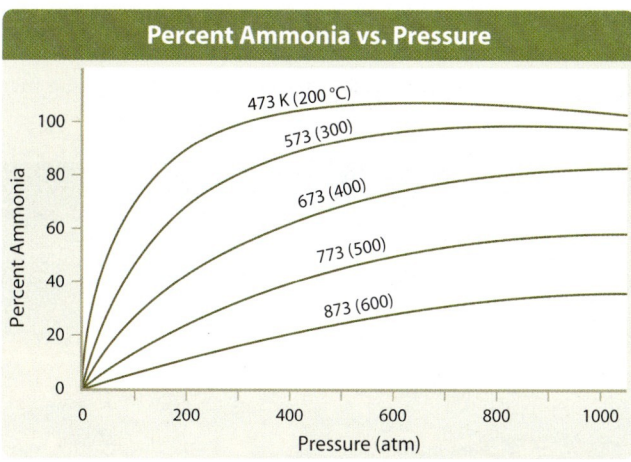

Figure 7.22 This graph represents the percent of ammonia that is produced at various temperatures and pressures. Haber performed thousands of experiments to find the best conditions to make ammonia.

Figure 7.22 shows how the yield of ammonia varies with the temperature and pressure of the reaction. Although the yield of ammonia increases with pressure, the cost of running a chemical plant also increases. A plant operating at higher pressure would incur higher costs, because more pumps are required. The reaction vessel and pipes would also need to be thicker to withstand the greater pressure. Safety risks increase with pressure, and repair and maintenance costs also increase. Haber decided that the higher overall reaction rate, due to increased temperature, and the higher yield of ammonia, due to increased pressure, were worth the associated higher production costs. However, he would need to increase the rate of the reaction even more.

Increasing the Yield of Ammonia

Finding a suitable catalyst for the production of ammonia would shorten the time taken for the mixture of gases to reach equilibrium. The removal of ammonia would also shift the equilibrium toward the production of more ammonia. Ammonia is removed from the reaction vessel by cooling the mixture of gases as shown in **Figure 7.23**. Once the ammonia has been removed, the gases are recycled back to the reaction vessel in a continuous operation. Haber performed more than 6500 experiments, changing the temperature and pressure of the mixture and varying the catalyst, to determine the rate and yield of ammonia in the reaction. Carl Bosch (1874–1940) was an engineer who solved the engineering problems associated with the high pressures used in the process that Haber had discovered. Haber won the Nobel Prize in chemistry in 1918, and Bosch won the prize in 1931.

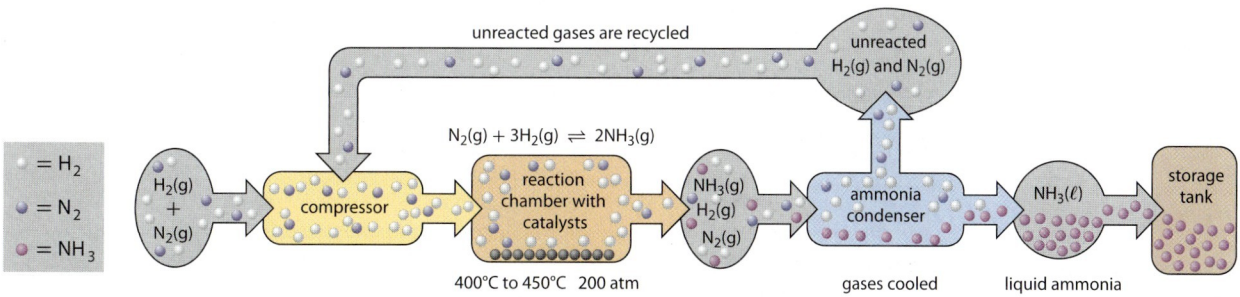

Figure 7.23 The catalyst that is often used with the Haber-Bosch process, shown in the diagram, is a mixture of MgO(s), Al_2O_3(s), and SiO_2(s), with embedded iron crystals.

Although ammonia is an inorganic compound, its synthesis depends greatly on a plentiful supply of methane. This is because modern ammonia production plants combine nitrogen from the air with hydrogen derived from methane. An ammonia manufacturing facility is shown in **Figure 7.24**.

Figure 7.24 This modern ammonia plant synthesizes ammonia using methane and air.

Manufacturing Sulfuric Acid

Sulfuric acid production is another chemical process that involves an equilibrium system. More sulfuric acid is produced than any other chemical in the world. Because sulfuric acid is used in so many processes, it is often said that the amount of sulfuric acid manufactured is a good indicator of the health of the country's general economy. **Figure 7.25** shows the many industrial processes that use sulfuric acid.

Activity 7.3 — The Haber-Bosch Process: Synthesizing Ammonia

Ammonia, $NH_3(g)$, is produced in the millions of tonnes each year. Among other things, it is used to prepare fertilizers and explosives. The procedure uses atmospheric nitrogen and hydrogen to produce ammonia in a process represented by the following equilibrium equation:

$$N_2(g) + 3H_2(g) \rightleftharpoons 2NH_3(g) \quad \Delta H_r = -92 \text{ kJ/mol}$$

Procedure

Look carefully at the equilibrium equation for the preparation of ammonia and at the boiling point data below. In small groups, use Le Châtelier's principle, and other concepts you have learned in this course, to answer the following questions.

Boiling Points of Three Compounds

Compound	Boiling Point (°C)
$N_2(\ell)$	−196
$H_2(\ell)$	−253
$NH_3(\ell)$	−33

Questions

1. In terms of Le Châtelier's principle, explain how increasing the pressure of the system will increase the yield of ammonia.

2. Use Le Châtelier's principle to explain why the amounts of hydrogen and nitrogen were kept high.

3. Given that a catalyst will increase both the forward and the reverse reaction rates, explain why Haber successfully used a catalyst in the production of ammonia.

4. What effect does a small K_{eq} have on the percentage yield of an equilibrium reaction?

5. Consider the data given.

    a. If $\Delta H_r = -92$ kJ/mol for the synthesis of ammonia, does Le Châtelier's principle favour the formation of ammonia at high or low temperature?

    b. Given your answer to part (a), why does the Haber-Bosch process use a high temperature to prepare ammonia? The answer to question 3 will be helpful.

6. Prepare a table to summarize the reaction conditions (temperature, pressure, use of catalyst, amounts of reactants and products present) required to produce ammonia on an industrial scale. Explain your reasoning in terms of Le Châtelier's principle and other chemistry concepts.

7. Research why Germany was interested in the production of ammonia prior to World War I.

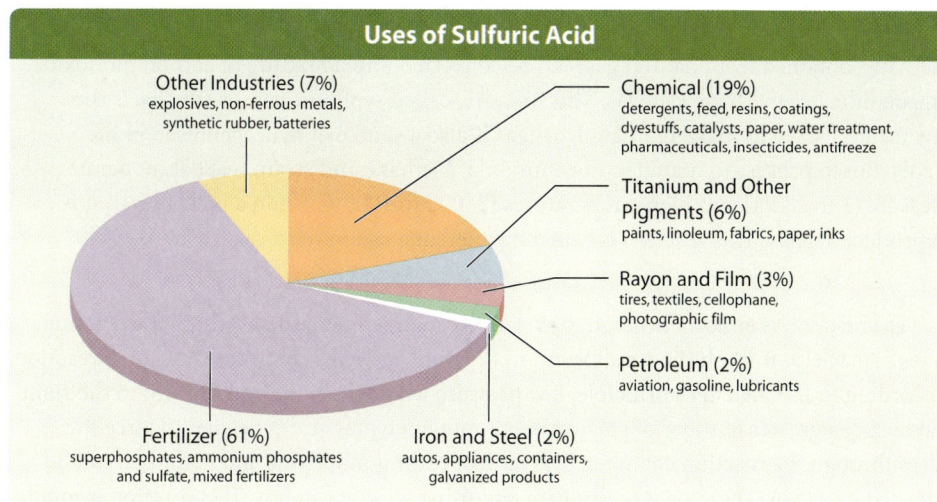

Figure 7.25 Sulfuric acid is used in the manufacturing processes that result in many products. The annual worldwide production of sulfuric acid is more than 150 million tonnes.

Sulfuric acid can be made from the waste gases formed during the smelting of ores that contain sulfur. Sulfuric acid can also be made from the sulfur removed from sour oil and gas. Canada is the second-largest producer of sulfur in the world, manufacturing about 8 million tonnes annually. Sulfur is made into sulfuric acid using air and water as raw materials. First, sulfur is burned in air:

$$S(s) + O_2(g) \rightarrow SO_2(g)$$

Then the sulfur dioxide reacts with oxygen over a catalyst containing the element vanadium, as you read in Chapter 6, to form sulfur trioxide:

$$2SO_2(g) + O_2(g) \rightleftharpoons 2SO_3(g) + 197 \text{ kJ/mol}$$

The reaction is exothermic, so Le Châtelier's principle predicts that the forward reaction is favoured at low temperatures. However, as you saw with the Haber-Bosch process to manufacture ammonia, lower temperatures slow the rate of reaction. As a compromise, a temperature of about 450°C is used. This gives a reasonable rate of reaction and a yield of 97 percent sulfur trioxide.

Le Châtelier's principle predicts greater yield if the pressure is increased. However, the yield is high enough that it does not justify the increased cost of pressurizing the gases more than is necessary to move the gas mixture through the reaction vessel. In the final two steps, the $SO_3(g)$ is dissolved in 98 percent sulfuric acid, $H_2SO_4(\ell)$, to create pyrosulfuric acid, $H_2S_2O_7(\ell)$. Water is then added to the pyrosulfuric acid to produce sulfuric acid. The reaction is completed as follows:

$$SO_3(g) + H_2SO_4(\ell) \rightarrow H_2S_2O_7(\ell)$$
$$H_2S_2O_7(\ell) + H_2O(\ell) \rightarrow 2H_2SO_4(\ell)$$

Notice that sulfuric acid is used as a reactant in this process to make more sulfuric acid. However, because 2 mol of sulfuric acid is produced for each mole used as a reactant, the process results in a net production of sulfuric acid.

Learning Check

44. Why was finding a method of producing ammonia without sodium nitrate important to Germany?
45. Why is the rate of the reaction between nitrogen and hydrogen at 25°C problematic for ammonia production?
46. What was Fritz Haber's solution for maximizing ammonia production?
47. What was Carl Bosch's role in the Haber-Bosch process?
48. Why is the amount of sulfuric acid manufactured in a country an indicator of the country's general economy?
49. Explain why increasing the pressure in the reaction vessel is unnecessary for sulfuric acid production.

Manufacturing Methanol

Methane, obtained from natural gas, can be converted into a mixture of carbon monoxide, carbon dioxide, and hydrogen gas. This mixture, called synthesis gas, or **syngas,** is the raw material used to make methanol. Syngas is also a source of hydrogen used in the Haber-Bosch process to manufacture ammonia. Methane and steam react at moderate pressure (1 to 2 kPa) and high temperatures (850°C to 1000°C), and a nickel catalyst is used to produce syngas. This reaction is called the methane-steam reaction:

$$CH_4(g) + H_2O(g) + \text{heat} \rightleftharpoons CO(g) + 3H_2(g)$$

The reaction is endothermic, so the relatively high temperature at which the reaction takes place helps to push the equilibrium to the right, as well as increase the rate of reaction. According to Le Châtelier's principle, low pressure would push the equilibrium to the right (favouring a greater number of particles), but moderate pressure is needed to force the gases through the reaction chamber. The ratio of carbon monoxide and hydrogen can be adjusted by mixing the syngas with steam and using an iron catalyst. This reaction is mildly exothermic, and the heat produced can be used for the methane-steam reaction:

$$CO(g) + H_2O(g) \rightleftharpoons CO_2(g) + H_2(g) + \text{heat}$$

The syngas is passed over a catalyst at a pressure of 5 to 10 MPa at about 250°C to form methanol:

$$CO(g) + 2H_2(g) \rightleftharpoons CH_3OH(g) + \text{heat}$$

In this reaction, higher pressures are used to shift the reaction to the right, according to Le Châtelier's principle. The reaction is highly exothermic and heat is removed from the reaction chamber. The heat can be used for the methane-steam reaction, because the position of equilibrium will shift to the left if the temperature increases.

The production of methanol consumes 2 mol of hydrogen gas, $H_2(g)$, for every mole of carbon monoxide gas, $CO(g)$. However, the methane-steam reaction to make syngas results in 3 mol of hydrogen gas for every mole of carbon monoxide gas. The excess hydrogen from the methane-steam reaction can be used to remove sulfur from gasoline and diesel at nearby plants.

Methanol was used in ancient times, as shown in **Figure 7.26,** and it is processed into a number of other chemicals today, as shown in **Figure 7.27.**

syngas the abbreviated form of "synthesis gas"; the end product of an industrial process in which a carbon-rich material, such as coal, natural gas, or biomass, is converted into a gas consisting of hydrogen, carbon monoxide, and smaller amounts of carbon dioxide and other trace gases; it is usually used to produce other products, such as ammonia, methanol, and synthetic petroleum

Figure 7.26 Methanol was used by the ancient Egyptians to prepare an embalming solution.

Figure 7.27 Methanol is a versatile chemical that can be processed into other chemicals that are used to make products that we commonly use.

medium density fibreboard

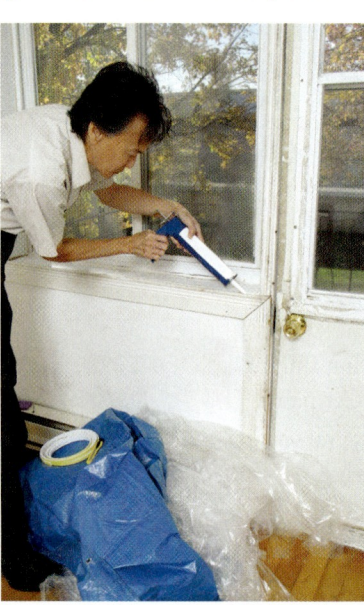

silicone sealant

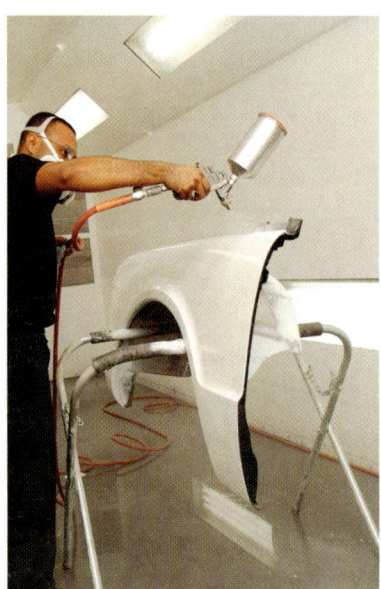

paints

Section 7.4 Review

Section Summary

- If a diver rapidly returns to the surface from a deep dive, the change in the equilibrium between dissolved and gaseous nitrogen causes bubbles to form in the blood vessels, causing a serious condition called "the bends."
- The equilibrium constant for the reaction of hemoglobin with carbon monoxide is about 250 times greater than the equilibrium constant for the reaction with oxygen.
- An understanding of the effects of pressure and temperature on the position of equilibrium between nitrogen and hydrogen gases and ammonia allowed the chemists Fritz Haber and Carl Bosch to develop an efficient method for synthesizing ammonia.
- Knowledge of the equilibrium reactions that are important in the production of sulfuric acid and of methanol makes it possible to produce these very important products in large amounts.

Review Questions

1. **K/U** Use your knowledge about scuba diving to answer the following questions.
   a. How does the solubility of a gas in water change as the pressure of the gas above the solution increases?
   b. How is this relevant to a scuba diver?
   c. What are the effects of increased concentrations of nitrogen and oxygen in the blood?
   d. Describe how a diver prevents "the bends."

2. **A** The snails that you might see in a garden have shells made of calcium carbonate. In deep crevasses on the ocean floor, hydrothermal vents emit very hot, acidic water. Explain why snails living near these vents do not have a shell, using two or three well-organized sentences.

3. **C** People die every year from carbon monoxide poisoning. Prepare a flyer that could be distributed to households in your neighbourhood describing the dangers of carbon monoxide. Describe specific ways in which the gas forms, and include precautions that should be taken to prevent carbon monoxide poisoning.

4. **A** When carbon monoxide, CO(g), is present in human lungs, the carbon monoxide behaves in a way that is similar to how oxygen gas behaves, in that it binds to hemoglobin (Hb) in the blood. The equilibrium reactions for oxygen and carbon monoxide are as follows:

   $$HHb(aq) + O_2(g) \rightleftharpoons H^+(aq) + HbO_2^-(aq)$$
   $$HHb(aq) + CO(g) \rightleftharpoons H^+(aq) + HbCO^-(aq)$$

   It is known that the equilibrium constant for the reaction involving carbon monoxide is approximately 250 times greater than that for the reaction involving oxygen gas. In two or three sentences, explain why this may cause serious health problems for someone in an area where carbon monoxide is present.

5. **T/I** A chemist studying the reaction below collected the data shown. Is the reaction in the forward direction endothermic or exothermic? Explain your answer.

   $$N_2(g) + O_2(g) \rightleftharpoons 2NO(g)$$

   Temperature vs. K_{eq}

Temperature (K)	K_{eq}
300	4×10^{-31}
700	5×10^{-13}
1100	4×10^{-8}
1500	1×10^{-5}

6. **C** Research an industry or a company that uses methanol as a raw material. Prepare a brief report (three or four paragraphs) on this industry. Include in your report the chemical process used by the industry or company and what conditions are used to optimize the manufacture of one of their final products.

7. **K/U** In the manufacturing process that produces methanol, $CH_3OH(g)$, the reaction used is as follows:

   $$CO(g) + 2H_2(g) \rightleftharpoons CH_3OH(g) + \text{heat}$$

   Apply Le Châtelier's principle to describe conditions that should be used to increase the yield of methanol.

8. **C** Create a flowchart or similar concept organizer that can be used to represent the process of increasing carbon dioxide gas levels in the atmosphere and how this increase ultimately causes a slowdown in coral reef growth.

9. **K/U** Of all the chemicals produced in the world, the chemical manufactured in the largest quantity is sulfuric acid. Describe the process by means of which sulfuric acid is produced in Canada and how Le Châtelier's principle is used in the process. Your answer should consist of two or three well-organized paragraphs.

Inquiry INVESTIGATION 7-A

Skill Check
- Initiating and Planning
- ✓ Performing and Recording
- ✓ Analyzing and Interpreting
- ✓ Communicating

Safety Precautions

- Wash your hands before and after this investigation.
- Gloves should be worn during this activity.

Materials
- 60 small objects such as buttons, pennies, or washers

Go to Significant Digits and Rounding in Appendix A for information about using significant digits and rounding numbers.

Go to Developing Research Skills in Appendix A for information about conducting research.

Simulating Dynamic Equilibrium

Chemical equilibrium consists of a reversible reaction in which reactants react to form products, while the products simultaneously react to form the reactants. In this investigation, you will model a chemical equilibrium using small objects. The results of the investigation will give you information about the exact nature of chemical equilibrium.

Pre-Lab Questions
1. Explain the terms *dynamic equilibrium* and *closed system*.
2. In a reversible reaction, is it necessary for the rates of the forward and reverse reactions to be equal? Briefly explain your answer.
3. Why is it important to sanitize the small objects before another student uses them?

Questions
1. What is the exact nature of chemical equilibrium?
2. How does the rate of the forward reaction compare with the rate of the reverse reaction?
3. Can equilibrium be reached only when the reactants are initially present?

Procedure
1. Work in small groups. One student will act as a recorder. Divide the remaining students into two teams: reactants (R) and products (P).
2. In Trial 1, Team R will begin with 40 items; Team P will have 0 items.
3. Each team will simultaneously make five transfers of items. Each time a transfer is made, Team R will transfer one half of the items that they have on hand; Team P will transfer one quarter of the items they have. If a fractional quantity needs to be transferred, round up. For example, one half of 15 is 7.5—*round up* to 8. This process will be repeated four more times. Copy the data table below into your notebook and record your results.

Table A Transfer Data for Trial 1

	Team R		Team P	
	Quantity of Items	Quantity Transferred	Quantity Transferred	Quantity of Items
Initial Quantities				
Transfer 1				
Outcome				
Transfer 2				
Outcome				
Transfer 3				
Outcome				
Transfer 4				
Outcome				
Transfer 5				
Outcome				

4. In Trial 2, Team R will begin with 40 items; Team P with 20 items. The transfer of items will be the same as in Procedure step 3. Copy the data table below into your notebook and record your results.

5. In Trial 3, each team will again make five simultaneous transfers of items. Team R will begin with 40 items; Team P will begin with 0 items. Each time a transfer is made, Team R will transfer *three quarters* of the items that they have on hand; Team P will transfer *one eighth* of the items they have. Again, if a fractional quantity needs to be transferred, round up. This process will be repeated four more times. The data table for Trial 3 is the same as for Trial 2. Copy the data table into your notebook and give it a correct title.

6. Return your collection of small objects to your teacher for disinfection.

Analyze and Interpret

1. Using your data in Trial 1, answer the following questions.
   a. In Trial 1, what happens to the ratio of $\frac{P}{R}$ after the third transfer?
   b. What does this suggest about the relative rates of forward and reverse "reactions."

2. Using your data in Trial 2, answer the following questions.
   a. In Trial 2, what happens to the ratio of $\frac{P}{R}$ after the third transfer?
   b. How does this compare with the ratio of $\frac{P}{R}$ from Trial 1?

3. Using your data in Trial 3, explain why the $\frac{P}{R}$ ratio in Trial 3 differs from that in Trial 1.

Conclude and Communicate

4. What do your results indicate about the nature of chemical equilibrium for a given "reaction"?
   a. Do the relative starting amounts of R and P affect the $\frac{P}{R}$ ratio? Explain your answer briefly.
   b. Do the relative rates of the forward and reverse reactions affect the amount of reactants and products present at equilibrium? Explain briefly.

Extend Further

5. **INQUIRY** Design another simulation of chemical equilibrium using two plastic basins or small aquaria, water, and two cups. Explain how to carry out the simulation; predict the results.

6. **RESEARCH** Use the Internet to research the history of chemical equilibrium. When was the first chemical equilibrium identified? What was the chemical reaction? Who is credited with the "discovery" of chemical equilibrium?

Table B Transfer Data for Trial 2

	Team R		Team P	
	Quantity of Items	Quantity Transferred	Quantity Transferred	Quantity of Items
Initial Quantities				
Transfer 1				
Outcome				
Transfer 2				
Outcome				
Transfer 3				
Outcome				
Transfer 4				
Outcome				
Transfer 5				
Outcome				

Plan Your Own INVESTIGATION 7-B

Skill Check
✓ Initiating and Planning
✓ Performing and Recording
✓ Analyzing and Interpreting
✓ Communicating

Safety Precautions

- Wear safety eyewear, protective gloves, and a lab coat or apron throughout this investigation.
- Inform your teacher and wash any spills on your skin or clothing with plenty of cool water. Also inform your teacher if you spill chemical compounds or solutions on the lab bench or floor.
- Wash your hands thoroughly when you have completed the investigation.

Suggested Materials
- soda water, fresh (not flat)
- 0.1 mol/L hydrochloric acid, HCl(aq)
- 0.1 mol/L ammonia solution, NH$_3$(aq)
- phenolphthalein solution
- a few small crystals of ammonium chloride, NH$_4$Cl(s)
- large hypodermic syringe with end cap or rubber stopper to seal the tip
- 2 small beakers (25 mL or 50 mL)
- 2 medicine droppers
- graduated cylinder
- 2 small test tubes
- test-tube rack
- white paper
- scoopula

How Does an Equilibrium System Respond to Changing Conditions?

In this investigation, you will use Le Châtelier's principle to predict the effect of changing one factor that affects a system at equilibrium. Then you will design a test to check your prediction by assessing a change of colour or the appearance (or disappearance) of a gas bubbles.

Pre-Lab Questions

1. State Le Châtelier's principle in your own words and explain how it can be used to predict equilibrium shifts when there are concentration, temperature, or pressure changes in a chemical system at equilibrium.

2. Describe three safety precautions that you must take while performing this investigation and explain the possible consequences of not following those precautions. Note: There are multiple caution statements listed in the steps of this investigation.

Question

How can Le Châtelier's principle qualitatively predict the effect of a change in a chemical equilibrium?

Plan and Conduct

Part 1: Investigating Gaseous Equilibrium

Soda water contains carbon dioxide dissolved in an aqueous solution. Carbon dioxide gas reacts with water and forms carbonic acid, H$_2$CO$_3$(aq). The equation representing this equilibrium system is shown below:

$$H_2CO_3(aq) \rightleftharpoons H_2O(\ell) + CO_2(aq)$$

1. With your partner or group, write a procedure to test the effect of pressure/volume changes on soda water. Use the syringe and soda water for this test.
2. Predict the changes in equilibrium that will occur during your test.
3. Construct a data table to record your observations.
4. Obtain your teacher's approval for your procedure, and then carry out your test. Record your observations.

474 MHR • Unit 4 Chemical Systems and Equilibrium

Part 2: Changes to Base Equilibrium System

When ammonia is mixed with water, a hydrogen atom from the water molecule attaches to the ammonia particle and forms the ammonium ion, $NH_4^+(aq)$. When the hydrogen atom is removed from the water molecule, water forms the hydroxide ion, $OH^-(aq)$. The chemical equation below represents the equilibrium system:

$$NH_3(aq) + H_2O(\ell) \rightleftharpoons NH_4^+(aq) + OH^-(aq)$$

1. Pour 10 mL of ammonia solution into a small beaker. **Caution! Hydrochloric acid and aqueous ammonia are corrosive and harmful if swallowed or inhaled.** Place the beaker on a sheet of white paper. Add two drops of phenolphthalein indicator. **Caution! Phenolphthalein solution may irritate skin, eyes, and mucous membranes. This solution is flammable. Keep away from flames.**

2. Divide the solution equally into two small test tubes. Given the list of materials, design a procedure to test Le Châtelier's principle. Describe how you will shift the equilibrium and predict the colour of the phenolphthalein indicator as a result of the shift. Include guidelines for the safe disposal of all materials. **Caution! Ammonium chloride is harmful if inhaled or swallowed and causes skin and eye irritation. Handle with care.**

3. Construct a data table to record your observations.

4. Obtain your teacher's approval for your procedure, and then carry out your test. Record your observations.

Analyze and Interpret

1. Compare your predictions and your actual results for the pressure/volume change test. Were your predictions correct? If not, explain the differences.

2. Do you think the value of K_{eq} changed or remained the same when the pressure changed and equilibrium re-established in the syringe? Explain your answer.

3. Briefly describe the test in which you increased or decreased the concentration of a reactant or product.

    a. Which reactant or product did you change?

    b. Did your observations indicate a shift in equilibrium to form more or less of the reactant or product? Explain your answer.

    c. Was the shift in equilibrium in your test predicted by Le Châtelier's principle? Explain any differences that might have occurred.

4. If you added hydrochloric acid to a test tube during your test in Part 2, what change did you notice? When hydrochloric acid mixes with water, a hydrogen ion and a chloride ion form. How would these additional ions affect the equilibrium system?

5. Do you think the value of K_{eq} changed or remained the same when the concentration changed and equilibrium re-established in the test tube? Explain your answer.

Conclude and Communicate

6. Considering all of the tests that you performed in this investigation, is Le Châtelier's principle reliable in predicting the shift in equilibrium when the conditions are changed for a system at equilibrium? Explain your answer.

Further

7. **INQUIRY** Design an investigation to study how changing the concentration of reactants and products would affect the following equilibrium:

    $$2CrO_4^{2-}(aq) + 2H^+(aq) \rightleftharpoons Cr_2O_7^{2-}(aq) + H_2O(\ell)$$
    yellow   orange

    You have available sodium chromate, $Na_2CrO_4(s)$, sodium dichromate, $Na_2Cr_2O_7(s)$, HCl(aq), NaOH(aq), $BaCl_2(aq)$, and any standard laboratory glassware.
    Hint: $Ba^{2+}(aq) + CrO_4^{2-}(aq) \rightarrow BaCrO_4(s)$

    For each step in your proposed procedure, provide an expected observation.

8. **RESEARCH** Use a print resource or the Internet to research the life and work of Henri Louis Le Châtelier, after whom Le Châtelier's principle is named. In particular, when and where was he born, what was his educational background, and on what work was his famous principle based and when was it first published?

Inquiry INVESTIGATION 7-C

Skill Check
- Initiating and Planning
- ✓ Performing and Recording
- ✓ Analyzing and Interpreting
- ✓ Communicating

Safety Precautions

- Wear safety eyewear throughout this investigation.
- Wear a lab coat or apron throughout this investigation.
- The iron(III) nitrate solution and nitric acid should be handled with care. Immediately wash any spills with plenty of water and inform your teacher.

Materials
- 30 mL of 0.0020 mol/L potassium thiocyanate, KSCN(aq)
- 30 mL of 0.0020 mol/L iron(III) nitrate, $Fe(NO_3)_3$(aq) (acidified)
- 25 mL of 0.200 mol/L iron(III) nitrate, $Fe(NO_3)_3$(aq) (acidified)
- distilled water
- labels or grease pencil
- 5 test tubes (18 mm × 150 mm)
- test-tube rack
- 5 flat-bottom vials or graduated cylinders
- 3 beakers (100 mL)
- 3 graduated pipettes
- pipette bulb
- stirring rod
- paper towel
- thermometer (alcohol or digital)
- strip of paper
- diffuse light source, such as a light box (used by doctors to look at X rays)
- medicine dropper

Using Experimental Data to Determine an Equilibrium Constant

The colour intensity of a solution is related to the type of ions present, their concentration, and the depth of the solution (the linear measure of the solution through which you are looking), as shown by the photographs on the next page. By adjusting the depth of a solution with an unknown concentration until it has the same intensity as a solution with known concentration, you can determine the concentration of the unknown solution. For example, if the concentration of a solution is lower than the standard, the depth of the solution has to be greater in order to have the same colour intensity. For this reason, the ratio of the concentrations of two solutions with the same colour intensity is in inverse ratio to their depths.

In this investigation, you will examine the homogeneous equilibrium between iron(III) ions and thiocyanate ions, and iron(III) thiocyanate ions, $Fe(SCN)^{2+}$(aq): Fe^{3+}(aq) + SCN^-(aq) $\rightleftharpoons$ $Fe(SCN)^{2+}$(aq)

You will prepare four equilibrium mixtures with different initial concentrations of Fe^{3+}(aq) and SCN^-(aq). You will calculate the initial concentrations of these reacting ions from the volumes and concentrations of the stock solution used and the total volumes of the equilibrium mixtures. Then you will determine the concentration of $Fe(SCN)^{2+}$(aq) ions in each mixture by comparing the colour intensity of the mixture with the colour intensity of a solution with known concentration. After you determine the concentration of $Fe(SCN)^{2+}$(aq) ions, you will use it to calculate the concentrations of the other two ions at equilibrium. You will substitute the three concentrations for each mixture into the equilibrium expression to determine the equilibrium constant.

Your teacher might choose to do this investigation as a demonstration. Alternatively, your teacher might have stations set up with solutions already prepared and you will make observations and record the data.

Pre-Lab Questions

1. Write the equilibrium constant expression for this reaction.
2. What data must a chemist have in order to calculate the equilibrium constant for a given equilibrium system?
3. Explain why it is necessary to specify the temperature when stating an equilibrium constant.
4. Describe the emergency procedures that you would follow if your lab partner accidentally got iron(III) nitrate solution in his or her eyes.

Question

What is the value of the equilibrium constant at room temperature for the following reaction? Fe^{3+}(aq) + SCN^-(aq) $\rightleftharpoons$ $Fe(SCN)^{2+}$(aq)

Prediction

Write the equilibrium expression for this reaction.

Procedure

1. Copy the following tables into your notebook, and give them titles. You will use the tables to record your measurements and calculations.

Test Tube #	$Fe(NO_3)_3(aq)$ (mL)	$H_2O(\ell)$ (mL)	KSCN(aq) (mL)	Initial $[SCN^-(aq)]$ (mol/L)
2	5.0	3.0	2.0	
3	5.0	2.0	3.0	
4	5.0	1.0	4.0	
5	5.0	0	5.0	

Vial #	Depth of Solution in Vial (mm)	Depth of Standard Solution (mm)	depth of standard solution / depth of solution in vial
2			
3			
4			
5			

2. Label five test tubes and five vials with the numbers 1 through 5. Label three beakers with the names and concentrations of the stock solutions: 0.0020 mol/L KSCN(aq), 0.0020 mol/L $Fe(NO_3)_3(aq)$, and 0.200 mol/L $Fe(NO_3)_3(aq)$. Pour about 30 mL of each stock solution into its labelled beaker. Be sure to distinguish between the different concentrations of the iron(III) nitrate solutions. Make sure you use the correct solution when needed in the investigation. Measure the volume of each solution as carefully as possible to ensure the accuracy of your results.

3. Prepare the standard solution of $Fe(SCN)^{2+}(aq)$ in test tube 1. Use the 20 mL pipette to transfer 18.0 mL of 0.200 mol/L $Fe(NO_3)_3(aq)$ into the test tube. Then use a 5 mL pipette to add 2.0 mL of 0.0020 mol/L KSCN(aq). The large excess of $Fe^{3+}(aq)$ is to help ensure that essentially all of the $SCN^-(aq)$ will react to form $Fe(SCN)^{2+}(aq)$.

4. Use the pipette to transfer 5.0 mL of 0.0020 mol/L $Fe(NO_3)_3(aq)$ into each of the other four test tubes (labelled 2 to 5).

5. Use the pipette to transfer 3.0, 2.0, 1.0, and 0 mL of distilled water into test tubes 2, 3, 4, and 5, respectively.

6. Use the pipette to transfer 2.0, 3.0, 4.0, and 5.0 mL of 0.0020 mol/L KSCN(aq) into test tubes 2, 3, 4, and 5, respectively. Each of these test tubes should now contain 10.0 mL of solution. Notice that the first table you prepared (in step 1) shows the volumes of the liquids you added to the test tubes. Use a stirring rod to mix each solution, being careful to rinse the rod with water and then dry it with a paper towel before stirring the next solution. Measure and record the temperature of one of the solutions. Assume that all the solutions are at the same temperature.

7. Pour about 5 mL of the standard solution from test tube 1 into vial 1.

8. Pour some of the solution from test tube 2 into vial 2. Look down through vials 1 and 2. Add enough solution to vial 2 to make its colour intensity appear about the same as the colour intensity in vial 1. Use a sheet of white paper as background to make your rough colour intensity comparison.

9. Wrap a sheet of paper around vials 1 and 2 to prevent light from entering the sides of the solutions. Looking down through the vials over a diffuse light source, adjust the volume of the standard solution in vial 1 until the colour intensity in the vials is the same. Use a medicine dropper to remove or add standard solution. Be careful not to add standard solution to vial 2.

10. When the colour intensity is the same in both vials, measure and record the depth of the solution in each vial as carefully as possible.

11. Repeat Procedure steps 9 and 10 using vials 3, 4, and 5.

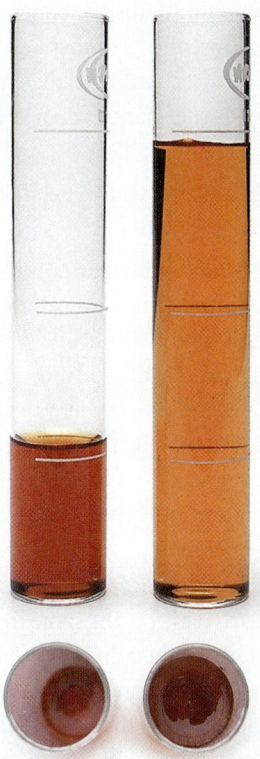

Which solution is the least concentrated? Why is the colour intensity the same when you look vertically through the solutions?

12. Discard the solutions into the container supplied by your teacher. Rinse the test tubes and vials with distilled water, and then return all the equipment. Remember to wash your hands when you have finished.

13. Copy the table below into your notebook to summarize the results of your calculations.

    a. Calculate the equilibrium concentration of $Fe(SCN)^{2+}(aq)$ in the standard solution you prepared in test tube 1. The $[Fe(SCN)^{2+}]_{standard}$ is essentially the same as the starting concentration of $SCN^-(aq)$ in test tube 1. The large excess of $Fe^{3+}(aq)$ ensured that the reaction of $SCN^-(aq)$ was almost complete. However, remember to include the volume of $Fe(NO_3)_3(aq)$ in the total volume of the solution for your calculation.

    b. Calculate the initial concentration of $Fe^{3+}(aq)$ in test tubes 2 to 5. $[Fe^{3+}]$ is the same in these four test tubes. They all contained the same volume of $Fe(NO_3)_3(aq)$, and the total final volume was the same. Remember to use the total volume of the solution in your calculation.

    c. Calculate the initial concentration of $SCN^-(aq)$ in test tubes 2 to 5. $[SCN^-]_i$ is different in each test tube.

    d. Calculate the equilibrium concentration of $Fe(SCN)^{2+}(aq)$ in test tubes 2 to 5. Use the following equation:

    $$[FeSCN^{2+}]_{eq} = \frac{\text{depth of standard solution}}{\text{depth of solution in vial}} \times [FeSCN^{2+}] \text{ standard}$$

    e. Based on the stoichiometry of the reaction, each mole of $Fe(SCN)^{2+}(aq)$ is formed by the reaction of 1 mol $Fe^{3+}(aq)$ with 1 mol $SCN^-(aq)$. Thus, you can determine the equilibrium concentrations of these ions by using the equations below:

    $$[Fe^{3+}]_{eq} = [Fe^{3+}]_i - [Fe(SCN)^{2+}]_{eq}$$
    $$[SCN^-]_{eq} = [SCN^-]_i - [Fe(SCN)^{2+}]_{eq}$$

    f. Calculate four values for the equilibrium constant, K_{eq}, by substituting the equilibrium concentrations into the equilibrium expression. Determine the average of your four values for K_{eq}.

Analyze and Interpret

1. Rank the colour intensity of the solutions in test tubes 2 to 5 from the least to the most intensely coloured. Explain your observations.

2. How consistent were the four K_{eq} values that you determined? Should they have all been the same? Suggest reasons for any differences.

3. What if the equilibrium reaction were as follows?

    $$Fe^{3+}(aq) + 2SCN^-(aq) \rightleftharpoons Fe(SCN)^{2+}(aq) + SCN^-(aq)$$

    a. How, if at all, would the equilibrium concentration of the product be different from the product in the actual reaction? Assume the identical experimental procedure.

    b. How, if at all, would the value of the calculated K_{eq} differ? Explain briefly.

Conclude and Communicate

4. State the equilibrium constant value that you calculated for the given equilibrium, specifying the temperature.

5. Write a conclusion for this investigation, summarizing your results.

6. Explain how Le Châtelier's principle was used in this investigation.

Extend Further

7. **INQUIRY** If you have access to a spectrophotometer, design a procedure to carry out this experiment spectrophotometrically. If your teacher approves your procedure, carry out the investigation.

8. **INQUIRY** How would you modify this investigation in order to determine the equilibrium constant at, say, 40°C? What equipment would be required? What would you do differently? What would you not change?

9. **RESEARCH** Use the Internet to look up the accepted value for the K_{eq} for this reaction at the specified temperature. Calculate the percentage error in your result.

Test Tube #	Initial Concentration (mol/L)		Equilibrium Concentration (mol/L)			Equilibrium Constant, K_{eq}
	$[Fe^{3+}]_i$	$[SCN^-]_i$	$[Fe^{3+}]_{eq}$	$[SCN^-]_{eq}$	$[Fe(SCN)^{2+}]_{eq}$	
1						
2						

STSE
CHEMISTRY Connections

Hemoglobin Rises to the Challenge

When people travel to the mountains, they often feel tired and light-headed for a time because the mountain air contains fewer oxygen molecules, as shown in the graph below. Over time, the fatigue lessens. The body adapts by producing more of the protein hemoglobin.

HEMOGLOBIN-OXYGEN EQUILIBRIUM Hemoglobin, Hb, binds with oxygen molecules that enter your bloodstream, producing oxygenated hemoglobin, $Hb(O_2)_4$. The equilibrium of hemoglobin and oxygen is represented as follows:

$$Hb(aq) + 4O_2(g) \rightleftharpoons Hb(O_2)_4(aq)$$

IN THE LUNGS When you breathe, oxygen molecules move into your blood. The equilibrium reacts to the stress by consuming oxygen molecules at an increased rate. The equilibrium shifts to the right, increasing the blood concentration of $Hb(O_2)_4(aq)$.

$$Hb(aq) + 4O_2(g) \rightleftharpoons Hb(O_2)_4(aq)$$

IN THE TISSUES When the $Hb(O_2)_4$ reaches body tissues where oxygen concentrations are low, the equilibrium shifts to the left, releasing oxygen to enable the metabolic processes that produce energy.

$$Hb(aq) + 4O_2(g) \leftrightharpoons Hb(O_2)_4(aq)$$

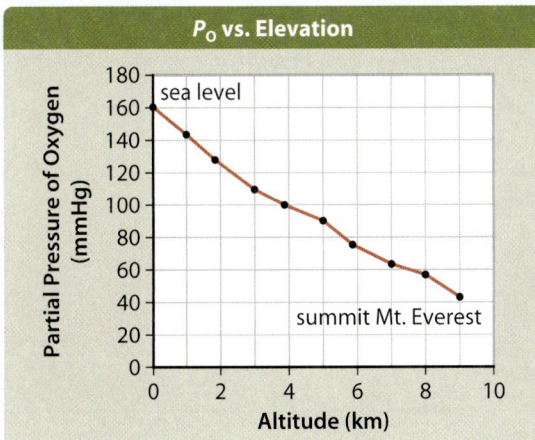

On the summit of Mount Everest, the partial pressure of O_2 is much lower than at the base of the mountain. Therefore, each breath that a person draws contains fewer O_2 molecules.

IN THE MOUNTAINS The equilibrium reacts to the stress of thin mountain air by producing oxygen at an increased rate. The equilibrium shift to the left releases oxygen molecules in your lungs, leaving less oxygenated hemoglobin in your blood.

$$Hb(aq) + 4O_2(g) \rightleftharpoons Hb(O_2)_4(aq)$$

The lower blood concentration of oxygenated hemoglobin means that fewer oxygen molecules are released in other parts of your body. Because less energy is produced, you feel tired.

THE BODY ADJUSTS Your body responds to the lower oxygen concentration by producing more hemoglobin, part of a process known as acclimatization. More hemoglobin shifts the equilibrium position back to the right.

$$Hb(aq) + 4O_2(g) \rightleftharpoons Hb(O_2)_4(aq)$$

The increased concentration of $Hb(O_2)_4(aq)$ means that more oxygen molecules can be released in your body tissues. The illustration below shows where climbers might adjust their bodies to high elevations before beginning their summit climb.

On Mount Everest, a climber might ascend to Camp II, descend to Base Camp, and then ascend to Camp III over the course of several days to prepare for a summit climb.

Connect to Society

1. Conduct research and write a brief summary describing the treatment for altitude sickness, including how equilibrium is restored.

2. Deliberately shifting equilibrium in the human body can provide advantages. Conduct research to find out why some athletes train at high altitudes. Present your findings in a brief report to the class.

3. Blood doping is a problem in many sports. What is blood doping and how is this related to equilibrium? What species in the equilibrium is altered? How does this affect an athlete's ability to compete?

Canadian Research in Action

Applying Equilibrium Principles to Improve Cancer Treatment

The Liu lab team. Back row, left to right: Ying Yi Zhang, Dr. Shijun Yue, Dr. Wei Shi, Lauren Chapman, Dr. Ken Yip, Dr. Philip Wong. Middle row, left to right: Christine How, Lusia Sepiashvili, Michelle Lenarduzzi, Dr. Angela Hui, Dr. Emma Ito, Ronald Wu, Derek Wong. Front row, left to right: Marissa Laureano, Dr. Fei-Fei Liu, Dr. Takashi Kawanaka. Not present: Justin Williams, Jeff Bruce, Mia Labitan.

> **Related Career**
> **Medical oncologists** are medical doctors who specialize in diagnosing and treating cancer. This type of doctor focuses on delivering treatments that reach cancer cells throughout the body, such as chemotherapy. When planning a patient's treatment, medical oncologists may involve other specialists, such as surgical oncologists or radiation oncologists. Becoming an oncologist in Canada involves completion of an undergraduate degree and a degree in medicine, followed by a period of further training, or residency.

Dr. Fei-Fei Liu is a radiation oncologist (a medical doctor who treats cancer through radiation therapy) and a senior scientist at the Princess Margaret Hospital in Toronto. She is also a professor of radiation oncology at the University of Toronto. Dr. Liu and her team of researchers are studying new approaches to cancer therapy.

Dr. Liu's team studied a variety of substances found in cells, such as enzymes, that may be involved in sensitizing cancerous cells to the effects of radiation. Promising results prompted them to look more closely at an enzyme called uroporphyrinogen decarboxylase (UROD).

Dr. Liu's team conducted tests to see what would happen if they blocked the activity of UROD in mice that have tumours. UROD is the fifth enzyme of eight different enzymes that are activated in sequence in the production of heme. Heme is an iron-containing molecule found in the cells of animals, including humans. In the final step of heme production, which occurs naturally in the bodies of animals, iron is added to a "carrier" molecule called protoporphyrin IX. The iron is added to protoporphyrin IX by an enzyme called ferrochelatase (the eighth enzyme involved in producing heme). This reaction releases protons and produces heme when the enzyme ferrochelatase is present in the following reversible reaction:

$$\text{protoporphyrin IX} + \text{iron} \rightleftharpoons \text{heme} + 2\text{H}^+$$

Dr. Liu's team members speculated that blocking UROD in mice would reduce the amount of protoporphyrin IX produced in the cells of the body. Because there is less protoporphyrin IX, the equilibrium shifts to the left. Iron that would normally be used to produce heme therefore accumulates in the cells. This excess iron may then interact with cellular hydrogen peroxide, H_2O_2, through a process called the Fenton reaction. This reaction generates free radicals, which are molecules that have incomplete electron shells, thus making them extremely chemically reactive.

When tumour cells are subsequently exposed to radiation, the free radicals that are normally produced by radiation alone interact with the excess iron in the course of the Fenton reaction. This interaction generates even more toxic radicals, leading ultimately to the destruction of cancerous cells.

Dr. Liu's team members believe that their work will have major implications for cancer therapy.

QUESTIONS

1. Erythropoietic protoporphpria is a disorder in which heme synthesis is disrupted when the enzyme ferrochelatase does not insert iron properly into protoporphyrin IX. Research this disorder and write the chemical reaction for heme synthesis under equilibrium conditions when the disorder is not present.

2. Write the chemical reaction for heme synthesis when this disorder is present.

3. Using Internet and/or print resources, research the roles of the team members who plan and deliver radiation treatment to people battling cancer and write a brief summary of how the skills involved in these careers are combined to provide patient care.

Chapter 7 SUMMARY

Section 7.1 Chemical Systems in Balance

Some reactions do not go to completion, but they reach a state of equilibrium in which the forward and reverse reactions occur at the same rate.

Key Terms

chemical equilibrium
dynamic equilibrium
equilibrium constant, K_{eq}
heterogeneous equilibrium
homogeneous equilibrium
law of chemical equilibrium or law of mass action
reversible reaction

Key Concepts

- A reversible reaction is a chemical reaction that proceeds in both forward and reverse directions.
- Chemical equilibrium is the state in a chemical system in which the forward reaction and the reverse reaction are balanced and occur at the same rates.
- When a chemical system at equilibrium is changing at the molecular level, but its macroscopic properties are constant, the system is said to have dynamic equilibrium.
- In a chemical system at equilibrium, there is a constant ratio between the concentrations of the products and the concentrations of the reactants and this ratio is the equilibrium constant, K_{eq}.
- Because K_{eq} is a ratio of product concentration to reactant concentration, a value of K_{eq} greater than 1 means that the concentration of products is greater than the concentration of reactants. A value of K_{eq} less than 1 means that the concentration of reactants is greater than the concentration of products. When K_{eq} is equal to 1, there are equal concentrations of reactants and products.

Section 7.2 The Effects of External Changes on Equilibrium

When a chemical system at equilibrium is disturbed, the system undergoes predictable changes.

Key Terms

Le Châtelier's principle

Key Concepts

- Le Châtelier's principle states that if an external stress (a change in concentration, pressure, volume, or temperature) is applied to a chemical system at equilibrium, the rates of the forward and reverse reactions are temporarily unequal because the stress affects the reaction rates. However, equilibrium is eventually restored in the chemical system.
- Only a temperature change affects K_{eq}. In a system that is endothermic in the forward direction, a temperature rise increases K_{eq}. If the forward reaction is exothermic, a temperature rise decreases K_{eq}.
- Adding a catalyst causes a system to reach equilibrium in a shorter period of time, but it does not shift the equilibrium in either direction.

Section 7.3 Calculating Equilibrium Constants

Equilibrium constants can be calculated and used to predict the concentrations of the components in a chemical system.

Key Terms

quadratic equation
quadratic formula
reaction quotient

Key Concepts

- The numerical value of the equilibrium constant is calculated by using the equilibrium constant expression.
- In a chemical equilibrium system composed of gases, the partial pressures of the gases can be used to calculate the equilibrium constant if the gases behave like ideal gases.
- You can determine information about an equilibrium system by organizing known information into an ICE table.
- If the equilibrium constant for a reaction is very small, you can make assumptions that will simplify the mathematical calculations for predicting the resultant concentrations of components in a chemical system.
- You can experimentally measure the macroscopic properties of an equilibrium system, such as colour intensity, and use them to calculate the equilibrium concentration of a product or reactant.

Chapter 7 | SUMMARY & REVIEW

Section 7.4 | Applications of Equilibrium Systems

Many chemical equilibrium systems occur in nature, and some industrial processes include chemical equilibrium systems.

Key Terms
hemoglobin
syngas

Key Concepts
- If a diver rapidly returns to the surface from a deep dive, the change in the equilibrium between dissolved nitrogen and gaseous nitrogen causes bubbles to form in the blood vessels, resulting in a serious condition called "the bends."
- The equilibrium constant for the reaction of hemoglobin with carbon monoxide is about 250 times greater than the equilibrium constant for the reaction with oxygen.
- An understanding of the effects of pressure and temperature on the position of equilibrium between nitrogen and hydrogen gases and ammonia allowed Haber and Bosch to develop an efficient method for synthesizing ammonia.
- Knowledge of the equilibrium reactions that are important in the production of sulfuric acid and of methanol makes it possible to produce these very important products in large amounts.

Knowledge and Understanding

Select the letter of the best answer below.

1. Which description best represents the process of equilibrium?
   a. a reaction with no macroscopic changes
   b. a reaction in which the reactants and products are in the gaseous phase
   c. a reaction that occurs in a closed container
   d. a reaction in which the rates of the forward and reverse processes are equal
   e. a reversible chemical reaction

2. Which of the following is most similar to a system at equilibrium?
   a. a shift change at an assembly plant involving two crews of 100 workers
   b. a popcorn maker when the popcorn starts to pop
   c. the water in a pool when swimmers start to splash the water out of the pool
   d. a burning candle
   e. salt concentrations in the oceans

3. Which is true of a reaction with a small value for K_{eq}?
   a. Reactants and products are approximately in the same concentration at equilibrium.
   b. Equilibrium is rarely established for the reaction.
   c. Most of the particles in the container are reactant particles.
   d. Most of the particles in the container are product particles.
   e. The reverse reaction occurs at a much slower rate than does the forward reaction.

4. Which can be used as a macroscopic property to monitor a reaction that could reach equilibrium?
   a. a change in colour intensity
   b. a change in pressure
   c. a change in concentration
   d. a change in temperature
   e. All of the above can be used.

5. Which is an example of a heterogeneous equilibrium system?
   a. $2H_2(g) + O_2(g) \rightleftharpoons 2H_2O(g)$
   b. $NO_2(g) + NO(g) \rightleftharpoons N_2O_3(g)$
   c. $PCl_5(g) \rightleftharpoons PCl_3(g) + Cl_2(g)$
   d. $Cu^{2+}(aq) + 2OH^-(aq) \rightleftharpoons Cu(OH)_2(s)$
   e. $Fe^{3+}(aq) + SCN^-(aq) \rightleftharpoons FeSCN^{2+}(aq)$

6. For the reaction $CO(g) + NO_2(g) \rightleftharpoons CO_2(g) + NO(g)$, which result will occur if the container experiences a decrease in volume?
   a. There will be no effect on the system.
   b. The reaction will shift to the left.
   c. The reaction will shift to the right.
   d. The reaction will heat up.
   e. The reaction will cool down.

7. When heat is added to a system at equilibrium, and the reaction shifts to the left, which statement is correct with respect to the reaction?
   a. It is endothermic as written.
   b. It is exothermic as written.
   c. It can be either endothermic or exothermic in the direction written.
   d. Nothing can be concluded with respect to the reaction being exothermic or endothermic.
   e. The reaction has a heat term on each side of the reaction.

8. A system at equilibrium has more of a reactant gas injected into the container. Which statement is most correct with respect to the reaction after the injection?
   a. A new equilibrium position is established with a new K_{eq} value that is larger than the original K_{eq}.
   b. A new equilibrium position is established with a new K_{eq} value that is smaller than the original K_{eq}.
   c. A new K_{eq} now exists and must be experimentally determined.
   d. A new equilibrium position is established with the same K_{eq} as the original system.
   e. The original equilibrium position is re-established with a slightly larger K_{eq} value.

9. In a chemical system at equilibrium, there is a constant ratio between the concentrations of the products and the concentrations of the reactants, according to
   a. Le Châtelier's principle.
   b. the law of chemical equilibrium.
   c. the law of mass action.
   d. two of the above choices.
   e. a, b, and c.

10. For the system below, which action will cause an equilibrium shift to the right?
$$N_2(g) + O_2(g) \rightleftharpoons 2NO(g)$$
   a. increasing [NO]
   b. increasing pressure
   c. decreasing volume
   d. adding a catalyst
   e. adding $O_2(g)$

11. For the system below, which action will cause an equilibrium shift to the left?
$$2NOCl(g) + energy \rightleftharpoons 2NO(g) + Cl_2(g)$$
   a. an increase in temperature
   b. a decrease in pressure
   c. a decrease in volume
   d. removal of $Cl_2(g)$
   e. All of these will cause a shift to the left.

12. For the reaction
$$2SO_2(g) + O_2(g) \rightleftharpoons 2SO_3(g),$$
K_{eq} equals K_1. For the reaction
$$SO_2(g) + \frac{1}{2}O_2(g) \rightleftharpoons SO_3(g),$$
K_{eq} equals K_2. Which relationship is true?
   a. $K_1 = \sqrt{K_2}$
   b. $K_2 = \sqrt{K_1}$
   c. $K_2 = \dfrac{K_1}{2}$
   d. $K_1 = \dfrac{K_2}{2}$
   e. $K_1 = K_2$

13. What is the name given to the manufacturing process that is used to generate ammonia?
   a. the Bends process
   b. Le Châtelier's process
   c. the Haber-Bosch process
   d. the Ammonia Fixation process
   e. the Bohr-Rutherford process

Answer the questions below.

14. Explain why a pot of boiling water on a stove can never reach equilibrium.

15. Does a small value for the equilibrium constant of a reaction indicate that the reaction proceeds slowly? Justify your answer.

16. Iodine crystals are placed in a stoppered flask as shown below. Explain why this chemical system has dynamic equilibrium.

17. The following system is at equilibrium:
$$2CO_2(g) \rightleftharpoons 2CO(g) + O_2(g)$$
Will an increase in pressure shift the equilibrium to the left or to the right? Explain your reasoning.

18. Consider the following reaction:
$$CO(g) + 3H_2(g) \rightleftharpoons CH_4(g) + H_2O(g)$$
The volume and temperature are kept constant, but adding argon, a non-reacting gas, increases the pressure on the system. Does this affect the equilibrium? If so, how? If not, explain your answer in one or two well-reasoned sentences.

Chapter 7 REVIEW

19. In a chemical system at equilibrium, are the concentrations of reactants and products in the same ratio as the coefficients in the chemical equation? Explain your answer.

20. At equilibrium, there is no overall change in the concentrations of reactants and products. Why is this state described as being dynamic?

21. Label each system as a homogeneous equilibrium or a heterogeneous equilibrium:
    a. $CaCO_3(s) + 2HF(g) \rightleftharpoons CaF_2(s) + H_2O(g) + CO_2(g)$
    b. $Na_2SO_4(aq) \rightarrow 2Na^+(aq) + SO_4^{2-}(aq)$
    c. $2NaHSO_3(s) \rightleftharpoons Na_2SO_3(s) + H_2O(g) + SO_2(g)$

22. Describe the changes that take place on a molecular level as a reversible reaction approaches equilibrium. Explain why the equilibrium that is reached is dynamic.

23. The graph below represents what is occurring in a closed reaction vessel. Explain the changes that occurred over time in the vessel.

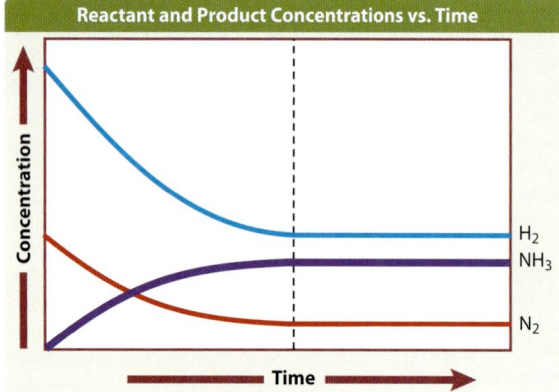

24. In the following reaction, the products are not favoured at room temperature, but are favoured at a much higher temperature.

    $$CO_2(g) + H_2(g) \rightleftharpoons CO(g) + H_2O(g)$$

    On the basis of this information, predict whether the reaction is exothermic or endothermic. Explain your answer.

25. A reaction is at equilibrium at a given temperature. The reaction is given as follows:

    $$aA(g) + bB(g) \rightleftharpoons cC(g) + dD(g) + heat$$

    Explain how this reaction can be at a constant temperature at equilibrium even when the reaction is exothermic as written.

26. Explain why a change in pressure in a container with the following equilibrium reaction will have no effect on the position of equilibrium.

    $$PbI_2(s) \rightleftharpoons Pb^{2+}(aq) + 2I^-(aq)$$

27. During an investigation of a heterogeneous reaction involving materials in all three states of matter, your lab partner removes the stopper of the flask to better observe the colour of the solution inside. Explain why doing this is not a good idea, using concepts studied in this chapter.

28. Write the equilibrium expression for each of the following homogeneous reactions:
    a. The reaction between propane and oxygen to form carbon dioxide and water vapour:
       $$C_3H_8(g) + 5O_2(g) \rightleftharpoons 3CO_2(g) + 4H_2O(g)$$
    b. The reaction between the rocket fuel hydrazine, $N_2H_4(g)$, and oxygen:
       $$N_2H_4(g) + 2O_2(g) \rightleftharpoons 2NO(g) + 2H_2O(g)$$
    c. The reaction to form a copper–ammonia complex:
       $$Cu^{2+}(aq) + 4NH_3(aq) \rightleftharpoons Cu(NH_3)_4^{2+}(aq)$$

29. When an equilibrium process is studied, it is found that the K_{eq} value is extremely large.
    a. What does this mean in terms of the favoured formation?
    b. What does this mean in terms of the K_{eq} of the reaction where reactant and product roles are reversed in this process? Fully explain your reasoning in three or four sentences.

30. Name the factors that can affect the equilibrium of a reaction.

31. Write K_p expressions for each of the following reactions:
    a. $C(s) + H_2O(g) \rightleftharpoons H_2(g) + CO(g)$
    b. $HSO_4^-(aq) + H_2O(\ell) \rightleftharpoons H_3O^+(aq) + SO_4^{2-}(aq)$
    c. $Fe_2O_3(s) + 3H_2(g) \rightleftharpoons 2Fe(s) + 3H_2O(g)$
    d. $PCl_5(g) + 2NO(g) \rightleftharpoons 2NOCl(g) + PCl_3(g)$

Thinking and Investigation

32. For the reaction below, which is the equilibrium concentration of $NO_2(g)$ if $[N_2O_4] = 4.18$ mol/L?
    $$N_2O_4(g) \rightleftharpoons 2NO_2(g) \quad K_{eq} = 0.21 \text{ at } 375 \text{ K}$$
    a. 1.07 mol/L
    b. 0.94 mol/L
    d. 1.14 mol/L
    c. 0.88 mol/L
    e. 4.18 mol/L

33. In each of the following reactions, explain the effect of increasing the concentration of oxygen gas on the position of equilibrium.
    a. $N_2(g) + 2O_2(g) \rightleftharpoons 2NO_2(g)$
    b. $4NO(g) + 6H_2O(g) \rightleftharpoons 4NH_3(g) + 5O_2(g)$
    c. $CH_4(g) + 2O_2(g) \rightleftharpoons CO_2(g) + 2H_2O(g)$

34. For the reaction below, $K_{eq} = 0.74$ at 600 K. If 1.41 mol of carbon dioxide, $CO_2(g)$, and 2.61 mol of hydrogen, $H_2(g)$, are placed into a 1.50 L container and then allowed to reach equilibrium at 600 K, what will be the equilibrium amount of CO(g) in the container?
$$CO_2(g) + H_2(g) \rightleftharpoons CO(g) + H_2O(g)$$

35. Consider an equilibrium system in which oxygen gas reacts with hydrogen chloride to form gaseous water and chlorine gas. At equilibrium, the gases have the following concentrations:

$[O_2] = 8.6 \times 10^{-2}$ mol/L
$[HCl] = 2.7 \times 10^{-2}$ mol/L
$[H_2O] = 7.8 \times 10^{-3}$ mol/L
$[Cl_2] = 3.6 \times 10^{-3}$ mol/L

a. Write the chemical equation for this reaction.
b. Calculate the value of the equilibrium constant.

36. In the reaction shown below, the oxidation of sulfur dioxide, $SO_2(g)$, to sulfur trioxide, $SO_3(g)$, is an important reaction in the process used to manufacture sulfuric acid. At 1000 K, the equilibrium constant for the reaction is 3.6×10^{-3}. If you add 3.8 mol/L of sulfur dioxide and the same concentration of oxygen into a closed container, what will be the concentration of sulfur trioxide at equilibrium when the reaction vessel is maintained at 1000 K?
$$2SO_2(g) + O_2(g) \rightleftharpoons 2SO_3(g)$$

37. The following results were collected for two investigations involving the reaction, at 600°C, between gaseous sulfur dioxide and oxygen to form gaseous sulfur trioxide. Show that the value of K_{eq} was the same in both investigations.

Experiment 1

Initial Concentration (mol/L)	Equilibrium Concentration (mol/L)
$[SO_2] = 2.00$	$[SO_2] = 1.50$
$[O_2] = 1.50$	$[O_2] = 1.25$
$[SO_3] = 3.00$	$[SO_3] = 3.50$

Experiment 2

Initial Concentration (mol/L)	Equilibrium Concentration (mol/L)
$[SO_2] = 0.500$	$[SO_2] = 0.590$
$[O_2] = 0$	$[O_2] = 0.0450$
$[SO_3] = 0.350$	$[SO_3] = 0.260$

38. A student has mixed two gases together in a closed container at a constant temperature and noted a colour change until the intensity of the colour reached a constant. The conclusion drawn was that the system had reached equilibrium. Is this conclusion correct? Explain your answer in a well-reasoned paragraph.

39. What is occurring on the molecular level in the reaction below to cause a shift in the forward direction due to a decrease in the volume of the container?
$$2NO_2(g) + O_2(g) \rightleftharpoons 2NO_3(g)$$

40. Hydrogen for the Haber-Bosch process can be obtained by the following endothermic reaction:
$$CH_4(g) + 2H_2O(g) \rightleftharpoons CO_2(g) + 4H_2(g)$$
How would the concentration of hydrogen be affected by each of the following changes to an equilibrium mixture of gases in a rigid container?

a. increasing the amount of methane
b. increasing the amount of carbon dioxide
c. decreasing the amount of water vapour
d. raising the temperature
e. adding a catalyst
f. adding helium gas to the mixture
g. transferring the mixture of gases to a container with greater volume

41. The reaction below is being studied in an investigation. Which condition should you alter to shift the reaction to the right: a decrease in volume or a decrease in temperature? Explain your answer.
$$H_2(g) + Cl_2(g) \rightleftharpoons 2HCl(g) + \text{heat}$$

42. Use reaction rate expressions to show how the K_{eq} expression is obtained for the following reaction:
$$2NO_2(g) \rightleftharpoons N_2O_4(g)$$

43. Write the chemical equation for the reversible reaction that has the following equilibrium expression (all are gases):
$$K_{eq} = \frac{[NO]^4[H_2O]^6}{[NH_3]^4[O_2]^5}$$
Assume that, at a certain temperature at equilibrium, [NO] and [NH$_3$] are equal. If $[H_2O] = 2.0$ mol/L and $[O_2] = 3.0$ mol/L at this temperature, what is the value of K_{eq}?

Chapter 7 REVIEW

Communication

44. Most equilibrium systems are monitored using a macroscopic property that can be measured. Create a chart or other similar graphic organizer to give some examples of macroscopic properties that can be used to monitor reactions as they proceed to equilibrium. Include a column in your chart to indicate how each property can be monitored.

45. Equal amounts of hydrogen gas and iodine vapour are heated in a sealed flask.
   a. Sketch a graph to show how [H_2] and [I_2] change over time.
   b. Would you expect a graph of [I_2] and [HI] to appear much different from your first graph? Explain why.

46. You work at a science centre that has opened a new exhibit area devoted to practical applications of chemistry. Write text for a sign for visitors explaining how the beverage below is preserved.

47. Draw a concentration-time graph to illustrate a reaction that goes to completion and a concentration-time graph to illustrate a reaction that reaches equilibrium.

48. Develop a short presentation for your class to explain the process of nitrogen narcosis. Include in your presentation similarities and differences between nitrogen narcosis and carbon monoxide poisoning.

49. Explain, with the use of a diagram, why changes to a macroscopic property occur more slowly as the reaction approaches and reaches equilibrium, compared with the changes that occur at the start of the reaction.

50. Draw a graphic organizer to illustrate how you could determine the difference between a reaction that has gone to completion and one that is at equilibrium.

51. Create a poster for your classroom to outline the interpretation for K_{eq} values in terms of concentrations of reactants and products for the following situations:

$$K_{eq} > 1, K_{eq} \approx 1, K_{eq} < 1$$

52. Write an e-mail to a classmate who is studying for an exam and has asked for your help in explaining, using Le Châtelier's principle, how temperature affects an equilibrium system with an exothermic forward reaction.

53. Research a biological system in the human body that is controlled by an equilibrium process. Present your findings in a fact sheet with diagrams for posting in the classroom.

54. Summarize your learning in this chapter using a graphic organizer. To help you, the Chapter 7 Summary lists the Key Terms and Key Concepts. Refer to Using Graphic Organizers in Appendix A to help you decide which graphic organizer to use.

55. **BIG IDEAS** Chemical systems are dynamic and respond to changing conditions in predictable ways. Develop a brief lesson, including appropriate visual support, designed to teach this concept to advanced Grade 11 chemistry students.

56. **BIG IDEAS** Applications of chemical systems at equilibrium have significant implications for nature and industry. Research one such application other than those described in this chapter and make a brief presentation of your findings to your class.

Application

57. In economics, the laws governing supply and demand suggest that if the price of a commodity such as a kilogram of sugar is constant, the market for this commodity is balanced. If the supply of sugar falls, the market adjusts by increasing the price per kilogram. This can cause the demand to fall and not as much sugar is purchased. The increased supply can cause a decrease in price. Explain, in a short, well-reasoned paragraph, how this situation is similar to an equilibrium system in a chemical process.

58. Agree or disagree with the following statement, and give reasons to support your answer: "In a sealed jar of water at equilibrium, the quantity of water molecules in the liquid state equals the quantity of molecules in the gaseous state."

59. Jacques Cousteau was a famous underwater explorer. When diving to depths of 100 m, he used a mixture of gases consisting of 98% helium and 2% oxygen. At 100 m below the surface, the pressure of water is 10 atm. Why did Cousteau use this particular mix of helium and oxygen?

60. Using a labelled flowchart, outline the process of manufacturing methanol, starting from the methane obtained from natural gas. Include all reactions involved in the steps of the process.

61. An industrial company is interested in using the reaction below as a way of generating nitrogen monoxide, NO(g), while not polluting the atmosphere (as oxygen gas is the only other product in the process). Describe five possible ways in which the company can increase the yield of their product.

$$2NO_2(g) + \text{energy} \rightleftharpoons 2NO(g) + O_2(g)$$

62. Dinitrogen monoxide, $N_2O(g)$ (also known as laughing gas), is used as an anesthetic in dentistry. It can be made in many ways, but once made, it has a tendency to decompose into nitrogen gas and oxygen gas according to the following equation:

$$2N_2O(g) \rightleftharpoons 2N_2(g) + O_2(g)$$

The K_{eq} for this reaction at 25°C is 7.3×10^{34}. What can be said about the tendency of dinitrogen monoxide to decompose into nitrogen gas and oxygen gas?

63. Ethyne, $C_2H_2(g)$ (also known as acetylene), is used in the process of oxyacetylene gas welding. It can be generated in an equilibrium reaction as follows:

$$2CH_4(g) \rightleftharpoons C_2H_2(g) + 3H_2(g)$$

At 500 K, $K_{eq} = 702$. At 500 K, a mixture of these gases has the following concentrations: $[CH_4] = 4.76$ mol/L, $[C_2H_2] = 15.74$ mol/L, and $[H_2] = 4.75$ mol/L.

  a. Determine Q_{eq} for the system.
  b. Is the system at equilibrium? If it is not, indicate the direction toward which the system will move to reach equilibrium.

64. Whenever fuels are burned at high temperatures, impurities in the fuels such as nitrogen gas cause air pollution (smog). The reaction is represented by the following equation:

$$N_2(g) + O_2(g) \rightleftharpoons 2NO(g)$$

At 1500 K, $K_{eq} = 1.1 \times 10^{-5}$. A 1.00 L sample of air is found to contain the following concentrations: $[N_2(g)] = 0.80$ mol/L and $[O_2(g)] = 0.20$ mol/L. When heated to 1500 K, what will be the equilibrium concentration of NO(g) in the container?

65. Research the sleep disorder apnea. How would an incident of sleep apnea affect the body's hemoglobin–oxygen equilibrium?

66. You are performing a reaction to generate hydrogen gas and iodine gas by decomposing hydrogen iodide gas in a lab. The reaction is as follows:

$$2HI(g) \rightleftharpoons H_2(g) + I_2(g)$$

K_{eq} equals 0.022 at the temperature you are using in the lab. Initially, 2.62 mol of hydrogen iodide is placed into a 1.15 L container. What will be the equilibrium concentrations of all substances?

67. One of the steps in the Ostwald process for the manufacture of nitric acid, HNO_3(aq), involves the oxidation of ammonia:

$$4NH_3(g) + 5O_2(g) \rightleftharpoons 4NO(g) + 6H_2O(g)$$
$$\Delta H_r = -905 \text{ kJ}$$

  a. State the reaction conditions that favour the production of nitrogen monoxide.
  b. A rhodium/platinum alloy is used as a catalyst. What effect does using a catalyst have on the position of equilibrium?
  c. Explain why the reaction temperature is relatively high, typically about 900°C.
  d. A relatively low pressure is used, about 7 atm. Suggest an explanation for this.

In the next step of the Ostwald process, nitrogen monoxide is mixed with oxygen to form nitrogen dioxide:

$$2NO(g) + O_2(g) \rightleftharpoons 2NO_2(g) \quad \Delta H_r = -115 \text{ kJ}$$

  e. Why are the gases cooled for this reaction? What do you think happens to the heat extracted?

Finally, the nitrogen dioxide reacts with water to form nitric acid:

$$3NO_2(g) + H_2O(\ell) \rightleftharpoons 2HNO_3(aq) + NO(g)$$

68. During an investigation of the reaction below, you obtained the following data. Which of the following experiments are at equilibrium when the measurements were taken at 373 K?

$$N_2O_4(g) \rightleftharpoons 2NO_2(g) \quad K_{eq} = 0.21 \text{ at } 373 \text{ K}$$

Experiment	Measured $[N_2O_4]$ (mol/L)	Measured $[NO_2]$ (mol/L)
1	0.052	0.104
2	0.082	0.074
3	0.018	0.630
4	0.0065	0.037

69. How could athletes apply knowledge of hemoglobin–oxygen equilibrium to design a program to enhance their cardiovascular fitness?

Chapter 7 | SELF-ASSESSMENT

Select the letter of the best answer below.

1. **K/U** For a system that involves a decomposition reaction in the forward direction, what must be true of the reverse reaction if the system can reach equilibrium?
   a. The reverse reaction is a synthesis reaction.
   b. The reverse reaction can occur when heated.
   c. The reverse reaction must be exothermic.
   d. The reverse reaction occurs in an open system.
   e. The reverse reaction must be a slower reaction.

2. **K/U** What is the most common reaction that generates carbon monoxide in homes?
   a. a complete combustion of hydrocarbons
   b. a single displacement reaction involving carbon and oxygen compounds
   c. oxygen removal from carbon dioxide
   d. an incomplete combustion of hydrocarbons
   e. simple synthesis between solid carbon and oxygen gases

3. **K/U** When is a system at equilibrium said to be dynamic?
   a. just prior to equilibrium being established
   b. at the start of the process when only reactants are present in the container
   c. when the system is changing at the molecular level with no change at the macroscopic level
   d. when the system is changing at the macroscopic level with no change at the molecular level
   e. when the system reaches constant pressure

4. **A** Which systems can reach equilibrium under proper conditions?
   a. a combustion reaction
   b. the reaction of hydrogen and oxygen gases to form water vapour
   c. baking soda and vinegar
   d. a solid dissolved into a solution
   e. Two of the above systems can reach equilibrium under proper conditions.

5. **K/U** What condition(s) is (are) required for a system to be at equilibrium?
   a. The system must be closed.
   b. The temperature must be constant.
   c. The forward and reverse reactions rates must be equal.
   d. There must be no changes of macroscopic properties.
   e. All of these are required.

6. **K/U** Which statement best describes the effect of a system moving toward equilibrium if a catalyst is added to the reaction?
   a. The K_{eq} will be larger.
   b. The K_{eq} will be smaller.
   c. The temperature increases.
   d. The temperature decreases.
   e. The system reaches equilibrium faster.

7. **K/U** "If an external stress is applied to a system at equilibrium, the rates of the forward and reverse reactions are temporarily unequal, until equilibrium is restored to the system." This is a statement of
   a. the law of chemical equilibrium.
   b. the law of mass action.
   c. Le Châtelier's principle.
   d. the law of stressed systems.
   e. the law of equilibrium restoration.

Use sentences and diagrams as appropriate to answer the questions below.

8. **T/I** For the reaction $CO_2(g) + H_2(g) \rightleftharpoons CO(g) + H_2O(g)$, $K_{eq} = 4.9 \times 10^{-3}$. At equilibrium, it is determined that $[CO] = [H_2O] = 0.11$ mol/L. If it is also known that $[CO_2] = [H_2]$ at equilibrium, what is this equilibrium concentration?

9. **T/I** In the preparation of ammonia, the reaction is $N_2(g) + 3H_2(g) \rightleftharpoons 2NH_3(g) +$ heat. What are the best conditions for a high yield of $NH_3(g)$?

10. **A** Explain why a deep-sea diver recovering artifacts from an ancient shipwreck must rise slowly to the surface.

11. **K/U** Briefly explain why solids and pure liquids are not included in equilibrium constant expressions.
12. **C** Write a paragraph to explain the historical significance of the Haber-Bosch process for producing ammonia.
13. **K/U** Explain why partial pressures can be used to write an equilibrium constant expression.
14. **A** Slush is a prominent feature of Canadian winters. Under what conditions do ice and water form an equilibrium mixture?
15. **K/U** In the photograph below, mixtures of $NO_2(g)$ and $N_2O_4(g)$ are at equilibrium. Explain why the contents of the sealed tubes are of different colours.

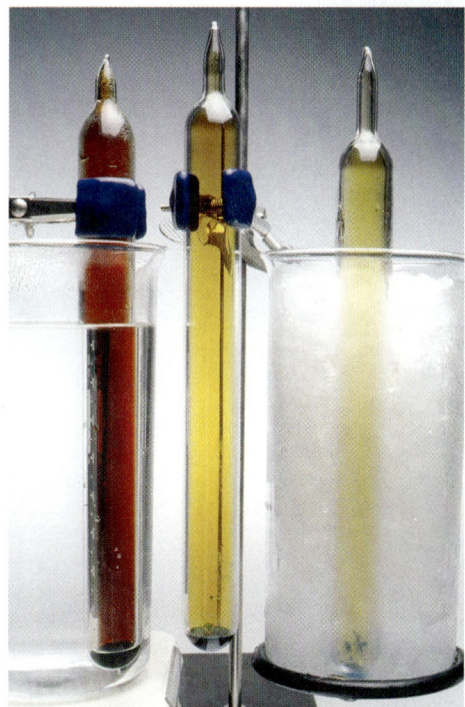

16. **T/I** Explain why a change in volume has no effect on the position of equilibrium in the following reaction: $H_2(g) + I_2(g) \rightleftharpoons 2HI(g)$
17. **C** Draw a diagram and explain what is occurring on the molecular level for the reaction given below, when the forward reaction rate increases after chlorine is added to the system.
$$PCl_3(g) + Cl_2(g) \rightleftharpoons PCl_5(g)$$

18. **K/U** Indicate the direction in which the reaction given below will shift under each of the given stresses: $H_2(g)$ is added, an inert gas is added, the volume is decreased, the system is heated, and $NH_3(g)$ is removed.
$$N_2(g) + 3H_2(g) \rightleftharpoons 2NH_3(g)$$
19. **K/U** Which change(s) in the previous question will cause a change to the K_{eq} value?
20. **T/I** Nitrosyl chloride, $NOCl(g)$, decomposes into nitrogen monoxide, $NO(g)$, and chlorine, $Cl_2(g)$, as described by the following reaction:
$$2NOCl(g) \rightleftharpoons 2NO(g) + Cl_2(g)$$
At 310 K, K_{eq} for this reaction is 1.6×10^{-5}. If 1.00 mol of nitrosyl chloride is placed into a 2.00 L container and the system is allowed to reach equilibrium at 310 K, what are the equilibrium concentrations of the products?
21. **T/I** An equilibrium mixture of dinitrogen oxide, $N_2O(g)$, nitrogen, $N_2(g)$, and oxygen, $O_2(g)$ is found to contain 0.14 mol $N_2O(g)$, 3.54 mol $N_2(g)$, and 4.41 mol $O_2(g)$ in a 3.50 L container. What is K_{eq} for the reaction?
$$2N_2O(g) \rightleftharpoons 2N_2(g) + O_2(g)$$
22. **T/I** During an investigation of the reaction given below, you analyze a mixture of gases at a given temperature and find the following partial pressures: $P_{SO_3} = 1.54$ atm, $P_{SO_2} = 4.54$ atm, and $P_{O_2} = 2.12$ atm.
$$2SO_3(g) \rightleftharpoons 2SO_2(g) + O_2(g)$$
Determine the Q_p for this system.
23. **A** Explain how your body controls the carbonic acid level in your blood governed by this reaction:
$$H_2CO_3(aq) \rightleftharpoons CO_2(g) + H_2O(\ell)$$
24. **T/I** At 1000 K, $K_p = 0.013$ for the following reaction:
$$2NO(g) + Br_2(g) \rightleftharpoons 2NOBr(g)$$
The partial pressures for the gases at equilibrium are $P_{NO} = 1.71$ atm and $P_{Br_2} = 0.71$ atm. What is the equilibrium partial pressure of $NOBr(g)$ at equilibrium in this mixture?
25. **C** Create a poster for the Haber-Bosch process outlining the reaction, the conditions used to optimize the product yield, and some everyday uses of the product.

Self-Check

If you missed question…	1	2	3	4	5	6	7	8	9	10	11	12	13	14	15	16	17	18	19	20	21	22	23	24	25
Review section(s)…	7.1	7.4	7.1	7.2	7.1	7.3	7.2	7.2	7.4	7.4	7.1	7.4	7.3	7.2, 7.3	7.1	7.2	7.2	7.2	7.3	7.3	7.3	7.4	7.3	7.3

CHAPTER 8
Acid-Base Equilibrium Systems

Specific Expectations

In this chapter, you will learn how to…

- **E1.1 analyze** the optimal conditions for a specific chemical process related to the principles of equilibrium that takes place in nature or is used in industry (8.4)

- **E1.2 assess** the impact of chemical equilibrium processes on various biological, biochemical, and technological systems (8.4)

- **E2.3 conduct** an inquiry to **determine** the value of an equilibrium constant for a chemical reaction (8.2, 8.4)

- **E2.4 solve** problems related to equilibrium by **performing** calculations involving concentrations of reactants and products (8.1, 8.2, 8.3, 8.4)

- **E2.5 solve** problems related to acid-base equilibrium, using acid-base titration data and the pH at the equivalence point (8.4)

- **E3.4 identify** common equilibrium constants including K_{eq}, K_{sp}, K_w, K_a, K_b, and K_p, and **write** the expressions for each (8.1, 8.2, 8.3, 8.4)

- **E3.5 use** the ion-product constant of water (K_w) to **calculate** pH, pOH, [H_3O^+], and [OH^-] for chemical reactions (8.1)

- **E3.6 explain** the Brønsted-Lowry theory of acids and bases (8.1, 8.2, 8.3)

- **E3.7 compare** the properties of strong and weak acids, and strong and weak bases, using the concept of dynamic equilibrium (8.2)

- **E3.8 describe** the chemical characteristics of buffer solutions (8.4)

Acid-base equilibrium has a significant impact on organisms inhabiting Earth's oceans. At the surface of the ocean, atmospheric carbon dioxide is in equilibrium with carbon dioxide dissolved in the ocean water. The dissolved carbon dioxide reacts with water and forms carbonic acid, $H_2CO_3(aq)$. As the level of carbonic acid increases, the acidity of the water increases. Many calcium-secreting organisms, such as coral, do not thrive in water that is acidic. However, jellyfish can thrive in some areas where changes in acid-base equilibrium are occurring. As these observations demonstrate, when the acid-base equilibrium of the oceans changes, the marine life also changes.

Launch Lab

A "Sponge" for Acids and Bases

In this activity, you will prepare a solution that can withstand the addition of considerable quantities of acid or base while maintaining a constant pH.

Safety Precautions

- Wear safety eyewear throughout this activity.
- Wear gloves and a lab coat or apron throughout this activity.
- If you get chemical compounds on your skin, flush with plenty of cold water.

Materials

- universal indicator, in dropper bottle
- 1 mol/L hydrochloric acid, HCl(aq), in dropper bottle
- 1 mol/L sodium hydroxide, NaOH(aq), in dropper bottle
- 20 mL of 1 mol/L sodium hydroxide, NaOH(aq)
- 50 mL of vinegar (0.83 mol/L acetic acid solution, CH_3COOH(aq))
- distilled water, in wash bottle
- 100 mL graduated cylinder
- three 150 mL or 200 mL beakers
- stirring rod
- pH meter or pH test strips

Procedure

1. Pour 50 mL of vinegar into an empty beaker. Add 4 to 5 drops of universal indicator. Observe and record the colour and the pH. Then add 20 mL of 1 mol/L sodium hydroxide. Observe and record the colour and the pH.
2. Divide this solution into two halves. To one half, add 1 mol/L hydrochloric acid drop-by-drop. Observe and record the colour and the pH after each drop.
3. Repeat step 2 using the solution in the second beaker, adding 1 mol/L sodium hydroxide instead of hydrochloric acid.
4. Dispose of all waste materials as directed by your teacher.

Questions

1. What did you observe regarding the pH of the solution when sodium hydroxide was added to the vinegar?
2. What did you notice when small amounts of either hydrochloric acid or sodium hydroxide were added to the vinegar/sodium hydroxide solution?
3. Write the balanced chemical equation for the reaction of acetic acid with sodium hydroxide.
4. Using the chemical equation from question 3, determine which compounds had a common polyatomic ion.

SECTION 8.1
Understanding Acid-Base Equilibrium

Key Terms

dissociation
hydronium ion, H_3O^+
ionization
hydroxide ion, OH^-
Brønsted-Lowry theory of acids and bases
conjugate acid-base pair
conjugate base
conjugate acid
amphiprotic
electrolyte
ion-product constant of water, K_w
pH
pOH

Acids and bases are substances that are used in industries, laboratories, and homes. If you read the content label for many household products, you would find that many of them contain acids and bases. **Figure 8.1** shows some common products found in homes that contain acids or bases.

Figure 8.1 Many household items contain acids or bases.

You learned in previous courses that acids and bases have distinctive properties. Acids taste sour and bases taste bitter. Bases are slippery to the touch. You can experience the sour taste of acids by tasting lemon juice and you can experience the slippery feel of a base the next time you use soap to wash your hands. *(Although these are defining characteristics of acids and bases, be careful to never taste or touch unknown substances.)*

In this chapter, you will review the Arrhenius definition of acids and bases, and then you will learn about another definition of acids and bases that developed as chemists gained more information about these compounds. In addition, you will learn how the principles of chemical equilibrium apply to acids and bases.

dissociation the process of breaking apart into smaller particles, such as ions or smaller neutral particles

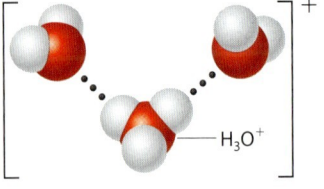

Figure 8.2 The hydrogen ion, which is a single proton, bonds covalently with water molecules. The resultant ion and the surrounding water molecules also form hydrogen bonds.
***Explain** what a hydrogen bond is.*

Acids, Bases, and Water

Many acid-base reactions occur in water, such as the reaction between hydrochloric acid, HCl(aq), and sodium hydroxide, NaOH(aq).

$$HCl(aq) + NaOH(aq) \rightarrow NaCl(aq) + H_2O(\ell)$$

The net ionic equation for this reaction is as follows:

$$H^+(aq) + OH^-(aq) \rightarrow H_2O(\ell)$$

Hydrochloric acid is a molecule consisting of a hydrogen atom and a chlorine atom that has formed a polar covalent bond. The hydrogen atom is made up of a single proton and a single electron. When the hydrogen atom loses its electron, the hydrogen ion is basically a proton. When hydrochloric acid breaks apart in water—a process known as **dissociation**— the positively charged hydrogen ion from the acid is attracted to the negatively charged electrons on the surrounding water molecules. The attraction is so strong that the hydrogen ion forms a covalent bond with the water molecule to produce H_3O^+(aq), shown in **Figure 8.2**.

The equation for the formation of H$_3$O$^+$(aq) is shown in the equation below:

$$\text{HCl(aq)} + \text{H}_2\text{O}(\ell) \rightarrow \text{Cl}^-\text{(aq)} + \text{H}_3\text{O}^+\text{(aq)}$$

This newly formed ion is called the **hydronium ion**. The process in which a charged particle is formed from an atom or a covalently bonded group of atoms is called **ionization**. During the formation of the hydronium ion, both dissociation and ionization occur*.

The hydronium ion and the surrounding water molecules form hydrogen bonds, as indicated by the dots in **Figure 8.2**. Sometimes, the notation H$_3$O$^+$(aq) for the hydronium ion is simplified to H$^+$(aq).

hydronium ion, H$_3$O$^+$ a proton bonded to a water molecule by a covalent bond

ionization** the process in which a charged particle (ion) is formed from a non-ionic species (an atom or a covalently bonded group of atoms)

hydroxide ion, OH$^-$ a negatively charged ion composed of a hydrogen atom and an oxygen atom

Brønsted-Lowry theory of acids and bases definitions of acids and bases based on the donation and acceptance of a proton

Limitations of the Arrhenius Theory of Acids and Bases

Swedish chemist Svanté Arrhenius (1859–1927) proposed an early definition of acids and bases. Arrhenius classified acids and bases according to their chemical formulas and according to how they dissociated in water.

- An Arrhenius acid is a substance that contains hydrogen in its chemical formula, and it ionizes in water to form the hydronium ion, as described above.
- An Arrhenius base is a substance that contains OH in its chemical formula, and it dissociates in water to form the **hydroxide ion**, OH$^-$.

Over time, as chemists learned more about acids and bases, they realized that these definitions were problematic. Some substances do not have OH in their chemical formulas, but nevertheless they yield hydroxide ions when they react with water. For example, ammonia, NH$_3$, reacts with water and forms the hydroxide ion, as shown in **Figure 8.3**. The Arrhenius definition is also limited by its assumption that all acid-base reactions occur in water.

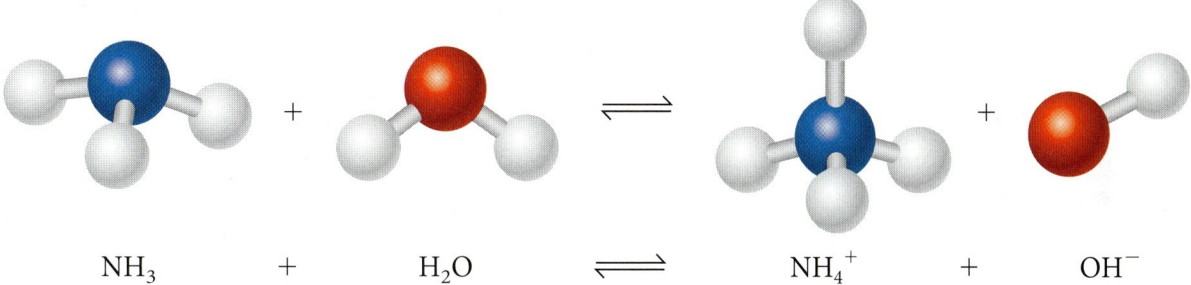

NH$_3$ +   H$_2$O   ⇌   NH$_4^+$ +   OH$^-$

Figure 8.3 Ammonia is not classified as a base by Arrhenius's definition, but it forms hydroxide ions when it reacts with water. This was a shortcoming in Arrhenius's definition of bases.

The Brønsted-Lowry Theory of Acids and Bases

The definition of acids and bases was broadened and improved when Danish chemist Johannes Brønsted (1879–1947) and British chemist Thomas Lowry (1874–1936) independently proposed a new definition in 1923. The **Brønsted-Lowry theory of acids and bases** defines acids and bases according to the donation and acceptance of a proton. According to the Brønsted-Lowry definition, acids and bases do not need to be in aqueous solution and their activity in water is not part of the definition.

---

*Some sources use the term "dissociate" to refer exclusively to the separation of ionic compounds into their component ions. In this sense, covalently bonded groups of atoms, such as molecules or polyatomic ions, do not dissociate; they separate into uncharged components, which become ions when they react with water. For simplicity, however, chemists often use the term "dissociate" to refer to any species, whether it contains ionic or covalent bonds, breaking up into its components. This textbook uses "dissociate" in this more general sense.

**Ionic compounds do not undergo ionization in water. That is, they do not react with water to form ions; they simply separate into their component ions.

Brønsted-Lowry Definitions of Acids and Bases

- A Brønsted-Lowry acid is a *proton donor* or any substance that donates a hydrogen ion. An acid must contain hydrogen in its formula, such as HCl and HNO_3. All Arrhenius acids are also Brønsted-Lowry acids.

- A Brønsted-Lowry base is a *proton acceptor* or any substance that accepts a hydrogen ion. A base must have a lone pair of electrons to bind with the hydrogen ion. All Arrhenius bases are Brønsted-Lowry bases because they contain the hydroxide ion, but the Brønsted-Lowry definition is much broader than the Arrhenius definition. The Brønsted-Lowry definition includes bases such as NH_3 that do not contain the hydroxide ion.

According to the Brønsted-Lowry definition of acids and bases, any substance that behaves as an acid can do so only if another substance behaves as a base at the same time. Similarly, according to this definition, if a substance behaves as a base, another substance must behave as an acid at the same time. Consider the reaction between hydrochloric acid and water shown in **Figure 8.4**. In this reaction, hydrochloric acid is an acid because it donates a proton, H^+, to water. The water molecule is a base because it accepts the proton.

HCl(aq) + H_2O(aq) → H_3O^+(aq) + Cl^-

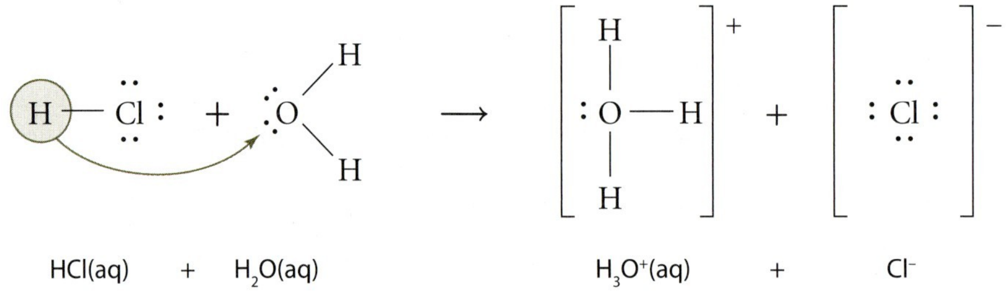

Figure 8.4 According to the Brønsted-Lowry definition of acids and bases, hydrochloric acid is an acid because it donates a proton, and water is a base because it accepts the proton. *Explain* whether or not the acid and base shown above are an Arrhenius acid and base too.

Conjugate Pairs

Two molecules or ions that differ because of the transfer of a proton are called a **conjugate acid-base pair**. (Conjugate means "linked together.")

- The **conjugate base** of an acid is the particle that remains when a proton is removed from the acid.
- The **conjugate acid** of a base is the particle formed when the base receives the proton from the acid.

The acid of an acid-base pair has one more proton than its conjugate base. An acid-base reaction always contains two conjugate acid-base pairs. In the reaction between hydrochloric acid and water, the chloride ion is the conjugate base of hydrochloric acid. Water acts as a base in this reaction, and the hydronium ion is its conjugate acid. Every acid has a conjugate base, and every base has a conjugate acid.

The ionization of ethanoic (acetic) acid, CH_3COOH (aq), in water is represented in **Figure 8.5** on the next page. Ethanoic acid is a Brønsted-Lowry acid because it donates a proton to the water. In receiving the proton, the water molecule is acting as a base in this reaction and becomes a hydronium ion. Notice that this reaction proceeds in both directions and equilibrium is established. When ethanoic acid reacts with water, only a few molecules react to form ions. The position of equilibrium lies to the left, and the equilibrium constant for the reaction is small. Because the equilibrium lies to the left, the reverse reaction is favoured.

conjugate acid-base pair two substances that are related by the gain or loss of a proton; the acid of an acid-base pair has one more proton than its conjugate base

conjugate base the particle that is produced when an acid donates a hydrogen ion to a base

conjugate acid the particle that is produced when a base accepts a hydrogen ion from an acid

In the reverse reaction, the hydronium ion gives up a proton to the ethanoate ion, $CH_3COO^-(aq)$. Thus, in the reverse reaction, the hydronium ion is a Brønsted-Lowry acid and the ethanoate ion is a Brønsted-Lowry base. The ethanoic acid on the left, $CH_3COOH(aq)$, and the base on the right, $CH_3COO^-(aq)$, differ by one proton, so they are a conjugate acid-base pair. Similarly, $H_2O(\ell)$ and $H_3O^+(aq)$ are a conjugate acid-base pair, because they too differ by one proton. The Sample Problems below demonstrate how to identify conjugate acid-base pairs. Use the Practice Problems that follow to practise this skill.

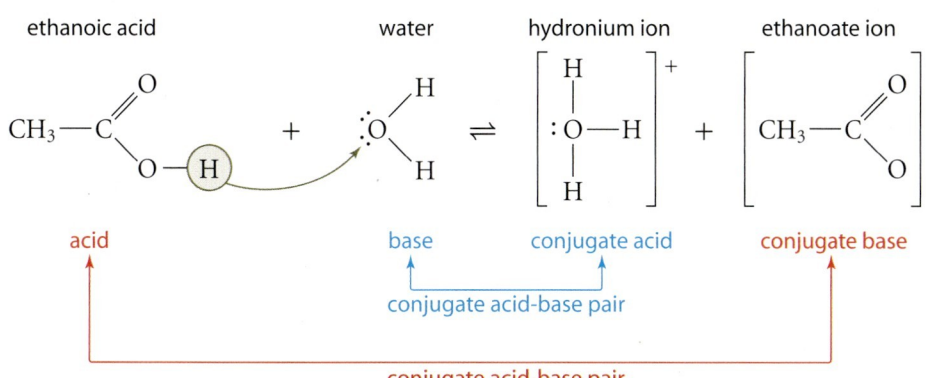

Figure 8.5 In the Brønsted-Lowry definition of acids and bases, every acid has a conjugate base and every base has a conjugate acid. *Identify the conjugate pairs in this diagram.*

Sample Problem

Identifying Conjugate Acid-Base Pairs

Problem
Hydrogen bromide, HBr(g), is a gas at room temperature that is soluble in water. Identify the conjugate acid-base pairs in the reaction between hydrogen bromide gas and water.

$$HBr(g) + H_2O(\ell) \rightarrow H_3O^+(aq) + Br^-(aq)$$

What Is Required?
You need to identify the two conjugate acid-base pairs.

What Is Given?
You know the balanced chemical equation.

Plan Your Strategy	Act on Your Strategy
On the left side of the equation, identify the acid as the molecule that donates a proton. Identify the base as the molecule that accepts the proton.	Hydrogen bromide donates a proton, so it is the Brønsted-Lowry acid in the reaction. Water accepts the proton, so it is the Brønsted-Lowry base.
Identify the conjugate base on the right side of the equation as the particle with one less proton than the acid on the left side of the equation. Identify the particle on the right side that has one proton more than the base on the left side as the conjugate acid.	The conjugate base is $Br^-(aq)$, and the conjugate acid is $H_3O^+(aq)$. The conjugate acid-base pairs are $HBr(g)/Br^-(aq)$ and $H_2O(\ell)/H_3O^+(aq)$. conjugate acid-base pair acid — conjugate base $HBr(aq) + H_2O(\ell) \rightarrow H_3O^+(aq) + Br^-(aq)$ base — conjugate acid conjugate acid-base pair

Check Your Solution
The formulas for the conjugate acid-base pairs differ by one proton, H^+.

Sample Problem

Identifying More Conjugate Acid-Base Pairs

Problem

Ammonia, $NH_3(g)$, is a pungent gas at room temperature. Its main use is in the production of fertilizers and explosives. You might be familiar with the odour of ammonia because it is used in some glass cleaners. Ammonia is extremely soluble in water and forms a solution with the properties of a base, such as turning red litmus paper blue. Use the Brønsted-Lowry definition of acids and bases to identify the conjugate acid-base pairs in the reaction between aqueous ammonia and water:

$$NH_3(aq) + H_2O(\ell) \rightleftharpoons NH_4^+(aq) + OH^-(aq)$$

What Is Required?

You need to identify the two conjugate acid-base pairs.

What Is Given?

You know the balanced chemical equation.

Plan Your Strategy	Act on Your Strategy
Identify the proton donor on the left side of the equation as the acid. Identify the proton acceptor on the left side of the equation as the base.	The conjugate acid-base pairs are $NH_3(aq)/NH_4^+(aq)$ and $H_2O(\ell)/OH^-(aq)$. 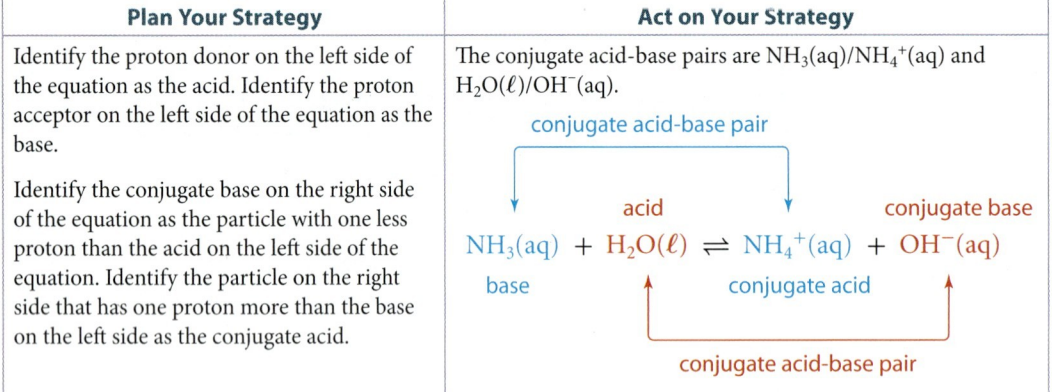
Identify the conjugate base on the right side of the equation as the particle with one less proton than the acid on the left side of the equation. Identify the particle on the right side that has one proton more than the base on the left side as the conjugate acid.	

Check Your Solution

The formulas for the conjugate acid-base pairs differ by one proton, H^+, as expected.

Practice Problems

Name and write the formula for the conjugate base of each molecule or ion below.

1. $HF(aq)$
2. $HCO_3^-(aq)$
3. $H_2SO_4(aq)$
4. $N_2H_5^+(aq)$

Name and write the formula for the conjugate acid of each molecule or ion below.

5. $NO_3^-(aq)$
6. $OH^-(aq)$
7. $H_2O(\ell)$
8. $HCO_3^-(aq)$

9. When perchloric acid, $HClO_4(aq)$, dissolves in water, the following reaction occurs:

$$HClO_4(aq) + H_2O(\ell) \rightarrow H_3O^+(aq) + ClO_4^-(aq)$$

Identify the conjugate acid-base pairs in the reaction above.

10. Identify the conjugate acid-base pairs in the following reactions:
    a. $HS^-(aq) + H_2O(\ell) \rightleftharpoons H_2S(aq) + OH^-(aq)$
    b. $O^{2-}(aq) + H_2O(\ell) \rightleftharpoons 2OH^-(aq)$
    c. $H_2S(aq) + NH_3(aq) \rightleftharpoons NH_4^+(aq) + HS^-(aq)$
    d. $H_2SO_4(aq) + H_2O(\ell) \rightleftharpoons H_3O^+(aq) + HSO_4^-(aq)$

> **Learning Check**
>
> 1. Define an Arrhenius acid and an Arrhenius base.
> 2. Describe a Brønsted-Lowry acid and a Brønsted-Lowry base.
> 3. What are conjugate acid-base pairs?
> 4. Explain the difference between a conjugate acid and a conjugate base.
> 5. Using **Figure 8.2**, describe how the hydronium ion forms.
> 6. What are two fundamental differences between the Arrhenius definition of acids and bases and the Brønsted-Lowry definition of acids and bases?

Both an Acid and a Base: Amphiprotic Substances

Water is a unique *solvent* and one of its properties is that it can act as an acid or as a base, meaning it is **amphiprotic**. Water acts as a Brønsted-Lowry base in reactions with acids, such as hydrochloric acid, because it is a proton acceptor, as shown in the reaction below:

$$HCl(aq) + H_2O(\ell) \rightarrow Cl^-(aq) + H_3O^+(aq)$$

Water functions as a Brønsted-Lowry acid, or a proton donor, in reactions with bases, such as ammonia, which is shown below.

$$NH_3(aq) + H_2O(\ell) \rightleftharpoons NH_4^+(aq) + OH^-(aq)$$

Amphiprotic substances can be molecules, as in the case of water, or ions with a hydrogen atom that can ionize, such as the hydrogen sulfate ion, $HSO_4^-(aq)$.

Water is a *very* weak electrolyte and it is a poor conductor of electric current, but it undergoes ionization to a small extent. An **electrolyte** is a substance that conducts electric current when it forms ions. The equation representing the ionization of water is shown below. This process is also called the autoionization or self-ionization of water.

$$H_2O(\ell) \rightleftharpoons H^+(aq) + OH^-(aq)$$

Consider the equations in **Figure 8.6** using the Brønsted-Lowry definition of acids and bases. The first conjugate acid-base pair is H_2O (acid) and OH^- (base). The second conjugate acid-base pair is H_3O^+ (acid) and H_2O (base). The molecular models represent the reactants and products in the equations above them. Two water molecules react to form hydronium and hydroxide ions. One water molecule acts as an acid and the other molecule acts as a base.

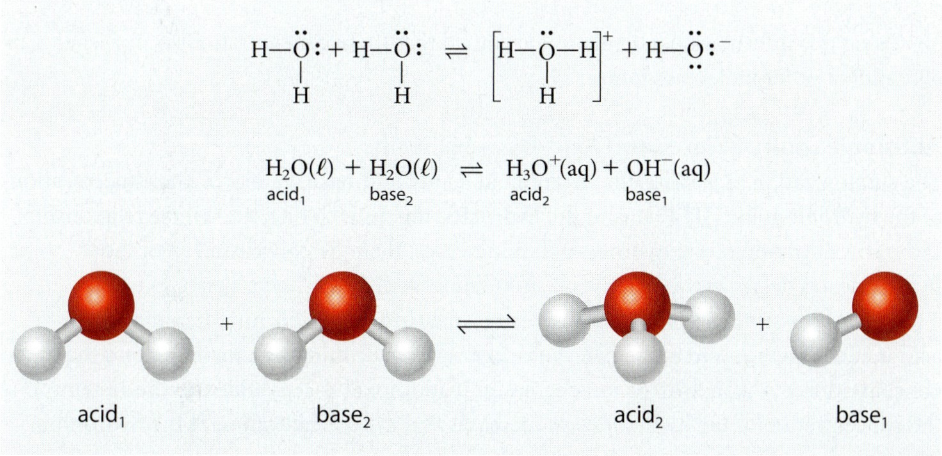

amphiprotic a molecule or ion that can accept or donate a proton, thus acting as an acid or a base

electrolyte a substance that conducts electric current when it forms ions

$$H_2O(\ell) + H_2O(\ell) \rightleftharpoons H_3O^+(aq) + OH^-(aq)$$
$$\text{acid}_1 \quad\quad \text{base}_2 \quad\quad\quad \text{acid}_2 \quad\quad \text{base}_1$$

Figure 8.6 These reactions illustrate the amphiprotic nature of water. Water molecules can act as both a Brønsted-Lowry acid and a Brønsted-Lowry base.

The Ion-Product Constant of Water, K_w

As you can see in the equation for the autoionization of water below, this process establishes equilibrium. Like all equilibrium processes, you can describe the process quantitatively using an equilibrium constant, as shown below:

$$H_2O(\ell) + H_2O(\ell) \rightleftharpoons H_3O^+(aq) + OH^-(aq)$$

$$K_{eq} = \frac{[H_3O^+][OH^-]}{[H_2O]^2}$$

As you learned in the previous chapter, concentrations of solids and liquids are essentially constant and they are included in the equilibrium constant, K_{eq}. For water, the equilibrium constant is simplified and is called the **ion-product constant of water, K_w**, as shown below:

$$K_{eq}[H_2O]^2 = [H_3O^+][OH^-] = K_w$$

$$K_w = 1.0 \times 10^{-14} \text{ (at 25°C)}$$

ion-product constant of water, K_w the equilibrium constant for the autoionization of water

The units for the ion-product constant of water are mol²/L². Like other equilibrium constants, the ion-product constant of water is usually written without units.

Examine the equilibrium equation again and note that one hydronium ion and one hydroxide ion are produced for every molecule of water that ionizes. You can use the ion-product constant of water, K_w, to determine the molar concentrations of the hydronium ions and the hydroxide ions. Use this equation to determine the molar concentrations of the ions at 25°C:

$$[H_3O^+][OH^-] = 1.0 \times 10^{-14}$$

You can see from the equilibrium equation that the concentrations of the positive and negative ions are equal. Therefore, the following applies:

$$[H_3O^+] = [OH^-]$$
$$[H_3O^+]^2 = 1.0 \times 10^{-14}$$
$$\sqrt{[H_3O^+]^2} = \sqrt{1.0 \times 10^{-14}}$$
$$[H_3O^+] = 1.0 \times 10^{-7} \text{ mol/L (at 25°C)}$$
$$[OH^-] = 1.0 \times 10^{-7} \text{ mol/L (at 25°C)}$$

Using this information, chemists determined that these concentrations occur when 1 in 555 million water molecules ionize.

Autoionization of Water and Acid-Base Solutions

The autoionization of water is important in aqueous acid-base reactions. The concentrations of the hydronium ion, $[H_3O^+]$, and the hydroxide ion, $[OH^-]$, have an inverse relationship. If the concentration of the hydronium ion increases, then the concentration of the hydroxide ion decreases and vice versa. You know from Le Châtelier's principle that a change of concentration in either ion results in a shift in equilibrium. If additional acid is added to the system, the concentration of the hydronium ion increases and the concentration of the hydroxide ion decreases. If additional base is added to the system, the concentration of the hydroxide ion increases and the concentration of the hydronium ion decreases. At a constant temperature, these concentration changes do not affect the equilibrium constant K_w. It remains a constant value.

Ion Concentrations and the Acidic-Basic Nature of Solutions

Because of the autoionization of water, hydronium ions and hydroxide ions are present in all aqueous systems. Therefore, in all acid-base aqueous solutions, both ions are present. The concentration of these ions is used to determine the relative acidic and basic nature of solutions. A solution with a high concentration of hydronium ions is acidic. A solution with a high concentration of hydroxide ions is basic. If the concentrations of the hydronium ions and the hydroxide ions are equal, then the solution is considered to be neutral. These relationships are shown below:

acidic solution	$[H_3O^+] > [OH^-]$
neutral solution	$[H_3O^+] = [OH^-]$
basic solution	$[H_3O^+] < [OH^-]$

The ion-product constant of water, K_w, can be used to determine the molar concentration of either the hydronium ion or the hydroxide ion if one of the concentrations is known. These equations are shown below, and the Sample Problem demonstrates how to use one of them. Complete the Practice Problems that follow to practise using these formulas.

$$K_w = [OH^-][H_3O^+] \quad\quad [H_3O^+] = \frac{K_w}{[OH^-]} \quad\quad [OH^-] = \frac{K_w}{[H_3O^+]}$$

Sample Problem

Calculating the $[H_3O^+]$ or $[OH^-]$ in Aqueous Solution

Problem
The concentration of hydroxide ions, $[OH^-]$, of household window cleaner is 0.0020 mol/L at 25°C. What is the concentration of hydronium ions, $[H_3O^+]$, in the sample? Is the window cleaner acidic, basic, or neutral? Explain your answer.

What Is Required?
You need to determine the hydronium ion concentration and compare it with the known hydroxide ion concentration.

What Is Given?
You know the concentration of hydroxide ions, $[OH^-]$.

Plan Your Strategy	Act on Your Strategy
Determine which equation you will need to use. Because the hydroxide ion concentration is known, you need to use the equation to determine the hydronium ion concentration. Remember that although K_w is expressed without units, the units are mol^2/L^2.	$[H_3O^+] = \dfrac{K_w}{[OH^-]}$ $= \dfrac{1.0 \times 10^{-14} \, \frac{mol^2}{L^2}}{0.0020 \, \frac{mol}{L}}$ $= 5.0 \times 10^{-12}$ mol/L
Compare the ionic concentrations to determine if the solution is acidic, basic, or neutral.	$[OH^-] = 2.0 \times 10^{-3}$ mol/L $[H_3O^+] = 5.0 \times 10^{-12}$ mol/L $[OH^-] > [H_3O^+]$; therefore, the solution is basic.

Check Your Solution
Multiply the concentration of the hydronium ion by the concentration of the hydroxide ion and see if the product is equal to 1.0×10^{-14}. The product is 1.0×10^{-14}; therefore, the solution is correct.

Practice Problems

11. The concentration of hydroxide ions, OH⁻(aq), in a solution at 25°C is 0.150 mol/L. Determine the concentration of hydronium ions, H_3O^+(aq), in the solution.

12. A solution of lithium hydroxide, LiOH(aq), is made by placing 2.00 mol of the base into 1.50 L of solution. What is the concentration of hydronium ions, H_3O^+(aq), in this solution at 25°C?

13. Two solutions at the same temperature are to be compared for their hydronium ion concentrations. Solution A has a hydroxide ion concentration of 0.335 mol/L and solution B has a hydroxide ion concentration of 0.285 mol/L. In which solution will the hydronium ion concentration be larger? Explain your answer.

14. Explain why the two solutions in question 13 need only to be at the same temperature for the comparison to be made, and do not necessarily have to be at 25°C.

15. In a solution at 25°C, 4.75 g of sodium hydroxide, NaOH(s), is added to enough water to create a volume of 2.40 L. What is the hydronium ion, H_3O^+(aq), concentration in this solution?

16. A drain cleaner is a mixture of soluble hydroxides in solution. Would the drain cleaner be acidic, basic, or neutral? Explain your answer using one or two well-reasoned sentences.

17. Verify that the hydronium ion, H_3O^+(aq), concentration in a solution at 25°C containing 0.455 mol/L of hydroxide ions, OH⁻(aq), is 2.20×10^{-14} mol/L.

18. A solution has a hydronium ion, H_3O^+(aq), concentration of 0.152 mol/L at 25°C. What is the hydroxide ion, OH⁻(aq), concentration of this solution?

19. What is the hydronium ion, H_3O^+(aq), concentration of a solution at 25°C that has a hydroxide ion, OH⁻(aq), concentration of 0.0025 mol/L?

20. A 1.55 mol/L hydrochloric acid solution, HCl(aq), is at 25°C. Determine the hydroxide ion, OH⁻(aq), concentration of this solution.

Establishing pH and pOH

As you can see from the Sample Problem on the previous page and the Practice Problems above, hydronium ion and hydroxide ion concentration values are very small numbers. To overcome this inconvenience, Søren Sørensen, a Danish chemist, introduced the idea of pH in 1909. The **pH** of a solution is the negative logarithm of the hydronium ion concentration (in mol/L). The equation is shown below:

$$pH = -\log [H_3O^+]$$

pH the negative common logarithm of the concentration of the hydronium ion, H_3O^+

If a solution has a hydronium ion concentration of 3.2×10^{-4} mol/L, what is the solution's pH? The equation below shows this calculation.

$$\begin{aligned} pH &= -\log [H_3O^+] \\ &= -\log (3.2 \times 10^{-4}) \\ &= 3.49 \end{aligned}$$

Go to **Logarithms and Calculating pH** in **Appendix A** for information about calculating the pH of a solution.

When you take the logarithm of the concentration, you take the logarithm of the numerical value only. You cannot take the logarithm of units. Therefore, the pH of a solution is written without units.

Significant digits must be used when writing a pH value just as they must be used for writing any calculated value derived from laboratory data. Significant digits communicate the precision of the measurement. To determine the number of significant digits in a logarithm, count the number of digits to the *right* of the decimal point. For example, if a solution has a hydronium ion concentration, $[H_3O^+]$, of 6.3×10^{-4} mol/L, what is its pH?

$$pH = -\log [H_3O^+] = -\log (6.3 \times 10^{-4}) = 3.20$$

The correct number of significant digits in the pH value is the number of significant digits in the molar concentration. In the above example, 6.3×10^{-4} mol/L has two significant digits, so the pH value must have two significant digits to the *right of the decimal.*

The pH equation can also be used to determine the concentration of hydronium ions, $[H_3O^+]$, if the pH is known. For example, if the pH of a solution is 4.85, set up the equation as shown below:

$$pH = -\log [H_3O^+] = 4.85$$
$$-\log [H_3O^+] = 4.85$$

Take the antilog of −4.85 on your calculator, which is usually the 10^x key. You can rewrite the antilog equation as follows:

$$[H_3O^+] = 10^{-pH} = 10^{-4.85}$$
$$[H_3O^+] = 1.4 \times 10^{-5} \text{ mol/L}$$

A high pH number corresponds to a low concentration of the hydronium ion or a basic solution. A low pH number corresponds to a high concentration of the hydronium ion or an acidic solution. Because the pH scale is logarithmic, an increase of one pH value is an increase of 10 times the ion concentration. **Figure 8.7** shows the pH values of some common solutions.

The same methods can be used to calculate the **pOH** of a solution, which is the negative logarithm of the hydroxide ion concentration (in mol/L). The equations are given below:

$$pOH = -\log [OH^-]$$
$$[OH^-] = 10^{-pH}$$

The equations above are used just like the pH equations. You can calculate the pOH, or the concentration of the hydroxide ion, $[OH^-]$, in the solution just as you calculated the pH and the concentration of the hydronium ion in a solution.

The Relationship Among pH, pOH, and pK_w

You can also take the logarithm of the ion-product constant of water, K_w, and obtain a useful relationship, as shown below:

$$K_w = [H_3O^+][OH^-] = 1.0 \times 10^{-14} \text{ (at 25°C)}$$
$$-\log K_w = (-\log [H_3O^+]) + (-\log [OH^-]) = -\log (1.0 \times 10^{-14})$$
$$pK_w = pH + pOH = 14.00 \text{ (at 25°C)}$$

The sum of pH and pOH is 14.00 for any aqueous solution at 25°C. The following Sample Problem illustrates how to use these relationships. Use the Practice Problems to practise these calculations.

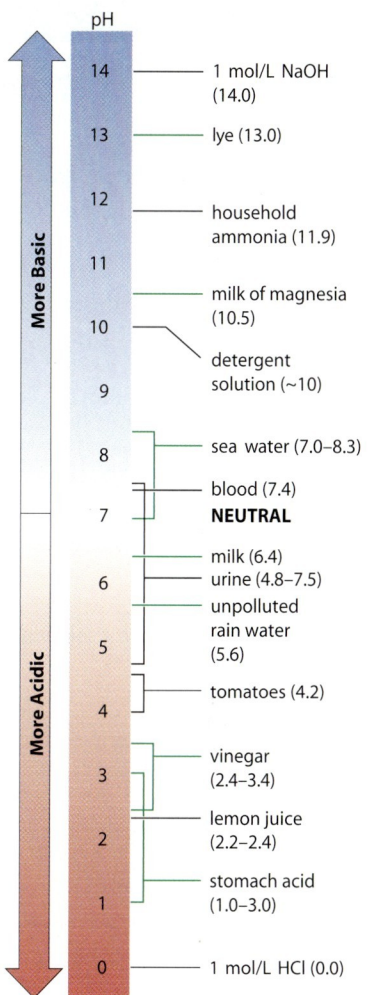

Figure 8.7 Mixtures that you encounter in daily life have a wide range of pH values.

pOH the negative common logarithm of the concentration of the hydroxide ion, OH^-

Sample Problem

Calculating pH, pOH, and [OH⁻]

Problem

A university chemistry instructor prepared a solution with the following [H$_3$O$^+$]: 0.50 mol/L. Calculate the pH, pOH, and [OH$^-$] of the solution. The solution is at 25°C.

What Is Required?

You need to calculate the pH, pOH, and [OH$^-$] of the solution.

What Is Given?

You know the hydronium ion concentration, [H$_3$O$^+$], of the solution: 0.50 mol/L

Plan Your Strategy	Act on Your Strategy

Calculate the pH of the solution.	[H$_3$O$^+$] = 0.50 mol/L
	pH = −log [H$_3$O$^+$]
	    = −log 0.50
	    = 0.30

Calculate the pOH of the solution.	pH + pOH = 14.00 0.30 + pOH = 14.00 pOH = 13.70

Calculate the hydroxide ion concentration, [OH$^-$].	[OH$^-$] = 10$^{-\text{pOH}}$
	       = 10$^{-13.70}$
	       = 2.0 × 10^{-14} mol/L

Check Your Solution

The hydronium ion concentration is high, so the pH should be low. The solution is highly acidic. The answers seem reasonable.

Practice Problems

21. An unknown solution has a pH of 5.84. If the solution is at 25°C, what is the pOH of the solution?

22. In a given solution, the pOH is 2.77. If the solution is at 25°C, what is the pH of the solution?

23. Determine the pH and pOH of a solution at 25°C with a hydronium ion, H$_3$O$^+$(aq), concentration of 3.20 × 10^{-10} mol/L.

24. A solution is made by dissolving 0.45 mol of sodium hydroxide, NaOH(s), in enough water to make 3.75 L of solution. Determine the pH and pOH of this solution at 25°C.

25. Determine the pH and pOH of a solution at 25°C that has 0.42 mol of hydroxide ions, OH$^-$(aq), in 2.00 L of solution.

26. Calculate the pH and pOH of a solution at 25°C that has a hydroxide ion, OH$^-$(aq), concentration of 1.74 × 10^{-9} mol/L.

27. What are the pH and pOH at 25°C of 0.097 mol/L nitric acid, HNO$_3$(aq), a strong acid?

28. A solution at 25°C is made by adding 0.083 g of calcium hydroxide, Ca(OH)$_2$(s) (a soluble solid), into enough water to make 125 mL of solution. What are the pH and pOH of the resulting solution?

29. What is the hydronium ion, H$_3$O$^+$(aq), concentration of a solution at 25°C with a pOH of 7.95?

30. Explain why pH + pOH is equal to 14.00 when any aqueous solution is at 25°C.

Section 8.1 Review

Section Summary

- The Arrhenius theory defines acids and bases based on their chemical formulas and on how they dissociate in water.
- The Brønsted-Lowry theory of acids and bases defines acids and bases based on the donation and acceptance of a proton.
- Water is amphiprotic and it can act as an acid or a base.
- pH and pOH are the negative common logarithms of the hydronium ion, H_3O^+, and the hydroxide ion, OH^-, respectively, and they are used to describe acids and bases.
- The sum of the pH and the pOH is 14.00 for any aqueous solution at 25°C.

Review Questions

1. **K/U** State the Arrhenius definitions of an acid and a base.

2. **K/U** Give two reasons why the Arrhenius definitions of acids and bases were not necessarily the best definitions to use for the two types of solutions.

3. **C** Use a chart to outline the similarities and differences between Arrhenius acids and bases and Brønsted-Lowry acids and bases.

4. **A** Identify the conjugate acid-base pairs in the following reactions:
   a. $HNO_3(aq) + H_2O(\ell) \rightarrow NO_3^-(aq) + H_3O^+(aq)$
   b. $HCO_3^-(aq) + H_2O(\ell) \rightleftharpoons CO_3^{2-}(aq) + H_3O^+(aq)$
   c. $HS^-(aq) + H_2O(\ell) \rightleftharpoons H_2S(aq) + OH^-(aq)$

5. **K/U** Which of the following molecules or ions can act as an acid or a base? Write the two possible chemical equations.
   a. dihydrogen phosphate, $H_2PO_4^-(aq)$
   b. sodium hydroxide, $NaOH(s)$
   c. water
   d. ammonia, $NH_3(aq)$

6. **C** Draw diagrams to illustrate how the ion hydrogen sulfate, $HSO_4^-(aq)$, can behave both as an acid and as a base in solution by proton transfer from or to water molecules.

7. **K/U** Is the following statement always true, regardless of the temperature of the solution? "A neutral aqueous solution will always have the same concentrations of hydronium and hydroxide ions." Explain your answer.

8. **T/I** A student uses a pH meter in the lab to test a solution and determines that the resulting pH is exactly 7.00. She suggests that this does not contain hydronium ions or hydroxide ions. Is this statement correct? Explain your answer in one or two well-reasoned sentences.

9. **C** Create a flowchart or similar graphic organizer that can be used as a checklist in calculating the pH of solutions that are either acidic or basic.

10. **K/U** Is the following statement true or false? "In all aqueous solutions, $[H_3O^+][OH^-] = 1.0 \times 10^{-14}$."

11. **K/U** Explain why the concentration of hydronium ions, $H_3O^+(aq)$, in the autoionization of water is not important when dealing with a strong acid of high concentration.

12. **A** The photograph below shows an aqueous solution at 25°C being studied in a lab.

    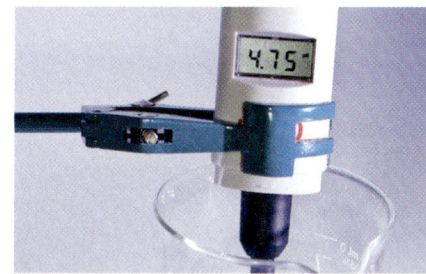

    a. Is the solution acidic, neutral, or basic?
    b. Determine the pOH of the solution.
    c. Calculate the concentrations of the hydronium ions and of the hydroxide ions in this solution.

13. **K/U** Explain why the ion-product constant of water can be 1.0×10^{-14} at 25°C if an acid is added to the solution.

14. **T/I** In a lab, a student decides that in order to neutralize a solution that was just analyzed to have a pH of 2.25, he needs to add a solution with a pOH of 2.25. Is this a correct approach to the neutralization? Explain why or why not in a well-reasoned paragraph.

15. **A** A 1500 L spill of a strong acid that donates one proton has occurred on the side of a highway when a tanker truck overturned. The pH of the acid was found to be 4.00. What pH of base would be needed, of equal volume, to neutralize the spill?

SECTION 8.2

Acid-Base Strength and Acid Dissociation

Key Terms

strong acid

weak acid

strong base

weak base

acid-dissociation constant, or acid-ionization constant, K_a

monoprotic acid

percent dissociation

polyprotic acid

If you have observed a metal in two different acids, like those in **Figure 8.8**, you know that all acids are not the same. Some acids are stronger than others, but what exactly does that mean?

In the test tubes in **Figure 8.8**, magnesium metal is added to two different acids. The acid in the left-side tube is hydrochloric acid, a strong acid. The acid in the right-side tube is ethanoic acid, a weak acid. The reaction between magnesium and the strong acid is more violent than the other reaction. Large bubbles of hydrogen gas, which is produced in the left-tube reaction, keep the magnesium powder buoyant on the surface of the acid. In the other test tube, the magnesium powder and tiny hydrogen bubbles are spread throughout the mixture, creating a milky appearance.

Figure 8.8 Small pieces of the metal magnesium were dropped into two test tubes. One test tube contains a strong acid and the other test tube contains a weak acid.
Describe briefly the chemical properties of the two acids with magnesium.

Strength of Acids

Some acids ionize almost completely in water and others ionize slightly. The strength of acids and bases depends on how much they ionize or dissociate in water and not on their pH values. For all practical purposes, a **strong acid** ionizes completely in water, which is represented by the equation below. The symbol HA represents a generic acid. The H in the symbol represents the hydrogen ion that is attached to the acid.

strong acid an acid that ionizes completely in water

$$HA(g \text{ or } \ell) + H_2O(\ell) \rightarrow H_3O^+(aq) + A^-(aq)$$
$$\text{acid} \qquad \text{water} \qquad \text{hydronium ion} \quad \text{conjugate base}$$

In a dilute solution of a strong acid, all of the acid ionizes. Once the acid dissolves in water, there are no intact acid molecules left in the solution. For a strong acid, the concentration of hydronium ions, $[H_3O^+]$, is approximately equal to the initial concentration of the acid. The bar graph and illustration in **Figure 8.9** on the next page illustrate how the solution changes when a strong acid is added to water.

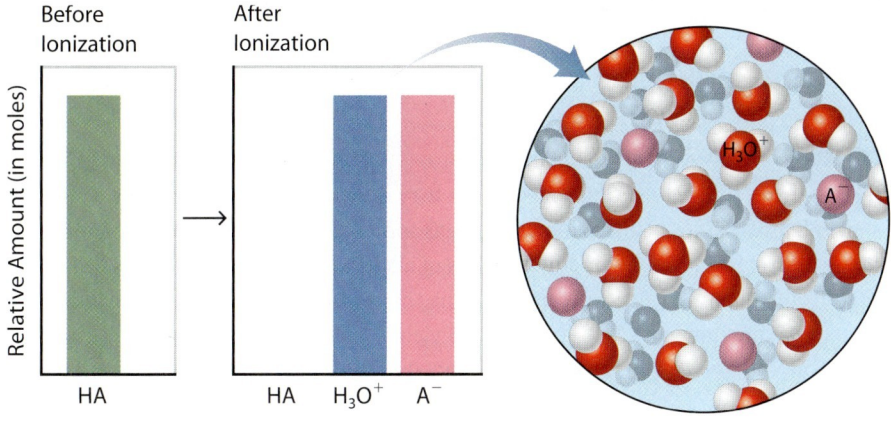

Strong acid: HA(g or ℓ) + H₂O(ℓ) ⟶ H₃O⁺(aq) + A⁻(aq)

Figure 8.9 The green bar on the left shows that the only particles in the solution are acid molecules. When the acid is added to water to form a dilute acid, the strong acid completely ionizes, as represented by the blue bar and the pink bar.

The ionization of a weak acid is different from the ionization of a strong acid. A **weak acid** ionizes slightly when dissolved in water. Most molecules of a weak acid remain intact and in equilibrium with only a few hydronium ions that form. As a result, the initial concentration of the weak acid is approximately equal to the concentration of the weak acid at equilibrium. The ionization of a weak acid in water is represented by the equation below:

$$\underset{\text{acid}}{\text{HA(g or } \ell)} + \underset{\text{water}}{\text{H}_2\text{O}(\ell)} \rightleftharpoons \underset{\text{hydronium ion}}{\text{H}_3\text{O}^+(\text{aq})} + \underset{\text{conjugate base}}{\text{A}^-(\text{aq})}$$

weak acid an acid that ionizes to a limited extent in water

The bar graph and illustration in **Figure 8.10** show the ionization of a weak acid.

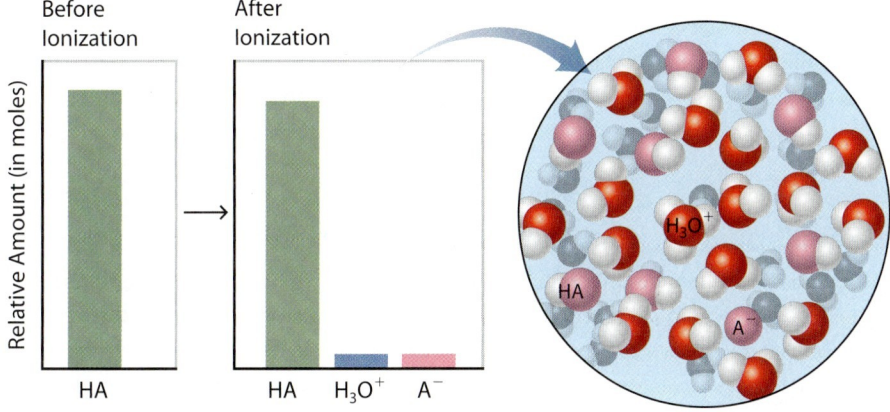

Weak acid: HA(aq) + H₂O(ℓ) ⟶ H₃O⁺(aq) + A⁻(aq)

Figure 8.10 The green bar in the graphs shows the change in the weak acid concentration as the acid ionizes. The blue bar and pink bar represent the ions that form.
***Describe** what occurs when a weak acid is added to water.*

When a weak acid is added to water, dynamic equilibrium is established in the solution. The solution contains a mixture of non-ionized acid molecules, water molecules, hydronium ions, and the conjugate base.

Consider **Figure 8.8** again. In a strong acid, the reaction proceeds rapidly, whereas the reaction is much slower in the weak acid. The strong acid has a much higher concentration of hydronium ions, $[H_3O^+]$, than does the weak acid.

Strength of Bases

Strong bases are similar to strong acids in that they dissociate completely in water. Strong bases include hydroxides of alkali metals, such as sodium hydroxide, NaOH(s), and potassium hydroxide, KOH(s), and hydroxides of alkaline-earth metals, such as $Ba(OH)_2$(s) and $Mg(OH)_2$(s). Sample equations representing the dissociation of three strong bases are shown below. Note that H_2O written above the yield arrow indicates that water is required as the solvent, but water is not considered a reactant.

strong base a base that dissociates completely in water

weak base a base that ionizes or dissociates to a limited extent in water

$$NaOH(s) \xrightarrow{H_2O} Na^+(aq) + OH^-(aq)$$
$$KOH(s) \xrightarrow{H_2O} K^+(aq) + OH^-(aq)$$
$$Ba(OH)_2(s) \xrightarrow{H_2O} Ba^{2+}(aq) + OH^-(aq)$$

The hydroxide ion forms when these metal hydroxides dissociate in water. They are Brønsted-Lowry bases because they can accept a proton. Thus, these substances are classified as bases because they form hydroxide ions when they dissociate.

Weak bases ionize or dissociate* slightly when dissolved in water, just as weak acids ionize slightly in water. Ammonia is an example of a weak base because it ionizes to a small extent in water, as shown below:

* Note that some weak bases, such as ammonia, NH_3, are molecules, which ionize in water. Other weak bases, such as ammonium hydroxide, NH_4OH, are ionic compounds, which dissociate in water. However, *all strong acids and weak acids ionize* in water, and *all strong bases dissociate* in water.

$$NH_3(aq) + H_2O(\ell) \rightleftharpoons NH_4^+(aq) + OH^-(aq)$$

Ammonia is classified as a Brønsted-Lowry base because it accepts a proton from water to form NH_4^+. Amines are another group of compounds that can act as Brønsted-Lowry bases. Recall from Chapter 1 that amines have the general formula R_3N, where R can be a hydrogen atom or a carbon group. Ammonia and amines have a lone pair of electrons on the nitrogen atom that can accept the proton from the hydrogen ion. The acceptance of this proton qualifies ammonia and amines as Brønsted-Lowry bases.

You can refer to the table, "Relative Strengths of Acids and Bases (concentration at 0.01 mol/L) at 25°C," in Appendix B for more information about the strength of acids and bases.

The Equilibrium Position of an Acid-Base Reaction

Acid-base reactions involve two conjugate acid-base pairs. The strength of the acids and bases involved in a chemical reaction determine the net direction, or shift, of the overall reaction. *In general, an acid-base equilibrium reaction shifts in the direction in which a stronger acid and a stronger base form a weaker acid and a weaker base.* For example, consider the following reaction:

$$H_2S(aq) + NH_3(aq) \rightleftharpoons HS^-(aq) + NH_4^+(aq)$$

This reaction shifts to the right because hydrogen sulfide, H_2S(aq), is a stronger acid than the ammonium ion, NH_4^+(aq), and ammonia, NH_3(aq), is a stronger base than the hydrogen sulfide ion, HS^-(aq).

Equilibrium Position and Strength of Acids and Bases

In the reaction below, hydrochloric acid completely dissociates and ionizes. Hydrochloric acid is a stronger acid than the hydronium ion, and water is a stronger base than the chloride ion. So the reaction shifts to the right. In some acid-base reactions, the equilibrium shift is so far to the right or left that it is inappropriate to use equilibrium arrows in the chemical equation. The reaction below is one of those reactions. Because hydrochloric acid is such a strong acid, the reaction is written as a completion reaction.

$$\underset{\substack{\text{acid} \\ \text{stronger acid}}}{\text{HCl(aq)}} + \underset{\substack{\text{base} \\ \text{stronger base}}}{\text{H}_2\text{O}(\ell)} \rightarrow \underset{\substack{\text{conjugate acid} \\ \text{weaker acid}}}{\text{H}_3\text{O}^+(\text{aq})} + \underset{\substack{\text{conjugate base} \\ \text{weaker base}}}{\text{Cl}^-(\text{aq})}$$

How does the strength of each particle determine the direction of the reaction? Consider the reaction above of hydrochloric acid and water. Because hydrochloric acid loses its proton more easily than does the hydronium ion, the hydrochloric acid is a stronger acid than the hydronium ion. You can also consider the reaction in terms of the bases—water and the chloride ion, $\text{Cl}^-(\text{aq})$. Water gains a proton more readily than the chloride ion does; therefore, water must be a stronger base than the chloride ion.

Over many years, chemists have performed countless experiments involving acids and bases. The data from these experiments have enabled chemists to rank acids and bases according to their strengths in relation to one another, as shown in **Table 8.1**. Observe in this table that an acid and its conjugate base are opposite in strength. A strong acid has a weak conjugate base and vice versa.

The Sample Problem on the next page demonstrates how to use the table below to predict the direction of an acid-base equilibrium reaction. Use the Practice Problems that follow the Sample Problem to practise this procedure.

Table 8.1 Relative Strengths of Conjugate Acid-Base Pairs

	Acid	Conjugate Base
Strong acids	HClO_4 (perchloric acid)	ClO_4^- (perchlorate ion)
	HI (hydroiodic acid)	I^- (iodide ion)
	HBr (hydrobromic acid)	Br^- (bromide ion)
	HCl (hydrochloric acid)	Cl^- (chloride ion)
	H_2SO_4 (sulfuric acid)	HSO_4^- (hydrogen sulfate ion)
	HNO_3 (nitric acid)	NO_3^- (nitrate ion)
	H_3O^+ (hydronium ion)	H_2O (water)
Weak acids	HSO_4^- (hydrogen sulfate ion)	SO_4^{2-} (sulfate ion)
	HF (hydrofluoric acid)	F^- (fluoride ion)
	HNO_2 (nitrous acid)	NO_2^- (nitrite ion)
	HCOOH (formic acid)	HCOO^- (formate ion)
	CH_3COOH (acetic acid)	CH_3COO^- (acetate ion)
	NH_4^+ (ammonium ion)	NH_3 (ammonia)
	HCN (hydrocyanic acid)	CN^- (cyanide ion)
	H_2O (water)	OH^- (hydroxide ion)
	NH_3 (ammonia)	NH_2^- (amide ion)

Acid strength increases ↑ (down the left) ; Base strength increases ↓ (down the right)

Sample Problem

Predicting the Direction of an Acid-Base Reaction

Problem
Predict the direction in which the following reaction will proceed.

$$SO_4^{2-}(aq) + CH_3COOH(aq) \rightleftharpoons HSO_4^-(aq) + CH_3COO^-(aq)$$

Briefly explain your answer.

Act on Your Strategy
You need to determine if the strong acid and strong base are on the left side or right side of the equation.

What Is Given?
You know the chemical equation. You have **Table 8.1** and the table in Appendix B as references.

Plan Your Strategy	Act on Your Strategy
Identify the acid and the conjugate acid on each side of the equation.	On the left side of the equation, $CH_3COOH(aq)$ is the acid. On the right side of the equation, $HSO_4^-(aq)$ acts as an acid.
Use Table 8.1 or Appendix B to determine the stronger acid. The reaction proceeds from the stronger acid toward the weaker acid.	In Table 8.1, $HSO_4^-(aq)$ is above $CH_3COOH(aq)$; therefore, $HSO_4^-(aq)$ is the stronger acid. The stronger acid more easily gives up a proton, so the equilibrium shift is to the left and reactants are favoured in this reaction. $$SO_4^{2-}(aq) + CH_3COOH(aq) \rightleftharpoons HSO_4^-(aq) + CH_3COO^-(aq)$$ weaker acid ⟶ stronger acid

Check Your Solution
In comparing the relative strengths of $HSO_4^-(aq)$ and $CH_3COOH(aq)$, ethanoic acid is weaker. The reaction proceeds from the stronger acid toward the weaker acid.

Practice Problems

Predict the direction for the following reactions. State whether reactants or products are favoured, and give reasons to support your decision.

31. $NH_4^+(aq) + H_2PO_4^-(aq) \rightleftharpoons NH_3(aq) + H_3PO_4(aq)$
32. $H_2O(\ell) + HS^-(aq) \rightleftharpoons OH^-(aq) + H_2S(aq)$
33. $HF(aq) + SO_4^{2-}(aq) \rightleftharpoons F^-(aq) + HSO_4^-(aq)$

In which direction will the following reactions proceed? In each case, explain your decision.

34. $HPO_4^{2-}(aq) + NH_4^+(aq) \rightleftharpoons H_2PO_4^-(aq) + NH_3(aq)$
35. $H_2SO_4(aq) + H_2O(\ell) \rightarrow HSO_4^-(aq) + H_3O^+(aq)$
36. $H_2S(aq) + NH_3(aq) \rightleftharpoons HS^-(aq) + NH_4^+(aq)$

Write equilibrium equations for each of the following reactions. State whether the reactants or the products are favoured. (Use **Table 8.1** or the table in Appendix B.)

37. Aqueous carbonic acid, $H_2CO_3(aq)$, is combined with ammonia, $NH_3(g)$.
38. Sodium hydrogen sulfite, $NaHSO_3(s)$, is dissolved in water. (**Hint:** The sodium hydrogen sulfite dissociates completely into sodium ions and hydrogen sulfite ions.) What happens to the hydrogen sulfite ion in water?
39. Hydrofluoric acid, $HF(aq)$, is mixed with potassium nitrate, $KNO_3(s)$. (Consider the hint in question 38.)
40. Write the reactions for the ionizations of the three hydrogen ions in $H_3PO_4(\ell)$.

> **Learning Check**
>
> 7. What is the difference between a strong acid and a weak acid?
> 8. What is the difference between a strong base and a weak base?
> 9. Describe a strong acid and a strong base in terms of protons.
> 10. Refer to **Table 8.1** and determine whether hydroiodic acid or water is the stronger acid. Explain your answer.
> 11. Draw four generic molecules of ammonia and amines showing the lone pair of electrons that accepts the proton. Explain why these compounds are classified as Brønsted-Lowry bases.
> 12. Use **Table 8.1** to write a chemical reaction showing a strong base reacting with water. Label the acids and bases on each side of the reaction equation and state whether reactants or products are favoured and why.

The Acid-Dissociation Constant, K_a

Acids vary in strength from strong to weak and these classifications are based on how much the acid molecule ionizes in water. Because strong acids ionize completely and the reaction between a strong acid and water essentially goes to completion, it makes no sense to write an equilibrium expression for the reaction. Weak acids, however, only ionize partially and a weak acid in water will establish equilibrium. A special equilibrium constant is used when working with weak acids. The equilibrium constant that is specific for the ionization of a weak acid is called the **acid-dissociation constant**, or **acid-ionization constant, K_a**. Consider the ionization of a generic weak acid, HA, that donates one proton and is a **monoprotic acid**.

$$HA(aq) + H_2O(\ell) \rightleftharpoons H_3O^+(aq) + A^-(aq)$$

The equilibrium expression for this generic reaction is given below:

$$K_{eq} = \frac{[H_3O^+][A^-]}{[H_2O][HA]} \qquad K_{eq}[H_2O] = K_a = \frac{[H_3O^+][A^-]}{[HA]}$$

Because the concentration of water, $[H_2O]$, does not change, the concentration of water is considered constant and is included in the value for K_{eq}. The acid-dissociation constant, K_a, is like other equilibrium constants and its value is temperature-dependent. So, to compare values of K_a or to calculate K_a, the temperature must be constant.

Look at the expression for the acid-dissociation constant. The more an acid ionizes, the higher the value of K_a. Thus, at a given temperature for the ionization of a weak acid at equilibrium, the stronger the acid is, the higher the hydronium ion concentration and the larger the value of K_a will be:

stronger acid → higher $[H_3O^+]$ → larger K_a value

For weak acids that only partially dissociate and ionize, percent dissociation is used to express how much the weak acid ionizes. **Percent dissociation** of a weak acid is the fraction of acid molecules that ionize at equilibrium compared with the initial concentration of the acid. The general equation for percent dissociation is shown below:

$$\text{percent dissociated} = \frac{[HA]_{dissociated}}{[HA]_{initial}} \times 100\%$$

acid-dissociation constant or **acid-ionization constant, K_a** an equilibrium constant for the ionization of an acid

monoprotic acid an acid that yields one proton, H^+, when it ionizes

percent dissociation the ratio of the concentration of ionized acid at equilibrium to the acid's initial concentration, expressed as a percent

> Go to **Relative Strengths of Acids and Bases (concentration = 0.01 mol/L) at 25°C** in **Appendix B** for more information about the K_a values of acids.

For a weak acid, the smaller the value of K_a is, the lower the percent dissociation of the acid will be:

weaker acid → lower percent dissociation of the acid → smaller K_a value

Selected values of the acid-dissociation constant are shown in **Table 8.2**.

Table 8.2 Selected Values of the Acid-Dissociation Constant, K_a

Acid Name	K_a
Hydronium ion, H_3O^+(aq)	1
Phosphoric acid, H_3PO_4(aq)	6.9×10^{-3}
Hydrocyanic acid, HCN(aq)	6.2×10^{-10}

Two assumptions are made when solving problems involving weak acids.

- The concentration of the hydronium ion from the autoionization of water is negligible, because it is so much smaller than the concentration of hydronium ions formed from the ionization of the weak acid.
- A weak acid dissociates into ions to such a small extent that in calculations to determine its equilibrium concentration, its change in concentration is ignored. In other words, the concentration of the acid at equilibrium is approximately equal to the initial concentration of the acid.

$$[HA]_{eq} = [HA]_{initial} - [HA]_{dissociation} \approx [HA]_{initial}$$

Study the Sample Problems that follow to learn how to calculate the acid-dissociation constant, K_a, and how to use the acid-dissociation constant to determine additional information about an acid-base reaction. Practise what you have learned by completing the Practice Problems.

Sample Problem

Determining the Acid-Dissociation Constant, K_a, and Percent Dissociation

Problem
Propanoic acid, C_2H_5COOH(aq), is a weak monoprotic acid that is used to inhibit mould formation in bread. A student prepared a 0.10 mol/L solution of propanoic acid and determined the pH to be 2.96. What is the acid-dissociation constant for propanoic acid? What is the percent dissociation of this weak acid?

What Is Required?
You need to determine K_a and the percent dissociation for propanoic acid.

What Is Given?
You know the initial $[C_2H_5COOH]$: 0.10 mol/L
You know the pH: 2.96

Plan Your Strategy	Act on Your Strategy
Write the equation for the dissociation of propanoic acid into ions when added to water. Then set up an ICE table. In the ICE table, [H_2O] is left blank because it is not included in the expression for K_a. The hydronium ion in pure water is 1.0×10^{-7} at 25°C. This is the initial concentration of the hydronium ion before the ionization of the acid. However, compared with the equilibrium concentration of hydronium ions from the dissociated acid, the initial concentration of the hydronium ion from the autoionization of water is not significant in this problem or in the other problems you will solve in this chapter. To show this, write ~0 ("almost zero") in the ICE table for the initial [H_3O^+].	See the ICE table below.

	$C_2H_5COOH(aq)$ +	$H_2O(\ell)$	⇌	$C_2H_5COO^-(aq)$ +	$H_3O^+(aq)$
	[C_2H_5COOH] (mol/L)	[H_2O] (mol/L)		[$C_2H_5COO^-$] (mol/L)	[H_3O^+] (mol/L)
Initial	0.10			0	~0
Change	−x			+x	+x
Equilibrium	0.10 − x			x	x

Plan Your Strategy	Act on Your Strategy
Write the expression for the acid-dissociation constant. Remember, pure water is not included in the expression for K_a.	$K_a = \dfrac{[C_2H_5COO^-][H_3O^+]}{[C_2H_5COOH]}$
Calculate [H_3O^+] using the given pH and the equation pH = −log [H_3O^+]. Because the hydronium ion is formed by the dissociation and ionization of the acid, [$C_2H_5COO^-$] = [H_3O^+]. Use the stoichiometry of the equation and [H_3O^+] to complete the ICE table.	pH = −log[H_3O^+] [H_3O^+] = 10^{-pH} = $10^{-2.96}$ = 1.1×10^{-3} mol/L
Calculate K_a. Remember that [$C_2H_5COO^-$] = [H_3O^+] = 1.1×10^{-3}.	$K_a = \dfrac{[C_2H_5COO^-][H_3O^+]}{[C_2H_5COOH]}$ $= \dfrac{(1.1 \times 10^{-3})^2}{0.10 - (1.1 \times 10^{-3})} = 1.2 \times 10^{-5}$
Calculate the percent dissociation.	percent dissociation = $\dfrac{[C_2H_5COOH]_{dissociated}}{[C_2H_5COOH]_{initial}} \times 100\%$ $= \dfrac{1.1 \times 10^{-3} \, \frac{mol}{L}}{0.10 \, \frac{mol}{L}} \times 100\%$ = 1.1%

Check Your Solution

In comparing the calculated value with other K_a values from Appendix B, the value for K_a seems reasonable for a weak acid.

Practice Problems

41. In low doses, barbiturates act as sedatives. Barbiturates are made from barbituric acid, a weak monoprotic acid that was first prepared by the German chemist Adolph von Baeyer in 1864. The formula for barbituric acid is $HC_4H_3N_2O_3(s)$. A chemist prepares a 0.10 mol/L solution of barbituric acid. The chemist measured the pH of the solution and recorded the value as 2.50. What is the acid-dissociation constant for barbituric acid? What percentage of its molecules dissociated into ions?

42. The word "butter" comes from the Greek *butyros*. Butanoic acid, $HC_4H_7O_2(aq)$ (common name butyric acid), gives rancid butter its distinctive odour. If the pH of a 1.00×10^{-2} mol/L solution of butanoic acid is 3.41, calculate the acid-dissociation constant for butyric acid. What percentage of butyric acid molecules in this solution ionized?

43. Wild almonds taste bitter (and are dangerous to eat!) because they contain hydrocyanic acid, HCN(aq). When a chemist prepared a 0.75 mol/L solution of HCN(aq), the pH was determined to be 4.67. What is the acid-dissociation constant, K_a?

44. Some sunscreen lotions contain salts of para-aminobenzoic acid (PABA). The structure of PABA is shown below. A saturated solution of PABA was prepared by dissolving 4.7 g in a 1.0 L solution. The pH of the solution was found to be 3.19. Calculate the acid-dissociation constant, K_a, for PABA.

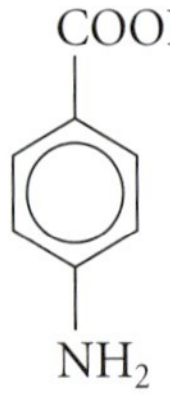

COOH

NH$_2$

45. Aspirin™ (acetylsalicylic acid) is a monoprotic acid with molar mass of 180 g/mol. An aqueous solution containing 3.3 g/L has a pH of 2.62. What percentage of acetylsalicylic acid molecules ionizes in the solution?

46. Quinoxaline is a heterocyclic compound with the molecular formula $C_8H_6N_2$. It is used in the manufacturing of dyes, pharmaceuticals, and antibiotics. When a chemist dissolved 7.19 g of quinoxaline in a 1.0 L solution, the pH of the solution was 1.33. Calculate the acid-dissociation constant, K_a, for quinoxaline.

47. Caprytic acid, also called octanoic acid, is an 8-carbon fatty acid that is used as a sanitizer on dairy equipment that comes in contact with milk. The acid has a molar mass of 144.21 g/mol. An aqueous solution of the sanitizer containing 12.25 g/L has a pH of 2.98. What is the acid-dissociation constant, K_a, for caprytic acid?

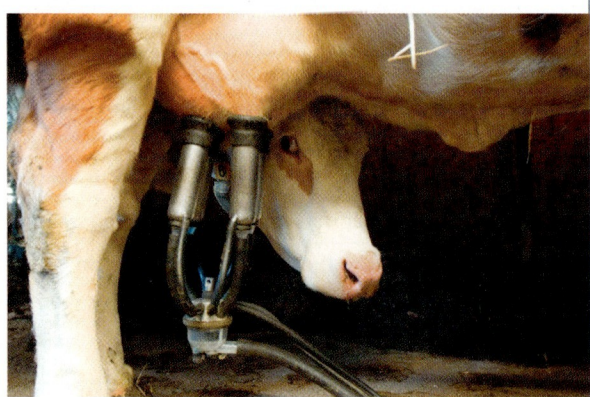

48. Citric acid, $C_6H_8O_7(aq)$, is used to add a sour taste to foods and soft drinks. It is prepared in a solution with a concentration of 0.52 mol/L, and has a pH of 1.72. Calculate the acid-dissociation constant for citric acid. What percentage of citric acid molecules ionizes in the solution?

49. Creatine is a naturally occurring organic acid that helps supply energy to all cells in the body, with particular emphasis on muscle cells. It has a molar mass of 131 g/mol. An aqueous solution containing 2.68 g/L has a pH of 2.23. What percentage of creatine molecules ionizes in the solution?

50. Uracil is one of the four nucleotide monomers that make up the nucleic acid RNA. It was originally isolated in 1900, by the hydrolysis of yeast nuclein found in bovine thymus and spleen. Uracil has a molar mass of 112 g/mol. A biologist prepares a solution of the acid by dissolving 1.24 g of the compound in 1.0 L of solution. The pH of the solution is 5.71. Calculate the acid-dissociation constant, K_a, for uracil.

Sample Problem

Determining pH Using K_a

Problem
An industrial chemist prepares a 0.050 mol/L solution of nitrous acid, $HNO_2(aq)$, which is represented by the equation below. What is the pH of the solution?

$$HNO_2(aq) + H_2O(\ell) \rightleftharpoons NO_2^-(aq) + H_3O^+(aq)$$

What Is Required?
You need to determine the pH of the nitrous acid solution.

What Is Given?
You know the initial concentration of nitrous acid: 0.050 mol/L
You know the balanced chemical equation.
You have the K_a value for nitrous acid from the table in Appendix B.

Plan Your Strategy	Act on Your Strategy
Evaluate the acid-base reaction. You know from **Table 8.1** that nitrous acid is a weak acid so it will partially ionize in water. You know that you can ignore the hydronium ions produced by the autoionization of water because the concentration of hydronium ions is negligible compared with the hydronium ions produced by the ionization of the acid. Set up an ICE table and let x represent the equilibrium concentration of the hydronium ion and the concentration of the nitrite ion, $[NO_2^-]$. You know from the balanced chemical equation that the molar concentrations of these two compounds are equal.	See the ICE table below.

	$HNO_2(aq)$	+	$H_2O(\ell)$	$\rightleftharpoons$	$NO_2^-(aq)$	+	$H_3O^+(aq)$
	$[HNO_2]$ (mol/L)		$[H_2O]$ (mol/L)		$[NO_2^-]$ (mol/L)		$[H_3O^+]$ (mol/L)
Initial	0.050				0.00		0.00
Change	$-x$				$+x$		$+x$
Equilibrium	$0.050 - x$				x		x

Write the acid-dissociation constant expression.	$K_a = \dfrac{[NO_2^-][H_3O^+]}{[HNO_2]}$
Use the table in Appendix B to find the value of K_a for nitrous acid. Use the information from the ICE table to fill in the known and unknown quantities in the acid-dissociation constant expression. This equation does not involve a perfect square. Use the quadratic equation to solve for x.	$K_a = \dfrac{[NO_2^-][H_3O^+]}{[HNO_2]}$ $5.6 \times 10^{-4} = \dfrac{(x)(x)}{0.050 - x}$ $(5.6 \times 10^{-4})(0.050 - x) = x^2$ $(2.8 \times 10^{-5}) - (5.6 \times 10^{-4}x) = x^2$ $x^2 + (5.6 \times 10^{-4}) - (2.8 \times 10^{-5}) = 0$

Continued on next page

	$x = \dfrac{-b \pm \sqrt{b^2 - 4ac}}{2a}$
	$= \dfrac{-5.6 \times 10^{-4} \pm \sqrt{(5.6 \times 10^{-4})^2 - (4)(1)(-2.8 \times 10^{-5})}}{2(1)}$
	$= \dfrac{-5.6 \times 10^{-4} \pm \sqrt{(3.136 \times 10^{-7}) + (1.12 \times 10^{-4})}}{2}$
	$= \dfrac{-5.6 \times 10^{-4} \pm \sqrt{1.123 \times 10^{-4}}}{2}$
	$= \dfrac{-5.6 \times 10^{-4} \pm 1.06 \times 10^{-2}}{2}$
	$= -5.58 \times 10^{-3}$ or 5.02×10^{-3}
Evaluate the two answers and determine which one is possible.	Because it is impossible to have a negative concentration, $x = 5.02 \times 10^{-3}$ mol/L. Thus, $[H_3O^+] = 5.02 \times 10^{-3}$ mol/L.
Use the formula that relates the hydronium ion concentration to pH to calculate the pH.	$\text{pH} = -\log [H_3O^+]$ $= -\log (5.02 \times 10^{-3})$ $= 2.30$

Check Your Solution

The calculated pH is reasonable for an acid. The number of significant digits in the original concentration is two, so the pH must have two significant digits to the right of the decimal.

Practice Problems

51. A 0.075 mol/L solution of chlorous acid, $HClO_2(aq)$, is made in a lab. It has a K_a value of 1.15×10^{-2}, with an equilibrium reaction as follows:

$HClO_2(aq) + H_2O(\ell) \rightleftharpoons ClO_2^-(aq) + H_3O^+(aq)$

What is the pH of the solution?

52. Cyanic acid, $HCNO(aq)$, has a K_a value of 3.47×10^{-4}. It ionizes according to the equation below:

$HCNO(aq) + H_2O(\ell) \rightleftharpoons CNO^-(aq) + H_3O^+(aq)$

Determine the pH of a 0.015 mol/L acid sample.

53. What is the change in pH of the cyanic acid solution from question 52, if the solution concentration triples from 0.015 mol/L to 0.045 mol/L?

54. Determine the pH of a 0.084 mol/L periodic acid solution, $HIO_4(aq)$. The K_a value for the reaction below is 2.29×10^{-2}.

$HIO_4(aq) + H_2O(\ell) \rightleftharpoons IO_4^-(aq) + H_3O^+(aq)$

55. Butylamine is a monoprotic organic acid used in the manufacturing of pesticides. It has a K_a value of 2.51×10^{-11}. A chemist prepares a solution of the acid with a concentration of 0.064 mol/L. Determine the pH of the solution.

56. Triclopyr is a weak monoprotic organic acid used to control broadleaf weeds while leaving grasses unaffected. It has a K_a value of 2.09×10^{-3}. A solution of this acid is prepared with an acid concentration of 0.072 mol/L. What is the pH of this solution?

57. Nitrobenzene is a monoprotic organic acid that has many uses, one of which is in the manufacturing of shoe and floor polishes. $K_a = 1.05 \times 10^{-4}$. The ionization of the acid is given by the following reaction:

$C_6H_5NO_2(aq) + H_2O(\ell) \rightleftharpoons C_6H_4NO_2^-(aq) + H_3O^+(aq)$

Determine the pH of a 0.10 mol/L solution of the acid.

58. Which solution is more acidic: a 0.045 mol/L solution of a weak monoprotic acid with $K_a = 7.74 \times 10^{-7}$ or a 0.087 mol/L solution of a weak monoprotic acid with $K_a = 9.81 \times 10^{-8}$?

59. Which solution is more acidic: a 0.15 mol/L solution of a weak monoprotic acid with $K_a = 0.025$ or a 0.34 mol/L solution of a weak monoprotic acid with $K_a = 0.018$?

Sample Problem

Determining Concentrations from K_a and Initial Weak Acid Concentration

Problem
Methanoic acid, which is also known as formic acid, is a weak acid that is found in the toxin of stinging ants. What is the $[H_3O^+]$ of a 0.10 mol/L solution if $K_a = 1.8 \times 10^{-4}$? The balanced chemical equation is given below:

$$HCOOH(aq) + H_2O(\ell) \rightleftharpoons HCOO^-(aq) + H_3O^+(aq)$$

What Is Required?
You need to determine the concentration of the hydronium ion, $[H_3O^+]$.

What Is Given?
You know the initial concentration of formic acid: 0.10 mol/L
You know the K_a value: 1.8×10^{-4}
You know the balanced chemical equation.

Plan Your Strategy	Act on Your Strategy
Evaluate the acid-base reaction. You know that methanoic acid is a weak acid, so it will partially ionize in water. You know that you can ignore the hydronium ions produced by the autoionization of water because the concentration of hydronium ions is negligible compared with the hydronium ions produced by the ionization of the acid. Set up an ICE table and let x represent the equilibrium concentration of the hydronium ion and the concentration of the formate ion, $[HCOO^-]$. You know from the balanced chemical equation that the molar concentrations of these two compounds are equal.	See the ICE table below.

	HCOOH(aq) +	H$_2$O(ℓ) $\rightleftharpoons$	HCOO$^-$(aq) +	H$_3$O$^+$(aq)
	[HCOOH] (mol/L)	[H$_2$O] (mol/L)	[HCOO$^-$] (mol/L)	[H$_3$O$^+$] (mol/L)
Initial	0.100		0.00	0.00
Change	$-x$		$+x$	$+x$
Equilibrium	$0.10 - x$		x	x

Write the acid-dissociation constant expression.	$K_a = \dfrac{[HCOO^-][H_3O^+]}{[HCOOH]}$
Fill in the known and unknown information in the equation. This equation does not involve a perfect square. Use the quadratic equation to solve for x.	$K_a = \dfrac{[HCOO^-][H_3O^+]}{[HCOOH]}$ $1.8 \times 10^{-4} = \dfrac{(x)(x)}{0.10 - x}$ $(1.8 \times 10^{-4})(0.10 - x) = x^2$ $(1.8 \times 10^{-5}) - (1.8 \times 10^{-4}x) = x^2$ $x^2 + (1.8 \times 10^{-4}x) - (1.8 \times 10^{-5}) = 0$

Continued on next page ❯

	$x = \dfrac{-b \pm \sqrt{b^2 - 4ac}}{2a}$
	$= \dfrac{-1.8 \times 10^{-4} \pm \sqrt{(1.8 \times 10^{-4})^2 - (4)(1)(-1.8 \times 10^{-5})}}{(2)(1)}$
	$= \dfrac{-1.8 \times 10^{-4} \pm \sqrt{(3.24 \times 10^{-8}) + (7.2 \times 10^{-5})}}{2}$
	$= -1.8 \times 10^{-4} \pm 8.487 \times 10^{-3}$
	$= 4.2 \times 10^{-3}$ or -8.7×10^{-3}
Evaluate the two answers and determine which one is possible.	Because it is impossible to have a negative concentration, $x = 4.2 \times 10^{-3}$ mol/L. The [H_3O^+] concentration at equilibrium is 4.2×10^{-3} mol/L.

Check Your Solution
Use your solution to calculate K_a and compare the answer with the K_a given in the problem. The numbers are equal within rounding error.

Practice Problems

60. Sulfamic acid, $NH_2SO_3H(aq)$, is the main ingredient in many household cleaners designed to remove calcium, lime, and rust stains. It has a K_a value of 0.089. What is the [H_3O^+] of a 0.15 mol/L solution of the acid? The chemical equation is given below:
$NH_2SO_3H(aq) + H_2O(\ell) \rightleftharpoons$
$\qquad NH_2SO_3^-(aq) + H_3O^+(aq)$

61. Dichloroacetic acid, $C_2H_2Cl_2O_2(aq)$, is a weak organic monoprotic acid with $K_a = 0.045$. It is used in cancer research, where researchers at the University of Alberta used the acid on cancer cells in mice. They found that the acid restored the function of the mitochondria in the cancerous cells, allowing these cells to self-destruct and cause the tumour to shrink. What is the [H_3O^+] of a 0.025 mol/L solution of the acid? The chemical equation is given below:
$C_2H_2Cl_2O_2(aq) + H_2O(\ell) \rightleftharpoons$
$\qquad C_2HCl_2O_2^-(aq) + H_3O^+(aq)$

62. Acetic acid, $C_2H_4O_2(aq)$, is the weak monoprotic acid found in vinegar. It has a K_a value of 1.75×10^{-5}. Determine the [H_3O^+] in a 0.84 mol/L acetic acid solution.

63. What is the non-ionized periodic acid, $HIO_4(aq)$, concentration at equilibrium if the initial concentration of the weak acid is 0.10 mol/L? The K_a for periodic acid is 2.29×10^{-2} and the reaction is written as follows:
$HIO_4(aq) + H_2O(\ell) \rightleftharpoons IO_4^-(aq) + H_3O^+(aq)$

64. How does the concentration of the hydronium ion for acetic acid change in question 62, if the solution concentration increases by a factor of 2 to a value of 1.68 mol/L?

65. Benzoic acid, $C_7H_6O_2(aq)$, is a weak monoprotic organic acid used in food preservation because it inhibits the growth of mould, yeast, and some bacteria. It has a $K_a = 6.25 \times 10^{-5}$. If, initially, a solution of the acid has a concentration of 0.074 mol/L, what will be the equilibrium concentration of the non-ionized benzoic acid? The chemical equation is given below:
$C_7H_6O_2(aq) + H_2O(\ell) \rightleftharpoons C_7H_5O_2^-(aq) + H_3O^+(aq)$

66. Heptanoic acid is used in the preparation of esters used in fragrances and as artificial flavours. It is a weak monoprotic acid with a K_a value of 1.29×10^{-5}. What is the hydronium ion concentration in a 0.12 mol/L solution of the acid? The chemical equation is given below:
$C_7H_{14}O_2(aq) + H_2O(\ell) \rightleftharpoons$
$\qquad C_7H_{13}O_2^-(aq) + H_3O^+(aq)$

67. Mandelic acid has long been used by doctors as an antibacterial medication, primarily for the treatment of urinary tract infections. It has a molecular formula of C_8H_8O and a K_a value of 4.27×10^{-5}. Initially, 1.84 g of the solid is used to make a 1.0 L solution of the weak acid. The chemical equation is given below:
$C_6H_5CH(OH)CO_2H(aq) + H_2O(\ell) \rightleftharpoons$
$\qquad C_6H_5CH(OH)CO_2^-(aq) + H_3O^+(aq)$
Determine the [H_3O^+] in this solution.

68. Tropine, $C_8H_{15}NO(aq)$, is a weak organic acid with a K_a value of 1.58×10^{-4}. It is used in the manufacture of atropine, a chemical used as a premedication for anesthesia in some patients. Tropine ionizes according to the equation below:

$$C_8H_{15}NO(aq) + H_2O(\ell) \rightleftharpoons C_8H_{14}NO^-(aq) + H_3O^+(aq)$$

What is the non-ionized tropine concentration at equilibrium in a 0.025 mol/L solution of the acid?

69. Which solution has a higher concentration of hydronium ion: a 0.042 mol/L solution of a weak monoprotic acid with $K_a = 1.58 \times 10^{-4}$ or a 0.035 mol/L solution of a weak monoprotic acid with $K_a = 2.27 \times 10^{-4}$?

Polyprotic Acids and Ionization

So far, all of the acids that you have read about are monoprotic acids. Some acids are **polyprotic acids**, which are acids with more than one ionizable proton. Diprotic acids have two protons that ionize, and triprotic acids have three protons that ionize. The protons in polyprotic acids ionize in steps. One proton ionizes at a time. Consider phosphoric acid, $H_3PO_4(aq)$. You can see from the chemical formula that it has three protons that can ionize. The first reaction and its acid-dissociation constant are shown below:

$$H_3PO_4(aq) + H_2O(\ell) \rightleftharpoons H_2PO_4^-(aq) + H_3O^+(aq)$$

$$K_{a1} = \frac{[H_2PO_4^-][H_3O^+]}{[H_3PO_4]} = 7.2 \times 10^{-3}$$

polyprotic acid an acid that yields two or more protons, H⁺, when it ionizes

When the second proton ionizes, the conjugate base in the first reaction becomes the acid in the second reaction, as shown below:

$$H_2PO_4^-(aq) + H_2O(\ell) \rightleftharpoons HPO_4^{2-}(aq) + H_3O^+(aq)$$

$$K_{a2} = \frac{[HPO_4^{2-}][H_3O^+]}{[H_2PO_4^-]} = 6.3 \times 10^{-8}$$

Suggested Investigation

Inquiry Investigation 8-B, Determining K_a for Ethanoic (Acetic) Acid

The third proton ionizes in the same manner as the second proton, and the conjugate base in the second reaction becomes the acid in the third reaction, as shown below:

$$HPO_4^{2-}(aq) + H_2O(\ell) \rightleftharpoons PO_4^{3-}(aq) + H_3O^+(aq)$$

$$K_{a3} = \frac{[PO_4^{3-}][H_3O^+]}{[HPO_4^{2-}]} = 4.2 \times 10^{-13}$$

Look closely at the acid-dissociation constants for the three steps. You can see that phosphoric acid is a much stronger acid than the other two acids. You can determine acid strength by looking at the K_a values. A smaller K_a value indicates a weaker acid. The decreasing K_a values for phosphoric acid are reasonable, because it is easier to remove a hydrogen ion, H^+, from a neutral atom than it is to remove a second or third hydrogen ion from a negatively charged ion. **Table 8.3** features some acid-dissociation constants for selected polyprotic acids.

Table 8.3 K_a Values for Selected Polyprotic Acids

Acid Name, Formula*	K_{a1}	K_{a2}	K_{a3}
Arsenic acid, $H_3AsO_4(aq)$	6×10^{-3}	1.1×10^{-7}	3×10^{-12}
Citric acid, $HOC(CH_2)_2(COOH)_3(aq)$	7.4×10^{-4}	1.7×10^{-5}	4.0×10^{-7}
Hydrosulfuric acid, $H_2S(aq)$	9×10^{-8}	1×10^{-17}	
Oxalic acid, $HOOCCOOH(aq)$	5.6×10^{-2}	5.4×10^{-5}	
Sulfurous acid, $H_2SO_3(aq)$	1.4×10^{-2}	6.5×10^{-8}	

*Ionizable protons in red type.

Section 8.2 Review

Section Summary

- Strong acids ionize almost completely in water, and strong bases dissociate almost completely in water. Weak acids partially ionize in water, and weak bases partially ionize or dissociate in water.
- In general, an acid-base equilibrium reaction shifts in the direction in which a stronger acid and a stronger base form a weaker acid and a weaker base.
- The acid-dissociation constant, or acid-ionization constant, K_a, is used for acid-base reactions.
- Percent dissociation of a weak acid is the fraction of acid molecules that ionizes at equilibrium compared with the initial concentration of the acid.
- Some acids are monoprotic and have one ionizable proton. Other acids are polyprotic and have more than one ionizable proton.

Review Questions

1. **K/U** Explain why the position of equilibrium in an acid-base equilibrium system is always toward the weaker acid.

2. **K/U** Use **Table 8.1** to give three examples of acid-base equilibrium systems and indicate the direction in which each reaction is favoured.

3. **C** Create a flowchart or similar graphic organizer that can be used to determine the direction in which an acid-base equilibrium system is favoured.

4. **T/I** For each of the following weak monoprotic acid concentrations, determine the percentage of molecules that ionize in solution.
    a. 0.01 mol/L, pH = 2.75
    b. 0.12 mol/L, pH = 2.31
    c. 0.027 mol/L, pH = 5.74

5. **T/I** When an investigation was performed, hydrogen sulfate ions, $HSO_4^-(aq)$, were combined with water. Using **Table 8.1**, determine the reaction that occurred and describe the position of equilibrium in the system.

6. **C** Draw the amide ion and illustrate how this ion can behave as a Brønsted-Lowry base in water.

7. **K/U** Write all possible reactions of sodium hydrogen carbonate in water. Recall that sodium hydrogen carbonate dissociates completely into sodium ions and hydrogen carbonate ions in solution.

8. **K/U** Write the acid-dissociation constant expressions for each of the following weak acids:
    a. ammonia, $NH_3(aq)$
    b. ethanoic acid, $CH_3COOH(aq)$
    c. perchloric acid, $HClO_4(aq)$

9. **C** Explain why the K_a value for the ionization of a strong acid is always larger than that for a weaker acid.

10. **T/I** An industrial chemist prepares a 0.025 mol/L solution of hydrazoic acid, $HN_3(aq)$, a weak monoprotic acid with $K_a = 7.94 \times 10^{-9}$. Calculate the concentration of hydronium ions in this solution.

11. **K/U** Determine the pH of a 0.35 mol/L hydrocyanic acid solution, $HNC(aq)$, prepared by a research chemist. For this acid, $K_a = 6.2 \times 10^{-10}$.

12. **A** The photograph below shows a pH meter in a solution of a weak monoprotic acid. Determine the K_a value of the acid if the initial concentration was 0.010 mol/L.

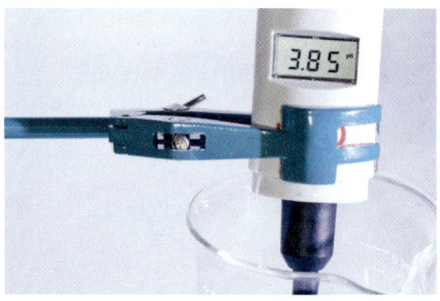

13. **T/I** A weak monoprotic acid has a K_a value of 7.54×10^{-6}. Determine the concentration of the hydronium ion in a 0.025 mol/L solution of acid.

14. **T/I** In general, when determining the percent dissociation for a weak acid, we assume that the ionization of the acid occurs to such a small extent that the initial acid concentration can be used. A weak monoprotic acid has a K_a value of 2.58×10^{-5}. The initial acid concentration is 0.10 mol/L.
    a. Determine the percent dissociation of the acid, assuming that the final acid concentration after the dissociation is still 0.10 mol/L.
    b. Determine the percent dissociation using the actual final acid concentration determined by calculations.
    c. Use the results of these calculations to discuss the validity of the assumption.

SECTION 8.3 Base Ionization

Thus far, the focus on ionization or dissociation constants has been on acids. Some weak bases also ionize in solution and form equilibrium systems. Just like acids, bases have equilibrium constants that convey information about the system. The ionization of weak bases is approached in a similar manner to that of acids.

The Base-Ionization Constant, K_b

Consider a generic weak base, B, dissolving in water. When the base dissolves in water, the base reacts with water, as represented by the equation below:

$$B(aq) + H_2O(\ell) \rightleftharpoons BH^+(aq) + OH^-(aq)$$

The base has a lone pair of electrons that accepts the donated proton. Recall that the ability to accept a proton is the Brønsted-Lowry definition of a base. Ammonia and amines are examples of Brønsted-Lowry bases that have a lone pair of electrons on the nitrogen atom that can accept a proton. The equation for ammonia reacting with water is shown below:

$$NH_3(aq) + H_2O(\ell) \rightleftharpoons NH_4^+(aq) + OH^-(aq)$$

Notice that this base does not dissociate, but it does become ionized. The equilibrium constant for a base is called the **base-ionization constant** or the **base-dissociation constant, K_b**. The generic equation for this constant is shown below. Just like other equilibrium constants, water is included in the value of K_b and is not part of the base-ionization expression because the concentration of water is almost constant. The base-ionization constant expression for ammonia is also shown below, and K_b values for selected bases are shown in **Table 8.4** on the next page.

$$K_b = K[H_2O] = \frac{[BH^+][OH^-]}{[B]} \qquad K_b = \frac{[NH_4^+][OH^-]}{[NH_3]} = 1.8 \times 10^{-5}$$

Compounds that contain nitrogen are not the only compounds that can act as a Brønsted-Lowry base. The conjugate base of a weak acid can also act as a base. For example, the fluoride ion, $F^-(aq)$, acts as a base because it can accept a proton, as shown in the equation below:

$$F^-(aq) + H_2O(\ell) \rightleftharpoons HF(aq) + OH^-(aq)$$

$$K_b = \frac{[HF][OH^-]}{[F^-]}$$

You can refer to the table, "Base-Ionization Constants for Nitrogen Bases," in Appendix B for more information about K_b values for bases.

To solve problems involving the base-ionization constant, you follow the same procedures as you do when working with acids, except that you calculate the concentration of the hydroxide ion, $[OH^-]$, first instead of calculating the concentration of the hydronium ion, $[H_3O^+]$. Study the Sample Problems on the following page and practise using base-ionization constants in the Practice Problems.

Key Terms

base-ionization constant, K_b

base-ionization constant, or base-dissociation constant, K_b*
an equilibrium constant for the ionization of a base

*The term "base-ionization constant" is used more commonly than "base-dissociation constant" because some weak bases become ionized without actually breaking apart, or dissociating, into their components.

Table 8.4 K_b Values for Selected Bases

Base Name, Formula	Molecular Structure*	K_b
Diethylamine, $(CH_3CH_2)_2NH(aq)$	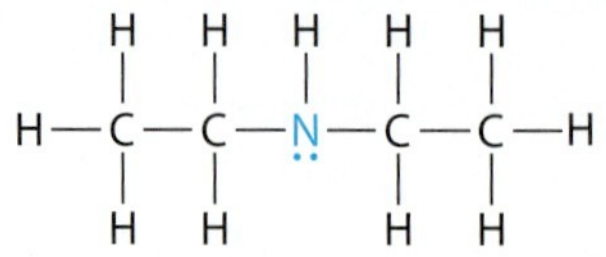	8.6×10^{-4}
Dimethylamine, $(CH_3)_2NH(aq)$	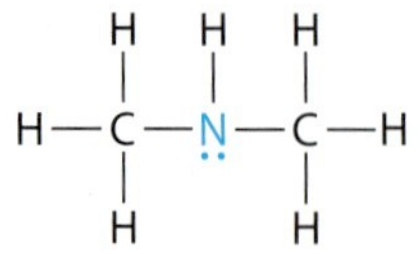	5.9×10^{-4}
Methylamine, $CH_3NH_2(aq)$	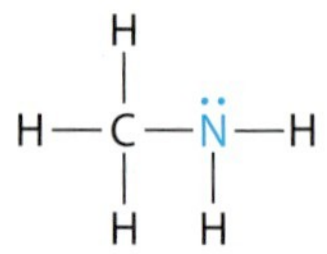	4.4×10^{-4}
Ammonia, $NH_3(aq)$	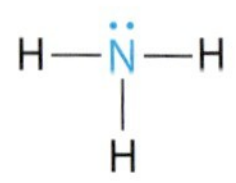	1.76×10^{-5}
Pyridine, $C_5H_5N(aq)$		1.7×10^{-9}
Aniline, $C_6H_5NH_2(aq)$	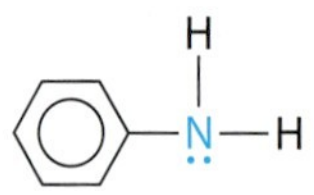	4.0×10^{-10}

Base strength increases ↑

*Nitrogen and its lone pair of electrons are shown in blue type.

Sample Problem

Calculating K_b for a Weak Base

Problem
One of the uses for aniline, $C_6H_5NH_2(\ell)$, is in the manufacture of dyes. Aniline is soluble in water and acts as a weak base. When a solution containing 5.0 g/L of aniline was prepared, the pH was determined to be 8.68. Calculate the base-ionization constant for aniline.

What Is Required?
You need to determine K_b for aniline.

What Is Given?
You know the formula for aniline: $C_6H_5NH_2(\ell)$
You know the concentration of the aniline solution, $C_6H_5NH_2(aq)$: 5.0 g/L
You know the pH of the solution: 8.68

Plan Your Strategy	Act on Your Strategy
Use the atomic masses from the periodic table for each atom present in aniline to calculate its molar mass.	$M_{C_6H_5NH_2} = 6M_C + 7M_H + 1M_N$ $= 6(12.01 \text{ g/mol}) + 7(1.01 \text{ g/mol}) + 1(14.01 \text{ g/mol})$ $= 72.06 \text{ g/mol} + 7.07 \text{ g/mol} + 14.01 \text{ g/mol}$ $= 93.14 \text{ g/mol}$
Calculate the molar concentration of the solution using the molar mass of aniline and the mass per litre used to make the solution.	$c = \dfrac{m}{V} \times \dfrac{1}{M}$ $= 5.0 \dfrac{\text{g}}{\text{L}} \times \dfrac{1 \text{ mol}}{93.14 \text{ g}} = 0.0537 \dfrac{\text{mol}}{\text{L}}$
Use an ICE table to organize the known and the unknown information. The first step is to write the balanced chemical equation across the top of the ICE table. Remember that aniline is an amine, and the lone pair of electrons on the nitrogen is a proton acceptor.	See the ICE table below.

	$C_6H_5NH_2(aq)$ +	$H_2O(\ell)$	⇌	$C_6H_5NH_3^+(aq)$ +	$OH^-(aq)$
	$[C_6H_5NH_2]$ (mol/L)	$[H_2O]$ (mol/L)		$[C_6H_5NH_3^+]$ (mol/L)	$[OH^-]$ (mol/L)
Initial	0.0537			0.00	0.00
Change	$-x$			$+x$	$+x$
Equilibrium	$0.0537 - x$			x	x

Plan Your Strategy	Act on Your Strategy
You are given the pH of the solution and it can be used to determine the concentration of the hydroxide ion, using the following relationships: $\text{pH} + \text{pOH} = 14.00$ $[OH^-] = 10^{-\text{pOH}}$	$\text{pOH} = 14.00 - \text{pH}$ $= 14.00 - 8.68$ $= 5.32$ $[OH^-] = 10^{-\text{pOH}}$ $= 10^{-5.32}$ $= 4.79 \times 10^{-6}$
Fill the known information into the ICE table.	

	$C_6H_5NH_2(aq)$ +	$H_2O(\ell)$	⇌	$C_6H_5NH_3^+(aq)$ +	$OH^-(aq)$
	$[C_6H_5NH_2]$ (mol/L)	$[H_2O]$ (mol/L)		$[C_6H_5NH_3^+]$ (mol/L)	$[OH^-]$ (mol/L)
Initial	0.0537			0.00	0.00
Change	$-(4.79 \times 10^{-6})$			$+(4.79 \times 10^{-6})$	$+(4.79 \times 10^{-6})$
Equilibrium	$(0.0537) - (4.79 \times 10^{-6})$ $= 0.0537$			4.79×10^{-6}	4.79×10^{-6}

Plan Your Strategy	Act on Your Strategy
Write the expression for the base-ionization constant. Substitute equilibrium terms into the expression and calculate K_b.	$K_b = \dfrac{[C_6H_5NH_3^+][OH^-]}{[C_6H_5NH_2]}$ $= \dfrac{(4.79 \times 10^{-6})(4.79 \times 10^{-6})}{0.0537} = 4.3 \times 10^{-10}$

Check Your Solution

Compare your calculated value to the values in **Table 8.4**. The calculated answer is reasonable and expressed with the correct number of significant digits.

Sample Problem

Calculating the pH of a Weak Base

Problem
The characteristic bitter taste of tonic water is due to the addition of quinine, $C_{20}H_{24}N_2O_2(s)$. Quinine is a naturally occurring white crystalline compound. It is used to treat malaria. The base-ionization constant, K_b, for quinine is 3.3×10^{-6}. What are the hydroxide ion concentration and pH of a 3.6×10^{-3} mol/L solution of quinine?

What Is Required?
You need to determine the [OH$^-$] and pH of quinine.

What Is Given?
You know the K_b value: 3.3×10^{-6}
You know the concentration of quinine: 3.6×10^{-3} mol/L

Plan Your Strategy	Act on Your Strategy
Let Q represent the formula for quinine. Write the equation for quinine acting as a base in water. Then set up an ICE table. If an acid or a base has a complex molecular formula, you can represent the formula using a shortened notation, such as Q for quinine. Remember that a Brønsted-Lowry acid always donates a proton to water, and a Brønsted-Lowry base always accepts a proton from water.	See the ICE table below.

$$Q(aq) + H_2O(\ell) \rightleftharpoons HQ^+(aq) + OH^-(aq)$$

	[Q] (mol/L)	[H$_2$O] (mol/L)	[HQ$^+$] (mol/L)	[OH$^-$] (mol/L)
Initial	3.6×10^{-3}		0.00	0.00
Change	$-x$		$+x$	$+x$
Equilibrium	$(3.6 \times 10^{-3}) - x$		x	x

Plan Your Strategy	Act on Your Strategy
Write the expression for the base-ionization constant. Substitute the values into the expression.	$K_b = \dfrac{[HQ^+][OH^-]}{[Q]}$ $3.3 \times 10^{-6} = \dfrac{(x)(x)}{(3.6 \times 10^{-3}) - x}$ $x^2 + (3.3 \times 10^{-6} x) - (1.188 \times 10^{-8}) = 0$
The equation is not a perfect square. The quadratic equation must be used to calculate x.	$x = \dfrac{-b \pm \sqrt{b^2 - 4ac}}{2a}$ $= \dfrac{-3.3 \times 10^{-6} \pm \sqrt{(3.3 \times 10^{-6})^2 - (4)(1)(-1.188 \times 10^{-8})}}{(2)(1)}$ $= \dfrac{-3.3 \times 10^{-6} \pm \sqrt{(1.089 \times 10^{-11}) + (4.752 \times 10^{-8})}}{2}$ $= \dfrac{-3.3 \times 10^{-6} \pm 2.180 \times 10^{-4}}{2}$ $x = 1.1 \times 10^{-4}$ or -1.1×10^{-4}

Evaluate the two answers and determine which one is possible.	Because it is impossible to have a negative concentration, $x = 1.1 \times 10^{-4}$ mol/L. The concentration of the hydroxide ion, [OH⁻], is 1.1×10^{-4} mol/L.
Use the formula that relates the hydroxide ion concentration to pOH to calculate the pOH. $\text{pOH} = -\log[\text{OH}^-]$	$\begin{aligned} \text{pOH} &= -\log[\text{OH}^-] \\ &= -\log(1.1 \times 10^{-4}) \\ &= 3.96 \end{aligned}$ $\begin{aligned} \text{pH} &= 14.00 - \text{pOH} \\ &= 14.00 - 3.96 \\ &= 10.04 \end{aligned}$

Check Your Solution

The pH of the solution is greater than 7, as expected for a basic solution. The answer has the correct number of significant digits to the right of the decimal point.

Practice Problems

70. Write the chemical equation for each base ionizing in an aqueous solution:
  a. ammonia, $NH_3(aq)$
  b. trimethylamine, $(CH_3)_3N(aq)$
  c. hydrogen sulfite ion, $HSO_3^-(aq)$
  d. carbonate ion, $CO_3^{2-}(aq)$

71. Write the K_b expression for each base in question 70.

72. When a 0.25 mol/L aqueous solution of methylamine was prepared, the pH of the solution was determined to be 10.04. What percentage of methylamine molecules ionized in the solution?

73. Codeine, $C_{18}H_{21}NO_3(s)$, is added to some cough medicines. When a 0.020 mol/L aqueous solution of codeine was prepared, the pH of the solution was determined to be 10.26. Calculate K_b for codeine.

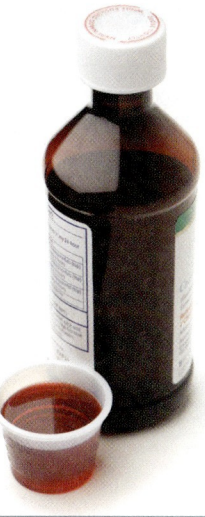

74. A material safety data sheet (MSDS) describes pyridine, $C_5H_5N(\ell)$, as a clear liquid with a putrid odour. A 16 g/L solution of pyridine has pH = 9.23. Use these data to calculate K_b for pyridine.

75. An aqueous solution of household ammonia, $NH_3(aq)$, has a molar concentration of 0.105 mol/L. Calculate the pH of the solution. K_b for ammonia is 1.8×10^{-5}.

76. Hydrazine, $N_2H_4(\ell)$, has been used as a rocket fuel. The concentration of an aqueous solution of hydrazine is 5.9×10^{-2} mol/L. Calculate the pH of the solution. The K_b for hydrazine is 1.3×10^{-6}.

77. Morphine, $C_{17}H_{19}NO_3(s)$, is a naturally occurring base found in opium poppy plants that is used to control pain. A 4.5×10^{-3} mol/L solution has a pH of 9.93. Calculate K_b for morphine.

78. Methylamine, $CH_3NH_2(g)$, is a fishy-smelling gas at room temperature. It is used in the manufacture of several prescription drugs, including methamphetamine. Calculate [OH⁻] and pOH of a 1.5 mol/L aqueous solution of methylamine. K_b for methylamine is 4.6×10^{-4}.

79. At room temperature, trimethylamine, $(CH_3)_3N(g)$, is a gas with a strong ammonia-like odour. Calculate [OH⁻] and the percentage of trimethylamine molecules that react with water in a 0.22 mol/L aqueous solution. K_b for trimethylamine is 6.3×10^{-5}.

80. An aqueous solution of ammonia has a pH of 10.85. What is the concentration of the solution?

Activity 8.1 The Chemistry of Oven Cleaning

Oven cleaning is not a job that most people enjoy. Removing baked-on grease from inside an oven requires a good cleaner and vigorous scrubbing. Traditional oven cleaners contain strong bases, such as sodium hydroxide, NaOH(aq), or potassium hydroxide, KOH(aq). Sodium hydroxide reacts with grease and oil to form, among other things, soap molecules. Organic chemists classify this reaction as the *hydrolysis of an ester*, even though the fatty acids in oil and grease are triesters of glycerol. Soap molecules have a long non-polar "tail" and a polar "head." The polar "head" is water-soluble. Because of its polarity, soap acts like a "bridge" between grease and water, thereby allowing the grease to be easily washed away with the soap.

Although traditional oven cleaners that contain sodium hydroxide or potassium hydroxide are effective, they are extremely caustic. If not used carefully, they are potentially a dangerous household chemical. Because the cleaners are so caustic, the user must wear rubber gloves when using them. Most traditional oven cleaners are aerosol sprays. Inhaling the vapours causes extreme discomfort and irritation of the nose and other airways. These oven cleaners also contain organic ingredients used to soften the baked-on residues. These organic ingredients also have problems. They create safety and disposal problems because the aerosol requires a propellant gas, which is butane in most cases. Butane is highly flammable. These strong bases are also corrosive to metals and they will damage paint and fabrics.

There are alternatives to traditional oven cleaners, which are commonly referred to as "green" oven cleaners. Green oven cleaners include applying a paste of baking soda (sodium hydrogen carbonate, $NaHCO_3(s)$) and water to the oven and leaving it for several hours, or leaving a bowl containing a household ammonia solution, $NH_3(aq)$, in the oven for a length of time. Each of these treatments still requires vigorous scrubbing to remove the grease and grime from the oven.

These green alternatives are considerably less toxic than traditional oven cleaners, but they are also problematic. Aqueous ammonia is volatile and is toxic if inhaled. The vapours irritate the eyes, lungs, and skin.

Questions

1. Explain why sodium hydroxide is described as an Arrhenius base.
2. Write the equation for the dissociation of sodium hydroxide in water.
3. Explain why ammonia is described as a Brønsted-Lowry base.
4. Write the equation for the ionization of ammonia in aqueous solution. Write the base-ionization expression and the value of K_b.
5. Explain why the hydrogen carbonate ion, HCO_3^-(aq), is described as a Brønsted-Lowry base.
6. Write the equation for the ionization of the hydrogen carbonate ion, HCO_3^-, in aqueous solution. Write the base-ionization expression and the value of K_b.
7. Rank the following in terms of increasing base strength: NaOH(aq), NH_3(aq), HCO_3^-(aq).
8. Based on your answers to question 7, explain why many people continue to use traditional oven cleaners rather than green oven cleaners, even though the green oven cleaners are environmentally friendly, readily available, and inexpensive?
9. Design an investigation to test the effectiveness of the oven cleaners discussed in this activity. If your teacher approves of your procedure, carry out the investigation.
   Note: A fume hood is required when working with oven cleaners.
10. Use the Internet or read the label of a can of traditional oven cleaner to determine the ingredients other than hydroxides. What health and safety issues are associated with these compounds?
11. Lately, more and more ovens are described as "self-cleaning." Use the Internet to research answers to the following questions: What does this mean? How does "self-cleaning" work? Is this an effective way to clean an oven? What, if any, are the drawbacks?

> **Learning Check**
>
> 13. What is a base-dissociation constant?
> 14. Would you expect a strong or a weak base to have a higher percent dissociation and why?
> 15. Is hydrofluoric acid, HF(aq), a monoprotic acid or a polyprotic acid? Explain your answer.
> 16. Explain why the term *base-dissociation constant* is misleading.
> 17. How many acid-dissociation constants would you expect to find in Appendix B for a triprotic acid? Explain your answer.
> 18. Using Appendix B, how many conjugate base-acid reactions would you expect the phosphate ion, PO_4^{3-} to have? Write the equations for each of these reactions.

The Relationship Among K_a, K_b, and K_w

An important relationship exists among the K_a of an acid, the K_b of its conjugate base, and the ion-product constant of water, K_w. Consider the reaction of acetic acid, $CH_3COOH(aq)$, dissolving in water, as shown below:

$$CH_3COOH(aq) + H_2O(\ell) \rightleftharpoons H_3O^+(aq) + CH_3COO^-(aq)$$

The conjugate base, $CH_3COO^-(aq)$, reacts with water, as shown below:

$$CH_3COO^-(aq) + H_2O(\ell) \rightleftharpoons OH^-(aq) + CH_3COOH(aq)$$

The acid-dissociation constant and the base-ionization constant are shown below:

$$K_a = \frac{[H_3O^+][CH_3COO^-]}{[CH_3COOH]} \qquad K_b = \frac{[CH_3COOH][OH^-]}{[CH_3COO^-]}$$

The product of these two constants yields the ion-product constant of water, as shown below:

$$K_a K_b = \frac{[H_3O^+][\cancel{CH_3COO^-}]}{[\cancel{CH_3COOH}]} \times \frac{[\cancel{CH_3COOH}][OH^-]}{[\cancel{CH_3COO^-}]}$$

$$= [H_3O^+][OH^-]$$

$$= K_w$$

If you treat the two reactions as a reaction sequence, as shown below, and add the reactions together, you see that the sum is the autoionization of water.

$$\cancel{CH_3COOH}(aq) + H_2O(\ell) \rightleftharpoons H_3O^+(aq) + \cancel{CH_3COO^-}(aq)$$
$$\underline{\cancel{CH_3COO^-}(aq) + H_2O(\ell) \rightleftharpoons OH^-(aq) + \cancel{CH_3COOH}(aq)}$$
$$2H_2O(\ell) \rightleftharpoons H_3O^+(aq) + OH^-(aq)$$

This illustrates an important principle for equilibrium reactions at a constant temperature: *For a reaction that is the sum of two or more reactions, the overall equilibrium constant is the product of the individual equilibrium constants.* Thus, the overall equilibrium constant for an acid and its conjugate base is as follows:

$$K_a K_b = K_w$$

This relationship allows you to calculate K_a if you know K_b, or you can calculate K_b if you know K_a. Study the Sample Problem on the next page and complete the Practice Problems that follow to practise using this equation.

Sample Problem

Equilibrium Constants for Conjugate Acid-Base Pairs

Problem

a. Calculate K_b for the conjugate base of benzoic acid, $C_6H_5COOH(aq)$.

b. Calculate K_a for the conjugate acid of ethylamine, $C_2H_5NH_2(aq)$.

What Is Required?

You have to calculate K_b for the conjugate base of benzoic acid, $C_6H_5COOH(aq)$, and calculate K_a for the conjugate acid of ethylamine, $C_2H_5NH_2(aq)$.

What Is Given?

You are given the chemical formulas for both compounds; values for the constants are found in Appendix B.

Plan Your Strategy	Act on Your Strategy
Identify the conjugate base of benzoic acid.	The conjugate base is the benzoate ion, $C_6H_5COO^-(aq)$.
Find the value of K_a for $C_6H_5COOH(aq)$ in Appendix B and use the equation $K_b = \dfrac{K_w}{K_a}$ to determine K_b.	$K_a = 6.3 \times 10^{-5}$ $K_b = \dfrac{K_w}{K_a} = \dfrac{1.0 \times 10^{-14}}{6.3 \times 10^{-5}} = 1.6 \times 10^{-10}$ K_b for the benzoate ion is 1.6×10^{-10}.
Identify the conjugate acid of ethylamine.	The conjugate acid of ethylamine is $C_2H_5NH_3^+(aq)$.
Find the value of K_b for $C_2H_5NH_2(aq)$ in Appendix B and calculate K_a for the conjugate acid using the following equation: $K_a = \dfrac{K_w}{K_b}$	$K_b = 4.5 \times 10^{-4}$ $K_a = \dfrac{K_w}{K_b} = \dfrac{1.0 \times 10^{-14}}{4.5 \times 10^{-4}} = 2.2 \times 10^{-11}$ K_a for $C_2H_5NH_3^+(aq)$ is 2.2×10^{-11}.

Check Your Solution

The calculations for K_a and K_b look reasonable compared with other values in Appendix B. Both answers have the correct number of significant digits.

Practice Problems

81. List the conjugate bases for each acid below:
  a. periodic acid, $HIO_4(aq)$
  b. cyanic acid, $HCNO(aq)$
  c. nitrous acid, $HNO_2(aq)$
  d. hydrofluoric acid, $HF(aq)$

82. Write the K_b expressions for each conjugate base in question 81.

83. Calculate the K_b value for the conjugate base of hydrosulfuric acid.

84. Calculate the K_b value for the conjugate base of the hydrogen citrate ion.

85. Calculate the K_b value for the conjugate base of acetic acid.

86. Calculate the K_a value for the conjugate acid of dimethylamine.

87. Calculate the K_a value for the conjugate acid of hydrazine.

88. Calculate the K_a value for the conjugate acid of hydroxylamine.

89. "The K_b expression for a conjugate base is simply the reciprocal expression of the K_a expression for the acid of that conjugate base." Is this statement true or false? Explain your reasoning.

90. Verify your answer to question 89 by writing the K_a and K_b expressions, using ammonia as the example.

Section 8.3 Review

Section Summary

- The equilibrium constant for a base is called the base-dissociation constant, or the base-ionization constant, K_b.
- The base-dissociation constant, or the base-ionization constant, K_b, is also used for acid-base reactions.
- Some weak bases do not dissociate, but they do become ionized in acid-base reactions.
- The overall equilibrium constant for an acid and its conjugate base is $K_a K_b = K_w$.

Review Questions

1. **K/U** Describe the process of proton acceptance by a base molecule in an aqueous solution. How can this process be extended to any solution?

2. **K/U** For each of the following weak base concentrations, determine the percentage of base molecules that ionized in the solution.
   a. 0.015 mol/L, pH = 10.15
   b. 3.1×10^{-4} mol/L, pH = 9.74
   c. 7.3×10^{-6} mol/L, pH = 7.04

3. **C** Create a flowchart or similar graphic organizer that can be used to calculate the K_b value for a weak acid.

4. **K/U** A solution containing 4.2 g/L of the weak base pyridine, C_5H_5N(aq), was determined to have a pH of 8.98. Calculate its base-ionization constant.

5. **C** Draw the diagram for the ions and molecules in the reaction of the weak base ammonia in water, and use arrows to illustrate the movement of the proton in the reaction, including the point where a proton would attach to the ion or molecule.

6. **T/I** Ethylamine is a weak organic base with many applications, including the production of some herbicides. For a 4.5×10^{-3} mol/L aqueous solution, what are the hydroxide ion concentration, pH, and pOH of this solution?

7. **K/U** Show that $K_a K_b = K_w$, using nitrous acid, HNO_2(aq), as the example.

8. **K/U** Write the base-dissociation constant expressions for the conjugate base of each of the following weak acids:
   a. oxalic acid, HOOCCOOH(aq)
   b. ascorbic acid, $C_6H_8O_6$(aq)
   c. sulfurous acid, H_2SO_3(aq)

9. **K/U** Explain why the K_b value for the dissociation of a strong base is always larger than that for a weaker base.

10. **T/I** Methanamine is a weak organic base that can be used to remove hydrogen sulfide from hydrocarbons. An industrial chemist prepares a 8.3×10^{-3} mol/L solution of methanamine with $K_b = 4.6 \times 10^{-4}$. Calculate the concentration of hydroxide ions in this solution.

11. **T/I** Determine the pH of a 0.25 mol/L ammonia solution prepared by a research chemist. For this base, $K_b = 1.8 \times 10^{-5}$.

12. **A** The photographs below show two solutions that have almost identical K_b values. Which of the solutions would have the higher solution concentration? Explain your answer.

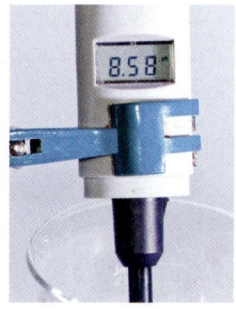

13. **T/I** A weak monoprotic acid has a K_b value of 2.9×10^{-4}. Determine the concentration of the hydronium ion in a 0.015 mol/L solution of acid.

14. **T/I** One way to approximate the percent ionization for a weak base is to assume that the ionization of the base occurs to such a small extent that the initial base concentration can be used in the calculation. A weak base has a K_b value of 1.8×10^{-6}. The initial solution concentration is 0.21 mol/L.
   a. Determine the percent ionization for the base, assuming that the final base concentration after the ionization is still 0.21 mol/L.
   b. Determine the percent ionization using the actual final base concentration determined by calculations.
   c. With the results of this in mind, do you think that the approximation for the percent ionization is a valid approach? Explain your answer.

SECTION 8.4
Salts, Buffers, Titrations, and Solubility

Key Terms

salt
neutralization reaction
anion
cation
salt hydrolysis
buffer solution
common-ion effect
endpoint
equivalence point
solubility
solubility-product constant, K_{sp}
precipitate
molar solubility

So far, you have learned basic information about acids and bases. In this section, you will learn more about the behaviour of these compounds.

Salt Hydrolysis

When an acid and a base react, water and a salt are formed, as shown in **Figure 8.11**. A **salt** is an ionic compound that results from an acid-base reaction. A chemical reaction between an acid and a base that yields a salt and water is called a **neutralization reaction**.

Salts are strong electrolytes that completely dissociate in water and they often affect the pH of a solution. The pH of the salt solution can be neutral, acidic, or basic. When the salt dissociates or splits apart in water, an **anion**, a negatively charged ion, and a **cation**, a positively charged ion, form. The process in which salt reacts with water is called **salt hydrolysis**.

Neutral Salt Solutions

When a salt consisting of an anion of a strong acid or a cation of a strong base reacts with water, hydrolysis, or a reaction with water, usually does not occur. For example, when a strong acid, such as nitric acid, $HNO_3(\ell)$, dissolves in water, the acid completely dissociates and ionizes as shown below:

$$HNO_3(\ell) + H_2O(\ell) \rightarrow NO_3^-(aq) + H_3O^+(aq)$$

Water is a much stronger conjugate base than the nitrate ion, $NO_3^-(aq)$, so the reaction essentially goes to completion. This is true for any strong acid: the negatively charged ion, or anion, of a strong acid is a weaker base than water, so the reaction goes to completion.

salt an ionic compound that results from an acid-base reaction

neutralization reaction a chemical reaction between an acid and a base that yields a salt and water

anion a negatively charged ion

cation a positively charged ion

salt hydrolysis the process in which a salt reacts with water

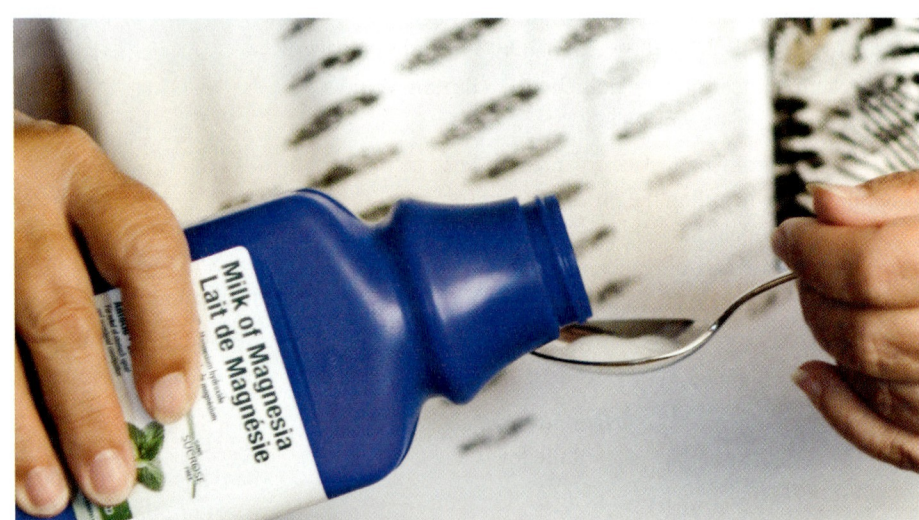

Figure 8.11 Hydrochloric acid in the stomach helps digest the foods you eat. Indigestion can be caused by too much hydrochloric acid in the stomach. Magnesium hydroxide is a base found in some medicines that neutralizes this excess acid. The chemical reaction is $Mg(OH)_2(s) + 2HCl(aq) \rightarrow MgCl_2(aq) + 2H_2O(\ell)$. Magnesium chloride, $MgCl_2$, is a salt.

Consider the dissociation of a strong base in water, such as sodium hydroxide, NaOH(s), as shown below:

$$NaOH(s) \xrightarrow{H_2O} Na^+(aq) + OH^-(aq)$$

Recall that the H_2O written above the yield arrow indicates that water is required as the solvent, but water is not considered a reactant. The sodium ion, $Na^+(aq)$, does not react further with water and cannot donate or accept a proton. The solution is neutral, with a pH of about 7. The positively charged ions, or cations, from all strong bases behave in this same way.

Acidic Salt Solutions

When a salt consisting of the anion of a strong acid and the cation of a weak base dissociates in water, the solution is acidic because the cation acts as a weak acid. When ammonium chloride, $NH_4Cl(s)$, dissolves in water, as shown below, the chloride ions, $Cl^-(aq)$, do not react with water because the ion is a very weak base.

$$NH_4Cl(s) \xrightarrow{H_2O} NH_4^+(aq) + Cl^-(aq)$$

The ammonium ion, $NH_4^+(aq)$, is a weak Brønsted-Lowry base that does react with water, as shown below:

$$NH_4^+(aq) + H_2O(\ell) \rightleftharpoons NH_3(aq) + H_3O^+(aq)$$

Because hydronium ions are produced, the solution is acidic.

Another group of salts that produce acidic solutions are small, highly charged metal ions, such as Al_3^{3+}, Cr_3^{3+}, Fe^{3+}, Bi^{3+}, and Be^{2+}. They yield hydronium ions when they react with water in solution, as demonstrated by the reaction below:

$$[Al(H_2O)_6]^{3+}(aq) + H_2O(\ell) \rightleftharpoons [Al(OH)(H_2O)_5]^{2+}(aq) + H_3O^+(aq)$$

Again, because hydronium ions are produced, the solution is acidic.

Basic Salt Solutions

When a salt consisting of the anion of a weak acid and the cation of a strong base dissociates in water, the solution is basic, as demonstrated below:

$$CH_3COONa(s) \xrightarrow{H_2O} Na^+(aq) + CH_3COO^-(aq)$$

In the above reaction, sodium acetate, $CH_3COONa(s)$, dissociates in water. The acetate ion, $CH_3COO^-(aq)$, produced in the first reaction reacts with water and forms the hydroxide ion, as shown in the second reaction below:

$$CH_3COO^-(aq) + H_2O(\ell) \rightleftharpoons CH_3COOH(aq) + OH^-(aq)$$

The resulting solution is basic because of the production of the hydroxide ion.

Acid-Base Solutions from Other Salts

There are other possible combinations of salt reactions in water. Those reactions are not explained in detail in this textbook, but **Table 8.5** shows additional reaction possibilities. Notice that some combinations require a comparison of the K_a and K_b values to determine the acidic-basic nature of the solution.

Table 8.5 Acid-Base Properties of Salts

Salt Solution: Examples	pH	Nature of Ions	Ion That Reacts with Water: Example
Neutral: NaCl, KBr, Ba(NO$_3$)$_2$	7.0	Cation of strong base Anion of strong acid	None
Acidic: NH$_4$Cl, NH$_4$NO$_3$, CH$_3$NH$_3$Br	<7.0	Cation of weak base Anion of strong acid	Cation: $NH_4^+ + H_2O \rightleftharpoons NH_3 + H_3O^+$
Acidic: Al(NO$_3$)$_3$, CrBr$_3$, FeCl$_3$	<7.0	Small, highly charged cation Anion of strong acid	Cation: $[Al(H_2O)_6]^{3+} + H_2O \rightleftharpoons [Al(H_2O)_5OH]^{2+} + H_3O^+$
Acidic/Basic: NH$_4$ClO$_2$, NH$_4$CN, Pb(CH$_3$COO)$_2$	<7.0 if $K_{a(cation)} > K_{b(anion)}$ >7.0 if $K_{b(anion)} > K_{a(cation)}$	Cation of weak base (or small, highly charged cation) Anion of weak acid	Cation and anion: $NH_4^+ + H_2O \rightleftharpoons NH_3 + H_3O^+$ $CN^- + H_2O \rightleftharpoons HCN + OH^-$
Acidic/Basic: NaH$_2$PO$_4$, KHCO$_3$, NaHSO$_3$	<7.0 if $K_{a(anion)} > K_{b(anion)}$ >7.0 if $K_{b(anion)} > K_{a(anion)}$	Cation of strong base Anion of polyprotic acid	Anion: $HSO_3^- + H_2O \rightleftharpoons SO_3^{2-} + H_3O^+$ $HSO_3^- + H_2O \rightleftharpoons H_2SO_3 + OH^-$

Buffered Solutions

buffer solution a solution that resists changes in pH when a limited amount of acid or base is added to the solution

You would expect a change in pH if you added an acid or base to a solution, as shown in **Figure 8.12** below.

Some solutions, however, resist changes to the pH. A **buffer solution** is a solution that resists changes in pH when a limited amount of acid or base is added to the solution. The pH meters in **Figure 8.13** on the next page show what happens when an acid or base is added to a buffered solution.

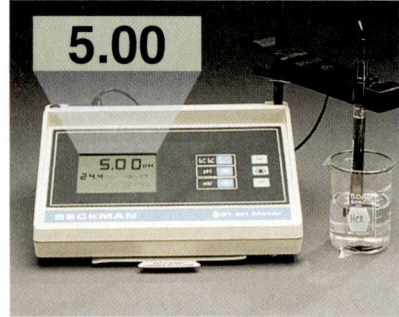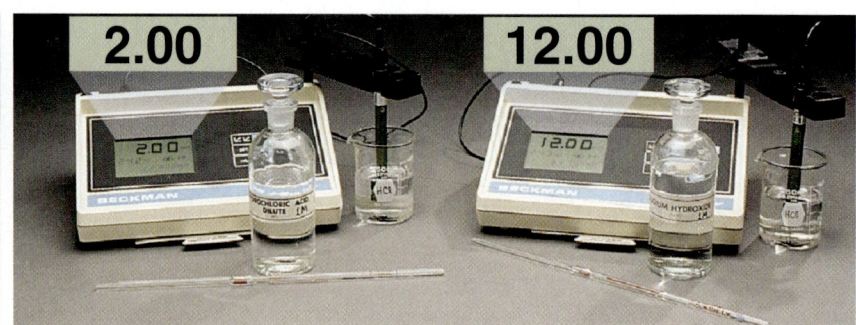

Figure 8.12 Each of the samples has a pH of 5.00 initially. One millilitre of 1 mol/L hydrochloric acid, HCl(aq), was added to the middle beaker, and 1 mL of 1 mol/L sodium hydroxide, NaOH(aq), was added to the beaker on the right. The new pH of each solution is shown on the pH meters.

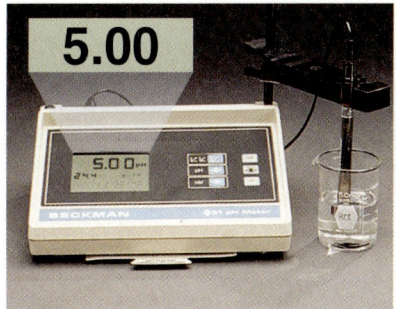
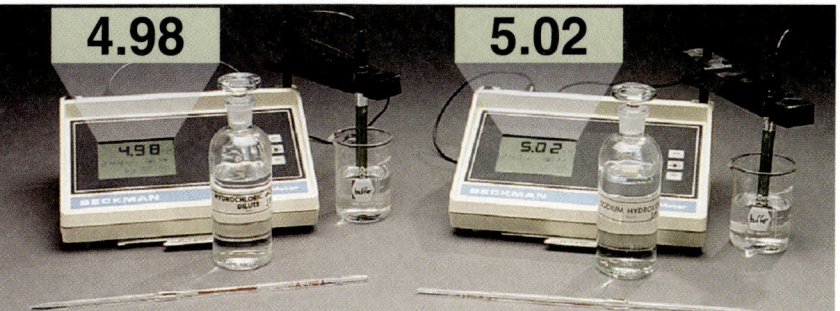

Figure 8.13 Each of the samples contains a buffered solution with an initial a pH of 5.00. One mL of 1 mol/L hydrochloric acid was added to the middle beaker. One mL of a 1 mol/L solution of sodium hydroxide was added to the beaker on the right. You can see from the readings on the pH meters that the pH change was minimal.

A buffer solution must contain a large quantity of acid to react with any base that is added to the solution, and it must contain a large quantity of base to react with any additional acid added to the solution. In addition, the acid and base components in the solution cannot react in a neutralization reaction. Buffered solutions contain a mixture of a weak acid and its conjugate base (supplied by a salt) or a weak base and its conjugate acid (supplied by a salt). Consider a buffered solution made by adding similar molar amounts of acetic acid, $CH_3COOH(aq)$, and its salt, sodium acetate, $CH_3COONa(s)$, to water. Sodium acetate dissociates completely in water, as represented by the reaction below:

$$CH_3COONa(s) \xrightarrow{H_2O} CH_3COO^-(aq) + Na^+(aq)$$

When an acid is added to the buffered solution, the acetate ion, $CH_3COO^-(aq)$, which is the conjugate base, reacts with the hydrogen ions in the acid, according to the reaction below, and neutralizes the additional acid.

$$CH_3COO^-(aq) + H^+(aq) \rightarrow CH_3COOH(aq)$$

When a base is added to the buffered solution, the hydroxide ions are neutralized by the acid in the solution, as shown below:

$$CH_3COOH(aq) + OH^-(aq) \rightarrow CH_3COO^-(aq) + H_2O(\ell)$$

Acetate is the common ion in both of these reactions in which the acid or base is consumed. When a given ion, such as acetate, is added to an equilibrium mixture that contains that ion, the equilibrium shifts away from forming more of the ion in a process called the **common-ion effect**.

The buffering capacity of a solution depends on how much acid or base the solution can absorb without a significant change in pH. The greater the amount that the solution can absorb, the greater the buffering capacity will be.

Suggested Investigation

Inquiry Investigation 8-C, Preparing a Buffer and Investigating Its Properties

common-ion effect the shift in equilibrium position caused by the addition of a compound that has an ion in common with one of the dissolved substances

Learning Check

19. Explain the relationship between a salt and a neutralization reaction.
20. Compare and contrast anions and cations.
21. When the chemical formula for water, H_2O, is written above the yield arrow, what does this indicate?
22. Referring to **Figure 8.11**, why is magnesium hydroxide used for acid indigestion?
23. Explain the concept of the common-ion effect in your own words, using Le Châtelier's principle.
24. Describe a scenario in real life in which a buffer solution might be used.

Acid-Base Titration

In a previous chemistry course, you probably titrated strong acids and bases to determine the concentration of an unknown acid or base. As a review, Appendix B, Performing an Acid-Base Titration, demonstrates how to perform a titration. In this section, you will use acid-base titration data to calculate additional information about the solution. You will learn about three types of titration reactions: (1) a strong acid and a strong base, (2) a weak acid and a strong base, and (3) a strong acid and a weak base. Titrations of a weak acid and a weak base are complicated because of the hydrolysis of the cation and anion of the salt formed. You will learn more about these titrations in a later course.

Endpoint Indicators

endpoint the pH at which the indicator changes colour in a titration

When you perform an acid-base titration, you use an indicator to determine the endpoint. The **endpoint** of a titration is the pH at which the indicator changes colour. There are many acid-base indicators, and together they cover the whole range of possible pH values. **Figure 8.14** shows the colours and endpoints of various indicators.

Indicators are weak acids. The acid is one colour and the conjugate base is another colour. You can write a general equilibrium equation for indicators, as follows, where HInd represents the acid form of the indicator and Ind$^-$ represents the conjugate base. The "H" in the HInd symbol represents the proton, H$^+$, which is donated in the reaction, as shown below:

$$\text{HInd(aq)} + \text{H}_2\text{O}(\ell) \rightarrow \text{H}_3\text{O}^+(\text{aq}) + \text{Ind}^-(\text{aq})$$
$$\text{colour 1} \qquad\qquad\qquad\qquad \text{colour 2}$$

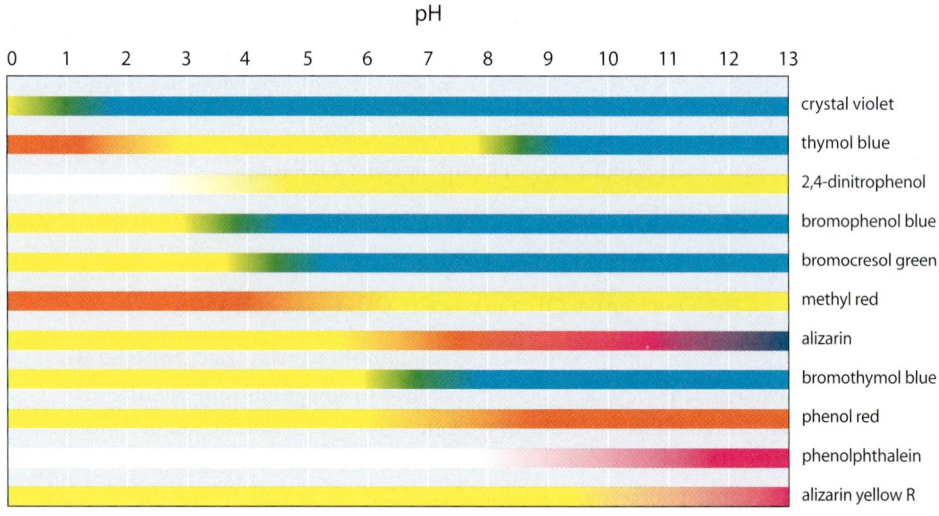

Figure 8.14 Indicators are used to estimate pH and to monitor acid-base titrations.
Explain *why it is important to select an indicator that has a clearly visible colour change.*

Strong Acid-Strong Base Titration

equivalence point the point in a titration at which the amount (in moles) of the substance added is stoichiometrically equivalent to the amount (in moles) present in the original test solution, or the point at which the acid and base have completely reacted

Often a titration is monitored using a pH meter. With a pH meter, you can monitor the titration reaction as it proceeds instead of merely estimating the pH with an indicator. Consider a titration reaction between a strong acid and a strong base that is monitored with a pH meter. A few drops of indicator are added to the solution that will change colour near the equivalence point. The **equivalence point** is the point in a titration at which the amount (in moles) of the substance added is stoichiometrically equivalent to the amount (in moles) present in the original test solution, or the point at which the acid and base have completely reacted. The endpoint of the titration is when the indicator changes colour.

Consider a titration in which a 40.00 mL solution of 0.1000 mol/L hydrochloric acid, HCl(aq), is titrated with 0.1000 mol/L sodium hydroxide, NaOH(aq), as represented by the equation below:

$$HCl(aq) + NaOH(aq) \rightarrow NaCl(aq) + H_2O(\ell)$$

The portion of the equation that involves the H$^+$ and OH$^-$ ions is shown below (the net ionic equation):

$$H^+(aq) + OH^-(aq) \rightarrow H_2O(\ell)$$

The volume of sodium hydroxide that is added to the flask and the pH of the resulting solution are plotted in **Figure 8.15**. A plot of this type is called a titration curve. Notice that the pH of the solution increases slowly at first. The low pH indicates a high concentration of hydronium ion, H_3O^+, or H^+, from the strong acid. As more sodium hydroxide is added, the concentration of hydroxide ion, OH$^-$, increases. Then near the equivalence point, the slope of the curve is almost vertical. In a strong acid-strong base titration, the concentrations of the hydrogen ion and the hydroxide ion are very small near the equivalence point. A small drop of sodium hydroxide can cause a large increase in the pH near this point. As more sodium hydroxide is added from the burette, the pH slowly increases as you go beyond the equivalence point.

It is possible to calculate the pH of the solution at various points during the titration. The Sample Problem on the next page shows how to do this. Use the Practice Problems that follow to practise this skill.

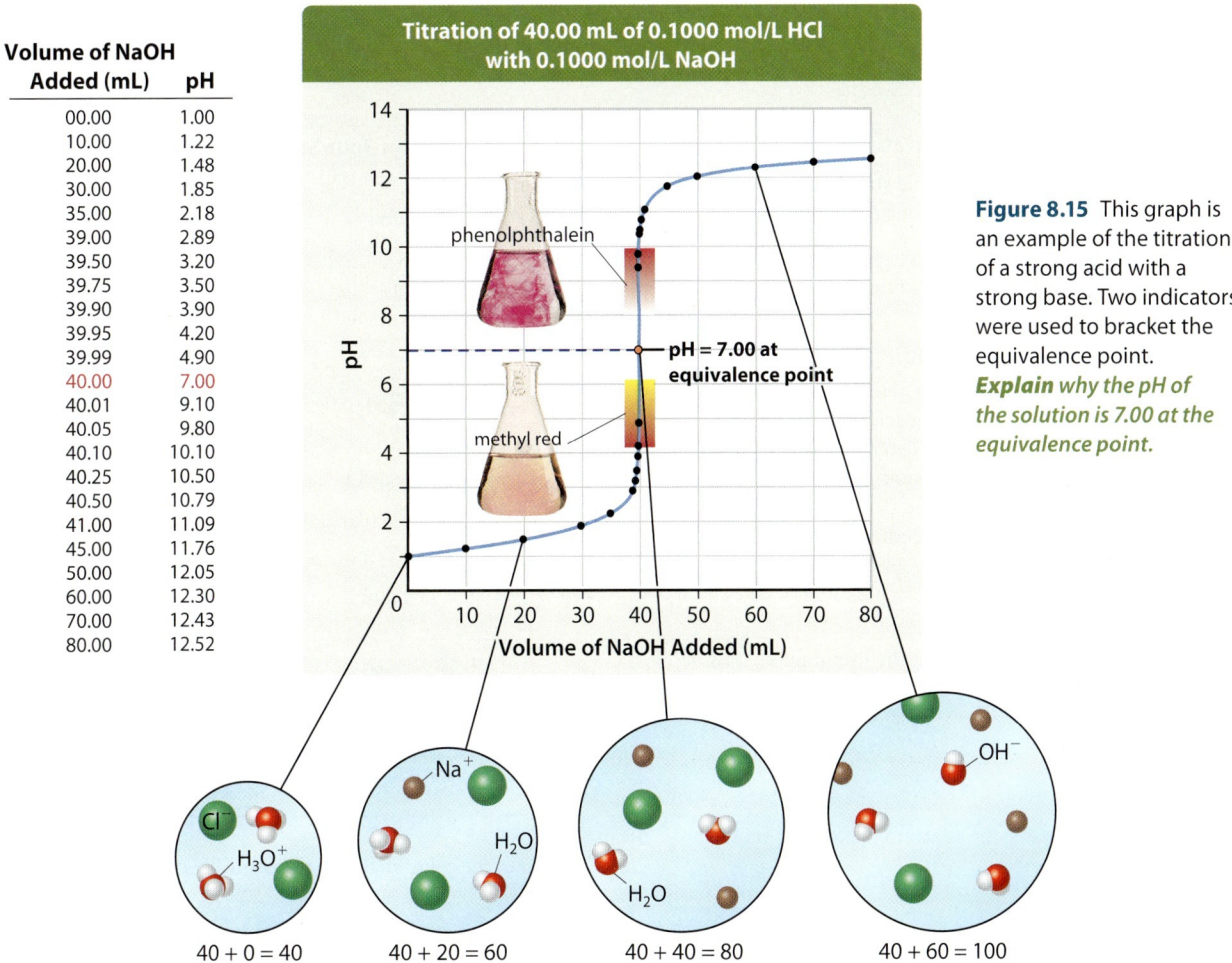

Figure 8.15 This graph is an example of the titration of a strong acid with a strong base. Two indicators were used to bracket the equivalence point. **Explain** why the pH of the solution is 7.00 at the equivalence point.

Volume of NaOH Added (mL)	pH
00.00	1.00
10.00	1.22
20.00	1.48
30.00	1.85
35.00	2.18
39.00	2.89
39.50	3.20
39.75	3.50
39.90	3.90
39.95	4.20
39.99	4.90
40.00	7.00
40.01	9.10
40.05	9.80
40.10	10.10
40.25	10.50
40.50	10.79
41.00	11.09
45.00	11.76
50.00	12.05
60.00	12.30
70.00	12.43
80.00	12.52

Sample Problem

Calculating pH During a Strong Acid-Strong Base Titration

Problem
A 40.00 mL solution of 0.1000 mol/L hydrochloric acid, HCl(aq), is titrated with 0.1000 mol/L sodium hydroxide, NaOH(aq), as represented by the equation below:

$$\text{NaOH(aq)} + \text{HCl(aq)} \rightarrow \text{NaCl(aq)} + \text{H}_2\text{O}(\ell)$$

Calculate the pH of the solution at various points in the titration:
a. the pH of the original solution of strong acid;
b. the pH of the solution before the equivalence point, after adding 20 mL of NaOH;
c. the pH of the solution at the equivalence point, after adding 40.00 mL of NaOH; and
d. the pH of the solution after the equivalence point, after adding 50.00 mL of NaOH.

What Is Required?
You need to calculate the pH of the solution at four different time points in the titration: original acid solution, before the equivalence point, at the equivalence point, and after the equivalence point.

What Is Given?
You know the chemical equation: $\text{NaOH(aq)} + \text{HCl(aq)} \rightarrow \text{NaCl(aq)} + \text{H}_2\text{O}(\ell)$
You know the net ionic equation: $\text{H}^+(\text{aq}) + \text{OH}^-(\text{aq}) \rightarrow \text{H}_2\text{O}(\ell)$
You know the volume of the original solution: 40.00 mL = 0.040 00 L
You know concentration of the strong acid, hydrochloric acid: 0.1000 mol/L
You know the concentration of the strong base, sodium hydroxide: 0.1000 mol/L
You know the volumes of strong base added at each point in question: 0.00, 20.00, 40.00, and 50.00 mL

Plan Your Strategy	Act on Your Strategy
a. Calculate the pH of the original strong acid solution. You know that a strong acid ionizes completely.	$[\text{HCl}] = [\text{H}_3\text{O}^+] = 0.1000$ mol/L
The pH of the original solution is calculated using the equation $\text{pH} = -\log[\text{H}_3\text{O}^+]$.	$\text{pH} = -\log(0.1000) = 1.00$ This is the pH of the original solution.
b. As base is added to the acid, two changes are occurring in the flask that will affect the pH. The strong base neutralizes some of the strong acid, and the volume of the solution is increasing. To determine $[\text{H}_3\text{O}^+]$ at any point up to the equivalence point, subtract the amount (in moles) of H_3O^+ neutralized (the amount of OH^- added) from the original concentration.	$n_{\text{initial H}_3\text{O}^+} = c_{\text{HCl}} V_{\text{HCl}}$ $= (0.100\ 00\ \tfrac{\text{mol}}{\text{L}})(0.040\ 00\ \text{L}) = 0.004\ 000$ mol $n_{\text{H}_3\text{O}^+\text{ reacted}} = n_{\text{OH}^-\text{ added}}$ $= c_{\text{NaOH}} V_{\text{NaOH added}}$ $= (0.1000\ \tfrac{\text{mol}}{\text{L}})(0.020\ 00\ \text{L}) = 0.002\ 000$ mol $n_{\text{H}_3\text{O}^+\text{ remaining}} = n_{\text{initial H}_3\text{O}^+} - n_{\text{OH}^-\text{ added}}$ $= 0.004\ 000\ \text{mol} - 0.002\ 000\ \text{mol} = 0.002\ 000\ \text{mol}$
Calculate the concentration of the hydronium ion, $[\text{H}_3\text{O}^+]$, accounting for the increase in volume.	$[\text{H}_3\text{O}^+] = \dfrac{n_{\text{H}_3\text{O}^+\text{ remaining}}}{V_{\text{original acid solution}} + V_{\text{base added}}}$ $= \dfrac{0.002\ 000\ \text{mol}}{0.040\ 00\ \text{L} + 0.020\ 00\ \text{L}} = 0.033\ 33$ mol/L
Calculate the pH using the equation $\text{pH} = -\log[\text{H}_3\text{O}^+]$.	$\text{pH} = -\log(0.033\ 33) = 1.48$ This is the pH of the solution before the equivalence point.

c. At the equivalence point, all of the H_3O^+ from the acid has reacted. The solution contains sodium ions, Na^+, and chloride ions, Cl^-, and neither of the ions reacts with water. The pH of the solution is due to the autoionization of water.	$[H_3O^+] = 1.0 \times 10^{-7}$ mol/L $pH = -\log [H_3O^+]$ $= -\log (1.0 \times 10^{-7}) = 7.00$
d. After the equivalence point, the pH of the solution is based on the excess OH^- present in the solution.	$n_{\text{total OH}^- \text{ added}} = c_{\text{NaOH}} V_{\text{NaOH added}}$ $= (0.1000 \tfrac{\text{mol}}{L}) (0.050\,00\,L) = 0.005\,000$ mol $n_{H_3O^+ \text{ consumed}} = c_{\text{HCl}} V_{\text{HCl solution}}$ $= (0.1000 \tfrac{\text{mol}}{L}) (0.040\,00\,L) = 0.004\,000$ mol $n_{\text{excess OH}^-} = n_{\text{total OH}^- \text{ added}} - n_{H_3O^+ \text{ consumed}}$ $= 0.005\,000$ mol $- 0.004\,000$ mol $= 0.001\,000$ mol
Calculate the concentration of the hydroxide ion, $[OH^-]$, accounting for the increase in volume.	$[OH^-] = \dfrac{n_{\text{excess OH}^-}}{V_{\text{to equivalence}} + V_{\text{over equivalence}}}$ $= \dfrac{0.001\,000 \text{ mol}}{0.040\,00 \text{ L} + 0.050\,00 \text{ L}} = 0.011\,11$ mol/L
Calculate the pOH using the equation $pOH = -\log [OH^-]$.	$pOH = -\log (0.01111)$ $= 1.95$
Calculate the pH of the solution using the equation $pH = pK_w - pOH$.	$pH = 14.00 - 1.95 = 12.05$

Check Your Solution

As expected, the pH of the solution increases as additional strong base is added to the solution at each step along the way.

Practice Problems

91. What is the pH of 35.00 mL of a 0.0225 mol/L hydrochloric acid solution, HCl(aq)?

92. During a titration using sodium hydroxide, NaOH(aq), and hydroiodic acid, HI(aq), 35.00 mL of 0.15 mol/L sodium hydroxide was added to 14.40 mL of 0.12 mol/L hydroiodic acid. At this point in the titration, what is the pH of the solution?

93. At the point in a titration when 5.00 mL of 0.225 mol/L hydrochloric acid, HCl(aq), is added to 40.00 mL of 0.175 mol/L potassium hydroxide, KOH(aq), what is the pH of the solution?

94. A beaker containing 31.50 mL of a 0.015 mol/L hydrobromic acid solution, HBr(aq), has been titrated with 24.53 mL of 0.012 mol/L potassium hydroxide, KOH(aq). Determine the pH of the solution at this point in the titration.

95. Determine the pH of a solution during a titration when 25.00 mL of 0.74 mol/L nitric acid, HNO_3(aq), has been added to 26.05 mL of 0.71 mol/L sodium hydroxide, NaOH(aq).

96. What are the pOH and pH of 25.00 mL of a 0.075 mol/L potassium hydroxide solution, KOH(aq)?

97. What volume of a 0.22 mol/L hydrochloric acid solution, HCl(aq), is needed to cause the pH of 25.00 mL of a 0.15 mol/L lithium hydroxide solution, LiOH(aq), to have a pH that is equal to 7.00?

98. What is the volume of 2.45 mol/L hydrochloric acid, HCl(aq), needed to completely neutralize 125.00 mL of 1.14 mol/L lithium hydroxide, LiOH(aq)?

99. At the equivalence point, 18.76 mL of 1.75 mol/L potassium hydroxide, KOH(aq), has been titrated with 28.65 mL of hydrochloric acid. What is the concentration of the original hydrochloric acid solution?

100. If 17.50 mL of 0.25 mol/L nitric acid, HNO_3(aq), is titrated to a pH of 7.00 with 11.27 mL of sodium hydroxide, NaOH(aq), what was the original concentration of the sodium hydroxide solution used in the titration?

Weak Acid-Strong Base Titration

The titration of a weak acid and strong base differs from the previous titration. You know that a weak acid only ionizes partially, whereas a strong acid ionizes completely. The partial ionization of the weak acid has to be considered in the calculations. First, observe the titration curve for a weak acid in **Figure 8.16**. The dotted line at the bottom of the curve is the strong acid-strong base curve from **Figure 8.15**, which is added to this graph for easy comparison. This graph illustrates the titration of the weak acid, propanoic acid, $CH_3CH_2COOH(aq)$, with the strong base, sodium hydroxide, $NaOH(aq)$. Propanoic acid is abbreviated HPr in the graph and the conjugate base, $CH_3CH_2COO^-$, is abbreviated Pr^-. The chemical reaction is shown in the equation below:

$$CH_3CH_2COOH(aq) + NaOH(aq) \rightarrow CH_3CH_2COONa(aq) + H_2O(\ell)$$

Notice that the initial pH is higher for a weak acid than it is for a strong acid. Because the weak acid only ionizes partially, there is less hydronium ion, H_3O^+, present than is present in a strong acid titration. Notice that there is also a buffer region identified on this graph. As the weak acid reacts with the strong base, more conjugate base forms. This creates an acid/conjugate base, HA/A^- (HPr/Pr^-), buffer. At the midpoint in the buffer reaction, half of the strong acid has reacted. Thus, $[HA] = [A^-]$ or $[HPr] = [Pr^-]$.

Note the pH of the equivalence point on the graph. It is greater than 7.00. The weak acid anion acts as a weak base and accepts a proton from water. This reaction yields OH^- ions that increase the pH of the solution. Beyond the equivalence point, the pH of the solution increases as excess base is added to the solution.

The Sample Problem following the graph demonstrates how to calculate pH values at various points in the weak acid-strong base titration. Use the Practice Problems that follow the Sample Problem to practise these calculations.

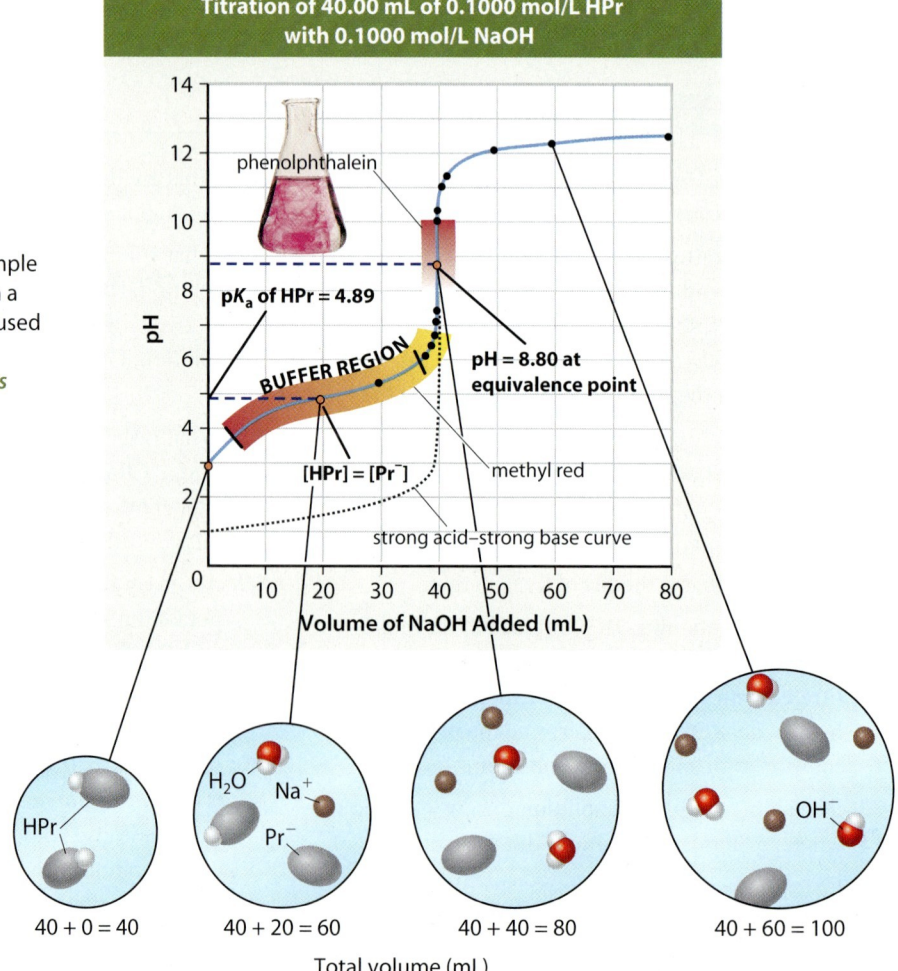

Figure 8.16 This graph is an example of the titration of a weak acid with a strong base. Two indicators were used to bracket the equivalence point. *Explain* why phenolphthalein was chosen as the indicator for this titration.

Sample Problem

Calculating pH During a Weak Acid-Strong Base Titration

Problem

A chemist titrated 25.00 mL of a 0.1000 mol/L solution of acetic acid, $CH_3COOH(aq)$, with a 0.1000 mol/L solution of sodium hydroxide, $NaOH(aq)$. Calculate the pH of the resulting solution after the addition of 10.00 mL and 25.00 mL of sodium hydroxide. The chemical reaction between these two substances is shown below:

$$CH_3COOH(aq) + NaOH(aq) \rightarrow CH_3COONa(aq) + H_2O(\ell)$$

What Is Required?

You need to determine the pH of the solution after the addition of the following volumes of sodium hydroxide: **a.** 10.00 mL and **b.** 25.00 mL.

What Is Given?

You know the volume of the weak acid: 25.00 mL
You know the concentration of the weak acid: 0.1000 mol/L
You know the concentration of the strong base: 0.1000 mol/L
You know the balanced chemical equation for the reaction:

$$CH_3COOH(aq) + NaOH(aq) \rightarrow CH_3COONa(aq) + H_2O(\ell)$$

You know that the values for K_a and K_b for many acids and bases are found in Appendix B.

Plan Your Strategy	Act on Your Strategy
a. The amount (in moles) is used to make calculations. As the solutions are mixed, the volume increases, but the amount (in moles) remains the same. Calculate the amount (in moles) of NaOH in 10.00 mL of solution.	$n_{NaOH} = cV$ $= \left(\dfrac{0.1000 \text{ mol}}{1 \text{ L}}\right)(10.00 \text{ mL})\left(\dfrac{1 \text{ L}}{1000 \text{ mL}}\right) = 1.000 \times 10^{-3}$ mol
Calculate the amount (in moles) of CH_3COOH originally present in 25.00 mL of solution.	$n_{CH_3COOH} = cV$ $= \left(\dfrac{0.1000 \text{ mol}}{1 \text{ L}}\right)(25.00 \text{ mL})\left(\dfrac{1 \text{ L}}{1000 \text{ mL}}\right) = 2.500 \times 10^{-3}$ mol
Use a table similar to an ICE table to organize your information. Use the balanced chemical equation to determine the relative amount (in moles) of each substance.	See table below. 1 mol of acetic acid reacts with 1 mol of sodium hydroxide to produce 1 mol of sodium acetate and 1 mol of water. Notice that sodium hydroxide is the limiting reagent in this reaction.

	$CH_3COOH(aq)$	+	$NaOH(aq)$	$\rightarrow$	$CH_3COONa(aq)$	+	$H_2O(\ell)$
Initial (mol)	2.500×10^{-3}		1.000×10^{-3}		0		
Change (mol)	$-(1.000 \times 10^{-3})$		$-(1.000 \times 10^{-3})$		$+(1.000 \times 10^{-3})$		
Final (mol)	1.500×10^{-3}		0		1.000×10^{-3}		

Plan Your Strategy	Act on Your Strategy
Determine the final volume of the solution.	$V = V_{CH_3COOH} + V_{NaOH}$ $= 25.00 \text{ mL} + 10.00 \text{ mL}$ $= 35.00 \text{ mL} \times \dfrac{1 \text{ L}}{1000 \text{ mL}} = 0.03500$ L
Use $c = \dfrac{n}{V}$ to determine the concentrations of $CH_3COOH(aq)$ and $CH_3COO^-(aq)$ in mol/L.	$c_{CH_3COOH} = \dfrac{n}{V}$ $= \dfrac{1.500 \times 10^{-3} \text{ mol}}{0.03500 \text{ L}} = 4.2857 \times 10^{-2}$ mol/L $c_{CH_3COO^-} = \dfrac{n}{V} = \dfrac{1.000 \times 10^{-3} \text{ mol}}{0.03500 \text{ L}} = 2.8571 \times 10^{-2}$ mol/L

Continued on next page ▶

Write equations for any equilibrium reactions occurring and determine whether the solution has buffering capacity.	$CH_3COOH(aq) + H_2O(\ell) \rightleftharpoons CH_3COO^-(aq) + H_3O^+(aq)$ $CH_3COO^-(aq) + H_2O(\ell) \rightleftharpoons CH_3COOH(aq) + OH^+(aq)$ The solution has buffering capacity. The reactions of CH_3COOH and CH_3COO^- with water balance each other, and very little change actually occurs. Therefore, you can use the amounts of CH_3COOH and CH_3COO^- present after the reaction with NaOH to find the concentration of hydronium ion, H_3O^+, present.
Write the equilibrium expression, substitute in the equilibrium constant and the calculated concentrations, and solve for the concentration of the hydronium ion.	$K_a = \dfrac{[CH_3COO^-][H_3O^+]}{[CH_3COOH]}$ $1.8 \times 10^{-5} = \dfrac{(2.8571 \times 10^{-2})(x)}{4.2857 \times 10^{-2}}$ $x = \dfrac{(1.8 \times 10^{-5})(4.2857 \times 10^{-2})}{2.8571 \times 10^{-2}} = 2.700 \times 10^{-5}$ $[H_3O^+] = x = 2.7 \times 10^{-5}$ mol/L
Calculate the pH using the equation $pH = -\log[H_3O^+]$.	$pH = -\log[H_3O^+] = -\log(2.7 \times 10^{-5}) = 4.57$
b. Calculate the amount (in moles) of sodium hydroxide in 25.00 mL of solution. When 25.00 mL of 0.1000 mol/L NaOH(aq) is added to 25.00 mL of 0.1000 mol/L CH_3COOH(aq), an equal amount of H_3O^+ and OH^- ions are in solution. This is the equivalence point.	$n_{NaOH} = cV$ $= \left(\dfrac{0.1000 \text{ mol}}{1 \text{ L}}\right)(25.00 \text{ mL})\left(\dfrac{1 \text{ L}}{1000 \text{ mL}}\right) = 2.500 \times 10^{-3}$ mol
Use a table to summarize the changes in the solution.	See the table below.

	CH_3COOH(aq)	+	NaOH(aq)	→	CH_3COONa(aq)	+	$H_2O(\ell)$
Initial (mol)	2.500×10^{-3}		2.500×10^{-3}		0		
Change (mol)	$-(2.500 \times 10^{-3})$		$-(2.500 \times 10^{-3})$		$+(2.500 \times 10^{-3})$		
Final (mol)	0		0		2.500×10^{-3}		

At equivalence, the concentrations of the weak acid and the strong base are zero and the weak acid anion acts as a weak base and accepts a proton from water. This reaction yields OH^- ions. First, determine the molar concentration of the salt.	$[CH_3COONa] = \left(\dfrac{2.500 \times 10^{-3} \text{ mol}}{50.0 \text{ mL}}\right)\left(\dfrac{1000 \text{ mL}}{1 \text{ L}}\right)$ $= 0.0500$ mol/L
As you learned earlier in this section, the acetate ion, CH_3COO^-, produced in the first reaction reacts with water and forms the hydroxide ion, OH^-, as shown below: $CH_3COO^-(aq) + H_2O(\ell) \rightleftharpoons CH_3COOH(aq) + OH^-(aq)$ Use an ICE table to organize your information.	See the ICE table below

	CH_3COO^-(aq)	+	$H_2O(\ell)$	⇌	CH_3COOH(aq)	+	OH^-(aq)
	$[CH_3COO^-]$ (mol/L)		$[H_2O]$ (mol/L)		$[CH_3COOH]$ (mol/L)		$[OH^-]$ (mol/L)
Initial	0.0500				0.00		0.00
Change	$-x$				$+x$		$+x$
Equilibrium	$0.0500 - x$				x		x

Write the base-ionization equation for the reaction using information from the ICE table.	$K_b = \dfrac{[CH_3COOH][OH^-]}{[CH_3COO^-]} = \dfrac{x^2}{0.0500 - x}$
The base-ionization constant, K_b, for acetic acid is not in the Appendix, but K_a is. Use the equation $K_a K_b = K_w$ to determine the value of K_b.	$K_b = \dfrac{K_w}{K_a}$ $= \dfrac{1.0 \times 10^{-14}}{1.8 \times 10^{-5}} = 5.6 \times 10^{-10}$

Solve for x. Only the positive root of the quadratic equation is a possible solution, because the concentration cannot be a negative number.	$5.6 \times 10^{-10} = \dfrac{x^2}{0.0500 - x}$ $(5.6 \times 10^{-10})(0.0500 - x) = x^2$ $(2.8 \times 10^{-11}) - (5.6 \times 10^{-10}x) = x^2$ $x^2 + (5.6 \times 10^{-10}x) - (2.8 \times 10^{-11}) = 0$ $x = \dfrac{-b \pm \sqrt{b^2 - 4ac}}{2a} = \dfrac{-5.6 \times 10^{-10} \pm \sqrt{(5.6 \times 10^{-10})^2 - (4)(1)(-2.8 \times 10^{-11})}}{(2)(1)}$ $= \dfrac{-5.6 \times 10^{-10} \pm \sqrt{(3.136 \times 10^{-19}) + (1.10 \times 10^{-10})}}{2}$ $= \dfrac{-5.6 \times 10^{-10} \pm 1.1 \times 10^{-5}}{2}$ $x = 5.3 \times 10^{-6}$ Therefore, $x = 5.3 \times 10^{-6}$ mol/L = [OH$^-$]
Calculate the pOH using the equation pOH = $-\log$ [OH$^-$].	pOH = $-\log (5.3 \times 10^{-6})$ = 5.38
Calculate the pH of the solution using the equation pH = pK_w − pOH.	pH = pK_w − pOH = 14.00 − 5.38 = 8.72

Check Your Solution
As expected, the pH of the solution increased as additional base was added to the solution.

Practice Problems

101. Determine the pH at a point in the titration when 20.00 mL of 0.2000 mol/L acetic acid, CH$_3$COOH(aq), has been added to 17.00 mL of 0.1500 mol/L potassium hydroxide, KOH(aq).

102. When hydrogen cyanide, HCN(g), is dissolved in water, it forms a very weak acid, $K_a = 6.2 \times 10^{-10}$. If a 50.00 mL sample of 0.1000 mol/L hydrocyanic acid, HCN(aq), is titrated with 8.00 mL of 0.1000 mol/L potassium hydroxide, KOH(aq), what is the pH of the solution after the base has been added?

103. What is the pH of the titration in question 102 at the equivalence point?

104. A chemist titrated 35.00 mL of a 0.150 mol/L solution of hypobromous acid, HBrO(aq), $K_a = 2.8 \times 10^{-9}$. Calculate the resulting pH after the addition of 15.00 mL of 0.1000 mol/L sodium hydroxide solution, NaOH(aq).

105. A solution of 50.00 mL of a 0.120 mol/L nitrous acid, HNO$_2$(aq), is titrated with 0.1000 mol/L of potassium hydroxide, KOH(aq). Determine the resulting pH of the solution after 11.25 mL of the base has been added. For the acid, $K_a = 5.6 \times 10^{-4}$.

106. If 100.00 mL of a 0.400 mol/L hydrofluoric acid solution, HF(aq), is titrated with a 0.2000 mol/L sodium hydroxide solution, NaOH(aq), determine the pH that results when 20.00 mL of the base is added. For the hydrofluoric acid solution, $K_a = 6.3 \times 10^{-4}$.

107. A chemist titrates 50.00 mL of a 0.350 mol/L solution of hypochlorous acid, HOCl(aq), with $K_a = 4.0 \times 10^{-8}$, with 0.150 mol/L of potassium hydroxide, KOH(aq). Calculate the pH after the addition of 5.00 mL of the base.

108. Determine the pH of 25.00 mL of a solution of 0.100 mol/L hypobromous acid, HBrO(aq), at the equivalence point, when titrated with a 0.100 mol/L sodium hydroxide solution, NaOH(aq).

109. A chemist titrated 50.00 mL of a 0.150 mol/L acetic acid solution, CH$_3$COOH(aq), with 0.300 mol/L sodium hydroxide solution, NaOH(aq). Determine the pH of the resulting solution when 25.00 mL of the base has been added.

110. If 50.00 mL of a 0.100 mol/L nitrous acid solution, HNO$_2$(aq), with $K_a = 5.6 \times 10^{-4}$, is titrated with 0.100 mol/L potassium hydroxide solution, KOH(aq), determine the resulting pH of the solution at the equivalence point in the titration.

Activity 8.2 Analyzing a Weak Acid-Strong Base Titration

A student used a pH meter to collect data for the titration of an unknown concentration of ethanoic (acetic) acid with a 0.150 mol/L solution of sodium hydroxide. The data table from the investigation is shown in the table below.

Titration of Ethanoic Acid with Sodium Hydroxide
Volume of ethanoic acid = 25.00 mL
[NaOH] = 0.150 mol/L

Volume of NaOH(aq) Added (mL)	pH
None	2.83
2.00	3.84
4.11	4.20
7.98	4.64
11.95	5.03
14.08	5.27
16.05	5.61
17.00	5.90
17.21	6.00
17.39	6.09
17.62	6.23
17.99	6.74
18.18	8.80
18.39	10.92
18.80	12.24
20.00	12.56
22.03	12.69

Procedure

1. Enter the data from the table into a spreadsheet program. Use the program to plot the results, with pH on the vertical axis and volume of base added on the horizontal axis. Make sure you enter labels for each axis, and provide a suitable title for your graph. Print your graph.

2. On your graph, shade the buffer region. Identify the pH range of an indicator suitable for this titration. Name two indicators that would have endpoints suitable for this titration.

3. The titration curve should show a steep change in pH near the equivalence point. Choose a point halfway along the portion of rapid change on the graph. Label this the equivalence point.

Analysis

1. From your graph, determine the pH and volume of base added at the equivalence point.

2. Calculate the concentration of the ethanoic (acetic) acid solution.

3. Explain why the pH at the equivalence point is not 7, the pH of neutral water.

4. What ions and molecules are in solution well before the equivalence point, such as at 10 mL of base added? How does this compare with the solution well after the equivalence point, such as at 20 mL of base added?

Learning Check

25. Distinguish between the equivalence point and the endpoint for a titration.

26. When choosing an indicator, should the pH at the equivalence point coincide exactly with the pH at the endpoint of the titration? Explain your answer.

27. Acid-base reactions are often called neutralization reactions. Although "neutral" water has a pH of 7, not every acid-base reaction results in a solution with a pH of this value. Explain the reason why.

28. Use **Figure 8.14** to estimate the pH of a solution in which bromocresol green is blue and methyl red is orange.

29. Suggest an indicator that could be used to titrate sodium hydroxide with nitric acid. Explain your choice.

30. Explain why the pH of the equivalence point of a weak acid-strong base titration is basic.

Weak Base-Strong Acid Titration

Now consider a weak base-strong acid titration. A graph of this type of titration is shown in **Figure 8.17**. Note the similarities between this graph and the one in **Figure 8.16**. The graphs have the same shape, but this is one is inverted compared with the graph in **Figure 8.16**. The pH in a weak base-strong acid titration decreases throughout the process. Notice that the initial pH of the solution is basic. This is because only the weak base is present in the flask at the beginning. The buffered region contains significant amounts of ammonia, $NH_3(aq)$, and its conjugate acid, the ammonium ion, $NH_4^+(aq)$. At the midpoint in the buffered region, the pH equals the pK_a of the conjugate acid. After the buffer region, the pH drops almost vertically. At the equivalence point, all of the ammonia, $NH_3(aq)$, has reacted with the strong acid, $HCl(aq)$, and the solution contains NH_4^+ and Cl^- ions. Note that the pH at the equivalence point is 5.27. The solution is acidic at the equivalence point because the ammonium ion reacts with water and forms the hydronium ion, $H_3O^+(aq)$. After the equivalence point, the pH continues to drop because the hydronium ion increases.

The initial reaction in the titration involves a strong acid (hydrochloric acid) and a weak base (ammonia), as shown below:

$$HCl(aq) + NH_3(aq) \rightarrow NH_4Cl(aq)$$
or
$$HCl(aq) + NH_3(aq) \rightarrow NH_4^+(aq) + Cl^-(aq)$$

The reaction can be simplified as follows:

$$H^+(aq) + NH_3(aq) \rightarrow NH_4^+(aq)$$

At the equivalence point, the hydrolysis of the NH_4^+ ion produces the hydronium ion, which lowers the pH. The equation is shown below:

$$NH_4^+(aq) + H_2O(\ell) \rightleftharpoons NH_3(aq) + H_3O^+(aq)$$

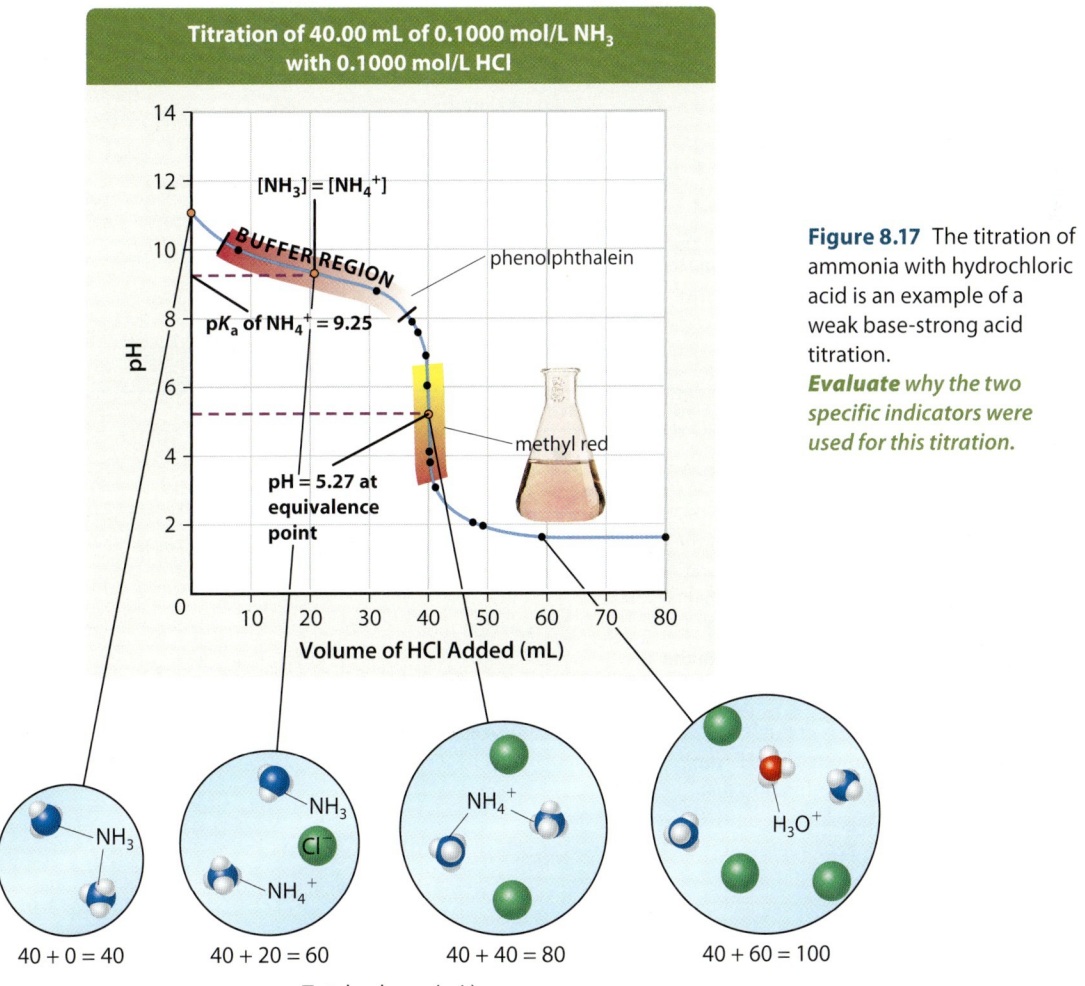

Figure 8.17 The titration of ammonia with hydrochloric acid is an example of a weak base-strong acid titration.
Evaluate why the two specific indicators were used for this titration.

The Sample Problem below demonstrates how to calculate the pH at the equivalence point for a weak base-strong acid titration. Use the Practice Problems that follow to practise solving this type of problem.

Sample Problem

Calculating the pH at the Equivalence Point

Problem
Calculate the pH at the equivalence point, when 40.00 mL of 0.1000 mol/L ammonia, $NH_3(aq)$, is titrated with a 0.1000 mol/L hydrochloric acid solution, $HCl(aq)$. The equations for the reaction are on the previous page.

What Is Required?
You need to calculate the pH at the equivalence point.

What Is Given?
You know the balanced chemical equations:

$$HCl(aq) + NH_3(aq) \rightarrow NH_4Cl(aq)$$
$$H^+(aq) + NH_3(aq) \rightarrow NH_4^+(aq)$$
$$NH_4^+(aq) + H_2O(\ell) \rightleftharpoons NH_3(aq) + H_3O^+(aq)$$

You know the concentration and the volume of the base: 0.1000 mol/L ammonia solution; 40.00 mL
You know the concentration of the strong acid: 0.1000 mol/L hydrochloric acid
You know that K_a and K_b values for many acids and bases are found in Appendix B.

Plan Your Strategy	Act on Your Strategy
Calculate the amount (in moles) of ammonia in solution.	$n_{NH_3} = cV$ $= \left(\dfrac{0.1000 \text{ mol}}{1 \text{ L}}\right)(40.00 \text{ mL})\left(\dfrac{1 \text{ L}}{1000 \text{ mL}}\right) = 4.000 \times 10^{-3}$ mol
You can see from the balanced chemical equation that the mole ratio of base to acid is 1:1. At the equivalence point, the amount (in moles) of $HCl(aq)$ added equals the amount (in moles) of $NH_3(aq)$. Set up a table similar to an ICE table to organize the known information.	See table below.

	HCl(aq)	+	NH$_3$(aq)	$\rightarrow$	NH$_4$Cl(aq)
Initial (mol)	4.000×10^{-3}		4.000×10^{-3}		0
Change (mol)	$-(4.000 \times 10^{-3})$		$-(4.000 \times 10^{-3})$		$+(4.000 \times 10^{-3})$
Final (mol)	0		0		4.000×10^{-3}

Plan Your Strategy	Act on Your Strategy
At the equivalence point, the concentrations of both the acid and the base are almost zero. Because the mole ratio is 1:1 and the concentrations are equal, you know that the total volume at the equivalence point is 40.00 mL + 40.00 mL = 80.00 mL. Calculate the concentration of the salt using information from your table.	$[NH_4Cl] = \left(\dfrac{4.000 \times 10^{-3} \text{ mol}}{80.00 \text{ mL}}\right)\left(\dfrac{1000 \text{ mL}}{1 \text{ L}}\right)$ $= 0.0500$ mol/L
At the equivalence point, the hydrolysis of the NH_4^+ ion produces the H_3O^+ ion, which lowers the pH. You have to determine the amount of hydronium ion that is in the solution at the equivalence point. Use an ICE table to organize your information. Let x represent the equilibrium concentration of NH_3 and H_3O^+ at the equivalence point.	The ICE table is at the top of the next page.

	NH$_4^+$(aq)	+	H$_2$O(ℓ)	$\rightleftharpoons$	NH$_3$(aq)	+	H$_3$O$^+$(aq)
	[NH$_4^+$] (mol/L)		[H$_2$O] (mol/L)		[NH$_3$] (mol/L)		[H$_3$O$^+$] (mol/L)
Initial	5.000×10^{-2}				0.0000		0.0000
Change	$-x$				$+x$		$+x$
Equilibrium	$(5.000 \times 10^{-2}) - x$ or $0.05000 - x$				x		x

You can use the known value of K_a for NH$_4^+$ and the acid-dissociation constant equation to determine x. Refer to Appendix B to determine the value of K_a.

$$K_a = \frac{[\text{NH}_3][\text{H}_3\text{O}^+]}{[\text{NH}_4^+]}$$

$$5.6 \times 10^{-10} = \frac{x^2}{0.05000 - x}$$

Use the quadratic equation to solve for x.

$$5.6 \times 10^{-10} = \frac{x^2}{0.050\,00 - x}$$

$$(5.6 \times 10^{-10})(0.050\,00 - x) = x^2$$

$$(2.8 \times 10^{-11}) - (5.6 \times 10^{-10}x) = x^2$$

$$x^2 + (5.6 \times 10^{-10}x) - (2.8 \times 10^{-11}) = 0$$

$$x = \frac{-b \pm \sqrt{b^2 - 4ac}}{2a}$$

$$= \frac{-5.6 \times 10^{-10} \pm \sqrt{(5.6 \times 10^{-10})^2 - (4)(1)(-2.8 \times 10^{-11})}}{(2)(1)}$$

$$= \frac{-5.6 \times 10^{-10} \pm 1.0583 \times 10^{-5}}{2}$$

$$x = 5.291 \times 10^{-6} \text{ or } -5.291 \times 10^{-6}$$

The concentrations of NH$_3$ and H$_3$O$^+$ cannot be a negative number. [NH$_3$] and [H$_3$O$^+$] at the equivalence point are 5.291×10^{-6} mol/L each. Extra digits are kept in the interim number to reduce rounding error in the final number. Calculate the pH using the equation pH = $-\log$ [H$_3$O$^+$].

$$\text{pH} = -\log [\text{H}_3\text{O}^+]$$
$$= -\log (5.291 \times 10^{-6})$$
$$= 5.27$$

Check Your Solution

The pH indicates an acidic solution. As stated in the chapter, this is expected from the hydrolysis of the ammonium ion.

Practice Problems

111. Determine the pH at the equivalence point when 50.00 mL of a 0.150 mol/L ammonia solution, NH$_3$(aq), is titrated with 0.150 mol/L hydrochloric acid solution, HCl(aq).

112. If 125.00 mL of a 0.100 mol/L hydrazine solution, N$_2$H$_4$(aq), $K_a = 7.94 \times 10^{-9}$, is titrated to the equivalence point with 0.100 mol/L nitric acid solution, HNO$_3$(aq), what is the pH at this point?

113. A 25.00 mL sample of a 0.200 mol/L pyridine solution, C$_5$H$_5$N(aq), $K_b = 1.7 \times 10^{-9}$, is titrated to the equivalence point using 0.200 mol/L hydrochloric acid solution, HCl(aq). What is the resulting pH of the solution?

114. Determine the pH at the equivalence point when 0.104 g of sodium acetate, NaC$_2$H$_3$O$_2$(s), $K_b = 5.6 \times 10^{-10}$, is added to enough water to make 25.00 mL of solution and is titrated with 0.100 mol/L solution of hydrochloric acid, HCl(aq).

Continued on next page

115. Determine the pH at the equivalence point of the titration involving 30.00 mL of a 0.150 mol/L solution of trimethylamine, $(CH_3)_3N(aq)$, and a 0.150 mol/L solution of the strong monoprotic acid perchloric acid, $HClO_4(aq)$. The K_b for trimethylamine is 6.3×10^{-5}.

116. If 18.00 mL of a 0.040 mol/L solution of methanamine, $(CH_3)_3N(aq)$, a weak base with $K_b = 4.6 \times 10^{-4}$, is titrated to the equivalence point using 0.40 mol/L hydrochloric acid, $HCl(aq)$, what is the pH of this solution at the equivalence point?

117. Calculate the pH at the equivalence point in the titration of 112.5 mL of a 0.075 mol/L aniline solution, $C_6H_5NH_2(aq)$, with a 0.075 mol/L solution of hydrobromic acid, $HBr(aq)$. Aniline has a K_b value of 7.4×10^{-10}.

118. Determine the pH at the equivalence point when 100.00 mL of a 0.200 mol/L ammonia solution, $NH_3(aq)$, is titrated with 0.400 mol/L hydrochloric acid solution, $HCl(aq)$.

119. If 60.00 mL of a 0.100 mol/L hydrazine solution, $N_2H_4(aq)$, $K_a = 7.94 \times 10^{-9}$, is titrated to the equivalence point with 0.200 mol/L hydrobromic acid solution, $HBr(aq)$, what is the pH at this point?

120. A 35.00 mL sample of a 0.250 mol/L pyridine solution, $C_2H_5N(aq)$, $K_b = 1.7 \times 10^{-9}$, is titrated to the equivalence point using 0.300 mol/L hydrochloric acid solution, $HCl(aq)$. What is the resulting pH of the solution?

Equilibrium of Slightly Soluble Ionic Compounds

solubility the maximum amount of solute that can dissolve in a given quantity of solvent at a particular temperature

Another type of equilibrium that has not been discussed is the equilibrium that exists in solutions of slightly soluble ionic compounds. Slightly soluble ionic compounds reach equilibrium with only small amounts of *solute* dissolved in a *solvent*. They are considered to have low solubility. **Solubility** is the maximum amount of solute that can dissolve in a given quantity of solvent at a particular temperature. An example of a slightly soluble ionic compound is shown in **Figure 8.18**.

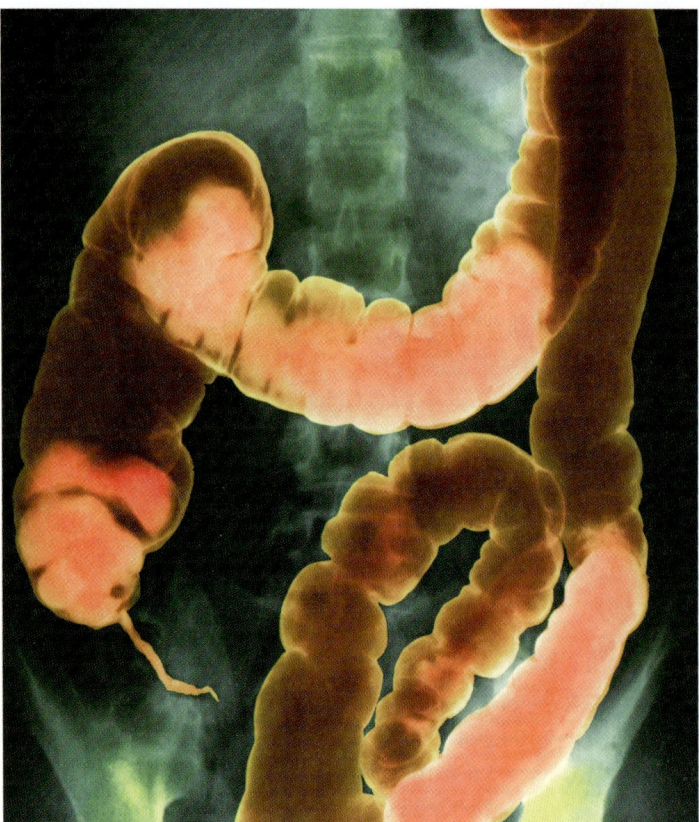

Figure 8.18 Barium sulfate is a toxic substance, but it is so insoluble that it can be safely ingested. The suspension of barium ions, Ba^{2+}, is opaque to X rays, and this characteristic improves the quality of the image.

When a soluble ionic compound dissolves in water, it dissociates completely into ions. This is not the case for slightly soluble ionic compounds. Only a small amount of slightly soluble ionic compounds dissolves in water. A variety of interactions occur among the particles in the solution. You will learn more about these complex behaviours in a higher-level chemistry course.

Silver chloride, $AgCl(s)$, is an example of a slightly soluble ionic compound. Consider a saturated solution of silver chloride that contains some solid silver chloride. It is assumed that the small amount of silver chloride that dissolves in water dissociates completely into silver ions, Ag^+, and chloride ions, Cl^-, as represented by the equation below:

$$AgCl(s) \rightleftharpoons Ag^+(aq) + Cl^-(aq)$$

The system can be expressed by a reaction quotient, as shown below:

$$Q_{eq} = \frac{[Ag^+][Cl^-]}{[AgCl]}$$

Just like the previous reaction quotients that you have studied, the constant concentration of the solid

Just like the previous reaction quotients that you have studied, the constant concentration of the solid is incorporated into the value of Q_{eq}. This expression is the ion-product expression, Q_{sp}, which is shown below:

$$Q_{sp} = Q_{eq}[AgCl]$$
$$= [Ag^+][Cl^-]$$

When the solution becomes saturated, the solid reaches equilibrium with the dissociated ions. In the above example, the solid silver chloride reaches equilibrium with the dissociated silver and chloride ions. At equilibrium, the value of the ion-product expression, Q_{sp}, becomes constant, and this constant value is called the **solubility-product constant**, K_{sp}.

The general chemical equation for a slightly soluble ionic compound, M_pX_q, that is composed of the ions M^{n+} and X^{z-}, is shown below:

$$M_pX_q \rightleftharpoons M^{n+} + X^{z-}$$

The ion-product constant expression and the solubility-product constant for this generic ionic compound have the following relationship:

$$Q_{sp} = [M^{n+}]^p [X^{z-}]^q = K_{sp}$$

Notice that each ion concentration is raised to an exponent equal to the subscript of each ion in the compound's formula. The solubility-product constant for the saturated silver chloride solution described previously is as follows:

$$K_{sp} = [Ag^+][Cl^-]$$

Other solubility-product constants are more complex, as shown below. Notice the use of superscripts in the solubility-product constant examples.

$BaSO_4(s) \rightleftharpoons Ba^{2+}(aq) + SO_4^{2-}(aq)$ $K_{sp} = [Ba^{2+}][SO_4^{2-}]$
$MgF_2(s) \rightleftharpoons Mg^{2+}(aq) + 2F^-(aq)$ $K_{sp} = [Mg^{2+}][F^-]^2$
$Ca_3(PO_4)_2(s) \rightleftharpoons 3Ca^{2+}(aq) + 2PO_4^{3-}(aq)$ $K_{sp} = [Ca^{2+}]^3 [PO_4^{3-}]^2$

solubility-product constant, K_{sp}
an equilibrium constant for slightly soluble ionic compounds

Suggested Investigation

Inquiry Investigation 8-A, Determining K_{sp} for Calcium Hydroxide

Solubility-Product Constant Values

Table 8.6 lists selected values of the solubility-product constant for several compounds. A more extensive list is found in Appendix B. These values are determined experimentally and they can also be found in chemistry handbooks. Notice the wide range of values represented in this table. The value of K_{sp} indicates the solubility of the compound. For example, a small K_{sp} value indicates that the compound is less soluble than a compound with a high value of K_{sp}. Like other equilibrium constants, the value of K_{sp} is temperature dependent. Unless otherwise stated, assume that the solvent is water and the temperature is 25°C for the examples and problems given in this section.

Table 8.6 Solubility-Product Constants of Some Slightly Soluble Ionic Compounds at 25°C

Compound	K_{sp}
Barium fluoride, $BaF_2(s)$	1.7×10^{-6}
Lead(II) chloride, $PbCl_2(s)$	2.4×10^{-4}
Zinc selenide, $ZnSe(s)$	3.6×10^{-26}
Silver chloride, $AgCl(s)$	1.6×10^{-10}

Go to **Solubility-Product Constants in Water at 25°C** in **Appendix B** for more information about K_b values of bases.

precipitate an insoluble product that forms from a reaction between two soluble ionic compounds

molar solubility the amount (in moles) of solute in 1 L of a saturated solution

Predicting the Formation of a Precipitate

In Chapter 7, you compared the values of Q_{eq} and K_{eq} to determine if a reaction had reached equilibrium. For solutions of slightly soluble ionic compounds, you can compare Q_{sp} and K_{sp} values to determine if a precipitate forms. A **precipitate** is an insoluble product formed in a reaction between two soluble ionic compounds, as shown in **Figure 8.19**.

There are three possible outcomes when these values are compared:

- If $Q_{sp} < K_{sp}$, the solution is unsaturated and no precipitate forms.
- If $Q_{sp} = K_{sp}$, the solution is saturated and no change occurs.
- If $Q_{sp} > K_{sp}$, a precipitate forms until the solution is saturated.

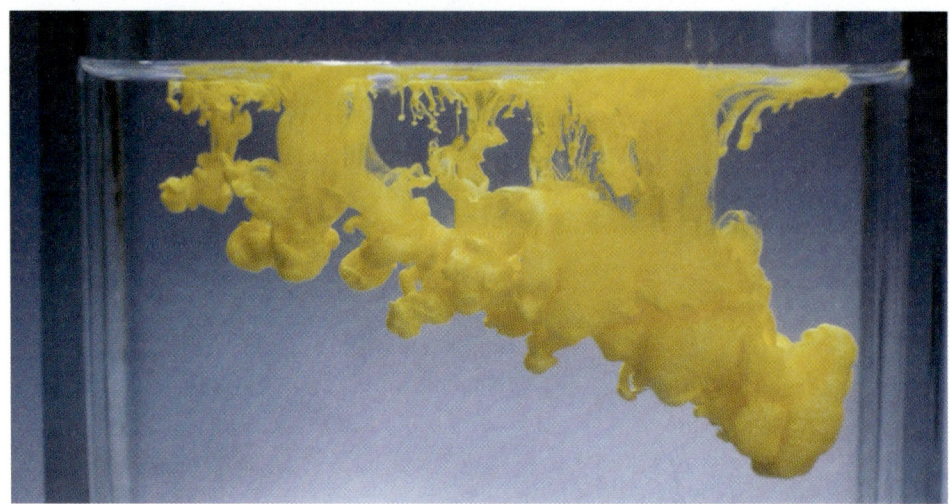

Figure 8.19 One drop of colourless lead(II) nitrate solution was added to a colourless potassium iodide solution, and the solid yellow precipitate lead(II) iodide formed.

Calculations Involving the Solubility-Product Constant

The solubility of a substance can be expressed as a molar solubility. **Molar solubility** is the amount (in moles) of solute in 1 L of a saturated solution. Often, the solubility is expressed as the mass (in grams) of solute dissolved in 100 g of water. Because the density of water is 1 g/mL at 25°C, this value is also the mass (in grams) of solute in 100 mL of water. The Sample Problems that follow demonstrate how to solve problems involving ion-product expressions and product-solubility constants. Use the Practice Problems to practise solving problems that involve slightly soluble ionic compounds.

Sample Problem

Calculating K_{sp} from Molar Solubility Data

Problem
A chemical technician determines that the solubility of silver carbonate, $Ag_2CO_3(s)$, is 1.3×10^{-4} mol/L. Calculate the solubility-product constant, K_{sp}, for silver carbonate.

What Is Required?
You need to calculate K_{sp} for silver carbonate.

What Is Given?
You know the solubility of silver carbonate: 1.3×10^{-4} mol/L

Plan Your Strategy	Act on Your Strategy
Write a balanced chemical equation for the solubility equilibrium. Remember that carbonate is a polyatomic ion and it stays intact.	$Ag_2CO_3(s) \rightleftharpoons 2Ag^+(aq) + CO_3^{2-}(aq)$

Write the expression for K_{sp}. Because silver carbonate is a solid, its concentration is included in the value of K_{sp}. In the balanced chemical equation, the coefficient of the silver ion is 2, so the concentration must be squared in the solubility-product constant.	$K_{sp} = [Ag^+]^2 [CO_3^{2-}]$
You know from the balanced chemical equation that 1 mol $Ag_2CO_3(s)$ dissociates and 2 mol $Ag^+(aq)$ and 1 mol $CO_3^{2-}(aq)$ form. Determine the value of each concentration using the given data.	$[Ag_2CO_3] = 1.3 \times 10^{-4}$ mol/L $[Ag^+] = 2[Ag_2CO_3] = (2)(1.3 \times 10^{-4}$ mol/L$) = 2.6 \times 10^{-4}$ mol/L $[CO_3^{2-}] = [Ag_2CO_3] = 1.3 \times 10^{-4}$ mol/L
Use the known concentrations to determine K_{sp}.	$K_{sp} = [Ag^+]^2 [CO_3^{2-}]$ $= (2.6 \times 10^{-4})^2 (1.3 \times 10^{-4})$ $= 8.8 \times 10^{-12}$

Check Your Solution
The calculated value is small, which is expected for slightly soluble ionic compounds, and the value has the correct number of significant digits.

Sample Problem

Determining Solubility from K_{sp}

Problem
From **Table 8.6**, you know that the value of K_{sp} for barium fluoride, BaF_2, is 1.7×10^{-6}. What is its molar solubility?

What Is Required?
You need to calculate the molar solubility of barium fluoride.

What Is Given?
You know the K_{sp} for barium fluoride: 1.7×10^{-6}

Plan Your Strategy	Act on Your Strategy
Write a balanced chemical equation.	$BaF_2(s) \rightleftharpoons Ba^{2+}(aq) + 2F^-(aq)$
Write the solubility-product constant equation.	$K_{sp} = [Ba^{2+}] [F^-]^2 = 1.7 \times 10^{-6}$
Set up an ICE table to organize your information.	See the ICE table below.

	$BaF_2(s)$	$\rightleftharpoons$	$Ba^{2+}(aq)$	$2F^-(aq)$
	$[BaF_2]$ (mol/L)		$[Ba^{2+}]$ (mol/L)	$2[F^-]$ (mol/L)
Initial				
Change	$-x$		$+x$	$+2x$
Equilibrium	$-x$		x	$2x$

Calculate the molar solubility of BaF_2.	$K_{sp} = [Ba^{2+}] [F^-]^2 = 1.7 \times 10^{-6}$ $(x)(2x)^2 = 4x^3 = 1.7 \times 10^{-6}$ $x = 7.5 \times 10^{-3}$ The solubility of barium fluoride is 7.5×10^{-3} mol/L.

Check Your Solution
The solubility of barium fluoride is low, which is expected of a slightly soluble ionic compound, and the correct number of significant digits is used.

Sample Problem

Calculating K_{sp} from Solubility Data

Problem

A student determined the solubility of calcium sulfate, $CaSO_4(s)$, to be 0.67 g/L. What is the value of K_{sp}?

What Is Required?

You need to calculate the K_{sp} of calcium sulfate.

What Is Given?

You know the solubility of calcium sulfate: 0.67 g/L

Plan Your Strategy	Act on Your Strategy
Write a balanced chemical equation for the solubility equilibrium. Remember that sulfate is a polyatomic ion and it stays intact.	$CaSO_4(s) \rightleftharpoons Ca^{2+}(aq) + SO_4^{2-}(aq)$
Convert the solubility to molar solubility so that you can use molar relationships. The molar mass of calcium sulfate is 136.15 g/mol.	molar solubility $CaSO_4 = \dfrac{0.67 \text{ g}}{1 \text{ L}} \times \dfrac{1 \text{ mol}}{136.15 \text{ g}} = 4.9 \times 10^{-3}$ mol/L
Set up an ICE table to organize your information.	See the ICE table below.

	$CaSO_4(s)$ $\rightleftharpoons$	$Ca^{2+}(aq)$ +	$SO_4^{2-}(aq)$
	$[CaSO_4]$ (mol/L)	$[Ca^{2+}]$ (mol/L)	$[SO_4^{2-}]$ (mol/L)
Initial	4.9×10^{-3}		
Change	$-x$	$+x$	$+x$
Equilibrium		x	x

Determine the equation for the solubility-product constant, K_{sp}. From the balanced chemical equation, you know that for every 1 mol $CaSO_4(s)$ that dissociates, 1 mol $Ca^{2+}(aq)$ and 1 mol $SO_4^{2-}(aq)$ form.	$K_{sp} = [Ca^{2+}][SO_4^{2-}] = x^2$
Solve for K_{sp}.	$K_{sp} = [Ca^{2+}][SO_4^{2-}]$ $= x^2$ $= (4.9 \times 10^{-3})^2 = 2.4 \times 10^{-5}$

Check Your Solution

The calculated value is small, which is expected for slightly soluble ionic compounds, and the value has the correct number of significant digits.

Sample Problem

Determining Whether a Precipitate Will Form

Problem

If exactly 200 mL of 0.0040 mol/L barium chloride solution, $BaCl_2(aq)$, is mixed with exactly 600 mL of 0.0080 mol/L potassium sulfate solution, K_2SO_4 (aq), the particles dissociate, and the only possible precipitate that can form is $BaSO_4$ (s). Will a precipitate form?

What Is Required?

You need to determine whether a precipitate will form.

What Is Given?
You know the volume and molarity of barium chloride: 200 mL of a 0.0040 mol/L solution
You know the volume and molarity of potassium sulfate: 600 mL of a 0.0080 mol/L solution
You know the only possible precipitate that can form: $BaSO_4(s)$.
You know that values of K_{sp} for selected compounds are listed in Appendix B.

Plan Your Strategy	Act on Your Strategy
Write a balanced chemical equation for the solubility equilibrium.	$BaSO_4(s) \rightleftharpoons Ba^{2+}(aq) + SO_4^{2-}(aq)$
Determine the amount (in moles) of barium ions, $Ba^{2+}(aq)$, in the original solution.	$n_{Ba^{2+}} = \left(\dfrac{0.0040 \text{ mol}}{1 \text{ L}}\right)(200 \text{ mL})\left(\dfrac{1 \text{ L}}{1000 \text{ mL}}\right) = 8.0 \times 10^{-4}$ mol
After the two solutions are mixed, the total volume is 800 mL. Determine the concentration of the barium ions in moles per litre.	$[Ba^{2+}] = \left(\dfrac{8.0 \times 10^{-4} \text{ mol}}{800 \text{ mL}}\right)\left(\dfrac{1000 \text{ mL}}{1 \text{ L}}\right) = 1.0 \times 10^{-3}$ mol/L
Determine the amount (in moles) of sulfate ions, $SO_4^{2-}(aq)$, in the original solution.	$n_{SO_4^{2-}} = \left(\dfrac{0.0080 \text{ mol}}{1 \text{ L}}\right)(600 \text{ mL})\left(\dfrac{1 \text{ L}}{1000 \text{ mL}}\right) = 4.8 \times 10^{-3}$ mol
Determine the concentration of sulfate ions in the final solution in moles per litre.	$[SO_4^{2-}] = \left(\dfrac{4.8 \times 10^{-3} \text{ mol}}{800 \text{ mL}}\right)\left(\dfrac{1000 \text{ mL}}{1 \text{ L}}\right) = 6.0 \times 10^{-3}$ mol/L
Refer to Appendix B to determine the value of K_{sp} for barium sulfate, and compare K_{sp} with Q_{sp}.	$K_{sp} = 1.08 \times 10^{-10}$ $Q_{sp} = [Ba^{2+}][SO_4^{2-}]$ $= (1.0 \times 10^{-3})(6.0 \times 10^{-3}) = 6.0 \times 10^{-6}$ $Q_{sp} > K_{sp}$ A precipitate forms until the solution is saturated.

Check Your Solution
Check your calculations to make sure that you did not make an error. The calculated values seem reasonable.

Practice Problems

121. It has been determined that the molar solubility of silver chloride, AgCl(s), is 1.3×10^{-5} mol/L. What is the value of the solubility-product constant for this solid?

122. Magnesium fluoride, $MgF_2(s)$, has a molar solubility of 2.7×10^{-3} mol/L. Use this information to determine the K_{sp} value for the solid.

123. Silver sulfide, $Ag_2S(s)$, has a K_{sp} value that is equal to 5.6×10^{-49}. What is the molar solubility of the solid?

124. The K_{sp} value for lead(II) bromide, $PbBr_2(s)$, is 6.6×10^{-6}. What is the solubility of this solid, in grams per litre?

125. Which solid can have more mass dissociate into 1.00 L of solution: silver chloride, AgCl(s), or copper(I) chloride, CuCl(s)?

126. The solubility of nickel(II) phosphate, $Ni_3(PO_4)_2(s)$, is 7.8×10^{-5} g/L. Determine the solubility-product constant for this solid.

127. The solubility of strontium fluoride, $SrF_2(s)$, is 12.2 mg/100 mL. What is K_{sp} for this solid?

128. Will a precipitate form if 1.00 mL of a 0.100 mol/L silver nitrate solution, $AgNO_3(aq)$, is added to 1.00 L of a 1.00×10^{-5} mol/L solution of sodium chloride, NaCl(aq)? Show your calculations.

Section 8.4 Review

Section Summary

- A reaction between an acid and a base is called a neutralization reaction, and a salt and water form in the reaction.
- A buffer is a solution that resists pH change when a limited amount of acid or base is added to it.
- The titration curve for an acid and base reaction depends on the strength of the acid and the strength of the base.
- Slightly soluble ionic compounds can establish equilibrium, and the equilibrium constant is called the solubility-product constant, K_{sp}.
- The values of the solubility-product constant, K_{sp}, and the ion-product expression, Q_{sp}, are compared for slightly soluble ionic compounds to determine if a precipitate forms.

Review Questions

1. **T/I** Two beakers studied in a lab contain the same weak monoprotic acid at the same concentration. Beaker A contains 225 mL of the acid and beaker B contains 425 mL of the acid. Will these two beakers show the same pH on a pH meter when tested? Explain why or why not.

2. **K/U** Which beaker in question 1 will have a greater amount (in moles) of hydronium ions? Explain your answer.

3. **A** Headache tablets were initially manufactured by first extracting salicin from the bark of the willow tree. Later this salicin was synthesized in a lab, but in the form of salicylic acid. Explain why modern headache tablets need to be buffered.

4. **K/U** Why does an indicator change from its base colour to its acid colour over a range of pH values?

5. **T/I** A chemist is titrating 30.00 mL of a 0.100 mol/L acetic acid solution, $CH_3COOH(aq)$, with a 0.100 mol/L solution of potassium hydroxide, $KOH(aq)$. Calculate the pH of the solution after the addition of 10.00 mL of the base.

6. **A** One of the buffering systems in the blood is the carbonic acid-hydrogen carbonate buffer system.

    $H_2CO_3(aq) + H_2O(\ell) \rightleftharpoons HCO_3^-(aq) + OH^-(aq)$

    Ideally, blood pH should be maintained at 7.4, with even the slightest deviation in pH leading to serious illness. However, the optimal pH for this buffer system is 6.4, which is much lower than the optimal pH of the blood.

    a. Determine the ratio of the hydrogen carbonate ion, $HCO_3^-(aq)$, to carbonic acid, $H_2CO_3(aq)$, at a pH of 7.4.
    b. Why is this buffer system excellent at dealing with the lactic acid build-up that occurs during exercise?
    c. How does the absorption of carbon dioxide aid this buffering system?

7. **A** Explain why less of solid iron(II) hydroxide, $Fe(OH)_2(s)$, can dissolve into a solution of 0.100 mol/L potassium hydroxide, $KOH(aq)$, compared with aqueous iron(III) hydroxide, $Fe(OH)_3(aq)$, dissolving into the same volume of pure water.

8. **A** The photograph on the right-hand side shows a beaker containing a weak acid. The photograph on the left-hand side shows the same beaker after 5.00 mL of a base was added to the solution. What conclusions can be drawn with respect to the contents of the beakers?

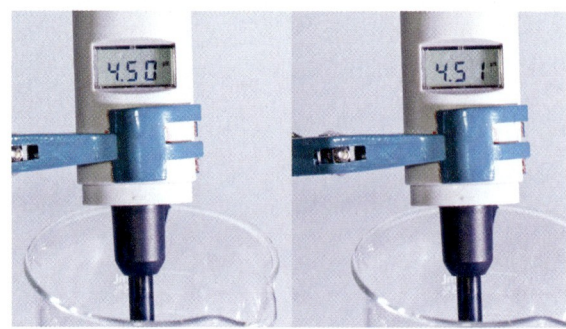

9. **A** A process called selective precipitation allows for one ion to be removed from a solution containing other ions, with only the ion of interest being precipitated out of solution. This process is used in the purification of drinking water. The process occurs by selecting an ion and then carefully controlling its concentration in the solution.

    A solution contains 0.010 mol/L silver ions, $Ag^+(aq)$, and 0.010 mol/L strontium ions, $Sr^{2+}(aq)$.

    a. Which ion will precipitate out first when a dilute solution of potassium chromate, $K_2CrO_4(aq)$, is added to the mixture? (**Hint:** Determine the concentrations of chromate ion, $CrO_4^{2-}(aq)$, needed for each solid to form. K_{sp} for $SrCrO_4$ is 2.2×10^{-5}.)
    b. What percentage of the ion that precipitates first will remain unprecipitated when the second ion starts to precipitate?

Inquiry INVESTIGATION 8-A

Skill Check
- Initiating and Planning
- ✓ Performing and Recording
- ✓ Analyzing and Interpreting
- ✓ Communicating

Determining K_{sp} for Calcium Hydroxide

The value of K_{sp} for a basic compound, such as calcium hydroxide, $Ca(OH)_2(aq)$, can be determined by performing an acid-base titration.

Pre-Lab Questions

1. Write the solubility equilibrium equation for calcium hydroxide, and write the K_{sp} equation.
2. Read the Procedure and make a list of the safety precautions that you should use.

Questions

What is the value of K_{sp} for calcium hydroxide?

Safety Precautions

- Wear safety eyewear, and a lab coat or apron throughout this activity.
- If you get acid or base on your skin, flush with plenty of cold water.
- Do not dispose of any chemicals down the drain.
- Phenolphthalein is flammable. Keep away from flames.
- Wash your hands thoroughly when you have completed this investigation.

Materials

- 10 mL of 0.050 mol/L hydrochloric acid, $HCl(aq)$
- phenolphthalein, in dropper bottle
- 10 mL of recently filtered saturated solution of calcium hydroxide, $Ca(OH)_2(aq)$
- distilled water, in wash bottle
- 100 mL beaker
- 2 identical microscale pipettes
- white sheet of paper
- glass stirring rod
- petri dish or watch glass

Procedure

1. Read the Procedure, and prepare a data table. Remember to give your table a title.
2. Add exactly 10 drops of 0.050 mol/L hydrochloric acid to a 100 mL beaker. To ensure uniform drop size, use the same type of pipette to dispense the acid and the base. Also, hold the pipette vertically when dispensing the solution. Always record the number of drops added. Place the beaker on the white sheet of paper.
3. To transfer a small amount of indicator to the acid solution, place one drop of phenolphthalein solution on a watch glass. Touch the drop with the glass rod. Transfer this small amount of indicator to the hydrochloric acid in the beaker.
4. Add the saturated calcium hydroxide solution, drop by drop, to the hydrochloric acid solution until the solution turns a permanent pale pink. Swirl the beaker, particularly as the pink colour begins to appear. Record the number of drops of calcium hydroxide that you added. Conduct as many trials as you can.
5. Dispose of all solutions as directed by your teacher.

Analyze and Interpret

1. Determine the average number of drops of calcium hydroxide solution that you needed to neutralize 10 drops of 0.050 mol/L hydrochloric acid.
2. Use the balanced chemical equation for the neutralization of hydrochloric acid with calcium hydroxide to determine the concentration of the hydroxide ion, in moles per litre. (**Hint:** Why do you not need to know the volume of one drop?) From $[OH^-]$, determine $[Ca^{2+}]$ in moles per litre.

Conclude and Communicate

3. Calculate K_{sp} for calcium hydroxide. If possible, look up the accepted value of K_{sp} and calculate your percent error.

Inquiry INVESTIGATION 8-B

Skill Check

Initiating and Planning
✓ Performing and Recording
✓ Analyzing and Interpreting
✓ Communicating

Determining K_a for Ethanoic (Acetic) Acid

To determine the concentration of an acid in a titration investigation, you can use a pipette to place a known volume of the acid into an Erlenmeyer flask and then add a few drops of an indicator to the flask. Next, you can use a burette to add a basic solution with known concentration to the Erlenmeyer flask until the indicator changes colour. In this investigation, you will be given a sample of ethanoic acid of unknown concentration. You will measure the pH of the solution using pH paper or a pH meter, whichever is available. Then you will perform a titration investigation to determine the molar concentration of the ethanoic acid solution. Using these data, you will calculate K_a for ethanoic acid and determine the percentage of ethanoic acid molecules that ionized in the solution.

Safety Precautions

- Wear safety eyewear, and a lab coat or apron throughout this activity.
- These solutions are harmful if inhaled, swallowed, or spilled on skin. Wash any spills on your skin or clothing with plenty of cool water and inform your teacher.
- Phenolphthalein is flammable. Keep away from flames.
- Wash your hands thoroughly when you have completed this investigation.

Materials

- ethanoic (acetic) acid solution, $CH_3COOH(aq)$, unknown concentration
- sodium hydroxide solution, $NaOH(aq)$, known concentration
- phenolphthalein, in dropper bottle
- distilled water
- 10 mL pipette
- labels
- two 150 mL beakers
- pH meter or pH paper
- 250 mL beaker for waste solutions
- burette and burette clamp
- retort stand
- meniscus reader
- funnel
- pipette bulb or pipette pump
- 125 mL Erlenmeyer flask
- sheet of white paper

Pre-Lab Questions

1. With respect to a titration, explain the terms *equivalence point* and *endpoint*.
2. Why is it necessary to rinse the burette with a few millilitres of the sodium hydroxide solution used in the titration before filling it with this solution?
3. When filling the burette, why must the solution fill the tip of the burette—below the burette tap—and contain no air bubbles?
4. When using phenolphthalein indicator in a titration, why is it necessary to have the sodium hydroxide solution in the burette, rather than in the Erlenmeyer flask?
5. Why must a piece of white paper be placed underneath the Erlenmeyer flask during a titration?
6. Explain why it is important to keep phenolphthalein away from open flames.

Questions

What is the acid-dissociation constant of ethanoic acid?
What percentage of the acid molecules ionize in an aqueous solution?

Prediction

Predict the value of K_a and the percent dissociation of ethanoic acid.

Procedure

1. Your teacher will give you the concentration of the sodium hydroxide solution. Record this concentration in your notebook, as well as the volume of the pipette. Design a table to record your titration data.
2. Label a clean, dry 150 mL beaker for each liquid. Obtain about 40 mL of ethanoic acid solution and approximately 70 mL of sodium hydroxide solution.

3. Measure the pH of the ethanoic acid solution using pH paper, or a pH meter if one is available. Record this value.

4. Rinse a clean burette with about 10 mL of sodium hydroxide solution. Discard the rinse into the 250 mL waste beaker. Then set up a retort stand, burette clamp, meniscus reader, and funnel, as shown in the diagram. Fill the burette with the sodium hydroxide solution. Make sure that the solution fills the tube below the burette tap and contains no air bubbles. Remove the funnel.

5. Your teacher will give you a clean 10 mL pipette and a suction bulb or pipette pump. Rinse the pipette with a few millilitres of ethanoic acid solution and discard the rinse. Pipette 10.00 mL of ethanoic acid solution into the Erlenmeyer flask. Add two or three drops of phenolphthalein indicator to the flask. Place a sheet of white paper under the flask.

6. Perform the titration. The endpoint is a faint pink colour that remains after swirling the contents of the Erlenmeyer flask for at least 10 s. Measure the volume of base required to reach the endpoint. Repeat the titration as time permits until you have at least two sets of data that agree with each other within 2 percent error.

7. Discard waste liquids into the beaker you have been using for this purpose. Give the beaker containing the waste liquids from your investigations to your teacher for safe disposal.

8. Rinse the pipette and burette with distilled water. Leave the burette tap open and store the burette upside down.

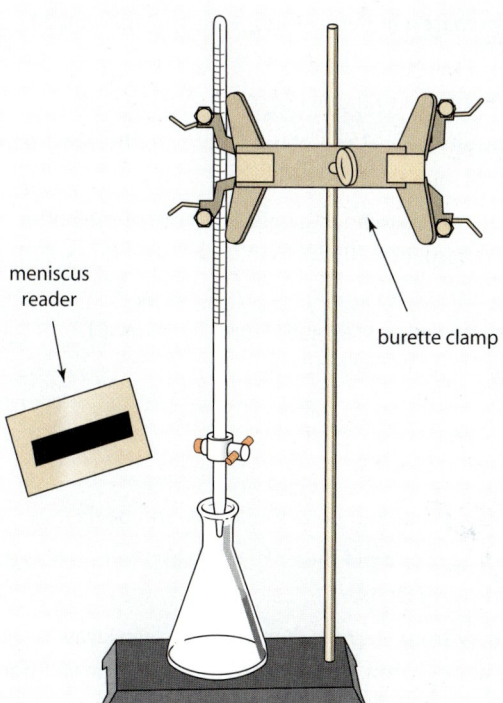

Analyze and Interpret

1. Write the balanced chemical equation for the neutralization reaction you performed.

2. Calculate the molar concentration of the ethanoic acid, [CH_3COOH]. Use the ratio in which the acid and base react, determined from the chemical equation.

3. Calculate [H_3O^+] using your measurement of the pH of the ethanoic acid solution.

4. Write the expression for K_a, the acid-dissociation constant, of ethanoic acid in water.

5. Set up an ICE table and substitute equilibrium concentrations into your expression for K_a. Calculate the value of K_a and the percentage of ethanoic acid molecules that ionized in solution.

Conclude and Communicate

6. Calculate the percent difference between your value for K_a of ethanoic acid and the accepted value. State two sources of error that might account for any differences in the results.

7. Compare your value for K_a and the percentage of ethanoic acid molecules that ionized with the values determined by others in your class. Discuss the results.

8. Do the values you calculated for [H_3O^+] and [CH_3COOH] demonstrate that ethanoic acid is a weak acid? Explain your answer.

Extend Further

9. **INQUIRY** Design an investigation to calculate the K_b value for ammonia, NH_3(aq). Assume that you have household aqueous ammonia and any other standard chemicals and laboratory equipment available.

10. **RESEARCH** If weak acids ionize only a few percent in aqueous solution, why is it possible to fully neutralize a weak acid by reacting it with the stoichiometric equivalent of sodium hydroxide solution, NaOH(aq)?

Inquiry INVESTIGATION 8-C

Skill Check
- Initiating and Planning
- ✓ Performing and Recording
- ✓ Analyzing and Interpreting
- ✓ Communicating

Safety Precautions

- Wear safety eyewear, and a lab coat or apron throughout this activity.
- Sodium hydroxide and hydrochloric acid are corrosive to the eye and skin and harmful if swallowed or inhaled. Wash any spills on your skin or clothing with plenty of cool water. Inform your teacher immediately if you spill hydrochloric acid or sodium hydroxide on yourself or on the lab bench or floor.
- Dispose of all materials as instructed by your teacher.
- Wash your hands when you have completed the investigation.

Materials
- 0.20 mol/L ethanoic (acetic) acid, $CH_3COOH(aq)$
- 0.20 mol/L sodium hydroxide, $NaOH(aq)$
- 0.20 mol/L hydrochloric acid, $HCl(aq)$
- distilled water
- 50 mL graduated cylinder
- four 50 mL beakers
- 100 mL beaker
- universal indicator paper (pH paper)
- pH meter (optional)
- two clean straws
- stirring rod
- burettes

Preparing a Buffer and Investigating Its Properties

In this investigation, you will first prepare a buffer solution. Then you will compare how the buffer resists a change in pH when an acid or a base is added and how water resists the same changes.

Pre-Lab Questions
1. Qualitatively describe the function of a buffer solution and how to prepare one.
2. In this investigation, sodium acetate is required, but is not directly provided. How is it produced?
3. List safety precautions that you should take while performing this investigation.

Questions
How much does the pH of a buffer change when a small amount of a strong acid or strong base is added? How much strong acid or base must be added to a buffer solution to change its pH by one unit?

Predictions
a. Calculate the volume of 0.20 mol/L sodium hydroxide, $NaOH(aq)$, needed to make the concentration of hydroxide ions, $OH^-(aq)$, equal to half the concentration in 40 mL of 0.20 mol/L of ethanoic acid, $CH_3COOH(aq)$.
b. The centre of the buffer region occurs at the half-titration point between a weak acid and a strong base. What volume of 0.20 mol/L sodium hydroxide solution is required to prepare a buffer solution with 40.0 mL of 0.20 mol/L ethanoic acid?
c. Make a reasonable prediction as to the pH of the buffer solution.
d. Calculate the pH that results when 1 mL of 0.20 mol/L sodium hydroxide solution is added to 20 mL of water.
e. Make a reasonable prediction as to how the pH of 20 mL of the buffer solution is affected when 1 mL of 0.20 mol/L sodium hydroxide solution is added to it.
f. Repeat your predictions for (d) and (e), substituting 0.20 mol/L hydrochloric acid for the sodium hydroxide.

Procedure

Part 1 Acid Bath
1. Measure 20 mL of distilled water and pour it into a 50 mL beaker.
2. Use universal indicator paper or a pH meter (if available) to measure the pH of the water. Record your results.
3. Obtain a fresh, clean straw from your teacher. Use the clean straw to gently blow into the water for about 2 min. Then record the pH of the solution again. Dispose of the straw when finished. Do not share straws.

Part 2 Preparing the Buffer

1. Rinse the graduated cylinder with a few millilitres of 0.20 mol/L ethanoic acid. Discard the rinse as directed by your teacher. Measure 40 mL of 0.20 mol/L ethanoic acid into a 100 mL beaker.
2. Rinse the graduated cylinder several times with tap water. Then rinse the graduated cylinder using a few millilitres of 0.20 mol/L sodium hydroxide solution. Discard the rinse as directed by your teacher.
3. Have your teacher check the volume of 0.20 mol/L sodium hydroxide solution that you calculated in (a), under Predictions. After receiving approval, add it to the contents of the beaker from Procedure step 1 to make the buffer solution.
4. Divide the buffer solution from Procedure step 3 into three equal portions, using the graduated cylinder and three 50 mL beakers.

Part 3 The Control

1. Copy the following table into your notebook. Give the table a suitable title.

Volume NaOH(aq) Added (mL)	pH of Water + Added NaOH(aq)	pH of Buffer + NaOH(aq)	pH of Buffer + HCl(aq)
0.0			
1.0			

2. Measure 20 mL of distilled water and pour it into a 50 mL beaker.
3. Record the pH of the water in the second column of the table (for 0.0 mL of added NaOH), measured with universal indicator paper or with a pH meter (optional).
4. Add 1.0 mL of sodium hydroxide solution from the burette that will be set up by your teacher. Stir thoroughly; then measure and record the pH of the solution. Record the value in the second column.
5. Repeat Procedure step 4 until the pH of the solution is at least one unit greater than the initial pH.

Part 4 Adding Base to the Buffer

1. Use one of the beakers containing buffer solution from Part 2. Measure the pH of the solution and record the value in the third column of the table (for 0.0 mL of NaOH added).
2. Add 1.0 mL of the sodium hydroxide solution to the buffer. Stir thoroughly, and then measure and record the pH of the solution in the third column of the table.
3. Repeat Procedure step 2 until the pH of the solution is at least one unit more than the initial pH.

Part 5 Adding Acid to the Buffer

1. Using a second beaker containing buffer solution, measure the pH of the solution and record the value in the last column of the table (for 0.0 mL HCl added).
2. Add 1.0 mL of hydrochloric acid solution to the buffer. Stir thoroughly, and then measure and record the pH of the solution in the last column of the table.
3. Repeat Procedure step 2 until the pH of the solution is at least one unit less than the initial pH.

Part 6 Controlling Acid Breath

1. Obtain the last beaker of buffer solution. Using another fresh, clean straw, gently blow into the solution for about 2 min. Then record the pH of the solution. Dispose of the straw.

Analyze and Interpret

1. The pH of distilled water may not be 7.0. Explain why this might be true.
2. How did the pH of the water change when you blew air into it? Explain by using a chemical equation.
3. What was the effect on pH of blowing air into the buffer solution?
4. Compare the pH calculated for 1 mL of 0.20 mol/L sodium hydroxide solution added to 20 mL of water, with the value you measured. If there is a difference, explain the reason for the difference.
5. Compare your estimate of the pH of the buffer solution with the value you measured. If it is outside of the range you estimated, explain the difference.
6. Use a spreadsheet program to graph the data in your table. Compare the effect on pH of adding base to water with the effect of adding the same amount of base to the buffer. Compare the effect on pH of adding acid to the buffer solution with the effect of adding the same amount of base to the buffer solution.

Conclude and Communicate

7. Write a statement about the effect of adding small amounts of either an acid or a base to a buffer solution.

Extend Further

8. **INQUIRY** Explain how you would prepare a basic buffer using a 0.20 mol/L ammonia solution, $NH_3(aq)$, and 0.20 mol/L hydrochloric acid, $HCl(aq)$. What would be the approximate pH of this buffer? If time permits and if your teacher approves, prepare about 100 mL of this buffer solution.
9. **RESEARCH** The pH of human blood is 7.4. Use the Internet to research the principal buffer system in blood, and how the body acts to maintain this buffer.

STSE
Case Study

Site Remediation
Equilibrium in Action

Scenario

Researchers at a university in your community have just issued a press release, shown on the next page, reporting findings that the inner harbour of the nearby Cataraqui River is contaminated with high levels of mercury. This area was once the site of at least 40 industries. Although many of these industries have shut down, their environmental footprint is still present. Contaminants detected over the years have included polychlorinated biphenyls (PCBs), polycyclic aromatic hydrocarbons (PAHs), and heavy metals such as chromium, copper, and lead. Prior to the university study, however, researchers had never looked closely at the distribution of mercury in the soil and how it was moving through the groundwater in the area.

The worst area of mercury contamination is near the Cataraqui Canoe Club just south of the former Davis Tannery. Most of the mercury contamination is in the shoreline soil, but rain is also washing the contaminated soil near the canoe club into the river. Because the river drains into Lake Ontario, there is risk of the mercury contamination spreading even farther into the environment. As a member of the rowing team at the Cataraqui Canoe Club and a resident of the area, you are concerned about the possible effects of mercury contamination on the environment, wildlife, and humans.

The Power of Community Activism

You recall a successful site remediation project undertaken in 2004 in Belleville, Ontario. The citizens of Belleville learned that waste from a former landfill and coal/fuel storage sites had caused contaminants including PAHs and heavy metals such as copper, lead, and zinc to leach into the groundwater. Like the Cataraqui Canoe Club near your home, the contaminated site in Belleville was located on prime land—an urbanized area on the waterfront. Citizens saw great potential in their harbour—if only they could clean up the land and make sure the waterline was kept free of harmful contaminants. By winning the attention and support of government agencies, members of the community succeeded in transforming what was once unusable space into a vibrant, revitalized marina and public park. These redevelopment efforts were part of a long-term project, now known as "Jane Forrester Park," that, to this day, continues to inspire investment in the waterfront area of Belleville, Ontario.

Jane Forrester Park was once a toxic contaminated area due to wastes from industries and from the coal storage site shown in the photograph on the left. It is now a safe marina and public park.

Queen's University News Centre

High Levels of Mercury Found in Cataraqui River, Kingston, Ontario

Researchers at Queen's University in Kingston, Ontario, have found mercury levels to be more than twice the level of the federal government's severe effect limit (>2000 microgram/kg) in the sediment around the inner harbour of the Cataraqui River.

Over the past 100 years, the area has been the site of many other industries, including a coal gasification plant, a lead smelter, a municipal dump, a textile mill, and a fuel depot.

Rain is washing contaminated shoreline soil near the canoe club into the river, adding to the sediment already contaminated by decades of industrial pollution.

Groundwater Treatment Using Equilibrium

One way to treat heavy metal contamination in groundwater is through a process called adsorption, shown in the diagram on the right. Adsorption involves incubating wastewater—the solvent, or liquid phase—with the solid phase of a substance—the "sorbent." A phase is a homogeneous part of a heterogeneous system in which there are well-defined boundaries between the system components. The solid phase can be made of various materials, such as activated carbon, or charcoal.

The key to the adsorption process is that the solid phase contains chemical groups, such as carboxyl, sulfhydryl, amino, phosphate, or hydroxyl groups, which bind to the metal ions, the "sorbate," in wastewater. The metal is attracted to the solid phase, and equilibrium is reached between the metal ions that bind to the solid and those that remain in solution. Once the metal species is bound to the solid phase, the sorbent can be incinerated or buried in a landfill.

Research and Analyze

1. Conduct research to find out more about the release of mercury into the environment. What are some possible effects on the health of people and organisms living within a region contaminated by mercury?

2. Research the regulations governing human and environmental exposure to mercury in Canada. What measures are used to assess mercury exposure in humans and the environment? What are the exposure limits for mercury in humans and the environment according to regulatory standards?

3. Citizens in Belleville, Ontario took action leading to revitalization of the land to create Jane Forrester Park. Locate other examples of remediation of sites that were once contaminated with mercury. Find out about the process by which environmental advocacy groups have alerted officials to their concerns and have ensured that action was taken to address those concerns.

Take Action

1. **PLAN** As a concerned citizen in your region, work in a group to identify key points that would help to win the attention and support of government agencies responsible for undertaking environmental clean-ups. Share the results of the research and analysis you conducted for questions 1 to 3 above.

2. **ACT** Prepare a letter to the City of Kingston to advocate for similar remediation efforts in your region. Your letter should propose possible solutions that may help to ensure the safety of your community. Support your recommendations with information from credible sources.

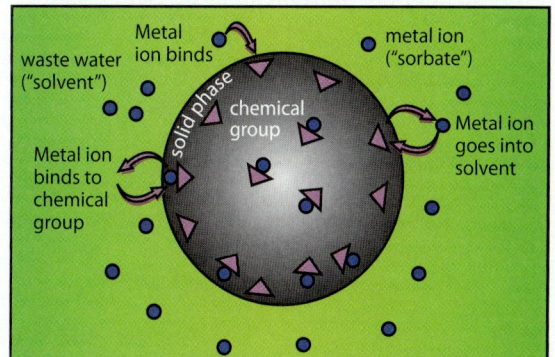

Adsorption of heavy-metal-contaminated water involves equilibrium processes.

Chapter 8 SUMMARY

Section 8.1 Understanding Acid-Base Equilibrium

The Brønsted-Lowry theory of acids and bases explains the behaviour of acids and bases.

Key Terms
amphiprotic
Brønsted-Lowry theory of acids and bases
conjugate acid
conjugate acid-base pair
conjugate base
dissociation
electrolyte
hydronium ion, H_3O^+
hydroxide ion, OH^-
ionization
ion-product constant of water, K_w
pH
pOH

Key Concepts
- The Arrhenius theory defines acids and bases based on their chemical formulas and on how they dissociate in water.
- The Brønsted-Lowry theory of acids and bases defines acids and bases based on the donation and acceptance of a proton.
- Water is amphiprotic and it can act as an acid or a base.
- pH and pOH are the negative common logarithms of the hydronium ion, H_3O^+, and the hydroxide ion, OH^-, respectively, and they are used to describe acids and bases.
- The sum of the pH and the pOH is 14.00 for any aqueous solution at 25°C.

Section 8.2 Acid-Base Strength and Acid Dissociation

The strength of acids and bases is based on how much they ionize or dissociate in water and not on their pH values; the equilibrium constant for the ionization of acids is represented by K_a.

Key Terms
acid-dissociation constant, or acid-ionization constant, K_a
monoprotic acid
percent dissociation
polyprotic acid
strong acid
strong base
weak acid
weak base

Key Concepts
- Strong acids ionize almost completely in water, and strong bases dissociate almost completely in water. Weak acids partially ionize in water, and weak bases partially ionize or dissociate in water.
- In general, an acid-base equilibrium reaction shifts in the direction in which a stronger acid and a stronger base form a weaker acid and a weaker base.
- The acid-dissociation constant, or acid-ionization constant, K_a, is used for acid-base reactions.
- Percent dissociation of a weak acid is the fraction of acid molecules that ionizes at equilibrium compared with the initial concentration of the acid.
- Some acids are monoprotic and have one ionizable proton. Other acids are polyprotic and have more than one ionizable proton.

Section 8.3 Base Ionization

Some weak bases do not dissociate, but they do ionize; the equilibrium constant for bases is represented by K_b.

Key Terms
base-ionization constant, or base-dissociation constant, K_b

Key Concepts
- The equilibrium constant for a base is called the base-ionization constant, or the base-dissociation constant, K_b.
- The base-ionization constant, K_b, is also used for acid-base reactions.
- In acid-base reactions, strong bases dissociate, but some weak bases ionize without dissociating.
- The overall equilibrium constant for an acid and its conjugate base is $K_a K_b = K_w$.

Chapter 8 SUMMARY & REVIEW

Section 8.4 Salts, Buffers, Titrations, and Solubility

When acids and bases react, they form a salt and water; some ionic compounds are only slightly soluble in water.

Key Terms

anion
buffer solution
cation
common-ion effect
endpoint
equivalence point
molar solubility
neutralization reaction
precipitate
salt
salt hydrolysis
solubility
solubility-product constant, K_{sp}

Key Concepts

- A reaction between an acid and a base is called a neutralization reaction, and a salt and water form in the reaction.
- A buffer is a solution that resists pH change when a limited amount of acid or base is added to it.
- The titration curve for an acid and base reaction depends on the strength of the acid and the strength of the base.
- Slightly soluble ionic compounds can establish equilibrium, and the equilibrium constant is called the solubility-product constant, K_{sp}.
- The values of the solubility-product constant, K_{sp}, and the ion-product expression, Q_{sp}, are compared for slightly soluble ionic compounds to determine if a precipitate forms.

Knowledge and Understanding

Select the letter of the best answer below.

1. "A weak acid has a low concentration." This statement is
   a. always true.
   b. never true.
   c. often true.
   d. often false.
   e. true or false, depending on the concentration of the weak acid.

2. Which of the following properties determines whether an acid is strong or weak?
   a. the percent dissociation
   b. the volume of water
   c. the amount of material dissolved in water
   d. the temperature of the water
   e. the number of protons that can be given off by the acid

3. What would be the conjugate acid of $CH_3^-(aq)$?
   a. $CH_2^{2-}(aq)$
   b. $CH_3^-(aq)$
   c. $CH_4(aq)$
   d. $CH_3COOH(aq)$
   e. $CH_3OH(aq)$

4. In the following reaction, which are conjugate acid-base pairs?
   $HC_2H_3O_2(aq) + H_2O(\ell) \rightleftharpoons C_2H_3O_2^-(aq) + H_3O^+(aq)$
   a. $HC_2H_3O_2(aq)$ and $H_2O(\ell)$
   b. $HC_2H_3O_2(aq)$ and $C_2H_3O_2^-(aq)$
   c. $C_2H_3O_2^-(aq)$ and $H_3O^+(aq)$
   d. $H_2O(\ell)$ and $H_3O^+(aq)$
   e. Two of these answers are conjugate acid-base pairs.

5. "The stronger the acid is, the weaker the corresponding conjugate base will be, and the stronger the base is, the weaker the corresponding conjugate acid will be." This statement is
   a. false.
   b. true.
   c. true, depending on the temperature of the solution.
   d. true only for amphiprotic ions.
   e. true only for polyprotic acids.

6. Which is the correct reaction for the second ionization of phosphoric acid?
   a. $H_3PO_4(aq) + H_2O(\ell) \rightleftharpoons H_2PO_4^-(aq) + H_3O^+(aq)$
   b. $H_2PO_4^-(aq) + H_3O^+(aq) \rightleftharpoons H_3PO_4(aq) + H_2O(\ell)$
   c. $H_2PO_4^-(aq) + H_2O(\ell) \rightleftharpoons HPO_4^{2-}(aq) + H_3O^+(aq)$
   d. $HPO_4^{2-}(aq) + H_3O^+(aq) \rightleftharpoons H_2PO_4^-(aq) + H_2O(\ell)$
   e. $HPO_4^{2-}(aq) + H_2O(\ell) \rightleftharpoons PO_4^{3-}(aq) + H_3O^+(aq)$

7. Which statement is true for a triprotic acid?
   a. $K_{a1} < K_{a2} > K_{a3}$
   b. $K_{a1} < K_{a2} < K_{a3}$
   c. $K_{a1} = 1, K_{a2} > K_{a3}$
   d. $K_{a1} > K_{a2} > K_{a3}$
   e. $K_{a1} > K_{a2}, K_{a3} = 1$

8. For a weak triprotic acid with $K_{a1} = 3.5 \times 10^{-4}$, $K_{a2} = 7.5 \times 10^{-9}$, and $K_{a3} = 1.8 \times 10^{-15}$, which ionization steps would determine the pH of the acid?
   a. the first ionization only
   b. the first and second ionizations
   c. the second ionization only
   d. the second and third ionizations
   e. all three ionizations

Chapter 8 REVIEW

9. Why is a solution of lithium carbonate, Li_2CO_3(aq), a basic solution?
   a. Lithium carbonate releases hydroxide ions into solution.
   b. Lithium carbonate absorbs hydronium ions from solution.
   c. The carbonate ion reacts with water to form hydroxide ions in solution.
   d. Lithium carbonate absorbs hydroxide ions from solution.
   e. The carbonate ions absorb protons in solution.

10. Which of the following statements is most correct with respect to an aqueous solution of a salt?
    a. The pH of an aqueous solution can be affected by the anion of the salt.
    b. The pH of an aqueous solution can be affected by the cation of the salt.
    c. The pH of an aqueous solution can be affected by the salt molecules.
    d. Two of these statements are correct.
    e. All three of these statements are correct.

11. A solution is said to be buffered when
    a. it has a pH of 7.00.
    b. $K_a = K_b$.
    c. it maintains a pH of 7.00, even when either a strong acid or a strong base is added.
    d. it maintains a constant pH, even when a strong acid or a strong base is added.
    e. it maintains a constant pH, only when weak acids or weak bases are added in small volumes.

12. Which factor affects the capacity of a buffer?
    a. the concentration of the acid-base pair
    b. the volume of the solution
    c. the concentration of the acid or base being added
    d. the volume of the acid or base being added
    e. the initial pH of the system

13. Which of the following statements is true with respect to a titration of a strong acid and a strong base?
    a. Any indicator that changes colour between a pH of 4 and a pH of 10 should be used for the titration.
    b. pH equals 7 at the equivalence point.
    c. The change in pH is dramatic around the equivalence point.
    d. Two of the above statements are true.
    e. All the statements above are true.

14. When two solutions are mixed, with the potential for the ions from each solution to form an insoluble solid, when will the solid form?
    a. when $Q_{sp} > K_{sp}$
    b. when $Q_{sp} < K_{sp}$
    c. when $Q_{sp} = K_{sp}$
    d. when $Q_{sp} \geq K_{sp}$
    e. This must be experimentally determined.

Answer the questions below.

15. Write the net ionic equation for each reaction:
    a. sulfuric acid and sodium hydroxide
    b. acetic acid and lithium hydroxide
    c. hydrochloric acid and potassium hydroxide

16. The hydrogen sulfide ion, HS^-(aq), is amphiprotic.
    a. Discuss the meaning of the term *amphiprotic*.
    b. Include reactions that will illustrate the term for the hydrogen sulfide ion.

17. Hydrofluoric acid, HF(aq), is a weak acid. Explain how you would determine a K_a value for the acid if a 0.100 mol/L solution undergoes a 5.9% dissociation.

18. Explain how the acid-base equilibrium in the oceans has affected the organism below.

19. Phosphoric acid, H_3PO_4(aq), has the following acid-dissociation constants: $K_{a1} = 7.1 \times 10^{-3}$, $K_{a2} = 6.3 \times 10^{-8}$, and $K_{a3} = 4.2 \times 10^{-13}$. Describe how you would determine the pH of a 0.210 mol/L solution of the acid.

20. In question 19, the value of the acid-dissociation constants gets smaller as each proton is removed from phosphoric acid. Explain why this is a common pattern for polyprotic acids.

21. Compare the molar solubilities of nickel carbonate, $NiCO_3$(s), and mercury(I) carbonate, Hg_2CO_3(s). The K_{sp} is 1.42×10^{-7} for nickel carbonate and 3.6×10^{-17} for mercury(I) carbonate.

22. Describe how you would determine if a precipitate will form if 200.00 mL of a 1.72×10^{-4} mol/L solution of magnesium nitrate is mixed with 225.00 mL of a 1.72×10^{-4} mol/L solution of sodium fluoride.

23. Compare and contrast conjugate acids and conjugate bases.

24. Explain why the Arrhenius definitions of acids and bases were inadequate and why the Brønsted-Lowry definitions were an improvement.

25. Describe how the hydronium ion forms when an acid is added to water.

26. Explain why pH is not used to classify acids and bases as strong or weak.

27. Define *common-ion effect* in your own words.

28. Compare and contrast *endpoint* and *equivalence point*.

Thinking and Investigation

29. Carbonic acid is a weak diprotic acid used in the manufacture of carbonated beverages. The acid has $K_{a1} = 4.5 \times 10^{-7}$ and $K_{a2} = 4.7 \times 10^{-11}$. Determine the concentrations of the carbonic acid, hydrogen carbonate ion, and carbonate ion, and the pH of a 0.100 mol/L solution of the acid. (**Hint:** Use the concentrations of the hydrogen carbonate ion and hydronium ion found in the first ionization in the calculations involving the second ionization.)

30. A student looks at the pH meter in the beaker below and makes the following statement:

    "Given how close the pH of the solution is to 7, this must be a weak acid." What must be added or changed to the statement to make it true? Explain your answer.

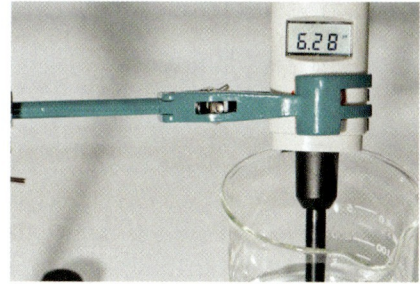

31. Explain why the common-ion effect is simply an application of Le Châtelier's principle.

32. What is the molar solubility of lead(II) chloride, $PbCl_2(s)$, with $K_{sp} = 1.7 \times 10^{-5}$, in
    a. pure water?
    b. a solution of 0.0185 mol/L sodium chloride?
    c. Explain the difference between the answers to parts (a) and (b).

33. Ascorbic acid, also known as vitamin C, is a weak diprotic acid of the form $H_2A(aq)$, with $K_{a1} = 7.89 \times 10^{-5}$ and $K_{a2} = 1.62 \times 10^{-12}$. Determine the following for the acid at equilibrium, if the initial concentration of ascorbic acid is 0.097 mol/L:
    a. $[HA^-]$
    b. $[A^{2-}]$
    c. pH

34. Write the three acid-dissociation constant expressions for arsenic acid, $H_3AsO_4(aq)$. Include the reactions that are used for these constant expressions.

35. Perform an Internet search on the process of liming lakes, rivers, and streams. Present your findings in a method of your choice. Include in your presentation the chemistry of liming and how the process is carried out.

36. A 1.00 L solution of 0.100 mol/L acetic acid is prepared and 5.00 g of sodium acetate is added to the acid. What will be the pH of the buffer system that this creates? The K_a value for the acid is 1.8×10^{-5}.

37. Develop a procedure that can be used to determine the pH of an unknown strong monoprotic acid, like the acid shown below.

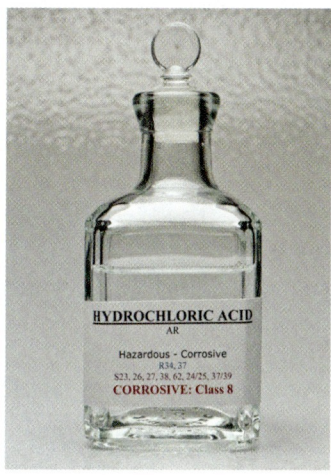

38. A weak base with a molecular mass of 146.21 g/mol is prepared by dissolving 7.25 g of the substance into 1.00 L of solution. The pH of the resulting solution was found to be 9.12. Calculate the base-ionization constant for this weak base.

39. In an investigation of an unknown solution, a chemist finds that when phenolphthalein is placed into a solution, the solution is clear and colourless. When alizarin is placed into a sample of the same solution, the solution is red. What is the pH range of the solution based on these results? Explain your answer.

Chapter 8 REVIEW

40. A student has determined in an investigation that the solubility of barium iodate, $Ba(IO_3)_2(s)$, is 0.36 g/L. What would be the solubility-product constant for this solid?

41. Research the history of the development of the pH scale. Include in your report the person responsible for inventing the scale, the reason for choosing pH to represent the scale, and any other important or interesting information that you find.

42. In the acid-base reaction below, does the position of equilibrium lie toward the reactants or toward the products? Justify your answer.
$F^-(aq) + CH_3COOH(aq) \rightleftharpoons HF(aq) + CH_3COO^-(aq)$

43. Design a procedure that can be used to determine which of two solutions has a higher concentration of lead(II) ions. Your procedure should include any equations and solutions needed.

44. A 1.00 L buffer system is created using 0.200 mol/L acetic acid and 0.200 mol/L sodium acetate at equilibrium.
    a. Determine the pH of the buffer system, with $K_a = 1.8 \times 10^{-5}$.
    b. If 0.100 mol of protons was to be added to the system with no change to the total volume, what would the pH of the system become?
    c. What would the pH of this system have been if the system was not buffered?
    d. Use your answers from parts (b) and (c) to explain the effect of the buffer in the system.

Communication

45. Conduct an Internet search on the research being done by Ronald Gillespie at McMaster University in Hamilton, Ontario on superacids. Write a press release that could be used on a local news broadcast.

46. Suppose that you were asked to explain the difference between an Arrhenius base and a Brønsted-Lowry base to a friend who had missed class on the day that this was covered. Use a software program to prepare slides that explains the difference.

47. Create a concept organizer for all terms and concepts studied in this unit. Include direction arrows to indicate how the concepts are related.

48. In calculating the pH of a weak monoprotic acid, the initial concentration of the acid can be used in the calculation, instead of the actual concentration at equilibrium. Make a poster that can be displayed in your classroom that explains why this is a valid procedure and the poster outlines the conditions required for this procedure to be accurate.

49. Your friend is confused as to why a triprotic acid has a pH that can be found using the first acid-dissociation constant, K_{a1}, only. In two or three sentences, describe what you would say to your friend to help clarify this concept.

50. Write a short two to three paragraph news report about an occupation that would involve an understanding of buffers. Include in your news report a brief explanation of the chemistry associated with the occupation.

51. Outline the similarities and differences between the values K_a and K_b for a weak monoprotic acid, using a chart or similar organizer.

52. **BIG IDEAS** Applications of chemical systems at equilibrium have significant implications for nature and industry. With specific reference to material covered in this chapter, write a short paragraph on the use of weak acids and bases in the pharmaceutical industry. Present your material in a method of your choice.

53. **BIG IDEAS** Chemical systems are dynamic and respond to changing conditions in predictable ways. With specific reference to material covered in this chapter, write a short script for a commercial that could be used to outline some of the considerations that are being implemented in the fight to clean up acidified lakes, rivers, and streams in Ontario.

54. Use sketches to illustrate the difference between the dissociation of hydrochloric acid and the dissociation of sulfuric acid.

55. In a small group, discuss the advantages and disadvantages of using the pH of an acid to describe the acid. Use a graphic organizer to organize the information.

56. Perform an Internet search on the use of buffers to calibrate a pH meter. Report on your findings. Be sure to include a brief description of the chemistry of the buffers and the two-point calibration technique used.

57. Summarize your learning in this chapter using a graphic organizer. To help you, the Chapter 8 Summary lists the Key Terms and Key Concepts. Refer to Using Graphic Organizers in Appendix A to help you decide which graphic organizer to use.

Application

58. A chemist titrated 15.00 mL of a 0.150 mol/L solution of acetic acid, $CH_3COOH(aq)$, with a 0.150 mol/L solution of sodium hydroxide, $NaOH(aq)$. Calculate the pH of the solution
    a. after the addition of 5.00 mL of the base.
    b. after the addition of 15.00 mL of the base.

59. A solution resulting from the combination of silver nitrate, $AgNO_3(aq)$, and sodium bromide, $NaBr(aq)$, has an ion-product constant value that is exactly equal to the solubility-product constant. Explain what this means in two or three well-organized sentences.

60. Research how gallstones, shown below, develop in the human body and assess the impact of chemical equilibrium in the process. Prepare a one or two paragraph report on your findings.

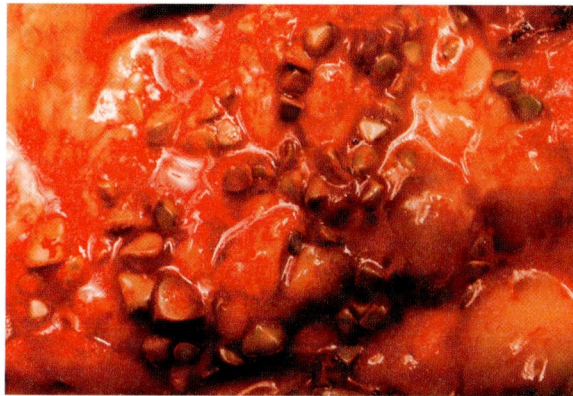

61. Draw diagrams of each molecule and ion involved in the reaction of acetic acid, $CH_3COOH(aq)$, and water in equilibrium with the acetate ion, $CH_3COO^-(aq)$, and the hydronium ion, $H_3O^+(aq)$. Indicate in your diagram the direction of the proton transfer.

62. In an investigation, you titrated 20.00 mL of a 0.100 mol/L ammonia solution, $NH_3(aq)$, with a 0.100 mol/L solution of hydrobromic acid, $HBr(aq)$, a strong acid. What would be the pH at the equivalence point?

63. Research how kidney stones form and assess the impact of chemical equilibrium on the process. Report your findings in a well-organized paragraph.

64. Atropine is found in a plant from the nightshade family, *Atropa belladonna*, shown below. Atropine is a medication currently used in the treatment of Parkinson's disease. It has a K_b value of 3.17×10^{-5}. What would be the pH of a 0.1000 mol/L solution of this medication?

65. Research the electrolyte balance in the human body. Analyze the optimal conditions for the balance of sodium and potassium in the cells. Summarize your findings in one or two paragraphs.

66. A research chemist determines that the solubility of a solid of the form $X_2Y(s)$ is 2.8×10^{-5} mol/L. What is the solubility-product constant for this solid?

67. In an investigation, ammonium nitrate, $NH_4NO_3(s)$, is dissolved into solution. Do you expect the resulting solution to be acidic, neutral, or basic? Explain your answer, including any equations needed to give a full explanation.

68. The K_{sp} for iron(II) hydroxide, $FeOH_2(s)$, is 4.9×10^{-17}. What mass (in grams) of the solid can be dissolved in 100.00 L of solution?

69. Will a precipitate form when 125.00 mL of 3.5×10^{-4} mol/L copper(I) nitrate, $CuNO_3(aq)$, is mixed with 75.00 mL of 8.1×10^{-4} mol/L sodium chloride, $NaOH(aq)$? The K_{sp} for copper chloride, $CuCl(s)$, is 1.7×10^{-7}. Justify your answer.

Chapter 8 SELF-ASSESSMENT

Select the letter of the best answer below.

1. **K/U** What is the conjugate base of $N_2H_5^+(aq)$?
   a. NH_3
   b. NH_4^+
   c. $N_2H_6^+$
   d. $N_2H_4^+$
   e. N_2H_4

2. **C** Which of the following is the conjugate acid of $SO_3^{2-}(aq)$ in the reaction below?
   $HSO_3^-(aq) + CH_3COO^-(aq) \rightleftharpoons SO_3^{2-}(aq) + CH_3COOH(aq)$
   a. $HSO_3^-(aq)$
   b. $CH_3COOH(aq)$
   c. $SO_3^{2-}(aq)$
   d. $CH_3COO^-(aq)$
   e. $H_2O(\ell)$

3. **T/I** Consider the following reaction:
   $NH_4^+(aq) + H_2O(\ell) \rightleftharpoons NH_3(aq) + H_3O^+(aq)$
   Which are the conjugate acid-base pairs?
   a. $NH_4^+(aq)$ and $NH_3(aq)$
   b. $H_2O(\ell)$ and $H_3O^+(aq)$
   c. $H_2O(\ell)$ and $NH_4^+(aq)$
   d. $NH_4^+(aq)$ and $NH_3(aq)$ and $H_2O(\ell)$ and $H_3O^+(aq)$
   e. $NH_3(aq) + H_3O^+(aq)$

4. **K/U** "Indicators are weak acids that act in a similar way to the components of the reaction that they are monitoring." This statement is
   a. true.
   b. false.
   c. true only in an acidic solution.
   d. true only in a basic solution.
   e. true only when the solution is a weak acid or base.

5. **K/U** What is the percent dissociation for hydrochloric acid, $HCl(aq)$?
   a. 0%
   b. 25%
   c. 50%
   d. 75%
   e. 100%

6. **T/I** In a titration of an unknown strong monoprotic acid, 25.00 mL of the acid was neutralized by 14.31 mL of a 0.0105 mol/L solution of sodium hydroxide, $NaOH(aq)$. What is the pH of the acid?
   a. 7.00
   b. 2.22
   c. 1.74
   d. 5.45
   e. −2.22

7. **K/U** Which of the following is the correct expression for the base ionization constant in water of the base shown in the photograph?

   a. $\dfrac{[OH^-][NH_4^+]}{[NH_3]}$
   b. $\dfrac{[OH^-][NH_4^+]}{[NH_3][H_2O]}$
   c. $\dfrac{[NH_3][H_2O]}{[OH^-][NH_4^+]}$
   d. $\dfrac{[NH_3]}{[OH^-][NH_4^+]}$
   e. $[NH_4^+]$

8. **K/U** Which of the following statements best describes a salt?
   a. any solid that dissolves in an aqueous solution
   b. any solid that dissolves in a weak acid
   c. the ionic compound that results from an acid-base reaction
   d. the molecular compound that results in the reaction between a strong acid and a strong base
   e. any solid that when dissolved into an aqueous solution produces a solution with a pH of 7.00

9. **K/U** Why does a solution of ammonium chloride, $NH_4Cl(aq)$, have a pH less that 7.00?
   a. Ammonium chloride releases hydroxide ions into solution.
   b. Ammonium chloride releases hydronium ions into solution.
   c. Ammonium chloride absorbs hydroxide ions from solution.
   d. Ammonium chloride absorbs hydronium ions from solution.
   e. $NH_4^+(aq)$ ions react with water to form hydronium ions.

10. **A** What type of solution will form when sodium acetate, $NaCH_3COO(s)$, dissolves in water?
    a. a neutral solution
    b. a strong acid
    c. a strong base
    d. a weak acid
    e. a weak base

Use sentences and diagrams as appropriate to answer the questions below.

11. **T/I** What is the pH of a 0.15 mol/L solution of $NaNO_2(aq)$, given that $K_a = 7.2 \times 10^{-4}$?

12. **C** Consider the following reaction:

    $$H_3PO_4(aq) + H_2O(\ell) \rightleftharpoons H_2PO_4^-(aq) + H_3O^+(aq)$$

    a. Identify the conjugate acid-base pairs.
    b. Draw diagrams of each molecule and ion and indicate the proton transfer for the conjugate acid-base pairs identified in part (a).

13. **K/U** The bicarbonate ion, $HCO_3^-(aq)$, can act as an acid or a base.
    a. Write equations to show each behaviour of the ion.
    b. What is the name given to this type of ion?

14. **T/I** What is the hydroxide ion concentration in a solution of 0.45 mol/L hydrochloric acid, a strong acid?

15. **T/I** Morphine is found in opium poppy flowers, shown in the photograph. Morphine is a weak base used as a very powerful painkiller. It has a K_b value of 7.47×10^{-7}. Determine the pH and pOH of a 0.035 mol/L solution of morphine.

16. **T/I** At 25°C, human blood contains a hydroxide ion concentration of 2.50×10^{-7} mol/L. What is the hydronium ion concentration of human blood and what is the pH?

17. **T/I** What is the pH of a 0.100 mol/L weak base solution with a K_b value of 1.68×10^{-6}?

18. **T/I** The K_{sp} for copper(I) chloride is 1.73×10^{-7}. What would be the maximum ion concentrations when copper(II) chloride is dissolved in pure water?

19. **T/I** Cyanic acid, HCNO(aq), is a weak acid that can be found in a variety of pesticides. A 0.100 mol/L solution of the acid is found to have ionized to 5.90%. What is the K_a value for the acid?

20. **A** A 1.00 L volume of a buffer system is made with ammonia, $NH_3(aq)$, and ammonium ion, $NH_4^+(aq)$, both present in a concentration of 0.350 mol/L. If 0.100 mol/L of hydrochloric acid, HCl(aq), is added to the 1 L solution, what is the change in pH of the system?

21. **T/I** At a given temperature, 2.12×10^{-3} g of magnesium fluoride, $MgF_2(s)$, can dissolve in 125.00 mL of solution. Determine the K_{sp} for magnesium fluoride at this temperature.

22. **T/I** You are given a solution that is either an acid or a base. In testing the solution, you add bromocresol green to a small sample of the solution, and the solution turns green. When you add methyl red to a small sample of the same solution, the solution turns orange.
    a. Consult the indicators in Appendix B to determine the pH range of the unknown solution you were given.
    b. Were these indicators good choices for the unknown solution? Explain your answer.

23. **C** Research the process of hemoglobin binding to oxygen in the human body, with particular attention to the role that the hydronium ion plays in this process. Report your findings in one or two well-structured paragraphs. Include the equation for the process in your report.

24. **T/I** Will a precipitate form if 750.00 mL of a 4.0×10^{-3} mol/L solution of cesium(III) nitrate, $Ce(NO_3)_3(aq)$, is mixed in a beaker with 300.00 mL of a 2.0×10^{-2} mol/L solution of potassium iodate, $KIO_3(aq)$? K_{sp} for cesium(III) iodate, $Ce(IO_3)_3(s)$, is 1.9×10^{-10}. Justify your answer.

25. **A** A lab technician determined that the solubility of silver chromate, $Ag_2CrO_4(s)$, is 21.7 mg/L. What is the solubility-product constant for this solid?

Self-Check

If you missed question …	1	2	3	4	5	6	7	8	9	10	11	12	13	14	15	16	17	18	19	20	21	22	23	24	25
Review section(s)…	8.1	8.1	8.3	8.4	8.2	8.4	8.3	8.4	8.2	8.3	8.3	8.1	8.1	8.2	8.3	8.2	8.3	8.4	8.2	8.4	8.4	8.2	8.2	8.4	8.4

Unit 4 Project

Conduct an Inquiry

Investigating the Lead Content of Drinking Water

Lead is a toxic metal that disrupts nervous system and organ functions when it exceeds certain levels in the body. Human exposure to lead has been reduced as a result of the phasing out of lead-containing products, such as gasoline and paints, over the last few decades. However, lead may still contaminate the drinking water in homes that were built before the 1950s. The lead is found in pipes that connect the houses to the city water main, as well as in pipes and other plumbing fixtures within the home. In 2007, the drinking water in some older homes in London, Ontario, was found to have elevated concentrations of lead. Older homes in other towns in Ontario were tested soon afterwards. The city of London met with environmental consultants and determined that the best course of action, given the source of the city's water and the nature of its distribution system, was to alter the pH of the water.

In this project, you will assume the role of a volunteer at a local environmental centre. The centre's co-ordinator asks you to give a presentation to citizens who are concerned about elevated lead levels in the drinking water in older homes and your municipality's plan to address this problem by changing the pH of the drinking water. Your presentation will clarify the relationship between pH and lead in drinking water. You will use Le Châtelier's principle to explain how pH affects the concentration of dissolved lead in drinking water. You will also design an investigation to test for lead in drinking water, which you will review in your presentation.

Older homes built before 1950 in Ontario, such as these, may contain lead in their plumbing fixtures or in the pipes that connect the houses to the city water main. As a result, lead may contaminate the drinking water in older homes.

How does pH affect the concentration of dissolved lead in drinking water and how could you test for this metal in the water?

Initiate and Plan

1. Use print and/or Internet resources to research information that will help you explain the relationship between pH and lead in drinking water. Consider the following questions as you conduct your research.
    - What factors can affect the pH of drinking water? How does the pH of drinking water vary naturally in Ontario and across Canada?
    - In homes with lead-containing pipes, how can a change in pH affect the level of dissolved lead in the drinking water? What other factors might affect the amount of lead dissolved in drinking water?
    - What is the maximum acceptable concentration (MAC) of lead in drinking water in Canada? Is changing the pH of drinking water always an effective way to reduce the concentration of dissolved lead when it exceeds this level?
    - How could you address citizens' concerns that changing the pH of drinking water might harm humans or ecosystems?

2. Use print and/or Internet resources to research ways in which you could test for dissolved lead in drinking water. Design an investigation based on your findings to test the lead content of a given water sample.

    a. Use the table below and the table "Solubility of Common Ionic Compounds in Water" in Appendix B to identify which compound could be added to the water to precipitate any dissolved lead.

Solubility Product Constants in Water at 25°C

Compound	Formula	K_{sp}
Lead(II) bromide	$PbBr_2$	6.60×10^{-6}
Lead(II) carbonate	$PbCO_3$	7.40×10^{-14}
Lead(II) chloride	$PbCl_2$	1.70×10^{-5}
Lead(II) chromate	$PbCrO_4$	3×10^{-13}
Lead(II) fluoride	PbF_2	3.3×10^{-8}
Lead(II) hydroxide	$Pb(OH)_2$	1.43×10^{-20}
Lead(II) iodide	PbI_2	9.8×10^{-9}
Lead(II) sulfate	$PbSO_4$	2.53×10^{-8}
Lead(II) sulfide	PbS	3×10^{-28}

b. List the chemicals and equipment you need. Calculate the concentration of substance needed to form a lead precipitate and any other values you require.

c. Describe all necessary safety precautions, including the safe handling and disposal of the lead precipitate. Refer to any relevant material safety data sheets (MSDS).

3. Write a detailed, step-by-step procedure for the investigation.

Perform and Record

4. Describe the observations you expect to make if you conducted the investigation. Include chemical equations to represent the chemical reactions that occur.

Analyze and Interpret

1. The series of balanced chemical equations below represents several chemical reactions that occur in drinking water exposed to lead. Including lead ions, several other ions, all of which are found naturally in drinking water, are involved in the reactions.

  i. $Pb(s) + 2H_3O^+(aq) \rightarrow Pb_2+(aq) + H_2(g) + 2H_2O(\ell)$
  ii. $Pb^{2+}(aq) + OH^-(aq) \rightarrow PbOH^+(aq)$
  iii. $H_2CO_3(aq) + H_2O(\ell) \rightarrow H_3O^+(aq) + HCO_3^-(aq)$
  iv. $HCO_3^-(aq) + H_2O(\ell) \rightarrow H_3O^+(aq) + CO_3^{2-}(aq)$
  v. $H_2O(\ell) + CO_2(g) \rightarrow H_2CO_3(aq)$
  vi. $PbCO_3(s) \rightarrow Pb^{2+}(aq) + CO_3^{2-}(aq)$
  vii. $Pb^{2+}(aq) + CO_3^{2-}(aq) \rightarrow PbCO_3(aq)$

  a. Referring to these reactions, use Le Châtelier's principle to explain whether the amount of lead dissolved in water would be greater at a higher or a lower pH. (**Hint:** Note that a concentration change in one reaction can affect other reactions.)

  b. Suppose that the pH of the drinking water in your town is slightly acidic. Based on your answer to question 1(a), how would your town alter the pH to reduce elevated lead levels in older homes? Explain your answer.

2. The city of London addressed the problem of elevated lead levels in the drinking water in older homes through a combination of public education, lead-pipe replacement, and pH adjustment. Explain why it was important that all three factors were addressed. What other factors might be relevant to this problem?

Communicate Your Findings

3. Choose an appropriate way to present your research. For instance, you may choose to create a video, an interactive website, or a poster.

4. Prepare a presentation that includes the following:
- an explanation of the relationship between pH and the dissolved lead content in drinking water, including any relevant chemical reactions
- an explanation, using Le Châtelier's principle, as to whether the amount of lead dissolved in water would be greater at a higher or a lower pH
- a summary of the design and expected results of your investigation to test the lead content of a water sample, along with any calculations you performed
- a literature citation section that documents the sources you used to complete your research, using an appropriate academic format

Assessment Criteria

Once you complete your project, ask yourself these questions. Did you...

☑ **K/U** explain the relationship between pH and the dissolved lead content in drinking water?

☑ **K/U** research ways in which you could test for dissolved lead in drinking water?

☑ **T/I** assess your information sources for accuracy and reliability?

☑ **T/I** design an investigation to test for lead in drinking water and describe your expected results?

☑ **C** record your calculations and any equations representing chemical reactions that would occur in your investigation?

☑ **A** explain, using Le Châtelier's principle, whether the amount of lead dissolved in drinking water would be greater at a higher or a lower pH?

☑ **A** explain why public education, lead-pipe replacement, and pH adjustment are important factors to consider when addressing the issue of the lead content in water, and identify other factors relevant to this issue?

☑ **C** communicate your findings in a form that is appropriate to your audience and purpose, using suitable instructional visuals and scientific vocabulary?

UNIT 4 SUMMARY

BIG IDEAS

- Chemical systems are dynamic and respond to changing conditions in predictable ways.
- Applications of chemical systems at equilibrium have significant implications for nature and industry.

Overall Expectations

In this unit, you will…

- **analyze** chemical equilibrium processes, and **assess** their impact on biological, biochemical, and technological systems
- **investigate** the qualitative and quantitative natures of chemical systems at equilibrium, and **solve** related problems
- **demonstrate** an understanding of the concept of dynamic equilibrium and the variables that cause shifts in the equilibrium of chemical systems

Chapter 7: Chemical Equilibrium

Key ideas

- Chemical equilibrium is the state of a chemical system in which the forward reaction and the reverse reaction are balanced and occur at the same rates.
- In a chemical system at equilibrium, there is a constant ratio between the concentrations of the products and the concentrations of the reactants, and this ratio is the equilibrium constant, K_{eq}.
- Because K_{eq} is a ratio of product concentration to reactant concentration, a large K_{eq} value means that the concentration of products is greater than the concentration of reactants. A small K_{eq} value means that the concentration of reactants is greater than the concentration of products. When K_{eq} is equal to 1, there are equal concentrations of reactants and products.
- Le Châtelier's principle states that if an external stress (a change in concentration, pressure, volume, or temperature) is applied to a chemical system at equilibrium, the rates of the forward and reverse reactions are temporarily unequal because the stress affects the reaction rates. However, equilibrium is eventually restored in the chemical system.
- Only a temperature change affects K_{eq}. In a system that is endothermic in the forward direction, a temperature rise increases K_{eq}. If the forward reaction is exothermic, then a temperature rise decreases K_{eq}.

- Adding a catalyst causes a system to reach equilibrium more quickly, but it does not shift the equilibrium in either direction.
- If a diver rapidly returns to the surface from a deep dive, the change in the equilibrium between dissolved and gaseous nitrogen causes bubbles to form in the blood vessels, causing a serious condition called "the bends."

- An understanding of the effects of pressure and temperature on the position of equilibrium between nitrogen and hydrogen gases and ammonia allowed the chemists Fritz Haber and Carl Bosch to develop an efficient method for synthesizing ammonia.
- Knowledge of the equilibrium reactions that are important in the production of sulfuric acid and of methanol makes it possible to produce these very important products in large amounts.

UNIT 4 SUMMARY & REVIEW

Chapter 8 Acid-Base Equilibrium Systems

Key ideas

- The Arrhenius theory defines acids and bases based on their chemical formulas and on how they dissociate in water.
- The Brønsted-Lowry theory of acids and bases defines acids and bases based on the donation and acceptance of a proton.
- The sum of the pH and the pOH is 14.00 for any aqueous solution at 25°C.
- Strong acids ionize almost completely in water, and strong bases dissociate almost completely in water. Weak acids partially ionize in water, and weak bases partially ionize or dissociate in water.
- In general, an acid-base equilibrium reaction shifts in the direction in which a stronger acid and a stronger base form a weaker acid and a weaker base.
- The acid-dissociation constant, or acid-ionization constant, K_a, is used for acid-base reactions.
- The equilibrium constant for a base is called the base-ionization constant, or the base-dissociation constant, K_b.
- The overall equilibrium constant for an acid and its conjugate base is $K_a K_b = K_w$.
- A reaction between an acid and a base is called a neutralization reaction, and a salt and water form in the reaction.
- A buffer is a solution that resists pH change when a limited amount of acid or base is added to it.
- The titration curve for an acid and base reaction depends on the strength of the acid and the strength of the base.
- Slightly soluble ionic compounds can establish equilibrium, and the equilibrium constant is called the solubility-product constant, K_{sp}.
- The values of the solubility-product constant, K_{sp}, and the ion-product constant, Q_{sp}, are compared for slightly soluble ionic compounds to determine if a precipitate forms.

Knowledge and Understanding

Select the letter of the best answer below.

1. All equilibrium reactions must be reversible. This statement is
   a. always true.
   b. never true.
   c. sometimes true.
   d. true only when all reactants are in the gas phase.
   e. true only when the system is heterogeneous.

2. Which of the following condition(s) is(are) necessary for a system to be at equilibrium?
   a. The system must be closed.
   b. The system must be at constant temperature.
   c. Observable properties of the system must be unchanging.
   d. Two of these are necessary.
   e. All of these are necessary.

3. When concentrations of products are increased in chemical reactions, the reverse reaction will proceed at a higher rate than the forward reaction rate. This statement is
   a. true.
   b. false.
   c. true only when all materials are in the gaseous phase.
   d. true only when the system is at equilibrium.
   e. impossible to determine, as rates must be experimentally determined.

4. In a system at equilibrium, the equilibrium constant is determined to be very large. What does this mean in terms of the position of equilibrium in the system?
   a. Product formation is favoured.
   b. Reactant formation is favoured.
   c. There is a balance in reactant and product formation.
   d. The reaction does not occur.
   e. No valid conclusion can be drawn from this information.

5. The equilibrium constant for a reaction at equilibrium is 4.00. If the reaction were written in the reverse direction, which number below would be the value of the equilibrium constant?
   a. 2.00
   b. 16.0
   c. 0.250
   d. 0.500
   e. 0.125

6. In which direction would a reaction with a $K_{eq} = 5.00$ proceed, if Q_{eq} was found to be 10.00?
   a. It would proceed in the forward direction.
   b. It would proceed in the reverse direction.
   c. The reaction would not move in any direction.
   d. The reaction would go to completion.
   e. The reaction would not occur at all.

UNIT 4 REVIEW

7. Which of the following is considered a Brønsted-Lowry base, but not an Arrhenius base?
   a. calcium hydroxide
   b. potassium hydroxide
   c. ammonia
   d. hydrogen fluoride
   e. two of the above

8. Which statement is correct with respect to determining the position of an acid-base equilibrium system?
   a. A reaction proceeds from the weaker acid to the stronger acid.
   b. A reaction proceeds from the stronger acid to the weaker acid.
   c. A reaction proceeds from the weaker acid to the stronger acid only when the pH is above 7.
   d. A reaction proceeds from the stronger acid to the weaker acid only when the pH is above 7.
   e. The position of the equilibrium must always be experimentally determined.

9. At 25°C, which statement is correct for weak acids and weak bases?
   a. $K_a K_b = 1 \times 10^{-14}$
   b. $K_a = \dfrac{1 \times 10^{-14}}{K_b}$
   c. $K_b = \dfrac{K_w}{K_a}$
   d. Two of the above are correct.
   e. All of the above are correct.

10. When $Q_{sp} < K_{sp}$,
    a. a precipitate will form.
    b. a precipitate will not form.
    c. a precipitate will form if the temperature is increased.
    d. the solution is saturated.
    e. a precipitate is just about to form.

Answer the questions below.

11. Write the equilibrium constant expressions for the following reactions.
    a. $CaCO_3(s) \rightleftharpoons CaO(s) + CO_2(g)$
    b. $Cl_2(g) + HI(g) \rightleftharpoons HCl(g) + I_2(s)$
    c. $HCl(aq) + NH_3(g) \rightleftharpoons NH_4Cl(s)$
    d. $2HCl(g) + \frac{1}{2}O_2(g) \rightleftharpoons H_2O(g) + Cl_2(g)$

12. State the conjugate acid-base pairs in the following reactions.
    a. $CH_3COO^-(aq) + HSO_3^-(aq) \rightleftharpoons SO_3^{2-}(aq) + CH_3COOH(aq)$
    b. $CN^-(aq) + H_2O(\ell) \rightleftharpoons HCN(aq) + OH^-(aq)$
    c. $HSO_4^-(aq) + HCO_3^-(aq) \rightleftharpoons SO_4^{2-}(aq) + H_2CO_3(aq)$
    d. $CH_3COOH(aq) + HPO_4^{2-}(aq) \rightleftharpoons CH_3COO^-(aq) + H_2PO_4^-(aq)$

13. Using **Table 8.1**, predict the direction that is favoured in the following reaction and explain your answer.
    $SO_4^{2-}(aq) + HNO_2(aq) \rightleftharpoons HSO_4^-(aq) + NO_2^-(aq)$

14. Write acid-dissociation equations and constant expressions for each weak acid dissociating in water.
    a. hydrocyanic acid, $HCN(aq)$
    b. ammonia, $NH_3(aq)$
    c. sodium hydrogen sulfate, $NaHSO_4(aq)$

15. Will the value of the equilibrium constant increase or decrease when the following reaction is heated?
    $2SO_2(g) + O_2(g) \rightleftharpoons 2SO_3(g) + \text{heat}$
    Explain your answer.

16. Use the image on the right to explain if there is a shift in equilibrium in the system $N_2O_4(g) \rightleftharpoons 2NO_2(g)$. Include a full explanation of your answer.

17. In a short paragraph, explain the process of carbon monoxide poisoning in terms of the chemistry and of the interaction of carbon monoxide with blood.

18. Use two or three well-reasoned sentences to explain the difference between dissociation and ionization with respect to weak acids and bases.

19. List three amphiprotic compounds or ions and state why these are considered amphiprotic.

20. Syngas is used in manufacturing processes in Canada.
    a. What is syngas and what is the main use of the mixture?
    b. How is syngas used in the Haber-Bosch process?
    c. What is the role of syngas in the manufacturing of methanol?

21. Explain why a pure liquid is not included in the equilibrium constant expression.

Thinking and Investigation

22. Determine the direction that the equilibrium will shift in the following reaction, based on the indicated changes below.

$$4NH_3(g) + 5O_2(g) \rightleftharpoons 4NO(g) + 6H_2O(g)$$

Include an explanation for each.
   a. increase in pressure
   b. addition of ammonia gas
   c. addition of water vapour
   d. addition of neon gas
   e. increase in total volume of the container

23. What four conditions will optimize the concentration of phosphorus pentachloride, $PCl_5(g)$, in the reaction below:

$$PCl_3(g) + Cl_2(g) \rightleftharpoons PCl_5(g)$$

24. For the reaction below, 1.00 mol each of $A_2(g)$ and $B_2(g)$ are placed in a 1.00 L container and allowed to reach equilibrium. At equilibrium, it is determined that the equilibrium concentration of AB(g) is 2.5×10^{-2} mol/L. What is the value of K_{eq} for this reaction?

$$A_2(g) + B_2(g) \rightleftharpoons 2AB(g)$$

25. Determine the percent dissociation for a weak monoprotic acid with an initial concentration of 0.100 mol/L and a pH of 4.15.

26. In the reaction of carbon dioxide gas and hydrogen gas, carbon monoxide and water vapour form. Initially, 2.34 mol of each reactant is placed into a 2.00 L container and allowed to reach equilibrium. If $K_{eq} = 1.29$ for this system, what will be the equilibrium concentration of carbon monoxide?

27. Determine the pH at the equivalence point when 30.00 mL of a 0.100 mol/L solution of ammonia is titrated with a 0.100 mol/L solution of hydrochloric acid.

28. For the reaction $XY(g) \rightleftharpoons X(g) + Y(g)$, predict the effect on the position of equilibrium when the indicated change is made to the system during a lab activity:
   a. The concentration of X(g) is increased.
   b. Y(g) is removed from the system.
   c. The total volume of the container is decreased.
   d. An inert gas is added to the system.
   e. A catalyst is added.

29. Design a procedure that could be used to determine if a system of gases was at equilibrium or had simply gone to completion. Include in the procedure any materials or equipment that would be needed.

30. The reaction of water vapour reacting in an equilibrium system to form oxygen gas and hydrogen gas is accomplished by adding energy to the system. What four changes could be made to this system in a lab to increase the amount of oxygen gas that forms?

31. In the reaction of $H_2(g) + Cl_2(g) \rightleftharpoons 2HCl(g)$, $K_{eq} = 50.0$. You perform an experiment where 1.00 mol $H_2(g)$ and 1.00 mol $Cl_2(g)$ are placed in a 0.500 L container and allowed to reach equilibrium. What is the concentration of the HCl(g) at equilibrium?

32. At a given temperature, the K_{eq} for the reaction of ammonia gas decomposing into nitrogen gas and hydrogen gas is 4.2×10^{-3}. If, initially, you were to place 1.00 mol of ammonia gas into a 1.00 L container and allow this equilibrium to establish, what amount (in moles) of hydrogen gas would be present in the equilibrium mixture?

33. Research a biological process involving equilibrium that deals with some system other than that found in the human body. Analyze the process and write a detailed report about the role of equilibrium in that process. Justify your conclusions. Present the report in a method of your choice.

34. Design an experimental procedure that can be used to determine if a solution was a strong acid or a weak acid, if the two solutions were the same concentration.

35. A chemist titrated 25.00 mL of a 0.100 mol/L hypochlorous acid, HOCl(aq), with a 0.100 mol/L lithium hydroxide solution. Calculate the pH of this solution
   a. after 10.00 mL of the base is added.
   b. at the equivalence point.

36. If 0.74 g of silver nitrate, $AgNO_3(s)$, is added to 1.75 L of solution that already contains 0.27 g of sodium chromate, $Na_2CrO_4(aq)$, will any solid silver chromate form? Show all work to justify your answer. For $Ag_2CrO_4(s)$, $K_{sp} = 1.12 \times 10^{-12}$.

UNIT 4 REVIEW

37. A solution may contain silver ions and/or copper(I) ions. The ions, if present, are in a concentration of 1.0×10^{-6} mol/L. Outline how a solution of sodium iodide could be used to determine which is present in the unknown solution. Include calculations where appropriate. K_{sp} is 1.27×10^{-12} for CuI and 8.52×10^{-17} for AgI.

38. During the titration of 32.00 mL of 0.225 mol/L hydrochloric acid with 0.185 mol/L of a sodium hydroxide solution, you reach the equivalence point. What volume of the base did you need to reach this point?

39. What mass (in grams) of magnesium carbonate can be dissolved into 0.500 L of water, if the K_{sp} for the solid is 6.82×10^{-6}?

40. You must plan and conduct an investigation to find the pH of a weak base at the equivalence point using a titration. You will use the equipment shown below:

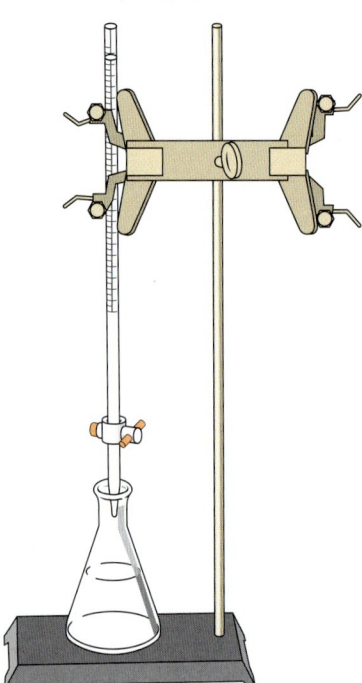

   a. What types of chemicals will you need to use?
   b. What do you predict will be the pH range of your final answer?
   c. What could you do to help demonstrate that you predicted the pH range correctly?

41. During a lab, you titrate 25.00 mL of a 0.100 mol/L ammonia solution to the equivalence point using 0.200 mol/L nitric acid, HNO$_3$(aq). What is the pH of the solution at the equivalence point?

42. During a lab activity, a student calculated the solubility of lithium fluoride to be 1.11 g/L. What is the solubility-product constant for the solid?

43. Does a precipitate form if you add 15.00 mL of a 2.50×10^{-3} mol/L solution of lead(II) nitrate to 10.00 mL of a 2.10×10^{-2} mol/L solution of potassium chloride? Justify your answer. K_{sp} for lead(II) chloride is 1.7×10^{-5}.

Communication

44. Create a flowchart that can be used to select a macroscopic property that could be used to monitor a reaction that is approaching equilibrium.

45. One of your classmates is having trouble understanding the conditions needed for a system to reach equilibrium. Use your own words to write a brief paragraph to help your classmate.

46. Suppose your friend missed the class on the equilibrium constants for homogeneous and heterogeneous equilibrium systems. Outline for your friend the similarities and differences between these two constants.

47. Why is it often more convenient to use a K_p expression for homogeneous reactions than to use K_{eq}? Write two or three well-reasoned sentences to explain your answer.

48. Create a graphic organizer to aid in the process of solving for an equilibrium concentration when the equilibrium constant and initial reactant concentrations are given.

49. Draw a diagram or build models to illustrate the reaction of a conjugate acid-base pair in water.

50. While calculating the pH of a weak base, a student is unable to find the concentration of the hydroxide ion in solution. The student realizes that there is some missing information that is preventing her from finding the pH of the base. Outline a procedure that the student can use to complete the calculation.

51. Write the text for a slide presentation that can be used in chemistry class that outlines the difference between a weak acid and a dilute acid.

52. Your classmate is confused about how to interpret K_a with respect to percent dissociation. Write a paragraph explaining to your classmate what a small K_a value for a weak monoprotic acid means and what this indicates about the percent dissociation of the acid.

53. Outline a procedure that can be used to determine the K_a and percent dissociation of a weak monoprotic acid, when the initial concentration of the acid and the pH of the resulting solution are known.

54. Create a graphic organizer that will help to classify a solution as a weak or strong acid or base.

55. Create a table that shows the similarities and differences between a weak acid and a weak base. Summarize this in three or four well-reasoned sentences.

56. Create a pamphlet that can be used to choose which acid-base indicator to use for a titration. In the pamphlet, briefly explain the chemistry of an acid-base indicator and how this helps to determine the equivalence point in a titration.

Application

57. **BIG IDEAS** Chemical systems are dynamic and respond to changing conditions in predictable ways. When a propane gas tank for a barbeque is filled at the filling station, the pressure inside the tank increases until the gas starts to liquefy. Is this system now at equilibrium? Explain your answer.

58. Why is it not enough to conclude that a system, in which all observable properties are unchanging, is at equilibrium?

59. Balance the following reactions and then write the equilibrium constant expressions.
    a. $NH_3(g) + O_2(g) \rightleftharpoons NO(g) + H_2O(g)$
    b. $Cl_2(g) + HI(g) \rightleftharpoons I_2(s) + HCl(g)$
    c. $NO_2(g) \rightleftharpoons N_2O_4(g)$
    d. $CO(g) + Cl_2(g) \rightleftharpoons COCl_2(g)$

60. Would you expect the K_w value to be larger or smaller than 1×10^{-14} at 75°C? Explain your answer.

61. The valve of a system at equilibrium is opened and a gaseous reactant is added. Is this system still at equilibrium? Explain your answer.

62. Explain why taking medication over a fixed amount of time is an application of Le Châtelier's principle.

63. When a catalyst is added to a system that can reach equilibrium, there is no shift in equilibrium, only that equilibrium is reached more quickly. An inhibitor is similar to a catalyst, but instead of speeding up a chemical process, it slows the process down. Comment on one application of an inhibitor that you have seen. If you have not seen an application of this, either ask a classmate or conduct an Internet search on inhibitors in chemical processes.

64. **BIG IDEAS** Applications of chemical systems at equilibrium have significant implications for nature and industry. Hydrogen gas is being developed as a non-polluting sustainable fuel source for internal combustion engines, such as the vehicle below that uses a fuel cell. There are several ways being looked at to generate the hydrogen gas. One such method is through the reaction of water vapour with solid carbon, represented by the reaction below:

$$H_2O(g) + C(s) \rightleftharpoons H_2(g) + CO(g)$$

At a given temperature, the equilibrium constant for this reaction is 1.15. Suppose that you start with 1.00 mol of each reactant in a 2.00 L container. What amount of hydrogen gas will be present at equilibrium at this temperature?

65. In another attempt to generate hydrogen gas as a fuel source, scientists have investigated using the decomposition of hydrogen iodide gas, represented by the reaction below:

$$2HI(g) \rightleftharpoons H_2(g) + I_2(g)$$

At 1100 K, the equilibrium constant for this reaction is 0.0400. If, initially, 2.00 mol of hydrogen iodide gas is placed into a 1.00 L container, what amount (in moles) of hydrogen gas will be present at equilibrium?

66. In the manufacturing of sulfuric acid, low temperatures and high pressures favour the formation of the acid. However, industries will normally use temperatures of approximately 450°C. In one or two sentences, explain why this would be the temperature used.

67. Lewis bases are defined as those compounds or ions that are electron-pair donors. Can Brønsted-Lowry bases be classified under the Lewis definition? Research the Lewis definitions of acids and bases to explain your answer.

68. Why does the autoionization of water not factor into pH and pOH calculations when dealing with weak acids and bases?

UNIT 4 SELF-ASSESSMENT

Select the letter of the best answer below.

1. **K/U** Which statement best describes the term *dynamic equilibrium*?
   a. a changing system that can reach equilibrium
   b. a system that changes at the molecular level, but macroscopic properties remain constant
   c. a system that changes at the molecular level and at the macroscopic level
   d. a system that does not change at the molecular level, and macroscopic properties remain constant
   e. a system that does not change at the molecular level, but macroscopic properties are changing

2. **T/I** Which change to the equilibrium system below will maximize the formation of product?
   $$2NO(g) + O_2(g) \rightleftharpoons 2NO_2(g)$$
   a. decrease the pressure
   b. increase the volume
   c. add helium gas
   d. add oxygen gas
   e. all of these changes

3. **T/I** For the reaction $2HCl(g) \rightleftharpoons H_2(g) + Cl_2(g)$, the following concentrations were found to exist at equilibrium:
   $[HCl] = 2.34 \times 10^{-2}$ mol/L, $[H_2] = 4.16 \times 10^{-4}$ mol/L, and $[Cl_2] = 6.37 \times 10^{-2}$ mol/L.
   What is the equilibrium constant for this reaction?
   a. 0.0484
   b. 20.7
   c. 0.00113
   d. 883.0
   e. 1.00

4. **T/I** In the following reaction at equilibrium, 50% of the reactants converted to products:
   $$2AB(g) \rightleftharpoons A_2(g) + B_2(g)$$
   What is the equilibrium constant for this reaction?
   a. 0.50
   b. 0.25
   c. 0.125
   d. 1.00
   e. 2.00

5. **T/I** Which condition produces a high yield of ammonia in the Haber-Bosch process?
   a. high pressure only
   b. high temperature only
   c. high temperature and high pressure
   d. low temperature and high pressure
   e. low pressure and high temperature

6. **K/U** What are the products of a reaction between an acid and a base?
   a. water
   b. salt
   c. a base and an acid
   d. water and salt
   e. The product depends on the acid and the base.

7. **A** Many household cleaning solutions contain bases to help convert organic fats to soaps. A solution of ammonia in water is used in this type of application because
   a. ammonia contains the hydroxide ion.
   b. ammonia is a strong base in high concentrations.
   c. ammonia makes water act like a base.
   d. liquid ammonia is a conjugate acid-base pair.
   e. ammonia releases hydroxide ions in solution when mixed with water.

8. **K/U** When comparing a concentrated weak acid with a dilute strong acid, which has the lower pH?
   a. the concentrated weak acid
   b. the dilute strong acid
   c. Both are equal in pH.
   d. This must be determined experimentally.
   e. This would depend on the volume of the containers.

9. **K/U** The K_a for a weak base is 7.2×10^{-9}. What is K_b for this weak base?
   a. 1.4×10^{-6}
   b. 1.4×10^{-6} at 25°C
   c. must be experimentally determined
   d. 7.2×10^{-9} at 25°C
   e. 7.2×10^{-9}

10. **A** In a household water purification system, hydroxide ions are removed from the water by the addition of iron(III) chloride. What is the precipitate that forms in this process?
    a. $Fe(OH)_3(s)$
    b. $Fe(OH)_2(s)$
    c. both $Fe(OH)_3(s)$ and $Fe(OH)_2(s)$
    d. $FeCl_3(s)$
    e. No precipitate forms; the hydroxide is simply neutralized.

Use sentences and diagrams as appropriate to answer the questions below.

11. **T/I** A weak monoprotic acid is prepared with a concentration of 0.150 mol/L. The pH of the solution is 3.17. What is K_a for this acid?

12. **K/U** Consider the following reactions:

$$N_2(g) + 2O_2(g) \rightleftharpoons 2NO_2(g)$$
$$\tfrac{1}{2} N_2(g) + O_2(g) \rightleftharpoons NO_2(g)$$

What is the relationship between the two equilibrium constant expressions for these reactions?

13. **K/U** State a property that can be used to monitor the reaction below to determine when equilibrium is established. Explain how the property changes as the system approaches equilibrium.

$$PCl_5(g) \rightleftharpoons PCl_3(g) + Cl_2(g)$$

14. **T/I** A student increases the pressure on a system believed to be at equilibrium, but there is no change observed in the reaction. The conclusion is that the reaction is not an equilibrium reaction; it has simply gone to completion. Is this a valid conclusion based on the observations? Explain your reasoning.

15. **C** In a well-reasoned paragraph, explain to a fellow student why the addition of an inert gas to a system at equilibrium does not affect the position of equilibrium.

16. **T/I** The reaction below is at equilibrium:

$$SO_2(g) + NO_2(g) \rightleftharpoons SO_3(g) + NO(g)$$

The components in the system have the following concentrations and are in a 1.50 L container: $[SO_2] = 4.00$ mol/L, $[NO_2] = 0.500$ mol/L, $[SO_3] = 3.00$ mol/L, and $[NO] = 2.00$ mol/L. With all other factors remaining the same, 1.50 mol $NO_2(g)$ is added to the system. What is the [NO] when equilibrium is re-established?

17. **T/I** When phosphorus pentachloride gas decomposes, an equilibrium system is established with the products of phosphorus trichloride gas and chlorine gas. In an experiment, you initially place 0.90 mol $PCl_5(g)$ into a 1.50 L container and allow equilibrium to be established. At this point, you determine that there is 0.48 mol $PCl_5(g)$ in the container. What is the equilibrium constant for this reaction?

18. **T/I** In the equilibrium system below, there were initially 2.00 mol of each reactant placed into a 0.50 L container.

$$Br_2(g) + Cl_2(g) \rightleftharpoons 2BrCl(g)$$

The K_{eq} value for this system is 47.5. What is the concentration of each component in the system?

19. **K/U** Why is it so important to have chemical balance within the human blood stream? Explain your reasoning in a well-structured paragraph, including comments regarding the blood chemistry equilibrium.

20. **C** Create a flowchart or similar graphic organizer for your peers that can be used to outline the steps needed to determine the pH of a weak base when you are given the K_a of the weak base and its initial concentration.

21. **T/I** A solution was prepared with a hydronium ion concentration of 0.00750 mol/L. Determine the pH, pOH, and concentration of hydroxide ions in the solution.

22. **A** Methanoic acid, also called formic acid, has the chemical formula HCOOH(aq) and is used as an antibacterial agent in livestock feed. It has an acid-dissociation constant of 1.70×10^{-4}. A student prepares a 0.100 mol/L solution of the acid. What is the pH of the resulting solution?

23. **T/I** A weak base used in the manufacturing of dyes has a molecular mass of 101.70 g/mol. When a chemist places 3.75 g of the material into enough water to make 1.00 L of solution, the pH is 9.14. What is the base-ionization constant for the base?

24. **T/I** At the endpoint of a titration between hydrochloric acid and sodium hydroxide, 25.00 mL of the acid is neutralized by 14.15 mL of a 0.0180 mol/L solution of the base. What was the pH of the original hydrochloric acid?

25. **K/U** Explain why water is an amphiprotic substance.

Self-Check

If you missed question …	1	2	3	4	5	6	7	8	9	10	11	12	13	14	15	16	17	18	19	20	21	22	23	24	25
Review section(s)…	7.1	7.2	7.3	7.4	7.4	8.1	8.1	8.2	8.3	8.4	8.2	7.1	7.2	7.2	7.2	7.3	7.3	7.3	8.4	8.2	8.1	8.2	8.3	8.1	8.1

UNIT 5 Electrochemistry

BIG IDEAS

- Oxidation and reduction are paired chemical reactions in which electrons are transferred from one substance to another in a predictable way.

- The control and applications of oxidation and reduction reactions have significant implications for industry, health and safety, and the environment.

Overall Expectations

In this unit, you will…

- **analyse** technologies and processes relating to electrochemistry, and their implications for society, health and safety, and the environment

- **investigate** oxidation-reduction reactions using a galvanic cell, and **analyse** electrochemical reactions in qualitative and quantitative terms

- **demonstrate** an understanding of the principles of oxidation-reduction reactions and the many practical applications of electrochemistry

Unit 5 Contents

Chapter 9
Oxidation-Reduction Reactions

Chapter 10
Electrochemical Cells

Focussing Questions

1. What are oxidation-reduction reactions and how are they characterized?

2. How do oxidation-reduction reactions apply to electrochemical cells?

3. How do galvanic and electrolytic cells function and what are some applications of these cells?

Go to **scienceontario** to find out more about electrochemistry

---

The first personal computer was officially demonstrated in 1968, but it was not until the early 1970s that desktop computers appeared on the market. Today, many personal computers literally fit in the palm of your hand. Their portability allows them to be used almost anywhere in the world, even in remote locations. As computers have shrunk in size, many batteries have become smaller as well. For example, the lithium-ion polymer batteries (commonly called LiPo batteries) that power portable computer devices, such as laptops, electronic books, and cell phones, are often less than one millimetre thick. Within this tiny battery, specific chemical reactions occur that enable electron flow to take place. It is this electron flow that powers the computer. Without electrochemical reactions, much of the technology we often take for granted today would be impossible. As you learn more about electrochemistry and batteries in this unit, think about their many applications in portable computers and other technologies that are now so common in everyday life.

As you study this unit, look ahead to the Unit 5 Project on pages 684 to 685. Complete the project in stages as you progress through the unit.

UNIT 5 Preparation

Safety in the Chemistry Laboratory and Classroom

- Be certain you understand the meaning of WHMIS symbols and use appropriate safety precautions when you see them on containers.
- Know the meaning of the safety symbols used in activities and investigations in *Chemistry 12* and follow any precautions they advise.
- Review relevant material safety data sheets (MSDS) before beginning an investigation.
- Be sure you know the location of the fire extinguisher, eyewash station, first aid kit, and other safety equipment in your classroom, as well as how to use them.
- EXTREME CAUTION should be used when working near an open flame. Take care to follow proper procedures when working with a Bunsen burner.

1. Describe the hazards represented by the symbols below and the precautions associated with them.

   a.

   b.

   c.

2. Draw a safety map of your classroom that includes the locations of three or more safety stations. Explain how to use the equipment found at each station.

3. An investigation involves working with several solutions. Your lab partner argues that she should not have to wear chemical safety goggles because she is wearing glasses.
   a. Are eyeglasses an acceptable substitute for chemical safety goggles? Explain your response.
   b. Describe the procedure you should follow if you get any material in your eyes in the chemistry laboratory.

4. An investigation requires you to use a Bunsen burner. How would you respond to your teacher's request to explain three procedures to follow when working with this apparatus?

Balancing Chemical Equations

- A chemical equation is a condensed method of representing a chemical reaction using numbers, symbols, and chemical formulas.
- A balanced chemical equation shows equal numbers of each type of atom involved in a chemical reaction. These numbers accurately reflect the ratios of the substances involved in the chemical reaction.
- When balancing chemical equations, begin by balancing the substance with the greatest number of atoms on each side of the equation first. Count polyatomic ions as a single item rather than counting the atoms within them.
- Do not change subscripts in chemical formulas when balancing chemical equations. Changing the subscripts would result in a formula that represents another substance.

5. A coefficient
   a. shows the relative number of atoms but not molecules in a chemical equation.
   b. is a positive number placed in front of a chemical formula to show the relative number of particles involved in a chemical reaction.
   c. is a ratio of substances involved in a chemical reaction.
   d. shows the relative number of atoms but not ions in a chemical equation.
   e. is all of the above.

6. Balance the following chemical equations.
   a. $SO_2(g) + O_2(g) \rightarrow SO_3(g)$
   b. $Na(s) + Fe_2O_3(s) \rightarrow Na_2O(s) + Fe(s)$
   c. $(NH_4)_2Cr_2O_7(s) \rightarrow N_2(g) + Cr_2O_3(s) + H_2O(g)$

7. Complete the steps in the following flowchart that shows how to balance chemical equations.

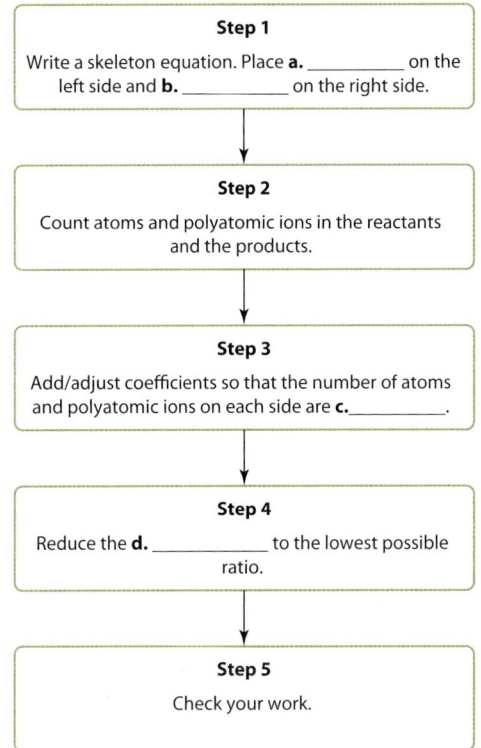

Step 1
Write a skeleton equation. Place **a.** _____ on the left side and **b.** _____ on the right side.

Step 2
Count atoms and polyatomic ions in the reactants and the products.

Step 3
Add/adjust coefficients so that the number of atoms and polyatomic ions on each side are **c.** _____.

Step 4
Reduce the **d.** _____ to the lowest possible ratio.

Step 5
Check your work.

8. Write a balanced chemical equation for each chemical reaction described below.
   a. Propane burns in the presence of oxygen to produce water vapour and carbon dioxide gas.
   b. Solid sodium and liquid water react to produce aqueous sodium hydroxide and hydrogen gas.
   c. Aqueous sodium hydroxide and sulfuric acid react to produce aqueous sodium sulfate and water.

9. A student is asked to balance the chemical equation shown in A below. The student's answer is shown in B. Explain whether the student's answer is correct. If it is not, balance the equation correctly.

   A $C_4H_{10}(g) + O_2(g) \rightarrow CO_2(g) + H_2O(g)$
   B $C_4H_{10}(g) + 4O_2(g) \rightarrow 4CO_2(g) + 5H_2(g)$

10. Aqueous silver nitrate and aqueous calcium chloride react to form solid silver chloride and aqueous calcium nitrate.
    a. Identify the polyatomic ion in this reaction.
    b. Explain how a polyatomic ion should be counted when balancing chemical equations.
    c. Write a balanced equation for this reaction.

Chemical Reactions and Activity Series

- Reactions may be classified as synthesis, decomposition, single displacement, double displacement, and combustion reactions.
- Understanding how chemical reactions are classified can help you predict the products of a chemical reaction when you know the reactants.
- Through experimentation, scientists have developed lists, called activity series, which indicate the reactivity of certain elements.
- The activity series of metals helps predict whether a single displacement reaction between a metal and an ionic compound will take place.

11. The general forms of various types of chemical reactions are show below. Name and describe each type of reaction.
    a.
    b.
    c.
    d.

12. The following chemical reaction occurs in car air bags. How would you classify this reaction?
    $$2NaN_3(s) \rightarrow 2Na(s) + 3N_2(g)$$

13. A scientist observes the following chemical reaction. What type of reaction has taken place?
    $$Cu(s) + 2AgNO_3(aq) \rightarrow Cu(NO_3)_2(aq) + 2Ag(s)$$

14. The flames in the photograph below are both fuelled by natural gas (mainly methane).

    a. Identify the types of chemical reactions taking place in the photograph and explain why the reactions differ.

    b. Write a skeleton equation for each reaction. (Hint: One reaction produces carbon monoxide gas and water vapour.)

15. Predict the products of the following chemical reactions and identify the type of reaction. Then write a balanced equation for the reaction.

    a. $Mg(s) + HCl(aq) \rightarrow$
    b. $Cu(s) + Cl_2(g) \rightarrow$
    c. $LiCl(aq) + Pb(NO_3)_2(aq) \rightarrow$

16. Explain why steel is no longer used to make water pipes, while copper pipes are still used in modern home plumbing. Refer to the activity series of metals in your response. (Hint: Steel is composed largely of iron.)

17. Acid precipitation affects both biotic and abiotic ecosystem components.

    a. Use the activity series of metals in Appendix B to explain how acid precipitation can leach metals such as magnesium out of the soil.

    b. Most acid precipitation contains sulfuric acid. Write a chemical equation for the reaction that takes place between acid precipitation and magnesium.

18. Use the activity series of metals in Appendix B to explain why silver metal will or will not react with copper(II) nitrate.

Electronegativity

- Electronegativity is an indicator of the relative ability of an atom to attract a shared electron.
- Because the noble gases do not share electrons, they have no electronegativity values.
- In the periodic table, the electronegativity of elements increases from left to right across a period. Electronegativity also increases up a group.
- Electronegativity difference—the difference in electronegativity between two atoms—affects the type of bond that forms between the two atoms.

Use the diagram below to answer questions 19 to 20.

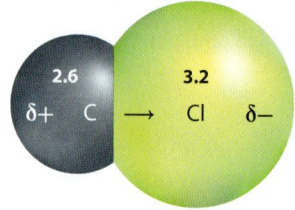

19. What do the symbols δ+ and δ– indicate in this diagram?

20. Write a caption that explains why the shared electrons in the bond between the atoms in this molecule spend more time near the chlorine nucleus.

21. Chlorine gas has an electronegativity of zero even though chlorine atoms have an electronegativity of 3.2. Use a diagram to explain why this is the case.

22. Your friend states that neon has a greater electronegativity than carbon because it lies farther to the right along a period in the periodic table. Explain whether this statement is correct or incorrect.

23. Use the periodic table to determine the electronegativity of the following atoms.

    a. oxygen
    b. lithium
    c. sulfur

24. Referring to the periodic table in your answer, explain why one atom in question 23 has a greater electronegativity than the other two atoms.

Concepts in Electricity

- Electricity is a form of energy that results from the interaction of charged particles.
- An electric circuit is a closed path along which electrons can flow. The rate at which the electrons flow is referred to as electric current.
- A voltaic (galvanic) cell generates electric current by chemical reactions involving two different metals or metal compounds separated by a solution that is a conductor.
- A battery is a connection of two or more cells.
- Electrical potential energy is potential energy (energy with the potential to perform work) that results from forces between charged particles.
- The difference between the electrical potential energy per unit of charge at two points in a circuit is the potential difference or voltage.

25. Use Venn diagrams to compare and contrast the following concepts.
    a. electrical insulators and conductors
    b. wet and dry cells
    c. primary and secondary cells
    d. electric charge and electric current

Use the diagram below to answer questions 26–29.

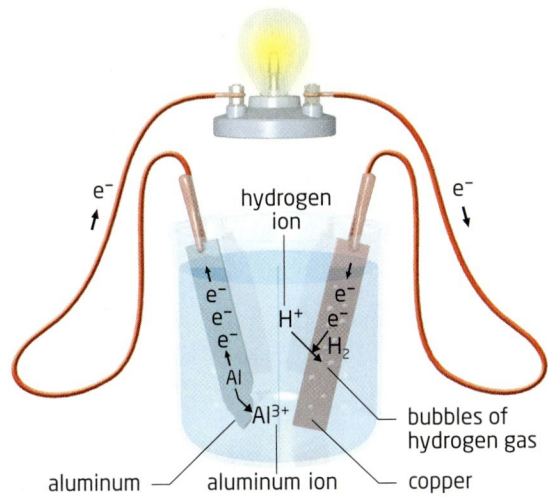

26. Describe the role played by the electrodes in the voltaic (galvanic) cell shown above.
27. Why is the presence of the electrolyte essential for generating an electric current?
28. Explain why electrodes in this cell must be made of different metals or metal compounds.
29. One of the electrodes shown in this diagram slowly disintegrates over time.
    a. Identify this electrode. Explain the reasoning for your choice.
    b. How does this change in the electrode affect the cell?

30. The units of potential difference are
    a. coulombs.
    b. joules.
    c. volts.
    d. watts.
    e. amps.

31. A friend, who has not studied chemistry, asks you several questions about the batteries (cells) shown below. Explain how you would respond to each question.

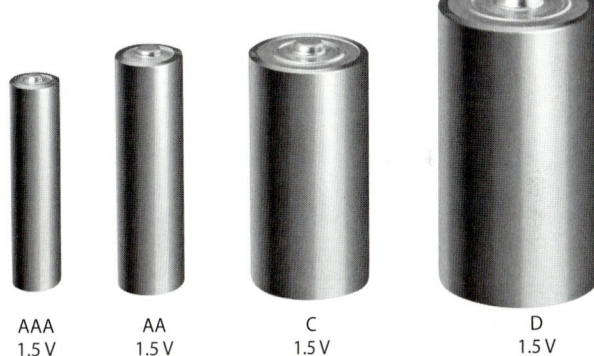

    a. Each cell has 1.5 V. What does this mean?
    b. Even though these cells all have 1.5 V, each one is a different size. What effect does size have on the performance of these cells?

32. A student builds an electric circuit using a flashlight bulb, two electrical wires with alligator clips, and a single lemon cell. The cell is made from a lemon, and zinc and copper electrodes.
    a. Use the concept of potential difference to explain why the flashlight bulb does not light up.
    b. Suggest a change to the design of the circuit that could cause the bulb to light up. Explain your reasoning.

CHAPTER 9
Oxidation-Reduction Reactions

Specific Expectations
In this chapter, you will learn how to...

- F2.1 **use** appropriate terminology related to electrochemistry (9.1, 9.2, 9.3)

- F2.2 **conduct** an inquiry to analyze, in qualitative terms, an oxidation-reduction (redox) reaction (9.1, 9.2)

- F2.3 **write** balanced chemical equations for oxidation-reduction reactions, using various methods including oxidation numbers of atoms and the half-reaction method of balancing (9.2, 9.3)

- F2.6 **predict** the spontaneity of redox reactions, based on overall cell potential as determined using a table of standard reduction potentials for redox half-reactions (9.1)

- F3.1 **explain** redox reactions in terms of the loss and gain of electrons and the associated change in oxidation number (9.1)

The chemical reactions that take place in burning logs, contracting muscles, and rusting metals are very similar. In each case, a compound reacts with oxygen and the reaction releases heat. In some reactions, large amounts of heat are released rapidly. In the reactions that occur in muscles, the overall reaction with oxygen takes place in many small steps; therefore, heat is released evenly over time. When metals rust, the reactions occur so slowly that it is difficult to detect the heat that is released. Because these reactions specifically use oxygen as a reactant, chemists originally called them "oxidation" reactions. As chemists continued to study these oxidation reactions, they learned exactly what happens to an atom that is oxidized. They also discovered the way in which oxidation reactions are related to another class of reactions that had previously been named "reduction" reactions.

In this chapter, you will begin your study of oxidation and reduction reactions. You will learn the modern definitions of oxidation and reduction. You will also learn about one way of predicting whether these reactions will be spontaneous.

Launch Lab

Penny Chemistry

Oxidation and reduction reactions are responsible for many familiar occurrences, such as the tarnishing of coins and other objects. In this activity, you will use some common substances to clean tarnished pennies.

Safety Precautions

- Wear safety eyewear throughout this activity.
- Wear a lab coat or apron throughout this activity.

Materials

- table salt
- white vinegar
- balance
- 100 mL graduated cylinder
- 1 small clear glass or plastic bowl
- stirring rod
- 6 pennies
- paper towel
- marker
- 1 steel screw or nail

Procedure

1. Measure 5 g of salt and 60 mL of vinegar and pour them into the bowl. Stir until the salt dissolves.
2. Hold a penny so that half of the penny is in the solution. After about 15 s, remove the penny. Record the appearance of the penny.
3. Put all the pennies in the solution and leave them for about 5 min.
4. Remove the pennies but leave the solution in the bowl for use in step 7.
5. Label one piece of paper towel "not rinsed" and lay half the pennies on it to dry.
6. Label a second piece of paper towel "rinsed." Rinse the remaining pennies thoroughly under running water and lay them on the paper towel to dry.
7. Position the screw (or nail) so that about half of it is in the solution and the other half is in air.
8. Observe the screw for a few minutes. Look for any evidence of a chemical reaction occurring. Record your observations.
9. Fully immerse the screw in the solution. At the end of the class period, examine the screw. Observe and record the appearance of the screw.

Questions

1. What do you think causes pennies to become dull?
2. Formulate a hypothesis about the chemical reaction that occurred when you placed the pennies in the vinegar-and-salt solution.
3. What chemical reaction might have caused the change in the unrinsed pennies that dried on the paper towel?
4. Provide a possible explanation for the change in appearance of the screw that was placed into the solution after the pennies had been removed.
5. After you have completed your study of this chapter, review your answers to these Launch Lab questions. If any of your answers need to be corrected, make those corrections.

Chapter 9 Oxidation-Reduction Reactions • MHR 583

SECTION 9.1 Characterizing Oxidation and Reduction

Key Terms

oxidation
reduction
oxidation-reduction reaction
redox reaction
ionic equation
spectator ions
net ionic equation
oxidizing agent
reducing agent

In chemistry, the terms *oxidation* and *reduction* are often used together to describe reactions. What is the origin of the term *reduction*, and what is its meaning as it relates to chemical reactions?

When metal is extracted from raw ore, as shown in **Figure 9.1**, the mass of the metal is much smaller than the mass of the mined ore. Thus, the process of extracting the metal was historically called reduction (a reduction in the amount of mass). The chemical reactions that remove the metals from the compounds were, therefore, called reduction reactions. How are these reduction reactions related to oxidation reactions? To answer this question and to see how chemists now define the terms *oxidation* and *reduction*, you will look more closely at some examples of oxidation and reduction reactions.

Figure 9.1 Many metals are extracted from the rock material (ore) in which they occur by a process that involves high temperatures, oxidation, and reduction. Examples of metals obtained in this way in Canada include copper, lead, nickel, and zinc.

Oxidation: The Loss of Electrons

As you read in the introduction to this chapter, chemists originally defined oxidation as any chemical reaction in which an atom or a compound reacted with molecular oxygen. As chemists made more observations and analyzed more data, they began to see similarities between reactions of atoms and compounds with oxygen and reactions of the same atoms and compounds with elements other than oxygen.

Consider the reaction between magnesium and oxygen. You might have observed this reaction in a laboratory activity. Magnesium burns very rapidly and emits a very bright light, as shown in **Figure 9.2**. The product of the reaction is magnesium oxide. The chemical equation is as follows:

$$2Mg(s) + O_2(g) \rightarrow 2MgO(s)$$

As you know, magnesium oxide is an ionic compound containing magnesium ions (Mg^{2+}) and oxide ions (O^{2-}). Magnesium atoms lose two electrons and become positively charged,

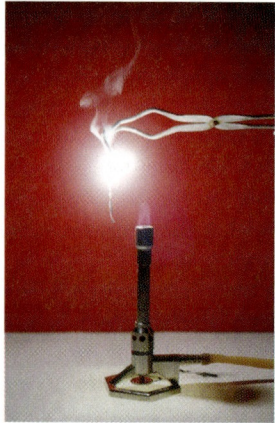

Figure 9.2 Magnesium burns in air with a bright white light and forms magnesium oxide.

while oxygen atoms gain two electrons and become negatively charged. Even in solid form, the elements exist as separate magnesium ions, as shown in the equation below.

$$2Mg(s) + O_2(g) \rightarrow 2Mg^{2+}(s) + 2O^{2-}(s)$$

Now compare the reaction between magnesium and oxygen with the reaction between magnesium and chlorine. The equation is shown here:

$$Mg(s) + Cl_2(g) \rightarrow Mg^{2+}(s) + 2Cl^-(s)$$

The product, magnesium chloride, is also an ionic compound. In this reaction, magnesium atoms lose two electrons and become ionized, while two chlorine atoms gain one electron each and become negatively charged chloride ions. As you can see, when solid magnesium reacts with either oxygen or chlorine, it loses two electrons and becomes a magnesium ion. This example illustrates the modern definition of **oxidation**, which is the loss of electrons.

Reduction: The Gain of Electrons

If one atom or ion in a reaction loses electrons, then another atom or ion must gain electrons, because electrons cannot exist free in a solution. Consider the reactions that occur when ores are reduced. Iron ore, for example, usually contains magnetite, $Fe_2O_3 \cdot FeO(s)$, or hematite, $Fe_2O_3(s)$, both of which are iron oxides. The process of converting the iron ions (Fe^{3+} or Fe^{2+}) in the oxides to metallic iron involves the addition of electrons to the ions. Since this process was historically called reduction, chemists now apply the term **reduction** to all cases in which atoms or ions gain electrons in a reaction.

To remember the definitions for oxidation and reduction, try using a memory aid such as "LEO the lion says GER." In this memory aid, LEO stands for "**L**oss of **E**lectrons is **O**xidation," and GER stands for "**G**ain of **E**lectrons is **R**eduction."

Redox Reactions

If one atom or ion is oxidized in a chemical reaction, another atom or ion must be reduced. Therefore, reactions in which electrons are gained by one atom or ion and lost by another are called **oxidation-reduction reactions** or, more briefly, **redox reactions**. Redox reactions do not comprise a separate set of reactions. On the contrary, redox reactions fit into several basic categories of reactions. The first reaction that you considered above, the oxidation of magnesium, is a synthesis reaction. Decomposition reactions are basically the reverse of synthesis reactions; thus, they are usually redox reactions. Since combustion reactions are defined as reactions in which a compound reacts with oxygen, they are also redox reactions. Single displacement reactions are always redox reactions. The reactants and products in single displacement reactions are often visibly different from each other, as shown in **Figure 9.3** on the following page. Each of the three test tubes shown in the photograph contains a zinc strip that has been placed in a copper(II) sulfate solution. In the first test tube, the reaction has progressed for the shortest time; in the second test tube, the reaction has progressed for a moderate time; and in the third test tube, the reaction has progressed for the longest time.

The single displacement reaction that is taking place between zinc and copper(II) sulfate is represented by the following complete balanced equation:

$$Zn(s) + CuSO_4(aq) \rightarrow Cu(s) + ZnSO_4(aq)$$

You can write this equation as an **ionic equation** in which all soluble ions are written separately.

$$Zn(s) + Cu^{2+}(aq) + SO_4^{2-}(aq) \rightarrow Cu(s) + Zn^{2+}(aq) + SO_4^{2-}(aq)$$

The sulfate ions are **spectator ions**, meaning they are ions that are not involved in the chemical reaction. By omitting the spectator ions (SO_4^{2-}), you obtain the following **net ionic equation**:

$$Zn(s) + Cu^{2+}(aq) \rightarrow Cu(s) + Zn^{2+}(aq)$$

oxidation the loss of electrons

reduction the gain of electrons

oxidation-reduction reaction a reaction in which electrons are gained by one atom or ion and lost by another atom or ion

redox reaction abbreviated form of oxidation-reduction reaction

ionic equation an equation in which soluble ionic compounds are written as individual ions

spectator ions ions that are present in a solution but do not change during a reaction

net ionic equation an ionic equation in which the spectator ions are omitted

Figure 9.3 A solid zinc strip reacts with a solution that contains blue copper(II) ions. The black material is Cu(s). When copper atoms deposit on the zinc strip, they do so one atom at a time, which results in a rough surface. As a result, you do not see the typical "copper colour" that you might expect.
Infer why the blue colour of the solution in the second test tube has faded and why the blue colour is absent in the third test tube.

The following equation shows how to track the electrons. In the reaction of zinc atoms with copper(II) ions, the zinc atoms *lose* electrons and undergo oxidation—the zinc atoms are *oxidized*. The copper(II) ions *gain* electrons and undergo reduction—the copper(II) ions are *reduced*.

$$\text{Zn(s)} + \text{Cu}^{2+}\text{(aq)} \rightarrow \text{Cu(s)} + \text{Zn}^{2+}\text{(aq)}$$

(gains 2e⁻ / loses 2e⁻)

oxidizing agent a reactant that accepts electrons and thus oxidizes another reactant

reducing agent a reactant that donates electrons and thus reduces another reactant

Since electrons are transferred from zinc atoms to copper(II) ions, the copper(II) ions are responsible for the oxidation of the zinc atoms. A reactant that oxidizes another reactant is called an **oxidizing agent**. The oxidizing agent receives electrons in a redox reaction and is therefore reduced. In this reaction, copper(II) is the oxidizing agent. The zinc atoms are responsible for the reduction of the copper(II) ions. A reactant that reduces another reactant is called a **reducing agent**. The reducing agent donates or loses electrons in a redox reaction and is therefore oxidized. In this reaction, zinc is the reducing agent.

A redox reaction can also be defined as a reaction between an oxidizing agent and a reducing agent, as illustrated in **Figure 9.4** on the following page.

Learning Check

1. Explain how a compound or atom can become oxidized in a reaction that does not involve oxygen.
2. What is the original definition of reduction? What is the modern definition of reduction? How do the two definitions of reduction differ? How are they the same?
3. State the original and modern definitions of oxidation.
4. Explain why an oxidation reaction must be accompanied by a reduction reaction.
5. Analyze the following equation for a single displacement reaction and identify the oxidizing agent and the reducing agent.

    $2\text{Al(s)} + 3\text{FeSO}_4\text{(aq)} \rightarrow \text{Al}_2(\text{SO}_4)_3\text{(aq)} + 3\text{Fe(s)}$

6. Analyze the following equation for a double displacement reaction. Using this reaction as a model, do you think that double displacement reactions are typically redox reactions or not? Explain why.

    $\text{BaCl}_2\text{(aq)} + \text{K}_2\text{CO}_3\text{(aq)} \rightarrow \text{BaCO}_3\text{(s)} + 2\text{KCl(aq)}$

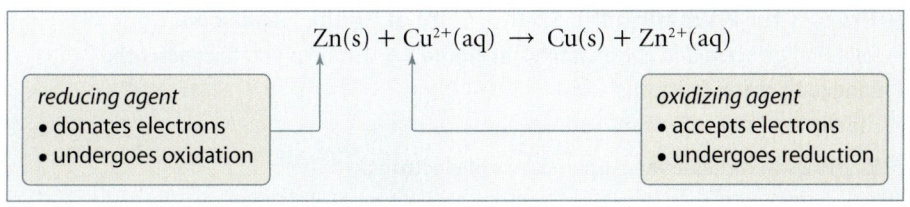

Figure 9.4 In a redox reaction, the reducing agent is oxidized and the oxidizing agent is reduced.

The Spontaneity of Redox Reactions

The reaction of zinc with copper(II) sulfate in **Figure 9.3** was spontaneous—it proceeded with no addition of energy or any other stimulus. When zinc displaced copper in the copper(II) sulfate compound, zinc acted as a reducing agent and reduced the copper(II) ion, while the zinc itself became oxidized. When metallic copper formed, it did not replace the zinc ions that had formed. That is, the reaction did not proceed in the reverse direction. This indicates that copper atoms cannot reduce zinc ions. Zinc atoms are a stronger reducing agent than are copper atoms, and copper(II) ions are a stronger oxidizing agent than are zinc ions. These concepts are expressed in **Table 9.1**.

Table 9.1 Strength of Oxidizing and Reducing Agents

Oxidizing Agent	Reducing Agent
Stronger oxidizing agent	*Weaker reducing agent*
Cu^{2+}	Cu
Zn^{2+}	Zn
Weaker oxidizing agent	*Stronger reducing agent*

Predicting the Spontaneity of Redox Reactions

Metal ions can act as oxidizing agents because they can remove electrons from certain metal atoms. Likewise, metal atoms act as reducing agents because they can donate electrons to certain ions. By performing experiments, chemists have determined the relative strengths of many ions as oxidizing agents and many atoms as reducing agents. **Table 9.2** lists the results of some of those experiments. Notice that the strength of the ions as oxidizing agents increases as you go up the list on the left. The strength of metal atoms as reducing agents increases as you go down the list on the right.

Be cautious, however, when using oxidation-reduction tables in other chemistry texts or reference books. Tables are not always written in the same direction as those in this textbook. Be sure to identify the direction of stronger versus weaker oxidizing or reducing agents. Use the concepts of oxidation and reduction instead of memorizing "up" or "down."

You can use **Table 9.2** to predict whether a reaction between atoms of one element and ions of another element will spontaneously undergo a redox reaction. Remember that a stronger reducing agent loses electrons more readily than a weaker reducing agent does. A stronger oxidizing agent gains electrons more readily than a weaker oxidizing agent does.

Suggested Investigation

Inquiry Investigation 9-A, Testing Relative Oxidizing and Reducing Strengths of Metal Atoms and Ions

Table 9.2 Relative Strengths of Oxidizing Agents and Reducing Agents

Strongest Oxidizing Agent	Weakest Reducing Agent
$Au^+(aq)$	Au(s)
$Pt^{2+}(aq)$	Pt(s)
$Ag^+(aq)$	Ag(s)
$Hg^{2+}(aq)$	$Hg(\ell)$
$Cu^{2+}(aq)$	Cu(s)
$Sn^{2+}(aq)$	Sn(s)
$Ni^{2+}(aq)$	Ni(s)
$Co^{2+}(aq)$	Co(s)
$Tl^+(aq)$	Tl(s)
$Cd^{2+}(aq)$	Cd(s)
$Fe^{2+}(aq)$	Fe(s)
$Cr^{3+}(aq)$	Cr(s)
$Zn^{2+}(aq)$	Zn(s)
$Al^{3+}(aq)$	Al(s)
$Mg^{2+}(aq)$	Mg(s)
$Ca^{2+}(aq)$	Ca(s)
$Ba^{2+}(aq)$	Ba(s)
Weakest Oxidizing Agent	Strongest Reducing Agent

The Process for Predicting the Spontaneity of Redox Reactions

The following process and the examples in **Figure 9.5** will help you to predict the spontaneity of redox reactions.

- Write the net ionic equation.
- Add arrows to indicate the gain and loss of electrons.
- By using **Table 9.2** or Appendix B, identify which of the two metals is the stronger reducing agent and which of the two ions is the stronger oxidizing agent.
- If the stronger reducing agent is losing electrons and the stronger oxidizing agent is gaining electrons, the reaction will proceed spontaneously as written.
- If the stronger reducing agent has gained electrons and the stronger oxidizing agent has lost electrons, the reaction will *not* proceed spontaneously in the forward direction.

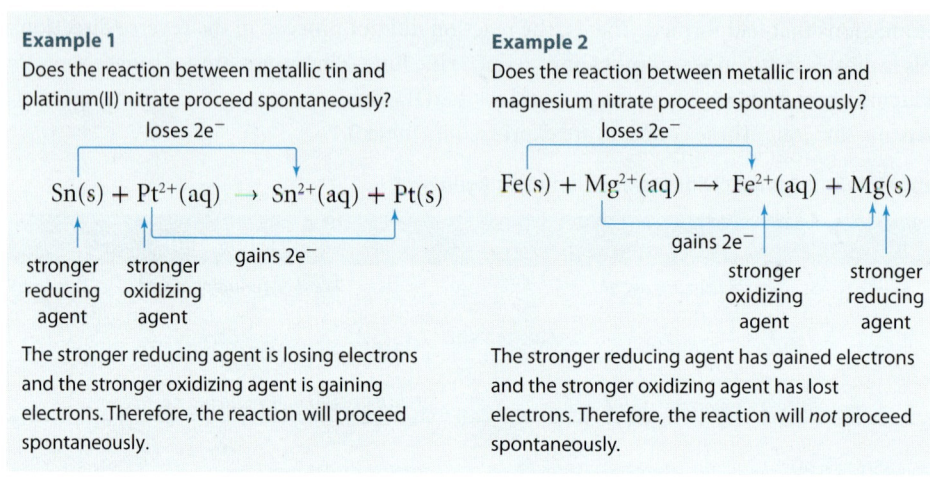

Figure 9.5 These examples show you the process, described above, for predicting the spontaneity of redox reactions.

Notice that when the stronger reducing agent and the stronger oxidizing agent are on the left of the equation, the reaction proceeds spontaneously. When the stronger reducing agent and the stronger oxidizing agent are on the right of the equation, the reaction does *not* proceed spontaneously.

Learning Check

Use **Table 9.2** to answer the following questions.

7. Which of the following reactions will proceed spontaneously?
   a. solid aluminum and aqueous copper(II) sulfate
   b. aqueous calcium nitrate and solid nickel
   c. solid chromium and aqueous silver nitrate
   d. aqueous barium sulfate and solid tin
   e. solid copper and aqueous magnesium chloride
   f. aqueous calcium bromide and solid tin

8. List three solid metals that, when placed in an aqueous solution of cadmium chloride, will react spontaneously.

9. If you want to use solid cobalt to demonstrate a spontaneous reaction between a solid and an ionic solution, which of the following aqueous solutions would you use? Explain why.
   a. silver nitrate
   b. zinc sulfate

10. Write net ionic equations for the three reactions referred to in question 8.

11. List three soluble salts that would react spontaneously with solid tin.

12. Write net ionic equations for the reactions that you listed in question 11.

Section 9.1 Review

Section Summary

- In the past, oxidation referred to any reaction involving molecular oxygen. The modern definition of oxidation, however, is the loss of electrons.
- In the past, reduction referred to the extraction of metals from their ores. The modern definition of reduction, however, is the gain of electrons.
- Reactions in which electrons are gained by one atom or ion and lost by another atom or ion are called oxidation-reduction reactions. (abbreviated to the term *redox reactions*).
- If one atom is oxidized in a reaction, then another atom must be reduced.
- An oxidizing agent accepts electrons from another compound and becomes reduced. A reducing agent donates electrons to another compound and becomes oxidized.
- You can determine experimentally whether one element is a stronger reducing agent or a stronger oxidizing agent than the other. From accumulated data, you can predict whether a given reaction will proceed spontaneously.

Review Questions

1. **K/U** Explain why oxidation and reduction reactions always occur together. Use the modern definitions of oxidation and reduction in your answer.

2. **K/U** Chemists originally defined an oxidation reaction as one in which an atom or compound reacted with molecular oxygen. Name three elements other than oxygen that can cause an oxidation reaction.

3. **K/U** Explain why the oxidizing agent in a redox reaction undergoes reduction.

4. **C** When metallic lithium is a reactant in a synthesis reaction, does the lithium act as an oxidizing agent or a reducing agent? Express and organize your ideas clearly and concisely as you explain your answer.

5. **T/I** In each of the following reactions, identify the oxidizing agent and the reducing agent.
   a. $Mg(s) + 2HCl(aq) \rightarrow H_2(g) + MgCl_2(aq)$
   b. $2Na(s) + 2H_2O(\ell) \rightarrow 2NaOH(aq) + H_2(g)$
   c. $FeSO_4(aq) + Cr(s) \rightarrow CrSO_4(aq) + Fe(s)$

6. **T/I** Write a net ionic equation for a spontaneous reaction in which
   a. $Fe^{2+}(aq)$ acts as an oxidizing agent
   b. $Al(s)$ acts as a reducing agent
   c. $Au^{+}(aq)$ acts as an oxidizing agent
   d. $Cu(s)$ acts as a reducing agent

7. **T/I** In the reaction of solid aluminum and aqueous iron(III) ions, solid iron and aqueous aluminum ions form.
   a. Write the chemical equation for this reaction.
   b. Identify what is being oxidized and what is being reduced in the reaction.
   c. Label the oxidizing agent and the reducing agent for the reaction in question 7a.

8. **T/I** For the following reactions, remove the spectator ions and write the redox reactions as net ionic equations. Track the electrons lost and gained in the reaction.
   a. copper(II) sulfate and solid calcium reacting to form solid copper and calcium sulfate
   b. mercury(II) nitrate and solid nickel reacting to form liquid mercury and nickel(II) nitrate
   c. silver chloride and solid thallium reacting to form solid silver and thallium(I) chloride

9. **T/I** Predict three solid metals that could be added to an aqueous solution of cobalt nitrate to cause a spontaneous redox reaction. Write net ionic equations for each reaction that would occur.

10. **K/U** Explain why combustion reactions are redox reactions.

11. **T/I** Explain why the following reaction is not possible:
    $Fe^{2+}(aq) + Cu(s) \rightarrow Fe^{3+}(aq) + Cu^{2+}(aq)$

12. **A** The photograph on the left shows a piece of metal in a beaker of aqueous silver(II) nitrate. The photograph on the right shows the same beaker after 15 min. Infer where the metal placed in the beaker would rank as a reducing agent compared with solid silver. Explain your answer.

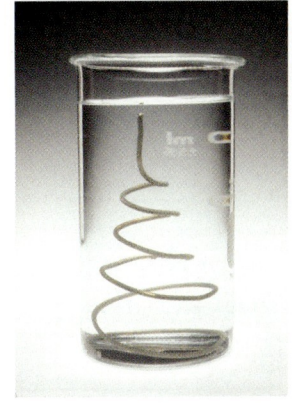

SECTION 9.2
Redox Reactions Involving Ionic Compounds

Key Terms

half-reaction
disproportionation reaction
smelting
refining

half-reaction an equation that describes changes in only the compound that is oxidized or the compound that is reduced

Most of the balanced chemical equations that you have seen represent redox reactions that can be balanced by inspection. Some reactions, however, require specific techniques for balancing the equations, particularly those reactions that take place under acidic or basic conditions. A common technique for balancing redox reactions uses half-reactions. A **half-reaction** is an equation that describes the changes in only the compound that is oxidized or only the compound that is reduced.

Writing Balanced Half-Reactions

Consider, again, the reaction of metallic zinc with aqueous copper(II) sulfate. Analyze the following net ionic equation:

$$\text{Zn(s)} + \text{Cu}^{2+}\text{(aq)} \rightarrow \text{Cu(s)} + \text{Zn}^{2+}\text{(aq)}$$

(gains 2e⁻ by Cu²⁺; loses 2e⁻ by Zn)

You can see that each neutral Zn atom is oxidized to form a Zn^{2+} ion. Thus, each Zn atom must lose two electrons. You can write an oxidation half-reaction to show this change.

Oxidation half-reaction: $\text{Zn(s)} \rightarrow \text{Zn}^{2+}\text{(aq)} + 2e^-$

Each Cu^{2+} ion is reduced to form a neutral Cu atom. Thus, each ion must gain two electrons. You can write a reduction half-reaction to show this change.

Reduction half-reaction: $\text{Cu}^{2+}\text{(aq)} + 2e^- \rightarrow \text{Cu(s)}$

Look again at each half-reaction above. Notice that the atoms and the charges are balanced. Like other types of balanced equations, half-reactions are balanced using the smallest possible whole-number coefficients.

Balancing Simple Equations Using Half-Reactions

For simple equations, such as the one for the reaction between zinc and copper(II) sulfate, you would simply add the half-reactions together to get a net ionic equation. Since the numbers of electrons on each side of the equation are the same, they can be cancelled. Finally, if you choose to do so, you can add back the spectator ions (SO_4^{2-}) as shown:

Oxidation half-reaction:	$\text{Zn(s)} \rightarrow \text{Zn}^{2+}\text{(aq)} + 2e^-$
Reduction half-reaction:	$\text{Cu}^{2+}\text{(aq)} + 2e^- \rightarrow \text{Cu(s)}$
Sum of half-reactions:	$\text{Zn(s)} + \text{Cu}^{2+}\text{(aq)} + 2e^- \rightarrow \text{Cu(s)} + \text{Zn}^{2+}\text{(aq)} + 2e^-$
Net ionic equation:	$\text{Zn(s)} + \text{Cu}^{2+}\text{(aq)} \rightarrow \text{Cu(s)} + \text{Zn(aq)}$
Ionic equation:	$\text{Zn(s)} + \text{Cu}^{2+}\text{(aq)} + \text{SO}_4^{2-}\text{(aq)} \rightarrow \text{Cu(s)} + \text{Zn}^{2+}\text{(aq)} + \text{SO}_4^{2-}\text{(aq)}$

Learning Check

Write balanced half-reactions based on each of the following ionic equations. (**Hint:** Remember to use the smallest possible whole-number coefficients in the reduction half-reaction.)

13. $\text{Al(s)} + \text{Fe}^{3+}\text{(aq)} \rightarrow \text{Al}^{3+}\text{(aq)} + \text{Fe(s)}$

14. $\text{Fe(s)} + \text{Cu}^{2+}\text{(aq)} \rightarrow \text{Fe}^{2+}\text{(aq)} + \text{Cu(s)}$

15. $\text{Cd(s)} + 2\text{Ag}^+\text{(aq)} \rightarrow \text{Cd}^{2+}\text{(aq)} + 2\text{Ag(s)}$

Write net ionic equations for each of the following equations. Then write balanced half-reactions for each of the equations.

16. $\text{Sn(s)} + \text{PbCl}_2\text{(aq)} \rightarrow \text{SnCl}_2\text{(aq)} + \text{Pb(s)}$

17. $\text{Au(NO}_3)_3\text{(aq)} + 3\text{Ag(s)} \rightarrow 3\text{AgNO}_3\text{(aq)} + \text{Au(s)}$

18. $3\text{Zn(s)} + \text{Fe}_2(\text{SO}_4)_3\text{(aq)} \rightarrow 3\text{ZnSO}_4\text{(aq)} + 2\text{Fe(s)}$

Balancing Equations Using Half-Reactions with Differing Numbers of Electrons

One additional step is needed when the numbers of electrons in the two half-reactions are not the same. For example, consider the synthesis of potassium chloride from its elements, as shown in **Figure 9.6**. Metallic potassium is oxidized to form potassium ions, and gaseous chlorine is reduced to form chloride ions. Each half-reaction can be balanced by writing the correct formulas for the reactant and the product, balancing the numbers of atoms, and then adding the correct number of electrons to balance the charges. The oxidation half-reaction is as follows:

$$\text{Oxidation half-reaction: } K(s) \rightarrow K^+(s) + e^-$$

The atoms are balanced. The net charge on each side is zero.
The reduction half-reaction is as follows:

$$\text{Reduction half-reaction: } Cl_2(g) + 2e^- \rightarrow 2Cl^-(s)$$

The atoms are balanced and the net charge on each side is 2−. There is one electron in the oxidation half-reaction and there are two electrons in the reduction half-reaction. In a balanced equation, the number of electrons lost in the oxidation half-reaction must be equal to the number of electrons gained in the reduction half-reaction. Therefore, before you can add the equations, you must multiply the entire oxidation half-reaction by 2 and then proceed as before. There are no spectator ions to add to this equation.

$$K(s) \rightarrow K^+(s) + e^-$$
$$2[K(s)] \rightarrow 2[K^+(s) + e^-]$$

$$2K(s) \rightarrow 2K^+(s) + 2e^-$$
$$Cl_2(g) + 2e^- \rightarrow 2Cl^-(s)$$
$$\overline{2K(s) + Cl_2(g) + \cancel{2e^-} \rightarrow 2K^+(s) + \cancel{2e^-} + 2Cl^-(s)}$$
or
$$2K(s) + Cl_2(g) \rightarrow 2KCl(s)$$

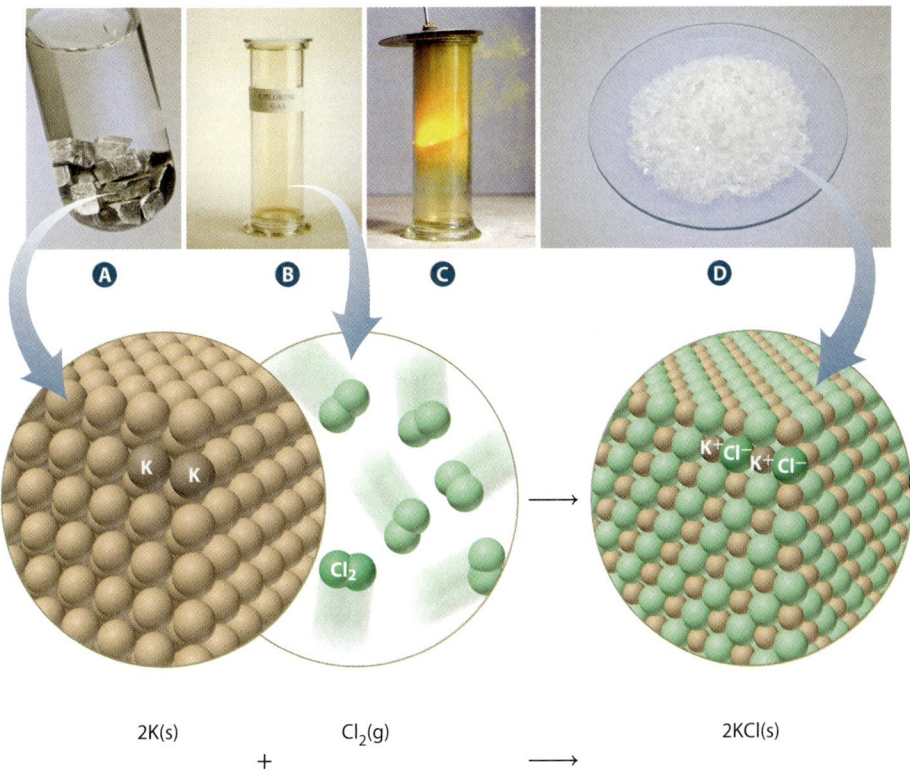

Figure 9.6 Potassium metal must be stored under oil (**A**) to prevent it from reacting with the oxygen and moisture in air. When exposed to the greenish-yellow chlorine gas (**B**), it reacts very vigorously (**C**) to form white potassium chloride (**D**).

2K(s) + Cl₂(g) → 2KCl(s)
potassium + chlorine → potassium chloride

Suggested Investigation

Inquiry Investigation 9-B, Redox Reactions and Balanced Equations

Balancing Equations for Reactions in Acidic or Basic Solutions

You could have balanced the two previous equations by inspection. However, when balancing equations for reactions that take place under acidic or basic conditions, you must account for the hydrogen, $H^+(aq)$, or hydroxide, $OH^-(aq)$, ions present in the solutions. The overall approach is similar, but a few additional steps are necessary.

The first box below lists the steps to follow when balancing the half-reactions. The second box lists the steps to follow when combining the two half-reactions to produce a balanced equation.

Read through the steps and then study the Sample Problems that follow on pages 593–598 to learn how to apply the rules to reactions that occur in acidic or basic solutions. Note that these steps allow you to balance equations, but they do not represent the actual mechanisms by which the reactions take place in the solutions. Nevertheless, your final result does represent the products of the reaction.

Balancing Half-Reactions Occurring in Acidic or Basic Solutions

Step 1 Write unbalanced half-reactions that show the formulas for the given reactant(s) and product(s).

Step 2 Balance any atoms other than oxygen and hydrogen first.

Step 3 Balance any oxygen atoms by adding water molecules.

Step 4 Balance any hydrogen atoms by adding hydrogen ions.

If your reaction is taking place in an acidic solution, skip to step 8.
If your reaction is taking place in a basic solution, proceed to step 5.

Step 5 Adjust for basic conditions by adding to both sides the same number of hydroxide ions as the number of hydrogen ions already present.

Step 6 For any hydrogen ions and hydroxide ions that appear on the same side of the equation, simplify the equation by combining these ions into water molecules.

Step 7 Cancel any water molecules present on both sides of the equation.

Step 8 Balance the charges by adding electrons.

Balancing Equations Using Half-Reactions

Step 1 Determine the lowest common multiple of the numbers of electrons in the oxidation and reduction half-reactions.

Step 2 Multiply one or both half-reactions by the number that will bring the number of electrons to the lowest common multiple.

Step 3 Add the balanced half-reactions.

Step 4 Cancel the electrons and any other identical molecules or ions present on both sides of the equation.

Step 5 If spectator ions were removed when forming half-reactions, add them back to the equation.

All these steps may seem challenging at first. However, you will find that you can combine some of the steps as you become more comfortable writing balanced equations. After you examine the following three Sample Problems, you can practise applying the rules for balancing equations for reactions in acidic or basic solutions by working through the Practice Problems on page 598.

Sample Problem

Balancing an Equation for a Reaction That Occurs in an Acidic Solution

Problem

Sulfur is oxidized by nitric acid in an aqueous solution, producing sulfur dioxide, nitrogen monoxide, and water, as shown by the unbalanced equation. Use the half-reaction method to balance the following equation:

$$S(s) + HNO_3(aq) \rightarrow SO_2(g) + NO(g) + H_2O(\ell)$$

Note: To reduce complexity, the subscript 8 has been omitted from the sulfur. After the final step, you will add the subscript to the sulfur and multiply all other coefficients by 8.

What Is Required?

You need to balance the equation using the half-reaction method occurring in an acidic solution.

What Is Given?

You are given the unbalanced equation:
$S(s) + HNO_3(aq) \rightarrow SO_2(g) + NO(g) + H_2O(\ell)$
You know that sulfur is oxidized.

Plan Your Strategy	Act on Your Strategy
First, write the ionic equation. Then follow the steps in Balancing Half-Reactions Occurring in Acidic or Basic Solutions on the previous page.	$S(s) + H^+(aq) + NO_3^-(aq) \rightarrow SO_2(g) + NO(g) + H_2O(\ell)$
Step 1 Write the unbalanced half-reactions. Include only those compounds that contain the atom that is oxidized or the atom that is reduced. (For this step, ignore the fact that one side of the equation might have oxygen atoms and the other side has none.)	*Oxidation half-reaction*: $S(s) \rightarrow SO_2(g)$ *Reduction half-reaction*: $NO_3^-(aq) \rightarrow NO(g)$
Step 2 Balance atoms other than oxygen and hydrogen.	The sulfur and nitrogen atoms are already balanced.
Step 3 Balance oxygen atoms by adding water molecules. *Oxidation half-reaction:* There are two oxygen atoms on the right side of the equation, so you must add two water molecules to the left side. *Reduction half-reaction:* There are three oxygen atoms on the left side of the equation and one on the right. Add two water molecules to the right side.	(Notice that the actions taken in each step are highlighted in blue.) $S(s) + 2H_2O(\ell) \rightarrow SO_2(g)$ $NO_3^-(aq) \rightarrow NO(g) + 2H_2O(\ell)$
Step 4 Balance hydrogen atoms by adding hydrogen ions. *Oxidation half-reaction:* There are four hydrogen atoms in the water on the left side of the equation, so add four hydrogen ions to the right side. *Reduction half-reaction:* There are four hydrogen atoms in the water molecules on the right side of the equation, so add four hydrogen ions to the left side.	$S(s) + 2H_2O(\ell) \rightarrow SO_2(g) + 4H^+(aq)$ $NO_3^-(aq) + 4H^+(aq) \rightarrow NO(g) + 2H_2O(\ell)$

Continued on next page

Plan Your Strategy	Act on Your Strategy
The nitric acid makes this an acidic solution, so skip to step 8. **Step 8** Balance the charges by adding electrons. *Oxidation half-reaction*: There are zero net charges on the left side of the equation and four positive charges on the right side. Therefore, give the right side a net charge of zero by adding four electrons to the right side. *Reduction half-reaction*: There are four positive charges and one negative charge on the left side of the equation, giving it a net charge of 3+. The net charge on the right side of the equation is zero. Add three electrons to the left side to give it a net zero charge.	$S(s) + 2H_2O(\ell) \rightarrow SO_2(g) + 4H^+(aq) + 4e^-$ $NO_3^-(aq) + 4H^+(aq) + 3e^- \rightarrow NO(g) + 2H_2O(\ell)$
The half-reactions are balanced. Now balance the entire equation by following the steps in Balancing Equations Using Half-Reactions on page 592. **Step 1** Determine the lowest common multiple of the numbers of electrons in the oxidation and reduction half-reactions. There are four electrons in the oxidation half-reaction and three electrons in the reduction half-reaction.	The lowest common multiple of 4 and 3 is 12.
Step 2 Multiply one or both half-reactions by the number that will bring the number of electrons to the lowest common multiple. *Oxidation half-reaction*: Multiply the reactants and products by 3. *Reduction half-reaction*: Multiply the reactants and products by 4.	$3[S(s) + 2H_2O(\ell) \rightarrow SO_2(g) + 4H^+(aq) + 4e^-]$ $3S(s) + 6H_2O(\ell) \rightarrow 3SO_2(g) + 12H^+(aq) + 12e^-$ $4[NO_3^-(aq) + 4H^+(aq) + 3e^- \rightarrow NO(g) + 2H_2O(\ell)]$ $4NO_3^-(aq) + 16H^+(aq) + 12e^- \rightarrow 4NO(g) + 8H_2O(\ell)$
Step 3 Add the balanced half-reactions. $3S(s) + 6H_2O(\ell) + 4NO_3^-(aq) + 16H^+(aq) + 12e^- \rightarrow 3SO_2(g) + 12H^+(aq) + 12e^- + 4NO(g) + 8H_2O(\ell)$	
Step 4 Cancel the electrons and any other identical molecules or ions present on both sides of the equation. $3S(s) + \cancel{6H_2O(\ell)} + 4NO_3^-(aq) + \cancel{16H^+(aq)} + \cancel{12e^-} \rightarrow 3SO_2(g) + \cancel{12H^+(aq)} + \cancel{12e^-} + 4NO(g) + \cancel{8H_2O(\ell)}$ $3S(s) + 4NO_3^-(aq) + 4H^+(aq) \rightarrow 3SO_2(g) + 4NO(g) + 2H_2O(\ell)$	
Step 5 If spectator ions were removed when forming half-reactions, add them back to the equation. There are no spectator ions to add back to the equation. However, you must place the subscript 8 beside S and multiply all other coefficients by 8. $3S_8(s) + 32NO_3^-(aq) + 32H^+(aq) \rightarrow 24SO_2(g) + 32NO(g) + 16H_2O(\ell)$	

Check Your Solution

The atoms of each element are balanced. There is a net charge of zero on both sides of the equation. The equation is balanced.

In the previous Sample Problem, you were told that sulfur was oxidized by nitric acid. In some problems, you might not know which compound is the oxidizing agent and which is the reducing agent. The next Sample Problem will demonstrate that you do not need to know which agent is which. If you follow the steps, the identity of the agents will be revealed. Examine the Sample Problem on pages 595–598 to see how to balance equations in which some information appears to be missing.

Sample Problem

Balancing an Equation for a Reaction That Occurs in an Acidic Solution

Problem

The unbalanced equation for the reaction between permanganate ions, $MnO_4^-(aq)$, and oxalate ions, $C_2O_4^{2-}(aq)$, in an acidic solution is shown below. Spectator ions have been omitted. Use the half-reaction method to balance the equation:

$MnO_4^-(aq) + C_2O_4^{2-}(aq) \rightarrow Mn^{2+}(aq) + CO_2(g)$

What Is Required?

You need to balance the equation for the reaction between $MnO_4^-(aq)$ and $C_2O_4^{2-}(aq)$.

What Is Given?

You are given the equation and know the reaction is taking place in an acidic solution.

Plan Your Strategy	Act on Your Strategy
Follow the steps in Balancing Half-Reactions Occurring in Acidic or Basic Solutions. **Step 1** Write the unbalanced half-reactions. *Carbon half-reaction*: *Manganese half-reaction*:	$C_2O_4^{2-}(aq) \rightarrow CO_2(g)$ $MnO_4^-(aq) \rightarrow Mn^{2+}(aq)$
Step 2 Balance any atoms other than oxygen and hydrogen. *Carbon half-reaction*: There are two carbon atoms on the left side of the equation and one carbon on the right. Multiply the right side by 2 to make the number of carbon atoms the same. *Manganese half-reaction*:	$C_2O_4^{2-}(aq) \rightarrow 2CO_2(g)$ Already balanced for Mn.
Step 3 Balance oxygen atoms by adding water molecules. *Carbon half-reaction*: *Manganese half-reaction*: There are four oxygen atoms on the left side of the equation and zero on the right. Add four water molecules to the right side.	Already balanced for oxygen. $MnO_4^-(aq) \rightarrow Mn^{2+}(aq) + 4H_2O(\ell)$
Step 4 Balance hydrogen atoms by adding hydrogen ions. *Carbon half-reaction*: *Manganese half-reaction*: There are eight hydrogen atoms in the water molecules on the right side of the equation, so add eight hydrogen ions to the left side.	There are no hydrogen atoms. $MnO_4^-(aq) + 8H^+(aq) \rightarrow Mn^{2+}(aq) + 4H_2O(\ell)$
The solution is acidic, so skip to step 8. **Step 8** Balance the charges by adding electrons. *Carbon half-reaction*: There are two negative charges on the left side and zero on the right side, so add two electrons to the right side. Since the oxalate is losing electrons, it is oxidized, making this the oxidation half-reaction. *Manganese half-reaction*: There are seven positive charges on the left side and two positive charges on the right side. Reduce the charge on the left side to two positive charges by adding five electrons to the left side. Since the permanganate is gaining electrons, it is being reduced, making this the reduction half-reaction.	$C_2O_4^{2-}(aq) \rightarrow 2CO_2(g) + 2e^-$ $MnO_4^-(aq) + 8H^+(aq) + 5e^- \rightarrow Mn^{2+}(aq) + 4H_2O(\ell)$
The half-reactions are balanced. Now balance the entire equation following the steps in Balancing Equations Using Half-Reactions.	

Continued on next page

Plan Your Strategy	Act on Your Strategy
Step 1 Determine the lowest common multiple of the numbers of electrons in the two half-reactions. There are two electrons in the oxidation half-reaction and five electrons in the reduction half-reaction.	The lowest common multiple of 2 and 5 is 10.
Step 2 Multiply one or both half-reactions by the number that will bring the number of electrons to the lowest common multiple. *Oxidation half-reaction*: Multiply the reactants and products by 5. *Reduction half-reaction*: Multiply the reactants and products by 2.	$5[C_2O_4^{2-}(aq) \rightarrow 2CO_2(g) + 2e^-]$ $5C_2O_4^{2-}(aq) \rightarrow 10CO_2(g) + 10e^-$ $2[MnO_4^-(aq) + 8H^+(aq) + 5e^- \rightarrow Mn^{2+}(aq) + 4H_2O(\ell)]$ $2MnO_4^-(aq) + 16H^+(aq) + 10e^- \rightarrow 2Mn^{2+}(aq) + 8H_2O(\ell)$
Step 3 Add the balanced half-reactions. $2MnO_4^-(aq) + 16H^+(aq) + 10e^- + 5C_2O_4^{2-}(aq) \rightarrow 2Mn^{2+}(aq) + 8H_2O(\ell) + 10CO_2(g) + 10e^-$	
Step 4 Cancel the electrons and any other identical molecules or ions present on both sides of the equation. $2MnO_4^-(aq) + 16H^+(aq) + \cancel{10e^-} + 5C_2O_4^{2-}(aq) \rightarrow 2Mn^{2+}(aq) + 8H_2O(\ell) + 10CO_2(g) + \cancel{10e^-}$ $2MnO_4^-(aq) + 16H^+(aq) + 5C_2O_4^{2-}(aq) \rightarrow 2Mn^{2+}(aq) + 8H_2O(\ell) + 10CO_2(g)$	

Check Your Solution
The atoms of each element are balanced and there is a net charge of 4+ on each side of the equation. The equation is balanced.

Sample Problem

Balancing an Equation for a Reaction That Occurs in a Basic Solution

Problem
Cyanide, $CN^-(aq)$, is oxidized by permanganate, $MnO_4^-(aq)$, in a basic solution, as shown in the following unbalanced equation. Use the half-reaction method to balance the equation:

$CN^-(aq) + MnO_4^-(aq) \rightarrow CNO^-(aq) + MnO_2(s)$

What Is Required?
You need to balance the equation for the reaction between $CN^-(aq)$ and $MnO_4^-(aq)$.

What Is Given?
You are given the unbalanced net ionic equation and know the reaction occurs in a basic solution.

Plan Your Strategy	Act on Your Strategy
Begin by balancing the half-reactions. **Step 1** Write the unbalanced half-reactions. *Oxidation half-reaction*: *Reduction half-reaction*:	$CN^-(aq) \rightarrow CNO^-(aq)$ $MnO_4^-(aq) \rightarrow MnO_2(s)$
Step 2 Balance any atoms other than oxygen and hydrogen. *Oxidation half-reaction*: *Reduction half-reaction*:	The carbon and nitrogen atoms are already balanced. The manganese atoms are already balanced.

Plan Your Strategy	Act on Your Strategy
Step 3 Balance oxygen atoms by adding water molecules. *Oxidation half-reaction*: There is one oxygen atom in the cyanate ion on the right side of the equation. Add one water molecule to the left side to balance the number of oxygen atoms. *Reduction half-reaction*: There are four oxygen atoms in the permanganate ion on the left side and two oxygen atoms in the manganese oxide on the right side. Therefore, add two water molecules to the right side.	$CN^-(aq) + H_2O(\ell) \rightarrow CNO^-(aq)$ $MnO_4^-(aq) \rightarrow MnO_2(s) + 2H_2O(\ell)$
Step 4 Balance hydrogen atoms by adding hydrogen ions. *Oxidation half-reaction*: There are two hydrogen atoms in the water molecule on the left side of the equation and zero on the right side. Therefore, add two hydrogen ions to the right side. *Reduction half-reaction*: There are four hydrogen atoms in the two water molecules on the right side of the equation and zero on the left side. Therefore, add four hydrogen ions to the left side.	$CN^-(aq) + H_2O(\ell) \rightarrow CNO^-(aq) + 2H^+(aq)$ $MnO_4^-(aq) + 4H^+(aq) \rightarrow MnO_2(s) + 2H_2O(\ell)$
Step 5 Adjust for basic conditions by adding to both sides the same number of hydroxide ions as the number of hydrogen ions already present. *Oxidation half-reaction*: There are two hydrogen ions on the right side of the equation, so add two hydroxide ions to both sides. $CN^-(aq) + H_2O(\ell) + 2OH^-(aq) \rightarrow CNO^-(aq) + 2H^+(aq) + 2OH^-(aq)$ *Reduction half-reaction*: There are four hydrogen ions on the left side of the equation, so add four hydroxide ions to both sides. $MnO_4^-(aq) + 4H^+(aq) + 4OH^-(aq) \rightarrow MnO_2(s) + 2H_2O(\ell) + 4OH^-(aq)$	
Step 6 Simplify the equation by combining the hydrogen ions and hydroxide ions that appear on the same side of the equation into water molecules. *Oxidation half-reaction*: $CN^-(aq) + H_2O(\ell) + 2OH^-(aq) \rightarrow CNO^-(aq) + 2H_2O(\ell)$ *Reduction half-reaction*: $MnO_4^-(aq) + 4H_2O(\ell) \rightarrow MnO_2(s) + 2H_2O(\ell) + 4OH^-(aq)$	
Step 7 Cancel any water molecules present on both sides of the equation. *Oxidation half-reaction*: $CN^-(aq) + H_2O(\ell) + 2OH^-(aq) \rightarrow CNO^-(aq) + 2H_2O(\ell)$ *Reduction half-reaction*: $MnO_4^-(aq) + 4H_2O(\ell) \rightarrow MnO_2(s) + 2H_2O(\ell) + 4OH^-(aq)$	$CN^-(aq) + 2OH^-(aq) \rightarrow CNO^-(aq) + H_2O(\ell)$ $MnO_4^-(aq) + 2H_2O(\ell) \rightarrow MnO_2(s) + 4OH^-(aq)$
Step 8 Balance the charges by adding electrons. *Oxidation half-reaction*: There are three negative charges on the left side of the equation and one on the right side. Balance the charges by adding two electrons to the right side. *Reduction half-reaction*: There is one negative charge on the left side of the equation and four on the right side. Balance the charges by adding three electrons to the left side.	$CN^-(aq) + 2OH^-(aq) \rightarrow CNO^-(aq) + H_2O(\ell) + 2e^-$ $MnO_4^-(aq) + 2H_2O(\ell) + 3e^- \rightarrow MnO_2(s) + 4OH^-(aq)$
The half-reactions are balanced, so proceed to balancing the entire equation.	
Step 1 Determine the lowest common multiple of the numbers of electrons in the oxidation and reduction half-reactions. There are two electrons in the oxidation half-reaction and three electrons in the reduction half-reaction.	The lowest common multiple of 2 and 3 is 6.

Continued on next page

Plan Your Strategy	Act on Your Strategy
Step 2 Multiply one or both half-reactions by the number that will bring the number of electrons to the lowest common multiple. *Oxidation half-reaction*: Multiply the reactants and products by 3. *Reduction half-reaction*: Multiply the reactants and products by 2.	$3[CN^-(aq) + 2OH^-(aq) \rightarrow CNO^-(aq) + H_2O(\ell) + 2e^-]$ $3CN^-(aq) + 6OH^-(aq) \rightarrow 3CNO^-(aq) + 3H_2O(\ell) + 6e^-$ $2[MnO_4^-(aq) + 2H_2O(\ell) + 3e^- \rightarrow MnO_2(s) + 4OH^-(aq)]$ $2MnO_4^-(aq) + 4H_2O(\ell) + 6e^- \rightarrow 2MnO_2(s) + 8OH^-(aq)$
Step 3 Add the balanced half-reactions. $2MnO_4^-(aq) + 4H_2O(\ell) + 6e^- + 3CN^-(aq) + 6OH^-(aq) \rightarrow 2MnO_2(s) + 8OH^-(aq) + 3CNO^-(aq) + 3H_2O(\ell) + 6e^-$	
Step 4 Cancel the electrons and any other identical molecules or ions present on both sides of the equation. $2MnO_4^-(aq) + 4H_2O(\ell) + 6e^- + 3CN^-(aq) + 6OH^-(aq) \rightarrow 2MnO_2(s) + 8OH^-(aq) + 3CNO^-(aq) + 3H_2O(\ell) + 6e^-$ $2MnO_4^-(aq) + H_2O(\ell) + 3CN^-(aq) \rightarrow 2MnO_2(s) + 2OH^-(aq) + 3CNO^-(aq)$	

Check Your Solution
The atoms of each element are balanced, and there is a net charge of 5− on each side of the equation. The equation is balanced.

Practice Problems

Balance each of the following ionic equations for acidic conditions. Identify the oxidizing agent and the reducing agent in each case.

1. $MnO_4^-(aq) + Ag(s) \rightarrow Mn^{2+}(aq) + Ag^+(aq)$
2. $Hg(\ell) + NO_3^-(aq) + Cl^-(aq) \rightarrow HgCl_4^{2-}(s) + NO_2(g)$
3. $AsH_3(s) + Zn^{2+}(aq) \rightarrow H_3AsO_4(aq) + Zn(s)$
4. $I_2(s) + ClO^-(aq) \rightarrow IO_3^-(aq) + Cl^-(aq)$

Balance each of the following ionic equations for basic conditions. Identify the oxidizing agent and the reducing agent in each case.

5. $MnO_4^-(aq) + I^-(aq) \rightarrow MnO_4^{2-}(aq) + IO_3^-(aq)$
6. $H_2O_2(aq) + ClO_2(aq) \rightarrow ClO^-(aq) + O_2(g)$
7. $ClO^-(aq) + CrO_2^-(aq) \rightarrow CrO_4^{2-}(aq) + Cl_2(g)$
8. $Al(s) + NO^-(aq) \rightarrow NH_3(g) + AlO_2^-(aq)$

Balance each of the following ionic equations for the conditions indicated. Identify the oxidizing agent and the reducing agent in each case.

9. $ClO_3^-(aq) + MnO_2(s) \rightarrow Cl^-(aq) + MnO_4^-(aq)$ (basic conditions)
10. $PbO_2(s) + I_2(s) \rightarrow Pb^{2+}(aq) + IO_3^-(aq)$ (acidic conditions)

Disproportionation Reactions

disproportionation reaction a reaction in which some atoms of an element are oxidized and other atoms of the same element are reduced

In most redox reactions, atoms of one element are oxidized and atoms of a different element are reduced. It is possible, however, for some atoms of an element to undergo oxidation and other atoms of the same element to undergo reduction in a single reaction called a **disproportionation reaction**. Examine the copper atoms and ions in the following equations.

Complete balanced equation: $Cu_2O(aq) + H_2SO_4(aq) \rightarrow Cu(s) + CuSO_4(aq) + H_2O(\ell)$
Ionic equation: $2Cu^+(aq) + O^{2-}(aq) + 2H^+(aq) + SO_4^{2-}(aq) \rightarrow Cu(s) + Cu^{2+}(aq) + SO_4^{2-}(aq) + H_2O(\ell)$
Net ionic equation: $2Cu^+(aq) + O^{2-}(aq) + 2H^+(aq) \rightarrow Cu(s) + Cu^{2+}(aq) + H_2O(\ell)$

(**Note:** Copper(I) oxide (Cu_2O) is nearly insoluble in water but it will react with sulfuric acid.)

Of the two copper(I) ions in the reactant, one is reduced to elemental copper, Cu(s), by gaining an electron and the other is oxidized to copper(II), Cu^{2+}(aq), by losing an electron. You can track the electrons as shown below.

$$Cu^+(aq) + Cu^+(aq) \rightarrow Cu(s) + Cu^{2+}(aq)$$

(gains 1e⁻ from second Cu^+ to product Cu; loses 1e⁻ from first Cu^+ to Cu^{2+})

The two half-reactions are as follows:

Oxidation half-reaction: $Cu^+(aq) \rightarrow Cu^{2+}(aq) + e^-$
Reduction half-reaction: $Cu^+(aq) + e^- \rightarrow Cu(s)$

Disproportionation reactions are balanced in the same way in which any other redox reaction is balanced.

Reducing Iron Ore

The term *reduction* originally came from the treatment of ore to produce metal. Today, however, the terms *smelting* and *refining* are often applied to processing and purifying ore. How are these terms related to the original term *reduction* and to the modern meaning of chemical reduction? A brief glimpse into the historical development of metal implements will tie these concepts together.

Copper artefacts, similar to those in **Figure 9.7**, that date back to about 3600 B.C.E. show that ancient peoples were extracting crude copper from copper ore, probably malachite, $CuCO_3 \cdot Cu(OH)_2$(s), and using it to make utensils. To extract the copper from the ore, the ore had to be exposed to very high temperatures—higher than a fire used for cooking could provide. Since the only way to generate such high temperatures at that time was by using the ovens in which clay pots were fired, archaeologists speculate that potters might have discovered the process of preparing copper. If ore had been placed in high-temperature ovens, the copper would have melted and thus separated from the other substances in the ore. The copper produced during that era could be shaped into very effective tools and other utensils.

Figure 9.7 These tools were made from raw copper by ancient peoples.

For about 1000 years after humans had learned how to prepare copper, the only source of iron for tool making was meteorites. Archaeologists have discovered evidence that ancient peoples began to process iron ore at about 2500 B.C.E. However, it was not a common practice until about 1200 B.C.E. By then, people had discovered that heating iron ore, probably hematite, Fe_2O_3(s), to very high temperatures and in contact with charcoal produced iron suitable for making ornaments and tools. The fact that the mass of iron obtained from ore was much smaller than the mass of the original ore was the basis of the term *reduction*.

Today, iron ore is still heated with a form of charcoal to extract metallic iron. The process is called **smelting** and it involves the chemical reduction of the iron ions to iron atoms with carbon as the reducing agent. The process takes place in several steps inside a large *blast furnace*, as shown in **Figure 9.8** on the following page.

smelting the melting of ore and reduction of metal ions to atoms, then separating the metal from non-metal substances

The chemistry of the reactions is somewhat complex, but it can be summarized by the equations in **Figure 9.8**. A mixture, called the *charge*, contains pulverized iron ore—usually hematite—limestone, $CaCO_3(s)$, and coke, $C(s)$. (Coke is prepared by heating coal in the absence of oxygen, which drives off most of the impurities; when an inexpensive process to prepare coke from coal was developed, it made iron smelting much less expensive and more efficient.) As the charge is poured onto the top of the blast furnace, blasts of hot air travel up through the particles as they fall.

At the lowest level of the furnace, where oxygen from injected air is available, carbon in the form of coke burns, heating the air to about 2000°C. By controlling the amount of air and coke, the burning of the coke can be made incomplete, producing carbon monoxide according to the following reaction:

$$2C(s) + O_2(g) \rightarrow 2CO(g) + \text{heat}$$

Carbon monoxide is the compound that acts as the reducing agent for the ore. As the carbon monoxide travels up the furnace, it reacts with the compounds from the iron ore that are falling. A variety of reduction reactions occur throughout the furnace. The important reactions are shown in **Figure 9.8**, along with the temperature range in which they occur. As you can see, complete reduction of the hematite occurs in three steps. Finally, the metallic iron melts and pools in the bottom of the furnace.

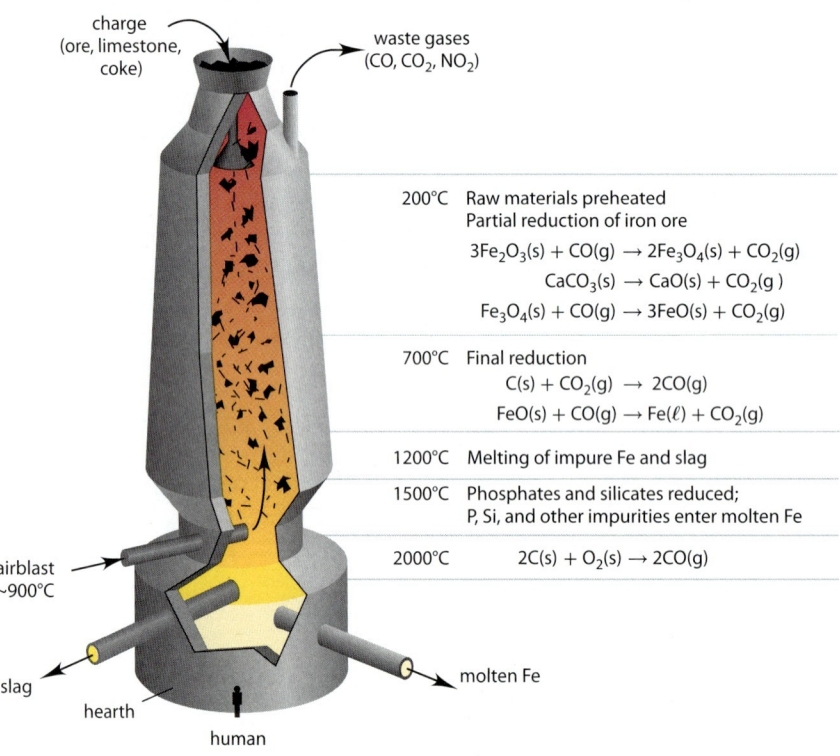

Figure 9.8 Important reactions that take place in a blast furnace are shown here. The human figure at the base of the illustration compares the size of a person with that of a blast furnace.
Explain how the air at the bottom of a blast furnace can reach 2000°C if the air that is injected is approximately 900°C.

The purpose of the lime, $CaO(s)$, which is produced by heating the limestone in the charge, is to react with impurities. Significant amounts of silicon dioxide and aluminum oxide are found in iron ore. The lime reacts with these compounds, according to the equations below, to produce a liquid called *slag*:

$$CaO(s) + SiO_2(s) \rightarrow CaSiO_3(\ell)$$
$$CaO(s) + Al_2O_3(s) \rightarrow Ca(AlO_2)_2(\ell)$$

The slag is less dense than the molten iron and thus floats on top of the iron. As shown in **Figure 9.8**, the slag and molten iron are drawn off at different levels.

The iron still contains contaminants—mainly carbon (about 5%), silicon, phosphorus, manganese, and sulfur. This molten iron is poured into long narrow moulds to form bars. In this form, the metal is called *pig iron* (see **Figure 9.9**). The pig iron is then transported to other locations, where most of it is converted into steel.

Making Steel

While the process of smelting reduced the iron ions in the ore to metallic iron, several contaminants were also reduced to their elemental form. Pig iron contains about 5 percent carbon from the coke. Some of the silicon and phosphorus, along with small amounts of manganese and sulfur from the ore, remain in the pig iron. Most of these impurities must be removed because they cause the iron to be brittle and granular. By the process of purifying or **refining**, pig iron is converted into steel. Many of the contaminants remain in the pig iron because they were reduced along with the iron. Thus, the reasonable way to remove them is by oxidation.

Molten pig iron is poured into an upright vessel. Oxygen gas is pumped into the vessel over the iron. Lime, called *flux*, is poured into the mixture. The impurities oxidize much more readily than does the iron. These oxidized compounds then react with the lime, according to the reactions shown here:

$$SiO_2(s) + CaO(s) \rightarrow CaSiO_3(\ell)$$
$$P_4O_{10}(\ell) + 6CaO(s) \rightarrow 2Ca_3(PO_4)_2(\ell)$$

The reactions produce a slag that is similar to the slag in the smelting process. The slag is less dense than the molten iron and therefore floats on it. When the reactions are complete, the vessel is tilted on its hinges, the slag is poured off the top, as shown in **Figure 9.10**, and the refined steel is recovered. Steel still contains some carbon (0.03% to 1.4%) but much less than pig iron does.

Figure 9.9 Pig iron was given its name because the bars cooling and solidifying in their moulds **(A)** resemble piglets nursing **(B)**.

refining the process of removing impurities

Figure 9.10 Slag can be poured off the top of molten iron because slag has a lower density compared to the density of iron.

Section 9.2 Review

Section Summary

- Oxidation half-reactions include only those atoms that become oxidized in a redox reaction.
- Reduction half-reactions include only those atoms that become reduced in a redox reaction.
- You can use a set of rules to balance oxidation and reduction half-reactions. You can then add the half-reactions to obtain a balanced redox reaction.
- In a disproportionation reaction, one or more atoms of an element are oxidized and one or more atoms of the same element are reduced in the same reaction.
- Iron ore is reduced in a series of reactions involving carbon monoxide to form pig iron. Pig iron is refined by oxidizing the impurities and reacting them with calcium oxide to form a liquid that floats on the molten iron.

Review Questions

1. **T/I** Balance each redox reaction using the half-reaction method. Label each half-reaction as an oxidation or reduction half-reaction.
    a. $Cl_2(g) + I^-(aq) \rightarrow Cl^-(aq) + I_2(s)$
    b. $Ag^+(aq) + Mg(s) \rightarrow Mg^{2+}(aq) + Ag(s)$
    c. $Al^{3+}(aq) + Ni(s) \rightarrow Ni^{2+}(aq) + Al(s)$

2. **C** In studying the reaction of solid copper in an aqueous solution of silver nitrate, a student is not sure what to do with the nitrate ions while balancing the redox reaction. What would you suggest to help the student? Explain your answer.

3. **C** Prepare a graphic organizer such as a flowchart that can be used to balance a half-reaction of a metal ion to a metal oxide in basic conditions.

4. **T/I** Balance each of the following half-reactions. Identify each reaction as an oxidation half-reaction or reduction half-reaction.
    a. $Cr_2O_7^{2-}(aq) \rightarrow Cr^{3+}(aq)$ (acidic conditions)
    b. $S_2O_3^{2-}(aq) \rightarrow S_2O_6^{2-}(aq)$
    c. $AsO_4^{3-}(aq) \rightarrow As_4O_6(aq)$ (acidic conditions)
    d. $Br_2(g) \rightarrow BrO_3^-(aq)$ (basic conditions)

5. **K/U** Explain why redox reactions that take place in acidic or basic conditions often cannot be balanced by inspection.

6. **T/I** Balance each of the following equations:
    a. $Au^{3+}(aq) + Co(s) \rightarrow Au(s) + Co^{3+}(aq)$
    b. $Cu(s) + NO_3^-(aq) \rightarrow Cu^{2+}(aq) + NO(g)$ (acidic conditions)
    c. $NO_3^-(aq) + Al(s) \rightarrow NH_3(g) + AlO_2^-(aq)$ (basic conditions)

7. **C** Prepare a graphic organizer such as a flowchart that shows how to balance a half-reaction of a solid metal oxide to a metallic ion in acidic conditions.

8. **C** Use a graphic organizer to explain the steps that are involved in producing steel from pig iron. What is this process called and why is it important in steel manufacturing?

9. **T/I** Write the net ionic equation and the half-reactions for the disproportionation of mercury(I) ions in aqueous solution to produce liquid mercury and aqueous mercury(II) ions. Assume that mercury(I) ions exist in solution as $2Hg^+(aq)$.

10. **T/I** Balance the following equations for a reaction that occurs in an acidic solution:
    a. $HClO_2(aq) + I^-(aq) \rightarrow Cl_2(g) + HIO(aq)$
    b. $P_4(s) + IO_3^-(aq) \rightarrow H_2PO_4^-(aq) + I^-(aq)$
    c. $Cr_2O_7^{2-}(aq) + Hg(\ell) \rightarrow Cr^{3+}(aq) + Hg^{2+}(aq)$
    d. $MnO_4^-(aq) + H_2O_2(\ell) \rightarrow Mn^{2+}(aq) + O_2(g)$

11. **K/U** Once a redox reaction is balanced for an acidic solution, describe how the reaction can be changed to a basic solution.

12. **T/I** Balance each of the equations from question 10 in a basic solution.

13. **T/I** Balance each equation using half-reactions in the given conditions, where necessary:
    a. $ClO_4^-(aq) + Br^-(aq) \rightarrow Cl^-(aq) + BrO_3^-(aq)$
    b. $N_2O_4(g) + TeO_3^{2-}(aq) \rightarrow Te(s) + NO_3^-(aq)$ (basic conditions)
    c. $H_2O_2(\ell) + Cr_2O_7^{2-}(aq) \rightarrow O_2(g) + Cr^{3+}(aq)$ (acidic conditions)

14. **A** The reverse of a disproportionation reaction is a comproportionation reaction. An example of such a reaction is one that occurs in volcanic eruptions in which sulfur compounds react:
    $H_2S(g) + SO_2(g) \rightarrow S(s) + H_2O(g)$
    Is this a redox reaction? Explain your answer.

SECTION 9.3
Redox Reactions Involving Molecular Compounds

The eerie glow in **Figure 9.11A**, which is sometimes visible in large bodies of water, is usually the result of light emitted by microscopic algae, such as the dinoflagellate *Lingulodinium polyedrum*, shown in **Figure 9.11B**. The light emitted by organisms such as certain kinds of algae is called bioluminescence. In the case of *Lingulodinium polyedrum*, the microorganisms emit light whenever they are disturbed by motion, such as waves crashing against a rocky shore. **Figure 9.11C** shows the reaction that produces light in bioluminescent organisms. This is a redox reaction, but there are no metal ions in this reaction. If you were asked, what would you need to know to write a half-reaction for this reaction?

Key Term

oxidation number

Figure 9.11 The glow in these ocean waves (**A**) is caused by the bioluminescent dinoflagellate, *Lingulodinium polyedrum* (**B**), which is a type of algae. The chemical reaction responsible for bioluminescence (**C**) involves a compound called luciferin, which is catalyzed by an enzyme, luciferase. (The names for the compound and its enzyme come from a Latin word that means "bringer of light.")
Infer why this redox reaction gives off visible light.

There are many other redox reactions for which it would be difficult to write half-reactions. For example, many of the reactions that occur in organisms involve molecular compounds and no ions or metal atoms. One familiar example is the set of reactions that comprise cellular respiration. The equation that summarizes cellular respiration is shown below:

$$C_6H_{12}O_6(aq) + 6O_2(g) \rightarrow 6CO_2(g) + 6H_2O(\ell)$$

In a cell of a living organism, cellular respiration takes place in many separate steps, some of which are redox reactions. How could you determine whether reactions that involve only molecular compounds are redox reactions? How could you write half-reactions for the equation for cellular respiration? There is a method that makes balancing redox reactions involving only molecular compounds much simpler than using half-reactions: the oxidation number method. To use this method, you must assign an oxidation number to each atom in the equation.

Balancing Redox Reactions Using the Oxidation Number Method

Oxidation numbers are, in general, the same as the charge that an atom in a compound would have if no electrons were shared but if, instead, the electrons were completely held

Suggested Investigation

ThoughtLab Investigation 9-C, Assessing Antioxidant Supplements

oxidation number a number equal to the charge that an atom would have if no electrons were shared but instead were possessed by the atom with the greatest electronegativity

by the atom with the greatest electronegativity. For example, you learned that, in a water molecule, oxygen is more electronegative than hydrogen. As a result, the oxygen atoms attract the shared electrons more strongly than do the hydrogen atoms. Therefore, to determine oxidation numbers, you would assign all the valence electrons to oxygen and none to hydrogen. Since the oxygen atom would then possess one extra electron from each of the two hydrogen atoms, in addition to its own valence electrons, it would have an oxidation number of -2. The hydrogen atoms would each have an oxidation number of $+1$ because their valence electrons are considered to "belong" to the oxygen atom. It is important to remember that oxidation numbers do *not* represent actual charges on atoms. Rather, oxidation numbers are a way to describe some properties of atoms in a compound. Also remember that charges are written as a superscript with the sign after the number, for example, O^{2-}. Conversely, with oxidation numbers, the sign is written before the number, for example, -2.

When electrons are equally shared by two identical atoms, such as chlorine atoms in a chlorine molecule, $Cl_2(g)$, half of the shared electrons are considered to be held by each atom of the atoms. In the chlorine molecule, neither atom "gained" or "lost" an electron, so each atom has an oxidation number of zero. To assign all oxidation numbers by using such a reasoning process would be very time consuming. However, you can assign oxidation numbers by following the rules listed in **Table 9.3** below.

Table 9.3 Rules for Assigning Oxidation Numbers

Rules	Examples
1. A pure element has an oxidation number of zero.	Na in Na(s), Br in $Br_2(\ell)$, and P in $P_4(s)$ all have an oxidation number of zero.
2. The oxidation number of an element in a monatomic ion equals the charge on the ion.	The oxidation number of aluminum in $Al^{3+}(aq)$ is $+3$. The oxidation number of selenium in $Se^{2-}(aq)$ is -2.
3. The oxidation number of hydrogen in compounds is $+1$, except in metal hydrides, where the oxidation number of hydrogen is -1.	The oxidation number of hydrogen in $H_2S(g)$ or in $CH_4(g)$ is $+1$. The oxidation number of hydrogen in NaH(s) or in $CaH_2(s)$ is -1.
4. The oxidation number of oxygen in compounds is usually -2, but there are exceptions. These include peroxides, such as $H_2O_2(\ell)$, superoxides, and the compound $OF_2(g)$.	The oxidation number of oxygen in $Li_2O(s)$ or $KNO_3(s)$ is -2.
5. In molecular compounds that do not contain hydrogen or oxygen, the more electronegative element is assigned an oxidation number equal to the negative charge it usually has when it is in ionic compounds.	The oxidation number of chlorine in $PCl_3(\ell)$ is -1. The oxidation number of sulfur in $CS_2(\ell)$ is -2.
6. The sum of the oxidation numbers of all the atoms in a neutral compound is zero.	In $CF_4(g)$, the oxidation number of fluorine is -1 and the oxidation number of carbon is $+4$. The oxidation numbers of 1 C atom + 4 F atoms = 0 $(+4) + 4(-1) = 0$ $+4 - 4 = 0$
7. The sum of the oxidation numbers of all the atoms in a polyatomic ion equals the charge on the ion.	In $NO_2^-(aq)$, the oxidation number of oxygen is -2 and the oxidation number of nitrogen is $+3$. The oxidation numbers of 1 N atom + 2 O atoms = -1 $(+3) + 2(-2) = -1$ $+3 - 4 = -1$

In the following Sample Problem, you will determine how to apply the rules in **Table 9.3** to molecular compounds and polyatomic ions. Note that when determining the oxidation numbers of elements in ionic compounds, you can work with the ions separately. For example, $Na_2Cr_2O_7$(aq) contains two Na^+(aq) ions, and sodium has an oxidation number of +1. The oxidation numbers of chromium and oxygen in the dichromate ion, $Cr_2O_7^{2-}$(aq), can then be calculated as shown in part C of the Sample Problem.

Sample Problem

Assigning Oxidation Numbers

Problem
Assign an oxidation number to each atom in the following compounds:
  a. $SiBr_4(\ell)$ **b.** $HClO_4$(aq)   **c.** $Cr_2O_7^{2-}$(aq)

What Is Required?
You must determine the oxidation number of every atom in three compounds.

What Is Given?
You are given three chemical formulas. You can refer to the rules in **Table 9.3**.

a. $SiBr_4(\ell)$

Plan Your Strategy	Act on Your Strategy
$SiBr_4(\ell)$ does not contain hydrogen or oxygen. Therefore, apply rule 5: the oxidation number of the more electronegative element is the same as the charge it would have as an ion. Determine the electronegativity of the two elements.	The electronegativity of Si is 1.9 and of Br is 3.0. Because bromine has a higher electronegativity, the bromine ion is assigned a charge of 1−. Therefore, the oxidation number of Br is −1.
The oxidation number of Si is unknown, but you know that the compound has a net charge of zero. Therefore, apply rule 6: the oxidation numbers must add to zero. Let x represent the oxidation number of Si.	1 Si atom + 4 Br atoms = 0 $x + 4(-1) = 0$ $x - 4 = 0$ $x = +4$

The oxidation number of Si is +4 and the oxidation number of Br is −1.

b. $HClO_4$(aq)

Plan Your Strategy	Act on Your Strategy
$HClO_4$(aq) contains oxygen and hydrogen. Apply rules 3 and 4.	The oxidation number of oxygen is −2 and the oxidation number of hydrogen is +1.
The oxidation number of chlorine is unknown, so call it x. $HClO_4$(aq) is a neutral compound. Therefore, apply rule 6: the oxidation numbers of all atoms must add to zero.	1 H atom + 1 Cl atom + 4 O atoms = 0 $1(+1) + 1(x) + 4(-2) = 0$ $1 + x - 8 = 0$ $x = +7$

The oxidation number of H is +1, the oxidation number of Cl is +7, and the oxidation number of O is −2.

c. $Cr_2O_7^{2-}$(aq)

Plan Your Strategy	Act on Your Strategy
$Cr_2O_7^{2-}$(aq) contains oxygen. Apply rule 4.	The oxidation number of oxygen is −2.
The oxidation number of chromium is unknown, so call it x. $Cr_2O_7^{2-}$(aq) is a polyatomic ion. Apply rule 7.	The sum of the oxidation numbers is −2. 2 Cr atoms + 7 O atoms = −2 $2x + 7(-2) = -2$ $2x - 14 = -2$ $2x = 12$ $x = +6$

Continued on next page

The oxidation number of O is −2 and the oxidation number of Cr is +6.

Check Your Solution

In every case, the oxidation numbers of all atoms add to zero for a molecule or to the indicated charge for an ion.

Practice Problems

Determine the oxidation number of the atoms of the specified element in each of the following:

11. N in $NF_3(g)$

12. S in $S_8(s)$

13. Cr in $CrO_4{}^{2-}(aq)$

14. P in $P_2O_5(s)$

15. C in $C_{12}H_{22}O_{11}(s)$

16. H in $CaH_2(s)$

Determine the oxidation number of each of the atoms in each of the following compounds:

17. $H_2SO_3(aq)$

18. $OH^-(aq)$

19. $HPO_4{}^{2-}(aq)$

Determine the oxidation number of oxygen in each of the following:

20. $O_2(g)$

21. the peroxide ion, $O_2{}^{2-}(aq)$

Determine the oxidation number of each element in each of the following ionic compounds by considering the ions separately. (**Hint:** One formula unit of the compound in question 24 contains two identical monatomic ions and one polyatomic ion.)

22. $Al(HCO_3)_3(s)$

23. $(NH_4)_3PO_4(aq)$

24. $K_2H_3IO_6(aq)$

Assigning Non-integer Oxidation Numbers

When you apply the rules in **Table 9.3**, you will discover that some oxidation numbers do not appear to be integers. This is not a problem because the reason becomes obvious when you analyze the compound thoroughly. For example, an important iron ore called magnetite has the formula $Fe_3O_4(s)$. Using the oxidation number rules, you can assign oxygen an oxidation number of −2 and calculate an oxidation number of $(+\frac{8}{3})$ for iron. When you analyze this compound more thoroughly, you determine that magnetite actually contains iron(III) ions and iron(II) ions in a 2:1 ratio. The formula for magnetite is sometimes written as $Fe_2O_3 \cdot FeO(s)$ to indicate that there are iron atoms with two different oxidation numbers present in the compound. The value of $(+\frac{8}{3})$ for the oxidation number of iron is an average value as shown:

$$\frac{2(\text{iron ions with oxidation number } +3) + 1(\text{iron ion with oxidation number } +2)}{3 \text{ iron ions}}$$

$$\frac{2(+3) + (+2)}{3} = +\frac{8}{3}$$

Now consider acetone, $H_6C_3O(\ell)$, a compound often found in nail polish remover. The oxidation number of each of the six hydrogen atoms is +1, and the oxidation number of the oxygen atom is −2. Acetone is a neutral molecule, so the oxidation numbers must add to zero. Let x be the average oxidation number of each of the three carbon atoms:

$$6(+1) + 3x + (-2) = 0$$
$$6 + 3x - 2 = 0$$
$$3x = -4$$
$$x = -\frac{4}{3}$$

Activity 9.1 | Using Lewis Structures to Assign Oxidation Numbers

You read that, for some compounds, the rules for assigning oxidation numbers give you only an average value for the oxidation numbers of atoms of a particular element. In some cases, you might want to know the oxidation number of each individual atom instead of an average value. Lewis structures can sometimes help you determine individual oxidation numbers. The two examples below show you the basic method for using Lewis structures to assign oxidation numbers.

Examples

	Chlorine molecule	Cyanide ion

1. Draw the Lewis structure of chlorine and cyanide.

2. Determine the electronegativities for each atom in your periodic table.

3. Circle the electrons that "belong" to each atom. Remember that the electrons in a bond belong to the atom with the largest electronegativity. For bonds between atoms of the same element, the electrons are shared equally between the atoms.

4. Count the valence electrons inside each circle.
   - chlorine atoms: 7 electrons each
   - carbon atom: 2 electrons
   - nitrogen atom: 8 electrons

5. Subtract the number of electrons in the circles from the number of valence electrons that the neutral atom would have. The answer is the oxidation number of the atom.
   - chlorine: $7 - 7 = 0$
   - The oxidation number of each chlorine atom is 0.
   - carbon: $+4 - 2 = +2$
   - The oxidation number of the carbon atom is $+2$.
   - nitrogen: $+5 - 8 = -3$
   - The oxidation number of the nitrogen atom is -3.

Procedure

Study the following example showing how to use Lewis structures to determine the oxidation numbers of each atom in acetone, $H_6C_3O(\ell)$. The structural formula for acetone is

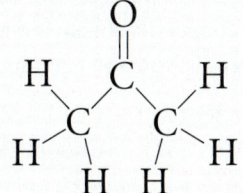

1. Draw the Lewis structure for acetone.

2. Determine and record the electronegativities of each atom.

3. Circle the electrons that "belong" to each atom.

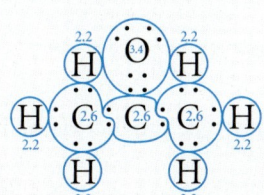

4. Count the electrons that are inside each circle.

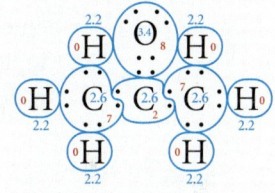

5. Subtract the number of electrons in the circle from the number of valence electrons for each neutral atom. These results are the oxidation numbers of the atoms.
   - all H atoms: $+1 - 0 = +1$
   - O atom: $+6 - 8 = -2$
   - central C atom: $+4 - 2 = +2$
   - two outer C atoms: $+4 - 7 = -3$

   Notice that the oxidation numbers of the carbon atoms are $+2, -3,$ and -3.

   The average is $\frac{+2 - 3 - 3}{3} = \frac{-4}{3}$, which agrees with the average value calculated on page 606.

Questions

1. Use Lewis structures and the rules for assigning oxidation numbers to determine the oxidation numbers of all atoms in the compounds below:
   a. methane, $CH_4(g)$
   b. carbon dioxide, $CO_2(g)$
   c. ammonium ion, $NH_4^+(g)$
   d. chloroform, $CHCl_3(\ell)$

Continued on next page

2. The following figures are a Lewis structure and a structural formula for glucose, $C_6H_{12}O_6$, in chain form. The structural formula is present to clarify the location of the bonds. Use the Lewis structure to determine the oxidation numbers of each atom in the glucose molecule.

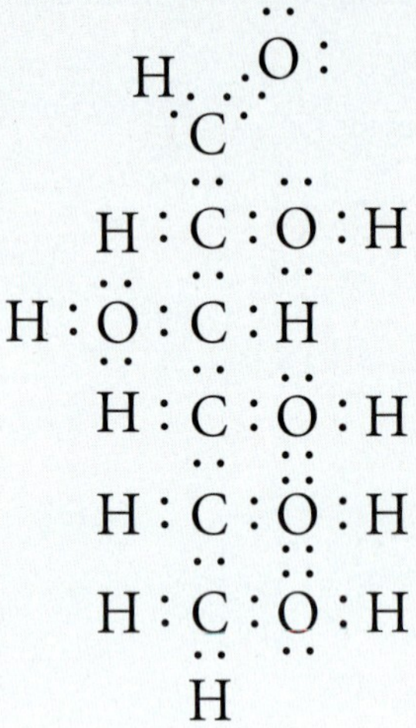

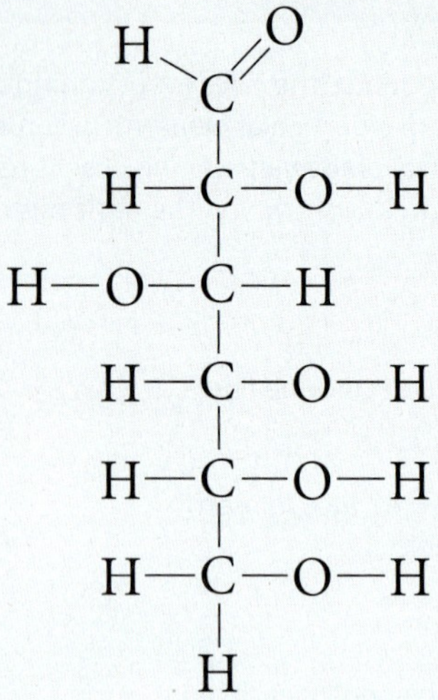

3. Describe what you can learn by using Lewis structures that you cannot determine by using the rules for assigning oxidation numbers listed in **Table 9.3**.

Applying Oxidation Numbers to Redox Reactions

You can use oxidation numbers to identify redox reactions and to identify the oxidizing and reducing agents. First, apply oxidation numbers to familiar equations to see how they can be used in more challenging equations.

The oxidation number for balancing equations can be applied to reactions involving ionic compounds as well as molecular compounds. You have seen that the single displacement reaction of zinc with copper(II) sulfate is a redox reaction, represented by the following complete balanced equation and net ionic equation:

$$Zn(s) + CuSO_4(aq) \rightarrow Cu(s) + ZnSO_4(aq)$$
$$Zn(s) + Cu^{2+}(aq) \rightarrow Cu(s) + Zn^{2+}(aq)$$

You can assign an oxidation number to each atom or ion in the net ionic equation, as follows:

- Solid Zn has an oxidation number of 0.
- Cu^{2+} has an oxidation number of +2.
- Solid Cu has an oxidation number of 0.
- Zn^{2+} has an oxidation number of +2.

Thus, there are changes in oxidation numbers in this reaction. The oxidation number of zinc increases, while the oxidation number of copper decreases:

oxidation number increases (loss of electrons)

$$\underset{0}{Zn} + \underset{+2}{Cu^{2+}} \rightarrow \underset{+2}{Zn^{2+}} + \underset{0}{Cu}$$

oxidation number decreases (gain of electrons)

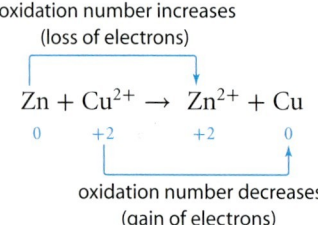

In the oxidation half-reaction, zinc undergoes an increase in its oxidation number from 0 to +2:

$$\underset{0}{Zn} \rightarrow \underset{+2}{Zn^{2+}} + 2e^-$$

In the reduction half-reaction, copper undergoes a decrease in its oxidation number from +2 to 0:

$$Cu^{2+} + 2e^- \rightarrow Cu$$
$$\phantom{Cu^{2+} + 2e^- \rightarrow} \text{+2} \text{0}$$

Therefore, you can describe redox reactions, oxidation, and reduction as follows. (See also **Figure 9.12**.)

- A *redox reaction* is a reaction in which the oxidation numbers of at least two atoms change.
- *Oxidation* is an increase in oxidation number.
- *Reduction* is a decrease in oxidation number.

You can also monitor changes in oxidation numbers in reactions that involve molecular compounds. For example, oxidation number changes occur in the reaction of hydrogen and oxygen to form water:

$$2H_2(g) + O_2(g) \rightarrow 2H_2O(\ell)$$
$$\ 0 \ 0 +1\ -2$$

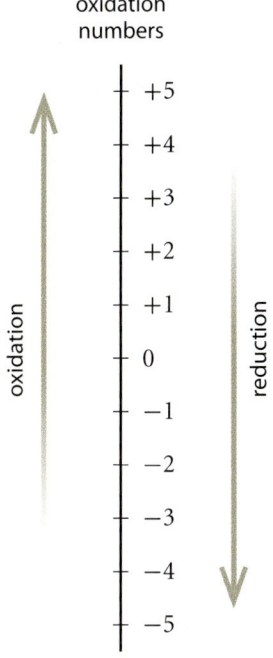

Figure 9.12 Oxidation and reduction are directly related to changes in oxidation numbers.

Because hydrogen combines with oxygen in this reaction, hydrogen undergoes oxidation, according to the original definition. Hydrogen also undergoes oxidation according to the modern definition, because the oxidation number of hydrogen increases from 0 to +1. Hydrogen is the reducing agent in this reaction. The oxygen undergoes reduction, because its oxidation number decreases from 0 to −2. Oxygen is the oxidizing agent in this reaction. The reaction is a redox reaction, because the oxidation numbers of three atoms—two hydrogen atoms and one oxygen atom—change.

The following Sample Problem illustrates how to use oxidation numbers to identify redox reactions, oxidizing agents, and reducing agents. You can practise using oxidation numbers to identify redox reactions, oxidizing agents, and reducing agents by working through the Practice Problems on page 611.

Sample Problem

Identifying Redox Reactions

Problem
Determine whether each of the following reactions is a redox reaction. For each redox reaction, identify the oxidizing agent and the reducing agent.

a. $CH_4(g) + Cl_2(g) \rightarrow CH_3Cl(g) + HCl(g)$
b. $CaCO_3(s) + 2HCl(aq) \rightarrow CaCl_2(aq) + H_2O(\ell) + CO_2(g)$
c. $3HNO_2(aq) \rightarrow HNO_3(aq) + 2NO(g) + H_2O(\ell)$

What Is Required?
You need to determine whether each chemical reaction, of the three that are given, is or is not a redox reaction.
For all reactions that are redox reactions, you need to identify the oxidizing agent and the reducing agent.

What Is Given?
You are given three balanced chemical equations.
You are given rules for assigning oxidation numbers in **Table 9.3**.

Continued on next page ▶

a. $CH_4(g) + Cl_2(g) \rightarrow CH_3Cl(g) + HCl(g)$

Plan Your Strategy	Act on Your Strategy
Apply the rules in **Table 9.3** to assign oxidation numbers to each atom in the equation.	$CH_4(g) + Cl_2(g) \rightarrow CH_3Cl(g) + HCl(g)$ ${-4+1}0{-2+1}\ {-1}{+1-1}$
Compare the oxidation numbers of the atoms of each element on both sides of the equation.	• The oxidation number of all hydrogen atoms is +1. • The oxidation number of carbon on the left side of the equation is −4 and on the right side of the equation is −2. • The oxidation number of chlorine atoms on the left side is 0 and on the right side is −1.
Determine whether the oxidation numbers of at least two atoms change during the reaction. If so, the reaction is a redox reaction. If oxidation numbers do not change, the reaction is not a redox reaction.	• The oxidation number of carbon changed from −4 to −2. • The oxidation number of chlorine changed from 0 to −1. • Therefore, the reaction is a redox reaction.
Determine which compound is the oxidizing agent by selecting the compound for which the oxidation number increased.	• The oxidation number of carbon increased from −4 to −2, which indicates that methane is oxidized. Therefore, chlorine is the oxidizing agent.
Determine which compound is the reducing agent by selecting the compound for which the oxidation number decreased.	• The oxidation number of chlorine decreased from 0 to −1, which indicates that chlorine is reduced. Therefore, methane is the reducing agent.

b. $CaCO_3(s) + 2HCl(aq) \rightarrow CaCl_2(aq) + H_2O(\ell) + CO_2(g)$

Plan Your Strategy	Act on Your Strategy
Apply the rules in **Table 9.3** to assign oxidation numbers to each atom in the equation. Because the reaction involves ionic compounds, you can simplify the process by writing the equation as a net ionic equation.	$CaCO_3(s) + 2H^+(aq) \rightarrow Ca^{2+}(aq) + H_2O(\ell) + CO_2(g)$ ${+2+4-2}{+1}{+2}\phantom{Ca^{2+}(aq)+}{+1\ -2}{+4-2}$
Compare the oxidation numbers of the atoms of each element on both sides of the equation.	• The oxidation number of all hydrogen atoms is +1. • The oxidation number of carbon is +4 on both sides of the equation. • The oxidation number of oxygen atoms on both sides of the equation is −2. • The oxidation number of calcium on both sides of the equation is +2.
Determine whether the oxidation numbers of at least two atoms change during the reaction. If so, the reaction is a redox reaction. If oxidation numbers do not change, the reaction is not a redox reaction.	• There was no change in any of the oxidation numbers. Therefore, the reaction is *not* a redox reaction.

c. $3HNO_2(aq) \rightarrow HNO_3(aq) + 2NO(g) + H_2O(\ell)$

Plan Your Strategy	Act on Your Strategy
Apply the rules in **Table 9.3** to assign oxidation numbers to each atom in the equation. Write the equation in ionic form. $3H^+(aq) + 3NO_2^-(aq) \rightarrow H^+(aq) + NO_3^-(aq) + 2NO(g) + H_2O(\ell)$ ${+1}{+3\ -2}{+1}{+5-2}{+2-2}{+1\ -2}$	
Compare the oxidation numbers of the atoms of each element on both sides of the equation.	• The oxidation number of all hydrogen atoms is +1. • The oxidation number of oxygen is −2 on both sides of the equation. • The oxidation number of all three nitrogen atoms on the left side of the equation is +3. • On the right side of the equation, one nitrogen atom has the oxidation number of +5 and the other two have an oxidation number of +2.

Plan Your Strategy	Act on Your Strategy
Determine whether the oxidation numbers of at least two atoms change during the reaction. If so, the reaction is a redox reaction. If oxidation numbers do not change, the reaction is *not* a redox reaction.	• The oxidation number of one nitrogen atom changed from +3 to +5. • The oxidation number of two other nitrogen atoms changed from +3 to +2. • Therefore, the reaction is a redox reaction.
Determine which compound is the oxidizing agent by selecting the compound for which the oxidation number increased.	• The oxidation number of one nitrogen atom increased from +3 to +5, indicating that it was oxidized. Therefore, nitrous acid is the reducing agent.
Determine which compound is the reducing agent by selecting the compound for which the oxidation number decreased.	• The oxidation number of two nitrogen atoms decreased from +3 to +2, indicating that they were reduced. Therefore, nitrous acid is also the oxidizing agent. • The reaction is a disproportionation reaction.

Check Your Solution

In every case, when one (or more) atom became oxidized, one (or more) other atom was reduced.

Practice Problems

Which of the reactions in questions 25-31 are redox reactions? Identify any disproportionation reactions. (**Hint:** Some of the oxidation numbers are averages.)

25. $2H_2(g) + O_2(g) \rightarrow 2H_2O(\ell)$

26. $PCl_3(\ell) + 3H_2O(\ell) \rightarrow H_3PO_3(aq) + 3HCl(aq)$

27. $2C_2H_6(g) + 7O_2(g) \rightarrow 4CO_2(g) + 6H_2O(\ell)$

28. $3NO_2(g) + H_2O(\ell) \rightarrow 2HNO_3(aq) + NO(g)$

29. $6HI(aq) + 2HMnO_4(aq) \rightarrow$
$3I_2(s) + 2MnO_2(s) + 4H_2O(\ell)$

30. $CH_3COOH(aq) + CH_3OH(aq) \rightarrow$
$CH_3COOCH_3(aq) + H_2O(\ell)$

31. $2NO_2(g) + 7H_2(g) \rightarrow 2NH_3(g) + 4H_2O(\ell)$

32. Identify the oxidizing agent and the reducing agent for the redox reaction(s) in questions 25 through 31.

33. For the following balanced net ionic equation, identify the reactant that undergoes oxidation and the reactant that undergoes reduction:

$Br_2(\ell) + 2ClO_2^-(aq) \rightarrow 2Br^-(aq) + 2ClO_2(aq)$

34. Nickel and copper ores usually contain the metals as sulfides, such as NiS(s) and Cu_2S(s). Does the extraction of these pure elemental metals from their ores involve redox reactions? Explain your reasoning.

Learning Check

19. How do oxidation numbers differ from numbers that are used to indicate charge?

20. What is the oxidation number of any pure element?

21. Under what circumstances does the oxidation number of an atom in a compound appear to be a fraction instead of an integer?

22. Write a general statement about the sum of the oxidation numbers for the atoms in a neutral molecule.

23. If the oxidation number of an atom increases during a reaction, what has happened to that atom?

24. In the reaction represented by the equation below, has the sulfur atom been oxidized or reduced? Explain your reasoning.

$$SO_3(g) + H_2O(\ell) \rightarrow H_2SO_4(aq)$$

Balancing Equations Using the Oxidation Number Method

Now that you know how to assign oxidation numbers to atoms in compounds and you can identify redox equations, you are ready to learn how to balance redox equations by using oxidation numbers. The critical step in balancing redox equations is to ensure that the total increase in the oxidation number of the oxidized element or elements equals the total decrease in the oxidation number of the reduced element or elements. This statement is the same as saying that the total number of electrons lost by the reducing agent must be the same as the total number of electrons gained by the oxidizing agent.

For example, the combustion of ammonia in oxygen produces nitrogen dioxide and water:

$$NH_3(g) + O_2(g) \rightarrow NO_2(g) + H_2O(\ell)$$
$${-3\ +1}{\ 0}{+4\ -2}{+1\ -2}$$

The oxidation number of nitrogen increases from -3 to $+4$, an increase of 7. The oxidation number of oxygen decreases from 0 to -2, a decrease of 2. Notice that there is one atom of nitrogen on the reactant side. Because the oxidation number of nitrogen increased by 7, you know that the nitrogen atom lost 7 electrons. Notice that there are two atoms of oxygen in the oxygen molecule on the reactant side. Because the oxidation number of the oxygen atoms decreased by 2, you know that each atom in the oxygen molecule gained 2 electrons, for a total of 4 electrons. You can then write the equation with lines connecting the oxidized and reduced atoms and write the number of electrons gained or lost above or below the lines, as shown in this unbalanced equation:

$$\overset{-7e^-}{NH_3(g) + O_2(g) \rightarrow NO_2(g) + H_2O(\ell)}$$
$$+4e^- \quad (2e^- \text{ per O atom})$$

Next, you balance the number of electrons gained and lost by determining the lowest common multiple of 7 and 4, which is 28. Multiply each number of electrons by the number that will bring it to the lowest common multiple, 28, as shown below:

$$4(-7e^-) = -28e^-$$
$$NH_3(g) + O_2(g) \rightarrow NO_2(g) + H_2O(\ell)$$
$$7(+4e^-) = +28e^-$$

Insert the numbers by which you multiplied the electrons as coefficients in front of the reactants in the equation.

$$4NH_3(g) + 7O_2(g) \rightarrow NO_2(g) + H_2O(\ell)$$

Finally, finish balancing the products side of the equation by inspection.

$$4NH_3(g) + 7O_2(g) \rightarrow 4NO_2(g) + 6H_2O(\ell)$$

This reaction was carried out under neutral conditions. In other cases, reactions are carried out under acidic or basic conditions. The following steps guide you through the oxidation number method of balancing equations under any of these conditions—neutral, acidic, or basic. A graphic organizer that outlines this same process is shown in **Figure 9.13** on page 615. Refer to these nine steps below and **Figure 9.13**, as necessary, as you work through the Sample Problem and Practice Problems that follow them.

Balancing Equations Using the Oxidation Number Method

Step 1 Write an unbalanced equation, if it is not given.

Step 2 Assign an oxidation number to each atom in the equation to determine whether it is a redox reaction.

Step 3 If the reaction is a redox reaction, identify the atom or atoms that undergo an increase in oxidation number and the atom or atoms that undergo a decrease in oxidation number.

Step 4 Determine the numerical values of the increase and the decrease in oxidation numbers.

Step 5 Determine the lowest common multiple of the number of electrons lost by the reducing agent (increase in oxidation number) and the number of electrons gained by the oxidizing agent (decrease in oxidation number).

Step 6 Apply the numbers determined in step 5 to balance the increase in oxidation number of one atom with the decrease in oxidation number of another atom.

Step 7 Balance the number of atoms of all elements by inspection unless the reaction takes place in an acidic or basic solution. If this is the case, balance everything except the hydrogen and oxygen atoms.

Step 8 For reactions that occur in an acidic solution, balance any oxygen atoms by adding water molecules. Then balance the hydrogen atoms by adding hydrogen ions.

Step 9 For reactions that occur in a basic solution, complete step 8, and then add hydroxide ions to both sides to neutralize the hydrogen ions. Cancel any water molecules that are on both sides of the equation.

Sample Problem

Balancing a Redox Equation for an Acidic Solution Using the Oxidation Number Method

Problem
The dichromate ion reacts with ethanol in an acidic solution to produce the chromium(III) ion and carbon dioxide. Write a balanced equation for the reaction using the oxidation number method.

What Is Required?
You must balance a redox equation for a reaction between a dichromate ion and ethanol, using the oxidation number method.

What Is Given?
You are given the reactants, dichromate and ethanol, and the products, chromium(III) and carbon dioxide.

You know that the reaction takes place in an acidic solution.

Plan Your Strategy	Act on Your Strategy
Step 1 Write an unbalanced equation from the given information.	$Cr_2O_7^{2-}(aq) + C_2H_5OH(aq) \rightarrow Cr^{3+}(aq) + CO_2(g)$
Step 2 Assign an oxidation number to each atom in the equation and determine whether it is a redox reaction.	$Cr_2O_7^{2-}(aq) + C_2H_5OH(aq) \rightarrow Cr^{3+}(aq) + CO_2(g)$ 　+6　−2　　−2 +1−2+1　　　+3　　　+4 −2 The oxidation numbers of chromium and carbon change during the reaction. It is a redox reaction.

Continued on next page

Plan Your Strategy	Act on Your Strategy
Step 3 Identify the atom or atoms that undergo an increase in oxidation number and the atom or atoms that undergo a decrease in oxidation number.	The oxidation number of chromium decreases from +6 to +3; therefore, it is reduced in the reaction. The oxidation number of carbon increases from an average of −2 to +4; thus, it is oxidized.
Step 4 Determine the numerical values of the increase and decrease in oxidation numbers. Write the numbers on arrows between the atom in the reactants and the atom in the products.	The oxidation number of chromium increases by 3 and the oxidation number of carbon decreases by 6, on the average. $+3e^-$ (from Cr in $Cr_2O_7^{2-}$ to Cr^{3+}) $Cr_2O_7^{2-}(aq) + C_2H_5OH(aq) \rightarrow Cr^{3+}(aq) + CO_2(g)$ $-6e^-$ (from C in C_2H_5OH to CO_2)
Step 5 Determine the lowest common multiple of the increase in oxidation number and the decrease in oxidation number.	The lowest common multiple of 3 and 6 is 6.
Step 6 Use the numbers you determined in step 5 to balance the increase in oxidation number (electrons added) of one element with the decrease in oxidation number (electrons lost) of the other element.	Multiply 3 by 2 and multiply 6 by 1 to equal 6. Give dichromate a coefficient of 2 and ethanol a coefficient of 1. $2(+3e^-)$ $2Cr_2O_7^{2-}(aq) + 1C_2H_5OH(aq) \rightarrow Cr^{3+}(aq) + CO_2(g)$ $1(-6e^-)$
Step 7 Balance the number of atoms of all elements by inspection, unless the reaction takes place in an acidic or basic solution. If this is the case, do not balance the hydrogen and oxygen atoms.	The reaction takes place in an acidic solution, so balance only the chromium and carbon atoms. There are 4 chromium atoms and 2 carbon atoms on the left side. Give chromium a coefficient of 4 and carbon a coefficient of 2 on the right side. $2Cr_2O_7^{2-}(aq) + 1C_2H_5OH(aq) \rightarrow 4Cr^{3+}(aq) + 2CO_2(g)$
Steps 8 and 9 For reactions that occur in acidic or basic solutions, include water molecules, hydrogen ions, or hydroxide ions as needed, to balance the equation. There are 15 oxygen atoms on the left side and 4 on the right side. Add 11 water molecules to the right side to balance the oxygen atoms. There are now 22 hydrogen atoms on the right side and 6 on the left side. Add 16 hydrogen ions to the left side to balance the hydrogen atoms. $16H^+(aq) + 2Cr_2O_7^{2-}(aq) + C_2H_5OH(aq) \rightarrow 4Cr^{3+}(aq) + 2CO_2(g) + 11H_2O(\ell)$	

Check Your Solution

Atoms of all of the elements are balanced. The total charge on the left side is $+16 + 2(-2) = +12$. The total charge on the right side is $4(+3) = +12$. The charge is balanced. There are hydrogen ions on the left side, in agreement with the solution being acidic. You are not given information about the spectator ions, so they are not included.

Practice Problems

35. Use the oxidation number method to balance the following equation for the combustion of carbon disulfide:

$$CS_2(g) + O_2(g) \rightarrow CO_2(g) + SO_2(g)$$

Use the oxidation number method to balance the following equations:

36. $B_2O_3(aq) + Mg(s) \rightarrow MgO(s) + Mg_3B_2(aq)$

37. $H_2S(g) + H_2O_2(aq) \rightarrow S_8(s) + H_2O(\ell)$

38. $ClO_2(aq) + SbO_2^-(aq) \rightarrow ClO_2^-(aq) + Sb(OH)_6^-(aq)$

Use the oxidation number method to balance each ionic equation in an acidic solution:

39. $Cr_2O_7^{2-}(aq) + Fe^{2+}(aq) \rightarrow Cr^{3+}(aq) + Fe^{3+}(aq)$

40. $I_2(g) + NO_3^-(aq) \rightarrow IO_3^-(aq) + NO_2(g)$

41. $PbSO_4(aq) \rightarrow Pb(s) + PbO_2(aq) + SO_4^{2-}(aq)$

Use the oxidation number method to balance each ionic equation in a basic solution:

42. $Cl^-(aq) + CrO_4^{2-}(aq) \rightarrow ClO^-(aq) + CrO_2^-(aq)$

43. $Ni(s) + MnO_4^-(aq) \rightarrow NiO(s) + MnO_2(s)$

44. $I^-(aq) + Ce^{4+}(aq) \rightarrow IO_3^-(aq) + Ce^{3+}(aq)$

The Oxidation Number Method for Balancing Redox Equations

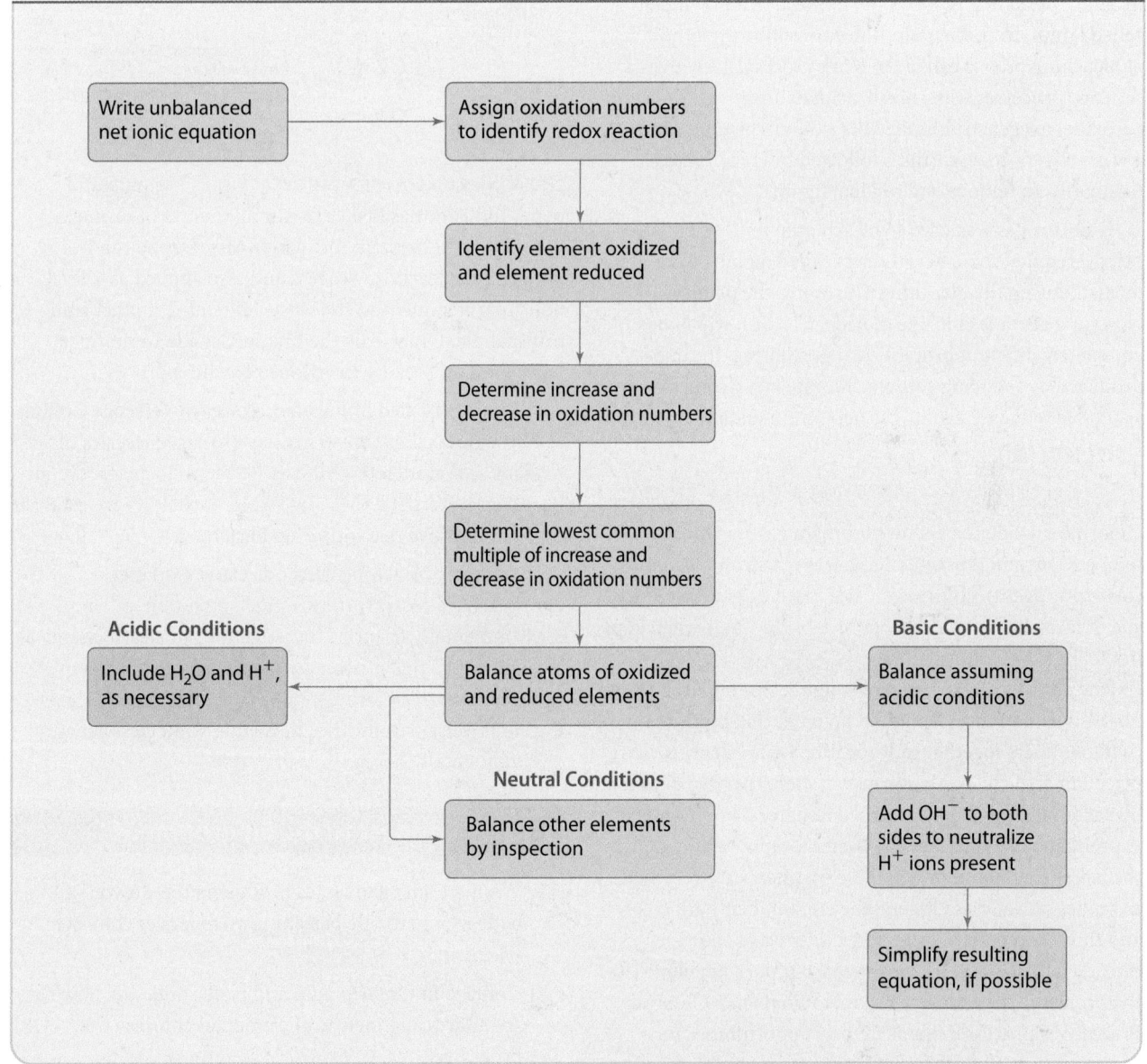

Figure 9.13 This graphic organizer outlines the steps for balancing redox equations using the oxidation number method.

STSE
CHEMISTRY Connections

How Green Is White Paper?

Wood pulp that is to be used for making paper is usually bleached not only to make it white but to make it more durable. The North American Paper Industry is enormous, producing 45–55 million tonnes of paper every year, about half of which is bleached. Canada produces 29% of the world's wood pulp and 49% of its newsprint. In Ontario, tree species commonly harvested to produce pulp include spruce, pine, and poplar.

BLEACHING PULP Bleaching not only whitens but also improves absorption, softness, flexibility, and resistance to aging. Bleaching involves the removal of a polymer, called lignin, from the pulp. The conventional method of bleaching pulp is called the Kraft process. It involves a series of processes using alkali, acid, hydrogen and sodium peroxide, oxygen, dithionite salts, sodium bisulfite, and a wash water process. This is followed by chlorinating treatments to remove any residual lignin.

Chlorine gas was used to bleach pulp until scientists discovered that toxic by-products called dioxins were formed during the bleaching. Currently, the primary bleaching agent is chlorine dioxide, $ClO_2(g)$, which has completely different properties than chlorine. It can be produced by reducing sodium chlorate in a strong acid with a suitable reducing agent. The net ionic equation is

$$2ClO_3^-(aq) + 2Cl^-(aq) + 4H^+(aq) \rightarrow 2ClO_2(g) + Cl_2(g) + 2H_2O(\ell)$$

Chlorine dioxide is a yellow-to-brown gas at standard temperature and pressure. Because it is a strong oxidant (oxidizing agent), chlorine dioxide must be generated on site. It is explosive as a gas, but is stable in water when kept in the dark.

The chlorine dioxide removes lignin from the cellulose fibers in wood pulp. Lignin is a polymer that binds the cellulose fibers together in wood. The lignin fragments are placed in artificial oxidation lakes, where they are digested by bacteria before being returned to natural bodies of water. A problem arises because the bacteria cannot easily digest the larger fragments. When these fragments are returned to bodies of water as effluent, they retain their dark color and thus stain natural waterways. The use of chlorine dioxide in place of chlorine lessens, but does not eliminate, the problem. The industry's move to Elemental Chlorine Free (ECF) processes opens up new opportunities for biotechnology and other competing technologies.

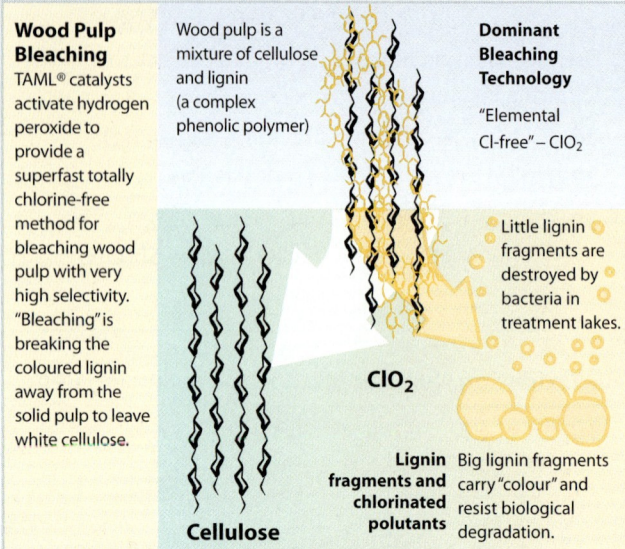

Wood Pulp Bleaching
TAML® catalysts activate hydrogen peroxide to provide a superfast totally chlorine-free method for bleaching wood pulp with very high selectivity. "Bleaching" is breaking the coloured lignin away from the solid pulp to leave white cellulose.

Wood pulp is a mixture of cellulose and lignin (a complex phenolic polymer)

Dominant Bleaching Technology
"Elemental Cl-free" – ClO_2

Little lignin fragments are destroyed by bacteria in treatment lakes.

Cellulose

ClO_2

Lignin fragments and chlorinated polutants
Big lignin fragments carry "colour" and resist biological degradation.

ENVIRONMENTALLY FRIENDLY BLEACHING The pulp and paper industry has been examining the use of ozone, a very powerful oxidant, for many years. Ozone can be used in the bleaching process and also applied as a final polishing treatment to the waste effluent. Domtar's mill in Espanola, Ontario, is the first in Canada to produce hardwood pulp using the ozone bleaching process.

Work performed in the laboratories of Terrence Collins at Carnegie Mellon University has produced a series of oxidant activators referred to as "tetraamido-macrocyclic ligand activators" (TAML™). TAML™ catalysts are catalysts that can improve peroxide pulp bleaching.

Enzymatic bleaching methods using oxidative enzymes have recently drawn much attention as being environmentally friendly. Investigations in electrochemical bleaching take this process further by replacing enzymes as oxidants with electrodes. Ultimately this research may lead to novel, cost-effective, bleaching strategies that are environmentally benign.

Connect to the Environment

1. What are some advantages of using the TAML™ / hydrogen peroxide bleaching system over chlorine systems?

2. Contact an Ontario pulp and paper mill. Ask how they are addressing the use of elemental chlorine free (ECF) processes.

Section 9.3 Review

Section Summary

- Some redox equations cannot be written as half-reactions. You can use the method of oxidation numbers to balance these equations.
- An oxidation number of an atom in a compound is the charge that the atom would have if, instead of sharing electrons, the electrons were held by the atom with the greatest electronegativity.
- You can assign oxidation numbers by following a set of rules. Sometimes the rules lead to fractional oxidation numbers.
- An increase in the oxidation number of an atom in a reaction indicates a loss of electrons. A decrease in the oxidation number of an atom in a reaction indicates a gain of electrons.
- You can balance an equation by determining the coefficients that make the number of electrons lost by one atom of one element equal to the number of electrons gained by atoms of another element. You then balance the rest of the equation by inspection.

Review Questions

1. **K/U** Explain why fluorine has an oxidation number of −1 in all its compounds other than fluorine gas, $F_2(g)$.

2. **K/U** Determine the oxidation number of manganese (Mn) in each of the following:
   a. manganese dioxide
   b. Mn_2O_7
   c. MnO_4^{2-}
   d. potassium permanganate

3. **C** Clearly identify and describe, using examples, the different oxidation numbers that an atom of oxygen can be assigned.

4. **T/I** Determine whether each of the following reactions is a redox reaction:
   a. $H_2(g) + I_2(s) \rightarrow 2HI(aq)$
   b. $2NaHCO_3(aq) \rightarrow Na_2CO_3(aq) + H_2O(\ell) + CO_2(g)$
   c. $2HBr(aq) + Ca(OH)_2(s) \rightarrow CaBr_2(aq) + 2H_2O(\ell)$
   d. $PCl_5(\ell) \rightarrow PCl_3(\ell) + Cl_2(g)$

5. **C** Write three different definitions for a redox reaction.

6. **K/U** When atoms of one element combine with atoms of another element, is the reaction a redox reaction? Explain your answer.

7. **K/U** Explain why, in redox reactions, the total increase in the oxidation numbers of the oxidized elements must equal the total decrease in the oxidation numbers of the reduced elements.

8. **T/I** The combustion of ammonia in oxygen to form nitrogen dioxide and water vapour involves molecular compounds in the gaseous phase. Use the oxidation number method for balancing the equation.

9. **A** Apply your knowledge of oxidation number rules. Questions 9 b-d refer to Activity 9.1.
   a. Determine the oxidation number of sulfur in a thiosulfate ion, $S_2O_3^{2-}(aq)$.
   b. The Lewis structure of a thiosulfate ion is given here. Use the Lewis structure to determine the oxidation number of each sulfur atom.

   $$\left[\begin{array}{c} \ddot{\underset{\cdot\cdot}{O}} \\ \ddot{\underset{\cdot\cdot}{O}} : \ddot{\underset{\cdot\cdot}{S}} : \ddot{\underset{\cdot\cdot}{S}} : \\ \ddot{\underset{\cdot\cdot}{O}} \end{array} \right]^{2-}$$

   c. Compare your results from questions 9a and 9b and explain any differences.
   d. What are the advantages and disadvantages of using Lewis structures to assign oxidation numbers?
   e. What are the advantages and disadvantages of using the oxidation number rules to assign oxidation numbers?

10. **T/I** Balance each equation by the method of your choice. Explain your choice of method in each case.
    a. $CH_3COOH(aq) + O_2(g) \rightarrow CO_2(g) + H_2O(\ell)$
    b. $O_2(g) + H_2SO_4(aq) \rightarrow HSO_4^-(aq)$ (acidic conditions)

11. **T/I** Use the oxidation number method to balance the following equations for neutral conditions:
    a. $NH_3(g) + Cl_2(g) \rightarrow NH_4Cl(aq) + N_2(g)$
    b. $Mn_3O_4(aq) + Al(s) \rightarrow Al_2O_3(aq) + Mn(s)$

12. **C** Explain what oxidation numbers are to a student who is not studying electrochemistry.

Inquiry INVESTIGATION 9-A

Skill Check

Initiating and Planning
✓ Performing and Recording
✓ Analyzing and Interpreting
✓ Communicating

Testing Relative Oxidizing and Reducing Strengths of Metal Atoms and Ions

By observing whether reactions occur between solid metals and metal ions in solution, you can determine the order of oxidizing and reducing agents according to strength.

Pre-Lab Questions

1. Define the following: oxidizing agent, reducing agent, complete ionic equation, and net ionic equation.
2. Define oxidation and reduction.
3. Explain how you would identify the oxidizing and reducing agents by analyzing a chemical equation.
4. What might you observe that indicates a chemical reaction has occurred?

Question

How can the presence or absence of a reaction provide information about the relative strength of oxidizing and reducing agents?

Safety Precautions

- Wear safety eyewear throughout this investigation.
- Tie back loose hair and clothing.
- Wear a lab coat or apron throughout this investigation.
- If you get any of the solutions in your eyes or on your skin, flush with plenty of water. Inform your teacher immediately.
- Wash your hands when you have completed the investigation.

Materials

- 4 small pieces of each of the following metals:
  - aluminum foil
  - thin copper wire or tiny copper beads
  - iron filings
  - magnesium
  - zinc
- dropper bottles containing dilute solutions of
  - aluminum sulfate
  - copper(II) sulfate
  - iron(II) sulfate
  - magnesium sulfate
  - zinc nitrate
- well plate
- white paper
- small test tube (optional)

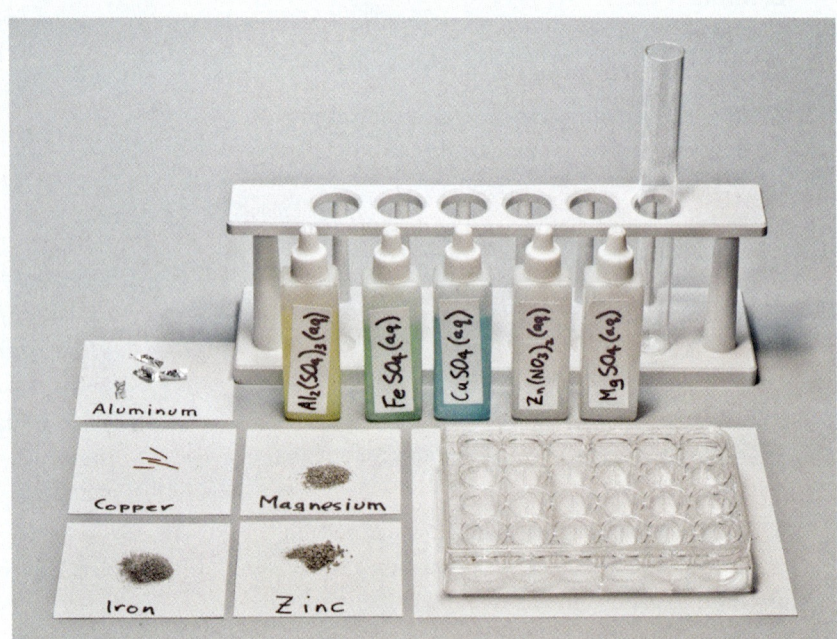

Procedure

1. Place the well plate on a piece of white paper. Label the paper to match the data table below.

Metal \ Compound	$Al_2(SO_4)_3$(aq)	$CuSO_4$(aq)	$FeSO_4$(aq)	$MgSO_4$(aq)	$Zn(NO_3)_2$(aq)
Al(s)					
Cu(s)					
Fe(s)					
Mg(s)					
Zn(s)					

2. Place the four small pieces of each metal, about the size of a grain of rice, into the well plate. Use the data table as a guide for placement of the metals. Cover each piece of metal with a few drops of the appropriate solution. Wait 3 to 5 min to observe whether a reaction occurs.

3. Look for evidence of a chemical reaction in each mixture. Record the results by using a "y" for a reaction and an "n" for no reaction. If you are unsure, repeat the process on a larger scale in a small test tube.

4. Discard the mixtures into the waste beaker supplied by your teacher. Do not pour anything down the drain.

Analyze and Interpret

1. For each single displacement reaction that proceeded spontaneously, write
   a. a complete balanced equation.
   b. an ionic equation.
   c. a net ionic equation.
2. Identify the oxidizing agent and the reducing agent in each of the reactions that proceeded spontaneously.

3. Make a simple redox table similar to **Table 9.1** that contains all the metal atoms and metal ions that you analyzed in this investigation. Note that the ion that was able to oxidize all other metal atoms is placed at the top of the left column. In the next row, place the ion that oxidized all but the first metal atom. Complete the table.

Conclude and Communicate

4. Based on your observations, do you think that there are any properties of metal atoms or ions that would allow a chemist to predict whether one would be a better oxidizing or reducing agent than another? Explain your reasoning.

Extend Further

5. **INQUIRY** Solutions of $NiSO_4$(aq), $Al_2(SO_4)_3$(aq), $CoSO_4$(aq), and $SnSO_4$(aq) are in bottles labelled A, B, C, and D.
   a. Design an experiment to identify which ionic sulfate solution is in which bottle. Give a list of equipment and chemicals required. Describe a step-by-step procedure for conducting the experiment.
   b. Explain why an activity series is required to identify each unknown solution.

6. **RESEARCH** Lithium, potassium, barium, calcium, and sodium react with cold water to produce hydrogen gas and the corresponding metal hydroxide solution. Lithium reacts with water slowly, while potassium reacts violently with water. Conduct research to determine why lithium, rather than potassium, is the most active metal and is at the top of the activity series of metals.

Inquiry INVESTIGATION 9-B

Skill Check

- Initiating and Planning
- ✓ Performing and Recording
- ✓ Analyzing and Interpreting
- ✓ Communicating

Safety Precautions

- Wear safety eyewear throughout this investigation.
- Tie back loose hair and clothing.
- Use EXTREME CAUTION when you are near an open flame.
- Wear a lab coat or apron throughout this investigation.
- Hydrochloric acid and sulfuric acid are corrosive. If you get any acid in your eyes or on your skin, flush with plenty of water. Inform your teacher immediately.
- Before lighting a Bunsen burner or candle, make sure that there are no flammable liquids in the laboratory.
- Wash your hands when you have completed the investigation.

Materials

- small pieces of each of the following metals:
  - magnesium
  - zinc
  - copper
  - aluminum
- 1 mol/L hydrochloric acid
- 1 mol/L sulfuric acid
- well plate
- 4 small test tubes
- test-tube rack
- Bunsen burner secured to a utility stand
- candle

Redox Reactions and Balanced Equations

You have practised balancing equations for redox reactions, but can you predict the products of a redox reaction? Can you determine whether a reaction has occurred and, if so, whether it was a redox reaction? In this investigation, you will develop these skills.

Pre-Lab Questions

1. In this experiment, what might you observe that indicates that a chemical reaction has occurred? State at least two possibilities.
2. What is responsible for the yellow colour in a candle flame?
3. List two safety precautions that you must take when working with an open flame in a laboratory.
4. What safety precautions must you take when you are working with a strong acid? What could happen if you did not take these precautions?

Question

How can you tell whether a redox reaction occurs when reactants are mixed? Can you observe the transfer of electrons in the mixture?

Predictions

- Predict which metals of magnesium, zinc, copper, and aluminum can be oxidized by aqueous hydrogen ions (acidic solution). Explain your reasoning.
- Predict whether metals that cannot be oxidized by hydrogen ions can be dissolved in acids. Explain your reasoning.
- Predict whether the combustion of a hydrocarbon is a redox reaction. What assumptions have you made about the products?

Procedure

Part 1: Reactions of Acids with Metals

1. Place one small piece of each metal into a well on the well plate. Add a few drops of hydrochloric acid to each metal. Record your observations. If you are unsure of your observations, repeat the procedure on a larger scale in a small test tube.
2. Place another small piece of each metal into clean sections of the well plate. Add a few drops of sulfuric acid to each metal. Record your observations. If you are unsure of your observations, repeat the procedure on a larger scale in a small test tube.
3. Dispose of the chemicals as directed by your teacher.

Part 2: Combustion of Hydrocarbons

4. Light a Bunsen burner and observe the combustion of natural gas. Adjust the colour of the flame by varying the quantity of oxygen admitted to the burner. Describe how the colour depends on the quantity of oxygen.

620 MHR • Unit 5 Electrochemistry

5. Light a candle and observe its combustion. Compare the colour of the flame with the colour of the Bunsen burner's flame. Which adjustment of the burner makes the colours of the two flames most similar?

Analyze and Interpret

Part 1 Reactions of Acids with Metals

1. Write a complete balanced equation for each of the reactions of an acid with a metal.
2. Write each equation from question 1 in net ionic form.
3. Determine which of the reactions from question 1 are redox reactions.
4. Write each redox reaction from question 3 as two half-reactions.
5. Describe and explain any trends that you see in your answers to question 4.
6. In the reactions you observed, are the hydrogen ions acting as an oxidizing agent, a reducing agent, or neither?
7. Write a balanced chemical equation for the neutralization reaction of hydrochloric acid and sodium hydroxide. Use the equation to help determine whether the hydrogen ions behave in the same way as you described in question 6. Explain your answer.
8. Your teacher might demonstrate the reaction of copper with concentrated nitric acid to produce copper(II) ions and brown, toxic nitrogen dioxide gas. Write a balanced net ionic equation for this reaction. Do the hydrogen ions behave in the same way as you described in question 7? Identify the oxidizing agent and the reducing agent in this reaction.
9. From your observations of the reaction of copper with hydrochloric acid in your investigation and the reaction of copper with nitric acid in the demonstration described above, can you tell whether hydrogen ions or nitrate ions are the better oxidizing agent? Explain your reasoning.

Part 2 Combustion of Hydrocarbons

10. The main component of natural gas is methane, $CH_4(g)$. The products of the combustion of this gas in a Bunsen burner depend on how the burner is adjusted. A blue flame indicates complete combustion. What are the products of complete combustion? Write a balanced chemical equation for this reaction.
11. A yellow or orange flame from a Bunsen burner indicates incomplete combustion and the presence of carbon in the flame. Write a balanced chemical equation for this reaction.
12. Name another possible carbon-containing product from the incomplete combustion of methane. Write a balanced chemical equation for this reaction.
13. Assume that the fuel in the burning candle is paraffin. Although paraffin is a mixture of hydrocarbons, you can represent it by the formula $C_{25}H_{52}$. Write a balanced chemical equation for the complete combustion of paraffin.
14. Write two different balanced equations that both represent a form of incomplete combustion of paraffin.
15. How do you know that at least one of the incomplete combustion reactions is taking place when a candle burns?
16. Are combustion reactions also redox reactions? Does your answer depend on whether the combustion is complete or incomplete? Explain your answer.

Conclude and Communicate

17. How could you tell whether a redox reaction occurred when the reactants were mixed? Could you observe the transfer of electrons in the mixture?

Extend Further

18. **INQUIRY** Natural gas, the same gas that you observed burning in Bunsen burners, is burned in gas furnaces. What products of incomplete combustion are toxic to people? What observations that you made in your investigation could you apply to the safe operation of gas furnaces? Discuss one way to ensure that a gas furnace burns safely.

19. **RESEARCH** Gold is very unreactive and does not dissolve in most acids. However, it does appear to dissolve in aqua regia (Latin for "royal water"), which is a mixture of concentrated hydrochloric acid and nitric acid. It does not really dissolve but, instead, reacts with the ions in the solution. The unbalanced ionic equation for the reaction is as follows:

$Au(s) + NO_3^-(aq) + Cl^-(aq) \rightarrow AuCl_4^-(s) + NO_2(g)$

Balance the equation, and identify the oxidizing agent and reducing agent.

Carry out research to find out how Niels Bohr used acid to protect the Nobel award medals for two friends during World War II.

ThoughtLab INVESTIGATION 9-C

Skill Check
- Initiating and Planning
- ✓ Performing and Recording
- ✓ Analyzing and Interpreting
- ✓ Communicating

Materials

access to the Internet

Assessing Antioxidant Supplements

Oxidation-reduction reactions play an important role in the body. Cellular respiration, for example, involves the oxidation of glucose by oxygen. However, these reactions can sometimes lead to the production of free radicals, which are characterized by the presence of one or more unpaired electrons. Because they are so reactive, free radicals can oxidize surrounding molecules. This oxidation can damage DNA, proteins, and other macromolecules. Such damage may contribute to aging and to cardiovascular disease, cataracts, and cancer.

Antioxidants are a class of compounds that remove potentially harmful oxidizing agents from the body. In recent years, antioxidant supplements have been promoted commercially as an effective way to improve human health.

Pre-Lab Questions

1. In terms of electron loss or gain, define an oxidant. In terms of electron loss or gain, define an antioxidant.
2. Provide a simple example of a free radical.
3. Explain why an antioxidant is a reducing agent.

Question

Do over-the-counter antioxidant supplements have a positive effect on human health?

Organize the Data

Conduct research into an antioxidant supplement of your choice.

1. Draw the molecular structure of the antioxidant supplement. For carotenoids and polyphenolic antioxidants, which describe a family of compounds, focus on one specific compound.
2. What are the (purported) benefits of the antioxidant as claimed by the manufacturer?

Analyze and Interpret

1. Summarize some key findings on the efficacy of the antioxidant supplement.
2. What is the annual cost of taking the antioxidant supplement at the recommended dosage? Perform a cost-benefit analysis related to the antioxidant supplement.

Conclude and Communicate

3. Would you recommend the use of the antioxidant supplement by a specific group of people—seniors, for example—or by people who have a particular disease? Explain your answer.

Many fruits and vegetables are rich in antioxidant compounds.

Examples of Over-the-counter Antioxidants
vitamin C
vitamin A
vitamin E
melatonin
carotenoids
glutathione
polyphenolic antioxidants

Extend Further

4. **INQUIRY** Suppose a company has just produced an antioxidant supplement that it claims can decrease the harmful effects of long-term cigarette smoking. Design an investigation to test this claim.
5. **RESEARCH** How much money do Canadians spend each year on antioxidant supplements? How has this amount changed over time?

Chapter 9 SUMMARY

Section 9.1 Characterizing Oxidation and Reduction

An atom or molecule is oxidized if it loses electrons and is reduced if it gains electrons. If an atom or molecule is oxidized in a chemical reaction, another atom or molecule must be reduced. Oxidation-reduction tables allow you to predict whether a redox reaction will be spontaneous.

Key Terms
ionic equation
net ionic equation
oxidation
oxidation-reduction reaction
oxidizing agent
redox reaction
reducing agent
reduction
spectator ions

Key Concepts
- In the past, oxidation referred to any reaction involving molecular oxygen. The modern definition of oxidation, however, is the loss of electrons.
- In the past, reduction referred to the extraction of metals from their ores. The modern definition of reduction, however, is the gain of electrons.
- Reactions in which electrons are gained by one atom or ion and lost by another atom or ion are called oxidation-reduction reactions. (abbreviated to the term *redox reactions*).
- If one atom is oxidized in a reaction, then another atom must be reduced.
- An oxidizing agent accepts electrons from another compound and becomes reduced. A reducing agent donates electrons to another compound and becomes oxidized.
- You can determine experimentally whether one element is a stronger reducing agent or a stronger oxidizing agent than the other. From accumulated data, you can predict whether a given reaction will proceed spontaneously.

Section 9.2 Redox Reactions Involving Ionic Compounds

Equations for redox reactions involving ionic compounds can be separated into an oxidation half-reaction and a reduction half-reaction. There are rules that allow you to balance a chemical equation using half-reactions. The smelting and refining of ores involves oxidation and reduction reactions.

Key Terms
disproportionation reaction
half-reaction
refining
smelting

Key Concepts
- Oxidation half-reactions include only those atoms that become oxidized in a redox reaction.
- Reduction half-reactions include only those atoms that become reduced in a redox reaction.
- You can use a set of rules to balance oxidation and reduction half-reactions. You can then add the half-reactions to obtain a balanced redox reaction.
- In a disproportionation reaction, one or more atoms of an element are oxidized and one or more atoms of the same element are reduced in the same reaction.
- Iron ore is reduced in a series of reactions involving carbon monoxide to form pig iron. Pig iron is refined by oxidizing the impurities and reacting them with calcium oxide to form a liquid that floats on the molten iron.

Section 9.3 Redox Reactions Involving Molecular Compounds

Oxidation numbers can be assigned to all atoms in a molecule or compound by applying a set of rules. You can balance chemical equations involving molecular compounds by assigning oxidation numbers to all atoms and then following the set of rules.

Key Term
oxidation number

Key Concepts
- Some redox equations cannot be written as half-reactions. You can use the method of oxidation numbers to balance these equations.
- An oxidation number of an atom in a compound is the charge that the atom would have if, instead of sharing electrons, the electrons were held by the atom having the greatest electronegativity.
- You can assign oxidation numbers by following a set of rules. Sometimes the rules lead to fractional oxidation numbers.
- An increase in the oxidation number of an atom in a reaction indicates a loss of electrons. A decrease in the oxidation number of an atom in a reaction indicates a gain of electrons.
- You can balance an equation by determining the coefficients that make the number of electrons lost by one atom of one element equal to the number of electrons gained by atoms of another element. You then balance the rest of the equation by inspection.

Chapter 9 REVIEW

Knowledge and Understanding

Select the letter of the best answer below.

1. In any balanced redox reaction, the total number of electrons gained by an atom, molecule, or ion must be equal to the total number of electrons lost by another atom, molecule, or ion. This is because electrons
   a. always require a place to go.
   b. are repelled by each other, and so are being forced to go somewhere.
   c. exist in pairs to help form bonds in molecules or ions.
   d. do not exist on their own anywhere.
   e. cannot exist free in solution.

2. "All single displacement reactions of the form A + BX → AX + B are redox reactions." This statement is
   a. always true.
   b. always false.
   c. only true if a metal displaces a metal.
   d. only true if a non-metal displaces a non-metal.
   e. only true if a metal displaces a non-metal.

3. Which of the following statements about the given reaction is correct?
   $Ca(s) + Br_2(\ell) \rightarrow Ca^{2+}(aq) + 2Br^-(aq)$
   a. Ca(s) is the oxidizing agent and $Br_2(\ell)$ is the reducing agent.
   b. $Br_2(\ell)$ is the oxidizing agent and Ca(s) is the reducing agent.
   c. Ca(s) is the oxidizing agent and Ca^{2+}(aq) is the reducing agent.
   d. $Br_2(\ell)$ is the oxidizing agent and $2Br^-$(aq) is the reducing agent.
   e. This is not a redox reaction, so there is no oxidizing agent or reducing agent.

4. Which of the following reactions is an example of a redox reaction?
   a. $CaO(s) + H_2O(\ell) \rightarrow Ca(OH)_2(aq)$
   b. $CuCl_2(aq) + Mg(s) \rightarrow MgCl_2(aq) + Cu(s)$
   c. $3Pb(NO_3)_2(aq) + 2AlCl_3(aq) \rightarrow 2Al(NO_3)_3(aq) + 2PbCl_2(aq)$
   d. $Ag^+(aq) + Cl^-(aq) \rightarrow AgCl(s)$
   e. These are all examples of redox reactions.

5. Which of the following reactions is an example of a disproportionation reaction?
   a. $CaCl_2(aq) + H_2CO_3(aq) \rightarrow CaCO_3(aq) + 2HCl(aq)$
   b. $Mg^{2+}(aq) + Cu(s) \rightarrow Cu^{2+}(aq) + Mg(s)$
   c. $Cu_2O(aq) + H_2SO_4(aq) \rightarrow Cu(s) + CuSO_4(aq) + H_2O(\ell)$
   d. $CH_4(g) + 2O_2(g) \rightarrow CO_2(g) + 2H_2O(g)$
   e. $Pb(s) + PbO_2(s) + H_2SO_4(aq) \rightarrow 2PbSO_4(s) + 2H_2O(\ell)$

6. In which of the following does the nitrogen have an oxidation number of +4?
   a. N_2O_5
   b. N_2
   c. N_2O_4
   d. NO_3
   e. NO_3^-

7. Chlorine has an oxidation number of −1 in all of the following *except*
   a. chloride ions
   b. HCl(aq)
   c. $MgCl_2$(aq)
   d. CCl_4(aq)
   e. ClO_2(aq)

8. Combustion reactions are redox reactions. This statement is
   a. always true.
   b. never true.
   c. often true.
   d. true only when a precipitate forms.
   e. true only when a gas forms.

9. Which of the following is the strongest oxidizing agent?
   a. hydrogen
   b. oxygen
   c. fluorine
   d. chlorine
   e. bromine

10. The oxidation number of an atom in a molecule or complex ion is equal to the charge that the atom would have if all bonds were to be considered ionic and the electrons were held by the more electronegative element. This statement is
    a. always true.
    b. always false.
    c. only true for ionic compounds.
    d. only true for complex ions.
    e. only true for molecular compounds.

11. Aluminum metal spontaneously reduces aqueous iron(III) ions to iron metal. Sodium metal spontaneously reduces aqueous aluminum ions to aluminum metal. Based on these statements, what is the correct order of the relative strengths of Na, Fe, and Al as reducing agents?
   a. Al > Fe > Na
   b. Fe > Na > Al
   c. Na > Fe > Al
   d. Fe > Al > Na
   e. Na > Al > Fe

12. In the half-reaction $Ag_2O(s) + H_2O(\ell) + 2e^- \rightarrow 2Ag(s) + 2OH^-(aq)$, what is the change in oxidation number of silver?
   a. +1 to 0
   b. 0 to +1
   c. −2 to 0
   d. 0 to −2
   e. There is no change in the oxidation number of silver.

13. What is the oxidation number of aluminum in tri ammonium aluminum hexafluoride, $(NH_4)_3AlF_6(s)$?
   a. +1
   b. +2
   c. +3
   d. +4
   e. −2

14. Consider the redox reaction $Cu(s) + NO_3^-(aq) \rightarrow Cu^{2+}(aq) + NO(g)$. Which of the following is the balanced form of the reaction?
   a. $Cu(s) + NO_3^-(aq) + H^+(aq) \rightarrow Cu^{2+}(aq) + NO(g) + H_2O(g)$
   b. $2Cu(s) + NO_3^-(aq) + 8H^+(aq) \rightarrow 2Cu^{2+}(aq) + NO(g) + 6H_2O(g)$
   c. $3Cu(s) + 2NO_3^-(aq) + 8H^+(aq) \rightarrow 3Cu^{2+}(aq) + 2NO(g) + 4H_2O(g)$
   d. $Cu(s) + NO_3^-(aq) + 2H^+(aq) \rightarrow Cu^{2+}(aq) + 2NO(g) + H_2O(g)$
   e. $Cu(s) + 2NO_3^-(aq) + 4H^+(aq) \rightarrow Cu^{2+}(aq) + 4NO(g) + 2H_2O(g)$

Answer the questions below.

15. The complete combustion of methane, which is an example of a redox reaction, occurs according to the following equation:
$$CH_4(g) + 2O_2(g) \rightarrow CO_2(g) + 2H_2O(g)$$
Identify what is being oxidized and what is being reduced in this reaction.

16. The synthesis reaction between hydrogen gas and oxygen gas to form water vapour is an example of a redox reaction. It occurs according to the following equation:
$$2H_2(g) + O_2(g) \rightarrow 2H_2O(g)$$
Identify what is being oxidized and what is being reduced in this reaction.

17. Explain why, in a redox reaction, the reducing agent undergoes oxidation.

18. In a single displacement reaction of the form A + BX → AX + B, which component is being oxidized and which component is being reduced? Support your answer with the half-reactions for each component.

19. Identify the oxidizing agent and the reducing agent in the synthesis of aluminum iodide.

20. Complete the following questions for the equation given below.
$$3Cu(s) + 2NO_3^-(aq) + 8H^+(aq) \rightarrow 3Cu^{2+}(aq) + 2NO(g) + 4H_2O(\ell)$$
   a. Write a balanced chemical equation by inspection.
   b. Write the ionic and net ionic equations.
   c. Identify the oxidizing agent and the reducing agent.
   d. Write the two half-reactions.
   e. Identify the change in oxidation number for an atom of copper.

21. When a metallic element reacts with a non-metallic element, which reactant is
   a. oxidized?
   b. reduced?
   c. the oxidizing agent?
   d. the reducing agent?

22. Determine the oxidation number of each element present in the following substances:
   a. $BaCl_2(s)$
   b. $Al_4C_3(s)$
   c. $Ag_2SO_4(s)$
   d. $NO_2(g)$
   e. $(NH_4)_2C_2O_4(s)$
   f. $S_8(s)$
   g. $AsO_3^{3-}(aq)$
   h. $VO^{2+}(aq)$
   i. $XeF_4(g)$
   j. $S_4O_6^{3-}(aq)$

23. Identify each of the following as reduction or oxidation.
   a. $MnO_4^-(aq)$ becomes $MnO_4^{3-}(aq)$
   b. $N_2(g)$ becomes $NO_3^-(aq)$
   c. $O_2(g)$ becomes $Na_2O(s)$
   d. $NH_3(g)$ becomes $N_2O(g)$
   e. $P_4O_{10}(s)$ becomes $P_4O_6(s)$

Chapter 9 REVIEW

24. Write an example of each of the following.
   a. a synthesis reaction that is a redox reaction
   b. a synthesis reaction that is not a redox reaction
   c. a decomposition reaction that is a redox reaction
   d. a decomposition reaction that is not a redox reaction

25. Phosphorus, $P_4(s)$, reacts with hot water to form phosphine, $PH_3(g)$, and phosphoric acid, $H_3PO_4(aq)$. Is the phosphorus oxidized or reduced? Explain your answer.

26. Potassium permanganate, $KMnO_4(aq)$, is a very strong oxidizing agent in acidic solutions. In acidic conditions, it oxidizes hydrogen halides to halogens. The net ionic equation for such a reaction is

$$2MnO_4^-(aq) + 10I^-(aq) + 16H^+(aq) \rightarrow$$
$$2Mn^{2+}(aq) + 5I_2(aq) + 8H_2O(\ell)$$

What is the reducing agent in this reaction? Explain your answer.

27. Consider the compounds $NO(g)$, $HNO_3(aq)$, $N_2(g)$, and $Li_3N(s)$.
   a. In which compound does an atom of nitrogen have the lowest oxidation number?
   b. In which compound does an atom of nitrogen have the highest oxidation number?

28. Explain how the change in oxidation number of an atom in a molecule relates to the loss or gain of electrons used in the half-reaction method.

Thinking and Investigation

29. Balance each of the following equations and identify which represent redox reactions. Identify any disproportionation reactions.
   a. $H_2O_2(aq) + Fe(OH)_2(s) \rightarrow Fe(OH)_3(s)$
   b. $PCl_3(\ell) + H_2O(\ell) \rightarrow H_3PO_3(aq) + HCl(aq)$
   c. $C_2H_6(g) + O_2(g) \rightarrow CO_2(g) + H_2O(\ell)$
   d. $NO_2(g) + H_2O(\ell) \rightarrow HNO_3(aq) + NO(g)$
   e. $MnO_2(s) + Cl^-(aq) \rightarrow Mn^{2+}(aq) + Cl_2(g)$
   (acidic conditions)

30. One half-reaction of a redox reaction is $Pb^{2+}(aq) \rightarrow Pb^{4+}(aq) + 2e^-$ and the other half-reaction is $Al^{3+}(aq) + 3e^- \rightarrow Al(s)$.
   a. Identify the oxidation half-reaction and the reduction half-reaction.
   b. What is the minimum number of lead(II) ions and aluminum ions that would need to react in order for the number of electrons to be balanced?

31. Four unknown metallic elements—W, X, Y, and Z—were combined with nitrate in aqueous solution. The table below shows whether or not there was a chemical reaction. Use this information to organize elements W, X, Y, and Z into a mini oxidation-reduction table.

Compound Metal	$W(NO_3)_2$ (aq)	$X(NO_3)_2$ (aq)	$Y(NO_3)_2$ (aq)	$Z(NO_3)_2$ (aq)
W		Reaction observed	Reaction observed	No reaction observed
X	No reaction observed		No reaction observed	No reaction observed
Y	No reaction observed	Reaction observed		No reaction observed
Z	Reaction observed	Reaction observed	Reaction observed	

32. Determine which of the following balanced chemical equations represent redox reactions. For each redox reaction, identify the oxidizing agent and the reducing agent.
   a. $2C_6H_6(\ell) + 15O_2(g) \rightarrow 12CO_2(g) + 6H_2O(\ell)$
   b. $CaO(s) + SO_2(g) \rightarrow CaSO_3(aq)$
   c. $H_2(g) + I_2(s) \rightarrow 2HI(aq)$
   d. $KMnO_4(aq) + 5CuCl(s) + 8HCl(aq) \rightarrow$
   $KCl(aq) + MnCl_2(aq) + 5CuCl_2(s) + 4H_2O(\ell)$
   e. $2Ag^+(aq) + Cu(s) \rightarrow 2Ag(s) + Cu^{2+}(aq)$
   f. $Pb^{2+}(aq) + S^{2-}(aq) \rightarrow PbS(s)$
   g. $2Mn^{2+}(aq) + 5BiO_3^-(aq) + 14H^+(aq) \rightarrow$
   $2MnO_4^-(aq) + 5Bi^{3+}(aq) + 7H_2O(\ell)$

33. Examples of molecules and ions composed only of vanadium and oxygen are listed below.

$V_2O_5(s)$ $VO(s)$ $VO_3^-(aq)$
$V_2O_3(s)$ $VO_2^+(aq)$ $VO_4^{3-}(aq)$
$VO_2(s)$ $VO^{2+}(aq)$ $V_3O_9^{3-}(aq)$

   a. In this list, identify the molecules and ions in which the oxidation number of vanadium is the same.
   b. Is the following reaction a redox reaction? Explain your reasoning.
   $2NH_4VO_3(aq) \rightarrow V_2O_5(s) + 2NH_3(g) + H_2O(\ell)$

34. Name a polyatomic ion in which chlorine has an oxidation number of +3, and explain your reasoning.

35. The following table shows the average formation, by volume, of the air that organisms inhale and exhale as part of a biochemical process called cellular respiration. (The values are rounded.) How do the data indicate that at least one redox reaction is involved in cellular respiration?

Average Formation, by Volume, of Inhaled and Exhaled Air

Gas	Inhaled Air (% by volume)	Exhaled Air (% by volume)
Oxygen	21	16
Carbon dioxide	0.04	4
Nitrogen and other gases	79	80

36. Balance each of the following net ionic equations. Then include the named spectator ions to write a balanced chemical equation.
   a. $Co^{3+}(aq) + Cd(s) \rightarrow Co^{2+}(aq) + Cd^{2+}(aq)$ (spectator ions are $NO_3^-(aq)$)
   b. $Ag^+(aq) + SO_2(g) \rightarrow Ag(s) + SO_4^{2-}(aq)$ (acidic conditions; spectator ions are $NO_3^-(aq)$)
   c. $Al(s) + CrO_4^{2-}(aq) \rightarrow Al(OH)_3(s) + Cr(OH)_3(s)$ (basic conditions; spectator ions are $Na^+(aq)$)

37. Iodine reacts with concentrated nitric acid to form iodic acid, gaseous nitrogen dioxide, and water.
   a. Write the balanced chemical equation.
   b. Explain why this reaction is a redox reaction.

38. In a laboratory investigation involving unknown elements A, B, C, and D, the following observations were made:
   - Element A reacts spontaneously with BNO_3 and with $DNO_3(aq)$ but does not react spontaneously with $CNO_3(aq)$.
   - Element B does not react spontaneously with any of the nitrate solutions of elements A, C, and D.
   - Element C reacts spontaneously with all of the nitrate solutions of the elements A, B, and D.
   - Element D reacts spontaneously with $BNO_3(aq)$.

   Using these observations, organize the unknowns in increasing strength as reducing agents.

39. The reaction $Ca^{2+}(aq) + Fe(s) \rightarrow Ca(s) + Fe^{2+}(aq)$ does not occur spontaneously.
   a. Explain why it is not a spontaneous reaction.
   b. What does this suggest about the reverse reaction, $Ca(s) + Fe^{2+}(aq) \rightarrow Ca^{2+}(aq) + Fe(s)$?

40. Determine the oxidation number of each atom in the equation $Ca(s) + 2H_2O(\ell) \rightarrow Ca(OH)_2(s) + H_2(g)$ to determine if the reaction is a redox reaction. If it is a redox reaction, identify which substance is oxidized and which substance is reduced.

41. In a laboratory, a sample of a rock containing several metal deposits has been identified to contain solid silver. The process of removing the silver involves the following reaction:
   $CN^-(aq) + 4Ag(s) + O_2(g) \rightarrow Ag(CN)_2^-(aq)$
   a. Is this reaction a redox reaction? Justify your answer.
   b. Balance the reaction using the half-reaction method. (**Hint:** You will need to first place water on the product side of the reaction to write and balance the half-reactions.)

42. Balance each redox reaction using the method of your choice. In one sentence, explain why you chose the method you used for each reaction.
   a. $Cr_2O_7^{2-}(aq) + I^-(aq) \rightarrow I_2(s) + Cr^{3+}(aq)$ (acidic conditions)
   b. $SeO_4^{2-}(aq) + Cl^-(aq) \rightarrow Cl_2(g) + SeO_3^{2-}(aq)$ (basic conditions)
   c. $MnO_4^-(aq) + SO_3^{2-}(aq) \rightarrow Mn^{2+}(aq) + SO_4^{2-}(aq)$ (acidic conditions)
   d. $Ag(s) + NO_3^-(aq) \rightarrow Ag^+(aq) + NO(g)$ (basic conditions)

Communication

43. Use a Venn diagram to compare and contrast oxidation and reduction.

44. Oxidation and reduction are paired in chemical reactions in which electrons are transferred from one substance to another in a predictable way. Explain, in the form of a well-phrased paragraph, how oxidation numbers allow for this *predictable way* of electron transfer to be monitored.

45. Explain, in the form of a well-reasoned paragraph, the difference between balancing a redox reaction in acidic conditions and balancing a redox reaction in basic conditions.

46. List three possible metallic solids that could be used to precipitate solid chromium from an ionic solution containing chromium(III) ions. Explain your reasoning, using two or three clearly written sentences.

Chapter 9 REVIEW

47. In a general synthesis reaction of the form A+B → AB,
  a. use words and two examples to discuss why this is an example of a redox reaction.
  b. identify the oxidizing agent and the reducing agent in this general reaction.

48. A redox reaction has been balanced in acidic conditions. In the process, H$^+$(aq) appears on the reactant side of the reaction. Use words and one example to clearly explain why hydroxide ions must be added to *both* sides of the reaction to change to basic conditions when the H$^+$(aq) ions can only be found as a reactant in the reaction.

49. **BIG IDEAS** The control and applications of oxidation and reduction reactions have significant implications for industry, health and safety, and the environment. With this in mind, write a short essay of three or four paragraphs, including the use of examples where appropriate, to discuss two situations for which this is true.

50. When an oxidation half-reaction is written, on which side of the reaction arrow are the electrons written? Explain your answer using words and one example to clarify your answer.

51. Create a mnemonic to help you remember the definitions for oxidizing agent and reducing agent.

52. A redox reaction of the general form A + B → C + D is found to be not spontaneous when the relative reducing agent strengths are determined. What would this indicate about the reverse of the reaction, C + D → A + B? Explain your answer, using an example and two or three sentences.

53. Explain why the oxidation number for fluorine atoms in a molecule is the charge on the elemental ion of the atom.

54. Outline, in the form of a numbered list, the steps that would be required to determine the oxidation number of sulfur in the molecule H$_2$SO$_3$(aq).

55. Would it be a good idea to store a solution of iron(II) sulfate in an aluminum container? Explain your answer using a short, well-reasoned paragraph.

56. Conduct research on the Internet and write a report on the various types of iron and steel that are in use today. Include in your report the redox chemistry used in their formation as well as the uses of the different types of iron and steel you studied.

57. Although compact disks (CDs) are fast becoming obsolete, for a few short decades these media were popular choices for recording and preserving audio and textual data. Conduct research to determine the role of redox reactions in the manufacture of CDs and present your findings in a report.

58. Summarize your learning in this chapter using a graphic organizer. To help you, the Chapter 9 Summary lists the Key Terms and Key Concepts. Refer to Using Graphic Organizers in Appendix A to help you decide which graphic organizer to use.

Application

59. The compound NaAl(OH)$_2$CO$_3$(s) is a component of some common stomach acid remedies.
  a. Determine the oxidation number of each element in the compound.
  b. Predict the products of the reaction of the compound with stomach acid (hydrochloric acid), and write a balanced chemical equation for the reaction.
  c. Were the oxidation numbers from question 59a useful in question 59b? Explain your answer.
  d. What type of reaction is this?

60. Two of the substances on the head of a safety match are potassium chlorate and sulfur. When the match is struck, the potassium chlorate decomposes to give potassium chloride and oxygen. The sulfur then burns in the oxygen and ignites the wood of the match.

  a. Write balanced chemical equations for the decomposition of potassium chlorate and for the burning of sulfur in oxygen.
  b. Identify the oxidizing agent and the reducing agent in each reaction in question 60a.
  c. Does any element in potassium chlorate undergo disproportionation in the reaction? Explain your answer.
  d. Research the history of the safety match to determine when it was invented, why it was invented, and what it replaced.

61. Sulfuric acid is usually commercially manufactured in North America in a three-step process:

$S_8(s) + 8O_2(g) \rightarrow 8SO_2(g)$
$2SO_2(g) + O_2(g) \rightarrow 2SO_3(g)$
$SO_3(g) + H_2O(\ell) \rightarrow H_2SO_4(aq)$

a. Which of these steps is (are) redox reaction(s)? Explain your answer in words and by identifying changes to oxidation numbers of the atoms in the reactions.

b. In the steps that are redox reactions, identify the atoms that are oxidized and the atoms that are reduced.

62. Clothing that has been stained with rust (iron(III) oxide) can be cleaned using a dilute solution of oxalic acid, $H_2C_2O_4(aq)$, according to the redox reaction
$Fe_2O_3(s) + H_2C_2O_4(aq) \rightarrow Fe(C_2O_4)_3^{3-}(aq) + H_2O(\ell)$.
Balance the reaction in acidic conditions using the method of your choice.

63. Explain, using words and an analysis of oxidation numbers, why the following reaction is not possible as written.

$Fe^{3+}(aq) + Sn^{4+}(aq) \rightarrow Fe^{2+}(aq) + Sn^{2+}(aq)$

64. The thermite reaction, which is highly exothermic, can be used to weld metals. In the thermite reaction, aluminum reacts with iron(III) oxide to form iron and aluminum oxide. The temperature becomes so high that the iron is formed as a liquid.

a. Write a balanced chemical equation for the reaction.

b. Is the reaction a redox reaction? If so, identify the oxidizing agent and the reducing agent.

65. Describe a laboratory investigation that you could perform to decide whether tin or nickel is the better reducing agent. Include in your description all the materials and equipment you would need, and describe the procedure you would follow. (**Safety note:** Do *not* perform the investigation.)

66. The catalytic converter on an automobile converts carbon monoxide gas, a product of incomplete combustion, into carbon dioxide gas in the presence of oxygen gas and with the aid of platinum that acts as a catalyst. Explain, in words and using oxidation numbers, why this is an example of a redox reaction.

67. When there is sufficient ethanol in a person's breath, the chromium ions in a police breathalyzer change from orange dichromate, $Cr_2O_7^{2-}(aq)$, to green $Cr^{3+}(aq)$. The carbon is oxidized from −2 in the ethanol molecule to 0 in the $C_2H_4O_2(aq)$ product molecule. Use the oxidation number method or the half-reaction method to write and balance the equation that occurs in acidic conditions for the reaction:

$Cr_2O_7^{2-}(aq) + C_2H_5OH(aq) \rightarrow Cr^{3+}(aq) + C_2H_4O_2(aq)$

68. The solid rocket boosters of the space shuttle use ammonium perchlorate, NH_4ClO_4 (aq), and powdered aluminum. This redox reaction releases a large amount of extra thrust to boost the shuttle rocket. The reaction is $Al(s) + NH_4ClO_4(g) \rightarrow Al_2O_3(g) + HCl(g) + N_2(g) + H_2O(g)$. Balance this reaction using the oxidation number method.

69. The Oswald process to commercially produce nitric acid occurs in three steps:

$4NH_3(g) + 5O_2(g) \rightarrow 4NO(g) + 6H_2O(g)$
$2NO(g) + O_2(g) \rightarrow 2NO_2(g)$
$3NO_2(g) + H_2O(\ell) \rightarrow 2HNO_3(aq) + NO(g)$

a. Which of the steps in the process are redox reactions?

b. In the steps that are redox reactions, identify the oxidizing agent and the reducing agent.

70. Referring to **Table 9.2** and conducting research as necessary, explain why contact between aluminum foil and dental amalgam results in a brief "shocking" and painful experience. (**Hint:** Dental amalgam contains small amounts of mercury and tin ions.)

Chapter 9 | SELF-ASSESSMENT

Select the letter of the best answer below.

1. **K/U** In which of the following does nitrogen have an oxidation number of +2?
   a. $NO_2(g)$
   b. $NO_3^-(aq)$
   c. $NO_3(g)$
   d. $NO(g)$
   e. Nitrogen has an oxidation number of +2 in all of the above.

2. **K/U** Xenon was long thought to be an inert gas, as it was considered to be incapable of forming chemical compounds. However, some xenon compounds have been created. One such compound is xenon hexafluoride, made according to the equation
   $Xe(g) + 3 F_2(g) \rightarrow XeF_6(g)$.
   What is the change in oxidation number for xenon?
   a. 0 to +6
   b. +1 to 0
   c. −6 to 0
   d. 0 to +1
   e. There is no change to the oxidation number of xenon.

3. **K/U** Which of the following is the balanced half-reaction for $MnO_4^-(aq) \rightarrow Mn^{2+}(aq)$ in basic conditions?
   a. $MnO_4^-(aq) + 8H^+(aq) \rightarrow Mn^{2+}(aq) + 4H_2O(\ell)$
   b. $MnO_4^-(aq) + 4H_2O(\ell) \rightarrow Mn^{2+}(aq) + 8OH^-(aq)$
   c. $MnO_4^-(aq) \rightarrow Mn^{2+}(aq) + 4H_2O(\ell) + 3e^-$
   d. $MnO_4^-(aq) + 4H_2O(\ell) + 5e^- \rightarrow Mn^{2+}(aq) + 8OH^-(aq)$
   e. $MnO_4^-(aq) + 8H^+(aq) + 5e^- \rightarrow Mn^{2+}(aq) + 4H_2O(\ell)$

4. **K/U** A chemist observes a chemical reaction in which some atoms of an element are oxidized and other atoms of the same element are reduced. This reaction is a
   a. half-reaction.
   b. displacement reaction.
   c. incomplete reaction.
   d. disproportionation reaction.
   e. spectator reaction.

5. **K/U** An oxidizing agent is a reactant that
   a. accepts electrons and oxidizes another reactant.
   b. donates electrons and reduces another reactant.
   c. donates electrons and oxidizes another reactant.
   d. accepts electrons and reduces another reactant.
   e. is a spectator ion.

6. **K/U** Most hearing aids and watches are powered with a zinc/silver oxide cell. The main redox reaction taking place in the cell is $Ag_2O(s) + H_2O(\ell) + 2e^- \rightarrow 2Ag(s) + 2OH^-(aq)$. What is the change in the oxidation number of silver?
   a. +1 to 0
   b. −2 to 0
   c. +2 to 0
   d. 0 to +2
   e. 0 to +1

7. **T/I** Which of the following half-reactions is the correct reduction half-reaction to the reaction of solid copper and silver ions?
   a. $Cu(s) \rightarrow Cu^{2+}(aq)$
   b. $Ag^+(aq) \rightarrow Ag(s)$
   c. $Cu(s) \rightarrow Cu^{2+}(aq) + 2e^-$
   d. $Ag^+(aq) + e^- \rightarrow Ag(s)$
   e. There is no reduction half-reaction as this is not a redox reaction.

8. **K/U** For the reaction $Zn(s) + CuSO_4(aq) \rightarrow ZnSO_4(aq) + Cu(s)$, which of the following statements is correct?
   a. Sulfur atoms are reduced.
   b. Copper gains one electron.
   c. Copper loses one electron.
   d. Zinc gains two electrons.
   e. Zinc loses two electrons.

9. **K/U** In which of the following substances does chlorine have the highest oxidation number?
   a. HCl
   b. HClO
   c. Cl_2
   d. ClO_4^-
   e. ClO_2

10. **K/U** Which statement describes what happens when a metal ore is reduced?
    a. There is a mass decrease from the ore to the metal.
    b. There is a gain in the number of electrons in the atoms of the metal.
    c. There is a decrease in the oxidation number of the atoms of the metal.
    d. Two of the above statements are correct.
    e. All three of the given statements are correct.

Use sentences and diagrams as appropriate to answer the questions below.

11. **K/U** Determine the oxidation number of the specified element in each of the following:
    a. N in $HNO_3(aq)$
    b. C in $C_2H_6(g)$
    c. Cl in $ClO_4^-(aq)$
    d. Cr in $Cr_2O_7^{2-}(aq)$

12. **C** Outline the steps in a numbered sequence that must be followed to determine the oxidation number of a sulfur atom in $S_3O_8(g)$.

13. **K/U** Use oxidation numbers to identify the change in carbon in the following reaction:
    $C_2H_5OH(\ell) + O_2(g) \rightarrow CO_2(g) + H_2O(\ell)$

14. **A** Batteries containing mercury are used to power small electronic devices. The overall reaction that occurs in the battery is
    $HgO(s) + Zn(s) \rightarrow ZnO(s) + Hg(\ell)$ (basic conditions).
    Show why this is an example of a redox reaction by writing and balancing each half-reaction and identifying the oxidizing agent and the reducing agent in the process.

15. **T/I** Predict whether each of the following single displacement reactions will proceed spontaneously. For those that will, write a complete balanced equation, an ionic equation, and a net ionic equation. (Refer to **Table 9.2** as necessary.)
    a. metallic iron and aluminum nitrate
    b. metallic tin and copper(II) sulfate
    c. metallic cobalt and magnesium sulfate

16. **T/I** Balance the following redox reactions using the half-reaction method:
    a. $Zn(s) + NO_3^-(aq) \rightarrow Zn^{2+}(aq) + NH_4^+(aq)$ (acidic conditions)
    b. $CN^-(aq) + CrO_4^{2-}(aq) \rightarrow CNO^-(aq) + Cr(OH)_3(s)$ (basic conditions)
    c. $BrO_3^-(aq) + I^-(aq) \rightarrow Br^-(aq) + I_2(s)$ (acidic conditions)

17. **C** Use one or two sentences to explain why you would not expect sulfide ions to act as an oxidizing agent.

18. **K/U** Balance the following redox reactions using the oxidation number method:
    a. $MnO_4^-(aq) + Fe^{2+}(aq) \rightarrow Mn^{2+}(aq) + Fe^{3+}(aq)$ (acidic conditions)
    b. $Cr^{3+}(aq) + ClO_3^-(aq) \rightarrow ClO_2(aq) + Cr_2O_7^{2-}(aq)$ (acidic conditions)
    c. $NO_3^-(aq) + Bi(s) \rightarrow Bi^{3+}(aq) + NO_2(aq)$ (basic conditions)

19. **T/I** Formaldehyde, $CH_2O(\ell)$, is used to preserve biological specimens. It is made from methanol, $CH_3OH(\ell)$, according to the following reaction:
    $CH_3OH(\ell) + O_2(g) \rightarrow CH_2O(\ell) + H_2O(\ell)$
    a. Using oxidation numbers, balance the reaction.
    b. Identify the oxidizing agent and the reducing agent in the process.

20. **T/I** Write three different spontaneous redox reactions in which zinc is oxidized.

21. **K/U** Explain how reduction and oxidation processes are used in the production of steel.

22. **K/U** For the following balanced net ionic equation, identify the reactant that undergoes oxidation and the reactant that undergoes reduction:
    $Br_2(\ell) + 2ClO_2^-(aq) \rightarrow 2Br^-(aq) + 2ClO_2(aq)$

23. **A** Ammonium ions, from fertilizers or animal waste, are oxidized by atmospheric oxygen. The reaction results in the acidification of soil on farms and the pollution of ground water with nitrate ions. Write a balanced net ionic equation for this reaction.

24. **A** An atom of an element in a substance on the reactant side of a reaction has been identified to have an oxidation number of +4. On the product side, an atom of the same element has been identified to have an oxidation number of +6. Explain what this change in oxidation number means in terms of electron transfer for the atom and the behaviour of the substance in the reaction.

25. **A** The rocket engines used in a space shuttle launch contain aluminum and ammonium perchlorate. The products of their reaction are aluminum oxide and ammonium chloride. Identify the oxidizing agent and reducing agent in the reaction.

Self-Check

If you missed question …	1	2	3	4	5	6	7	8	9	10	11	12	13	14	15	16	17	18	19	20	21	22	23	24	25
Review section(s)…	9.3	9.3	9.2	9.2	9.1	9.3	9.2	9.1	9.3	9.1	9.3	9.3	9.3	9.1, 9.2	9.1	9.2	9.1	9.3	9.1, 9.3	9.1, 9.2	9.1, 9.3	9.1, 9.3	9.1, 9.2	9.1	9.1

CHAPTER 10
Electrochemical Cells

Specific Expectations

In this chapter, you will learn how to . . .

- F1.1 **assess**, on the basis of research, the viability of using electrochemical technologies as alternative sources of energy, and **explain** their impact on society and the environment (10.3)

- F1.2 **analyze** health and safety isssues involving electrochemistry (10.2)

- F2.4 **build** a galvanic cell and **measure** its cell potential (10.1)

- F2.5 **analyze** the processes in galvanic cells, and **draw** labelled diagrams of these cells (10.1, 10.2)

- F2.6 **predict** the spontaneity of redox reactions (10.1, 10.2)

- F3.2 **identify** the components of a galvanic cell, and **explain** how each component functions in a redox reaction (10.1)

- F3.3 **describe** galvanic half-cells in terms of oxidation and reduction half-cells whose voltages can be used to determine the overall cell potential (10.1, 10.2)

- F3.4 **explain** how the hydrogen half-cell is used as a standard reference to determine the voltage of another half-cell (10.2)

- F3.5 **explain** some applications of electrochemistry in common industrial processes (10.1, 10.2, 10.3)

- F3.6 **explain** the corrosion of metals in terms of an electrochemical process, and **describe** some common corrosion-inhibiting techniques (10.2)

Batteries come in a wide range of sizes and shapes, from batteries large enough to operate forklifts and golf carts to the tiny button batteries in watches and hearing aids. Some batteries, such as the ones powering the "exoskeleton" device worn by the person in the photograph, can be recharged. Exoskeletons are being developed to enhance the mobility of people with physical disabilities. Various types of batteries generate different voltages. For example, automobile batteries generate 12 V. Flashlight batteries come in many sizes (AAA to D), but they all provide 1.5 V. What is the difference between a large battery and a small battery that provide the same voltage? What is the relationship between batteries and the redox reactions that you studied in Chapter 9? This chapter will help you to determine answers to these questions.

Launch Lab

What Determines Voltage?

In this activity, you will test some of the characteristics of lemon batteries and make predictions about commercial batteries.

Safety Precautions

- Wear safety eyewear throughout this activity.

Materials

- 4 zinc strips (1 cm × 5 cm)
- 4 copper strips (1 cm × 5 cm)
- 4 lemons
- fine sandpaper
- 8 electrical leads with alligator clips
- voltmeter (high sensitivity)
- small flashlight bulb

Procedure

1. Clean the zinc and copper strips with the sandpaper. Roll each lemon on the table with your hand on top, pressing down on the lemon to break open the pockets of juice inside.
2. Insert one zinc strip and one copper strip into one lemon. Attach one electrical lead to each strip by using the alligator clips. Connect the other end of each lead to the voltmeter. Read and record the voltage displayed by the voltmeter.
3. Disconnect the leads from the voltmeter and connect them to the flashlight bulb. If you see any light, describe its intensity.
4. Insert one zinc strip and one copper strip into each of the lemons. Connect the strips as shown in the diagram labelled "Series."
5. Connect the final leads to the voltmeter. Read and record the voltage. Repeat step 3.
6. Disconnect and then reconnect the lemons as shown in the diagram labelled "Parallel." Connect the leads to the voltmeter and record the voltage. Then connect the leads to the light bulb and describe the light intensity of the bulb, if any.

Questions

1. Which connection—single lemon, series lemons, or parallel lemons—produced the highest voltage?
2. In which case (if any) did the system cause the flashlight bulb to produce the brightest light?
3. Based on your observations, what do you think is the difference between a cell and a battery?
4. Why do you think that some batteries are larger than others?

SECTION 10.1
Galvanic Cells

Key Terms

electric current
electrochemistry
galvanic cell
external circuit
salt bridge
electrode
electrolyte
anode
cathode
inert electrode
cell notation
electrical potential difference
voltage
cell potential
standard cell potential
standard reduction potential

Batteries provide power to operate mobile devices or devices that are located far from electrical power lines. For example, battery packs are used to operate camera traps set up in remote locations to capture photographs of animals such as the one shown in **Figure 10.1**. Many of these animals are otherwise hard to study because their numbers are small, they avoid all traces of humans, and they are active mainly at night. A sensor detects an animal's presence, triggering the camera. The energy that the battery provides depends on redox reactions.

Figure 10.1 Battery-operated camera traps are non-invasive ways of collecting data on endangered species and other animals in their natural habitat.

You learned in Chapter 9 that a zinc strip reacts with a solution containing copper(II) ions to form zinc ions and metallic copper. The redox reaction is spontaneous, meaning that it occurs by itself, without an ongoing input of energy. In fact, the reaction releases energy in the form of heat—it is exothermic:

$$Zn(s) + Cu^{2+}(aq) \rightarrow Zn^{2+}(aq) + Cu(s) + \text{energy}$$

The very first "battery" contained these two metals. In 1800, an Italian physicist, Alessandro Volta, put a layer of saltwater-soaked paper between a zinc disk and a copper disk, as shown in **Figure 10.2**. He showed that the copper disk became positively charged and the zinc disk became negatively charged. If he attached wires to the two disks and then connected the wires, the electrons would flow away from the negatively charged zinc disk to the positively charged copper disk. Volta knew nothing about the chemical reaction that was occurring. He simply knew that the combination of metals could generate electrical energy.

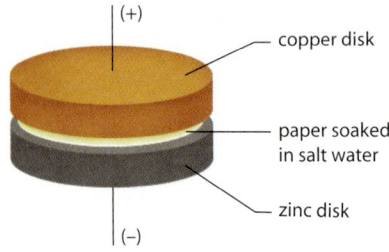

Figure 10.2 A model of Volta's charge-generating device. When many of these disk assemblies were stacked one on top of another, they were termed a voltaic pile.

A flow of electric charges, such as electrons, is called an **electric current**. The concepts of redox reactions and electric current form the basis of the field of **electrochemistry**: the study of the processes involved in converting chemical energy into electrical energy and in converting electrical energy into chemical energy.

The Galvanic Cell

Volta was inspired to research the interaction between two unlike metals after reading a scientific paper written by Luigi Galvani (1737–1798), an Italian physician. When Galvani was dissecting a frog, he touched a brass pin with a steel scalpel and noticed that the frog muscle twitched. He and his students were able to reproduce the reaction whenever they touched different metals together while they were touching a frog muscle. Galvani believed that the living tissue was necessary in order to cause this interaction between the two metals, but Volta showed that the electrical energy was obtained by the contact between the two unlike metals alone.

Scientists continued to study and develop these electrical energy-producing cells, with some people calling them "voltaic cells" and others calling them "galvanic cells." This textbook will use the term galvanic cell throughout.

A **galvanic cell** is a device that uses redox reactions, such as the reaction between copper(II) ions and zinc atoms, to transform chemical potential energy into electrical energy. The key to the operation of the galvanic cell is the prevention of direct contact between the reactants in a redox reaction. Volta accomplished this by placing saltwater-soaked paper between the metal disks. Copper and zinc ions could move into the moist medium, but electrons could not escape the metal disks.

However, when metal wires connected the disks, electrons could move through the wire, from one disk to the other. The electrons flowed through an **external circuit**. The energy carried by the electric current could then be used for other purposes, such as lighting a light bulb.

The Daniell Cell

One of the first practical galvanic cells was developed by the English chemist John Frederic Daniell (1790–1845). A Daniell cell, shown in **Figure 10.3**, consists of a zinc strip in zinc sulfate solution and a copper strip in a copper(II) sulfate solution.

electric current a directional motion of electric charges

electrochemistry the study of processes involved in converting chemical energy into electrical energy and converting electrical energy into chemical energy

galvanic cell a device that uses redox reactions to transform chemical potential energy into electrical energy

external circuit a circuit outside the reactions vessel in which redox reactions are occurring

Figure 10.3 In a Daniell cell, a salt bridge connects the two beakers while not allowing the solutions in the beakers to mix.

salt bridge an electrical connection between half-cells that contains an electrolyte solution, allowing a current to flow but preventing contact between the oxidizing agent and the reducing agent

electrode a conductor that carries electric current into and out of electrochemical cells

electrolyte a substance that, when dissolved in water, conducts an electric current

anode the electrode at which oxidation occurs

cathode the electrode at which reduction occurs

The two solutions shown in **Figure 10.3** are connected by a **salt bridge**, which is a U-shaped glass tube filled with potassium chloride. The ends of the tube are plugged with a porous material such as cotton or glass wool. Ions can diffuse through the plugs, but the plugs prevent the solutions from mixing. A wire is connected to the copper and zinc rods. The other ends of the wire can be connected to any electrical device. In **Figure 10.3**, they are connected to a voltmeter.

A diagrammatic representation of a Daniell cell is shown in **Figure 10.4**. In a Daniell cell, or any other type of galvanic cell, the metal strips act as electrical conductors. Conductors that carry electrons into and out of a cell are called **electrodes**. The solutions in a galvanic cell contain electrolytes, such as the zinc sulfate and copper(II) sulfate solutions in the Daniell cell. **Electrolytes** are substances that, when dissolved in water, conduct an electric current in the form of moving ions.

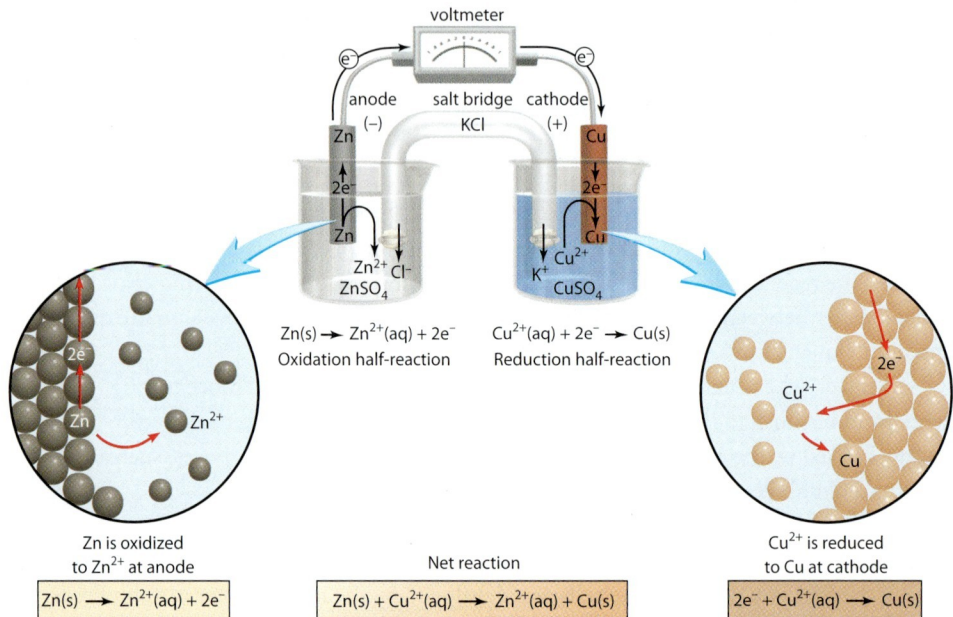

Figure 10.4 By convention, galvanic cells, such as this Daniell cell, are drawn with the anode on the left and the cathode on the right.

In any galvanic cell, oxidation occurs at the electrode called the **anode**, and reduction occurs at the electrode called the **cathode**. In the Daniell cell shown in **Figure 10.4**, the zinc electrode is the anode because it is where the zinc atoms undergo oxidation. The copper electrode is the cathode because it is where copper(II) ions undergo reduction.

As you know, if the zinc atoms in the zinc electrode and the copper(II) ions in the copper(II) sulfate solution were in direct contact, zinc atoms would spontaneously transfer electrons to the copper(II) ions. In the Daniell cell, the zinc strip is separated from the copper(II) ions, so electrons cannot escape the metal conductors. Only ions, such as K^+, Cl^-, Zn^{2+}, and Cu^{2+}, can move through the solutions. Thus, the only path for electrons to travel from the zinc electrode to the copper(II) ions is through the conductors that make up the external circuit. The arrows labelled e^- show the path of the electrons from the zinc electrode, through the connecting wires, and to the copper electrode where they contact the copper(II) ions in the solution. The copper(II) ions accept the electrons and form copper atoms, which then deposit on the copper electrode. Because the solution has lost some positive charge, positive potassium ions diffuse from the salt bridge into the copper(II) sulfate solution, replacing the lost positive charges. At the same time, the zinc ions that formed when the electrons moved out of the zinc electrode go into solution. These additional zinc ions make the solution positive, so chloride ions diffuse from the salt bridge and neutralize the positive charges in the solution.

The electrolyte solution in the salt bridge—in this case, KCl(aq)—is selected so that it does not interfere in the reaction. For example, if one of the solutions contained silver nitrate, you would not use KCl(aq) in the salt bridge because, when the chloride ions diffused into the silver nitrate solution, silver chloride would precipitate out of the solution.

As you can see, there is a complete circuit around which current is flowing. In some parts of the circuit, the moving charges are electrons. In other parts of the circuit, the moving charges are ions. The energy that maintains the current comes from the reaction

$$Zn(s) + Cu^{2+}(aq) \rightarrow Zn^{2+}(aq) + Cu(s) + energy$$

Current flows until the concentration of the solutions and the changes in the electrodes are so great that the processes can no longer continue. For example, as copper accumulates on the copper electrode, the concentration of copper(II) ions in the solution decreases. As well, potassium ions are accumulating in the solution, and the zinc electrode is dissolving as zinc ions are formed and go into solution. **Figure 10.5** shows electrodes after they have been used for a long period of time.

When a zinc strip is in a copper(II) sulfate solution, the energy is converted into heat. In a galvanic cell, the chemical energy is converted into electrical energy. In **Figure 10.4**, the external circuit is connected to a voltmeter. However, you could replace the voltmeter with a light bulb and convert the electrical energy into light energy. Activity 10.1 provides an example that demonstrates the conversion of chemical energy into electrical energy.

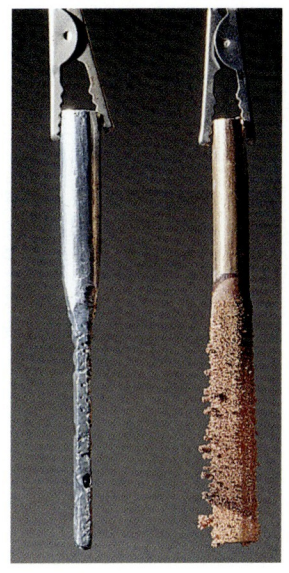

Figure 10.5 The mass of the zinc anode decreases as the zinc is oxidized and the ions go into solution. The mass of the copper cathode increases as the copper(II) ions are reduced and become copper atoms that become part of the electrode.

Explain *what happens to the copper(II) ion concentration in the copper(II) sulfate solution and to the zinc ion concentration in the zinc sulfate solution after the cell has been operating for a long period of time.*

Activity 10.1 | Make a Potato Clock

How long can a "potato juice" electrolyte keep a low-voltage LED clock running? Find out in this activity.

Materials
- 1 potato cut in half
- 2 pieces of copper wire
- 3 alligator clips
- 2 galvanized nails
- low-voltage LED clock

Procedure
1. Insert a nail in each piece of potato.
2. Insert each piece of copper wire into a potato, as far from the nail as possible.
3. Use an alligator clip to connect one copper wire to the positive terminal in the clock.
4. Use another alligator clip to connect the nail in the other potato to the negative terminal in the clock.
5. Use the last alligator clip to connect the nail in the first potato to the copper wire in the second potato.
6. Set the clock, and keep a log of how long it continues to operate.

Questions
1. Explain why the potato set-up is a type of electrochemical cell.
2. How could you modify this set-up so that the clock can operate longer?
3. What other devices do you think could be operated with a one-potato cell? Explain your reasoning.

Types of Electrodes

Galvanic cells can be made with a wide variety of electrodes other than the copper and zinc of the Daniell cell. For example, **Figure 10.6** on the following page shows a galvanic cell with chromium and silver electrodes. Notice that the electrolyte in the salt bridge is potassium nitrate rather than potassium chloride. Although the chloride ions would, in general, migrate to the chromium(III) nitrate cell, a small amount could diffuse into the silver nitrate cell and form a precipitate with the silver ions. It is always best to avoid such possibilities.

Figure 10.6 Chromium is the anode and silver is the cathode because chromium is a stronger reducing agent than silver.

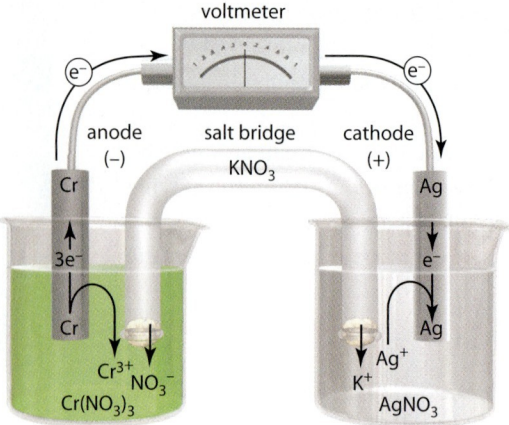

Inert Electrodes

inert electrode a conductor that consists of neither the reactant nor the product but provides a surface on which redox reactions can occur.

The zinc anode and copper cathode of a Daniell cell and the silver and chromium electrodes in **Figure 10.6** are all metals and can act as electrical conductors. However, some redox reactions involve oxidizing or reducing agents that are not solid metals. Instead, they are dissolved electrolytes or gases, so they cannot be used as electrodes. To construct a galvanic cell that will use these oxidizing and reducing agents, you have to use inert electrodes. An **inert electrode** is an electrode made from a material that is neither a reactant nor a product of the redox reaction. Instead, the inert electrode can carry a current and provide a surface on which redox reactions can occur. **Figure 10.7** shows a cell that contains one example of an inert electrode—a platinum electrode. The complete balanced equation, net ionic equation, and half-reactions for this cell are given below.

Complete balanced equation: $Pb(s) + 2FeCl_3(aq) \rightarrow 2FeCl_2(aq) + PbCl_2(aq)$
Net ionic equation: $Pb(s) + 2Fe^{3+}(aq) \rightarrow 2Fe^{2+}(aq) + Pb^{2+}(aq)$
Oxidation half-reaction: $Pb(s) \rightarrow Pb^{2+}(aq) + 2e^-$
Reduction half-reaction: $Fe^{3+}(aq) + e^- \rightarrow Fe^{2+}(aq)$

Figure 10.7 This cell uses an inert electrode to conduct electrons.

Explain why you think that platinum is often chosen as an inert electrode.

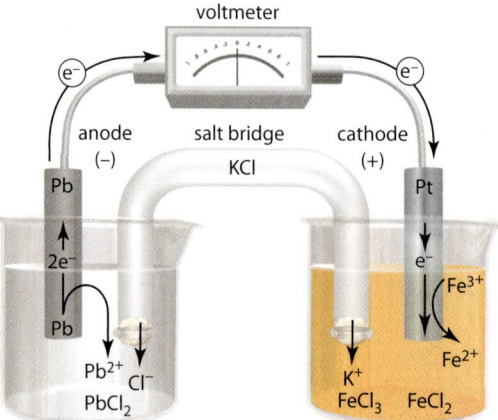

The lead electrode is the anode. Lead atoms lose electrons that travel through the electrode while the lead(II) ions dissolve in the solution in the same way that the anode did in the previous example. However, the reduction half-reaction involves dissolved iron(III) ions that accept an electron from the platinum inert electrode and become dissolved iron(II) ions. The platinum atoms in the platinum electrode (cathode) remain unchanged. In the following Sample Problem and Practice Problems, you can practise sketching and visualizing the processes that take place in a galvanic cell.

Sample Problem

Using Half-Reactions to Sketch a Galvanic Cell

Problem

Sketch a galvanic cell based on the half-reactions shown below.

$Al^{3+}(aq) + 3e^- \rightarrow Al(s)$

$Ni^{2+}(aq) + 2e^- \rightarrow Ni(s)$

a. Label the anode and the cathode.
b. Indicate where oxidation and reduction are occurring.
c. Show the direction of flow of the electrons.
d. Show the direction of the movement of the ions.
e. Write a balanced ionic equation for the reaction.

What Is Required?

You need to sketch a galvanic cell for the reaction between aluminum and nickel, label the anode and the cathode, show the direction of motion of electrons and of ions, indicate where an oxidation reaction is occurring, and indicate where a reduction reaction is occurring.

What Is Given?

You are given two half-reactions.

Plan Your Strategy	Act on Your Strategy
Sketch the apparatus including the beakers, electrodes, conducting wires, voltmeter, and salt bridge.	
a. Label the anode and the cathode, and **b.** indicate where oxidation and reduction are occurring. Use Table 9.2 Relative Strengths of Oxidizing Agents and Reducing Agents to determine which metal will be the anode and which will be the cathode. Label the electrodes in the sketch.	Aluminum is a stronger reducing agent than nickel, so it is oxidized, making it the anode. Label the anode, on the left of the galvanic cell, Al. Nickel is a stronger oxidizing agent than aluminum is, so it is reduced, making it the cathode. Label the cathode, on the right of the galvanic cell, Ni. 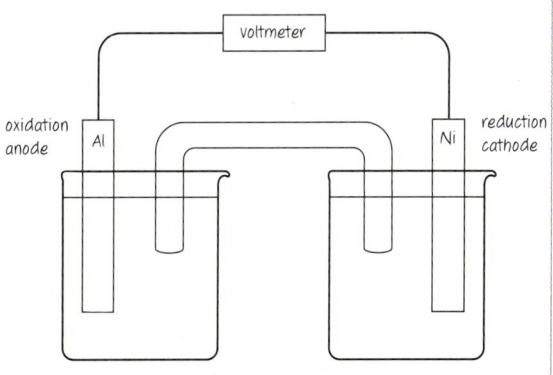

Continued on next page ❯

Plan Your Strategy	Act on Your Strategy
c. Show the direction of flow of electrons. Show the half-reactions that occur at each electrode and, using that information, show the direction of flow of electrons.	Aluminum is losing electrons, which go into the external circuit, and aluminum ions are going into solution. Electrons are entering the nickel electrode, and nickel ions are accepting the electrons at the surface of the electrode. The nickel atoms are depositing onto the electrode. Thus, electrons are moving in a clockwise direction around the external circuit. 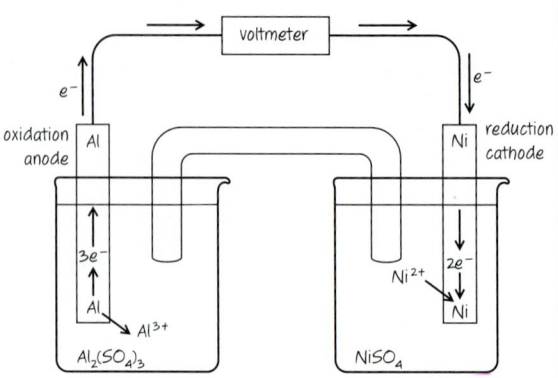
d. Show the direction of the movement of the ions. Select a salt for the salt bridge, and analyze the direction in which the ions must diffuse in order to maintain a neutral charge in the solutions. Using this information, determine the direction of the movement of ions. **Note:** Be sure that no insoluble salts will form. Also be sure that the metal ion from the salt bridge will not accept electrons from the cathode more readily than will the metal ions in the solution.	Potassium chloride will be in the salt bridge. Chloride will not cause either aluminum or nickel to precipitate, because aluminum chloride and nickel(II) chloride are soluble. Potassium will not accept electrons from the cathode as strongly as will nickel. When positively charged aluminum ions from the anode go into solution, negatively charged chloride ions move into the solution to balance the charge. When positively charged nickel ions accept electrons and deposit on the electrode, positively charged potassium ions move into the solution to replace the positive charge. 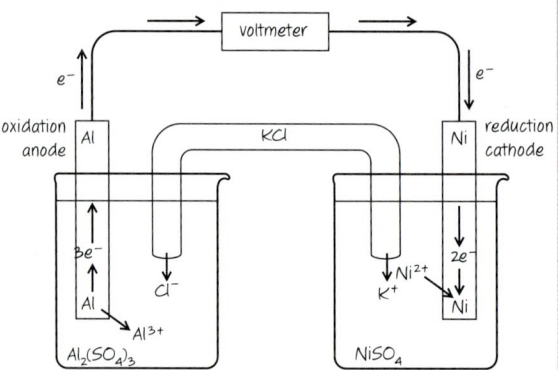
e. Write a balanced ionic equation.	Because aluminum is losing electrons, reverse the direction of the equation as written in the problem statement. $Al(s) \rightarrow Al^{3+}(aq) + 3e^-$ $Ni^{2+}(aq) + 2e^- \rightarrow Ni(s)$ The lowest common multiple of 2 and 3 is 6. Multiply the terms in the first equation by 2 to get 6 electrons, and multiply the second equation by 3 to get 6 electrons. $2Al(s) \rightarrow 2Al^{3+}(aq) + 6e^-$ $3Ni^{2+}(aq) + 6e^- \rightarrow 3Ni(s)$ Add the equations and cancel the electrons. $3Ni^{2+}(aq) + \cancel{6e^-} + 2Al(s) \rightarrow 2Al^{3+}(aq) + \cancel{6e^-} + 3Ni(s)$ $3Ni^{2+}(aq) + 2Al(s) \rightarrow 2Al^{3+}(aq) + 3Ni(s)$

Check Your Solution

The equation is balanced. According to **Table 9.2** on page 587, the reaction will proceed as written. Therefore, the direction of the movement of electrons and ions is correct. All questions have been answered.

Practice Problems

The following questions relate to a galvanic cell involving zinc and magnesium.

1. Which electrode will be the anode and which will be the cathode in this galvanic cell?
2. Explain where the oxidation and the reduction are occurring.
3. Draw a diagram of the cell and indicate the direction of electron flow.
4. Indicate the direction of the ionic movement in this cell.
5. Write a balanced ionic equation that represents this reaction.

The following questions relate to a galvanic cell involving nickel and silver.

6. Which electrode will be the anode and which will be the cathode in this galvanic cell?
7. Explain where the oxidation and the reduction are occurring.
8. Draw a diagram of the cell and indicate the direction of electron flow.
9. Indicate the direction of the ionic movement in this cell.
10. Write a balanced ionic equation that represents this reaction.

Cell Notation

Sketching entire cells helps you to visualize and learn about the movement of ions and electrons in a galvanic cell. However, it becomes tedious when you are trying to communicate quickly. Chemists have therefore developed a shorthand method for representing galvanic cells, called **cell notation**. The cell notation of a Daniell cell is as follows:

$$Zn(s) \mid Zn^{2+}(aq) \parallel Cu^{2+}(aq) \mid Cu(s)$$

In the cell notation, as in the sketch of the entire cell, the anode is usually shown on the left side and the cathode on the right side. Each single vertical line, |, represents a phase boundary between the electrode and the solution in a half-cell. For example, the first single vertical line shows that the solid zinc and aqueous zinc ions are in different phases or states—solid and aqueous. The double vertical line, ||, represents the salt bridge between the half-cells.

Inert electrodes, such as the platinum electrode in the cell shown in **Figure 10.7**, do not appear in the chemical equation or in half-reactions. However, they are included in the cell notation. The cell notation for the cell in **Figure 10.7** is shown here.

$$Pb(s) \mid Pb^{2+}(aq) \parallel Fe^{3+}(aq), Fe^{2+}(aq) \mid Pt(s)$$

A comma separates the formulas Fe^{3+} and Fe^{2+} ions involved in the reduction half-reaction to indicate that they are in the same phase—the aqueous phase.

cell notation
a shorthand method of representing galvanic cells

Learning Check

1. How can zinc atoms reduce copper(II) ions when the two metals are not in contact?
2. Explain the function of the salt bridge in a galvanic cell.
3. How do the anode and cathode in a galvanic cell differ?
4. Consider the processes of oxidation and reduction in a reaction of zinc with copper(II) ions.
   a. If the reaction of zinc with copper(II) ions is carried out in a test tube, what is the oxidizing agent and what is the reducing agent?
   b. In a Daniell cell, what is the oxidizing agent and what is the reducing agent? Explain your answer.

Continued on next page

5. Sketch and label galvanic cells for each of the following cell notations. Write the oxidation half-reaction, the reduction half-reaction, and the overall cell reaction. Identify the anode and the cathode in each case. Identify any inert electrodes.

   a. $Sn(s) \mid Sn^{2+}(aq) \parallel Tl^{+}(aq) \mid Tl(s)$
   b. $Cd(s) \mid Cd^{2+}(aq) \parallel H^{+}(aq) \mid H_2(g) \mid Pt(s)$

6. Pushing a zinc electrode and a copper electrode into a lemon makes a "lemon cell." In the following representation of the cell, $C_6H_8O_7$ is the formula for citric acid. Explain why the representation does not include a double vertical line.

   $Zn(s) \mid C_6H_8O_7(aq) \mid Cu(s)$

Cell Potentials

electrical potential difference between two points, is the amount of energy that a unit charge would gain by moving from one point to the other

voltage a common term for electrical potential difference

cell potential the electrical potential difference between the two electrodes of a cell

standard cell potential the cell potential when the salt concentrations of all salt solutions are 1.0 mol/L under standard conditions of temperature and pressure

You read that the oxidation reaction at the anode causes the anode to become negatively charged and the reduction reaction that occurs at the cathode causes the cathode to become positively charged. Whenever a separation of charge exists, a force acts on the charged particles. Therefore, they have potential energy. The amount of energy conferred on a unit of charge when it moves from one point to another is called the **electrical potential difference** between those two points. In the case of galvanic cells, these two points are the two electrodes. In the sketches of the galvanic cells, you saw a voltmeter. A voltmeter measures the potential difference (also called **voltage**) between two points. The magnitude of the electrical potential difference between the electrodes in a galvanic cell is an important property of a cell because it determines how much energy can be conferred on the moving charges. For any given cell, the electrical potential difference between the electrodes is called the **cell potential**.

The cell potential depends on many factors, including the nature of the oxidizing and reducing agents, the concentrations of the salt solutions in the half-cells, the temperature of the solutions, and the atmospheric pressure. Chemists have agreed on a set of standard conditions for reporting cell potentials. The **standard cell potential**, symbolized by $E°_{cell}$, is the potential difference between the electrodes of a galvanic cell when the concentrations of the salt solutions are 1.0 mol/L, the atmospheric pressure is 101.325 kPa (1.0 atm), the electrodes are pure metals, the temperature is 25°C, and there is no electric current flowing in the cell. When all of these variables are held constant, the only factor affecting the cell potential is the identity of the oxidizing and reducing agents.

You can measure a standard cell potential for any combination of oxidizing and reducing agents. However, it would be convenient to be able to describe half-cell potentials. Because any type of electrical potential difference always reports a difference between two points, you can define a half-cell potential only by choosing an arbitrary reference point. This situation is analogous to defining an altitude. When you note the altitude at which an airplane is flying, you are using sea level as a reference point. You are not referring to the distance that the airplane is above the ground. For example, if you were to land at the Bangda Airport in Tibet, the highest airport in the world, you would be at an altitude of more than 4 km. The altitude at sea level is *defined* as zero and all other altitudes are measured in relation to sea level. Chemists have likewise agreed on a reference half-cell to which all other half-cells are related. This reference point is defined as the half-reaction between hydrogen gas and hydrogen ions, as shown below:

$$H_2(g) \rightarrow 2H^{+}(aq) + 2e^{-}$$

Since hydrogen is a gas, standard conditions are defined as a platinum electrode immersed in a 1.0 mol/L solution of a monoprotic acid with hydrogen gas being bubbled past the electrode at 1.0 atm pressure (see **Figure 10.8**). The half-cell potential of the hydrogen half-cell is defined as zero. The half-cell potential of all other cells is defined as the potential difference between the hydrogen half-cell and the chosen cell.

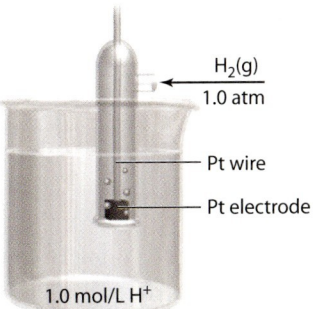

Figure 10.8 The potential of this standard hydrogen half-cell is arbitrarily assigned to be zero. This half-cell is the reference against which all other half-cell potentials are measured.

The hydrogen half-cell can be either the reducing half-cell or the oxidizing half-cell, depending on whether hydrogen is a stronger or weaker reducing agent than the compound in the opposite half-cell. **Figure 10.9** shows that the hydrogen half-cell is the reducing half-cell (cathode) when connected to a zinc half-cell and is the oxidizing half-cell (anode) when connected to the copper half-cell.

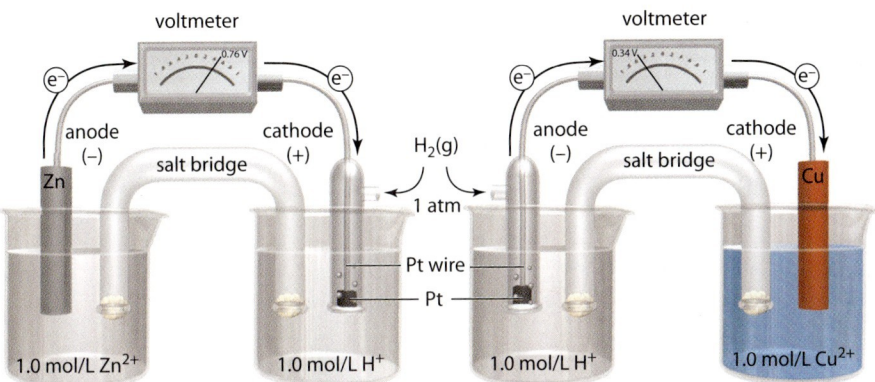

Figure 10.9 Zinc is a stronger reducing agent than hydrogen is. Therefore, the hydrogen electrode is the cathode when connected to a zinc electrode. Hydrogen is a stronger reducing agent than copper is, so the hydrogen electrode is the anode when connected to the copper electrode.

If you used an apparatus, such as the one in **Figure 10.9**, and measured the standard cell potentials of the two cells, you would determine that the cell potential for the first cell is 0.76 V. The cell notation for that cell is shown here:

$$Zn(s) \mid Zn^{2+}(aq) \parallel H^{+}(aq) \mid H_2(g) \mid Pt(s)$$

Since the hydrogen half-cell potential is defined as zero, the zinc half-cell potential is 0.76 V. Similarly, if you measured the cell potential of the second cell, you would determine a potential difference of 0.34 V. The cell notation is shown here:

$$Pt(s) \mid H_2(g) \mid H^{+}(aq) \parallel Cu^{2+}(aq) \mid Cu(s)$$

Notice that zinc is being oxidized in the first cell, and copper(II) ions are being reduced in the second cell. To be consistent and to make calculations more uniform, half-cell potentials should be reported for oxidation and reduction.

Standard Reduction Potential

The standard cell potentials for a large number of compounds have been measured and the values listed in tables. Chemists have generally agreed to list the half-reactions as reduction reactions. How, then, would you write a reduction half-cell potential for a compound that is not reduced by a hydrogen half-cell, such as the zinc half-cell?

As you saw in **Figure 10.9**, zinc is oxidized when a zinc half-cell is connected to a hydrogen half-cell. The reaction goes spontaneously in a direction opposite to the reduction of zinc. Therefore, you would consider the potential difference to be negative. You would

standard reduction potential the potential difference between a given half-cell and a hydrogen half-cell, written as a reduction reaction, when all solutes are present at 1.0 mol/L concentrations at SATP and hydrogen gas is at 1.0 atm of pressure

write the reduction standard half-cell potential, called the **standard reduction potential**, for copper and zinc as shown below:

$$Zn^{2+}(aq) + 2e^- \rightarrow Zn(s) \qquad E° = -0.76 \text{ V}$$
$$Cu^{2+}(aq) + 2e^- \rightarrow Cu(s) \qquad E° = +0.34 \text{ V}$$

More examples of standard reduction potentials are listed in **Table 10.1**. A more complete table appears in Appendix B.

If you compare the sequence of the metals in **Table 10.1** with the those of the oxidizing and reducing agents in **Table 9.2** on page 587, you will discover that the sequences are the same. **Table 9.2** showed the relative strengths of the ions and atoms as oxidizing or reducing agents. In **Table 10.1**, however, you have numerical values that tell you how much stronger the atoms, ions, or compounds are as oxidizing or reducing agents.

Table 10.1 Standard Reduction Potentials (298 K, 1.0 atm)

Half-reaction	$E°$ (V)
$F_2(g) + 2e^- \rightarrow 2F^-(aq)$	+2.87
$Br_2(\ell) + 2e^- \rightarrow 2Br^-(aq)$	+1.07
$Ag^+(aq) + e^- \rightarrow Ag(s)$	+0.80
$I_2(s) + 2e^- \rightarrow 2I^-(aq)$	+0.54
$Cu^{2+}(aq) + 2e^- \rightarrow Cu(s)$	+0.34
$2H^+(aq) + 2e^- \rightarrow H_2(g)$	0.00
$Fe^{2+}(aq) + 2e^- \rightarrow Fe(s)$	−0.45
$Cr^{3+}(aq) + 3e^- \rightarrow Cr(s)$	−0.74
$Zn^{2+}(aq) + 2e^- \rightarrow Zn(s)$	−0.76
$Al^{3+}(aq) + 3e^- \rightarrow Al(s)$	−1.66
$Na^+(aq) + e^- \rightarrow Na(s)$	−2.71

(Increasing strength as oxidizing agent ↑ ; Increasing strength as reducing agent ↓)

Another important application of these data is in choosing the salts for a salt bridge in a galvanic cell. Re-examine the Daniell cell as it is reproduced in **Figure 10.10**. Suppose, for example, that you had chosen silver nitrate, $AgNO_3(aq)$, for the salt bridge. Silver, ions, rather than potassium ions, would diffuse into the copper(II) sulfate solution. Silver ions are stronger oxidizing agents than are copper(II) ions, so the silver ions would migrate to the copper anode and accept the electrons in place of copper(II) ions. As a result, the reading on the voltmeter would be incorrect. A different chemical reaction would be occurring at the anode.

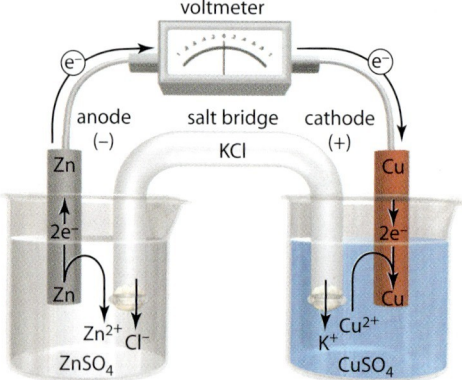

Figure 10.10 When potassium diffuses into the copper(II) sulfate solution, it has no effect on the reduction reaction of copper. However, any ion that has a more positive standard reduction potential than does copper(II) will displace the copper(II) ions at the cathode.

Calculating Standard Cell Potentials

Using the formula below, you can calculate the standard cell potential of any cell for which the standard reduction potentials of the oxidizing and reducing agents are listed in a table, such as **Table 10.1**.

$$E°_{cell} = E°_{cathode} - E°_{anode}$$

$E°_{cell}$: standard cell potential
$E°_{cathode}$: standard reduction potential for the reduction (cathode) half-reaction
$E°_{anode}$: standard reduction potential for the oxidation (anode) half-reaction

A positive standard cell potential tells you that the reaction will proceed spontaneously, in the direction indicated. A reaction will always proceed spontaneously if the reducing agent on the left side is stronger than the reducing agent on the right side of the chemical equation. These concepts are summarized below, using the reaction between the zinc metal and copper(II) ion.

$Zn(s)$	+	$Cu^{2+}(aq)$	→	$Zn^{2+}(aq)$	+	$Cu(s)$
stronger reducing agent than $Cu(s)$		stronger oxidizing agent than $Zn^{2+}(aq)$		weaker oxidizing agent than $Cu^{2+}(aq)$		weaker reducing agent than $Zn(s)$

Suggested Investigation

Inquiry Investigation 10-A, Measuring Cell Potentials of Galvanic Cells

If your calculated standard cell potential is negative, the reaction will not proceed spontaneously in the direction indicated. In fact, the reaction proceeds in the reverse direction.

Study the following Sample Problems for calculating standard cell potentials and then complete the Practice Problems that follow. To remember which reaction occurs at which electrode, think of the phrase, "an ox and a red cat." The "an ox" part refers to oxidation occurring at the anode. The "red cat" part refers to reduction occurring at the cathode.

Sample Problem

Calculating a Standard Cell Potential, Given a Net Ionic Equation

Problem
a. Calculate the standard cell potential for the galvanic cell in which the following reaction occurs:
$2I^-(aq) + Br_2(\ell) \rightarrow I_2(s) + 2Br^-(aq)$
b. Predict whether the reaction will proceed spontaneously as written.

What Is Required?
a. You need to determine the standard cell potential for the reaction between iodide ions and liquid bromine.
b. You need to predict whether the reaction is spontaneous as written.

What Is Given?
You are given the balanced net ionic equation.
You have a table of standard reduction potentials.

Plan Your Strategy	Act on Your Strategy
a. Calculate the standard cell potential for the galvanic cell. Write the oxidation and reduction half-reactions.	*Oxidation half-reaction* (occurs at the anode): $2I^-(aq) \rightarrow I_2(s) + 2e^-$ *Reduction half-reaction* (occurs at the cathode): $Br_2(\ell) + 2e^- \rightarrow 2Br^-(aq)$
Locate the relevant reduction potentials in a table of standard reduction potentials.	The relevant reduction potentials in the table of standard reduction potentials are as follows: $I_2(s) + 2e^- \rightarrow 2I^-(aq)$ $E°_{anode} = +0.54$ V $Br_2(\ell) + 2e^- \rightarrow 2Br^-(aq)$ $E°_{cathode} = +1.07$ V

Continued on next page

Plan Your Strategy	Act on Your Strategy
Subtract the reduction potentials to determine the cell potential by using the formula $E°_{cell} = E°_{cathode} - E°_{anode}$	Calculate the cell potential. $E°_{cell} = E°_{cathode} - E°_{anode}$ $= +1.07 \text{ V} - (+0.54 \text{ V})$ $= +0.53 \text{ V}$
b. Predict whether the reaction will proceed spontaneously.	The overall cell potential is positive (+0.53 V), so the reaction is spontaneous.

Check Your Solution

The equations were checked and are written correctly. The standard reduction potential values were rechecked and agree with the values in **Table 10.1**. The calculated value for the overall cell potential is positive, so the reaction should proceed spontaneously.

A standard cell potential depends only on the identities of the reactants and products in their standard states. As you will see as you work through the following Sample Problem, you do not need to consider the amounts of reactants or products present, or the reaction stoichiometry, when calculating a standard cell potential. Therefore, you do not need to multiply the cell potential by any factors. However, you must make sure that the species match.

Sample Problem

Calculating a Standard Cell Potential, Given a Chemical Reaction

Problem
a. Calculate the standard cell potential for the galvanic cell in which the following reaction occurs:
$2Na(s) + 2H_2O(\ell) \rightarrow 2NaOH(aq) + H_2(g)$
b. Predict whether the reaction will proceed spontaneously.
(**Note:** Sodium reacts violently with water, so these reactants could not be used to construct an electrochemical cell. Nevertheless, you can still calculate a " theoretical cell" potential for the chemical reaction.)

Reaction of sodium with water

646 MHR • Unit 5 Electrochemistry

What Is Required?

You need to calculate a standard cell potential for the reaction between sodium and water.
You need to determine whether the reaction will proceed spontaneously.

What Is Given?

You are given the balanced chemical equation.
You can refer to the table of standard reduction potentials for half-reactions.

Plan Your Strategy	Act on Your Strategy
a. Calculate the standard cell potential for the galvanic cell. Write the equation in ionic form to identify the half-reactions.	$2Na(s) + 2H_2O(\ell) \rightarrow 2Na^+(aq) + 2OH^-(aq) + H_2(g)$
Write the oxidation and reduction half-reactions.	*Oxidation half-reaction* (occurs at the anode): $Na(s) \rightarrow Na^+(aq) + e^-$ *Reduction half-reaction* (occurs at the cathode): $2H_2O(\ell) + 2e^- \rightarrow 2OH^-(aq) + H_2(g)$
Locate the relevant reduction potentials in a table of standard reduction potentials.	$Na^+(aq) + e^- \rightarrow Na(s) \quad E^°_{anode} = -2.71$ V $2H_2O(\ell) + 2e^- \rightarrow 2OH^-(aq) + H_2(g) \quad E^°_{cathode} = -0.83$ V
Subtract the standard reduction potentials to calculate the cell potential.	$E^°_{cell} = E^°_{cathode} - E^°_{anode}$ $= -0.83$ V $- (-2.71$ V$)$ $= +1.88$ V The standard cell potential is $+1.88$ V.
b. Predict whether the reaction will proceed spontaneously.	The overall cell potential is positive ($+1.88$ V), so the reaction is spontaneous as written.

Check Your Solution

You know that the reaction between metallic sodium and water is violently spontaneous and thus the calculated cell potential should be positive, which it is.

Practice Problems

For each of the following reactions
  a. write the oxidation and reduction half-reactions.
  b. determine the standard cell potentials for galvanic cells in which these reactions occur.
  c. predict whether the reaction will proceed spontaneously as written.

(**Note:** Obtain the necessary standard reduction potential values from **Table 10.1** or the table in Appendix B.)

11. $Cl_2(g) + 2Br^-(aq) \rightarrow 2Cl^-(aq) + Br_2(\ell)$
12. $Mg(s) + 2AgNO_3(aq) \rightarrow Mg(NO_3)_2(aq) + 2Ag(s)$
13. $Sn(s) + 2HBr(aq) \rightarrow SnBr_2(aq) + H_2(g)$
14. $Cr(s) + 3AgCl(s) \rightarrow CrCl_3(aq) + 3Ag(s)$
15. $3Fe(s) + 2Cr(NO_3)_3(aq) \rightarrow 2Cr(s) + 3Fe(NO_3)_2(aq)$
16. $2Al(s) + 3ZnCl_2(aq) \rightarrow 3Zn(s) + 2AlCl_3(aq)$
17. $2AgNO_3(aq) + Zn(s) \rightarrow 2Ag(s) + Zn(NO_3)_2(aq)$
18. $3Cu(NO_3)_2(aq) + 2Al(s) \rightarrow 2Al(NO_3)_3(aq) + 3Cu(s)$
19. $CuSO_4(aq) + 2Ag(s) \rightarrow Ag_2SO_4(aq) + Cu(s)$
20. $Br_2(\ell) + 2NaI(aq) \rightarrow 2NaBr(aq) + I_2(s)$

Section 10.1 Review

Section Summary

- A galvanic cell is a device that uses the energy from spontaneous redox reactions to generate an electrical potential difference, or voltage. In any galvanic cell, the oxidation half-reaction occurs at the anode, and the reduction half-reaction occurs at the cathode.
- If the oxidizing or reducing agent is not a solid, inert electrodes are used to provide a surface on which the reactions can occur and also carry the electrons to and from the external circuit.
- The standard reduction potential of a half-cell is the potential difference between any chosen half-cell and the hydrogen half-cell under conditions of 1.0 atm of pressure, 25°C, and 1.0 mol/L concentrations of electrolyte solutions, and hydrogen gas is pumped into the half-cell at 1.0 atm of pressure.
- The standard cell potential can be calculated by using the following formula:

$$E°_{cell} = E°_{cathode} - E°_{anode}$$

Review Questions

1. **K/U** To construct a galvanic cell, why is it necessary to prevent any direct contact between the reactants in a redox reaction?

2. **K/U** In three or four detailed sentences, explain why a salt bridge is necessary in a galvanic cell. Include an explanation of how the salt bridge works during the operation of the cell.

3. **C** Create a graphic organizer such as a flowchart that can be used to determine a cell potential for a spontaneous redox reaction in a galvanic cell.

4. **T/I** Determine the standard cell potential for each of the following redox reactions:
   a. $CuSO_4(aq) + Ni(s) \rightarrow NiSO_4(aq) + Cu(s)$
   b. $4Au(OH)_3(s) \rightarrow 4Au(s) + 6H_2O(\ell) + 3O_2(g)$
   c. $3Cu(s) + 2Al^{3+}(aq) \rightarrow 3Cu^{2+}(aq) + 2Al(s)$

5. **T/I** Use the calculated cell potentials for the redox reactions in question 4 to predict the spontaneity of each reaction.

6. **T/I** Look at the half-cells in the table of standard reduction potentials in Appendix B. Explain whether you could use two of the standard half-cells to build a galvanic cell with a standard cell potential of 7 V.

7. **K/U** Explain the difference between a standard reduction potential and a cell potential.

8. **T/I** The cell potential for the following galvanic cell is given:

    $Zn(s) | Zn^{2+}(aq)(1\ mol/L) || Pd^{2+}(aq)(1\ mol/L) | Pd(s)$
    $E°_{cell} = +1.750\ V$

    Determine the standard reduction potential for the following half-reaction:

    $Pd^{2+}(aq) + 2e^- \rightarrow Pd(s)$

9. **A** The diagram shown below is of a galvanic cell involving zinc and silver.

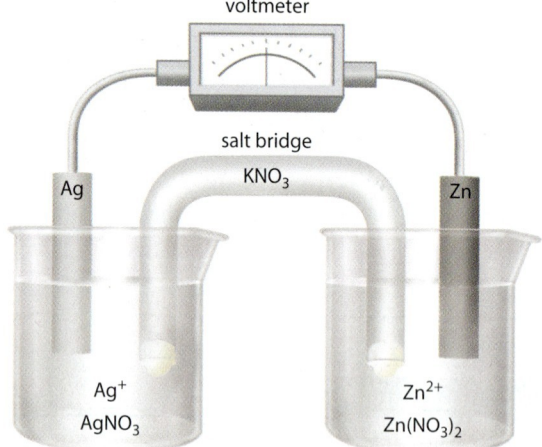

   a. Write the half-reactions and the overall reaction for the cell.
   b. Use standard half-cell potentials to determine the cell potential.
   c. Identify the oxidizing agent and the reducing agent.
   d. Identify which electrode will increase in mass and which electrode will decrease in mass.

10. **K/U** Explain the difference between an electrode that participates in the redox reaction of a galvanic cell and an inert electrode.

11. **T/I** If a half-reaction other than the hydrogen half-reaction had been chosen as the standard potential of 0.00 V, how would the overall cell potential values calculated for any cell have been affected?

12. **C** Outline the steps needed to determine a cell potential. After identifying the steps, create a graphic organizer of your choice to summarize the process.

SECTION 10.2
Applications of Galvanic Cells

Galvanic cells are fairly large and filled with liquid. You could not use a galvanic cell to power a cell phone, a remote control, or a flashlight. How are the common batteries that you use daily related to the galvanic cells about which you have been learning?

Dry Cells

A **dry cell** is a galvanic cell in which the electrolyte has been thickened into a paste. The first dry cell was invented in 1866 by the French chemist Georges Leclanché, who used starch to thicken the electrolyte. The cell was called the Leclanché cell.

Modern dry cells are closely modelled on the Leclanché cell and also contain electrolyte pastes. You have probably used inexpensive dry cells in many kinds of electrical devices, such as a flashlight, a remote control, or an iPod™. The lowest priced 1.5 V batteries (sizes AAA, AA, A, C, and D) are dry cells.

A **battery** is defined as a set of galvanic cells connected in series. In a series connection, the negative electrode of one cell is connected to the positive electrode of the next cell. *The voltage of a set of cells connected in series is the sum of the voltages of the individual cells.* Thus, a 9 V battery contains six 1.5 V dry cells connected in series. Often, the term battery is (incorrectly) used to describe a single cell. For example, a 1.5 V dry cell "battery" contains only a single cell. It is not, in fact, a battery.

A dry cell stops producing electrical energy when the reactants are used up. For many years, all batteries were disposable and were discarded after they had run down completely. A disposable battery is known as a **primary battery**. Some newer batteries, known as **secondary batteries**, are rechargeable. You will learn more about these batteries in Section 10.3.

A typical dry cell contains a zinc anode and an inert graphite cathode, as shown in **Figure 10.11**. The electrolyte is a moist paste of manganese(IV) oxide, $MnO_2(s)$; zinc chloride, $ZnCl_2(s)$; ammonium chloride, $NH_4Cl(s)$; and "carbon black," $C(s)$.

Key Terms
dry cell
battery
primary battery
secondary battery
alkaline battery
button battery
fuel cell
corrosion
galvanizing
sacrificial anode
cathodic protection

dry cell a galvanic cell in which the electrolyte has been thickened into a paste

battery a set of galvanic cells connected in series

primary battery a disposable battery that cannot be recharged

secondary battery a rechargeable battery

Figure 10.11 The D-size dry cell battery is shown both whole and cut in half. The anode is the zinc container, located just inside the outer paper, steel, or plastic case. The graphite cathode runs through the centre of the cylinder.

You are already familiar with the oxidation half-reaction at the zinc anode:

$$Zn(s) \rightarrow Zn^{2+}(aq) + 2e^-$$

The reduction half-reaction at the cathode is somewhat more complicated. A simplified equation is shown here:

$$2MnO_2(s) + H_2O(\ell) + 2e^- \rightarrow Mn_2O_3(s) + 2OH^-(aq)$$

Therefore, a simplification of the overall cell reaction is

$$2MnO_2(s) + Zn(s) + H_2O(\ell) \rightarrow Mn_2O_3(s) + Zn^{2+}(aq) + 2OH^-(aq)$$

The more expensive alkaline cell, shown in **Figure 10.12**, is an improved, longer-lasting version of the dry cell.

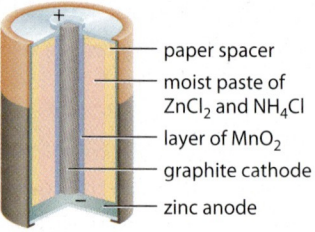

Figure 10.12 The structure of an alkaline cell is similar to the structure of a dry cell. Each type produces a voltage of 1.5 V.

Billions of **alkaline batteries**, each containing a single alkaline cell, are made every year. The ammonium chloride and zinc chloride used in a dry cell are replaced by strongly alkaline (basic) potassium hydroxide, KOH. The half-reactions and the overall reaction in an alkaline cell are given here.

Figure 10.13 Button batteries are small and long lasting.

Oxidation (at the anode): $Zn(s) + 2OH^-(aq) \rightarrow ZnO(s) + H_2O(\ell) + 2e^-$
Reduction (at the cathode): $MnO_2(s) + 2H_2O(\ell) + 2e^- \rightarrow Mn(OH)_2(s) + 2OH^-(aq)$
Overall cell reaction: $Zn(s) + MnO_2(s) + H_2O(\ell) \rightarrow ZnO(s) + Mn(OH)_2(s)$

alkaline battery a dry cell that has an alkaline (basic) electrolyte in the paste

button battery a very small dry cell, usually having an alkaline electrolyte in the paste and either zinc and mercury or zinc and silver electrodes

A **button battery** is much smaller than an alkaline battery. Button batteries are commonly used in small devices, as shown in **Figure 10.13**. Because it is so compact, the button battery is used for hearing aids, pacemakers, and some calculators and cameras. The development of smaller batteries has had an enormous impact on portable devices.

Two common types of button batteries both use a zinc container, which acts as the anode, and an inert stainless steel cathode, as shown in **Figure 10.14**. In the mercury button battery, the alkaline electrolyte paste contains mercury(II) oxide, HgO(s). In the

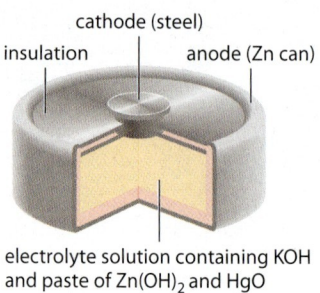

Figure 10.14 A common type of button battery, shown here, contains silver oxide or mercury(II) oxide. Mercury is cheaper than silver, but discarded mercury batteries release toxic mercury metal into the environment.

650 MHR • Unit 5 Electrochemistry

silver button battery, the electrolyte paste contains silver oxide, $Ag_2O(s)$. The batteries have similar voltages of about 1.3 V for the mercury cell and about 1.6 V for the silver cell.

The reaction products in a mercury button battery are solid zinc oxide and liquid mercury. The two half-reactions and the overall equation are as follows.

Oxidation half-reaction:	$Zn(s) + 2OH^-(aq) \rightarrow ZnO(s) + H_2O(\ell) + 2e^-$
Reduction half-reaction:	$HgO(s) + H_2O(\ell) + 2e^- \rightarrow Hg(\ell) + 2OH^-(aq)$
Overall reaction:	$Zn(s) + HgO(s) \rightarrow ZnO(s) + Hg(\ell)$

Health and Safety Concerns Involving Batteries

Canadians have known for many years that batteries can become dangerous. They can corrode and the alkaline substances can leak out. They can also explode if they are incinerated, releasing not only alkaline material but also the toxic heavy metals that are in some batteries.

Another hazard associated with using batteries involves accidental swallowing of button batteries, such as those shown in **Figure 10.15**. As the number and type of button batteries increase, the number of swallowing cases is expected to increase. More than 60 percent of these cases involve children under five years old, with a peak between the ages of one and two years of age. One reason for the increase in the number of cases is the accessibility of the batteries. Several years ago, most button batteries were used in hearing aids, calculators, and camera equipment. Today they are appearing in remote controls, and even in musical or lighted jewellery, greeting cards, shoelaces, and pens.

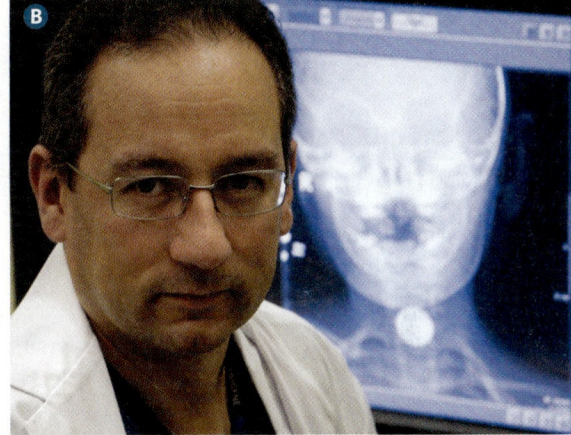

Figure 10.15 Button batteries come in a variety of sizes (**A**) to suit the type of device for which they have been designed. As button batteries have become more common, the number of cases of accidentally swallowed batteries has increased. If a battery gets stuck in the esophagus (**B**), it can cause severe injuries.

The danger in swallowing button batteries does not come from choking or from toxic substances leaking out of the batteries. Most of the time, when someone swallows a battery, it passes quickly through the digestive system and causes no harm. However, if the battery lodges in the esophagus, it can cause serious damage or even death. The button batteries that are most likely to lodge in the esophagus are the lithium batteries, which are about the size of a five-cent coin. They are large enough to get caught in a small child's esophagus, and these batteries generate more power than most others.

When lodged in the esophagus, the body fluids provide an electrolyte for the battery. A current then flows through the fluids, which causes chemical reactions that produce strongly alkaline compounds. These compounds cause severe burns to the tissues. In some cases, the compounds burnt holes completely through the esophagus. The resulting injuries were extremely serious and, in a few cases, were fatal. Serious damage can begin within two hours after swallowing the battery.

fuel cell a battery in which reactants can be added and products can be removed while the battery is operating

Fuel Cells

Fuel cells offer great promise for the future by providing clean electrical energy for transportation as well as for industries and homes. A **fuel cell** is, fundamentally, a battery that can be refuelled. Instead of a container with chemical reactants sealed inside, the reactants flow into a fuel cell and the products flow out of it. Although this sounds similar to an internal combustion engine or a fossil fuel-burning electrical generator, fuel cells convert the energy in the fuel directly into electrical energy, as does a battery, instead of burning the fuel and using the heated gases to drive an engine or generator. Fuel cells are more efficient than are engines or generators that burn fuel and, in addition, they are much cleaner. The major "waste" product is water.

So, if fuel cells are so clean and efficient, why are they not in everyday use? The simple answer is cost. Nevertheless, many government and industry research projects are finding ways to reduce the cost and improve the technology. For example, the bus in **Figure 10.16** is part of a testing, demonstration, and development program. Many more buses similar to this have been used for public transportation in cities throughout the world.

Figure 10.16 This city bus in Vancouver, British Columbia, is part of a fleet of buses in a development program. The buses are powered by fuel cells produced by Ballard Power Systems located in Burnaby, British Columbia. The buses are fuelled by hydrogen and the only emission is pure water.

Considering the stage of the development of fuel cells, you might think that the concept was only recently developed. On the contrary, the first demonstration of a working fuel cell was carried out by Sir William Robert Grove in 1839. He did not pursue the development of the "gas battery" as he called it. In 1889, Ludwig Mond and Charles Langer tried to modify Grove's design but were unable to produce a practical device. It was Mond and Langer who coined the term fuel cell. In 1932, Dr. Francis Thomas Bacon made modifications to Mond and Langer's fuel cell and created one that was able to power a welding machine. Although a proven concept, the fuel cell had not yet become practical or economical.

In 1960, NASA (National Aeronautics and Space Administration) began to look for a safe, efficient, light-weight source of electrical energy for space flights that had crews. Funded by NASA, several companies carried out intensive research and the first practical—though expensive—fuel cells were developed. Not only could the fuel cells produce electrical energy efficiently but also the "waste" product was pure water that the astronauts could consume (**Figure 10.17**).

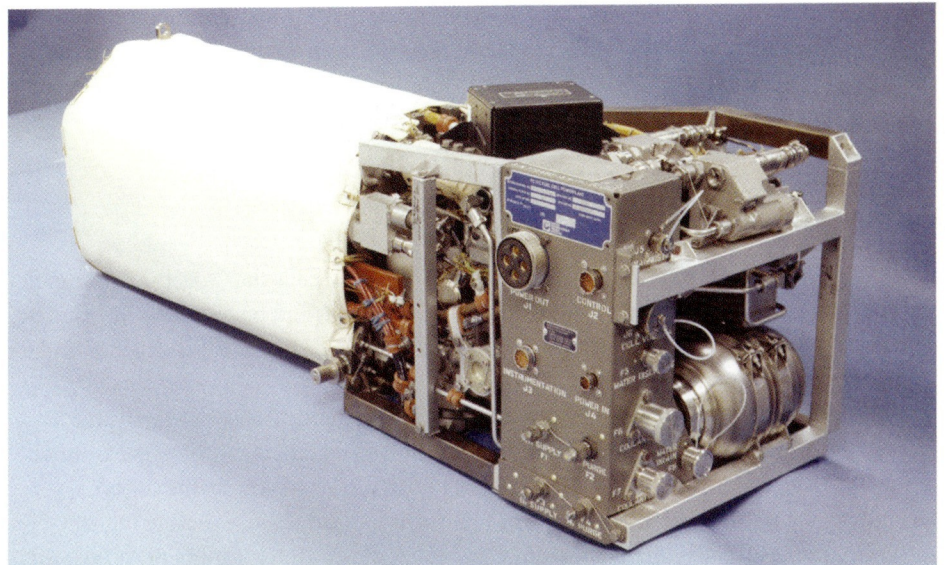

Figure 10.17 This fuel cell provides electrical energy for instruments and equipment on the space shuttle, as well as water for the astronauts to drink.

Fuel Cell Technology

Various types of fuel cells are currently being developed, but they are all based on the same principle—the principle of the galvanic cell. The main difference is that the chemical reactants are gases that flow past the anode and cathode where the oxidation and reduction half-reactions occur. An electric current then flows through an external circuit. Finally, the gaseous products are eliminated from the cell.

The type of fuel cell that was first used by NASA on space flights for their Gemini program is called the *proton exchange membrane* (PEM) *fuel cell*. A schematic diagram of a PEM fuel cell is shown in **Figure 10.18**.

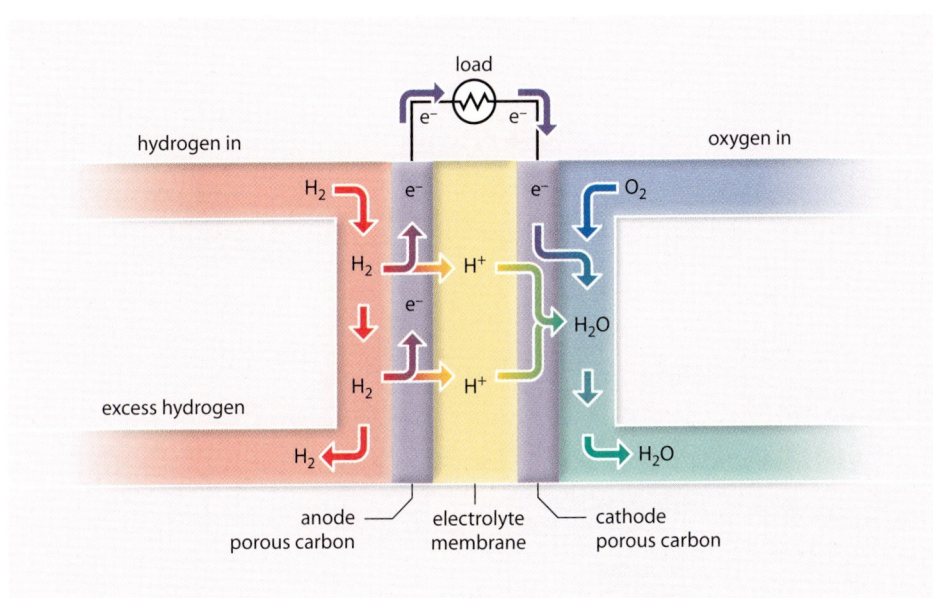

Figure 10.18 Hydrogen gas from tanks and oxygen in air provide a continuous supply of fuel for the PEM fuel cell. The electrolyte is a solid polymer that allows hydrogen ions to pass through.

The anode of the PEM fuel cell is porous carbon coated with platinum to catalyze the oxidation half-reaction. A thin solid polymer acts as the electrolyte, allowing the positively charged hydrogen ions, formed in the oxidation half-reactions, to pass through but blocking the passage of negatively charged electrons. The electrons move from the anode, through an external circuit, to the cathode. The source of oxygen for the cathode is air. As air passes beside the porous carbon cathode, oxygen combines with the electrons returning to the cathode from the external circuit and protons that have passed through the membrane. The oxygen, hydrogen ions, and electrons combine to form water. The reactions that take place at the electrodes are shown below. Notice that the hydrogen ions are in the solid phase because they bind to the solid membrane as they pass through it.

Oxidation half-reaction (anode):	$H_2(g) \rightarrow 2H^+(s) + 2e^-$
Reduction half-reaction (cathode):	$O_2(g) + 4H^+(s) + 4e^- \rightarrow 2H_2O(\ell)$
Overall reaction:	$2H_2(g) + O_2(g) \rightarrow 2H_2O(\ell)$

A complete fuel cell consists of many layers of individual cells that, together, are called a fuel cell stack. PEM fuel cells are about 40% to 50% efficient and operate at temperatures between 60°C and 100°C. PEM fuel cells are currently being tested in buses and cars and for electrical energy for homes.

Another type of fuel cell that is being tested for use in public transportation is the *phosphoric acid fuel cell*. The oxidation and reduction half-reactions are the same as those for the PEM fuel cell. However, the electrolyte is phosphoric acid. These fuel cells run at slightly higher temperatures than the PEM fuel cells but can achieve slightly higher efficiencies. Also, they can tolerate fuels that are not as pure as those for the PEM fuel cells.

A third type of fuel cell, called the *alkaline fuel cell*, was developed for NASA's Apollo program and is still used in space shuttles. In an alkaline fuel cell (see **Figure 10.19**), the electrolyte is aqueous potassium hydroxide. When hydrogen reaches the anode, it combines with the hydroxide ions from the electrolyte and forms water. The electrons travel along the electrode to the external circuit. At the cathode, oxygen gas combines with the electrons that are returning from the external circuit and with water. The anode, cathode, and overall reactions are shown here.

Oxidation half-reaction (anode):	$2H_2(g) + 4OH^-(aq) \rightarrow 4H_2O(\ell) + 4e^-$
Reduction half-reaction (cathode):	$O_2(g) + 2H_2O(\ell) + 4e^- \rightarrow 4OH^-(aq)$
Overall reaction:	$2H_2(g) + O_2(g) \rightarrow 2H_2O(\ell)$

Figure 10.19 In an alkaline fuel cell, the hydroxide ions that are used in the oxidation half-reaction at the anode are replenished by the reduction half-reaction at the cathode.

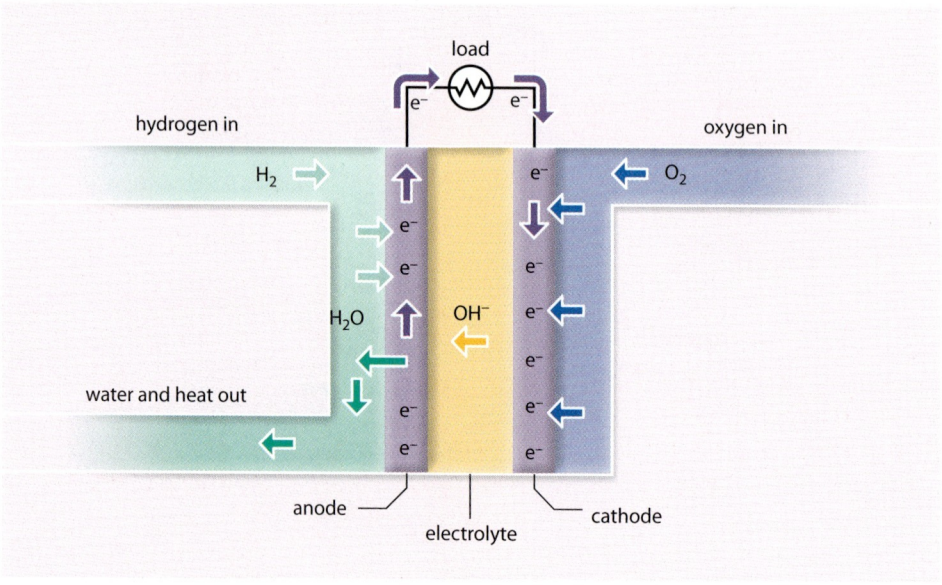

Alkaline fuel cells operate at temperatures around 90°C to 100°C and are about 40% to 50% efficient. Their use will probably remain with the space program and the military.

Source of Hydrogen Gas

Only trace amounts of hydrogen gas are found in the atmosphere. Hydrogen for use in fuel cells must be extracted from other compounds, and any extraction processes requires energy. For example, electrical energy can split water into hydrogen and oxygen. Also, hydrogen can be chemically removed from hydrocarbons by processes called *reforming*. Once again, all these processes require energy. If the energy used to extract hydrogen is obtained from the burning of fossil fuels, there would be no benefit in using fuel cells. If, however, wind and solar energies are used to produce the hydrogen, the entire process is still environmentally friendly.

Research is under way to develop fuel cells that have internal reformers—systems that remove hydrogen from hydrocarbons. These fuel cells can use a variety of fuels, such as methane or other hydrocarbons. Some carbon dioxide is produced, but for the amount of energy generated, much less carbon dioxide is released than from internal combustion engines or fossil fuel-burning power plants.

Progress is being made in the development of another unique fuel cell—the direct methanol fuel cell (DMFC). The reactions that take place at the electrodes are shown below. This fuel cell can use methanol rather than hydrogen, as shown in **Figure 10.20**.

Oxidation half-reaction (anode):	$CH_3OH(\ell) + H_2O(\ell) \rightarrow CO_2(g) + 6H^+ + 6e^-$
Reduction half-reaction (cathode):	$O_2(g) + 4H^+ + 4e^- \rightarrow 2H_2O(\ell)$
Overall reaction:	$2CH_3OH(\ell) + 3O_2(g) \rightarrow 2CO_2(g) + 4H_2O(\ell)$

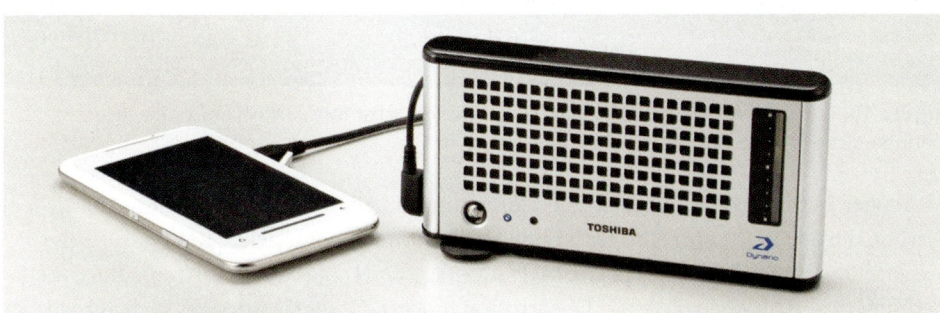

Figure 10.20 This direct methanol fuel cell serves as a power source for mobile digital devices. The fuel cell converts a methanol solution supplied from a cartridge into electricity.

Learning Check

7. Describe the similarities and differences between a Daniell cell and a dry cell.

8. What is the difference between a cell and a battery?

9. You read about two common button batteries that produce voltages of 1.3 V and 1.6 V. Why do they produce different voltages?

10. Calculate $E°_{cell}$ for a PEM fuel cell.

11. Reactions that occur in fuel cells are sometimes referred to as "flameless combustion reactions." Explain how the reactions are similar to combustion and how they differ from combustion.

12. What is the source of hydrogen for fuel cells?

Corrosion: Unwanted Galvanic Cells

Rusting is an example of **corrosion**, which is a spontaneous redox reaction of materials with substances in their environment. Many metals are easily oxidized by a powerful oxidizing agent in the atmosphere—oxygen. Because metals are constantly in contact with oxygen, they are vulnerable to corrosion. In fact, the term corrosion is sometimes defined as the oxidation of metals exposed to the environment. In North America, about 20 to 25 percent of the iron and steel produced is used to replace objects that have been damaged or destroyed by corrosion. However, not all corrosion is harmful. For example, the green layer formed by the corrosion of a copper roof is considered attractive by many people. Once this layer, called patina, is formed, it protects the copper beneath it from further corrosion. Some sculptors and other artists who work with metals make deliberate use of patinated (corroded) copper for artistic effect. An example is shown in **Figure 10.21**.

Rust is a hydrated iron(III) oxide, $Fe_2O_3 \cdot xH_2O(s)$. (Note that the "x" signifies a variable number of water molecules per formula unit.) The surface of a piece of iron behaves as though it consists of many small galvanic cells in which electrochemical

corrosion a spontaneous redox reaction between materials and substances in their environment

reactions form rust. In each small cell, iron acts as the anode. The cathode is inert and may be an impurity that exists in the iron or is deposited onto it. For example, the cathode could be a piece of soot that has been deposited onto the iron surface from the air.

Figure 10.21 Susan A. Point, a Coast Salish First Nation artist from British Columbia, uses patinated copper and bronze in her artwork.

Water, in the form of rain, is needed for rusting to occur, as shown in **Figure 10.22**. Carbon dioxide in the air reacts with rainwater to form carbonic acid, $H_2CO_3(aq)$. This weak acid partially dissociates into ions, $H_2CO_3(aq) \rightleftharpoons H^+(aq) + HCO_3^-(aq)$. Thus, the carbonic acid is an electrolyte for the corrosion process. Other electrolytes, such as road salt, may also be involved. The circuit is completed by the iron itself, which conducts electrons from the anode to the cathode.

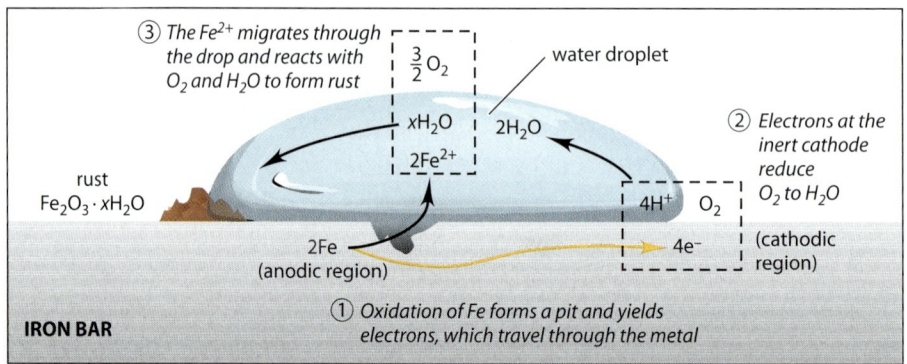

Figure 10.22 The rusting of iron involves the reaction of iron, oxygen, and water in a naturally occurring galvanic cell on the exposed surface of the metal. There are usually many of these small cells on the surface of the same piece of iron.

The rusting process is complex, and the equations can be written in various ways. A simplified description of the half-reactions and the overall cell reaction is given here.

Oxidation half-reaction (occurs at the anode):	$Fe(s) \rightarrow Fe^{2+}(aq) + 2e^-$
Reduction half-reaction (occurs at the cathode):	$O_2(g) + 2H_2O(\ell) + 4e^- \rightarrow 4OH^-(aq)$
Overall reaction:	$2Fe(s) + O_2(g) + 2H_2O(\ell) \rightarrow$ $2Fe^{2+}(aq) + 4OH^-(aq)$

There is no barrier in the cell, so nothing stops the dissolved Fe^{2+} and OH^- ions from mixing. The iron(II) ions produced at the anode and the hydroxide ions produced at the cathode react to form a precipitate of iron(II) hydroxide, $Fe(OH)_2(s)$. Therefore, the overall cell reaction could be written as follows:

$$2Fe(s) + O_2(g) + 2H_2O(\ell) \rightarrow 2Fe(OH)_2(s)$$

The iron(II) hydroxide undergoes further oxidation through reaction with the oxygen in the air to form iron(III) hydroxide:

$$4Fe(OH)_2(s) + O_2(g) + 2H_2O(\ell) \rightarrow 4Fe(OH)_3(s)$$

Iron(III) hydroxide readily breaks down to form hydrated iron(III) oxide, $Fe_2O_3 \cdot xH_2O(s)$, more commonly known as rust:

$$2Fe(OH)_3(s) \rightarrow Fe_2O_3 \cdot 3H_2O(s)$$

Both $Fe(OH)_3(s)$ and $Fe_2O_3 \cdot xH_2O(s)$ are reddish-brown, or "rust-coloured." A rust deposit may contain a mixture of these compounds.

Not all metals corrode to the same extent as iron. In fact, many metals corrode in air to form a surface coating of metal oxide that, in many cases, adheres to the metal surface and forms a protective layer that prevents the metal from further corrosion. For example, aluminum, chromium, and magnesium are readily oxidized in air to form their oxides, $Al_2O_3(s)$, $Cr_2O_3(s)$, and $MgO(s)$. Unless the oxide layer is broken by a cut or a scratch, the layer prevents further corrosion. In contrast, rust easily flakes off from the surface of an iron object and provides little protection against further corrosion.

Corrosion Prevention

Corrosion, and especially the corrosion of iron, can be very destructive. For this reason, a great deal of effort goes into corrosion prevention. If an iron object is kept cool, dry, and clean, it will not corrode. However, iron objects are often outside, exposed to the atmosphere, and it is not possible to keep them cool, clean, and dry. So more measures must be taken. The simplest method of preventing corrosion is to paint an iron object. The protective coating of paint prevents air and water from reaching the metal surface. Other effective protective layers include grease, oil, plastic, or a metal that is more resistant to corrosion than is iron. For example, a layer of chromium protects bumpers and metal trim on cars. An enamel coating is often used to protect metal plates, pots, and pans. *Enamel* is a shiny, hard, and very unreactive type of glass that can be melted onto a metal surface. A protective layer is effective as long as it completely covers the iron object. If a hole or scratch breaks the layer, the metal underneath can corrode.

It is also possible to protect iron against corrosion by forming an alloy with a different metal. *Stainless steel* is an alloy of iron that contains at least 10% chromium, by mass, in addition to small quantities of carbon and occasionally other metals, such as nickel. Stainless steel is much more resistant to corrosion than is pure iron. Therefore, stainless steel is often used for cutlery, taps, and various other applications where rust resistance is important. However, chromium is much more expensive than iron. As a result, stainless steel is too expensive for use in large-scale applications, such as for building bridges.

Galvanizing is a process in which iron is covered with a protective layer of zinc. Galvanized iron is often used to make metal buckets and chain-link fences. Galvanizing protects iron in two ways. First, the zinc acts as a protective layer. If this layer is broken, the iron is exposed to air and water. When this happens, however, the iron is still protected. Zinc is more easily oxidized than is iron. Therefore, zinc, not iron, becomes the anode in the galvanic cell. The zinc metal is oxidized to zinc ions. In this situation, zinc is called a **sacrificial anode**, because it is destroyed (sacrificed) to protect the iron. Iron acts as the cathode when zinc is present. Thus, iron does not become oxidized, until all the zinc has reacted.

Cathodic protection, shown in **Figure 10.23**, is another method of preventing rusting that is similar to galvanizing, in that a more reactive metal is attached to the iron object.

galvanizing the process of covering iron with a protective layer of zinc

sacrificial anode a metal that oxidizes more easily than iron and is destroyed to protect an iron object

cathodic protection the process of attaching a more reactive metal to an iron object that will act as an anode and prevent the iron object from corroding

Figure 10.23 In the city of Peterborough, the water mains are preserved by cathodic protection. Every summer, Peterborough Utilities installs more magnesium anodes and connects them to the water mains as shown here. They protect the water main from rusting for 15 to 25 years after installation.

Suggested Investigation

ThoughtLab Investigation 10-B, Health and Safety Issues involving Corrosion

This reactive metal acts as a sacrificial anode, and the iron becomes the cathode of a galvanic cell. Unlike galvanizing, the metal used in cathodic protection does not completely cover the iron. Because the sacrificial anode is slowly destroyed by oxidation, it must be replaced periodically.

If iron is covered with a protective layer of a metal that is less reactive than iron, there can be unfavourable results. A "tin" can is actually a steel can coated with a thin layer of tin. While the tin layer remains intact, it provides effective protection against rusting. If the tin layer is broken or scratched, however, the iron in the steel corrodes faster in contact with the tin than the iron would on its own. Since tin is less reactive than iron is, tin acts as a cathode in each miniature galvanic cell on the surface of the can. Therefore, the tin provides a large area of available cathodes for the small galvanic cells involved in the rusting process. Iron acts as the anode of each cell, which is its normal role when rusting.

Sometimes, the rusting of iron is promoted accidentally. For example, by connecting an iron pipe to a copper pipe in a plumbing system, an inexperienced plumber could accidentally speed up the corrosion of the iron pipe. Copper is less reactive than iron. Therefore, copper acts as the cathode and iron as the anode in numerous small galvanic cells at the intersection of the two pipes.

Learning Check

13. Use the two half-reactions for the rusting process and a table of standard reduction potentials to determine the standard cell potential for this reaction.

14. Do you think that your calculated value for question 13 is the actual cell potential for each of the small galvanic cells on the surface of a rusting iron object? Explain your reasoning.

15. Explain why aluminum provides cathodic protection to an iron object.

16. In 2000, Transport Canada reported that thousands of cars sold in the Atlantic provinces between 1989 and 1999 had corroded engine cradle mounts. Failure of these mounts can cause the steering shaft to separate from the car. The manufacturer recalled the cars so that repairs could be made, where necessary. The same cars were sold in other parts of the country but had little corrosion damage. Why do you think that the corrosion problems showed up in the Atlantic provinces?

17. A "tin" can is actually a steel can coated with a thin layer of tin. Explain how the tin keeps the can from rusting.

18. Referring to your answer in question 17, explain what happens if the layer of tin covering a "tin" can becomes scratched.

Activity 10.2 | Modelling Corrosion Prevention

Materials
- 4 iron nails
- 2 pieces of magnesium ribbon (about 5 cm long each)
- 2 thick copper wires (about 5 cm long each)
- four 150 mL beakers
- distilled water
- saltwater solution
- sandpaper

Procedure

1. Sand the surfaces of each nail. Wrap two nails with the magnesium ribbon, and wrap the other two nails with the copper wire. Make sure you wrap the metals tightly so the nails cannot slip out.

2. Put each nail in a beaker. Add distilled water to one beaker with a copper-wrapped nail and to a second beaker with a magnesium-wrapped nail. Add enough distilled water to just cover the nails. Then do the same using saltwater for the other two beakers. Record your observations of the nails and the liquids.

3. Leave the beakers overnight in a warm location.

4. Record your observations of the nails and the liquids.

Questions

1. Compare the two copper-wrapped nails and the two magnesium-wrapped nails after they have stood overnight. Write a general statement that explains the differences.

Section 10.2 Review

Section Summary

- Galvanic cells are made more portable and practical by thickening the electrolyte into a paste and sealing the components of the cell. The resulting cell is called a dry cell. A battery is a set of cells connected in series.
- A fuel cell is based on the concept of a galvanic cell. For most fuel cells, hydrogen is the reducing agent and oxygen is the oxidizing agent. The by-product is pure water. The hydrogen and oxygen flow into the fuel cell and the excess hydrogen and water flow out of the cell.
- Corrosion is caused by the spontaneous formation of galvanic cells on the surface of metals.
- Corrosion can be reduced or eliminated by covering an iron surface with paint or some other material, by galvanizing, or by cathodic protection.

Review Questions

1. **K/U** Describe the oxidizing agent and the reducing agent in a typical dry cell.

2. **K/U** Explain why the top of a commercial 1.5 V dry cell "battery" is always marked with a plus sign, as shown in the photograph below.

3. **T/I** The reaction products in a silver button battery are solid zinc oxide and solid silver.
   a. Write the two half-reactions and the equation for the overall reaction in the battery.
   b. Name the materials used to make the anode and the cathode.

4. **K/U** Explain why button batteries containing silver oxide are preferred over those made of mercury(II) oxide from an environmental point of view.

5. **T/I** How many dry cells are needed to make a 6 V battery? Explain your answer.

6. **A** Many 9 V batteries are very small, whereas some 1.5 V dry cells are very large. Explain how a small battery can create a large voltage (potential difference) whereas a large cell can produce a small voltage. What is the advantage of a large size for a 1.5 V dry cell?

7. **K/U** When a dry cell produces an electric current, what happens to the container? Explain your answer.

8. **T/I** Use the following cell notation to sketch a possible design of the cell. Include as much information as you can. Identify the anode and cathode, and write the half-reactions and the overall cell reaction: Fe(s) | Fe^{2+}(aq) || Ag^+(aq) | Ag(s)

9. **C** Use a table or graphic organizer such as a Venn diagram to explain how a fuel cell is similar to a dry cell and how a fuel cell differs from a dry cell.

10. **K/U** Name three ways in which fuel cells are superior to other possible methods of producing electrical energy for space flights, and explain your reasoning.

11. **C** Sketch a PEM fuel cell.
    a. Label the parts of the fuel cell.
    b. Write the reactions that occur at the anode and cathode.
    c. Describe how the fuel cell provides electrical energy.

12. **K/U** Why does the use of road salt cause motor vehicles to rust faster than they otherwise would?

13. **K/U** Explain why zinc acts as a sacrificial anode in contact with iron.

14. **A** Identify two metals that do not corrode easily in the presence of oxygen and water.
    a. Explain why the metals do not corrode.
    b. How are these metals useful? How do the uses of these metals depend on their resistance to corrosion?

15. **A** A silver utensil is said to "tarnish" when its surface corrodes to form a brown or black layer of silver sulfide.
    a. Research and describe a chemical procedure that can be used to remove the layer of silver sulfide.
    b. Write balanced half-reactions and an overall chemical equation for the process.

SECTION 10.3

Driving Non-spontaneous Reactions

Key Terms

electrolytic cell
electrolysis
chlor-alkali process

In the first section of this chapter, you learned more about redox reactions and how spontaneous redox reactions release energy. In the second section, you learned how galvanic cells harness that energy in the form of electrical energy. Would it be possible to introduce electrical energy from an external source and cause redox reactions to proceed in the opposite direction? If so, what could you accomplish by reversing the direction of redox reactions?

Electrolytic Cells

A cell that uses an external source of electrical energy to drive a non-spontaneous redox reaction is called an **electrolytic cell**. You could describe an electrolytic cell as a cell that converts electrical energy into chemical energy. The process that takes place in an electrolytic cell is called **electrolysis**.

Electrolytic cells can look very much like galvanic cells. In fact, some galvanic cells can be converted into electrolytic cells. **Figure 10.24** shows how a Daniell cell can be converted into an electrolytic cell by adding a power source.

In **Figure 10.24A**, zinc is spontaneously oxidized, and electrons flow through the external circuit to the copper electrode, on the surface of which copper(II) ions are reduced to copper atoms. In **Figure 10.24B**, a power source was added to the external circuit, making the cell an electrolytic cell. The power supply "pulls" electrons from the copper electrode, thus oxidizing copper atoms in the electrode to copper(II) ions that go into solution. The copper electrode is therefore the anode, because oxidation half-reactions occur there.

At the same time, the power supply is forcing electrons onto the zinc electrode, causing zinc ions in the solution to become reduced to zinc atoms that become part of the zinc electrode. Since zinc ions are becoming reduced at the zinc electrode, that electrode is the cathode. The entire system is operating opposite to the Daniell cell.

The processes happening in the galvanic cell and the electrolytic cell are compared in **Table 10.2** on the following page.

electrolytic cell an electrochemical cell that uses an external source of energy to drive a non-spontaneous redox reaction

electrolysis the process of using electrical energy to drive a non-spontaneous redox reaction

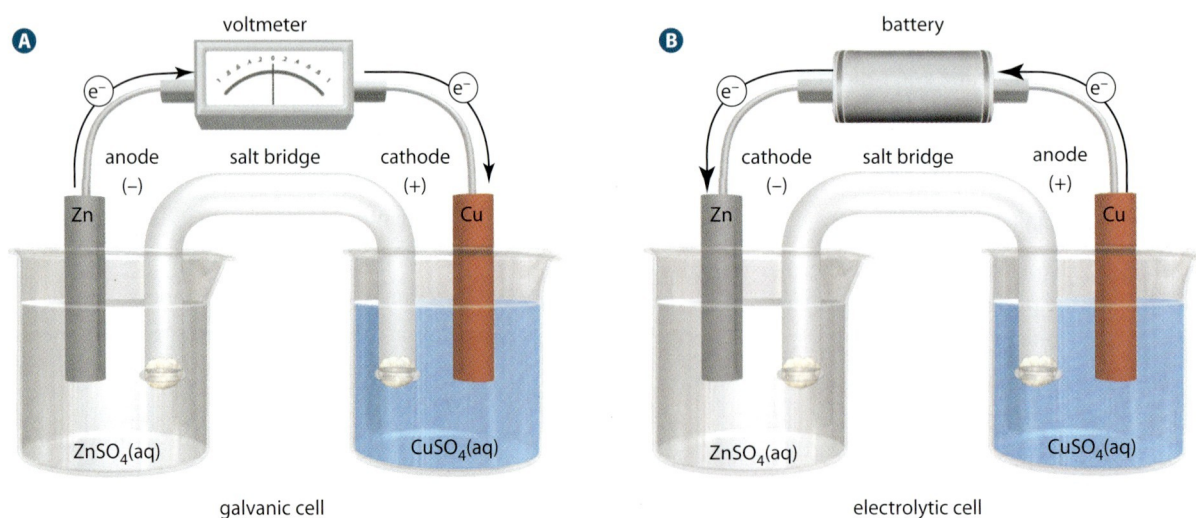

Figure 10.24 Adding an external voltage to reverse the electron flow converts a Daniell cell (**A**) from a galvanic cell into an electrolytic cell (**B**).

Table 10.2 Comparison of Galvanic Cell and Electrolytic Cell

Galvanic Cell	Electrolytic Cell
Spontaneous reaction	Non-spontaneous reaction
Converts chemical energy to electrical energy	Converts electrical energy to chemical energy
Anode (negatively charged): zinc electrode	Anode (positively charged): copper electrode
Cathode (positively charged): copper electrode	Cathode (negatively charged): zinc electrode
Oxidation (at anode): $Zn(s) \rightarrow Zn^{2+}(aq) + 2e^-$	Oxidation (at anode): $Cu(s) \rightarrow Cu^{2+}(aq) + 2e^-$
Reduction (at cathode): $Cu^{2+}(aq) + 2e^- \rightarrow Cu(s)$	Reduction (at cathode): $Zn^{2+}(aq) + 2e^- \rightarrow Zn(s)$
Cell reaction: $Zn(s) + Cu^{2+}(aq) \rightarrow Zn^{2+}(aq) + Cu(s)$	Cell reaction: $Cu(s) + Zn^{2+}(aq) \rightarrow Cu^{2+}(aq) + Zn(s)$

Previously, you calculated the standard cell potential for the redox reaction between zinc atoms and copper(II) ions and found it to be +1.10 V.

$$\begin{aligned} E°_{cell} &= E°_{cathode} - E°_{anode} \\ &= E°_{copper} - E°_{zinc} \\ &= +0.34 \text{ V} - (-0.76 \text{ V}) \\ &= +1.10 \text{ V} \end{aligned}$$

Similarly, if you calculated the standard cell potential for the reverse reaction, you would obtain −1.10 V.

$$\begin{aligned} E°_{cell} &= E°_{cathode} - E°_{anode} \\ &= E°_{zinc} - E°_{copper} \\ &= -0.76 \text{ V} - (+0.34 \text{ V}) \\ &= -1.10 \text{ V} \end{aligned}$$

The negative sign means that the reaction is not spontaneous. This negative value represents the minimum potential difference that you would have to apply from the external power source to drive the cell reaction for the electrolytic cell.

Electrolysis in Aqueous Solutions

When you convert some galvanic cells into electrolytic cells, the reactions are effectively the reverse of those in the galvanic cell, as in the example above. However, depending on the nature of the electrolyte that is dissolved in the aqueous solution, the reaction that occurs might not be the reverse of the reaction that would occur in the galvanic cell.

Shortly after Volta invented the galvanic cell (1800), Sir Humphry Davy (1778–1829) built a large galvanic cell and used it to perform electrolysis experiments. He wanted to reduce metal ions in salts to produce the pure metals. At this time, few pure metals had been discovered. Davy first tried to carry out the electrolysis of salts, such as sodium chloride and potassium chloride, in aqueous solutions. The reactions that he hoped would occur when using sodium chloride are shown below in the form in which chemists now express them.

Oxidation half-reaction (anode): $2Cl^-(aq) \rightarrow Cl_2(g) + 2e^-$
Reduction half-reaction (cathode): $Na^+(aq) + e^- \rightarrow Na(s)$

Davy observed that chlorine gas did, in fact, form at the anode. However, hydrogen gas formed at the cathode. The only source of hydrogen in the electrolytic cell was the water in which the sodium chloride was dissolved. Water was being reduced at the cathode rather than sodium ions. Chemists now understand how and why that process occurred. To learn how to predict the products of electrolysis in aqueous solutions, you need to first understand the electrolysis of water itself.

Electrolysis of Water

When water is subjected to electrolysis, some water molecules are oxidized at the anode and other water molecules are reduced at the cathode. The half-reaction equations that occur at each electrode and their standard reduction potentials are shown below. (Because the reaction that occurs at the anode is written as an oxidation half-reaction, a negative sign is needed in front of the standard reduction potential.)

Oxidation (anode): $\quad 2H_2O(\ell) \rightarrow O_2(g) + 4H^+(aq) + 4e^- \quad -E° = -1.23$ V
Reduction (cathode): $\quad 2H_2O(\ell) + 2e^- \rightarrow H_2(g) + 2OH^-(aq) \quad E° = -0.83$ V

Oxygen gas is generated at the anode and hydrogen gas is generated at the cathode. To prevent the oxygen and hydrogen gases from mixing, the electrodes are usually positioned below or in the closed end of glass tubes, as shown in **Figure 10.25**.

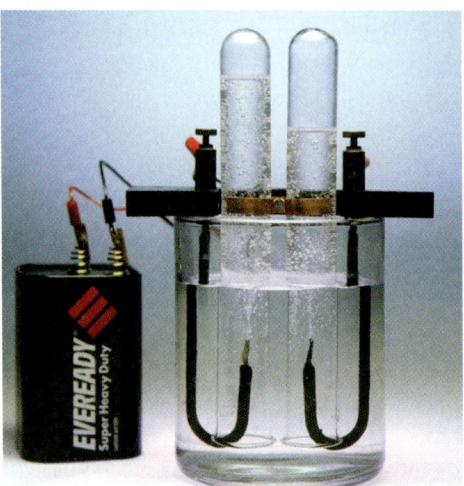

Figure 10.25 When water is subjected to electrolysis, the volume of the hydrogen gas is twice as great as the volume of the oxygen gas.
Explain why the volume of the hydrogen is twice that of the oxygen.

Several factors that affect the electrolysis of water must be considered when you are performing an experiment, making predictions about reactions, or carrying out calculations. Pure water is a poor conductor of electric current, so the electrolysis of pure water proceeds very slowly. If you use a salt that will conduct current but will not interfere with the reactions, you can increase the rate of the reaction. Sodium sulfate, $Na_2SO_4(aq)$, is often used for this purpose. A second factor that affects the electrolysis of water is the fact that the concentrations of the reactants and products —$H^+(aq)$, $OH^-(aq)$, and $H_2O(\ell)$—are not 1.0 mol/L. The concentrations of hydrogen ions and hydroxide ions are 1.0×10^{-7} mol/L. Water has a concentration of about 55 mol/L. Therefore, standard reduction potentials cannot be used for predictions or calculations in this case. The reduction potentials for the half-reactions of water under the non-standard concentrations are as shown below. Notice that there are no superscripts on the symbol E for the reduction potentials, because the values do not represent standard conditions.

Oxidation: $\quad 2H_2O(\ell) \rightarrow O_2(g) + 4H^+(aq) + 4e^- \quad -E = -0.82$ V
Reduction: $\quad 2H_2O(\ell) + 2e^- \rightarrow H_2(g) + 2OH^-(aq) \quad E = -0.42$ V

The Chlor-Alkali Process

Sodium hydroxide and chlorine are two of the most extensively produced commercial chemicals, with billions of kilograms of each produced every year in North America.

Chlorine is used to make laundry bleach, to bleach pulp for paper, to make compounds for treating water, to use as a disinfectant, and to make hydrochloric acid. A large portion of the chlorine that is produced every year goes into making polyvinyl chloride (PVC), a type of plastic. Large amounts of sodium hydroxide are used in the pulp and paper industry to break down the lignin in wood that holds fibres together. Sodium hydroxide is also used in making soaps and detergents, in the production of aluminum, and in the manufacturing of many different chemicals.

Most of the chlorine and sodium hydroxide that are used commercially are produced by the **chlor-alkali process**. The complete balanced equation for the redox reaction is $2NaCl(aq) + 2H_2O(\ell) \rightarrow Cl_2(g) + H_2(g) + 2NaOH(aq)$. In this process, brine (aqueous sodium chloride) is electrolyzed in a cell, like the one shown in **Figure 10.26**.

chlor-alkali process an electrolysis procedure for making chlorine gas and sodium hydroxide from brine, which is an aqueous solution of sodium chloride

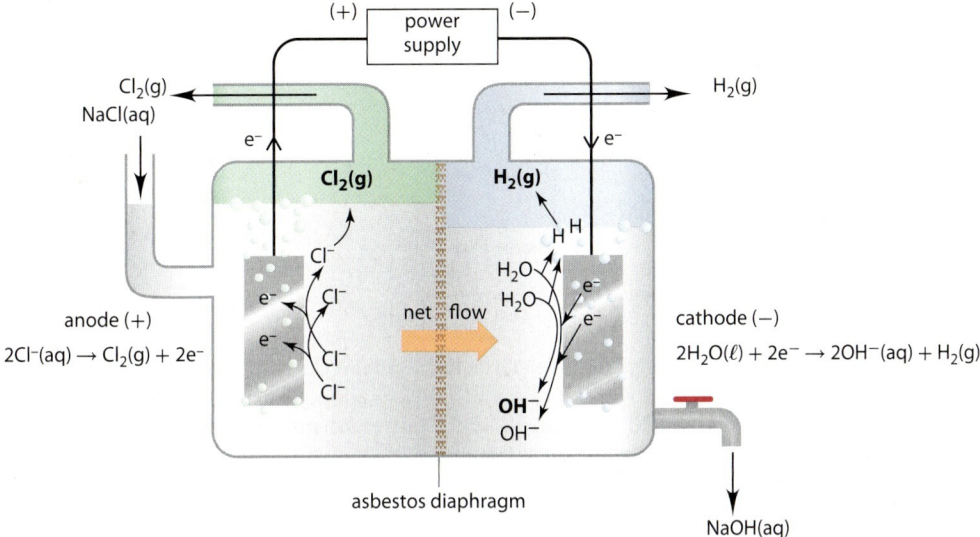

Figure 10.26 In the chlor-alkali process, chloride ions from sodium chloride lose their electrons at the anode and become neutral atoms that combine to form chlorine molecules. Water molecules pick up electrons from the cathode and form hydroxide ions and hydrogen atoms. The hydrogen atoms combine to form hydrogen molecules.

Chlorine gas, hydrogen gas, and sodium hydroxide are all highly reactive with one another and must be separated as they are being produced. The difference in the liquid level between the compartments results in a net movement of solution into the cathode compartment in which hydrogen gas is produced. Chlorine gas is produced at the anode, where it is removed and prevented from mixing with the hydroxide ions produced at the cathode. Sodium hydroxide solution is removed from the cell periodically, and fresh brine is added to the cell. The aqueous sodium hydroxide is later dried by evaporation and packaged as a solid.

Hydrogen gas is not as widely used commercially as are chlorine gas and sodium hydroxide. Sometimes hydrogen gas is used as fuel to heat and thus dry the sodium hydroxide. However, if hydrogen fuel cell automobiles and electrical generators become economical, more hydrogen produced in the chlor-alkali industry might be distributed for use in fuel cells.

Electrolysis of Molten Salts

Since sodium cannot be purified by electrolysis in an aqueous solution, how is pure sodium obtained? Sir Humphry Davy found the answer. Salts are solid at standard temperatures and will not conduct electric current. So Davy heated the salts until they melted and applied electrolysis to the molten solids. Since there was no water present, it could not interfere with the reactions. Davy was successful in using electrolysis to isolate sodium, potassium, magnesium, calcium, strontium, and barium.

The electrolysis of molten sodium chloride is an important industrial reaction. The half-reactions are shown below. **Figure 10.27** shows the large electrolytic cell that is used in the industrial production of chlorine.

Reduction half-reaction (cathode): $Na^+(\ell) + e^- \rightarrow Na(\ell)$
Oxidation half-reaction (anode): $2Cl^-(\ell) \rightarrow Cl_2(g) + 2e^-$

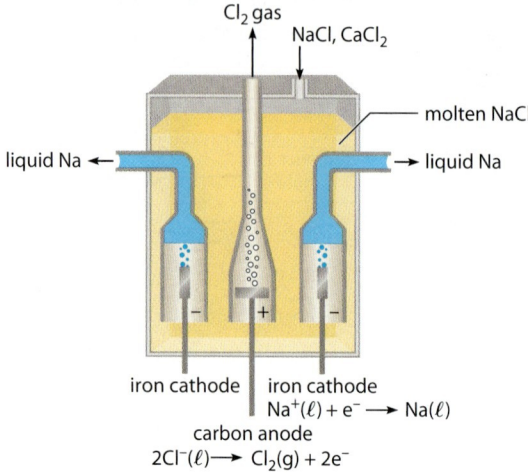

Figure 10.27 The large cell used for the electrolysis of sodium chloride in industry is known as a Downs cell. To decrease heating costs, calcium chloride is added to lower the melting point of sodium chloride from about 800°C to about 600°C. The reaction produces sodium by reduction at the cathode, and chlorine by oxidation at the anode.

Learning Check

19. What is the fundamental difference between a galvanic cell and an electrolytic cell?

20. The electrolysis of molten calcium chloride produces calcium and chlorine. Write
    a. the half-reaction that occurs at the anode.
    b. the half-reaction that occurs at the cathode.
    c. the complete balanced equation for the overall cell reaction.

21. For the electrolysis of molten lithium bromide, write
    a. the half-reaction that occurs at the negative electrode.
    b. the half-reaction that occurs at the positive electrode.
    c. the net ionic equation for the overall cell reaction.

22. The standard cell potential for an electrolytic cell is -1.10V. What does the negative sign mean?

23. A galvanic cell produces direct current, which flows in one direction. The main electrical supply at your home is a source of alternating current, which changes direction 120 times a second. Explain why the external electrical supply for an electrolytic cell must be a direct current rather than an alternating current.

24. Explain why Sir Humphry Davy could only isolate sodium from sodium chloride at high temperatures.

Rechargeable Batteries

In Section 10.2, you learned about several primary (disposable) batteries that contain galvanic cells. Now that you have learned about electrolytic cells, you might have figured out how secondary batteries can be recharged. One of the most common secondary (rechargeable) batteries is found in car engines. Most cars contain a lead-acid battery, similar to the one shown in **Figure 10.28**. When you turn the ignition, a surge of electric current from the battery starts the engine.

Figure 10.28 A typical car battery consists of six 2 V cells. The cells are connected in series to give a total potential of 12 V.

When in use, a lead-acid battery partially discharges. In other words, the cells in the battery operate as galvanic cells and produce electrical energy. The reaction in each cell proceeds spontaneously in one direction. To recharge the battery, an alternator, driven by the car engine, supplies electrical energy to the battery. The external voltage of the alternator reverses the reaction in the cells. The reaction in each cell now proceeds non-spontaneously, and the cells operate as electrolytic cells. All secondary batteries, including the lead-acid battery, operate some of the time as galvanic cells and some of the time as electrolytic cells.

As the name suggests, the materials used in a lead-acid battery include lead and an acid. **Figure 10.29** shows that the electrodes in each cell are constructed using lead grids. One electrode consists of powdered lead packed into one grid. The other electrode consists of powdered lead(IV) oxide packed into the other grid. The electrolyte solution is sulfuric acid at a concentration of about 4.5 mol/L.

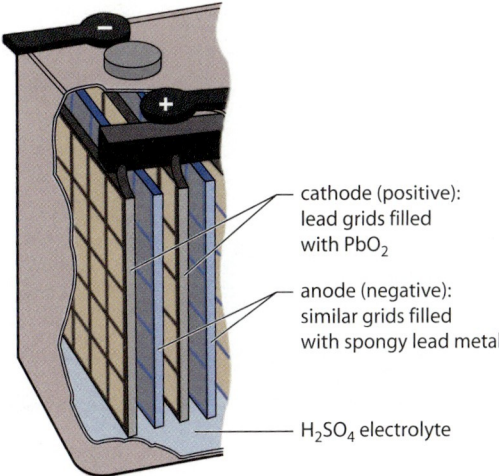

cathode (positive): lead grids filled with PbO_2

anode (negative): similar grids filled with spongy lead metal

H_2SO_4 electrolyte

Figure 10.29 Each cell of a lead-acid battery is a single compartment, with no porous barrier or salt bridge. Fibreglass or wooden sheets are placed between the electrodes to prevent them from touching.

When the battery supplies electrical energy, the half-reactions and overall cell reaction are as follows:

Oxidation (at the Pb anode):
$$Pb(s) + SO_4^{2-}(aq) \rightarrow PbSO_4(s) + 2e^-$$

Reduction (at the PbO$_2$ cathode):
$$PbO_2(s) + 4H^+(aq) + SO_4^{2-}(aq) + 2e^- \rightarrow PbSO_4(s) + 2H_2O(\ell)$$

Overall cell reaction:
$$Pb(s) + PbO_2(s) + 4H^+(aq) + 2SO_4^{2-}(aq) \rightarrow 2PbSO_4(s) + 2H_2O(\ell)$$

The reaction consumes some of the lead in the anode, some of the lead(IV) oxide in the cathode, and some of the sulfuric acid. A precipitate of lead(II) sulfate forms.

When the battery is recharged, the half-reactions and the overall cell reaction are reversed. In this reverse reaction, lead and lead(IV) oxide are re-deposited in their original locations, and sulfuric acid is re-formed.

Reduction (at the Pb cathode):
$$PbSO_4(s) + 2e^- \rightarrow Pb(s) + SO_4^{2-}(aq)$$

Oxidation (at the PbO$_2$ anode):
$$PbSO_4(s) + 2H_2O(\ell) \rightarrow PbO_2(s) + 4H^+(aq) + SO_4^{2-}(aq) + 2e^-$$

Overall cell reaction:
$$2PbSO_4(s) + 2H_2O(\ell) \rightarrow Pb(s) + PbO_2(s) + 4H^+(aq) + 2SO_4^{2-}(aq)$$

In practice, this reversibility is not perfect. Nevertheless, the battery can go through many charge/discharge cycles before it eventually wears out.

Many types of rechargeable batteries are much more portable than a lead-acid battery. For example, a rechargeable version of the alkaline battery is now available. Another example is the rechargeable nickel-cadmium (nicad) battery, which is commonly used in portable devices such as the drill shown in **Figure 10.30**.

Figure 10.30 Billions of rechargeable nicad batteries are produced every year. They are used in portable devices, such as cordless razors and cordless power tools.

Figure 10.31 shows a nickel-cadmium cell, which has a potential difference of about 1.4 V. A typical nicad battery contains three cells in series to produce a suitable voltage for electronic devices. When the cells in a nicad battery operate as galvanic cells, the half-reactions and the overall cell reaction are as follows:

Oxidation (at the Cd anode):
$$Cd(s) + 2OH^-(aq) \rightarrow Cd(OH)_2(s) + 2e^-$$

Reduction (at the NiO(OH) cathode):
$$NiO(OH)(s) + H_2O(\ell) + e^- \rightarrow Ni(OH)_2(s) + OH^-(aq)$$

Overall cell reaction:
$$Cd(s) + 2NiO(OH)(s) + 2H_2O(\ell) \rightarrow Cd(OH)_2(s) + 2Ni(OH)_2(s)$$

Like many technological innovations, nickel-cadmium batteries carry risks as well as benefits. After being discharged repeatedly, they eventually wear out. In theory, worn-out nicad batteries should be recycled. In practice, however, many end up in landfills.

Over time, discarded nicad batteries release toxic cadmium. The toxicity of this substance makes it hazardous to the environment, as cadmium can enter the food chain. Long-term exposure to low levels of cadmium can have serious medical effects on humans, such as high blood pressure and heart disease.

Industrial Extraction and Refining of Metals

Some metals, such as iron, are smelted. However, reactive metals, including sodium, lithium, beryllium, magnesium, calcium, and radium, are also extracted industrially by the electrolysis of their molten chlorides. One of the most important electrolytic processes is the extraction of aluminum from an ore called bauxite.

In industry, the process of purifying a material is known as refining. After the extraction stage, some metals are refined in electrolytic cells. For example, copper is about 99 percent pure after extraction. This copper is pure enough for some uses, such as the manufacture of copper pipes for plumbing. However, the copper is not pure enough for one of its principal uses, electrical wiring. Therefore, some of the impure copper is refined electrolytically, as shown in **Figure 10.32**. Nickel can be refined electrolytically in a similar way.

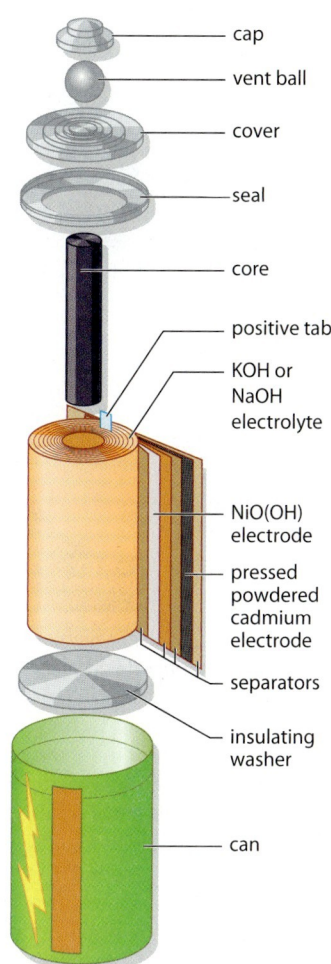

Figure 10.31 A nicad cell has a cadmium electrode and another electrode that contains nickel(III) oxyhydroxide, NiO(OH). When the cell is discharging, cadmium is the anode. When the cell is recharging, cadmium is the cathode. The electrolyte is a base—either sodium hydroxide or potassium hydroxide.

Figure 10.32 This electrolytic cell is used to refine copper. The anode is impure copper, and the cathode is pure copper. During electrolysis, the impure copper anode dissolves, and pure copper is plated onto the cathode. The resulting cathode is 99.99 percent pure metal. Most impurities that were present in the anode either remain in solution or fall to the bottom of the cell as sludge.

Canadian Research in Action

Energizing a Greener World

Dr. Linda Nazar is a fellow of the Royal Society of Canada and was named a Distinguished Woman in Chemistry in 2011 by IUPAC and UNESCO, the scientific agency of the United Nations. She holds a Tier 1 Canada Research Chair in Solid State Materials.

▶ **Related Career**
Materials engineers work with the characteristics, structures, and properties of materials at the atomic level to help create materials and products that meet desired chemical, electrical, and mechanical requirements. Materials engineers have strong science backgrounds, often with undergraduate degrees in disciplines including mathematics, physics, and chemistry. They study further to acquire specialized knowledge of engineering and apply their expertise in areas such as metallurgy, biomaterials, and nanotechnology.

Global demand for reliable, efficient, and reasonably priced energy is growing, especially for applications related to communications technology and transportation. At the same time, countries are under mounting pressure to address challenges posed by climate change and dwindling supplies of non-renewable resources. One response to this dilemma has been to boost the power and capacity of energy storage systems such as batteries. There is now considerable focus on lithium-based battery systems, in part because lithium is highly electropositive, which is why it is the predominant element used in rechargeable batteries. Across the globe, chemists, materials engineers, and other specialists are working to develop and commercialize breakthrough technologies in lithium-based battery systems.

Dr. Linda Nazar, a professor of chemistry at the University of Waterloo in Waterloo, Ontario, is an internationally recognized leader in research to improve the efficiency of batteries based on lithium technology.

In 2009, Dr. Nazar and her team of researchers reported an important development in their attempts to overcome limitations in lithium-sulfur (Li-S) batteries. In theory, the energy density—the product of capacity and voltage—of a Li-S battery is up to five times greater than that of a lithium-ion battery because the chemical reactions in the batteries are different. Despite this apparent advantage, however, certain factors limit the performance of Li-S batteries. For example, because sulfur on its own is an insulator, it must remain in close contact with an electrically conductive additive such as carbon in order to generate battery power. As well, the capacity of a Li-S battery degrades in the course of repeated discharge-charge cycles. Using nanotechnology, Dr. Nazar and her team created a positive electrode based on an interwoven composite of sulfur and mesoporous carbon—carbon that has pores between 2 nm and 50 nm in diameter. The cathode's unique framework provides essential electrical contact for the insulating sulfur while promoting the lithium-sulfur reaction. The process to create the framework is relatively simple and, in concept, can be extended to a range of materials that can serve as electrodes.

In an earlier breakthrough, Dr. Nazar and her team developed a new material for cathodes for lithium-ion batteries. The material, a sodium iron fluorophosphate, can be exchanged with lithium and substituted for lithium metal oxide cathodes. The result is a battery that has higher energy capacity, is less costly to manufacture, and sidesteps toxicity issues arising from either the synthesis of the cathode material or final disposal of the battery. These characteristics have important implications for the development of large-scale storage systems linked to solar power and wind power and to the potential development of more efficient batteries for use in electric and hybrid vehicles.

As the demand for clean energy accelerates, so too will the research to improve battery technologies. The continuing development of new materials and new approaches is essential in the quest to create the next generation of lithium batteries.

QUESTIONS

1. Do some research to find out and describe what occurs at the cathode and anode ends of a Li-S battery.
2. Compare and contrast Li-S batteries with conventional lithium-ion batteries.
3. Use Internet and/or print resources to find another career related to the research covered in this feature. Briefly describe the nature of this career and any required training or education.

Section 10.3 Review

Section Summary

- An electrolytic cell is a device that converts electrical energy into chemical potential energy. A galvanic cell can be turned into an electrolytic cell by inserting a battery or electrical power source into the external circuit and driving the reactions backward.
- In an electrolytic cell, the electrode that would be the anode in a galvanic cell becomes the cathode, and the electrode that would be the cathode in the galvanic cell becomes the anode.
- The electrolysis of brine is used commercially to produce chlorine gas, hydrogen gas, and sodium hydroxide base in a process known as the chlor-alkali process.
- Metallic sodium and chlorine gas are produced by electrolysis of molten sodium chloride in a large cell called a Downs cell.
- Electrolysis is used to recharge batteries. By driving the chemical reactions in a battery backward, the original compounds can be regenerated.

Review Questions

1. **T/I** The overall reaction for a lead-acid battery is
   $Pb(s) + PbO_2(s) + 4H^+(aq) + SO_4^{2-}(aq) \rightarrow 2PbSO_4(aq) + 2H_2O(\ell)$.
   a. Which material acts as the anode and which acts as the cathode in the reaction?
   b. What name is given to the $SO_4^{2-}(aq)$ ion?

2. **K/U** An external source of electrical energy can reverse the cell reaction in a Daniell cell so that the products are zinc atoms and copper (II) ions.
   a. What does the battery do to cause the change from the galvanic cell to the electrolytic cell?
   b. What changes does this cause in the salt bridge?

3. **T/I** Predict whether each of the following reactions is spontaneous or non-spontaneous under standard conditions:
   a. $2FeI_3(aq) \rightarrow 2Fe(s) + 3I_2(s)$
   b. $2Ag^+(aq) + H_2SO_3(aq) + H_2O(\ell) \rightarrow 2Ag(s) + SO_4^{2-}(aq) + 4H^+(aq)$

4. **K/U** Write the two half-reactions and the overall cell reaction for the process that occurs when a nicad battery is being recharged.

5. **T/I** What external voltage is required to recharge a lead-acid car battery?

6. **K/U** The equation for the overall reaction in an electrolytic cell does not include any electrons. Why is an external source of electrical energy needed for the reaction to proceed?

7. **A** What are the advantages and disadvantages of the lead-acid battery used in cars and trucks? Why is it extremely important to use caution when recharging a lead-acid car battery?

8. **K/U** In the chlor-alkali process, two of the most extensively produced commercial chemicals are produced.
   a. Identify these two chemicals.
   b. List some of their uses.

9. **C** Sketch this chlor-alkali cell. Add labels, arrows to indicate flow of matter, and chemical equations to show what is taking place at each electrode. Explain how this chlor-alkali cell works.

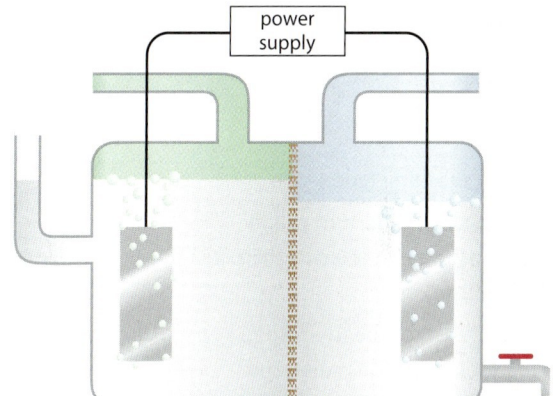

10. **K/U** Your lab partner suggests that most galvanic cells can be converted into electrolytic cells. Explain why this is or is not a correct statement.

11. **C** Draw a diagram to show the arrangement of a nicad battery. Label which electrode is the anode and which is the cathode when the battery is being used.

12. **K/U** Describe the industrial production of sodium and chlorine in a Downs cell.

Inquiry INVESTIGATION 10-A

Measuring Cell Potentials of Galvanic Cells

Skill Check
- Initiating and Planning
- ✓ Performing and Recording
- ✓ Analyzing and Interpreting
- ✓ Communicating

A galvanic cell consists of separate oxidation and reduction half-cells. The oxidation half-cell contains both the oxidized and the reduced forms of the oxidizing agent, whereas the reduction half-cell contains both the oxidized and the reduced forms of the reducing agent. The half-cells are joined by an ion-porous salt bridge; electrons travel through an external wire. In this investigation, you will construct several galvanic cells and measure the cell potential (voltage) of each one.

Pre-Lab Questions

1. From your knowledge of the activity series of metals, predict which metal will act as the anode in each galvanic cell.
2. Explain the function of the graphite electrode.
3. What determines the direction of electron flow in a galvanic cell?
4. What precautions do the MSDS require you to take when working with a strong acid such as nitric acid?
5. How are the solutions used in this experiment to be disposed of?

Question

What factors affect the cell potential of a galvanic cell?

Safety Precautions

- Wear safety eyewear throughout this investigation.
- Wear a lab coat or apron throughout this investigation.
- Nitric acid is corrosive. If you get any nitric acid or any of the solutions of metal salts in your eyes or on your skin, flush with plenty of water. Inform your teacher immediately.
- Dispose of solutions according to your teacher's directions.
- Locate the nearest eyewash station or drench shower.

Materials

- six 50 mL beakers
- 10 cm masking tape
- 25 cm clear aquarium rubber tubing (Tygon®; internal diameter 4 to 6 mm)
- 15 mL each of the following 0.1 mol/L aqueous solutions: $Mg(NO_3)_2$, $Cu(NO_3)_2$, $Zn(NO_3)_2$, $Al(NO_3)_3$, HNO_3
- strips (1 cm × 5 cm) of the following metals: Cu, Zn, Al, Mg
- 5 cm of thick graphite pencil lead or graphite rod
- sandpaper (5 cm × 5 cm)
- cotton batting
- 15 mL of 1.0 mol/L KNO_3 solution
- disposable plastic (Beral) pipette
- one black and one red electrical lead, each with alligator clips
- voltmeter (set to a scale of 0 to 20 V)

Procedure

1. Use masking tape to label the outer surface of five beakers. Four beakers should correspond to one of the four different metal/metal ion pairs: $Al(s)/Al^{3+}(aq)$, $Cu(s)/Cu^{2+}(aq)$, $Mg(s)/Mg^{2+}(aq)$, $Zn(s)/Zn^{2+}(aq)$. Label the fifth beaker $H^+(aq)/H_2(g)$.

2. In your notebook, prepare a 5 × 5 grid. Label each column to match the half-cells you labelled above. Label the five rows in the same way. You will use this chart to record the positive cell potentials you obtain when you connect two half-cells to build a galvanic cell. You will also identify which half-cell contains the anode and which half-cell contains the cathode for each galvanic cell you build. (You may not need to fill out the entire chart.)

3. Sand each piece of metal to remove any oxide coating from its surface.

4. Pour 15 mL of each metal salt solution into the appropriate beaker. Pour 15 mL of the nitric acid into the beaker labelled $H^+(aq)/H_2(g)$. (Your teacher might do the parts of this investigation that involve nitric acid as a demonstration.)

5. Prepare the salt bridge as follows:
   a. Roll a small piece of cotton batting so that it forms a plug about the size of a grain of rice. Insert the plug into one end of the aquarium tubing, leaving a small amount of the cotton hanging out, so that you can easily remove the plug later.
   b. Fill the disposable pipette as full as possible with the KNO_3 electrolyte solution. Fit the tip of the pipette firmly into the open end of the tubing.

670 MHR • Unit 5 Electrochemistry

Slowly inject the solution into the tubing. Make sure that the previously inserted cotton plug becomes wet.

   c. With the tubing completely full, insert another plug of cotton into the other end. There should be no air bubbles. (You will have to repeat this step from the beginning if air bubbles are present.)

6. Insert each metal strip into the appropriate beaker. Place the graphite rod into the beaker containing the nitric acid. (**Note:** The graphite rod is fragile—be careful!)

7. Attach the alligator clip of the red lead to the red probe of the voltmeter. Attach the black lead to the black probe.

8. Choose two beakers to test. Insert one end of the salt bridge into the solution in the first beaker; insert the other end into the solution in the second beaker. Attach a free alligator clip to the electrode in each beaker. You have built a galvanic cell.

9. If you get a negative voltage, switch the alligator clips. Once you obtain a positive voltage, record it in the appropriate place on your chart. Also record which metal is acting as the anode and which is acting as the cathode in this galvanic cell.

10. Remove the salt bridge and wipe any excess solution from the outside of the tubing. Remove the alligator clips from the electrodes.

11. Repeat steps 8 to 10 for all other combinations of electrodes. Record your results in the chart.

12. Rinse the metal electrodes, the graphite rod, and the beakers with water. Dispose of the salt solutions in the designated waste beaker; do not pour solutions of metal salts down the drain. Remove the cotton plugs from the salt bridge; dispose of the KNO_3 solution in the same waste beaker. Return all equipment as directed by the teacher.

Analyze and Interpret

1. For each cell in which you measured a cell potential, identify
   a. the anode and the cathode.
   b. the positive and the negative electrodes.

2. For each cell in which you measured a cell potential, write a balanced equation for the reduction half-reaction, the oxidation half-reaction, and the overall cell reaction.

3. For any one cell in which you measured a cell potential, describe
   a. the direction in which electrons flow through the external circuit.
   b. the movement of anions and cations through the salt bridge.

4. Use your observations to decide which of the metals used as an electrode is the most effective reducing agent. Briefly describe your reasoning.

5. List all the reduction half-reactions you wrote in question 2 so that the metallic elements in the half-reactions appear in order of their strength as reducing agents. Put the least effective reducing agent at the top of the list and the most effective reducing agent at the bottom of the list.

6. In your list from question 5, which metal ion is the best oxidizing agent? Briefly explain your answer.

7. How did your observed cell potentials correlate with the predictions you made using the activity series of metals?

Conclude and Communicate

8. Identify the factors that affect the cell potential of a galvanic cell.

Extend Further

9. **INQUIRY** Predict any factors, other than those you were able to observe, that you think might affect the cell potential of a galvanic cell. Design a procedure that could be used to test your prediction(s). (Do not carry out any procedure unless your teacher has checked it and given you permission to proceed.)

10. **RESEARCH** Galvanic cells were named after the Italian physicist Luigi Galvani (1738–1798). Research how Galvani "discovered" electrical cells while dissecting frog legs. These cells are also called voltaic cells, named after Italian physicist Count Alessandro Volta (1745–1827). Research how Volta built the first chemical batteries. Discuss how Galvani's and Volta's interpretations of their observations differed.

ThoughtLab INVESTIGATION 10-B

Skill Check

Initiating and Planning
✓ Performing and Recording
✓ Analyzing and Interpreting
✓ Communicating

Materials
- print resources
- access to the Internet

Health and Safety Issues Involving Corrosion

In a study that was published in 2001 and jointly authored by two agencies of the United States Federal Government and one private company specializing in corrosion and engineering, the direct cost of corrosion to the United States was estimated to be 276 billion dollars per year. An earlier study, adjusted for inflation, put the cost estimate at 350 billion dollars. Following similar estimates for developed countries, the annual cost of corrosion to Canada would be about 52 billion dollars per year. Clearly, the economic impact of corrosion to a country is enormous. What kinds of issues related to health and safety are part of this cost?

Pre-Lab Questions

1. What are at least five different objects and structures in urban and rural environments that can, and do, experience corrosion with the passage of time?
2. Why is corrosion a natural and expected event for objects and structures that are made of and from metals?
3. What methods can be used to slow the corrosion process?

Question

What are some societal consequences of corrosion, and how can they be minimized?

Organize the Data

1. For at least one structure or object identified in the Pre-Lab Questions, collect and tabulate data relating to corrosion.
2. Graph the data as a function of time to determine if corrosion is becoming more of a problem in recent years.
3. Make a list, table, or graph of some societal consequences of corrosion, aside from financial concerns.

Corrosion is reducing the structural integrity of this bridge support.

Analyze and Interpret

1. How has corrosion affected the Canadian economy?
2. What potential positive economic effects might the occurrence of corrosion have on certain sectors of the economy?
3. In terms of public safety, what do you think are the most important effects of corrosion?
4. Use examples to illustrate how corrosion can affect worker safety.

Conclude and Communicate

5. What methods will best allow society as a whole to cope with the problem of corrosion? Consider whether preventative methods are more effective than dealing with corrosion issues as they arise. Explain your answers.
6. If you were appointed the new Public Works Minister of Ontario, what policies would you put forth to deal with corrosion-related problems effectively in the short term and in the long term?

Extend Further

7. **INQUIRY** Corrosion affects the safety of structures and the longevity of metal products.
    a. Design a study to determine the effectiveness of different types of corrosion protection on roads and bridges.
    b. Design a study to determine the effectiveness of different types of corrosion protection in the automotive sector.
8. **RESEARCH** Use Internet or print resources to research the use of galvanization of metal as a method of corrosion protection in the automotive industry or in another industry.

STSE Case Study

Electrochemical Technologies
Assessing Green Alternatives

Scenario

You are a consultant in energy efficiency and green building design. The board of directors of a seniors' residential complex has hired you to recommend an emergency power system for a new building. The building to be constructed is a small multipurpose facility, and the directors want it to meet the latest environmental standards in design and energy efficiency.

The facility will have a kitchen with refrigerators and freezers. Therefore, it will need a back-up energy supply to protect refrigerated and frozen food in the event of a power failure. You estimate that a small power system with a capacity of about 20 kW of electricity would be sufficient to run the kitchen equipment as well as standby lighting in the building's corridors and function rooms.

The complex's main residential building has a gas-fired standby generator. The directors are considering a similar generator for the new facility, but they want to evaluate other options that might provide a greener source of emergency power. They have asked you to research and assess the viability of other options (such as fuel cells and solar power) and to make recommendations concerning the type of power source to use.

A Life-Cycle Approach

One of the directors is a retired chemical technologist. She told the other board members that electrochemistry is at the forefront of research into developing sources of clean, renewable energy. She explained that, although technologies differ in design and materials used, they share a common process. Chemical reactions known as reduction and oxidation (redox reactions) take place in galvanic cells, converting chemical energy into electrical energy and electrical energy into chemical energy. A galvanic cell consists in part of two electrodes, an anode and a cathode. Each electrode is made of a different metal and is placed in an electrolyte, which is a solution of a substance dissolved in water that can carry an electric current. Oxidation at the anode releases electrons that flow across an external circuit to the cathode, where reduction occurs. To keep the reactions in balance, ions move in the opposite direction across a barrier known as a salt bridge. The bridge allows a current to flow but prevents contact between the oxidizing agent and the reducing agent in their respective halves of the cell. The flow of electrons along the circuit is electrical energy that can then be converted to other purposes, such as running a motor or illuminating a light bulb.

Advocates of electrochemical technologies (e.g., fuel cells, solar power, rechargeable batteries, and deep-cycle batteries) emphasize positive benefits associated with the efficient and pollution-free delivery of the energy provided by these power sources. The technologist stated that, although she generally agrees with the technology, she questions how green these energy sources really are.

This building uses solar panels not only as a power source but also as an attractive architectural feature.

She says that a life-cycle approach can help clarify the benefits and risks of emerging technologies. To support her position, she has conducted research into several metals commonly used in electrochemical processes and presented her findings to the directors. The directors have asked you to incorporate this approach in your research and analysis, and they have provided you with a copy of the technologist's notes, shown on the next page.

Research and Analyze

1. Using a life-cycle analysis approach (see the Unit 1 Case Study in this textbook), compare and contrast various electrochemical technologies. Use the following criteria: key raw materials used in manufacturing each technology; the costs of operating and maintaining each technology; the energy efficiency of each technology; and materials end-of-life management issues, including recycling and waste disposal. Construct a matrix table to organize the results of your research and to compare and contrast the impacts you assess.

2. Based on your research and comparative analysis, assess which electrochemical technology appears to be the best choice as a green source of emergency power for the seniors' facility.

Take Action

3. **PLAN** In a group, prepare a synopsis of each electrochemical technology as an alternative source of emergency power, based on your life-cycle analysis. Rank each option in terms of the most preferred to the least preferred technology. Justify each choice.

4. **ACT** Prepare a presentation to the board of directors to communicate your findings and recommendations. Use the presentation to

   - describe each of the electrochemical technologies you researched and assessed, using principles and concepts related to electrochemistry
   - explain how you evaluated the options
   - summarize your conclusions and make a recommendation

Overview of Metals Used in Galvanic Cells

Here are some facts associated with the mining and refining of some metals used in batteries and other galvanic cells, and with the use and disposal of products that contain these metals.

Platinum is mined from nickel and copper ores. Because platinum is resistant to corrosion, it is suitable as a catalyst in fuel cell electrodes. The environmental effects of platinum mining and refining include the pollution of groundwater and air.

Mining operations tend to marginalize indigenous peoples. However, the Bafokeng people in South Africa, who live on the world's biggest platinum deposit, have benefited from "a resource that has transformed the once-traditional tribe into a mini-state with its own investment company" (*Mail & Guardian Online – February 13, 2011*)

Cadmium is a toxic heavy metal. It is usually a by-product of zinc production. Cadmium is used as an electrode in nickel-cadmium batteries. Along with lead and mercury, cadmium is considered in the European Union (EU) to be the most problematic substance in the battery waste stream. EU Directive 2006/66 (the "Batteries Directive") essentially bans household nickel-cadmium batteries.

Chromium is extracted from chromite ore. It can be combined with lanthanum to make a type of anode suitable for high-temperature solid oxide fuel cells.

A major chromite deposit has been discovered in Northern Ontario's Ring of Fire region. Mining and refining operations must be carefully planned, with the full involvement of First Nations communities, to preserve sensitive ecosystems.

Lanthanum is a rare earth metal usually refined from monazite and bastnäsite ores. Between 10 and 15 kg of lanthanum are needed to make the nickel-metal hydride battery used in some hybrid cars. In addition, lanthanum is combined with chromium (and other metals) for use in galvanic cell anodes.

The Bafokeng people of South Africa use revenues from platinum mining to fund economic, educational, and social programs, including sports training for young people.

Chapter 10 | SUMMARY

Section 10.1 | Galvanic Cells

Galvanic cells can convert chemical potential energy into electrical energy, which can then be used to power other devices.

Key Terms

anode
cathode
cell notation
cell potential
electric current
electrical potential difference
electrochemistry
electrode
electrolyte
external circuit
galvanic cell
inert electrode
salt bridge
standard cell potential
standard reduction potential
voltage

Key Concepts

- A galvanic cell is a device that uses the energy from spontaneous redox reactions to generate an electrical potential difference, or voltage. In any galvanic cell, the oxidation half-reaction occurs at the anode, and the reduction half-reaction occurs at the cathode.
- If the oxidizing or reducing agent is not a solid, inert electrodes are used to provide a surface on which the reactions can occur and also carry the electrons to and from the external circuit.
- The standard reduction potential of a half-cell is the potential difference between any chosen half-cell and the hydrogen half-cell under conditions of 1.0 atm of pressure, 25°C, and 1.0 mol/L concentrations of electrolyte solutions, and hydrogen gas is pumped into the half-cell at 1.0 atm of pressure.
- The standard cell potential can be calculated by using the following formula:

$$E^\circ_{cell} = E^\circ_{cathode} - E^\circ_{anode}$$

Section 10.2 | Applications of Galvanic Cells

All batteries are essentially galvanic cells or a set of galvanic cells connected in series.

Key Terms

alkaline battery
battery
button battery
cathodic protection
corrosion
dry cell
fuel cell
galvanizing
primary battery
sacrificial anode
secondary battery

Key Concepts

- Galvanic cells are made more portable and practical by thickening the electrolyte into a paste and sealing the components of the cell. The resulting cell is called a dry cell. A battery is a set of cells connected in series.
- A fuel cell is based on the concept of a galvanic cell. For most fuel cells, hydrogen is the reducing agent and oxygen is the oxidizing agent. The by-product is pure water. The hydrogen and oxygen flow into the fuel cell and the excess hydrogen and water flow out of the cell.
- Corrosion is caused by the spontaneous formation of galvanic cells on the surface of metals.
- Corrosion can be reduced or eliminated by covering an iron surface with paint or some other material, by galvanizing, or by cathodic protection.

Section 10.3 | Driving Non-spontaneous Reactions

The direction of flow of current in a galvanic cell can be reversed by applying an external source of electrical energy.

Key Terms

chlor-alkali process
electrolysis
electrolytic cell

Key Concepts

- An electrolytic cell is a device that converts electrical energy into chemical potential energy. A galvanic cell can be turned into an electrolytic cell by inserting a battery or electrical power source into the external circuit and driving the reactions backward.
- In an electrolytic cell, the electrode that would be the anode in a galvanic cell becomes the cathode, and the electrode that would be the cathode in the galvanic cell becomes the anode.
- The electrolysis of brine is used commercially to produce chlorine gas, hydrogen gas, and sodium hydroxide base in a process known as the chlor-alkali process.
- Metallic sodium and chlorine gas are produced by electrolysis of molten sodium chloride in a large cell called a Downs cell.
- Electrolysis is used to recharge batteries. By driving the chemical reactions in a battery backward, the original compounds can be regenerated.

Chapter 10 REVIEW

Knowledge and Understanding

Select the letter of the best answer below.

1. Which of the following bests describes the term *electrochemistry*?
   a. the study of processes involved in converting chemical energy to electrical energy
   b. the study of processes involved in converting electrical energy to chemical energy
   c. the study of chemically generated electricity
   d. Two of the above statements are correct.
   e. All three statements are correct.

2. In a galvanic cell involving zinc and copper electrodes, which electrode is the anode and which electrode is the cathode?
   a. Zinc is the anode and copper is the cathode.
   b. Copper is the anode and zinc is the cathode.
   c. Copper is both the anode and the cathode.
   d. Zinc is both the anode and the cathode.
   e. The salt bridge would act as both the cathode and the anode.

3. In the cell notation $Zn(s) \mid Zn^{2+}(aq) \parallel Cu^{2+}(aq) \mid Cu(s)$, what does the double vertical line represent?
   a. a boundary between the anode and its aqueous solution
   b. a boundary between the cathode and its aqueous solution
   c. the salt bridge between the half-cells
   d. the wires that lead through the voltmeter
   e. the boundary between the anode and cathode half-reactions

4. Another name for potential difference is
   a. amperage.
   b. voltage.
   c. static potential.
   d. current.
   e. resistance.

5. Research is currently under way to develop fuel cells that have internal reformers. The process of reforming
   a. takes up carbon dioxide that is produced in fuel cells.
   b. removes hydrogen from hydrocarbons for use in fuel cells.
   c. adds hydrogen to hydrocarbons for use in fuel cells.
   d. uses solar energy and wind energy to produce hydrogen for use in fuel cells.
   e. produces methanol and other alcohol-based fuels that can be burnt in fuel cells.

6. A battery that is disposable and cannot be recharged is known as a(n)
   a. anode.
   b. cathode.
   c. dry cell.
   d. primary battery.
   e. secondary battery.

7. Fuel cells are clean and efficient, yet they are not yet part of our everyday use. Why is this?
   a. They cannot yet be mass-produced.
   b. There is not yet a large demand for them.
   c. They are still too large and heavy to be effective.
   d. They do not last for long periods of time.
   e. They are still too costly.

8. Which of the following is an example of a fuel cell?
   a. button cell
   b. DMFC
   c. dry cell
   d. Daniell cell
   e. voltaic cell

9. Which metal corrodes in air to form a surface coating of metal oxide that prevents further corrosion?
   a. gold
   b. carbon
   c. iron
   d. magnesium
   e. none of the above

10. What are the products of the chlor-alkali process?
    a. chlorine gas and sodium hydroxide
    b. sodium chloride, chlorine gas, hydrogen gas, and sodium hydroxide
    c. chlorine gas, hydrogen gas, and sodium hydroxide
    d. chlorine gas and water
    e. chloride ions, hydroxide ions, and hydrogen ions

11. Which of the following statements is correct with respect to a galvanic cell?
    a. The mass of the anode decreases while the mass of the cathode increases.
    b. The mass of the anode increases while the mass of the cathode decreases.
    c. Both the anode and the cathode increase in mass.
    d. Both the anode and cathode decrease in mass.
    e. Neither the anode nor the cathode experience a change in mass.

Chapter 10 REVIEW

12. Which of the following statements is correct with respect to an inert electrode?
    a. An inert electrode will gain mass.
    b. An inert electrode will lose mass.
    c. The mass of an inert electrode will always remain constant.
    d. An inert electrode will either lose mass or gain mass, depending on the other half-cell reaction.
    e. All galvanic cells require the use of an inert electrode.

13. Which statement best describes the difference between a galvanic cell and a battery?
    a. A battery is a set of galvanic cells connected in series to each other.
    b. A battery is a set of galvanic cells connected in parallel to each other.
    c. A galvanic cell is a set of batteries connected in series to each other.
    d. A galvanic cell is a set of batteries connected in parallel to each other.
    e. There is no difference between the two terms.

14. In cathodic protection, what happens to the metal that is the sacrificial anode?
    a. It is oxidized.
    b. It is reduced.
    c. It is either oxidized or reduced, based on the metal it is designed to protect.
    d. It is neither oxidized nor reduced; it just coats the metal it is designed to protect.
    e. It is oxidized and reduced at the same time.

Answer the questions below.

15. A D-size dry cell flashlight battery is much bigger than a AAA-size dry cell calculator battery, as shown in the photograph below. However, both batteries have cell potentials of 1.5 V. Do the two batteries supply the same amount of charge? Explain your answer.

16. What advantages does a dry cell have over a galvanic cell that uses a salt bridge?

17. A student sets up a galvanic cell with silver and zinc electrodes and silver nitrate and zinc nitrate aqueous solutions in each half-cell. The salt bridge is assembled with a solution of sodium chloride. Are there any issues with the set-up used by the student? If so, what can be done to improve the procedure?

18. Reactions that are the reverse of each other have standard cell potentials that are equal in size but opposite in sign. Explain why.

19. Use a labelled diagram to represent each of the following:
    a. a galvanic cell in which the hydrogen electrode is the anode
    b. a galvanic cell in which the hydrogen electrode is the cathode

20. It is possible to measure and describe a voltage between two electrodes. How, then, is it possible to define half-cell potentials?

21. Lithium, sodium, beryllium, magnesium, calcium, and radium are all made industrially by the electrolysis of their molten chlorides. These salts are all soluble in water, but aqueous solutions are not used for the electrolytic process. Explain why.

22. Can zinc be used to protect a copper pipe from oxidizing? Explain your answer.

23. If the standard cell potential for a given reaction is negative, will the reverse of the reaction given be spontaneous?

24. Explain the function of the following parts of an electrolytic cell:
    a. electrodes
    b. electrolyte
    c. external voltage

25. In a galvanic cell, one half-cell has a cadmium electrode in a 1.0 mol/L solution of cadmium nitrate. The other half-cell has a magnesium electrode in a 1.0 mol/L solution of magnesium nitrate. Write the cell notation for the cell.

26. Explain why sodium metal cannot be purified from solid sodium chloride at standard temperatures. Include an explanation of what can be done to purify the metal from solid sodium chloride.

27. Use a diagram to explain what happens if a plumber accidentally connects an iron pipe to a copper pipe in a plumbing system.

28. Sketch the PEM fuel cell shown below. Add the following labels and explain how the fuel cell works.

   anode (porous carbon)
   electrolyte membrane
   cathode (porous carbon)
   hydrogen in
   excess hydrogen
   oxygen in
   load
   H_2 (4 times)
   e^- (5 times)
   H_2O (2 times)
   O_2
   H^+ (2 times)

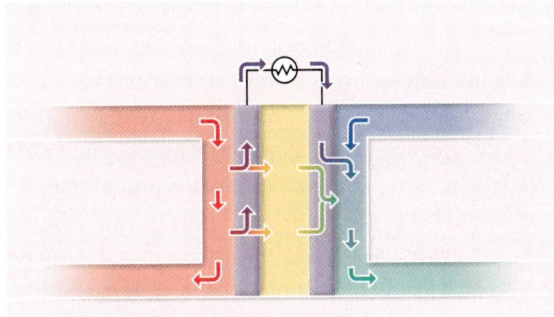

29. Rank the following in order of most effective to least effective oxidizing agents under standard conditions:

   $Zn^{2+}(aq)$, $Co^{3+}(aq)$, $Br_2(\ell)$, $H^+(aq)$

Thinking and Investigation

30. Consider the following galvanic cell:

    $Sn(s) \mid Sn^{2+}(aq)(1.0 \text{ mol/L}) \parallel Pb^{2+}(aq)(1.0 \text{ mol/L}) \mid Pb(s)$

    a. Describe a method to measure the standard cell potential.
    b. Why is this cell unlikely to find many practical uses?

31. Identify the oxidizing agent and the reducing agent in a lead-acid battery that is
    a. discharging.
    b. recharging.

32. Use the half-cells shown in a table of standard reduction potentials. Could you build a battery with a potential of 8 V? If your answer is yes, give an example.

33. In the oxidation half-cell of a galvanic cell, ions from the anode enter the solution as the cell is in operation. At the same time, ions from solution migrate onto the cathode in the reduction half-cell. Looking at the two half-cells, write a detailed paragraph to explain why the ion movements will cause a drop in voltage over the time that the cell is being used.

34. In planning a set-up to illustrate a galvanic cell for a reaction between zinc and copper, your lab partner suggests using a copper electrode for both the anode and the cathode in a copper(II) nitrate solution and a zinc nitrate solution. Is this a good idea? Explain using one or two sentences.

35. Consider a half-cell composed of $Mg(NO_3)_2(aq)/Mg(s)$ connected to a $AgNO_3(aq)/Ag(s)$ half-cell.
    a. Predict the anode and the cathode half-reactions.
    b. When a solution of NaCl is added to the $AgNO_3(aq)/Ag(s)$ half-cell, the voltage is seen to drop to zero. Propose an explanation for this; include a chemical equation in your answer.

36. Rank the following in order of most effective to least effective reducing agents under standard conditions:

    $H_2(g)$, $Cl^-(aq)$, $Al(s)$, $Ag(s)$

37. How rapidly do you think iron would corrode on the surface of the moon? Explain your answer.

38. The two half-cells in a galvanic cell consist of one iron electrode in a 1.0 mol/L iron(II) sulfate solution, and a silver electrode in a 1.0 mol/L silver nitrate solution.
    a. Assume the cell is operating as a galvanic cell. State the cell potential, the oxidation half-reaction, the reduction half-reaction, and the overall cell reaction.
    b. Repeat question 38a, but assume this time that the cell is operating as an electrolytic cell.
    c. For the galvanic cell in question 38a, do the mass of the anode, the mass of the cathode, and the total mass of the two electrodes increase, decrease, or stay the same while the cell is operating?
    d. Repeat question 38c, for the electrolytic cell in question 38b.

39. Answer the following for the galvanic cell
    $C(s), I_2(s) \mid I^-(aq) \parallel Ag^+(aq) \mid Ag(s)$:
    a. Identify the anode, the cathode, the positive electrode, and the negative electrode.
    b. Write the two half-reactions and the overall cell reaction.
    c. Identify the oxidizing agent and the reducing agent.
    d. Determine the standard cell potential.

Chapter 10 REVIEW

40. In the electrolysis of water, the following half-reactions occur.
    Oxidation:
    $2H_2O(\ell) \rightarrow O_2(g) + 4H^+(aq) + 4e^-$ $-E = -0.82$ V
    Reduction:
    $2H_2O(\ell) + 2e^- \rightarrow H_2(g) + 2OH^-(aq)$ $E = -0.42$ V
    a. Calculate the cell potential in this process.
    b. What does the sign of the cell potential indicate? Explain your answer.
41. The ions Fe^{2+}(aq), Ag^+(aq), and Cu^{2+}(aq) are present in the half-cell that contains the cathode of an electrolytic cell. The concentration of each of these ions is 1.0 mol/L. If the external voltage is very slowly increased from zero, in what order will the three metals Fe, Ag, and Cu begin to be plated onto the cathode? Explain your answer.
42. A student has set up a galvanic cell as follows to determine the cell potential of the zinc-copper cell:
    anode: zinc with an aqueous zinc nitrate solution
    cathode: copper with an aqueous copper(II) nitrate solution
    salt bridge: silver nitrate
    What is the error associated with this set-up, and how can it be corrected?

Communication

43. Conduct an Internet search on how rechargeable batteries are recycled. Write two or three well-planned paragraphs to summarize your findings. Include in your report a brief discussion of the Rechargeable Battery Recycling Corporation's Call2Recycle program.
44. Suppose you live in a small town with a high rate of unemployment. A company plans to build a smelter in your town. The smelter will produce copper and nickel by roasting their sulfide ores and reducing the oxides formed. Use a graphic organizer of your choice to present the arguments in favour of building the smelter and the arguments against building the smelter.
45. Construct a graphic organizer that can be used to help identify which electrode is the anode and which electrode is the cathode in an electrolytic cell.
46. Describe the internal arrangement of the six cells in a lead-acid battery in two or three well-organized sentences.
47. Humphry Davy and Michael Faraday were fascinated with the development of galvanic cells. Davy used his homemade galvanic cells to perform some of the first electrolysis experiments. However, Davy and Faraday could not describe their experiments and ideas in terms of electron transfers, because the electron was not discovered and named until after their deaths. Choose either a galvanic cell or an electrolytic cell, and write a description of how it works as you think Davy and Faraday might have described it.
48. Your friend is confused as to why a zinc electrode is an anode in a zinc/silver galvanic cell, but is a cathode in a magnesium/zinc galvanic cell. In two or three sentences, describe what you would say to your friend to help clarify this concept.
49. Write a short two to three paragraph report on an occupation that would involve galvanic and electrolytic cells. Include in your report a brief explanation of the chemistry associated with the occupation.
50. List the similarities and differences between a galvanic cell and an electrolytic cell, using a chart or similar organizer.
51. **BIG IDEAS** The control and applications of oxidation and reduction reactions have significant implications for industry, health and safety, and the environment. With specific reference to material covered in this chapter, write a short script for a commercial that could be used to explain some of the improvements made to battery technology in order to lessen the effect of pollutants in used batteries when they are thrown away.
52. Use sketches to illustrate the difference between a galvanic cell and an electrochemical cell that both involve a zinc/copper redox reaction.
53. In a small group, discuss the advantages and disadvantages of rechargeable batteries. Use a graphic organizer to organize the information.
54. Use the Internet to research a new type of battery or fuel cell being looked at today as a future source of energy. Make a brochure describing the energy source, including the chemical processes involved.
55. Summarize your learning in this chapter using a graphic organizer. To help you, the Chapter 10 Summary lists the Key Terms and Key Concepts. Refer to Using Graphic Organizers in Appendix A to help you decide which graphic organizer to use.

Application

56. A galvanic cell involves the overall reaction of iodide ions with acidified permanganate ions to form manganese(II) ions and iodine. The salt bridge contains potassium nitrate. Both electrodes are inert and are made of graphite.
    a. Write the half-reactions and the overall cell reaction.
    b. Identify the oxidizing agent and the reducing agent.
    c. Solid iodine forms on one of the electrodes. Does it form on the anode or the cathode? Explain.
    d. Sketch and label the entire galvanic cell.

57. Calculate the standard cell potential of a galvanic cell that uses Ag(s)/Ag$^+$(aq) and Al(s)/Al^{3+}(aq) half-cell reactions. State which half-cell is the oxidation half-cell and which is the reduction half-cell.
58. Write the oxidation half-reaction, the reduction half-reaction, and the overall cell reaction for the following galvanic cell:
K(s) | K$^{+(aq)}$ || Fe^{3+}(aq), Fe^{2+}(aq) | Pt(s)
59. Write the half-reactions and calculate the standard cell potential for each reaction.
   a. Zn(s) + Fe^{2+}(aq) → Zn^{2+}(aq) + Fe(s)
   b. Cr(s) + AlCl$_3$(aq) → CrCl$_3$(aq) + Al(s)
   c. 2AgNO$_3$(aq) + H$_2$O$_2$(aq) → 2Ag(s) + 2HNO$_3$(aq) + O$_2$(g)
60. Identify each reaction in question 59 as spontaneous or non-spontaneous.
61. Estimate the number of used batteries you discard in a year. Survey the class to determine an average number.
   a. Estimate the number of used batteries discarded by all the high-school students in your province in a year.
   b. Prepare an action plan suggesting ways of decreasing the number of batteries discarded each year.
62. A newly opened company advertises a device that can be attached to your car and can provide cathodic protection to the vehicle. Consider concepts studied in this chapter to comment on the effectiveness of such a device, using a well-reasoned paragraph. (**Note:** An Internet search on such devices may help in forming an opinion on such a device.)
63. Use the following two half-reactions to write balanced net ionic equations for one spontaneous reaction and one non-spontaneous reaction. State the standard cell potential for each reaction:
N$_2$O(g) + 2H$^+$(aq) + 2e$^-$ → N$_2$(g) + H$_2$O(ℓ) $E°$ = +1.770 V
CuI(s) + e$^-$ → Cu(s) + I$^-$(aq) $E°$ = −0.185 V
64. A gutter carries rainwater from a roof.
   a. Would you use aluminum nails to attach an iron gutter to a house? Explain your answer.
   b. Would you use iron nails to attach aluminum siding to a house? Explain your answer.
65. In designing a new battery, what considerations must be taken into account to ensure that it will be a useful energy source?
66. Electroplating is a process where a more valuable metal can be coated onto the surface of a less expensive metal. Research this process and report on it, using diagrams.
67. Research why there is a need for different sizes of batteries, in the size designations of A, AA, AAA, C, and D cells, when they all seem to provide approximately the same voltage. Report your findings.
68. If rechargeable batteries are more environmentally friendly, in that they do not need to be replaced as often, why does an alkaline battery that cannot be recharged still exist?
69. Research the aluminum-air battery and the sodium-sulfur battery. Both are rechargeable batteries that have been used to power electric cars. In each case, describe the design of the battery, the half-reactions that occur at the electrodes, and the overall cell reaction. Also, describe the advantages and disadvantages of using the battery as a power source for a car.
70. Is painting a steel bridge an effective way of protecting the metal from corrosion? Explain why or why not.

71. Suggest a valid way to protect the steel hull of a submersible drilling rig in the North Atlantic.
72. Every year, corrosion is responsible for the failure of many thousands of water mains. These are the pipes that transport water to Canadian homes and businesses. Research and describe the economic, environmental, health, and safety issues associated with the rupture and repair of water mains. Describe the methods that are being used to improve the situation.
73. In designing a new battery, what considerations would you need to take into account to ensure that the battery will be commercially successful in today's society? Explain your answer.
74. Nicad batteries are made in various sizes.
   a. Why is it not as important to make smaller and smaller nicad batteries for power tools as it is for electronic devices?
   b. What is important in the power tool industry with respect to cordless power tools?
75. Most electronic devices in use today contain rechargeable batteries. Manufacturers have gone to great lengths to improve the rechargeable cells used in these devices, to the point where most high-quality devices have the battery built into the device. Thus, the user cannot replace the battery if it wears down and it can no longer recharge. Why do you think this is done?

Chapter 10 SELF-ASSESSMENT

Select the letter of the best answer below.

1. **K/U** What is meant by *standard conditions* in a standard cell potential?
   a. 1.0 mol/L aqueous solution concentrations
   b. 1.0 atm pressures on gases and the system
   c. temperatures of 25°C
   d. pure metal electrodes
   e. All of the above are needed for standard conditions.

2. **C** Which of the following is the correct cell notation for a zinc/chromium galvanic cell?
   a. $Zn^{2+}(aq) \mid Zn(s) \parallel Cr(s) \mid Cr^{3+}(aq)$
   b. $Cr(s) \mid Cr^{3+}(aq) \parallel Zn^{2+}(aq) \mid Zn(s)$
   c. $Zn^{2+}(aq) \mid Zn(s), Pt(s) \parallel Cr(s) \mid Cr^{3+}(aq), Pt(s)$
   d. $Zn(s) \mid Zn^{2+}(aq) \parallel Cr^{3+}(aq) \mid Cr(s)$
   e. $Cr(s) \mid Cr^{3+}(aq), Pt(s) \parallel Zn^{2+}(aq), Pt(s) \mid Zn(s)$

3. **T/I** In the redox reaction in a galvanic cell, $Pb(s) + 2FeCl_3(aq) \rightarrow 2FeCl_2(aq) + PbCl_2(aq)$, which would be a choice for the cathode of the cell?
   a. a solid piece of lead
   b. a solid piece of iron
   c. a solid piece of copper
   d. a solid piece of platinum
   e. There would be no cathode in this cell.

4. **C** In the following diagram, which statement below correctly identifies the anode and cathode?

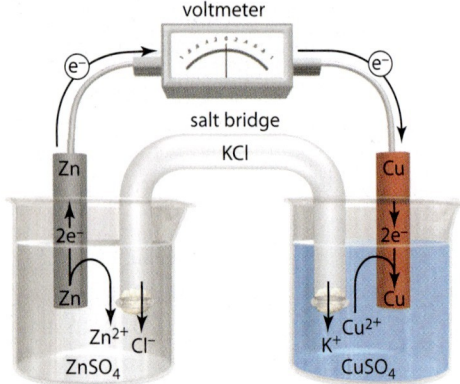

   a. The anode is Cu(s) and the cathode is Zn(s).
   b. The anode is $Cu^{2+}(aq)$ and the cathode is $Zn^{2+}(aq)$.
   c. The cathode is Cu(s) and the anode is Zn(s).
   d. The cathode is $Cu^{2+}(aq)$ and the anode is $Zn^{2+}(aq)$.
   e. The anode is $K^+(aq)$ and the cathode is $Cl^-(aq)$.

5. **T/I** What is the standard cell potential for the redox reaction involving a zinc electrode in a zinc nitrate solution, and a cadmium electrode in a cadmium nitrate solution?
   a. −1.16 V
   b. +1.16 V
   c. −0.76 V
   d. −0.36 V
   e. +0.36 V

6. **T/I** Element A has a half-reaction reduction potential of +0.74 V, whereas element B has a half-reaction reduction potential of −1.15 V. Which of the following statements is correct with respect to a galvanic cell formed with these two elements?
   a. A will be the cathode, B will be the anode, and the cell potential will be +1.89 V.
   b. A will be the cathode, B will be the anode, and the cell potential will be +0.41 V.
   c. A will be the anode, B will be the cathode, and the cell potential will be −0.41 V.
   d. A will be the anode, B will be the cathode, and the cell potential will be +0.41 V.
   e. The anode, cathode, and cell potential must all be experimentally determined.

7. **K/U** Which of the following is an example of a technique used to prevent corrosion?
   a. galvanizing
   b. cathodic protection
   c. anodic protection
   d. Two of the above techniques can be used.
   e. All three of the above techniques can be used.

8. **K/U** What is the fundamental difference between a battery and a fuel cell?
   a. A fuel cell is not reversible.
   b. A battery is not reversible.
   c. A fuel cell is a battery that can be refuelled.
   d. A battery is a fuel cell that can be refuelled.
   e. There is no difference between the two.

9. **K/U** Which statement below is most correct with respect to the electrolysis of water?
   a. Oxygen gas will collect in the oxidation half-cell, and hydrogen gas will collect in the reduction half-cell.
   b. Oxygen gas will collect in the reduction half-cell, and hydrogen gas will collect in the oxidation half-cell.
   c. The volume of hydrogen produced is half that of the volume of oxygen produced.
   d. The reduction half-cell will be slightly acidic, and the oxidation half-cell will be slightly basic.
   e. All of the above statements are correct.

10. **K/U** Why does a sacrificial anode need to be replaced?
    a. It tends to lose its oxidizing power over time.
    b. It tends to lose its reducing power over time.
    c. Its mass decreases over time.
    d. Its mass increases over time.
    e. The cell potential decreases to zero over time.

Use sentences and diagrams as appropriate to answer the questions below.

11. **K/U** In two or three sentences, explain why sodium iodide should not be used as the salt bridge electrolyte in a lead/zinc galvanic cell.

12. **K/U** How many 1.5 V dry cells need to be connected in series to create a 9 V battery? Explain how you determined your answer.

13. **A** Rechargeable nicad batteries help to reduce the number of disposable batteries that end up in our landfill sites. Comment on why the nicad battery still ends up being an environmental issue.

14. **T/I** Determine the standard cell potential for each galvanic cell. Include the half-reactions and the overall reaction for each cell.
    a. zinc/iron
    b. copper/chromium
    c. silver/aluminum

15. **T/I** What are the products of the electrolysis of molten potassium chloride?

16. **T/I** In a button battery, the half-reactions are
    $Zn(s) + 2OH^-(aq) \rightarrow ZnO(s) + H_2O(\ell) + 2e^-$
    $HgO(s) + H_2O(\ell) + 2e^- \rightarrow Hg(\ell) + 2OH^-(aq)$
    a. Which is the reduction half-reaction and which is the oxidation half-reaction?
    b. What is the overall reaction for the button battery?
    c. What are some uses of the button battery?

17. **K/U** Explain why it is beneficial to cars and trucks for municipalities to use more sand on the roads in the winter than salt.

18. **T/I** Determine the standard cell potential for the following reactions. Use this standard cell potential to determine if the cells are spontaneous or non-spontaneous.
    a. $Cl_2(g) + 2I^-(aq) \rightarrow I_2(s) + 2Cl^-(aq)$
    b. $3Br_2(\ell) + 2Cr^{3+}(aq) + 7H_2O(\ell) \rightarrow Cr_2O_7^{2-}(aq) + 14H^+(aq) + 6Br^-(aq)$

19. **A** Explain why the recycling of aluminum is more economically viable than the recycling of many other metals.

20. **T/I** A fuel cell called the direct methanol fuel cell is being developed. The half-reactions for this cell are given below:
    $CH_3OH(\ell) + H_2O(\ell) \rightarrow CO_2(g) + 6H^+(aq) + 6e^-$
    $O_2(g) + 4H^+(aq) + 4e^- \rightarrow 2H_2O(\ell)$
    a. Which half-reaction will occur at the cathode and which will occur at the anode?
    b. What is the overall reaction in this fuel cell?

21. **K/U** For the cell where zinc and copper are being used as electrodes, which will be the anode and which will be the cathode in
    a. a galvanic cell?
    b. an electrolytic cell?

22. **C** In a brief paragraph, describe some of the benefits of a fuel cell that are not shared by batteries.

23. **K/U** Aluminum is a more reactive metal than any of the metals present in steel. However, discarded steel cans disintegrate much more quickly than discarded aluminum cans, when both are left exposed to the environment in the same location. Give an explanation for this.

24. **T/I** Since the corrosion of iron is such an expensive problem, why do you think that iron is still used for so many purposes?

25. **A** In a D-size battery, the oxidation half-reaction is $Zn(s) \rightarrow Zn^{2+}(aq) + 2e^-$. The reduction half-reaction is $2MnO_2(s) + H_2O(\ell) + 2e^- \rightarrow Mn_2O_3(s) + 2OH^-(aq)$. This battery generates a voltage of 1.50 V. If the reduction potential of the zinc half-cell is -0.76 V, what would be the reduction half-cell potential of the manganese dioxide half-reaction?

Self-Check

If you missed question …	1	2	3	4	5	6	7	8	9	10	11	12	13	14	15	16	17	18	19	20	21	22	23	24	25
Review section(s)…	10.1	10.1	10.1, 10.2	10.2	10.1	10.1	10.3	10.2	10.3	10.3	10.1	10.2	10.3	10.1	10.3	10.2	10.2	10.1	10.3	10.2	10.3	10.2	10.1	10.3	10.1, 10.2

Unit 5 Project

Conduct an Inquiry

The Making of an Oscar

While working as a summer student at the Academy of Motion Picture Arts and Sciences, the Academy learns that you have studied electrochemistry. You are asked to help create a short film that documents how an Oscar statuette is made. In your initial research, you learn that the first step in creating an Oscar involves making a mould. Britannium (an alloy of tin, antimony, and copper) is added to the mould to create the body of the statuette. The Oscar then undergoes a chemical process known as *electroplating*. During electroplating, a thin layer of a specific metal is plated (coated) onto a conductive object in an electrolytic cell. The Oscar is electroplated with four different metals: copper, nickel, silver, and gold.

The Academy has arranged access to a chemistry laboratory and a supervisor so that you can carry out a general demonstration of electroplating to be included in the film. You will also describe how each of the metals listed above is electroplated onto the Oscar. Finally, to promote the film, you will prepare a presentation that explains your demonstration and the processes used to electroplate the Oscar.

How can you safely and effectively demonstrate electroplating—both in a general demonstration and as it applies to an Oscar statuette?

Part 1: Demonstrating Electroplating

Initiate and Plan

1. Use print and Internet resources, along with your knowledge of electrochemistry, to research the chemical processes involved in electroplating.
   - What is the role of the electrolytic cell in electroplating?
   - How does the flow of ions and electrons in the cell result in the object being electroplated?
2. Research how you could demonstrate electroplating in the chemistry laboratory.
   - Write a brief overview of your experimental design.
   - Draw a labelled diagram to show the components of your electrolytic cell, illustrating the electron and ion flow that will take place in the cell. Include the cathode, anode, electrolyte (specify the solution), and power source in your diagram.
   - Write a detailed, step-by-step procedure, listing all materials, equipment, and safety precautions.
3. Your teacher will act as the supervisor in this scenario. Have your teacher check and approve your design, materials, procedures, and safety precautions.

Perform and Record

4. Carry out your electroplating demonstration, repeating the demonstration at least once.
5. Record your observations, made during and after the electroplating process, into a data table. Be sure that you observe both the electrodes and the solution.

Analyze and Interpret

1. In a brief paragraph, describe the flow of ions and electrons that take place in the electrolytic cell, and explain the relationship between this flow and the electroplating process that you observed.
2. Evaluate your demonstration, focussing on ways in which it might be improved.
3. Answer the following questions for the electrolytic cell.
   a. Identify the anode and the cathode.
   b. Write the equation for the half-reaction that occurs at each electrode.
   c. Identify whether oxidation or reduction has occurred at each electrode. Explain your reasoning.
   d. Identify the oxidizing agent and reducing agent in each half-reaction.
   e. Identify the electrode at which electroplating occurs. Explain your reasoning.

4. Is it possible to write a chemical equation for the overall reaction that occurred in the cell? Explain your answer.

Communicate Your Findings

5. Prepare a presentation that outlines the key steps of your demonstration. Your presentation should include

- an overview of the chemical processes involved in electroplating, including a description of the role of the electrolytic cell and the flow of electrons and ions
- a description that summarizes the electroplating demonstration, including a brief overview of your experimental design, a labelled diagram of the electrolytic cell, and an outline of the procedure steps, noting any safety precautions
- a description of your observations, including an explanation of the chemical reactions that took place during the demonstration
- a literature citation section that documents the resources you used to complete your research

Part 2: Electroplating an Oscar

Initiate and Plan

Use print and Internet resources to research how to electroplate an Oscar with the four metals described in the introduction: copper, nickel, silver, and gold.

- Write a brief overview of your experimental design.
- Draw a labelled diagram to show the electrolytic cell for each plated metal, illustrating the flow of ions and electrons that will take place in each cell. Include the cathode, anode, electrolyte (specify the solution), and power source for each metal.
- Write a detailed, step-by-step procedure that you would follow for plating each metal, including a materials list and safety procedures.

Analyze and Interpret

1. Describe any problems that you might encounter with your experimental design and how you might overcome them.

2. Complete question 3 in Analyze and Interpret Part 1 for each metal that was electroplated onto the Oscar.

3. Is the Oscar the anode or the cathode during electroplating? Explain your reasoning.

4. Could an Oscar be electroplated if it were made of carbon (a non-reactive, conductive material) or of plastic? Explain your answer.

5. Infer why an Oscar is electroplated successively in the sequence of copper, nickel, silver, and, finally, gold.

Communicate Your Findings

6. Add to your presentation from Part 1 to explain how the four metals can be electroplated onto an Oscar. Include a brief overview of your experimental design, a labelled diagram of the electrolytic cell used for each metal, and an outline of the procedure, noting any safety precautions. Explain how the chemical reactions will take place. Update your literature citation section.

Assessment Criteria

Once you complete your project, ask yourself these questions. Did you…

- ✓ **T/I** assess your information sources for accuracy and reliability?
- ✓ **K/U** describe the chemical processes involved in electroplating?
- ✓ **K/U** describe how you will perform a demonstration of electroplating?
- ✓ **T/I** carry out your demonstration of electroplating, meeting all safety precautions?
- ✓ **C** draw labelled diagrams and use tables to record your observations?
- ✓ **T/I** evaluate your demonstration and suggest ways in which it might be improved?
- ✓ **K/U** describe how each metal can be electroplated onto an Oscar?
- ✓ **A** make a recommendation based on supporting evidence as to whether or not an Oscar could be electroplated if it were made of carbon or of plastic?
- ✓ **A** propose an explanation as to why an Oscar is successively electroplated according to the following sequence: copper, nickel, silver, and, finally, gold?
- ✓ **C** communicate the electroplating process in an appropriate form, using suitable instructional visuals and scientific vocabulary?

UNIT 5 SUMMARY

BIG IDEAS

- Oxidation and reduction are paired chemical reactions in which electrons are transferred from one substance to another in a predictable way.
- The control and applications of oxidation and reduction reactions have significant implications for industry, health, and safety, and the environment.

Overall Expectations

In this unit you learned how to…

- **analyse** technologies and processes relating to electrochemistry, and their implications for society, health and safety, and the environment
- **investigate** oxidation-reduction reactions using a galvanic cell, and **analyse** electrochemical reactions in qualitative and quantitative terms
- **demonstrate** an understanding of the principles of oxidation-reduction reactions and the many practical applications of electrochemistry

Chapter 9 — Oxidation-Reduction Reactions

Key ideas

- Reactions in which electrons are gained by one atom or ion and lost by another atom or ion are called oxidation-reduction reactions. (abbreviated to the term redox reactions).
- If one atom is oxidized in a reaction, then another atom must be reduced.
- An oxidizing agent accepts electrons from another compound and becomes reduced. A reducing agent donates electrons to another compound and becomes oxidized.
- Oxidation half-reactions include only those atoms that become oxidized in a redox reaction.
- Reduction half-reactions include only those atoms that become reduced in a redox reaction.

- You can use a set of rules to balance oxidation and reduction half-reactions. You can then add the half-reactions to obtain a balanced redox reaction.
- In a disproportionation reaction, one or more atoms of an element are oxidized and one or more atoms of the same element are reduced in the same reaction.
- An increase in the oxidation number of an atom in a reaction indicates a loss of electrons. A decrease in the oxidation number of an atom in a reaction indicates a gain of electrons.
- You can balance an equation by determining the coefficients that make the number of electrons lost by one atom of one element equal to the number of electrons gained by atoms of another element. You then balance the rest of the equation by inspection.

Chapter 10 — Electrochemical Cells

Key ideas

- A galvanic cell is a device that uses the energy from spontaneous redox reactions to generate an electrical potential difference, or voltage. In any galvanic cell, the oxidation half-reaction occurs at the anode, and the reduction half-reaction occurs at the cathode.
- The standard cell potential can be calculated by using the following formula:

$$E^\circ_{cell} = E^\circ_{cathode} - E^\circ_{anode}$$

- Galvanic cells are made more portable and practical by thickening the electrolyte into a paste and sealing the components of the cell. The resulting cell is called a dry cell. A battery is a set of cells connected in series.
- A fuel cell is based on the concept of a galvanic cell. For most fuel cells, hydrogen is the reducing agent and oxygen is the oxidizing agent. The by-product is pure water.

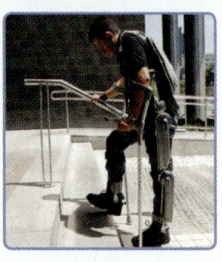

- Corrosion is caused by the spontaneous formation of galvanic cells on the surface of metals.
- An electrolytic cell is a device that converts electrical energy into chemical potential energy.
- Metallic sodium and chlorine gas are produced by electrolysis of molten sodium chloride in a large cell called a Downs cell.
- Electrolysis is used to recharge batteries. By driving the chemical reactions in a battery backward, the original compounds can be regenerated.

UNIT 5 REVIEW

Knowledge and Understanding

Select the letter of the best answer below.

1. For the reaction below, which of the following statements is correct?

   $Pb(s) + 2FeCl_3(aq) \rightarrow 2FeCl_2(aq) + PbCl_2(aq)$

   a. Lead is oxidized, and iron is reduced.
   b. Lead is reduced, and iron is oxidized.
   c. Lead is reduced, and chlorine is oxidized.
   d. Chlorine is reduced, and iron is oxidized.
   e. This is not a redox reaction.

2. What is the single oxidation number for nitrogen in dinitrogen pentoxide?
   a. +3
   b. +4
   c. +5
   d. −3
   e. −4

3. Which term is the reverse of a corresponding reduction half-reaction?
   a. a redox reaction
   b. a spontaneous reaction
   c. a non-spontaneous reaction
   d. a potential reaction
   e. an oxidation half-reaction

4. What is the change in the oxidation number of nitrogen when nitrogen dioxide becomes nitrogen gas in a redox reaction?
   a. an increase of 4
   b. a decrease of 4
   c. an increase of 2
   d. a decrease of 2
   e. There is no change to the oxidation number of nitrogen.

5. What is a Downs cell?
   a. a galvanic cell involving zinc and magnesium electrodes
   b. any cell that requires the use of an inert electrode
   c. a large cell used for the industrial electrolysis of sodium chloride
   d. a cell used for the electrolysis of water
   e. a rechargeable fuel cell

6. By definition, an electrolyte is
   a. a substance that participates in a redox reaction as an ion.
   b. a spectator ion.
   c. a reducing agent.
   d. an oxidizing agent.
   e. a substance that conducts electricity when dissolved in water.

7. The photograph below shows a whole dry cell battery and one that has been cut in half. Why is this type of battery referred to as *dry*?
   a. It contains no electrolytes.
   b. The electrolytes have been thickened into a paste.
   c. Electrolytes have been replaced with conducting wires.
   d. Electrolytes have been replaced with graphite powder.
   e. There are no ions present in the cell.

8. Which of the following is an example of a fuel cell?
   a. a galvanic cell
   b. a dry cell
   c. a car battery
   d. a PEM cell
   e. All of the above are examples of fuel cells.

9. For the redox reaction in a galvanic cell shown below, which of the following is the correct notation for the cell?

   $Pb(s) + 2FeCl_3(aq) \rightarrow 2FeCl_2(aq) + PbCl_2(aq)$

   a. $Pb(s) \mid Pb^{2+}(aq) \parallel Fe^{3+}(aq) \mid Fe^{2+}(aq)$
   b. $Pb(s) \mid Pb^{2+}(aq) \parallel Fe^{3+}(aq), Fe^{2+}(aq) \mid Fe(s)$
   c. $Pb(s) \mid Pb^{2+}(aq) \parallel Fe^{3+}(aq), Fe^{2+}(aq) \mid Pt(s)$
   d. $Fe^{3+}(aq), Fe^{2+}(aq) \mid Pt(s) \parallel Pb(s) \mid Pb^{2+}(aq)$
   e. $Fe^{3+}(aq), Fe^{2+}(aq) \parallel Pb(s) \mid Pb^{2+}(aq)$

10. Which statement is correct with respect to the following redox reaction?

    $FeO(s) + CO(g) \rightarrow Fe(\ell) + CO_2(g)$

    a. FeO(s) is the reducing agent, and CO(g) is the oxidizing agent.
    b. FeO(s) is the oxidizing agent, and CO(g) is the reducing agent.
    c. FeO(s) is both the oxidizing agent and the reducing agent.
    d. Fe(ℓ) is the oxidizing agent, and CO_2(g) is the reducing agent.
    e. Fe(ℓ) is the reducing agent, and CO_2(g) is the oxidizing agent.

UNIT 5 REVIEW

Answer the questions below.

11. Identify the oxidation number of the element underlined in each of the following compounds:
    a. $K_2\underline{S}O_3$
    b. $\underline{Mn}_2O_7$
    c. $\underline{P}_4O_{10}$
    d. $\underline{N}_2O_3$

12. What is the difference between a primary battery and a secondary battery?

13. What is an inert electrode, and when must one be used? Name two materials that are commonly used as inert electrodes.

14. Explain the meaning of the standard reduction potentials that are listed in Appendix B. How can a half-cell have a potential when a potential must be measured between two points or two electrodes?

15. Metals and non-metals can be displaced in single displacement reactions.
    a. Metal A displaces metal B in a single displacement reaction. Explain which metal is the more effective reducing agent. Give an example of this type of reaction.
    b. Non-metal A displaces non-metal B in a single displacement reaction. Explain which non-metal is the more effective oxidizing agent. Give an example of this type of reaction.

16. List all the information you can obtain from a balanced half-reaction. In your answer, include two examples of balanced half-reactions.

17. Explain how electronegativity factors into determining if an atom will be oxidized or reduced during a redox reaction.

18. Are oxygen atoms present in a redox reaction always involved in the oxidation of an atom? If they are, explain why, and if they are not, include an example of when they are not involved in oxidation.

19. Looking at the anode of a cell used in the electrolysis of water, you notice gas bubbles are forming.
    a. What is the identity of this gas?
    b. What test can be performed to verify this identity?

20. The early definition of oxidation described the process as any chemical reaction in which an atom or compound reacted with molecular oxygen. Use one or two sentences to explain why the definition needed to be changed.

21. Describe one step in the production of steel that is a reduction reaction and one step that is an oxidation reaction.

22. Describe the characteristics of a disproportionation reaction.
    a. Give an example of a disproportionation reaction.
    b. Write the oxidation half-reaction and the reduction half-reaction for the example you gave in part (a).

23. When a student applied the oxidation number rules to the compound $H_6C_3O(\ell)$, the oxidation number for a single atom of carbon was found to be $-\frac{4}{3}$. How can this be correct if oxidation numbers are designed to help count electrons as they move in a redox process?

24. When are inert electrodes used, and why must they be used in a galvanic cell? Provide your answer in one or two sentences.

25. When balancing a reduction half-reaction, a student first balances all atoms other than oxygen and hydrogen. The student adds water molecules to balance the oxygen atoms. Then the student needs to balance the half-reaction in a basic solution. Write a procedure that this student could follow to complete the balancing of the half-reaction.

Thinking and Investigation

26. The diagrams below show a galvanic cell and an electrolytic cell. Describe how you could build these cells, using a lead electrode and a silver electrode. Include the electrolytes you would require.

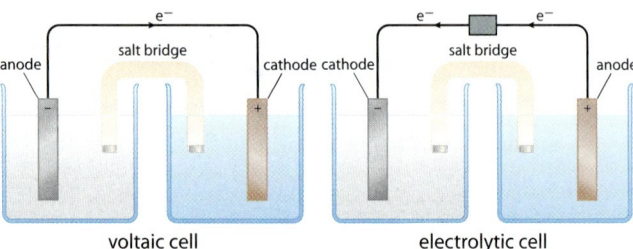

voltaic cell   electrolytic cell

27. Balance each of the following half-reactions:
    a. $MnO_4^-(aq) \rightarrow Mn^{2+}(aq)$ (acidic conditions)
    b. $SO_3^{2-}(aq) \rightarrow SO_4^{2-}(aq)$ (basic conditions)
    c. $NO_3^-(aq) \rightarrow NH_4^+(aq)$ (basic conditions)
    d. $Re^-(aq) \rightarrow ReO_3^-(aq)$ (acidic conditions)

28. Identify each half-reaction in question 27 as a reduction half-reaction or an oxidation half-reaction.

29. Balance the following redox reactions using the half-cell method:
    a. $Cd(s) + NO_3^-(aq) \rightarrow Cd^{2+}(aq) + NO(g)$ (acidic conditions)
    b. $Fe(OH)_2(aq) + H_2O_2(\ell) \rightarrow Fe(OH)_3(aq)$
    c. $I_2(s) \rightarrow IO_3^-(aq) + I^-(aq)$ (basic conditions)

30. Balance the following redox reactions using the oxidation number method:
   a. $Cr^{3+}(aq) + ClO_3^-(aq) \rightarrow Cr_2O_7^{2-}(aq) + ClO_2$ (acidic conditions)
   b. $I^-(aq) + MnO_4^-(aq) \rightarrow I_2(s) + Mn^{2+}(aq)$ (acidic conditions)
   c. $CN^-(aq) + Cu(NH_3)_4^{2+}(aq) \rightarrow Cu(CN)_3^{2-}(aq) + NH_3(g) + CNO^-(aq)$ (basic conditions)

31. Determine the standard cell potential for each of the following reactions:
   a. $2Fe^{2+}(aq) + I_2(s) \rightarrow 2Fe^{3+}(aq) + 2I^-(aq)$
   b. $Au(NO_3)_3(aq) + 3Ag(s) \rightarrow 3AgNO_3(aq) + Au(s)$
   c. $H_2O_2(aq) + 2HCl(aq) \rightarrow Cl_2(g) + 2H_2O(\ell)$

32. For each cell in question 31, state whether the reaction is spontaneous or non-spontaneous.

33. Write the following equation as an ionic equation and then as a net ionic equation:
   $Cd(s) + Sn(NO_3)_2(aq) \rightarrow Cd(NO_3)_2(aq) + Sn(s)$
   a. Use the equation to explain the meaning of "spectator ion."
   b. Identify the reducing agent.
   c. Identify the oxidizing agent.
   d. Which element is oxidized?
   e. Which element is reduced?

34. Outline an investigation that can be used to determine if a copper/aluminum cell can be set up as a galvanic cell with the copper as the anode and the aluminum as the cathode. Include in your procedure the indicators you will use to determine if the cell can run as a galvanic cell.

35. Considering that the balanced half-reactions for a redox reaction might include different numbers of electrons, explain how a balanced equation for a redox reaction supports the fact that electrons cannot be created or destroyed during the reaction.

36. In an investigation, you see that limewater, $Ca(OH)_2(aq)$, turns cloudy in the presence of carbon dioxide.
   a. Write a balanced chemical equation for the reaction. Include the states of the substances.
   b. State whether the reaction is a redox reaction. Explain how you arrived at your conclusion.

37. Design and describe a procedure you could use to galvanize an iron nail. Explain your reasons for choosing each of the materials required for your procedure.

38. Some metals can have different oxidation numbers in different compounds. In the following reactions of iron with concentrated nitric acid, assume that one of the products *in each case* is gaseous nitrogen monoxide. Include the states of all the reactants and products in the equations.
   a. Use the principles of redox reactions to write a balanced chemical equation for the reaction of iron with concentrated nitric acid to form iron(II) nitrate.
   b. Use the principles of redox reactions to write a balanced chemical equation for the reaction of iron(II) nitrate with concentrated nitric acid to form iron(III) nitrate.
   c. Use the principles of redox reactions to write a balanced chemical equation for the reaction of iron with concentrated nitric acid to form iron(III) nitrate.
   d. What process do the equations in parts (a), (b), and (c) represent?

39. The diagram below shows the structure of a typical alkaline cell. When the cell is connected, the overall reaction that takes place is given by the following unbalanced redox reaction:
   $MnO_2(s) + Zn(s) \rightarrow Mn_2O_3(s) + Zn^{2+}(aq)$
   a. Balance this reaction in basic conditions.
   b. Identify the anode and cathode in this process.

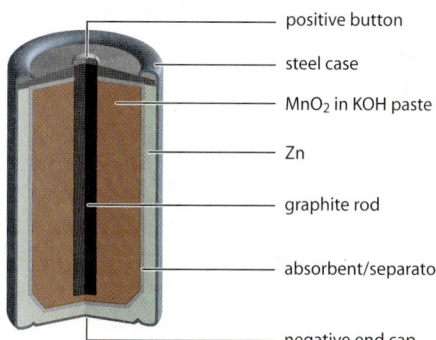

40. State whether the reaction shown in each of the following unbalanced equations is a redox reaction. If the reaction is a redox reaction, identify the oxidizing agent and the reducing agent. Balance each equation.
   a. $Cl_2O_7(\ell) + H_2O(\ell) \rightarrow HClO_4(aq)$
   b. $I_2(s) + ClO_3^-(aq) \rightarrow IO_3^-(aq) + Cl^-(aq)$ (acidic conditions)
   c. $S^{2-}(aq) + Br_2(\ell) \rightarrow SO_4^{2-}(aq) + Br^-(aq)$ (basic conditions)
   d. $HNO_3(aq) + H_2S(g) \rightarrow NO(g) + S(s) + H_2O(\ell)$

UNIT 5 REVIEW

41. Identify the oxidizing agent and the reducing agent in each of the following unbalanced redox reactions:
    a. $AgNO_3(aq) + Cu(s) \rightarrow Cu(NO_3)_2(aq) + Ag(s)$
    b. $Mg(s) + IO_3^-(aq) \rightarrow Mg^{2+}(aq) + I^-(aq)$

42. Determine if the following redox reactions will proceed spontaneously as written:
    a. $Cu^{2+}(aq) + Sn(s) \rightarrow Sn^{2+}(aq) + Cu(s)$
    b. $Ba(s) + Cr^{3+}(aq) \rightarrow Cr(s) + Ba^{2+}(aq)$

43. In a lab, a piece of metallic element A is placed into a beaker that contains metallic ions of $B^{2+}(aq)$. Instantly, a reaction can be seen to occur.
    a. Which element is the stronger reducing agent?
    b. Which element is likely to have the larger electronegativity?

44. Consider the following reaction:
    $$16H^+(aq) + 2Cr_2O_7^{2-}(aq) + C_2H_5OH(\ell) \rightarrow 4Cr^{3+}(aq) + 2CO_2(g) + 11H_2O(\ell)$$
    a. Which method was most likely used to balance the reaction? Explain your answer.
    b. Identify the oxidizing and the reducing agents.
    c. Balance the reaction for basic conditions.

45. In the electrolysis of potassium fluoride, outline the reaction that will occur at the anode, the reaction that will occur at the cathode, and the overall reaction.

46. The diagram below shows a cross-section of a lead-acid storage battery of the type commonly used in cars. State the composition of the electrolyte, anode, and cathode in the cells.

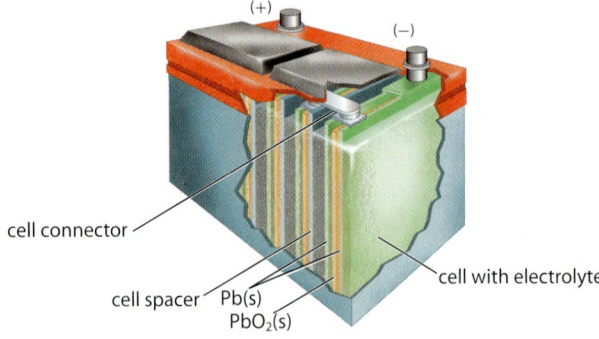

47. When aqueous solutions of potassium permanganate, $KMnO_4(aq)$, and sodium oxalate, $Na_2C_2O_4(aq)$, react in acidic solution, the intense purple colour of the permanganate ion fades and is replaced by the very pale-pink colour of manganese(II) ions. Gas bubbles are observed as the oxalate ions are converted to carbon dioxide. Complete and balance the equation for acidic conditions:
    $$MnO_4^-(aq) + C_2O_4^{2-}(aq) \rightarrow Mn^{2+}(aq) + CO_2(g)$$

Communication

48. **BIG IDEAS** Oxidation and reduction are paired chemical reactions in which electrons are transferred from one substance to another in a predictable way. Draw and label a galvanic cell that has magnesium and zinc electrodes. Indicate the path of electron transfer.

49. In a well-organized paragraph, explain the process of smelting iron ores in a blast furnace.

50. Create a labelled diagram and write a paragraph to explain the process of how smelted iron is converted to steel.

51. One of your classmates is having trouble understanding some of the main concepts in this unit, which are listed below. Use your own words to write an explanation for each of the following concepts. Include any diagrams or examples that will help to make the concepts clear to your classmate.
    a. oxidation and reduction
    b. galvanic and electrolytic cells

52. Use the diagram below to explain how an iron object rusts.
    a. Copy the sketch and add labels to show the rusting process. Include the half-reactions that occur at the anode and the cathode.
    b. Write the overall reaction for the process.

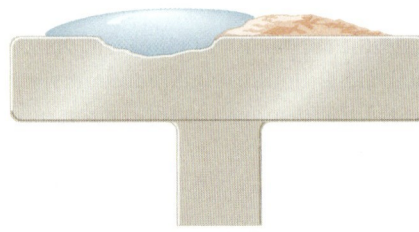

53. A friend in your class has difficulty recognizing disproportionation reactions.
    a. Write a clear explanation for your friend on how to recognize a disproportionation reaction.
    b. Write a balanced chemical equation that represents a disproportionation reaction.

54. Write an advertisement as part of a child safety campaign that explains how button batteries can harm children if they are accidentally ingested.

55. Sketch a cell that has a standard cell potential of 0 V.
    a. Write an explanation for a classmate to explain why the cell potential is zero.
    b. Explain whether the cell could be operated as an electrolytic cell.

56. Use the Internet to research the fuel cells used on the International Space Station. Write several well-organized paragraphs to describe your findings to a class of younger students.

57. A piece of coiled solid copper wire is left overnight in a beaker of silver nitrate.
    a. What changes would you expect to see in this beaker on the following day?
    b. Are the changes a result of a redox reaction? Explain your answer.

58. Create a flowchart or similar graphic organizer outlining the steps that can be used to balance a half-reaction in acidic conditions.

59. Draw a diagram to illustrate the flow of electrons in a galvanic cell, starting at the anode and returning to the anode.

60. Outline the similarities and differences between an alkaline battery and a button battery. Describe the overall reaction that occurs in each battery.

61. Write a descriptive paragraph to compare the reactions that occur in a Downs cell and a chlor-alkali cell. Describe the similarities and differences.

62. Copy the diagram of the voltaic cell shown below. Assume that one half-cell consists of a magnesium electrode in 1.0 mol/L magnesium nitrate, and the other half-cell consists of a silver electrode in 1.0 mol/L silver nitrate.
    a. Label the electrodes and solutions.
    b. Label the anode, the cathode, and the direction of the electric current.
    c. Choose an appropriate solution for the salt bridge and label it.
    d. Write half-reactions for each half-cell.
    e. Write the overall reaction.
    f. Calculate the cell potential.
    g. Write the cell notation for the voltaic cell.

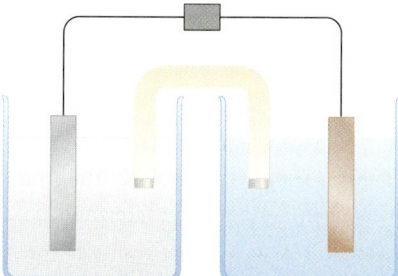

Application

63. If most galvanic cells can be reversed to an electrolytic cell by applying a potential of the correct voltage, why are all batteries not rechargeable? Explain the reason, using two or three sentences.

64. An electrolytic cell contains a standard hydrogen electrode as the anode and another standard half-cell.
    a. Is the standard reduction potential for the half-reaction that occurs in the second half-cell greater than or less than 0 V? Explain your answer.
    b. Will your answer for part (a) change if the hydrogen electrode is the cathode of the electrolytic cell? Explain your reasoning.

65. Describe a situation in which it is easier to use the oxidation number method for balancing a redox equation than it is to use the half-reaction method.

66. Electric cars might become common in the future. At present, however, the technology is not progressing quickly. Perform an Internet search to outline some of the barriers to the widespread use of electric cars. Organize your findings in a paragraph.

67. Will the mass increase of the cathode be equal to the mass decrease of the anode in a galvanic cell? Explain your answer.

68. A tin can is usually a steel can that has been coated with a thin layer of tin. Explain why this layer of tin is needed for a can that is used for tomatoes.

69. In the electrolysis of water, the two half-reactions are as follows:

    Oxidation: $2H_2O(\ell) \rightarrow O_2(g) + 4H^+(aq) + 4e^-$
    $-E = -0.82$ V
    Reduction: $2H_2O(\ell) + 2e^- \rightarrow H_2(g) + 2OH^-(aq)$
    $E = -0.42$ V

    a. Write the overall redox reaction.
    b. Determine the cell potential.
    c. What does the sign on the cell potential indicate about the reaction?
    d. Why are there no superscripts on the symbol E for the reduction potentials?

70. **BIG IDEAS** The control and applications of oxidation and reduction reactions have significant implications for industry, health and safety, and the environment. Research a biological process that involves a redox reaction. Write a report consisting of two or three paragraphs that include a description of the chemistry of the process and its effects on human health and the environment.

UNIT 5 SELF-ASSESSMENT

Select the letter of the best answer below.

1. **T/I** Which of the following is the coefficient for $Fe_2(SO_4)_3(aq)$ in the balanced redox reaction for the reaction below?

   $KMnO_4(aq) + FeSO_4(aq) + H_2SO_4(aq) \rightarrow$
   $K_2SO_4(aq) + MnSO_4(aq) + Fe_2(SO_4)_3(aq) + H_2O(\ell)$

   a. 1
   b. 2
   c. 3
   d. 4
   e. 5

2. **K/U** For any given cell, the electrical potential difference between the electrodes is called the
   a. voltage.
   b. cell potential.
   c. standard cell potential.
   d. standard reduction potential.
   e. redox potential.

3. **K/U** A galvanic cell can become an electrochemical cell if
   a. the system is heated.
   b. the salt bridge is reversed.
   c. an external voltage is applied.
   d. the wires are reversed.
   e. the electrodes are placed in opposite half-cells.

4. **K/U** The change in oxidation number for an atom of nitrogen in the half-reaction $NO_2 \rightarrow NH_4^+(aq)$ is
   a. a decrease of 5.
   b. a decrease of 1.
   c. an increase of 1.
   d. an increase of 7.
   e. a decrease of 7.

5. **T/I** The following reaction is found to be non-spontaneous as written:
   $$A(s) + B^{2+}(aq) \rightarrow A^{2+}(aq) + B(s)$$
   Based on this, which of the following statements is correct?
   a. B(s) is the stronger reducing agent and $A^{2+}(aq)$ is the stronger oxidizing agent.
   b. A(s) is the stronger reducing agent and $B^{2+}(aq)$ is the stronger oxidizing agent.
   c. A(s) is both the stronger oxidizing agent and stronger reducing agent.
   d. B(s) is both the stronger oxidizing agent and stronger reducing agent.
   e. There is no difference in reducing agent strength between A(s) and B(s).

6. **K/U** A battery that is disposable and cannot be recharged is known as
   a. an anode.
   b. a cathode.
   c. a dry cell.
   d. a primary battery.
   e. a secondary battery.

7. **K/U** Another name for the battery used in a flashlight is
   a. a dry cell.
   b. a wet cell.
   c. a fuel cell.
   d. an electrochemical cell.
   e. a voltaic cell.

8. **T/I** Which is the equation for the following oxidation half-reaction?
   $$Al(s) + Fe^{3+}(aq) \rightarrow Fe(s) + Al^{3+}(aq)$$
   a. $Fe(s) \rightarrow Fe^{3+}(aq) + 3e^-$
   b. $Fe^{3+}(aq) + 3e^- \rightarrow Fe(s)$
   c. $Al^{3+}(aq) + 3e^- \rightarrow Al(s)$
   d. $Al(s) \rightarrow Al^{3+}(aq) + 3e^-$
   e. $Al(s) \rightarrow Al^{3+}(aq) + e^-$

9. **K/U** The oxidation number for carbon in a molecule of $C_5H_{10}O$ is
   a. $+\frac{8}{5}$
   b. $+8$
   c. $+5$
   d. $-\frac{8}{5}$
   e. 0

10. **K/U** Many metals corrode when exposed to the atmosphere. Which of the following best describes the process of corrosion?
    a. a spontaneous reaction involving oxygen
    b. a non-spontaneous reaction made to occur by adding a voltage
    c. the spontaneous reaction between materials and substances in their environment
    d. a spontaneous reaction between materials and oxygen
    e. another term for rusting

Use sentences and diagrams as appropriate to answer the following questions.

11. **A** State the modern definition for oxidation reactions. Write ionic equations for the complete balanced equations given below. Use the equations to explain why chemists developed the modern definition that you stated.
    $$4Na(s) + O_2(g) \rightarrow 2Na_2O(s)$$
    $$2Na(s) + Cl_2(g) \rightarrow 2NaCl(s)$$

692 MHR • Unit 5 Electrochemistry

12. **K/U** Determine the oxidation number of the specified atom in each of the following compounds:
    a. N in N_2O_3
    b. P in $H_4P_2O_7$
    c. Si in SiF_6^{2-}
    d. each atom in $(NH_4)_2SO_4$

13. **K/U** Explain why the reaction below is an example of a redox reaction.
$$4Al(s) + 3O_2(g) \rightarrow 2Al_2O_3(s)$$

14. **C** Both a galvanic cell and an electrolytic cell can have silver and zinc electrodes.
    a. Draw and fully label a galvanic cell involving silver and zinc electrodes.
    b. Draw and fully label an electrolytic cell involving silver and zinc electrodes.

15. **A** Portions of the Alaskan pipeline are buried. The pipeline has a zinc wire buried alongside the steel pipe. In a paragraph, describe the purpose of the zinc wire.

16. **T/I** Balance each of the following half-reactions:
    a. $Hg_2^{2+} \rightarrow Hg$
    b. $TiO_2 \rightarrow Ti^{2+}$ (acidic conditions)
    c. $I_2 \rightarrow H_3IO_6^{3-}$ (basic conditions)

17. **K/U** Does the fact that you can assign oxidation numbers of +1 to hydrogen and −2 to oxygen in water mean that water is an ionic substance? Explain your answer.

18. **T/I** Which of the following reactions will proceed spontaneously?
    a. aqueous calcium chloride and metallic silver
    b. aqueous nickel sulfate and metallic zinc

19. **C** Create a flowchart or similar graphic organizer outlining the steps that can be used to balance a half-reaction in basic conditions.

20. **C** Draw a diagram to indicate the process of the formation of rust on a metallic surface that is exposed to the environment. Include labels for the cathode, anode, air, water, iron, $Fe^{2+}(aq)$, $O_2(g)$, and rust.

21. **T/I** Balance the following reactions using the oxidation number method:
    a. $Cr^{3+}(aq) + ClO_3^-(aq) \rightarrow CrO_4^{2-}(aq) + Cl^-(aq)$ (acidic conditions)
    b. $ClO_2(g) + SbO_2^-(aq) \rightarrow ClO_2^-(aq) + Sb(OH)_6^-(aq)$ (basic conditions)
    c. $HNO_3(aq) + H_3AsO_3(aq) \rightarrow NO(g) + H_3AsO_4(aq)$

22. **C** Explain, in one or two well-organized sentences, the importance of the chlor-alkali process.

23. **C** Write the cell notation for the spontaneous reaction in which Sn(s) goes to $Sn^{2+}(aq)$ at the anode and $Fe^{3+}(aq)$ goes to $Fe^{2+}(aq)$ at the cathode.

24. **T/I** A student performs a lab involving a galvanic cell operating for a period of 5 min. After the cell is disconnected, the student removes the electrodes and determines that the mass of electrode 1 increased whereas the mass of electrode 2 decreased. Using this information, how can the anode and cathode be determined? Explain your answer in three or four sentences.

25. **K/U** Consider a Downs cell.
    a. Identify all of the reactants and products of the reactions taking place in the cell.
    b. Write the anode half-reaction and the cathode half-reaction for the process that occurs in the cell.

Self-Check

If you missed question …	1	2	3	4	5	6	7	8	9	10	11	12	13	14	15	16	17	18	19	20	21	22	23	24	25
Review section(s)…	9.2	9.1	10.3	9.3	9.1	10.1	10.2	9.2	9.3	10.2	9.2	9.1	9.1	10.3	10.2	9.2	9.3, 9.1	9.1	9.2	10.2	9.3	10.2	10.1	10.1	10.3

Guide to the Appendices

Guide to the Appendices

Appendix A: Science Skills **695**

Green Chemistry 695
Green Engineering 696
Analyzing STSE Issues 697
Scientific Inquiry 700
Developing Research Skills 704
Writing a Lab Report 706
Organizing Data in a Table 707
Constructing Graphs 708
Using Graphic Organizers 712
Measurement 715
Significant Digits and Rounding 718
Scientific Notation 720
Using Experimental Data to Determine Rate Laws 721
Logarithms and Calculating pH 725
Preparing Solutions 726
Performing an Acid-Base Titration 728

Appendix B: Useful References **730**

Hydrocarbon Derivatives with Multiple Functional Groups 730
Chemistry Data Tables 739
Alphabetical List of Elements 749
Periodic Table of the Elements 750

Appendix C: Answers to Selected Questions and Problems **751**

Appendix A — Science Skills

Green Chemistry

Green chemistry refers to a movement within chemistry and the chemical industry to improve safety and efficiency in chemical processes while reducing waste generation, as well as energy and resource consumption. To achieve these goals, green chemistry focusses on improving the entire life cycle of a chemical product or process, from planning and synthesis through to re-use, disposal, and clean-up. For instance, in order to reduce the amount of toxic waste produced by a chemical process, green chemistry would complete a life-cycle analysis to determine how the generation of such waste can be minimized during each stage of the process, rather than focusing on post-process waste clean-up.

The 12 Principles of Green Chemistry*

1. **Prevention**
   It is better to prevent waste than to treat or clean up waste after it has been created.

2. **Atom Economy**
   Synthetic methods should be designed to maximize the incorporation of all materials used in the process into the final product.

3. **Less Hazardous Chemical Syntheses**
   Wherever practicable, synthetic methods should be designed to use and generate substances that possess little or no toxicity to human health and the environment.

4. **Designing Safer Chemicals**
   Chemical products should be designed to affect their desired function while minimizing their toxicity.

5. **Safer Solvents and Auxiliaries**
   The use of auxiliary substances (e.g., solvents, separation agents, etc.) should be made unnecessary whenever possible and innocuous when used.

6. **Design for Energy Efficiency**
   Energy requirements of chemical processes should be recognized for their environmental and economical impacts and should be minimized. If possible, synthetic methods should be conducted at ambient temperature and pressure.

7. **Use of Renewable Feedstocks**
   A raw material or feedstock should be renewable rather than depleting whenever technically and economically practicable.

8. **Reduce Derivatives**
   Unnecessary derivatization (modifications that temporarily change a compound for various purposes) should be minimized or avoided if possible, because such steps require additional reactants and can generate waste.

9. **Catalysis**
   Catalytic reactants (as selective as possible) are superior to stoichiometric reactants.

10. **Design for Degradation**
    Chemical products should be designed so that at the end of their function they break down into innocuous degradation products and do not persist in the environment.

11. **Real-Time Analysis for Pollution Prevention**
    Analytical methodologies need to be further developed to allow for the real-time, in-process monitoring and control prior to the formation of hazardous substances.

12. **Inherently Safer Chemistry for Accident Prevention**
    Substances and the form of a substance used in a chemical process should be chosen to minimize the potential for chemical accidents, including releases, explosions, and fires.

*Anastas, P. T. and Warner, J. C. *Green Chemistry: Theory and Practice*. Oxford University Press: New York, 1998, p. 30.

Instant Practice

Using print and/or Internet resources, describe how the principles of green chemistry have been applied to the entire life cycle of a chemical process or chemical product. What improvements, if any, occurred when these principles were applied?

Appendix A

Green Engineering

Like green chemistry, green engineering attempts to maximize safety, cost effectiveness, and efficiency, while minimizing waste generation and harm to both humans and the environment. In green engineering, however, these goals focus on the conceptualization, creation, and use of products and processes that have practical applications in human lives. As is the case with green chemistry, green engineering focusses on improving the entire life cycle of a process or product, from initial design to the end of a product's life.

The 12 Principles of Green Engineering*

1. **Inherent Rather Than Circumstantial**
   Designers need to strive to ensure that all material and energy inputs and outputs are as inherently non-hazardous as possible.

2. **Prevention Instead of Treatment**
   It is better to prevent waste than to treat or clean up waste after it is formed.

3. **Design for Separation**
   Separation and purification operations should be designed to minimize energy consumption and materials use.

4. **Maximize Efficiency**
   Products, processes, and systems should be designed to maximize mass, energy, space, and time efficiency.

5. **Output-Pulled Versus Input-Pushed**
   Products, processes and systems should be "output-pulled" rather than "input-pushed" through the use of energy and materials.

6. **Conserve Complexity**
   Embedded entropy and complexity must be viewed as an investment when making design choices on recycle, reuse, or beneficial disposition.

7. **Durability Rather Than Immortality**
   Targeted durability, not immortality, should be a design goal.

8. **Meet Need, Minimize Excess**
   Design for unnecessary capacity or capability (e.g., "one size fits all") solutions should be considered a design flaw.

9. **Minimize Material Diversity**
   Material diversity in multicomponent products should be minimized to promote disassembly and value retention.

10. **Integrate Local Material and Energy Flows**
    Design of products, processes, and systems must include integration and interconnectivity with available energy and material flows.

11. **Design for Commercial "Afterlife"**
    Products, processes, and systems should be designed for performance in a commercial "afterlife."

12. **Renewable Rather Than Depleting**
    Material and energy inputs should be renewable rather than depleting.

* Anastas, P.T., and Zimmerman, J.B., "Design through the Twelve Principles of Green Engineering", *Env. Sci. Tech.* 2003, 37(5), 94A-101A.

Instant Practice

You must build a galvanic cell that will be used to power a communications radio at an isolated research station in northern Ontario. The cell must last for 10 days until bad weather passes and a back-up generator can be delivered. Suggest how the principles of green engineering might be applied to the entire life cycle of your galvanic cell, from initial design through construction and materials used, to eventual recycling or disposal.

Appendix A

Analyzing STSE Issues

STSE is an abbreviation for **s**cience, **t**echnology, **s**ociety, and the **e**nvironment. An issue is a topic that can be seen from more than one point of view. In *Chemistry 12*, you are frequently asked to make connections between scientific, technological, social, and environmental issues. Making such connections could involve, for example, assessing the impact of science on developments in consumer goods, medical devices, or industrial processes; on people, social policy, or the economy; or on air, soil, and water quality, the welfare of organisms, or overall ecosystem health. Analyzing STSE issues involves researching background information about a problem related to science, technology, society, and the environment; evaluating differing points of view concerning the problem; deciding on the best response to the problem; and proposing a course of action to deal with the problem.

The following flowchart outlines one process that can help you to focus your thinking and organize your approach to analyzing STSE issues. The most effective analyses result in decision making and, ultimately, an action plan. Group discussion and collaborative analysis can also play roles in analyzing an STSE issue.

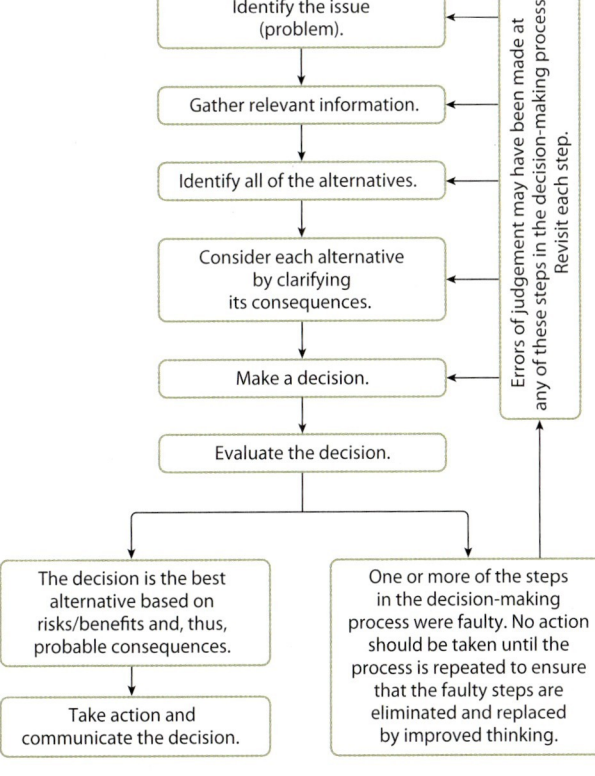

A Process for Analyzing Issues

Identify the Issue (Problem)

An STSE issue is a topic that is debatable—it can be viewed from more than one perspective. When you encounter an issue related to STSE, such as a medical breakthrough, a health-care policy, or an environmental regulation, you need to try to understand it from multiple points of view.

> Suppose you have learned that despite Ontario's ban on pesticide use for cosmetic purposes, use of chemical pesticides is allowed for golf course maintenance.

Assess whether there is any controversy associated with this situation. Could there be different viewpoints concerning the cause of the situation and how to respond to it?

> You read a webzine article that argues that pesticides are harmful to human health and the environment. The article says pesticides should not be used to maintain golf courses under any circumstances. You decide that this situation represents an STSE issue, because it lends itself to multiple points of view and there are both risks and benefits to be considered when analyzing this issue.

Try to sum up the issue in a specific question.

> For example, "What steps, if any, should the Ontario provincial government take to reduce pesticide use for golf course maintenance?"

Gather Relevant Information

You will need to do some research to gain a better understanding of the issue. Go to Developing Research Skills in Appendix A for help with finding information.

> For example, why are golf courses exempt from Ontario's ban on cosmetic pesticide use? What rules must golf courses in Ontario follow with regard to pesticide use, and how are they enforced? What role, if any, can municipal governments play in regulating pesticide use on golf courses?

Identify Possible Solutions to the Problem

In order to make an informed decision about how to respond to the issue, you will need to assess the possible solutions to the problem. Your research should reveal some alternative solutions.

> For example, you read a letter to the editor in your local paper in which a citizen proposes that the provincial government provide grants to help golf courses make the transition to pesticide-free course maintenance. You read a golf blog about pesticide-free golf courses. One article you read describes a golf course in North America where predatory insects are used successfully to reduce numbers of turf-destroying insects. Perhaps the Ontario government should also ban pesticide use for golf course maintenance.

Clarify the Consequences of Each Possible Solution

You may need to do additional research to identify potential consequences of each alternative solution and the reactions of the various stakeholders (that is, the individuals or groups affected by the issue).

For example:
- How do pesticides used for golf course maintenance affect the environment and human health?
- How are golf courses in other parts of the world being maintained without using pesticides, and how successful is this approach?
- What are the disadvantages of pesticide-free course maintenance, and how might they affect golf courses and golfers?

You can sort the potential consequences of an alternative into benefits (positive outcomes) and risks (negative outcomes). Use a risk-benefit analysis table like the one below to help you analyze the alternative solutions. For each possible solution, assess the impact on various stakeholders. The potential consequences of each solution could be different for each stakeholder. For some issues, you might choose to assess differing perspectives rather than differing effects on stakeholders. For example, you could assess benefits and risks from economic, environmental, social, scientific, and ethical perspectives. Each perspective could reveal different consequences.

Risk-Benefit Analysis

Issue: What steps, if any, should the Ontario provincial government take to reduce pesticide use for golf course maintenance?			
Possible Solutions	**Stakeholders**	**Potential Benefits (positive outcomes)**	**Potential Risks (negative outcomes)**
1. The Ontario government should ban pesticide use for golf course maintenance.	Government	• Reduced amounts of pesticides entering the environment lower remediation costs • Less pesticide exposure reduces health care costs	• Possible increases in golf course maintenance costs could cause golf club owners and other entrepreneurs to criticize the government • Some golf course owners and golfers may lobby for removal of the ban
	Golfer	• Less exposure to pesticides • Satisfaction of playing on a course that is maintained by less environmentally harmful methods	• Increases in maintenance costs could be transferred to golfers in the form of higher course fees • Turf changes due to non-toxic maintenance methods may make golfing less pleasurable
	Golf course owner	• Positive public relations • Possible increase in membership due to decreased health risks and improved public profile	• Reduction in revenue if maintenance costs increase
	Citizen	• Ban on pesticides results in less harm to the environment and human health, increasing quality of life	• Reduction in revenue may cause golf courses to close, reducing sports facilities available to the community
2. The Ontario government should continue to allow pesticide use for golf course maintenance but with strict regulations in place.			

Make a Decision

Once you have identified potential outcomes for each possible solution, you are faced with the task of making a decision. Which alternative promises the greatest benefits and the least risks or lowest costs? Your personal values will influence your assessment. You will need to decide whether the benefits of a particular alternative are major or minor. You will also need to decide what an acceptable level of risk is. You might find it helpful to write down a list of questions to help you evaluate the alternative solutions. Some factors to consider are listed here:

- How likely is it that a potential outcome will occur?
- Is there evidence to support the likelihood of a potential outcome?
- How many people (or other organisms) will the proposed course of action affect?
- Is there an estimated sum of money associated with the benefits or costs of each solution?
- Is the outcome of a proposed solution short-term (a one-time benefit/risk) or long-term (ongoing)?
- According to your analysis, how important are the risks of a possible solution compared with its potential benefits?
- How do the benefits and risks of one possible solution compare with the risks and benefits of other possible solutions?

> After considering all the alternatives, you might decide that the benefits of banning pesticide use for golf course maintenance in Ontario outweigh the disadvantages. This solution will have the desired effect of reducing the environmental and health impacts of pesticide use. Your research has shown that golf courses are able to maintain current course standards without the use of pesticides, and that the cost of turf maintenance does not increase significantly when non-toxic methods are adopted. However, because such maintenance requires specialized knowledge, golf courses should be given a reasonable amount of time to make these adjustments before the ban comes into effect.

Evaluate the Decision

Once you have made a decision, evaluate whether you can justify it with logic and verifiable information. If you discover that some of the information you used to make the decision was incorrect, you should reconsider the alternatives. If new information becomes available, then that could also affect your decision.

> Suppose a new study reveals that invasive insects from Europe are destroying turf at an unprecedented rate at many North American golf courses. How might this new information affect your decision?

Also, assess whether you have taken all perspectives into account in your analysis. Is there another stakeholder that is strongly affected by a particular alternative? If you decide that you are not confident in the decision you have made, you will need to revisit each step in your analysis.

Act on Your Decision

If you are confident in your decision, the next step is to propose and implement a course of action.

> For example, you could e-mail the results of your analysis to your Member of the Legislative Assembly and ask this MLA to propose that pesticide use be banned for golf course maintenance in Ontario.

Instant Practice

1. Consider the second possible solution listed in the risk-benefit analysis table on the previous page. Create a table in your notes to analyze the benefits and risks of this possible solution. Fill in the "Stakeholders," "Potential Benefits," and "Potential Risks" columns.
2. Look for a chemistry-related STSE issue in the news. Apply the analysis method outlined in this appendix to determine your response to the issue. Write a brief paragraph to explain your viewpoint and a proposed course of action.

Appendix A

Scientific Inquiry

Scientific inquiry is a process that involves making observations, asking questions, performing investigations, and drawing conclusions.

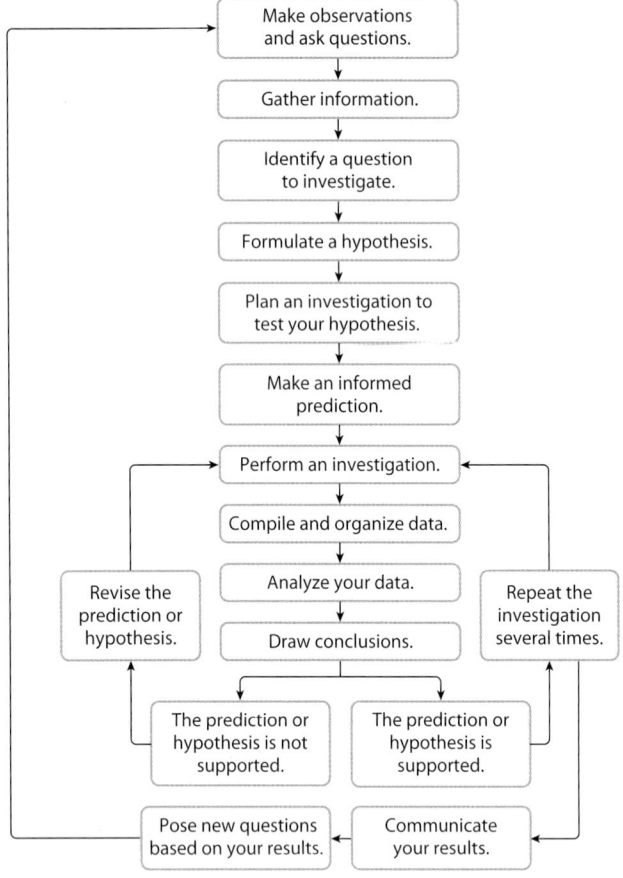

A Process for Scientific Inquiry

Make Observations and Ask Questions

Scientific inquiry usually starts with observations. You notice something that sparks your curiosity and prompts you to ask questions. You try to make sense of your observations by connecting them to your existing knowledge. When your existing knowledge cannot explain your observations, you ask more questions.

> For example, suppose that a train derailment has resulted in an acid spill near the shore of a local lake. You wonder what effect the spill will have on the fish and other organisms that live there. Has the spill killed all of the organisms in the lake? How have other organisms, such as aquatic plants, been affected by the spill? How can you find answers to your questions without endangering your safety?

Gather Information

Background research may help you to understand your observations and answer some of your questions. Go to Developing Research Skills in Appendix A for guidance on conducting research. You may also be able to gather information by making additional observations.

> For example, you read a news report about an environmental assessment of the spill site. You discover that the pH of the lake water before the accident was 6.7. Measurements taken after the accident indicate that the pH has dropped to 4.1. You do additional research to find out what kinds of organisms inhabit the lake and the optimal pH for their survival and growth.

Identify a Question to Investigate

You need to have a clear purpose and decide on a specific question that you are able to investigate with the resources available. If a question is provided for you, make sure you understand the science behind the question.

> You decide to investigate the effect of acidity on living organisms. You do not wish to risk harming fish or other animals, so you decide to use aquatic plants as your test organism. You pose the scientific question, "What effect will increasing acidity have on aquatic plants grown in an aquarium?"

Formulate a Hypothesis

A hypothesis attempts to answer the question being investigated. It often proposes a relationship that is based on background information or an observed pattern of events.

> You hypothesize that because plants can remove some impurities from polluted water, aquatic plants will be able to reduce the effect of small amounts of acid. However, because highly acidic water will damage or kill most organisms, you hypothesize that the aquatic plants will not be able to counteract the addition of large quantities of acid.

Plan an Investigation

Some investigations lay out steps for you to follow in order to answer a question, analyze a set of data, explore an issue, or solve a problem. In planning your own investigation, however, *you* must decide how to approach a scientific question. Taking time to plan your approach thoroughly will ensure that you address the question appropriately.

Design a Procedure Write out step-by-step instructions for performing the investigation. Include instructions for repeat trials, if appropriate. Ensure that the procedure is written in a logical sequence, and that it is complete and clear enough that someone else could carry it out. Create diagrams, if necessary. Ask someone else to read through the procedure and explain it back to you, to ensure you have not omitted any important details.

> You decide to investigate the effect of the pH change of water when you add acid to a large glass bottle containing water and aquatic plants. You will measure the pH of the water and observe the physical appearance of the plants twice a day for three days.

Identify Variables Many investigations study relationships between variables (quantities or factors that can change). An *independent variable* is changed by the person conducting the investigation. A *dependent variable* is affected by changes in the independent variable. *Controlled variables* are kept the same throughout an experiment.

A simple, controlled experiment shows relationships especially clearly because it has a single independent variable and a single dependent variable. All other variables are controlled. Changes in the dependent variable occur only in response to changes in the independent variable. When you are planning your investigation, you will need to identify the variables and decide which ones to control.

If possible, investigations include a *control*: a situation identical to the one being tested, except that the independent variable is not changed in any way. There is no reason, therefore, for the dependent variable to change. If it does, the reasoning behind your hypothesis, prediction, and variable analysis may be faulty. Look at the illustration at the top of the next column to see some examples of independent and dependent variables, as well as two examples of a control (no independent variable).

a. A test to find the best filter for muddy water

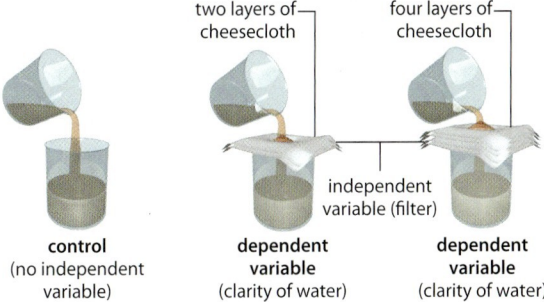

b. A test to find the best plant food for plant growth

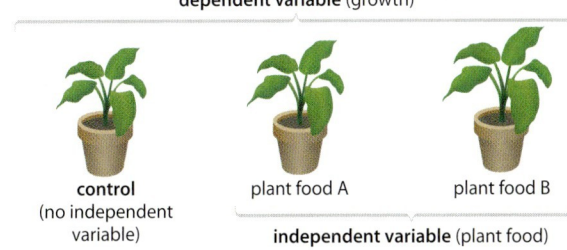

In planning your investigation, you decide to manipulate (change) the quantity of acid added to the aquarium you have made. Therefore, the quantity of acid is the independent variable. The pH of the water will be the dependent variable. Water temperature, lighting conditions, the particular species of aquatic plant used, and nutrients will be the controlled variables. In addition, you decide to set up an identical aquarium as a control. No acid will be added to the water in this aquarium, so you expect the pH of the water to stay constant.

You decide to set up three different experimental aquariums. You plan to add a different amount of acid to the water in each of these aquariums. You will add no acid to the fourth aquarium (the control). Your teacher suggests using 1.0 mol/L hydrochloric acid. You will add five drops of hydrochloric acid to Aquarium 1, 10 drops to Aquarium 2, and 15 drops to Aquarium 3. You will measure the pH of the water in each aquarium at 9:00 A.M. on the first day, immediately before adding the acid, and then at 2:00 P.M. You will measure the pH again at 9:00 A.M. and 2:00 P.M. on Day 2 and Day 3.

List Materials and Safety Precautions Develop a list of materials and apparatus you will need. Include measuring and recording instruments. Examine your procedure for safety hazards and plan any necessary precautions. (Go to Safety in Your Chemistry Lab and Classroom at the front of this book for information about safety hazards and precautions.) **Note:** Before doing any experimental work, ask your teacher to examine and approve your plan.

> Your materials list will include four glass jars, a dropper, aquatic plants, hydrochloric acid, water, and a pH meter. Safety precautions include handling glassware carefully to avoid breakage; wearing safety eyewear, gloves, and protective clothing to protect yourself from any acid spillage; storing the acid safely after use; and disposing of the aquarium water at the end of the investigation according to your teacher's instructions.

Make an Informed Prediction

A clear hypothesis often leads to a specific, testable prediction about what the investigation will reveal. You need to determine how to test your question before you can predict what will happen.

> You predict that an aquarium full of a certain species of aquatic plants will maintain a stable pH of about 7 when a small quantity of acid is added. When greater quantities of acid are added, however, you predict that the plants will be damaged. The pH of the water will decrease rapidly and the plants will eventually die.

Perform an Investigation

Be responsible whenever you conduct an investigation. Think before acting, and follow all safety precautions. Carry out your procedure carefully. Ask for assistance if you are unsure how to proceed or if you encounter an unexpected difficulty. Report any accidents to your teacher immediately. Keep your work area neat and clean it up when you have finished your investigation.

Compile and Organize Data

Record your results carefully and organize them in a logical way. Go to Organizing Data in a Table in Appendix A for help with recording and organizing the results of an investigation. As part of your observations, keep careful notes of any unexpected occurrences, problems with equipment, or unusual circumstances that might affect your results. If you are working with a partner, ensure that both of you have a copy of all observations and results.

Your results may include either qualitative or quantitative observations, or both. *Quantitative observations* are measurable and involve numbers. *Qualitative observations* involve descriptions rather than numbers or measurements. When making qualitative observations, try to record specific characteristics so that you can make comparisons between different trials.

In your investigation, you will record both qualitative and quantitative results. The pH values that you record are quantitative observations. Your descriptions of the physical appearance of the aquatic plants are qualitative observations. Looking at specific plant characteristics such as colour (green or brown) and vigour (robust or spindly) will help you to compare the physical appearance of the plants in each aquarium.

You might use a table like the one below to record and organize the data from your investigation.

Effect of Increasing Acidity on the Physical Appearance of Aquatic Plants in an Aquarium

	Physical Appearance of Plants (colour and vigour)			
	Control	+ 5 drops of acid	+ 10 drops of acid	+ 15 drops of acid
Day 1, 9:00 A.M. (before addition of acid)	green, robust	green, robust	green, robust	green, robust
Day 1, 2:00 P.M.	green, robust	green, robust	green, robust	brownish spots, spindly
Day 2, 9:00 A.M.	green, robust	green, robust	brownish spots, less robust	brown, spindly (looks dead)
Day 2, 2:00 P.M.	green, robust	green, robust	mostly brown, less robust	brown, spindly (looks dead)
Day 3, 9:00 A.M.	green, robust	green, robust	brown, spindly (looks dead)	brown, spindly (looks dead)
Day 3, 2:00 P.M.	green, robust	green, robust	brown, spindly (looks dead)	brown, spindly (looks dead)

Analyze Your Data

Perform any necessary graph work or calculations. Go to Constructing Graphs in Appendix A for help with graphing. Then consider and interpret your results. Do your data and observations support or refute your hypothesis and prediction? Are additional data needed before you can draw definite conclusions? Identify any possible sources of error or bias in your investigation. Does the procedure or apparatus need to be modified to obtain better data?

Using the pH data from your investigation, you construct the graph shown below.

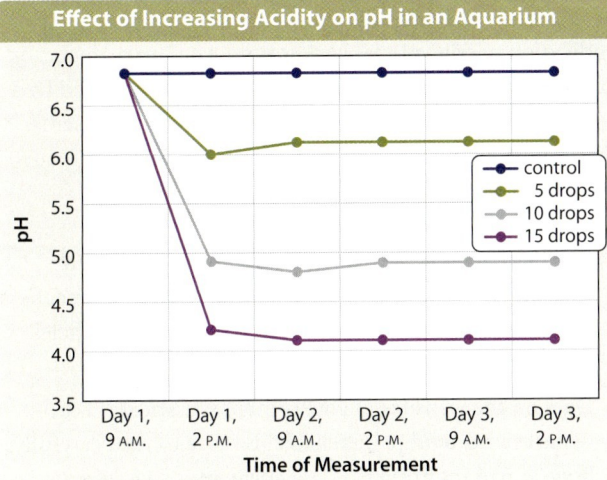

Draw Conclusions

Conclusions usually answer several questions:

- What has the investigation revealed about the answer to the question?
- How well does your prediction agree with the data?
- How well is your hypothesis supported by the data? Are the observations explained by the hypothesis?
- How precise were the measuring instruments and resulting observations?
- What improvements could be made to the investigation?

Relate your conclusions to your background knowledge of the scientific principles involved.

You conclude that your hypothesis and prediction were supported by the data. The aquatic plants were able to survive the addition of small amounts of hydrochloric acid (5 drops), but when more acid was added to the aquarium, the pH decreased rapidly and the plants soon looked brown and spindly.

However, you are unsure whether the plants in the highly acidic water are actually dead. You think perhaps you could place them in fresh water to see whether they could recover.

Now you can relate your results to the original problem of the acid spill in the lake. Are the aquatic plants in the lake likely to survive? Do your results reflect the conditions in the lake? What other factors might you need to consider?

Communicate Your Results

Communicate the results of your investigation. Always include a summary of your findings and an evaluation of the investigation. Be sure to round answers to the proper number of significant digits. Go to Significant Digits and Rounding in Appendix A for help with reporting numerical answers. Demonstrate your results clearly using graphs, tables, or diagrams, as appropriate. Go to Constructing Graphs or Organizing Data in a Table in Appendix A for help with communicating your results. Be sure to include units when expressing measurements. Go to Measurement in Appendix A for information on units and measurements.

Pose New Questions Based on Your Results

The conclusion of an investigation is not the end of scientific inquiry. Scientific inquiry is a continuous process in which results and conclusions lead to new questions. What new research questions might arise from your investigation? How might you find an answer to one of these questions?

After performing this investigation, you wonder how much the aquatic plants themselves affected the pH of the water. Would the decrease in pH have been more noticeable if there were no plants present? How would you test this?

Instant Practice

You are asked to plan an investigation to determine how temperature affects the rate of the reaction that occurs when an effervescent tablet is placed in water. Think about how you could test a hypothesis related to this question.

1. Will your results include qualitative or quantitative observations, or both? Explain your answer.
2. State a hypothesis for this investigation.
3. What will your independent variable be? What will your dependent variable be? What control will you set up?

Appendix A

Developing Research Skills

In this course, you will need to conduct research to answer specific questions and to explore broad research topics. The following skills will take you through the research process from start to finish:

- focussing your research
- searching for resources that contain information related to your topic
- evaluating the reliability of your information sources
- gathering, recording, and organizing information in an appropriate format
- presenting your work

Focussing Your Research

- Start by carefully reading your assignment. Pick out key words and phrases, such as *apply, analyze, argue, compare and contrast, describe, discuss, evaluate, explain, identify, infer, interpret,* and *predict*. These key words and phrases will guide you on what kind of information you need to collect, and what you need to do with the information.
- Jot down ideas on your own, and then get additional input from others, including your teacher.
- Once you have done some general research, narrow down your topic until you can express it in one specific question. This will help you focus your research.
- Ensure that the question you are researching fulfills the guidelines of the assignment provided by your teacher.

Searching for Resources

- It is important to find reliable resources to help you answer your question. Potential sources of information include print and on-line resources such as encyclopedias, textbooks, non-fiction books, journals, websites, and newsgroups.
- The library and the Internet can both provide information for your search. Whether you are looking at print or digital resources, you need to evaluate the accuracy and objectivity of the information.

Evaluating the Reliability of Your Information Sources

Assess the reliability of your information sources to help you decide whether the information you find is likely to be accurate. To determine the validity of a source, check that the author is identified, a recent publication date is given, and the source of facts or quotations is identified. An author's credentials are important. Look for an indication of educational background, work experience, or professional affiliation. If the information is published by a group, try to find out what interests the group represents. The following guidelines may be helpful in assessing your information sources:

- On-line and print scientific journals provide data that have been reviewed by experts in a field of study (peer-reviewed), so they are usually a reliable source. Be aware, however, that the conclusions in journal articles may contain opinions as well as facts.
- Data on the websites of government statistical departments tend to be reliable. Be sure to read carefully, however, to interpret the data correctly.
- University resources, such as websites ending in ".edu" are generally reliable.
- Reliable experts in a field of study often have a PhD or MSc degree, and their work is regularly cited in other publications.
- Consumer and corporate sources may present a biased view. That is, they may only present data that support their side of an issue. Look for sources that treat all sides of an issue equally and fairly, or that clearly specify which perspective(s) they are presenting.
- Some sources, such as blogs and editorials, provide information that represents an individual's point of view or opinion. Therefore, the information is not objective. However, opinion pieces can alert you to controversy about an issue and help you consider various perspectives. The opinion of an expert in a field of study should carry more weight than that of an unidentified source.
- On-line videos and podcasts can be dynamic and valuable sources of information. However, their accuracy and objectivity must be evaluated just as thoroughly as all other sources.

- A piece of information is generally reliable if you can find it in two other sources. However, be aware that several on-line resources might use the same incorrect source of information. If you see identical wording on multiple sites, try to find a different source to verify the information.

Gathering, Recording, and Organizing Information

- As you locate information, you may find it useful to jot it down on large sticky notes or make colour-coded entries in a digital file so that you can group similar ideas together. Remember to document the source of your information for each note or data entry.

  Avoid Plagiarism Copying information word-for-word and then presenting it as your own work is called *plagiarism*. Instead, you must cite every source you use for a research assignment. This includes all ideas, information, data, and opinions, other than your own, that appear in your work. If you include a quotation, be sure to indicate it as such, and supply all source information. Avoid direct quotations whenever possible—put information in your own words. Remember, though, that even when you paraphrase, you need to cite your sources.

  Record Source Information A research paper should always include a bibliography—a list of relevant information sources you have consulted while writing the paper. Bibliographic entries include information such as the author, title, publication year, name of the publisher, and city in which the publisher is located. For magazine or journal articles, the name of the magazine or journal, the name of the article, the issue number, and the page numbers should be recorded. For on-line resources, you should record the site URL, the name of the site, the author or publishing organization, and the date on which you retrieved the information. Remember to record source information while you are taking notes to avoid having to search it out again later! Ask your teacher about the preferred style for your references.

- You might find it helpful to create a chart to keep track of detailed source information. For on-line searches, a tracking chart is useful to record the key words you searched, the information you found, and the URL of the website where you found the information.
- Write down any additional questions that you think of as you are researching. You may need to refine your topic if it is too broad, or take a different approach if there is not enough information available to answer your research question.

Presenting Your Work

- Once you have organized all of your information, you should be able to summarize your research so that it provides a concise answer to your original research question. If you cannot answer this question, you may need to refine the question or do a bit more research.
- Check the assignment guidelines for instructions on how to format your work.
- Be sure that you fulfill all of the criteria of the assignment when you communicate your findings.

> **Instant Practice**
>
> 1. Your assignment asks you to research chemical waste generation during the production of pharmaceuticals and present your opinion on how this waste can be reduced.
>   a. What search terms might you use for your initial research on the Internet or at the library?
>   b. How might you narrow down this assignment into a research question?
> 2. How could you determine the validity of a posting on a pharmaceutical company's website that states how the adoption of green chemistry principles has reduced its use of toxic solvents?
> 3. How would you record the online source in question 2 in the bibliography of your research paper?

Appendix A

Writing a Lab Report

Use the following headings and guidelines to create a neat and legible lab report.

Title

- Choose a title that clearly states the independent variable and the dependent variable, but not the outcome of the investigation. For example, "A Comparison of the Neutralizing Ability of Different Antacid Ingredients."
- Under the title, write the names of all participants and the date(s) of the investigation.

Introduction

- Summarize the background of the problem.
- Cite any relevant scientific principles or literature related to the question being investigated.

Question/Problem

- Clearly state the question being investigated or the problem for which you are seeking a solution. For example, "Which ingredient in antacids is most effective at neutralizing acid?"

Hypothesis

- State, in general terms, the relationship that you believe exists between the independent variable and the dependent variable. For example, "Calcium carbonate, an ingredient in many antacids, is more effective at neutralizing acid than sodium hydrogen carbonate, another ingredient found in antacids."

Prediction

- State, in detailed terms, the specific results you expect to observe. For example, "Calcium carbonate will neutralize more hydrochloric acid than the same mass of sodium hydrogen carbonate will."

Materials

- List all of the materials and equipment you used, or refer to the appropriate page number in your textbook and note any additions, deletions, or substitutions you have made.

Procedure

- Write your procedure in the form of precise, numbered steps, or refer to the appropriate page number in your textbook and note any changes to the procedure. Include any safety precautions.

Results

- Set out the observations and/or data in a clearly organized table(s). Give your table(s) a title.
- If appropriate, construct a graph that shows the data accurately. Label the x-axis and the y-axis of the graph clearly and accurately, and use the correct scale and units. Give your graph a title.

Data Analysis

- Analyze all the results you have gathered and recorded, and ensure that you can defend your analysis. For example, "As shown in the following calculations, the volume of hydrochloric acid neutralized by calcium carbonate was 1.5 mL more on average than that neutralized by sodium hydrogen carbonate."
- Show sample calculations for any mathematical data analysis.

Conclusion

- State a conclusion based on your data analysis. Relate your conclusion to your hypothesis. For example, "Based on the results of this investigation, calcium carbonate has a greater neutralizing ability than sodium hydrogen carbonate."
- Compare the results you obtained with those you expected, or those obtained by other researchers.
- Examine and comment on experimental error.
- Assess the effectiveness of the experimental design.
- Indicate how the data support your conclusion.
- Make recommendations for how your conclusion could be applied, or for further study of the question you investigated.

References

- Cite your information sources according to the reference style your teacher suggests.
- Sources that need to be cited include background information for your introduction, a materials list or procedure from a textbook, any specialized methods of data analysis, results from other studies that you used for comparison with your own results, and any other sources used in your conclusion.

Appendix A

Organizing Data in a Table

Scientific investigation is about collecting information to help you answer a question. In many cases, you will develop a hypothesis and collect data to see if your hypothesis is supported. An important part of any successful investigation is recording and organizing your data. Often, scientists create tables in which to record data.

Planning to Record Your Data Suppose you are doing an investigation on the water quality of a stream that runs near your school. You will take water samples at three different locations along the stream. You need to decide how to record and organize your data. Begin by making a list of what you need to record. For this experiment, you will need to record the sample site, the pH of the water at each sample site, the chemicals found in the water at each sample site, and the concentration of these chemicals.

Creating Your Data Table Your data table must allow you to record your data neatly. To do this, you need to create

- headings to show what you are recording
- columns and rows that you will fill with data
- enough cells to record all the data
- a title for the table

In this investigation, you will find several chemicals in the water at each site, so you must make space for multiple recordings at each site. This means every row representing a sample site will have at least four rows associated with it for the different chemicals.

If you think you might need extra space, create a special section. In this investigation, leave space at the bottom of your table, in case you find more than four chemicals in the water at a sample site. Remember, if you use the extra rows, make sure you identify which sample site the extra data are from. Finally, give your table an appropriate title. Your data table might look like the one in the next column.

Reading a Table A table can be used to organize observations and measurements so that data are represented neatly and clearly. However, a table can also show relationships among the data presented. When you are reading a table, be sure to start by reading the column and row headings carefully. If the table contains measurements, look for the units in which they are reported. Follow vertically down a column or horizontally across a row to look for trends in the data. If the table contains numbers, do the numbers increase or decrease as you look down the column or across the row?

Water Quality Observations Made at Three Sample Stream Sites

Sample Site	pH	Type of Chemical	Concentration of Chemical (mg/L)
1	6.9	sulfate	30.7
		nitrate	0.11
		phosphate	0.001
2	7.2	sulfate	31.2
		nitrate	0.35
		phosphate	0.002
3	7.1	sulfate	30.9
		nitrate	0.07
		phosphate	0.001
		iron	0.1

Also look for relationships between columns or rows. Do the numbers in one column increase as the numbers in another column decrease? Is there one piece of datum that does not fit the pattern in the rest of the table? Think about why this might be the case.

Instant Practice

1. An investigation instructs you to place a sample of magnesium in three different solutions of hydrochloric acid. The concentrations of the solutions are as follows:
   - 0.25 mol/L HCl(aq)
   - 0.5 mol/L HCl(aq)
   - 1.0 mol/L HCl(aq)

   Construct a table to record and compare your observations. Give your table a title.

2. The next part of the investigation asks you to determine how each concentration of hydrochloric acid affects two other metals, zinc and aluminum. Draw a new table to record these data.

3. Read the table at the top of this page to determine which sample site has the lowest concentration of nitrate.

Appendix A

Constructing Graphs

A graph is a diagram that shows relationships among variables. Graphs help you to interpret and analyze data. The three basic types of graphs used in science are the line graph, the bar graph, and the circle graph.

The instructions given here describe how to construct graphs using paper and pencil. You can also use computer software to generate graphs. Whichever method you use, the graphs you construct should have the features described in the following pages.

Line Graphs

A line graph is used to show the relationship between two variables. The independent variable is plotted on the horizontal axis, called the x-axis. The dependent variable is plotted on the vertical axis, called the y-axis. The dependent variable (y) changes as a result of a change in the independent variable (x).

Suppose a chemist carried out an investigation to determine the relationship between the temperature and volume of an unknown gas at a specific pressure (P_1). She measured the volume (in mL) of the gas upon heating it to various temperatures (in K), as shown in the table below.

Temperature and Volume for an Unknown Gas at P_1

Temperature (K)	Volume (mL)
300	38
400	49
500	62
600	75

To make a graph of volume versus temperature measurements for this gas, start by determining the dependent and independent variables. The volume of the gas is the dependent variable and is plotted on the y-axis. The independent variable, or the temperature to which the the gas was heated, is plotted on the x-axis.

Give your graph a title and label each axis, indicating the units if appropriate. In this example, label the temperature on the x-axis. Your x-axis will need to be numbered to at least 600 K. Because the lowest volume of gas measured was 38 mL and the highest was 75 mL, you know that you will have to start numbers on the y-axis from at least 38 and number to at least 75 mL. For instance, you could decide to number 20 to 80 by intervals of 10, spaced at equal distances. Look at the example at the top of the page to see how you could label your axes.

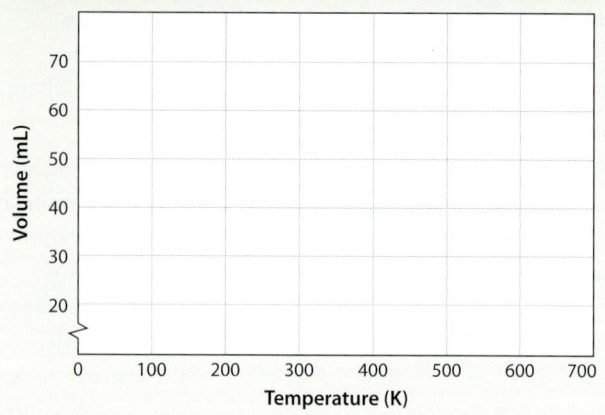

Begin plotting points by locating 300 on the x-axis and 38 on the y-axis. Where an imaginary vertical line from the x-axis and an imaginary horizontal line from the y-axis meet, place the first data point. Place the other data points using the same process. After all the points are plotted, draw a "best-fit" straight line through the points.

A best-fit line should be drawn to represent the general trend of the data. Try to draw the line so that there are as many points above it as there are below. Do not change the position or slope of the line dramatically just to include an outlier—a single data point that does not seem to be in line with all the others.

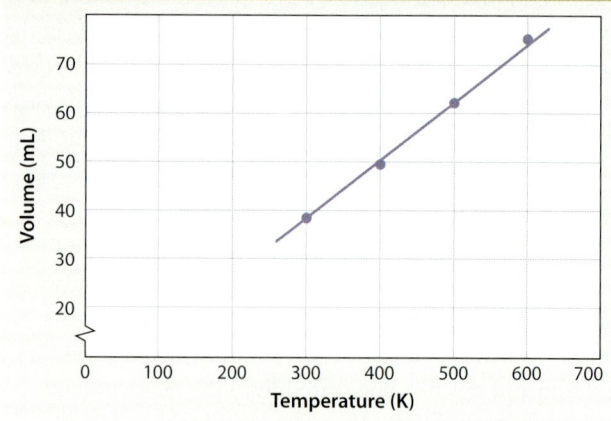

The chemist then repeated the investigation at a different pressure (P_2), using the same amount of gas. Her observations are shown in the table at the top of the next page.

Volume and Temperature for an Unknown Gas at P_2

Volume (mL)	Temperature (K)
21	300
28	400
36	500
43	600

What if you want to compare the relationship between the volume and temperature of the gas at these two different pressures? The P_2 data can be plotted on the same graph as the data for P_1. Label the different lines indicating different sets of data as P_1 and P_2.

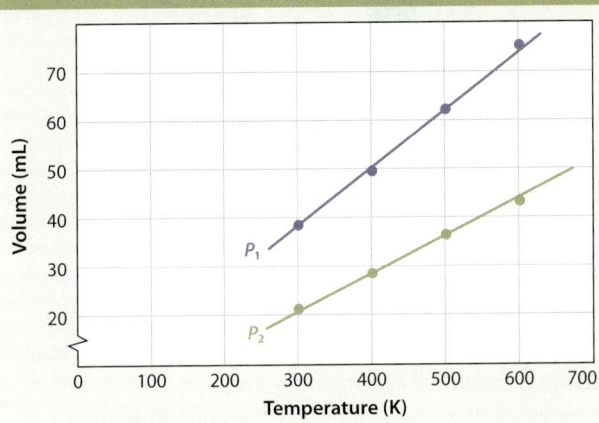

The Relationship between Volume and Temperature at P_1 and P_2

Instant Practice

1. At P_2, what change in temperature caused a volume change from 20 mL to 30 mL?
2. At which pressure would the volume of the gas decrease the most if temperature were decreased from 500 K to 400 K?
3. Construct a line graph for the following data:

Solubility of Sodium Nitrate at Various Temperatures

Temperature (°C)	Solubility (g/100 mL H_2O)
0	64
10	80
20	87
30	96
40	104

Slope of a Linear Graph The slope of a line is a number determined by any two points on the line. This number describes how steep the line is. The greater the absolute value of the slope, the steeper the line. Slope is the ratio of the change in the *y*-coordinates (rise) to the change in the *x*-coordinates (run) as you move from one point to the other.

The graph below shows a line that passes through points (5, 4) and (9, 6).

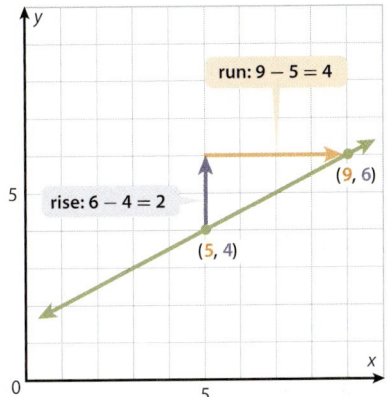

$$\text{slope} = \frac{\text{rise}}{\text{run}}$$
$$= \frac{\text{change in } y\text{-coordinates}}{\text{change in } x\text{-coordinates}}$$
$$= \frac{6-4}{9-5}$$
$$= \frac{2}{4} \text{ or } \frac{1}{2}$$

So, the slope of the line is $\frac{1}{2}$.

A positive slope indicates that the line climbs from left to right. A negative slope indicates that the line descends from left to right. A slope of zero indicates that there is no change in the dependent variable as the independent variable increases. A horizontal line has a slope of zero.

Linear and Non-Linear Trends Two types of trends that you are likely to see when you graph data in chemistry are linear trends and non-linear trends. A linear trend has a constant increase or decrease in data values. For a non-linear trend, the degree to which the data values are increasing or decreasing is not constant. The graphs shown on the next page are examples of these two common trends.

In the graph below, there are two lines describing the solubility of salts at various temperatures. Both lines show an increasing, linear trend. As the temperature increases, so too does the solubility of each salt. The rate of increase is constant.

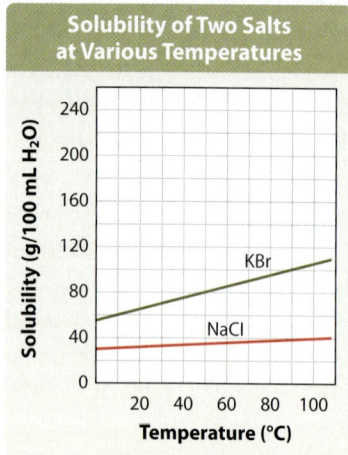

The graph below also shows two lines describing the solubility of salts at various temperatures. Both lines show an increasing, non-linear trend. As in the graph above, the solubility of each salt increases as the temperature increases. However, for the graph below, the rate of increase is not constant. For instance, for potassium nitrate, you will see that the compound's solubility increases more as the temperature increases 20°C from 60°C to 80°C than it does as it increases 20°C from 30°C to 50°C.

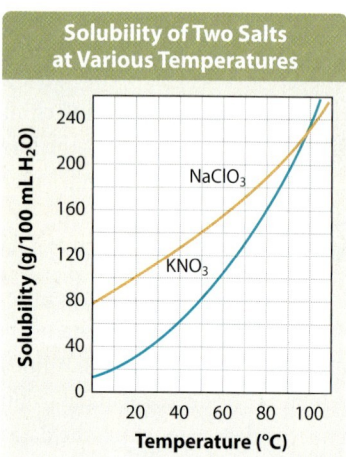

When you are drawing a curve to represent a non-linear trend, you should not connect the data points. Instead, draw a smooth best-fit curve that shows the general trend of the data. Try to draw the curve so there are as many points above it as there are below. The curve should change smoothly. It should not have a dramatic change in direction just to include a single data point that does not fit with the others.

Bar Graphs

A bar graph displays a comparison of different categories of data by representing each category with a bar. The length of the bar is related to the category's frequency. To make a bar graph, set up the x-axis and y-axis as you did for the line graph. Plot the data by drawing thick bars from the x-axis up to an imaginary line representing the y-axis point.

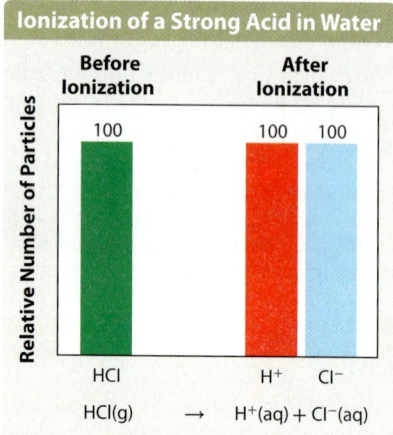

Look at the graph above. The independent variable is the type of particle. The dependent variable is the relative number of particles.

Bar graphs can also be used to display multiple sets of data in different categories at the same time, as shown in the graph below. Bar graphs, like the one below, have a legend to denote which bars represent each set of data.

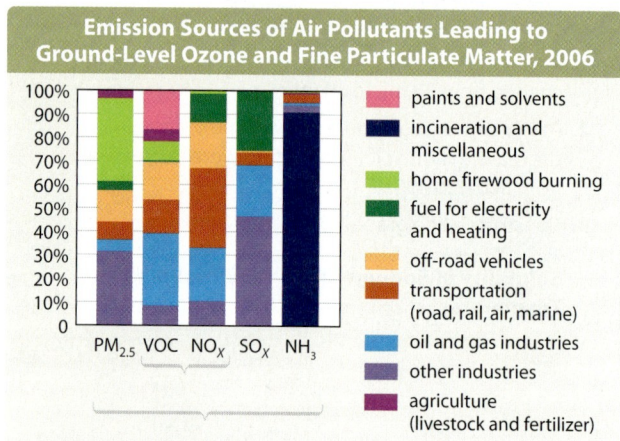

Instant Practice

In the graph at the bottom of this column, what percentage of VOC air pollution is generated by the oil and gas industries?

Circle Graphs

A circle graph is a circle divided into sections that represent parts of a whole. When all the sections are placed together, they equal 100 percent of the whole.

Consider the circle graph shown below. This graph shows the anthropogenic sources of the air contaminant sulfur dioxide. Each component of the graph, electrical utilities, industry, and other, add up to 100 percent of all sources of sulfur dioxide air pollution.

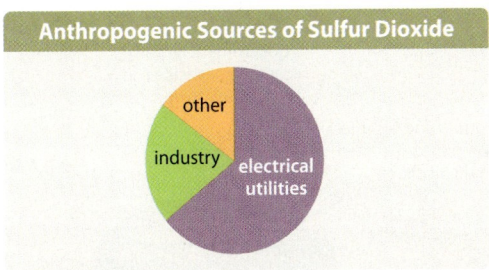

Suppose you wanted to make a circle graph to represent data you observed or calculated, such as the percentage composition of a compound. For instance, if you determine the percentage composition of copper(I) sulfide, $Cu_2S(s)$, to be 79.9% copper and 20.1% sulfur by mass, you can represent this graphically with a circle graph.

To begin, you know that the percentages of the different elements in the compound must add up to 100. This 100 percent is represented by the 360° (the number of degrees in a circle) that make up the circle graph.

To find out how much of the circle each element should cover in the graph, first multiply the percent of copper by 360. Then, round your answer to the nearest whole number.

$$79.9\% \times 360° = 0.799 \times 360°$$
$$= 287.64°$$
$$= 288°$$

The sum of all the segments of the circle graph should add up to 360°. Therefore, you can calculate the segment of the circle that represents the percentage of sulfur by subtracting the degrees representing copper from 360°.

$$360° - 288° = 72°$$

To draw your circle graph, you will need a compass and a protractor. First, use the compass to draw a circle. Then, draw a straight line from the centre to the edge of the circle. Place your protractor on this line, and mark the point on the circle where an angle of 72° will intersect the circle. Draw a straight line from the centre of the circle to the intersection point. This is the section representing the percentage of sulfur in the compound. The remaining section represents the percentage of copper.

Complete the graph by labelling the sections of the graph with percentages and giving the graph a title. Your completed graph should look similar to the one below.

If your circle graph has more than two sections, you will need to construct a segment for each entry. Place your protractor on the last line segment that you have drawn and mark off the appropriate angle. Draw a line segment from the centre of the circle to the new mark on the circle. Continue this process until all of the segments have been drawn.

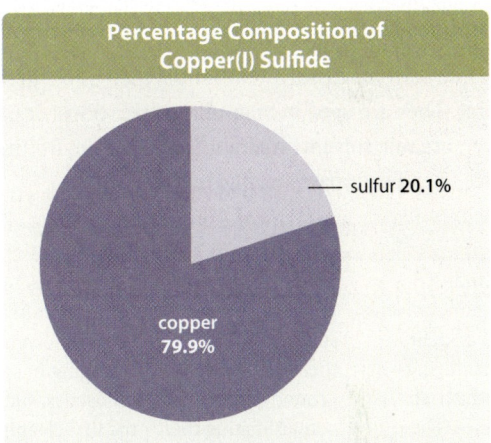

Instant Practice

Copper is often used as the cathode of a galvanic cell. It is a relatively abundant element in Earth's crust. The percentages of copper produced around the world are as follows: 35% in Chile, 8% in Peru, 8% in the United States, 6% in China, and 6% in Australia. The rest of the world's copper production is distributed among other nations to a lesser extent. Create a circle graph to illustrate these percentages.

Appendix A

Using Graphic Organizers

When deciding which type of graphic organizer to use, consider your purpose. It may be to brainstorm, to show relationships among ideas, to summarize a section of text, to record research notes, or to review what you have learned before writing a test. Several different graphic organizers are shown here. The descriptions indicate the function or purpose of each organizer.

PMI Chart

PMI stands for Plus, Minus, and Interesting. A PMI chart is a simple three-column table that can be used to state the positive and negative aspects of an issue, or to describe advantages and disadvantages related to the issue. The third column in the chart is used to list interesting information related to the issue. PMI charts help you to organize your thinking after reading about a topic that is up for debate or that can have positive or negative effects. They are useful when analyzing an issue.

Organic solvents dissolve substances such as oil, grease, and paint. They are used in many Canadian industries. However, organic solvents may also harm the environment and have negative impacts on human health.

P	M	I
Many industries use organic solvents as part of their manufacturing and industrial processes. These industries are important to the Canadian economy.	These industries may leak organic solvents into the soil and groundwater, contaminating the environment and threatening human health. Industrial spills may pose similar risks.	Alternatives to using harmful organic solvents are emerging in some industries, such as the dry-cleaning industry.
Jobs in industries that use organic solvents provide a livelihood for thousands of Canadians.	Workers who come into contact with organic solvents on a regular basis may experience negative long-term health effects, which affect quality of life and job performance.	Some of these industries are the major employers in small Canadian towns. Finding other jobs in these towns may be difficult.

Main Idea Web

A main idea web shows a main idea and several supporting details. The main idea is written in the centre of the web, and each detail is written at the end of a line extending from the centre. This organizer is useful for brainstorming or for summarizing text.

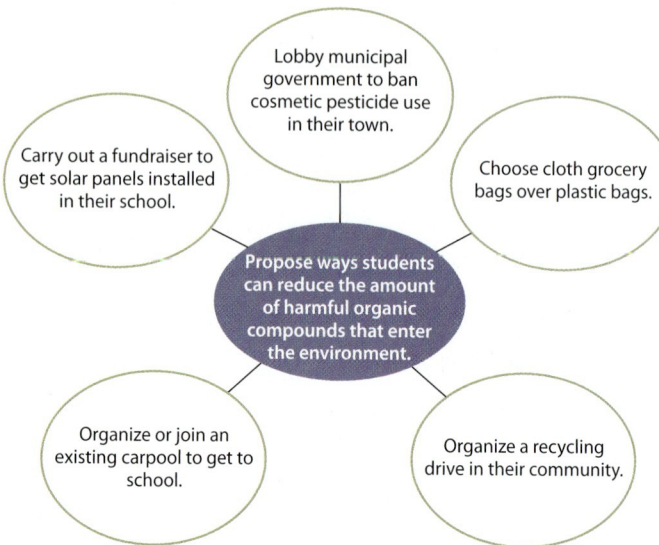

Spider Map

A spider map shows a main idea and several ideas associated with the main idea. It does not show the relationships among the ideas. A spider map is useful when you are brainstorming or taking notes.

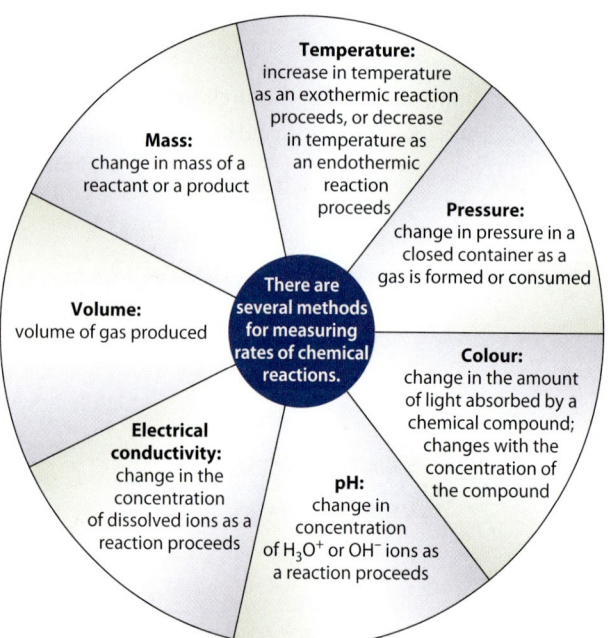

Fishbone Diagram

A fishbone diagram looks similar to a spider map, but it organizes information differently. A main topic, situation, or idea is placed in the middle of the diagram. This is the "backbone" of the "fish." The "bones" (lines) that extend from the backbone can be used to list reasons why the situation exists, factors that affect the main idea, or arguments that support the main idea. Finally, supporting details further extend outward from these issues. Fishbone diagrams are useful for planning and organizing a research project. You can clearly see when you do not have enough details to support an issue, which indicates that you need to do additional research.

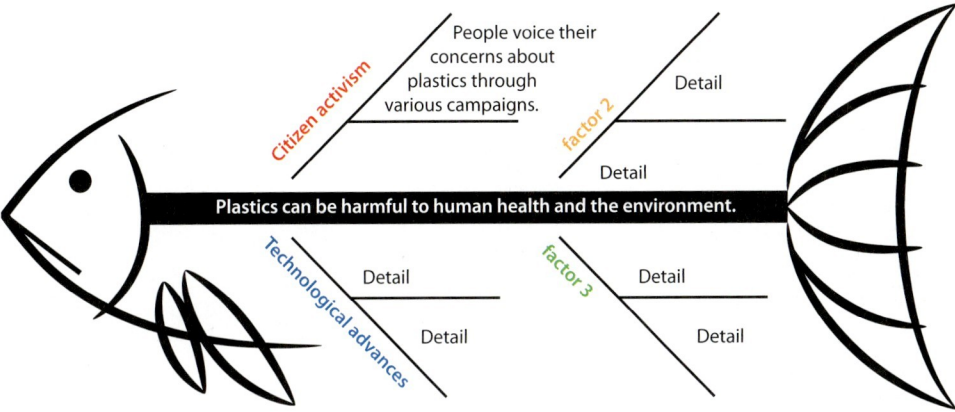

Concept Map

A concept map uses shapes and lines to show how ideas, concepts, or formulas are related. Each idea, concept, or formula is written inside a circle, a square, a rectangle, or another shape. Lines and arrows that connect the shapes indicate the relationships between them. In some cases, words that explain how the concepts are related are written on the lines that connect the shapes.

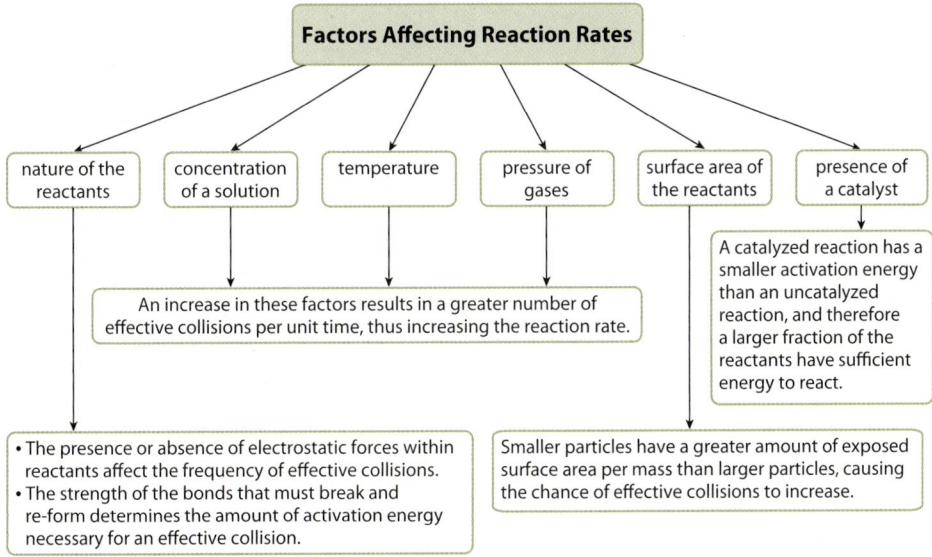

Flowchart

A flowchart shows a sequence of events or the steps in a process. An arrow leads from an initial event or step to the next event or step, and so on, until the final outcome is reached. Side arrows may also provide further explanation.

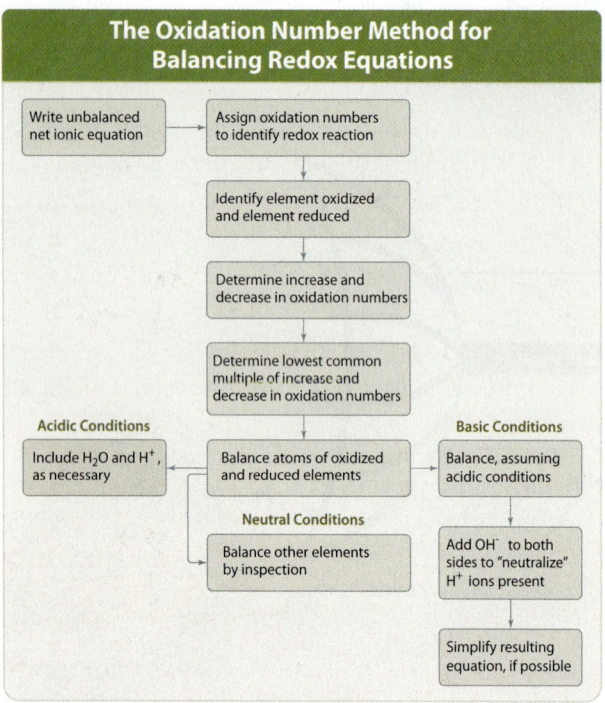

Cycle Chart

A cycle chart is a flowchart that has no distinct beginning or end. All the events are shown in the order in which they occur, as indicated by arrows, but there are no first and last events. Instead, the events occur again and again in a continuous cycle. In the photosynthesis/cellular respiration cycle, shown below, arrows branch off to show energy entering and leaving the cycle.

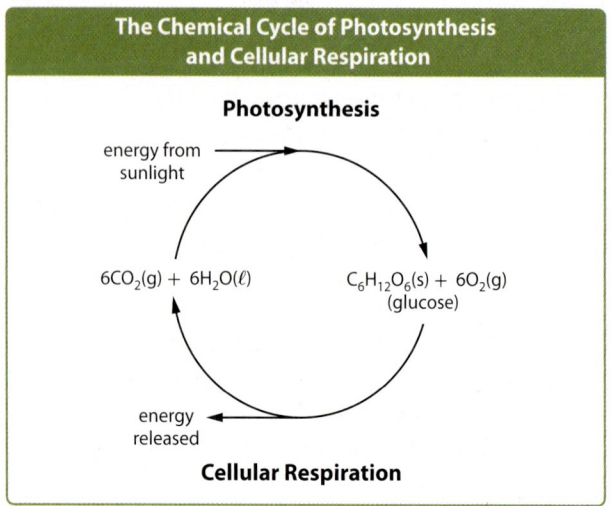

Venn Diagram

A Venn diagram uses overlapping shapes to show similarities and differences among concepts.

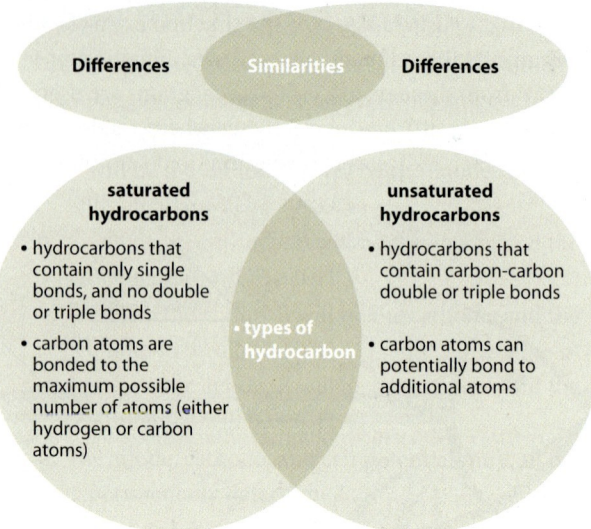

Cause-and-Effect Map

The first cause-and-effect map below shows one cause that results in several effects. The second map shows one effect that has several causes.

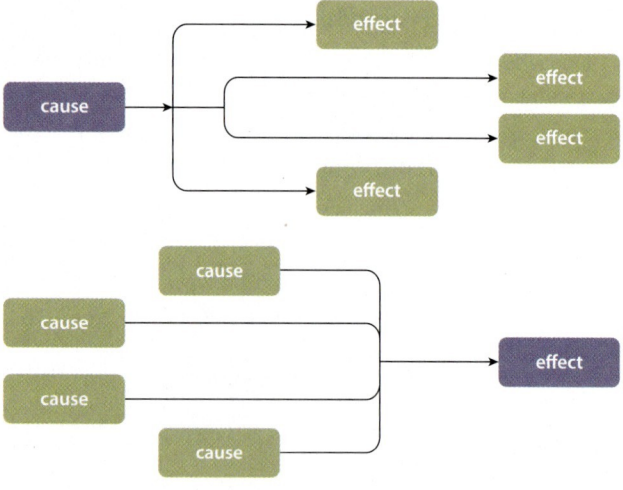

Instant Practice

1. Use information in this textbook to create a main idea web or spider map. Exchange your organizer with a partner and assess the effectiveness of each organizer.
2. Create a Venn diagram to compare and contrast oxidation and reduction.

Appendix A

Measurement

Scientists have developed globally agreed-upon standards for measurement, and for recording and calculating data. These are the standards that you will use throughout this science program.

Units of Measurement

When you take measurements for scientific purposes, you use the International System of Measurement (commonly know as SI, from the French *Système international d'unités*). SI includes the metric system and other standard units, symbols, and prefixes, which are reviewed in the tables on this page.

In SI, the base units include the metre, the kilogram, and the second. The size of any particular unit can be determined by the prefix used with the base unit. Larger and smaller units of measurement can be obtained by either multiplying or dividing the base unit by a multiple of 10.

For example, the prefix *kilo-* means multiplied by 1000. So, one kilogram is equivalent to 1000 grams:

$$1 \text{ kg} = 1000 \text{ g}$$

The prefix *milli-* means divided by 1000. So, one milligram is equivalent to one thousandth of a gram:

$$1 \text{ mg} = \frac{1}{1000 \text{ g}}$$

The following tables show the most commonly used metric prefixes, as well as some common metric quantities, units, and symbols.

Commonly Used Metric Prefixes

Prefix	Symbol	Relationship to the Base Unit
tera-	T	$10^{12} = 1\,000\,000\,000\,000$
giga-	G	$10^{9} = 1\,000\,000\,000$
mega-	M	$10^{6} = 1\,000\,000$
kilo-	k	$10^{3} = 1\,000$
hecto-	h	$10^{2} = 100$
deca-	da	$10^{1} = 10$
—	—	$10^{0} = 1$
deci-	d	$10^{-1} = 0.1$
centi-	c	$10^{-2} = 0.01$
milli-	m	$10^{-3} = 0.001$
micro-	μ	$10^{-6} = 0.000\,001$
nano-	n	$10^{-9} = 0.000\,000\,001$
pico-	p	$10^{-12} = 0.000\,000\,000\,001$

Commonly Used Metric Quantities, Units, and Symbols

Quantity	Unit	Symbol
Length	nanometre	nm
	micrometre	μm
	millimetre	mm
	centimetre	cm
	metre	m
	kilometre	km
Mass	gram	g
	kilogram	kg
	tonne	t
Area	square metre	m^2
	square centimetre	cm^2
	hectare	ha (10 000 m^2)
Volume	cubic centimetre	cm^3
	cubic metre	m^3
	millilitre	mL
	litre	L
Time	second	s
Temperature	degree Celsius	°C
	kelvin	K
Force	newton	N
Energy	joule	J
	kilojoule*	kJ
Pressure	pascal	Pa
	kilopascal**	kPa
Electric current	ampere	A
Quantity of electric charge	coulomb	C
Frequency	hertz	Hz
Power	watt	W

* Many dieticians in North America continue to measure nutritional energy in Calories, also known as kilocalories or dietetic Calories. In SI units, 1 Calorie = 4.186 kJ.

** In current North American medical practice, blood pressure is measured in millimetres of mercury, symbolized as mmHg. In SI units, 1 mmHg = 0.133 kPa.

Accuracy and Precision

In science, the terms accuracy and precision have specific definitions that differ from their everyday meanings.

Scientific *accuracy* refers to how close a given quantity is to an accepted or expected value. For example, under standard (defined) conditions of temperature and pressure, 5 mL of water has a mass of 5 g. When you measure the mass of 5 mL of water under the same conditions, you should, if you are accurate, find that the mass is 5 g.

Scientific *precision* refers to the exactness of your measurements. The precision of your measurements is directly related to the instruments you use to make the measurements. Although faulty instruments (for example, a balance that is not working properly) will likely affect both the accuracy and the precision of your measurements, the calibration of the instruments you use is the factor that most affects precision. For example, a ruler calibrated in millimetres will allow you to make more precise measurements than one that shows only centimetres.

Precision also describes the repeatability of measurements. The closeness of a series of data points on a graph is an indicator of repeatability. Data that are close to one another, as in graph A, below, are said to be precise.

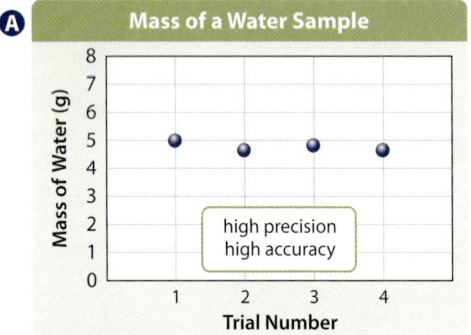

Graph A shows a group of data with high accuracy, since the data points are all grouped around 5 g.

There is no guarantee, however, that the data are accurate until a comparison with an accepted value is made. For example, graph B shows a group of measurements that are precise, but not accurate, since they report the mass of a 5 g sample of water as approximately 7 g.

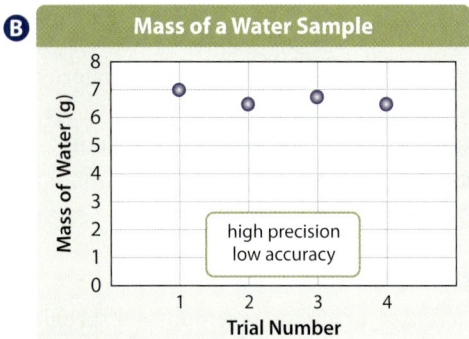

Graph B shows data with low accuracy, since the data points are grouped around 7 g.

In graph C, the data points give an accurate value for average mass, but they are not precise.

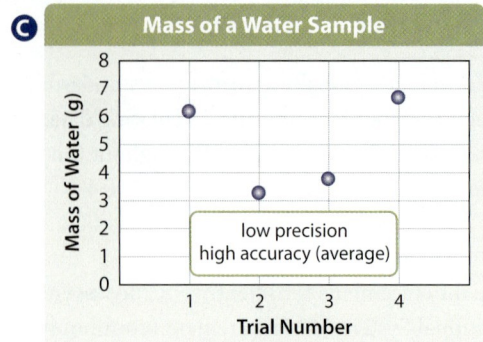

In graph C, the individual data points are not very accurate, since they are all more than 1 g away from the expected value of 5 g. However, taken as a group, the data set in graph C has high accuracy, since the average mass from the four trials is 5 g.

Error

Error exists in every measured or experimentally obtained value. Even the most careful scientist cannot avoid having error in a measurement. *Random error* results from uncontrollable variation in how we obtain a measurement. For example, human reflexes vary, so it is not possible to push the stem of a stopwatch exactly the same way every time. No measurement is perfect. Repeating trials will reduce but never eliminate the effects of random error. Random error affects precision and, usually, accuracy.

Systematic error results from consistent bias in observation. For example, a scale might consistently give a reading that is 0.5 g heavier than the actual mass of a sample, or a person might consistently read the scale of a measuring instrument incorrectly. Repeating trials will not reduce systematic error. Systematic error affects accuracy.

Percent Error

The amount of error associated with a measurement can be expressed as a percentage, which can help you to evaluate the accuracy of your measurement. The higher the *percent error* is, the less accurate the measurement will be. Percent error is calculated using the following equation:

$$\text{percent error} = \left| \frac{\text{measured value} - \text{expected value}}{\text{expected value}} \right| \times 100\%$$

(Note that the vertical lines surrounding the fraction mean *the absolute value of* the expression within the lines. That is, the expression's numerical value should be reported without a positive or negative sign.) As an example, a student measures a 5 mL sample of water and finds the volume to be 4.6 mL.

$$\text{percent error} = \left| \frac{4.6 \text{ mL} - 5 \text{ mL}}{5 \text{ mL}} \right| \times 100\%$$

$$= \left| \frac{-0.4 \text{ mL}}{5 \text{ mL}} \right| \times 100\%$$

$$= 8\%$$

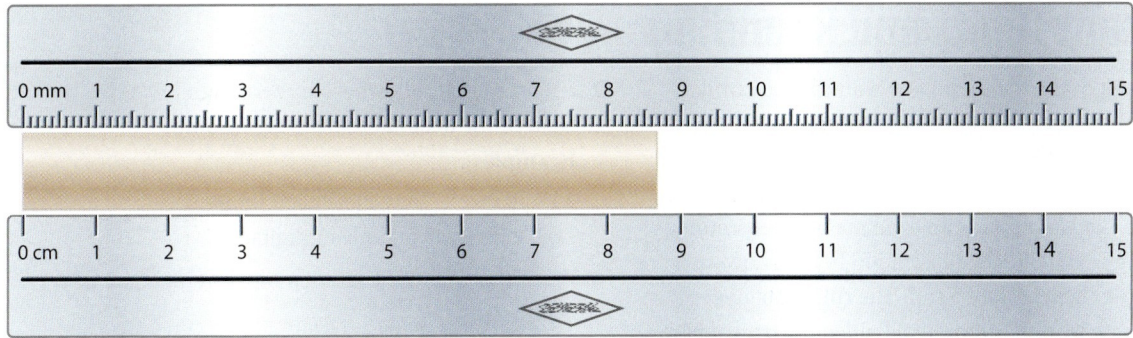

Estimated uncertainty is half of the smallest visible division. In this case, the estimated uncertainty is ±0.5 mm for the top ruler and ±0.5 cm for the bottom ruler.

Uncertainty

Estimated uncertainty describes the limitations of a measuring device. It is defined as half of the smallest division of the measuring device. For example, a metre stick with only centimetres marked on it would have an error of ±0.5 cm. A ruler that includes millimetre divisions would have a smaller error of ±0.5 mm (0.05 cm, or a 10-fold decrease in error). A measurement can be recorded with its estimated uncertainty. In the diagram at the top of the page, for example, the top ruler gives a measurement of 8.69 ±0.05 cm, whereas the bottom ruler gives a measurement of 8.7 ±0.5 cm.

You can convert the estimated uncertainty into a percentage of the actual measured value using the following equation:

$$\text{relative uncertainty} = \frac{\text{estimated uncertainty}}{\text{actual measurement}} \times 100\%$$

Example

Convert the error represented by 22.0 ±0.5 cm to a percentage.

$$\text{relative uncertainty} = \frac{0.5 \text{ cm}}{22.0 \text{ cm}} \times 100\%$$
$$= 2\%$$

Estimating

Sometimes it is not practical or possible to make an accurate measurement of a quantity. You must instead make an *estimate*—an informed judgement that approximates a quantity. For example, if you were conducting an experiment to compare the number of weeds in a field treated with herbicide with the number of weeds in an untreated field, counting the weeds would be impractical, if not impossible. Instead, you could count the number of weeds in a typical square metre of each field. You could then estimate the number of weeds in the entire field by multiplying the number of weeds in a typical square metre by the number of square metres in the field. To make a reasonable estimate of the number of weeds in the field, however, you would need to sample many areas, each 1 m^2, and then calculate an average to determine the number of weeds in a typical square metre for each field.

Estimating can be a valuable tool in science. It is important to keep in mind, however, that the number of samples you take can greatly influence the reliability of your estimate. To make a good estimate, include as many samples as is practical.

Instant Practice

1. Describe the relationships between the prefixes *mega*, *deci*, and *micro* and the SI base unit of the metre.

2. You and your lab partner each measure the volume of a 25.0 mL sample of water given to you by your teacher, who asks you to measure it twice in a graduated cylinder. Your lab partner records the measurements 26.1 mL and 26.0 mL, whereas you record 25.3 mL and 24.8 mL.
   a. Analyze these results in terms of accuracy and precision.
   b. Determine the percent error for each measurement.
   c. Provide the estimated uncertainty for each measurement.

Appendix A

Significant Digits and Rounding

You might think that a measurement is an exact quantity. In fact, all measurements involve uncertainty. The measuring device is one source of uncertainty, and you, as the reader of the device, are another. Every time you take a measurement, you are making an estimate by interpreting the reading. For example, the illustration below shows a ruler measuring the length of a rod. The ruler can give quite an accurate reading, since it is divided into millimetre marks. But the end of the rod falls between two marks. There is still uncertainty in the measurement. You can be certain that if the ruler is accurate, the length of the rod is between 5.2 cm and 5.3 cm. However, you must estimate the distance between the 2 mm and 3 mm marks.

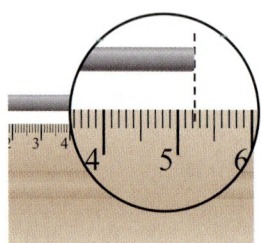

Significant Digits

Significant digits are the digits you record when you take a measurement. The significant digits in a measured quantity include all the certain digits plus the first uncertain digit. In the example above, suppose you estimate the length of the rod to be 5.23 cm. The first two digits (5 and 2) are certain (those marks are visible), but the last digit (0.03) is estimated. The measurement 5.23 cm has three significant digits.

Determining the Number of Significant Digits

The following rules will help you determine the number of significant digits in a given measurement.

1. All non-zero digits (1–9) are significant.
   Examples:
   - 123 m—three significant digits
   - 23.56 km—four significant digits

2. Zeros between non-zero digits are also significant.
   Examples:
   - 1207 m—four significant digits
   - 120.5 km/h—four significant digits

3. Any zero that follows a non-zero digit *and* is to the right of the decimal point is significant.
   Examples:
   - 12.50 m/s^2—four significant digits
   - 6.0 km—two significant digits

4. Zeros that are to the left of a measurement are not significant.
   Examples:
   - 0.056—two significant digits
   - 0.007 60—three significant digits

5. Zeros used to indicate the position of the decimal are not significant. These zeros are sometimes called spacers.
   Examples:
   - **500 km—one significant digit** (the decimal point is assumed to be after the final zero)
   - 0.325 m—three significant digits
   - 0.000 34 km—two significant digits

6. In some cases, a zero that appears to be a spacer is actually a significant digit. All counting numbers have an infinite number of significant digits.
   Examples:
   - 6 apples—infinite number of significant digits
   - 125 people—infinite number of significant digits
   - 450 deer—infinite number of significant digits

> **Instant Practice**
>
> Determine the number of significant digits in each measurement.
>
> a. 10 molecules
> b. 23.4 mL
> c. 40.08 g
> d. 9.60 mol
> e. 0.04 L
> f. 0.570 mol/L
> g. 320 m
> h. −89.4 kJ

Using Significant Digits in Mathematical Operations

When you use measured values in mathematical operations, the calculated answer cannot be more certain than the measurements on which it is based. Often the answer on your calculator will have to be rounded to the correct number of significant digits.

Rules for Rounding

1. When the first digit to be dropped is less than 5, the preceding digit is not changed.

   Example:
   - 6.723 m rounded to two significant digits is 6.7 m. The digit after the 7 is less than 5, so the 7 does not change.

2. When the first digit to be dropped is 5 or greater, the preceding digit is increased by one.

   Example:
   - 7.237 m rounded to three significant digits is 7.24 m. The digit after the 3 is greater than 5, so the 3 is increased by one.

3. When the first digit to be dropped is 5, and there are no following digits, increase the preceding number by 1 if it is odd, but leave the preceding number unchanged if it is even.

   Examples:
   - 8.345 L rounded to three significant digits is 8.34 L, because the digit before the 5 is even.
   - 8.375 L rounded to three significant digits is 8.38 L, because the digit before the 5 is odd.

Adding or Subtracting Measurements

Perform the mathematical operation, and then round off the answer so it has the same number of decimal places as the value that has the fewest decimal places.

Example:
Add the following measured lengths and express the answer to the correct number of significant digits.

$x = 2.3$ cm $+ 6.47$ cm $+ 13.689$ cm
$ = 22.459$ cm
$ = 22.5$ cm

Since 2.3 cm has only one decimal place, the answer can have only one decimal place.

Multiplying or Dividing Measurements

Perform the mathematical operation, and then round off the answer so it has the same number of significant digits as the value that has the least number of significant digits.

Example:
Multiply the following measured lengths and express the answer to the correct number of significant digits.

$x = (2.342 \text{ m})(0.063 \text{ m})(306 \text{ m})$
$ = 45.149\,076 \text{ m}^3$
$ = 45 \text{ m}^3$

Since 0.063 m has only two significant digits, the final answer must also have two significant digits.

> **Instant Practice**
>
> Perform the following calculations, rounding off your answer to the correct number of significant digits.
>
> a. 0.003 mL + 3.84 mL
> b. 6.75 g + 0.4 g − 1.20 g
> c. 14.0 s × 1.956 s
> d. $\dfrac{2.87 \text{ m}}{0.056 \text{ m}}$
> e. $\dfrac{(10 \text{ km})(5.70 \text{ km})}{0.02 \text{ km}}$

Appendix A

Scientific Notation

An exponent is the symbol or number denoting the power to which another number or symbol is to be raised. The exponent shows the number of repeated multiplications of the base. In 10^2, the exponent is 2 and the base is 10. The expression 10^2 means 10×10.

Powers of 10

Digits	Standard Form	Exponential Form
Ten thousands	10 000	10^4
Thousands	1 000	10^3
Hundreds	100	10^2
Tens	10	10^1
Ones	1	10^0
Tenths	0.1	10^{-1}
Hundredths	0.01	10^{-2}
Thousandths	0.001	10^{-3}
Ten thousandths	0.0001	10^{-4}

Why use exponents? Consider this: One molecule of water has a mass of 0.000 000 000 000 000 000 000 029 9 g. Using such a number for calculations would be quite awkward. The mistaken addition or omission of a single zero would make the number either 10 times larger or 10 times smaller than it actually is. Scientific notation allows scientists to express very large and very small numbers more easily, to avoid mistakes, and to clarify the number of significant digits.

Expressing Numbers in Scientific Notation

In scientific notation, a number has the form $x \times 10^n$, where x is greater than or equal to 1 but less than 10, and 10^n is a power of 10. To express a number in scientific notation, use the following steps:

1. To determine the value of x, move the decimal point in the number so that only one non-zero digit is to the left of the decimal point.
2. To determine the value of the exponent n, count the number of places the decimal point moves to the left or right. If the decimal point moves to the right, express n as a positive exponent. If the decimal point moves to the left, express n as a negative exponent.
3. Use the values you have determined for x and n to express the number in the form $x \times 10^n$.

Examples

Express 0.000 000 000 000 000 000 000 029 9 g in scientific notation.

1. To determine x, move the decimal point so that only one non-zero number is to the left of the decimal point:
$$2.99$$

2. To determine n, count the number of places the decimal moved:

Since the decimal point moved to the right, the exponent will be negative.

3. Express the number in the form $x \times 10^n$:
$$2.99 \times 10^{-23} \text{ g}$$

Express 602 000 000 000 000 000 000 000 in scientific notation.

1. To determine x, move the decimal point so that only one non-zero number is to the left of the decimal point:
$$6.02$$

2. To determine n, count the number of places the decimal moved:

6.02 000 000 000 000 000 000 000.
    23 21 18 15 12 9 6 3

Since the decimal point moved to the left, the exponent will be positive.

3. Express the number in the form $x \times 10^n$:
$$6.02 \times 10^{23}$$

> **Instant Practice**
>
> 1. Express 0.000 000 000 000 000 088 m in scientific notation.
> 2. Express 12 345 670 000 000 000 000 000 J in scientific notation.

Appendix A

Using Experimental Data to Determine Rate Laws

The Sample Problems below show how the order of reaction, rate constant, and rate law for specific reactions can be determined mathematically from experimental data. Study the Sample Problems and then complete the Practice Problems that follow.

Sample Problem

Calculating the Order of Reaction and the Rate Constant

Problem

The decomposition of dinitrogen pentoxide, $N_2O_5(g)$, occurs according to the following reaction:

$$2N_2O_5(g) \rightarrow 4NO_2(g) + O_2(g)$$

The general equation for the rate law for this reaction is as follows:

$$\text{rate} = k[N_2O_5]^m$$

The data in the table below are from four experiments conducted to determine the initial rate of the reaction at different initial concentrations of dinitrogen pentoxide. Determine the value of m and then determine the value of the rate constant, k.

Initial Rates of Dinitrogen Pentoxide Reactions

Experiment	Initial [N₂O₅] (mol/L)	Initial Rate (mol/L•s)
1	0.050	2.4×10^{-5}
2	0.100	4.8×10^{-5}
3	0.150	7.2×10^{-5}
4	0.200	9.6×10^{-5}

What Is Required?

You need to calculate the value of the exponent m and the value of the rate constant in the rate law for the reaction.

What Is Given?

You know the general equation for the rate law: $\text{rate} = k[N_2O_5]^m$
You are given a data table with the initial rates of reaction for different initial concentrations of dinitrogen pentoxide.

Plan Your Strategy	Act on Your Strategy
Determine the value of m. Using the data in the table and the general equation for the rate law, you can set up four equations. Since you are looking for two unknowns, you need only two equations. Write equations using the data from the first two rows of the table.	$\text{rate} = k[N_2O_5]^m$ $2.4 \times 10^{-5} \dfrac{\text{mol}}{\text{L} \cdot \text{s}} = k\left(0.050 \dfrac{\text{mol}}{\text{L}}\right)^m$ $4.8 \times 10^{-5} \dfrac{\text{mol}}{\text{L} \cdot \text{s}} = k\left(0.100 \dfrac{\text{mol}}{\text{L}}\right)^m$

Continued on next page

Combine the two equations in a way that will eliminate one of the variables.	$$\dfrac{2.4 \times 10^{-5}\,\dfrac{\text{mol}}{\text{L}\cdot\text{s}}}{4.8 \times 10^{-5}\,\dfrac{\text{mol}}{\text{L}\cdot\text{s}}} = \dfrac{k\left(0.050\,\dfrac{\text{mol}}{\text{L}}\right)^m}{k\left(0.100\,\dfrac{\text{mol}}{\text{L}}\right)^m}$$
Dividing one by the other will allow you to cancel k.	
When the numerator and denominator of a fraction have the same exponent, you write the entire fraction in brackets and put the exponent outside the brackets.	$$0.5 = \dfrac{\left(0.050\,\dfrac{\text{mol}}{\text{L}}\right)^m}{\left(0.100\,\dfrac{\text{mol}}{\text{L}}\right)^m}$$ $$0.5 = \left(\dfrac{0.050\,\dfrac{\text{mol}}{\text{L}}}{0.100\,\dfrac{\text{mol}}{\text{L}}}\right)^m$$ $$0.5 = 0.5^m$$
You now have an equation with one variable. Write both sides of the equation to a power. If the base on both sides of an equality is the same, then the exponents are the same.	$0.5^m = 0.5^1$ $m = 1$ The decomposition of dinitrogen pentoxide is a first-order reaction.
Use the value of m and data from one of the experiments to calculate the value of k.	$$\text{rate} = k[\text{N}_2\text{O}_5]^1$$ $$2.4 \times 10^{-5}\,\dfrac{\text{mol}}{\text{L}\cdot\text{s}} = k\left(0.050\,\dfrac{\text{mol}}{\text{L}}\right)$$ $$k = \dfrac{2.4 \times 10^{-5}\,\dfrac{\text{mol}}{\text{L}\cdot\text{s}}}{0.050\,\dfrac{\text{mol}}{\text{L}}}$$ $$k = 4.8 \times 10^{-4}\,\text{s}^{-1}$$ The rate constant for the temperature at which the experiments were carried out is $4.8 \times 10^{-4}\,\text{s}^{-1}$.

Check Your Solution

To check your value for m, set up a ratio for two different experiments. Solve for m, and compare your results. To check your value for k, substitute data from a different experiment and compare your results.

Sample Problem

Determining a Rate Law

Problem

Chlorine dioxide, $\text{ClO}_2(aq)$, reacts with hydroxide ions to produce a mixture of chlorate and chlorite ions as follows:

$$2\text{ClO}_2(aq) + 2\text{OH}^-(aq) \rightarrow \text{ClO}_3^-(aq) + \text{ClO}_2^-(aq) + \text{H}_2\text{O}(\ell)$$

The rate data in the table on the right were determined at a constant temperature. Find the rate law for this reaction.

Initial Rates of Chlorine Dioxide Reactions

Experiment	Initial [ClO$_2$] (mol/L)	Initial [OH$^-$] (mol/L)	Initial Rate (mol/L•s)
1	0.0150	0.0250	1.30×10^{-3}
2	0.0150	0.0500	2.60×10^{-3}
4	0.0450	0.0250	1.16×10^{-2}

What Is Required?
You need to find the value of the exponents m and n, and the value of the rate constant, k, to determine the rate law for the reaction.

What Is Given?
You know the general equation for the rate law: rate $= k[\text{ClO}_2]^m[\text{OH}^-]^n$
You are given the initial rate of reaction data for different initial concentrations of chlorine dioxide and hydroxide ions.

Plan Your Strategy	Act on Your Strategy
Write three equations using the data in the table and the general equation for the rate law.	rate $= k[\text{ClO}_2]^m[\text{OH}^-]^n$ $1.30 \times 10^{-3}\ \dfrac{\text{mol}}{\text{L}\cdot\text{s}} = k\left(0.0150\ \dfrac{\text{mol}}{\text{L}}\right)^m \left(0.0250\ \dfrac{\text{mol}}{\text{L}}\right)^n$ $2.60 \times 10^{-3}\ \dfrac{\text{mol}}{\text{L}\cdot\text{s}} = k\left(0.0150\ \dfrac{\text{mol}}{\text{L}}\right)^m \left(0.0500\ \dfrac{\text{mol}}{\text{L}}\right)^n$ $1.16 \times 10^{-3}\ \dfrac{\text{mol}}{\text{L}\cdot\text{s}} = k\left(0.0450\ \dfrac{\text{mol}}{\text{L}}\right)^m \left(0.0250\ \dfrac{\text{mol}}{\text{L}}\right)^n$
You have three unknowns (k, m, n) and three equations. Combine equations 1 and 3 to eliminate k and n by dividing the third equation by the first equation.	$\dfrac{1.16 \times 10^{-2}\ \frac{\text{mol}}{\text{L}\cdot\text{s}}}{1.30 \times 10^{-3}\ \frac{\text{mol}}{\text{L}\cdot\text{s}}} = \dfrac{k\left(0.0450\ \frac{\text{mol}}{\text{L}}\right)^m \left(0.0250\ \frac{\text{mol}}{\text{L}}\right)^n}{k\left(0.0150\ \frac{\text{mol}}{\text{L}}\right)^m \left(0.0250\ \frac{\text{mol}}{\text{L}}\right)^n}$ $\dfrac{1.16 \times 10^{-2}}{1.30 \times 10^{-3}} = \dfrac{\left(0.0450\ \frac{\text{mol}}{\text{L}}\right)^m}{\left(0.0150\ \frac{\text{mol}}{\text{L}}\right)^m}$ $8.9231 = 3^m$
Solve the final equation for m by determining what power of 3 gives a value close to 8.9231.	$3^2 = 9$, which is very close to 8.9231. Therefore, $3^m = 3^2$, giving $m = 2$. The reaction is second order with respect to chlorine dioxide.
To find n, identify two experiments in which [ClO$_2$] remains constant while [OH$^-$] changes. Divide the second equation by the first equation.	$\dfrac{2.60 \times 10^{-3}\ \frac{\text{mol}}{\text{L}\cdot\text{s}}}{1.30 \times 10^{-3}\ \frac{\text{mol}}{\text{L}\cdot\text{s}}} = \dfrac{k\left(0.0150\ \frac{\text{mol}}{\text{L}}\right)^m \left(0.0500\ \frac{\text{mol}}{\text{L}}\right)^n}{k\left(0.0150\ \frac{\text{mol}}{\text{L}}\right)^m \left(0.0250\ \frac{\text{mol}}{\text{L}}\right)^n}$ $\dfrac{2.60 \times 10^{-3}}{1.30 \times 10^{-3}} = \dfrac{\left(0.0500\ \frac{\text{mol}}{\text{L}}\right)^n}{\left(0.0250\ \frac{\text{mol}}{\text{L}}\right)^n}$ $2 = 2^n$ $n = 1$ The reaction is first order with respect to the hydroxide ion.

Continued on next page

Substitute $m = 2$ and $n = 1$ into any of the rate equations and solve for k.	Choose the first equation. $$1.3 \times 10^{-3} \frac{\text{mol}}{\text{L}\cdot\text{s}} = k\left(0.0150 \frac{\text{mol}}{\text{L}}\right)^m \left(0.0250 \frac{\text{mol}}{\text{L}}\right)^n$$ $$1.3 \times 10^{-3} \frac{\text{mol}}{\text{L}\cdot\text{s}} = k\left(0.0150 \frac{\text{mol}}{\text{L}}\right)^2 \left(0.0250 \frac{\text{mol}}{\text{L}}\right)^1$$ $$1.3 \times 10^{-3} \frac{\text{mol}}{\text{L}\cdot\text{s}} = k\left(0.000225 \frac{\text{mol}^2}{\text{L}^2}\right)\left(0.0250 \frac{\text{mol}}{\text{L}}\right)$$ $$1.3 \times 10^{-3} \frac{\text{mol}}{\text{L}\cdot\text{s}} = k\left(5.625 \times 10^{-6} \frac{\text{mol}^3}{\text{L}^3}\right)$$ $$k = \frac{1.3 \times 10^{-3} \frac{\text{mol}}{\text{L}\cdot\text{s}}}{5.625 \times 10^{-6} \frac{\text{mol}^3}{\text{L}^3}}$$ $$= 231.11 \frac{\text{L}^2}{\text{mol}^2 \cdot \text{s}}$$ $$= 231 \frac{\text{L}^2}{\text{mol}^2 \cdot \text{s}}$$
Write the rate law by substituting the values of m, n, and k into the general equation for the rate law.	rate = $k[\text{ClO}_2]^m [\text{OH}^-]^n$ rate = 231 L^2/(mol$^2 \cdot$s) [ClO$_2$] [OH$^-$]

Check Your Solution

To check your values of m and n, solve by inspection. When [OH$^-$] is constant and [ClO$_2$] triples, the rate increases by a factor of 9. Recall that $3^2 = 9$, indicating a second-order relationship. When [ClO$_2$] is constant and [OH$^-$] doubles, the rate also doubles, so the reaction is first order with respect to hydroxide ions. To check your value for k, substitute data from Experiment 2 or 3. You should get the same answer. Also check the units and the number of significant digits for k.

Practice Problems

1. For a reaction with a single reactant, the reaction rate is determined to be 1.4×10^{-2} mol/L·s when the initial concentration of the reactant is 0.020 mol/L. When the initial concentration of the reactant is increased to 0.080 mol/L, the rate increases to 2.24×10^{-1} mol/L·s.

   a. Based upon this result, how is the change in the initial reaction rate related to the change in the initial concentration of the reactant?

   b. Using the answer from (a), what would be the expected rate if the initial concentration of the reactant increased by 5 times?

2. The general equation for the rate law of a reaction is rate = $k[\text{Cl}_2][\text{NO}]^2$.

   a. What is the overall order of the reaction?

   b. The initial rate of this reaction is 2.42×10^{-2} mol/L·s when the initial concentrations of Cl$_2$ and NO are 0.20 mol/L. What is the value of the rate constant?

   c. What is the initial rate of reaction expected to be when the initial concentration of Cl$_2$ = 0.20 mol/L and NO = 0.10 mol/L?

3. Examine the data in the table below for a reaction between I$^-$(aq) and OCl$^-$(aq).

Experiment	Initial [I$^-$] (mol/L)	Initial [OCl$^-$] (mol/L)	Initial Rate (mol/L·s)
1	0.16	0.10	6.5×10^{-2}
2	0.080	0.10	3.26×10^{-2}
3	0.16	0.050	1.63×10^{-2}

   Find the value of k and the rate law.

Appendix A

Logarithms and Calculating pH

An understanding of logarithms is essential for calculating the pH of a solution.

Logarithms

The logarithm of a number is the power to which you must raise a base to equal that number. By convention, we usually use 10 as the base. Every positive number has a logarithm. For example, the logarithm of 10 is 1, because $10^1 = 10$. The logarithm of 100 is 2, because $10^2 = 100$. This can be understood by examining the following equation:

$$\log_a x = y; \text{ where } a^y = x$$

Therefore, since $10^1 = 10$, we know $\log_{10} 10 = 1$. This can also be written as $\log 10 = 1$, since it is understood that 10 is used as the base by convention unless otherwise indicated. Similarly, since $10^2 = 100$, we know $\log_{10} 100 = 2$ or $\log 100 = 2$.

All numbers that are greater than 1 have a positive logarithm. Numbers that are between 0 and 1 have a negative logarithm. For instance, since $10^{-3} = 0.001$, we know $\log 0.001 = -3$. Note also that the number 1 has a logarithm of 0. The table below shows several examples of numbers and their logarithms.

Some Numbers and Their Logarithms

Number	Scientific Notation	As a Power of 10	Logarithm
1 000 000	1×10^6	10^6	6
7 895 900	7.8959×10^6	$10^{6.89740}$	6.897 40
1	1×10^0	10^0	0
0.000 01	1×10^{-5}	10^{-5}	-5
0.004 276	4.276×10^{-3}	$10^{-2.3690}$	-2.3690

Logarithms are a convenient method for communicating large and small numbers, and are especially useful for expressing values that span a range of powers of 10. For instance, the Richter scale for earthquakes, the decibel scale for sound, and the pH scale for acids and bases all use logarithmic scales.

Calculating pH

The pH of an acid solution is defined as $-\log[H^+]$, where the square brackets mean *concentration*. In the figure below, the "p" in pH represents "the negative logarithm of..." As the logarithm of a number refers to an exponent or "power," the "p" can be thought of as "power." The power referred to is exponential power: the power of 10. Similarly, the "H" stands for the concentration of hydrogen ions, measured in mol/L.

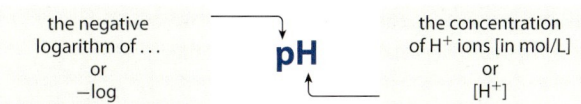

The concept of pH allows hydrogen ion concentrations to be expressed as positive numbers, rather than negative exponents. For example, the $[H^+]$ of neutral water at 25°C is 1.0×10^{-7} mol/L. You can find the pH of water (and of any solution) by taking the negative logarithm of the concentration of hydrogen ions.

$$\begin{aligned}
\therefore \text{pH} &= -\log[H^+] \\
&= -\log(1.0 \times 10^{-7}) \\
&= -(-7.00) \\
&= 7.00
\end{aligned}$$

For a logarithm, only the digits to the right of the decimal place are significant. The numbers to the left of the decimal place reflect the power of base 10, and are, therefore, not significant.

Example:

1. Find the pH of a solution with a hydrogen ion concentration of 0.004 76 mol/L.

$$\begin{aligned}
\text{pH} &= -\log[H^+] \\
&= -\log(0.004\ 76 \text{ mol/L}) \\
&= 2.322
\end{aligned}$$

Note that the pH scale is a negative log scale. Thus, a decrease from pH 7 to pH 4 is actually an increase of 10^3, or 1000 times, in the acidity of a solution. An increase from pH 3 to pH 6 is a decrease in acidity of 10^3 times.

> **Instant Practice**
>
> Find the pH of a solution with the following hydrogen ion concentrations.
>
> a. 1.0×10^{-8} mol/L
> b. 0.0054 mol/L

Appendix A

Preparing Solutions

Using a Volumetric Flask to Prepare a Standard Aqueous Solution

1. Place the known mass of solute in a clean beaker. Use distilled water to dissolve the solute completely.

2. Rinse a clean volumetric flask of the required volume with a small quantity of distilled water. Discard the rinse water. Repeat the rinsing several times.

3. Transfer the solution from the beaker to the volumetric flask using a funnel.

4. Using a wash bottle, rinse the beaker with distilled water, and pour the rinse water into the volumetric flask. Repeat this rinsing several times.

5. Using a wash bottle or a beaker, add distilled water to the volumetric flask until the level is just below the graduation mark. Then remove the funnel from the volumetric flask.

6. View the neck of the volumetric flask straight on from the side, so that the graduation mark looks like a line, not an ellipse. Add distilled water, drop by drop, until the bottom of the *meniscus* (the curved surface of the solution) appears to touch the graduation mark.

Using a Volumetric Pipette to Measure the Volume of a Stock Solution for Dilution

1. Make sure that the outside of the pipette, especially the tip, is dry. If not, wipe it with a paper towel.

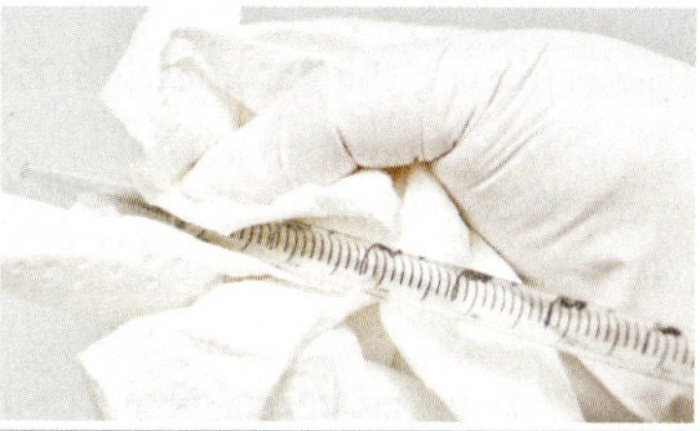

2. Squeeze the pipette bulb, and then place it over the top of the pipette. If using a pipette pump, place it over the top of the pipette.

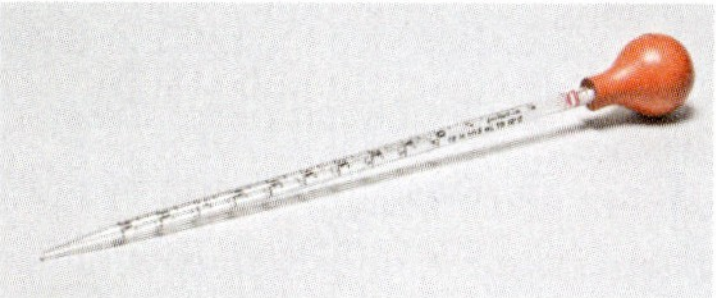

3. Rinse the pipette as follows. Place the tip of the pipette below the surface of the stock solution. Release the bulb carefully to draw up some liquid until the pipette is about half full. Remove the pipette bulb, invert the pipette, and drain the liquid into a beaker for waste. Repeat this rinsing two or three times.

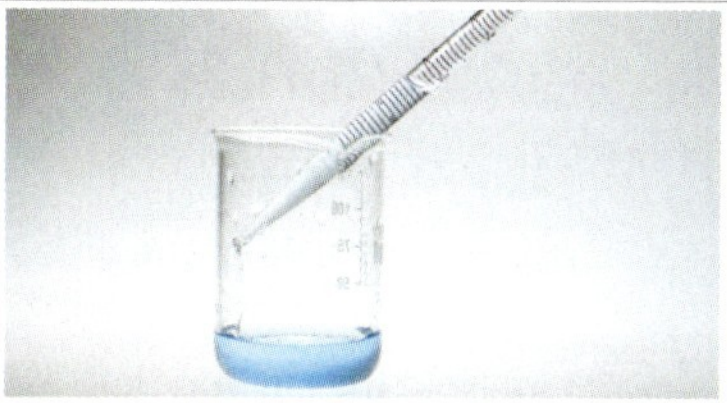

4. Fill the pipette with stock solution so that the level is past the graduation mark, but do not allow stock solution into the pipette bulb.

5. Remove the pipette bulb, and quickly seal the top of the pipette with your finger or thumb.

6. Remove the tip of the pipette from the stock solution. Lift your finger slightly, and let stock solution drain out slowly until the meniscus reaches the graduation mark. Wipe the tip of the pipette with a piece of paper towel.

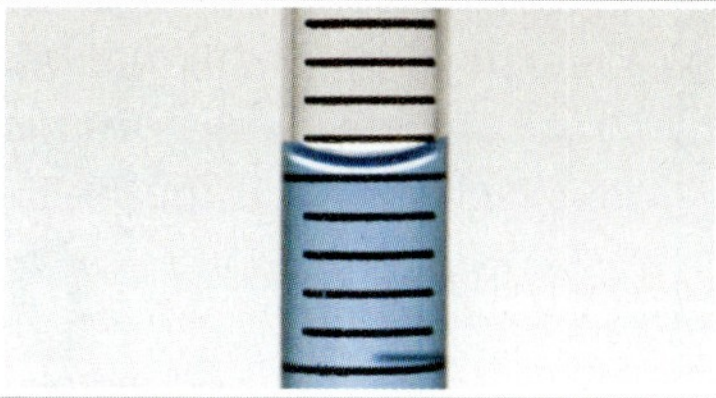

7. Move the pipette to the container into which you want to transfer the stock solution. Touch the tip of the pipette against the inside of the container, and release your finger to allow the liquid to drain. A small volume of liquid will remain inside the pipette. The pipette has been calibrated to allow for this volume of liquid. *Do not* force this liquid from the pipette.

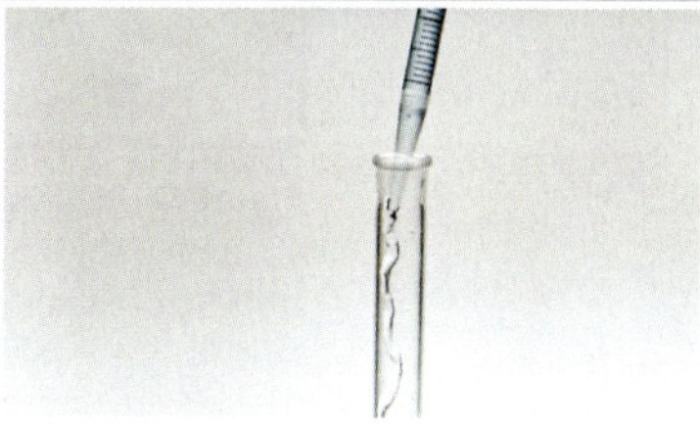

Appendix A

Performing an Acid-Base Titration
The following steps describe how to prepare for and perform a titration.

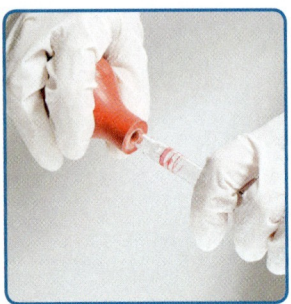

Figure A Squeeze the pipette bulb as you put it on the stem of the pipette.

Rinsing the Volumetric or Graduated Pipette
Rinse a pipette with the solution whose volume you are measuring. This will ensure that any drops remaining inside the pipette will form part of the measured volume.

1. Put the pipette bulb on the pipette, as shown in **Figure A**. Place the tip of the pipette into a beaker of distilled water.
2. Relax your grip on the bulb to draw up a small volume of distilled water.
3. Remove the bulb, and discard the water by letting it drain out.
4. Pour a sample of the solution with the unknown concentration into a clean, dry beaker.
5. Rinse the pipette by drawing several millilitres of the solution with the unknown concentration from the beaker into the pipette. Coat the inner surface with the solution, as shown in **Figure B**. Discard the rinse. Rinse the pipette twice in this way. The pipette is now ready to be filled with the solution that has the unknown concentration.

Filling the Pipette
6. Place the tip of the pipette below the surface of the solution with the unknown concentration.
7. Hold the suction bulb loosely on the end of the glass stem. Use the suction bulb to draw the solution up to the point shown in **Figure C**.
8. As quickly and smoothly as you can, slide the bulb off the glass stem and place your index finger over the end.
9. Roll your finger slightly away from end of the stem to let the solution slowly drain out.
10. When the bottom of the meniscus aligns with the etched mark, as in **Figure D**, press your finger back over the end of the stem. This will prevent more solution from draining out.
11. Touch the tip of the pipette to the side of the beaker to remove any clinging drops. The measured volume inside the pipette is now ready to transfer to an Erlenmeyer flask.

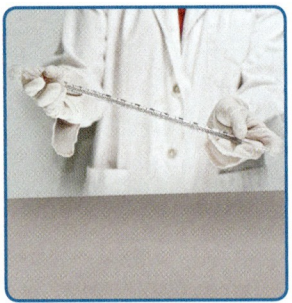

Figure B Cover the ends of the pipette so that none of the solution spills out as you rock the pipette back and forth to coat its inner surface with solution.

Transferring the Solution
12. Place the tip of the pipette against the inside glass wall of the flask, as shown in **Figure E**. Let the solution drain slowly, by removing your finger from the stem.
13. After the solution drains, wait several seconds and then touch the tip to the inside wall of the flask to remove any drops on the end. **Note:** Do not remove the small amount of solution shown in **Figure F**.

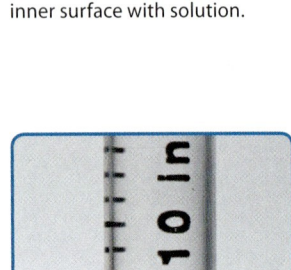

Figure C Start with more of the unknown solution than you need. You will drain out the excess solution in the next two steps.

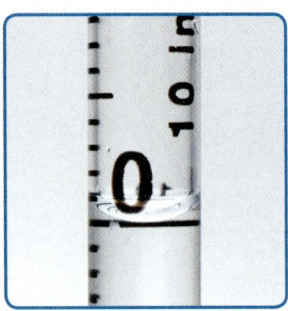

Figure D Always read the volume of the solution at the bottom of the meniscus.

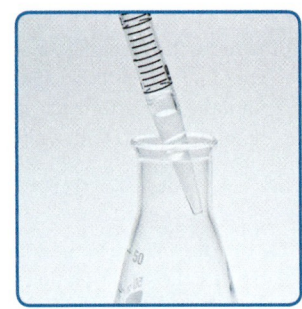

Figure E Draining the pipette with the tip against the wall of the flask will prevent splashing.

Adding the Indicator

14. Add two or three drops of the indicator to the flask and its contents. Do not add too much indicator. Using more indicator does not make the colour change easier to see. Also, most indicators are weak acids. Too much indicator can change the amount of base needed for the neutralization. You are now ready to prepare the apparatus for the titration.

Rinsing the Burette

15. To rinse the burette, close the tap and add about 10 mL of distilled water from a wash bottle.
16. Tip the burette to one side, and roll it gently back and forth so that the water comes in contact with all the inner surfaces.
17. Hold the burette over a sink. Let the water drain out, as shown in **Figure G**. While you do this, check that the tap does not leak. Make sure that the tap turns smoothly and easily.
18. Rinse the burette twice, with 5 to 10 mL of the titrant. Remember to open the tap to rinse the lower portion of the burette. Discard the rinse solution each time.

Filling the Burette

19. Assemble a retort stand and burette clamp to hold the burette. Place a funnel in the top of the burette, and put a beaker under the burette.
20. With the tap closed, add the solution until it is above the zero mark. Remove the funnel. Carefully open the tap. Drain the solution into the beaker until the bottom of the meniscus is at or below the zero mark.
21. Touch the tip of the burette against the beaker to remove any clinging drops. Check that the part of the burette below the tap is filled with solution and contains no air bubbles. **Figure H** shows the air bubbles that you should avoid.
22. Find the initial burette reading using a meniscus reader, as shown in **Figure I**. Record the initial volume to the nearest 0.05 mL.

Titrating the Unknown Solution

23. Replace the beaker with the Erlenmeyer flask that contains the solution you want to titrate. Place a sheet of white paper under the flask to help you see the colour change.
24. Add titrant from the burette to the Erlenmeyer flask by opening the tap, as shown in **Figure J**. You may start by adding the titrant quickly, but slow down when you start to see a colour change in the solution in the flask.
25. At first, the colour change will disappear as you mix the solution in the flask. Add a small amount of titrant, and swirl thoroughly before adding any more. Stop adding titrant when the solution in the Erlenmeyer flask has a persistent colour change. If you are using phenolphthalein as an indicator, stop when the solution is a faint pink colour.
26. Use the meniscus reader to read the final volume. Record this volume, and subtract the initial volume from it to find the volume of the titrant needed to reach the end point.

Figure J Always swirl the flask as you add the titrant. If you have trouble swirling and adding titrant at the same time, use a magnetic stirrer or have your laboratory partner swirl the flask as you add the titrant.

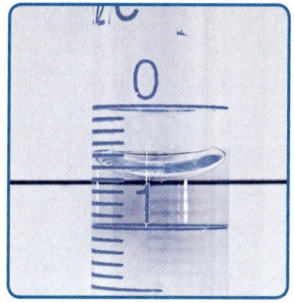

Figure I Hold the meniscus reader so that the line is under the meniscus.

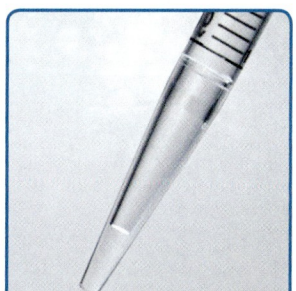

Figure F A small amount of solution will always remain in the tip of the pipette. Do not remove this.

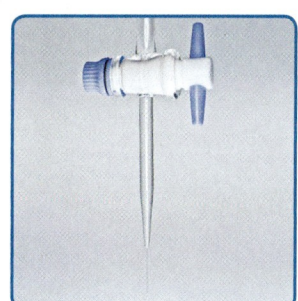

Figure G The tap is fully open when the handle on the tap is parallel to the burette and the solution inside the burette comes out quickly.

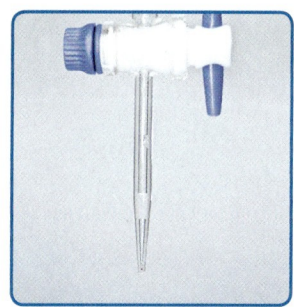

Figure H Do NOT start a titration if you have air bubbles like these in the tip of the burette. They will cause errors in your measurements.

Appendix B | Useful References

Hydrocarbon Derivatives with Multiple Functional Groups

The table below lists the common functional groups in order of their priority, from highest to lowest. The priority of a functional group is used to determine how to classify and name a compound when more than one functional group is present. For example, amides are higher on the list than alcohols. Therefore, if a compound contains both an amide group and a hydroxyl group, the compound is classified as an amide and not an alcohol. The hydroxyl group is treated as a side group.

This table also provides a variety of other data that will help you name and draw molecules with multiple functional groups. This includes the name of the prefix that is used to denote each functional group when it is a side group. You will only be asked to use those prefixes that are listed in red.

Common Functional Groups in Order of Priority

Priority	Functional Group	Name of Functional Group	Name of Compound	Suffix or Prefix	Name as a Side Group
Highest	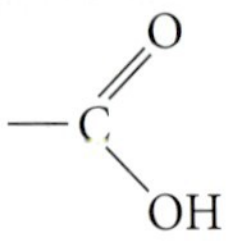 —C(=O)OH	carboxyl group	carboxylic acid	-oic acid	carboxy-
	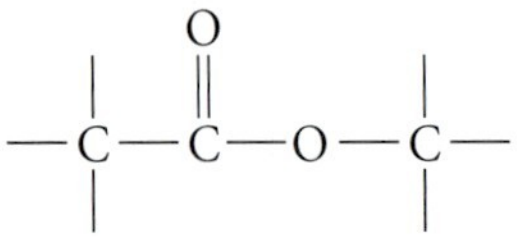 —C(=O)—O—C—	ester linkage	ester	-oate	alkoxycarbonyl-
	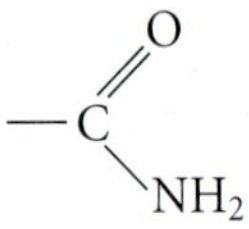 —C(=O)NH$_2$	amide group	amide	-amide	amido- or carbamoyl-
	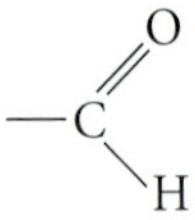 —C(=O)H	formyl group	aldehyde	-al	oxo- or formyl-
	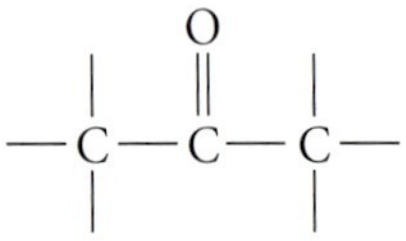 —C—C(=O)—C—	carbonyl group	ketone	-one	oxo-
	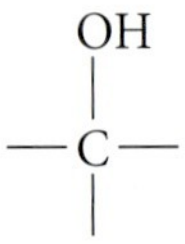 —C(OH)—	hydroxyl group	alcohol	-ol	hydroxy-
	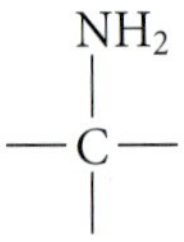 —C(NH$_2$)—	amino group	amine	-amine	amino-
↓	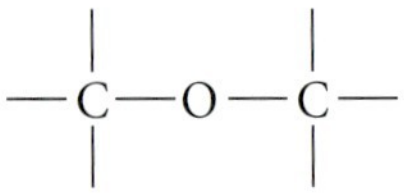 —C—O—C—	alkoxy group	ether	-oxy	alkoxy-

Priority	Functional Group	Name of Functional Group	Name of Compound	Suffix or Prefix	Name as a Side Group
↓	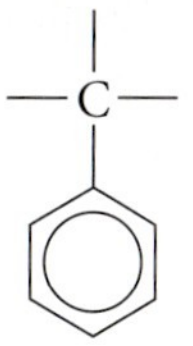 —C— attached to benzene ring	N/A	benzene	N/A	phenyl-
	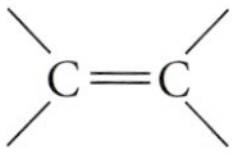 C=C	N/A	alkene	-ene	alkenyl-
	 —C≡C—	N/A	alkyne	-yne	alkynl-
	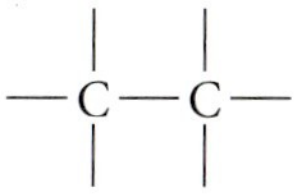 —C—C—	alkyl group	alkane	-ane	alkyl-
Lowest	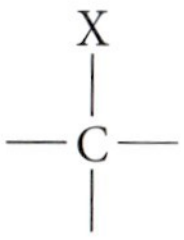 X—C— (X = any halogen)	N/A	haloalkane	fluoro- chloro- bromo- iodo-	fluoro- chloro- bromo- iodo-

The table on the next page outlines the steps to follow when naming straight-chain hydrocarbon derivatives with multiple functional groups, using glucosamine as the example molecule. For each step, first read the description in the left-hand column. Next, study the example in the right-hand column. Then develop your skills in naming compounds by completing the Sample Problem and Practice Problems that follow.

Steps in Naming Hydrocarbon Derivatives with Multiple Functional Groups

1. Identify the highest priority functional group. **a.** Find all of the functional groups in the compound.	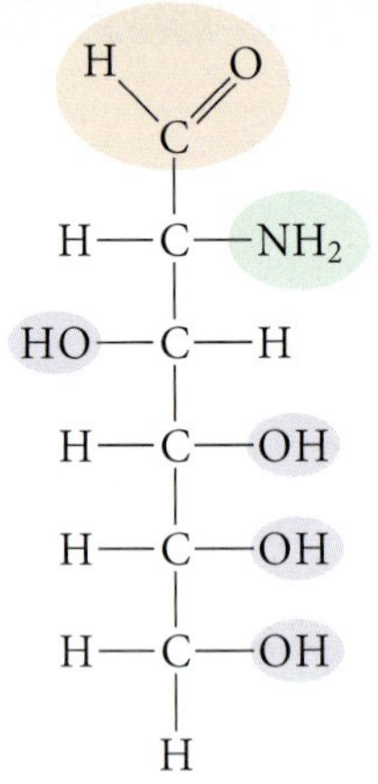 (structure of glucosamine shown with formyl group, amino group, and hydroxyl groups highlighted)
b. Use the table of common functional groups to determine which group has the highest priority. The highest priority functional group determines the type of compound.	The compound has a formyl group, an amino group, and four hydroxyl groups. The formyl group has the highest priority. That makes the compound an aldehyde.
2. Identify and number the parent portion of the compound. **a.** The parent portion of the compound is the longest carbon chain that includes the highest priority functional group. If there are two chains of the same length, choose the chain with the largest number of functional groups on it.	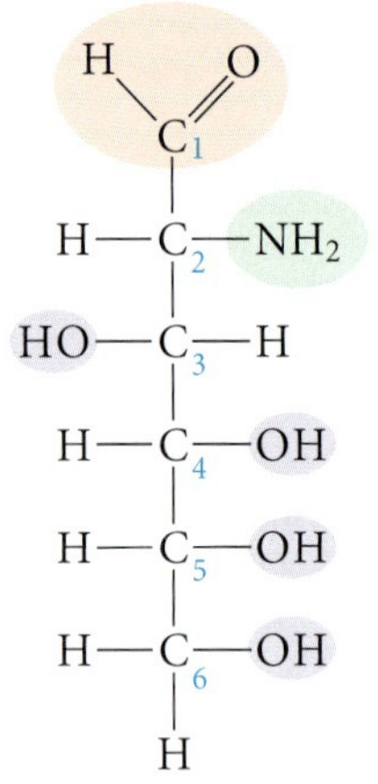 (same structure with carbons numbered C_1 through C_6 from top to bottom)
b. Numbering is done in the same way that you would number the carbon atoms if the highest priority functional group were the only functional group present.	The longest chain containing the formyl group is six carbon atoms long. The parent is hexanal. Numbering is carried out according to the rules for numbering an aldehyde. The carbon atom of the formyl group is number 1.
3. Identify and assign numbers to the side groups. **a.** Identify each functional group other than the parent group and use the table of common functional groups to determine the prefix that describes that group when it is considered a side group.	The amino group is on carbon atom 2 so it contributes -2-amino- to the name.
b. Each functional group is given the number of the carbon atom to which it is attached. If there is more than one of the same type of functional group, list all of its numbers and use a prefix to describe the number of times it appears. This step is done in exactly the same way as for alkyl groups.	There are hydroxyl groups on carbon atoms 3, 4, 5, and 6. They contribute -3,4,5,6-tetrahydroxy- to the name.
4. Assemble the parts of the name of the compound. Combine all of the parts of the name contributed by the side groups and order them alphabetically. Add the parent name.	The IUPAC name for glucosamine is 2-amino-3,4,5,6-tetrahydroxyhexanal.

Sample Problem

Problem

Name the hydrocarbon derivatives in (a) and (b) and draw the condensed structural formula for compound (c).

a.

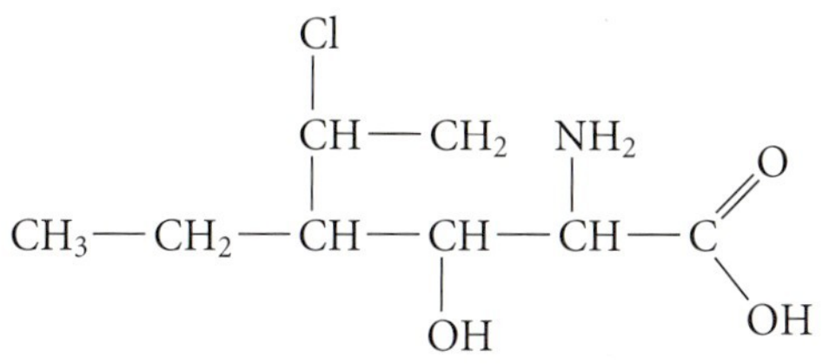

$$CH_3-CH_2-\underset{\underset{CH_3}{|}}{CH}-\underset{\underset{OH}{|}}{CH}-\underset{\underset{}{|}}{CH}-\underset{}{C}\underset{\diagdown OH}{\overset{\diagup O}{}}$$
(with Cl on top of the CH group that also bears CH₂, and NH₂ on the CH next to the carboxyl)

b.

$$H_2N-CH_2-\underset{\underset{}{|}}{CH}-\underset{\underset{Cl}{|}}{CH}-CH=CH-CH_3$$
(with OH on the first CH)

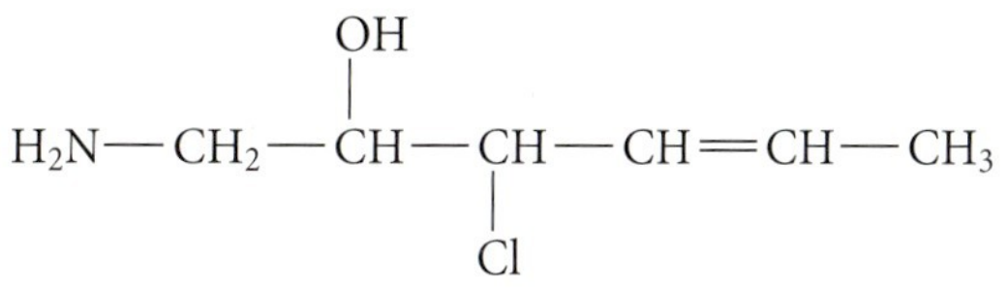

c. 4-hydroxy-4-propylhept-2,5-dieneamide

What Is Required?

You must name two hydrocarbon derivatives and draw a third.

What Is Given?

You are given two structures and one name.

Plan Your Strategy	Act on Your Strategy
a. Identify the highest priority group.	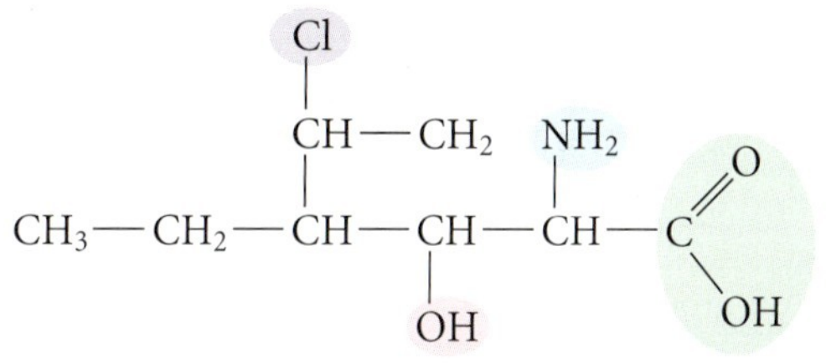 (structure shown with carboxyl group highlighted) Of the different functional groups, chloro, amino, hydroxyl, and carboxyl, the carboxyl group has the highest priority. Therefore, the compound is named as a carboxylic acid. There will be an alkyl group, but until the parent chain is selected, it cannot be identified.
Identify and number the parent portion of the compound. (Remember that for esters and amides, the parent compound contains *only* those carbon atoms that are in the chain containing the carbonyl carbon atom.)	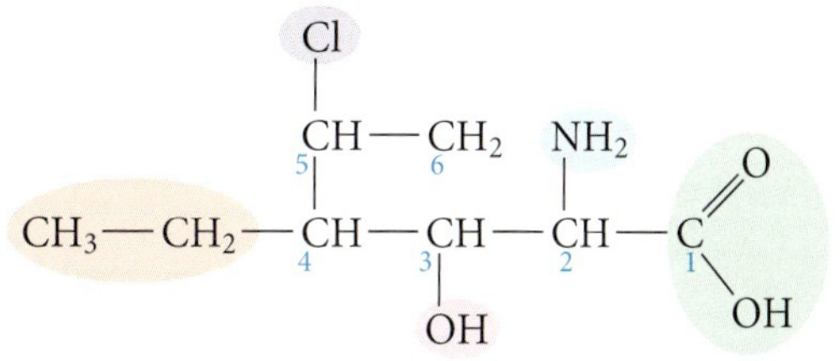 (structure shown with carbons numbered 1–6 and ethyl group highlighted) There are two chains that are six carbon atoms long. The parent is hexanoic acid. The chain with the most functional groups is numbered in the structure above. This defines the ethyl group as a side group. The carbon atom of the carboxyl group is carbon atom 1.
Identify and assign numbers to the side groups.	There is a 5-chloro, a 2-amino, a 3-hydroxy, and a 4-ethyl group.
Assemble the parts of the name of the compound.	Name the side groups in alphabetical order. The compound is 2-amino-5-chloro-4-ethyl-3-hydroxyhexanoic acid.

Continued on next page

Plan Your Strategy	Act on Your Strategy
b. Identify the highest priority group.	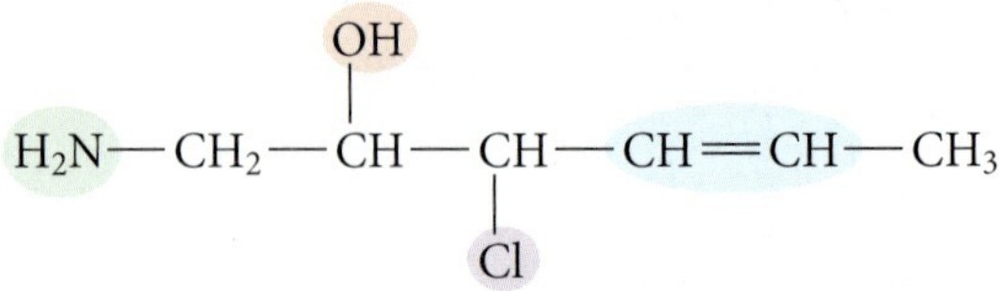 $H_2N-CH_2-CH(OH)-CH(Cl)-CH=CH-CH_3$ Of the groups, amino, hydroxyl, chloro, and ene, the hydroxyl group has the highest priority. Therefore, the compound is named as an alcohol.
Identify and number the parent portion of the compound.	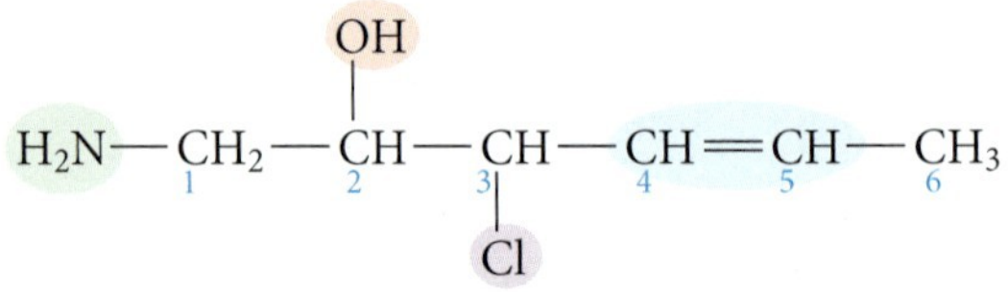 $\underset{}{H_2N}-\underset{1}{CH_2}-\underset{2}{CH(OH)}-\underset{3}{CH(Cl)}-\underset{4}{CH}=\underset{5}{CH}-\underset{6}{CH_3}$ There is only one carbon chain and it is six carbon atoms long. Because the hydroxyl group takes priority, numbering must start at the end of the carbon chain nearest the hydroxyl group. The parent is hexan-2-ol.
Identify and assign numbers to the side groups.	There is a 1-amino group, a 3-chloro group, and a 4-ene.
Assemble the parts of the name of the compound.	Name the side groups in alphabetical order. When you have two suffixes such as –ene and –ol, for which positions must be defined, the one with the higher priority must end the name. Because alcohol has the higher priority, the 2-ol must come last. The name of the compound is 1-amino-3-chlorohex-4-ene-2-ol.
c. Identify the highest priority group.	The name ends in –amide so the compound is an amide.
Identify and number the parent chain.	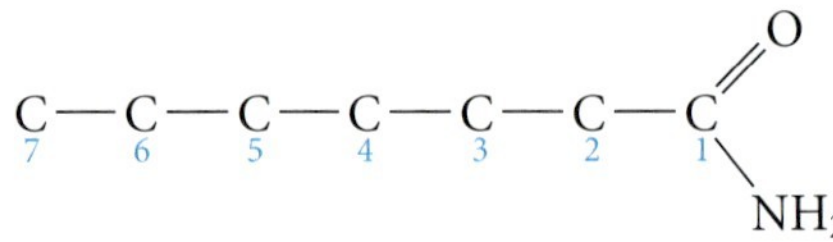 $\underset{7}{C}-\underset{6}{C}-\underset{5}{C}-\underset{4}{C}-\underset{3}{C}-\underset{2}{C}-\underset{1}{C}(=O)(NH_2)$ The -hept- indicates that the parent chain is seven carbon atoms long. Draw a seven-carbon amide.
Identify and add the side groups.	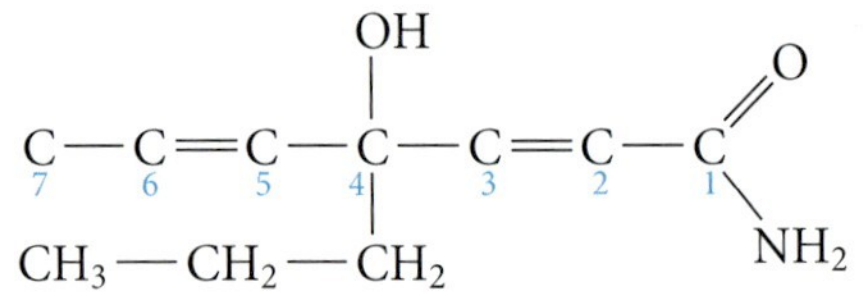 $\underset{7}{C}-\underset{6}{C}=\underset{5}{C}-\underset{4}{C}(OH)(CH_2CH_2CH_3)-\underset{3}{C}-\underset{2}{C}=\underset{1}{C}(=O)(NH_2)$ The 4-hydroxy- means that there is a hydroxyl group on carbon atom 4. The -4-propyl- means that there is a three-carbon chain on carbon atom 4. The -2,5-diene- means that there are two double bonds, one between carbon atoms 2 and 3 and a second between carbon atoms 5 and 6.
Add enough hydrogen atoms to give each carbon atom a total of four bonds.	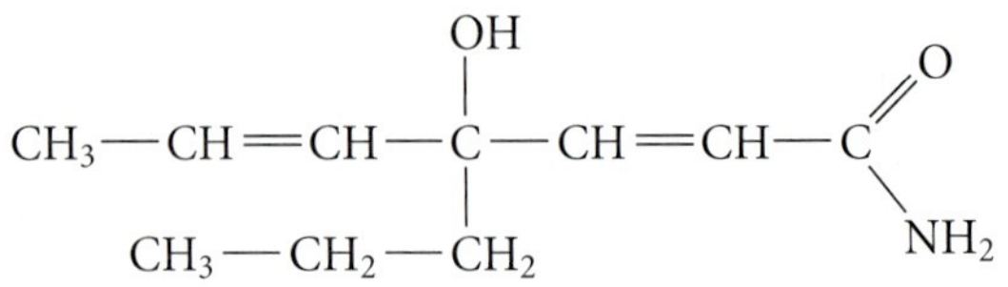 $CH_3-CH=CH-C(OH)(CH_2CH_2CH_3)-CH=CH-C(=O)NH_2$

Check Your Solution

a. The carboxyl group has the highest priority and the main chain has six carbon atoms, so the parent name is correct. There is a chlorine atom on carbon 5, an amino group on carbon 2, a hydroxyl group on carbon 3, and an ethyl group on carbon 4. The name reflects these groups in the correct order.

b. The hydroxyl group has the highest priority. It is bonded to the second carbon on a main chain of six carbon atoms, so the parent name is correct. There is a chlorine atom on carbon 3, an amino group on carbon 1, and a double bond between carbons 4 and 5. The name reflects this structure.

c. The parent chain is seven carbon atoms long and begins with an amide group. There is a hydroxyl group and a propyl group on carbon atom 4. There are two double bonds, one between carbon atoms 2 and 3 and a second between carbon atoms 5 and 6. The structure is drawn correctly.

Practice Problems

1. Name the following hydrocarbon derivatives.
   a. $H_3C-CH(OH)-CH_2-CH_2-C(=O)OH$
   b. $H_2C(NH_2)-CH_2-HC(CH_3)-C(=O)NH_2$
   c. $H_3C-CH_2-HC(F)-CH=CH-HC(OH)-CH_3$
   d. $H_3C-CH_2-CH(OH)-HC(CH_2CH_3)-C(=O)-CH_3$

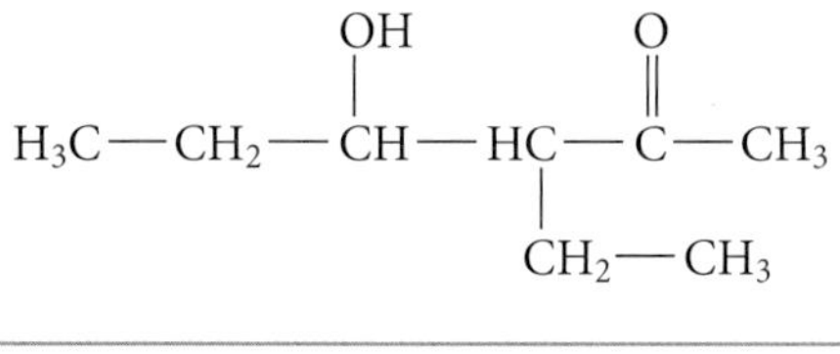

2. Draw the condensed structural formulas for the following hydrocarbon derivatives.
   a. 2-aminopropan-1-ol
   b. 4-chloro-2-ethylpentanal
   c. N-ethyl-3-hydroxybutanamide
   d. 3-chloro-4-methylpent-3-ene-2-ol

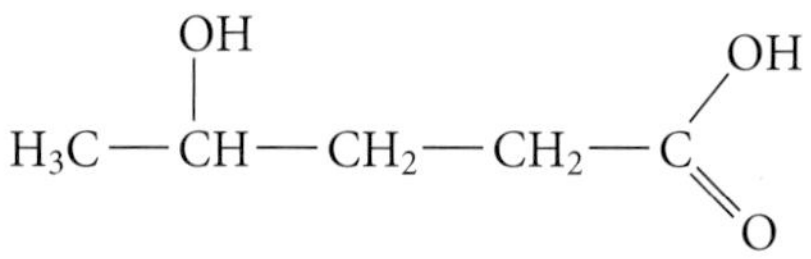

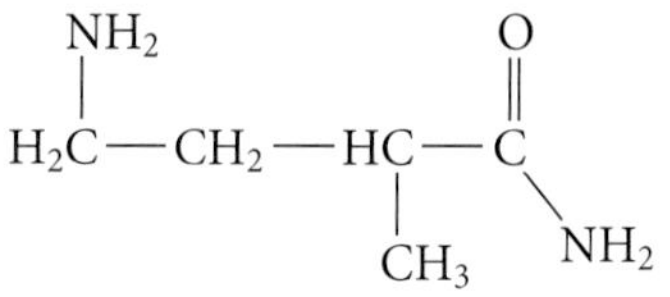

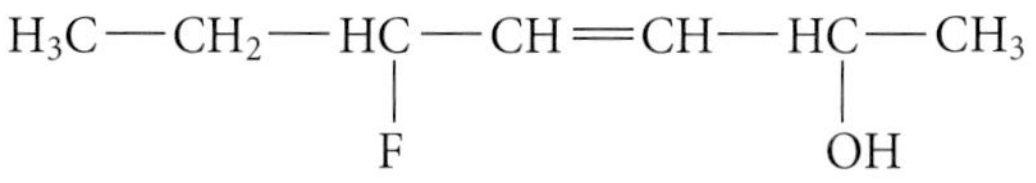

3. Name the following hydrocarbon derivatives.
   a. (structure with NH$_2$ and OH on central carbon)
   b. (structure with HO, Cl, OH and C=O)
   c. (structure with ethyl branch, OH OH and C=O)
   d. (structure with triple bond, C=O, NH and NH$_2$)

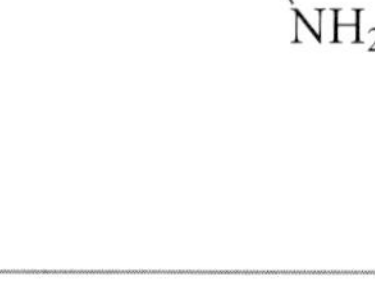

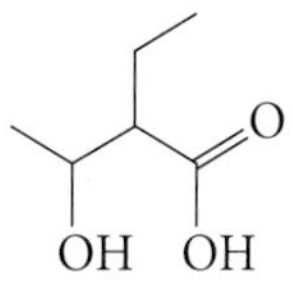

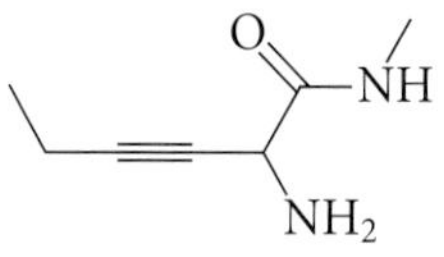

Benzene Derivatives with Substituted Functional Groups

The table below lists the trivial IUPAC accepted names, the IUPAC preferred names, and the structures of several common benzene derivatives that you may encounter in your studies.

Common Benzene Derivatives with Substituted Functional Groups

Trivial Name (IUPAC Accepted)	IUPAC Preferred Name	Structure
phenol	benzenol	benzene ring with OH
aniline	benzenamine	benzene ring with NH_2
benzoic acid	benzenecarboxylic acid	benzene ring with COOH

IUPAC Preferred Naming of Benzene Derivatives

Many of the IUPAC rules for naming aliphatic hydrocarbon derivatives with multiple functional groups also apply to naming benzene derivatives with multiple functional groups. Similarly, the methods that you learned for numbering the carbon atoms of a benzene ring for alkyl side groups also apply to benzene derivatives. The steps for naming substituted benzene compounds are listed in the table below and examples are given with each step. (**Note:** High priority functional groups, above alcohol, will not be discussed because these groups require the use of new terminology is needed.)

Steps for Naming Benzene Derivatives with Multiple Functional Groups

Step	Example
1. Identify the highest priority functional group. **a.** Find all of the functional groups bonded to the benzene ring. **b.** Use the table of common functional groups to determine which group has the highest priority. This functional group determines the identity of the parent compound.	There is a hydroxyl group and a methyl group on the benzene ring. The hydroxyl group has the higher priority, so the compound is an alcohol. The root plus suffix is benzenol.
2. Identify and assign numbers to the side groups. **a.** Identify each functional group other than the parent group and use the table of common functional groups to determine the prefix that describes that group when it is a side group. **b.** Numbering begins at the carbon atom to which the highest priority group is bonded and goes in the direction that will generate the smallest numbers for the side groups. While the highest priority group is always on carbon 1 and receives no number, each lower priority functional group is given the number of the carbon atom to which it is attached. If there is more than one of the same type of functional group, list all of its numbers and use a prefix to describe its frequency.	There is a methyl group attached as a side group. Numbering begins at the hydroxyl group and goes in the direction of the methyl group. The prefix is 2-methyl-.
3. Assemble the parts of the name of the compound. Drop the terminal e on benzene and add the suffix determined by the highest priority side group. Combine all parts of the name contributed by the side groups and order them alphabetically.	The only side group other than the highest priority group is a methyl group. The name of the compound is 2-methylbenzenol.

Sample Problem

Problem
Name the benzene derivatives in (a) and (b) and draw the structure for compound (c).

a. [benzene ring with F, Cl, and NH_2 substituents]

b. [benzene ring with $O-CH_2-CH_3$ and CH_2-CH_3 substituents]

c. 3-amino-2,6-diiodobenzenol

What Is Required?
You must name two benzene derivatives and draw a third.

What Is Given?
You are given two structures and one name.

Plan Your Strategy	Act on Your Strategy
a. Identify the highest priority functional group.	There is a fluorine, a chlorine, and an amino group bonded to the benzene ring. The amino group has the highest priority so the compound is an amine. The root plus suffix is benzenamine.
Identify and assign numbers to the side groups.	Numbering starts at the amino group. The numbers will be 3,5- no matter which direction you take. Because chloro- comes before fluoro- alphabetically, give chlorine the lower number. The prefix will be 3-chloro-5-fluoro-.
Assemble the parts of the name of the compound.	The name of the compound is 3-chloro-5-fluorobenzenamine.
b. Identify the highest priority functional group.	There is an ethyl group and an ethoxy group on the benzene ring. The ethoxy group has the highest priority, making the compound an ether. Ethers are named by making the alkoxy group a prefix, so the compound is an ethoxybenzene
Identify and assign numbers to the side groups.	Start numbering at the ethoxy group and number in the direction that gives the ethyl group the lower number. This places the ethyl group on carbon atom 3. Thus, the prefix contains 3-ethyl.
Assemble the parts of the name of the compound.	The name of the compound is 3-ethylethoxybenzene.

Appendix B • MHR **737**

c. Identify the highest priority functional group.	The name ends with –benzenol, so the highest priority group is a hydroxyl group. The hydroxyl group will be bonded to carbon atom 1.	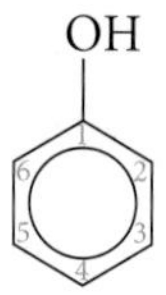
Determine the locations of the side groups and complete the structure.	There is an amino group on carbon atom 3 and there are two iodine atoms, one on carbon 2 and the other on carbon atom 6.	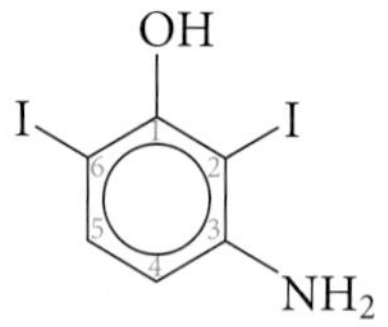

Check Your Solution

Each compound is named and numbered according to the highest priority side group.

All other groups are on the carbon atoms that are described in the names.

Practice Problems

4. Name the following benzene derivatives.
   a. 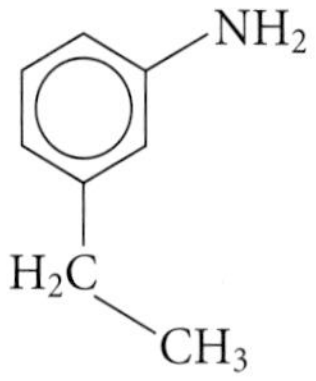
   b. 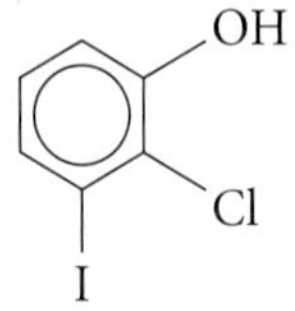
   c. 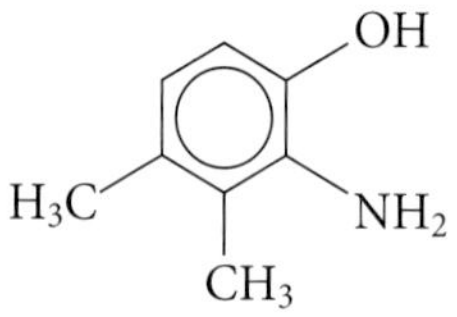
   d.

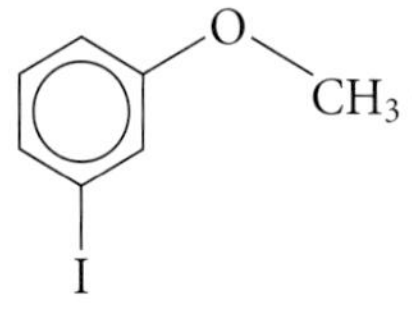

5. Draw the structures for the following benzene derivatives.
   a. 2-aminobenzenol
   b. 2-ethyl-4-fluorobenzenamine
   c. 3-fluoroethoxybenzene
   d. 2-ethenylbenzenol

6. Identify any errors in the following names by drawing the structure for each benzene derivative. Give the correct name, as appropriate.
   a. 5-chlorobenzenamine
   b. 2-hydroxybenzenamine
   c. 2-methoxy-4-aminobenzene
   d. 3-fluoro-4-chloroethoxybenzene

Chemistry Data Tables

Names and Formulas of Ions

Some Common Polyatomic Ions

Name	Formula
ammonium	NH_4^+
acetate or ethanoate	CH_3COO^-
benzoate	$C_6H_5COO^-$
borate	BO_3^{3-}
carbonate	CO_3^{2-}
hydrogen carbonate	HCO_3^-
perchlorate	ClO_4^-
chlorate	ClO_3^-
chlorite	ClO_2^-
hypochlorite	ClO^-
chromate	CrO_4^{2-}
dichromate	$Cr_2O_7^{2-}$
cyanide	CN^-
hydroxide	OH^-
iodate	IO_3^-

Name	Formula
nitrate	NO_3^-
nitrite	NO_2^-
oxalate	$OOCCOO^{2-}$
hydrogen oxalate	$HOOCCOO^-$
permanganate	MnO_4^-
phosphate	PO_4^{3-}
hydrogen phosphate	HPO_4^{2-}
dihydrogen phosphate	$H_2PO_4^-$
sulfate	SO_4^{2-}
hydrogen sulfate	HSO_4^-
sulfite	SO_3^{2-}
hydrogen sulfite	HSO_3^-
cyanate	CNO^-
thiocyanate	SCN^-
thiosulfate	$S_2O_3^{2-}$

Prefixes and Suffixes for Families of Polyatomic Ions

Relative Number of Oxygen Atoms	Prefix	Suffix	Example	
Family of Four				
most	per-	-ate	ClO_4^-	perchlorate
second most	(none)	-ate	ClO_3^-	chlorate
second fewest	(none)	-ite	ClO_2^-	chlorite
fewest	hypo-	-ite	ClO^-	hypochlorite
Family of Two				
most	(none)	-ate	NO_3^-	nitrate
fewest	(none)	-ite	NO_2^-	nitrite

Names and Formulas for Compounds

Rules for Naming Binary Ionic Compounds
1. The name of the metal ion is first, followed by the name of the non-metal ion.
2. The name of the metal ion is the same as the name of the metal atom.
3. If the metal is a transition metal, it might have more than one possible charge. In these cases, a roman numeral is written in brackets after the name of the metal to indicate the magnitude of the charge.
4. The name of the non-metal ion has the same root as the name of the atom, but the suffix is changed to -ide.

Rules for Writing Chemical Formulas for Ionic Compounds
1. Identify the positive ion and the negative ion.
2. Find the chemical symbols for the ions, either in the periodic table or in the table of polyatomic ions. Write the symbol for the positive ion first and the symbol for the negative ion second.
3. Determine the charges of the ions. If you do not know the charges, you can find them in the periodic table.
4. Check to see if the charges differ. If the magnitudes of the charges are the same, the formula is complete. If they differ, determine the number of each ion that is needed to create a zero net charge. Write the numbers of ions needed as subscripts beside the chemical symbols, with one exception. When only one ion is needed, leave the subscript blank. A blank means 1. If a polyatomic ion needs a subscript, the formula for the ion must be in brackets and the subscript must be outside the brackets.

Names of Some Common Acids without Oxygen

Pure Substance (name)	Formula H(negative ion)(aq)	Classical Name hydro(root)ic acid	IUPAC Name aqueous hydrogen (negative ion)
hydrogen fluoride	HF(aq)	hydrofluoric acid	aqueous hydrogen fluoride
hydrogen cyanide	HCN(aq)	hydrocyanic acid	aqueous hydrogen cyanide
hydrogen sulfide	H_2S(aq)	hydrosulfuric acid	aqueous hydrogen sulfide

Classical Naming System for Families of Oxoacids

		Examples	
Name of Ion	Name of Acid (dissolved in water)	Name of Ion	Name of Acid (dissolved in water)
hypo(root)ite	hypo(root)ous acid	hypochlorite, ClO^-	hypochlorous acid, $HClO$
(root)ite	(root)ous acid	chlorite, ClO_2^-	chlorous acid, $HClO_2$
(root)ate	(root)ic acid	chlorate, ClO_3^-	chloric acid, $HClO_3$
per(root)ate	per(root)ic acid	perchlorate, ClO_4^-	perchloric acid, $HClO_4$

Rules for Naming Binary Molecular Compounds
1. Name the element with the lower group number first. Name the element with the higher group number second.
2. The one exception to the first rule occurs when oxygen is combined with a halogen. In this situation, the halogen is named first.
3. If both elements are in the same group, name the element with the higher period number first.
4. The name of the first element is unchanged.
5. To name the second element, use the root name of the element and add the suffix *-ide*.
6. If there are two or more atoms of the first element, add a prefix to indicate the number of atoms.
7. Always add a prefix to the name of the second element to indicate the number of atoms of this element in the compound. (If the second element is oxygen, an "o" or "a" at the end of the prefix is usually omitted.)

Prefixes for Binary Molecular Compounds

Number	Prefix
1	mono-
2	di-
3	tri-
4	tetra-
5	penta-
6	hexa-
7	hepta-
8	octa-
9	nona-
10	deca-

Names and Formulas for Some Common Hydrocarbons

Name	Formula
methane	$CH_4(g)$
ethane	$C_2H_6(g)$
propane	$C_3H_8(g)$
butane	$C_4H_{10}(g)$
acetylene (ethyne)	$C_2H_2(g)$
benzene	$C_6H_6(\ell)$

Ion Properties

Colours of Some Common Ions in Aqueous Solution

Ionic Species	Solution Concentration	
	1.0 mol/L	0.010 mol/L
chromate	yellow	pale yellow
chromium(III)	blue-green	green
chromium(II)	dark blue	pale blue
cobalt(II)	red	pink
copper(I)	blue-green	pale blue-green
copper(II)	blue	pale blue
dichromate	orange	pale orange
iron(II)	lime green	colourless
iron(III)	orange-yellow	pale yellow
manganese(II)	pale pink	colourless
nickel(II)	blue-green	pale blue-green
permanganate	deep purple	purple-pink

The Flame Colour of Selected Metal Ions

Ion	Symbol	Colour
lithium	Li^+	red
sodium	Na^+	yellow
potassium	K^+	violet
cesium	Cs^+	violet
calcium	Ca^{2+}	red
strontium	Sr^{2+}	red
barium	Ba^{2+}	yellowish-green
copper	Cu^{2+}	bluish-green
lead	Pb^{2+}	bluish-white

Bond Character

Predicting Bond Character from Electronegativity Difference Values

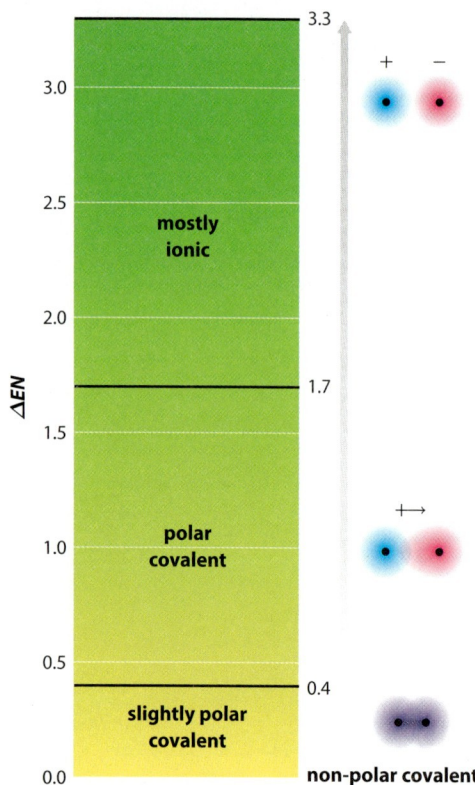

Character of Bonds

Electronegativity Difference	0.00	0.65	0.94	1.19	1.43	1.67	1.91	2.19	2.54	3.03
Percent Ionic Character	0	10	20	30	40	50	60	70	80	90
Percent Covalent Character	100	90	80	70	60	50	40	30	20	10

Energy and Chemical Reactions

Specific Heat Capacities of Common Substances and Materials

Substance	Specific Heat Capacity (J/g·°C at SATP)
Elements	
aluminum	0.897
carbon (graphite)	0.709
copper	0.385
gold	0.129
hydrogen (gas)	14.304
iron	0.449
Compounds	
ammonia (liquid)	4.70
ammonia (gas)	2.06
ethanol	2.44
water (solid)	2.00
water (liquid)	4.19
water (gas)	2.02
Mixtures	
air	1.01
concrete	0.88
glass	0.84
granite	0.79
wood	1.26

Selected Standard Molar Enthalpies of Formation

Substance	ΔH_f° (kJ/mol)	Substance	ΔH_f° (kJ/mol)	Substance	ΔH_f° (kJ/mol)
$Al_2O_3(s)$	−1675.7	$HBr(g)$	−36.3	$NH_3(g)$	−45.9
$CaCO_3(s)$	−1207.6	$HCl(g)$	−92.3	$N_2H_4(\ell)$	+50.6
$CaCl_2(s)$	−795.4	$HF(g)$	−273.3	$NH_4Cl(s)$	−314.4
$Ca(OH)_2(s)$	−985.2	$HCN(g)$	+135.1	$NH_4NO_3(s)$	−365.6
$CCl_4(\ell)$	−128.2	$H_2O(\ell)$	−285.8	$NO(g)$	+91.3
$CCl_4(g)$	−95.7	$H_2O(g)$	−241.8	$NO_2(g)$	+33.2
$CHCl_3(\ell)$	−134.1	$H_2O_2(\ell)$	−187.8	$N_2O(g)$	+81.6
$CH_4(g)$	−74.6	$HNO_3(\ell)$	−174.1	$N_2O_4(g)$	+11.1
$C_2H_2(g)$	+227.4	$H_3PO_4(s)$	−1284.4	$PH_3(g)$	+5.4
$C_2H_4(g)$	+52.4	$H_2S(g)$	−20.6	$PCl_3(g)$	−287.0
$C_2H_6(g)$	−84.0	$H_2SO_4(\ell)$	−814.0	$P_4O_6(s)$	−2144.3
$C_3H_8(g)$	−103.8	$FeO(s)$	−272.0	$P_4O_{10}(s)$	−2984.0
$C_6H_6(\ell)$	+49.1	$Fe_2O_3(s)$	−824.2	$KBr(s)$	−393.8
$CH_3OH(\ell)$	−239.2	$Fe_3O_4(s)$	−1118.4	$KCl(s)$	−436.5
$C_2H_5OH(\ell)$	−277.6	$FeCl_2(s)$	−341.8	$KClO_3(s)$	−397.7
$CH_3COOH(\ell)$	−484.3	$FeCl_3(s)$	−399.5	$KOH(s)$	−424.6
$CO(g)$	−110.5	$FeS_2(s)$	−178.2	$Ag_2CO_3(s)$	−505.8
$CO_2(g)$	−393.5	$PbCl_2(s)$	−359.4	$AgCl(s)$	−127.0
$COCl_2(g)$	−219.1	$MgCl_2(s)$	−641.3	$AgNO_3(s)$	−124.4
$CS_2(\ell)$	+89.0	$MgO(s)$	−601.6	$Ag_2S(s)$	−32.6
$CS_2(g)$	+116.7	$Mg(OH)_2(s)$	−924.5	$SF_6(g)$	−1220.5
$CrCl_3(g)$	−556.5	$HgS(s)$	−58.2	$SO_2(g)$	−296.8
$Cu(NO_3)_2(s)$	−302.9	$NaCl(s)$	−411.2	$SO_3(g)$	−395.7
$CuO(s)$	−157.3	$NaOH(s)$	−425.6	$SnCl_2(s)$	−325.1
$CuCl(s)$	−137.2	$Na_2CO_3(s)$	−1130.7	$SnCl_4(\ell)$	−511.3
$CuCl_2(s)$	−220.1				

Note: The enthalpy of formation of an element in its standard state is defined as zero.

Reactivity and Solubility

Activity Series of Metals

Metal	Displaces Hydrogen…	Reactivity
lithium		most reactive
potassium		
barium		
calcium		
sodium	from cold water	
magnesium		
aluminum		
zinc		
chromium		
iron		
cadmium		
cobalt		
nickel		
tin		
lead	from acids	
hydrogen		
copper		
mercury		
silver		
platinum		
gold		least reactive

Activity Series of Halogens

Halogen	Reactivity
fluorine	most reactive
chlorine	
bromine	
iodine	least reactive

Solubility of Common Ionic Compounds in Water

	Anion	+	Cation	→	Solubility of Compound*
1.	Most		Alkali metal ions: Li^+, K^+, Rb^+, Cs^+, Fr^+		Soluble
	Most		hydrogen ion, H^+		Soluble
	Most		ammonium ion, NH_4^+		Soluble
2.	nitrate, NO_3^-		Most		Soluble
	acetate (ethanoate), CH_3COO^-		Ag^+		Low solubility
			Most others		Soluble
3.	chloride, Cl^- bromide, Br^- iodide, I^-		Ag^+, Pb^{2+}, Hg_2^{2+}, Cu^+, Tl^+		Low solubility
			All others		Soluble
4.	fluoride, F^-		Mg^{2+}, Ca^{2+}, Ba^{2+}, Pb^{2+}		Low solubility
			Most others		Soluble
5.	sulfate, SO_4^{2-}		Ca^{2+}, Sr^{2+}, Ba^{2+}, Pb^{2+}		Low solubility
			All others		Soluble
6.	sulfide, S^{2-}		Alkali ions and H^+, NH_4^+, Be^{2+}, Mg^{2+}, Ca^{2+}, Sr^{2+}, Ba^{2+}		Soluble
			All others		Low solubility
7.	hydroxide, OH^-		Alkali ions and H^+, NH_4^+, Sr^{2+}, Ba^{2+}, Tl^+		Soluble
			All others		Low solubility
8.	phosphate, PO_4^{3-} carbonate, CO_3^{2-} sulfite, SO_3^{2-}		Alkali ions and H^+, NH_4^+		Soluble
			All others		Low solubility

*Compounds listed as soluble have solubilities of at least 1 g/100 mL of water at 25°C and 100 kPa.

Concentration Calculations

Measures of Concentration

Type of Concentration	Formula	Common Application
Concentration as a Percent • mass/volume percent • mass percent • volume percent	$\text{percent (m/v)} = \dfrac{\text{mass of solute [in grams]}}{\text{volume of solution [in millilitres]}} \times 100\%$ $\text{percent (m/m)} = \dfrac{\text{mass of solute}}{\text{mass of solution}} \times 100\%$ $\text{percent (v/v)} = \dfrac{\text{volume of solute}}{\text{volume of solution}} \times 100\%$	• intravenous solutions, such as a saline drip • concentration of metals in an alloy • solutions prepared by mixing liquids
Very Small Concentrations • parts per million • parts per billion	$\text{ppm} = \dfrac{\text{mass of solute}}{\text{mass of solution}} \times 10^6$ $\text{ppb} = \dfrac{\text{mass of solute}}{\text{mass of solution}} \times 10^9$	• safety limits for contaminants, such as mercury or lead in food or water
Molar Concentration	$\text{molar concentration} = \dfrac{\text{amount of solute [in moles]}}{\text{volume of solution [in litres]}}$ $c = \dfrac{n}{V}$	• solutions used as reactants

Acids, Bases, Indicators, and Constants

The Most Common Strong Acids

Name	Formula
hydrochloric acid	HCl(aq)
hydrobromic acid	HBr(aq)
hydroiodic acid	HI(aq)
perchloric acid	$HClO_4$(aq)
nitric acid	HNO_3(aq)
sulfuric acid	H_2SO_4(aq)

Some Common Strong Bases

Name	Formula
lithium hydroxide	LiOH(aq)
sodium hydroxide	NaOH(aq)
potassium hydroxide	KOH(aq)
calcium hydroxide	$Ca(OH)_2$(aq)
barium hydroxide	$Ba(OH)_2$(aq)

Ionization Constants for Nitrogen Bases

Base	Formula	Conjugate acid	K_b
1,2-diaminoethane (ethylenediamine)	$NH_2CH_2CH_2NH_2$	$NH_2CH_2CH_2NH_3^+$	8.4×10^{-5}
dimethylamine (N-methylmethanamine)	$(CH_3)_2NH$	$(CH_3)_2NH_2^+$	5.4×10^{-4}
ethanamine	$C_2H_5NH_2$	$C_2H_5NH_3^+$	4.5×10^{-4}
methanamine	CH_3NH_2	$CH_3NH_3^+$	4.6×10^{-4}
trimethylamine (N-N-dimethyl-methanamine)	$(CH_3)_3N$	$(CH_3)_3NH^+$	6.4×10^{-5}
ammonia	NH_3	NH_4^+	1.8×10^{-5}
hydrazine	N_2H_4	$N_2H_5^+$	1.3×10^{-6}
hydroxylamine	NH_2OH	NH_3OH^+	8.8×10^{-9}
pyridine	C_5H_5N	$C_5H_5NH^+$	1.7×10^{-9}
aniline	$C_6H_5NH_2$	$C_6H_5NH_3^+$	7.5×10^{-10}
urea	NH_2CONH_2	$NH_2CONH_3^+$	1.3×10^{-14}

Solubility Product Constants in Water at 25°C

Bromates
$AgBrO_3$	5.38×10^{-5}
$TlBrO_3$	1.10×10^{-4}

Bromides
AgBr	5.35×10^{-13}
CuBr	6.27×10^{-9}
$PbBr_2$	6.60×10^{-6}

Carbonates
Ag_2CO_3	8.46×10^{-12}
$BaCO_3$	2.58×10^{-9}
$CaCO_3$	3.36×10^{-9}
$MgCO_3$	6.82×10^{-6}
$PbCO_3$	7.40×10^{-14}

Chlorides
AgCl	1.77×10^{-10}
CuCl	1.72×10^{-9}

Chromates
Ag_2CrO_4	1.12×10^{-12}
$BaCrO_4$	1.12×10^{-10}
$PbCrO_4$	2.3×10^{-13}

Cyanides
AgCN	5.97×10^{-17}
CuCN	3.47×10^{-20}

Fluorides
BaF_2	1.84×10^{-7}
CdF_2	6.44×10^{-3}
CaF_2	3.45×10^{-11}
FeF_2	2.36×10^{-6}

Hydroxides
$Be(OH)_2$	6.92×10^{-22}
$Cd(OH)_2$	7.2×10^{-15}
$Ca(OH)_2$	5.02×10^{-6}
$Co(OH)_2$	5.92×10^{-15}
$Eu(OH)_3$	9.38×10^{-27}
$Fe(OH)_2$	4.87×10^{-17}
$Fe(OH)_3$	2.79×10^{-39}
$Pb(OH)_2$	1.43×10^{-20}
$Mg(OH)_2$	5.61×10^{-12}
$Ni(OH)_2$	5.48×10^{-16}
$Sn(OH)_2$	5.45×10^{-27}
$Zn(OH)_2$	3×10^{-17}

Iodates
$Ba(IO_3)_2$	4.01×10^{-9}
$Ca(IO_3)_2$	6.47×10^{-6}
$Sr(IO_3)_2$	1.14×10^{-7}
$Y(IO_3)_3$	1.12×10^{-10}

Iodides
CuI	1.27×10^{-12}
PbI_2	9.8×10^{-9}
AgI	8.52×10^{-17}

Phosphates
$AlPO_4$	9.84×10^{-21}
$Ca_3(PO_4)_2$	2.07×10^{-33}
$Co_3(PO_4)_2$	2.05×10^{-35}
$Cu_3(PO_4)_2$	1.40×10^{-37}
$Ni_3(PO_4)_2$	4.74×10^{-32}

Sulfates
$BaSO_4$	1.08×10^{-10}
$CaSO_4$	4.93×10^{-5}
Hg_2SO_4	6.5×10^{-7}

Thiocyanates
CuSCN	1.08×10^{-13}
$Pd(SCN)_2$	4.39×10^{-23}

Endpoint Indicators

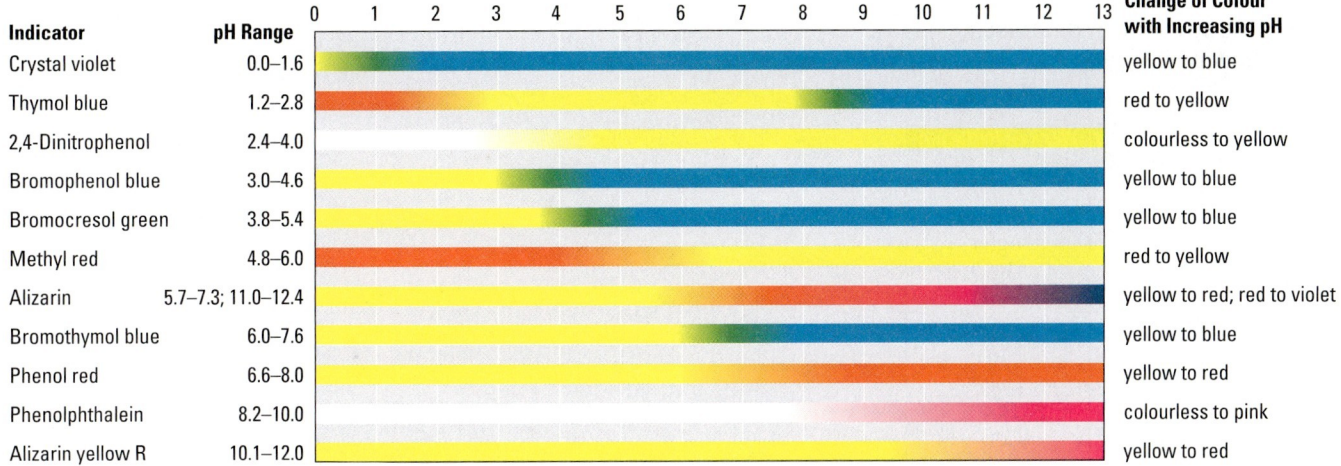

Indicator	pH Range	Change of Colour with Increasing pH
Crystal violet	0.0–1.6	yellow to blue
Thymol blue	1.2–2.8	red to yellow
2,4-Dinitrophenol	2.4–4.0	colourless to yellow
Bromophenol blue	3.0–4.6	yellow to blue
Bromocresol green	3.8–5.4	yellow to blue
Methyl red	4.8–6.0	red to yellow
Alizarin	5.7–7.3; 11.0–12.4	yellow to red; red to violet
Bromothymol blue	6.0–7.6	yellow to blue
Phenol red	6.6–8.0	yellow to red
Phenolphthalein	8.2–10.0	colourless to pink
Alizarin yellow R	10.1–12.0	yellow to red

Relative Strengths of Acids and Bases (concentration = 0.10 mol/L) at 25°C

Acid Name	Acid Formula	Formula of Conjugate Base	K_a
perchloric acid	$HClO_4(aq)$	$ClO_4^-(aq)$	very large
hydroiodic acid	$HI(aq)$	$I^-(aq)$	very large
hydrobromic acid	$HBr(aq)$	$Br^-(aq)$	very large
hydrochloric acid	$HCl(aq)$	$Cl^-(aq)$	very large
sulfuric acid	$H_2SO_4(aq)$	$HSO_4^-(aq)$	very large
nitric acid	$HNO_3(aq)$	$NO_3^-(aq)$	very large
hydronium ion	$H_3O^+(aq)$	$H_2O(\ell)$	1
oxalic acid	$HOOCCOOH(aq)$	$HOOCCOO^-(aq)$	5.6×10^{-2}
sulfurous acid ($SO_2 + H_2O$)	$H_2SO_3(aq)$	$HSO_3^-(aq)$	1.4×10^{-2}
hydrogen sulfate ion	$HSO_4^-(aq)$	$SO_4^{2-}(aq)$	1.0×10^{-2}
phosphoric acid	$H_3PO_4(aq)$	$H_2PO_4^-(aq)$	6.9×10^{-3}
citric acid	$H_3C_6H_5O_7(aq)$	$H_2C_6H_5O_7^-(aq)$	7.4×10^{-4}
hydrofluoric acid	$HF(aq)$	$F^-(aq)$	6.3×10^{-4}
nitrous acid	$HNO_2(aq)$	$NO_2^-(aq)$	5.6×10^{-4}
methanoic acid	$HCOOH(aq)$	$HCOO^-(aq)$	1.8×10^{-4}
hydrogen oxalate ion	$HOOCCOO^-(aq)$	$OOCCOO^{2-}(aq)$	1.5×10^{-4}
ascorbic acid	$C_6H_8O_6(aq)$	$C_6H_7O_6^-(aq)$	9.1×10^{-5}
benzoic acid	$C_6H_5COOH(aq)$	$C_6H_5COO^-(aq)$	6.3×10^{-5}
ethanoic (acetic) acid	$CH_3COOH(aq)$	$CH_3COO^-(aq)$	1.8×10^{-5}
dihydrogen citrate ion	$H_2C_6H_5O_7^-(aq)$	$HC_6H_5O_7^{2-}(aq)$	1.7×10^{-5}
carbonic acid ($CO_2 + H_2O$)	$H_2CO_3(aq)$	$HCO_3^-(aq)$	4.5×10^{-7}
hydrogen citrate ion	$HC_6H_5O_7^{2-}(aq)$	$C_6H_5O_7^{3-}(aq)$	4.0×10^{-7}
hydrosulfuric acid	$H_2S(aq)$	$HS^-(aq)$	8.9×10^{-8}
hydrogen sulfite ion	$HSO_3^-(aq)$	$SO_3^{2-}(aq)$	6.3×10^{-8}
dihydrogen phosphate ion	$H_2PO_4^-(aq)$	$HPO_4^{2-}(aq)$	6.2×10^{-8}
hypochlorous acid	$HOCl(aq)$	$OCl^-(aq)$	4.0×10^{-8}
hydrocyanic acid	$HCN(aq)$	$CN^-(aq)$	6.2×10^{-10}
ammonium ion	$NH_4^+(aq)$	$NH_3(aq)$	5.6×10^{-10}
hydrogen carbonate ion	$HCO_3^-(aq)$	$CO_3^{2-}(aq)$	4.7×10^{-11}
hydrogen ascorbate ion	$C_6H_7O_6^-(aq)$	$C_6H_6O_6^{2-}(aq)$	2.0×10^{-12}
hydrogen phosphate ion	$HPO_4^{2-}(aq)$	$PO_4^{3-}(aq)$	4.8×10^{-13}
water (55.5 mol/L)	$H_2O(\ell)$	$HO^-(aq)$	1.0×10^{-14}

Increasing Acid Strength →

Increasing Base Strength →

Oxidation and Reduction

Relative Strengths of Oxidizing Agents and Reducing Agents

Strongest Oxidizing Agent	Weakest Reducing Agent
$Au^+(aq)$	$Au(s)$
$Pt^{2+}(aq)$	$Pt(s)$
$Ag^+(aq)$	$Ag(s)$
$Hg^{2+}(aq)$	$Hg(\ell)$
$Cu^{2+}(aq)$	$Cu(s)$
$Sn^{2+}(aq)$	$Sn(s)$
$Ni^{2+}(aq)$	$Ni(s)$
$Co^{2+}(aq)$	$Co(s)$
$Tl^+(aq)$	$Tl(s)$
$Cd^{2+}(aq)$	$Cd(s)$
$Fe^{2+}(aq)$	$Fe(s)$
$Cr^{3+}(aq)$	$Cr(s)$
$Zn^{2+}(aq)$	$Zn(s)$
$Al^{3+}(aq)$	$Al(s)$
$Mg^{2+}(aq)$	$Mg(s)$
$Ca^{2+}(aq)$	$Ca(s)$
$Ba^{2+}(aq)$	$Ba(s)$
Weakest Oxidizing Agent	**Strongest Reducing Agent**

Standard Reduction Potentials (298 K, 1.0 atm)

Reduction Half-reaction	$E°(V)$
$F_2(g) + 2e^- \rightleftharpoons 2F^-(aq)$	2.87
$Co^{3+}(aq) + e^- \rightleftharpoons Co^{2+}(aq)$	1.92
$H_2O_2(aq) + 2H^+(aq) + 2e^- \rightleftharpoons 2H_2O(\ell)$	1.78
$Ce^{4+}(aq) + e^- \rightleftharpoons Ce^{3+}(aq)$	1.72
$PbO_2(s) + 4H^+(aq) + SO_4^{2-}(aq) + 2e^- \rightleftharpoons PbSO_4(s) + 2H_2O(\ell)$	1.69
$MnO_4^-(aq) + 8H^+(aq) + 5e^- \rightleftharpoons Mn^{2+}(aq) + 4H_2O(\ell)$	1.51
$Au^{3+}(aq) + 3e^- \rightleftharpoons Au(s)$	1.50
$PbO_2(s) + 4H^+(aq) + 2e^- \rightleftharpoons Pb^{2+}(aq) + 2H_2O(\ell)$	1.46
$Cl_2(g) + 2e^- \rightleftharpoons 2Cl^-(aq)$	1.36
$Cr_2O_7^{2-}(aq) + 14H^+(aq) + 6e^- \rightleftharpoons 2Cr^{3+}(aq) + 7H_2O(\ell)$	1.36
$O_2(g) + 4H^+(aq) + 4e^- \rightleftharpoons 2H_2O(\ell)$	1.23
$MnO_2(s) + 4H^+(aq) + 2e^- \rightleftharpoons Mn^{2+}(aq) + 2H_2O(\ell)$	1.22
$IO_3^-(aq) + 6H^+(aq) + 6e^- \rightleftharpoons I^-(aq) + 3H_2O(\ell)$	1.08
$Br_2(\ell) + 2e^- \rightleftharpoons 2Br^-(aq)$	1.07
$AuCl_4^-(aq) + 3e^- \rightleftharpoons Au(s) + 4Cl^-(aq)$	1.00
$NO_3^-(aq) + 4H^+(aq) + 3e^- \rightleftharpoons NO(g) + 2H_2O(\ell)$	0.96
$2Hg^{2+}(aq) + 2e^- \rightleftharpoons Hg_2^{2+}(aq)$	0.92
$Ag^+(aq) + e^- \rightleftharpoons Ag(s)$	0.80
$Hg_2^{2+}(aq) + 2e^- \rightleftharpoons 2Hg(\ell)$	0.80
$Fe^{3+}(aq) + e^- \rightleftharpoons Fe^{2+}(aq)$	0.77
$O_2(g) + 2H^+(aq) + 2e^- \rightleftharpoons H_2O_2(aq)$	0.70
$I_2(s) + 2e^- \rightleftharpoons 2I^-(aq)$	0.54
$Cu^+(aq) + e^- \rightleftharpoons Cu(s)$	0.52
$O_2(g) + 2H_2O(\ell) + 4e^- \rightleftharpoons 4OH^-(aq)$	0.40

Reduction Half-reaction	$E°(V)$
$Cu^{2+}(aq) + 2e^- \rightleftharpoons Cu(s)$	0.34
$AgCl(s) + e^- \rightleftharpoons Ag(s) + Cl^-(aq)$	0.22
$4H^+(aq) + SO_4^{2-}(aq) + 2e^- \rightleftharpoons H_2SO_3(aq) + H_2O(\ell)$	0.17
$Cu^{2+}(aq) + e^- \rightleftharpoons Cu^+(aq)$	0.15
$2H^+(aq) + 2e^- \rightleftharpoons H_2(g)$	0.000
$Fe^{3+}(aq) + 3e^- \rightleftharpoons Fe(s)$	−0.04
$Pb^{2+}(aq) + 2e^- \rightleftharpoons Pb(s)$	−0.13
$Sn^{2+}(aq) + 2e^- \rightleftharpoons Sn(s)$	−0.14
$Ni^{2+}(aq) + 2e^- \rightleftharpoons Ni(s)$	−0.26
$Cd^{2+}(aq) + 2e^- \rightleftharpoons Cd(s)$	−0.40
$Cr^{3+}(aq) + e^- \rightleftharpoons Cr^{2+}(aq)$	−0.41
$Fe^{2+}(aq) + 2e^- \rightleftharpoons Fe(s)$	−0.45
$Cr^{3+}(aq) + 3e^- \rightleftharpoons Cr(s)$	−0.74
$Zn^{2+}(aq) + 2e^- \rightleftharpoons Zn(s)$	−0.76
$2H_2O(\ell) + 2e^- \rightleftharpoons H_2(g) + 2OH^-(aq)$	−0.83
$Al^{3+}(aq) + 3e^- \rightleftharpoons Al(s)$	−1.66
$Mg^{2+}(aq) + 2e^- \rightleftharpoons Mg(s)$	−2.37
$La^{3+}(aq) + 3e^- \rightleftharpoons La(s)$	−2.38
$Na^+(aq) + e^- \rightleftharpoons Na(s)$	−2.71
$Ca^{2+}(aq) + 2e^- \rightleftharpoons Ca(s)$	−2.87
$Ba^{2+}(aq) + 2e^- \rightleftharpoons Ba(s)$	−2.91
$K^+(aq) + e^- \rightleftharpoons K(s)$	−2.93
$Li^+(aq) + e^- \rightleftharpoons Li(s)$	−3.04

Appendix B

Alphabetical List of Elements

Element	Symbol	Atomic Number
actinium	Ac	89
aluminum	Al	13
americium	Am	95
antimony	Sb	51
argon	Ar	18
arsenic	As	33
astatine	At	85
barium	Ba	56
berkelium	Bk	97
beryllium	Be	4
bismuth	Bi	83
bohrium	Bh	107
boron	B	5
bromine	Br	35
cadmium	Cd	48
calcium	Ca	20
californium	Cf	98
carbon	C	6
cerium	Ce	58
cesium	Cs	55
chlorine	Cl	17
chromium	Cr	24
cobalt	Co	27
copernicium	Cn	112
copper	Cu	29
curium	Cm	96
darmstadtium	Ds	110
dubnium	Db	105
dysprosium	Dy	66
einsteinium	Es	99
erbium	Er	68
europium	Eu	63
fermium	Fm	100
flerovium	Fl	114
fluorine	F	9
francium	Fr	87
gadolinium	Gd	64
gallium	Ga	31
germanium	Ge	32
gold	Au	79
hafnium	Hf	72
hassium	Hs	108
helium	He	2
holmium	Ho	67
hydrogen	H	1
indium	In	49
iodine	I	53
iridium	Ir	77
iron	Fe	26
krypton	Kr	36
lanthanum	La	57
lawrencium	Lr	103
lead	Pb	82
lithium	Li	3
livermorium	Lv	116
lutetium	Lu	71
magnesium	Mg	12
manganese	Mn	25
meitnerium	Mt	109
mendelevium	Md	101
mercury	Hg	80
molybdenum	Mo	42
moscovium	Mc	115
neodymium	Nd	60
neon	Ne	10
neptunium	Np	93
nickel	Ni	28
nihonium	Nh	113
niobium	Nb	41
nitrogen	N	7
nobelium	No	102
oganesson	Og	118
osmium	Os	76
oxygen	O	8
palladium	Pd	46
phosphorus	P	15
platinum	Pt	78
plutonium	Pu	94
polonium	Po	84
potassium	K	19
praseodymium	Pr	59
promethium	Pm	61
protactinium	Pa	91
radium	Ra	88
radon	Rn	86
rhenium	Re	75
rhodium	Rh	45
roentgenium	Rg	111
rubidium	Rb	37
ruthenium	Ru	44
rutherfordium	Rf	104
samarium	Sm	62
scandium	Sc	21
seaborgium	Sg	106
selenium	Se	34
silicon	Si	14
silver	Ag	47
sodium	Na	11
strontium	Sr	38
sulfur	S	16
tantalum	Ta	73
technetium	Tc	43
tellurium	Te	52
tennessine	Ts	117
terbium	Tb	65
thallium	Tl	81
thorium	Th	90
thulium	Tm	69
tin	Sn	50
titanium	Ti	22
tungsten	W	74
uranium	U	92
vanadium	V	23
xenon	Xe	54
ytterbium	Yb	70
yttrium	Y	39
zinc	Zn	30
zirconium	Zr	40

Appendix B

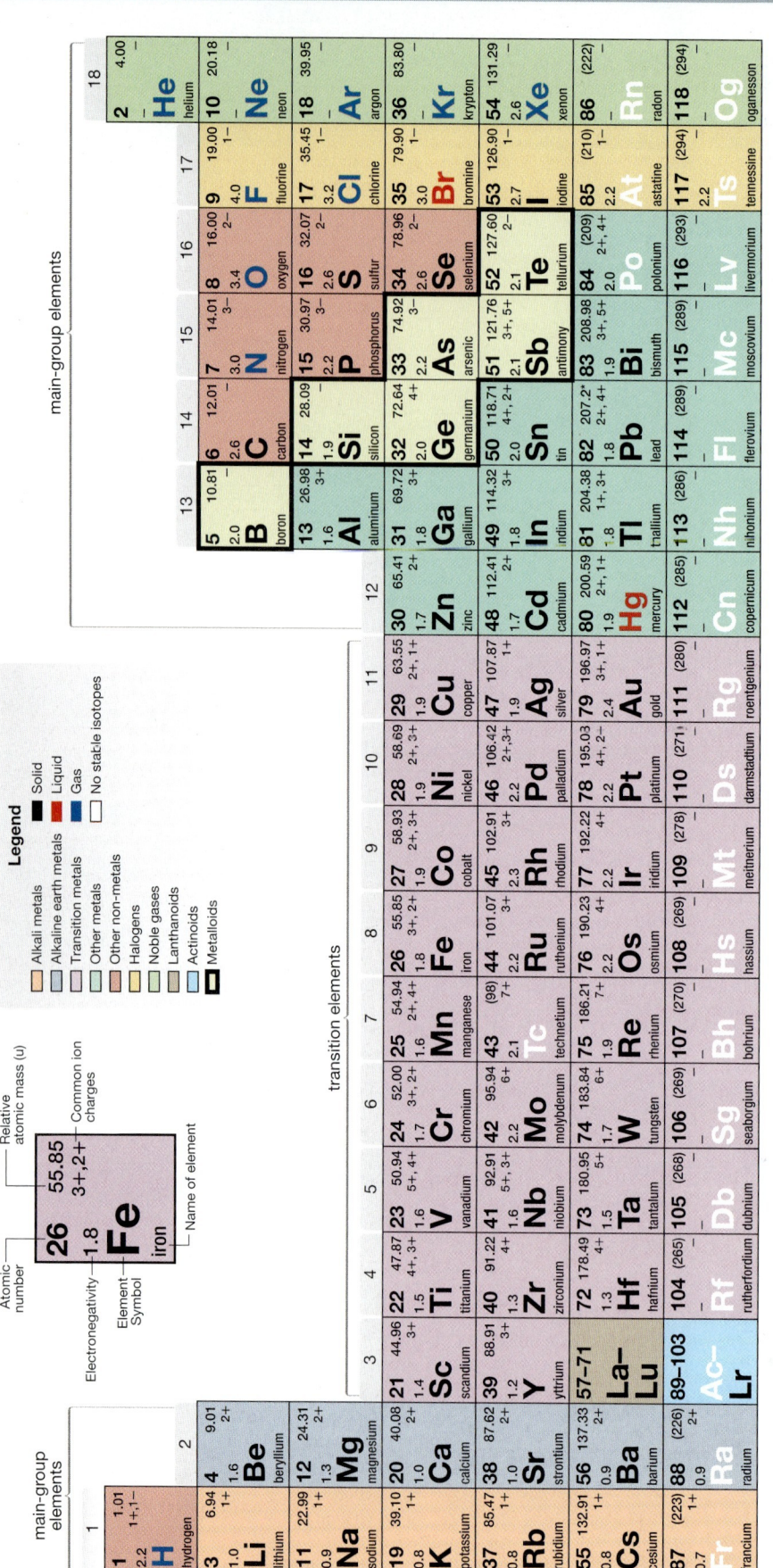

Periodic Table of the Elements

Appendix C — Answers to Selected Questions and Problems

Answers are provided for all caption questions and multiple choice questions. Answers are provided for selected Learning Check questions, Practice Problems, Section Review, Chapter Review, Chapter Self-Assessment, Unit Review, and Unit Self-Assessment questions. Data sources for calculating numerical answers are from tables in Appendix B in this textbook and from the *CRC Handbook*, 87th Edition (2006-2007).

UNIT 1
Chapter 1

Answers to Learning Check Questions

1. Up to and including the 1800s, the term *organic* was used to describe matter that came from living matter that contained a "vital energy," and *inorganic* was used to describe matter that came from non-living matter. The analysis and synthesis of carbon compounds led to the modern definition of an organic compound as one in which carbon atoms are bonded to each other, to hydrogen atoms, and sometimes to a few specific elements, usually oxygen, nitrogen, sulfur, or phosphorus.

2. The key to carbon's ability to bond with several atoms is found in its atomic structure. A carbon atom has four valence electrons, and a half-filled outer shell of electrons. It has an intermediate electronegativity and is much more likely to share electrons than to gain or lose enough electrons to form ions. Its four valence electrons can be shared with up to four other atoms. This leads to the potential for the formation of a wide variety of molecules.

3. Any molecule that contains C-C or C-H could be considered organic, and molecules or ions such as CO_2 and CO_3^{2-} that contain no C-C or C-H bonds could be considered inorganic.

4. Atomic systems arrange themselves to minimize their potential energy. For methane, this occurs if the four bonds are as far apart as possible (because the electron pairs repel each other), which the molecule achieves by adopting the symmetrical, tetrahedral arrangement of its bonds.

6. There are nine constitutional isomers of heptane.

7. Examples include methane (CH_4) found in natural gas to heat homes, propane (C_3H_8) used in barbeques and as a heating fuel, butane (C_4H_8) found in lighters and portable burners, octane (C_8H_{18}) found in gasoline, waxes ($C_{20}H_{42}$) found in candles, and tars ($C_{40}H_{82}$) used in paving.

8. In a saturated hydrocarbon, each carbon atom is bonded to as many other atoms as possible. Unsaturated hydrocarbons have at least one multiple bond and are therefore not completely saturated with hydrogens. Unsaturated alkenes generally have lower melting and boiling points when compared with saturated hydrocarbons of the same length, although alkynes will be slightly higher.

9. A homologous series is a set of molecules in which each member differs from the next by an additional specific structural unit. The alkane series can be represented by a general formula, C_nH_{2n+2}. Ethane, C_2H_6, differs from the next member of the series, propane, C_3H_8, by $-CH_2$.

10. 3 carbon atoms: C_3H_8; 7 carbon atoms: C_7H_{16}; 9 carbon atoms: C_9H_{20}; 12 carbon atoms: $C_{12}H_{26}$

11. All reasonable answers should show that an atom or group of atoms on an alkane has been substituted in place of a hydrogen atom on the parent chain of carbons.

12. The root is *pent-*, the prefix is *2-methyl*, and the suffix is *-ane*.

14. They are insoluble in water but soluble in non-polar solvents.

15. **a.** Alkanes that are liquids have between 5 and 16 carbon atoms inclusive. **b.** Alkanes that are gases have between 1 and 4 carbon atoms inclusive.

16. C_nH_{2n}

17. They are similar in that they have the same number and sequence of carbon atoms as the corresponding alkane. They are different in that there are fewer hydrogen atoms in an alkene, there is a double bond in an alkene, and the shape is different.

20. alkenes < alkanes < alkynes

21. The linear structure of alkynes allows them to attract one another more strongly than corresponding alkanes and alkenes.

22. Testosterone and estrogen are two examples of steroid hormones containing cyclic hydrocarbons.

23. Straight-chain alkanes have the general formula C_nH_{2n+2}. Cyclic alkanes have the general formula C_nH_{2n}. Alkenes have the general formula C_nH_{2n}. Alkynes have the general formula C_nH_{2n-2}.

24. At least three carbon atoms are necessary and the molecular formula is C_3H_6.

25. Cyclic hydrocarbons have higher boiling points and melting points than straight-chain hydrocarbons. There is a greater difference in terms of melting point.
26. Aromatic hydrocarbons contain a benzene ring; aliphatic hydrocarbons do not contain a benzene ring.
27. Benzene is more stable than cyclohexene (therefore, less reactive) and it has fewer hydrogen atoms.
28. All the bonds in benzene are identical and have an intermediate length compared with single and double bonds.
29. Electrons in the "double bonds" of a benzene ring are in fact shared by all six carbon atoms.

Answers to Practice Problems

1. 2-methylpropane
2. 2,2-dimethylpentane
3. 5-ethyl-3,4-dimethylnonane
4. 3,3,5-trimethylheptane
5. 2,2,5-trimethylhexane
6. 2-methylbutane
7. dimethylpropane or 2,2-dimethylpropane
8. 2,2,4,4-tetramethylhexane
9. pentane
10. 2,3-dimethylpentane
11. 3,3-dimethylheptane
16. pentane
17. 4-ethyloctane
18. 3,3-diethyl-4-methylhexane
22. 4-ethyl-4-propylheptane
23. pent-2-ene
24. 3-methylbut-1-ene
25. 4,4-dimethylhex-2-ene
26. 2-ethylpent-1-ene
27. 3,4-diethylhex-2-ene
28. but-1-ene
29. 5,6-dimethylhept-3-ene
30. 4-ethyl-3-methylhex-2-ene
31. 2,5-dimethyloct-3-ene
32. propene
33. 4-methylpent-2-ene
34. 2-ethyl-3-methylpent-1-ene
40. hex-2-ene
41. 5-ethyloct-2-ene
42. 2-methylbut-2-ene
44. 3-ethyl-3-propyl-4-methylhex-1-ene
45. hex-3-yne
46. 4-methylpent-1-yne
47. 5-ethyloct-2-yne
48. 4,4,5-trimethylhex-1-yne
51. but-1-yne
52. but-1-yne
53. 4-methylpent-2-yne
54. 3-ethyl-5-methyl-3-propylhex-1-yne
55. cyclopentane
56. 1-ethyl-3-methylcyclobutane
57. 4-methylcycloheptene
58. 3-methyl-5-propylcyclopentene
59. 3-cyclopentyloctane
65. methylbenzene, historically known as toluene
66. 1,2,4-trimethylbenzene
67. 1-ethyl-3-propylbenzene
68. 2,4-diphenyloctane
74. 1-ethyl-4-methylbenzene
75. butan-2-ol
76. pentane-2,3-diol
77. propan-2-ol
78. 3-methylbutane-1,3-diol
79. 2-ethyl-6-phenylheptan-1-ol
85. 2-fluorobutane
86. 3-bromo-3-methylpentane
87. 4-chloro-2-methylhexane
88. 1,3-dichloro-2-fluorobutane
89. 1,3-dibromo-2-chlorocyclohexane
95. a. 2-chlorobutane
    b. 3-bromo-4-chlorohexane
    c. 1,3-dichlorocyclopentane
    d. 2-chloro-3,3-dimethylbutane
96. propanal
97. 2-methylbutanal
98. 3-ethyl-4-methylhexanal
99. 2,4-dibromopentanal

105. a. The correct name is ethanal. The aldehyde group should be placed on the number 1 carbon (unless there are other higher priority functional groups also present such as carboxylic acids). It is not necessary to include a number in this case as it is assumed the aldehyde is on the first carbon.

b. The correct name is 5-methylheptanal. The longest chain would include the ethyl group, and the methyl group would be a side branch.

c. Since carbon only forms four bonds, an aldehyde could not be inside a cyclic hydrocarbon as well as having hydrogen and double-bonded oxygen. Therefore, this compound does not exist.

d. Since the terminal carbon would need to have a hydrogen and a double-bonded oxygen, and be joined to the hydrocarbon chain, there would be no room for a fluorine to bond. This compound does not exist.

106. butan-2-one

107. 2-methyl-pentan-3-one

108. 3-ethyl-4-methyl-hexan-2-one

112. The ketone group lies on a carbon attached to two other carbons and therefore would never have a numerical assignment of 1. This compound does not exist.

113. The correct name is pentan-2-one. Numbering of the longest carbon chain gives the ketone group the lowest number.

114. The correct name is 5-methyloctane-3,4-dione. Numbering should begin with giving the ketone groups the lowest possible numbers. The longest continuous chain containing these groups is eight carbons long.

115. Since carbon forms only four bonds and the linkage between carbons in the benzene ring is considered the intermediate of a single and double bond, the carbon atom with the ketone group would not be able to form a double bond with oxygen. This compound does not exist.

116. propanoic acid

117. 4-ethylhexanoic acid

122. The correct name is hexanoic acid. The carboxylic acid gets the lowest number on the longest hydrocarbon and is assumed to be on carbon 1.

123. Owing to carbon only being able to form four bonds, a carboxylic acid functional group would always be at the end of a hydrocarbon chain. This compound does not exist.

124. The correct name is 3-ethylheptanoic acid. Numbering should begin with giving the carboxylic acid groups the lowest possible numbers. The longest continuous chain containing these groups is seven carbons long.

125. Since carbon forms only four bonds, a carboxylic acid group could never be inside a cyclic hydrocarbon. This compound does not exist.

126. methylethanoate

127. ethylmethanoate

128. butyl 3-chlorobutanoate

136. 1-ethoxypropane

137. 2-ethoxypropane

138. ethoxycyclohexane

143. The correct name is methoxyethane. The root name should be the longest hydrocarbon chain.

144. The correct name is 2-propoxybutane. The numbering of the root name should give the ether linkage the lowest number possible on its hydrocarbon chain.

145. The correct name is 2-methoxypentane. The numbering of the root name should be made to give the longest possible chain to which the R′ group is attached.

146. The correct name is ethoxybenzene. It is assumed that the R′ group is first attached to the number 1 carbon of the benzene ring and it is not necessary to number it.

147. ethanamine

148. pentan-3-amine

149. N-ethylbutan-2-amine

150. N-methyl-N-propylhexan-2-amine

159. methanamide

160. 3-ethylhexanamide

161. N-propylpentanamide

162. N,N-dimethylbutanamide

167. propanamide

168. N-propyl-2,2-dimethylbutanamide

169. N,N-dimethyl-2-propylhexanamide

Answers to Caption Questions

Figure 1.10 Triple bonds are linear and rigid.

Figure 1.13 They all contain only carbon and hydrogen atoms. All contain only single bonds. Except for methane, the carbon atoms are bonded to other carbon atoms. Each compound has one more carbon atom than the one before.

Figure 1.15 The compound on the left is unsaturated because the carbon atoms are not bonded to the maximum number of atoms possible, owing to the double bond. The compound on the right is saturated because the carbon atoms are bonded to the maximum number of atoms; all of the bonds are single bonds.

Figure 1.16 These two alkenes are isomers. The double bond can join an end carbon atom to another carbon atom, or the double bond can join the two middle carbon atoms.

Figure 1.25 Possible response: The CFCs take a long time to naturally degrade in the atmosphere. Also, older products, such as old refrigerators, may still emit CFCs. Also, there are other compounds that damage the ozone layer.

Figure 1.36 The citric acid neutralizes the amines in the fish.

Figure 1.43 Possibly an amine because it does have an amine group and it has the suffix-*amine* in its name.

Answers to Section 1.2 Review Questions

4. **a.** C_nH_{2n+2}
   b. C_nH_{2n}
   c. C_nH_{2n-2}

11. C_nH_{2n}; The alkenes also have this general formula.

Answers to Chapter 1 Review Questions

1. b
2. c
3. a
4. d
5. e
6. d
7. b
8. d
9. e
10. e
11. a
12. c
13. e
14. b

21. **a.** C_nH_{2n+2}
    b. C_nH_{2n}
    c. C_nH_{2n-2}
    d. C_nH_{2n}

29. **a.** CH_4
    b. C_2H_6
    c. C_6H_{14} or C_6H_{12} as a cycloalkane
    d. Pure alkanes do not contain oxygen atoms.

40. **a.** hexane-3,4-diol
    b. 4-chloro-2,3-dimethylpentane
    c. 3-ethyl-6-methyldecan-2-one
    d. 3-ethyl-3-methylpentan-2-one

42. **b.** $C_{11}H_{24}$ about 200°C; $C_{12}H_{26}$ about 215°C

44. **a.** 2-methylbutanoic acid
    b. 7-methyl-7-phenylnonan-3-one
    c. ethylpentanoate
    d. N-methyl-N-propylbutanamine

50. **a.** methanal
    b. methylbenzene
    c. 1,2-dimethylbenzene
    d. phenylamine
    e. chloroform or trichloromethane

53. **a.** butane-1,4-diamine; pentane-1,5-diamine

54. **a.** N,N-diethyl-3-methylbenzamide

58. **a.** adrenaline: $C_9H_{13}NO_3$; amphetamine: $C_9H_{13}N$

Answers to Chapter 1 Self-Assessment Questions

1. a
2. c
3. e
4. e
5. d
6. c
7. a
8. c
9. c
10. e

13. **a.** 2-methylbutane
    b. 2,3-dimethylpentane
    c. This molecule is named correctly.
    d. 5-ethyl-6-methylhept-3-ene

17. **a.** 3-methylbutanoic acid
    b. N,N-dimethylpropan-2-amine

Chapter 2

Answers to Learning Check Questions

1. Both are examples of reactions of organic compounds. In an addition reaction, atoms are added to an organic compound at the site of a double or triple bond. In elimination reactions, atoms are removed from an organic molecule and a double bond is formed. Elimination reactions are the opposite of addition reactions.

2. They act as catalysts.
3. a. More than one product is possible with an asymmetric molecule.
   b. The major product occurs when the hydrogen atom is removed from the carbon atom that has the most carbon-carbon bonds.
4. The hydrogen atoms of the small molecule will attach to the carbon of a double bond that is already bonded to the most hydrogen atoms. The rule is used when two products can be formed from an addition reaction.
5. No, if there is a limited amount of X-X, then a substituted alkene will be produced.
6. Carbons can only have up to four bonds, and alkanes are already fully saturated. Therefore, the carbons cannot accept any more bonding partners. Alkenes and alkynes are unsaturated and can break a double or triple bond in order to bond with another element/compound.
7. A substitution reaction occurs when the reactants are an alkane with a substituent of a halogen or an alcohol, and the other reactant is X-X or OH–. A condensation reaction occurs when the reactants are a carboxylic acid and an ammonia or amine. An esterification reaction occurs when the reactants are a carboxylic acid and an alcohol.
8. In a condensation reaction, two large molecules combine and form one larger molecule and a very small molecule, usually water. An esterification reaction is a special type of condensation reaction in which a carboxylic acid reacts with an alcohol to form an ester and water. In both reactions, two large molecules form one large molecule and one small molecule, which is typically water.
9. They are reactions that form large biomolecules that make up carbohydrates, fats, and DNA, which are essential to living things.
10. acetylsalicylic acid, artificial flavours, and artificial aromas
11. 9 esters; Each alcohol will react with each of the carboxylic acids. The ester names are methyl methanoate, methyl ethanoate, methyl propanoate, ethyl methanoate, ethyl ethanoate, ethyl propanoate, propyl methanoate, propyl ethanoate, and propyl propanoate.
12. a. esterification, because the product is an ester
    b. condensation, because the product is an amide
    c. substitution, because a halogen could replace an alcohol
13. A polymer is a large, long-chain molecule with repeating units of small molecules called monomers. Some uses are plastics, adhesives, and chewing gum.
14. In an addition reaction, the monomers are alkenes. In a condensation reaction, the monomers contain an OH group on either end of the molecule that is released. In both addition and condensation polymerizations, monomers join together to form polymers.
15. polyurethane
16. addition polymer: carbon atoms single-bonded together; condensation polymer: amide or ester linkages
17. amino acids
18. stronger and less flexible
19. cracking; The ethane is heated (800°C) to produce ethene.
20. The petrochemical is more reactive, and can therefore be converted more easily into other important compounds.
21. Ethene is reacted with chlorine to make dichloroethane. This is then cracked to produce HCl and chloroethane. Chloroethane is reacted in an addition polymerization reaction to make PVC.
22. advantages: very useful for industrial products such as windows, piping, and doors; disadvantage: vinyl chloride is a carcinogen
23. toxic by-products from the disposal of PVC
24. recycle plastics and purchase degradable plastics

Answers to Practice Problems
1. $H_3CCH_2CH_2CH_3$
3. Only one product is possible because if I (iodine) is added to carbon 1 or carbon 2, the same product is formed.
9. a. $H_2C=CHCH_2CH_3$, or $H_3CCH=CHCH_3$, or $HC\equiv CCH_2CH_3$, or $H_3CC\equiv CCH_3$
   b. $CH_2=CHCH_2CH_3$
13. $H_2C=CH-CH_3 + HOCH_2CH_3 + NaCl$
14. There are four products. Two are $HOCH_2CH_3$ and NaBr. The third occurs when the H is removed from carbon 2, and the fourth occurs when the hydrogen is removed from carbon 4.

22. Cl$_2$ and either HC≡C–CH$_2$CH$_3$ or H$_3$C–C≡C–CH$_3$
24. nine
26. bromobenzene + H$_2$O
27. bromobenzene + H$_2$
28. 2-hydroxypropane + Cl$^-$
31. CH$_3$CH$_2$CH$_3$ + Br$_2$
33. condensation reaction
34. esterification reaction
35. esterification reaction
36. esterification reaction
37. condensation reaction
38. octanol and ethanoic acid
39. methanol and butanoic acid
40. methanol and salicylic acid
41. 3,3-dimethylheptanoic acid + propan-1,2-diol
42. butanoic acid + propan-1-ol
43. oxidation
44. reduction
45. reduction
46. oxidation
47. addition and reduction
48. esterification and reduction
49. CH$_4$ + 2O$_2$ → CO$_2$ + 2H$_2$O + energy
50. C$_4$H$_8$ + 6O$_2$ → 4CO$_2$ + 4H$_2$O + energy
51. C$_3$H$_8$ + 5O$_2$ → 3CO$_2$ + 4H$_2$O + energy
52. C$_6$H$_{12}$O$_6$ + 6O$_2$ → 6CO$_2$ + 6H$_2$O + energy
53. addition
54. addition
55. condensation
56. polyamide
57. polyester
58. polyester

Answers to Chapter 2 Review Questions

1. d	8. b
2. d	9. b
3. a	10. b
4. d	11. a
5. d	12. d
6. a	13. e
7. c	14. a

35. **a.** 2C$_2$H$_6$ + 7O$_2$ → 4CO$_2$ + 6H$_2$O
    b. 2C$_2$H$_5$OH + 6O$_2$ → 4CO$_2$ + 6H$_2$O
66. **b.** 2C$_8$H$_{18}$(ℓ) + 25O$_2$(g) → 16CO$_2$(g) + 18H$_2$O(ℓ)

Answers to Chapter 2 Self-Assessment Questions

1. d	6. e
2. c	7. b
3. b	8. d
4. d	9. b
5. a	10. c

19. (CH$_3$)2CHCH=CHCH$_3$ + 9O$_2$ → 6CO$_2$ + 6H$_2$O

Answers to Unit 1 Review Questions

1. c	8. c
2. c	9. b
3. b	10. e
4. b	11. a
5. a	12. e
6. d	13. a
7. b	14. c

Answers to Unit 1 Self-Assessment Questions

1. b	6. b
2. e	7. d
3. b	8. b
4. b	9. b
5. e	10. a

Answers to Caption Questions

Figure 2.3 The carbon atoms in the product are bonded to more atoms than the carbon atoms in the organic reactant.
Figure 2.14 Possible responses: train cars linked together to form a long train, linking building blocks together

Answers to Section 2.1 Review Questions

5. **a.** C$_3$H$_8$(g) + 5O$_2$(g) → 3CO$_2$(g) + 4H$_2$O(ℓ)
   b. 2C$_4$H$_{10}$(ℓ) + 13O$_2$(g) → 8CO$_2$(g) + 10H$_2$O(ℓ)
   c. C$_{13}$H$_{28}$(ℓ) + 20O$_2$(g) → 13CO$_2$(g) + 14H$_2$O(ℓ)

Unit 2
Chapter 3

Answers to Learning Check Questions

1. Thomson's discovery of the electron in 1897 invalidated Dalton's atomic theory.

2. Alpha particles would have passed straight through the foil with minimal or no deflection from encounters or collisions with nearby electrons. There would be no deflection caused by the positive charge because Thomson's model postulates a uniform, positive charge spread throughout the atom.

3. Some radioactive elements emit positively charged alpha particles. Rutherford studied them and then used the alpha particles to bombard thin foils including gold foils. This led to the model in which all of the positive charge and most of the atom's mass were confined to a very small region at the centre of the atom, which Rutherford called the nucleus.

4. Diagrams should be based on Figures 3.3 and 3.6. Both models are spherical and include electrons and the positive charge. In Thomson's model, the positive charge is spread throughout the sphere and electrons are embedded in the sphere like raisins in a muffin. In Rutherford's model, the positive charge is found in a tiny, extremely dense nucleus and the electrons orbit the nucleus like planets.

5. Scientists tend to name their models, or other discoveries, after something that is common to their own everyday lives. Rutherford's model is sometimes called the planetary model.

6. In Thomson's model, negative charges were scattered evenly throughout a large positively charged mass. The alpha particles were highly energetic and would not be expected to be deflected very much by such atoms.

7. In a hydrogen atom, orbital energy depends only on n. For example, electrons in $2s$ and $2p$ have the same energy. In multi-electron atoms, orbitals in different sublevels have different energies associated with them, even if they have the same value of n. For example, $2s$ and $2p$ are associated with different energies.

8. a. $2s$, $2p$, $3s$, $3p$
   b. $3p$, $4s$, $3d$, $4p$
   c. $5s$, $4d$, $5p$, $6s$, $4f$, $5d$, $6p$, $5f$

9. An orbital is "full" when it contains two electrons.

10. Method one: There are five possible orbitals for $n = 1$ and $n = 2$: one $1s$ orbital, one $2s$ orbital, and three $2p$ orbitals. Each of these can contain a maximum of two electrons. Therefore, 10 electrons can occupy all possible orbitals with $n = 1$ and $n = 2$. Method two: Using the formula $2n^2$, $n = 1$ can contain two electrons and $n = 2$ can contain eight electrons, for a total of 10.

11. No. Two arrows pointing in the same directions would indicate that two electrons in the same orbital have the same spin quantum number. This violates the statement made in the Pauli exclusion principle that no two electrons can have the same four quantum numbers.

12. a. ☐ b. ↑ c. ↑↓

13. Orbitals fill in order of increasing energy. At energy levels above $n = 3$, the different sublevels overlap. As a result, the $5s$ orbital has a lower energy than the $4d$ orbitals.

14. boron: $1s^22s^22p^1$; [He]$2s^22p^1$
    neon: $1s^22s^22p^6$; [He]$2s^22p^6$

15. $1s^22s^22p^63s^23p^4$

16. ↑↓ | ↑ | ↑ | ☐
    $3s$ $3p$

17. a. sodium: $1s^22s^22p^63s^1$
    b. vanadium: $1s^22s^22p^63s^23p^64s^23d^3$

18. titanium: [Ar]$4s^23d^2$

Answers to Practice Problems

1. l can be 0, 1, or 2; for $l = 0$, $m_l = 0$; for $l = 1$, m_l can be -1, 0, or $+1$; for $l = 2$, m_l can be -2, -1, 0, 1, or 2; There are 9 orbitals.

2. $5d$; m_l can be -2, -1, 0, $+1$, or $+2$; There are five orbitals.

3. a. $n = 2$, $l = 0$, $m_l = 0$
   b. $n = 3$, $l = 1$, $m_l = -1$, 0, or $+1$
   c. $n = 5$, $l = 2$, $m_l = -2$, -1, 0, $+1$, or $+2$
   d. $n = 4$, $l = 3$, $m_l = -3$, -2, -1, 0, $+1$, $+2$, or $+3$

4. a. $2s$
   b. $5f$

5. a. 1
   b. 7
   c. 7
   d. 3

6. $n = 4$, $l = 2$, $m_l = -2$; $n = 4$, $l = 2$, $m_l = -1$; $n = 4$, $l = 2$, $m_l = 0$; $n = 4$, $l = 2$, $m_l = +1$; $n = 4$, $l = 2$, $m_l = +2$

7. **a.** $m_l = -1$
   b. $l = 3$
8. $n = 6, l = 1, m_l = -1$;
   $n = 6, l = 1, m_l = 0$ (many more)
9. Sample answers:
   a. $l = 2$ does not exist with $n = 1$;
   change $n = 1$ to $n = 3$
   b. $m_l = -2$ does not exist with $l = 1$;
   change $l = 1$ to $l = 2$
10. **a.** Allowed
    b. Not allowed; $l = 1$ does not exist with $n = 1$
    c. Not allowed; $n = 0$ does not exist
    d. Not allowed; m_l can be only -1, 0, or $+1$ when $l = 1$
11. $1s^2 2s^2 2p^6 3s^2 3p^6 4s^2 3d^{10} 4p^6 5s^2 4d^1$; [Kr]$5s^2 4d1$
12. $1s^2 2s^2 2p^6 3s^2 3p^6 4s^2 3d^{10} 4p^6 5s^2 4d^{10} 5p^6 6s^2 4f^{14} 5d^{10} 6p^2$;
    [Xe]$6s^2 4f^{14} 5d^{10} 6p^2$
13. Group 2 elements
14. Group 5; V, Nb, Ta, Db
15. The two exceptions are copper and chromium. The expected diagram for chromium would have a filled 4s orbital and four 3d orbitals containing one electron each (the fifth 3d orbital would be empty.) The expected diagram for copper would have a filled 4s orbital, four filled 3d orbitals, and one 3d orbital with one electron. The actual diagram for chromium has one electron in its 4s orbital and one electron in each of its five 3d orbitals. The actual diagram for copper has one electron in its 4s orbital and five filled 3d orbitals. The discrepancy arises because the predicted electron configurations have a slightly higher energy than the actual electron configurations. When the 3d orbitals are either all half-filled or all completely filled, the configuration becomes stable.
16. The configuration for the valence electrons, s^2, indicates that strontium is in Group 2.
17. **a.** nickel: [Ar]$4s^2 3d^8$
    b. lanthanum, La: [Xe]$6s^2 5d^1$
18. The value of 4 in $4s^2$ indicates that titanium is in Period 4.
19. The configuration of the valence electrons shows full s and d orbitals, but a half-full p orbital, so arsenic must be in the p block.
20. **a.** The electron configuration of the valence electron is s^1, so francium must be in Group 1 and belong to the s block. Because of the 7 in $7s^1$, francium must be in Period 7.
    b. The electron configuration of the valence electrons is $s^2 f^{14} d^4$, so tungsten must be in Group 6 (2 + 4) and belong to the d block. Because of the 6 in $6s^2$, tungsten must be in Period 6.
    c. The electron configuration of the valence electrons is $s^2 d^{10} p^3$, so antimony must be in Group 15 (2 + 10 + 3) and belong to the p block. Because of the 5 in $5s^2$, antimony must be in Period 5.

Answers to Caption Questions

Figure 3.3 These descriptions act as models for real structures that are complex or incapable of being seen. Each part of the model is related to a part of the real structure (for example, raisins represent electrons), so that it is easier to visualize the whole structure and its component parts.

Figure 3.16 4s is higher since it has the higher principal quantum number (even though it is filled before the 3d)

Answers to Section 3.1 Review Questions

11. **a.** $n = 2$
    b. $n = 5$

Answers to Section 3.2 Review Questions

8. **a.** 1
   b. 7
   c. 3
   d. 5
   e. 1
   f. infinite
9. Three sets: $n = 3, l = 1, m_l = 0$; $n = 3, l = 1, m_l = -1$; $n = 3, l = 1, m_l = 1$
18. **a.** 2
    b. 8
    c. 18
    d. 32

Answers to Chapter 3 Review Questions

1. b
2. a
3. c
4. a
5. e
6. d
7. a
8. a
9. b
10. d
11. e
12. a
13. c
14. d
69. [Uuo]$8s^2 5g^7$

Answers to Chapter 3 Self-Assessment Questions

1. c
2. a
3. d
4. e
5. d
6. a
7. e
8. d
9. c
10. a

Chapter 4

Answers to Learning Check Questions

1. Three types of bonding are ionic, covalent, and metallic. All chemical bonds involve the electrons of atoms interacting with the other atoms of the same or different elements.

2. The general trend is for electronegativity to decrease down a group and increase across a period from left to right. Electronegativity values are a measure of how strongly an atom of a given element attracts shared electrons in a bond. A comparison of the electronegativity of two elements that are bonded gives information about the characteristics of the bond.

3. Bonds with a ΔEN between 1.7 and 3.3 are classified as mostly ionic. Bonds with a ΔEN between 0.4 and 1.7 are classified as polar covalent. Bonds with a ΔEN between 0.0 and 0.4 are classified as mostly (non-polar) covalent.

4. Since metal atoms cannot attract and hold electrons of other atoms well enough to form filled valence shells, the valence electrons of metals in the solid or liquid state have the ability to move freely from one atom to the next. The electrons are said to be *delocalized*, because they do not remain in one location. This is often referred to as the electron-sea model of metals, in which a metal is described as being a relatively ordered array of cations in a "sea" of freely moving electrons, with the positively charged ions all being attracted to many of the electrons in the "sea" simultaneously.

5. False. Change "disordered" to "relatively ordered" array of cations.

6. Metals are made up of aggregates of millions of tiny crystals, called grains, which range in size from a few nanometres to several millimetres, depending on the metal and the conditions under which it has formed. The atoms of the crystals (grains) form precise, regularly repeating patterns, whereas the atoms at the boundaries between grains are arranged randomly.

7. High melting and boiling points indicate strong attractions between atoms. A large amount of kinetic energy is required to pull the particles apart. The kinetic energy of the particles is directly related to the temperature of the substance. A high temperature will be required to provide sufficient kinetic energy to cause melting and boiling.

8.

Periodic Table	Trend	Explanation
Down a group	Decrease	As you go down a group, the atoms have one more electron shell than atoms in the previous group. Therefore, the free valence electrons are progressively farther from the nucleus and the strength of the attractive forces decreases, resulting in lower melting and boiling points.
Across a period (except for metals with electrons in d orbitals)	Increase	The number of valence electrons increases across a period and the ions have a larger positive charge. The larger number of electrons in the "electron sea" and the larger charge on the ions result in a stronger attractive force. As the ions are held in place more tightly, the melting and boiling points increase.
Group 12	Decrease	Since d shells in Group 12 are filled, electrons cannot freely move away from the atom. There are fewer electrons in the "electron sea." There will be less attraction between the positively charged ions and the electrons in the "electron sea." The melting and boiling points decrease.

9. The valence electrons in metals are free to move from one atom to another. When a potential difference is applied to a piece of metal, the electrons are drawn toward the positive end and repelled from the negative end. Similarly, metals conduct heat when freely moving electrons receive kinetic energy from the source of heat and pass the energy along to other electrons.

10. Metals can be hammered or stretched without breaking, because the ions in the metal crystals can slide past one another without a change in the sea of electrons that surrounds them. Refer to **Figure 4.6**.

11. The hardness of a metal depends on the size of its crystalline grains. Metals are malleable because the atoms in a crystal can slide over one another. The boundaries of grains resist this sliding, because the atoms are not aligned in layers that slide smoothly. A metal that has a very large number of small crystals has a greater boundary surface and is harder than a metal that has a larger grain size with fewer boundaries.

12. Similarity (overlap): In both types of alloys, electrons attract any kind of positive ion so that all the ions are held together in the same "sea."

    Differences: In a substitutional alloy, the atoms of the different metals are similar in size and one kind of atom readily takes the place of a different kind. In an interstitial alloy, atoms of one or more of the alloy metals are smaller than those of another metal and will fit into spaces between the larger atoms, making this type of alloy stronger.

13. A crystal lattice is a three-dimensional pattern of alternating positive and negative ions in an ionic solid. The ratio of positive to negative ions in a crystal lattice is the smallest whole-number ratio of ions in the crystal and is called a formula unit.

14. The relative size and the charge on ions affect how they pack together so that oppositely charged ions are as close together as possible.

15. Similarities: In one formula unit of each compound, the ratio of positive ion to negative ion is 1:1 and both form cubic-shaped crystals.

    Differences: In NaCl, each Na^+ is surrounded by 6 Cl^-, and each Cl^- is surrounded by 6 Na^+; the Na^+ and Cl^- alternate in a row; Na^+ and Cl^- alternate above and below one another; the Na^+ is about half as large as Cl^-. In CsCl, each Cs^+ is surrounded by 8 Cl^-, and each Cl^- is surrounded by 8 Cs^+; layers of Cs^+ alternate with layers of Cl^-; layers of oppositely charged ions are offset so that Cs^+ is not directly above a Cl^-; Cs^+ is more than twice as large as Cl^-.

16. **a.** High melting point in 900°C range and boiling point in 1500°C range
    b. Hard and brittle
    c. Not malleable
    d. Good electrolyte, conducts an electric current
    e. Non-conductor of electric current

17. This is a cut-away three-dimensional image in which the ions on the sides of each unit cell are shared by the next unit cell. If you add up the "halves" and "eights" of the ions, you will find a total of four sodium ions and four chloride ions.

18. For an ionic compound to be soluble in water, the attractive forces between the ions and the water molecules must be stronger than the attractive forces among the ions themselves. For ionic solids of low solubility, the attractive forces between the ions are stronger that the attractive forces between the ions and the water molecules.

19. A covalent bond exists because of electrostatic forces. The nuclei of both atoms exert attractive forces on both of the shared electrons. Repulsive forces exist between positive nucleus and positive nucleus, and between negative electron and negative electron. The bond between two atoms occurs at a distance where the repulsive forces balance the attractive forces.

20. A σ bond is a bond that is formed by the overlap of half-filled atomic orbitals that are symmetrical around the bond axis of the two nuclei; for example, overlap of two half-filled s orbitals, two half-filled p orbitals, or half-filled s and p orbitals. The σ bond formed has an energy level that is lower than the energy of the half-filled atomic orbitals, making the molecule more stable than the separate atoms.

21. [Ne] $3s^2 3p^2$

    Mix one $3s$ orbital with three $3p$ orbitals to produce four $3sp^3$ orbitals.

22. Ethene is a planar molecule, meaning that all of its atoms lie in the same plane. All of the bond angles in the molecule are approximately 120° and there are three orbitals of the carbon atoms that form a plane. This planar structure is explained by three sp^2 hybrid orbitals formed by mixing the $2s$ orbital and two of the $2p$ orbitals of carbon. One σ bond forms by the overlap of a half-filled sp^2 hybrid orbital along the axis between the two carbon atoms, and the other sp^2 hybrid orbitals from each carbon overlap with the half-filled s orbital

from a hydrogen atom. These are also σ bonds. The lobes of the half-filled pure *p* atomic orbital not hybridized from each carbon atom overlap above and below the axis of the σ bond to form a π bond between the two carbon atoms.

23. Like a hybrid offspring resulting from crossing two species, a hybrid orbital results from the combination of atomic orbitals of the valence electrons. For example, a sp^2 hybrid orbital results from combining one *s* atomic orbital and two *p* atomic orbitals.

24. $$H—C≡N:$$
    The triple bond between the carbon atom and the nitrogen atom consists of one sigma bond and two pi bonds.
    One σ bond forms by the overlap of a half-filled *sp* orbital of C with a half-filled 2*p* orbital of N. Two π bonds form from the overlap of the half-filled *p* orbital from C with two of the half-filled 2*p* orbitals of N. The second half-filled *sp* orbital of C overlaps with the half-filled 1*s* orbital of H to form a σ bond.

25. Drawing a Lewis structure for a molecule shows how many electrons are involved in each bond, as well as how many, if any, lone pairs of electrons are present.

26. A line represents a shared pair of electrons or a covalent (or polar covalent) bond.

27. A co-ordinate covalent bond is a covalent bond in which one of the atoms contributes both of the shared electrons. Refer to **Figure 4.27**.

28. An expanded valence refers to more than eight electrons in the valence shell of a bonded atom. This is possible for a central atom that forms hybrid orbitals that include *d* orbitals, such as sp^3d and sp^3d^2 hybrids. Refer to $SF_6(g)$ in **Figure 4.28**.

29. Carbon cannot have an expanded valence as a central atom because it does not have *d* orbitals in the second energy level, and the *d* orbitals in its third energy level are too high in energy to combine with *s* or *p* orbitals in the second energy level.

30. This Lewis structure is not accurate because experimental evidence has indicated that all of the oxygen–oxygen bonds are the same in length and energy. In this depiction of the molecule, there are single and double bonds that would be of different bond lengths. The structure is explained by using two Lewis diagrams, which if "averaged," would give the accurate picture. These representations are called hybrid resonance structures.

31. $$\left[\begin{array}{c} H—\ddot{O}—H \\ | \\ H \end{array} \right]^+$$
    Oxygen is sp^3 hybridized from mixing one 2*s* orbital with three 2*p* orbitals producing four sp^3 orbitals. Three of the sp^3 orbitals form a bond with hydrogen atoms and the fourth sp^3 orbital becomes the lone pair.

32. sp^3d

33. sp^2

34. **a.** sp^3, the N–H bond angle is a little less than the tetrahedral angle, about 107°.
    b. sp^3, the N–H bond angle is the tetrahedral angle of 109.5°.

35. The condensed configuration for Br is $[Ar]4s^23d^{10}4p^5$. To form hybrid orbitals, the bromine atom uses the 4*s* orbital, three 4*p* orbitals, and two 4*d* orbitals to give six sp^3d^2 hybrid orbitals. Five of these hybrid orbitals are half-filled and bond with the five F atoms. The other contains a lone pair of electrons. The overall shape is square pyramidal.

36. The condensed configuration for Cl is $[Ne]3s^23p^5$. To form hybrid orbitals, the chlorine atom uses the 3*s* orbital, three 3*p* orbitals, and one 3*d* orbital to give five sp^2d hybrid orbitals. Three of these hybrid orbitals are half-filled and bond with the three F atoms. The other two contain two non-bonding electrons. The overall shape is T shaped.

Answers to Practice Problems

11. **a.** trigonal planar
    b. square pyramidal
12. **a.** 32
    b. 24
13. **a.** 4 BP, 0 LP
    b. 2 BP, 0 LP
    c. 4 BP, 2 LP
    d. 2 BP, 1 LP
14. bent
15. trigonal pyramidal
16. tetrahedral
17. tetrahedral, 109.5°
18. trigonal planar
19. OF_2, NF_3, CF_4, BF_3, BeF_2
20. trigonal bipyramidal; seesaw; octahedral

Answers to Caption Questions

Figure 4.1 For the transition elements, electrons are added to d orbitals, which are filled after the $(n + 1)s$ orbital in any period. The effect of the nuclear charge on this shell will vary, depending on the number of electrons, affecting the size of the atom and the atom's electronegativity to varying degrees.

Figure 4.15 Current will flow through a solution if charged particles are free to move independently. When an ionic compound is dissolved in water, the ions are free to move past one another and will migrate to the electrodes. This will be registered as current flow on the conductivity meter.

Figure 4.35 The molecule CH_3OH is polar. The molecular shape is tetrahedral but the C–O and O–H bonds are polar. This results in a permanent dipole in the molecule.

Figure 4.36 The strength of a dipole-dipole force depends on the size of the charge difference between the two poles of the molecule. This depends on the difference in the electronegativity of the two atoms in the molecule that results in it being polar. For example, the polarity of the F–Cl molecule is different from the polarity of the F–Br molecule because Cl and Br have different electronegativity values.

Answers to Section 4.1 Review Questions

7. a. H–N is the most covalent; ΔEN for H–N $= 0.9$; ΔEN for H–O $= 1.4$; ΔEN for H–F $= 1.9$
 b. O–O is the most covalent; ΔEN for O–O $= 0.00$; ΔEN for O–N $= 0.5$; ΔEN for O–C $= 1.0$

8. a. mostly ionic; $\Delta EN = 3.2$
 b. mostly covalent; $\Delta EN = 0.0$
 c. polar covalent; $\Delta EN = 0.5$
 d. mostly ionic; $\Delta EN = 2.5$

9. a. One s orbital, three p orbitals, and one d orbital
 b. Five hybrid orbitals

Answers to Chapter 4 Review Questions

1. e
2. d
3. c
4. a
5. d
6. b
7. c
8. d
9. a
10. c
11. b
12. c
13. a
14. e

32. a. H–F is the most ionic; ΔEN for H–Cl $= 0.9$; ΔEN for H–Br $= 0.7$; ΔEN for H–F $= 1.9$
 b. K–O is the most ionic; ΔEN for Na–O $= 2.6$; ΔEN for Li–O $= 2.5$; ΔEN for K–O $= 2.7$

33. a. ionic; $\Delta EN = 2.0$
 b. covalent; $\Delta EN = 0.0$
 c. polar covalent; $\Delta EN = 0.5$
 d. ionic; $\Delta EN = 2.6$

Answers to Chapter 4 Self-Assessment Questions

1. d
2. b
3. e
4. e
5. b
6. d
7. b
8. a
9. b
10. e

14. a. CaO
 b. KCl
 c. RbCl

15. a. $\Delta EN = 1.8$, therefore ionic
 b. $\Delta EN = 3.1$, therefore ionic
 c. $\Delta EN = 1.0$, therefore polar covalent
 d. $\Delta EN = 0.0$, therefore covalent

21. a. trigonal pyramidal
 b. trigonal planar
 c. linear
 d. square pyramidal

Answers to Unit 2 Review Questions

1. b
2. a
3. d
4. e
5. e
6. a
7. a
8. c
9. c
10. b
11. e
12. e
13. a
14. b
15. d
31. **a.** B: [He]$2s^22p^1$; B^{3+}: $1s^2$
    b. Mg: [Ne]$3s^2$; Mg^{2+}: [He]$2s^22p^6$
    c. S: [Ne]$3s^23p4$; S^{2-}: [Ne]$3s^23p^6$
    d. K: [Ar]$4s^1$; K$^+$: [Ne]s^23p^6
    e. H: $1s^1$; H$^+$: no electrons
32. **i.** c
    ii. a
    iii. b
    iv. c
    v. b
34. carbon
35. iodine
36. **a.** Group 1
    b. i. [Uuo 118]$8s^1$
    ii. $n = 8, l = 0, m_l = 0, ms = +\frac{1}{2}$ or $-\frac{1}{2}$
42. **a.** nitrogen (1), oxygen (2), fluorine (3), neon (4)
    b. beryllium (1), boron (1), carbon (1), nitrogen (1), oxygen (2), fluorine (3), neon (4)
43. **a.** polar covalent; $\Delta EN = 1.3$
    b. mostly covalent; $\Delta EN = 0.0$
    c. polar covalent; $\Delta EN = 1.4$
    d. mostly ionic; $\Delta EN = 3.1$
57. **a.** [Kr]$5s^24d^{10}5p^4$

59. **i.** d
    ii. c
    iii. b
    iv. a
    v. b
    vi. c
    vii. a
    viii. d
    SiF$_4$ forms a tetrahedron; XeF$_4$ forms a square plane
60. **a.** [Xe]$6s^2$
    b. Group: 2; period: 6; block: *s*
61. **a.** iron
    b. Group: 8; period: 4
62. **a.** oxygen
    b. [He]$2s^22p^4$
    c. Group: 16; period: 2; block: *p*

Answers to Unit 2 Self-Assessment Questions

1. b
2. d
3. e
4. b
5. c
6. a
7. e
8. d
9. c
10. d
14. Co
16. **a.** $m_l = -1, 0, +1$
    b. $5p$
    c. 3

UNIT 3

Chapter 5

Answers to Learning Check Questions

1. Sample answer: The heating element on an electric stove transfers heat to a pot of water; hot water in a wash basin transfers heat to your hands; a person exercising transfers body heat to the surrounding air.

2. A closed system can exchange energy with its surroundings in forms such as thermal energy, mechanical energy, and chemical energy.

3. Constant pressure and volume

4. The burning of fuel in an automobile occurs in an open system. It is not possible to isolate the combustion reaction that occurs in an automobile engine. Under laboratory conditions, the combustion of a fuel could be studied in a controlled manner. The second law of thermodynamics would be valid. This tells us that when studying chemical reactions, the immediate surroundings must be isolated from the system for the results to be accurate.

5. An endothermic process is one in which the enthalpy or heat content of the system increases. Thermal energy is added to the system. An exothermic process is one in which the enthalpy or heat content of the system decreases. Thermal energy is given off from the system.

6. a. The products have greater potential energy.
   b. The enthalpy of the system is increasing; the reaction is endothermic; the enthalpy change is positive.

7. The enthalpy term is a product in a thermochemical equation. This is because it is a negative value, which means the energy is released.

8. Energy is given off from the system, so the products have less potential energy than the reactants.

9. $C_2H_6(g) + \frac{7}{2}O_2(g) \rightarrow 2CO_2(g) + 3H_2O(\ell) + 1560.7$ kJ

10. The diagram should indicate that the vertical scale measures enthalpy in kilojoules per mole. The reactants, $C_3H_6(\ell) + \frac{9}{2}O_2(g)$, are at a higher energy level than the products, $3CO_2(g) + 3H_2O(\ell)$, by 2091.3 kJ.

11. $C_7H_6O_2(s) + \frac{15}{2}O_2(g) \rightarrow 7CO_2(g) + 3H_2O(\ell) + 3228.2$ kJ

    $\Delta H°_{comb} = -3228.2$ kJ/mol of $C_7H_6O_2(s)$

12. (1) $C_2H_4O_2(\ell) + 2O_2(g) \rightarrow 2CO_2(g) + 2H_2O(\ell) + 972.6$ kJ

    (2) $2C_3H_6O_2(\ell) + 7O_2(g) \rightarrow 6CO_2(g) + 6H_2O(\ell) + 3184.4$ kJ

    (3) $C_3H_6O_2(\ell) + \frac{7}{2}O_2(g) \rightarrow 3CO_2(g) + 3H_2O(\ell) + 1592.2$ kJ

    More heat is given off for $C_3H_6O_2(\ell)$ than for $C_2H_4O_2(\ell)$; 972.6 kJ/mol. The standard molar enthalpy of combustion for $C_3H_6O_2(\ell)$ is −1592.2 kJ/mol.

13. For any physical or chemical process, the overall enthalpy change is the sum of the enthalpy changes of its individual steps and depends only on the initial and final conditions. The enthalpy change can be determined for reactions that are either very slow or are too dangerous to carry out under laboratory conditions.

14. The standard conditions are SATP (25°C or 298.15 K, and 100 kPa) and aqueous solutions have a concentration of 1 mol/L.

15. The amount (in moles) of product must be the same in both reactions.

16. The enthalpy diagram should have the same shape. Since the process is reversed, the arrows point upward to show the absorption of energy, an endothermic process. ΔH for the reaction $CO(g) + \frac{1}{2}O_2(g) \rightarrow CO_2(g)$ will be +110.5 kJ, and ΔH for the overall reaction will be +393.5 kJ.

17. Calorimetry experiments can be used to find the enthalpy of reaction for simpler steps. No, as data for a large number of reactions is known. Any combination of these reactions that total to the overall reaction can be used.

18. Hess's law is valid because the enthalpy change is determined only by the initial and final conditions of the system.

19. $C_2H_4(g) + H_2O(\ell) \rightarrow C_2H_5OH(\ell)$ $\Delta H = -74.4$ kJ

    In the enthalpy diagram, the reactants, $C_2H_4(g) + H_2O(\ell)$, are 74.4 kJ higher in energy than the product, $C_2H_5OH(\ell)$.

20. efficiency $= \frac{\text{energy output}}{\text{energy input}} \times 100\%$

21. In Canada, there are large reserves of natural gas, and the infrastructure to deliver and use this energy source is firmly established. It is more economical to look at how we can conserve use of energy, rather than switch from this readily available source.

22. The use has a low efficiency (as low as 30%) and there are serious environmental issues both in the production and use, such as the emissions of greenhouse gases that increase global warming and nitrogen oxides that contribute to the formation of acid rain and smog.

23. Advantages: use of nuclear energy produces no greenhouse gas emissions; once set up, the reactor is efficient to maintain; is a reliable and long-term source; radioactive isotopes can be a by-product from related nuclear reactions that are important for treatment of some diseases Disadvantages: must store radioactive waste by-product for thousands of years; high initial set-up cost; susceptibility to environmental disasters that can result in radioactive leaks into the air and water

24. Deforestation (strip mining for coal); thermal pollution of natural habitats (warming of water in lakes and rivers used to cool power plants); hazardous to birds and creates noise pollution (wind turbines) and air pollution (burning of fossil fuels)

25. A non-renewable energy source is effectively gone once it is used up; for example, oil, natural gas, coal, uranium. A renewable energy source can be replenished or is so large a source that it will not be used up; for example, wind, solar, geothermal, biomass.

Answers to Practice Problems

1. +4.06 kJ
2. +16.5 kJ
3. +6.10 kJ
4. The liquid in beaker B absorbs twice as much heat because it has twice the mass.
5. $+2.14 \times 10^2$ kJ
6. Specific heat capacity is 0.7899 J/g·°C; it is granite.
7. 11.1 g
8. 1.95°C
9. +3.154 kJ
10. **a.** ΔT for hydrogen is 3.496°C; the temperature change of the hydrogen gas is much less than the change for air.
    b. The molecules that make up air have a greater mass than hydrogen molecules. There will be more molecules in 10.0 g of $H_2(g)$ than in 10.0 g of air. The absorbed energy will be distributed among a larger number of $H_2(g)$ molecules and each will gain less energy than in the air sample.
11. **a.** −438.62 kJ
    b. −701.80 kJ
    c. −584.83 kJ
12. −136.7 kJ
13. **a.** −2742 kJ
    b. -6.51×10^4 kJ
    c. -1.126×10^6 kJ
14. −55.5 kJ
15. 12.43 g
16. 23.8 kg
17. **a.** −2058.0 kJ/mol
    b. +244 kJ
18. **a.** -2.2×10^3 kJ/mol
    b. propane
19. 20.2 g
20. **a.** $CH_3CH(OH)CH_3(\ell) + \frac{9}{2}O_2(g) \rightarrow 3CO_2(g) + 4H_2O(\ell) + 2006$ kJ
    b. −695.8 kJ
21. −75.5 kJ/mol
22. −55.0 kJ/mol
23. -2.9×10^2 kJ/mol
24. −27.4 kJ/mol
25. The temperature increases by 0.853°C.
26. −41.9 kJ/mol
27. The temperature increases by 1.31°C.
28. The initial temperature was 21.8°C.
29. The temperature increases by 30.9°C.
30. −54.47 kJ/mol KOH
31. 616°C
32. -3.9×10^3 kJ/mol
33. 2.00 g
34. +20.3 kJ/g
35. −25 kJ/g
36. −711 kJ/mol
37. **a.** -1.38×10^3 kJ/mol
    b. $C_2H_4(g) + 3O_2(g) \rightarrow 2CO_2(g) + 2H_2O(g) + 1.38 \times 10^3$ kJ
38. The temperature will increase by 8.81°C.
39. 2.93 g
40. −1780 kJ/mol
41. **a.** −55.3 kJ
    b. $2NO_2(g) \rightarrow N_2O_4(g) + 55.3$ kJ

42. −635.7 kJ
43. −817.6 kJ
44. −147.5 kJ
45. −219.6 kJ
46. −205.9 kJ
47. −1124.0 kJ
48. −395 kJ
49. +52.6 kJ
50. −128.8 kJ
51. a. $C_2H_5OH(\ell) + 3O_2(g) \rightarrow 2CO_2(g) + 3H_2O(g)$
    b. −1235 kJ/mol $C_2H_5OH(\ell)$
52. −176.2 kJ
53. a. −158.3 kJ
    b. 52.3 g
54. −902 kJ
55. −102.7 kJ/mol
56. −224.2 kJ/mol
57. −130.8 kJ
58. +20.4 kJ/mol
59. −1857.3 kJ/mol
60. − 478.8 kJ/mol
61. 16%
62. 69.5%
63. 38.7%
64. 0.812 g
65. a. +13.4 kJ
    b. $+7.36 \times 10^3$ kJ
66. a. $+1.82 \times 10^4$ kJ
    b. $+3.18 \times 10^4$ kJ; 36.4%
67. +155 MJ
68. a. 2.2×10^4 J
    b. 3.6×10^4 J
    c. 62%
69. a. 2.78 g
    b. +273 kJ
    c. 4.92 g
70. 77.9%

Answers to Caption Questions

Figure 5.2 Equipment, air, water (that will be added to the beaker)
Figure 5.3 An open system can exchange both energy and matter with its surroundings. Water vapour and heat escape into the air (surroundings). A closed system can exchange energy, but not matter, with its surroundings. Water and potatoes do not escape, but heat energy does escape into the air. An isolated system cannot exchange anything with its surroundings. Since the pot is insulated and there is a lid, neither heat nor matter can escape to the surroundings.
Figure 5.16 In addition to gases, thermal energy can also escape through the holes.
Figure 5.18 To maximize the transfer of heat to the can rather than to the air around the can
Figure 5.24 Graphite is the more stable form of carbon, because diamond has a greater potential energy, as shown by its higher standard molar enthalpy of formation.
Figure 5.30 2010: coal + gas = 43%

Answers to Section 5.1 Review Questions

2. $+2.4 \times 10^4$ J
3. a. $^{14}_{6}C \rightarrow ^{14}_{7}N + ^{0}_{-1}e$
   b. $^{1}_{0}n \rightarrow ^{1}_{1}p + ^{0}_{-1}e$
   c. $^{55}_{26}Fe + ^{0}_{-1}e \rightarrow ^{55}_{25}Mn +$ energy
5. −6.6 kJ
6. −67.4°C
7. The air temperature will change by 41.5°C.

Answers to Section 5.2 Review Questions

3. 5.0×10^2 J
8. a. −55.3 kJ/mol
   b. $KOH(aq) + HNO_3(aq) \rightarrow$
      $KNO_3(aq) + H_2O(\ell) + 55.5$ kJ
11. −14.8 kJ/g

Answers to Section 5.3 Review Questions

2. $\frac{1}{2}N_2(g) + \frac{5}{2}H_2(g) + C(s) + \frac{3}{2}O_2(g) \rightarrow$
   $NH_4HCO_3(s) + 849.4$ kJ
3. $H_2(g) + \frac{1}{8}S_8(s) + 2O_2(g) \rightarrow H_2SO_4(\ell) + 814.0$ kJ
4. −103.0 kJ
5. −277 kJ
6. −549 kJ/mol
9. a. −3347.6 kJ
   b. $+6.660 \times 10^6$ kJ
11. −266 kJ/mol
13. +895.2 kJ

Answers to Section 5.4 Review Questions

10. a. $CO_2(g)$ (primarily)
    b. $CO_2(g), NO_2(g), SO_2(g)$
    c. $NO_2(g)$

12. 72.0%

14. 0.2801 g

Answers to Chapter 5 Review Questions

1. b
2. c
3. b
4. c
5. c
6. e
7. a
8. d
9. b
10. d
11. a
12. c
13. c
14. d
29. −1128.4 kJ
30. −96.7 kJ
32. a. $Cu(NO_3)_2(s) + 302.9 \text{ kJ} \rightarrow Cu(s) + N_2(g) + 3O_2(g)$
 b. +181 kJ
34. a. +327 kJ/mol
 b. $Pb(\ell) \rightarrow Pb(s) + 327 \text{ kJ}$
35. $\frac{1}{4}P_4(s) + \frac{3}{2}Cl_2(g) \rightarrow PCl_3(g)$, $\Delta H_f° = -71.9$ kJ/mol
36. −289.2 kJ
37. −601.6 kJ/mol
38. −319.5 kJ
40. The calorimeter will change temperature by 88.3°C.
41. a. −45.4 kJ/mol
 c. 29.3%
42. 4.59 g
43. a. 309 kJ/mol
 b. $C_2N_2(g) \rightarrow 2C(s) + N_2(g) + 309 \text{ kJ}$
45. +32.8 kJ/mol
46. 90%
61. −31.9 kJ/g
62. a. The temperature of the water is expected to increase by 50.2°C.

Answers to Chapter 5 Self-Assessment Questions

1. d
2. c
3. d
4. b
5. b
6. c
7. e
8. a
9. e
10. a
13. $+1.1 \times 10^8$ kJ
14. 30.7°C
15. $I_2(s) + 20.85 \text{ kJ} \rightarrow I_2(\ell)$
16. −58.2 kJ/mol
17. 400.0 mL
18. −109.5 kJ
21. $+1.2 \times 10^3$ kJ
22. a. −33.15 kJ/g
 b. +22.36 kJ
23. 17 g

Chapter 6

Answers to Learning Check Questions

1. Measure the change in mass of the reactant, limestone, over a period of time or the amount of product, $CO_2(g)$, generated over a period of time.

2. It does not give information about the concentration of the reactants or products and does not indicate whether the reaction will proceed by itself or if additional energy will be required.

3. Since the concentration increases from 0.25 mol/L to 0.420 mol/L, product was measured.

4. The graph should show that the tangent is a line drawn between two points on a concentration vs. time graph that are brought closer and closer until they converge to one point in time. The instantaneous rate is calculated by measuring the slope of this tangent. This is done by determining the rise and the run and dividing the rise by the run. The rise is the change in concentration and the run is the change in time.

5. a. A = 30; B = 10
 b. The average rate of reaction can be determined using the number of molecules of A that are

consumed or the number of molecules of B that are formed over a period of time. Draw a secant from $t = 0$ s to $t = 10$ s on either curve. The slope of this secant represents the average rate of change in the number of molecules of A and B, respectively.

c. The average rate of change in the number of molecules of A and of B is the same.

6. The average rate. It represents how long the fruit could be left on the shelf. The instantaneous rate indicates how fast the fruit was spoiling at one point in time.

7. The particles must collide with the proper orientation to one another and have sufficient kinetic energy to overcome the potential energy barrier between reactants and products.

8. Many collisions have the wrong collision geometry, and only a fraction of the collisions are between particles with sufficient energy to overcome the potential energy barrier.

9. The angle at which the reactants collide must be the same as the new bond will be when the products form.

10. Diagrams for exothermic reactions show reactants with a higher potential energy than the potential energy for the products. Diagrams for endothermic reactions show reactants with a lower potential energy than that for the products.

11. a. The minimum collision energy required for reaction between reactant particles.
    b. Only the particles having kinetic energy equal to or greater than E_a will react when collision occurs. For a reaction at room temperature with a high E_a, there will be few particles having sufficient energy to overcome the energy barrier.

12. The enthalpy change, the activation energy, and whether the reaction is endothermic or exothermic. The enthalpy change is the difference between the initial (reactants) and final (products) potential energies. The activation energy is the difference between the initial potential energy and the maximum potential energy. The relative values of the potential energy of the reactants and products indicate whether it is an endothermic or exothermic reaction.

13. The greater the activation energy, the slower the rate; the lower the activation energy, the faster the rate

14. a. The flame increases the energy of a few reactant particles so that when collisions occur, the reactant particles have energy equal to or greater than the activation energy. After a few reactions occur, they release enough energy to provide energy for the rest of the paper particles.
    b. It is an exothermic process. The thermal energy given off provides the energy for more particles to react.

15. It does not show the activation energy, which is expected to be high. Graphite and diamond have a different arrangement of carbon atoms. Carbon–carbon bonds must be broken and the atoms re-arranged.

16. a. An unstable, temporary chemical species, including the reactant and product; it will break apart to form product or return to reactants.
    b. The nitrogen atom in the NO collides with an oxygen atom in the NO_3. Student sketches should show dotted lines indicating new bonds forming between the N of NO and the O of NO_3 and dotted lines indicating the breaking of bonds between the O and N of NO_3.

17. Exothermic; $\Delta H = E_{a(fwd)} - E_{a(rev)}$
    $= 45$ kJ $- 50$ kJ $= -5$ kJ

18. Since the reaction is endothermic, student sketches should indicate the products with higher potential energy than the reactants; the difference between the two values is 89 kJ.

19. Any change that increases the number of collisions between reactant particles will increase the rate of reaction. Any change that decreases the number of collisions between reactant particles will decrease the rate of reaction.

20. A change in the nature of the reactant(s); a change in the concentration of the reactant(s); a change in temperature; a change in pressure, if the reactants are gases; a change in the total surface area of the reactant material; and by introducing a catalyst

21. Only collisions between reactant particles having kinetic energy equal to or exceeding the activation energy will lead to formation of product. At lower temperatures, there are fewer reactant particles with sufficient kinetic energy.

22. The rate of rusting could be slowed down by reducing the number of collisions between Fe(s) and O_2(g). A decrease in temperature and covering the iron with a protective coating would do this.

23. Sawdust and plant material have a larger total exposed surface area than the pellets and there will be many more collisions between reactant particles.

As successful collisions occur, heat is given off, which rapidly leads to more collisions between particles having kinetic energy greater than the activation energy. The result is a rapid, uncontrollable, and possibly explosive burning. This is not desirable for a fuel. It is more important for fuels to burn slowly so that the heat from this burning can be distributed for a required use.

24. Since the temperature is already high, an increase in temperature would not be expected to have much effect. The high temperature suggests that there are sufficient collisions for a reaction to occur, so changing the concentration of the reactants would not be expected to have much effect. Introducing a catalyst would seem to have the best chance of changing the rate.

25. A catalyst will lower the activation energy of a reaction. This can make it possible for a reaction to occur at conditions that are safer and less costly. A catalyst may also speed up a very slow reaction to make a process more economical.

26. The shape of the surface will be important in determining if a substance can act as a catalyst. The surface of the catalyst must have sites to which a reactant particle can attach. These sites provide an alternate way for the reactants to combine that has a lower activation energy.

27. **a.** Diagrams should have the following: "Potential Energy" represented on the y-axis and "Reaction Progress" represented on the x-axis; products with lower potential energy than reactants; potential energy of products the same for catalyzed and uncatalyzed reactions; potential energy of reactants the same for catalyzed and uncatalyzed reactions; the transition state at a lower potential energy for the catalyzed reaction than for the uncatalyzed reaction.
    b. For both the forward and reverse reactions, the activation energy is lower in the presence of a catalyst so that more of the collisions have the energy necessary to overcome the energy barrier and thus form products.
    c. The catalyst has no effect on the potential energy of the reactants or products, so there is no change in ΔH.

28. Petroleum refineries, pulp and paper mills, and steel mills are closely monitored for emissions because the by-products of their processes are environmentally harmful. Oxides of carbon, sulfur, and nitrogen lead to such problems as global warming, smog formation, acid rain, and ozone depletion, and they are often major contributors to respiratory problems in humans.

29. **a.** $N_2(g) + 3H_2(g) \rightleftharpoons 2NH_3(g) + 92.6 \text{ kJ}$
    b. The reaction is slow at room temperature. A higher temperature increases the rate of reaction. This also increases the rate of the reverse reaction.
    c. The catalyst is composed of iron and small amounts of potassium oxide and aluminum oxide. It provides an alternate path for the reaction that has a lower activation energy. Molecules of $H_2(g)$ and $N_2(g)$ form bonds with the metal catalyst, weakening the covalent bonds that hold the molecules together. The reactant molecules split into atoms and these atoms recombine to form $NH_3(g)$. The $NH_3(g)$ quickly leaves the surface of the metal.

30. A chemist studies why and how a reaction occurs. Fritz Haber was a chemist and was able to determine the temperature and type of catalyst for the conversion of $N_2(g)$ and $H_2(g)$ to $NH_3(g)$. A chemical engineer determines how a reaction can be made efficient and profitable on a large scale. Carl Bosch was a chemical engineer. Both scientists contributed to different aspects of this process. A team of researchers can contribute expertise from a variety of disciplines, resulting in a greater chance of developing a product.

31. The observed rate of a reaction is affected by the rate of the reverse reaction that may occur. The only accurate datum for the relationship between the concentration of a reactant and the reaction rate is the point at which there is no product—at time zero.

32. The reaction rate at a time at which there is no product present—time zero

33. A graph of concentration of reactant vs. time is plotted for a reaction. The initial rate of reaction is measured by drawing a line tangent to this curve at $t = 0$ and then determining the slope of this line.

34. Carry out several experiments, each one starting with a different concentration of reactant. Draw graphs of concentration vs. time for each experiment and determine the initial rate by measuring the slope of the tangent for each at $t = 0$. Plot a graph of initial rate vs. starting concentration.

35. If the curve is linear, rate = $k[A]$; the reaction is first order. If the curve is parabolic, rate = $k[A]^2$; the reaction is second order.

36. m is the order of the reaction with respect to reactant A, n is the order of the reaction with respect to reactant B, and the proportionality constant, k, is called the *rate constant*. The order of the overall reaction is $m + n$. For a reaction, k, m, and n can be determined graphically. Carry out several investigations, each one starting with a different concentration of reactant. Draw graphs of concentration vs. time for each investigation and determine the initial rate by measuring the slope of the tangent for each at $t = 0$. Plot a graph of initial rate vs. starting concentration. The type of curve indicates if the reaction is first or second order.

Answers to Practice Problems

1. -4.74×10^{-5} mol/L·s
2. 7×10^{-4} mol/L·s
3. **a.** 0.165 mol
   b. 0.165 mol $Br_2(aq)$
4. 1.4 mol/L
5. 5.0×10^{-4} L/s
6. rate of formation of $BrO_3^-(aq) = 0.060$ mol/L·s; rate of consumption of $BrO^-(aq) = 0.18$ mol/L·s
7. **a.** 0.0032 mol/L·s
   b. 0.080 mol/L
8. 1.40×10^2 mol/L
9. **a.** 2.42×10^{-4} mol/s
   b. 2.98×10^{-3} L/s
10. 0.70 mol/L·s $Cl_2(g)$ consumption; NOCl(g) is produced at a rate of 1.4 mol/L·s
11. Diagrams should contain the following: "Potential Energy" on y-axis; "Reaction Progress" on x-axis; $E_{a(fwd)}$ is the energy between the reactants and the transition state; $E_{a(rev)}$ is the energy between the transition state and the products; ΔH_r is the energy between the reactants and the products.
    a. Endothermic
    b. Products
12. Diagrams should indicate the following: the reactants have a lower potential energy than the products; $E_{a(fwd)}$ is the energy between the reactants and the transition state (+99 kJ); Ea(rev) is the energy between the transition state and the products (+34 kJ); and ΔH_r is the enthalpy of reaction between the reactants and the products (+65 kJ).
13. Diagrams should indicate the following: the reactants have a higher potential energy than the products; $E_{a(fwd)}$ is the energy between the reactants and the transition state (+61 kJ); $E_{a(rev)}$ is the energy between the transition state and the products (+150 kJ); and ΔH_r is the enthalpy of reaction between the reactants and the products (−89 kJ).
14. $E_{a(fwd)} = +42$ kJ; $E_{a(rev)} = +67$ kJ; $\Delta H_r = -25$ kJ; exothermic
15. $E_{a(rev)} = +411$ kJ; energy diagrams should indicate the reactants having higher potential energy than the products with $E_{a(fwd)}$ being the energy between the reactants and the transition state (+19.0 kJ); $E_{a(rev)}$ is the energy between the transition state and the products (+411 kJ); and ΔH_r is the enthalpy of reaction between the reactants and the products (−392 kJ).
16. **a.** $E_a = 112$ kJ − 36 kJ = +76 kJ; $\Delta H = 78$ kJ − 36 kJ = +42 kJ
    b. Potential energy diagrams should indicate the reactants having lower potential energy than the products and the activated complex having the highest potential energy, positioned between the reactants and products.
17. **a.** $CH_4(g) + 2O_2(g) \rightarrow CO_2(g) + 2H_2O(\ell) + 890.8$ kJ
    b. Since $CH_4(g)$ easily ignites with a spark, the activation energy for the combustion reaction would be expected to be small. The activated complex would be an unstable association of $CH_4(g)$ and $O_2(g)$.
18. Diagrams should indicate the reactants having higher potential energy than the products and the activated complex having the highest potential energy, positioned between the reactants and products. $\Delta H_r = E_{a(fwd)} − E_{a(rev)}$; $E_{a(fwd)} = +49.5$ kJ
19. Diagrams should indicate the reactants having lower potential energy than the products and the activated complex having the highest potential energy, positioned between the reactants and products.
20. $\Delta H_r = E_{a(fwd)} − E_{a(rev)}$; $E_{a(fwd)} = +320$ kJ

Answers to Caption Questions

Figure 6.7 Some of the aqueous solution could escape from the flask, increasing the mass lost and making the reaction rate appear to be faster than it actually is.

Figure 6.8 The first four collisions shown are ineffective because the orientations of the reactants do not allow a reaction to occur and products to form. In the effective collision, the best orientation of the collision creates the same geometry that will exist in the products.

Figure 6.15 The T_1 curve uses blue cross-hatching to indicate the area that represents the relative number of collisions with sufficient activation energy, and the T_2 curve uses a red cross-hatched area to indicate the same.

Figure 6.16 A catalyst does not change the enthalpy, ΔH.

Figure 6.17 Part A: the hydrogen and nitrogen molecules bind to the surface of the catalyst; part B: the molecules dissociate into H and N atoms; part C: the highly reactive H and N atoms react to form ammonia molecules.

Figure 6.18 The reaction can proceed more quickly because there are more sites available on which a reaction can occur.

Answers to Section 6.1 Review Questions

3. -2.9×10^{-4} mol/L·s
4. 6.37×10^{-7} g/s
5. 132 s
12. Consumption of $O_2(g)$: 0.10 mol/L·s; formation of $H_2O(g)$: 0.12 mol/L·s

Answers to Section 6.2 Review Questions

11. -160 kJ

Answers to Section 6.3 Review Questions

10. a $Cl_2(g) + CHCl_3(g) \rightarrow CCl_4(g) + HCl(g)$
11. b. $+80.0$ kJ
    d. $+60.0$ kJ
    e. $+20.0$ kJ
    f. -30.0 kJ

Answers to Chapter 6 Review Questions

1. d
2. b
3. c
4. a
5. e
6. d
7. d
8. b
9. d
10. e
11. a
12. d
13. c
14. d
16. a. mL/s
    b. kPa/s
    c. pH/s
29. $+5.0 \times 10^2$ kJ
30. $+3.1 \times 10^2$ kJ
32. $+7 \times 10^2$ kJ
33. $+4.7 \times 10^2$ kJ
34. -1.7×10^2 kJ
35. $+1.7 \times 10^2$ kJ
36. 0.26 mol/L·min
37. 0.018 g/s
38. a. III
    b. IV
    c. III
    d. II
40. 1.6×10^{-5} mol/s
42. a. $+20$ kJ
61. 59 g/s
62. a. 1.14×10^{-3} mol/L·s
63. 1.54×10^2 mol/min

Answers to Chapter 6 Self-Assessment Questions

1. a
2. e
3. b
4. d
5. d
6. e
7. c
8. d
9. d
10. b
13. 22 mL/s
16. -64 kJ
19. 4.7×10^{-3} mol/L·s

Answers to Unit 3 Review Questions

1. a
2. d
3. c
4. a
5. c
6. b
7. e
8. d
9. b
10. e
12. c. $H_2O(g) \rightarrow H_2O(\ell) + 40.7$ kJ

15. b. Step 3
    c. C to E
    d. B, C, F
26. −285.4 kJ
27. a. $NH_4NO_3(s) + 25.69 \text{ kJ} \rightarrow NH_4^+(aq) + NO_3^-(aq)$
    b. $C_5H_{11}OH(\ell) + \frac{15}{2}O_2(g) \rightarrow$
       $\quad 5CO_2(g) + 6H_2O(\ell) + 3330.9 \text{ kJ}$
    c. $6C(s) + 3H_2(g) + \frac{1}{2}O_2(g) \rightarrow$
       $\quad C_6H_5OH(s) + 164.9 \text{ kJ}$
28. −2.14 kJ
29. a. $CH_4(g) \rightarrow CH_4(\ell) + 8.19 \text{ kJ/mol}$
    b. +51.0 kJ
30. For NH_3: −226 kJ/mol; for O_2: −181 kJ/mol; for NO: −226 kJ/mol; for H_2O: −151 kJ/mol
31. 7.8°C
32. a. −1367 kJ/mol
    b. ethanol
33. b. 112.2 g
34. 1.11 kg
35. a, b, d, e, and f
36. a. +25.8 kJ
    b. −41.69 kJ
    d. 61.8%
37. −455.2 kJ/mol
38. 181 kg
39. +197.8 kJ
40. a. −49.5 kJ
    b. +49.5 kJ
    c. 38.6°C
    d. 2.31×10^{-4} mol/s
41. a. 1.00×10^{-5} mol/L·s
    b. 5.00×10^{-6} mol/L·s
42. $t = 0$ s: 0.0050 mol/L·s; $t = 30$ s: 0.00020 mol/L·s; average rate: 0.00075 mol/L·s
44. 3.00×10^{-2} mol/L·s
45. a. $H_2O_2(aq) + 2I^-(aq) + 2H^+(aq) \rightarrow$
       $\quad 2H_2O(\ell) + I_2(aq)$
46. b. $N(g)$ and $N_2O(g)$
    c. $2H_2(g) + 2NO(g) \rightarrow N_2(g) + 2H_2O(g)$
47. $\dfrac{\text{mol}^{\frac{2}{3}}}{L^{\frac{2}{3}} \cdot s}$
48. $2I^-(aq) + S_2O_8^{2-}(aq) \rightarrow I_2(aq) + 2SO_4^{2-}(aq)$
49. 3.2×10^{-3} mol/L·s
50. a. rate = $k[NO][H_2]^2$
51. +14.4 kJ
52. a. rate = $k[A][B]$
    b. 2
67. a. 16.2 kg
    b. 3.71 mol/min
69. −44 kJ
70. a. $NO_2Cl_2 \rightarrow NO_2Cl + Cl$
71. c. $k = 0.19$ L/mol·s
    d. rate = 4.5×10^{-2} mol/L·s
73. b. −98.0 kJ

Answers to Unit 3 Self-Assessment Questions

1. e
2. d
3. c
4. b
5. a
6. d
7. b
8. d
9. b
10. c
12. +33.8 kJ/mol
15. -2.22×10^{14} kJ
16. −538.0 kJ/mol
17. 67.0 %
22. a. $2NO_2(g) + Br_2(g) \rightarrow 2NO_2Br(g)$
    b. step 2
    c. 1

UNIT 4
Chapter 7

Answers to Learning Check Questions

1. A reversible reaction is a reaction that can proceed in both the forward and the reverse directions.
2. The double arrows indicate that the reaction is reversible.
3. The rope-pulling team as a whole (comparable to a chemical system) may not appear to be moving, but the individual participants (comparable to particles in a chemical system) are engaged in movement to maintain their position.
4. Equilibrium does not mean an equal balance in concentrations of reactants and products but, rather, a balance in the reaction rates of the forward and reverse processes.
5. Changing: the reaction is still occurring, so reactants still form products while products are re-forming reactants

   Balanced: these two processes are occurring at the same rate
6. $CO(g) + 3H_2(g) \rightleftharpoons CH_4(g) + H_2O(g)$
7. Only the liquid and the water vapour in the sealed jar can reach equilibrium, because it is the only system that is closed to the surroundings.
8. Similarities: both involve a balance in forward and reverse reaction rates, and both involve constant macroscopic properties.

   Differences: different states of matter exist in the heterogeneous equilibrium, whereas all substances in a homogeneous equilibrium are in the same state.
9. If the stopper were removed, the iodine gas would escape, thus preventing the reverse reaction from occurring. As a result, the open system could not reach equilibrium.
10. The law of mass action states that there is a constant ratio between the concentrations of products and the concentrations of reactants. This ratio (where the balanced coefficients of the reaction are used as exponents) is the equilibrium constant.
11. If a chemical system is not at equilibrium, then it is not accurate to write an equilibrium constant expression or a constant. A reaction quotient is written for chemical systems when they are not at equilibrium.
12. If $K_{eq} > 1$, the denominator of the equilibrium constant is less than the numerator, and since the denominator contains information regarding reactants, product formation is favoured. If $K_{eq} \approx 1$, the numerator is approximately equal to the denominator, and approximately equal concentrations of reactants and products exist. If $K_{eq} < 1$, the denominator of the equilibrium constant is greater than the numerator, and since the denominator contains information regarding reactants, reactant formation is favoured.
13. When an external influence (such as a change in temperature or pressure) on a system at equilibrium causes a change, the system will eventually move to a new equilibrium.
14. The forward reaction is favoured, as initially more reactant particle collisions will occur, which temporarily increases the rate of the forward reaction, until equilibrium is restored.
15. You exhale $CO_2(g)$, which causes a decrease in the carbon dioxide gas concentration in the system. As a result, the reaction will shift in the forward direction to form more $CO_2(g)$ and this causes a decrease in the carbonic acid level in the blood.
16. The addition of the inert gas will increase the pressure inside the container, but it does not have an effect on the equilibrium, as this increase in pressure affects the reactants and products equally, so both rates of reaction remain the same.
17. With a pressure increase (due to a volume decrease), the system will shift to favour the reaction that takes up the smaller volume, which will be in the direction of the lesser amount in moles of gas. With a pressure decrease (due to a volume increase), the system will shift to favour the reaction that takes up the larger volume, which will be in the direction of the greater amount in moles of gas.
18. a. No change d. No change
    b. No change e. No change
    c. No change f. No change
19. Similarities: both involve a difference in thermal energy during the reaction. Differences: exothermic reactions give off thermal energy, whereas endothermic reactions absorb thermal energy.
20. a. When heated, the endothermic reaction (that is, forward reaction) is favoured to absorb the heat added, and more heat is available to enable the reaction to occur.
    b. The product concentrations will increase and the reactant concentrations will decrease.

21. The time needed to reach equilibrium is reduced when a catalyst is added, but the equilibrium is not shifted in either direction.

22. There is no change in the K_{eq} value when a catalyst is added, because there is no change in the amount of reactant or product; rather, the rate of the reaction changes.

23. a. The endothermic reaction (that is, the reverse reaction) is favoured to absorb the heat added.
b. The product concentration will decrease and the reactant concentration will increase.

24. In question 20, the forward reaction is an endothermic reaction. When the system is heated, the product concentrations increase and the reactant concentrations decrease. Because the equation for K_{eq} involves product concentrations divided by reactant concentrations, K_{eq} increases. In question 23, the forward reaction is exothermic. When the system is heated, the reverse reaction is favoured and the reactant concentrations increase and the product concentrations decrease. K_{eq} decreases because the numerator is decreasing and the denominator is increasing.

25. Pressure can be used to monitor this reaction, or colour intensity can be used (dinitrogen tetroxide is colourless, whereas nitrogen dioxide is a dark-brown colour).

26. K_{eq} is calculated using the equilibrium concentrations of the products and reactants at a given temperature.

27. Within experimental error, the investigation reveals that K_{eq} is a constant for a reaction, even when concentrations vary.

28. K_p represents the equilibrium constant calculated using partial pressures of the gases in the system.

29. K_p uses partial pressures of all gases at a constant temperature, unlike K_{eq} that uses concentrations.

30. The units of partial pressure and the units for pressure in R must be the same.

31. When initial concentrations of reactants and K_{eq} are given, an ICE table should be used to calculate equilibrium concentrations.

32. Any equation of the form $ax^2 + bx + c = 0$ is a quadratic equation.

33. When the expression involving the x is not a perfect square or cannot be factored, the quadratic formula must be used to solve the problem.

34. Any negative roots (as a negative concentration has no meaning) and any root that exceeds initial concentrations must be eliminated, leaving the other root as the correct answer.

35. The approximation method can be used to solve equilibrium calculations when the K_{eq} value is extremely small.

36. In general, if the initial concentrations are at least 1000 times greater than the value of K_{eq}, the approximation method can be used.

37. If $K_{eq} = 4.7 \times 10^{-9}$ and the initial concentrations of reactants are approximately 1.0 mol/L, the approximation method can be used.

38. Nitrogen narcosis occurs with an elevated concentration of nitrogen in the blood, which can cause a diver to experience symptoms of intoxication.

39. To avoid the bends, a diver must surface slowly, allowing the extra dissolved gases in the blood to leave solution slowly.

40. If inhaled, carbon monoxide binds the hemoglobin protein (which would normally bind to the oxygen that cells need). The carbon monoxide binds more readily than does the oxygen and thus does not let go as easily. As a result, there is a decreased capacity for the blood to carry oxygen to the cells in need of the oxygen. This can lead to death.

41. Since the carbon monoxide binds more readily to the hemoglobin, the equilibrium constant for the reaction with $CO(g)$ would be larger than that for the reaction with oxygen.

42. The increased pressure in the chamber, coupled with an increased oxygen level in the chamber, causes a shift in the equilibrium process and the toxic gases are removed from the blood.

43. Increased amounts of carbon dioxide in the atmosphere cause less calcium carbonate to be available because of a shift in the equilibrium reaction of calcium carbonate, calcium ions, and carbonate ions, and as a result, there is less calcium carbonate available to coral polyps for making shells. Thus, the corals grow more slowly.

44. The supply of sodium nitrate from Chile to Germany could easily have been interrupted or even cut off in the years around 1900, and so a method of producing ammonia without sodium nitrate was important.

45. At this temperature, the reaction occurs too slowly to be economically viable.

46. Haber ran the reaction at relatively high pressures and low temperature, but also added a catalyst to reduce the time needed for the reaction to reach a position of equilibrium.

47. Carl Bosch was an engineer who solved the engineering problems associated with the high pressures used in the process.

48. The amount of sulfuric acid manufactured in a country is an indicator of the general economy of the country, because sulfuric acid is used in so many processes; an increase in its production is an indicator that the manufacturing processes that require the acid are doing well.

49. Since the final steps in the production of sulfuric acid occur in an aqueous solution, increasing pressure will have no effect on the system.

Answers to Practice Problems

1. $K_{eq} = \dfrac{[CH_3COOCH_2CH_3][H_2O]}{[CH_3CH_2OH][CH_3COOH]}$

2. $K_{eq} = \dfrac{[NO]^2}{[N_2][O_2]}$

3. $K_{eq} = \dfrac{[H_2O]^2}{[H_2]^2[O_2]}$

4. $K_{eq} = \dfrac{[NO]^4[H_2O]^6}{[NH_3]^4[O_2]^5}$

5. $K_{eq} = \dfrac{[H_2]^4[CS_2]}{[H_2S]^2[CH_4]}$

6. $K_{eq} = \dfrac{[Cl_2][SbCl_3]}{[SbCl_5]}$

7. $K_{eq} = \dfrac{[N_2][H_2O]^2}{[H_2]^2[NO]^2}$

8. a. $2SO_3(g) \rightleftharpoons 2SO_2(g) + O_2(g)$

   b. $K_{eq} = \dfrac{[SO_2]^2[O_2]}{[SO_3]^2}$

9. a. $2NO(g) + O_2(g) \rightleftharpoons 2NO_2(g)$

   b. $K_{eq} = \dfrac{[NO_2]^2}{[NO]^2[O_2]}$

10. a. $4HCl(g) + O_2(g) \rightleftharpoons 2H_2O(g) + 2Cl_2(g)$

   b. $K_{eq} = \dfrac{[H_2O]^2[Cl_2]^2}{[HCl]^4[O_2]}$

11. $K_{eq} = [NH_3][HCl]$

12. $K_{eq} = \dfrac{[H_2S]}{[H_2]}$

13. $K_{eq} = \dfrac{1}{[CO_2]}$

14. $K_{eq} = \dfrac{[CO]^2}{[CO_2]}$

15. $K_{eq} = [CO_2][H_2O]$

16. $K_{eq} = \dfrac{[NH_4^+][OH^-]}{[NH_3]}$

17. $K_{eq} = \dfrac{[Fe_3O_4][H_2]^4}{[H_2O]^4}$

18. $2Mg(s) + O_2(g) \rightleftharpoons 2MgO(s)$

$K_{eq} = \dfrac{1}{[O_2]}$

19. $H_2(g) + I_2(s) \rightleftharpoons 2HI(g)$

$K_{eq} = \dfrac{[HI]^2}{[H_2]}$

20. $K_{eq} = \dfrac{[CO_2]}{[O_2]}$

21. The reaction shifts to the left, because the reverse reaction is endothermic.

22. As the reaction proceeds, there is no change in the number of gas molecules on each side of the equation. Therefore, increasing the volume of the container has no effect on the position of equilibrium.

23. There are more gas molecules on the left side of the equation. Therefore, increasing the volume of the container causes the reaction to shift to the left.

24. There are more gas molecules on the right side of the equation. Therefore, increasing the volume of the container causes the reaction to shift to the right.

25. There are more gas molecules on the right side of the equation. Therefore, increasing the volume of the container causes the reaction to shift to the right.

26. Increase the concentration of methyl cyclohexane; increase the temperature to increase the rate of the endothermic reaction; remove some of either product from the equilibrium system; increase the volume or decrease the pressure of the reaction container

27. a. Right
   b. No change
   c. Left

28. Only change (c) affects the value of K_{eq}. A change in pressure, or the addition of an inert gas, does not change K_{eq}. A temperature change affects the forward and reverse reactions differently. So the value of K_{eq} changes when the temperature changes.

29. **a.** Left
    b. No change

30. Neither change affects K_{eq} because changing the concentration of reactants and products or adding a catalyst does not affect K_{eq}.

31. **a.** $K_{eq} = \dfrac{[N_2][H_2]^3}{[NH_3]^2}$
    b. 0.017

32. 0.060 mol/L

33. 1.2×10^2

34. 83.3 mol/L

35. 0.046 mol/L

36. 0.11 mol/L

37. The concentration of NO(g) is very small at this temperature, owing to the small value of K_{eq}.

38. 0.013

39. 1.9×10^{-2}

40. 8.90×10^{-2} mol

41. 8.9

42. 42

43. 3.74

44. 2.7

45. 8.99

46. 0.48

47. 5.61 atm

48. 4.4 atm

49. 2.3 atm

50. 1.38 atm

51. 3.0×10^1

52. $[I_2] = [Cl_2] = 0.015$ mol/L; $[ICl] = 0.14$ mol/L

53. 4.7

54. $[H_2] = [Br_2] = 2.9 \times 10^{-6}$ mol/L; $[HBr] = 0.045$ mol/L

55. $[PCl_3] = [NO_2] = 0.42$ mol/L; $[POCl_3] = [NO] = 0.82$ mol/L

56. $[N_2] = [O_2] = 3.3 \times 10^{-2}$ mol/L; $[NO] = 0.23$ mol/L

57. Amount of $H_2(g)$ = amount of $I_2(g) = 0.78$ mol; amount of HI(g) = 5.47 mol

58. Amount of CO(g) = amount of $H_2O(g) = 0.74$ mol; amount of $CO_2(g)$ = amount of $H_2(g) = 1.51$ mol

59. Amount of $Br_2(g)$ = amount of $Cl_2(g) = 2.36$ mol; amount of BrCl(g) = 12.70 mol

60. Amount of $O_3(g)$ = amount of NO(g) = 0.45 mol; amount of $NO_2(g)$ = amount of $O_2(g) = 1.17$ mol

61. $[H_2] = [CO] = 2.07$ mol/L; $[H_2O] = 0.18$ mol/L

62. $[N_2O_4] = 0.15$ mol/L; $[NO_2] = 0.37$ mol/L

63. $[C_2H_4] = 0.24$ mol/L; $[H_2] = 0.43$ mol/L; $[C_2H_6] = 0.10$ mol/L

64. Amount of hydrogen gas = 0.180 mol; amount of iodine gas = 1.16 mol; amount of hydrogen iodide gas = 3.40 mol

65. $[CO] = 1.25$ mol/L; $[Cl_2] = 0.04$ mol/L; $[COCl_2] = 1.10$ mol/L

66. Amount of $PCl_3(g) = 0.86$ mol; amount of $NO_2(g) = 0.64$ mol; amount of $POCl_3(g)$ = amount of NO(g) = 1.00 mol

67. $[PCl_3] = 0.08$ mol/L; $[Cl_2] = 0.64$ mol/L; $[PCl_5] = 0.73$ mol/L

68. Amount of $N_2(g) = 0.286$ mol; amount of $O_2(g) = 1.76$ mol; amount of NO(g) = 2.09 mol

69. $[CO] = 0.73$ mol/L; $[H_2O] = 1.48$ mol/L; $[CO_2] = [H_2] = 0.74$ mol/L

70. $[SO_2] = 2.11$ mol/L; $[Cl_2] = 1.10$ mol/L; $[SO_2Cl_2] = 1.04$ mol/L

71. $[CO] = [Cl_2] = 1.8 \times 10^{-4}$ mol/L

72. $[H_2] = 9.5 \times 10^{-2}$ mol/L

73. $[CO_2] = 0.60$ mol/L; $[CO] = 1.1 \times 10^{-2}$ mol/L; $[O_2] = 5.6 \times 10^{-3}$ mol/L

74. 6.1×10^{-5} mol/L

75. $[NO] = 1.2 \times 10^{-5}$ mol/L

76. 1.8×10^{-4} mol/L

77. $[O_2(g)] = 1.71 \times 10^{-9}$ mol/L; $[SO_2(g)] = 3.41 \times 10^{-9}$ mol/L

78. $[CO] = 1.05 \times 10^{-2}$ mol/L; $[O_2] = 5.25 \times 10^{-3}$ mol/L

79. 2.7×10^{-5} mol/L

80. 2.1×10^{-3} mol/L

81. $Q_{eq} = 95.9$; therefore, the reaction is not at equilibrium and is shifting to the left.

82. $Q_{eq} = 3.00$; therefore, the reaction is not at equilibrium and is shifting to the right.

83. $Q_{eq} = 0.77$; therefore, the reaction is not at equilibrium and is shifting to the left.

84. $Q_{eq} = 6.0 \times 10^{-2}$; therefore, the reaction is approximately at equilibrium.

85. $Q_{eq} = 12.8$; therefore, the reaction will shift to the right.

86. $Q_p = 27.2$; therefore, the reaction is not at equilibrium and is shifting to the left.

87. $Q_p = 2.60$; therefore, the reaction is not at equilibrium and is shifting to the right.

88. The reaction will shift to the right, as the Q_{eq} would be equal to 1.0.

Answers to Caption Questions

Figure 7.1: Initially, only nitrogen and hydrogen molecules are in the container. Some of these molecules collide and form ammonia molecules. As the number of ammonia molecules increases, the frequency of collisions that occur among ammonia and the other molecules increases and some of the ammonia molecules break apart and nitrogen and hydrogen molecules re-form. At the same time, there are fewer nitrogen and hydrogen molecules present, so the frequency of their collisions decreases. At equilibrium, the collisions that form ammonia occur at the same rate as the collisions that re-form the nitrogen and hydrogen molecules.

Figure 7.4: The diagram should show a pile of solid iodine crystals with gaseous iodine molecules above the pile of crystals. The diagram should have labels identifying these two groups of particles. The diagram should show gaseous iodine molecules with low kinetic energy combining with particles of the solid iodine crystals with high kinetic energy, forming gaseous iodine molecules. There should be labels on the diagram identifying and describing these two processes.

Figure 7.6 At the beginning of the reaction, there are no nitrogen dioxide molecules present in the bottle; only dinitrogen tetroxide molecules are present. Over time, the dinitrogen tetroxide molecules decompose and the concentration of nitrogen dioxide increases. At equilibrium, the processes of the molecules composing and decomposing are balanced.

Figure 7.17: When thermal energy is added to an endothermic reaction, the rate of the reaction increases, because more thermal energy is available for the reaction. When thermal energy is removed from an endothermic reaction, the rate of the reaction slows down because there is less energy available for the reaction. The rate changes in an exothermic reaction are not as dramatic as those in an endothermic reaction. An exothermic reaction will occur at a slightly faster rate when thermal energy is added to the system, but because energy is not required for the reaction to occur, the change is not as significant as in an endothermic reaction.

Figure 7.18: Initially, the concentrations of N_2O_4 and NO_2 are equal. As the reaction proceeds, some N_2O_4 molecules break apart and form two NO_2 molecules. The concentration of NO_2 is greater because two molecules of it form from every molecule of N_2O_4 that breaks apart.

Answers to Section 7.3 Review Questions

1. a. $K_{eq} = \dfrac{[H_2]^4[CS_2]}{[H_2S]^2[CH_4]}$

b. $K_{eq} = \dfrac{[P_2O_3]^2}{[P_4][O_2]^3}$

c. $K_{eq} = \dfrac{[N_3S_4]^2[N_2S_2]^4}{[N_2]^7[S_8]^2}$

2. 3.32 mol/L

4. 1.2 mol

5. a. 3.5×10^{-7} mol/L

6. a. $K_p = \dfrac{P_{H_2O}}{P_{CO} P_{H_2}}$

b. $K_p = \dfrac{P_{HI}^2}{P_{H_2} P_{I_2}}$

c. $K_p = \dfrac{P_{CO_2} P_{H_2}}{P_{CO} P_{H_2O}}$

d. $K_p = \dfrac{P_{CH_4}}{P_{H_2}^2}$

8. a. $K_{eq} = [As_4][CO]^6$

b. 15.3

Answers to Chapter 7 Review Questions

1. d
2. a
3. c
4. e
5. d
6. a
7. b
8. d
9. d
10. e
11. c
12. b
13. c

28. a. $K_{eq} = \dfrac{[CO_2]^3[H_2O]^4}{[C_3H_8][O_2]^5}$

b. $K_{eq} = \dfrac{[NO]^2[H_2O]^2}{[N_2H_4][O_2]^2}$

c. $K_{eq} = \dfrac{[Cu(NH_3)_4^{2+}]}{[Cu^{2+}][NH_3]^4}$

31. a. $K_p = \dfrac{P_{CO}\, P_{H_2}}{P_{H_2O}}$

b. Since no substances are in the gas phase, a K_p expression does not exist for this system.

c. $K_p = \dfrac{P_{H_2O}^3}{P_{H_2}^3}$

d. $K_p = \dfrac{P_{NOCl}^2\, P_{PCl_3}}{P_{PCl_5}\, P_{NO}^2}$

32. b

34. 0.85 mol

35. a. $4HCl(g) + O_2(g) \rightleftharpoons 2H_2O(g) + 2Cl_2(g)$

b. $K_{eq} = 1.7 \times 10^{-2}$

36. 0.39 mol/L

37. In experiment 1, $K_{eq} = 4.35$; in experiment 2, $K_{eq} = 4.31$. Within experimental error, these two can be considered the same value.

42. At equilibrium, $\text{rate}_{forward} = \text{rate}_{reverse}$
$\text{rate}_{forward} = k_{forward}[NO_2]^2$
$\text{rate}_{reverse} = k_{reverse}[N_2O_4]$
The equilibrium constant expression is defined as the ratio of reaction rates:
$k_{forward}[NO_2]^2 = k_{reverse}[N_2O_4]$

$\dfrac{k_{forward}}{k_{reverse}} = \dfrac{[N_2O_4]}{[NO_2]^2}$

$K_{eq} = \dfrac{[N_2O_4]}{[NO_2]^2}$

43. $4NH_3(g) + 5O_2(g) \rightleftharpoons 4NO(g) + 6H_2O(g); K_{eq} = 0.26$

63. a. $Q_{eq} = 74.5$

64. 1.3×10^{-3} mol/L

66. $[H_2] = [I_2] = 0.261$ mol/L; $[HI] = 1.76$ mol/L

Answers to Chapter 7 Self-Assessment Questions

1. a
2. d
3. c
4. e
5. e
6. e
7. c
8. 1.57 mol/L
20. $[NO] = 2.0 \times 10^{-2}$ mol/L; $[Cl_2] = 1.0 \times 10^{-2}$ mol/L
21. $K_{eq} = 806$
22. $Q_p = 18.4$
24. $P_{NOBr} = 0.16$ atm

Chapter 8

Answers to Learning Check Questions

1. An Arrhenius acid is a substance that contains hydrogen in its chemical formula, and it ionizes in water to form the hydronium ion, H_3O^+(aq). An Arrhenius base is a substance that contains OH in its chemical formula, and it ionizes in water to form the hydroxide ion, OH^-(aq).

2. A Brønsted-Lowry acid is a proton donor or any substance that donates a hydrogen ion. Such acid must contain hydrogen in its formula, for example, HCl and HNO_3. A Brønsted-Lowry base is a proton acceptor or any substance that accepts a hydrogen ion. Such base must have a lone pair of electrons to bind with the hydrogen ion. The hydroxide ion, OH^-(aq), does not have to be present.

3. Two molecules or ions that differ because of the transfer of a proton are called a conjugate acid-base pair. The acid of an acid-base pair has one more proton than its conjugate base.

4. The conjugate base of an acid is the particle that remains when a proton is removed from the acid. The conjugate acid of a base is the particle formed when the base receives the proton from the acid.

5. A proton or hydrogen ion, H^+(aq), is released from the acid. This positively charged hydrogen ion from the acid is attracted to the negatively charged electrons on the surrounding water molecules. This results in the formation of a hydronium ion, H_3O^+(aq).

6. Arrhenius acids all contain a hydrogen ion, and Arrhenius bases all contain the hydroxide ion. Brønsted-Lowry acids are proton donors, and Brønsted-Lowry bases are proton acceptors. The definitions of Arrhenius acids and bases depend upon the presence of water to produce hydronium and hydroxide ions, whereas the Brønsted-Lowry definitions for acid and bases do not.

7. A strong acid fully dissociates in water, whereas a weak acid partially dissociates, setting up an equilibrium system.

8. A strong base fully dissociates in water, whereas a weak base partially dissociates, setting up an equilibrium system.

9. A strong acid readily donates a proton to solution, whereas a strong base readily accepts a proton in solution.

10. Hydroiodic acid is a much stronger acid than water, as it is located more toward the top of the acid column of the table, which is organized with the stronger acids at the top of the column.

11. Multiple answers exist, as long as the amine is of the form R3N, with R representing either a hydrogen atom (in the case of ammonia) or carbon groups (in the case of amines). These are classified as Brønsted-Lowry bases, because they all accept protons in solution from the hydrogen ion.

12. Multiple possible reactions exist here, as long as the base chosen is from the bottom of the conjugate base side of the table (where the stronger bases are found).

13. A base-dissociation constant is the equilibrium constant for the ionization of a base in water.

14. A strong base would form more ions in solution, causing it to have a higher percent dissociation in solution.

15. Hydrofluoric acid is a monoprotic acid, as it can only donate one proton into solution per acid molecule.

16. A base forms ions in solution, but it does not dissociate in solution.

17. A triprotic acid would have three acid-dissociation constants, as the triprotic acid can go through three processes in which a proton is donated to solution in each step.

18. There would be three reactions for this ion:
$$PO_4^{3-}(aq) + H_2O(\ell) \rightleftharpoons HPO_4^{2-}(aq) + OH^-(aq)$$
$$HPO_4^{2-}(aq) + H_2O(\ell) \rightleftharpoons H_2PO_4^-(aq) + OH^-(aq)$$
$$H_2PO_4^-(aq) + H_2O(\ell) \rightleftharpoons H_3PO_4(aq) + OH^-(aq)$$

19. In a neutralization reaction, an acid and a base combine to form water and a salt.

20. Both have charges, but their charges are opposite to each other. Cations are positive and anions are negative.

21. This indicates that water is a requirement of the reaction, but is not considered a reactant in the process.

22. It neutralizes excess stomach acid (HCl) that may be present. As $OH^-(aq)$ reacts, more of the $Mg(OH)_2(s)$ dissolves. There is never excess $OH^-(aq)$ present in the stomach.

23. The common-ion effect is the effect on an equilibrium system of adding a substance that provides an ion that is part of the equilibrium system. The direction of the equilibrium shift can be predicted by Le Châtelier's principle.

24. *Sample Answer*: Our blood is buffered with a carbonate ion/hydrogen carbonate ion system. If the hydronium ion concentration becomes too high, the following reaction occurs:
$$H_3O^+(aq) + HCO_3^-(aq) \rightleftharpoons CO_2(g) + 2H_2O(\ell)$$
Excess $OH^-(aq)$ can be removed as shown in the following reaction:
$$OH^-(aq) + HCO_3^-(aq) \rightleftharpoons CO_3^{2-}(aq) + H_2O(\ell)$$

25. The equivalence point is the point in a titration when the amount (in moles) of the substance added is stoichiometrically equivalent to the amount (in moles) present in the original test solution. The endpoint of the titration is simply when the indicator changes colour.

26. Since a titration is performed to determine properties associated with an unknown solution by reaching a pH of 7, the two should coincide.

27. Neutralization can only occur as long as there are hydroxide and hydronium ions from the base and acid molecules in solution. When a weak acid or a weak base is involved in the titration, the anion of the salt that is produced can react with water (hydrolysis) to give a solution that is not neutral.

28. Between a pH of 5 and 6

29. Since nitric acid is a strong acid and sodium hydroxide is a strong base, an indicator with a colour change close to 7 should be used. Many possibilities exist, but indicators such as bromothymol blue, phenol red, or even phenolphthalein can be used.

30. At the equivalence point, the weak acid anion acts as a weak base and accepts a proton from water. This yields hydroxide ions that increase the pH of the solution; thus the pH is above 7, indicating that the solution is basic at the equivalence point.

Answers to Practice Problems

1. fluoride ion, $F^-(aq)$

2. carbonate ion, $CO_3^{2-}(aq)$

3. hydrogen sulfate ion, $HSO_4^-(aq)$

4. hydrazine, N_2H_4(aq)
5. nitric acid, HNO_3(aq)
6. water, $H_2O(\ell)$
7. hydronium ion, H_3O^+(aq)
8. carbonic acid, H_2CO_3(aq)
9. Acid 1, $HClO_4$(aq); base 2, $H_2O(\ell)$; acid 2, H_3O^+(aq); base 1, ClO_4^-(aq)
10. Identify the conjugate acid-base pairs in the following reactions:
    a. Base 2, HS^-(aq); acid 1, $H_2O(\ell)$; acid 2, H_2S(aq); base 1, OH^-(aq)
    b. Base 2, O_2^-(aq); acid 1, $H_2O(\ell)$; acid 2, OH^-(aq); base 1, OH^-(aq)
    c. Acid 1, H_2S(aq); base 2, NH_3(aq); acid 2, $NH4^+$(aq); base 1, HS^-(aq)
    d. Acid 1, H_2SO_4(aq); base 2, $H_2O(\ell)$; acid 2, H_3O^+(aq); base 1, HSO_4^-(aq)
11. 6.67×10^{-14} mol/L
12. 7.52×10^{-15} mol/L
13. The solution with the larger hydroxide ion concentration will have the smaller hydronium ion concentration, and so solution B will have a slightly higher hydronium ion concentration.
14. $[H_3O^+]$ and $[OH^-]$ will still be inversely proportional even though the K_w will be different at other temperatures.
15. 2.02×10^{-13} mol/L
16. Since the hydroxides are soluble, the solution would have a high concentration of hydroxide ions in solution. As a result, the hydronium ion concentration would be very low, which means that the solution is basic.
17. Verified by multiplying the two concentrations together to obtain 1.0×10^{-14}
18. 6.58×10^{-14} mol/L
19. 4.0×10^{-12} mol/L
20. 6.45×10^{-15} mol/L
21. 8.16
22. 11.23
23. pH = 9.495; pOH = 4.505
24. pH = 13.08; pOH = 0.92
25. pH = 13.32; pOH = 0.68
26. pH = 5.241; pOH = 8.759
27. pH = 1.01; pOH = 12.99
28. pH = 12.25; pOH = 1.75
29. 8.91×10^{-7} mol/L
30. Water undergoes autoionization:
    $2H_2O(\ell) \rightleftharpoons H_3O^+(aq) + OH^-(aq)$
    Regardless of the temperature, the hydronium ion concentration and the hydroxide ion concentration in pure water are always equal.
    At 25°C, $[H_3O^+] = [OH^-] = 1.0 \times 10^{-7}$ mol/L
    $K_w = [H_3O^+][OH^-]$
    $1.0 \times 10^{-14} = (1.0 \times 10^{-7})(1.0 \times 10^{-7})$
    $-\log K_w = (-\log[H_3O^+]) + (-\log[OH^-])$
    $pK_w = pH + pOH$
    $14.00 = 7.00 + 7.00$
    At another temperature, the value of K_w will be different and pH + pOH ≠ 14.
31. H_3PO_4(aq) is a stronger acid than NH_4^+(aq), so the reaction will favour the formation of reactants over products.
32. H_2S(aq) is a stronger acid than water, so the reaction will favour the formation of reactants over products.
33. HSO_4^-(aq) is a stronger acid than HF(aq), so the reaction will favour the formation of reactants over products.
34. $H_2PO_4^-$(aq) is a stronger acid than NH_4^+(aq), so the reaction will favour the formation of reactants over products.
35. H_2SO_4(aq) is a stronger acid than H_3O^+(aq), so the reaction will favour the formation of products over reactants.
36. H_2S(aq) is a stronger acid than NH_4^+(aq), so the reaction will favour the formation of products over reactants.
37. $H_2CO_3(aq) + NH_3(g) \rightleftharpoons HCO_4^-(aq) + NH_4^+(aq)$, with the formation of products favoured
38. $HSO_3^-(aq) + H_2O(\ell) \rightleftharpoons SO_3^{2-}(aq) + H_3O^+(aq)$
    $\quad$ Acid₁ $\qquad\qquad\qquad\qquad$ Acid₂
    Acid₂ is stronger than Acid₁. The formation of reactants is favoured.
39. $NO_3^-(aq) + HF(aq) \rightleftharpoons HNO_3(aq) + F^-(aq)$, with the formation of reactants favoured
40. $H_3PO_4(aq) + H_2O(\ell) \rightleftharpoons H_2PO_4^-(aq) + H_3O^+(aq)$
    $H_2PO_4^-(aq) + H_2O(\ell) \rightleftharpoons HPO_4^{2-}(aq) + H_3O^+(aq)$
    $HPO_4^{2-}(aq) + H_2O(\ell) \rightleftharpoons PO_4^{3-}(aq) + H_3O^+(aq)$
41. $K_a = 1.0 \times 10^{-4}$, with a percent dissociation of 3.2%

42. $K_a = 1.6 \times 10^{-5}$, with a percent dissociation of 3.9%
43. $K_a = 6.1 \times 10^{-10}$
44. $K_a = 1.2 \times 10^{-5}$
45. 13%
46. $K_a = 0.26$
47. $K_a = 1.3 \times 10^{-5}$
48. $K_a = 7.2 \times 10^{-4}$, with a percent dissociation of 3.7%
49. 29%
50. $K_a = 3.4 \times 10^{-10}$
51. pH = 1.62
52. pH = 2.67
53. The pH changes from 2.67 to 2.42, a change of −0.25.
54. pH = 1.47
55. pH = 5.90
56. pH = 1.95
57. pH = 2.50
58. The first solution has a pH of 3.73, whereas the second solution has a pH of 4.03, making the first solution more acidic.
59. The first solution has a pH of 1.30, whereas the second solution has a pH of 1.16, making the second solution more acidic.
60. 0.079 mol/L
61. 0.018 mol/L
62. 3.8×10^{-3} mol/L
63. 0.062 mol/L
64. The concentration changes from 3.8×10^{-3} mol/L to 5.4×10^{-3} mol/L, an increase by a factor of approximately $\sqrt{2}$.
65. 0.072 mol/L
66. 1.2×10^{-3} mol/L
67. 7.9×10^{-4} mol/L
68. 0.023 mol/L
69. The first solution has a hydronium ion concentration of 2.5×10^{-3} mol/L, whereas the second solution has a hydronium ion concentration of 2.7×10^{-3} mol/L, which is a higher concentration.
70. a. $NH_3(aq) + H_2O(\ell) \rightleftharpoons NH_4^+(aq) + OH^-(aq)$
    b. $(CH_3)_3N(aq) + H_2O(\ell) \rightleftharpoons (CH_3)_3NH^+(aq) + OH^-(aq)$
    c. $HSO_3^-(aq) + H_2O(\ell) \rightleftharpoons H_2SO_3(aq) + OH^-(aq)$
    d. $CO_3^{2-}(aq) + H_2O(\ell) \rightleftharpoons HCO_3^-(aq) + OH^-(aq)$

71. a. $K_b = \dfrac{[NH_4^+][OH^-]}{[NH_3]}$
    b. $K_b = \dfrac{[(CH_3)_3NH^+][OH^-]}{[(CH_3)_3N]}$
    c. $K_b = \dfrac{[H_2SO_3][OH^-]}{[HSO_3^-]}$
    d. $K_b = \dfrac{[HCO_3^-][OH^-]}{[CO_3^{2-}]}$

72. 0.044%
73. $K_b = 1.67 \times 10^{-6}$
74. $K_b = 1.4 \times 10^{-9}$
75. pH = 11.14
76. pH = 10.44
77. $K_b = 1.6 \times 10^{-6}$
78. $[OH^-] = 0.026$ mol/L; pOH = 1.58
79. $[OH^-] = 3.7 \times 10^{-3}$ mol/L; 1.7%
80. equilibrium concentration: 0.028 mol/L; initial concentration: 0.029 mol/L
81. a. $IO_4^-(aq)$
    b. $CNO^-(aq)$
    c. $NO_2^-(aq)$
    d. $F^-(aq)$
82. a. $K_b = \dfrac{[HIO_4][OH^-]}{[IO_4^-]}$
    b. $K_b = \dfrac{[HCNO][OH^-]}{[CNO^-]}$
    c. $K_b = \dfrac{[HNO_2][OH^-]}{[NO_2^-]}$
    d. $K_b = \dfrac{[HF][OH^-]}{[F^-]}$
83. $K_b = 1.1 \times 10^{-7}$
84. $K_b = 2.5 \times 10^{-8}$
85. $K_b = 5.6 \times 10^{-10}$
86. $K_a = 1.9 \times 10^{-11}$
87. $K_a = 7.7 \times 10^{-9}$
88. $K_a = 1.1 \times 10^{-6}$
89. This statement is false. The reaction of the acid and conjugate base either losing or gaining a proton are the reverse processes of each other, but not in terms of their equations for K_a and K_b, as these both involve the combination of the acid or conjugate base with water. In the K_a situation, the hydronium ion is produced and in the K_b situation, the hydroxide ion is produced.

90. $K_b = \dfrac{[NH_4^+][OH^-]}{[NH_3]}$ $K_a = \dfrac{[NH_3][H_3O^+]}{[NH_4^+]}$

91. pH = 1.648
92. pH = 12.85
93. pH = 13.116
94. pH = 2.50
95. pH = 4.05
96. pOH = 1.12; pH = 12.88
97. 17.05 mL
98. 58.2 mL
99. 1.15 mol/L
100. 0.39 mol/L
101. pH = 4.99
102. pH = 8.49
103. pH = 10.96
104. pH = 8.15
105. pH = 2.61
106. pH = 2.25
107. pH = 6.05
108. pH = 10.63
109. pH = 8.87
110. pH = 7.98
111. pH = 5.19
112. pH = 4.70
113. pH = 3.12
114. pH = 3.11
115. pH = 5.46
116. pH = 6.18
117. pH = 3.15
118. pH = 5.06
119. pH = 4.65
120. pH = 3.05
121. $K_{sp} = 1.7 \times 10^{-10}$
122. $K_{sp} = 7.9 \times 10^{-8}$
123. 5.2×10^{-17} mol/L
124. 4.34 g/L
125. CuCl
126. $K_{sp} = 4.7 \times 10^{-32}$
127. $K_{sp} = 3.7 \times 10^{-9}$
128. Yes

Answers to Caption Questions

Figure 8.2 A hydrogen bond is a type of intermolecular, electrostatic attraction between an exposed hydrogen nucleus of a H atom covalently bonded to a highly electronegative atom (F, Cl, O, N, S) and the electronegative atom on an adjacent molecule.

Figure 8.4 The acid (HCl) is an Arrhenius acid, because it contains a hydrogen atom in its chemical formula. It ionizes in water to form the hydronium ion, $H_3O^+(aq)$. The H_2O is not an Arrhenius base. An Arrhenius base is a substance that contains OH in its chemical formula and it ionizes in water to form the hydroxide ion, $OH^-(aq)$. H_2O contains OH but it does not form the $OH^-(aq)$ ion in this example.

Figure 8.5 Acid 1, $CH_3COOH(aq)$; base 2, $H_2O(\ell)$; acid 2, $H_3O^+(aq)$; base 1, $CH_3COO^-(aq)$

Figure 8.8 The acid on the left side, HCl, has ionized to a much higher degree than the acid on the right, CH_3COOH, to produce a larger concentration of hydronium ions, $H_3O^+(aq)$.

Figure 8.10 When a weak acid is added to water, a dynamic equilibrium is established in the solution because some acid molecules donate a proton to water molecules. The solution contains a mixture of non-ionized acid molecules, water molecules, hydronium ions, and the conjugate base. The equilibrium favours the non-ionized acid molecules.

Figure 8.14 In a titration, the indicator should turn from one colour to another at the equivalence point. This point could be missed if the colour change is not clearly visible.

Figure 8.15 The reaction in this titration is between a strong acid and a strong base. The salt produced is a "neutral" salt, meaning that it does not undergo a hydrolysis reaction to produce either $H^+(aq)$ or $OH^-(aq)$.

Figure 8.16 At the equivalence point, this reaction yields $OH^-(aq)$ ions that increase the pH of the solution to 4.89. Phenolphthalein changes colour at pH = 4.9.

Figure 8.17 At the equivalence point, pH = 5.27. The endpoint range of phenolphthalein does not include this value. The endpoint range for methyl red includes this endpoint.

Answers to Section 8.1 Review Questions

4. **a.** Acid: $HNO_3(aq)$; conjugate base: $NO_3^-(aq)$
   Base: $H_2O(\ell)$; conjugate acid: $H_3O^+(aq)$
   b. Acid: $HCO_3^-(aq)$; conjugate base: $CO_3^{2-}(aq)$
   Base: $H_2O(\ell)$; conjugate acid: $H_3O^+(aq)$
   c. Base: $HS^-(aq)$; conjugate acid: $H_2S(aq)$
   Acid: $H_2O(\ell)$; conjugate base: $OH^-(aq)$

5. a. $H_2PO_4^-(aq) + H_2O(\ell) \rightarrow HPO_4^{2-}(aq) + H_3O^+(aq)$
$H_2PO_4^-(aq) + H_2O(\ell) \rightarrow H_3PO_4(aq) + OH^-(aq)$
b. No
c. $H_2O(\ell) + H_2O(\ell) \rightarrow H_3O^+(aq) + OH^-(aq)$
d. $NH_3(aq) + H_2O(\ell) \rightarrow NH_2^-(aq) + H_3O^+(aq)$
$NH_3(aq) + H_2O(\ell) \rightarrow NH_4^+(aq) + OH^-(aq)$

12. b. pOH = 9.25
c. $[H_3O^+] = 1.8 \times 10^{-5}$ mol/L;
$[OH^-] = 5.6 \times 10^{-10}$ mol/L

15. 10.00

Answers to Section 8.2 Review Questions

4. a. 17.8%
b. 4.08%
c. 0.0067%

5. $HSO_4^-(aq) + H_2O(\ell) \rightleftharpoons SO_4^{2-}(aq) + H_3O^+(aq)$

Hydrogen sulfate is a stronger acid than the hydronium ion is, and therefore the position of equilibrium will be toward the formation of products in this equilibrium system.

7. $HCO_3^-(aq) + H_2O(\ell) \rightleftharpoons H_2CO_3(aq) + OH^-(aq)$ or
$HCO_3^-(aq) + H_2O(\ell) \rightleftharpoons CO_3^{2-}(aq) + H_3O^+(aq)$

8. a. $K_a = \dfrac{[NH_2^-][H_3O^+]}{[NH_3]}$

b. $K_a = \dfrac{[CH_3COO^-][H_3O^+]}{[CH_3COOH]}$

c. $K_a = \dfrac{[ClO_4^-][H_3O^+]}{[HClO_4]}$

10. 1.4×10^{-5} mol/L
11. pH = 4.83
12. $K_a = 2.02 \times 10^{-6}$
13. 4.3×10^{-4} mol/L
14. a. 1.61%
b. 1.62%

Answers to Section 8.3 Review Questions

2. a. 0.94%
b. 17.7%
c. 1.5%
4. $K_b = 1.7 \times 10^{-9}$
6. $[OH^-] = 1.2 \times 10^{-3}$ mol/L;
pOH = 2.92; pH = 11.08

8. a. $K_b = \dfrac{[HOOCCOOH][OH^-]}{[HOOCCOO^-]}$

b. $K_b = \dfrac{[C_6H_8O_6][OH^-]}{[C_6H_7O_6^-]}$

c. $K_b = \dfrac{[H_2SO_3][OH^-]}{[HSO_3^-]}$

10. 1.7×10^{-3} mol/L
11. pH = 11.32
13. 7.2×10^{-7} mol/L
14. a. 0.29%
b. 0.29%

Answers to Section 8.4 Review Questions

5. pH = 4.44

6. a. $\dfrac{[HCO_3^-]}{[H_2CO_3]} = \dfrac{4.3 \times 10^{-7}}{10^{-7.4}} = 10.8$

9. a. Ag^+ will precipitate first.
b. 0.22% of the Ag^+ ions remain in solution when $SrCrO_4$(s) starts to precipitate.

Answers to Chapter 8 Review Questions

1. e
2. a
3. c
4. e
5. b
6. c
7. d
8. a
9. c
10. d
11. d
12. a
13. e
14. a
15. In all cases, the net ionic equation should be
$H^+(aq) + OH^-(aq) \rightleftharpoons H_2O(aq)$
17. $K_a = 3.7 \times 10^{-4}$
19. pH = 1.41
29. $[H_2CO_3] = 0.100$ mol/L; $[HCO_3^-] = 2.1 \times 10^{-4}$ mol/L; $[CO_3^{2-}] = 4.7 \times 10^{-11}$ mol/L; pH = 3.68
32. a. 0.0162 mol/L
b. 5.0×10^{-2} mol/L
c. Owing to the fact that the solution in (b) has the common ion of chloride, there will be a dramatic decrease in the solubility of the solid, as explained by Le Châtelier's principle.

33. a. $[HA^-] = 2.8 \times 10^{-3}$ mol/L
    b. $[A^{2-}] = 1.62 \times 10^{-12}$ mol/L
    c. pH = 2.55
34. $H_3AsO_4(aq) + H_2O(\ell) \rightleftharpoons H_2AsO_4^-(aq) + H_3O^+(aq)$

$$K_{a1} = \frac{[H_2AsO_4^-][H_3O^+]}{[H_3AsO_4]}$$

$H_2AsO_4^-(aq) + H_2O(\ell) \rightleftharpoons HAsO_4^{2-}(aq) + H_3O^+(aq)$

$$K_{a2} = \frac{[HAsO_4^{2-}][H_3O^+]}{[H_2AsO_4^-]}$$

$HAsO_4^{2-}(aq) + H_2O(\ell) \rightleftharpoons AsO_4^{3-}(aq) + H_3O^+(aq)$

$$K_{a3} = \frac{[AsO_4^{3-}][H_3O^+]}{[HAsO_4^{2-}]}$$

36. pH = 4.52
38. $K_b = 3.51 \times 10^{-9}$
40. $K_{sp} = 1.61 \times 10^{-9}$
44. a. pH = 4.74
    b. pH = 4.27
    c. pH = 1.00
58. a. pH = 4.44
    b. pH = 8.81
62. pH = 5.27
64. pH = 11.25
66. $K_{sp} = 8.8 \times 10^{-14}$
68. 0.021 g

Answers to Chapter 8 Self-Assessment Questions

1. e
2. a
3. d
4. a
5. e
6. b
7. a
8. c
9. e
10. c
11. pH = 8.16.
13. a. $HCO_3^-(aq) + H_2O(\ell) \rightleftharpoons H_2CO_3(aq) + OH^-(aq)$
    (acting as a base)
    $HCO_3^-(aq) + H_2O(\ell) \rightleftharpoons CO_3^{2-}(aq) + H_3O^+(aq)$
    (acting as an acid)
14. 2.2×10^{-14} mol/L
15. pH = 10.21; pH = 3.79

16. $[H_3O^+] = 4.00 \times 10^{-8}$ mol/L; pH = 7.40
17. pH = 10.61
18. $[Cu^+] = [Cl^-] = 4.16 \times 10^{-4}$ mol/L
19. $K_a = 3.7 \times 10^{-4}$
20. The pH would change from 9.26 to 9.00, which shows the buffering effect of the system.
21. $K_{sp} = 8.07 \times 10^{-11}$
25. $K_{sp} = 1.12 \times 10^{-12}$

Answers to Unit 4 Review Questions

1. a
2. e
3. d
4. a
5. c
6. b
7. e
8. a
9. e
10. b
11. a. $K_{eq} = [CO_2]$

    b. $K_{eq} = \dfrac{[HCl]^2}{[Cl_2][HI]^2}$

    c. $K_{eq} = \dfrac{1}{[HCl][NH_3]}$

    d. $K_{eq} = \dfrac{[H_2O][Cl_2]}{[HCl]^2 [O_2]^{\frac{1}{2}}}$

12. a. CH_3COO^-(aq) and CH_3COOH(aq); HSO_3^-(aq) and SO_3^{2-}(aq)
    b. CN^-(aq) and HCN(aq); $H_2O(\ell)$ and OH^-(aq)
    c. HSO_4^-(aq) and SO_4^{2-}(aq); HCO_3^-(aq) and H_2CO_3(aq)
    d. CH_3COOH(aq) and CH_3COO^-(aq); HPO_4^{2-}(aq) and $H_2PO_4^-$(aq)

14. a. $HCN(aq) + H_2O(\ell) \rightleftharpoons H_3O^+(aq) + CN^-(aq)$

    $$K_a = \frac{[H_3O^+][CN^-]}{[HCN]}$$

    b. $NH_3(aq) + H_2O(\ell) \rightleftharpoons H_3O^+(aq) + NH_2^-(aq)$

    $$K_a = \frac{[H_3O^+][NH_2^-]}{[NH_3]}$$

    c. $HSO_4^-(aq) + H_2O(\ell) \rightleftharpoons H_3O^+(aq) + SO_4^{2-}(aq)$

    $$K_a = \frac{[H_3O^+][SO_4^{2-}]}{[HSO_4^-]}$$

24. $K_{eq} = 6.4 \times 10^{-4}$
25. 0.071%
26. 0.622 mol/L
27. pH = 5.27
31. 3.12 mol/L
32. 0.300 mol
35. a. pH = 7.22
    b. pH = 10.13
36. $Q_{eq} = 5.9 \times 10^{-9}$, which exceeds the actual K_{sp} value, so a solid will form.
38. 38.92 mL
39. 0.11 g
41. pH = 5.21
42. $K_{sp} = 1.83 \times 10^{-3}$
43. A precipitate will not form, as the Q_{sp} value is 1.06×10^{-7}, which is smaller than the K_{sp} value for the solid.
59. a. $4NH_3(g) + 5O_2(g) \rightleftharpoons 4NO(g) + 6H_2O(g)$

$$K_{eq} = \frac{[NO]^4[H_2O]^6}{[NH_3]^4[O_2]^5}$$

b. $Cl_2(g) + 2HI(g) \rightleftharpoons I_2(s) + 2HCl(g)$

$$K_{eq} = \frac{[HCl]^2}{[Cl_2][HI]^2}$$

c. $2NO_2(g) \rightleftharpoons N_2O_4(g)$

$$K_{eq} = \frac{[N_2O_4]}{[NO_2]^2}$$

d. $CO(g) + Cl_2(g) \rightleftharpoons COCl_2(g)$

$$K_{eq} = \frac{[COCl_2]}{[CO][Cl_2]}$$

64. 0.75 mol
65. 0.333 mol

Answers to Unit 4 Self-Assessment Questions
1. b
2. d
3. a
4. b
5. c
6. d
7. e
8. d
9. b
10. a
11. $K_a = 3.05 \times 10^{-6}$
16. 2.59 mol/L
17. $K_{eq} = 0.25$
18. $[Br_2] = 0.90$ mol/L; $[Cl_2] = 0.90$ mol/L; $[BrCl] = 6.20$ mol/L
21. pH = 2.12; pOH = 11.88; $[OH^-] = 1.33 \times 10^{-12}$ mol/L
22. pH = 2.39
23. $K_b = 5.17 \times 10^{-9}$
24. pH = 1.99

UNIT 5
Chapter 9

Answers to Learning Check Questions

1. By definition, oxidation involves the loss of electrons, so a compound or atom can become oxidized if it loses electrons, without the need to combine with oxygen.

2. The original definition of reduction is the process of extracting metals from ores. The modern definition of reduction is the process of ions, atoms, or molecules gaining electrons. They are the same in that both definitions can refer to reactions involving metals. They differ in that the modern definition states that reduction involves a gain of electrons, and that materials other than metals can be reduced, whereas the original definition involves a loss of mass and refers only to metals.

3. Originally, oxidation was defined as any chemical reaction in which atoms or compounds react with molecular oxygen. The modern definition is the process in which an atom, ion, or molecule loses electrons.

4. If an atom, ion, or molecule loses electrons (that is, is oxidized), another atom, ion, or molecule in the reaction must gain the electrons (that is, be reduced), as electrons cannot exist free in solution.

5. Oxidizing agent: $Fe^{2+}(aq)$; reducing agent: Al(s)

6. Using this reaction as a model for double displacement reactions, these reactions do not experience an exchange of electrons, and so double displacement reactions tend not to be redox reactions.

7. a and c

8. Sample answer: zinc, barium, and magnesium.

9. You would use silver nitrate because silver ions are stronger oxidizing agents than cobalt ions and cobalt metal is a stronger reducing agent than silver metal. Under these conditions, the reaction will occur spontaneously.

10. $Cd^{2+}(aq) + Zn(s) \rightarrow Zn^{2+}(aq) + Cd(s)$
    $Cd^{2+}(aq) + Ba(s) \rightarrow Ba^{2+}(aq) + Cd(s)$
    $Cd^{2+}(aq) + Mg(s) \rightarrow Mg^{2+}(aq) + Cd(s)$

11. Sample answer: copper(II) nitrate, platinum nitrate, and mercury(II) nitrate.

12. $Cu^{2+}(aq) + Sn(s) \rightarrow Sn^{2+}(aq) + Cu(s)$
    $Pt^{2+}(aq) + Sn(s) \rightarrow Sn^{2+}(aq) + Pt(s)$
    $Hg^{2+}(aq) + Sn(s) \rightarrow Sn^{2+}(aq) + Hg(\ell)$

13. $Al(s) \rightarrow Al^{3+}(aq) + 3e^-$
    $Fe^{3+}(aq) + 3e^- \rightarrow Fe(s)$

14. $Fe(s) \rightarrow Fe^{2+}(aq) + 2e^-$
    $Cu^{2+}(aq) + 2e^- \rightarrow Cu(s)$

15. $Cd(s) \rightarrow Cd^{2+}(aq) + 2e^-$
    $Ag^+(aq) + e^- \rightarrow Ag(s)$

16. $Sn(s) + Pb^{3+}(aq) \rightarrow Sn^{3+}(aq) + Pb(s)$
    $Sn(s) \rightarrow Sn^{3+}(aq) + 3e^-$
    $Pb^{3+}(aq) + 3e^- \rightarrow Pb(s)$

17. $Au^{3+}(aq) + 3Ag(s) \rightarrow 3Ag^+(aq) + Au(s)$
    $Ag(s) \rightarrow Ag^+(aq) + e^-$
    $Au^{3+}(aq) + 3e^- \rightarrow Au(s)$

18. $3Zn(s) + 2Fe^{3+}(aq) \rightarrow 3Zn^{3+}(aq) + 2Fe(s)$
    $Zn(s) \rightarrow Zn^{2+}(aq) + 2e^-$
    $Fe^{3+}(aq) + 3e^- \rightarrow Fe(s)$

19. Oxidation numbers are usually (but not always) the same as the charge that an atom in a compound would have if the electrons were completely held by the atom with the greatest electronegativity instead of being shared. Unlike the numbers used to indicate charge, oxidation numbers do not represent a charge. Also, the plus/minus signs for charges are written as a superscript after the number, whereas the plus/minus signs for oxidation numbers are written before the number. Additionally, oxidation numbers can be non-integers, whereas the numbers used to indicate the charge are not.

20. The oxidation number of any pure element is zero.

21. An oxidation number may be a fraction if an atom or ion with two or more different oxidation numbers, such as iron(III) and iron(II), is present in a compound. The fraction is the average of these oxidation numbers. Sometimes, the rules lead to fraction oxidation numbers in other cases as well. For instance, the oxidation numbers in a neutral molecule must add to zero. In acetone, $H_6C_3O(\ell)$, hydrogen has an oxidation number of +1 and that of oxygen is −2. Thus, carbon must have an oxidation number of $-\frac{4}{3}$.

22. The sum of the oxidation numbers for the atoms in a neutral molecule must be zero.

23. The atom has lost electrons or undergone oxidation.

24. In $SO_3(g)$, sulfur has an oxidation number of +6, and in $H_2SO_4(aq)$, the sulfur has an oxidation number of +6. With no change to the oxidation number, sulfur is neither oxidized nor reduced in this reaction.

Answers to Practice Problems

1. $MnO_4^-(aq) + 5Ag(s) + 8H^+(aq) \rightarrow$
   $\qquad Mn^{2+}(aq) + 5Ag^+(aq) + 4H_2O(\ell)$
   Oxidizing agent: $MnO_4^-(aq)$; reducing agent: $Ag(s)$

2. $Hg(\ell) + 2NO_3^-(aq) + 4Cl^-(aq) + 4H^+(aq) \rightarrow$
   $\qquad HgCl_4^{2-}(s) + 2NO_2(g) + 2H_2O(\ell)$
   Oxidizing agent: $NO_3^-(aq)$; reducing agent: $Hg(\ell)$

3. $4H_2O(\ell) + AsH_3(s) + 4Zn^{2+}(aq) \rightarrow$
   $\qquad H_3AsO_4(aq) + 4Zn(s) + 8H^+(aq)$
   Oxidizing agent: $Zn^{2+}(aq)$; reducing agent: $AsH_3(s)$

4. $I_2(s) + 5ClO^-(aq) + H_2O(\ell) \rightarrow$
   $\qquad 2IO_3^-(aq) + 5Cl^-(aq) + 2H^+(aq)$
   Oxidizing agent: $ClO^-(aq)$; reducing agent $I_2(s)$

5. $6MnO_4^-(aq) + I^-(aq) + 6OH^-(aq) \rightarrow$
   $\qquad 6MnO_4^{2-}(aq) + IO_3^-(aq) + 3H_2O(\ell)$
   Oxidizing agent: $MnO_4^-(aq)$; reducing agent: $I^-(aq)$

6. $3H_2O_2(aq) + 2ClO_2(aq) + 2OH^-(aq) \rightarrow$
   $\qquad 2ClO^-(aq) + 3O_2(g) + 4H_2O(\ell)$
   Oxidizing agent: $ClO_2(aq)$; reducing agent: $H_2O_2(aq)$

7. $6ClO^-(aq) + 2CrO_2^-(aq) + 2H_2O(\ell) \rightarrow$
   $\qquad 2CrO_4^{2-}(aq) + 3Cl_2(g) + 4OH^-(aq)$
   Oxidizing agent: $ClO^-(aq)$; reducing agent: $CrO_2^-(aq)$

8. $4Al(s) + 3NO^-(aq) + 4H_2O(\ell) + OH^-(aq) \rightarrow$
   $\qquad 3NH_3(g) + 4AlO_2^-(aq)$
   Oxidizing agent: $NO^-(aq)$; reducing agent: $Al(s)$

9. $ClO_3^-(aq) + 2MnO_2(s) + 2OH^-(aq) \rightarrow$
   $\qquad Cl^-(aq) + 2MnO_4^-(aq) + H_2O(\ell)$
   Oxidizing agent: $ClO_3^-(aq)$; reducing agent: $MnO_2(s)$

10. $5PbO_2(s) + I_2(s) + 8H^+(aq) \rightarrow$
    $\qquad 5Pb^{2+}(aq) + 2IO_3^-(aq) + 4H_2O(\ell)$
    Oxidizing agent: $PbO_2(s)$; reducing agent: $I_2(s)$

11. +3
12. 0
13. +6
14. +5
15. 0
16. −1
17. H +1, S +4, O −2
18. O −2, H +1
19. H +1, P +5, O −2
20. 0
21. −1
22. Al +3, H +1, C +4, O −2
23. N −3, H +1, P +5, O −2
24. K +1, H +1, I +7, O −2
25. redox reaction
26. not a redox reaction
27. redox reaction
28. disproportionation redox reaction
29. redox reaction
30. not a redox reaction
31. redox reaction
32. (25) reducing agent: $H_2(g)$, oxidizing agent: $O_2(g)$
    (27) reducing agent: $C_2H_6(g)$, oxidizing agent: $O_2(g)$
    (28) $NO_2(g)$ is both the oxidizing and reducing agent.
    (29) reducing agent: HI(aq), oxidizing agent: $HMnO_4(aq)$
    (31) reducing agent: $H_2(g)$, oxidizing agent: $NO_2(g)$
33. Bromine liquid is reduced and $ClO_2^-(aq)$ is oxidized.
34. The oxidation number of nickel decreases from +2 in the sulfide to 0 in its elemental form. This is a reduction. A reducing agent must be used to achieve this change, so this is a redox reaction. The same analysis can be used with copper sulfide and copper metal, with the same conclusion.
35. $CS_2(g) + 3O_2(g) \rightarrow CO_2(g) + 2SO_2(g)$
36. $B_2O_3(aq) + 6Mg(s) \rightarrow 3MgO(s) + Mg_3B_2(aq)$
37. $8H_2S(g) + 8H_2O_2(aq) \rightarrow S_8(s) + 16H_2O(\ell)$
38. $2OH^-(aq) + 2H_2O(\ell) + 2ClO_2(aq) + SbO_2^-(aq) \rightarrow 2ClO_2^-(aq) + Sb(OH)_6^-(aq)$
39. $14H^+(aq) + Cr_2O_7^{2-}(aq) + 6Fe^{2+}(aq) \rightarrow 2Cr^{3+}(aq) + 6Fe^{3+}(aq) + 7H_2O(\ell)$
40. $I_2(g) + 10NO_3^-(aq) + 8H^+(aq) \rightarrow 2IO_3^-(aq) + 10NO_2(g) + 4H_2O(\ell)$
41. $2PbSO_4(aq) + 2H_2O(\ell) \rightarrow Pb(s) + PbO_2(aq) + 2SO_4^{2-}(aq) + 4H^+(aq)$
42. $H_2O(\ell) + 3Cl^-(aq) + 2CrO_4^{2-}(aq) \rightarrow 3ClO^-(aq) + 2CrO_2^-(aq) + 2OH^-(aq)$
43. $H_2O(\ell) + 3Ni(s) + 2MnO_4^-(aq) \rightarrow 3NiO(s) + 2MnO_2(s) + 2OH^-(aq)$
44. $6OH^-(aq) + I^-(aq) + 6Ce^{4+}(aq) \rightarrow IO_3^-(aq) + 6Ce^{3+}(aq) + 3H_2O(\ell)$

Answers to Caption Questions

Figure 9.3 The blue colour is characteristic of $Cu^{2+}(aq)$. In the second test tube, some of the $Cu^{2+}(aq)$ has been reduced to Cu(s), so there is less of this ion in solution and the blue colour has faded. In the third test tube, all of the $Cu^{2+}(aq)$ has been reduced and there is no colour.

Figure 9.8 The reaction $2C(s) + O_2(g) \rightarrow 2CO(g)$ is exothermic.

Figure 9.11 When chemical bonds are broken and re-formed, energy, in the form of visible light, is released.

Answers to Section 9.1 Review Questions

6. Sample answers:
   a. $Zn(s) + Fe^{2+}(aq) \rightarrow Zn^{2+}(aq) + Fe(s)$
   b. $Al(s) + Cr^{3+}(aq) \rightarrow Al^{3+}(aq) + Cr(s)$
   c. $Tl(s) + Au^+(aq) \rightarrow Tl^+(aq) + Au(s)$
   d. $Cu(s) + Pt^{2+}(aq) \rightarrow Cu^{2+}(aq) + Pt(s)$
7. a. $Al(s) + Fe^{3+}(aq) \rightarrow Al^{3+}(aq) + Fe(s)$
   b. Al(s) is oxidized and $Fe^{3+}(aq)$ is reduced.
   c. $Fe^{3+}(aq)$ is the oxidizing agent and Al(s) is the reducing agent.
8. a. $Cu^{2+}(aq) + Ca(s) \rightarrow Ca^{2+}(aq) + Cu(s)$;
      Ca(s) loses 2e⁻, $Cu^{2+}(aq)$ gains 2e⁻
   b. $Hg^{2+}(aq) + Ni(s) \rightarrow Ni^{2+}(aq) + Hg(\ell)$;
      Ni(s) loses 2e⁻, $Hg^{2+}(aq)$ gains 2e⁻
   c. $Ag^+(aq) + Tl(s) \rightarrow Tl^+(aq) + Ag(s)$;
      Tl(s) loses 1e⁻, $Ag^+(aq)$ gains 1e⁻

Answers to Section 9.2 Review Questions

1. a. *Oxidation:* $2I^-(aq) \rightarrow I_2(s) + 2e^-$
      Reduction: $Cl_2(g) + 2e^- \rightarrow 2Cl^-(aq)$
      Balanced redox reaction:
      $Cl_2(g) + 2I^-(aq) \rightarrow 2Cl^-(aq) + I_2(s)$
   b. *Oxidation:* $Mg(s) \rightarrow Mg^{2+}(aq) + 2e^-$
      Reduction: $Ag^+(aq) + 1e^- \rightarrow Ag(s)$
      Balanced redox reaction:
      $2Ag^+(aq) + Mg(s) \rightarrow Mg^{2+}(aq) + 2Ag(s)$
   c. *Oxidation:* $Ni(s) \rightarrow Ni^{2+}(aq) + 2e^-$
      Reduction: $Al^{3+}(aq) + 3e^- \rightarrow Al(s)$
      Balanced redox reaction:
      $2Al^{3+}(aq) + 3Ni(s) \rightarrow 3Ni^{2+}(aq) + 2Al(s)$

4. a. $14H^+(aq) + Cr_2O_7^{2-}(aq) + 6e^- \rightarrow 2Cr^{3+}(aq) + 7H_2O(\ell)$; reduction

  b. $S_2O_3^{2-}(aq) + 3H_2O(\ell) \rightarrow S_2O_6^{2-}(aq) + 6H^+(aq) + 6e^-$; oxidation

  c. $20H^+(aq) + 4AsO_4^{3-}(aq) + 8e^- \rightarrow As_4O_6(aq) + 10H_2O(\ell)$; reduction

  d. $12OH^-(aq) + Br_2(g) \rightarrow 2BrO_3^-(aq) + 6H_2O(\ell) + 10e^-$; oxidation

6. a. $Au^{3+}(aq) + Co(s) \rightarrow Au(s) + Co^{3+}(aq)$

  b. $3Cu(s) + 2NO_3^-(aq) + 8H^+(aq) \rightarrow$
  $ 3Cu^{2+}(aq) + 2NO(g) + 4H_2O(\ell)$

  c. $3NO_3^-(aq) + 8Al(s) + 2H_2O(\ell) + 5OH^-(aq) \rightarrow$
  $ 3NH_3(g) + 8AlO_2^-(aq)$

9. *Half-reactions:* $Hg^+(aq) + e^-(aq) \rightarrow$
  $ Hg(\ell)$ and $Hg^+(aq) \rightarrow Hg^{2+}(aq) + e^-(aq)$

  Net ionic equation: $2Hg^+(aq) \rightarrow Hg(\ell) + Hg^{2+}(aq)$

10. a. $2HClO_2(aq) + 3I^-(aq) + 3H^+(aq) \rightarrow$
  $ Cl_2(g) + 3HIO(aq) + H_2O(\ell)$

  b. $3P_4(s) + 10IO_3^-(aq) + 18H_2O(\ell) \rightarrow$
  $ 12H_2PO_4^-(aq) + 10I^-(aq) + 12H^+(aq)$

  c. $Cr_2O_7^{2-}(aq) + 3Hg(\ell) + 14H^+(aq) \rightarrow$
  $ 2Cr^{3+}(aq) + 3Hg^{2+}(aq) + 7H_2O(\ell)$

  d. $2MnO_4^-(aq) + 5H_2O_2(\ell) + 6H^+(aq) \rightarrow$
  $ 2Mn^{2+}(aq) + 5O_2(g) + 8H_2O(\ell)$

12. a. $2HClO_2(aq) + 3I^-(aq) + 2H_2O(\ell) \rightarrow$
  $ Cl_2(g) + 3HIO(aq) + 3OH^-(aq)$

  b. $3P_4(s) + 10IO_3^-(aq) + 12OH^-(aq) + 6H_2O(\ell) \rightarrow$
  $ 12H_2PO_4^-(aq) + 10I^-(aq)$

  c. $Cr_2O_7^{2-}(aq) + 3Hg(\ell) + 7H_2O(\ell) \rightarrow$
  $ 2Cr^{3+}(aq) + 3Hg^{2+}(aq) + 14OH^-(aq)$

  d. $2MnO_4^-(aq) + 5H_2O_2(\ell) \rightarrow$
  $ 2Mn^{2+}(aq) + 5O_2(g) + 6OH^-(aq) + 2H_2O(\ell)$

13. a. $3ClO_4^-(aq) + 4Br^-(aq) \rightarrow 3Cl^-(aq) + 4BrO_3^-(aq)$

  b. $2N_2O_4(g) + TeO_3^{2-}(aq) + 2OH^-(aq) \rightarrow$
  $ Te(s) + 4NO_3^-(aq) + H_2O(\ell)$

  c. $3H_2O_2(\ell) + Cr_2O_7^{2-}(aq) + 8H^+(aq) \rightarrow$
  $ 3O_2(g) + 2Cr^{3+}(aq) + 7H_2O(\ell)$

Answers to Section 9.3 Review Questions

2. a. +4 **b.** +7 **c.** +6 **d.** +7

8. $4NH_3(g) + 7O_2(g) \rightarrow 4NO_2(g) + 6H_2O(\ell)$

9. a. +2

  b. central sulfur, +6; sulfur atom bonded to central sulfur atom, −1; total oxidation number, +5

10. a. $CH_3COOH(aq) + 2O_2(g) \rightarrow 2CO_2(g) + 2H_2O(\ell)$

  b. $O2(g) + 2H_2SO_3(aq) \rightarrow 2HSO_4^-(aq) + 2H^+(aq)$

11. a. $8NH_3(g) + 3Cl_2(g) \rightarrow 6NH_4Cl(aq) + N_2(g)$

  b. $3Mn_3O_4(aq) + 8Al(s) \rightarrow 4Al_2O_3(aq) + 9Mn(s)$

Answers to Chapter 9 Review Questions

1. e **8.** a
2. a **9.** c
3. b **10.** a
4. b **11.** e
5. c **12.** a
6. c **13.** c
7. e **14.** c

20. a. $3Cu(s) + 8HNO_3(aq) \rightarrow$
  $ 3Cu(NO_3)_2(aq) + 2NO(g) + 4H_2O(\ell)$

  b. *Ionic equation:* $3Cu(s) + 8NO_3^-(aq) + 8H^+(aq) \rightarrow$
  $ 3Cu^{2+}(aq) + 6NO_3^-(aq) + 2NO(g) + 4H_2O(\ell)$

  Net ionic equation: $3Cu(s) + 2NO_3^-(aq) + 8H^+(aq)$
  $ \rightarrow 3Cu^{2+}(aq) + 2NO(g) + 4H_2O(\ell)$

  c. *Oxidizing agent:* $HNO_3(aq)$; reducing agent: $Cu(s)$

  d. *Oxidation:* $Cu(s) \rightarrow Cu^{+2}(aq) + 2e^-$
  Reduction:
  $NO_3^-(aq) + 4H^+(aq) + 3e^- \rightarrow NO(g) + 2H_2O(\ell)$

  e. 0 to +2.

22. a. Ba +2, Cl −1
  b. Al +3, C −4
  c. Ag +1, S +6, O −2
  d. N +4, O −2
  e. N −3, H +1, C +3, O −2
  f. S 0
  g. As +3, O −2
  h. V +4, O −2
  i. Xe +4, F −1
  j. S $+\frac{9}{4}$, O −2

24. a. $2H_2(g) + O_2(g) \rightarrow 2H_2O(\ell)$
  b. $CaO(s) + H_2O(\ell) \rightarrow Ca(OH)_2(aq)$
  c. $2C_7H_5(NO_2)_3(s) \rightarrow$
  $ 12CO(g) + 2C(s) + 5H_2(g) + 3N_2(g)$
  d. $CaCO_3(s) \rightarrow CaO(s) + CO_2(g)$

27. a. $Li_3N(s)$
  b. $HNO_3(aq)$

29. a. $H_2O_2(aq) + 2Fe(OH)_2(s) \rightarrow 2Fe(OH)_3(s)$;
  a redox reaction

  b. $PCl_3(\ell) + 3H_2O(\ell) \rightarrow H_3PO_3(aq) + 3HCl(aq)$;
  not a redox reaction

  c. $2C_2H_6(g) + 7O_2(g) \rightarrow 4CO_2(g) + 6H_2O(\ell)$;
  a redox reaction

d. $3NO_2(g) + H_2O(\ell) \rightarrow 2HNO_3(aq) + NO(g)$; a redox and disproportionation reaction

e. $MnO_2(s) + 2Cl^-(aq) + 4H^+(aq) \rightarrow Mn^{2+}(aq) + Cl_2(g) + 2H_2O(\ell)$; a redox reaction

30. a. *Oxidation*: $Pb^{2+}(aq) \rightarrow Pb^{4+}(aq) + 2e^-$
   Reduction: $Al^{3+}(aq) + 3e^- \rightarrow Al(s)$

   b. *Balanced equation*: $3Pb^{2+}(aq) + 2Al^{3+}(aq) \rightarrow 3Pb^{4+}(aq) + 2Al(s)$; $3Pb^{2+}(aq)$ ions and $2Al^{3+}(aq)$ are required

33. a. oxidation number +5 in $V_2O_5(s)$, $VO_2^+(aq)$, $VO_3^-(aq)$, $VO_4^{3-}(aq)$, and $V_3O_9^{3-}(aq)$; oxidation number +4 in $VO_2(s)$ and $VO^{2+}(aq)$

36. a. $2Co(NO_3)_3(aq) + Cd(s) \rightarrow 2Co(NO_3)_2(aq) + Cd(NO_3)_2(aq)$

   b. $2AgNO_3(aq) + SO_2(g) + 2H_2O(\ell) \rightarrow 2Ag(s) + H_2SO_4(aq) + 2HNO_3(aq)$

   c. $Al(s) + Na_2CrO_4(aq) + 4H_2O(\ell) \rightarrow Al(OH)_3(s) + Cr(OH)_3(s) + 2NaOH(aq)$

37. a. $I_2(s) + 10HNO_3(aq) \rightarrow 2HIO_3(aq) + 10NO_2(g) + 4H_2O(\ell)$

40. Oxidation numbers (left to right): Ca 0, H +1, O −2; Ca +2, O −2, H +1, H 0.
   Redox reaction: Ca is oxidized and H is reduced

41. b. $8CN^-(aq) + 4Ag(s) + O_2(g) + 2H_2O(\ell) \rightarrow 4Ag(CN)_2^-(aq) + 4OH^-(aq)$

42. a. $Cr_2O_7^{2-}(aq) + 6I^-(aq) + 14H^+(aq) \rightarrow 3I_2(s) + 2Cr^{3+}(aq) + 7H_2O(\ell)$

   b. $SeO_4^{2-}(aq) + 2Cl^-(aq) + H_2O(\ell) \rightarrow Cl_2(g) + SeO_3^{2-}(aq) + 2OH^-(aq)$

   c. $2MnO_4^-(aq) + 5SO_3^{2-}(aq) + 6H^+(aq) \rightarrow 2Mn^{2+}(aq) + 5SO_4^{2-}(aq) + 3H_2O(\ell)$

   d. $3Ag(s) + NO_3^-(aq) + 2H_2O(\ell) \rightarrow 3Ag^+(aq) + NO(g) + 4OH^-(aq)$

59. a. Na +1, Al +3, O −2, H +1, C +4

   b. $NaAl(OH)_2CO_3(s) + 4HCl(aq) \rightarrow NaCl(aq) + AlCl_3(aq) + 3H_2O(\ell) + CO_2(g)$

60. a. $2KClO_3(s) \rightarrow 2KCl(s) + 3O_2(g)$; $S(s) + O_2(g) \rightarrow SO_2(g)$

62. $Fe_2O_3(s) + 6H_2C_2O_4(aq) \rightarrow 2Fe(C_2O_4)_3^{3-}(aq) + 3H_2O(\ell) + 6H^+(aq)$

64. a. $2Al(s) + Fe_2O_3(s) \rightarrow 2Fe(\ell) + Al_2O_3(s)$

67. $16H^+(aq) + 2Cr_2O_7^{2-}(aq) + 3C_2H_5OH(aq) \rightarrow 4Cr^{3+}(aq) + 3C_2H_4O_2(aq) + 11H_2O(\ell)$

68. $10Al(s) + 6NH_4ClO_4(g) \rightarrow 5Al_2O_3(g) + 6HCl(g) + 3N_2(g) + 9H_2O(g)$

Answers to Chapter 9 Self-Assessment Questions

1. d
2. a
3. d
4. d
5. a
6. a
7. d
8. e
9. d
10. e

11. a. N +5 b. C −3 c. Cl +7 d. Cr +6

13. Carbon changes from −2 to +4.

14. *Oxidation*:
   $Zn(s) + 2OH^-(aq) \rightarrow ZnO(s) + H_2O(\ell) + 2e^-$
   Reduction:
   $HgO(s) + H_2O(\ell) + 2e^- \rightarrow Hg(\ell) + 2OH^-(aq)$
   Oxidizing agent: $HgO(s)$; reducing agent: $Zn(s)$

15. a and c do not proceed spontaneously

   b. *Balanced equation*: $Sn(s) + CuSO_4(aq) \rightarrow SnSO_4(aq) + Cu(s)$
   Ionic equation: $Sn(s) + Cu^{2+}(aq) + SO_4^{2-}(aq) \rightarrow Sn^{2+}(aq) + SO_4^{2-}(aq) + Cu(s)$
   Net ionic equation: $Sn(s) + Cu^{2+}(aq) \rightarrow Sn^{2+}(aq) + Cu(s)$

16. a. $4Zn(s) + NO_3^-(aq) + 10H^+(aq) \rightarrow 4Zn^{2+}(aq) + NH_4^+(aq) + 3H_2O(\ell)$

   b. $3CN^-(aq) + 2CrO_4^{2-}(aq) + 5H_2O(\ell) \rightarrow 3CNO^-(aq) + 2Cr(OH)_3(s) + 4OH^-(aq)$

   c. $BrO_3^-(aq) + 6I^-(aq) + 6H^+(aq) \rightarrow Br^-(aq) + 3I_2(s) + 3H_2O(\ell)$ (acid conditions)

18. a. $MnO_4^-(aq) + 5Fe^{2+}(aq) + 8H^+(aq) \rightarrow Mn^{2+}(aq) + 5Fe^{3+}(aq) + 4H_2O(\ell)$

   b. $2Cr^{3+}(aq) + 6ClO_3^-(aq) + H_2O(\ell) \rightarrow 2H^+(aq) + 6ClO_2(aq) + Cr_2O_7^{2-}(aq)$

   c. $3NO_3^-(aq) + Bi(s) + 3H_2O(\ell) \rightarrow Bi^{3+}(aq) + 3NO_2(aq) + 6OH^-(aq)$

19. a. $2CH_3OH(\ell) + O_2(g) \rightarrow 2CH_2O(\ell) + 2H_2O(\ell)$

   b. Reducing agent: $CH_3OH(\ell)$; oxidizing agent: $O_2(g)$

20. Sample answers:
   $Zn(s) + Cu^{2+}(aq) \rightarrow Zn^{2+}(aq) + Cu(s)$
   $Zn(s) + 2Au^+(aq) \rightarrow Zn^{2+}(aq) + 2Au(s)$
   $Zn(s) + Ni^{2+}(aq) \rightarrow Zn^{2+}(aq) + Ni(s)$

23. $NH^{4+}(aq) + 2O_2(g) \rightarrow NO_3^-(aq) + H_2O(\ell) + 2H^+(aq)$

Chapter 10

Answers to Learning Check Questions

1. The zinc atoms can reduce the copper(II) ions even though the two metals are not in contact, because the electrons from the zinc travel through the electrodes via the connecting wire before coming into contact with the copper(II) ions in solution. Ions migrate through a salt bridge to maintain a balance of ionic charge.

2. The salt bridge in a galvanic cell allows movement of the anions and cations, as oxidation and reduction half-reactions occur. This prevents a build-up of charge in each half-cell.

3. At the anode, atoms are converted into cations by an oxidation reaction, and the electrode loses mass. At the cathode, cations are converted into atoms by a reduction reaction, and the electrode gains mass.

4. **a.** In a test tube, the zinc would be the reducing agent and the copper(II) ions would be the oxidizing agent.
   b. In a Daniell cell, the zinc would be the reducing agent and the copper(II) ions would be the oxidizing agent. In this cell, the two half-cell reactions are in separate compartments but the overall reaction is the same.

5. **a.** *Oxidation (anode):* $Sn(s) \rightarrow Sn^{2+}(aq) + 2e^-$
   Reduction (cathode): $Tl^+(aq) + 1e^- \rightarrow Tl(s)$
   Overall cell reaction:
   $Sn(s) + 2Tl^+(aq) \rightarrow Sn^{2+}(aq) + 2Tl(s)$
   b. *Oxidation (anode):* $Cd(s) \rightarrow Cd^{2+}(aq) + 2e^-$
   Reduction (cathode): $2H^+(aq) + 2e^- \rightarrow H_2(g)$
   Overall cell reaction:
   $Cd(s) + 2H^+(aq) \rightarrow Cd^{2+}(aq) + H_2(g)$
   Platinum is an inert electrode.

6. There is no double vertical line in the notation because there is no salt bridge in the lemon to separate the two half-cell reactions.

7. The dry cell and Daniell cell are both galvanic cells. They are similar in that both use a zinc anode and the same reaction will occur at the anode. They differ as follows: The Daniell cell uses a copper cathode in a solution containing Cu^{2+} that is separated from the anode by a salt bridge. The dry cell uses a paste of MnO_2, $ZnCl_2$, NH_4Cl, and carbon black as the electrolyte between the two half-cells. The cathode in the dry cell is made of graphite. The reduction reactions at the cathodes in the two cells are different.

   Daniell cell: $Cu^{2+}(aq) + 2e^- \rightarrow Cu(s)$
   Dry cell:
   $2MnO_2(s) + H_2O(\ell) + 2e^- \rightarrow Mn_2O_3(s) + 2OH^-(aq)$

8. A battery consists of several cells connected in series.

9. Different voltages are produced, because the reduction reactions are different and therefore the overall reactions and voltages will not be the same.

10. $2H^+(aq) + 2e^- \rightarrow H_2$ $E°_{anode} = 0.00$ V
    $O_2(g) + 4H^+(aq) + 4e^- \rightarrow 2H_2O(\ell)$
    $E°_{cathode} = +1.23$ V
    $E°_{cell} = E°_{cathode} - E°_{anode}$
    $= +1.23$ V $- 0.00$ V
    $= +1.23$ V

11. They are similar in that the overall reaction in a fuel cell is a combustion reaction. They are different because fuel cell reactions convert the energy in the fuel directly into electrical energy. A combustion reaction converts the energy in the fuel into heat, which is used to drive an engine or generator to produce electricity. Fuel cell reactions are more efficient than combustion reactions and they are cleaner. The major "waste" product produced by fuel cells is water.

12. Electrical energy can split water into hydrogen and oxygen. Hydrogen can also be chemically removed from hydrocarbons by reforming. Additionally, wind and solar energies are used to produce the hydrogen. Research is also under way to develop fuel cells that have internal reformers.

13. $Fe^{2+}(aq) + 2e^- \rightarrow Fe(s)$ $E°_{anode} = -0.45$ V
    $O_2(g) + 2H_2O(\ell) + 4e^- \rightarrow 4OH^-(aq)$
    $E°_{cathode} = +0.40$ V
    $E°_{cell} = E°_{cathode} - E°_{anode}$
    $= +0.40$ V $- (-0.45$ V$)$
    $= +0.85$ V

14. The standard cell potentials are based on 1.0 mol/L concentrations and SATP conditions. The concentrations and conditions in the environment where corrosion occurs will be different. The cell potentials will be different to those calculated.

15. Aluminum is a stronger reducing agent than iron is and will act as the anode, protecting the iron cathode.

16. The proximity to the Atlantic ocean results in a climate where salt-laden fog and generally humid conditions are common. This provides an electrolyte to connect dissimilar metals, making corrosion more common.

17. The tin covers the steel so that water and oxygen from the environment cannot reach the steel. This keeps the iron in the steel from corroding.

18. If the can is scratched, water and oxygen from the environment can now reach the steel under the tin. The iron in the steel now corrodes faster in contact with the tin than it would on its own. This happens because tin is less reactive than iron is and acts as a cathode in each miniature galvanic cell on the surface of the can. The tin provides a large area of available cathodes for the small galvanic cells, and iron acts as the anode of each cell, and thus rusting is facilitated.

19. A galvanic cell converts chemical energy into electrical energy, whereas an electrolytic cell converts electrical energy into chemical energy.

20. **a.** Reaction at anode: $2Cl^-(\ell) \rightarrow Cl_2(g) + 2e^-$
    b. Reaction at cathode: $Ca^{2+}(\ell) + 2e^- \rightarrow Ca(\ell)$
    c. $CaCl_2(\ell) \rightarrow Ca(\ell) + Cl_2(g)$

21. **a.** Reaction at negative electrode:
    $Li^+(\ell) + 1e^- \rightarrow Li(\ell)$
    b. Reaction at positive electrode:
    $2Br^-(\ell) \rightarrow Br_2(g) + 2e^-$
    c. $2Li^+(\ell) + 2Br^-(\ell) \rightarrow 2Li(\ell) + Br_2(\ell)$

22. The negative sign means that the reaction is not spontaneous. This negative value represents the minimum potential difference that you would have to apply from an external power source to drive the cell reaction for the electrolytic cell.

23. The current in the electrolytic cell flows in one direction. Because alternating current constantly changes direction, it would not be able to drive the redox reaction in the electrolytic cell.

24. Sodium is solid at standard temperatures and will neither conduct an electric current nor be purified by electrolysis in an aqueous solution. Thus, Davy heated the salts until they melted and applied electrolysis to the molten solids to isolate sodium.

Answers to Practice Problems

1. Magnesium is the anode and zinc is the cathode.

2. Oxidation occurs at the magnesium electrode and reduction occurs at the zinc electrode.

3. The diagram should be similar to the one in the previous Sample Problem, but with magnesium instead of aluminum and zinc instead of nickel. Electron flow will be from the magnesium electrode to the zinc electrode.

4. Magnesium ions will flow into the magnesium half-cell, and zinc ions will flow onto the zinc electrode in the zinc half-cell.

5. $Mg(s) + Zn^{2+}(aq) \rightarrow Mg^{2+}(aq) + Zn(s)$

6. The anode is nickel and the cathode is silver.

7. Oxidation occurs at the nickel electrode and reduction occurs at the silver electrode.

8. The diagram should be similar to the one in the previous Sample Problem, but with nickel instead of aluminum (anode) and silver instead of nickel (cathode). Electron flow will be from the nickel electrode to the silver electrode.

9. $Ni^{2+}(aq)$ will flow into the nickel half-cell, and $Ag^+(aq)$ will flow onto the silver electrode in the silver half-cell.

10. $Ni(s) + 2Ag^+(aq) \rightarrow 2Ag(s) + Ni^{2+}(aq)$

11. **a.** Oxidation: $2Br^-(aq) \rightarrow Br_2(\ell) + 2e^-$
    Reduction: $Cl_2(g) + 2e^- \rightarrow 2Cl^-(aq)$
    b. $Br_2(\ell) + 2e^- \rightarrow 2Br^-(aq)$ $E°_{anode} = +1.07$ V
    $Cl_2(g) + 2e^- \rightarrow 2Cl^-(aq)$ $E°_{cathode} = +1.36$ V
    c. +0.29 V
    The reaction is spontaneous in the direction written.

12. **a.** Oxidation: $Mg(s) \rightarrow Mg^{2+}(aq) + 2e^-$
    Reduction: $Ag^+(aq) + 1e^- \rightarrow Ag(s)$
    b. $Mg^{2+}(aq) + 2e^- \rightarrow Mg(s)$ $E°_{anode} = -2.37$ V
    $Ag^+(aq) + 1e^- \rightarrow Ag(s)$ $E°_{cathode} = +0.80$ V
    c. +3.17 V
    The reaction is spontaneous in the direction written.

13. **a.** Oxidation: $Sn(s) \rightarrow Sn^{2+}(aq) + 2e^-$
    Reduction: $2H^+ + 2e^- \rightarrow H_2(g)$
    b. $Sn^{2+}(aq) + 2e^- \rightarrow Sn(s)$ $E°_{anode} = -0.14$ V
    $2H^+(aq) + 2e^- \rightarrow H_2(g)$ $E°_{cathode} = 0.000$ V
    c. 0.14 V
    The reaction is spontaneous in the direction written.

14. **a.** Oxidation: $Cr(s) \rightarrow Cr^{3+}(aq) + 3e^-$
    Reduction: $Ag^+(aq) + 1e^- \rightarrow Ag(s)$
    b. $Cr^{3+}(aq) + 3e^- \rightarrow Cr(s)$ $E°_{anode} = -0.74$ V
    $Ag^+(aq) + 1e^- \rightarrow Ag(s)$ $E°_{cathode} = +0.80$ V
    c. +1.54 V
    The reaction is spontaneous in the direction written.

15. a. Oxidation: Fe(s) → Fe^{2+}(aq) + 2e⁻
    Reduction: Cr^{3+}(aq) + 3e⁻ → Cr(s)
    b. Fe^{2+}(aq) + 2e⁻ → Fe(s) $E°_{anode} = -0.45$ V
    Cr^{3+}(aq) + 3e⁻ → Cr(s) $E°_{cathode} = -0.74$ V
    c. −0.29 V

    The reaction is not spontaneous in the direction written.

16. a. Oxidation: Al(s) → Al^{3+}(aq) + 3e⁻
    Reduction: Zn^{2+}(aq) + 2e⁻ → Zn(s)
    b. Al^{3+}(aq) + 3e⁻ → Al(s) $E°_{anode} = -1.66$ V
    Zn^{2+}(aq) + 2e⁻ → Zn(s) $E°_{cathode} = -0.76$ V
    c. +0.90 V

    The reaction is spontaneous in the direction written.

17. a. Oxidation: Zn(s) → Zn^{2+}(aq) + 2e⁻
    Reduction: Ag^+(aq) + 1e⁻ → Ag(s)
    b. Zn^{2+}(aq) + 2e⁻ → Zn(s) $E°_{anode} = -0.76$ V
    Ag^+(aq) + 1e⁻ → Ag(s) $E°_{cathode} = +0.80$ V
    c. +1.56 V

    The reaction is spontaneous in the direction written.

18. a. Oxidation: Al(s) → Al^{3+}(aq) + 3e⁻
    Reduction: Cu^{2+}(aq) + 2e⁻ → Cu(s)
    b. Al^{3+}(aq) + 3e⁻ → Al(s) $E°_{anode} = -1.66$ V
    Cu^{2+}(aq) + 2e⁻ → Cu(s) $E°_{cathode} = +0.34$ V
    c. +2.00 V

    The reaction is spontaneous in the direction written.

19. a. Oxidation: Ag(s) → Ag^+(aq) + 1e⁻
    Reduction: Cu^{2+}(aq) + 2e⁻ → Cu(s)
    b. Ag^+(aq) + 1e⁻ → Ag(s) $E°_{anode} = +0.80$ V
    Cu^{2+}(aq) + 2e⁻ → Cu(s) $E°_{cathode} = +0.34$ V
    c. −0.46 V

    The reaction is not spontaneous in the direction written.

20. a. Oxidation: 2I⁻(aq) → I_2(s) + 2e⁻
    Reduction: Br_2(ℓ) + 2e⁻ → 2Br⁻(aq)
    b. I_2(s) + 2e⁻ → 2I⁻(aq) $E°_{anode} = +0.54$ V
    Br_2(ℓ) + 2e⁻ → 2Br⁻(aq) $E°_{cathode} = +1.07$ V
    c. +0.53 V

    The reaction is spontaneous in the direction written.

Answers to Caption Questions

Figure 10.5 Cu^{2+}(aq) ions gain electrons and deposit on the copper electrode. This causes the concentration of Cu^{2+}(aq) to decrease. The Zn(s) atoms lose electrons, and Zn^{2+}(aq) ions go into solution, causing the concentration of Zn^{2+}(aq) to increase.

Figure 10.7 Solid platinum is a very weak reducing agent, so it is less likely to participate in the reaction.

Figure 10.25 The non-standard reduction potentials for the reactions that occur at each electrode are as follows:

Oxidation:
$2H_2O(\ell) \rightarrow O_2(g) + 4H^+(aq) + 4e^-$ $-E = -0.82$ V

Reduction:
$2H_2O(\ell) + 2e^- \rightarrow H_2(g) + 2OH^-(aq)$ $E = -0.42$ V

The number of electrons gained during reduction must be the same as the number of electrons lost during oxidation. The equations show that the reduction reaction occurs twice for every oxidation reaction. Therefore, 2 mol H_2(g) is produced for every 1 mol O_2(g).

Answers to Section 10.1 Review Questions

4. a. +0.60 V
   b. +1.90 V
   c. −2.00 V
8. +0.99 V
9. a. Oxidation: Zn(s) → Zn^{2+}(aq) + 2e⁻
   Reduction: Ag^+(aq) + 1e⁻ → Ag(s)
   Overall cell reaction:
   Zn(s) + 2Ag^+(aq) → Zn^{2+}(aq) + 2Ag(s)
   b. +1.56 V

Answers to Section 10.2 Review Questions

3. a. Oxidation:
   Zn(s) + 2OH⁻(aq) → ZnO(s) + $H_2O(\ell)$ + 2e⁻
   Reduction:
   Ag_2O(s) + $H_2O(\ell)$ + 2e⁻ → 2Ag(s) + 2OH⁻(aq)
   Overall cell reaction:
   Zn(s) + Ag_2O(s) → ZnO(s) + 2Ag(s)
5. 4 dry cells at 1.5 V each
8. Oxidation (anode): Fe(s) → Fe^{2+}(aq) + 2e⁻
   Reduction (cathode): Ag^+(aq) + 1e⁻ → Ag(s)
   Overall cell reaction:
   Fe(s) + 2Ag^+(aq) → Fe^{2+}(aq) + 2Ag(s)
11. b. Oxidation (anode): H_2(g) → $2H^+$(s) + 2e⁻
    Reduction (cathode):
    O_2(g) + $4H^+$(s) + 4e⁻ → $2H_2O(\ell)$

15. b. $3Ag_2S(s) + 2Al(s) \rightarrow 6Ag(s) + Al_2S_3(s)$
Oxidation half-reaction: $Al(s) \rightarrow Al^{3+}(aq) + 3e^-$
Reduction half-reaction: $Ag^+(aq) + 1e^- \rightarrow Ag(s)$

Answers to Section 10.3 Review Questions

4. On discharging, the half-reactions are
$Cd(s) + 2OH^-(aq) \rightarrow Cd(OH)_2(s) + 2e^-$
$NiO(OH)(s) + H_2O(\ell) + e^- \rightarrow$
$\qquad Ni(OH)_2(s) + OH^-(aq)$
On recharging, therefore, the half-reactions are
$Cd(OH)_2(s) + 2e^- \rightarrow Cd(s) + 2OH^-(aq)$
$Ni(OH)_2(s) + OH^-(aq) \rightarrow$
$\qquad NiO(OH)(s) + H_2O(\ell) + e^-$
To balance the charges, multiply the oxidation equation by 2:
$2Ni(OH)_2(s) + 2OH^-(aq) \rightarrow$
$\qquad 2NiO(OH)(s) + 2H_2O(\ell) + 2e^-$
The overall reaction for recharging a nicad battery can then be written as
$Cd(OH)_2(s) + 2Ni(OH)_2(s) \rightarrow$
$\qquad Cd(s) + 2NiO(OH)(s) + 2H_2O(\ell)$

5. > 12 V

Answers to Chapter 10 Review Questions

1. d
2. a
3. c
4. b
5. b
6. d
7. e
8. b
9. d
10. c
11. a
12. c
13. a
14. a
25. $Mg(s) | Mg^{2+}(aq) \| Cd^{2+}(aq) | Cd(s)$
35. a. Oxidation at anode: $Mg(s) \rightarrow Mg^{2+}(aq) + 2e^-$
Reduction at cathode: $Ag^+(aq) + e^- \rightarrow Ag(s)$
b. Overall reaction:
$Mg(s) + 2Ag^+(aq) \rightarrow Mg^{2+}(aq) + 2Ag(s)$

38. a. $E°_{cell} = +1.25$ V
Oxidation at anode: $Fe(s) \rightarrow Fe^{2+}(aq) + 2e^-$
Reduction at cathode: $Ag^+(aq) + e^- \rightarrow Ag(s)$
Overall cell reaction:
$2Ag^+(aq) + Fe(s) \rightarrow 2Ag(s) + Fe^{2+}(aq)$
b. $E°_{cell} = -1.25$ V (not spontaneous)
Oxidation at anode: $Ag(s) \rightarrow Ag^+(aq) + e^-$
Reduction at cathode: $Fe^{2+}(aq) + 2e^- \rightarrow Fe(s)$
Overall cell reaction:
$2Ag(s) + Fe^{2+}(aq) \rightarrow 2Ag^+(aq) + Fe(s)$
c. mass of anode decreases; mass of cathode increases; total mass increases
d. mass of anode decreases; mass of cathode increases; total mass decreases

39. a. anode – inert carbon electrode (negative); cathode – silver electrode (positive)
b. Oxidation at anode: $2I^-(aq) \rightarrow I_2(s) + 2e^-$
Reduction at cathode: $Ag^+(aq) + 1e^- \rightarrow Ag(s)$
Overall cell reaction:
$2I^-(aq) + 2Ag^+(aq) \rightarrow I_2(s) + 2Ag(s)$
d. $E°_{cell} = +0.26$ V

40. a. $E°_{cell} = -1.24$ V

41. Ag(s), Cu(s), then Fe(s)

56. a. Oxidation: $2I^-(aq) \rightarrow I_2(s) + 2e^-$
Reduction: $MnO_4^-(aq) + 8H^+(aq) + 5e^- \rightarrow$
$\qquad Mn^{2+}(aq) + 4H_2O(\ell)$
Overall cell reaction:
$10I^-(aq) + 2MnO_4^-(aq) + 16H^+(aq) \rightarrow$
$\qquad 5I_2(s) + 2Mn^{2+}(aq) + 8H_2O(\ell)$

57. $E°_{cell} = +2.46$ V; oxidation, Al/Al^{3+}; reduction, Ag/Ag$^+$

58. Oxidation: $K(s) \rightarrow K^+(aq) + 1e^-$
Reduction: $Fe^{3+}(aq) + 1e^- \rightarrow Fe^{2+}(aq)$
Overall cell reaction:
$K(s) + Fe^{3+}(aq) \rightarrow K^+(aq) + Fe^{2+}(aq)$

59. a. $Zn(s) \rightarrow Zn^{2+}(aq) + 2e^-$ (anode)
$Fe^{2+}(aq) + 2e^- \rightarrow Fe(s)$ (cathode)
$E°_{cell} = +0.31$ V
b. $Cr(s) \rightarrow Cr^{3+}(aq) + 3e^-$ (anode)
$Al^{3+}(aq) + 3e^- \rightarrow Al(s)$ (cathode)
$E°_{cell} = -0.92$ V
c. $2H_2O_2(\ell) \rightarrow O_2(g) + 2H^+(aq) + 2e^-$ (anode)
$Ag^+(aq) + e^- \rightarrow Ag(s)$ (cathode)
$E°_{cell} = +0.10$ V

63. *net ionic equation* (spontaneous):
$$N_2O(g) + 2H^+(aq) + 2Cu(s) + 2I^-(aq) \rightarrow$$
$$N_2(g) + H_2O(\ell) + 2CuI(s)$$
$E°_{cell} = +1.955$ V

net ionic equation (non-spontaneous):
$$N_2(g) + H_2O(\ell) + 2CuI(s) \rightarrow$$
$$N_2O(g) + 2H^+(aq) + 2Cu(s) + 2I^-(aq)$$
$E°_{cell} = -1.955$ V

Answers to Chapter 10 Self-Assessment Questions

1. e
2. d
3. d
4. c
5. e
6. a
7. d
8. c
9. a
10. c
12. 6
14. a. *Oxidation:* $Zn(s) \rightarrow Zn^{2+}(aq) + 2e^-$
  Reduction: $Fe^{2+}(aq) + 2e^- \rightarrow Fe(s)$
  Overall cell reaction:
  $Fe^{2+}(aq) + Zn(s) \rightarrow Fe(s) + Zn^{2+}(aq)$
  Cell potential = +0.31 V
b. *Oxidation:* $Cr(s) \rightarrow Cr^{3+}(aq) + 3e^-$
  Reduction: $Cu^{2+}(aq) + 2e^- \rightarrow Cu(s)$
  Overall cell reaction:
  $3Cu^{2+}(aq) + 2Cr(s) \rightarrow 3Cu(s) + 2Cr^{3+}(aq)$
  Cell potential = +1.08 V
c. *Oxidation:* $Al(s) \rightarrow Al^{3+}(aq) + 3e^-$
  Reduction: $Ag^+(aq) + e^- \rightarrow Ag(s)$
  Overall cell reaction:
  $3Ag^+(aq) + Al(s) \rightarrow 3Ag(s) + Al^{3+}(aq)$
  Cell potential = +2.46 V
16. a. *Oxidation:*
  $Zn(s) + 2OH^-(aq) \rightarrow ZnO(s) + H_2O(\ell) + 2e^-$
  Reduction:
  $HgO(s) + H_2O(\ell) + 2e^- \rightarrow Hg(\ell) + 2OH^-(aq)$
b. *Overall cell reaction:*
  $Zn(s) + HgO(s) \rightarrow ZnO(s) + Hg(\ell)$
18. a. +0.82 V, spontaneous
b. −0.29 V, non-spontaneous

20. a. *Anode:*
  $CH_3OH(\ell) + H_2O(\ell) \rightarrow CO_2(g) + 6H^+(aq) + 6e^-$
  Cathode: $O_2(g) + 4H^+(aq) + 4e^- \rightarrow 2H_2O(\ell)$
b. Overall cell reaction:
  $2CH_3OH(\ell) + 3O_2(g) \rightarrow 2CO_2(g) + 4H_2O(\ell)$
25. +0.74 V

Answers to Unit 5 Review Questions

1. a
2. c
3. e
4. b
5. c
6. e
7. b
8. d
9. c
10. b
11. a. +4
  b. +7
  c. +5
  d. +3
15. a. $Mg(s) + Zn(NO_3)_2(aq) \rightarrow Zn(s) + Mg(NO_3)_2(aq)$
  b. $F_2(g) + 2NaCl(aq) \rightarrow 2NaF(aq) + Cl_2(g)$
22. a. $2Cu^+(aq) \rightarrow Cu(s) + Cu^{2+}(aq)$
  b. *Oxidation:* $Cu^+(aq) \rightarrow Cu^{2+}(aq) + e^-$
  Reduction: $Cu^+(aq) + e^- \rightarrow Cu(s)$
27. a. $8H^+(aq) + MnO_4^-(aq) + 5e^- \rightarrow$
  $Mn^{2+}(aq) + 4H_2O(\ell)$
  b. $SO_3^{2-}(aq) + 2OH^-(aq) \rightarrow$
  $SO_4^{2-}(aq) + H_2O(\ell) + 2e^-$
  c. $NO_3^-(aq) + 7H_2O(\ell) + 8e^- \rightarrow$
  $NH_4^+(aq) + 10OH^-(aq)$
  d. $Re^-(aq) + 3H_2O(\ell) \rightarrow$
  $ReO_3^-(aq) + 6H^+(aq) + 6e^-$
29. a. $3Cd(s) + 2NO_3^-(aq) + 8H^+(aq) \rightarrow$
  $3Cd^{2+}(aq) + 2NO(g) + 4H_2O(\ell)$
  b. $2Fe(OH)_2(aq) + H_2O_2(\ell) \rightarrow 2Fe(OH)_3(aq)$
  c. $3I_2(s) + 6OH^-(aq) \rightarrow$
  $IO_3^-(aq) + 5I^-(aq) + 3H_2O(\ell)$
30. a. $2Cr^{3+}(aq) + 6ClO_3^-(aq) + H_2O(\ell) \rightarrow$
  $Cr_2O_7^{2-}(aq) + 6ClO_2 + 2H^+(aq)$
  b. $10I^-(aq) + 2MnO_4^-(aq) + 16H^+(aq) \rightarrow$
  $5I_2(s) + 2Mn^{2+}(aq) + 8H_2O(\ell)$

c. $7CN^-(aq) + 2Cu(NH_3)_4^{2+}(aq) + 2OH^-(aq) \rightarrow$
$2Cu(CN)_3^{2-}(aq) + 8NH_3(g) + CNO^-(aq) + H_2O(\ell)$

31. a. −0.23 V
b. +0.70 V
c. +0.42 V

33. *Ionic equation:* $Cd(s) + Sn^{2+}(aq) + 2NO_3^-(aq) \rightarrow$
$Cd^{2+}(aq) + 2NO_3^-(aq) + Sn(s)$

Net ionic equation:
$Cd(s) + Sn^{2+}(aq) \rightarrow Cd^{2+}(aq) + Sn(s)$
b. Cd(s)
c. $Sn(NO_3)_2(aq)$
d. cadmium
e. tin

36. a. $Ca(OH)_2(aq) + CO_2(g) \rightarrow CaCO_3(s) + H_2O(\ell)$

38. a. $3Fe(s) + 8HNO_3(aq) \rightarrow$
$3Fe(NO_3)_2(aq) + 2NO(g) + 4H_2O(\ell)$
b. $3Fe(NO_3)_2(aq) + 4HNO_3(aq) \rightarrow$
$3Fe(NO_3)_3(aq) + NO(g) + 2H_2O(\ell)$
c. $Fe(s) + 4HNO_3(aq) \rightarrow$
$Fe(NO_3)_3(aq) + NO(g) + 2H_2O(\ell)$

39. a. $2MnO_2(s) + Zn(s) + H_2O(\ell) \rightarrow$
$Mn_2O_3(s) + Zn^{2+}(aq) + 2OH^-(aq)$
b. Anode: Zn(s); cathode: $MnO_2(s)$

40. a. Not redox; $Cl_2O_7(aq) + H_2O(\ell) \rightarrow 2HClO_4(aq)$
b. Redox; oxidizing agent:
$ClO_3^-(aq)$; reducing agent: $I_2(s)$
$3I_2(s) + 3H_2O(\ell) + 5ClO_3^-(aq) \rightarrow$
$6IO_3^-(aq) + 5Cl^-(aq) + 6H^+(aq)$
c. Redox; oxidizing agent: Br_2; reducing agent: S^{2-}
$8OH^-(aq) + S^{2-}(aq) + 4Br_2(\ell) \rightarrow$
$SO_4^{2-}(aq) + 8Br^-(aq) + 4H_2O(\ell)$
d. Redox; oxidizing agent: HNO_3; reducing agent: H_2S
$3H_2S(aq) + 2HNO_3(aq) \rightarrow$
$3S(s) + 2NO(g) + 4H_2O(\ell)$

44. c. $5H_2O(\ell) + 2Cr_2O_7^{2-}(aq) + C_2H_5OH(\ell) \rightarrow$
$4Cr^{3+}(aq) + 2CO_2(g) + 16OH^-(aq)$

45. Cathode: $K^+(\ell) + e^- \rightarrow K(\ell)$
Anode: $2F^-(\ell) \rightarrow F_2(g) + 2e^-$
Overall reaction: $2K^+(\ell) + 2F^-(\ell) \rightarrow 2K(\ell) + F_2(g)$

46. Electrolyte: $H_2SO_4(aq)$; anode: Pb(s); cathode: $PbO_2(s)$

47. $2MnO_4^-(aq) + 5C_2O_4^{2-}(aq) + 16H^+(aq) \rightarrow$
$2Mn^{2+}(aq) + 10CO_2(g) + 8H_2O(\ell)$

52. a. Anode: $Fe(s) \rightarrow Fe^{2+}(aq) + 2e^-$
Cathode: $O_2(g) + 2H_2O(\ell) + 4e^- \rightarrow 4OH^-(aq)$
b. Overall reaction: $2Fe(s) + O_2(g) + 2H_2O(\ell) \rightarrow$
$2Fe^{2+}(aq) + 4OH^-(aq)$

53. b. $3ClO^-(aq) \rightarrow 2Cl^-(aq) + ClO_3^-(aq)$

60. Alkaline battery: $Zn(s) + MnO_2(s) + H_2O(\ell) \rightarrow$
$ZnO(s) + Mn(OH)_2(s)$
Button battery: $Zn(s) + HgO(s) \rightarrow ZnO(s) + Hg(\ell)$

62. d. Anode: $Mg(s) \rightarrow Mg^{2+}(aq) + 2e^-$
Cathode: $Ag^+(aq) + e^- \rightarrow Ag(s)$
e. $Mg(s) + 2Ag^+(aq) \rightarrow Mg^{2+}(aq) + 2Ag(s)$
f. +3.17 V
g. $Mg(s) \mid Mg^{2+}(aq) \parallel Ag^+(aq) \mid Ag(s)$

69. a. $6H_2O(\ell) \rightarrow O_2(g) + 2H_2(g) + 4OH^-(aq) + 4H^+(aq)$
b. −1.24 V

Answers to Unit 5 Self-Assessment Questions

1. e
2. b
3. c
4. e
5. a
6. d
7. a
8. d
9. d
10. c

11. *Ionic equation:* $4Na(s) + O_2(g) \rightarrow 4Na^+(s) + 2O^{2-}(s)$
Ionic equation: $2Na(s) + Cl_2(g) \rightarrow 2Na^+(s) + 2Cl^-(s)$

12. a. N = +3
b. P = +5
c. Si = +4
d. N = −3, H = +1, S = +6, O = −2

16. a. $Hg_2^{2+}(aq) + 2e^- \rightarrow 2Hg$
b. $4H^+(aq) + TiO_2(s) + 2e^- \rightarrow Ti^{2+}(aq) + 2H_2O(\ell)$
c. $18OH^-(aq) + I_2(s) \rightarrow$
$2H_3IO_6^{3-}(aq) + 6H_2O(\ell) + 12e^-$

18. b

21. a. $2Cr^{3+}(aq) + 5H_2O(\ell) + ClO_3^-(aq) \rightarrow$
$2CrO_4^{2-}(aq) + Cl^-(aq) + 10H^+(aq)$
b. $2ClO_2(g) + SbO_2^-(aq) + 2H_2O(\ell) + 2OH^-(aq) \rightarrow$
$2ClO_2^-(aq) + Sb(OH)_6(aq)$
c. $2HNO_3(aq) + 3H_3AsO_3(aq) \rightarrow$
$2NO(g) + 3H_3AsO_4(aq) + H_2O(\ell)$

23. $Sn(s) \mid Sn^{2+}(aq) \parallel Fe^{3+}(aq), Fe^{2+}(aq) \mid Pt(s)$

25. b. Anode: $2Cl^-(\ell) \rightarrow Cl_2(g) + 2e^-$
Cathode: $Na^+(\ell) + e^- \rightarrow Na(\ell)$

Glossary

How to Use This Glossary
This Glossary provides the definitions of the key terms that are shown in **boldface** type in the text. Definitions for terms that are *italicized* within the text are included as well. Each glossary entry also shows the number(s) of the sections where you can find the term in its original context.

acid-dissociation constant, or acid ionization constant, K_a an equilibrium constant for the ionization of an acid (8.2)

activated complex a chemical species temporarily formed by the colliding reactant molecules before the final product of the reaction is formed (6.2)

activation energy, E_a the minimum amount of energy (collision energy) required to initiate a chemical reaction (6.2)

addition polymerization a reaction in which alkene monomers are joined through multiple addition reactions to form a polymer (2.2)

addition reaction a reaction in which atoms are added to a carbon-carbon double or triple bond (2.1)

alcohol a hydrocarbon derivative that contains a hydroxyl group (1.3)

aldehyde a hydrocarbon derivative that contains a formyl group (1.3)

aliphatic compound a compound containing only carbon and hydrogen in which carbon atoms form chains and/or non-aromatic rings (1.2)

alkaline battery a dry cell that has an alkaline (basic) electrolyte in the paste (10.2)

alkaline fuel cell a fuel cell developed for NASA's Apollo program that is still used in space shuttles; the electrolyte is aqueous potassium hydroxide (10.2)

alkane a hydrocarbon molecule in which the carbon atoms are joined by single covalent bonds (also considered saturated hydrocarbons because they contain no double or triple bonds) (1.2)

alkene a hydrocarbon molecule that contains one or more carbon-carbon double bonds (1.2)

alkoxy group a side group found in an ether that includes the oxygen atom and the shorter alkyl group bonded to it (1.3)

alkyl group a side group that is based on an alkane (1.2)

alkyne a hydrocarbon molecule that contains one or more carbon-carbon triple bonds (1.2)

allotrope one of two or more structurally different forms of the same element having different physical properties (4.1)

alloy a solid mixture of two or more different types of metal atoms (4.1)

alpha linkage a chemical bond between monomers forming polymers such as starch; can be broken by digestive enzymes (2.2)

amide a hydrocarbon derivative that contains a carbonyl group bonded to a nitrogen atom (1.3)

amide linkage amide groups that link amino acids in polymers (2.1)

amine a hydrocarbon derivative that contains a nitrogen atom bonded to at least one carbon atom, although it may be bonded to up to three carbon atoms (1.3)

amphiprotic describes a molecule or ion that can accept or donate a proton, thus acting as an acid or a base (8.1)

amylase a straight-chain starch (2.2)

amylopectin a branched-chain starch (2.2)

anhydrous describes a compound with all water removed, especially water of hydration (5.1)

anion a negatively charged ion (8.4)

anode the electrode at which oxidation occurs (10.1)

aromatic hydrocarbon a compound containing only carbon and hydrogen and based on the aromatic benzene ring (1.2)

atomic orbital a region in space around a nucleus that is related to a specific wave function (3.2)

atomic radius half the distance between the nuclei of two adjacent atoms; for metals, between atoms in a crystal, and for molecules, between atoms chemically bonded together (3.3)

aufbau principle a principle underlying an imaginary process of building up the electronic structure of the atoms, in order of atomic number (3.3)

average rate of reaction the change in the concentration of a reactant or product per unit time over a given time interval as a chemical reaction proceeds (6.1)

base-ionization constant, or base dissociation constant, K_b an equilibrium constant for the ionization of a base (8.3)

battery a set of galvanic cells connected in series (10.2)

benzene a cyclic, aromatic hydrocarbon, C_6H_6, in which all six carbon-carbon bonds are intermediate in length between a single and double bond; delocalized electrons are shared by all six carbon atoms (1.2)

blast furnace a vertical-shaft furnace used to smelt iron ore, copper, lead, and other minerals; air is blown through a blast furnace from below (9.2)

bomb calorimeter a device that measures heat released during a combustion reaction at a constant volume (5.2)

bond angle the angle formed between the nuclei of two atoms that surround the central atom of a molecule (4.2)

bond dipole polar covalent bonds that have a positive pole and a negative pole (4.2)

Brønsted-Lowry theory of acids and bases the definitions of acids and bases based on the donation and acceptance of a proton (8.1)

buffer solution a solution that resists changes in pH when a limited amount of acid or base is added to the solution (8.4)

button battery a very small dry cell, usually having an alkaline electrolyte in the paste and either zinc and mercury or zinc and silver electrodes (10.2)

calorie the amount of heat needed to increase the temperature of one gram of water by one degree Celsius (5.2)

calorimeter a device used to measure the heat released or absorbed during a chemical or physical process occurring within it (5.2)

calorimetry the technological process of measuring the heat released or absorbed during a chemical or physical process (5.2)

carbonyl group a functional group in which a carbon atom is double bonded to an oxygen atom (1.3)

carboxyl group a functional group made up of a carbonyl group with a hydroxyl group attached to it (1.3)

carboxylic acid a hydrocarbon derivative that contains a carboxyl group (1.3)

catalyst a substance that increases the rate of a chemical reaction without being consumed by the reaction (6.2)

catalyzed reaction a reaction in which a catalyst has been used to speed up the rate of the reaction (6.2)

cathode the electrode at which reduction occurs (10.1)

cathodic protection the process of attaching a more reactive metal to an iron object that will act as an anode and prevent the iron object from corroding (10.2)

cation a positively charged ion (8.4)

cell notation a shorthand method of representing galvanic cells (10.1)

cell potential the electrical potential difference between the two electrodes of a cell (10.1)

cellulose the natural polymer that provides most of the structure of plants (2.2)

charge a mixture used in the smelting process that contains pulverized iron ore (9.2)

chemical equilibrium a state in a chemical system in which the forward reaction and the reverse reaction are occurring at the same rate (7.1)

chemical kinetics the field of chemistry that investigates the rate at which reactions occur (6.1)

chlor-alkali process an electrolysis procedure for making chlorine gas and sodium hydroxide from brine, which is an aqueous solution of sodium chloride (10.2)

closed system a system that can exchange only energy with the surroundings (5.1)

collision geometry the orientation of reacting particles in a collision relative to each other; the collision must be in a precise orientation if a reaction is to take place (6.2)

collision theory a theory that proposes that a reaction occurs between two particles (atoms, molecules, or ions) if they collide at the correct orientation and with certain minimum energy (6.2)

combustion reaction a type of reaction in which a compound reacts with oxygen to produce the oxides of elements that make up the compound (2.1)

common-ion effect the shift in equilibrium position caused by the addition of a compound that has an ion in common with one of the dissolved substances (8.4)

complete balanced equation an equation for a chemical reaction showing all the reactants and products as if they were intact compounds that had not dissociated in solution (9.2)

complete combustion reaction a reaction in which an excess of oxygen reacts with a hydrocarbon and produces carbon dioxide and water vapour, and releases energy (2.1)

condensation polymerization a reaction in which monomers are combined through multiple condensation reactions to form a polymer (2.2)

condensation reaction a reaction in which two molecules combine to form a larger molecule, producing a small, stable molecule, usually water, as a second product or functional group (2.1)

condensed electron configuration condensed notation used to reduce the length of electron configurations; this notation places the electron configuration of the noble gas of the previous period in square brackets, using its atomic symbol only, followed by the configuration of the next energy level being filled (3.3)

conjugate acid-base pair two substances that are related by the gain or loss of a proton; the acid of an acid-base pair has one more proton than its conjugate base (8.1)

conjugate acid the particle that is produced when a base accepts a hydrogen ion from an acid (8.1)

conjugate base the particle that is produced when an acid donates a hydrogen ion to a base (8.1)

constitutional isomers (structural isomers) molecules that have the same molecular formula but their atoms are bonded together in a different sequence (1.1)

contact process an industrial process for the manufacture of sulfuric acid based on the catalyzed oxidation of SO_2 (6.2)

continuous spectrum all the wavelengths in the visible region of the electromagnetic spectrum; produced by sunlight (3.1)

co-ordinate covalent bond a covalent bond in which one atom contributes both electrons to the shared pair of electrons (4.2)

corrosion a spontaneous redox reaction between materials and substances in their environment (10.2)

cross-linking in a polymer, the formation of bonds from one strand to another at several points along the polymer strand (2.2)

crystal lattice the three-dimensional pattern of alternating positive and negative ions (4.1)

cyclic hydrocarbon an aliphatic hydrocarbon chain that forms a ring (but not a benzene ring); can be a cycloalkane, cycloalkene, or cycloalkyne; is nonpolar and has physical properties similar to its straight chain counterpart; compare *aromatic hydrocarbon* (1.2)

degradable plastics polymers that break down over time when exposed to environmental conditions, such as light and bacteria (2.2)

delocalized as applied to the electron-sea model of metals, describes valence electrons that are not associated with a specific atom but move among many metal ions (4.1)

delocalized electron an electron in the second bond of a double bond, shared equally by all carbon atoms; e.g., as found in benzene rings (1.2)

diastereomer a stereoisomer based on a double bond, in which different types of atoms or groups are bonded to each carbon in the double bond (1.1)

dioxin a class of chlorinated aromatic hydrocarbons, which are highly toxic chemicals (2.2)

dipole-dipole force an intermolecular attraction between opposite partial charges of polar molecules (4.2)

dipole-induced dipole force an intermolecular attraction due to the distortion of electron density of a non-polar molecule by a nearby polar molecule; a force of attraction between a polar molecule and a temporary dipole of a non-polar molecule (4.2)

dispersion force (London force) a weak intermolecular attraction between all molecules, including non-polar molecules, due to temporary dipoles (4.2)

disproportionation reaction a reaction in which some atoms of an element are oxidized and other atoms of the same element are reduced (9.2)

dissociation the process of breaking apart into smaller particles, such as ions or smaller neutral particles (8.1)

dry cell a galvanic cell in which the electrolyte has been thickened into a paste (10.2)

dynamic equilibrium a chemical system at equilibrium that is changing at the molecular level, while its macroscopic properties remain constant (7.1)

efficiency the ratio of useful energy produced (energy output) to energy used in its production (energy input), expressed as a percentage (5.4)

electric current a directional motion of electric charges (10.1)

electrical potential difference between two points, is the amount of energy that a unit charge would gain by moving from one point to the other (10.1)

electrochemistry the study of processes involved in converting chemical energy into electrical energy and converting electrical energy into chemical energy (10.1)

electrode a conductor that carries electric current into and out of electrochemical cells (10.1)

electrolysis the process of using electrical energy to drive a non-spontaneous redox reaction (10.2)

electrolyte a substance that conducts electric current when it forms ions (8.1); a substance that, when dissolved in water, conducts an electric current (10.1)

electrolytic cell an electrochemical cell that uses an external source of energy to drive a non-spontaneous redox reaction (10.2)

electromagnetic radation oscillating, perpendicular electric and magnetic fields moving through space as waves (3.1)

electromagnetic spectrum the continuum of wavelengths of radiant energy (3.1)

electron affinity a change in energy that accompanies the addition of an electron to an atom in the gaseous state (3.3)

electron configuration a shorthand notation that shows the number and arrangement of electrons in an atom's orbitals (3.3)

electron-group arrangement the ways in which groups of valence electrons are positioned around a specific atom (4.2)

electron-sea model of metals a model of metallic bonding that proposes that the valence electrons of metal atoms move freely among the ions, thus forming a "sea" of delocalized electrons that hold the metal ions rigidly in place (4.1)

electronegativity the relative ability of the atoms of an element to attract shared electrons in a chemical bond (4.1)

elementary steps a series of simple reactions that represent the progress of an overall chemical reaction at the molecular level (6.3)

elimination reaction a reaction in which atoms are removed from an organic molecule to form a double bond (2.1)

emission spectrum (line spectrum) a series of separate lines of different colours of light emitted by atoms of a specific element as they lose excitation energy (3.1)

enamel a shiny, hard, and very unreactive type of glass that can be melted onto a metal surface (10.2)

enantiomer a stereoisomer in which molecules are mirror images of each other around a single carbon atom bonded to four different types of atoms or groups (1.1)

endpoint the pH at which the indicator changes colour in a titration (8.4)

energy input energy used (5.4)

energy output useful energy produced (5.4)

endothermic describes the process during which heat enters a system (5.1)

enthalpy, *H* (heat content) the total energy of the system plus the pressure times the volume, or $H = E + PV$ (5.1)

enthalpy of condensation energy released when a gas becomes a liquid (5.1)

enthalpy of freezing energy released when a liquid becomes a solid (5.1)

enthalpy of melting energy needed to change a solid into a liquid (5.1)

enthalpy of solution, $\Delta H_{solution}$ the enthalpy change associated with a solute dissolving in a solvent (5.1)

enthalpy of vaporization energy needed to change a liquid into a gas (5.1)

enzyme a biological catalyst (usually a protein) (6.2)

equilibrium a state that is reached when opposing forces or processes are in balance (7.1)

equilibrium constant, K_{eq} the ratio of equilibrium concentrations for a particular chemical system at a particular temperature (7.1)

equivalence point the point in a titration at which the amount (in moles) of the substance added is stoichiometrically equivalent to the amount (in moles) present in the original test solution, or the point at which the acid and base have completely reacted (8.4)

ester a hydrocarbon derivative that contains a functional group with a carbon atom double bonded to one oxygen atom and single bonded to another (1.3)

ester linkage a linkage between alcohol groups and acid groups to form a polymer by esterification (2.2)

esterification reaction a reaction of a carboxylic acid with an alcohol to form an ester and water; a specific type of condensation reaction (2.1)

ether a hydrocarbon derivative in which an oxygen atom is single bonded to two carbon atoms (1.3)

ethyl group the univalent hydrocarbon radical C_2H_5 derived from ethane by the removal of one hydrogen atom (1.2)

exothermic describes the process during which heat leaves a system (5.1)

expanded valence (expanded octet) a valence energy level of a central atom that has more than eight electrons (4.2)

external circuit a circuit outside the reaction vessel in which redox reactions are occurring (10.1)

fatty acids long-chain carboxylic acids (2.1)

first-order reaction a reaction the rate of which is proportional to the concentration of the single substance undergoing change (6.3)

first electron affinity, EA_1 the change in energy that results in the formation of a gaseous anion with a charge of 1− (3.3)

first ionization energy the least amount of energy required to remove an electron from the outermost occupied energy level (3.3)

first law of thermodynamics (law of conservation of energy) a law stating that energy can be converted from one form to another but cannot be created or destroyed; can be represented as $E_{system} = -E_{surroundings}$ (5.1)

flux a mineral added to the metals in a furnace to promote fusing or to prevent the formation of oxides (9.2)

formula unit the smallest ratio of ions in a crystal (4.1)

formyl group a functional group in which a carbon atom is double bonded to an oxygen atom and single bonded to a hydrogen atom (1.3)

forward direction the convention of reading the equation that represents a reversible chemical reaction from left to right as the reactants form products (7.1)

frequency, v the number of wave cycles that pass a given point in a unit of time (3.1)

fuel cell a battery in which reactants can be added and products can be removed while the battery is operating (10.2)

fullerenes a class of spherical allotropes of carbon discovered by chemists Robert F. Curl Jr., Richard E. Smalley, and Sir Harold W. Kroto in 1985 (4.1)

functional group in a molecule, a certain group of atoms responsible for chemical reactions that are characteristic of that molecule (1.3)

galvanic cell a device that uses redox reactions to transform chemical potential energy into electrical energy (10.1)

galvanizing the process of covering iron with a protective layer of zinc (10.2)

gel electrophoresis a technique used to separate and analyze samples of proteins and DNA fragments (2.2)

glycogen a third glucose polymer; the energy storage unit in animals (2.2)

ground state the electron configuration of an atom or ion that is lowest in energy (3.1)

half-reaction an equation that describes changes in only the compound that is oxidized or the compound that is reduced (9.1)

haloalkane a hydrocarbon derivative that contains at least one halogen atom (1.3)

heat content of a fuel, the amount of energy released per kilogram of the fuel (5.4)

Heisenberg uncertainty principle a principle stating that it is impossible to simultaneously know the exact position and speed of a particle (3.2)

hemoglobin a protein in the blood of vertebrates that aids in the transport of oxygen to cells (7.4)

Hess's law a law stating that the enthalpy change of a physical or chemical process depends only on the initial and final conditions of the process; the enthalpy change of the overall process is the sum of the enthalpy changes of its individual steps (5.3)

heterogeneous equilibrium a chemical system in equilibrium in which the components are in different physical states (7.1)

homogeneous equilibrium a chemical system in equilibrium in which all of the components are in the same physical state (7.1)

homologous series a series of molecules in which each member differs from the next by an additional specific structural unit such as —CH_2— (1.2)

Hund's rule a rule stating that the lowest energy state for an atom has the maximum number of unpaired electrons allowed by the Pauli exclusion principle in a given energy sublevel (3.3)

hybrid orbital an orbital that is formed by the combination of two or more orbitals in the valence shell of an atom (4.1)

hydration a process that involves an ion or molecule being surrounded by water molecules that are arranged in a specific manner (4.2)

hydrocarbon a compound that contains only carbon atoms and hydrogen atoms (1.2)

hydrocarbon derivative a compound made up of carbon atoms and at least one other atom that is not hydrogen (1.3)

hydrogen bonding a strong intermolecular attraction between molecules with a hydrogen atom that is covalently bonded to a highly electronegative atom, often oxygen or nitrogen; a type of dipole-dipole attraction between a partially positive hydrogen and partially negative atom, such as oxygen or nitrogen (4.2)

hydroxide ion, OH^- a negatively charged ion composed of a hydrogen atom and an oxygen atom (8.1)

hydrolysis the decomposition of a substance during a chemical reaction with water (2.1)

hydrolysis reaction a reaction in which a molecule is broken apart by adding the hydroxyl group from a water molecule to one side of a bond and the hydrogen atom of a water molecule to the other side of the bond (2.1)

hydronium ion, H_3O a proton bonded to a water molecule by a covalent bond (8.1)

hydroxyl group a functional group consisting of an oxygen atom and a hydrogen atom (1.3)

incomplete combustion reaction a reaction that occurs when insufficient oxygen is present, such that all of the elements in the fuel will not combine with oxygen to the greatest extent possible (2.1)

inert electrode a conductor that consists of neither the reactant nor the product but provides a surface on which redox reactions can occur (10.1)

initial rate the rate of a chemical reaction at time zero (6.2)

inorganic compound a type of compound that includes carbonates, cyanides, carbides, and oxides of carbon, along with all compounds that do not contain carbon atoms (1.1)

instantaneous rate of reaction the rate of a chemical reaction at a particular point in time (6.1)

intermediate a chemical species that appears in the elementary steps of a chemical reaction but not in the overall balanced chemical equation (6.3)

intermolecular force a force that exists between molecules or between ions and molecules to influence the physical properties of substances (4.2)

interstitial alloy a compound that is formed when an atom of sufficiently small radius sits in an interstitial "hole" in a metal lattice (4.1)

intramolecular force a force that holds atoms or ions together; in metals, a force between metal cations and free electrons; forms the basis of chemical bonding (4.2)

ion-dipole force an intermolecular attraction between partial charges of polar molecules and ions (4.2)

ion-induced dipole force an intermolecular attraction due to the distortion of electron density of a non-polar molecule caused by a nearby ion; a force of attraction between an ion and a temporary dipole of a non-polar molecule (4.2)

ion-product constant of water, K_w the equilibrium constant for the autoionization of water (8.1)

ionic equation an equation in which soluble ionic compounds are written as individual ions (9.1)

ionization the process in which a charged particle (ion) is formed from an atom or a covalently bonded group of atoms (8.1)

ionization energy the energy required to remove an electron from a ground-state atom in the gaseous state (3.3)

isolated system a system that cannot exchange either energy or matter with the surroundings (5.1)

isomers molecules that have the same molecular formula but their atoms are in a different arrangement (1.1)

joule, J SI unit of energy; one joule equals work done by a force of one newton when the force's point of application moves one metre in the direction of the force (5.1)

K_{eq} (equilibrium constant) the ratio of equilibrium concentrations for a particular chemical system at a particular temperature

ketone a hydrocarbon derivative that contains a carbonyl group that is bonded to two carbon atoms or carbon chains (1.3)

kilojoule, kJ SI unit for measuring energy; 1000 joules (5.1)

kinetic energy, E_k the energy of motion (in chemistry, this usually means the energy of the motion of particles or thermal energy) (6.2)

law of chemical equilibrium or law of mass action a law that states that in a chemical system at equilibrium, there is a constant ratio between the concentrations of the products and the concentrations of the reactants (7.1)

law of conservation of energy (first law of thermodynamics) a law stating that energy can be converted from one form to another but cannot be created or destroyed; can be represented as $E_{system} = -E_{surroundings}$ (5.1)

Le Châtelier's principle a principle stating that if a chemical system in a state of equilibrium is disturbed, the system will undergo a change that shifts its equilibrium position in a direction that reduces the effect of the disturbance (7.2)

life-cycle approach the study of a product, process, or organism within the context of its impact on the environment throughout its life cycle; life-cycle assessment (LCA) is a method used to account for and evaluate the environmental impacts of products, from the extraction of raw materials through manufacturing, distribution, use, and disposal (4.2)

line spectrum (emission spectrum) a series of separate lines of different colours of light emitted by atoms of a specific element as they lose excitation energy (3.1)

luciferase a generic term for the class of oxidative enzymes that is used in bioluminescence and that is distinct from a photoprotein (6.1)

macroscopic property an observable or measurable property such as concentration, colour, temperature, pressure, and pH (7.1)

magnetic quantum number, m_l an integer that indicates the orientation of an orbital in the space around the nucleus of an atom (3.2)

Markovnikov's rule the rule stating that the hydrogen atom of the small molecule will attach to the carbon of the double bond that is already bonded to the most hydrogen atoms (2.1)

Maxwell-Boltzmann distribution curve a curve resulting from plotting the number of molecules against the speed of the molecules at a given temperature (6.2)

medically-intractable epilepsy epilepsy that does not respond to current medical treatments (3.3)

methyl group the chemical group or radical $-CH_3$ (1.2)

molar solubility the amount (in moles) of solute in 1 litre of a saturated solution (8.4)

molecular orbital theory a quantum mechanically based theory that explains covalent bond formation and molecular shapes based on the formation of new molecular orbitals (4.1)

molecular shape the relative positions of the atomic nuclei in an entire molecule (4.2)

monomer a small molecule, linked covalently to others of the same or similar type to form a polymer (2.2)

monoprotic acid an acid that yields one proton, H^+, when it ionizes (8.2)

mostly covalent (non-polar covalent) describes bonds with a ΔEN from 0.0 to 0.4 (4.1)

mostly ionic describes bonds with a ΔEN from 1.7 to 3.3 (4.1)

net ionic equation an ionic equation in which the spectator ions are omitted (9.1)

network solid a substance in which all atoms are covalently bonded together in a continuous two- or three-dimensional array; no natural beginning or end exists (4.1)

neutralization reaction a chemical reaction between an acid and a base that yields a salt and water (8.4)

newton, N SI unit of force; force required to give an acceleration of one metre per second squared to a mass of one kilogram

noble gases atoms of elements in Group 18 which have very high ionization energies and very low electron affinities; in nature, they do not gain, give up, or share electrons at all (3.3)

nuclear fission a process in which a heavier nucleus is split into smaller, lighter nuclei with the release of energy (5.1)

nuclear model a model of the atom in which electrons move around an extremely small, positively charged nucleus; also called a *planetary model* (3.1)

nucleotide a monomer of DNA, consisting of a ribose sugar, a phosphate group, and one of four possible nitrogenous bases (2.2)

open system a system that can exchange both matter and energy with its surroundings (5.1)

orbital diagram a diagram that uses a box for each orbital in any given principal energy level (3.3)

orbital-shape quantum number, l an integer that describes the shape of atomic orbitals within each principal energy level (3.2)

organic compound a type of compound in which carbon atoms are nearly always bonded to each other, to hydrogen atoms, and occasionally to atoms of a few specific elements (1.1)

oxidation the loss of electrons (2.1) (9.1)

oxidation number a number equal to the charge that an atom would have if no electrons were shared but instead were possessed by the atom with the greatest electronegativity (9.3)

oxidation-reduction reaction a reaction in which electrons are gained by one atom or ion and lost by another atom or ion (9.1)

oxidizing agent a reactant that accepts electrons and thus oxidizes another reactant (9.1)

packing efficiency the percentage of total volume occupied by spheres (4.1)

parent alkane the alkane having the same basic carbon structure as a hydrocarbon derivative (1.3)

Pauli exclusion principle a principle that states that a maximum of two electrons can occupy an orbital, and that the electrons must have opposite spins (3.2)

peptide bond the bond formed when the amine group of one amino acid reacts with the carboxyl (acid) group of the next (2.1)

percent dissociation the ratio of the concentration of ionized acid at equilibrium to the acid's initial concentration, expressed as a percent (8.2)

periodic trends recurring patterns in the periodic table (3.3)

petrochemical a product derived from petroleum; a basic hydrocarbon, such as ethene or propene, that is converted into plastics and other synthetic materials (2.2)

petroleum a fossil fuel that contains a mixture of hydrocarbons, such as alkanes and alkenes (2.2)

pH the negative common logarithm of the concentration of the hydronium ion, H_3O^+ (8.1)

phase any physically distinct, homogenous part of a system (5.1)

phenyl group the term used for a benzene ring that forms a substituent group on a hydrocarbon chain (1.2)

phosphoric acid fuel cell a fuel cell in which the oxidation and reduction half-reactions are the same as those for the proton exchange membrane (PEM) fuel cell, but the electrolyte is phosphoric acid; runs at slightly higher temperatures than the PEM fuel cells but can achieve slightly higher efficiencies and can tolerate fuels that are not as pure as those for the PEM fuel cells (10.2)

photon a packet, or quantum, of electromagnetic energy (3.1)

pig iron bars formed from molten iron being poured into long narrow moulds (9.2)

plasticizer a substance (typically a solvent) added to a synthetic resin to produce or promote plasticity and flexibility and to reduce brittleness (2.2)

plastics synthetic polymers that can be heated and moulded into specific shapes and forms (2.2)

pOH the negative common logarithm of the concentration of the hydroxide ion, OH^- (8.1)

polar covalent describes bonds with a ΔEN from 0.4 to 1.7

polyamides (nylons) condensation polymers that contain amide linkages (2.2)

polymer a large, long-chain molecule with repeating units of small molecules called monomers (2.2)

polyprotic acids an acid that yields two or more protons, H^+, when it ionizes (8.2)

polysaccharides polymers comprising sugar monomers (2.2)

position of equilibrium a term related to a chemical system that reaches equilibrium; when referring to a reaction with a value of K_{eq} greater than 1, chemists often say that the position of equilibrium lies to the right (in the direction of the forward reaction) or that it favours product formation; similarly, if K_{eq} is less than 1, the concentration of reactants is larger than the concentration of products at equilibrium and the position of equilibrium lies to the left (in the direction of the reverse reaction)— that is, it favours reactant formation (7.1)

potential energy, E_p energy that is stored (in chemistry, usually energy stored in chemical bonds) (6.2)

precipitate an insoluble product that forms from a reaction between two soluble ionic compounds (8.4)

prefix the part of the IUPAC name of any organic compound that gives the positions and names of any branches from the main chain (1.2)

primary amines amines that have one carbon atom bonded to the nitrogen atom (1.3)

primary battery a disposable battery that cannot be recharged (10.2)

principal quantum number, n a positive whole number (integer) that indicates the energy level and relative size of an atomic orbital (3.2)

proton acceptor any substance that accepts a hydrogen ion (8.1)

proton donor any substance that donates a hydrogen ion (8.1)

proton exchange membrane (PEM) fuel cell type of fuel cell in which the electrolyte is a membrane that will allow protons to pass through but not electrons; first used by NASA on space flights for their Gemini program; also under development by Ballard Power Systems for use in cars and buses (10.2)

quadratic equation an algebraic equation in the form $ax^2 + bx + c = 0$, where a, b, and c are real numbers and $a \neq 0$ (7.3)

quadratic formula an algebraic equation used to determine the possible solutions to algebraic equations in the form $ax_2 + bx + c = 0$, where a, b, and c are real numbers and $a \neq 0$ (7.3)

quantum (plural quanta) an indivisible packet of energy that must be absorbed or emitted in an "all or none" manner (3.1)

quantum mechanical model of the atom the atomic model in which electrons are treated as having wave characteristics (3.2)

quantum numbers integers arising from the solutions to the wave equation that describe specific properties of electrons in atoms (3.2)

rate-determining step (rate-limiting step) the slowest step among all the elementary steps in a specific multistep reaction, which determines the rate of the overall chemical reaction (6.3)

rate constant the proportionality constant, k (6.3)

rate law the equation representing the relationship between reaction rates and the concentration of reactants for the overall reaction (6.3)

reaction a chemical change that forms a new substance or substances (5.2)

reaction mechanism a series of elementary steps that add to the overall reaction (6.3)

reaction quotient a numerical value determined by using the same formula as the equilibrium constant, using data for a reversible reaction that may or may not be at equilibrium (7.3)

reaction rate the speed at which a reaction occurs, or the amount of reactants consumed or products formed over a given time interval (6.1)

reactive metals atoms of elements in Group 1 and Group 2 that have low ionization energies and low electron affinities; atoms of these elements give up electrons easily but attract them poorly (3.3)

reactive non-metals atoms of elements in Group 17, and to a lesser degree Group 16, that have high ionization energies and high electron affinities (3.3)

redox reaction the abbreviated form of *oxidation-reduction reaction* (9.1)

reducing agent a reactant that donates electrons and thus reduces another reactant (9.1)

reduction the gain of electrons (2.1) (9.1)

refining the process of removing impurities (9.2)

resonance hybrid an average of two different Lewis structures or a structure that is in between two structures (1.2)

resonance structure one of two or more Lewis structures that show the same relative position of atoms but different positions of electron pairs (4.2)

reverse direction the convention of reading the equation that represents a reversible chemical reaction from right to left as the product decomposes to form the reactants (7.1)

reversible reaction a chemical reaction that proceeds in both the forward and reverse directions (7.1)

root the part of the IUPAC name of any organic compound that denotes the number of carbon atoms in the longest continuous chain of carbon atoms for alkanes or the longest continuous chain that includes the functional group (1.2)

saccharide a sugar monomer (2.2)

sacrificial anode a metal that oxidizes more easily than iron and is destroyed to protect an iron object (10.2)

salt an ionic compound that results from an acid-base reaction (8.4)

salt bridge an electrical connection between half-cells that contains an electrolyte solution, allowing a current to flow but preventing contact between the oxidizing agent and the reducing agent (10.1)

salt hydrolysis the process in which salt reacts with water (8.4)

saturated hydrocarbon a hydrocarbon that contains only single bonds, and no double or triple bonds; that is, each carbon atom is bonded to the maximum possible number of atoms (either hydrogen or carbon atoms) (1.2)

second-order reaction a reaction whose rate of reaction is determined by the concentration of two chemical species (6.3)

second ionization energy energy that is always greater than the first ionization energy because the electron must be removed from a positively charged ion (3.3)

second law of thermodynamics a law stating that when two objects are in thermal contact, heat is always transferred from the object at a higher temperature to the object at a lower temperature until the two objects are at the same temperature (5.1)

secondary amines amines that have two carbon atoms bonded to the nitrogen atom (1.3)

secondary battery a rechargeable battery (10.2)

shell the main energy level associated with a given value of n (the principal quantum number) (3.2)

simple calorimeter a calorimeter made of two stacked vessels covered by a lid with holes in the top just large enough for a thermometer and a stirrer (5.2)

slag a molten waste product formed in a blast furnace by the reaction of acidic silica with a basic metal oxide (9.2)

smelting the melting of ore and reduction of metal ions to atoms, then separating the metal from non-metal substances (9.2)

solubility the maximum amount of solute that can dissolve in a given quantity of solvent at a particular temperature (8.4)

solubility-product constant, K_{sp} an equilibrium constant for slightly soluble ionic compounds (8.4)

solute a substance that is dissolved in a solvent (8.4)

solvent the component of a solution that is present in the greatest amount (8.1) (8.4)

specific heat capacity, c the amount of energy needed to increase the temperature of one gram of a substance by one degree Celsius (5.1)

spin quantum number, m_s the quantum number that specifies the orientation of the axis on which the electron is spinning (3.2)

spectator ions ions that are present in a solution but do not change during a reaction (9.1)

stainless steel an alloy of iron that contains at least 10% chromium, by mass, in addition to small quantities of carbon and occasionally metals, such as nickel; stainless steel is often used for cutlery, taps, and various other applications where rust resistance is important (10.2)

standard cell potential the cell potential when the salt concentrations of all salt solutions are 1.0 mol/L under standard conditions of temperature and pressure (10.1)

standard molar enthalpy of formation, ΔH_f° the change in enthalpy when 1 mol of a compound is formed directly from its elements in their most stable state at standard ambient temperature and pressure (SATP: 25°C and 100 kPa) and all solutions have a 1.0 mol/L concentration (5.3)

standard reduction potential the potential difference between a given half-cell and a hydrogen half-cell, written as a reduction reaction, when all solutes are present at 1.0 mol/L concentrations at SATP and hydrogen gas is at 1.0 atm of pressure (10.1)

starch the energy storage unit in plants (2.2)

stereoisomers molecules that have the same molecular formula and their atoms are bonded together in the same sequence but differ in the three-dimensional orientations of their atoms in space (1.1)

strong acid an acid that ionizes completely in water (8.2)

strong base a base that dissociates completely in water (8.2)

sublevel the energy subshell associated with a given value of l (the orbital-shape quantum number) (3.2)

substituent group an atom or group of atoms substituted in place of a hydrogen atom on the parent chain of an organic compound; commonly referred to as a *side group* (1.2)

substitution reaction a reaction in which a hydrogen atom or functional group is replaced by a different atom or functional group (2.1)

substitutional alloy an alloy where the atoms of the materials that make up the alloy have equal or very similar dimensions (4.1)

suffix the part of the IUPAC name of any organic compound that indicates the series to which the molecule belongs; sometimes includes position number of functional group (1.2)

syngas the abbreviated form of "synthesis gas"; the end product of an industrial process in which a carbon-rich material, such as coal, natural gas, or biomass, is converted into a gas consisting of hydrogen, carbon monoxide, and smaller amounts of carbon dioxide and other trace gases; it is usually used to produce other products, such as ammonia, methanol, and synthetic petroleum (7.4)

temperature a measure of the average kinetic energy of all the particles of a sample of matter (5.1)

tertiary amines amines that have three carbon atoms bonded to the nitrogen atom (1.3)

tetrahedral describes the specific shape of the molecule that results from the bonding of a carbon atom to four differerent atoms (1.1)

thermal energy the sum of all the kinetic energies of all the particles of a sample of matter (5.1)

thermal equilibrium the state that exists when two systems have reached the same temperature (5.1)

thermal stability the ability of a substance to resist decomposition when heated (5.3)

thermochemistry the study of the energy changes involved in chemical and physical processes (5.1)

total ionic equation an equation showing all the high-solubility compounds dissociated into ions (9.2)

trans fat a type of unsaturated fat in which the double bonds have a trans configuration; not produced by living systems (2.1)

transition state the changed state of the substances involved in a chemical reaction when they are neither reactants nor products and could change into either one (6.2)

unit cell the smallest group of ions in a crystal for which the pattern is repeated over and over (4.1)

unsaturated hydrocarbon a hydrocarbon that contains carbon-carbon double or triple bonds, whose carbon atoms can potentially bond to additional atoms (1.2)

valence-shell electron-pair repulsion (VSEPR) theory a theory that proposes particular three-dimensional arrangements of electron groups around a central atom based on repulsions between the electron groups; a model used to predict molecular shapes (4.2)

valence bond theory a quantum mechanically based theory that explains covalent bond formation and molecular shapes based on orbital overlap (4.1)

vapor pressure the pressure exerted by a vapor at equilibrium with its liquid in a closed system (7.1)

voltage a common term for electrical potential difference (10.1)

wavelength, λ the shortest distance between equivalent points on a continuous wave (3.1)

weak acid an acid that ionizes to a limited extent in water (8.2)

weak base a base that ionizes or dissociates to a limited extent in water (8.2)

Index

Note: "f" in a page reference indicates material found in a figure; "t" in a page reference indicates material found in a table; and "n" in a page reference indicates material found in a clarifying note at the bottom of the page.

accuracy, 715–716
acetic acid. *See* ethanoic acid
acetone, 53, 53f
acid-base equilibrium
    acid-base reaction, 506–508
    acid-base strength, 504–506
    acid-base titration, 532–544, 728–729
    acid-dissociation constant (K_a), 509–517, 525–526, 552–553
    amphiprotic substances, 497
    Arrhenius theory of acids and bases, 493
    autoionization of acid-base solutions, 498
    base ionization, 519–526
    base-ionization constant (K_b), 519–521, 520t, 525–526
    Brønsted-Lowry theory of acids and bases, 493–495, 494f
    buffer solution, 530–531, 531f
    conjugate acid-base pair, 494–496, 507t, 526
    ion-product constant of water (K_w), 498–499, 501, 525–526
    percent dissociation, 509–511
    pH. *See* pH
    pOH, 501–502
    polyprotic acids, 517, 517t
    salt hydrolysis, 528–530, 530t
    site remediation, 556–557
    slightly soluble ionic compounds, 544–549
    solubility-product constant (K_{sp}), 545, 545t, 546–548, 551
    understanding, 492–502
    water, 492–493
acid-base reaction, 506–508
acid-base titration, 532–544, 728–729
acid-dissociation constant (K_a), 509–517, 525–526, 552–553
acid-ionization constant (K_a), 509–517, 525–526, 552–553
acidic solutions
    see also acids
    acidic salt solutions, 529

balancing redox equations using oxidation number method, 613–614
acids, 416, 491, 492–493
    see also acid-base equilibrium
    acid-base titration, 532–544
    amphiprotic substances, 497
    Arrhenius theory, 493
    Brønsted-Lowry theory, 493–495, 494f, 495f
    common acids without oxygen, 740t
    conjugate base of an acid, 494
    half-reactions, 592–596
    monoprotic acid, 509
    oxoacids, 740t
    polyprotic acids, 517, 517t
    strength of, 504–506, 747t
    strong acids, 504, 505f, 746t
    weak acids, 505, 505f, 510
activated complex, 368
activation energy (E_a), 366, 367–369, 385f
activity series, 579, 744t
addition polymerization, 117–118, 118f, 118t
addition reactions, 96–100, 97f
alcohols, 42–46, 42t, 43t
    drawing, 45
    elimination reactions, 100
    esterification reaction, 106
    naming, 43–44, 43t
    oxidation, 128–129
    physical properties, 46
    substitution reactions, 103
    aldehydes, 42t, 50–53
    drawing, 52
    naming, 50–51, 50t
    physical properties, 53
aliphatic compounds, 35
alkaline batteries, 650, 650f
alkanes, 15–21
    alkyl group, 16
    boiling point, 21t, 30t
    drawing alkanes, 20–21, 20t
    modelling alkanes, 15, 16t
    naming alkanes, 16–19, 17t
    parent alkane, 43
    physical properties, 21
    root and side group names, 16, 17t
    size, 21t
    substitution reactions, 103
alkenes, 22–27, 22f
    addition reaction, 98

boiling point, 30t
    drawing alkenes, 26–27
    modelling alkenes, 23, 23f
    naming alkenes, 24–26, 24f
    physical properties, 27
alkoxy group, 66
alkyl group, 16
alkynes, 28–30, 98
allotropes, 224–225
alloys, 214
alpha decay, 288
alpha linkages, 124–125, 125f
alpha particles, 166–167
amide linkage, 119
amide linkages, 105
amides, 42t, 75–80, 75f, 76f
    boiling and melting points, 80, 80t
    condensation reactions, 105
    drawing, 78–79
    hydrolysis reaction, 107
    naming, 76–78, 76t, 77f
amines, 42t, 70–75, 70f
    boiling point, 75t
    drawing, 73–74
    naming, 71–73, 71t, 72f
    physical properties, 74
amino acids, 105, 105f, 126, 126f
ammonia, 375, 375f, 418, 432, 432f, 466–468, 467f
amphiprotic, 497
amplitude of a wave, 168f
amylopectin, 125
anion, 528
anode, 636
antioxidant supplements, 622
aqueous solutions
    acidic-basic nature of, and ion concentrations, 499
    balancing chemical equations in, 415
    buffer solution, 530–531, 554–556
    colours of common ions in, 742t
    electrolysis in, 661–663
    preparation of, 414, 726–727
    salt solutions, 528–530
    thermodynamics of, 310
aromatic hydrocarbons, 35–39
benzene, 35, 35f, 39
    drawing, 38
    naming, 36–37, 36t
    physical properties, 39
    substitution reactions, 103

Arrhenius, Svanté, 493
Arrhenius theory of acids and bases, 493
asymmetric molecules
    addition reaction, 98
    elimination reaction, 101
atom
    atomic radius, 189–190, 189f, 190f
    electronegativity values, 209f
    ground state, 171
    ionization energy, 191–192, 191f
    many-electron atoms, 181–182, 182f
    overall shape, 176
    quantum numbers, 175–178, 177t
atomic models
    Bohr model of hydrogen atom, 171–172, 171f, 172f
    Dalton's model, 164, 164f
    nuclear model, development of, 164–172
    quantum mechanical model, 164, 174–179
    Rutherford's model, 166–167, 167f
    Thomson's model, 164–165, 165f, 166
atomic orbital, 174, 177
    energies for many-electron atoms, 181–182, 182f
    orbital diagrams, 182–186
    quantum mechanical model. *See* quantum mechanical model
    shape, 176, 177f
    shell, 176
atomic radius, 189–190, 189f, 190f
atomic spectra, 170, 170f
aufbau principle, 184
autoionization, 498
average rates of reaction, 356, 358–359

Bader, Richard, 246
balanced chemical equations, 578, 590–598, 620–621
balanced half-reactions, 590–598
ball and stick model, 11
bar graphs, 710

base-dissociation constant (K_b), 519–521, 520t, 525–526
base ionization, 519–526
base-ionization constant (K_b), 519–521, 520t, 525–526
bases, 416, 491, 492–493
  see also acid-base equilibrium
  acid-base titration, 532–544
  amphiprotic substances, 497
  Arrhenius theory, 493
  basic salt solutions, 529
  Brønsted-Lowry theory, 493–495, 494f, 495f
  conjugate acid of a base, 494
  half-reactions, and basic solutions, 592, 596–598
  ionization constants for nitrogen bases, 746t
  strength of, 506, 747t
  strong bases, 506, 746t
  weak bases, 506, 520–523
basic solutions. See bases
battery, 632, 634, 634f, 649–651
  alkaline batteries, 650, 650f
  button battery, 650–651, 650f
  lead-acid battery, 665–666, 665f
  lithium-based battery systems, 668
  lithium-ion polymer batteries, 576
  nickel-cadmium cell, 667, 667f
  primary battery, 649
  rechargeable batteries, 664–667
  secondary batteries, 649
Becquerel, Henri, 166
benzene, 35, 35f, 39
benzene derivatives, 80, 736–738
beta decay, 288
beta linkages, 124–125
binary ionic compounds, 740
binary molecular compounds, 741, 741t
biochemical equilibrium processes, 463–464
biodiesel, 340–341
biological equilibrium processes, 465
bioluminescent intensity, 352
bioplastics, 123, 123f, 144–145
birch bark, 6
bisphenol A (BPA), 134–135
bleaching, 616
Bohr, Niels, 164, 171–172
Bohr model of hydrogen atom, 171–172, 171f, 172f
Bohr radius, 171

boiling point, 5
  alkanes, 21t, 30t
  alkenes, 30t
  alkynes, 30t
  amines, 75t
  carbon compounds, 61t
  carbon derivatives, 80, 80t
  cyclic alkanes, 35t
  ionic compounds, 216–217, 217t
  metal, 212
bomb calorimeter, 306–308, 307f
bond angle, 232
bond-breaking, 292, 292f
bond character, 742, 742t
bond dipole, 238
Born, Max, 174
Bosch, Carl, 467
Brønsted, Johannes, 493
Brønsted-Lowry theory of acids and bases, 493–495, 494f, 495f
buffer solution, 530–531, 531f, 554–556
Burneo, Jorge, 194
button battery, 650–651, 650f

C

calcium hydroxide, 551
calorie, 299
calorimeter, 299
calorimetry, 299–308
  bomb calorimeter, 306–308, 307f
  endothermic process, 300f
  enthalpy of combustion, 306–308
  enthalpy of reaction, 303–304
  exothermic process, 300f
  flame calorimetry, 306, 306f
  simple calorimeter, 300–302, 301f
  theoretical basis, 300
cancer, 23, 480
carbon atom
  bonding of, 224
  isomers, 10–13
  special nature of, 9
carbon-based life, 2
carbon dioxide emissions, 333t
carbon monoxide poisoning, 464
carbonyl group, 50, 50f
carboxyl group, 57, 57f
carboxylic acids, 42t, 57–61
  boiling point, 61t
  condensation reactions, 105
  drawing, 60
  esterification reaction, 106
  naming, 57–59, 58t
  physical properties, 61

case studies
  electrochemical technologies, 674–675
  ethanol vs. biodiesel, 340–341
  nanoparticles, 250–251
  organic compounds in everyday life, 134–135
  site remediation, 556–557
catalyst, 372, 374–377, 374f, 389, 390, 437
catalytic converter, 378
catalyzed reaction, 374
cathode ray tubes, 164–165, 165f, 636
cathodic protection, 657
cation, 528
cause-and-effect map, 714
cell notation, 641
cell potential, 642–643, 670–671
cellulose, 124–125
chelation, 441
chemical bonding, 208–225
  see also chemical bonds
  covalent bonding, 208t, 219–225
  electronegativity, 208–210, 209f
  hydrogen bonding, 242–243, 242f, 243f
  ionic bonding, 208t, 214–216
  metallic bonding, 208t, 211
  and quantum mechanics, 220
  in solids, 248–249
  types of, 208t
chemical bonds, 5
  see also chemical bonding; specific types of chemical bonds
  covalent bond, 5, 96, 219–225
  double bonds, 11, 11f, 24, 222
  physical properties, 5
  range in, 210f
  single bonds, 220–221
  test for multiple bonds, 97, 97f
  triple bond, 12, 12f, 30, 223
chemical engineers, 81
chemical equations, 415, 578
chemical equilibrium, 420, 420f
  acid-base equilibrium. See acid-base equilibrium
  cancer treatments, and equilibrium principles, 480
  catalyst, 437
  colour, 458–459
  common factors, 424
  concentration changes, 432–433
  conditions for, 423

and dynamic equilibrium, 421, 472–473
equilibrium constant expression, 424–427, 428, 430
equilibrium constant (K_{eq}). See equilibrium constant (K_{eq})
equilibrium equations, 421
equilibrium systems, 463–470, 474–475
  see also equilibrium systems
external changes, effects of, 432–439, 437t
hemoglobin-oxygen equilibrium, 479
heterogeneous equilibrium, 423, 429, 430
homogeneous equilibrium, 423, 427, 428, 443
law of chemical equilibrium, 424
Le Châtelier principle, 432–439, 466, 469, 470
molar concentrations, 443–444
physical systems, 422–423, 422f
position of equilibrium, 427
pressure changes, 434–435
quadratic formula, 452–453
and reversible reactions, 420–421
stress, response to, 439
temperature changes, 436, 436f
volume changes, 434–435
chemical kinetics, 354
  see also reaction rate
chemical reactions, 579
  see also specific chemical reactions
  activation energy (E_a), 366, 367–369
  calculations related to, 416
  catalyzed reaction, 374
  order of reaction, 721–722
  potential energy diagram, 366, 366f, 369, 370
  reaction rate. See reaction rate
  reversible reactions, 368, 420–421, 423, 425f
  standard cell potential, calculation of, 646–647
chemistry data tables, 739t–748t
  acids, 746t, 747t
  bases, 746t, 747t
  bond character, 742, 742t

concentration calculations, 745*t*
constants, 746*t*
energy and chemical reactions, 743*t*
indicators, 746*t*
ion properties, 742*t*
ions, names and formulas, 739*t*
names and formulas for compounds, 740–741, 740*t*, 741*t*
oxidation, 748*t*
polyatomic ions, prefixes and suffixes, 739*t*
reactivity and solubility, 744*t*–745*t*
reduction, 748*t*
chlor-alkali process, 662–663, 663*f*
chlorofluorocarbons (CFCs), 46, 376
chloroform, 46
cholesterol, 114
circle graphs, 711
cis isomer, 12, 12*f*, 101
"clean" fuel, 333
closed system, 279, 279*f*, 422
co-ordinate covalent bond, 229, 231
cold packs, 287
Collins, Terrence, 616
collision theory, 365–366
colour, 362*t*, 458–459
colour change, 419
combustion, 306–308, 322, 338–339
combustion reaction, 110–111, 294, 295*t*
combustion reactions, 5
common-ion effect, 531
complete combustion reaction, 110
concentration
from acid-ionization constant (K_a), 515–516
calculations, 745*t*
and equilibrium, 432–433
measures of, 745*t*
and reaction rate, 372, 380–383, 386*f*
concept map, 713
condensation, 285, 285*f*
condensation reactions, 105, 119–120, 120*t*
condensed structural formula
alkanes, 16*t*
alkenes, 23*f*
alkynes, 28*f*

conductivity. *See* electrical conductivity
Confuciusornis sanctus, 162
conjugate acid, 494
conjugate acid-base pair, 494–496, 507*t*, 526
conjugate base, 494
constitutional isomers, 10–11, 11*f*
contact process, 313*f*, 375
coral reefs, 465
corrosion, 655–658, 672–673
covalent bond, 5, 96, 219–225
see also covalent bonding
co-ordinate covalent bond, 229
covalent bonding, 208*t*, 219–225
see also covalent bond
allotropes, 224–225
bond dipole, 238
co-ordinate covalent bond, 231
forces in covalent bonds, 220
hybridization, types of, 224
network solids, 225
and quantum mechanics, 220
crystal lattice, 215, 215*f*
Curie, Marie and Pierre, 166
Curl, Robert F., Jr., 225
cycle chart, 714
cyclic hydrocarbons, 30–35, 31*f*
boiling point, 35*t*
drawing, 33–34
naming, 31–33, 31*t*
properties, 35

Dalton, John, 164
Dalton's model, 164, 164*f*
Daniell, John Frederic, 635
Daniell cell, 635–637, 636*f*
Davy, Humphry, 661
de Broglie, Louis, 174
decomposition reactions, 381, 389
decompression sickness, 463–464
deep water cooling, 334
delocalized electrons, 35, 211
diastereomers, 12, 12*f*
dioxins, 123, 123*f*
dipole-dipole forces, 242–243
dipole-induced dipole forces, 244, 244*f*
dipoles
bond dipole, 238
dipole-dipole forces, 242–243
induced dipoles, 244, 244*f*
ion-dipole forces, 243, 243*f*
ion-induced dipole forces, 244

dispersion forces, 244–245, 245*f*
disproportionation reaction, 598–599
dissociation, 492, 493*n*
DNA (2-deoxyribonucleic acid), 126, 126*f*
double bonds, 11, 11*f*, 24, 222
see also chemical bonds
dry cells, 649–651
ductibility of metal, 213
dynamic equilibrium, 421, 472–473

Earth Summit, 46
effective collisions, 365–366
efficiency, 325–333
Einstein, Albert, 170, 171
electric current, 635
electrical conductivity, 212, 218, 218*f*, 362*t*
electrical potential difference, 642
electricity, 581
electrochemical cells
electrolytic cell, 660–661, 660*f*, 661*t*
galvanic cells. *See* galvanic cells
industrial extraction and refining of metals, 667
non-spontaneous reactions, 660–667
rechargeable batteries, 664–667
electrochemical technologies, 674–675
electrochemistry, 635
electrodes, 636, 637–638
electrolysis, 660
in aqueous solutions, 661–663
chlor-alkali process, 662–663, 663*f*
of modern salts, 663–664, 664*f*
of water, 662
electrolytes, 497, 636
electrolytic cell, 660–661, 660*f*, 661*t*
electromagnetic radiation, 168–169, 169*f*
electron affinity, 192, 192*f*
electron configuration, 182–184
aufbau principle, 184
condensed electron configuration, 185
filling orbitals for Period 4 elements, 186, 186*t*

filling orbitals for Periods 1 and 2 elements, 184
for first ten elements, 185*t*
helium, 182*f*
Hund's rule, 184
hydrogen, 182*f*
for Period 3 elements, 185
periodic table to predict, 187, 187*t*
and periodic trends in atomic properties, 189–192
writing, 183, 184
electron-sea model of metals, 211, 214
electron sharing, 209–210
electron-spin quantum number (m_s), 177, 177*t*
electronegativity, 208–210, 209*f*, 580
electrons
delocalized electrons, 35, 211
electron groups, and molecular shapes, 232–233, 233*t*
half-reactions with differing numbers of electrons, 591
in lithium, 183, 183*t*
electroplating, 684
element
alphabetical list, 749*t*
inferring characteristics of, 188
periodic table. *See* periodic table
elementary step, 383
elimination reactions, 100–102
emission spectrum, 170
empirical molecular formula
alkanes, 16*t*
alkenes, 23*f*
alkynes, 28*f*
enantiomers, 13, 13*f*
endothermic process, 283, 284*f*, 293, 300*f*
endpoint, 532, 532*f*, 747*f*
energy
bond-breaking, 292, 292*f*
efficiency, 325–333
electrical potential difference, 642
electromagnetic radiation, 168–169, 169*f*
enthalpy (H). *See* enthalpy (H)
first law of thermodynamics, 282–283
forms and transfer of, 273
input and output, 325, 367
ionization energy, 191–192, 191*f*

joule (J), 278
  of light, 169
  photons, 169, 170
  second law of thermodynamics, 283, 300, 334
  shell, 176
  sources, 329–333
  sublevels, 176
  thermal energy, 280, 308
enthalpy (*H*), 282–283
  and activation energy (E_a), 36
  calculation of enthalpy change, 296–297
  changes, categories of, 284–286
  chemical changes, 288
  of combustion, 306–308, 322, 338–339
  comparison of changes, 290, 290*t*
  of condensation, 285, 285*f*
  diagrams, 293, 294*f*
  of formation, 319–322
  of freezing, 285, 285*f*
  heating curve of water, 286, 287*f*
  Hess's law, 312–322, 338–339
  mass of products, 298
  of melting, 285, 285*f*, 286*t*
  molar enthalpy of combustion, 294, 295*t*
  neutralization reaction, 336–337
  notation, 293
  nuclear changes, 288–290
  phase changes, 285, 285*f*
  of reaction, 296, 303–304
  of solution, 284, 284*f*
  standard molar enthalpy of formation, 317–318, 318*t*
  terminology differences, 286
  of vaporization, 285, 285*f*, 286, 286*t*
enthalpy of solution, 284, 284*f*
environmental issues
  bioplastics, 123, 123*f*, 144–145
  catalytic converter, 378
  chlorofluorocarbons (CFCs), 46, 376
  deep water cooling, 334
  electrochemical technologies, 674–675
  energy sources, 329–330
  ethanol vs. biodiesel, 340–341
  "green" alternatives, 84
  green chemistry, 40, 695
  green engineering, 696
  green oven cleaners, 524

green solvents, 226
hexane use, 40
ozone depletion, 376
paper production, 616
plastics, 94, 95
polymer production, 123
polystyrene alternatives, 124
renewable energy sources, 332
site remediation, 556–557
Enwave Energy Corporation, 334
enzymes, 377
epilepsy, 194
equilibrium. *See* chemical equilibrium
equilibrium constant expression, 424–427, 428, 430
equilibrium constant (K_{eq}), 424–427, 426*f*
  approximation method, 456–457
  calculation of, 442–461
  colour, 458–459
  experimental data, 476–478
  gas partial pressures, 445–446
  homogeneous chemical system, 443
  ICE tables, 448–449
  molar concentrations, 443–444
  quadratic formula, 452–453
  reaction quotient, 459–461
  small equilibrium constant, 456
  stoichiometry, 450–451
equilibrium equations, 421
equilibrium systems, 463–470
  biochemical equilibrium processes, 463–464
  biological equilibrium processes, 465
  changing conditions, 474–475
  methanol, 470
  technological equilibrium systems, 466–469
equivalence point, 532, 542–543
error, 716–718
ester linkages, 119, 119*f*, 120
esterification reaction, 106–107, 106*f*, 108, 130
esters, 42*t*, 61–65, 61*f*
  artificial esters, 130
  drawing, 64–65
  esterification reaction, 106, 130
  hydrolysis of an ester, 524
  hydrolysis reaction, 107
  naming, 61–64, 62*t*
  physical properties, 65
  preparation of, 130–131

estimate, 717
estimated uncertainty, 717
ethanoic acid, 494–495, 552–553
ethanol, 340–341
ethene, 222, 222*f*
ethers, 42*t*, 66–70
  drawing, 69
  naming, 66–68, 67*t*
  physical properties, 70, 70*f*
ethyl ethanoate, 455
ethyne, 223, 223*f*
exoskeletons, 632
exothermic process, 283, 284*f*, 293, 300*f*
expanded molecular formula
  alkanes, 16*t*
  alkenes, 23*f*
  alkynes, 28*f*
expanded valence, 229
exponents, 417
external circuit, 635

fatty acids, 114
femtochemistry, 384
fireflies, 352
first ionization energy, 191
first law of thermodynamics, 282–283
first-order reactions, 381
fishbone diagram, 713
flame calorimeter, 306, 306*f*
flame tests, 163
flowchart, 714
formaldehyde, 50, 52
formation, 319–322
formation reactions, 319
formula unit, 215
formyl group, 50, 50*f*
fossil fuels, 331–332, 331*f*, 333*t*, 340
freezing, 285, 285*f*
frequency, 168, 168*f*
fuel cell, 652–655
Fuller, R. Buckminster, 225
fullerenes, 225
functional group, 42, 42*t*
  carbonyl group, 50, 50*f*
  carboxyl group, 57, 57*f*
  formyl group, 50, 50*f*
  hydroxyl group, 42
  multiple functional groups, 80, 730–738
  in order of priority, 730*t*
  substituted functional groups, 80
fusible alloys, 207

Galvani, Luigi, 635
galvanic cells, 634–647
  applications of, 649–658
  cell notation, 641
  cell potentials, 642–643, 670–671
  corrosion, 655–658
  Daniell cell, 635–637, 636*f*
  dry cells, 649–651
  electrodes, types of, 637–638
  vs. electrolytic cell, 661*t*
  fuel cell, 652–655
  half-reactions, 639–641
  inert electrode, 638, 638*f*
  standard cell potential, 642, 644–647
  standard reduction potential, 643–644, 644*t*
galvanizing, 657
gasoline, 330
gel electrophoresis, 118
Gillespie, Ronald, 232, 246
glucosamine, 80, 80*f*
glycogen, 125
graphic organizers, 712–714
graphite, 224, 225*f*
graphs, 708–711
green chemistry, 40, 226, 695
  see also environmental issues
green engineering, 696
green solvents, 226
ground state, 171

H

Haber, Fritz, 466
Haber-Bosch process, 466
Hakin, Andrew, 310
half-reaction, 590–598
  acidic or basic solutions, 592–598
  balancing equations, 590–598
  with differing numbers of electrons, 591
  galvanic cell, 639–641
  writing balanced half-reactions, 590
haloalkanes, 42*t*, 46–49
  drawing, 48–49
  elimination reactions, 100
  naming, 47–48, 47*t*
  physical properties, 49
  substitution reactions, 103
halogens, 744*t*
hardness of metal, 213
hazardous products, alternatives for, 84–85

heat
  capacities of common substances and materials, 280t, 743t
  entering or leaving an object, 280, 281
  enthalpy, 283
  temperature. *See* temperature
  thermochemistry, 278–280
heat content, 333
heating curve of water, 286, 287f
heavy metals, 441
Heisenberg, Werner, 175
Heisenberg uncertainty principle, 175
helium, 178t, 181, 182f
hemoglobin, 464, 479
Hess, Germain Henri, 312
Hess's law, 312–322
  combining sets of chemical equations, 313–314
  enthalpy of combustion of magnesium, 338–339
  enthalpy of formation, 319–322
  formation reactions and thermal stability, 319
  manipulation of equations, 314
  standard molar enthalpy of formation, 317–318
heterogeneous equilibrium, 423, 429, 430
hexane, 40
high-density lipoprotein (HDL), 114
Hoffmann, Felix, 6
Hojabri, Leila, 81
homogeneous equilibrium, 423, 427, 428, 443
homologous series, 15
horseshoe, 206
hot packs, 287
Hund's rule, 184
hybrid orbitals, 221, 221f, 222f, 223f, 237t
hybridization
  central atom of molecule or ion, 237
  of orbitals, 224
hydration, 243
hydrocarbon derivative, 42
  alcohols, 42–46, 42t
  aldehydes, 42t, 50–53
  amides, 42t, 75–80, 75f, 76f
  amines, 42t, 70–75, 70f
  carboxylic acids, 42t, 57–61
  esters, 42t, 61–65, 61f

ethers, 42t, 66–70
haloalkanes, 42t, 46–49
ketones, 42t, 53–57, 53f
with multiple functional groups, 80, 730–738
polyurethane, 81
hydrocarbons, 5, 15
  alkanes, 15–21
  alkenes, 22–27
  alkynes, 28–30
  aromatic hydrocarbons, 35–39
  common, names and formulas for, 741t
  complete combustion reaction, 110
  cyclic hydrocarbons, 30–35
  derivatives. *See* hydrocarbon derivative
  saturated hydrocarbons, 15
  unsaturated hydrocarbons, 22
hydrochloric acid, 492
hydroelectric power, 332
hydrogen atom
  Bohr model, 171–172, 171f, 172f
  electron configuration, 182f
  energies of its orbitals, 181
  line spectrum, 172
  probability map or orbital, 175, 175f
  quantum numbers, 178t
hydrogen bonding, 242–243, 242f, 243f
hydrogen gas, 654–655
hydrogen half-cell, 642–643, 643f
hydrogen sulfide, 412
hydrolysis of an ester, 524
hydrolysis reaction, 107–108, 107f
hydronium ion, 493
hydroxide ion, 493
hydroxyl group, 42

ICE tables, 448–449
incomplete combustion reaction, 111
industrial extraction, 667
inert electrode, 638, 638f, 641
initial rate, 380
inorganic compounds, 9
instantaneous rate of reaction, 356
intermediate, 384
intermolecular forces, 5, 241
International Union of Pure and Applied Chemistry (IUPAC), 16
  see also IUPAC name

interstitial alloy, 214, 214f
intramolecular forces, 241
ion-dipole forces, 243, 243f
ion-induced dipole forces, 244
ion-product constant of water (K_w), 498–499, 501, 525–526
ionic bond, 5
ionic bonding, 208t, 214–216
ionic compounds, 5, 216–218
  binary ionic compounds, 740
  chemical formulas for, 740
  oxidation-reduction reactions, 590–601
  slightly soluble ionic compounds, 544–549
  solubility, 217, 217t, 745t
ionic crystals, 216
ionic equation, 585
ionization, 493, 493n
  base ionization, 519–526
  and polyprotic acids, 517
ionization constants for nitrogen bases, 746t
ionization energy, 191–192, 191f
ions
  see also specific types of ions
  anion, 528
  cation, 528
  colours, 742t
  common-ion effect, 531
  concentrations of, and acidic-basic nature of solutions, 499
  flame colour, 742t
  hybridization of central atom, 237
  ion-dipole forces, 243, 243f
  ion-induced dipole forces, 244
  names and formulas, 739t
  polyatomic ions, 228, 739t
  properties, 742t
  spectator ions, 585
iron, 206
iron ore, 599–600, 600f
isolated system, 279, 279f
isomers, 10–13
  cis isomer, 12, 12f, 101
  constitutional isomers, 10–11, 11f
  defined, 10
  diastereomers, 12, 12f
  enantiomers, 13, 13f
  stereoisomers, 11
  structural isomer, 10
  trans isomer, 12, 12f, 101
IUPAC name, 16, 44, 116, 736

jellyfish, 490
Jessop, Philip, 40
joule (J), 278

Kawah Ijen Lake, 412
ketones, 42t, 53–57, 53f
  drawing, 56
  naming, 54–55, 54t
  physical properties, 57
kinetic molecular theory, 274
Kroto, Harold W., 225

lab reports, 706
law of chemical equilibrium, 424
law of conservation of energy, 282–283
law of mass action, 424
Le Châtelier, Henri, 432
Le Châtelier principle, 432–439, 466, 469, 470
Le Roy, R.J., 246
lead, 441, 566–567
lead-acid battery, 665–666, 665f
Lesperance, Cathy, 206
Lewis structures, 228–231, 229f, 607–608
life-cycle approach, 250–251, 674
line graphs, 708–710
line spectrum, 170, 172
line structural formula
  alkanes, 16t
  alkenes, 23f
  alkynes, 28f
Lingulodinium polyedrum, 603
liquids, and intermolecular forces, 241
lithium, 181, 183, 183t
lithium-based battery systems, 668
lithium-ion polymer batteries, 576
Liu, Fei-Fei, 480
logarithms, 417, 725
London, Fritz, 245
London forces, 245
low-density lipoproteins (LDL), 114
Lowry, Thomas, 493

macroscopic property, 421
magnesium, 338–339
magnetic quantum number (m_l), 176–177, 177t

Index • MHR **809**

magnetic resonance spectroscopy (MRS), 194
main idea web, 712
malleability of metal, 213
mass, 362, 362t
materials engineers, 668
mathematical calculations, 275, 417, 718–719, 725
matter waves, 174–175
Maxwell-Boltzmann distribution, 366, 366f
measurement, 715–717, 719
medical oncologists, 480
melt-away metals, 207
melting, enthalpy of, 285, 285f, 286t
melting point, 5
   carbon derivatives, 80, 80t
   ionic compounds, 216–217, 217t
   metal, 207, 212, 212f
metallic bonding, 208t, 211
metals
   activity series, 744t
   alloys, 214
   boiling point, 212
   ductility, 213
   electrical conductivity, 212
   electron-sea model of metals, 211, 214
   flame colour of metal ions, 742t
   hardness, 213
   heavy metals, 441
   industrial extraction and refining, 667
   malleability, 213
   melt-away metals, 207
   melting point, 212, 212f
   oxidizing and reducing strengths, 618–619
   properties of, 212–213
   reactivity of metals, 192
   structure of, 211, 211f
   thermal conductivity, 212
methane, 9f, 15, 15f, 221f
methanol, 470
methylethylketone, 53f
metric measurements, 715
molar enthalpy of combustion, 294, 295t
molar entropies of formation, 743t
molar solubility, 546–547
molecular compounds
   see also molecules
   binary molecular compounds, 741, 741t

oxidation-reduction reactions, 603–615
structure of, 228
molecular orbital (MO) theory, 220
molecules
   dipole-dipole forces, 242–243
   dipole-induced dipole forces, 244, 244f
   dispersion forces, 244–245, 245f
   hybridization of central atom, 237
   intermolecular forces, 241
   intramolecular forces, 241
   ion-dipole forces, 243, 243f
   Lewis structures, 228–231, 229f, 237, 237f
   physical properties, 241t
   polar or non-polar, determination of, 238–239
   polarity, and molecular shape, 238–239, 239t
   resonance structures, 229–230
   shapes, 232–236, 233t, 234f, 238–239, 239t
   two-dimensional structures, 228
   valence-shell electron-pair repulsion theory (VSEPR), 232–236, 240–241
monomers, 116
monoprotic acid, 509
Montreal Protocol, 46
MRI (magnetic resonance imaging), 194
MRI technicians, 194
multiple functional groups, 80, 730–738
Murchison meteorite, 4f

nanoparticles, 250–251
NASA, 652, 653
natural gas, 329, 329f
natural polymers, 124–127
Nazar, Linda, 668
net ionic equation, 585, 645–646
network solids, 225
neutral salt solutions, 528–529
neutralization reaction, 336–337, 528
Newton, Isaac, 207
nickel-cadmium cell, 667, 667f
nitric acid, 376
noble gases, 192
non-polar compounds, 5
non-spontaneous reactions, 660–667

nuclear energy, 331
nuclear engineers, 310
nuclear fission, 288–289
nuclear fusion, 289–290, 289f
nuclear model, 164–172
nucleotides, 126
nucleus, 288–290
Nyholm, Ronald, 232
nylons, 119

Ontario, energy sources in, 331–332
open system, 279, 279f, 422
orbital diagram, 182–186
   aufbau principle, 184
   filling orbitals for Period 4 elements, 186, 186t
   filling orbitals for Periods 1 and 2 elements, 184
   for first ten elements, 185t
   Hund's rule, 184
   for Period 3 elements, 185
   writing, 183, 184
orbital-shape quantum number (l), 176, 177t
organic compounds
   see also specific organic compounds
   carbon atom, special nature of, 9
   defined, 9
   in everyday life, 134–135
   homologous series, 15
   introduction to, 8–13
   IUPAC name, 16
   modelling, 83
   prefix, 16
   root, 16
   suffix, 16
organic molecules, 2
organic reactions
   addition reactions, 96–100, 97f
   combustion reaction, 110–111
   complete combustion reaction, 110
   condensation reaction, 105
   elimination reactions, 100–102
   esterification reaction, 106–107, 106f, 108
   hydrolysis reaction, 107–108, 107f
   incomplete combustion reaction, 111
   oxidation, 109, 112
   reduction, 110, 112
   substitution reaction, 102–104

types of, 96–113
Oscar statuette, 684
oven cleaning, 524
oxidation, 109, 112, 128–129, 584–585, 609, 618–619, 748t
   see also redox reactions
oxidation half-reaction, 590
oxidation numbers, 603–614, 605–606, 615f
   application to redox reactions, 608–609
   balancing equations, 612–614, 615f
   Lewis structures, 607–608
   non-integer oxidation numbers, 606
   rules for assigning, 604t
oxidation-reduction reactions. *See* redox reactions
oxidizing agent, 586, 587t, 748t
oxoacids, 740t
ozone depletion, 376
ozone layer, 46, 46f

paper production, 377, 616
parent alkane, 43
partially hydrogenated oils, 114
Pauli, Wolfgang, 178
Pauli exclusion principle, 178, 196
penny, 583
peptide bonds, 105
percent dissociation, 509–511
percent error, 716
periodic table, 750t
   d block elements, 187
   electron configuration, prediction of, 187, 187t
   electronic structures for Period 3 elements, 196
   extension of, 197
   f block elements, 187
   group and period numbers, patterns of, 188
   p block elements, 187
   periodic trends in atomic properties, 189–192
   s block elements, 187
periodic trends in atomic properties, 189–192
personal computers, 576
petrochemicals, 122
pH
   calculating, 725
   determining using K_a, 513–514
   establishing, 500–502

measurement of reaction rate, 362t
solutions resistant to changes in pH, 530–531
strong acid-strong base titration, 534–535
weak acid-strong base titration, 537–539
weak base, 522–523
phenyl group, 36
phosphoric acid fuel cell, 654
photons, 169, 170
physical changes, 284
physical systems, 422–423, 422f
pig iron, 601
Planck, Max, 169, 170, 171
Planck's constant, 169
planetary model, 167
see also nuclear model
plasticizer, 116
plastics, 94, 95, 116, 117f, 123
see also polymers
Plunkett, Roy, 260
PMI chart, 712
pOH, 501–502
polar molecules, 5, 238–239, 242, 242f
polarity, and molecular shape, 238–239, 239t
polyamides, 119
polyatomic ions, 228, 739t
polybrominated diphenyl ethers (PBDEs), 66
polyethylene, 119
polyethylene terephthalate (PET), 116f, 119, 119f
polymers, 116–117, 116f, 117f
addition polymerization, 117–118, 118f, 118t
common name, 116
condensation reactions, 105, 119–120, 120t
cross links, 118
and industry, 122–124
modelling and making polymers, 132–133
natural polymers, 124–127
risks and solutions in production of, 123
synthetic polymers, 117–121, 123
polyparaphenylene terephthalamide (Kevlar®), 119, 119f
polyprotic acids, 517, 517t
polysaccharides, 124–125
polystyrene, 124
polyurethane, 81
polyvinyl alcohol (PVA), 132

polyvinyl chloride (PVC), 122, 123
potato clock, 637
potential energy diagram, 366, 366f, 369, 370
precipitate, 546, 548–549
precision, 715–716
prefix, 16
alcohols, 43t
aldehydes, 50t
alkanes, 17t
alkenes, 24t
alkynes, 29
amides, 76t
amines, 71t
aromatic hydrocarbons, 36t
binary molecular compounds, 741, 741t
carboxylic acids, 58t
cyclic hydrocarbons, 31t
esters, 62t
ethers, 67t
haloalkanes, 47t
ketones, 54t
polyatomic ions, 739t
pressure, 362t, 373
pressure changes, 434–435
primary amide, 75
primary amines, 70, 70f
primary battery, 649
principal quantum number (*n*), 176, 177t
propane, 330
proteins, 126, 126f
proton exchange membrane (PEM) fuel cell, 653–654
Pyykkö, Pekka, 197

quadratic equations, 452
quadratic formula, 417, 452–453
quantum, 170
quantum mechanical model, 174–179
atomic orbital, 174
development of, 164
magnetic quantum number (m_l), 176–177, 177t
orbital-shape quantum number (*l*), 176, 177t
Pauli exclusion principle, 178
principal quantum number (*n*), 176, 177t
quantum numbers, 175–178, 177t
spin quantum number (m_s), 177, 177t
quantum mechanics, and bonding, 220

quantum numbers, 175–178, 177t, 178t

random error, 716
rate constant, 383, 721–722
rate-determining step, 385, 386f
rate law, 383
rate laws, 721–724
rate-limiting step. *See* rate-determining step
rate of reaction. *See* reaction rate
reactant amounts, 296
reaction mechanism, 383–386
reaction quotient, 459–461
reaction rate, 354
activation energy (E_a), 366, 367–369
average rates of reaction, 356, 358–359
calculation of, 357
catalyst, 372, 374–377, 374f, 389, 390
collision theory, 365–366
concentration, 372, 380–383, 386f
determination of, 354–355
from experimental data, 363
factors affecting, 353, 372–374
instantaneous rate of reaction, 356
investigation, 388
methods of measurement of, 361–362, 362t
nature of the reactants, 372
pressure, 373
progress of a chemical reaction, 366, 366f
rate law, 383
remaining mass, measurement of, 362, 362t
reversible reactions, 425f
surface area, 373
temperature, 373, 373f
in terms of reactants or products, 358, 359–360
volume of gas produced, measurement of, 361, 362t
reactive metals, 192
reactive non-metals, 192
reactivity, 744t
rechargeable batteries, 664–667
redox reactions, 585–588, 587f
antioxidant supplements, 622
balancing equations, 590–598, 603–614, 615f, 620–621
corrosion, 655–658
disproportionation reaction, 598–599

half-reaction, 590–598
identification of, 609–611
ionic compounds, 590–601
molecular compounds, 603–615
oxidation number method, 603–614, 615f
spontaneity of, 587–588
reducing agent, 586, 587t, 748t
reduction, 110, 112, 585, 609, 618–619, 748t
see also redox reactions
reduction half-reaction, 590
refining, 599, 601, 667
renewable energy sources, 332
research skills, 704–705
resonance hybrid, 35, 35f, 229
resonance structures, 229–230
reversible reactions, 368, 420–421, 423, 425f
risk-benefit analysis, 698
room temperature ionic liquids (RTILs), 226
root, 16
alcohols, 43t
aldehydes, 50t
alkanes, 17t
alkenes, 24t
alkynes, 29t
amides, 76t
amines, 71t
aromatic hydrocarbons, 36t
carboxylic acids, 58t
cyclic hydrocarbons, 31t
esters, 62t
ethers, 67t
haloalkanes, 47t
ketones, 54t
rounding, 719
rust, 655–658, 656f
Rutherford, Ernest, 164, 166–167
Rutherford's model, 166–167, 167f

saccharides, 124–125
sacrificial anode, 657, 658
safety, 4, 272, 414, 578, 651, 672–673
salicylic acid, 6
salt bridge, 636
salt hydrolysis, 528–530
salts, 530t, 663–664, 664f
saturated hydrocarbons, 15
Schrödinger, Erwin, 174
Schrödinger wave equation, 174, 181
Schultz, Emeric, 493n

science skills
　acid-base titration, 728–729
　graphic organizers, 712–714
　graphs, 708–711
　green chemistry, 695
　green engineering, 696
　lab reports, 706
　logarithms, 725
　measurement, 715–717
　organization of data in table, 707
　pH, calculating, 725
　rate laws, 721–724
　research skills, 704–705
　rounding, 719
　scientific inquiry, 700–703
　scientific notation, 720
　significant digits, 718–719
　solutions, preparation of, 726–727
　STSE issues, analysis of, 697–699
scientific inquiry, 700–703
scientific notation, 417, 720
scuba diving, 463–464
second ionization energy, 191
second law of thermodynamics, 283, 300, 334
second-order reactions, 382
secondary amide, 75
secondary amines, 70, 70f
secondary batteries, 649
shell, 176
side groups, 15
　alkoxy group, 66
　alkyl group, 16
　names, 17t
significant digits, 718–719
silicon dioxide, 225, 225f
simple calorimeter, 300–302, 301f
single bonds, 220–221
site remediation, 556–557
Smalley, Richard E., 225
smelting, 599
solar energy, 332
solids
　bonding in, 241–249
　and intermolecular forces, 241
solubility, 217, 217t, 544–549, 744t
solubility-product constant (K_{sp}), 545, 545t, 546–548, 551
solubility product constants, 746t
solutions. See aqueous solutions
space-filling model, 9, 9f
specific heat capacity (c), 280

spectator ions, 585
spectra, observation of, 195
spheres, 219
spider map, 712
spin quantum number (m_s), 177, 177t
standard cell potential, 642, 644–647
standard molar enthalpy of formation, 317–318, 318t
standard reduction potential, 643–644, 644t, 748t
starch, 124–125
steel, 601
stereoisomers, 11
stoichiometry, 450–451
strong acid-strong base titration, 532–535
strong acids, 504, 505f, 746t
strong bases, 506, 746t
structural formula
　alkanes, 16t
　alkenes, 23f
　alkynes, 28f
structural isomer, 10
STSE issues, 697–699
sublevels, 176
substituent groups, 15
substituted functional groups, 80
substitution reaction, 102–104
substitutional alloy, 214, 214f
suffix, 16
　alcohols, 43t
　aldehydes, 50t
　alkanes, 17t
　alkenes, 24t
　alkynes, 29t
　amides, 76t
　amines, 71t
　aromatic hydrocarbons, 36t
　carboxylic acids, 58t
　cyclic hydrocarbons, 31t
　esters, 62t
　ethers, 67t
　haloalkanes, 47t
　ketones, 54t
　polyatomic ions, 739t
sulfuric acid, 375, 400, 468–469, 469f
surface area, 373
synchrotron, 162
syngas, 470
synthetic polymers, 117–121, 123
system, 279, 301
　equilibrium systems. See equilibrium systems

heat, amount entering and leaving, 280, 281
heat content, 282
measurable and calculated variables, 280
physical systems, and equilibrium, 422–423, 422f
systematic error, 716

tables, 707
　see also chemistry data tables
technological equilibrium systems, 466–469
Teflon® (polytetrafluoroethylene), 260
temperature, 270, 280
　see also heat
　of bunsen burner flame or hot plate, 302
　changes, and equilibrium, 436, 436f
　measurement of reaction rate, 362t
　reaction rate, influence on, 373, 373f
tertiary amide, 75
tertiary amines, 70, 70f
tetrahedral, 9, 9f
tetrahedral electron groups, 233, 233t
thermal conductivity, 212
thermal energy, 280, 308, 423
thermal equilibrium, 283
thermal stability, 319
thermochemistry, 278–280
　aqueous solutions, thermodynamics of, 310
　enthalpy (H). See enthalpy (H)
　first law of thermodynamics, 282–283
　second law of thermodynamics, 283, 300, 334
　thermochemical equations, 293
Thomson, George P., 174
Thomson, Joseph John, 164–165
Thomson's model, 164–165, 165f, 166
thorny devil (Moloch horridus), 270
titration, 532–544, 728–729
trans fats, 114
trans isomer, 12, 12f, 101
trichloromethane, 46

triple bond, 12, 12f, 30, 223
　see also chemical bonds

uncertainty, 717
unit cell, 216, 216f
units of measurement, 715
unsaturated fats, 114
unsaturated hydrocarbons, 22
urea, 8

valence bond (VB) theory, 220
valence-shell electron-pair repulsion theory (VSEPR), 232–236, 240–241
vaporization, 285, 285f, 286, 286t
Venn diagram, 714
volatile organic compounds (VOCs), 226
Volta, Alessandro, 634, 635
voltage, 633, 642
voltaic cells. See galvanic cells
volume, 361, 362t
volume changes, 434–435
volumetric flask, 726
volumetric pipette, 727
VSEPR theory, 232–236, 240–241

water
　acid-base reactions, 492–493
　amphiprotic nature of, 497f
　autoionization, 498
　as conjugate base, 528
　electrolysis of, 662
　heating curve of water, 286, 287f
　ion-product constant of water (K_w), 498–499, 501, 525–526
　lead content of drinking water, 566–567
wave function, 174
wavelength, 168f
weak acid-strong base titration, 536–540
weak acids, 505, 505f, 510
weak base-strong acid titration, 541–543, 541f
weak bases, 506, 520–523
wind energy, 332
Wöhler, Friedrich, 8

Credits

PP iv-v NASA/JPL/CalTech/S.Willner/Harvard/Smithsonian; vi-vii Carsten Peter/Speleoresearch & Films/National Geographic/Getty Images; viii-ix Olivier Grunewald; x-xi Life Style/Tom George/All Canada Photos; xii-xiii Art Wolfe/Photo Researchers, Inc.; pp2-3 NASA/JPL/CalTech/S. Willner/Harvard/Smithsonian, inset Creative Commons License/ Basilicofresco; p4 David Tanaka; p5 Christy Scott/iStock; pp6-7 Layne Kennedy/Corbis; p8, 22, David Tanaka; p28 Dejan Saman/iStock; p40 David Tanaka; p46 NASA/Goddard Space Flight Center Scientific Visualization Studio; p57 left David Tanaka, RedHelga/iStock, David Tanaka; p70, 75, 80, David Tanaka; p81 Photo courtesy of Dr. Leila Hojabri; p84 left mark wragg/iStock, David Tanaka, Vasiliki Varvaki/ iStock, David Tanaka; p89 Oliver Childs/iStock; pp94-95 Paul Miller/epa/ Corbis; p95 Greenpeace/Alex Hofford; p96 left Will & Deni McIntyre/ Photo Researchers, Inc., David Tanaka; p97 Dave Scarrett; p106 Madmickandmo/iStock; p111 left David Tanaka, Karl-Friedrich Hohl/ iStock; p116 Philippe Hallé/iStock; p117 left Carolyn A. McKeone/Photo Researchers, Inc., Gaertner/All Canada Photos, Mona Makela/iStock; p118 Explorer/Photo Researchers, Inc.; p119 top Today ago kids/shutterstock, goce risteski/iStock; p122 Joseph Sohm/Visions of America/Corbis; p123 left Michał Modzelewski/iStock, Hank Morgan/Photo Researchers, Inc., Angela Hampton Picture Library/All Canada Photos; Ramin Talaie/ Corbis; p125 Michael Abbey/Photo Researchers, Inc.; pp134-135 background A. Klammt/plainpicture/Corbis; pp144-145 background David Tanaka, p144 Roger Russmeyer/Corbis; p146 top Layne Kennedy/ Corbis, Paul Miller/epa/Corbis; p152 Perennou Nuridsany/Photo Researchers, Inc.; pp156-157 Carsten Peter/Speleoresearch & Films/ National Geographic/Getty Images; p160 Haveseen/iStock; pp162-163 Drawing of C. sanctus is by Richard Hartley, University of Manchester. Photo by T. Larson, courtesy of the Black Hills Institute. Image created by Gregory Stewart, SLAC National Accelerator Laboratory for the U.S. Dept. of Energy Office of Science; p164 Science Museum/Science & Society Picture Library; p165 Charles D. Winter/Photo Researchers, Inc.; p194 Photo provided by Schulich School of Medicine & Dentistry, used by permission of Jorge Burneo; p203 top left clockwise Photo courtesy of Lutfi Ozkok, Bettman/Corbis, Photo courtesy of Bertrand Pullman, Emilio Segre Visual Archives/American Institute of Physics/Science Photo Library, Photo courtesy of Sigrid Peyerimhoff; pp206-207 Used by permission of Cathy Lesperance, photo by David Meyer. Courtesy of the Wellington Advertiser. Inset, Lee Rees Photography/Photographers Direct; p207 Jimmi Larsen/iStock; p211 Sciencephotos/All Canada Photos; p214 Buquet Christophe/shutterstock, T.W. van Urk/shutterstock; p226 ITAR-TASS/Yuri Belinsky/The Canadian Press; p245 Andrew Lambert Photography/Photo Researchers, Inc.; p246 left Photo courtesy of Ronald J. Gillespie, Professor Emeritus, B.Sc., Ph.D., D.Sc. (London), F.R.S., F.R.S.C., F.R.S.C. (U.K.), F.C.I.C., Dr. Richard Bader from the *Canadian Journal of Chemistry*, Vol. 74, Issue 6. Photo courtesy of the *Canadian Journal of Chemistry*, Canadian Science Publishing (NRC Research Press), Photo courtesy of Robert J. Le Roy, B.Sc., M.Sc., Ph.D., Professor of Chemistry, University of Waterloo; p250-251 Georgy Shafeev/shutterstock; p258 Jane Norton/iStock; p259 kyoshino/iStock; pp260-261 NASA; pp270-271 Art Wolfe/Photo Researchers, Inc.; p272 David Tanaka; p273 top Luca Bruno/AP/The Canadian Press, Alessandro Trovati/AP/The Canadian Press; p274 Masterfile; pp276-277 Tim Tadder/New Sport/ Corbis; p277 Martyn F.Chillmaid/Photo Researchers, Inc.; p278 Janusz Wrobel/All Canada Photos; p279 David Tanaka; p290 Lawrence Livermore National Laboratory. Photo No. NIF-0109-15881; p296 Chris Beddoe/ iStock; p308 Stephen Frisch Photography; p309 left Ocean/Corbis, David Tanaka; p310 Photo courtesy of Andrew W. Hakin, Ph.D, Department of Chemistry and Biochemistry, University of Lethbridge; p318 top Minerals in Your World, United States Geological Survey and the Mineral Information Institute, U.S. House Subcommittee on Energy and Natural Resources, Photo courtesy Diavik Diamond Mines Inc.; p321 Anders Aagesen/iStock; p325 David Tanaka; p332 Creative Commons License/ wiki; p334 Enwave Corporation; p338 Andrew Lambert Photography/ Photo Researchers, Inc.; p340 Ron Stroud/Masterfile; p345 Christy Scott/ iStock; pp352-353 Phil Degginger/All Canada Photos; p354 Eye of Science/Photo Researchers, Inc.; p361 Andrew Lambert Photography/ Photo Researchers, Inc.; p362 Andrew Lambert Photography/Science Photo Library; p376 James L. Amos/Corbis; p377 David Tanaka; p385 Tupungato/bigstock; pp400-401 background Manfred Mehlig/Corbis; p400 Northern News/Rick Owen/The Canadian Press; p402 top Tim Tadder/New Sport/Corbis, Phil Degginger/All Canada Photos; pp412-413 Olivier Grunewald; p415 David Tanaka, p416 Charles D.Winters/Photo Researchers, Inc.; p417 David Tanaka; p418-419 China Photos/Getty Images; p421 PhotosIndia/MaXximages.com; p423 Charles D.Winters/ Photo Researchers, Inc.; p425 NASA; p427 Bill Bachman/All Canada Photos; p429 Reuters/Mark Blinch/Corbis; p431 Charles D.Winters/Photo Researchers, Inc.; p433 David Vintiner/Corbis; p435 David Tanaka; p436 Charles D.Winters/Photo Researchers, Inc.; p439 Ian Crysler; p441 Andrew Sawicki/Toronto Star/The Canadian Press; p463 Kennet Havgaard/Aurora Photos/Corbis; p464 Frances M. Roberts/All Canada Photos; p465 Stephen Frink/Corbis; p468 Peter Hendri/Getty Images; p470 top Steven Vidler/Eurasia Press/Corbis, bottom left age fotostock/ MaXximages.com, tan510jomast/dreamstime, Paul Morton/iStock; p474, 477 David Tanaka; p480 Photo courtesy of Dr. Fei-Fei Liu; p483 Charles D.Winters/Photo Researchers, Inc.; p486 David Tanaka; p488 Imagebroker/MaXximages.com; p489 Charles D.Winters/Photo Researchers, Inc.; pp490-491 Jon Arnold Images/Masterfile; p492 David Tanaka; p503 David Tanaka; p504 Martyn F. Chillmaid/Science Photo Library; p512 left Levente Varga/iStock, Imagebroker/All Canada Photos; p518 David Tanaka; p523 Jill Fromer/iStock; p527 David Tanaka; p528 David Tanaka; p544 CNRI/Photo Researchers, Inc.; p546 Charles D. Winters/Photo Researchers, Inc.; p550 David Tanaka; pp556-557 Images courtesy of Stantec Consulting and the City of Belleville, Economic & Strategic Initiatives; p560 Ron Niebrugge/All Canada Photos; p561, 562 David Tanaka; p563 left Delalande/Photo Researchers, Inc., CCL/Tom Oates at the English Language Wikipedia; p564 David Tanaka; p565 BasieB/iStock; p566-567 Michael N. Paras/maXximages.com; p566 Peter Spiro/iStock; p568 China Photos/Getty Images; p569 Jon Arnold Images/ Masterfile; p573 John James/All Canada Photos; pp576-577 Life Style/Tom George/All Canada Photos; p580 Leslie Garland Picture Library/All Canada Photos; pp582-583 Oliveromg/shutterstock; p584 left Charles D. Winters/Photo Researchers, Inc., Charles O'Rear/Corbis; p586, 589 Charles D.Winters/Photo Researchers, Inc.; p591 left David Tanaka, Martyn F. Chillmaid/Photo Researchers, Inc., David Tanaka; p593 David Tanaka; p599 Bridgeman Art Library/Getty Images; p601 top left clockwise Adam Woolfitt/Corbis, Jeff Nagy/iStock, Caroline/Corbis; p603 StockTrek Images/Getty Images, Steve Morton/NOAA; p618, 619 , 622 David Tanaka; p628 Photos.com; p629 The Canadian Press/Darryl Dick; pp632-633 Baz Ratner/Reuters; p634 Michael Durham/Minden Pictures; p635 Joel Gordon; p637 McGraw-Hill Higher Education/Stephen Frisch, photographer; p646 Charles D.Winters/Photo Researchers, Inc.; p649 Tedd Foxx/All Canada Photos; p650 David Tanaka; p651 left Metta foto/ All Canada Photos, The Canadian Press/Adrian Wyld; p652 Photo courtesy of Ballard Power Systems; p653 Used with permission of UTC Power Corporation; p655 Toshiba Corporation; p656 Image courtesy of the artist, Susan A. Point; p657 Peterborough Utilities; p659 David Tanaka; p662 Charles D.Winters/Photo Researchers, Inc.; p665 Joe Belanger/ iStock; p666 AdShooter/iStock; p667 Chris R. Sharp/Photo Researchers, Inc.; p668 Photo courtesy of Dr. Linda Nazar; p672 Ewald Froech/iStock; p674 Paul Matthew Photography/shutterstock; p675 Football Foundation of South Africa; p678 David Tanaka; p681 Adrian Sherratt/All Canada Photos; pp684-685 background Bill Noll/iStock, inset Jason DeCrow/AP/ The Canadian Press; p686 top Oliveromg/shutterstock, Baz Ratner/ Reuters; p687 Tedd Foxx/All Canada Photos; p693 Barry Williams/Getty Images; p694 David Tanaka; p726-729 David Tanaka.

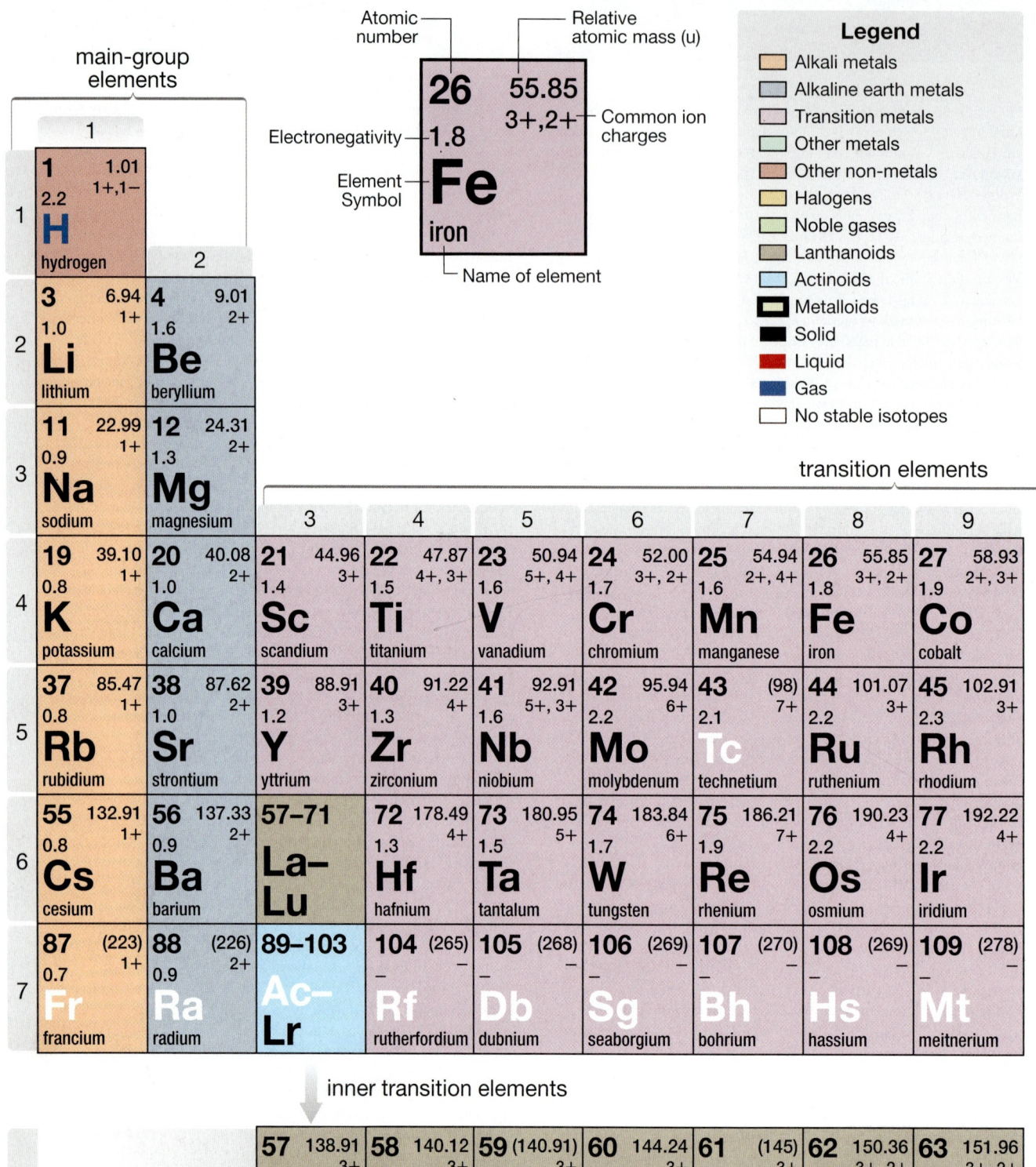

main-group elements

13	14	15	16	17	18
					2 4.00 — He helium
5 10.81 — 2.0 B boron	6 12.01 — 2.6 C carbon	7 14.01 3− 3.0 N nitrogen	8 16.00 2− 3.4 O oxygen	9 19.00 1− 4.0 F fluorine	10 20.18 — Ne neon
13 26.98 3+ 1.6 Al aluminum	14 28.09 — 1.9 Si silicon	15 30.97 3− 2.2 P phosphorus	16 32.07 2− 2.6 S sulfur	17 35.45 1− 3.2 Cl chlorine	18 39.95 — Ar argon

10	11	12					
28 58.69 2+,3+ 1.9 Ni nickel	29 63.55 2+,1+ 1.9 Cu copper	30 65.41 2+ 1.7 Zn zinc	31 69.72 3+ 1.8 Ga gallium	32 72.64 4+ 2.0 Ge germanium	33 74.92 3− 2.2 As arsenic	34 78.96 2− 2.6 Se selenium	35 79.90 1− 3.0 Br bromine	36 83.80 — Kr krypton
46 106.42 2+,3+ 2.2 Pd palladium	47 107.87 1+ 1.9 Ag silver	48 112.41 2+ 1.7 Cd cadmium	49 114.32 3+ 1.8 In indium	50 118.71 4+,2+ 2.0 Sn tin	51 121.76 3+,5+ 2.1 Sb antimony	52 127.60 2− 2.1 Te tellurium	53 126.90 1− 2.7 I iodine	54 131.29 — 2.6 Xe xenon
78 195.08 4+,2+ 2.2 Pt platinum	79 196.97 3+,1+ 2.4 Au gold	80 200.59 2+,1+ 1.9 Hg mercury	81 204.38 1+,3+ 1.8 Tl thallium	82 207.2* 2+,4+ 1.8 Pb lead	83 208.98 3+,5+ 1.9 Bi bismuth	84 (209) 2+,4+ 2.0 Po polonium	85 (210) 1− 2.2 At astatine	86 (222) — Rn radon
110 (271) — Ds darmstadtium	111 (280) — Rg roentgenium	112 (285) — Cn copernicum	113 (286) — Nh nihonium	114 (289) — Fl flerovium	115 (289) — Mc moscovium	116 (293) — Lv livermorium	117 (294) 2.2 Ts tennessine	118 (294) — Og oganesson

64 157.25 3+ 1.2 Gd gadolinium	65 158.93 3+ — Tb terbium	66 162.50 3+ 1.2 Dy dysprosium	67 164.93 3+ 1.2 Ho holmium	68 167.26 3+ 1.2 Er erbium	69 168.93 3+ 1.2 Tm thulium	70 173.04 3+,2+ 1.3 Yb ytterbium	71 174.97 3+ 1.0 Lu lutetium
96 (247) — — Cm curium	97 (247) 3+,4+ — Bk berkelium	98 (251) 3+ — Cf californium	99 (252) 3+ — Es einsteinium	100 (257) 3+ — Fm fermium	101 (258) 3+ — Md mendelevium	102 (259) 2+,3+ — No nobelium	103 (262) 3+ — Lr lawrencium